# Money and Capital Markets

## Financial Institutions and Instruments in a Global Marketplace

# The McGraw-Hill/Irwin Series in Finance, Insurance and Real Estate

**Stephen A. Ross**
*Franco Modigliani Professor of Finance and Economics*
*Sloan School of Management*
*Massachusetts Institute of Technology*
Consulting Editor

## FINANCIAL MANAGEMENT

Adair
**Excel Applications for Corporate Finance**
*First Edition*

Benninga and Sarig
**Corporate Finance: A Valuation Approach**

Block and Hirt
**Foundations of Financial Management**
*Twelfth Edition*

Brealey, Myers, and Allen
**Principles of Corporate Finance**
*Eighth Edition*

Brealey, Myers, and Marcus
**Fundamentals of Corporate Finance**
*Fifth Edition*

Brooks
**FinGame Online 5.0**

Bruner
**Case Studies in Finance: Managing for Corporate Value Creation**
*Fifth Edition*

Chew
**The New Corporate Finance: Where Theory Meets Practice**
*Third Edition*

Chew and Gillan
**Corporate Governance at the Crossroads: A Book of Readings**
*First Edition*

DeMello
**Cases in Finance**
*Second Edition*

Grinblatt (editor)
**Stephen A. Ross, Mentor: Influence Through Generations**

Grinblatt and Titman
**Financial Markets and Corporate Strategy**
*Second Edition*

Helfert
**Techniques of Financial Analysis: A Guide to Value Creation**
*Eleventh Edition*

Higgins
**Analysis for Financial Management**
*Eighth Edition*

Kester, Ruback, and Tufano
**Case Problems in Finance**
*Twelfth Edition*

Ross, Westerfield, and Jaffe
**Corporate Finance**
*Eighth Edition*

Ross, Westerfield, Jaffe, and Jordan
**Corporate Finance: Core Principles and Applications**
*First Edition*

Ross, Westerfield, and Jordan
**Essentials of Corporate Finance**
*Fifth Edition*

Ross, Westerfield, and Jordan
**Fundamentals of Corporate Finance**
*Eighth Edition*

Shefrin
**Behavioral Corporate Finance: Decisions That Create Value**
*First Edition*

White
**Financial Analysis with an Electronic Calculator**
*Sixth Edition*

## INVESTMENTS

Adair
**Excel Applications for Investments**
*First Edition*

Bodie, Kane, and Marcus
**Essentials of Investments**
*Sixth Edition*

Bodie, Kane, and Marcus
**Investments**
*Seventh Edition*

Hirt and Block
**Fundamentals of Investment Management**
*Eighth Edition*

Hirschey and Nofsinger
**Investments: Analysis and Behavior**
*First Edition*

Jordan and Miller
**Fundamentals of Investments: Valuation and Management**
*Fourth Edition*

## FINANCIAL INSTITUTIONS AND MARKETS

Rose and Hudgins
**Bank Management and Financial Services**
*Seventh Edition*

Rose and Marquis
**Money and Capital Markets: Financial Institutions and Instruments in a Global Marketplace**
*Tenth Edition*

Saunders and Cornett
**Financial Institutions Management: A Risk Management Approach**
*Fifth Edition*

Saunders and Cornett
**Financial Markets and Institutions: An Introduction to the Risk Management Approach**
*Third Edition*

## INTERNATIONAL FINANCE

Eun and Resnick
**International Financial Management**
*Fourth Edition*

Kuemmerle
**Case Studies in International Entrepreneurship: Managing and Financing Ventures in the Global Economy**
*First Edition*

## REAL ESTATE

Brueggeman and Fisher
**Real Estate Finance and Investments**
*Thirteenth Edition*

Corgel, Ling, and Smith
**Real Estate Perspectives: An Introduction to Real Estate**
*Fourth Edition*

Ling and Archer
**Real Estate Principles: A Value Approach**
*Second Edition*

## FINANCIAL PLANNING AND INSURANCE

Allen, Melone, Rosenbloom and Mahoney
**Retirement Plans: 401(k)s, IRAs, and Other Deferred Compensation Approaches**
*Tenth Edition*

Altfest
**Personal Financial Planning**
*First Edition*

Harrington and Niehaus
**Risk Management and Insurance**
*Second Edition*

Kapoor, Dlabay, and Hughes
**Focus on Personal Finance: An Active Approach to Help You Develop Successful Financial Skills**
*First Edition*

Kapoor, Dlabay, and Hughes
**Personal Finance**
*Eighth Edition*

# Money and Capital Markets

## Financial Institutions and Instruments in a Global Marketplace

Tenth Edition

**Peter S. Rose**
*Texas A&M University*

**Milton H. Marquis**
*Florida State University*

Boston   Burr Ridge, IL   Dubuque, IA   New York   San Francisco   St. Louis
Bangkok   Bogotá   Caracas   Kuala Lumpur   Lisbon   London   Madrid   Mexico City
Milan   Montreal   New Delhi   Santiago   Seoul   Singapore   Sydney   Taipei   Toronto

*To our families*

*PETER S. ROSE*

*MILTON H. MARQUIS*

**McGraw-Hill Irwin**

MONEY AND CAPITAL MARKETS

Published by McGraw-Hill/Irwin, a business unit of The McGraw-Hill Companies, Inc., 1221 Avenue of the Americas, New York, NY, 10020. Copyright © 2008, 2006, 2003, 2000, 1997, 1994, 1992, 1989, 1986, 1983 by The McGraw-Hill Companies, Inc. All rights reserved. No part of this publication may be reproduced or distributed in any form or by any means, or stored in a database or retrieval system, without the prior written consent of The McGraw-Hill Companies, Inc., including, but not limited to, in any network or other electronic storage or transmission, or broadcast for distance learning.

Some ancillaries, including electronic and print components, may not be available to customers outside the United States.

This book is printed on acid-free paper.

2 3 4 5 6 7 8 9 0 VNH/VNH 0 9 8

ISBN 978-0-07-340516-2
MHID 0-07-340516-7

Executive editor: *Michele Janicek*
Editorial assistant: *Elizabeth Hughes*
Marketing director: *Dan Silverburg*
Senior project manager: *Harvey Yep*
Senior production supervisor: *Debra R. Sylvester*
Lead designer: *Matthew Baldwin*
Lead media project manager: *Cathy L. Tepper*
Cover image: *© Getty Images*
Typeface: *10.5/12 Times Roman*
Compositor: *Laserwords Private Limited*
Printer: *Von Hoffmann Corporation*

**Library of Congress Cataloging-in-Publication Data**

Rose, Peter S.
   Money and capital markets : financial institutions and instruments in a
global marketplace / Peter S. Rose, Milton H. Marquis.
     p. cm.—(The McGraw-Hill/Irwin Series in Finance, Insurance, and Real Estate)
   Includes bibliographical references and index.
   ISBN-13: 978-0-07-340516-2 (alk. paper)
   ISBN-10: 0-07-340516-7 (alk. paper)
   1. Finance—United States. 2. Money market—United States. 3. Capital
market—United States. I. Marquis, Milton H., 1948- II. Title.
  HG181.R66 2008
  332.0973—dc22                  2007037981

www.mhhe.com

## About the Authors

### Peter S. Rose

In his professional career Peter S. Rose has served as a professor of finance, as a financial economist with the Federal Reserve System, as an author, and as an advisor for a wide variety of different financial institutions. He has published more than 200 articles in journals and proceedings in the United States, Canada, Great Britain, France, Brazil, India, and Mexico. He has served as author, co-author, or editor for numerous books, including *Money and Capital Markets* (McGraw-Hill/Irwin) now in its tenth edition, *Banking and Financial Services* (McGraw-Hill/Irwin) now in its seventh edition, *Financial Institutions* (Richard D. Irwin, Inc.) which passed through five editions, *Banking Across State Lines* (Quorum Books), *The Changing Structure of American Banking* (Columbia University Press), and *Japanese Banking and Investment in the United States* (Quorum Books). Some of these texts have been translated into Chinese, Russian, and other languages and used in classrooms around the globe.

### Milton H. Marquis

Milton H. Marquis received a Bachelor of Science degree from Purdue University in Mechanical Engineering in 1972 and subsequently worked as a project engineer for American Electric Power. He received a Master of Arts degree in Economics in 1982 and a Ph.D. in Economics in 1985 from Indiana University. He has taught economics and finance at St. Olaf College in Northfield, MN and at Florida State University, where he has been a member of the faculty since 1985. He worked as an Economist in the Monetary Affairs Division of the Federal Reserve Board from 1993 to 1995, and as a Senior Economist in the Research Department of the Federal Reserve Bank of San Francisco from 2000 to 2003. He was also a Visiting Scholar at the Bank of Japan in 1997. Mr. Marquis has authored a textbook in 1996 entitled *Monetary Theory and Policy,* and has published over thirty articles on monetary theory, monetary policy, and macroeconomic theory in academic journals, including the *Journal of Monetary Economics, Economica,* the *Review of Economics and Statistics,* and the *Economic Journal.*

# Preface to the Tenth Edition

The twenty-first century is still young as its opening decade moves toward closure. Yet we can begin to see the broad outlines of this new millennium and have at least a sense of what the world may look like as this new era gradually unfolds. Sadly, the new millennium has not yet ushered in an era of peace, mutual respect, and rising living standards for all as many of us had hoped.

The Cold War between superpowers has been replaced by a war on terror, spearheaded by the tragedy of 9/11 and punctuated by ongoing wars in Iraq, Afghanistan, and in Africa and other portions of the Middle East. Scores are hurt or killed every day and the struggle threatens to spread into other nations. The awesome threat posed by the great nuclear face-off between the former Soviet Union and the United States has been largely supplanted by nuclear proliferation in which more nations, large and small, are either armed with destructive nuclear weapons or seem to be working toward that goal.

Somehow, the world of friendly economic competition between nations that we thought the new millennium might usher in appears instead to be pockmarked by disease, drought, military confrontation, and abject poverty for millions. Many of us had hoped that the rapidly evolving technology of communications—satellites, personal computers, cell phones, and the like—would bring us all closer together. Instead, the fundamental values we cherish—personal freedom, liberty, respect for law and the rights of others—seem to be under assault in many parts of the globe at levels not seen in decades.

Now we find ourselves wondering if our most important institutions, those that have served us well for generations, can continue to function well and provide us the benefits they have brought us before. One of the most important of these institutions is the *financial system*—the vast complex of banks, security dealers, mutual funds, insurance and finance companies, and thousands of other financial-service providers and the dynamic money and capital markets that surround them. The great financial marketplace today encircles the globe and may look solid and secure. But, it too faces great uncertainty and the pressures of ongoing turmoil. As we learned from the tragedy of 9/11, the global financial system like the rest of the economy is vulnerable in a tumultuous world, and we must find ways to ensure its soundness and guarantee that the financial services it provides are available as demanded every single day.

No other institution on our planet provides us with as many critically important services as the global financial system. Every day of our existence the great system of money and capital markets:

- *Supplies us with credit* when we require borrowed funds to supplement our incomes and enhance our standard of living.

- *Encourages our saving,* enabling us to set extra funds aside in popular savings instruments (such as bank deposits and mutual funds) and add to those funds in order to meet future financial needs (such as education and retirement).

- *Transforms our savings into investments* that include building new plants and equipment, construction of new office buildings and shopping centers, stocking the shelves of businesses with new goods to sell, and, ultimately, providing new jobs and a better standard of living.

- *Provides a channel for payments* through which flow trillions of currency units (dollars, euros, pounds, yen, yuan, rupees, etc.) every day in order to make payments for purchases of goods and services possible, so that spendable funds move rapidly and safely between buyers and sellers.
- *Creates liquidity in the economy* so that each of us can convert our assets (stocks, bonds, etc.) into spendable cash to help satisfy our immediate spending needs.
- *Supplies risk protection for individuals and institutions* in the guise of insurance policies, derivative contracts, and other financial services aimed at protecting our well-being and shielding that which we value highly from loss.
- *Provides a channel for public policy to promote growth and prosperity* as governments and central banks work through the financial system to regulate the condition of their economies and fulfill important economic objectives, such as maximum employment, price stability with low or nonexistent inflation, and sustainable economic growth.

If you scan the foregoing list of vital tasks performed by modern financial systems, you will get at least a feel for how awesome the system of money and capital markets and financial institutions must be. How truly fortunate we are to be living in an era where this one sector of our economy rises daily to meet so many critical needs for us, personally and professionally—credit, savings, investments, payments, liquidity, risk protection, and public policy aimed at providing jobs, protecting us from the ravages of inflation, and promoting a growing economy.

Indeed, how utterly different our circumstances would be if the system of financial markets and institutions were seriously disrupted and suddenly did not function as efficiently as we have experienced in the past. A dramatic example of the extreme consequences that could occur if our financial system is significantly damaged occurred on September 11, 2001, when New York's World Trade Center was destroyed as a consequence of terrorist attacks. It was terrible enough that more than 3,000 people lost their lives from terrorist violence in New York City and Washington, D.C., but adding to the chaos and distress were the number of financially oriented businesses—principally security dealers, credit-card and check clearing systems, and banks—that were destroyed or damaged. Thousands of customers suddenly became concerned about whether their savings were adequately protected and about the credit and cash balances they required to carry out daily transactions. Major institutions like the New York Stock Exchange briefly shut down their operations. Soon the pubic began to curtail its spending and jobs disappeared as the economy slipped into a recession.

Following these terrible events, our system of money and capital markets recovered rapidly (for most individuals and institutions, in a matter of hours or days). Records were reconstructed, vital operations were transferred to new locations, and additional cash quickly flowed through the banking system with the aid of the Federal Reserve System. The money and capital markets and the financial institutions within them recovered with amazing speed, beyond anything we imagined possible, restoring the flow of critical financial services to thousands of financial-service customers.

And, we were supplied with an important lesson we dare not forget. Our financial system today is so deeply integrated with our economy and with the rest of the world that when it stumbles, for whatever reason, it affects the whole planet—individuals, families, businesses, governments, and institutions on every continent.

Indeed, that is one of the reasons the authors wrote this book. We need to understand and appreciate what the money and capital markets and the financial system that surrounds them do for us, both personally and professionally. We must learn how vital it is to preserve and protect our global system of financial markets and institutions and how we can contribute to the task of improving the functioning of that system for the public's benefit. In short, through the pages of this book there is an adventure that lies in front of us. We are asked to take the challenge and learn as much as possible about our vital money and capital markets and the great financial system that embraces them.

## Key Features of the Tenth Edition of Money and Capital Markets

*Money and Capital Markets* remains one of the most comprehensive texts covering the entire financial system, including all major types of financial institutions and instruments.

As in previous editions, the new tenth edition is extensively updated from front to back, including new financial data and new laws and regulations reshaping the financial system as well as new financial scandals and identity theft affecting millions of consumers.

Numerous new end-of-chapter problems, including the addition of EXCEL-based problems in many chapters.

Expanded treatment of URLs with key Web addresses placed in the chapter margins near the locations where related topics are presented.

Numerous new boxes, including discussions of ethical issues (such as backdating stock options), behavioral finance, and market microstructure.

Expanded discussion of the rapid rise of China, India, and the European Union as global forces in the financial system and the economy.

Inclusion of major new changes in financial-sector laws and regulations, including the Pension Protection Act of 2006, the FDIC Reform and Deficit Reduction Act, the Financial Services Regulatory Relief Act of 2006, the USA Patriot Act, and the Bankruptcy Abuse Prevention and Consumer Protection Act.

New reference materials listed at each chapter's end to provide readers with in-depth, updated material for further study and allow them to pursue deeper research on semester and term projects.

New presentation on the history of financial panics around the globe.

Expanded discussion of new financial instruments and institutions, such as new housing futures and option contracts, hedge funds, and subprime loans that have recently led to serious credit quality problems.

Expanded discussion of advances in electronic technology, especially in the transfer of financial information via computer, Web sites, direct deposits, cell phones, radio frequency transactions, and so on.

## Different Approaches to Teaching about the Financial System Using This Book

*Money and Capital Markets: Financial Institutions and Instruments in a Global Marketplace,* now in its tenth edition, discusses all of the major financial marketplaces, instruments, and institutions that belong to our financial system. This book is arranged to be flexible in order to accommodate the needs of different instructors, students, and other readers who often approach the financial marketplace from unique perspectives. In short, this book offers multiple ways to tackle this important subject and master our understanding of the global financial system.

Readers may choose to orient their course of study in their own way, creating quite different approaches to a study of the financial marketplace each term or semester. To illustrate:

## Teaching a Financial Institutions' Course with This Book

Some teachers and other readers may choose to use this text as the basis for a course on *financial institutions,* focusing principally on the leading financial-service providers in our financial system—commercial and investment banks, mutual and pension funds, life and property-casualty insurers, finance companies, and security brokers and dealers, to name a few key examples. Parts of the new edition useful for such a course include:

- Part 1, including Chapters 1 through 4 on the current and emerging financial system, including a discussion of the critical roles played by financial intermediation and financial assets in the money and capital markets.
- Part 3, including Chapters 10 through 13, dealing with financial firms operating in the money market and the great central banks at work to regulate the economy around the globe.
- Part 4, including Chapters 14 through 17 that examine significant features of all major financial institutions, accompanied by a detailed discussion of the regulations that surround the financial institutions' sector.
- Part 5, including Chapters 18 through 20 that focus on businesses and governments operating in the money and capital markets.
- Part 6, including Chapters 21 and 22 on the most important consumer lending institutions in the financial sector.
- Part 7, especially Chapter 24 that explores recent trends in international banking.

## Teaching a Security Markets Course with This Book

Other instructors and readers may prefer a course oriented mainly around the leading *security markets and the trading of key financial instruments,* such as bonds, stocks, and shares in mutual funds. Key sections of the book useful to support such a course include:

- Part 1, especially Chapters 2–4 on the creation of financial assets, the key sources of financial information, and trends unfolding in the security markets.
- Part 2, including Chapters 5 through 9 on interest rate determination and asset pricing for both short- and long-term security markets.
- Part 3, especially Chapters 10 through 13 on trading Treasury bills and other money market instruments and the role of the Federal Reserve and other central banks and security dealer firms in influencing security market conditions.
- Part 4, particularly Chapter 16 dealing with mutual funds and investment bankers.
- Part 5, including Chapters 18–20 on the issuance and trading of corporate and government securities.
- Part 6, especially Chapter 22 focusing on the operations of the largest of all domestic security markets—the residential mortgage market.
- Part 7, particularly Chapter 23 that focuses on the biggest of all global financial marketplaces—the currency or foreign-exchange market.

## Teaching a Public Policy or Regulations-Oriented Course with This Book

For instructors and other readers interested in *public policy issues* and *government regulation of the financial sector,* key sections of the text for such a public policy–oriented course would include:

- Part 1, especially Chapters 3 and 4 on laws shaping the financial system and unfolding trends in government regulation.
- Part 2, particularly Chapters 5 and 7 dealing with government policies that mold the structure of interest rates and Chapter 8 which, among other topics, focuses on security tax law.
- Part 3, including Chapters 10–13 on central banking policy and government rules for conducting trading in the money market.
- Part 4, especially Chapter 17 that provides a detailed explanation of the philosophy and scope of government regulations affecting all major financial institutions.
- Part 6, particularly Chapter 21 on privacy and financial disclosure issues in the consumer finance sector and Chapter 22 that looks at the massive structure of regulation surrounding the trading of residential mortgages.
- Part 7, including Chapter 23 that discusses government policy applying to foreign exchange rates, and Chapter 24 that explores the rules governing international banks and other multinational financial-service providers.

## Teaching an Internationally Focused Course Using This Book

For teachers and others looking for a global view of the financial marketplace *an internationally focused or global finance course* could be put together using the following text parts and chapters:

- Part 1, especially Chapters 3 and 4 on domestic and global information sources and unfolding trends in financial markets across continents.
- Part 2, particularly Chapters 5, 7, and 9 where the determinants of market interest rates, the structure of yield curves, inflation, and futures and options exchanges all over the globe are discussed.
- Part 3, including Chapters 10–13 focusing on the money market with its substantial international component as well as the goals and operations of leading central banks that span Asia, Europe, and the United States.
- Part 4, especially Chapters 14 and 17 on banking, security firms, insurance companies, pension funds, and finance companies and the regulation of financial firms around the globe.
- Part 7, including Chapters 23 and 24 on international transactions, foreign currency prices, and international banking services.

## Teaching a Financial Market Theory Course Using This Book

For those instructors and other users of this book seeking basic *theoretical concepts and research findings* about the financial marketplace the following sections would appear to be on target for such a theory-based course:

- Part 1, especially Chapters 1–3 that explore such concepts as saving, investment, financial asset creation and destruction, intermediation and disintermediation, the efficient markets hypothesis, and the debate over asymmetric market influences within the financial system.

- Part 2, especially Chapters 5, 7, 8, and 9 on conceptual issues surrounding the determinants of interest rates, asset prices, and the risk structure of rates and prices.

- Part 3, especially Chapters 10, 12, and 13 dealing with the theory of money market trading and monetary policy.

- Part 5, especially Chapters 18 and 20 on the theoretical impact of government borrowing on the economy and financial system and on the controversial issue of stock market anomalies.

- Part 7, particularly Chapter 23 that unfolds the theory of exchange rate determination and international currency standards.

Clearly this book offers several different approaches to a study of the money and capital markets. Instructors and other readers can pick and choose the particular direction they wish to take in maximizing the opportunity to learn about the powerful forces that are reshaping the structure and functioning of modern financial systems.

## Learning Tools in the New Tenth Edition

*Money and Capital Markets: Financial Institutions and Instruments in a Global Marketplace* in this new edition contains several important learning tools for its readers. Specifically:

- Each chapter opens with a list of its *learning objectives*—a few brief sentences that let the reader know what he or she is about to explore and understand in the chapter that follows.

- Placed alongside the learning objectives on the opening page of each chapter is a box labeled *What's in This Chapter? Key Topics Outline,* alerting the reader about the most important subjects he or she will encounter in the chapter.

- Following the initial listing of learning objectives and key topics the text material in each chapter is divided up into *numbered sections,* each accompanied by a descriptive title of the topics discussed therein. This feature permits instructors to easily designate which numbered sections they want their classes to read and which parts should be omitted or postponed.

- Every chapter contains *key terms* that appear in bold in the text and also appear in the left-hand margin, also in bold, near the point where first discussed. Finally, due to their importance to the book and its readers these same key terms are listed near each chapter's end in a section entitled *Key Terms Appearing in This Chapter,* together with the page numbers where they first emerge in text discussion.

- To give readers one last crack at the key terms, there is a *Money and Capital Markets Dictionary* at the back of the book, where each term is briefly defined and the chapter(s) where it appears cited.

- *Exhibits, graphs, and examples* appear throughout in an effort to reinforce key points and principles and help the reader remember the central ideas the book works hard to develop and communicate.

- Numerous *information boxes* appear in nearly all chapters. These boxes are titled *Financial Developments, Ethics in the Money and Capital Markets,* and *E-Commerce in the Financial Marketplace.* Boxes focusing on ethical issues deal with several of the most notorious scandals recently affecting financial-services businesses. E-Commerce sections concentrate on the rapidly growing role of electronic equipment and electronic networks that store and convey financial information and direct flows of funds between buyers and sellers of financial services.

- Web sites appear in the text margins along the left side of many chapter pages, labeled *Key URLs,* and placed parallel to the text's discussion of financial-service issues and institutions. These URLs offer readers clues as to where to look in the Web's domain for additional information on important topics presented within each chapter.

- At selected key points within each chapter the text pauses to assess whether the reader is learning what each chapter presents through boxes marked *Questions to Help You Study.* The reader is encouraged to reread any section where he or she has difficulty in answering the study questions posed.

- At the conclusion of each chapter appears an important section entitled *Summary of the Chapter's Main Points* in which the central ideas and concepts are restated in bullet-point format. These summary points aid readers in quickly determining if they missed any key ideas while exploring a chapter, offering a useful review for exams and giving instructors an outline for the preparation of lecture material.

- Following the summary, readers will find two sections labeled *Problems and Issues* and *Web-Based Problems.* These particular sections carry over many of the best problems from earlier editions as well as numerous new problems constructed specially for this tenth edition. Web-based problems typically contain multiple parts and often guide the reader into multiple areas on the World Wide Web.

- At the ultimate conclusion of every chapter are *Selected References to Explore* which contain several of the most up-to-date articles and research studies bearing on selected chapter topics. These sources provide excellent material for research projects and term papers, giving readers an excellent opportunity to expand their knowledge beyond what is already contained in each chapter of this new edition.

## Supplements to Maximize Your Learning Experience with This Text

Supplementary learning tools help improve the effectiveness and efficiency of *Money and Capital Markets* as a channel through which to understand how the financial marketplace operates and how it is put together, The supplements help to make both students' and instructors' experience with this text more enjoyable and rewarding.

These important supplements include:

### Instructor's Manual and Test Bank

The Instructor's Manual is one of the most effective and sought-after tools for teachers, providing an outline of each chapter and supplying hundreds of questions and problems useful for class presentation, class discussion, or the construction of exams.

### Text Web Site (www.mhhe.com/rose10e08)

The text Web site provides problems, questions, and solutions for instructors and, indeed, for all those who read this book. An *Updates* section on the Web site attempts to track new developments since publication of the previous edition.

**Power Point Presentations**

This supplementary tool provides a collection of slides for each chapter, suitable for class lectures, giving explanations of key ideas, usually in outline form for display on a screen. The slides encompass numerous graphs, charts, examples, and bullet-point outlines. Teachers and other users can easily edit or rearrange each slide to satisfy the needs of each reader and each class.

## New and Expanded Discussions of Issues in the Financial Marketplace and Emerging Concepts in the Tenth Edition of *Money and Capital Markets*

A large number of new issues as well as expanded discussions of continuing controversies and concepts are included in this new edition of *Money and Capital Markets.* Examples include:

- The rapid rise of *China* as a global force in trade and finance and the struggle to remedy weaknesses in the Chinese economy and financial system, including more effective regulatory controls over China's financial institutions. (See in particular, Chapters 23 and 24.)

- The continuing growth of the *European Union* and its newest members from Eastern Europe and around the Mediterranean region, offering a strong competitive challenge to the economies and financial systems of Asia and United States. (See especially Chapters 23 and 24.)

- The growing use of *interest-only* and other types of *option mortgages* that pose new opportunities for would-be home buyers and mortgage banks, but also present more daunting risks to both lenders and borrowers as interest rates and loan default records surge. (See, in particular, Chapter 22.)

- The nature and role of *behavioral finance research* in designing, testing, and sometimes challenging financial theory and concepts. (See especially Chapter 3.)

- The *declining U.S. household savings rate* and the possible reasons the United States has such a low personal-savings-to-income ratio, potentially decreasing future investment activity and productivity that might otherwise increase American living standards in the long run. (See, in particular, Chapters 1 and 21.)

- The *decline of checks and other paper-based means of payment* for purchases of goods and services, increasingly replaced with credit and debit cards, cell phones, direct deposits, point-of-sale terminals, radio-frequency noncontact payments devices, and Web-based payments channels, especially in Europe, the United States, and Asia. (See especially Chapters 1, 2, 14, 15, 18, and 21.)

- The exploration of *new housing futures and options contracts* designed to protect housing values and stimulate the growth of residential construction. (See in particular, Chapter 22.)

- Expanded discussion of *domestic and foreign stock indexes* and the differences in their composition, behavior, and interpretation. (See especially Chapters 3 and 20.)

- Recent discussion surrounding the drafting and eventual passage of the *FDIC Reform and Deficit Reduction Act of 2005* has raised public awareness of the controversy over indexing deposit insurance coverage to inflation and increasing overall insurance coverage for each deposit account (including qualified retirement accounts whose insurance protection was increased from $100,000 to $250,000 in 2006). (See in particular, Chapters 4, 14, and 17.)

- An exploration of the *history of financial panics around the globe,* including problems in the early Roman financial system and historic European financial schemes and their implications for today's market for financial information. (See especially Chapter 3.)

- The *differences between market-dominated and bank-dominated financial systems* and why that distinction can be important today. (See, in particular, Chapter 2.)

- The new tougher banking regulations beginning in 2007 that are designed to provide *greater protection for customer privacy through more stringent authentication procedures for customers seeking access to their financial accounts.* (See, especially, Chapters 14, 17, and 21.)

- A new discourse on the reasons behind recent *historically low long-term interest rates* and how the Federal Reserve views and deals with this "conundrum" concerning the relative behavior of long- and short-term interest rates. (See in particular, Chapter 7.)

- New numerical examples explaining *how security dealers can ride the yield curve.* (See especially Chapter 7.)

- Updates on the *cross-border consolidation of international security exchanges* and recent *technological advances in the price discovery process.* (See in particular, Chapters 9 and 20.)

- Expanded and more complete explanation of *convexity* and numerical examples on how to measure and interpret the convexity concept. (See, in particular, Chapter 7.)

- Expanded discussion of the *characteristics and impact of credit-rating agencies (CRAs),* including the Securities and Exchange Commission's recent regulation of their activities. (See especially Chapter 8.)

- An expanded discussion of controversial *cash-balance pension plans* and the new Pension Protection Act of 2006 which demands stronger and more complete funding of future pension claims and promotes improved employee retirement education programs. (See in particular, Chapters 16 and 17.)

- New presentation on the ethical issues surrounding the practice of *backdating stock options* to enhance corporate managerial compensation. (See especially Chapters 3 and 20.)

- Expanded discussion of *hedge funds,* their growth, recent challenges they present to regulators, and occasional hedge fund failures. (See, in particular, Chapters 16 and 17.)

- Added material on the *history of savings and loans and savings banks.* (See especially Chapter 15.)

- A new exposition covering *loan risk and loan-loss allowances* in the banking community. (See, in particular, Chapter 14.)

- An expanded overview of *economies of scale in the credit union industry*—the results of recent research. (See especially Chapter 15.)

- Exploration of the nature and changing roles of *financial holding companies (FHCs)* in the United States. (See, in particular, Chapter 14.)

- Expanded discussion of the problems and the rapid growth of the *Pension Benefit Guarantee Corporation* (PBGC), known as *Penny Benny* or the federal pension insurance fund, and the issues raised by recent Congressional action to strengthen PBGC. (See especially Chapters 16 and 17.)

- Opening of a new presentation on *government-sponsored enterprises* (GSEs), their programs, problems, and recent regulatory issues. (See, in particular, Chapters 16, 17, and 22.)

- Expanded discussion of *Basel II*—the current worldwide standard for determining the volume of required bank capital—and its implications for the future growth and profitability of small banks versus large banks around the globe. (See especially Chapter 17.)

- Greater exploration of the *Treasury auction process,* the when-issued market, and U.S. Treasury marketing techniques. (See, in particular, Chapter 18.)

- New material on the differences between "*on-the-run*" and "*off-the-run*" *Treasury securities* and their importance to investors. (See especially Chapters 6 and 18.)

- Expanded discussion of *the role of U.S. Treasury securities as global benchmarks for loans and fixed-income securities worldwide.* (See, in particular, Chapters 18 and 22.)

- Exploration of the provisions and probable impact of the *2005 Bankruptcy Abuse Prevention and Consumer Protection Act*—the most comprehensive set of revisions in the U.S. bankruptcy code in more than a generation, limiting consumers' access to more lenient parts of the bankruptcy code and raising the average cost of bankruptcy relief. (See especially Chapter 21.)

- An expanded presentation on the *federal mortgage agencies,* their performance problems and changing roles in the residential mortgage market. (See, in particular, Chapter 22.)

- Greater analysis and a clearer explanation of the *wealth effect* and its probable impact on household consumption spending and savings behavior. (See especially Chapter 5.)

- Major revisions in the presentation of the *unbiased expectations theory of the yield curve* along with new numerical yield-curve problems to unravel. (See, in particular, Chapter 7.)

Many more fascinating and important topics are also new to this edition, but the above list gives you some idea concerning the scope of concepts, ideas, and financial behavior in the tenth edition of *Money and Capital Markets: Financial Institutions and Instruments in a Global Marketplace.*

## Thanks to the Numerous Professionals Who Have Worked to Make This Text Better over the Years

The authors want to express their profound gratitude to the many teachers, researchers, and other professionals in the financial markets field who have criticized and offered suggestions in an effort to strengthen this book. Indeed, there have been so many professional comments and contributions as the book has passed through its ten editions that the authors are especially concerned they may have misplaced or forgotten the identities of some of those who have made significant contributions to the quality and breadth of this book. We hope our readers will understand in case we have omitted the names of one or more deserving professionals in the financial field and promise to make corrections as we become aware of those deserving individuals accidentally left off our list of important contributors.

Among the leading contributors to this book include James C. Baker of Kent State University; Ivan T. Call of Brigham Young University; Eugene F. Drzycimski of the University of Wisconsin System; Mona J. Gardner of Illinois Wesleyan University; David Mills of Illinois State University; Richard Rivard of the University of South Florida; Paul Bolster, Colleen C. Pantalone, and Rick Swasey of Northeastern University; John O. Olienyk of Colorado State University; Robert M. Crowe formerly of the American College at Bryn Mawr; Joseph P. Ogden of SUNY-Buffalo; Donald A. Smith of Pierce College; Oliver G. Wood, Jr., and Timothy Koch of the University of South Carolina; Larry Lang of the University of Wisconsin—Oshkosh; Jeffrey A. Clark of Florida State University; James F. Gatti of the University of Vermont; Gloria P. Bales of Hofstra University; Ahmed Sohrabian of California State Polytechnic University at Pomona; Thomas A. Fetherston of the University of Alabama at Birmingham; Mary Piotrowski of Northern Arizona University; Owen K. Gregory of the University of Illinois at Chicago; Thomas Dziadosz of The American College; Tom Potter of the University of North Dakota; Lester Hadsell of the State University of New York, Albany; John Hysom of George Mason University; Frank Ohara of the University of San Francisco; Robert Sweitzer of the University of Delaware; Donald J. Smith and Jack Aber of Boston University; Bonnie Buchanan of the University of Georgia; Samuel Bulmash of Stockton College; Krishnan Dandapani of Florida International University; John Halstead of Southern Connecticut State University; Bento Lobo of the University of Tennessee at Chattanooga; Tim Michael of James Madison University; and Walter Perlick of California State University at Sacramento.

The authors would also like to record a special note of gratitude to those professionals in the financial markets field who provided suggestions for this newest (tenth) edition of the text. Specifically we thank:

Bill Curtis, *Hardin-Simmons University*

Shokoofeh Fazel, *Montana State University, Billings*

Jonathan Godbey, *James Madison University*

Charles Guez, *University of Houston*

Steve Henry, *Sam Houston State Unversity*

Shawn Howton, *Villanova University*

John Kallianiotis, *University of Scranton*

Joseph Reising, *Minnesota State University, Mankato*

Luis Rivera, *Dowling College*

Arthur Wilson, *George Washington University*

Fred Wu, *University of South Alabama*

These instructors made countless valuable suggestions as we progressed from the ninth to the tenth edition of *Money and Capital Markets*.

In addition, the authors want to extend their deep appreciation to the professionals at McGraw-Hill/Irwin Publishers, especially Harvey Yep, Dan Wiencek, Michelle Driscoll, Elizabeth Hughes, Katherine Mau, and Executive Editor Michele Janicek. Their guidance and effort throughout the revision and production processes have been invaluable. Literally they made this newest edition possible.

A special acknowledgement of gratitude must be passed along to Joseph Reising at Minnesota State University, Ron Carlson at American Intercontinental University, and Wuttipan Tantivong at Florida State University, who skillfully prepared the PowerPoint Slides, Test Bank, Instructor's Manual, and online quizzes that are essential supplements for this tenth edition.

Moreover, several associations and institutions have contributed to the makeup of this book over the years, including the American Council of Life Insurance, *The Canadian Banker* (published by the Canadian Bankers Association), the Chicago Board of Trade, the Credit Union National Association, the Insurance Information Institute, Moody's Investors Service, and Standard & Poor's Corporation.

Finally, the authors gratefully acknowledge the support and, ultimately, the extreme patience of friends and family who made the preparation and ultimate completion of this latest edition feasible. The shortcomings that still persist are attributable to the authors alone who continue to work at improving this learning tool.

## Note to the Readers of This Textbook in Its Tenth Edition

The money and capital markets and the financial system that surrounds them are an exciting and important area for study. What goes on every day in the financial marketplace has a powerful effect on our lives. Indeed, our ability to function as human beings and as professionals in our chosen fields is shaped in so many different ways by the functioning of the global financial system. Moreover, the money and capital markets are constantly changing. Broad changes are constantly in motion, leading to the rise of new financial institutions, new financial methods, new problems to solve, and new financial services.

The rapidity of change that characterizes our financial system today gives us no choice but to work vigilantly to keep up with our unfolding financial world. Reading this book will get you started, but it cannot be the end of the road. A great American poet, Robert Frost, once declared that we "cannot stop here" for we have "promises to keep" and "miles to go before we sleep." For the sake of your own future success, personally and professionally, plan to enjoy what you discover in the pages that follow, but view this book as only the *first step* in what must be a lifetime journey of learning about the financial system and its effects on our everyday existence.

As you tackle each new chapter and section of *Money and Capital Markets: Financial Institutions and Instruments in a Global Marketplace* set your sights on true *mastery* of the subject. Make the most of the time you spend with this text. Plan for success and hit your target with determination and well-organized study techniques. How can you do this? How can you learn what you need to know in today's complex financial world?

First, begin with the *Learning Objectives* and the *Key Topics Outline* that open each chapter. These are road signs, alerting you to the key questions and issues that each chapter will address. They tell you what you should *expect to learn* in the pages that follow. It is a useful idea to review the list of Learning Objectives and the Key Topics Outline as you sit down to tackle each new chapter and then to revisit them when you are finished reading.

Have you touched base with each learning objective and each key topic as you explore the material? If you are not sure about one or more of them, please go back and review the relevant portions of the chapter that apply to that particular topic or objective. Ask yourself if the learning objective or key topic you are focusing upon makes sense to you and if you now feel better informed about it.

Next, examine the list of *Key Terms* at the close of each chapter. There are page numbers telling you where each key term is defined and discussed. Return to the pages where any key terms appear that still seem a mystery to you. We suggest that you make a list of these key terms in your PC or notebook and accumulate them as the assigned chapters and sections roll by. This is much more than an act of memorizing terms. Rather, this is reaching out to learn the "language" of the financial marketplace.

Your aim is to make the "lingo" of the money and capital markets second nature to you so, for everything you subsequently read and hear about the financial system, you will understand and be able to make that new information work for you. You may even want to write out or type into your PC a definition of each key term and then double-check that definition or explanation against the meaning that appears in the *Money and Capital Markets Dictionary* at the end of this book.

Every chapter contains *Questions to Help You Study*. These study questions encourage you to pause briefly after reading several pages and ask yourself: Do I really understand what I just read? Please try to answer each of these study questions, either verbally or by writing out a brief answer in your PC and then double-checking the accuracy of your answers by referring back to the relevant portion of the chapter. You may wish to store the answers you develop for future reference, especially as you approach the time for an exam.

In each chapter of this new tenth edition several useful Web sites appear in the left-hand margins, labeled *Key URLs*. These Web sites offer you the opportunity to go beyond what the textual material gives you to the far more detailed world of the World Wide Web. Check out these sites and learn as much as possible about the subject matter of the chapter from a different perspective—from the point of view of the authors of each suggested Web site. Thus, by reading both the text and the material in many of the associated Web sites, you are following one of the most famous ideas about how we learn—that *repetition is the key to learning.*

At the end of each chapter there are two sets of problems to unravel—one set titled *Problems and Issues*—exercises that are relatively short in most cases and frequently call for calculating numerical answers—and a second set marked *Web-Based Problems,* which are generally longer, multipart problems that ask you to explore the World Wide Web, gather new information, and come to some conclusions. These two problem sets will add another important dimension to your learning experience. Finance is about problem solving and the better and more accomplished you become at this skill, the greater your chances for success in this field. As you work through each problem consider saving the solution and the conclusions you reach for future reference, either in your PC or in some other convenient file.

On the last page of every chapter is a section entitled *Selected References to Explore.* This section supplies up-to-date reference materials in the form of publicly accessible articles and research studies that explore some of the issues raised in each chapter. Many of the articles listed are printed on the World Wide Web at sites maintained by a publishing house or publishing agency. These readings frequently provide greater depth than is available in this book on a given topic and present a different viewpoint on what you have been studying. The *Selected References* represent an excellent way to help you achieve mastery over your subject area.

Finance in general and the money and capital markets in particular are moderately difficult disciplines to master. Yet, finance does have its challenges. Therefore, *group study sessions* are often helpful in tackling its hardest issues and problems. See if you can form a study group that periodically meets and goes over some of the more difficult concepts and problems. Resolve to be a contributor to these sessions and take the lead in explaining and helping others. *Teaching others* is one of the best ways to learn a new subject for yourself.

Remember that this text has two fundamental purposes: (1) to give you an arsenal of *analytical tools* that you can apply to any financial problem so as to make better financial decisions; and (2) to make you feel more comfortable with the *language of the financial marketplace* so you can speak this language with comfort and maximum understanding. A truly successful course of study will develop *both* the tools and the language of the financial system and get you started along the road to mastery and personal success.

This course can be a foundation stone for many promising future careers. Perhaps you have considered becoming a financial manager or CFO of a large corporation; the head of the financial division of an important unit of government; a member of the legislature or of Congress where financial issues are nearly always among the main topics of discussion; a trader (dealer or broker) in securities or derivative contracts; a consultant or adviser to those who wish to enter the global financial marketplace; or an active investor in your own right, striving to build up your own personal wealth and to prepare for a rewarding lifestyle. Wherever your career path leads you, superior knowledge and understanding of the financial marketplace will be an essential companion on your journey.

However, as you probably already know from prior experience with other challenging fields of study, mastering the money and capital markets and the financial system that surrounds them will *not* be easy. In the words of Robert Frost, your future success in keeping the "promises" you have made and traveling successfully the many "miles to go" before you reach your goals will depend crucially upon the energy and enthusiasm, the commitment to excellence, and the hard work that you bring to this subject. By any measure it is a challenge worthy of your best efforts. Good luck and good fortune on your journey!

*Peter S. Rose*

*Professor Emeritus of Finance*

*Texas A&M University*

*September 2007*

*Milton H. Marquis*

*Professor of Economics and Finance*

*Florida State University*

# Brief Contents

# Contents

PART 2

Interest Rates and the Prices of Financial Assets  117

# Part 1

# The Global Financial System in Perspective

Try to imagine living in a world in which there are no financial institutions, no financial markets, and no financial assets. In such a world, there would be no opportunity to borrow against future income in order to purchase a home or an automobile, or to finance an education. Nor would you be able to save some of your current income (and, thereby, accumulate wealth over time) to handle the future expenses of a growing family or retirement. Businesses could not come up with the resources needed to produce the goods and services you like to consume. There would be no way to acquire insurance against sickness and death. Even the simple act of buying food would become extremely difficult, requiring you to barter simply to survive.

The financial system has emerged to fill these and many other critical needs that require some separation in time between the use of resources (such as capital and labor), the production of goods and services, and the actual consumption of those goods and services desired. Financial markets and institutions deal with these issues and provide for the smooth functioning of modern economies, enabling resources to find their way to their most highly valued use. In so doing, the financial system dramatically enhances the efficiency of the economy and raises our standard of living.

In order to set the stage for our study of the global financial system, Part 1 of *Money and Capital Markets* takes up essential topics—the linkage between financial and nonfinancial markets, the mechanism by which financial assets are created, valued, and traded, and the critical importance of public and private information in determining the value of a financial asset. Finally, any study of the financial system would be hopelessly ill-informed if it were not conducted against the backdrop of the fast-paced, ever-changing world of finance. Spurred on by technology and the creativity of those working in the financial marketplace, the financial system has rapidly evolved to better perform its traditional roles and meet new challenges. This rapid pace of financial innovation is unlikely to slow in the future, requiring all of us to learn how to adapt to a dynamic and changing financial marketplace.

# Chapter 1

# Functions and Roles of the Financial System in the Global Economy

## Learning Objectives

in This Chapter

- You will understand the functions performed and the roles played by the system of financial markets and financial institutions in the global economy and in our daily lives.

- You will discover how important the money and capital markets and the whole financial system are to increasing our standard of living, generating new jobs, and building our savings to meet tomorrow's financial needs.

## What's in This Chapter?
## Key Topics Outline

How the Financial System Interfaces with the Economy

The Importance of Savings and Investment

The Nature of Financial Claims and Money and Capital Markets

Functions of the Money and Capital Markets: Savings, Wealth, Liquidity, Credit, Payments, Risk Protection, and Pursuing Public Policy

Types of Financial Markets within the Global Financial System

Factors Tying All Financial Markets Together

The Dynamic Financial System: Key Emerging Trends

## 1.1   Introduction to the Financial System

**financial system**

This book is devoted to the study of the **financial system**—the collection of markets, institutions, laws, regulations, and techniques through which bonds, stocks, and other securities are traded, interest rates are determined, and financial services are produced and delivered around the world. The financial system is one of the most important creations of modern society. *Its primary task is to move scarce loanable funds from those who save to those who borrow to buy goods and services and to make investments in new equipment and facilities so that the global economy can grow and increase the standard of living enjoyed by its citizens.* Without the global financial system and the loanable funds it supplies, each of us would lead a much less enjoyable existence.

The financial system determines both the cost and the quantity of funds available in the economy to pay for the thousands of goods and services we purchase daily. Equally important, what happens in this system has a powerful impact upon the health of the global economy. When funds become more costly and less available, spending for goods and services falls. As a result, unemployment rises and the economy's growth slows as businesses cut back production and lay off workers. In contrast, when the cost of funds declines and loanable funds become more readily available, spending in the economy often increases, more jobs are created, and the economy's growth accelerates. In truth, the global financial system is an integral part of the global economic system. We cannot understand one of these systems without understanding the other.

## 1.2   The Global Economy and the Financial System

### *Flows within the Global Economic System*

To better understand the role played by the financial system in our daily lives, we begin by examining its position within the global economy.

The basic function of the global economic system is to allocate scarce resources— land, labor, management skill, and capital—to their most highly valued use, producing the goods and services needed by society. The high standard of living most of us enjoy today depends on the ability of the global economy to turn out each day an enormous volume of food, shelter, and other essentials of modern living. This is an exceedingly complex task because scarce resources must be procured in just the right amounts to provide the raw materials of production and combined at just the right time with labor, management, and capital to generate the products and services demanded by consumers. In short, any economic system must combine inputs—land and other natural resources, labor and management skill, and capital equipment—to produce output—goods and services. The global economy generates a flow of production in return for a flow of payments.

**Key URLs:**
If you are interested in following the financial system on a daily basis, consider following such sites as **money.cnn.com/ markets**; **ftbusiness.com**; and **money.aol.com/**

We can depict the flows of payments and production within the global economic system as a *circular flow* between producing units (mainly businesses and governments) and consuming units (principally households). (See Exhibit 1.1.) In the modern economy, households provide labor, management skill, and natural resources to business firms and governments in return for income in the form of wages, salaries, and other payments. Most of the national income that is generated by the economy— which averaged more than $11.6 trillion in 2006—is spent on consumption of goods and services. The remainder—nearly $2 trillion of the $11.6 trillion—is saved. The

EXHIBIT 1.1

Circular Flow
of Income,
Payments, and
Production in the
Global Economic
System

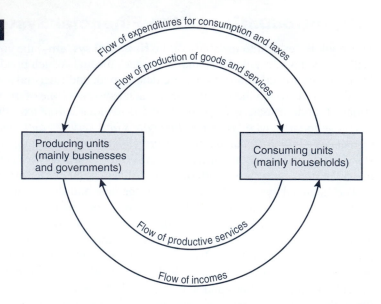

result of this spending is a flow of funds back to the producing units as income, which stimulates them to produce more goods and services by modernizing and expanding their production facilities. The circular flow of production and income is interdependent and never ending.

## The Role of Markets in the Global Economic System

Most economies around the world rely principally upon *markets* to carry out this complex task of allocating scarce resources, making possible the production and sale of goods and services that are in demand by businesses and households. What is a **market**? It is an institution through which buyers and sellers meet to exchange goods, services, and productive resources. This exchange determines what goods and services will be produced and in what quantity.

market

The marketplace is *dynamic*. It must respond continuously not only to changes in consumers' tastes, but also to the introduction of new goods and services, often associated with new technology. Today, cell phones and DVDs are part of our everyday lives, yet they barely existed a few years ago. How did the resources of the economy get redeployed to produce those new goods?

This shift in production was accomplished in the marketplace through changes in the *prices* of goods and services being offered. If the price of an item rises, for example, this stimulates business firms to produce and supply more of it to consumers. In the long run, new firms may enter the market to produce those goods and services experiencing increased demand and rising prices. A decline in price, on the other hand, usually leads to reduced production of a good or service, and in the long run some less-efficient suppliers may leave the marketplace.

Markets also distribute *income*. In a pure market system, the income of an individual or a business firm is determined solely by the contribution each makes to producing goods and services demanded by the marketplace. Markets reward superior productivity and sensitivity to consumer demands with increased profits, higher wages, and other economic benefits. Of course, in all economies, government policies also affect the distribution of income and the allocation of other economic benefits.

## Types of Markets

There are essentially three *types of markets* at work within the global economic system: (1) factor markets, (2) product markets, and (3) financial markets (see Exhibit 1.2). In factor markets, consuming units sell their labor and other resources to those producing units offering the highest prices. The *factor markets* allocate factors of production—land, labor, managerial skills, and capital—and distribute income—wages, salaries, rental payments, and so on—to the owners of productive resources.

Consuming units use most of their income from factor markets to purchase goods and services in *product markets*. Food, shelter, automobiles, theater tickets, and clothing are among the many goods and services sold in product markets.

## The Financial Markets and the Financial System: Channel for Savings and Investment

Of course, households' consumption of goods and services seldom matches their factor income. In most years a portion of after-tax income received by households is earmarked for *personal savings*. However, households will sometimes have zero or even negative savings, in which case they must have either sold off some of their assets and/or gone into debt to maintain their standard of living. For example, personal savings for 2006 averaged a *negative* $102 billion. Historically, this negative figure for personal savings is very unusual and would be a major impediment to the economy's ability to invest in updating and expanding its production facilities to support continued economic growth *if* households were the only source of savings in the economy. Fortunately, this is not the case. Businesses are also a major source of savings. For example, in 2006 U.S. corporations earned slightly more than $1.3 trillion on an annualized basis, of which about half (about $700 billion) was set aside (undistributed) for possible future needs as *business savings*.

**EXHIBIT 1.2**    **Three Types of Markets in the Global Economic System**

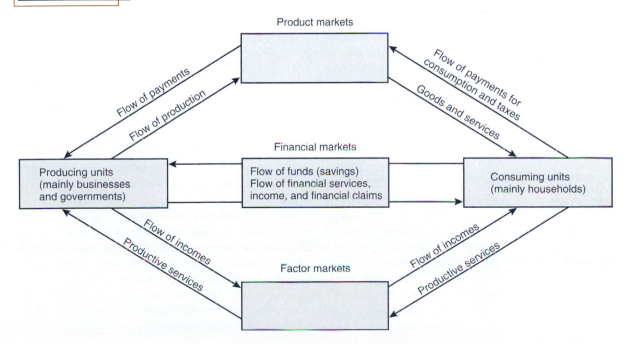

**financial market**

It is here that the third kind of market, the **financial market**, performs a vital function within the global economic system. The financial markets channel savings to those individuals and institutions needing more funds for spending than are provided by their current incomes. The financial markets are the heart of the global financial system, attracting and allocating savings and setting interest rates and the prices of financial assets (stocks, bonds, etc.).

**savings**

*Nature of Savings*     The definition of **savings** differs depending on what type of unit in the economy is doing the saving. For households, savings are what is left from current income after current consumption expenditures and tax payments are made. In the business sector, savings include current earnings retained inside business firms after payment of taxes, stockholder dividends, and other cash expenses. Government savings arise when there is a surplus of current revenues over current expenditures in a government's budget.

**investment**

*Nature of Investment*     Most of the funds set aside as savings flow through the global financial markets to support **investment** by business firms, governments, and households. Investment generally refers to the acquisition of capital goods, such as buildings and equipment, and the purchase of inventories of raw materials and goods to sell. The makeup of investment varies with the particular unit doing the investing. For a business firm, expenditures on *capital goods* (fixed assets, such as buildings and equipment) and *inventories* (consisting of raw materials and goods offered for sale) are investment expenditures. In contrast to businesses, for *households,* current accounting procedures in the United States stipulate that only the purchase of a home may be counted as an *investment.* All other household expenditures on durable goods (such as autos and furniture), as well as expenditures on nondurable goods (for example, food and fuel) and services (such as having your hair styled) are lumped together as *consumption spending* (i.e., expenditures on current account), rather than investment spending. Government spending to build and maintain public facilities (such as buildings, monuments, and highways) is another form of investment.

**Key URL:**
To learn more about savings and investment see Bankrate.com at **bankrate.com/brm**

Modern economies require enormous amounts of investment to produce the goods and services demanded by consumers. Investment increases the productivity of labor and leads to a higher standard of living. However, investment often requires huge amounts of funds, far beyond the resources available to a single individual or institution. By selling financial claims (such as stocks and bonds) in the financial markets, large amounts of funds can be raised quickly from the pool of savings accumulated by households, businesses, and governments. The unit carrying out the investment then hopes to repay its loans from the financial marketplace by generating future income. Indeed, the money and capital markets make possible the *exchange of current income for future income* and the *transformation of savings into investment* so that production, employment, and income can grow, and living standards can improve.

**Key URLs:**
Information about savings and investment options in the money and capital markets may be found in such popular Web sites as **businessweek.com;** **forbes.com;** **fortune.com;** **moneyline.com;** **kiplinger.com;** and **smartmoney.com**

Those who supply funds to the financial markets receive only *promises* in return for the loan of their money. These promises are packaged in the form of attractive financial claims and financial services, such as stocks, bonds, deposits, and insurance policies (see Exhibit 1.3). *Financial claims* promise the supplier of funds a future flow of income in the form of dividends, interest, or other returns. But there is no guarantee that the expected income will ever materialize. However, suppliers of funds to the financial system expect not only to recover their original funds but also to earn additional income as a reward for waiting and for assuming risk.

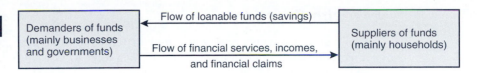

The role of the financial markets in channeling savings into investment is absolutely essential to the health of the economy. Indeed, countries with better-developed financial systems tend to grow faster. However, if households set aside savings and those funds are not returned to the spending stream through investment by businesses and governments, the economy will begin to contract. The amount of income paid out by business firms and governments will *not* be matched by funds paid back to those same sectors by households. As a result, income payments will decline, leading, in turn, to reduced consumption spending. The public's standard of living will fall. Moreover, with less spending, the need for labor will be curtailed, resulting in fewer jobs and rising unemployment.

---

### QUESTIONS TO HELP YOU STUDY

1. Why is it important for us to understand how the global financial system works?
2. What are the principal links between the financial system and the economy? Why is each important to the other?
3. What are the principal functions or roles of the global financial system? How do the money and capital markets fulfill those roles or functions?
4. What exactly is *savings? Investment?* Are these terms often misused by people on the street? Why do you think this happens?
5. How and why are savings and investment important determinants of economic growth? Do they impact our standard of living? How?

---

## 1.3 Economic Functions Performed by the Global Financial System and the Financial Markets

The great importance of the financial system in our daily lives can be illustrated by reviewing the different functions that it performs. The global financial system has *seven* basic economic functions that create a need for the money and capital markets.

### Savings Function

The global system of financial markets and institutions provides a *conduit for the public's savings.* Bonds, stocks, and other financial claims sold in the money and capital markets provide a profitable, relatively low-risk outlet for the public's savings. By acquiring these financial assets, households may choose to forego consumption today in order to increase their consumption opportunities in the future. In the process, this flow of savings through the financial markets into investment allows the economy to increase production while raising productivity, thereby increasing the world's standard of living. In contrast, when savings decline, investment and living standards begin to fall in those nations where savings are in short supply.

## *Wealth Function*

While current savings represent a *flow* of funds, accumulated savings built up over time represent a *stock* of assets that we often refer to as *wealth*. For those businesses and individuals choosing to save, the financial instruments sold in the money and capital markets provide an excellent way to *store wealth* (i.e., preserve the value of assets we hold) until funds are needed for spending. Although we might choose to store our wealth in "things" (e.g., automobiles), such items are subject to depreciation and often carry great risk of loss. However, bonds, stocks, and other financial instruments do *not* wear out over time and usually generate income; moreover, their risk of loss often is much less than for many other forms of stored wealth.

**wealth**

Incidentally, what specifically is **wealth**? For any individual, business firm, or government, wealth is the sum of the values of all assets we hold at any point in time. Thus, our wealth at the moment equals the combined value of the automobiles, homes, clothing, and hundreds or thousands of other assets we have managed to accumulate and hold up to the present day.

Our wealth is built up over time (unless we make bad decisions and squander it away!) by a combination of current savings plus income earned from all our previously accumulated wealth. The increase (or decrease) in the total wealth we own in the current time period equals our current savings plus the value of all previously accumulated wealth multiplied by the average rate of return on all previously accumulated wealth. For example, suppose our wealth (accumulated assets) at the end of the previous period was $1,000. In the current time period we manage to save an additional $50 and also earn an average rate of return on our previously accumulated wealth of 10 percent or $100 (that is, $1,000 × 0.10). Then our wealth will increase from $1,000 in the previous period to $1,150 in the current period (that is, $1,000 + $50 + $100).

**financial wealth**

The portion of wealth held by society in the form of stocks, bonds, and other financial assets—that is, **financial wealth**—is created by the financial system and the money and capital markets within that system. The volume of financial wealth is huge and growing nearly every year. For example, in 2006 nearly $60 trillion in securities, deposits, and other financial assets were held by domestic nonfinancial businesses, households, and governments in the United States, while foreign investors held just over $12 trillion in financial instruments issued inside the United States during the same year. Individuals and families (households) alone held more than $42 trillion in stocks, bonds, and other financial assets.

**net financial wealth**

If we subtract total debts owed by U.S. nonfinancial businesses, households, and governments, which amounted to about $37 trillion in 2006, we obtain what is called **net financial wealth**. The total *net* financial wealth (Financial assets − Debts) held by U.S. individuals and nonfinancial institutions was about $22 trillion in 2006.

Wealth holdings represent *stored purchasing power* that will be used in future periods as income to finance purchases of goods and services and to increase society's standard of living. Therefore, income is generated from the wealth function of the global financial system. Income emerges from the average rate of return that our current wealth holdings (including any marketable skills—*human capital*—we have) generate for us times the amount of our current wealth. For example, if our wealth totals $1,000 at the moment and yields an average rate of return of 10 percent, we can expect our current wealth holdings to generate $100 in income in the current period. In turn, wealth-created income leads to *both* increased consumption spending and to new savings, resulting in a higher standard of living for those who hold wealth in income-generating forms.

## *Liquidity Function*

liquidity

For wealth stored in financial instruments, the global financial marketplace provides a means of converting those instruments into cash with little risk of loss. The world's financial markets provide **liquidity** (immediately spendable cash) for savers who hold financial instruments but are in need of money. In modern societies, *money* consists mainly of currency and spendable deposits held in banks, credit unions, and other depository institutions, amounting to almost $1.4 trillion in the United States in 2006, and is the only financial instrument possessing *perfect liquidity*. Money can be spent as it is without the necessity of converting it into some other form. However, money generally earns the lowest rate of return of all assets traded in the financial system, and its purchasing power is seriously eroded by inflation. That is why savers generally minimize their holdings of money and hold other, higher-yielding financial instruments until they really need spendable funds. Of course, money is not the only means of making purchases of goods and services. In many lesser-developed economies, simple bartering—exchanging one good or service for another—performs many of the same services that money provides in a developed economy.

## *Credit Function*

credit

In addition to providing liquidity and facilitating the flow of savings into investment to build wealth, the global financial markets furnish **credit** to finance current consumption and investment spending by pledging future income, thus reducing spending opportunities in the future. It thus represents the flipside of savings. Credit consists of a loan of funds in return for a promise of future payment. Consumers need credit to purchase a home, buy groceries, repair the family automobile, and retire outstanding debts. Businesses draw on their lines of credit to stock their shelves with inventory, construct new buildings, meet payrolls, and grant dividends to their stockholders. State, local, and federal governments borrow to construct buildings and other public facilities and to cover daily cash expenses until tax revenues flow in.

The volume of credit extended by the money and capital markets today is huge and growing. In the United States alone total credit funds raised in U.S. financial markets in 2006 amounted to more than $3.5 trillion—more than double the amount raised in the money and capital markets only a decade before. Growth of the economy, inflation, and the tax deductibility of some interest payments all appear to have fueled this rapid growth in credit usage by businesses, households, and governments.

## *Payments Function*

The global financial system also provides *a mechanism for making payments for purchases of goods and services.* Certain financial assets—including *currency, noninterest-bearing checking accounts (referred to as demand deposits), and interest-bearing checking accounts (often referred to as negotiable order of withdrawal or NOW accounts)*—still serve as a popular medium of exchange in making payments all over the globe (especially in the United States).

Also high on the payments list and growing rapidly are debit and credit cards issued by banks, credit unions, and retail stores. In the case of *debit cards,* a customer pays immediately for purchases by electronically debiting his or her account in a depository institution. On the other hand, in the case of *credit cards* the customer receives instant access to short-term credit when contracting for purchases of goods and services.

On September 11, 2001, the United States experienced one of the most devastating tragedies in its history when hijackers took control of four commercial airliners and crashed two of the four into the World Trade Center in New York City and one into the Pentagon in Washington, D.C. More than 3,000 people lost their lives.

The assault on the World Trade Center was an attack on a key trading center within the financial system—a place where major dealers in securities, large banks, and other financial-service institutions served clients around the globe. When the trade center collapsed, several financial firms faced severe disruption, losing their communications links and suffering death or serious injury to their employees.

Still the flexibility and resilience of the money and capital markets in adjusting to this terrible tragedy proved to be remarkable. Within a handful of days the New York Stock Exchange was reopened and major security, banking, and insurance firms found new space from which to serve their customers.

Of course, even with the remarkable "bounce back" of the financial system from terror, significant damages to the economy and financial system were felt. Lenders and investors became more concerned about *risk*. Stock prices around the globe fell for a time as investors sold riskier securities and fled into government bonds and insured bank deposits. Insurance companies braced for an unprecedented volume of financial claims related to deaths and destruction. Layoffs of workers rose and business sales fell.

These tragic events remind us of several key points. First, the economy and the financial system are intimately connected to each other—an external shock that affects one affects the other. Second, though a great institution, the money and capital markets are fragile and need the support of governments and the confidence of the public to operate efficiently and perform their essential functions. Third, the financial marketplace is now unquestionably global rather than belonging to a single nation—significant events in any nation, either good or bad, quickly spread around the world and eventually affect all markets.

Also on the rise are *stored-value cards* that many workers now receive on payday instead of a payroll check; *direct deposits* in which funds are transferred electronically from the payor's account to the account of the payee (now representing close to two-thirds of all payments to employees in the United States); *ATM cards* that give the holder access to cash machines and the ability to check account balances and transfer funds to cover any payments due; *contactless payment devices* that communicate purchases and payments through radio frequencies without physical contact; *electronic bill presentment* in which a purchaser is issued a bill online and can make payments online at the purchaser's convenience; and *preauthorized debits,* permitting a customer to authorize automatic funds transfers from his or her account on a specific date each month to pay recurring bills (including payments due on home mortgages, auto loans, and utility bills).

If present trends continue, electronic means of payment, including *computer terminals in homes, offices, and stores* and *digital cash* (accessed by an encoded plastic card) eventually may completely replace checks and other pieces of paper as the principal means of paying in the future. Indeed, electronic means of payment are growing rapidly today (especially in Europe), while checks and other paper-based means of payment are declining in volume.

## Risk Protection Function

The financial markets offer businesses, consumers, and governments *protection against life, health, property, and income risks.* This is accomplished, first of all, by the sale of insurance policies. Policies marketed by life insurance companies indemnify a

**Key URLs:**
For further exploration of the many risks often present in the financial system and markets, see, for example,
**Standardandpoor.com**; **moodys.com**; and **cbot.com**

family against possible loss of income following the death of a loved one. Property-casualty insurers protect their policyholders against an incredibly wide array of personal and property risks, ranging from ill health and storm damage to negligence on the highways. In addition to making possible the sale of insurance policies, the money and capital markets have been used by businesses and consumers to "self-insure" against risk; that is, holdings of wealth are built up as protection against future losses.

The financial system permits individuals and institutions to engage in both *risk sharing* and *risk reduction*. Risk sharing occurs when an individual or institution transfers risk exposure to someone willing to accept that risk (such as an insurance company), while risk reduction usually takes place when we diversify our wealth across a wide variety of different assets so that our overall losses are likely to be more limited.

Overall, the risk protection business is huge. In the United States, for example, life insurance and pension fund reserves to protect individuals and families against loss due to death and old age tallied more than $13 trillion in 2006.

## Policy Function

Finally, in recent decades, the financial markets have been *the principal channel through which government has carried out its policy of attempting to stabilize the economy and avoid inflation.* By manipulating interest rates and the availability of credit, government can affect the borrowing and spending plans of the public, impacting the growth of jobs, production, and prices. As we will see later on, this task of economic stabilization has been given largely to central banks, such as the Federal Reserve System in the United States, the Bank of England, the Bank of Japan, and the new European Central Bank (the ECB).

---

**QUESTIONS TO HELP YOU STUDY**

6. What seven vital *functions* does the financial system of money and capital markets perform?

7. Why is each function of the financial system important to households, businesses, and governments? What kinds of lives would we be living today if there were no financial system or no financial markets?

8. What exactly do we mean by the term *wealth*? Why is it important?

9. What is *net financial wealth*? What does it reveal about each of us?

10. Can you explain what factors determine the current volume of financial wealth and net financial wealth each of us has?

---

## 1.4 Types of Financial Markets within the Global Financial System

The global financial system fulfills its various roles mainly through *markets* where financial claims and financial services are traded (though in some lesser-developed economies government dictation and even barter are used). These markets may be viewed as *channels* through which moves a vast flow of loanable funds that is continually being drawn upon by demanders of funds and continually being replenished by suppliers of funds.

## The Money Market versus the Capital Market

The flow of funds around the world may be divided into different segments, depending on the characteristics of financial claims being traded and the needs of different investors. One of the most important divisions in the financial system is between the *money market* and the *capital market*.

**money market**

The **money market** is designed for the making of short-term loans. It is the institution through which individuals and institutions with *temporary* surpluses of funds meet the needs of borrowers who have *temporary* funds shortages (deficits). Thus, the money market enables economic units to manage their liquidity positions. By convention, a security or loan maturing within one year or less is considered to be a money market instrument. One of the principal functions of the money market is to finance the working capital needs of corporations and to provide governments with short-term funds in lieu of tax collections. The money market also supplies funds for speculative buying of securities and commodities.

**capital market**

In contrast, the **capital market** is designed to finance long-term investments by businesses, governments, and households. Trading of funds in the capital market makes possible the construction of factories, highways, schools, and homes. Financial instruments in the capital market have original maturities of *more than one year* and range in size from small loans to multimillion dollar credits.

Who are the principal suppliers and demanders of funds in the money market and the capital market? In the money market, commercial banks are the most important institutional supplier of funds (lender) to both business firms and governments. Nonfinancial business corporations with temporary cash surpluses also provide substantial short-term funds to the money market. On the demand-for-funds side, the largest borrower in the U.S. money market is the Treasury Department, which borrows billions of dollars weekly. Other governments around the world are often among the leading borrowers in their own domestic money markets. The largest and best-known corporations and securities dealers are also active borrowers in money markets around the world. Due to the large size and strong financial standing of these well-known money market borrowers and lenders, money market instruments are considered to be high-quality, "near money" IOUs.

In contrast, the principal suppliers and demanders of funds in the capital market are more varied than those in the money market. Families and individuals, for example, tap the capital market when they borrow to finance a new home. Governments rely on the capital market for funds to build schools and highways and provide essential services to the public. The most important borrowers in the capital market are businesses of all sizes that issue long-term debt instruments representing claims against their future revenues in order to cover the purchase of equipment and the construction of new facilities. Ranged against these many borrowers in the capital market are financial institutions, such as insurance companies, mutual funds, security dealers, and pension funds, which supply the bulk of capital market funds.

## Divisions of the Money and Capital Markets

The money market and the capital market may be further subdivided into smaller markets, each important to selected groups of demanders and suppliers of funds. Within the money market, for example, is the huge *Treasury bill* market. Treasury bills—short-term IOUs issued by many governments around the world—are a safe and popular investment medium for financial institutions, corporations of all sizes, and wealthy individuals.

The financial system performs the economic functions described in this section by providing financial services to the public. Therefore, it can be viewed as a collection of financial-service firms (FSFs) that produce and sell those financial services most in demand by the public. Among the financial services most widely sought by the public and distributed by the money and capital markets are:

- *Payments services*, providing payments accounts against which the customer can write checks, wire funds, or use encoded cards or cell phones to pay for purchases of goods and services.

- *Thrift services*, providing attractive financial instruments with adequate safety and yield to encourage people, businesses, and governments to save for their future financial needs.

- *Insurance services*, providing protection from loss of income or property in the event of death, disability, negligence, or other adverse developments.

- *Credit services*, providing loanable funds to supplement current income through borrowing in order to sustain current living standards.

- *Hedging services*, providing protection against loss due to unfavorable movements in market prices or interest rates through such devices as futures, options, and other hedging instruments.

- *Agency services*, acting on behalf of a customer in managing retirement funds or other property (as a bank trust department or security dealer might do).

**Key URL:**
An interesting source of information on ongoing trends in financial services and the financial marketplace is *The Economist* from London at
**economist.com**

Somewhat larger in volume is the market for *certificates of deposit* (CDs) issued by banks and other depository institutions to raise funds in order to carry on their lending activities. Two other important money market instruments that arise from large corporations borrowing money are *bankers' acceptances* and *commercial paper*. In another corner of the money market, *federal funds*—the reserve balances of banks plus other immediately transferable monies—are traded daily in huge volume. Another segment of the money market reaches around the globe to encompass suppliers and demanders of short-term funds in Europe, Asia, and the Middle East. This is the vast, largely unregulated *Eurocurrency market,* in which deposits denominated in the world's major trading currencies—for example, the dollar and the euro—are loaned to corporations and governments around the globe.

The capital market, too, is divided into several sectors, each having special characteristics. For example, one of the largest segments of the capital market is devoted to residential and commercial *mortgage loans* to support the building of homes and business structures, such as factories and shopping centers. In the United States, state and local governments sell their *tax-exempt (municipal) bonds* in another sector of the capital market. Households borrow in yet another segment, using *consumer loans* to make purchases ranging from automobiles to home appliances. There is also an international capital market for borrowing by large corporations represented by *Eurobonds* and *Euronotes*.

Probably the best-known segment of the capital market is the market for *corporate stock* represented by the major exchanges, such as the New York Stock Exchange (NYSE) and the Tokyo Exchange, and a vast over-the-counter (OTC) market, including electronic stock trading over the Internet. No matter where it is sold, however, each share of stock (equity) represents a certificate of ownership in a corporation, entitling the holder to receive any dividends paid out of current company earnings and to lay claim to any residual value left in the firm's assets after all its obligations are met. Businesses also sell a huge quantity of *corporate notes* and *bonds* in the capital market each year to raise long-term funds. These securities, unlike shares of stock, are pure IOUs, evidencing a debt owed by the issuing company. Each of these financial instruments will be examined in detail in the chapters that lie ahead.

## Open versus Negotiated Markets

**open markets**

**negotiated markets**

**Key URLs:**
For interesting and often useful information about corporate stocks and bonds, see such sites as **finance.yahoo.com; wsj.com; financenter.com;** and **bloomberg.com**

Another distinction between markets in the global financial system focuses on **open markets** versus **negotiated markets.** For example, some corporate bonds are sold in the open market to the highest bidder and are bought and sold any number of times before they mature and are paid off. In contrast, in the negotiated market for corporate bonds, securities generally are sold to one or a few buyers under private contract.

An individual who goes to his or her local banker to secure a loan for new furniture enters the negotiated market for personal loans. In the market for corporate stocks there are the major stock exchanges, which represent the open market. Operating at the same time, however, is the negotiated market for stock, in which a corporation may sell its entire stock issue to one or a handful of buyers.

## Primary versus Secondary Markets

**primary markets**

**secondary markets**

**Key URLs:**
For further discussion of the importance of savings see **bankrate. com/brm** and **frbsf. org/publications/ economics/letter/2002/ e/2002-09.html**

The global financial markets also may be divided into **primary markets** and **secondary markets.** The primary market is for the trading of *new* securities. Its principal function is raising financial capital to support new investment in buildings, equipment, and inventories. You engage in a primary-market transaction when you purchase shares of stock just issued by a company or borrow money through a new mortgage to purchase a home.

In contrast, the secondary market deals in securities previously issued. Its chief function is to provide *liquidity* to security investors—that is, provide an avenue for converting financial instruments into cash. If you sell shares of stock or bonds you have been holding for some time to a friend or call a broker to place an order for shares currently being traded on the American, London, or Tokyo stock exchanges, you are participating in a secondary-market transaction.

The volume of trading in the secondary market is far larger than in the primary market. However, the secondary market does *not* support new investment. Nevertheless, the primary and secondary markets are closely intertwined. For example, a rise in security prices in the secondary market usually leads to a similar rise in prices on primary-market securities, and vice versa. This happens because many investors readily switch from one market to another in response to differences in price or yield.

## Spot versus Futures, Forward, and Option Markets

We may also distinguish between *spot markets, futures* or *forward markets,* and *option markets.* A spot market is one in which assets are traded for immediate delivery (usually within one or two business days). If you pick up the telephone and instruct your broker to purchase Telecon Corporation stock at today's price, this is a spot market transaction. You expect to acquire ownership of Telecon shares today.

A *futures* or *forward market,* on the other hand, is designed to trade contracts calling for the *future delivery* of financial instruments. For example, you may call your broker and ask to purchase a contract calling for delivery to you of $1 million in government bonds six months from today. The purpose of such a contract would be to shift risk to some individual or institution willing to bear that risk by agreeing upon a delivery price today rather than waiting six months when government bonds might cost a lot more.

*Saving* is vital to support the growth of *investment* in new capital equipment and new technologies so that economies can grow and increase the standard of living of their citizens. Unfortunately, the United States (along with Australia and New Zealand) posts one of the lowest personal savings rates in the world, with a savings-to-gross-domestic-product ratio well below that of Germany, France, and Japan, for example. In 2005 and 2006 the personal savings rate was *negative* for the first time in U.S. history since the Great Depression of the 1930s, and the percentage of U.S. families saving any funds at all dropped significantly. We should note too that several other nations (including Britain, Italy, Japan, and South Korea), while posting higher savings rates than the United States, are likewise experiencing declining personal savings ratios.

One reason for these lower savings rates may simply be changing public attitudes toward saving itself. Older generations remember the Great Depression when millions of people were out of work. Younger savers, however, are more likely to have experienced extended periods of prosperity and low unemployment and see less need for the protection savings offer. At the same time the values of new homes—the principal asset of most individuals and families—have risen substantially in recent periods, making homeowner households feel wealthier with less pressure to save.

Then, too, the U.S. government's Social Security and Medicare systems promise workers at least a minimal level of retirement income, reducing the apparent need for maximizing personal savings, at least in the minds of many savers. Moreover, when inflation rises, many consumers prefer to buy *now* rather than add to their savings. Further encouraging the "buy now" philosophy have been the comparatively low rewards for saving as nominal interest rates have recently been among the lowest in history.

Unfortunately, the current low U.S. savings rate may come back to haunt Americans in the future. For example, should a relatively low personal savings rate translate into a low investment rate in the economy, then the capacity to produce goods and services would be impaired and the living standards of individuals and families would likely grow more slowly in the future, or even decline.

However, many economists believe our measures of savings fail to adequately capture the *total* volume of savings actually carried out by businesses, households, and governments. For example, the U.S. Department of Commerce derives personal savings of households by deducting personal consumption spending from after-tax disposable income. But this measure of household savings doesn't figure in any market-value appreciation in the public's holdings of securities or in its housing values. Yet, American business and household wealth is rising rapidly in value, indicating that total savings volume in the United States may be more adequate than many realize. Then, too, some economists argue, the U.S. personal savings rate may *rise* in the future as the population *ages* because there will be more Americans concerned about building their savings for retirement. Let's hope they are right!

Finally, *options markets* also offer investors in the money and capital markets an opportunity to reduce risk. These markets make possible the trading of contracts that give an investor the right to either buy designated securities from or sell designated securities to the writer of the option at a guaranteed price at any time during the life of the contract. Options make it possible to lock in prices of assets no matter which way those prices move before the options expire. We will see more clearly how and why such transactions take place when we explore the financial futures and options markets in Chapter 9 and the forward markets for foreign currencies in Chapter 23.

## 1.5  Factors Tying All Financial Markets Together

Each corner of the financial system represents a market segment with its own special characteristics. Each segment is insulated from the others to some degree by investor preferences and by rules and regulations. Yet when interest rates and security prices change in one corner of the financial system, *all* of the financial markets likely will be affected eventually. This implies that, even though the financial system is split up into many different markets, there must be forces at work to tie all the financial markets together.

## Credit, the Common Commodity

One unifying factor is the fact that the basic commodity being traded in most financial markets is *credit*. Borrowers can switch from one credit market to another, seeking the most favorable credit terms wherever they can be found. It is not uncommon, for example, for an oil company to finance the construction of a drilling rig through short-term loans from the money market when interest rates in the capital market are unusually high, but to seek long-term financing of the project later on when capital market conditions are more favorable. The shifting of borrowers between markets helps to weld the parts of the financial system together and to bring credit costs in different markets into balance with one another.

## Speculation and Arbitrage

Another unifying element is profit seeking. *Speculators* are continually on the lookout for opportunities to profit from their forecasts of future market developments. The speculator in the financial marketplace gambles that security prices or interest rates will move in a direction that will result in quick gains due to his or her ability to outguess the market's collective judgment. Speculators perform an important function in the markets by leveling out the prices of assets, buying those they believe are underpriced and selling those thought to be overpriced.

Still another unifying force in the financial markets comes from investors who watch for profitable opportunities to **arbitrage** funds—moving funds from one market to another whenever the prices of assets in different markets appear to be out of line with each other. *Arbitrageurs* often buy assets in markets where assets seem to be undervalued and sell in those markets where assets appear to be overvalued. They help to maintain *consistent prices between markets,* aiding other buyers in finding the best prices with minimal effort.

**arbitrage**

**KEY URL:**
For an overview of the concept of arbitrage, see especially **finpipe. com/derivglossary.htm**

## 1.6  The Dynamic Financial System

There is an old saying: "You cannot step into the same river twice, for rivers are ever flowing onward." That statement can be applied to the global financial system—it is rapidly changing into a *new* financial system powered by *innovation,* as new financial services and instruments continually appear to attract customers. Major trends are under way to convert smaller national financial systems into an integrated global system, at work 24 hours a day to attract savings, extend credit, and fulfill other vital roles. Satellites, computers, and other automated systems now tie together financial-service trading centers as widely dispersed as London, New York, Tokyo, Singapore, and Sydney. This process of integrating financial systems globally has been aided by gradual deregulation of financial institutions and services on the part of leading industrialized nations (such as the United States, Japan, and members of the European Economic Union). Many of these countries have begun to "harmonize" their regulations so that financial-service firms operate under similar rules no matter where they are located. Nonfinancial companies (such as Wal-Mart, GE, and Toyota) are invading the financial-services field in growing numbers, tying the performance of the economy even more closely to the performance of the financial marketplace. The results

Unethical behavior—the violation of a written or unwritten moral code—is nearly everywhere in our world, even in the money and capital markets. A prime example emerged recently among some prominent *mutual funds* that attract money from millions of investors and invest in stocks, bonds, and other assets having income or growth potential. They are among the simplest of businesses, consisting of shareholders and a board of directors and with most of their daily operations—portfolio management, recordkeeping, and the like—handled by outsiders. Sadly, this loose organizational structure can lead to unethical behavior.

Mutual funds have a reputation for being "customer friendly," especially to small investors with limited knowledge of the financial marketplace. Recently, many customers were in shock, not really believing that their fund manager might take part in such questionable games as "front running" (placing an order for stock just ahead of an order for the same shares from a customer, hoping to benefit from a price change) or "after hours trading" (allowing favorite clients to trade *after* the closing bell but at the previously established closing price—a privilege not available to most customers).

In the wake of this kind of behavior, millions of customers suddenly realized that mutual funds are not as heavily scrutinized from stem to stern like banks, life insurers, and other financial intermediaries. Instead, the funds' principal regulators (e.g., the states and the U.S. Securities and Exchange Commission) have limited control and few investigatory resources. Ethics are a powerful moral force, however, and it seems likely that tougher rules will continue to unfold as a result of this recent scandal.

have been increasingly intense competition for customers, the development of many new financial services, and a wave of mergers among financial firms, many of which extend beyond national boundaries. One of the purposes of this book is to help you understand why these global trends are occurring and what they are likely to mean for all of us in the future.

### QUESTIONS TO HELP YOU STUDY

11. Can you distinguish between the following institutions?

    *Money market* versus *capital market*

    *Open market* versus *negotiated market*

    *Primary market* versus *secondary market*

    *Spot market* versus *forward or futures market*

12. If we follow the money and capital markets around the world each day it soon becomes apparent that interest rates and asset prices in different markets tend to move together, albeit with leads and lags. Why do you think this is so?

13. What are some of the forces that appear to tie all the financial markets together and often result in common movements in prices and interest rates across the whole financial system?

14. What is meant by the *dynamic financial system?* What trends appear to be reshaping the system?

## 1.7 The Plan of This Book

This text is divided into seven parts, each devoted to a particular segment of the financial system. Part One provides an overview of the global financial system—its role in the world's economy and basic characteristics. The vital processes of saving and investing and lending and borrowing are described. Part One surveys the principal sources of information available today on the workings of the worldwide financial marketplace and presents an overview of how the financial system is likely to look in the future.

Part Two examines forces that shape interest rates and the prices of financial instruments. Because the rate of interest is the key price in the financial system, this section begins in Chapter 5, with a presentation encompassing a variety of views about how interest rates are determined. Subsequent chapters address such important topics as the measurement of interest rates and financial asset prices, yield curves and duration, and the impact of inflation, the risk of default, and taxes, among other factors, on interest rates and asset prices. Part Two concludes with a review of methods for hedging against interest rate and asset price changes, including swaps, futures, and options.

Part Three draws our attention to the money market—its principal institutions and instruments—and to a government institution that often dominates the tone of the money market—the central bank. Chapters in this section examine the characteristics of Treasury bills, federal funds, repurchase agreements, certificates of deposit, commercial paper, federal agency securities, bankers' acceptances, and Eurocurrency deposits. Part Three also presents a thorough examination of the many roles and functions of a central bank within the financial system, including an in-depth look at the history, organizational structure, and policy tools of the Federal Reserve System as well as the policy tools used by other central banks around the world. Part Three concludes with a review of the goals and targets for implementing central bank monetary policy.

In Part Four, the spotlight turns to private financial institutions—commercial banks, credit unions, savings associations, money market funds, insurance companies, pension funds, mutual funds, investment banks, and other financial-service firms. The reader is presented with an overview of their characteristics, regulation, current problems, and management tools designed to deal with those problems.

Part Five turns to the role of governments (federal, state, and local) and business firms within the global financial system. The opening chapter of this section explores the fiscal and debt management policies of the U.S. government, followed by an overview of state and local government borrowing, spending, and taxation. Then Chapter 19 takes up the topic of business borrowing, including the pricing and marketing of corporate bonds and asset-backed securities. Part Five concludes with an exploration of the many facets of the corporate stock market.

The financial characteristics of consumers—individuals and families—are considered in Part Six. Chapter 21 looks at the types of consumer debt and savings instruments available today and reviews current laws that protect the financial-services consumer. This section closes with an overview of the residential mortgage market—one of the largest of all financial markets. Chapter 22 explores the array of different types of home loans that have appeared in recent years and how this huge market has expanded lately under the umbrella of government support and aggressive private innovation.

Finally, Part Seven focuses upon the international financial system and future trends in global finance. Topics covered include international trade and the balance of payments, the markets for foreign currencies, hedging against currency risk, and international banking.

Throughout this text there is a strong emphasis on the innovative character of modern financial systems and institutions. A veritable explosion of new services and trading techniques has occurred in recent years. Moreover, the pace of innovation in financial services appears to be accelerating under the combined pressure of increased competition and rising costs. As we will see in the pages that follow, the forces of innovation, competition, cost, and other factors are profoundly reshaping the structure and the operations of our whole financial system today.

## Summary of the Chapter's Main Points

The opening chapter of *Money and Capital Markets* presents us with an introduction to the global financial system in which the money and capital markets play central roles. It also highlights the principal institutions that shape the character and functioning of the world's financial marketplace.

- The *financial system* produces and distributes financial services to the public. Among its most important services is a supply of *credit* that allows businesses, households, and governments to invest and acquire assets they need to carry on daily economic activity. The financial system of money and capital markets determines both the amount and cost of credit available. In turn, the supply and cost of credit affect the health and growth of the global economy and our own economic welfare.

- Credit and other financial services are offered for sale in the institution we call a *market*. Markets price and allocate financial and physical resources that are scarce relative to demand.

- Another key role played by markets operating within the financial system is to generate an adequate volume of *savings* (i.e., funds left over after current consumption spending by households and earnings retained by businesses) and to transform those savings into an adequate volume of *investment* (i.e., the purchase of capital goods and the buildup of inventories of goods to sell). In turn, investment generates new products and services and creates new jobs and new businesses, resulting in faster economic growth and a higher standard of living. By determining interest rates within the financial system, the money and capital markets bring the volume of savings generated by the public into balance with the volume of investment in new plant and equipment and in inventories of goods and resources available for sale.

- One important way to view the financial system is by examining its seven key functions or roles in meeting the financial-service needs of individuals and institutions, including generating and allocating savings, stimulating the accumulation of wealth, providing liquidity for spending, providing a mechanism for making payments, supplying credit to aid in the purchase of goods and services, providing risk protection services, and supplying a channel for government policy in helping achieve the nation's economic goals (including maximum employment, low inflation, and sustainable economic growth).

- The markets that serve the financial system may be classified in several different ways, including *money markets,* supplying short-term loans (credit) of less than a year, and *capital markets,* supplying long-term loans (credit) lasting longer than a year. There are also *open markets* where anyone may participate as buyer or seller versus *negotiated markets* where only a few bidders seek

www.mhhe.com.rose10e

to trade assets. There are *primary* versus *secondary* markets; in the former, *new* financial instruments are traded in contrast to the latter where existing instruments are exchanged. Additional types of financial markets that make up the global financial system include markets that deal in the immediate purchase or sale of goods or services, called *spot markets,* and those that promise future delivery, known as *futures, forward,* or *option markets.*

- While many different segments make up the money and capital markets around the globe, all these markets share the common purpose of supplying credit to answer global demands for borrowed funds and all encourage saving to make investment (and, therefore, economic growth) possible. Funds flow easily and, for the most part, smoothly from one segment of the marketplace to another, spurred by such forces as *arbitrage* and *speculation.* For example, *arbitrage* causes credit, savings, and investment to flow toward those market segments that offer the most favorable returns, helping different markets to price resources more consistently and to eliminate price disparities for the same goods and services. Prices are also brought into balance from market to market by the force of *speculation,* which seeks out underpriced and overpriced services and assets.

- The financial system of money and capital markets is rapidly becoming a new financial system due to dynamic trends sweeping through the system. Among the most prominent trends are innovation, improvements in communications technology, deregulation to reduce the burden of government rules, and increasingly intense competition to find and hold new customers.

## Key Terms Appearing in This Chapter

**financial system,** 3

**market,** 4

**financial market,** 6

**savings,** 6

**investment,** 6

**wealth,** 8

**financial wealth,** 8

**net financial wealth,** 8

**liquidity,** 9

**credit,** 9

**money market,** 12

**capital market,** 12

**open markets,** 14

**negotiated markets,** 14

**primary markets,** 14

**secondary markets,** 14

**arbitrage,** 16

## Problems and Issues

1.  *None* of the following statements are correct. In each case, identify the error and correct the statement.

    a. A household's current savings includes its current purchases of corporate stock as well as prior holdings of corporate stock and its current investment includes the equity it currently has in its house.

    b. The change in a household's wealth over a quarter is given by its wealth at the beginning of the quarter plus its savings during the quarter.

c. The ability of a household to borrow money from a bank to purchase a new PC is an example of the payments function of the financial markets, while the ability of the bank to make the loan is an example of the liquidity function.

d. The ability of Treasury bills to retain their value over time is an example of the savings function of the economy, while the ability of a household to sell a Treasury bill on short notice with little risk of loss is an example of the liquidity function.

e. The ability of the Federal Reserve to manipulate interest rates is an example of the policy function of the financial markets, while the ability of households to earn interest on those investments affected by the Fed's decision is an example of the risk-protection function of the financial markets.

**2.** George Wilkins checked the spreadsheet where he keeps track of his assets and liabilities. He discovered that (i) he owes $80,000 on his house, which he believes to be worth $150,000; (ii) his car is worth $20,000, against which there is $2,000 on the remaining bank loan; (iii) his stock portfolio has risen to $50,000; (iv) he has a $10,000 balance in his bank account, which is earning a 1.2 percent annual interest rate; and (v) the value of his other belongings is $45,000. He has just received his monthly paycheck for $6,000 and he is trying to decide about taking a vacation and whether or not to pay off his car loan. His monthly expenses are $3,000 which includes the interest expense on his auto loan. He has two possible vacation choices: the Bahamas for $2,000 or a local beach for $1,000. If he has any money left over at the end of the month, it will go into his bank account. If he doesn't have enough money to cover all of his expenses for the month, he will sell enough of his stock to cover the excess expenses.

a. Use a spreadsheet to input each of George's assets, (i) to (v), in the first column; the value of these assets in the second column; and the liabilities (if any) against those assets in the third column. In the fourth column compute the net asset value of each of the assets. Total the fourth column to determine George's net worth at the beginning of the month.

b. Compute the additional net income that George will have from his paycheck plus the interest on his bank account minus the monthly expenses. Use this information to answer parts (c) through (f) below.

c. Repeat part (a) for the end of the month assuming George does not take a vacation and pays off his auto loan.

d. Repeat part (a) for the end of the month assuming George takes the Bahamas vacation and only pays $1,000 on the principal of the auto loan.

e. Repeat part (a) for the end of the month assuming that George takes the local beach vacation and pays off his auto loan.

f. Repeat part (a) for the end of the month assuming George takes the Bahamas vacation and pays off the auto loan.

**3.** James Jenkins walks into a Big Box electronics store in search of a new HDTV. He finds exactly what he wants. The price is $2,000 and the HDTV has a $100 maintenance contract that ensures against component failures. He has $1,000 in cash, $3,500 in his checking account that pays 2 percent interest, a credit card with a 7 percent interest charge on unpaid balances, and a savings account paying 5 percent (all annual rates). Discuss which of the functions that the money and capital markets perform are important to Jim Jenkins as he considers various options for purchasing the HDTV.

4. Roberto begins the year with $5,000 in a savings account earning a 6 percent interest return annually. He decides to add $1,000 to that savings account today and he assumes interest rates will not change in the future. He also owns a car whose market value is $20,000 but he expects it will depreciate by $5,000 over the course of the year. Based on these two items alone, describe his annual savings and his total wealth at the beginning and end of the year. How might your answers change if Roberto had to wait 6 months before he could add that $1,000 to his savings account?

5. Classify the *market* in which each of the following financial transactions takes place as: (a) money versus capital; (b) primary versus secondary; (c) open versus negotiated; and (d) spot versus futures/forward.

   a. A three-year auto loan from a bank.

   b. A share of Google stock bought at its initial public offering (IPO).

   c. A six-month CD purchased from your local credit union.

   d. A contract for the delivery of hog bellies six months from today.

   e. A municipal bond purchased from a broker.

6. At the end of the calendar year, a firm has total financial assets amounting to $3.78 billion, while its total liabilities are $3.63 billion. What is this firm's *net* financial wealth? If the firm saved $50 million dollars over the previous year, representing the amount by which its financial assets rose relative to its liabilities, and it had begun the year with $3.63 billion in total financial assets, how much did it earn on its previously accumulated assets?

7. One definition of *pure arbitrage* is to combine a series of investments with a series of debts such that the net dollar investment is zero, no risk is taken, and a profit is made. How does this differ from *pure speculation* in the financial markets? Do you think that arbitrage opportunities can really exist? If so, do you think the opportunities for pure arbitrage would be long-lived? Please explain.

## Web-Based Problems

1. Your text defines the wealth of a business firm as the sum of all its assets. To determine its *net* wealth (or total equity) you have to subtract the firm's liabilities from its assets. Net wealth is the value of the firm and should be reflected in its market capitalization (or stock price times the number of shares outstanding). Firms in different industries will require different amounts of wealth to create the same market value (or market capitalization). In this problem you are asked to compare the wealth (total assets), net wealth (assets less liabilities), and market capitalization of a large firm in each of the following industries: Financial Services (Citigroup, ticker symbol C); Manufacturing (Caterpillar, CAT); and High Tech (Microsoft, MSFT). Using

the financial resources of the World Wide Web, key in each firm's ticker symbol and find its most recent balance sheet and market capitalization. Are you surprised by how different these firms are in terms of the dollar value of assets required to create $1 of market value?

2. A large share of household wealth is held in the form of corporate stock. How much wealth does the entire stock market represent? To find an approximate answer, go to the Web site for Wilshire Associates at **www.wilshire.com** and click Indexes from the menu. Locate the information that explains how the Wilshire 5000 Index is constructed. This index is weighted by the market capitalization of the firms included in it, such that if you add the right amount of zeros to the index, you obtain the total value of all the firms represented in the index. Why is this number a good approximation to the entire U.S. stock market? Now obtain a chart for the index. How much stock market wealth has been created or destroyed over the past 12 months? Determine how much stock market wealth was created or lost *per person* in the United States over this period. (Hint: You can find the U.S. population at **census.gov/main/www/ popclock.html**). Compare this with the average after-tax annual income *per person* in the United States. Use the disposable personal income figure that can be found under "Selected NIPA Tables: Table 2.1" at **bea.gov/national/ nipaweb/Index.asp** to make the comparison.

3. One of the world's most important financial markets that we will study throughout this book is the market for U.S. Treasury securities. It is important because it is one of the few default-free, highly liquid debt instruments available anywhere in the financial marketplace. To determine the size of this market go to the Treasury Department's Web site at **publicdebt.treas.gov** and find the *Monthly Statement of the Public Debt.* How much debt does the U.S. government owe *per person* in the United States? (See the previous problem on how to find the U.S. population figure.) How much of this debt is held by the public and how much by government agencies? Only a portion of this debt—termed "marketable"—is traded daily in the money and capital markets. The remainder is held by the buyer until it matures. How much of this public debt is "marketable"?

## Selected References to Explore

1. Duca, John V. "The Democratization of America's Capital Markets," *Economic and Financial Review,* Federal Reserve Bank of Dallas, Second Quarter 2001, pp. 10–19.

2. Emmons, William R. "Wealth Gains Don't Offset Decline in Savings," *The Regional Economist,* Federal Reserve Bank of St. Louis, July 2006, pp. 10–11.

3. Garner, S. Alan. "Should the Decline in the Personal Saving Rate Be a Cause for Concern?" *Economic Review,* Federal Reserve Bank of Kansas City, Second Quarter 2006, pp. 5–28.

4. Kliesen, Kevin L. "Families Digging Deeper Into Debt," *The Regional Economist,* Federal Reserve Bank of St. Louis, July 2006, pp. 12–13.

5. Lansing, Kevin J. "Spendthrift Nation," *FRBSF Economic Letter,* Federal Reserve Bank of San Francisco, November 10, 2005, pp. 1–3.

6. Leach, Richard, and Charles Steindel. "A Nation of Spendthrifts? An Analysis of Trends in Personal and Gross Savings," *Current Issues in Economics and Finance,* Federal Reserve Bank of New York, September 2000.

7. Poole, William, and David C. Wheelock. "The Real Population Problem: Too Few Working, Too Many Retired," *The Regional Economist,* Federal Reserve Bank of St. Louis, April 2005, pp. 5–9.

8. Valderrame, Diego. "Financial Development, Productivity and Economic Growth," *FRBSF Economic Letter,* Federal Reserve Bank of San Francisco, June 27, 2003.

# Chapter 2

# Financial Assets, Money, Financial Transactions, and Financial Institutions

## Learning Objectives

### in This Chapter

- You will see the most important channels through which funds flow from lenders to borrowers and back again within the global system of money and capital markets.

- You will discover the nature and characteristics of *financial assets*—how they are created and destroyed by decision makers within the financial system.

- You will explore the critical roles played by *money* within the financial system and the linkages between money and inflation in the prices of goods and services.

- You will examine the important jobs carried out by *financial intermediaries* in lending and borrowing and in creating and destroying financial assets.

## What's in This Chapter?
## Key Topics Outline

Financial Assets: What Are They? What Are Their Features?

Balance Sheet Identities: Assets, Liabilities, and Net Worth

Deficit- and Surplus-Budget Units

Money: What Is It? What Are Its Principal Functions?

Inflation, Deflation, and Money: Thinking in Real Terms

Types of Financial Transactions: Direct, Semidirect, and Indirect

Financial Intermediation and Types of Financial Institutions

The Disintermediation and Reintermediation of Funds

Bank-Dominated vs. Market-Dominated Financial Systems

## 2.1  Introduction: The Role of Financial Assets

The financial system is the mechanism through which loanable funds reach borrowers. Through the operation of the financial markets, money is exchanged for financial claims in the form of stocks, bonds, and other securities. And through the exchange of money for financial claims, the economy's capacity to produce goods and services is increased. This happens because the global money and capital markets provide the financial resources needed for real investment. Although it is true that the financial markets deal mainly in the exchange of paper claims and computer entries evidencing the transfer of funds, these markets provide an indispensable conduit for the transformation of savings into investment, accelerating the economy's growth and developing new businesses and new jobs.

This chapter looks closely at the essential role played by the financial markets in converting savings into investment and how that role has changed over time. We begin by observing that nearly all financial transactions between buyers and sellers involve the creation or destruction of a special kind of asset: a *financial asset*. Moreover, financial assets possess a number of characteristics that make them unique among all assets held by individuals and institutions. In the next section, we consider the nature of financial assets and how they are created and destroyed through the workings of the global financial system.

## 2.2  The Nature and Characteristics of Financial Assets

**financial asset**

What is a **financial asset?** It is a *claim* against the income or wealth of a business firm, household, or unit of government, represented usually by a certificate, receipt, computer record file, or other legal document, and usually created by or related to the lending of money. Familiar examples include stocks, bonds, insurance policies, futures contracts, and deposits held in a bank or credit union.

### *Characteristics of Financial Assets*

Financial assets do *not* provide a continuing stream of services to their owners as a home, an automobile, or a washing machine would do. These assets are sought after because they promise *future* returns to their owners and serve as a *store of value* (purchasing power). Their value rests on *faith* that their issuer will honor his or her contractual promise to pay.

A number of other features make financial assets unique. They *cannot be depreciated* because they do not wear out like physical goods. Moreover, their physical condition or form usually is *not* relevant in determining their market value (price). A stock certificate is not more or less valuable, for example, because of the size or quality of paper it may be printed on, because it may be frayed around the edges, or because of the type and format of the computer file in which it may appear.

Because financial assets are generally represented by a piece of paper (certificate or contract) or by information stored in a computer, they have little or no value as a commodity and their cost of transportation and storage is low. Indeed, the cost of the storage and transfer of funds and other bits of financial information declined sharply as the twenty-first century began due to rapid advances in computer and electronic technology, causing financial assets to grow faster than world trade and faster than the economy as a whole. Finally, financial assets are *fungible*—they can be easily changed in form and substituted for other assets. Thus, a bond or share of stock often can be quickly converted into any other asset the holder desires.

## Types of Financial Assets

Although there are thousands of different financial assets, they generally fall into four categories: money, equities, debt securities, and derivatives.

**money**

Any financial asset that is generally accepted in payment for purchases of goods and services is **money.** Thus, checkable accounts and currency are financial assets serving as payment media and, therefore, are forms of money. In the modern world, money— even the forms of money issued by the government—depends for its value only upon the issuer's pledge to pay as promised. **Equities** (more commonly known

**equities**

as *stock*) represent ownership shares in a business firm and, as such, are claims against the firm's profits and against proceeds from the sale of its assets. We usually further subdivide equities into *common stock,* which entitles its holder to vote for the members of a firm's board of directors and, therefore, determine company policy, and *preferred stock,* which normally carries no voting privileges but does entitle its holder to a fixed share of the firm's net earnings ahead of its common stockholders.

**debt securities**

**Debt securities** include such familiar instruments as *bonds, notes, accounts payable,* and *savings deposits.* Legally, these financial assets entitle their holders to a priority claim over the holders of equities to the assets and income of an individual, business firm, or unit of government. Usually, that claim is fixed in amount and time (maturity) and, depending on the terms of the *indenture* (contract) that accompanies most debt securities, may be backed up by the pledge of specific assets as collateral. Financial analysts usually divide debt securities into two broad classes: (1) *negotiable,* which can easily be transferred from holder to holder as a marketable security, and (2) *nonnegotiable,* which cannot legally be transferred to another party. Passbook savings accounts and U.S. savings bonds are good examples of nonnegotiable debt securities.

**derivatives**

Finally, **derivatives** are among the newest kinds of financial instruments that are closely linked to financial assets. These unique financial claims have a market value that is tied to or influenced by the value or return on a financial asset, such as stocks (equities) and bonds, notes, and other loans (debt securities). Examples include futures contracts, options, and swaps. As we will see in future chapters, these particular instruments are often employed to manage risk in the assets to which they are tied or related.

**Key URL:**
One of the most popular sites today for tracking the changing values of financial assets is *Money Magazine's* **money.cnn.com**

## 2.3 How Financial Assets Are Created

How are financial assets created? We may illustrate this process using a rudimentary financial system in which there are only two economic units: a household and a business firm.

Assume that this financial system is *closed,* so no external transactions with other units are possible. Each unit holds certain assets accumulated over the years as a result of its saving out of current income. The household, for example, has accumulated furniture, an automobile, clothes, and other items needed to provide entertainment, food, shelter, and transportation. The business firm holds inventories of goods to be sold, raw materials, machinery and equipment, and other assets required to produce its product and sell it to the public.

| EXHIBIT 2.1 | Balance Sheets of Units in a Simple Financial System |
|---|---|

**HOUSEHOLD**
**Balance Sheet**

| Assets | | Liabilities and Net Worth | |
|---|---|---|---|
| Accumulated uses of funds: | | Accumulated sources of funds: | |
| Cash | $13,000 | Net worth (accumulated savings) | $20,000 |
| Furniture | 1,000 | | |
| Clothes | 1,500 | | |
| Automobile | 4,000 | | |
| Other assets | 500 | | |
| Total assets | $20,000 | Total liabilities and net worth | $20,000 |

**BUSINESS FIRM**
**Balance Sheet**

| Assets | | Liabilities and Net Worth | |
|---|---|---|---|
| Accumulated uses of funds: | | Accumulated sources of funds: | |
| Inventories of goods | $ 10,000 | Net worth (accumulated savings) | $100,000 |
| Machinery and equipment | 25,000 | | |
| Building | 60,000 | | |
| Other assets | 5,000 | | |
| Total assets | $100,000 | Total liabilities and net worth | $100,000 |

The financial position of these two economic units is presented in the form of balance sheets, shown in Exhibit 2.1. A balance sheet, of course, is a financial statement prepared as of a certain date, showing a particular unit's assets, liabilities, and net worth. *Assets* represent *accumulated uses of funds* made by an economic unit; *liabilities* and *net worth* represent the *accumulated sources of funds* that an economic unit has drawn upon to acquire the assets it now holds. The net worth (equity) account reflects total savings accumulated over time by each economic unit.

A balance sheet must balance. Total assets (accumulated uses of funds) must equal total liabilities plus net worth (accumulated sources of funds).

The household in our example holds total assets currently valued at $20,000, including an automobile, clothes, furniture, and cash. Because the household's financial statement must balance, total liabilities and net worth also add up to $20,000, all of which in this instance happens to come from net worth (accumulated savings). The business firm holds total assets amounting to $100,000, including a building housing the firm's offices, equipment, and inventory. The firm's only source of funds currently is net worth (accumulated savings), also valued at $100,000.

By today's standards, the two balance sheets shown in Exhibit 2.1 look very strange. Neither the household nor the business firm has any outstanding debt (liabilities). Each unit is entirely *self-financed,* because each has acquired its assets by saving and by spending within its current income, not by borrowing. In the terminology of finance, **internal financing** both the household and the business firm have engaged in **internal financing:** the use of current income and accumulated savings to acquire assets. In the case of the household, savings have been accumulated by taking some portion of each period's income and setting money aside rather than spending all income on current consumption. The business firm has abstained from paying out all of its current revenues in the form of expenses (including stockholder dividends), retaining some of its current earnings in its net worth account.

For most businesses and households, internally generated funds are still the most important resources for acquiring assets. For example, in the U.S. economy well over half of all investments in plant, equipment, and inventories carried out by business firms each year is financed internally rather than by borrowing. Households as a group may save substantially more than they borrow in a given year, with the savings flowing into purchases of real assets (such as homes and automobiles) and into purchases of financial assets (such as stocks, bonds, and bank deposits).

Suppose that the business firm in our rudimentary financial system wishes to purchase new equipment in the form of a drill press. Due to inflation and shortages of key raw materials, however, the cost of the new drill press has been increasing rapidly. Internal sources of funds are not sufficient to cover the equipment's full cost. What can be done? There are four likely alternatives: (1) postpone the purchase of the new equipment until sufficient savings can be accumulated, (2) sell off some existing assets to raise the necessary funds, (3) borrow all or a portion of the needed funds, or (4) issue new stock (equity).

*Time* is frequently a determining factor here. Postponement of the equipment purchase probably will result in lost sales and lost profits. A competing company may rush ahead to expand its operations and capture some share of this firm's market. Moreover, in an environment of inflation, the new drill press surely will cost even more in the future than it does now. Selling some existing assets to raise the necessary funds is a distinct possibility, but this may take time, and there is risk of substantial loss, especially if fixed assets must be sold. The third alternative—borrowing—has the advantage of raising funds quickly, and the interest cost on the loan is tax deductible.[1] The firm could sell additional stock if it hesitated to take on debt, but equity financing is often more expensive than borrowing and requires more time to arrange.

If the business firm decides to borrow, who will lend the funds it needs? Obviously, in this two-unit financial system, the household must provide the needed funds. The **external financing** firm must engage in **external financing** by issuing to the household securities evidencing a loan of money. In general, if any economic unit wishes to add to its holdings of assets but lacks the necessary resources to do so, it can raise additional funds by issuing financial liabilities (borrowing)—provided that a buyer of those IOUs can be found. The buyer will regard the IOUs as an asset—a financial asset—that may earn income unless the borrower goes out of business and defaults on the loan.

Suppose that the business firm decides to borrow by issuing a liability (debt security) in the amount of $10,000 to pay for its new drill press. Because the firm is promising an attractive interest rate on the new IOU, the household willingly acquires it as a financial asset. This asset is *intangible:* a mere promise to pay $10,000 at maturity

---

[1]An added advantage associated with issuing debt is the *leverage effect.* If the firm can earn more from purchasing and using the new equipment than the cost of borrowing funds, the surplus return will flow to the firm's owners in the form of increased earnings, increasing the value of the company's stock. The result is positive financial leverage. Unfortunately, leverage is a two-edged sword. If the firm earns less than the cost of borrowed funds, the owners' losses will be magnified as a result of unfavorable (negative) financial leverage.

| EXHIBIT 2.2 | Unit Balance Sheets Following the Purchase of Equipment and the Issuance of a Debt Security (Financial Asset) |
|---|---|

### HOUSEHOLD
#### Balance Sheet

| Assets | | Liabilities and Net Worth | |
|---|---|---|---|
| Cash | $ 3,000 | Net worth (accumulated savings) | $20,000 |
| Financial asset | 10,000 | | |
| Furniture | 1,000 | | |
| Clothes | 1,500 | | |
| Automobile | 4,000 | | |
| Other assets | 500 | | |
| Total assets | $20,000 | Total liabilities and net worth | $20,000 |

### BUSINESS FIRM
#### Balance Sheet

| Assets | | Liabilities and Net Worth | |
|---|---|---|---|
| Inventories of goods | $ 10,000 | Liabilities | $ 10,000 |
| Machinery and equipment | 35,000 | Net worth | 100,000 |
| Building | 60,000 | | |
| Other assets | 5,000 | | |
| Total assets | $110,000 | Total liabilities and net worth | $110,000 |

plus a promised stream of interest payments over time. The borrowing and creation of this financial asset will impact the balance sheets of these two economic units. As shown in Exhibit 2.2, the household has purchased the firm's IOU by using up some of its accumulated cash. Its total assets are unchanged. Instead of holding $13,000 in noninterest-bearing cash, the household now holds an interest-bearing financial asset in the form of a $10,000 security and $3,000 in cash. The firm's total assets and total liabilities *increase* due to the combined effect of borrowing (*external finance*) and the acquisition of a productive real asset.

What would happen to the balance sheet shown in Exhibit 2.2 if the business firm in our small financial system decided to issue stock (*equities*), rather than debt, to finance the purchase of its new equipment? Selling stock is usually more expensive than borrowing and any dividend payments to stockholders are not usually a tax-deductible expense. While equity financing generally requires more time to arrange, it does have the advantage of making a business firm financially stronger because the owners (stockholders) are committing more of their funds to the firm, thereby giving it greater protection against failure. As Exhibit 2.3 shows, the household in our rudimentary financial system would record its purchase of the firm's newly issued stock as a financial asset in the amount of $10,000. And, on the business firm's balance sheet, net worth would rise to $110,000, from $100,000. There would *not* be a liability account on the business's balance sheet because the household in this particular case is not a creditor, but rather a shareholder (part owner) of the business firm.

| EXHIBIT 2.3 | Unit Balance Sheets Following the Purchase of Equipment and the Issuance of Stock (a Financial Asset) to Pay for That Purchase |
|---|---|

**HOUSEHOLD**
**Balance Sheet**

| Assets | | Liabilities and Net Worth | |
|---|---|---|---|
| Cash | $ 3,000 | Net worth (accumulated savings) | $20,000 |
| Financial asset | 10,000 | | |
| Furniture | 1,000 | | |
| Clothes | 1,500 | | |
| Automobile | 4,000 | | |
| Other assets | 500 | | |
| Total assets | $20,000 | Total liabilities and net worth | $20,000 |

**BUSINESS FIRM**
**Balance Sheet**

| Assets | | Liabilities and Net Worth | |
|---|---|---|---|
| Inventories of goods | $ 10,000 | Net worth (including the issuance of new stock in the amount of $10,000) | $110,000 |
| Machinery and equipment | 35,000 | | |
| Building | 60,000 | | |
| Other assets | 5,000 | | |
| Total assets | $110,000 | Total liabilities and net worth | $110,000 |

## 2.4  Financial Assets and the Financial System

This simple example illustrates several important points concerning the operation and role of the financial system within the economy. First, the act of borrowing or of issuing new stock simultaneously gives rise to the creation of an equal volume of financial assets. In the foregoing example, the $10,000 financial asset held by the household lending money is exactly matched by the $10,000 liability of the business firm borrowing money. This suggests another way of defining a financial asset: *Any asset held by a business firm, government, or household that is also recorded as a liability or claim on some other economic unit's balance sheet is a financial asset.* As we have seen, many different kinds of assets satisfy this definition, including stocks, bonds, bank loans, and deposits held with a credit union.

*For the entire financial system, the sum of all financial assets held must equal the total of all financial liabilities (claims) outstanding.* In contrast, real assets, such as automobiles, are not necessarily matched by liabilities (claims) somewhere in the financial system.

This distinction between *financial assets* and *liabilities,* on the one hand, and *real assets,* on the other, is worth pursuing with an example. Suppose that you borrow $10,000 from the bank to purchase an automobile. Your balance sheet will now contain a liability in the amount of $10,000. The bank from which you borrowed the funds will record the transaction as a loan—an interest-bearing financial asset—appearing on the asset side of its balance sheet in the like amount of $10,000. On the asset side of your balance sheet appears the market value of the automobile—a real asset. The value of the real asset probably exceeds $10,000 since most banks expect a borrower to supply some of his or her own funds rather than borrowing the full purchase price. Let's say the automobile was sold to you for $15,000, with $5,000 of the cost coming out of your savings account and $10,000 from the bank loan. Then, your balance sheet will contain a new real asset (automobile) valued at $15,000, a liability (bank loan) of $10,000, and your savings account (a financial asset) will decline by $5,000.

Clearly, there are two equalities that hold not only for this transaction but whenever funds are loaned and borrowed in the financial system. First,

$$
\begin{array}{ccc}
\text{Volume of financial} & = & \text{Volume of liabilities} \\
\text{assets created for lenders} & & \text{issued by borrowers}
\end{array}
$$

$$
\begin{array}{ccc}
\text{In this case, a bank} & = & \text{A borrower's IOU of} \\
\text{loan of \$10,000} & & \text{\$10,000}
\end{array} \qquad (2.1)
$$

Second,

$$
\text{Total uses of funds} \quad = \quad \text{Total sources of funds}
$$

$$
\begin{array}{ccc}
 & & \text{Issuance of a \$10,000} \\
\text{Purchase of \$15,000} & = & \text{borrower IOU} + \text{\$5,000} \\
\text{automobile} & & \text{drawn from a savings} \\
 & & \text{account}
\end{array} \qquad (2.2)
$$

Every financial asset in existence represents the lending or investing of funds transferred from one economic unit to another.

Because the sum of all financial assets created must always equal the amount of all liabilities (claims) outstanding, the amount of lending in the financial system must always equal the amount of borrowing going on. In effect, *financial assets and liabilities (claims) cancel each other out across the whole financial system.* We illustrate this fact by reference to the balance sheet of any unit in the economy—business firm, household, or government. The following must be true for *all* balance sheets:

$$
\text{Total assets} = \text{Total liabilities} + \text{Net worth} \qquad (2.3)
$$

Then, because all assets may be classified as either real assets or financial assets, it follows that

$$
\text{Real assets} + \text{Financial assets} = \text{Total liabilities} + \text{Net worth} \qquad (2.4)
$$

Because the volume of financial assets outstanding must always equal the volume of liabilities (claims) in existence, it follows that the aggregate volume of real assets held in the economy must equal the total amount of net worth. Therefore, for the economy and financial system *as a whole:*

$$
\text{Total financial assets} = \text{Total liabilities} \qquad (2.5)
$$

$$
\text{Total real assets} = \text{Net worth (i.e., accumulated savings)} \qquad (2.6)
$$

This means that the value of all buildings, machinery, and other real assets in existence matches the total amount of *accumulated savings* carried out by all businesses, households, and units of government. We *are not* made better off in real terms by the mere creation of financial assets and liabilities. These are only pieces of paper or blips on a computer screen evidencing a loan or the investment of funds. Rather, society increases its wealth only by saving and increasing the quantity of its real assets, for these assets enable the economy to produce more goods and services in the future.

Does this suggest that the creation of financial assets and liabilities—one of the key functions of the global financial system—is a useless exercise? Not at all. The mere act of saving by one economic unit does not guarantee that those savings will be used to build or purchase real assets that add to society's stock of wealth. In modern economies, saving and investment usually are carried out by different groups of people. For example, most saving is usually carried out by households (individuals and families) and business firms account for the majority of investments in productive real assets. Some mechanism is needed to ensure that savings flow from those who save to those who wish to invest in real assets, and the system of money and capital markets is that mechanism.

The *financial system* provides the essential channel necessary for the creation and exchange of financial assets between savers and borrowers so that real assets can be acquired. Without that channel for savings, the total volume of investment in the economy surely would be reduced. All investment by individual economic units would have to depend on the ability of those same units to save (i.e., engage in internal financing). Many promising investment opportunities would have to be forgone or postponed due to insufficient savings. Society's scarce resources would be allocated less efficiently than is possible with a system of financial markets. Growth in society's income, employment, and standard of living would be seriously impaired without a vibrant financial system at work. In short, the financial system matters in reducing the barriers to external financing, lowering the cost of capital, and accelerating economic growth. Nations with more fully developed financial systems tend to grow faster and enjoy a higher standard of living.

---

### QUESTIONS TO HELP YOU STUDY

1. Exactly what do we mean by the term *financial asset*?
2. How do financial assets come about within the functioning of the financial system?
3. Carefully explain why the volume of financial assets outstanding must always equal the volume of liabilities outstanding.
4. What is the difference between *internal finance* and *external finance?*
5. When a business, household, or unit of government is in need of additional funding, what are its principal alternatives? What factors should these different economic units consider when they have to choose among different sources of funds?
6. What is the relationship between the process of creating financial assets and liabilities and the acts of saving and investment? Why is that relationship important to your financial and economic well-being?

---

## 2.5 Lending and Borrowing in the Financial System

Business firms, households, and governments play a wide variety of roles in modern financial systems. It is quite common for an individual or institution to be a lender of funds in one period and a borrower in the next, or to do both simultaneously. Indeed, financial intermediaries, such as banks and insurance companies, operate on *both sides* of the financial markets, borrowing funds from customers by issuing attractive financial claims and simultaneously making loans available to other customers. Virtually all of us at one point or another in our lifetimes will be involved in the financial system as both a borrower and a lender of funds.

A number of years ago, economists John Gurley and Edward Shaw [4] pointed out that each business firm, household, or unit of government active in the financial system must conform to the following identity:

$$R - E \quad = \quad \Delta FA - \Delta D$$

$$
\begin{array}{ccc}
\text{Current income receipts} & & \text{Change in holdings of} \\
\text{— Expenditures out of} & = & \text{financial assets —} \\
\text{current income} & & \text{Change in debt and} \\
& & \text{equity outstanding}
\end{array}
\quad (2.7)
$$

If, on the one hand, our current expenditures ($E$) exceed our current income receipts ($R$), we usually make up the difference by (1) reducing our holdings of financial assets ($\Delta FA < 0$) such as by drawing money out of a savings account; (2) issuing debt or stock ($\Delta D > 0$); or (3) using some combination of both. For example, suppose our expenditures this month exceed our current income receipts by $200. We can make up the difference by such steps as drawing down our savings account by $200, borrowing an additional $200, or doing a bit of each to cover the financial gap.

If, on the other hand, our receipts ($R$) in the current period are larger than our current expenditures ($E$), we can (1) build up our holdings of financial assets ($\Delta FA > 0$), for example, by placing money in a savings account or buying a few shares of stock; (2) pay off some outstanding debt or retire stock previously issued by our business firm ($\Delta D < 0$); or (3) do some combination of both of these steps. For example, if our receipts this month tally up to $200 more than our expenditures we now have the opportunity to increase our savings balance by $200 (perhaps because we are worried that next month will bring a budget deficit and we want to be ready), reduce any debt outstanding by $200, or elect to add some of the expected excess income to savings and the rest to debt repayment.

It follows that for any given period of time (e.g., day, month, or year), the individual economic unit must fall into one of three groups:

**deficit-budget unit**

**Deficit - budget unit (DBU):**    $E > R$; and so $\Delta D > \Delta FA$
  (net borrower of funds)

**surplus-budget unit**

**Surplus - budget unit (SBU):**    $R > E$; and thus $\Delta FA > \Delta D$
  (net lender of funds)

**balanced-budget unit**

**Balanced - budget unit (BBU):**   $R = E$; and, therefore, $\Delta D = \Delta FA$
  (neither net lender nor
  net borrower)

A *net lender of funds (SBU) is really a net supplier of funds to the financial system.* He or she accomplishes this function by purchasing financial assets, paying off debt, or retiring equity (stock). In contrast, a *net borrower of funds (DBU) is a net demander of funds from the financial system,* selling financial assets, issuing new debt, or selling new stock to raise new money. The business and government sectors of the economy

| EXHIBIT 2.4 | Net Acquisitions of Financial Assets and Liabilities by Major Sectors of the U.S. Economy, 2006* ($ Billions) | | |
|---|---|---|---|
| Major Sectors of the Economy | Net Acquisitions of Financial Assets during the Year | Net Increase in Liabilities during the Year | Net Lender (+) or Net Borrower (−) of Funds |
| Households | $865.1 | $1,411.1 | $−546.0 |
| Nonfinancial business firms | 599.0 | 680.5 | −81.5 |
| State and local governments | 80.0 | 144.0 | −64.0 |
| Federal government | −13.6 | 634.6 | −648.2 |
| International sector: Foreign investors and borrowers | 1491.9 | 545.3 | +946.6 |

Source: Board of Governors of the Federal Reserve System, *Flow of Funds Accounts.*

*Figures in the tables are for the first quarter of 2006.

tend to be net borrowers (demanders) of funds (DBUs) in most periods; the household sector, composed of all families and individuals, tends to be a net lender (supplier) of funds (SBU) in most (though not all) years.

Net lending and borrowing sectors in the U.S. economy early in 2006 reflected some of the patterns discussed above, but there were some important exceptions as well. For example, as shown in Exhibit 2.4, households during 2006 were significant net borrowers of funds in the financial system, declining to play their historic role as net lender. That is, U.S. households borrowed an amount from other sectors of the economy—recorded as their "Net Increase in Liabilities"—that was $546 billion *more* than the amount they loaned to other sectors—recorded as "Net Acquisitions of Financial Assets." The biggest borrowers in 2006 were governments. State and local governments were net borrowers to the tune of $64 billion, while the federal government sold off nearly $14 billion in previously acquired financial assets to raise new money and then borrowed nearly $635 billion on top of that! Nonfinancial businesses also joined the borrowing parade, issuing liabilities that exceeded the financial assets they purchased by nearly $82 billion.

If businesses, households, and governments were net borrowers in the money and capital markets in 2006, who loaned them the money? As Exhibit 2.4 clearly shows, it was foreign investors who supplied most of the funds these domestic borrowers were seeking. Foreign participants active in U.S. financial markets sought out U.S. dollar-denominated assets, buying up corporate stock, government bonds, and thousands of other American financial instruments, resulting in total net lending to U.S. domestic borrowers of more than $946 billion. Many of these overseas lenders of funds saw the United States as a relatively safe haven for their money, in contrast to the turmoil that characterized many foreign markets at the time.

Finally, if we look across all sectors in Exhibit 2.4 we note that early in 2006 total funds borrowed exceeded total funds loaned by about $393 billion. How could that be? Where did the extra funds borrowed come from? Some of those excess funds came from sectors not shown in the exhibit—for example, funds provided by the financial institutions' sector of the economy. Still other funds flowed in from "unrecorded transactions" (sometimes referred to as a "statistical discrepancy"). Many experts believe that some of these mysterious transactions probably reflect unreported money flows across national borders—money that is very hard to trace.

Of course, over any given period of time, any one household, business firm, or unit of government may be a deficit-, surplus-, or balanced-budget unit. In fact, from day to day and week to week, many households, businesses, and governments fluctuate from being deficit-budget units (DBUs) to surplus-budget units (SBUs) and back again. Consider a large corporation such as Ford or General Electric. Such a firm may be a net lender one week, supplying monies to deficit-budget units in the financial system for short periods of time through purchases of Treasury bills, bank Euro-deposits and CDs, and other financial assets. The following week, a dividend payment may be due company stockholders, bonds must be refunded, or purchases must be made to increase inventories and expand plant and equipment. At this point, the firm may become a net borrower of funds, drawing down its holdings of financial assets, securing loans by issuing liabilities, or selling equity (stock). Most of the large institutions that interact in the global financial marketplace continually fluctuate from one side of the market to the other. *One of the most important contributions of the global financial system to our daily lives is in permitting businesses, households, and governments to adjust their financial position from that of net borrower (DBU) to net lender (SBU) and back again, smoothly and efficiently.*

## 2.6   Money as a Financial Asset

### What Is Money?

The most important financial asset in the economy is *money*—one of the oldest and most useful inventions in the history of the world. Metallic coins served as money for many centuries until paper notes (currency) first appeared in China during the Tang Dynasty over a thousand years ago (618–907 C.E.) and in Sweden in 1661. The federal government of the United States did not issue paper money until 1861 in the form of "greenbacks," named for the green ink on the back of each note. Many other assets besides currency and coin have served as money in earlier periods, including beads, seashells, cigarettes, and even playing cards.

All financial assets are valued in terms of money, and flows of funds between lenders and borrowers occur through the medium of money. Money itself *is* a financial asset, because all forms of money in use today are claims against some institution, public or private. For example, one of the largest components of the money supply today is the checking account, which is the debt of a depository institution (although today check-writing volume is declining relative to electronic payments). Another important component of the money supply is the sum of all currency and coin—pocket money—held by the public. The bulk of currency in use today in the United States, for example, consists of Federal Reserve notes, representing debt obligations of the 12 Federal Reserve banks. In fact, if the Federal Reserve ever closed its doors (a highly unlikely event!), Federal Reserve notes held by the public would be a first claim against the assets of the Federal Reserve banks. Other forms of money that are growing rapidly in popularity include credit and debit cards to allow instant borrowing or the withdrawal of funds from a bank deposit; stored-value ("smart") cards that are encoded via computer with a fixed amount of money available for spending; and digital cash available through the Internet computer network from a variety of financial-service providers. As we will see in the accompanying box on alternative definitions of the money supply, some concepts of what money is today include savings accounts at banks, credit unions, and money market funds—all forms of debt to their issuers, giving rise to financial assets.

Money performs multiple functions in the financial system, serving as a medium of exchange, a store of value (purchasing power), a standard for valuing goods and services (unit of account), and a source of liquidity (spending power). These different functions of money have given rise to a variety of different definitions of the actual money supply available to the public, with each definition reflecting a different function that money performs for those who hold it. For example, in the United States the principal definitions of money in use today are:

M1 = Currency and coin held by the public outside bank vaults, plus various kinds of payments accounts at depository institutions, such as checkable deposits and travelers' checks. M1 emphasizes the role of money as a medium of exchange. In 2006, M1 totaled close to $1.4 trillion in the United States.

M2 = M1 plus small savings and time deposits (less than $100,000) and share accounts at retail money market mutual funds. Thus, M2 adds in primarily short-term household savings to the money supply. In 2006, M2 amounted to just over $7 trillion.

MZM (money, zero maturity) = M2 minus small-denomination time deposits plus institutional money market funds (excluded from M2). In 2006 MZM, developed by the Federal Reserve Bank of St. Louis as a money measure close to the transactions demand for money, climbed in the vicinity of $7 trillion.

Clearly, each of the foregoing definitions reflects the many different roles money performs in the economy and financial system.

## The Functions of Money

**Key URLs:**
Want to know more about the money supply and what makes it up? See especially **frbatlanta.org/publica** and **research.St Louisfed .org/fred 2/**

Money performs a wide variety of important services. It serves as a *standard of value* (or *unit of account*) for all the goods and services we might wish to trade. Without money, the price of every good or service would have to be expressed in terms of exchange ratios with all other goods and services—an enormous information burden for both buyers and sellers. We would need to know, for example, how many loaves of bread would be required to purchase a quart of milk, or what quantity of firewood might be exchanged for a suit of clothes. To trade just 12 different goods and services, we would have to remember 66 different exchange ratios! In contrast, the existence of money as a common standard of value permits us to express the prices of all goods and services in terms of only one item—the *monetary unit*. In the United States and Canada that unit is the dollar; in Japan, the yen; in China, the yuan; and in Europe, the euro. But whatever the monetary unit is called, it always has a constant price in terms of itself (e.g., a dollar always exchanges for a dollar). The prices of all other goods and services are expressed in multiples of the monetary unit.

**Key URLs:**
The importance of money within the financial system is discussed further in **encarta.msn.com**

Money also serves as a *medium of exchange*. It is usually the only financial asset that virtually every business, household, and unit of government will accept in payment for goods and services. By itself, money typically has little or no use as a commodity (except when gold or silver, for example, is used as the medium of exchange). People accept money only because they know they can exchange it at a later date for something else. This is why modern governments have been able to separate the monetary unit from precious metals (such as gold and silver) and successfully issue *fiat money* (i.e., pieces of paper or data stored in a computer file or on a plastic card) not tied to any particular commodity. Money's service as a medium of exchange frees us from the terrible constraints of barter, allowing us to separate the act of selling goods and services from the act of buying goods and services. With a medium of exchange, buyers and sellers no longer need to have an exact coincidence of wants in terms of quality, quantity, time, and location.

Money serves also as a *store of value*—a reserve of future purchasing power. Purchasing power can be stored in currency and coin, in a checking account, on a plastic card, or in a computer file until the time is right to buy. Of course, money is not always a good store of value. The value of money, measured by its purchasing power, can experience marked fluctuations. For example, the prices of consumer goods represented in the U.S. cost-of-living index rose more than five times over between 1960 and 2006 and jumped almost a third during the most recent decade, on average. Individuals and families purchasing the identical market basket of goods represented in the cost-of-living index would have experienced a steep decline in their purchasing power unless their incomes rose rapidly enough to keep up with inflation.

Money functions as the *only perfectly liquid asset* in the financial system. An asset is liquid if it can be converted into cash quickly with little or no loss in value. A liquid asset possesses three essential characteristics: *price stability, ready marketability,* and *reversibility.* An asset must be considered *liquid* if its price tends to be relatively stable over time, if it has an active resale market, and if it is reversible so investors can recover their original investment without loss.

All assets—real and financial—differ in their *degrees of liquidity.* Generally, financial assets, especially bank deposits and stocks and bonds issued by major corporations, tend to be highly liquid; on the other hand, real assets, such as a home or an automobile, may be difficult to sell in a hurry without taking a substantial loss. *Money is the most liquid of all assets because it need not be converted into any other form to be spent.* Unfortunately, the most liquid assets, including money, tend to carry the lowest rates of return. One measure of the "cost" of holding money is the income forgone by the owner who fails to convert his or her money balances into more profitable investments in real or financial assets. The *rate of interest* determined by the financial system is a measure of the penalty suffered by an investor for not converting money into income-earning assets.

## The Value of Money and Other Financial Assets and Inflation

**inflation**

The value of money—its *purchasing power*—changes due to **inflation,** defined as a rise in the average price level of all goods and services. Inflation lowers the value or purchasing power of money and is a special problem in the money and capital markets because it can damage the value of financial contracts (such as a bond or a deposit). Financial loss due to inflation is particularly likely where the amount of price inflation has not been fully anticipated or if the people and institutions who agreed to a financial contract were simply not able to adjust fully to the inflation that subsequently occurred.

**deflation**

The opposite of inflation is **deflation,** where the average level of prices for goods and services actually declines. Less common than inflation, deflation benefits those whose income doesn't also decline with prices and, therefore, can buy more goods and services than they could in the past. Unfortunately, deflation may be accompanied by a troubled economy and loss of jobs so that, even though living costs are less, many people may still find themselves with sharply reduced income (purchasing power).

**price indexes**

Today most economists measure inflation using popular **price indexes,** such as the Consumer Price Index (CPI) or the Gross Domestic Product (GDP) Deflator Index. The CPI, a cost of living index, measures the cost of a market basket of goods and

**Key URL:**
To learn more
about the Producer
Price Index, see
especially **bls.gov**

**Key URL:**
Additional information
concerning personal
consumption and
GDP deflator price
indexes may be found
at **bea.doc.gov**

**Key URL:**
To learn more about
U.S. inflation and how
to adjust costs for
inflation's effects see
**stats.bls.gov**

services normally purchased by an urban family of four people. To determine this measure of the cost of living, the actual prices of designated items are collected from thousands of stores in cities across the United States each month, averaged, and combined into one index number. The U.S. CPI is widely used to make cost-of-living adjustments (COLAs) in labor contracts, Social Security payments, and in other government and private programs. A number of other nations, especially in Europe, have begun in recent years to compile their own CPIs in order to monitor the effects of inflation on their economies. An even broader price index is the GDP deflator series, which gathers both business and consumer prices on goods and services produced each year by labor and property inside the United States.

We can use the foregoing indexes to measure percentage changes in price levels (and inflation) relative to some base year employing the following relationship:

$$\Delta P = \frac{(PI_t - PI_{t-1})}{PI_{t-1}} \times 100 \qquad (2.8)$$

where $\Delta P$ is the percentage change in prices or in the price index we are following between two time periods ($t$ and $t-1$), $PI_t$ is the price or price index in period $t$, and $PI_{t-1}$ is the price index in some previous time period ($t-1$).

For example, suppose the U.S. CPI rises from 100 to 125 over a five-year period. We know that this cost of living index has climbed

$$\frac{(125 - 100)}{100} = 0.25 \text{ or } 25 \text{ percent}$$

over the five-year period we are studying. Unless the value of our incomes and our investments in financial assets and other forms of wealth has also gone up at least 25 percent during the same time period, we would have suffered a decline in purchasing power and in the true value of our wealth in terms of the goods and services we can now buy.

What else can a price index tell us? In 2006 the U.S. Consumer Price Index (CPI) averaged just over 200. This index value was based on the base period 1982–84 when the CPI was set at 100. This means that between 1982–84 and 2006 consumer prices in U.S. urban communities climbed an average of about 100 percent [that is, (200–100)/100 times 100 percent]. We can use numbers such as these to help figure out what has happened recently to the purchasing power of the basic monetary unit.

For example, suppose we wish to know what has happened to the purchasing power of the U.S. dollar recently. We could use this relationship:

$$\frac{\text{Purchasing power}}{\text{of the U.S. dollar}} = \frac{1}{\substack{\text{Cost of living index} \\ \text{where goods and services} \\ \text{are sold in U.S. dollars}}} \times 100 \qquad (2.9)$$

As an illustration, if the American CPI stood just above 200 in 2006 and was equal to 100 in 1982–84, the U.S. dollar's relative purchasing power would have fallen to

$$\frac{1}{200} \times 100 = 0.50$$

between 1982–84 and 2006. In other words, in 2006, one dollar bought only about 50 percent of what it would have purchased just over two decades earlier.

**real values**

**nominal values**

These dramatic changes in the purchasing power of money, even in the United States where inflation is relatively modest, give us a stern warning. We should get into the habit of thinking in terms of the **real** ("purchasing power adjusted") **values** of things—incomes, goods, services, financial assets such as bonds, stocks, bank deposits, and so on—rather than only in terms of their **nominal** (or face) **values,** which can be highly misleading (sometimes referred to as a "money illusion") in periods of significant inflation or deflation.

---

### QUESTIONS TO HELP YOU STUDY

7. What do the following terms mean?

    Deficit-budget unit (DBU)

    Surplus-budget unit (SBU)

    Balanced-budget unit (BBU)

8. Which were you last year—a deficit-, surplus-, or balanced-budget unit? Why is it important to know?

9. Explain what *money* is. What are its principal functions within the system of money and capital markets? within the economy?

10. Does money have any serious limitations as a financial asset? What are these limitations?

11. Can you distinguish between *inflation* and *deflation?* What do they have to do with money, if anything?

12. Would you expect to find a relationship between money supply growth and inflation or deflation? What kind of relationship?

---

## 2.7   The Evolution of Financial Transactions

Financial systems are *never* static. They change constantly in response to shifting demands from the public, the development of new technology, and changes in laws and regulations. Competition in the financial marketplace forces financial institutions to respond to public need by developing more convenient and more efficient financial services. Over time, the global system of financial markets has evolved from simple to more complex ways of carrying out financial transactions. The growth of industrial centers with enormous capital investment needs and the emergence of a huge middle class of savers have played major roles in the gradual evolution of the financial system.

Whether simple or complex, all financial systems perform at least one basic function. They move scarce funds from those who save and lend (surplus-budget units) to those who wish to borrow and invest (deficit-budget units). In the process, money is exchanged for financial assets. However, the transfer of funds from savers to borrowers can be accomplished in at least three different ways. We label these methods of funds transfer: (1) direct finance, (2) semidirect finance, and (3) indirect finance. Most financial systems have evolved gradually over time from direct and semidirect finance toward greater reliance on indirect finance.

### Direct Finance

With the direct financing technique, borrower and lender meet each other and exchange funds in return for financial assets without the help of a third party to bring

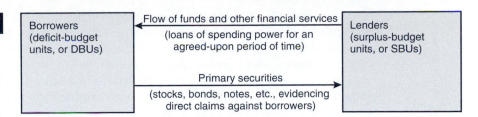

**EXHIBIT 2.5**

**Direct Finance (direct lending gives rise to direct claims against borrowers)**

**direct finance**

them together. You engage in **direct finance** when you borrow money from a friend and give him or her your IOU or when you purchase stocks or bonds directly from the company issuing them. We usually call the claims arising from direct finance *primary securities* because they flow directly from the borrower to the ultimate lender of funds. (Exhibit 2.5 illustrates the process of direct financing.)

Direct finance is the simplest method of carrying out financial transactions and probably the most efficient if conditions are right. Indeed, most financial systems in history started out using direct finance. However, it has a number of serious limitations. For one thing, both borrower and lender must desire to exchange the *same amount* of funds at the *same time*. More important, the lender must be willing to accept the borrower's IOU, which may be quite risky or slow to mature. Clearly, there must be a coincidence of wants between surplus- and deficit-budget units in terms of the amount and form of a loan. Without that fundamental coincidence, direct finance breaks down.

Another problem is that both lender and borrower must frequently incur substantial *information costs* simply to find each other. The borrower may have to contact many lenders before finding the one surplus-budget unit (SBU) with just the right amount of funds and a willingness to take on the borrower's IOU. Not surprisingly, direct finance soon is joined by other methods of carrying out financial transactions as money and capital markets develop.

## *Semidirect Finance*

**semidirect finance**

Early in the history of most financial systems, a new form of financial transaction called **semidirect finance** appears. Some individuals and business firms become securities brokers and dealers whose essential function is to bring surplus-budget (SBU) and deficit-budget (DBU) units together, thereby reducing information costs (see Exhibit 2.6).

**EXHIBIT 2.6**

**Semidirect Finance (direct lending with the aid of market makers who assist in the sale of direct claims against borrowers)**

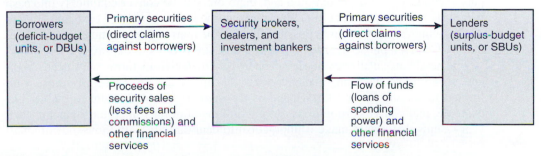

We must distinguish here between a broker and a dealer in securities. A *broker* is merely an individual or financial institution who provides information concerning possible purchases and sales of securities. Either a buyer or a seller of securities may contact a broker, whose job is simply to bring buyers and sellers together. A *dealer* also serves as a service channel between buyers and sellers, but the dealer actually acquires the seller's securities in the hope of marketing them to buyers at a later time at a favorable price. Dealers take a "position of risk" because, by purchasing securities outright for their own portfolios, they are subject to losses if those securities decline in value.

Semidirect finance may have some advantages over direct finance if conditions are right. It lowers the search (information) costs for participants in the financial markets. Frequently, a dealer will split up a large issue of primary securities into smaller units affordable by even buyers of modest means and, thereby, expand the flow of savings into investment. In addition, brokers and dealers facilitate the development of secondary markets in which securities can be offered for resale.

Despite the important contribution of brokers and dealers to the functioning of the global financial system, the semidirect finance approach is not without its limitations. The ultimate lender still winds up holding the borrower's securities, and, therefore, the lender must be willing to accept the risk and maturity characteristics of the borrower's IOUs. There still must be a *coincidence* of wants and needs between surplus-and deficit-budget units for semidirect financial transactions to take place.

## Indirect Finance and Financial Intermediation

**indirect finance**

The limitations of direct and semidirect finance under certain conditions stimulated the development of **indirect finance** carried out with the help of *financial intermediaries.* Financial intermediaries include commercial banks, insurance companies, credit unions, finance companies, savings and loan associations, savings banks, pension funds, mutual funds, and similar organizations. (See Exhibit 2.7.) Their fundamental role in the financial system is to serve both ultimate lenders and borrowers but in a different way than brokers and dealers do. Financial intermediaries issue securities of their own—often called **secondary securities**—to ultimate lenders and at the same time accept IOUs from ultimate borrowers—**primary securities** (see Exhibit 2.8).

**secondary securities**

**primary securities**

The *secondary securities* issued by financial intermediaries include such familiar instruments as checking and savings accounts, life insurance policies, annuities, and shares in a mutual fund. For the most part, these securities share several common characteristics. They generally carry *low risk of default.* For example, most deposits held in banks and credit unions are insured by an agency of government (in the United States, for amounts up to $100,000). Moreover, the majority of secondary securities can be acquired in *small denominations,* affordable by savers of limited means. For the most part, secondary securities are liquid and, therefore, can be converted quickly into cash with little risk of significant loss. Financial intermediaries in recent years have tried to make savings as convenient as possible through the mail and by plastic card, computer terminal, and telephone in order to reduce transactions costs to the saver.

Financial intermediaries accept *primary securities* from those who need credit and, in doing so, take on financial assets that many savers, especially those with limited funds and limited knowledge of the market, would find unacceptable. For example, many large corporations require billions of dollars in credit financing each year—sums that would make it impractical to deal directly with thousands of small

| EXHIBIT 2.7 | Major Financial Institutions Active in the Money and Capital Markets |
|---|---|

| Financial Intermediaries | |
|---|---|
| Depository institutions: | Contractual institutions: |
| Commercial banks | Life insurance companies |
| Nonbank thrifts: | Property-casualty insurers |
| Savings and loan associations | Pension funds |
| Savings banks | Investment institutions: |
| Credit unions | Investment companies (mutual funds) |
| Money market funds | Real estate investment trusts |
| Other financial intermediaries: | |
| Finance companies | |
| Government credit agencies | |
| Mortgage banking companies | |

| Other Financial Institutions | | |
|---|---|---|
| Investment bankers | Security brokers | Security dealers |

savers. By pooling the resources of scores of small savings accounts, however, a large financial intermediary frequently can service the credit needs of several large firms simultaneously. In addition, many primary securities are not readily marketable and carry sizable risk of borrower default—a situation usually not acceptable to the small saver. By issuing its own securities attractive to ultimate lenders (SBUs), and accepting primary securities from ultimate borrowers (DBUs), the financial intermediary acts to satisfy the financial needs of *both* surplus-and deficit-budget units in the economy.

**Key URL:**
To learn more about the role of financial intermediaries in the economy see **ny.frb.org**

One of the benefits of the development of efficient financial intermediation (indirect finance) has been to smooth out consumption spending by households and investment spending by businesses over time, despite variations in income, because intermediation makes saving and borrowing easier and safer. Financial intermediation permits a given amount of saving in the global economy to finance a greater amount of investment than probably would have occurred without intermediation.

| EXHIBIT 2.8 | Indirect Finance (the financial intermediation of funds) |
|---|---|

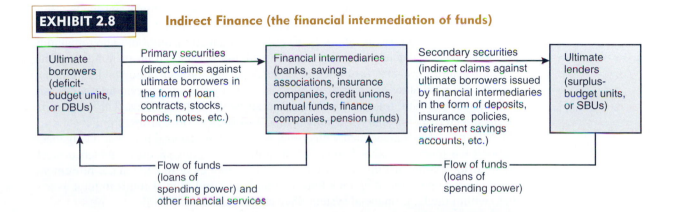

Interestingly enough, finance theory suggests that in a perfect world with perfect competition and where the public has access to information at little or no cost, financial intermediaries probably would *not* exist. Rather, it is *imperfections* in the financial system (where, for example, some groups do not have access to relevant financial information or face prohibitive information costs) that help explain why there are financial intermediaries and why they have grown to be such huge and important institutions within the financial system. Financial intermediaries overcome inefficiencies in the financial marketplace and reduce the cost to society of moving information and wealth among households, businesses, and governments, thereby providing access to economies of scale (information cost savings) that would otherwise not be available to smaller units in the economy. Financial intermediaries improve the real world efficiency of the money and capital markets in allocating the daily flow of capital toward its best possible uses. How well financial intermediaries work is a key determinant of which countries have the largest and strongest economies.

## 2.8   Relative Sizes and Types of Major Financial Institutions

### *Comparative Sizes of Key Financial-Service Providers*

Financial intermediaries and other financial institutions differ greatly in their relative importance within any nation's financial system. Measured by total financial assets, for example, *commercial banks* dominate the United States's financial system (as shown in Exhibit 2.9) and most other financial systems around the globe. The more than $9.5 trillion in financial assets held by U.S. banks represent about one-quarter of the total resources of all U.S. financial institutions. By some measures banks appear to have lost some of their market share to some nonbank financial institutions (such as mutual funds and credit unions), which may be less regulated or offer more flexible service options. In most countries, however, banks still represent the dominant financial institution.

Lagging well behind banks are *savings and loans associations*—another deposit-type financial intermediary active primarily in the U.S. mortgage market, financing the building and purchase of new homes. Very similar in sources and uses of funds to savings and loans are *savings banks,* which attract small savings deposits from individuals and families and make a wide variety of household loans. The fourth major kind of deposit-type financial intermediary, the *credit union,* was also created to attract small savings deposits from individuals and families and make loans to credit union members.

When the assets of all four deposit-type intermediaries—commercial banks, savings and loans, savings banks, and credit unions—are combined, they make up about one-third of the total financial assets of all U.S. financial institutions. The remainder of the sector's financial assets are held by a highly diverse group of nondeposit financial institutions. *Life insurance companies,* which protect policyholders against the risks of premature death and disability, are among the most important nondeposit institutions and rank fourth behind commercial banks in total assets. The other type of insurance firm—*property-casualty insurers*—offers a wider array of policies to reduce the risk of loss associated with crime, weather damage, and personal negligence. Among the most specialized financial institutions are *pension funds,* which protect their customers against the risk of outliving their sources of income in the retirement years. Private pensions now rank third behind banks and mutual funds in total assets held within the U.S. financial system. (See again Exhibit 2.9.)

| EXHIBIT 2.9 | Total Financial Assets Held by U.S. Financial Institutions, Selected Years ($ Billions at Year-End) | | | | |
|---|---|---|---|---|---|
| Financial Institutions | 1970 | 1980 | 1990 | 2000 | 2006* |
| **Financial intermediaries:** | | | | | |
| Commercial banks | $ 489 | $1,248 | $3,340 | $6,488 | $9,528 |
| Savings and loan associations and savings banks | 252 | 794 | 1,358 | 1,219 | 1,829 |
| Life insurance companies | 201 | 464 | 1,367 | 3,204 | 4,479 |
| Private pension funds | 110 | 413 | 1,629 | 4,587 | 4,876 |
| Investment companies (mutual funds) | 47 | 64 | 602 | 4,457 | 6,473 |
| State and local government pension funds | 60 | 198 | 820 | 2,290 | 2,791 |
| Finance companies | 63 | 199 | 611 | 1,138 | 1,300 |
| Property-casualty insurance companies | 50 | 174 | 534 | 872 | 1,280 |
| Money market funds | — | 74 | 498 | 1,812 | 2,014 |
| Credit unions | 18 | 72 | 202 | 441 | 703 |
| Mortgage banks | — | 16 | 49 | 36 | 32 |
| Real estate investment trusts | 4 | 6 | 13 | 62 | 385 |
| **Other financial institutions:** | | | | | |
| Security brokers and dealers | 16 | 36 | 262 | 1,221 | 2,296 |

*Figures are for the first quarter of 2006.

Source: Board of Governors of the Federal Reserve System, *Flow of Funds Accounts: Financial Assets and Liabilities,* selected years.

Other important financial institutions include finance companies, investment companies (mutual funds), and real estate investment trusts. *Finance companies* lend money to businesses and consumers to meet short-term working capital and long-term investment needs. *Investment companies* pool the funds contributed by thousands of savers by selling shares and then investing in securities sold in the open market and are particularly important in holding and investing the public's retirement savings. A specialized type of investment company is the *money market fund,* which accepts savings (share) accounts from businesses and individuals and places those funds in high-quality, short-term (money market) securities. Also related to investment companies are *real estate investment trusts,* one of the smallest members of the financial institutions sector, which invest mainly in commercial and residential properties. Finally, near the bottom of the list, size-wise, are *mortgage banks,* which facilitate the raising of credit to construct new businesses and homes.

## Classifying Financial Institutions

**depository institutions**
**contractual institutions**
**investment institutions**

Financial institutions may be grouped in a variety of different ways. One of the most important distinctions is between **depository institutions** (commercial banks, savings and loan associations, savings banks, and credit unions); **contractual institutions** (insurance companies and pension funds); and **investment institutions** (mutual funds and real estate investment trusts). Depository institutions derive the bulk of their loanable funds from deposit accounts sold to the public. Contractual institutions attract funds by offering legal contracts to protect the saver against risk (such as an insurance policy or retirement account). Some investment institutions, particularly mutual funds, sell shares to the public and invest the proceeds in stocks, bonds, and other assets in the hope of providing higher returns to their shareholders. Other investment institutions facilitate the buying and selling of securities and other assets as in the case of brokers and dealers.

## Portfolio (Financial-Asset) Decisions by Financial Institutions

The management of a financial institution is called on daily to make *portfolio decisions*—that is, *deciding what financial assets to buy or sell.* A number of factors affect these critical decisions. For example, the *relative rate of return and risk* attached to different financial assets will affect the composition of each financial institution's portfolio. Obviously, if management is interested in maximizing profits and has minimal aversion to risk, it will tend to pursue the highest yielding financial assets available, such as corporate bonds and stocks. A more risk-averse institution, on the other hand, is likely to surrender some yield in return for the greater safety available from acquiring government bonds and high-quality money market instruments.

The *cost, volatility, and maturity of incoming funds* provided by surplus-budget units (ultimate savers) also have a significant impact on the financial assets acquired by financial institutions. Banks, for example, derive a substantial portion of their funds from checkable deposits, which are relatively inexpensive but highly volatile. Such an institution will tend to concentrate its lending activities in short- and medium-term loans to avoid an embarrassing shortage of cash (liquidity). On the other hand, a financial institution such as a pension fund, which receives a stable and predictable inflow of savings, is largely freed from concern over short-term liquidity needs. It is able to invest heavily in long-term financial assets. Thus, the *hedging principle*—the approximate matching of the maturity of financial assets held with liabilities taken on—is an important guide for choosing those financial assets that a financial institution wants to hold in its portfolio.

Decisions on what financial assets to acquire and what financial assets to issue to the public are also influenced by the *size* of the individual financial institution. Larger institutions frequently can take advantage of greater *diversification* in their sources and uses of funds. This means that the overall risk of a portfolio of financial assets can be reduced by acquiring financial assets from many different deficit-budget units (DBUs or ultimate borrowers). Similarly, a larger financial institution can contact a broader range of surplus-budget units (SBUs or ultimate savers) and achieve greater stability in its incoming flows of funds. At the same time, through *economies of scale* (size), larger financial institutions can often sell financial services at a lower cost per unit and pass those cost savings along to their customers.

Finally, *regulations and competition,* two external forces, play major roles in shaping the financial assets acquired and issued by financial institutions. Because they hold the bulk of the public's savings and are so crucial to economic growth, financial intermediaries are among the most heavily regulated of all business firms. Commercial banks are prohibited from investing in low-quality or highly volatile loans and securities in many countries. Insurance companies and pension funds must restrict asset purchases to those a "prudent person" would most likely choose. Most government regulations in this sector pertain to the assets that can be acquired, the adequacy of net worth, and the services that can be offered to the public. Such regulations are designed primarily to ensure the safety of the public's funds.

## 2.9   The Disintermediation of Funds

**disintermediation**

One factor that has influenced the financial assets selected by financial institutions for their portfolios from time to time is the phenomenon of **disintermediation.** Exactly opposite from the intermediation of funds, disintermediation means the withdrawal of funds from a financial intermediary by ultimate lenders (SBUs) and the lending of those funds directly to ultimate borrowers (DBUs). In other words, disintermediation involves the shifting of funds from indirect finance to direct and semidirect finance (see Exhibit 2.10).

**Key URLs:**
To learn more about disintermediation see, in particular, **http://en.wikipedia.org** and answers.com/topic/disintermediation

You engage in disintermediation when you remove funds from a savings account at the local bank and purchase common stock or other financial assets through a broker. The phenomenon is more likely to occur during periods of high and rapidly rising interest rates, when the higher returns demanded by savers may outpace the interest rates offered by financial intermediaries. Disintermediation forces a financial institution to surrender funds and, if severe, may lead to losses of assets and ultimate failure.

A good example of disintermediation was provided by banks and savings associations which, during the 1980s and early 1990s, lost billions of dollars in assets due to massive withdrawals of funds by worried depositors who feared the loss of their savings. Although intermediaries are forced to be more liquid and reduce their credit-granting activities during periods of disintermediation, there is no evidence that the *total* flow of credit through the financial system is necessarily reduced during such periods. Moreover, particularly when interest rates are low or declining or the riskiness of financial instruments appears to be rising in the marketplace, disintermediation may reverse itself as funds flow back into the perceived "safe haven" of financial

**reintermediation**

intermediaries—a process called **reintermediation**.

### New Types of Disintermediation

Some authorities argue that new forms of disintermediation have appeared in recent years, some initiated by financial intermediaries themselves and some by their borrowing customers. For example, some banks in recent years have sold off some of their loans because of difficulties in raising enough capital. At the same time, some of their largest borrowing customers have learned how to raise funds directly from the open market (i.e., through direct and semidirect finance) rather than borrowing from a bank or other traditional financial intermediary.

**Key URL:**
For additional discussion of the differences between bank-dominated and market-dominated financial systems see especially **http://ideas.repec.org**

In recent years many traditional financial intermediaries, such as banks and credit unions, have been challenged by nonfinancial retail and industrial firms attempting to draw financial-service customers away. Prominent examples include General Electric,

**EXHIBIT 2.10**

**Financial Disintermediation**

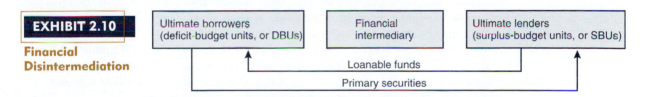

General Motors, Target, and Toyota which recently set up industrial loan companies (ILCs) that offer services similar to those provided by smaller banks and finance companies. Recently the world's largest retailer, Wal-Mart, submitted an application for a charter to the state of Utah and to the FDIC for deposit insurance (later withdrawn) in an effort to set up their own ILC, creating a storm of controversy that such a step might weaken public confidence in the financial system and drive many traditional financial intermediaries out of business.

These new forms of disintermediation have tended not only to slow the growth of some financial institutions but also to gradually reduce the overall importance of traditional financial intermediaries within the global financial system. A substantial volume of funds today flow around traditional financial intermediaries toward other financial-service providers and through direct and semidirect financial market channels.

## 2.10.  Bank-Dominated versus Market-Dominated Financial Systems

**bank-dominated financial systems**

Many countries financial systems today are called **bank-dominated financial systems** because of the prominent role that banks play in supplying credit and attracting savings. Examples include China, Japan, and South Korea as well as Germany and other countries in Eastern and Western Europe where banks account for more than half the assets of all financial institutions. Bank-denominated systems tend to emerge where there is less protection for the rights of small investors and rules are not well defined or enforced, impeding the development of security markets for stocks and bonds. Without adequate investor protection and rules those in need of capital tend to avoid the open market and develop strong relationships with banks and other traditional lenders.

While bank-dominated systems emerged centuries ago, today a change is underway. A growing number of financial systems appear to be gradually moving toward **market-dominated financial systems,** in which traditional financial intermediaries are gradually playing somewhat lesser roles and growing numbers of borrowers (particularly the largest corporations) are selling securities (e.g., stocks and bonds) in the open market to get the funds they need. Prominent examples of such systems include those in Great Britain and the United States.

**market-dominated financial systems**

In short, early financial systems have tended to be bank-dominated. However, as financial sophistication grows and effective legal systems appear, financial systems tend to become more market oriented. Such a change is especially evident today in Western Europe where national financial systems are becoming more integrated with each other and debt and equity capital flow more smoothly across political boundaries.

Is this emerging trend in financial-system architecture beneficial? No one knows for sure, but there is at least limited evidence that such a change in the structure of the financial system could be helpful to the public and especially to those borrowing money. With the emergence of market-dominated systems there may be greater competition to attract the public's savings, higher returns for savers, increased competition among lenders, and more funds available to loan. Some experts believe the financial system may become more stable, so that troubles in the banking sector will have less of a negative impact on the system as a whole. On the other hand, if traditional financial intermediaries begin to decline, they may become less efficient and more prone to failure. Hopefully the passage of time will reveal what the real benefits and costs are of less bank and more market domination of the financial system.

## QUESTIONS TO HELP YOU STUDY

13. What is *direct finance? Semidirect finance? Indirect finance?*

14. In the evolution of the financial system, which do you think came first—direct, indirect, or semidirect finance? Why do you think this is so?

15. What are the essential differences between *primary* and *secondary securities?* Why are these instruments important to the operation of the financial system?

16. In what different ways are financial institutions classified or grouped? Why are such classifications or groupings important in helping us understand what different financial institutions do and what kinds of financial assets they prefer to hold?

17. Which financial institutions are the *largest* within the financial system? Why do you think this is so?

18. What factors influence the particular financial assets each financial institution acquires?

19. What is *disintermediation* and why is it important? How has disintermediation changed in recent years? What is meant by the term *reintermediation?*

20. Explain the difference between a *bank-dominated financial system* and a *market-dominated financial system.* What trends in the structure of the financial system appear to be ongoing in the more highly developed economies around the world?

## Summary of the Chapter's Main Points

The global financial system of money and capital markets performs the important function of channeling savings into investment. In that process a unique kind of asset—a *financial asset*—is created.

- Financial assets represent *claims against the income and assets* of individuals and institutions issuing those claims. There are three major categories of financial assets—*money, debt,* and *equities.* A fourth instrument, *derivatives,* is closely related to financial assets, deriving its value from these assets.

- *Money* is among the most important financial assets because it serves as a medium of exchange to facilitate purchases of goods and services, a standard for valuing all items bought and sold, a store of value (purchasing power) for the future, and a reserve of liquidity (immediate spending power). Despite all these advantages, money has a weakness—susceptibility to inflation (i.e., a rising price level), because its rate of return is normally so low. In contrast, the financial assets represented by *debt* or *equity* securities, and often by *derivatives* as well, carry greater average yields but, unlike money, may incur loss when converted into immediately spendable funds.

- The creation of financial assets occurs within the financial system through three different channels—direct, semidirect, or indirect finance. *Direct finance* involves the direct exchange of financial assets for money in which borrowers (deficit-budget units, or DBUs) and lenders (surplus-budget units or SBUs) meet directly with each other to conduct their business. *Semidirect finance* involves the use of a broker or dealer to help bring borrower and lender together and reduce information costs. *Indirect finance* refers to the creation of financial assets by financial intermediaries who accept *primary securities* from ultimate borrowers (DBUs) and issue *secondary securities* to ultimate savers (SBUs) to raise funds.

- *Financial intermediaries* (such as banks, pension funds, and insurance companies) have grown to dominate most financial systems today due to their greater expertise and efficiency in diversifying away some of the risks involved in lending money.

- One of the most serious management problems encountered by some financial intermediaries is *disintermediation*—the loss of funds from an intermediary to direct or semidirect finance. Much of the disintermediation experienced by modern intermediaries has occurred due to *financial innovation.* Borrowers have found new ways to obtain the funds they need without going through an intermediary. However, in times of heightened uncertainty, this process may be reversed with *reintermediation* occurring as funds flow back into financial intermediaries from direct and semidirect finance as investors seek a "safe haven" for their investments.

- Finally, financial systems around the world appear to fall into one of two broad categories—*bank-dominated financial systems* and *market-dominated financial systems.* In bank-dominated systems the majority of financial assets arise from the banking system. When banks get into trouble the financial system itself may experience difficulties with risk exposure and slower growth. In market-dominated financial systems, by contrast, security brokers and dealers tend to be leaders in the financial system and often provide the greatest volume of funds to those in need of new capital. Market-dominated financial systems are heavily dependent upon direct and semidirect finance (i.e., the open market), while bank-dominated systems tend to rely upon financial intermediaries (indirect finance) for raising funds.

## Key Terms Appearing in This Chapter

## Problems and Issues

1. In a recent year, the various sectors of the economy listed below reported the following *net* changes in their financial assets and liabilities (measured in billions of dollars):

| | Net Acquisitions of Financial Assets | Net Increase in Liabilities |
|---|---|---|
| Households | $ 434.6 | $ 292.0 |
| Farm businesses | 2.7 | −2.5 |
| Nonfarm noncorporate businesses | 8.7 | 35.0 |
| Nonfinancial corporations | 84.9 | 127.8 |
| State and local governments | 74.8 | 60.6 |
| U.S. government | 13.0 | 236.3 |
| Foreign individuals and institutions | 150.7 | 29.0 |
| Federal Reserve System | 32.0 | 31.2 |
| Commercial banking | 256.0 | 245.7 |
| Private nonbank financial institutions | 556.9 | 590.7 |

Using these figures, indicate which sectors were deficit-budget sectors (DBUs) and which were surplus-budget sectors (SBUs) for the year under study. Were there any balanced-budget sectors? Which sectors were the largest net lenders and the largest net borrowers during the year? For all these sectors *combined*, were more funds loaned or more funds borrowed? Why do you think there is a discrepancy between total funds loaned and total funds borrowed?

2. In this chapter, a number of different types of financial transactions were discussed: *direct finance, semidirect finance, indirect finance* (intermediation), *disintermediation* and *reintermediation*. Examine each of the following financial transactions and indicate which type it is. (*Note:* Some of the transactions described below involve more than one type of financial transaction. Be sure to identify *all* types involved.)

   a. Borrowing money from a bank.
   b. Purchasing a life insurance policy.
   c. Selling shares of stock through a broker and returning the proceeds of the sale to your checking account.
   d. Withdrawing money from a savings deposit account and lending it to a friend.
   e. Selling shares of stock to a colleague at work.
   f. Your corporation's contracting with an investment banker to help sell its bonds.
   g. Writing a bank check to purchase stock from your broker.

3. ITT Corporation in the most recent period reported current sales receipts of $542 million, current operating expenditures of $577 million, and net new debt issued of $5 million. What change in holdings of financial assets must have occurred over the period? Was ITT a deficit-, surplus-, or balanced-budget unit in the most recent period? Explain why.

4. What would happen to the purchasing power of the U.S. dollar if the base period for the cost of living index were 1980 = 100 and the index reached the following levels in the indicated years?

   a. 1985—116

   b. 1990—127

   c. 1995—134

   d. 2000—151

   e. 2005—170

5. A household receives $6,000 in income for the month of September. Which of the following could have been true of the household's financial assets and liabilities (debt) if its total expenditures for the month amounted to $7,000?

   a. Its financial assets grew by $1,000 and its debt grew by $2,000.

   b. Its financial assets fell by $2,000 and its debt grew by $1,000.

   c. Its financial assets grew by $2,000 and its debt grew by $1,000.

   d. Its financial assets grew by $2,000 and its debt fell by $1,000.

6. Marvin purchases a $2,000 computer online using his credit card. His wife, Jane, purchases an identical computer with a check. For Marvin and Jane's combined household balance sheet. What is true?

   a. Total assets have increased by $4,000, but there has been no change in net worth.

   b. Total assets have increased by $4,000, while total liabilities rose by $2,000.

   c. Total financial assets fell by $2,000, while total liabilities rose by $2,000.

   d. Total financial assets fell by $2,000, while net worth remained unchanged.

 7. Jack and Jill are small business owners who run a hot dog stand licensed to operate outside a business shopping district. They have been so successful that they believe a second hot dog stand in the area also would be profitable. The capital expense to set it up would be $10,000 and they are considering several options. Use a spreadsheet to evaluate these options by inserting (i) their receipts in column 1; (ii) expenses in column 2; (iii) change in financial assets in column 3; and (iv) change in their debt in column 4. State whether they would be a surplus-budget unit or a deficit-budget unit under each option.

   a. Their sales for the month turn out to be $12,000 and their expenses are $9,500; they borrow $10,000 for the new hot dog stand.

   b. Their sales for the month turn out to be $15,000 and their expenses $9,500; they sell $5,000 in stock and borrow the remaining funds needed to finance the new hot dog stand.

   c. Their sales for the month turn out to be $8,000 and their expenses are $9,500; they choose neither to borrow any funds nor build the second hot dog stand.

   d. Their sales for the month turn out to be $9,500 and their expenses also are $9,500; they use $5,000 in their bank account (with no other asset sales) to help finance the new hot dog stand.

## Web-Based Problems

1. The total volume of *primary securities* created by the banking system as a whole is referred to as *bank credit.* The total volume of *secondary securities* issued by the banking system is given by the banks' *total liabilities* minus any interbank lending, referred to as either "borrowings from other banks" or "federal funds purchased."

   a. Go to the Web site of the Federal Reserve System and find its H.8 statistical release: **federalreserve.gov/releases/h8/Current/.** Identify the total volume of primary and secondary securities for the banking system as a whole for the most recent quarter.

   b. Compute the *difference* between the total amount of credit created by the banking system in the form of primary securities and the banking system's liabilities in the form of secondary securities. What does this difference represent? What is this difference expressed as a percentage of total assets in the banking system?

   c. See if you can find annual balance sheets for at least two of the largest U.S. banks—for example, Bank of America (BAC) and Wells Fargo (WFC). Identify the total amount of primary securities (investment securities plus loans, claims, and advances) and secondary securities (customer deposits plus short-term borrowings less federal funds purchased) for each bank. Perform similar calculations as in part (b) to determine what percentage of the total assets for each of these banks is the difference between primary and secondary securities on their books. Does this tell you anything about these very large banks relative to the banking industry as a whole?

2. Most major security dealers houses engage in both *semidirect* and *indirect* financing in their roles as *financial intermediaries.*

   a. Identify which of these two types of financing should show up on the intermediary's balance sheet and which should not. Explain.

   b. How would you expect these two different types of financial transactions to show up on the intermediary's income statement?

   c. Consult the World Wide Web for the annual balance sheet and income statement of a major dealer house such as Lehman Brothers (www.lehman.com) or Goldman Sachs (www.gs.com).

   d. Identify the *semidirect* and *indirect* finance activities of these or other dealer houses.

## Selected References to Explore

1. Bauer, Paul W. "When Is Checkout Time?" *Economic Commentary,* Federal Reserve Bank of Cleveland, September 1, 2004, pp. 1–4.

www.mhhe.com.rose10e

2. Beck, Thorsten, and Ross Levine. "Industry Growth and Capital Allocation: Does Having a Market- or Bank-Based System Matter?" *NBER Working Papers 8982,* National Bureau of Economic Research, Inc., 2002.
3. Fitzgerald, Terry J. "Money Growth and Inflation," *Economic Commentary,* Federal Reserve Bank of Cleveland, August 1, 1999, pp. 1–4.
4. Gurley, John, and Edward S. Shaw. *Money in a Theory of Finance.* Washington, DC: Brookings Institution, 1960.
5. Levine, Ross. "More on Finance and Growth: More Finance, More Growth?" *Review,* Federal Reserve Bank of St. Louis, July/August 2003, pp. 31–52.
6. Revell, Jack. *The Recent Evolution of the Financial System.* New York: MacMillan, May 1997.
7. Santomero, Anthony M. "The Changing Patterns of Payments in the United States," *Business Review,* Federal Reserve Bank of Philadelphia, Third Quarter 2005, pp. 1–8.

# Chapter 3

# The Financial Information Marketplace

## Learning Objectives

### in This Chapter

- You will be able to identify the most important sources of information about the money and capital markets and the financial system.

- You will discover why the efficient distribution of information within the financial system is so important and what can happen when relevant financial information is not readily available to all market participants.

- You will understand how any individual or institution active in the financial marketplace can keep track of the prices of financial assets, interest rates, and other financial variables.

- In an appendix to the chapter you will learn about the *Flow of Funds Accounts of the United States* and discover what is meant by "social accounting."

## What's in This Chapter?
## Key Topics Outline

**The Efficient Markets Hypothesis: Assumptions and Forms**

**Insider Trading**

**Asymmetric Information**

**Problems of Asymmetry: Lemons, Adverse Selection, Moral Hazard**

**Remedies for Asymmetry**

**Sources of Information for Bonds, Notes, and Corporate Stock**

**Information on Security Issuers and the Economy**

**Appendix: The Flow of Funds in the Financial System**

## 3.1    Introduction: The Importance of Information in the Financial Marketplace

Every day in the money and capital markets, individuals and institutions must make important financial decisions. For those who plan to borrow, for example, key decisions must be made concerning the timing of a request for credit and exactly where the necessary funds should be raised. Lenders of funds must make decisions on when and where to invest their limited resources, considering such factors as the risk and expected return on loans and securities available in the financial marketplace. Government policymakers also are intimately involved in the financial decision-making process. It is the responsibility of government to ensure that financial markets function smoothly in channeling savings into investment and in creating a volume of credit sufficient to support business and commerce.

Sound financial decisions require adequate and reliable *financial information.* Borrowers, lenders, and those who make financial policy require data on the prices and yields attached to individual loans and securities today and the prices and yields likely to prevail in the future. A borrower, for example, may decide to postpone taking out a loan if it appears that the cost of credit will be significantly lower six months from now than it is today. Moreover, because economic conditions exert a profound impact on the money and capital markets, the financial decision maker must also be aware of economic data series that reflect trends in employment, prices, and related types of information.

Where do financial decision makers go to find the data they need? We may divide the sources of information relied upon by financial decision makers into four broad groups: (1) debt security prices and yields, (2) stock prices and dividend yields, (3) information on security issuers, and (4) general economic and financial conditions across the entire economy and financial system. In this chapter, we will discuss several of the most important sources of each of these different kinds of information.

## 3.2    The Great Debate over Efficient Markets and Asymmetric Information

Before we examine the principal sources of information available to financial market participants, however, we need to be aware of a great debate going on in the field of finance today concerning the availability and cost of information. One view, referred **efficient markets hypothesis** to as the **efficient markets hypothesis,** contends that information relevant to the pricing (valuation) of loans, securities, and other financial assets is readily available to *all* borrowers and lenders at *negligible cost.* The other view, called the *asymmetric information hypothesis,* argues that the financial marketplace contains pockets of inefficiency in the availability and use of information. Some market players—for example, professional lenders of funds, auditors, attorneys, journalists, or members of management and the boards of directors of corporations—may possess special information that enables them to get a more accurate picture of the value and risk of certain assets. These "insiders" allegedly can earn excess returns by selectively trading financial assets based on the special information they have been able to acquire—information that would be costly for others to obtain.

In this chapter, we briefly sketch out how these two contrasting views of the information marketplace—efficient markets and asymmetric information—differ in terms of the cost and availability of relevant information to decision makers in the financial marketplace and ultimately affect the prices (values) of all financial assets.

## The Efficient Markets Hypothesis (EMH)

*What Is an Efficient Market?* The efficient markets hypothesis (hereafter EMH) suggests that *all* information that has a bearing on the market value of stocks, bonds, and other financial assets will be used to value (price) those assets. *An efficient market neither wastes nor misuses information.* Under the terms of the EMH, the money and capital markets will not consistently ignore information that can earn profits. Because financial markets today may encompass large numbers of profit-maximizing, well-informed, intelligent investors there won't be any profitable trades of assets not made (at least not for very long) and there will be no systematic mispricing of assets.

For example, if an individual has savings to invest in stocks and bonds, he or she will seek out information on the financial condition of the business firms issuing those particular financial assets, the quality of their management and products, the strength of their industry, and the condition of the economy in which each firm operates. Each individual investor will rationally use *all* of the available information relevant to valuing the stocks and bonds he or she might wish to buy. Because all investors are likely to be seeking the same information for the same reasons, the current market price of any financial asset will reflect all relevant information that investors as a group have been able to obtain regarding that asset's true value. Because all information available has been used to establish the value of financial assets, no single user of that same information can consistently earn "excess returns" or "abnormal returns" by trading on information available to all. Rather, in an efficient marketplace, each financial asset will generate an "ordinary," "normal," or "expected" rate of return commensurate with its level of risk.

*If the EMH is correct, any temporary deviation of actual returns from expected returns* (i.e., excess positive or excess negative returns) *should be quickly eliminated as investors react to temporary underpricing* (when a financial asset's actual return rises *above* its expected return) *or temporary overpricing of assets* (when a financial asset's actual return falls *below* its expected return) *and make changes in their asset portfolios.* Investors in the money and capital markets will react to financial assets they perceive to be *underpriced* (with positive excess returns) or *overpriced* (with negative excess returns) by buying or selling the temporarily mispriced assets.

In short, the discovery of a financial asset whose expected return lies consistently above or below its "expected," "ordinary," or "normal" return would be a signal of possible market inefficiency, inconsistent with the EMH. This may be true because rational market participants use *all* relevant information available. Because all financial asset prices may instantaneously incorporate all relevant information few excess returns from trading assets will be available.

Moreover, when *new* relevant information reaches the marketplace, the prices (value) of financial assets normally *will change quickly* as investors possessing this new information move rapidly to seize any profitable opportunities that appear, bidding up the prices of some assets and lowering the prices of others. And because market prices respond only to *new* information, which by its nature is unpredictable, the value of financial assets cannot be predicted consistently. If we could consistently predict asset values, this would be evidence of an inefficient market in which not all information is being fully utilized.

The essential contribution that the EMH makes to our understanding of the money and capital markets is to suggest that the current prices of all financial assets represent the *optimal use* of available information. And each asset's price, determined by demand-and-supply forces in the marketplace, is an optimal forecast of each asset's fundamental or intrinsic value.

In fact, a financial asset's current market price may be the *best estimate* of that asset's expected fundamental or intrinsic value. However, each asset's fundamental value will vary with the state of the world (e.g., the condition of the economy and the current concerns of asset buyers about risk) prevailing at the time the asset is being traded. Therefore, the current price of a financial asset equals its expected fundamental value given all possible states of the world recognized by buyers and sellers. Under the terms of the EMH, the price of a financial asset must embody *all* of the information relevant to the valuation of that asset, including all present and past information.

*Different Forms of the EMH*    In recent years, the EMH has been split into three different versions based on what each assumes to be true about the availability and cost of information. These three versions are:

**Key URL:**
To examine the evidence for and against the efficient markets hypothesis see, for example, **investorhome.com/ emh.htm**

1. *Weak form of the EMH,* which argues that the current prices of financial assets contain all information that buyers and sellers have been able to obtain on the past trading of those assets: their *price history and past volume of trading.* Moreover, this past price and trading information is available freely to all market participants. No one buyer or seller can consistently earn excess profits beyond those that are "normal" or "expected" for the amount of risk taken on from trading on this historical price and volume information. If this were not true, investors would have figured out long ago how to profit from historical data and asset prices would have been adjusted accordingly, eliminating further opportunities for exceptional returns.

2. *Semistrong form of the EMH,* which contends that the current prices of financial assets already reflect *all publicly available information* affecting the value of these instruments, including information about past prices and volume, the financial condition and credit rating of each issuer, any published forecasts, the condition of the economy, and all other relevant information. All buyers and sellers are rational and use all publicly available information to help them value financial assets. No one buyer or seller will, therefore, find consistent opportunities for exceptional profits by trading on publicly available information.

3. *Strong form of the EMH,* which argues that the current prices of financial assets capture *all* the information—*both public and private*—that is relevant to the value of financial instruments. This includes the information possessed by "insiders," such as the officers, directors, and principal owners of a corporation issuing stocks and bonds or even accountants, attorneys, or journalists who work with the company and have access to its privileged information.

**Key URLs:**
To sample the long-term debate over the random walk hypothesis see especially **en.wikipedia.org; investopedia.com/ university/concepts; and answers.com/ topic/random-walk- hypothesis**

Repeated research studies tend to support the weak and semistrong forms of the EMH. Only limited opportunities for exceptional profits flowing from trading on past or present publicly available information appear to exist. According to the related concept of *random walk,* successive changes in asset prices often appear as unpredictable as a sequence of random numbers so that smaller, less-well-informed investors should, on average, do about as well as more well-informed financial analysts in anticipating asset price changes.

The strong form of the EMH, however, has aroused the most controversy and resulted in mixed research findings. This may be due to the existence of insider trading activities and because of the apparent presence of pockets of special information asymmetrically scattered throughout the financial system.[1]

*Insiders and Insider Trading*   The word "insiders" has come to have a sinister meaning for most of us. It smacks of something illegal or unfair. Someone has special knowledge or special privileges and can, at will, take advantage of that knowledge or privilege and profit from it, perhaps at our expense. Nowhere is the term "insider" more recognized and more often condemned than in the money and capital markets.

*What Is Insider Trading?*   The board of directors of a company, its officers or managers, and even many of its staff employees may know something about its condition the public doesn't know, and as such, they may be able to benefit from that knowledge, perhaps by buying or selling the firm's stock before the public becomes aware of what's really going on. Section 10(b)-5 of the U.S. Securities and Exchange Act forbids any "manipulative or deceptive device" in trading securities and other financial assets, and Section 16(c) of the Securities and Exchange Act requires all trading by insiders to be reported to the Securities and Exchange Commission (SEC) within the first 10 days of the month following the particular month an insider trade has occurred. These insider trades are reported in the SEC's *Official Summary of Insider Transactions.* Recent federal laws have raised the maximum criminal penalties for insider trading up to a million dollars and have made it possible for judges to set jail terms for offenders of up to 10 years in certain cases. Those harmed by insider trading may file civil suits for recovery of losses.

*When Is Insider Trading Legal or Illegal?*   Recent research suggests that **insider trading** frequently "works" in the sense that insiders often win exceptional ("abnormal" or "excess") returns on the trading of financial assets. For example, approximately one-half of the increase in the price of a firm's stock associated with the appearance of "new" information occurs *prior* to the release of that information to the public. These "early" price movements suggest that trading is taking place by insiders or by others privy to the "new" information before it becomes public knowledge.

insider trading

One of the most famous insider trading cases in history involved Michael Milken, a securities dealer and broker who worked with numerous companies to arrange their new bond and stock offerings and used some of the information he gained to earn millions of dollars in the financial markets. Ultimately, Milken paid fines in the hundreds of millions of dollars and went to prison for a time, eventually receiving a presidential pardon.

Actually, insiders can use privileged information legally if they provide that information to the public *before* they go into the money and capital markets to trade financial assets. However, the number of insider trading cases prosecuted has been rising, despite doubts expressed by some experts that anyone is really consistently hurt by insider trading activity. In fact, insider deals may, under certain circumstances, actually be beneficial to the efficient functioning of the financial marketplace.

For example, consider managers who produce performance gains for their company. Shouldn't they be able to benefit from trading in their firm's stock? Governments that penalize insider trading may actually discourage business managers from taking on risk and demonstrating their superior managerial capabilities. Other experts argue that businesses themselves, not the government, should decide if they want to permit or prohibit insiders from trading in their bonds, stocks, or other financial instruments.

[1] For further discussion of research findings regarding the EMH and the random walk hypothesis see Chapter 20 on the market for corporate stock.

Moreover, they argue, insider-trading activity may actually *improve* market efficiency by encouraging more rapid information flows and quicker adjustments in the prices of financial assets to the appearance of *new* information. As a result, financial assets may be more correctly priced more quickly. This would tend to reduce risk to investors who hold ownership (equity) shares in a particular business.

Nonetheless, corporations today, especially those whose stock is publicly traded, are encouraged to monitor closely employees trading their stock. The criminal and civil penalties can be onerous, including the negative publicity that often surrounds these cases (as illustrated in recent years by the damages associated with alleged insider transactions involving associates of AT&T, Enron, IBM, ImClone, and Tyson Foods). Moreover, insider trading seems more difficult to get away with today due to the growing use of electronic surveillance systems by corporations themselves, major stock exchanges, and security trading firms.

## The Asymmetric Information Hypothesis (AIH)

What if, contrary to the efficient markets hypothesis, we lived in a world where *all* relevant information about the true value of financial assets was *not* readily available or was expensive to obtain? What would happen if some important information pertinent to financial decision making were distributed *asymmetrically?* Suppose *some* individuals and institutions had access to pockets of information concerning the true value and risk of financial assets and others simply did not. This is the basic premise of the **asymmetric information hypothesis** (here after AIH).

asymmetric
information
hypothesis

The asymmetric view says that there *are* pockets of special information—a "lumpiness" in the supply of relevant information about financial assets. These pockets may include corporate insiders, journalists, security dealers, and financial analysts who possess unique analytical skills in spotting profitable trades. These possessors of special knowledge need not be operating illegally. Indeed, they may come by their unique talents in assessing value and risk through rigorous schooling and on-the-job training or by virtue of the special location they occupy within the financial system. For example, every year hundreds of corporations flock to college campuses to hire graduates whom they believe have the potential to become expert judges of the quality of financial assets.

Attempts to exploit asymmetries in information could have great consequences for the financial marketplace as a whole. For example, under the terms of the AIH there will be variations in both the quantity and the quality of information available. Unfortunately, most users of financial information cannot easily assess its quality at the time they must pay for it. Thus, considerable incentive exists in the money and capital markets for sellers of information to make wild claims about the quality of the information they are selling. It is not clear that the financial markets have yet developed an effective mechanism for policing the quality and truthfulness of information (as exemplified recently by the financial problems of such firms as Enron Corp. and Global Crossing), although, over time, those who provide misleading information may suffer a loss of reputation and eventually exit the industry due to lack of demand for their services. In short, the presence of imperfect or "bad" information may lead to market inefficiency, thwart the making of optimal decisions, and lead to more government intervention in the marketplace in an effort to fix the problems that asymmetrically distributed and poor quality information can create.

The AIH does not necessarily contradict the weak and semistrong forms of the EMH. It concedes that the value of financial assets will capture all publicly available

**ETHICS IN THE MONEY AND CAPITAL MARKETS**

What Is Legal and Illegal Insider Trading in the Money and Capital Markets?

Defining what types of insider activity are legal and what forms are illegal is one of the toughest distinctions to make, and many experts in the field flatly disagree. One problem is deciding who an "insider" really is. Certainly the board of directors, management, and employees of a company whose financial assets are publicly traded would qualify as privileged "insiders." These individuals are said to owe a *fiduciary duty* to act in their company's best interest and the best interests of its stockholders (owners). If these people personally benefit from inside information, they may be charged with breaching their fiduciary duty or with *misappropriating information* that belongs to their employer.

However, government lawyers often argue that outside consultants, investment bankers, and lawyers under contract to provide services to a firm also owe a fiduciary duty to that company and could be considered illegal "insiders," breaching their fiduciary duty if they use the information they receive to engage in asset trading.

Beyond these particular groups of individuals, however, the law is badly split today. Generally speaking, those who clearly have a fiduciary duty because they are paid to work for a firm and benefit personally from using its inside information to score profits in the market run the risk of prosecution. However, if you do *not* work for such a firm and use its insider information to score trading profits, there may be no legal violation because there may be no fiduciary responsibility.

This happened to a print shop worker in the *Chiarella vs. the United States* case (1986) because of profit-generating information that Mr. Chiarella allegedly obtained while setting copy for the corporate clients of his printing firm. However, Mr. Chiarella went free because the Supreme Court found no evidence that he had a fiduciary duty to the firms whose reports he read.

On the other hand, you might be brought to trial on misappropriation of information if you are working for a company that has a relationship with another firm and just happen to overhear nonpublic information and proceed to trade on it. This happened in the case of *James H. O'Hagan* vs. *the United States* (1996). Mr. O'Hagan allegedly found out about a proposed acquisition of Pillsbury—a case being worked on by attorneys in his law firm—and allegedly used that information to generate trading profits. Ultimately, the Supreme Court ruled that misappropriation of information had occurred with respect to the defendant's law firm. Unfortunately, the courts have mixed records on whether misappropriation of information or the existence of fiduciary duty can be broadly applied to individuals who are *not* employees or owners of a business firm, such as family members, psychiatrists, golfing partners, security dealers, or, in the Martha Stewart case, friends.

information. However, it is inconsistent with the strong form of the EMH in believing that some market participants have sufficient access to special (private) information that they can, at times, profit from, thereby earning excess returns. Moreover, where asymmetries are very strong, a financial market can misfire, misallocate resources, and even collapse.

## Problems Asymmetries Can Create: Lemons and Plums

Asymmetries can create many difficulties in the availability and distribution of information. One of the most familiar—often called the *lemons problem*—has confronted used car buyers ever since the automobile was invented. Everyone who has ever purchased a used car is aware of the risks involved in the process. The buyer does not know whether the used automobile he or she is looking at is a real "lemon"—a continuing source of trouble and grief as repair bills mount—or if the car is a "plum"—a solid piece of transportation that runs and runs with few problems. The seller, in hopes of getting a higher price, has a strong incentive to misrepresent the car as a *plum*. Unless he or she is convinced this is true, the buyer will probably be unwilling to pay the full price for a plum due to the risk that the car will ultimately turn out to be a lemon. The seller possesses special ("inside") information built up by personal experience with the vehicle; the buyer cannot obtain this information except at considerable cost (such as by hiring a mechanic to do an inspection of the vehicle).

A similar problem confronts the loan officer of a bank. Dozens of customers come in every day asking for loans, pledging they will use the requested funds for a good purpose that meets the lending institution's credit standards, and promising they will repay their loans on time. Clearly, the loan officer can't be sure without incurring substantial costs which of his or her customers is a lemon or a plum. Equally frustrating, some customers who were plums when they took out their first loan may now be lemons due to changing circumstances, such as the loss of a job or the failure of a business. This asymmetry problem helps explain why credit rating agencies have become so important to lending institutions that willingly pay to have someone accumulate and evaluate the credit histories of borrowing businesses and households.

Given the right circumstances, it can be shown that a market divided between lemons and plums can eventually become largely a market in which *only lemons are offered for sale.* This can happen because buyers will be unwilling to pay a premium price for plums if there is a substantial probability they will, in fact, be purchasing lemons. However, the seller, possessed of inside information, knows whether he owns a plum and will usually be unwilling to sell a plum for the price of a lemon. If there is no low-cost way around this asymmetry problem, the ultimate result over time is that the plums will be driven from the market and only lemons will remain to be sold. *Lower-value assets will drive out higher-value assets.*

What can happen to used cars also can happen to financial assets. Lower-quality borrowers can drive away higher-quality borrowers who are unwilling to borrow at the higher interest rates that lower-quality borrowers must pay. This is a situation in which one price alone (such as the interest rate on a loan) cannot effectively separate the lemons from the plums. Something else is needed to insure that markets function efficiently, including independent audits, warranties, loan commitment fees, and other devices.

Incidentally, if mispricing tends to drive higher-quality borrowers out of a particular market, where might those borrowing institutions go to get the funds they need? One way of escaping this dilemma is to turn to other markets where informational asymmetries may be less of an issue. As we noted in the previous chapter, a new form of *disintermediation* has occurred in recent years in which top-quality borrowers are avoiding traditional lending institutions, such as banks and insurance companies. Instead, they are going straight to the *open market,* selling their bonds, stocks, and other financial assets directly to global investors. In contrast, smaller borrowers with significant informational problems (such as unaudited financial statements) have frequently come to depend upon banks and other traditional lenders for the credit they need. In short, the existence of informational asymmetries has helped to restructure some of our most important marketplaces.

## *Problems Asymmetries Can Create: Adverse Selection*

A related problem revolves around differences in risk presented by different groups of customers who want to enter into contracts with financial institutions. In this case, information asymmetry exists *before* the parties to a contract reach an agreement. When an asymmetrical distribution of information is already present, it can drastically alter the nature of contracts that a business firm is willing to write in order to serve its customers.

For example, banks face an *adverse selection* problem with one of their most important services: checking accounts. To a banker, there are two principal categories of checking account customers: (1) those who hold high deposit balances and write few checks, giving the bank more money to lend while the low level of account activity keeps bank costs down, and (2) those customers who keep low balances in their account but write lots of checks, giving the bank few funds to invest while heavy account activity runs up bank costs. When a customer walks in to open a new account, the banker doesn't know what kind of customer she will be. Only the customer has the "inside" information on what kind of checking account user she is likely to be.

If the banker sets a single, average price for all checking account customers the bank runs the risk of being *adversely selected against* by its potentially most profitable customers. The preferred high-balance, low-activity customers will leave because the one price set by the bank is likely to be too high for them, but that price may be too low to cover the bank's operating costs in serving the less preferred low-balance, high-activity checking account customers. Another bank could simply enter the market with a checking account service that is more attractive to high-balance customers and attract away the most profitable accounts. The first bank would be "adversely selected against" by those particular customers it most wanted to attract.

How does the first bank mitigate this problem of adverse selection? The most common technique used today is to set up a *conditional price schedule* in which the prices vary based on how much money each customer keeps on deposit and how many checks are written each month. The customer then chooses the most appropriate checking account plan. Such an array of different prices (rather than having only one price) for the same service, based on each customer's usage level and deposit balance, helps a bank to ensure that low-balance, high-activity customers will pay higher service fees and that low-activity, high-balance customers will pay lower fees. In effect, the customer "self-selects" his or her own checking account plan according to the "inside" information he or she possesses. Moreover, the customer's choice of any particular deposit plan signals to the banker what kind of customer he or she is likely to be.

Thus, in some situations the problem of asymmetric information can be mitigated by *signaling:* letting participants in the marketplace who possess inside information take actions that will reveal the nature of that unique information to other potential participants. For example, an insider in a corporation who knows that her company is in trouble can signal the problem to the public by selling the company's stock. If the public happens to see insiders selling out, they too may begin to sell, driving the value of the company's stock lower in the financial marketplace.

## *Problems Asymmetries Can Create: Moral Hazard*

Another problem in information asymmetry often arises *after* contracts are agreed to between buyers and sellers. One party to a contract may decide to pursue his own self-interest at the expense of other parties to the agreement. This is known as **moral hazard** and it often arises because of poorly drafted contracts or ineffective monitoring activity by the principal parties involved.

**moral hazard**

For example, the managers of a corporation, instead of managing the company for the benefit of the firm's stockholders, may grant themselves generous benefit packages and lavish offices, boosting their firm's expenses well beyond what is necessary to efficiently produce and sell the firm's products. Management may also conceal bad performance, take on excessive risk, misrepresent the outcomes of projects, or simply shirk in doing their jobs. The result is that management—the *agent* of the stockholders—optimizes its own well-being, while the stockholders—the *principals* in this instance—receive less than optimal returns on their stock. Because information on what is happening inside the firm is often difficult and expensive to obtain, the stockholders (principals) may not be aware for a long time (if ever) of the unnecessary expenses that their agent—the firm's management—is creating. (The act of running up operating costs higher than they need to be is often called *expense preference behavior.*) In this instance the agents are creating a "moral hazard" problem for a company's principals (its shareholders).

Elimination of moral hazard problems can be costly, both in discovering the problem and in rewriting contracts between principals and agents to get rid of it. Usually, moral hazard problems are dealt with by placing appropriate incentives in principal-agent contracts so agents will want to act more in line with the interests of principals. For example, the board of directors of a corporation, representing its stockholders, might tie management salaries to the actual performance of the firm, such as its profitability or sales growth, or to other performance measures linked to the firm's stock price.

## Asymmetry, Efficiency, and Real-World Markets

No market in the real world is either completely efficient or completely asymmetric. Rather, all real-world markets contain elements of *both* efficiency and asymmetry. Recent research has found some evidence that appears to be inconsistent with the pure efficient markets hypothesis. For example, some investors appear to earn excess returns at times from trading the stock of *small firms.* Moreover, some market anomalies seem to run counter to a truly efficient market, such as unusually high stock returns on Fridays and unusually low stock returns on Mondays (known as the *weekend effect*). Stock prices also appear to display exceptionally high volatility in the short run, with some traders apparently buying on the basis of a stock's past performance (*momentum*) rather than buying on the basis of its fundamental value, temporarily driving its price higher, and then, subsequently, selling the stock as its price returns to its former level (a phenomenon called *mean reversion,* which also seems inconsistent with the efficient markets hypothesis). Perhaps real-world markets are split into segments: (1) a highly efficient segment, in which well-informed individuals and institutions (the "smart money") trade, and (2) a segment in which less-well-informed small investors trade, where information *is* asymmetrically distributed, more costly to acquire, and often of poorer quality.

We will see in subsequent chapters of this book how market participants have moved to counter informational asymmetries by developing special kinds of expertise, forming special kinds of organizations (such as credit rating agencies and auditing firms), writing unique contractual agreements (such as detailed insurance and loan contracts that contain deductibles and commitment fees), using multiple prices for the same service to separate profitable from unprofitable clients, and striving continually to become more efficient and reduce the cost of gathering relevant information. It is also useful to bear in mind that the possession of special or inside information does not always result in an advantage for its possessors. Research suggests that, at times, there may be a "curse of knowledge": *Some market participants may be so overloaded with information they cannot effectively sort out what is relevant and what is irrelevant in order to make a profitable decision.*

In this chapter we are exploring the damage that can be done to individuals and institutions in a situation where information is asymmetrically distributed. The classic case, as we saw earlier in this chapter, is the *lemons problem*—sellers have knowledge about the true worth of an asset, but buyers cannot access that information without incurring significant costs. As a result, quality items may be driven from the marketplace, leaving flawed merchandise for people to bid on.

The global online marketer, eBay, which auctions off everything from autos to baseball cards, confronts this quality issue every day. eBay has attacked the "lemons" problem from several different directions. It warns sellers of the consequences of misrepresenting what they sell in terms of damage to their reputation, possible legal action, and loss of access to eBay's market. The firm cooperates with N.E.W. Customer Service in offering warranties to cover at least a portion of a buyer's loss. Moreover, complaints that qualify may receive some reimbursement from eBay itself. Finally, eBay has set up an online dispute mechanism called *SquareTrade* where buyers and sellers attempt to mediate their dispute. As eBay has demonstrated, there are ways of dealing with an uneven distribution of quality information so that markets *can* function effectively.

## Informational Asymmetries and the Law

One way to deal with information asymmetries is to pass laws and regulations designed to improve the flow of information between buyers and sellers, reduce the cost of obtaining quality information, and protect the public against deception in valuing assets. However, as the history of the financial marketplace clearly shows this is not easy to do. For example, a rumor-fed banking panic in 33 CE almost destroyed the global banking system as mobs of frightened depositors descended upon leading Roman banks, fearing their connections with troubled businesses. During the eighteenth century deceptive information and lavish promises helped attract huge sums of money into the highly speculative South Seas bubble, in which the stock of the South Seas Company soared upward before sinking like a stone, ultimately resulting in huge losses when the true value of this scheme finally became known.[2]

In the United States prior to the Great Depression of the 1930s, the public was often victimized by misinformation about the true condition and intent of companies entering the market with new stock and bond issues. More recently, misleading information about the accounting practices and debt loads of Enron Corporation and WorldCom resulted in unprecedented financial losses for individual and institutional investors, including wiping out many workers' pensions. Today scores of Internet hoaxes, including investors hoping to profit by sending out false statements about selected firms, threaten the public's trust of electronic sources of information.

---

[2] In the South Seas bubble, known today as the "Enron of England," the British government made a deal with South Seas Company to help ease Britain's debt burden. Buoyed by this connection South Seas promoted itself as having a profitable monopoly in trading with Latin America and hyped its prospects for future success. Its stock soared before better-informed investors realized the company was substantially overvalued, eventually sending its shares tumbling. The great physicist, Sir Isaac Newton, sold his shares before South Seas collapsed, but couldn't resist reinvesting when the company's stock continued to rise. Sir Isaac lost close to 20,000£ and is reported to have said: "I can calculate the motions of the heavenly bodies but not the madness of people."

In an effort to improve the flow of information about securities offered for public sale and prohibit misinformation and securities fraud, Congress in 1933 passed the Securities Act, requiring companies selling financial assets across state lines to submit a *prospectus* to a federal agency, the Securities and Exchange Commission (SEC), giving detailed economic and financial information about the firm's condition and prospects. Once the prospectus is approved, the SEC requires that the issuer of stocks, bonds, and other financial assets supply a prospectus to any investor interested in buying those assets. Misrepresentation or fraud in a prospectus can trigger lawsuits by the SEC and by investors against a business selling financial assets, its directors, and any public accounting firms involved, as well as dealers handling the sale of those assets.

In 1934 the Securities Exchange Act was passed, requiring corporate insiders to follow guidelines in trading the financial instruments of firms with which they are affiliated in order to avoid excessive profit taking from privileged information. This law also moved to outlaw fraud and misrepresentation in trading financial assets already issued, requiring assets traded on exchanges and trading firms themselves to register with the SEC, providing detailed annual reports to the SEC and to their own shareholders. Shortly thereafter, the Maloney Act was passed, requiring trade associations, such as the National Association of Securities Dealers (NASD), to register with the SEC. Today, NASD tries to discourage cheating and deception by enforcing an ethics code and by licensing dealers.

The Investment Company Act, passed in 1940, required mutual funds (investment companies) to register with the SEC and provide the shareholding public with reports on their activities and performance. The Investment Advisers Act, passed in the same year, required the registration of professional investment advisers, who also must report their procedures for analyzing and recommending investments. In 1970, the Securities Investor Protection Act set up the Securities Investor Protection Corporation (SIPC) to insure an investor against losses of up to $500,000 in securities and up to $100,000 in lost cash should his or her brokerage firm fail. The SIPC agrees to replace any assets lost due to the collapse of a brokerage firm, although it does not guarantee the value of those assets.

In the fall of 2000 the U.S. Securities and Exchange Commission passed Regulation FD (for Fair Disclosure). This required companies to disclose material financial information broadly rather than only to selected viewers (such as stockbrokers or security dealers). This supposedly gives *all* possible investors roughly equal access to market-moving information. Even more recently a settlement between the New York Attorney General's Office and major brokerage companies restricted the exchange of privileged information between security brokers and their wealthiest clients who often pay large brokerage commissions and expect special treatment in return. At about the same time the SEC moved to block mutual funds from releasing inside information about the funds' portfolio strategies to hedge funds and other large investors. Rules such as these help to protect the public by giving them equal access to pertinent information as an aid to sound financial decision making.

While government regulations and controls recently put in place to mitigate the damaging effects of asymmetric information may be helpful in improving the efficiency of the financial markets, many observers think we have a long way to go in solving asymmetric information problems. They point, for example, to the case of Enron Corporation, a huge energy firm that filed for bankruptcy in 2001 and whose alleged insider dealings and questionable accounting practices cost investors billions in stock market losses and destroyed the retirement savings of many Enron employees. The accounting practices of major corporations need a closer look today to make sure

**Key URL:**
Information for investors on current financial scams, on the rights of defrauded investors, and on how to file a complaint dealing with deceptive marketing practices can be found on the Securities and Exchange Commission's Web site: **sec.gov**

The financial markets provide more detailed information every day than any other sector of the economy. Literally millions of data bytes flow through the financial system hourly, with the sheer volume of information often leading to confusion and poor decisions. In recent decades the field of *behavioral and experimental finance* has provided opportunities to test fundamental principles that often get covered up in the daily chaos of real-world markets. Moreover, many financial theories are based on *expectations* which real-world data do not directly provide us.

Researchers in behavioral and experimental finance often design simple experiments in uncomplicated settings away from the bustle of real-world markets, such as in a classroom, laboratory, or through suveys. (One prominent example is the CalTech Laboratory for Experimental Finance (CLEF) in which individuals may trade for real money and communicate their decisions to researchers over the Internet.) This far-less-complicated setting makes it possible to examine one or a few isolated factors while holding everything else constant, just as researchers in biological, chemical, or physics labs work in a controlled environment. The subjects surveyed may be supplied with assets to trade or bytes of information and asked to make financial decisions that can be tracked.

Behavioral and experimental researchers have discovered numerous fundamental principles. For example:

- Only the best-informed traders (i.e., insiders) appear to significantly outperform less-informed traders.

- Investors who purchase market research information do not appear, on average, to achieve greater net returns than investors who do not buy such information.

- Financial markets are able to dispense information efficiently to investors through *both* verbal and nonverbal communication (e.g., through prices and trading volume).

- Financial assets tend to gravitate toward those market participants who assign the highest values to those assets based on the latest information available.

Using simple tools in controlled settings and armed with the principles of economics and psychology, these researchers have affirmed many old ideas about human behavior, but also have challenged some existing theories. They are able to compare the behavior of rational decision makers versus those who may act irrationally when making financial decisions and to examine the behavioral basis of *market anomalies* (such as mispriced assets and seasonal trading patterns) that existing efficient markets theories do not seem to adequately explain. This field remains highly promising as a diagnostic check on the work of theorists and field researchers studying real-world markets.

**Key URLs:**
To explore the issues and findings of behavioral and experimental finance see, for example, ssrn.com; http://ideas.repec.org; and hss.caltech.edu/~pbs/Labfinance.htm

---

that capital-market investors are getting the full amount of reliable and relevant information they need to make rational buy-sell decisions.

In response to the troubles at Enron and other widely publicized corporate scandals the Sarbanes-Oxley Accounting Practices Act (SARBOX) was signed into law in July 2002. The new law set up the Public Company Accounting Oversight Board (PCAOB) to oversee the conduct of corporate auditors, enhance the accuracy and disclosure to the public of corporate insider information, and reduce the incidence of accounting and corporate fraud. SARBOX makes chief executive officers (CEOs) and chief financial officers (CFOs) of public companies responsible when their firms dispense inaccurate or misleading information about the financial condition of the businesses they manage. Sarbanes-Oxley represents a step toward a more information-rich and information-reliable financial marketplace, but it is only a step in what is still a long road to travel. We turn now to look at some of the most important sources of financial information currently available to the public as a whole.

## QUESTIONS TO HELP YOU STUDY

1. Why is the availability and reliability of financial information important to both borrowers and lenders of funds? What can happen when relevant information is missing?

2. Can you explain why financial information that is accurate and reliable is of great significance to government policymakers and regulators within the financial system?

3. Carefully explain what is meant by the term *efficient market*. Are there different *levels* of market efficiency? What are these levels?

4. Explain what is meant by *informational asymmetries*. What problems can these asymmetries create for participants in the money and capital markets?

5. What does it mean to say a financial asset is "temporarily overpriced" or "temporarily underpriced"? How can such a situation happen? Why is such overpricing or underpricing likely to be only temporary?

6. As you look at the real world around you, do you see examples of what seem to be efficient markets? Can you detect any real-world examples of what seem to be informational asymmetries? How did you identify these market situations?

7. What steps have been taken recently to promote greater accuracy and reliability of information concerning the financial marketplace and the valuation of individual assets?

## 3.3 Debt Security Prices and Yields: Sources of Information

**Key URL:**
Investors can get lots of information on investing in bonds through such sources as the Bond Market Association at **investinginbonds.com**

**note**

**bond**

The concept of "efficient" markets assumes that information relevant to the valuation of *all* financial assets is readily available to the public at comparatively low cost. What kinds and what depth of information about the financial marketplace *does* the public receive? Let's begin with a look at some of the most popular information sources for debt securities, usually referred to as *bonds* and *notes.*

*Bonds and Notes*    Bonds and notes are debt obligations issued by governments and corporations, usually in units (par values) of $1,000. A **note** is a shorter-term written promissory obligation, usually not exceeding 5 years to maturity; a **bond** is a longer-term promissory note, at least 5 to 10 years to maturity and sometimes much longer. Although bonds and notes generally pay a fixed amount of interest income to their owners, their prices fluctuate daily as interest rates change. Therefore, although bonds and notes are often referred to as *fixed-income securities,* the investor may experience significant capital gains or losses on these instruments as their prices change if he or she chooses to sell an asset before it matures. Bonds and notes generally carry a set maturity date, at which time the issuer must pay the holder the assets' par value. These debt securities are generally identified by the name of the issuing company or governmental unit, their coupon (fixed interest) rate, and their maturity date.

*Bid and Asked Prices and Pricing Information*    Bonds and notes can be bought and sold through dealers who manage portfolio holdings of these securities. The dealers are referred to as "market makers" because each dealer creates a market

| EXHIBIT 3.1 | Indicators of Average Bond Yields (Average Annual Yields in Percent) | | | | | | | |
|---|---|---|---|---|---|---|---|---|
| **Yield Series** | **1992** | **1994** | **1996** | **1998** | **2000** | **2002** | **2004** | **2006** |
| State and local government notes and bonds: | | | | | | | | |
| Aaa-Moody's series | 6.09% | 5.77% | 5.52% | 4.93% | 5.58% | 4.87% | 4.50% | 4.15% |
| Bond buyer series | 6.48 | 6.18 | 5.76 | 5.09 | 5.71 | 5.04 | 4.68 | 4.40 |
| Corporate bonds: | | | | | | | | |
| Seasoned issues, all industries | 8.55 | 8.26 | 7.66 | 6.87 | 7.98 | 7.10 | 6.00 | 5.98 |
| Moody's corporate bond indexes classified by rating: | | | | | | | | |
| Aaa | 8.14 | 7.97 | 7.37 | 6.53 | 7.62 | 6.49 | 5.63 | 5.59 |
| Aa | 8.46 | 8.15 | 7.55 | 6.80 | 7.83 | 6.93 | 5.91 | 5.80 |
| A | 8.62 | 8.28 | 7.69 | 6.93 | 8.11 | 7.18 | 6.08 | 6.06 |
| Baa | 8.98 | 8.63 | 8.05 | 7.22 | 8.36 | 7.80 | 6.39 | 6.48 |

Source: Board of Governors of the Federal Reserve System, *Federal Reserve Bulletin* and *Statistical Supplement to the Federal Reserve Bulletin,* selected issues.

**bid price**
**asked price**

for the securities he or she holds by posting a **bid price,** the price at which the dealer is willing to purchase additional securities to add to his portfolio, and an **asked price,** the price at which the dealer is willing to sell from his portfolio.

Today traders require information regarding the prices and availability of debt securities on an up-to-the-minute basis. Computer networks report instant price quotations on the most actively traded bonds and similar financial instruments, supplemented by reports from television channels such as Bloomberg and CNBC. One of the most complete listings of daily price and yield quotations on bonds and notes appears in *The Wall Street Journal* (*WSJ*), published by Dow Jones & Company. In addition, most daily newspapers contain prices and yields on the most actively traded bonds.

**Key URLs:**
Additional information on bond market investing and bond market behavior may be found in **http:// money.cnn.com; bloomberg .com;** and **cnbc.com; investinginbonds.com; bondsonline.com;** and **tradingedge.com**

Recent changes in various bond yield indexes as reported in the quarterly *Federal Reserve Bulletin* and the more recent monthly *Statistical Supplement to the Federal Reserve Bulletin* are shown in Exhibit 3.1. Note the fluctuations in bond yields, which reflect significant changes in economic and credit conditions during this period. This is why bond buyers pay a great deal of attention to announcements of new economic data each week, such as new information on auto sales, manufacturing employment, price inflation, or the construction of new homes. Any hint of softening in the economy or of reduced inflation may result in a bond market price rally, pulling interest rates down and pushing bond prices higher.

## 3.4 Stock Prices and Dividend Yields: Sources of Information

**stocks**

Of all the financial assets traded in the money and capital markets, **stocks** are among the most popular with active investors. Stock prices can be extremely volatile (especially the stock of smaller companies), offering the prospect of substantial capital gains if prices rise but also significant capital losses if prices tumble. Several corporations (such as General Electric and Verizon) pay dividends on their stock regularly, thus offering the buyer a relatively steady source of income as well as the opportunity for capital gains if prices go up. Unlike a bond, however, a share of stock is a certificate of ownership in a corporation, not a debt obligation. No corporation need pay dividends to its stockholders. In fact, some never have, preferring to retain all after-tax earnings in the business. In this section we summarize the kinds of public information that stock market investors have access to on a regular basis.

*Price and Yield Information*    As in the case of bonds, price and yield data on the most actively traded stocks are reported daily in the financial press as well as over television, radio, and the Internet. Most daily newspapers, along with *The Wall Street Journal,* list current stock prices. Each stock price quotation is identified by the abbreviated name of the company issuing it. High and low prices at which the stock has been traded during the past year and the most recent annual dividend declared by the issuing company are normally given. The dividend yield—the ratio of dividends to current price—often appears, along with the ratio of the stock's current price to the past 12 months of company earnings (the P-E ratio). Remaining entries in a financial newssheet may provide a summary of the previous business day's transactions in the markets where that particular stock is bought and sold. The one-day sales volume, expressed in hundreds of shares, may also be shown. The closing price for which the stock was traded in the last sale of the day is often reported, usually expressed in dollars and decimal fractions of a dollar.

**Key URLs:**
Information on daily stock market developments for active investors may be found on the World Wide Web at such sites as **moneycentral. msn.com/; fool.com; quote.com; nyse.com;** and **nasdaq.com**

Stock prices for more than 1,700 companies in over 100 industries are provided by *The Value Line Investment Survey,* published weekly by Arnold Bernhard & Company of New York. Each company's business is described, and basic financial information, such as sales, net earnings, and long-term indebtedness, is provided for at least a decade. Individual stocks are also rated by *Value Line,* from those expected to be top performers down to those expected to be the poorest performers. Stock prices and basic financial data for individual companies are also presented in comprehensive reports compiled by Standard & Poor's Corporation (S&P). The performance of the shares issued by mutual funds is reported by Morningstar, which rates each fund's performance using a star system of one to five. Five-star-rated mutual funds are considered by Morningstar to be the best-performing and best-managed investment companies among those mutual funds whose shares are available to investors.

The stock market is watched closely by investors as a barometer of expectations in the business community. A rising trend in stock prices generally signals an optimistic assessment of future business prospects and expectations of higher corporate earnings. A declining market, on the other hand, is often a harbinger of adverse economic news and may signal a cutback in business investment and lower corporate earnings. Among the most important factors watched by stock traders are reports of corporate earnings, merger and dividend announcements, changes in corporate management, announcements of new products being introduced, changes in government policy that might affect interest rates (with the prospect of lower interest rates generally favorable for stocks), and apparent changes in the strength of the economy (as reflected in such data series as new orders to manufacturers of durable goods, new housing construction, the growth of business investment expenditures, changes in the level of business inventories, and measures of inflation).

**Key URLs:**
For further information on stocks, bonds, and mutual funds see the Investment Company Institute at **ici.org;** Morningstar at **morningstar.com;** and ValueLine at **valueline.com**

*Stock Price Indexes and Foreign Stock Prices*    Many students of the financial marketplace follow several broad stock indexes that reflect price movements in groups of similar quality stocks. One of the most popular indexes is the Dow Jones Industrial Average of 30 stocks, including shares of such leading companies as ExxonMobil, Wal-Mart, McDonald's, Boeing, and Citigroup. Dow Jones also reports a transportation index of 20 stocks (including such industry leaders as Federal

**Key URL:**
A full description
of the Wilshire
5000 Index and its
relationship to the
market value of
publicly traded U.S.
corporations can be
found at **wilshire.com**

**Key URL:**
To learn more
about stock price
indexes see, for
example, Standard &
Poor's Corporation
at **standardandpoors
.com**

**Key URL:**
For additional
information regarding
Standard & Poor's
stock price indexes
see, for example,
**investopedia.com/
terms/s**

**Key URLs:**
You can track
foreign stock price
movements at such
sites as **stocksmart
.com** and **finix.at**

Express) and a utility index composed of the shares of 15 leading utility companies (such as Pacific Gas & Electric). The Dow utility index is of special importance because it tends to be highly sensitive to interest-rate fluctuations; some analysts regard it as a barometer of interest-rate expectations.

The Dow-Jones Industrial Average is more than 100 years old, but its authors, the Dow Jones Company, have since dramatically expanded the number of stock and bond indexes which now number more than 5,000 and cover markets around the globe. Additional Dow indexes encompass energy prices, commodities and precious metals, Internet-based firms, futures and options, foreign currencies, mutual funds, annuities, and selected debt instruments, as well as scores of custom-made financial indexes requested by DJ clients.

Among other comprehensive stock market indicators are Standard & Poor's 400 Industrial and S&P's 500 Composite Stock Price Indexes, both of which include the most actively traded U.S. equity shares. The S&P 500 includes the shares of 40 utility, 20 transportation, and 40 financial company stocks not present in the S&P 400 Industrial Index. More recently, S&P has developed an S&P 600 Index, consisting of small-cap businesses, and an S&P 400 series for midsize companies. All S&P stock series are regarded as sensitive barometers of general stock price movements.

An even broader price index than S&P's Composite is the New York Stock Exchange Composite Index, which gives the greatest weight to stocks with the highest market values. Considered an indicator of total market performance, the NYSE Composite is often used to compare the performance of major institutional investors, such as mutual funds and pension funds, against the market as a whole. Other broad market indicators include the NASDAQ Composite that measures price movements in stocks sold over the counter (OTC) rather than on the major exchanges, and the Wilshire 5,000, which has among the broadest measures of stock market performance and includes more than 6,300 stocks—most of them publicly traded U.S. corporations. The Wilshire is considered the best measure currently available of overall stock market wealth in the United States and has recently been expanded to help track stock market wealth around the globe.

Many newspapers and financially oriented magazines contain daily stock market diaries or summaries. Such summaries of recent market developments indicate both price movements and the volume of trading on the major exchanges. Examples may be found in *Barron's, Forbes, Fortune, Money,* and *The Wall Street Journal.* Market diaries or summaries usually report the total number of shares traded on a given day or week and the number of stocks advancing or declining in price.

Finally, with the spreading globalization of markets, more and more savers and borrowers are turning to foreign markets to invest their savings and raise needed funds. Therefore, key information sources increasingly are reporting daily changes in security prices and interest rates in foreign trading centers, such as London, Frankfurt, Hong Kong, Singapore, Tokyo, and Sydney. To help foreign investors who deal predominantly in their own home currencies, there are also listings of currency exchange rates in various publications (such as the *Statistical Supplement to the Federal Reserve Bulletin* and *The Wall Street Journal*) so that they can translate a security's current price from one currency into another.

## 3.5    Information on Security Issuers

*Moody's and Standard & Poor's Reports*    Lenders of funds have a pressing need to secure accurate financial information on those individuals and institutions that seek to borrow funds or to sell their stock. Fortunately, financial information on

Key URLs:
Want to know more
about Moody's and
Standard & Poor's?
Try **moodys.com** or
**standandpoor.com**

many individual companies and other security issuers, particularly for the largest issuing institutions, is available from a wide variety of published sources.

Two of the most respected sources of information on major security issues and issuers are Moody's Investor Service and Standard & Poor's Corporation, both headquartered in New York City.

For more than a century, Moody's has assigned credit risk ratings to borrowing institutions and supplied advice on investment decisions around the globe. Moody's offers research studies focusing upon the performance and financial condition of thousands of businesses, financial institutions, and government authorities; provides opinions on economic and credit trends; and offers training seminars for credit analysts in the Americas, Europe, and Asia. A long-time competitor of Moody's, Standard & Poor's Corporation, provides many similar services, including credit research and ratings and investment portfolio recommendations, making it possible for thousands of corporate and governmental institutions as well as individuals to make better-informed portfolio decisions.

Key URL:
For further
information about
data and other
types of information
available from the
SEC, see **sec.gov.**
This site includes the
EDGAR database that
discloses documents
that publicly owned
companies must file
with the SEC.

### Securities and Exchange Commission (SEC) Reports

Even more extensive financial data are provided by the reports that corporations must file with the Securities and Exchange Commission (SEC). These SEC reports are available in many libraries on microfiche or microfilm. One company, Disclosure Incorporated, provides its subscribers with microfiche copies of more than 100,000 corporate documents filed each year by well over 10,000 companies. The most important of these corporate documents is the SEC's 10-K report, an annual statement that must be filed by most companies within 90 days after their fiscal year-end. These 10-K reports identify the principal products or services of each firm, provide a summary of its recent operations, note any securities outstanding, and list the names of key officers. The SEC's overall mission is to protect investors, facilitate investment, and maintain efficient markets.

Key URL:
To learn more
about Disclosure
Incorporated
see **disclosure.com**

### Company Histories

The backgrounds on thousands of businesses all over the world can be found by searching through a wide variety of private information sources. For example, *The International Directory of Company Histories* provides brief historical sketches of nearly 3,000 firms worldwide, while through a service on a CD-ROM called *Global Researcher* the *SEC* provides information on the directors, officers, and leading shareholders for over 12,000 companies whose securities are traded in U.S. markets. A related CD-ROM source known as *Global Researcher Worldscope* provides financial data and news headlines for almost 15,000 firms that trade on leading stock exchanges around the world.

Key URL:
Learn more about
Dun & Bradstreet
at **dnb.com**

### Dun & Bradstreet Ratings and Risk Management

Another useful source of data on individual firms comes from Dun & Bradstreet, Inc. (D&B). This credit rating and risk management company collects information on millions of businesses, making detailed financial reports on these firms available to its subscribers all over the world. D&B also supplies industrywide financial data so that the financial condition of an individual business borrower can be compared with that of other firms in the same industry for more than 800 industry lines. D&B offers guidelines for assessing and managing risk and for unraveling supply chain management issues.

Key URL:
To discover more
about information
sources available from
RMA, see especially
**rmahq.org** and the
*Annual Statement
Studies* link.

Similar industrywide performance indicators are prepared and published by Risk Management Associates (RMA) in its *Annual Statement Studies* that covers smaller firms in more than 400 industries. This information can be supplemented with news concerning individual investors and businesses by checking *The Wall Street Journal Index,* the *New York Times Index,* and *Barron's Index.* Recently an Internet database called *Investext,* a component of the Thomson Financial network, was added with financial reports and forecasts from thousands of companies in more than 50 different industries scattered around the globe.

*Financial Institutions*    Information on banks and other financial institutions is available from a wide variety of sources, including trade associations in each industry and federal and state regulatory agencies. For example, the American Bankers Association, Life Insurance Association of America, Insurance Information Institute, Investment Company Institute, and Credit Union National Association frequently provide annual reports or pamphlets describing recent industry trends. Studies of financial institutions' problems are found in specialized journals and magazines, such as the *Bankers Magazine, Financial Analysts Journal, Euromoney, The Economist, Forbes, Fortune, BusinessWeek,* and the *Journal of Portfolio Management.*

Among key government agencies that provide annual reports and special studies of financial institutions' trends and problems are the Federal Deposit Insurance Corporation, Federal Reserve Board and Federal Reserve Banks, the Federal Home Loan Banks, and the Comptroller of the Currency. For example, the Federal Deposit Insurance Corporation (FDIC) has a detailed Web site that identifies all FDIC-insured depositories and provides financial data for each insured institution. Many government reports are available in university libraries or through the Superintendent of Documents in Washington, DC.

*Credit Bureaus*    Finally, information on individuals and families who seek credit is assembled and disseminated to institutional lenders by *credit bureaus.* The files of these bureaus include such information as the individual's place of residence and occupation, debts owed, and the promptness with which an individual pays his or her bills. Most credit bureaus maintain files on an individual's bill-paying record for up to seven years and may release that information only to lenders, employers, or licensing agencies who have a legitimate right to know the individual's credit standing. Individuals also have a right to see their credit files and verify their accuracy.

## 3.6   General Economic and Financial Conditions

A number of different sources provide market participants with information on developments in the economy, prevailing trends in the money and capital markets, and actions by the government that may affect economic and financial conditions worldwide.

*The Federal Reserve System*    The Federal Reserve System releases large quantities of financial information to the public on request. Statistical releases available on a weekly, monthly, or quarterly basis cover such items as interest rates, money supply measures, industrial output, and international transactions. Information of this sort is summarized each month in the *Statistical Supplement to the Federal Reserve Bulletin,* published by the Board of Governors of the Federal Reserve System in Washington, DC. The Board also publishes the results of internal staff studies that examine recent financial trends or address major issues of public policy. Within the Federal Reserve System, the Federal Reserve banks scattered around the United States are also major suppliers of financial and economic information. Addresses for the Federal Reserve Board and all the Federal Reserve banks appear at the back of each quarterly *Federal Reserve Bulletin,* as well as on the Internet.

*Other Domestic and International Sources of Information*   A number of published sources regularly report on the status of the economy. Daily financial newspapers, such as *The Wall Street Journal* and the *Financial Times,* nearly always include important economic data. The U.S. Department of Commerce (USDC) maintains one of the most comprehensive collections of U.S. economic data available anywhere, including the latest statistics on consumer, government, and business spending, and on exports and imports. The USDC publishes several convenient compilations of business data, including the annual *Statistical Abstract of the United States.*

Forecasts of *future* economic and financial developments are available from a wide variety of sources. For example, the Federal Reserve Bank of Philadelphia publishes the quarterly *Survey of Professional Forecasters,* which compiles a summary of the forecasts of leading economists regarding production, unemployment, inflation, and interest rates. Forecasts of annual capital spending based on repeated industry surveys are prepared by the U.S. Department of Commerce and McGraw-Hill Publications Company. Businesses often subscribe to the services of one or more of a number of economic consulting firms that prepare detailed forecasts of income and interest rates.

The growing internationalization of the financial markets has led to dramatic increases in new sources of information regarding foreign markets and institutions. Up-to-date security price and interest rate data are published in *The Wall Street Journal/Europe* from Brussels and a corresponding *Asian Wall Street Journal* issued from Hong Kong. *The Financial Times* of London is considered one of the finest daily newspapers in the world. *The Economist,* also published in London, deals with foreign business and political developments throughout the world. Of comparable quality is *Euromoney* (London), which monitors Europe's ongoing economic integration. For businesspersons interested in Asia and the Pacific Rim, such magazines as *Asiaweek,* the *Far Eastern Economic Review,* and *Asiamoney* offer greater understanding of Pacific economies and institutions.

**Key URL:**
For an excellent source of economic and financial data that can be easily downloaded into an Excel spreadsheet see the Federal Reserve Bank of St. Louis's Web site: **research. stlouisfed.org/fred2/**

**Key URL:**
For a comprehensive source of U.S. economic data, see the Department of Commerce at **commerce.gov** and the Bureau of Labor Statistics at **bls.gov/**

**Key URLs:**
Important and interesting international Web sites include the International Monetary Fund at **imf.org;** the Bank for International Settlements at **bis.org;** the *Financial Times* at **ft.com;** and *Euromoney* at **Euromoney.com**

## QUESTIONS TO HELP YOU STUDY

8. If you needed to gather information for a possible stock or bond purchase, where would you go to get such information? What are the principal sources to check?

9. Suppose you wanted to evaluate the financial condition of a business firm. What major sources exist that could assist you in getting that kind of information?

10. Suppose you were planning to take a job with a particular company. What would you want to know about the company and where could you find that information?

11. If you wanted to gather information about the state of the U.S. economy, which information sources would likely be most helpful to you?

12. Where could you go to gather information about the global economy?

13. Why would information about the global and domestic economies be of assistance to investors in stocks, bonds, and other financial assets?

# Summary of the Chapter's Main Points

This chapter examines the key role that *information* plays in the money and capital markets. Among its key points are the following:

- An unimpeded flow of relevant, low-cost information is vital to efficient functioning of the financial markets. If the scarce resource of credit is to be allocated efficiently and an ample flow of savings made available for investment, accurate financial information must be made readily available at low cost to all market participants.

- Two different types of markets operate within the financial system every day: an *information market* and a *market for financial assets.* The two types of markets must work together in coordinated fashion to accomplish the desired result—directing the flow of scarce funds (coming primarily from savings) toward their most beneficial uses (primarily into investments that help create jobs, expand the economy, and improve our standard of living).

- If the market for financial information is truly *efficient,* so that all relevant information for valuing financial assets is readily available at negligible cost, these assets will be correctly priced based on their expected return and risk. Scarce resources will flow to those uses of funds promising the highest expected returns.

- When *asymmetries* exist in the flow and availability of information, however, the financial marketplace will operate imperfectly. Some market participants, armed with special information not available to all participants, will earn *excess profits* (that is, they will generate returns that exceed the *normal* or *expected* rate of return for the amount of risk taken on).

- With imperfections in the quality and availability of information, scarce resources will be allocated less efficiently than otherwise might be the case. Research evidence to date suggests that most financial markets tend to be relatively efficient at some level but that important asymmetries (information imperfections) still remain.

- Some of the key problems informational asymmetries can create include (1) *the lemons problem,* in which vital information about the quality of assets is costly and difficult to obtain, with the possible result that lesser-quality assets may drive superior-quality assets from the marketplace; (2) the *adverse selection problem,* in which sellers of some services have difficulty in correctly pricing what they offer because of inadequate information about the riskiness and other relevant characteristics of buyers, often resulting in multiple prices for the same service; and (3) the *moral hazard problem,* in which agents possessing superior-quality information (for example, the management of a corporation) may use it to their advantage at the expense of principals (for example, the stockholders of the same corporation), unless suitable arrangements can be worked out that better align the interests of agents and principals.

- In this chapter, the principal focus has been on four broad categories of financial information available today: debt security prices and yields, stock prices and dividend yields, the financial condition of security issuers, and general conditions in the economy and financial system. This chapter gives the reader a broad overview of the kinds and quality of information currently available to the public. Knowing where to find relevant, up-to-date information is an essential ingredient in the process of solving economic and financial problems.

## Key Terms Appearing in This Chapter

efficient markets hypothesis
  (EMH), 56
insider trading, 59
asymmetric information hypothesis
  (AIH), 60
moral hazard, 63

note, 68
bond, 68
bid price, 69
asked price, 69
stocks, 69

## Problems and Issues

1. Which is true? Trading on inside information would not yield excess returns to investors if the stock market:

   a. were efficient according to the *weak form* of market efficiency, but not efficient according to either the *semistrong form* or the *strong form* of market efficiency.

   b. were efficient according to the *weak form* of market efficiency and the *semistrong form* of market efficiency, but not efficient according to the *strong form* of market efficiency.

   c. were not efficient according to any of the *weak form, semistrong form,* or *strong form* of market efficiency.

   d. were efficient according to all of the *weak form, semistrong form,* or *strong form* of market efficiencies.

2. A manager of Accurate Info, Inc., decides to purchase a golf membership for the senior executives of his firm. If he does not believe that this decision will raise shareholder value, then his decision is an example of:

   a. adverse selection, but not an agency problem.

   b. adverse selection and an agency problem.

   c. moral hazard, but not an agency problem.

   d. moral hazard and an agency problem.

3. Insider trading by corporate executives that yields abnormal profits:

   a. is a violation of the *semistrong form* of the efficient market hypothesis (EMH) and is subject to investigation by the Federal Reserve.

   b. is a violation of the *strong form* of the efficient market hypothesis (EMH) and is subject to investigation by the Securities and Exchange Commission (SEC).

   c. is not a violation of the *semistrong form* of the efficient market hypothesis (EMH) and is subject to investigation by the Federal Reserve.

   d. is not a violation of the *strong form* of the efficient market hypothesis (EMH) and is subject to investigation by the Securities and Exchange Commission (SEC).

4. In the appendix to this chapter (especially Exhibit 3A.2) you are given household balance sheet information relating to the U.S. household sector's financial assets and liabilities. Households also possess nonfinancial assets,

the bulk of which is housing. Use the information presented below along with the information in Exhibit 3A.2 to examine how housing has affected U.S. household wealth since 1980.

| U.S. Household Balance Sheet Items ($ Billions) | 1980 | 1990 | 2000 | 2006 |
|---|---|---|---|---|
| Total household sector assets | $10,914.7 | $23,915.6 | $48,772.2 | $65,705.9 |
| Total nonfinancial assets of households | 4,359.7 | 9,353.0 | 15,806.8 | 25,780.4 |
| Value of housing assets | 2,943.2 | 6,578.5 | 11,411.9 | 19,926.1 |

   a. For each of the years: 1980, 1990, 2000, and 2006, please place into a spreadsheet the following information: Total assets, Total nonfinancial assets, Total housing, Total liabilities, and Total mortgages.

   b. For each year, determine what percentage of Total assets is made up of Housing.

   c. For each year, determine what percentage of Total liabilities is made up of Mortgages.

   d. For each year compute the net equity that U.S. households have in their home by subtracting Mortgages (liability) from Housing (asset).

   e. For each year, compute U.S. households' Net worth = Total assets less Total liabilities.

   f. For each year, compute the percentage of households' Net worth that is made up of net equity in their homes.

   g. Describe the *principal trends* in the makeup of U.S. households' balance sheets that you observe and try to explain why these trends are occurring. What role might the development of the financial information marketplace play in the trends you observe?

5. The following situations *may* be covered by *insider trading laws* in the United States. Examine each situation described and indicate whether, in your opinion, a violation of insider trading laws might have occurred. If you think a violation occurred, what kind of violation was it?

   a. The chief financial officer of Start Corporation reads an internal memorandum criticizing the firm's recent oil field development investments and picks up his phone to call his broker, placing an order to sell his holdings of the firm's shares when the market opens in the morning.

   b. Corren Professional Corporation, a CPA firm, assists Selkirk Industrial Corporation with its quarterly and annual financial reports. Jim Roberts, a CPA with Corren, after reviewing the latest information provided by Selkirk's CEO, calls a friend and suggests making certain stock and bond trades involving Selkirk's securities. Roberts will not benefit financially from these suggested trades and refuses to get involved.

   c. James Smith works for Cohen and Cooper, a local law firm, and while browsing in his firm's law library, he discovers a new report from a legal client of his colleague, Roscoe Adams, that predicts serious financial problems if the client proceeds with its recently drafted strategic plan. Smith subsequently discovers discreetly that the strategic plan is to be launched next week. He also learns that Roscoe is selling the client's stock short through his broker. Smith quietly advises Roscoe not to make the short sale and lets the matter drop.

**d.** Samuel Joule learns from conversations with Sarah Conklin, a bartender at a local bar, that neighboring Locket Corporation has recently developed a warning device that may help prevent air collisions and may be worth tens of millions of dollars once announced to the public. Neither Joule nor Conklin works for Locket, though he has been dating Miss Conklin. Both of these individuals decide to purchase 1,000 shares of Locket's stock before Locket holds a press conference to announce the new air collision device. Joule and Conklin will use a bank loan to finance the purchase of Locket's shares. A wedding is planned if the transaction pays off.

6. In this chapter we discussed three different forms or levels of *market efficiency.* Refer to the appropriate forms of market efficiency in answering the following questions:

   **a.** Why is insider trading illegal?

   **b.** Why and how do small investors benefit from efficient markets?

   **c.** If you were a stock trader and markets were *not* efficient, how would this influence your trading activity? What does this tell you about *why* markets may be efficient?

   **d.** Consider the case of a day trader who looks only at the past history of stock prices in conducting his or her trades. How likely would it be for such a person to "beat the market"? What does this suggest about investing in the "entire market" (such as by purchasing shares in an index fund) rather than attempting to pick individual stocks?

7. Based on the material in the appendix to this chapter construct sources and uses of funds statements for each sector and for the whole economy using the following information:

| | Households ($ Billions) | Business Firms ($ Billions) | Banks and Other Financial Institutions ($ Billions) | Governmental Units ($ Billions) |
|---|---|---|---|---|
| Current saving | $428.8 | $280.0 | $35.0 | −$35.0 |
| Current real investment | 332.5 | 350.0 | 17.5 | — |
| Current financial investment | 306.3 | 78.8 | 43.8 | 8.8 |
| Current borrowing | 210.0 | 148.8 | 26.3 | 43.8 |

Assume that the four sectors listed above are the only sectors in the economy and that there are no international transactions. Is there a statistical discrepancy? Where? Referring to the discussion in Chapter 2, which sectors are deficit-budget sectors (DBUs) and which are surplus-budget sectors (SBUs)? Are there any balanced-budget sectors (BBUs)?

## Web-Based Problems

1. Go to the Internet and use such Web sources as **www.federalreserve.gov, www.bea.gov,** and **www.bls.gov**—in order to obtain the following information:

   **a.** The latest stock price for IBM.

   **b.** The average yield on highly rated long-term bonds.

    **c.** The interest rate on newly issued three-month U.S. Treasury bills.

    **d.** The size of the U.S. money supply (measured as M1 and M2).

    **e.** The annualized growth rate of the U.S. economy for the most recent quarter (real GDP).

    **f.** The size of the U.S. budget deficit (or surplus) for the last fiscal year.

    **g.** Total business fixed investment in the United States during the last calendar year.

    **h.** Total employment in the nonfarm business sector.

    **i.** The inflation rate in the United States for the past year, measured in terms of the growth rate of the CPI.

**2.** Track the performance of a stock issued by a company included in the Dow Jones Industrial Average (DJIA) Index (such as IBM or Microsoft) over the course of the semester and compare the performance of the stock you have selected relative to the performance of a broad stock market index of your own choosing (such as the S&P 500 Stock Index, the Vanguard Total Stock Market Index Fund, or the Wilshire 5000 Index). There is a wide variety of sources you might consult for the information you will need, including *The Wall Street Journal* (**www.WSJ.com),** the New York Stock Exchange (**www.nyse.com),** and other sources mentioned in this chapter.

At the end of each week, find the closing price of your stock and the stock index you have chosen. Keep a running account of the percentage gains and losses that you would have experienced had you (a) bought the stock, or (b) "bought the market" by buying an index fund representing a whole basket of stocks (such as an S&P 500 index fund). At the semester's end, compute the return you would have made had you invested $10,000 in your chosen stock or in your chosen index fund. Did your stock outperform or underperform the index fund? What information can you point to that seems to account for the over- or under-performance of your stock relative to the market?

## Selected References to Explore

**1.** Akerlof, George. "The Market for Lemons: Quality Uncertainty and the Market Mechanism," *Quarterly Journal of Economics,* 84 (1970). pp. 488–500.

**2.** Craig, Ben. "Bubble, Toil and Trouble," *Economic Commentary,* Federal Reserve Bank of Cleveland, October 15, 2003, pp. 1–4.

**3.** Ergungor, O. Emre, and Joseph G. Haubrich. "Information and Prices," *Economic Commentary,* Federal Reserve Bank of Cleveland, May 1, 2003, pp. 1–3.

**4.** Hersh, Shefrin. *Beyond Greed and Fear: Understanding Behavioral Finance and the Psychology of Investing,* Oxford University Press, 2002.

**5.** Lehmann, Michael B. *The Irwin Guide to The Wall Street Journal,* 7th ed., McGraw-Hill Companies, Inc., 2005.

**6.** Stiglitz, Joseph, and Andrew Weiss. "Credit Rationing in Markets with Imperfect Information," *American Economic Review,* 71 (1981), pp. 393–419.

# Appendix 3A: The Flow of Funds in the Financial System

Students of the economy and the financial markets make use of social accounting systems to keep track of broad trends in economic and financial conditions. *Social accounting* refers to a system of record keeping that reports transactions between the principal sectors of the economy, such as households, financial institutions, corporations, and units of government. The two most closely followed social accounting systems in the United States are the National Income Accounts and the Flow of Funds Accounts.

## National Income and Product Accounts

The *National Income and Product Accounts* (NIPAs) are compiled and released quarterly by the U.S. Department of Commerce. These accounts present data on the nation's production of goods and services, income flows, investment spending, consumption, and savings. Probably the best-known account in the NIPA series is gross domestic product (GDP)—a measure of the market value of all goods and services produced within the geographical boundaries of the United States. It is the most important barometer of overall U.S. economic activity. GDP may be broken down into the uses to which the nation's output of goods and services are put. For example, Exhibit 3A.1, drawn

**Key URLs:**
Data on the U.S. economy may be found at such Web sites as **economagic.com.** In addition, the American Economic Association sponsors a Web site that includes *Resources for Economists on the Internet,* which contains an extensive list of links to Web sites with data and analysis, at **http://rfe.org**

from the U.S. Department of Commerce, indicates the size of the U.S. GDP and its major components for 2006.

The National Income and Product Accounts provide valuable information on the level and growth of the nation's economic activity. However, these accounts provide little or no information on financial transactions themselves. This task is left to the *Flow of Funds Accounts* prepared by the Board of Governors of the Federal Reserve System.

## The Flow of Funds Accounts

Flow of funds data are published quarterly by the Federal Reserve System and include data back to 1955. Monthly issues of the *Statistical Supplement to the Federal Reserve Bulletin* contain the latest summary reports of flow of funds transactions, and detailed break-downs of financial transactions among major sectors of the economy are available from the Federal Reserve Board in Washington, DC.

| EXHIBIT 3A.1 | National Income and Product Accounts: The Components of U.S. Gross Domestic Product (GDP), 2006* ($ Billions, Current) | | |
|---|---|---|---|
| Personal consumption expenditures | | | $ 9,084.4 |
| Durable goods | $ 1,047.9 | | |
| Nondurable goods services | 2,686.7 | | |
| Gross private domestic investment | 5,349.7 | | 2,273.4 |
| Fixed investment | 2,239.8 | | |
| Change in private inventories | 33.7 | | |
| Net U.S. exports of goods and services | | | −794.2 |
| Exports | 1,394.5 | | |
| Imports | 2,188.7 | | |
| Government consumption expenditures and gross investment | | | 2,473.8 |
| Federal | 924.7 | | |
| State and local | 1,549.2 | | |
| Gross domestic product (GDP) | | | $13,037.4 |

Source: U.S. Department of Commerce and the Board of Governors of the Federal Reserve System's *Flow of Funds Accounts.*

*Figures are for the first quarter of 2006 and annualized. Figures may not add to totals due to rounding.

The basic purposes of the Flow of Funds Accounts are to: (1) trace the flow of savings by businesses, households, and governments into purchases of financial assets; (2) show how the various parts of the financial system interact with each other; and (3) highlight the interconnections between the financial sector and the rest of the economy.

Construction of the Flow of Funds Accounts takes place in *four* basic steps.

### Constructing the Flow of Funds Accounts: Sectoring the Economy

**Key URL:**
More information on the Federal Reserve's Flow of Funds Accounts may be found at **federalreserve.gov/ releases**

The first step is to divide the economy into several broad *sectors,* each consisting of economic units (transactors) with similar balance sheets. Among the major sectors in the current account series are:

- Households.
- Farm businesses.
- Nonfarm nonfinancial businesses.
- Governments.
- Federally sponsored credit agencies.
- Monetary authorities (i.e., the Federal Reserve System and monetary accounts of the U.S. Treasury).
- Commercial banks.
- Nonbank financial institutions.
- Rest of the world (U.S. international transactions).

### Constructing the Flow of Funds Accounts: Building Sector Balance Sheets

The second step in assembling the Flow of Funds Accounts is to construct *balance sheets* for each of the sectors listed above at the end of each quarter. Like any balance sheet for a business firm or household, sector balance sheets contain estimates of the assets, liabilities, and net worth held by each sector at a single point in time. The assets held by each sector are divided into financial assets and tangible real (nonfinancial) assets.

An example of such a balance sheet—in this case, a partial balance sheet containing only the financial assets and liabilities for the household

sector for the years 1980, 1990, 2000, and 2006—is shown in Exhibit 3A.2. We note, for example, that U.S. households held total financial assets of nearly $40 trillion in 2006 (shown in line 1), more than five times their financial asset holdings in 1980. A substantial part of this total was represented by household deposits—checking (demand) accounts and time and savings deposits placed in commercial banks and savings institutions. These liquid financial assets totaled nearly $6.3 trillion in 2006 (line 2). An even larger volume of financial assets held by households took the form of pension fund reserves (line 20), accumulated to prepare individuals and families for the retirement years. These reserves amounted to more than $11 trillion in 2006, followed by direct holdings of corporate stock (equities), which totaled almost $5.7 trillion in 2006 (line 16). Direct holdings of debt securities (credit market instruments), including U.S. Treasury notes and bonds, federal agency securities, state and local government bonds, mortgages, and similar assets, amounted to a little over $3 trillion (line 7) in 2006.

It is interesting that the total indebtedness of individuals and families in the United States is *far less* than their holdings of financial assets. Exhibit 3A.2 indicates that the household sector's liabilities totaled more than $12 trillion in 2006 (line 23), or less than a third of its total financial asset holdings. Most household indebtedness was in the form of home mortgages and home equity loans (line 25) and installment (consumer credit) debt obligations (line 26), which include automobile and education loans that are gradually retired in a series of payments stretching over months or years.

Just as the liabilities of households substantially trail their holdings of financial assets, so do their tangible (real or physical) assets. For example, if we add the values of all the automobiles, homes and other real estate, clothing, furniture, iPods, and thousands of other tangible or real assets that were possessed by American households in 2006, the total amount is close to $26 trillion versus nearly $40 trillion in the households' financial assets. This significant edge for financial assets compared to liabilities and real assets reflects the fact that, in most years, the household sector has been a net lender of funds to the rest of the economy. Moreover, if we combine the financial and real assets of households together, totaling about $66 trillion, and subtract

| EXHIBIT 3A.2 | Statement of Financial Assets and Liabilities for the Household Sector, 1980, 1990, 2000, and 2006* ($ Billions, Outstanding at Year-End) | | | |
|---|---|---|---|---|
| Asset and Liability Items | 1980 | 1990 | 2000 | 2006* |
| 1. Total Financial Assets | $6,602.2 | $14,827.7 | $33,108.4 | $39,806.3 |
| 2.  Deposits | 1,520.7 | 3,259.3 | 4,394.9 | 6,251.4 |
| 3.    Foreign deposits | 0.0 | 13.4 | 48.3 | 66.9 |
| 4.    Checkable deposits and currency | 219.5 | 412.4 | 279.4 | 338.5 |
| 5.    Time and savings deposits | 1,239.0 | 2,465.0 | 3,062.4 | 4,889.2 |
| 6.    Money market fund shares | 62.2 | 368.6 | 959.8 | 956.7 |
| 7.  Credit market instruments | 425.4 | 1,555.3 | 2,345.7 | 3,215.9 |
| 8.    Open market paper | 38.3 | 63.2 | 97.3 | 169.3 |
| 9.    Treasury securities | 160.0 | 471.2 | 584.0 | 464.2 |
| 10.    Savings bonds | 72.5 | 126.2 | 184.8 | 205.9 |
| 11.    Other Treasury securities | 87.5 | 345.0 | 399.3 | 258.2 |
| 12.    Federal agency securities | 5.3 | 68.9 | 509.0 | 691.3 |
| 13.    Municipal securities | 104.5 | 575.0 | 539.3 | 860.1 |
| 14.    Corporate and foreign bonds | 30.0 | 233.5 | 548.8 | 854.2 |
| 15.    Mortgages | 87.2 | 143.5 | 117.3 | 176.8 |
| 16.  Corporate equities | 875.4 | 1,781.4 | 8035.6 | 5,684.5 |
| 17.  Mutual fund shares | 45.6 | 456.6 | 2,855.9 | 4,537.4 |
| 18.  Security credit | 16.2 | 62.4 | 412.4 | 589.5 |
| 19.  Life insurance reserves | 220.6 | 391.7 | 819.1 | 1096.8 |
| 20.  Pension fund reserves | 970.4 | 3,376.3 | 9,163.7 | 11,108.6 |
| 21.  Equity in noncorporate businesses | 2,183.1 | 3,150.5 | 4,990.6 | 6,786.3 |
| 22.  Miscellaneous financial assets | 344.8 | 794.2 | 1,466.7 | 535.8 |
| 23. Total Liabilities | 1,453.0 | 3,719.3 | 7,356.7 | 12,198.8 |
| 24.  Credit market instruments | 1,401.5 | 3,597.2 | 6,966.7 | 11,760.5 |
| 25.    Home mortgages and home equity loans | 932.0 | 2,504.1 | 4,770.1 | 8,943.6 |
| 26.    Consumer credit | 358.0 | 824.4 | 1,735.8 | 2,149.6 |
| 27.    Municipal securities | 16.7 | 86.6 | 143.0 | 212.4 |
| 28.    Bank loans (not elsewhere classified) | 27.8 | 17.9 | 77.2 | 117.9 |
| 29.    Other loans and advances | 52.1 | 81.7 | 119.8 | 119.5 |
| 30.    Commercial mortgages | 14.8 | 82.5 | 120.7 | 217.6 |
| 31.  Security credit | 24.7 | 38.8 | 235.1 | 249.4 |
| 32.  Trade payables | 13.8 | 66.8 | 134.7 | 166.4 |
| 33.  Deferred and unpaid life insurance premiums | 12.9 | 16.5 | 19.6 | 22.5 |

Source: Board of Governors of the Federal Reserve System's *Flow of Funds Accounts.*

Note: As used here, the term "households" includes personal trusts and nonprofit organizations as well as individuals and families. It excludes corporate entities.

*Figures for 2006 are for the first quarter, annualized.

households' total liabilities of about $12 trillion, we get a rough estimate of the combined net worth (accumulated savings) of all American households—a figure close to $54 trillion (or about $180,000 per person).

## Sources of Balance Sheet Data

Where does information come from to build sector balance sheets in the Flow of Funds Accounts? It comes from a wide variety of public and private sources. For example, information on lending and borrowing by nonfinancial businesses is derived from such sources as the Securities and Exchange Commission and the U.S. Department of Commerce. Various trade groups provide financial data on their respective industries, such as the Investment Company Institute, which provides data on mutual funds, and the Securities Industry Association, which provides selected information on gross offerings of securities. Inevitably, inconsistencies arise in classifying financial transactions due to differences in accounting procedures among the groups contributing data. Moreover, in an economy as vast and complex as that of the United States, some financial transactions fall between the cracks. To deal with problems in data consistency and coverage, the Federal Reserve includes a *statistical discrepancy* account that brings each sector into balance.

## Constructing the Flow of Funds Accounts: Preparing Sources and Uses of Funds Statements

After balance sheets are constructed for each sector of the economy, the third step in the construction of the Flow of Funds Accounts is to prepare a *sources and uses of funds statement* for each sector. This statement shows changes in net worth and changes in holdings of financial assets and liabilities taken from each sector's balance sheet at the beginning and end of a calendar quarter or year.

An example of such a statement for the U.S. commercial banking sector for 2006 is shown in Exhibit 3A.3. The first portion of the sources and uses statement (lines 1–21) shows changes in the banking sector's net worth (gross saving), real assets (net fixed investment in plant and equipment),

| EXHIBIT 3A.3 | Sources and Uses of Funds Statement for the U.S. Banking Sector, 2006[*] ($ Billions) | | |
|---|---|---|---|
| **Changes in Asset and Liability Items** | | | |
| 1. Gross saving | 138.3 | 22. Net increase in liabilities | 928.7 |
| 2. Fixed nonresidential investment | 25.3 | 23.  Net interbank liabilities | 73.9 |
| 3. Net acquisition of financial assets | 968.8 | 24.   To monetary authority | −4.9 |
| 4.  Vault cash | 1.0 | 25.   To domestic banks | −2.7 |
| 5.  Reserves at Federal Reserve | −4.9 | 26.   To foreign banks | 81.5 |
| 6.  Checkable deposits and currency | −1.3 | 27.  Checkable deposits | 35.6 |
| 7.  Total bank credit | 957.0 | 28.   Federal government | −26.5 |
| 8.    Treasury securities | −9.1 | 29.   Rest of the world | 57.6 |
| 9.    Agency and GSE-backed securities[†] | 154.3 | 30.   Private domestic | 4.5 |
| 10.   Municipal securities | 16.2 | 31.  Small time and savings deposits | 115.3 |
| 11.   Corporate and foreign bonds | 97.0 | 32.  Large time deposits | 318.8 |
| 12.  Total loans | 701.3 | 33.  Federal funds and RPs (net) | 164.3 |
| 13.    Open market paper | 0.0 | 34.  Credit market instruments | 77.4 |
| 14.    Bank loans (n.e.c.)[‡] | 245.4 | 35.   Open market paper | 6.4 |
| 15.   Mortgages | 370.3 | 36.   Corporate bonds | 47.0 |
| 16.   Consumer credit | 26.5 | 37.   Other loans and advances | 24.0 |
| 17.   Security credit | 59.1 | 38.  Corporate equity issues | −26.6 |
| 18.  Corporate equities | 1.8 | 39.  Taxes payable | 3.6 |
| 19.  Mutual fund shares | −4.3 | 40.  Miscellaneous liabilities | 166.4 |
| 20.  Customer liabilities on acceptances | 0.0 | 41.  Statistical discrepancy | 72.9 |
| 21.  Miscellaneous assets | 16.9 | | |

Source: Board of Governors of the Federal Reserve System's *Flow of Funds Accounts.*

[*]Data are for the first quarter of 2006, annualized.

[†]GSE-backed securities are issued by government-sponsored agencies, such as the Federal National Mortgage Association (FNMA) and the Federal Home Loan Mortgage Corporation (FHLMC).

[‡]n.e.c. means "not elsewhere classified".

and net acquisitions of financial assets. The second portion of the sources and uses statement (lines 22–41) reflects net borrowing as illustrated by an increase in the liabilities carried by U.S. commercial banks and their affiliates.[1]

We note, for example, that banks operating in the United States increased their holdings of financial assets by more than $968 billion in 2006 (line 3). Bank loans to businesses, households, and other borrowers rose by just over $700 billion (line 12) as the U.S. economy enjoyed a period of positive growth following a recession at the beginning of the decade. With the U.S. economy continuing to expand in 2006, more individuals and businesses demanded bank credit to help them increase their standard of living and increase the economy's output of goods and services. Bank holdings of U.S. government and agency securities (including issues of mortgage-backed securities guaranteed by a federal government agency) also rose significantly, by almost $155 billion (line 9), reflecting bankers' search for higher-quality assets and the increased availability of government securities in the wake of large government budget deficits. Banks with offices in the United States invested more than $25 billion (line 2) in new plant and equipment (fixed nonresidential investment) during the year as the industry continued to automate many of its facilities and establish branch offices.

Where did the banking sector get the funds it needed to make new loans and security purchases and increase its investment in new plant and equipment? A portion of the necessary funds came from a rise of about $115 billion in small-denomination (under $100,000 each) time and savings deposits (line 31), while the largest time deposits (each over $100,000 in amount) that banks sell—often called money market CDs—rose by nearly $320 billion (line 32). Deposits in checking accounts by households and firms barely budged (line 30), while the federal government significantly cut back on its deposits at commercial banks by more than $26 billion (line 28). This loss of funds was more than offset by the sizeable increase in federal funds and RPs (or short-term loans backed by government securities owned by the banks). The banking sector therefore drew on a wide range of sources in 2006 to support the industry's substantial increase in financial and real assets.

Banks often supplement their deposit growth with borrowing in the money market through such instruments as federal funds borrowings, security repurchase agreements, and sales of other IOUs in the open market. This particular source of bank funding increased more than $170 billion in 2006 (lines 33 and 35). U.S. banks also added to their savings (shown as gross savings) by just over $138 billion (line 1), thereby opening up another source of cash that bankers could draw upon in the future to respond to their customers' service needs and help their industry grow.

### Balancing Out a Sources and Uses of Funds Statement

As we have seen, sources and uses of funds statements in the Flow of Funds Accounts are derived from the aggregated balance sheets of each sector of the economy. Because balance sheets must always balance, we would also expect a sources and uses of funds statement to balance (except, of course, for discrepancies in the underlying data). In a sources and uses statement,

$$\begin{matrix} \text{Net investment} \\ \text{in plant and} \\ \text{equipment} \end{matrix} + \begin{matrix} \text{Net acquisitions} \\ \text{of financial} \\ \text{assets} \end{matrix} = \begin{matrix} \text{Net increase in} \\ \text{liabilities} + \text{Change in} \\ \text{current surplus} \\ \text{account (or gross savings)} \end{matrix} \qquad (3A.1)$$

---

[1]All changes on a sources and uses of funds statement are shown *net* of purchases and sales. When purchases of an asset exceed sales of that asset, the resulting figure is reported as a *positive* increase in the asset. When sales exceed purchases, an asset item will carry a *negative* sign. A nonnegative liability item on the sources and uses statement indicates that net borrowing (i.e., total borrowings larger than debt repayments) has occurred during the period under study. If a liability item is negative, debt repayments exceed new borrowings during the period covered by the statement.

Net acquisitions of financial assets are frequently referred to as *financial investment;* net purchases of plant and equipment may be labeled *real investment.* Both are *uses of funds* for a sector or economic unit. Net increases in liabilities represent *current borrowing,* while changes in the current surplus account reflect *current savings.* These latter two items are *sources of funds.* Therefore, the relationship shown above may be written:

$$\text{Net real investment } + \text{ Net financial investment}$$
$$= \text{Net borrowing } + \text{ Net current saving} \tag{3A.2}$$

or

$$\text{Total uses of funds } = \text{ Total sources of funds} \tag{3A.3}$$

For each unit—business, household, or government—and for each sector of the economy, the above statement *must* be true—it is an accounting identity. For example, in the U.S. commercial banking sector in 2006 we have the following figures drawn from Exhibit 3A.3.

Once the statistical discrepancy account is considered, total uses and total sources of funds should be equal for this and for all other sectors of the economy (except for small remaining discrepancies in column totals due to rounding error).

**SOURCES AND USES OF FUNDS STATEMENT
FOR THE BANKING SECTOR, 2006\* ($ Billions)**

| Uses of Funds | | Sources of Funds | |
|---|---|---|---|
| Net investment in plant and equipment (net increase in real assets) | $ 25.3 | Net borrowing (net increase in liabilities) | $ 928.7 |
| Net financial investment (net acquisitions of financial assets) | 968.8 | Net current saving (net change in net worth) | 138.3 |
| Statistical discrepancy | 72.9 | | |
| Total uses of funds | $1,067.0 | Total sources of funds | $1,067.0 |

*Data are for the first quarter of 2006, annualized.

### Constructing the Flow of Funds Accounts: Building a Flow of Funds Matrix for the Whole Economy

The final step in the construction of the Flow of Funds Accounts is to combine the sources and uses of funds statement for each sector into a flow of funds matrix for the entire economy. An example of such a matrix is shown in Exhibit 3A.4, which lists borrowings by each major sector and total borrowings by all sectors combined. Another example appears in Exhibit 3A.5, which shows funds raised by all sectors through the issuance of debt (credit market borrowing) and through the issuance of corporate equities (stock). The majority of funds sought by businesses, households, and governments in the financial marketplace clearly were raised by issuing debt instruments (primarily bonds and notes), as shown in Exhibit 3A.5. The total of all debt instruments outstanding rose by just over $4.5 trillion (line 1 in Exhibit 3A.5) in the year 2006 (as of the first quarter of that year, annualized).

Corporations were heavy borrowers of funds in the American economy, issuing more than $1 trillion in debt instruments (line 5 in Exhibit 3A.5). Also

among the heaviest borrowers were debtors taking on mortgage loans (both new home mortgages and commercial mortgages), who borrowed nearly $1.6 trillion (line 8). Borrowings by governments at all levels ranked high in volume as well at around $731 billion (lines 3 and 4). Of course, borrowing—issuing debt—is not the only possible source of funds from the money and capital markets. Substantial funds also can be raised by issuing stock (corporate equities), which in 2006 totaled almost $100 billion, net, including about $400 billion in retired corporate stock and just over $500 billion in shares offered by mutual funds (lines 10, 11, and 15 in Exhibit 3A.5).

Exhibit 3A.4 looks at borrowing in the economy from *both* the lenders' and borrowers' points of view. From Chapter 2 we know that what is borrowed by one sector just equals the credit extended to that sector by other sectors. For example, line 27 in Exhibit 3A.4 shows that total funds *loaned* in U.S. credit markets during 2006 (through the first quarter, annualized) amounted to about $4.5 trillion. This amount exactly matches total net borrowing by all sectors reported in line 1 of Exhibit 3A.4 and in line 1 of Exhibit 3A.5 for the same time period.

| EXHIBIT 3A.4 | Total Net Borrowing and Lending in Credit Markets and Borrowing by Sector ($ Billions)) | | |
|---|---|---|---|
| | **1993** | **2000** | **2006**[†] |
| | Total Net Borrowing and Lending in Credit Markets[*] | | |
| 1. Total net borrowing | $930.6 | $1,668.6 | 4,503.7 |
| 2. Domestic nonfinancial sectors | 566.6 | 826.6 | 2,913.6 |
| 3. Federal government | 256.1 | −295.9 | 607.7 |
| 4. Nonfederal sectors | 310.5 | 1,122.6 | 2,305.9 |
| 5. Household sector | 236.6 | 551.7 | 1,333.9 |
| 6. Nonfinancial corporate business | 34.4 | 347.0 | 509.4 |
| 7. Nonfarm noncorporate business | −20.5 | 197.1 | 336.3 |
| 8. Farm business | 2.3 | 11.3 | 18.3 |
| 9. State and local governments | 57.7 | 15.5 | 107.7 |
| 10. Rest of the world | 69.8 | 63.0 | 111.0 |
| 11. Financial sectors | 294.2 | 779.0 | 1,479.2 |
| 12. Commercial banking | 13.4 | 60.0 | 77.4 |
| 13. U.S.-chartered commercial banks | 9.7 | 36.8 | 40.9 |
| 14. Foreign banking offices in U.S. | −5.1 | 0.0 | 0.1 |
| 15. Bank holding companies | 8.8 | 23.2 | 36.4 |
| 16. Savings institutions | 11.3 | 27.3 | −22.7 |
| 17. Credit unions | 0.2 | 0.0 | −6.2 |
| 18. Life insurance companies | 0.2 | −0.7 | 2.8 |
| 19. Government-sponsored enterprises | 80.6 | 235.2 | 144.8 |
| 20. Federally related mortgage pools | 84.7 | 199.7 | 348.2 |
| 21. ABS issuers | 85.2 | 157.8 | 662.7 |
| 22. Finance companies | −1.4 | 81.9 | 16.7 |
| 23. Mortgage companies | 0.0 | 0.0 | 0.0 |
| 24. REITs | 1.7 | 2.6 | 94.8 |
| 25. Brokers and dealers | 12.0 | 15.6 | 35.1 |
| 26. Funding corporations | 6.3 | −0.3 | 119.6 |
| 27. Total net lending | 930.6 | 1,668.6 | 4,503.7 |

Source: Board of Governors of the Federal Reserve System, *Flow of Funds Accounts.*
[*]Excludes corporate equities and mutual fund shares.
[†]Figures are for the first quarter of 2006, annualized.

*The flow of funds matrix reminds us that, for all sectors of the economy combined into one, the amount of saving must equal the total amount of real investment in the economy, and, therefore, the amount of borrowing in total must equal total financial investment* (i.e., the total amount of financial assets acquired by all sectors).

### Limitations and Uses of the Flow of Funds Accounts

It should be clear by now that the Flow of Funds Accounts provide a vast amount of information on trends in the financial system. These accounts provide indispensable aid in tracing the flow of savings through the money and capital markets. Estimates of flow of funds data can be used to help make forecasts of lending, borrowing, and interest rates. However, these social accounts have a number of limitations that must be kept firmly in mind.

First, the Flow of Funds Accounts present no information on transactions among economic units *within* each sector. If a household sells stock to another household, this transaction will *not* be picked up in the accounts, because both units are in the same sector. However, if a household sells stock to a business firm, this transaction *will* be captured by the flow of funds bookkeeping system.

| EXHIBIT 3A.5 | **Funds Raised in Credit and Equity Markets ($ Billions)** | | |
|---|---|---|---|
| | **1993** | **2000** | **2006*** |
| **Credit Market Borrowing, All Sectors, by Instrument** | | | |
| 1. Total net debt taken on | $ 930.6 | $ 1,668.6 | $4,503.7 |
| 2.  Open market paper | −5.1 | 211.6 | 351.4 |
| 3.  U.S. government securities | 421.4 | −294.9 | 608.7 |
| 4.  Municipal securities | 66.3 | 23.6 | 122.3 |
| 5.  Corporate and foreign bonds | 281.0 | 345.1 | 1,013.2 |
| 6.  Bank loans n.e.c. | −7.2 | 113.3 | 245.4 |
| 7.  Other loans and advances | −8.9 | 120.8 | 27.0 |
| 8.  Mortgages | 121.8 | 546.8 | 1,595.7 |
| 9.  Consumer credit | 61.4 | 168.4 | 48.1 |
| **Funds Raised through Corporate Equities and Mutual Fund Shares** | | | |
| 10. Total net issues of stock | $ 425.4 | $ 242.9 | $ 98.9 |
| 11.  Corporate equities | 133.4 | 5.3 | −401.5 |
| 12.   Nonfinancial | 21.3 | −118.2 | −586.8 |
| 13.   Foreign shares purchased by U.S. residents | 63.4 | 106.7 | 172.0 |
| 14.   Financial | 48.7 | 16.8 | 13.3 |
| 15.  Mutual fund shares | 292.0 | 237.6 | 500.4 |

Source: Board of Governors of the Federal Reserve System, *Flow of Funds Accounts.*

*Figures are for the first quarter of 2006, annualized. Columns may not add to totals due to rounding.

Second, the Flow of Funds Accounts show only *net* flows between one point in time and another point in time. These accounts do *not* show any changes that occur *between* the beginning and ending points of the period under study.

Finally, all flow of funds data are expressed in terms of current *market values.* Therefore, these accounts measure not only the flow of savings in the economy but also capital gains and losses. This market-value bias distorts estimates of the amount of actual savings and investment activity that occur from year to year.

Despite these limitations, however, the Flow of Funds Accounts are among the most comprehensive sources of information available to students of the financial system. These accounts provide vital clues on the demand and supply forces that shape movements in interest rates and the prices of financial assets. The Flow of Funds Accounts indicate which types of financial assets are growing or declining in volume and which sectors finance other sectors. One of the principal uses of flow of funds data today is to forecast interest rates and build models to simulate future conditions in the credit markets. Combined with other sources of information, Flow of Funds Accounts provide us with the raw material from which to make important financial decisions.

## QUESTIONS TO HELP YOU STUDY THE APPENDIX TO CHAPTER 3

3A-1. What is meant by the term *social accounting*? Why is such an accounting system needed?

3A-2. Compare and contrast the Flow of Funds Accounts with the National Income and Product Accounts. What types of information does each system of accounts provide that could be useful for making financial decisions?

3A-3. How are the Flow of Funds Accounts constructed?

3A-4. What is a *sources and uses of funds statement*? Why is it important?

3A-5. Discuss the principal limitations of flow of funds data. Why must a user of flow of funds information keep these limitations in mind?

# Chapter 4

# The Future of the Financial System and Trends in the Money and Capital Markets

## Learning Objectives

### in This Chapter

- You will explore the economic, demographic, social, and technological forces reshaping financial institutions, financial markets, and the financial system today.

- You will learn about recent trends in the financial system and how they may affect each one of us in the future, both personally and professionally.

- You will learn how your behavior and decisions, along with millions of others, may play an important role in shaping the future of the financial system.

## What's in This Chapter?
## Key Topics Outline

**Forces and Trends Reshaping the Financial System**

**Financial Innovation, Technological Change, Homogenization**

**Consolidation, Convergence, Globalization, and Market Broadening**

**Deregulation and Harmonization**

**Demographic and Economic Forces Reshaping the Financial System**

**New Types of Financial Institutions and Regulations**

**Risk in the Financial System: Possible Remedies**

**Financial Disclosure, Personal Privacy, and the Gramm-Leach-Bliley Act**

**Competition: Leveling the Playing Field**

## 4.1  Introduction: The Financial Markets in Change

The money and capital markets and the financial system that surrounds them are continually in transition, always moving toward something *new*. As we observed in the opening chapter, you cannot step into the same river twice, for rivers are ever flowing onward. So it is with the financial system. Today's financial marketplace differs radically from that of a decade ago and will be still more different as we move forward into the future.

Powerful forces and trends are reshaping financial institutions and services today. These forces for change include powerful trends within the financial sector itself, major changes in the structure and functioning of the economy that surrounds the financial system, and new demographic trends that are altering the public's need for financial services. In this chapter we focus upon these tidal changes that are refashioning the financial system we see today and helping to build a new financial marketplace for the future.

## 4.2  Financial Forces Reshaping the Money and Capital Markets Today

The money and capital markets we see today will soon be very different as the financial marketplace continues to transform itself. Vast changes now under way will demand that we continue to study the money and capital markets throughout our lives for greater understanding and personal benefit.

**financial innovation**

One of the most important changes currently sweeping through the financial system is **financial innovation**—the development of *new* financial services and instruments. Every year new financial services and instruments expand rapidly in variety and volume. Home equity credit lines, international mutual funds, currency and interest-rate swaps, loan securitizations, along with other exotic new services and financial instruments that we may have heard about (and will discuss later in this book) are only the vanguard of a wave of invention and change sweeping through the money and capital markets. Moreover, with rapidly growing innovation has come **service proliferation** as each financial institution expands the menu of services it is willing to offer customers.

**service proliferation**

**competition**

One of the causes of the ongoing rush to innovate and develop new services and techniques is the rise of intense **competition** among financial-service providers. Banks, insurance companies, securities dealers, mutual funds, and thrift institutions are locked in an intense struggle for the customer's business that is unparalleled in history. Many of these financial institutions are engaged in *mergers and acquisitions* aimed at creating bigger financial firms out of numerous smaller financial-service providers—giant companies that are able to compete more effectively due to lower costs and offer one-stop shopping convenience for those customers that value that feature. Ultimately, these larger firms will win bigger shares of the financial-service marketplace. In short, a major trend toward the **consolidation** of smaller financial firms into fewer, but much larger financial-service providers is well under way as competitors seek any possible advantage over their rivals.

**consolidation**

**deregulation**

The rise of greater financial-services competition has been fueled, in part, by **deregulation**—a trend set in motion over the years by several governments. Major nations around the globe, especially the United States, Japan, and the countries of the European Union, are gradually freeing portions of their financial sector from the burden of so many government rules. As government regulations are lightened or eliminated, the *private marketplace* is becoming more and more important in shaping

**privatization**

how financial-service providers perform in order to serve the public. Financial-service competition is increasingly taking the place of government rules—a strategy of **privatization** of the financial sector, allowing privately owned firms to decide what services to provide and in what quantity, driven by the expectation that the public will, ultimately, benefit in the form of more convenient services at lower cost.

The expanding competitive struggle in a deregulated financial marketplace has given rise to new services and new financial instruments, as well as new types of financial institutions—large, multiproduct, multimarket, technologically sophisticated, sales-oriented organizations designed to weather the risks inherent in today's volatile financial marketplace. As a result, financial institutions and industries have come to closely resemble each other and are organized in much the same ways and this includes industrial and retail companies (like Wal-Mart and General Electric) which are reaching out to invade the financial-services marketplace.

**convergence**

Reflecting this trend toward **convergence** among financial firms and industries, traditional distinctions between one type of financial institution and another have become hopelessly blurred. Today many banks, thrifts, and credit unions clearly look like each other; the same is true for some of the largest security dealers and insurance companies. Increasingly, their service menus are mirror images of each other—a trend

**homogenization**

called **homogenization.** This has created a real challenge for marketing professionals, who must try to convince the public that their particular financial institution is truly different from its rivals.

More financial institutions are establishing interstate operations and expanding their marketing programs to cover whole regions or the whole globe (usually referred

**globalization**

to as **globalization**). The results are falling geographic barriers to international competition and strong pressure to consolidate smaller institutions into larger ones in order to deal with intense competitive pressure and rising costs. At the same time, financial markets that have traditionally been local in character are expanding to become

**market broadening**

regional, national, and even international in scope. This **market broadening** reflects recent advances in communications technology. Such breakthroughs offer the prospect of reducing service delivery costs, improving employee productivity, bringing new financial services online more rapidly, and expanding the effective marketing area for both old and new services.

As new financial-service markets develop, many of the larger businesses and governments will have less reason to borrow from traditional financial intermediaries and more reason to sell debt and equity securities directly to investors in the open market. Indeed, the role of the traditional financial intermediary in the channeling of savings into investment seems to be shrinking somewhat. Moreover, the development of a market for *securitized assets*—pools of loans—allows almost any large firm with a strong market reputation to package its loans and issue new securities against them, thereby generating more cash to make *new* loans and investments. Thus, there is less need for traditional loans from traditional financial institutions, although many banks and insurance companies have learned that they can benefit from this trend by selling advice, acting as agents for new security offerings, and issuing standby credit guarantees in case something goes wrong in the fund-raising process.

Of course, the trends we observe in today's financial system are *not* a completely new story. Their roots lie deep in history. For example, today's trend toward deregulation of financial institutions counteracts the excesses of a much earlier era—the Great Depression of the 1930s—when comprehensive regulation of financial institutions promised *safety* but tended to stifle competition and innovation. Furthermore, the current emphasis in the financial sector on new product development and research, frequent technological updating, elaborate marketing programs to sell financial services, and strategic planning is a carryover from manufacturing and industrial firms that have used such techniques for decades. There is a growing awareness that the challenges and techniques of managing a financial-service institution are *not* fundamentally different from those of managing any other business. The products are different, but the methods of control and decision making are much the same.

## 4.3 Economic and Demographic Forces Reshaping the Financial System

We must recognize that much of what is happening in the financial system today is a response to broad economic and demographic trends that span generations. These trends are affecting not just financial institutions but also governments, businesses, and households in every corner of society and every nation on the globe.

For example, fundamental changes in the age makeup of the population are having profound effects on savings habits, consumption, and borrowing decisions worldwide. The population is *rapidly aging,* due primarily to better medical care, nutrition, and changing attitudes about childbearing. The *life-cycle hypothesis*—developed by Modigliani and Ando [10] and expanded later by others—suggests that, as individuals age, they reduce their expectations of lifetime income, mainly because their expected time in the labor force is decreasing. With retirement looming closer, personal savings rates should rise and, correspondingly, per-capita consumption spending may fall in real terms, possibly lowering living standards. Thus, the boom in recent years of runaway consumer borrowing and spending may eventually moderate, resulting in a more moderate-growth economy, lower average interest rates, and less inflation. The challenge faced by financial-service providers in the future will be to find better ways to accommodate the demands of older savers, including the greater need for retirement and estate planning.

The basic family unit is also changing, with *more single-parent households, a rising age at which first marriages occur,* and *a declining fertility rate in most industrialized countries*—all of which have profound implications for spending and borrowing and accessing financial services. However, in the United States, population growth estimates have recently been revised upward due to greater-than-expected immigration, an increase in fertility, and greater longevity, reaching an estimated 300 million in 2007 and about 400 million by 2043, with close to half white and close to a quarter Hispanic. A high divorce rate marks many industrialized nations, although married couples make up a majority of all U.S. households. But less than half of these have children living in the home. People living alone make up the remainder of households, although this number appears to be rising. Also on the rise are dual-earner couples with above-average incomes, who are becoming one of the most important segments of the population in terms of their contributions to the economy and demand for financial services.

The general population has stronger educational backgrounds than at any other time in history. Today, a roughly *equal* proportion of young women and young men (ages 25 to 29) have completed at least four years of college. Educational levels have risen so much that almost half of the U.S. labor force (in the 25 to 64 age group) has been enrolled in college at one time or another. High school diplomas are becoming the minimal educational achievement an individual needs to avoid poverty. Financial-service institutions must be prepared to deal with a more educated clientele, more aware of their financial-services needs and options, and more willing to shop around for competitive pricing and quality service.

- Aging population (with wealthier retirees and a growing volume of funds transfers over time to their heirs).

- Larger corporate customers going directly to the open market to raise funds, bypassing traditional financial institutions (such as banks and finance companies).

- Growing demands for retirement planning and long-term saving by millions of workers and their families not covered adequately by existing retirement programs.

- Increasing numbers of nontraditional families (including single-parent homes) who have credit-access problems and a need for lower-cost financial services.

- Greater ethnic diversity in the populations of the world's leading countries, resulting in a range of different customer attitudes and philosophies about managing money and the need for financial services.

- More volatile job markets, with customers switching jobs and residential locations more frequently so that financial-service providers need greater product-line and geographic flexibility.

- Increased need for personal budgeting and debt management education for individuals, families, and businesses.

- Growing need for financial planning programs to aid individuals and families in managing their retirement assets and their inheritances.

Although many of the foregoing demographic trends have slowed or paused recently, most demographers do not anticipate a significant *reversal* anytime soon, and so demands will continue to grow for new forms of housing, flexible work schedules, less expensive medical care and more effective financial budgeting and planning for businesses and consumers. The result is a new matrix of financial-service needs, including demands for new savings instruments and loans that support retraining and relocation, provide education, and supply more venture capital to support new businesses struggling to be born.

Added to the demographic changes are broad *economic* movements. For example, manufacturing industries are being displaced by service industries in more developed economies. The computer has transformed the economy from a system primarily reliant on manufacturing to one centered increasingly upon the flow of *information*. The expansion of service firms is creating most of the new jobs, and these businesses have their own unique financing needs. Accelerated growth in automation, computer systems, telecommunications, and biotechnology is creating the need for new kinds of credit and risk protection that financial-service providers must respond to.

The broader and faster dissemination of information today is contributing to the *internationalization* of markets, which spurs competition and heightens the need for international cooperation among financial institutions and among the government agencies that regulate them. One of the most dramatic examples is the emergence of the European Union (EU), creating a common market with more than 400 million customers. A similar trend toward establishing a "free trade zone" is under way among many nations in North and South America.

Many financial institutions are licensed to offer their services throughout Western Europe and the Americas, leading to the free and open marketing of financial services. These reforms have already set in motion a wave of mergers and joint ventures among

**Key URL:**
For further discussion of recent demographic trends, see U.S. Bureau of the Census at **census.gov**

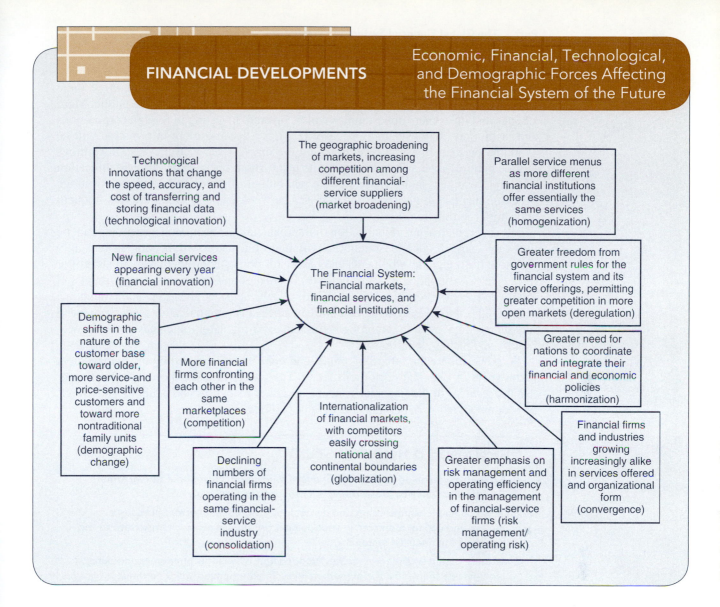

leading banks, insurance companies, and other firms in order to survive in a more open financial marketplace.

Similar developments loom on the horizon for Eastern Europe and the nations that comprise the former Soviet Union now that the Cold War has ended. Huge amounts of venture capital as well as funding for education are desperately needed in Russia and the other nations that belonged to the old Warsaw Pact in order to improve their living standards and retrain their workers to be competitive in a global marketplace. In one positive step taken early in the new century, several Eastern European nations were admitted to the European Union (EU).

In Asia parallel changes are unfolding as expanding populations migrate to the cities to become part of a rapidly expanding industrial sector. Moreover, Asian economies, led by China and India, are opening their doors (in some cases, slowly) to foreign business ventures, including the banking and financial-service sector. However, if economic growth is to continue at its current rapid pace, this sector must expand and modernize along with the rest of Asia's economic system.

Clearly, as the *internationalization* of economies and the *globalization* of the financial sector continue, along with steady advances in *communications technology,* there will be a wide range of possible benefits for the financial system and the public. More savings and investment opportunities will be opened. Investing in foreign corporations and institutions may eventually become less risky because more information will be available on their financial condition, and the markets serviced by these institutions will be better known and understood. The result should be a more efficient allocation of scarce resources and increases in the real output of goods and services. Arbitrage opportunities due to discrepancies in prices between markets should be less frequent and shorter in duration.

However, increasing globalization of the financial and economic system will not be without its costs. Economic conditions within any one nation will become increasingly sensitive to foreign developments and harder for domestic policymakers to control or influence. Confirmation of security trades (*clearing*) and getting proper payment and timely delivery of securities bought and sold (*settlement*) will be more challenging in a globalized financial system, at least until advances in communications technology and international cooperation among governments and regulatory agencies catch up with rapidly advancing globalization.

So powerful are the foregoing trends that *none* can be ignored by the management and owners of financial institutions today. The choice now for those who work in or use the services of the financial system is to either recognize and adapt to such trends or become a victim, rather than a beneficiary, of change.

---

### QUESTIONS TO HELP YOU STUDY

1. Explain the meaning of the term *financial innovation.* How about *deregulation? Privatization? Service proliferation? Consolidation? Convergence?*

2. Why are financial innovation and deregulation significant factors in today's money and capital markets? In your opinion are they likely to be important to the future of the financial system?

3. What is meant by the term *market broadening?* Why is this phenomenon taking place inside today's financial marketplace? In your opinion will it continue?

4. Explain the reasoning behind the *life-cycle hypothesis.* How will the life-cycle idea affect the financial system of the future, in your opinion? Why?

5. What changes in the financial markets' *customer base* are underway? What are the implications of these projected changes for managers of financial-service institutions?

6. What is meant by the term *homogenization?* What do you think is motivating this trend toward service homogenization today?

---

## 4.4 The Challenges and Opportunities Presented by Recent Trends

There is little question now that the demographic, economic, and financial trends mentioned above will continue into the foreseeable future. But we must recognize that these trends have unleashed new problems of their own—great unresolved issues that must somehow be dealt with as we rush toward the future. We turn now to these critical issues for the future of the financial system in the sections that follow.

## Dealing with Risk in the Financial System: Ensuring the Strength of Financial Institutions and Increasing Public Confidence

The money and capital markets and the financial institutions that operate within them depend heavily on *public confidence*. The financial system works to channel scarce loanable funds (credit) to their most productive uses only if individuals and businesses are willing to save and entrust their savings to financial institutions, and only if other businesses and individuals are willing to rely on the financial system to provide credit to support their consumption and investment. When *any* financial institution develops serious problems that reach public notice, the public's confidence in other financial institutions may be damaged as well. The result can be a smaller flow of savings and restrictions on the availability of credit. Jobs and economic growth could be adversely affected.

*The Consequences of Reduced Public Confidence*  The close of the twentieth century and the opening of the twenty-first brought new concerns on the part of the public regarding the strength of both financial and nonfinancial businesses. Inaccurate and even illegal financial reporting on the part of companies such as Enron, WorldCom, and other prominent firms weakened not only those firms but also some of their financial-service providers. At the same time, apparent misconduct on the part of several investment bankers and mutual fund managers led to deep public skepticism about the honesty and reliability of many financial institutions. As a result, financial-service customers today appear to be more sensitive to the risk of losing their funds and are, therefore, less loyal in dealing with any *one* financial institution. Financial-service *honesty* and *reliability* have become as important as price to many customers today.

Loss of public confidence not only produces adverse consequences for individual financial institutions but also damages the *efficiency* of financial market processes. A flight of funds from financial institutions reduces their size, threatening to make them less efficient in using resources. That portion of the public continuing to rely on the financial system is forced to pay higher prices for financial services that may be fewer in quantity and inferior in quality.

*Ways to Promote Public Confidence in Financial Institutions and Reduce Risk in the Financial System*  How can we ensure the continued viability of financial institutions and promote public confidence in them? Both government and the private sector may offer effective remedies.

**Key URLs:**
To learn more about government insurance systems for financial institutions in the United States see, for example, **fdic.gov** and **pbgc.gov**

**Government-Sponsored Insurance Systems to Manage Risk**  Governments have taken major steps over the years to ensure the safety of financial institutions in order to protect the public's savings. For example, during the 1930s, with thousands of banks failing, the U.S. Congress created the Federal Deposit Insurance Corporation (FDIC) to provide insurance coverage for smaller deposits (initially up to $2,500). Then, in 1980 in the wake of significant inflation and government deregulation of the U.S. financial sector, the Congress increased federal deposit insurance coverage to a maximum of $100,000 per depositor. Most recently, as a result of the passage of the FDIC Insurance Reform Act of 2005, federal insurance coverage of qualified retirement deposits was increased from $100,000 to $250,000.

In the mid-1970s Congress decided to copy the government-sponsored deposit insurance idea and extend similar protection to selected employee retirement plans. In 1974, the Pension Benefit Guaranty Corporation (PBGC) was set up to insure retirement income promised to employees having certain types of defined-benefit pension programs. It did not take long for similar proposals to be brought forward for public debate, including the possibility of offering government-sponsored insurance protection for certain kinds of insurance policies, annuities, and security investments.

There is, however, serious concern today with the idea of further extending government-sponsored insurance to promote greater public confidence in the financial system. A government-provided insurance program, unless skillfully crafted, can do more harm than good. It can distort risk-taking decisions by the managements of privately owned financial institutions. Federal deposit insurance, for example, has protected small depositors but led many banks and thrifts in prior decades to take on greater risk with the public's money. In brief, government-provided insurance can lead to a *moral hazard* problem in which agents (such as managers of insured financial firms) take advantage of a guarantee underwritten by principals (in this case, the taxpayers).

This moral hazard problem resulting from government-subsidized insurance can be mitigated somewhat by using an insurance system modeled after some of those used by selected nations in the European Union. In several of these national insurance systems, no rescue fund is built up by the taxpayers or even by participating banks over time as happens with the FDIC in the United States. In other words, there is *no* emergency reserve. Rather, when a failure occurs among many insured European banks, the remaining institutions are expected to provide the resources necessary to cover any losses of insured depositors. While this system may *reduce* moral hazard, it may not completely eliminate the problem, particularly if there is an implicit guarantee that government (i.e. the taxpayers) will rush in should the volume of failures threaten to swamp the current insurance system.

One solution mandated by the U.S. Congress for the FDIC was to tie the size of government insurance premiums charged an insured bank or thrift institution directly to the amount of risk taken on. Thus, risk exposure to the insurance fund becomes the determinant of the cost of insurance paid by private financial institutions. Unfortunately, we aren't sure how to accurately measure the failure risk of an individual financial institution.

Ideally, we would like to have a *risk index* that correctly *ranks* financial institutions from most risky to least risky. This way we could be sure the most risky financial-service firms are paying the highest insurance premiums. Our preferred risk index ought to tell us that if one financial firm is twice as risky as another, the former will pay insurance premiums twice as high as the latter. Moreover, the difference in risk premiums must be significant enough to modify the behavior of riskier institutions, providing a strong incentive for them to manage the public's money more prudently.

Unfortunately, no such ideal risk measure has yet been identified. Moreover, history indicates that private entrepreneurs usually possess great skill in finding loopholes in nearly all the regulatory rules that have been devised.

**Regulation of Capital to Limit Risk**    Another step governments have taken to promote greater public confidence in the financial system is to impose at least *minimum capital requirements* on financial-service firms. The stockholders' equity (net worth) in each financial institution provides a cushion to absorb losses until management can correct weaknesses. When a financial institution has insufficient capital to cover its current and anticipated risk exposure, it faces a *capital adequacy problem*. By imposing minimum capital requirements on financial institutions, regulators can force a financial firm's *stockholders* to accept a substantial share of the risks taken on by their firm. The bigger the stockholders' share of each financial institution's total capital, presumably the more watchful the stockholders will be over the firm's risk exposure and the policies pursued by its management. In this instance, the burden of controlling risk would be vested in a financial institution's stockholders, who must supply more high-cost capital if the institution suffers so many losses that it has a real capital adequacy problem.

**Key URLs:**
For further discussion of trends in the financial system, see such sources as **apra. gov.au**; **gcn.com**; and **heovers.com**

Governments must be careful in imposing capital requirements on financial institutions, however. The international financial markets have become so competitive that if institutions in one nation face high minimum capital requirements while those in another face low or no capital requirements, the latter institutions will possess an unfair competitive advantage. Funds will tend to flow out of an area with burdensome regulations toward an area with less strict rules (often called *regulatory arbitrage*). This fact of international life led the 12 leading industrialized nations to adopt a revolutionary international agreement, known as the Basel Agreement on Bank Capital Standards (discussed fully in Chapter 17). This regulatory agreement pledged supervisory authorities in all participating countries to require their banks to hold at least a minimum amount of capital relative to the size of their risk-exposed assets, thereby providing greater protection for depositors around the world. Important breakthroughs like the Basel Agreement that bring nations together to cooperate in global financial-sector regulation—

**harmonization**

sometimes referred to as **harmonization** of regulatory rules—must continue in the future if public confidence in the global financial marketplace is to be maintained.

**Market Discipline: A Vehicle to Control Risk Taking**   Is government the only vehicle that can limit risk in the financial system? Could the private marketplace itself be a competent police officer to control risk taking and promote public confidence in the financial system?

In theory at least, the private marketplace *is* its own regulator. Financial institutions choosing to accept greater risk in managing their customers' and their owners' funds must pay the penalty for risk that the market imposes: a higher cost for any funds they raise from the public. Thus, the financial markets will squeeze the earnings of riskier financial institutions through the mechanism of a rising cost of capital. This phenomenon is called *market discipline.*

One of the most important ways the private market deals with greater risk of failure is by encouraging the development of *larger* financial institutions that diversify themselves geographically and by product line in order to spread risk over a greater number of markets and services. This development is most evident, as we will see in Part Four of this text, in the recent rise of interstate banking in the United States and the emergence of highly service-diversified financial holding companies. This trend toward market-expanding operations has encompassed not only financial firms that have traditionally served broad markets (such as insurance companies, money-center banks, and security brokerage firms) but also locally oriented financial institutions (such as credit unions and savings banks).

**Key URLs:**
For a discussion of risk management techniques in the modern world see especially **www. business.com/ directory/management** and **finpipe.com/ derivglossary.htm**

*Developing Better Management Tools to Deal with Risk*   Another way for financial institutions to deal with risk in the financial system is to develop and use **risk-management tools.** Managers of successful financial institutions today must be intimately familiar with such risk-management tools as:

**risk-management tools**

- *Interest rate SWAPs,* which permit institutions to trade interest payments with each other (as discussed in Chapter 9).

- *Currency swaps,* which permit borrowers to trade currencies with each other and limit exchange rate risk (as discussed in Chapter 23).

- *Financial futures and option contracts,* which allow the setting of prices today for future security purchases or sales (as discussed in Chapter 9).

- *Stress-testing of balance sheets,* through which financial firms employ computer simulations to better understand the risks inherent in their investment portfolio under various market conditions (as discussed in Chapter 17).

Although these risk-management tools are useful, *new* tools must continually be added to the financial manager's arsenal in order to identify and hedge effectively the risks that will challenge tomorrow's financial-service institutions. Mere knowledge of existing risk-management tools does not guarantee that all risk exposures will be adequately dealt with, however. Continuing innovation in the risk-management field is absolutely essential to the future smooth operation of the financial system and the continuing maintenance of public confidence in that system.

*The Information Problem*    Unfortunately, relying *exclusively* on the private marketplace to ensure the strength of financial institutions is open to serious question. Given adequate information, an efficient market can correctly value individual financial institutions and provide effective ways to deal with risk. But does the financial marketplace receive *all* of the information it needs to make optimal decisions? The answer is probably *no*. Depository institutions, for example, still provide only limited information to buyers of the claims they issue against their earnings and assets. Key information regarding the quality of their assets (particularly their individual loans) is often known in detail only to government regulatory agencies.

Capital market investors can only *approximately* price the securities of financial institutions that do not fully disclose their financial condition and prospects. Serious consideration needs to be given to greater financial disclosure of the risk exposure of individual financial institutions, especially for the protection of the public's savings. In 1991, the U.S. Congress passed the FDIC Improvement Act, requiring regular full-scope, on-site examinations of each U.S.-insured depository institution. Moreover, federally insured depository institutions must supply regulatory agencies with annual reports, including an annual audit by an independent public accountant. The FDIC Improvement Act called for more public disclosure of auditor information and of the market values of institutional assets and capital.

---

### QUESTIONS TO HELP YOU STUDY

7. How can we *reduce risk* in the financial sector?

8. What are the principal *types of risk* encountered by financial institutions?

9. In what ways can we promote and protect *public confidence* in the financial-service sector of the economy ? Why is this important to the public and to financial institutions?

10. Can *government-sponsored insurance* help to preserve and protect public confidence in our financial institutions? What are its advantages and disadvantages?

11. How can the private marketplace work to control a financial institution's assumption of risk and promote greater public confidence in the financial system as a whole?

12. How might common capital rules among all financial institutions, improved risk-management tools, and greater disclosure to the public help promote public confidence in financial institutions?

Similar legislation may be needed to promote disclosure among other types of financial institutions as well. In combination with a strong, risk-adjusted insurance program, increased public information about the true condition of financial-service firms could unleash the powerful economic force of *informed investing* to control risk taking by financial institutions more effectively and promote public confidence in the financial system.

## The Effect of New Technology on the Design and Delivery of Financial Services

*The Information Revolution*   Providing financial services to the public involves the analysis, storage, and transfer of *financial information*. A checking account or debit card, for example, conveys information that an individual or business firm has claim to assets managed by a financial institution offering payment services. The writing of a check or the swiping of a debit card through an electronic reader at a store counter is a new information item, designating what amount of funds are to be removed from one account and transferred to another. The advent of computers and the Internet has taught us that information can be transferred in microseconds via computer through Web sites, and via wire, satellite, and other electronic networks that offer greater speed, lower cost, and greater accuracy. The technological revolution in information analysis, storage, and transfer is moving at an accelerating pace. Newer, smaller, and faster electronic-based communications systems appear every year, impacting the money and capital markets and the financial-services industry.

*Recent Technological Advances*   One area of continuing growth will be in *networking,* or *systems integration,* in which computers and other electronic devices are linked via a global communications network. The *Internet* offers financial-service firms a low-cost channel through which to advertise their services and offer expanding service packages. Leading financial firms today typically have extensive sites on the Internet that describe the services they offer and their facilities. Web customers can file requests for transfers of funds, pay bills electronically, file credit applications, receive price or rate quotes, check on available balances, and, in many cases, carry out online purchases of goods and services. Once fully adequate safety measures are in place to protect the customer's privacy, access to an even wider array of goods and services will be available through the nearest networked computer, via digitized communication through the Internet, and through smart phones that send text messages, load video information and entertainment, and view and edit documents.

Also exerting a growing influence on financial-market transactions are *cellular* or *pocket telephones* that allow financial-service customers to communicate with individuals and institutions from almost any location on the globe, 24 hours a day. Cell phones are increasingly being employed to transfer funds between established financial accounts, make online bill payments (such as through eBay's Pay Pal), carry out purchases from retail stores by waving these phones in front of a merchant's card reader, accessing financial and medical records, storing and accessing credit card account numbers on demand, carrying television and audio broadcasts, and communicating with mobile and other Web sites.

Accompanying the development of full-service pocket telephones is the *pocket* or *handheld computer.* As faster and lighter computer chips continue to emerge, pocket-size and palm-size PCs are able to more rapidly merge information storage, information retrieval, telecommunications, and extensive computing power into one lightweight,

**Key URL:**
For a good example of an extensive Web site maintained by a financial-service institution, see
**wellsfargo.com**

**Key URLs:**
To learn more about mobile-enabled versions of Web sites that can be reached from a PDA or telephone, see, for example,
**www.google.com/xhtml; www.wap.oa.yahoo.com; www.imenu.com/wireless;** and
**www.mobileanswers.com.**
Currently China leads the world in mobile-phone communications (including third-generation (3G) wireless networks that promote the use of wireless video, net surfing, and instant messaging). Phone access to the internet may soon outstrip computer access to the net, especially in China, while sending and receiving money via mobile phones is becoming increasingly common through so-called mobile-wallet services.

eminently portable, information-gathering resource, available at lower cost. Pocket and handheld computers will allow an increasing number of managers of financial-service firms, and more of their customers as well, to instantly record transactions, notes, and memos; fax documents; and send and retrieve financial data. Financial decision makers increasingly are being equipped with powerful new tools, permitting 24-hour global market monitoring and decision making and the rapid implementation of financial decisions from any location.

New financial technologies are making it possible for customers to literally do away with their checkbooks and other paper media. Growing numbers of depository institutions are offering telephone-bill-paying services as well as home and office personal computer (PC) links to a financial institution's computer through which the customer can authorize payments from his or her account with the touch of a button. Equally significant is the spread of "smart cards" encoded with "digitized cash" that allow the customer to pay for goods and services at the point of sale by merely presenting a plastic card. When inserted into a suitable terminal, the amount of a purchase is automatically subtracted from the remaining balance of "digitized cash." Smart cards have grown rapidly in Europe, but more slowly in the United States, though these cards seem to have a bright future.

These and other technological advances in information technology literally make every financial-service customer a mobile "branch office." There will be less and less need to visit the brick-and-mortar office facilities of a financial institution. Fewer employees are also likely to be needed in the financial institutions sector. The financial-service business is in transition from a labor-intensive industry to a capital-intensive one that increasingly relies upon automation and electronic processing.

*Public Attitudes and Cost* The adjustment of people and institutions to the unfolding technological revolution probably will be slower than the revolution itself. For example, many consumers and businesses still prefer the security and privacy of cash and checkbook transactions to pay for their purchases of goods and services, even though checkbook volume in the United States has been falling since the mid-1990s in the face of increasingly widespread use of electronic payments devices. Personal communication between financial institutions and their customers will always be important in the delivery of some financial services, especially to older customers and smaller businesses. However, the cost of these traditional communication methods is rising, and their economic advantage over electronic methods continues to decline.

*All* financial institutions must be prepared for the continuing spread of new information technology. Otherwise, their competitors will wrest the "high ground" of new markets and new services away from them. But there are major challenges in this technological high ground for all financial institutions, including the following:

- Customer access to financial information and the transfer of financial information must be as user friendly as possible.

- Operating costs and service prices must be kept low relative to more conventional paper-based or in-person information systems so that there is sufficient economic incentive for the customer to use the most modern, cost-efficient service-delivery systems available.

- Adequate technological flexibility must be built in so that, as improved technologies for service production and delivery appear, they can be quickly pressed into service in order to keep each financial-service institution current and competitive.

- Auditing and internal control programs must be strengthened to reduce the probability of loss due to computer error or computer fraud, which can drive away customers and endanger the viability of any financial institution.
- Finally, managers must recognize and adapt to the great power the Internet gives consumers today to evaluate the quality and convenience of the financial products they offer and share those service evaluations with millions of other consumers through blogs, podcasts, mashups, and a myriad of other developing information channels.

## The Changing Mix of Financial-Service Suppliers in the Financial System

*Who* will offer the financial services of the future? When the customer wishes to purchase a life insurance policy, a retirement plan, or a checking account, who will be the most likely provider? One thing that is clear now is that the traditional walls between different financial-service industries have eroded so far that they are almost nonexistent today. For example, the cash management accounts and savings plans that an insurance company sells to its customers are fully competitive with the cash-management and savings instruments offered by banks and securities firms. Going forward, most of the remaining vestiges of the traditional distinctions between one type of financial-service institution and another are likely to be swept away, as the service menus of different financial institutions look increasingly alike and different financial-service industries rush toward each other.

### Price Sensitivity and Local Competition
Financial services will be purchased from the financial firm offering the lowest price and best nonprice features (such as service quality). That low-cost supplier may differ from one market to another, depending on the level and intensity of competition in each marketplace. In smaller cities and rural communities, the local bank may turn out to be the most advantageous supplier of most financial services. Larger urban markets, in contrast, will continue to be characterized by multiple financial-service suppliers, usually locked in an intense competitive struggle. Moreover, financial-service firms will face a customer increasingly sensitized to differing terms of sale and more ready to transfer his or her business to the cheapest source for the quantity and quality of service desired.

### Importance of Established Delivery Systems
Because cost control and productivity will be key factors for the future success of financial-service firms, financial institutions with extensive service delivery systems already in place will have a competitive advantage. This feature will clearly favor financial-service institutions possessing established computer, telephone, and full-service office networks. These cost and productivity advantages are likely to lead to still more mergers and consolidations among smaller financial-service companies so that service providers converge and consolidate into larger and larger producing units.

### New Financial Institutions and Instruments
The future will usher in *new* financial institutions to deal with newly emerging financial-service needs. For example, additional secondary (resale) markets for many loans will emerge so that lenders of funds can even more readily than today sell their older assets and gain the cash needed to make new loans and investments. Just as high-grade common stocks, bonds, and futures and options contracts are traded on national exchanges or in the open market today, freer and more open trading of many other financial instruments will eventually become a reality. The unfolding new markets will require new types of

financial institutions and new financial services. A few of the newer financial instruments and services that appear to have good prospects for continuing rapid development in the future include:

1. Loans to remodel residential dwellings (due to the aging of existing homes and greater availability of home equity credit).
2. Small business loans (as numerous new firms emerge to replace failing ones).
3. Credit risk derivatives (including credit swaps), which permit a lending institution to seek protection against loan defaults and depreciation in asset values (as discussed in depth in Chapter 8).

*Securitization*    There will be a need for new institutions to facilitate the continuing trend toward *securitization* of many of the credit-related assets held by lending institutions and other corporations. The success of mortgage-backed securities over the past three decades demonstrates that a financial institution can more easily take some of the loans it has made and use them as collateral for borrowing money through the sale of securities. Today, there are loan-backed securities collateralized by such diverse assets as commercial and residential mortgage loans, mobile home loans, credit-card receivables, auto and boat loans, home equity loans, and computer equipment leases, to name just a few (see, for example, Chapters 8, 11, 22, and 24). Securitization is likely to support the ongoing shift of nonfinancial companies away from traditional types of credit obtained through a financial intermediary, such as a bank, and toward self-financing and self-borrowing directly from investors in the open market.

## Consolidations and Convergences within the Financial System

As we noted at this chapter's beginning, acquisitions and mergers have recently come to dominate the financial-service business, as the largest financial firms have moved to expand in size in the fastest way possible, usually through megamergers involving multibillion-dollar institutions. These megamergers are generally of two types: (1) *consolidations,* which bring together financial firms serving the same industry, and (2) *convergences,* wherein firms from different industries combine their operations. Familiar examples include the *consolidation* of JPMorgan Chase with Bank One in 2004, creating the second trillion-dollar banking organization in the United States (following Citigroup) and the more recently proposed mergers of ABN Amro Bank of the Netherlands with either Barclays of Great Britain or a group of banks led by the Royal Bank of Scotland. A good example of *convergence* was the 2002 acquisition of Household Finance—a consumer finance company—with HSBC Bank Plc—a British bank.

Many strong economic and technological forces are propelling these consolidating and converging changes, including a better-informed, more-demanding customer, the globalization of financial transactions made possible by the rapidly changing technology of information and communication over great distances, and the development of many new financial instruments and services that only the largest financial-service providers can produce and deliver efficiently at low cost. Some of the key players in this race for market size and dominance argue that these consolidation and convergence trends will bring about at least some of the following changes:

• Substantial cost savings (through the elimination of duplicate offices and other overlapping resources).

- Acceleration of revenue growth (as new services are developed in both new and old markets in order to reach out to broader customer segments).

- Greater diversification and, therefore, reduction of risk by widening the service lines offered to the public and spreading out geographically into many different local markets.

- Increased professional expertise, developed by combining the best talents of two or more companies, so that customers get higher-quality services.

- Increased affordability of the latest information storage and transfer technology so that a wide variety of financial-service firms can remain up-to-date in developing new services and in reaching their customers, no matter how distant those customers may be.

- Greater efficiency in producing and selling a mix of services that can be jointly marketed and cross-sold so that the same customers are encouraged to buy more than one service from the same financial firm (i.e., one-stop shopping), helping to tie a larger proportion of customers more closely to the particular financial-service companies with which they trade.

However, other experts in the field warn that today's trend toward consolidation and convergence is a "mixed blessing." There are key *disadvantages* that may prove to be as powerful as the alleged advantages of these major structural trends among financial-service institutions, including:

- Higher operating costs may result due to the greater complexities of managing and controlling a highly diversified, giant company that may have grown too fast.

- Many financial-service managers may have overestimated the public's real demand for "one-stop" financial shopping, because many consumers seem less interested in the convenience of receiving all their financial services from one supplier and more interested in shopping around for the best terms available for each major service they buy. This process has been enhanced by the growing volume of financial services being offered on the Internet.

- The possibility of damaging competition for the largest financial firms from smaller financial-service companies, which can provide more personalized financial services (including making the most sensitive customers seem like valued clients, not simply a number in a computer file).

- The ability of smaller financial companies to compete effectively in the range of services they are able to offer, even against financial-service giants, by using *outsourcing*—that is, selling services provided to the offering firm by other suppliers (similar to the franchising concept in retailing).

The foregoing potential disadvantages of consolidation and convergence suggest that not every financial firm needs to be huge, national, or international in scope. Smaller, specialized financial-service companies may still be able to hold onto a solid niche in tomorrow's financial marketplace. This will be especially true if smaller, more specialized firms can keep their operating costs under control and not be undersold by stronger financial-service giants. Indeed, there is little evidence that economies of scale in financial services favor only the largest firms. Some of the best-run financial-service companies lie somewhere in the middle ground, being neither the largest nor the smallest suppliers of financial services.

QUESTIONS TO HELP YOU STUDY

13. What *technological changes* are likely to have the greatest impact on the production and delivery of financial services to the public in future years?

14. Why do you think *consolidation* and *convergence* are taking place today in the financial-services sector? What are the consequences for the managers of financial institutions and for the public?

## 4.5  A New Role for Regulation in an Age of Financial-Services Consolidation and Convergence

The growing consolidation and convergence of financial-service companies pose major new challenges for government regulators charged with maintaining a safer and more stable financial system. Regulators cannot stop the powerful market forces that are bringing about the rise of massive financial-service conglomerates, such as Citigroup and Deutsche Bank, because the financial-services industry is now worldwide and much of its growth technologically driven, which recognizes no artificially erected boundaries. However, government regulators must find a way to make safety and soundness principles work and preserve at least something of the "safety net" that protects less financially sophisticated consumers from mistreatment and the loss of their savings.

This dual concern—letting markets and competition work to benefit consumers, while preserving safety and soundness to protect the most vulnerable customers—has led to the development of several different regulatory approaches, any one of which may come to dominate the future of government regulation of the financial-service business. For example, the recent Financial-Services Modernization (Gramm-Leach-Bliley) Act, passed in the United States in November 1999, allows banks, insurance companies, and securities firms to enter each other's backyard through a well-known type of financial structure, the *holding company,* where different affiliated firms offer different groups of services, but all are owned by one controlling company at the top of the organization. (See Exhibit 4.1A.) Yet another possibility permitted under the new Gramm-Leach-Bliley Act is to allow one financial-service provider, such as a bank, insurance company, or security dealer, to sell other services through its own *subsidiary firms.* (See Exhibit 4.1B.)

Under the *financial holding company organizational form,* each financial firm has its own capital and management and its own net earnings or earnings losses, which are independent of the earnings or losses of other affiliated companies belonging to the same holding company. With the *subsidiary organizational form,* on the other hand, the earnings or losses of each subsidiary company also affect the parent firm. Nevertheless, regulators can develop walls of protection to shelter financial firms they wish to protect, such as by insisting upon stronger capitalization for one or more of the businesses belonging to the same parent company (especially any banks that serve small savers) or by legally limiting transactions between more-regulated and less-regulated affiliates of the same holding company.

There is also a movement toward establishing new *regulatory* structures—a different approach to government supervision of the financial sector that matches the changing features of the financial-services industry. One such model—known as the *single regulator approach*—calls upon one regulatory agency to oversee an entire

**EXHIBIT 4.1**

**A. Financial Holding Company—Growing Organizational Form in the Financial-Services Industry**

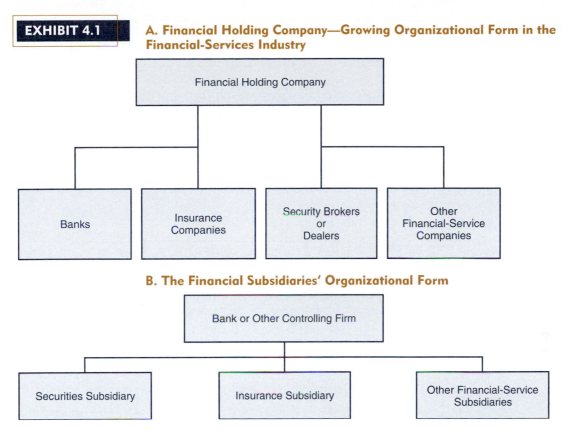

**B. The Financial Subsidiaries' Organizational Form**

financial-service company with all of its component parts. The challenge here is that such a regulator has to know many different businesses well in order to do a good job of supervising the safety of complex financial institutions. Nevertheless, the "single regulator" strategy may work well in certain situations—for example, in the oversight of small banks, credit unions, and insurance companies. (See Exhibit 4.2A.)

A different approach calls for *functional regulation*—letting specialized regulators oversee those financial firms about which they know the most and then pooling their regulatory reports to get an overall picture of the condition of a large, complex financial company. For example, state insurance commissions could regulate and supervise a financial holding company's insurance affiliates or subsidiaries, while the Securities and Exchange Commission could oversee the activities of the securities dealers and brokers belonging to that same company, and the Comptroller of the Currency could track the soundness of any bank that belongs to the large, complex financial firm we are describing. Finally, a single regulatory agency may act as overall or "umbrella" supervisor, receiving regulatory reports from the other regulatory agencies involved and making a general assessment of the strength or weakness of the entire financial-services company. (See Exhibit 4.2B.)

Unfortunately, each of these regulatory models is cumbersome, may be costly to manage, and could lead to regulatory conflicts. In the case of the single regulator model, the same government agency must learn how to examine and supervise many different types of financial firms—a potentially costly endeavor—and could easily miss major problems. On the other hand, functional regulation may not allow any one supervisor to get an accurate picture of the true condition of the *whole* financial-services organization. This is one of the reasons the U.S. Congress, when it passed

**EXHIBIT 4.2**

**A. The Single Regulator Model for the Oversight of Financial-Service Firms**

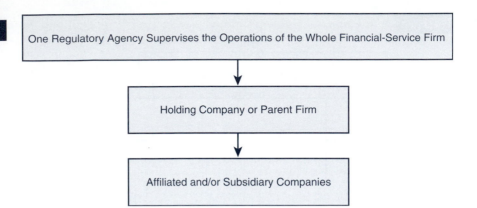

**B. The Functional Regulator Model for the Oversight of Financial-Service Firms**

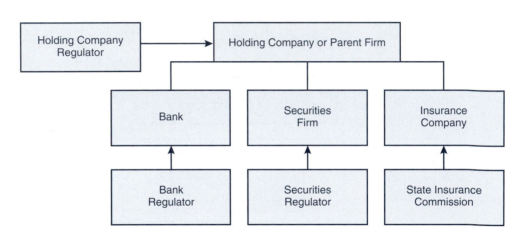

the Financial Services Modernization (Gramm-Leach-Bliley) Act in 1999, adopted a portion of *both* the single regulator model (with the Federal Reserve System normally serving as overall or "umbrella" regulatory supervisor for each financial-services company as a whole) and a form of functional regulation (with two or more different regulators looking at different units within the same financial-services company).

There is also the danger that some financial firms, if allowed to acquire many different types of companies without safeguards on the quality of management they are hiring, will simply become "too big to fail," requiring regulators to spread out (and possibly thin down) the government's safety net, which was originally set up to protect small savers. If the biggest financial-service providers are not allowed by government to fail, not only does this give financial companies an incentive to expand their size as fast as possible, it also does not fully allow the discipline of the marketplace to work in order to control the assumption of risk by financial institutions. We may easily lose sight of the fact that the most vulnerable financial institutions are probably those that manage the public's savings deposits and carry out payments for businesses, households, and governments—two financial-service areas that we can ill afford to have break down due to reckless management behavior because these services impact the whole economy and, if poorly done, threaten the public's confidence in the financial system.

We need more disclosure of information to the public on the true condition of financial institutions, and we also need more international regulatory cooperation (*harmonization*) to prevent global panics by investors and the public at large. We need to use recent technological advances to improve monitoring systems so that regulators can spot troubled financial firms earlier and have a chance to head off problems quickly. We need to have owners of financial institutions bear more of their institutions' risk and encourage large account holders to play a bigger role in the market disciplining of poorly managed financial firms, stimulating management and owners of financial-services companies to pay increasing attention to measuring and managing risk in order to protect the public from needless financial losses.

## 4.6 The Payments System: Current and Future

Tomorrow's marketplace will depend crucially upon the continuing ability of the world's *payments system* to function efficiently and accurately. Unless businesses that sell goods and services can be confident they will be paid promptly for what they sell, the economy will begin to slow, production will fall, and unemployment will rise. A good example of partial payment system breakdown occurred in 2001 when the terrorist attacks of 9/11 caused several of the largest financial-service firms to shut down temporarily. Ultimately, unless restored, the economy may collapse, because a well-functioning payments system is the lifeblood of a modern economy. A major breakdown in the flow of payments can result in disaster for millions of people who will lose income and their standard of living.

There are, in reality, *two* payments systems at work in the economy today—one for *retail* (or small) payments flowing largely between individuals, and business firms; and one for *wholesale* (or large) transactions that flow mainly between banks, business firms, and agencies of government and typically pass through automated clearinghouses (ACHs), the Federal Reserve's wire network (Fedwire), and regional clearing institutions (such as the New York Clearinghouse, known as CHIPS) that connect thousands of payors and payees every day. Technological change has affected *both* of these payments systems, as a rapidly growing volume of payments are being made today electronically through computers, via telephone, with plastic debit and credit cards inserted in point-of-sale terminals in stores, with radio-frequency cards waved in front of payments terminals, through electronic wire networks between depository institutions, and through the Internet.

The retail payments system in the United States continues to lag behind wholesale payments in converting from paper transactions to electronic systems. However, Smart cards (plastic wafers with an encoded computer chip aboard that lists how much is available to spend and identifies the account owner) are gaining ground (especially in Europe), as are online accounts inside the Internet and telephone payments via verbal authorization or through the use of a credit card number. What the public must have for the future, if our financial system is to avoid the burgeoning cost of paper transactions, is a retail payments network that is fast, cheap, and convenient. Countries such as Denmark and Norway have raised their use of electronic payments media to account for a majority of their daily payments, while China leads the world in payments by mobile phone. Meanwhile, the United States still remains a heavy user of paper, due, in part, to the fact the U.S. banking system, through most of its history, has been dominated numerically by small depository institutions, making it difficult to bring together all banks within a single electronic system.

To be fair, however, we must note that electronic payments in the United States have grown about fivefold in the past two decades and payments by wire now exceed the number of checks written each year. Moreover, the U.S. Congress passed new legislation in 2003, known as the Check 21 Act, which no longer requires a check to be

**Key URL:**
You can explore further the trends unfolding in the payments system through such sites as ftc.gov/bcp/workshops/techade/trends.htm/

**Key URLs:**
One of the most controversial payments devices developed recently has been radio-frequency identification cards (RFIDs) which users can simply pass in front of a scanner to pay for goods and services, but whose signal may be intercepted by thieves. See, for example, ManagingAutomation.com and rfidjournal.com/

physically transported in order to be processed. Financial institutions can now make an image of a check, use that image to create a *substitute check*, and electronically transfer the substitute. Thus, electronic checks can now be processed faster and more cheaply than with the old paper-driven system in which the original check had to travel from the bank of deposit to the bank upon which it was drawn. Check 21 should reduce the blizzard of paper that used to be needed to move money.

However, big problems still lie ahead for the payments system, especially in the processing of wholesale payments where transactions exceed a trillion dollars a day. It is the *size* of individual wholesale transactions—many of these denominated in multimillions of dollars apiece—that poses a substantial threat for the future. If a few of these supersize transactions fail to *settle* (clear) because of credit risk (i.e., the failure of one party to fully comply), liquidity risk (i.e., a temporary cash shortage on the part of one or more large transactors), or unwinding risk (where payment instructions are subsequently reversed and, therefore, someone is left unpaid), the result could be a panicky chain reaction of failed payments spreading around the globe. Eventually, the *whole* payments system could break down as institutions expecting payments do not receive them and, therefore, cannot meet all of their own promises to pay. To help head off such a calamity in the United States, the Federal Reserve has set limits upon how much in total a payments-system participant can owe to everyone else who belongs to the same clearing system.

---

### QUESTIONS TO HELP YOU STUDY

15. What exactly is meant by *functional regulation?* What are its advantages and disadvantages for financial institutions and their customers?

16. In what ways is regulation of the financial-service sector changing?

17. What is happening to the global *payments system* today? What changes in the payments system seem likely for the future?

18. Why was passage of the Gramm-Leach-Bliley (Financial Services Modernization) Act so important for American financial-service institutions?

---

## 4.7  The Current and Future Need for Regulation of Financial Institutions

The recent trend toward *deregulation*—the gradual removal of government restrictions on the freedom of the financial markets to trade and allocate resources—of the worldwide financial sector is likely to continue. Governments will be under continuing pressure to relax regulations against the development of new services and the geographic expansion of various financial institutions. If governments do not act to free more completely the financial institutions they supervise from today's regulatory rules, nonregulated financial institutions will move in and eventually drive out the more heavily regulated institutions from one market after another.

The most likely future developments in government deregulation of the financial system will be the following:

- Reduced barriers to geographic expansion in order to allow financial institutions to find new customers anywhere.

- Reduced restrictions on the portfolio choices made by financial institutions except as may be required to preserve public confidence in the financial system, allowing the private marketplace to play a larger role in shaping a financial-service firm's portfolio choices.

- Reorganization of regulatory agencies to avoid duplication and to minimize the burden of regulation upon financial institutions.

- Reduced barriers to the development and offering of new services to the public.

Within the United States, one of the most contentious regulatory debates focuses on the issue of *what new services* banks and other depository institutions should be allowed to offer, consistent with the public's interest in a sound banking and financial system. For example, in the fall of 1999 the U.S. Congress lifted restrictions in place since the 1930s and allowed financial holding companies the power to combine menus of banking, insurance, and security underwriting services under the same financial-services organization. It allowed regulators to expand the permissible list of financial services for banks and financial holding companies as market conditions change in the future. Thus, the United States recognized that financial-service institutions are not frozen in time and must adjust their service menus and service delivery methods to changing circumstances in the markets they serve.

Overall, the pace of government deregulation of our financial system appears to be accelerating. For example, at the recent Uruguay Round of the General Agreement on Tariffs and Trade (GATT), with 105 nations participating, both Australia and the United States proposed a global free-trade agreement in financial services. In 1993 Mexico, Canada, and the United States crafted a free-trade agreement (NAFTA) parallel to the one signed by the United States and Canada in 1987. The move toward freer trade in financial services has been accompanied by banking and securities deregulation in Britain; liberalization of bank service offerings in Germany; and the licensing of European financial firms to offer their services throughout Western Europe as part of the continuing expansion of the European Union.

## *Financial-Service Regulations That Could Grow*

**Key URLs:**
Information on financial disclosure protection for the modern consumer may be found at such Web sites as **consumerlaw.org** and **fdic.gov/consumers**

Not all government regulations in the financial-service field will be eliminated. Indeed, the regulation of financial institutions is shifting to a different ground. There will continue to be great concern over the safety of the public's savings and over maintaining public confidence in financial institutions and the financial system in which they operate. But there is also likely to be continuing and possibly increasing regulatory attention to the issues of financial disclosure, customer privacy, social responsibility, and a level playing field for financial-service competitors.

**financial disclosure**

*Financial Disclosure*    One important area of regulatory emphasis for the future will be **financial disclosure.** Financial institutions will be expected to divulge more completely their terms of service and their financial condition to investors and to the customers they serve in order to promote better financial decision making. Good examples of this trend in the United States in the recent past are the Competitive Banking Equality Act (1987), the Truth in Savings Act (1991), and the FDIC Improvement Act (1991). These laws require increased public disclosure of deposit terms and withdrawal penalties, as well as guaranteeing customers more rapid credit for their deposits and greater disclosure concerning the risks of losing one's home if it is used as collateral for a loan.

There is potential gain here as well as risk. With greater disclosure, more financial institutions will be subject to the risk of public disfavor. Ultimately the "discipline of the market" will be more completely unleashed to help ensure prudent management and to control risk taking. Increased disclosure will enable both investors in and customers of financial institutions to make more intelligent decisions and make the most economical use of available resources.

*Privacy Protection and Identity Theft*    The new century has ushered in a hotly debated issue centered around the disclosure of individuals' personal information (such as their social security number, driver's license number, deposit account numbers, etc.). Scores of proposed new laws have been introduced at federal and state levels to protect so-called "nonpublic information" about individuals and families.

**Key URL:**
For further discussion of consumer privacy issues, see especially
**ftc.gov**

The principal cause of this explosion in privacy legislation is *identity theft*. Each year, thousands of consumers have become victims of fraud and theft as their personal information is stolen and used to access their bank accounts and other assets. Frequently before the thieves can be stopped, victimized consumers have lost their access to credit, found that their credit reputations have been severely damaged, or discovered that their savings have disappeared.

Worse still, identity theft appears to have been used by terrorist groups to steal money and credit in an effort to fund terrorism around the globe.

Under the terms of the Gramm-Leach-Bliley (Financial Services Modernization) Act covered financial-service entities were ordered to develop procedures to protect the privacy of their customers' nonpublic information. Moreover, customers were granted the authority to stop a financial institution from sharing their private information with nonaffiliated firms if those customers did so in writing or by some other acceptable method. However, the new law permitted companies that are part of the same overall organization to share private customer information with each other unless they voluntarily agreed not to do so. Subsequently more than 20 states passed legislation requiring businesses with sensitive customer data to notify customers if their employees have lost their customers' private information.

**Key URLs:**
To learn about the ways private financial firms deal with identity theft and protect their customers see, for example, Citi Identity Theft solutions at
**citibank.com/us/cards/ cardserv/advice/victim. htm**; the Identity Theft assistance Center at
**identitytheftassistance. org**; and Identity theft 911 LLC at
**identitytheft911.org**

The future is likely to bring even more debate as well as real changes in laws and regulations to enhance *customer privacy protection*. For example, beginning in 2007 the Federal Financial Institutions Examination Council ordered U.S. depository institutions to tighten entry requirements for getting into customers' online accounts by asking for more than just a name and password. Several leading banking companies have begun to require customers to answer one or more personal questions (such as friends' or pets' names) that, presumably, only the true account owner would know while others are experimenting with tokens or biometric devices (such as finger- or voiceprints) that are difficult to copy. In addition, several proposed new privacy laws call for requiring financial firms to protect consumer information and not share it unless the customer grants explicit permission to do so. This would be a far more strict standard than the current rule which allows information sharing unless customers notify their financial-service institution that they wish to put a stop to this practice. While consumer groups tend to support strict privacy legislation, many financial-service firms oppose these proposals because of the added cost and risk involved. Indeed, the debate over protecting the privacy of financial-service consumers is likely to persist far into the future as consumer interests are balanced against the demands for efficiency, innovation, and cost control within the financial-service marketplace.

*Social Responsibility*　Another area of regulatory emphasis likely to grow in the future is the *social responsibility* of financial institutions. The financial-service industry will find itself under increasing regulatory scrutiny concerning the fairness of its use of resources and the distribution of its services, particularly access to credit. For example, are all loan customers subjected to the same credit standards? Is there any evidence that the age, race, religion, the neighborhood where someone lives or does business, or other irrelevant characteristics of a credit customer have entered into the decisions of what loans a financial institution has chosen to make or not make, resulting in illegal discrimination? Are some communities and neighborhoods losing convenient access to financial services as neighborhood financial-service facilities are closed, forcing some households and businesses to travel great distances in order to obtain the services they require? Are these closings due solely to economic factors or do they reflect hidden discrimination? How can the regulatory agencies who supervise these changes balance economic forces with social issues? Pressure will grow on *all* financial firms to make an "affirmative effort" to serve *all* of their customers, consistent with sound financial practice but with due regard for economic necessity and the fact that most financial-service firms are privately owned and must earn competitive returns for their owners in order to survive.

*Promoting a Level Playing Field*　Finally, the *fair and equal regulatory treatment* of all financial institutions offering essentially the same services will continue to be a burning issue in future years. Bankers, who have labeled this the *level playing field* issue, will continue to be among its strongest advocates, pressing for more equal taxation of the earnings of different financial institutions and more equal powers to offer a full range of services in order to be competitive with other financial-service firms. As long as some financial firms are taxed and regulated differently than other financial firms, the so-called level playing field issue will never go away. It will continue to be a bone of contention that divides the financial sector into the "more regulated" and the "less regulated" firms. Inevitably, financial-service businesses that are "more regulated" and see these added rules as a real burden will strive to bend or change the rules in order to close the gap between them and their less-regulated competitors.

## QUESTIONS TO HELP YOU STUDY

19. What regulations in the financial sector are likely to grow in the future?
20. What is the *financial disclosure* issue and what is its significance?
21. What is *privacy protection* and why is it important to customers of financial institutions? To financial-service institutions themselves?
22. What does a *level playing field* mean to financial institutions and the public?

## Summary of the Chapter's Main Points

The focus of this chapter is the future of the money and capital markets and the financial system that surrounds them. We have highlighted several powerful trends that are reshaping the financial marketplace today, including the following.

- Among the most important broad trends affecting the financial system today are *financial innovation* (i.e., the development of many new services and new service delivery mechanisms), *service proliferation* (as the service menu offered by most financial firms grows), *homogenization* (as the service menus of different financial institutions increasingly look alike), *deregulation* (as governments pull back and let the private marketplace play a bigger role in controlling the financial system), *market broadening* (as recent advances in communications technology allow financial firms to serve wider market areas, bringing more financial firms into direct competition with each other), *globalization (*as financial-service firms reach across national and continental boundaries), *consolidation* (as surviving financial firms grow larger in size but fewer in number through acquisitions and mergers), *convergence* (as financial-service providers from different industries make acquisitions and combine operations across traditional industry boundaries), and *competition* (as broader markets, better technology, and longer service menus bring more financial firms into intense rivalry with each other as they compete for the customers' business).

- This chapter also portrays the broad *economic* and *demographic* trends that are restructuring financial institutions today. The chapter highlights major shifts in the character of the population—the consumers of today's and tomorrow's financial services. That population is not only growing older with a need for a somewhat different menu of services, but is also more focused on risk exposure and the need for long-term, relatively stable sources of income. Financial institutions must learn how to better serve this older, most rapidly growing segment of the world's population.

- This chapter examines the broad *technological* and *economic* changes that are likely to make the financial markets look very different in the era ahead. Service-oriented industries are expanding, while manufacturing units are becoming less important, particularly in the United States and Europe. Automation, telecommunications, and remarkable advances in biotechnology have opened up new areas for capital investment and accelerated economic growth, provided the financial system can generate more savings to fund these activities.

- Each of the foregoing trends must be dealt with by the management and owners of financial institutions. These trends call for new managerial and technical skills, including greater knowledge of marketing and planning techniques, greater sensitivity to customers' financial-service needs, greater knowledge of how to integrate new technology into the financial-service business, and the capacity to deal with the ongoing information revolution.

- *Government regulation* of the financial sector is changing in content and focus, with the *private marketplace* playing a larger role, disciplining financial firms to control risk and become more efficient. While many regulations may be reduced, eliminated, or simplified in the future, other rules governing the behavior of financial institutions may become more important. Some of the government regulations likely to become more significant in future years include *financial disclosure* rules, *privacy protection* for customers, rules to promote greater *social responsibility,* and regulatory changes designed to bring about a *level playing field* so that the rules of the game are essentially the same for *all* competing financial institutions.

• No one knows for sure what the financial system of the future will look like. However, it seems safe for us to predict fewer, but larger financial-service institutions and more highly diversified financial firms operating within an increasingly competitive financial marketplace.

• Financial institutions of the future will pay more attention to *risk management* and to training their employees to be more effective salespeople. Managers and their staffs inside financial firms will have to work harder to control expenses, improve productivity, and manage risk more effectively.

## Key Terms Appearing in This Chapter

**financial innovation,** 89

**service proliferation,** 89

**competition,** 89

**consolidation,** 89

**deregulation,** 89

**privatization,** 90

**convergence,** 90

**homogenization,** 90

**globalization,** 90

**market broadening,** 90

**harmonization,** 97

**risk-management tools,** 97

**financial disclosure,** 109

## Problems and Issues

1. Please describe how each of the following terms discussed in this chapter could affect the availability and cost of financial services to the public:

| | | |
|---|---|---|
| deregulation | financial innovation | financial disclosure |
| consolidation | convergence | privacy protection |
| risk-management tools | homogenization | market broadening |
| globalization | harmonization | technological change |

2. *Privacy protection* has become an important public policy issue in the financial-service industry. Why does this issue appear to be more important today than in the past? What are the costs and benefits of additional legislation and regulation designed to protect customer privacy? Is there evidence as to how these regulations benefit the public?

3. If you were managing a small bank or insurance agency in your local community, what current and future trends in financial services and institutions would likely have the greatest impact on your institution? Why? What responses could you make to each trend you have listed?

4. What is the significance of the *life-cycle hypothesis* for the management of financial institutions? Of an aging population? Of ongoing changes in the basic family unit and the spread of universal education?

5. Why are government regulations to enforce *financial disclosure* and a *level playing field* important to the success of the financial system?

6. What is *functional regulation* and why does it appear to be needed in the modern financial system?

7. What are the advantages and the disadvantages of having government-sponsored insurance in the financial system? Why is *moral hazard* often a problem with a government-sponsored system?

8. How might the regulation of *capital* serve to limit and control risk-taking by financial institutions?

## Web-Based Problems

1. One of the interesting consequences of the growing internationalization of markets is the migration of more and more workers across national borders—most of whom send at least a portion of their paychecks back home to families and friends. This trend has spawned a huge volume of relatively small, individual remittances flowing across geographical boundaries (especially between Mexico and the United States). What problems has this created for the financial system and for the workers and families involved? See, for example, **usinfo.state.gov/regional/ar/mexico/02093002.htm.**

2. According to the U.S. Bureau of the Census (especially the Web site **census. gov**) what appear to be the major demographic trends affecting the population of the United States? Do these trends appear to have important implications for the production and delivery of financial services?

3. How does the bank deposit insurance system and the pension plan insurance system work in the United States (as discussed in such Web sites as **fdic.gov** and **pbgc.gov**)? What appear to be the strengths and weaknesses of these two insurance systems?

4. As reflected in such Web sites as **consumerlaw.org** and **fdic.gov/consumers** how and why do we need to protect personal consumer information in the financial-services field?

5. Antifraud measures taken by financial institutions to protect consumers from identity theft have become a major concern for the financial-services industry. Scams such as *phishing* and *pretexting* have become commonplace, but new scams are always being invented. Go to the Web site of the American Bankers Association (ABA) at **www.aba.com** and click on the

link to "Fraud/Security" on their home page. What are the principal concerns the ABA has listed relating to current fraud schemes and what is being done about them?

6. Globalization of the financial system and the rapid pace with which information is now being transmitted has allowed capital to flow quickly from one country to another, essentially ignoring geographic boundaries. As discussed in this chapter, international capital mobility has resulted, among other things, in "regulatory arbitrage," whereby financial-service firms are seeking to place their funds in the least heavily regulated markets around the world, and in heightened "international liquidity" risk, that could cause financial crises in one part of the world to spread globally. One implication of these changes is that regulation of financial-service firms needs to become harmonized around the world. Go to the Web site of the Bank for International Setttlements (BIS), **http://www.bis.org/bcbs/index.htm,** and learn how regulators from the major industrialized economies are coordinating their efforts, under the aegis of the Basel Committee on Banking Supervision, to deal with the changing nature of international financial institutions. By reviewing the responsibilities of each of the six major "subcommittees" the Basel Committee has established, describe the principal areas of cooperation that have been targeted by this international group of regulators.

## Selected References to Explore

1. Baily, Martin Neil, and Robert Z. Lawrence. "Do We Have a New E-conomy?" *American Economic Review*, 91 (May 2001), pp. 308–12.

2. Bauer, Paul W. "When Is Checkout Time?" *Economic Commentary*, Federal Reserve Bank of Cleveland, September 1, 2004.

3. Bodie, Zvi. "On Asset-Liability Matching and Federal Deposit and Pension Insurance," *Review*, Federal Reserve Bank of St. Louis, July/August 2006, Vol. 88, No. 4, pp. 323–30.

4. Cummins, J. David. "Should the Government Provide Insurance for Catastrophes?" *Review*, Federal Reserve Bank of St. Louis, July/August 2006, Vol. 88, No. 4, pp. 337–80.

5. Federal Deposit Insurance Corporation. "Checks and Balances: New Rules, New Strategies for Bank Customers in the 21st Century," *FDIC Consumer News*, Summer 2004, pp.1–4.

6. Kwan, Simon. "Banking Consolidation," *FRBSF Economic Letter*, Federal Reserve Bank of San Francisco, June 18, 2004.

7. Litan, Robert E., and Alice M. Rivlin. "Projecting the Economic Impact of the Internet," *American Economic Review*, 91 (May 2001), pp. 313–17.

8. Litan, Robert E., and Joseph E. Stiglitz. "What Is the Appropriate Role of the Federal Government in the Private Markets for Credit and Insurance? What Is the Outlook?" *Review*, Federal Reserve Bank of St. Louis, July/August 2006, Vol. 88, No. 4, pp. 387–95.

9. Mester, Loretta J. "Changes in the Use of Electronic Payments," *Business Review*, Federal Reserve Bank of Philadelphia, Third Quarter 2003.

10. Modigliani, Franco, and Albert Ando. "The Permanent Income and the Life Cycle Hypothesis of Saving Behavior," in *Proceedings of the Conference on Consumption and Saving*, The University of Pennsylvania, 1960, pp. 49–174.

11. Quigley, John M. "Federal Credit and Insurance Programs: Housing," *Review*, Federal Reserve Bank of St. Louis, July/August 2006, Vol. 88, No. 4, pp. 281–310.

12. Strahan, Philip E. "The Real Effects of U.S. Banking Deregulation," *Review,* Federal Reserve Bank of St. Louis, July/August 2003, pp. 111–28.

# Part 2

# Interest Rates and the Prices of Financial Assets

There is an old adage that says, "It takes money to make money!" When it comes to saving and investing, this is certainly true. But how much money can you make? The smart investor will have done his or her homework and have a pretty good idea. However, this same smart investor also knows there are few sure bets in the world. As Humphrey Bogart said in *The African Queen*, "You pays your money and you takes your chances." It is the smart investor who understands how much "chance" is being taken, and just what the nature of this "chance" is. The purpose of Part 2 of this book is to help you become a smart investor—which is a status worth achieving because, quite literally, it pays!

How much money can an investor expect to earn? The answer depends on which financial asset he or she chooses to buy. But regardless of the choice made, when the asset is acquired, the investor gives up his or her ability to consume the amount of that investment today. A smart investor must be compensated fully for that loss of consumption power, even if there is no risk that the investment will turn sour. The amount of this compensation per dollar invested is referred to as the "risk-free real interest rate" and it plays a central role in determining the price of *every* financial asset. How the economy arrives at this fundamental interest rate is the subject of Chapter 5.

Understanding the risk-free real interest rate is only the first step toward becoming a smart investor. There are literally thousands of interest rates in the financial marketplace! And to complicate matters, there is no single way to compute an interest rate. The smart investor must understand exactly how the interest rate he or she has been quoted was computed and how to compute the right interest rate that he or she really needs to know when evaluating any investment. Chapter 6 develops the tools you will need to understand and compute the various interest rates in common usage in the financial marketplace today.

Chapters 7 and 8 are devoted to analyzing the "chances" investors take when they "pays their money." Should you invest in short-term or long-term assets? How can inflation turn a good investment into a loser? What other risks does the investor face and how do these risks differ across different financial assets? The smart investor must decide not only how much and what types of risk to accept, but also how much compensation for risk he or she requires in order to make the investment. Of course, many risks are unavoidable. Chapter 9 describes the rapidly growing number of special financial assets—referred to as *financial derivatives*—that enable these risks to be transferred from one investor to another. Therefore, smart investors also may choose to hedge the risks they face when they "takes their chances" in the financial marketplace.

# Chapter 5

# The Determinants of Interest Rates: Competing Ideas

## Learning Objectives

### in This Chapter

- You will see the important roles that *interest rates* play within the economy.
- You will explore the most important ideas about what determines the level of interest rates and asset prices within the financial system.
- You will learn what economists believe are the key forces that set market interest rates and asset prices in motion.

## What's in This Chapter?
## Key Topics Outline

Interest Rates: Nature and Roles within the Financial System

The Classical Theory of Interest: Assumptions and Conclusions

The Substitution Effect and Investment Demand

Liquidity Preference Theory: Demand and Supply of Cash Balances

Central Banking and Interest Rates

The Credit Theory of Interest Rates: Demand and Supply of Loanable Funds

Rational Expectations and the Public's Changing Outlook for Interest Rates

## 5.1   Introduction: Interest Rates and the Price of Credit

In the opening chapter of this book, we described the money and capital markets as one vast pool of funds, depleted by the borrowing activities of households, businesses, and governments and replenished by the savings these sectors supply to the financial system. The money and capital markets make saving possible by offering the individual saver a wide menu of choices where funds may be placed at attractive rates of return. By committing funds to one or more financial instruments (assets), the saver, in effect, becomes a lender of funds. The financial markets also make borrowing possible by giving the borrower a channel through which securities (IOUs) can be issued to lenders. And the money and capital markets make investment and economic growth possible by providing the funds needed for the purchase of machinery and equipment and the construction of buildings, highways, and other productive facilities.

**rate of interest**

**price of credit**

Clearly, then, the acts of saving and lending, borrowing and investing are intimately linked through the entire financial system. And one factor that significantly influences and ties all of them together is the **rate of interest.** The rate of interest is the price a borrower must pay to secure scarce loanable funds from a lender for an agreed-upon time period. Some authorities refer to it as the **price of credit.** But unlike other prices in the economy, the rate of interest is really a *ratio* of two quantities: the money cost of borrowing divided by the amount of money actually borrowed, usually expressed on an *annual percentage* basis.

Interest rates send *price signals* to those who ultimately supply funds to the economy through saving and lending and to those who ultimately demand funds by borrowing to make capital investments in the economy. Higher interest rates provide incentives to increase the supply of funds, but at the same time they reduce the demand for those funds. Lower interest rates have the opposite effects. Because (as we saw in Chapter 2) the total amount of funds supplied by the financial system must just equal the total amount borrowed—that is, quantity supplied equals quantity demanded, then whether an increase in interest rates increases the total amount of funds available in the economy depends on whether the supply response of savers and lenders is greater or less than the demand response of borrowers. In this chapter, we will discuss the forces that are believed by economists and financial analysts to underlie the supply and demand factors that ultimately determine interest rates in the financial marketplace.

## 5.2   Functions of the Rate of Interest in the Economy

The *rate of interest* performs a number of important functions to support the smooth, efficient functioning of the economy:

1. It facilitates the flow of current savings into investments that promote economic growth. For example, banks can attract household savings by offering interest on deposits. These funds can then be made available to small businesses to expand their operations, thus increasing employment and output.

2. Interest rates allocate the available supply of credit to those investment projects with the highest returns. A firm computes the rate of return on a project that would expand its production line. If the interest rate is too high, then the cost of borrowing could cause an otherwise profitable project to become a loser. Therefore, interest rates allow only those projects with the greatest profit potential to be funded.

3. Adjustments in interest rates can bring the supply of money into balance with demand. A household needs money to conduct its purchases of goods and

services. If there is more money in supply in the economy than is demanded by households, a decrease in the interest rate would occur that would reduce the opportunity cost of holding money and thereby increase the demand for money.

4. Finally, interest rates are an important tool of government policy through their influence on the volume of saving and investment. If the economy is growing too slowly and unemployment is rising, the government can use its policy tools to lower interest rates in order to stimulate borrowing and investment. On the other hand, an economy experiencing rapid inflation has traditionally called for a government policy of higher rates to slow borrowing and spending and encourage more saving.

In the pages of the financial press, the phrase "the interest rate" is frequently used. In truth, there is no such thing as *the* interest rate, for there are thousands of different interest rates in the financial system. Even securities issued by the same borrower may carry a variety of interest rates. How many of these interest rates are computed and reported in the financial press is the subject of Chapter 6. In this chapter, we focus on the basic economic forces that influence the level of *all* interest rates.

To understand these basic rate-determining forces, we need to make a simplifying assumption. For now, assume there is *one* fundamental interest rate that is commonly known as the *pure* or **risk-free rate of interest,** and this risk-free rate is a component of *all* interest rates. While the pure or risk-free interest rate exists only in theory, its properties are shared with market rates of interest on government bonds. An investor can earn a minimal rate of return on government bonds while incurring almost no risk to his or her investment. Therefore, the rate of return on government bonds represents the opportunity cost of holding idle cash, which is also a risk-free asset but pays no interest. Why government bonds themselves have different interest rates is a very important topic that we will study in Chapter 7. Interest rates on securities issued by borrowers in the economy other than the government must reflect the different types and degrees of risk that investors in those securities must assume, such as default or credit risk, term risk, marketability risk, and so on. These additional risk factors are discussed in Chapters 7 and 8.

First, however, we must examine the forces that determine the pure or risk-free interest rate itself. In this chapter we present the four most popular views—the classical theory, the liquidity preference theory, the loanable funds theory, and the rational expectations theory of interest—about how the pure or risk-free rate of interest is determined. We will also note which of these views about interest rates is the most widely followed today by practitioners and active investors "on the street," keeping in mind, however, that there are some important truths to consider in every one of the interest-rate theories discussed in this chapter.

*(margin note: **risk-free rate of interest**)*

## 5.3  The Classical Theory of Interest Rates

One of the oldest theories concerning the determinants of the pure or risk-free interest rate is the **classical theory of interest rates,** developed during the nineteenth and early twentieth centuries by a number of British economists and elaborated on by Irving Fisher [2] more recently. The classical theory argues that the rate of interest is determined by two forces: (1) the supply of savings, derived mainly from households, and (2) the demand for investment capital, coming mainly from the business sector. Let us examine these rate-determining forces of savings and investment demand in detail.

*(margin note: **classical theory of interest rates**)*

### *Saving by Households*

What is the relationship between the rate of interest and the volume of savings in the economy? Most saving in modern economies is carried out by individuals and families. For these households, saving is simply abstinence from consumption spending. *Current savings, therefore, are equal to the difference between current income and current consumption expenditures.*

In making the decision on the timing and amount of saving to be done, households typically consider several factors: the size of current and future expected income, their wealth (or net worth), a desired savings target, and what proportion of their income they are able to put aside in the form of savings (referred to as the *propensity to save*). Generally, the volume of saving rises with income, with higher-income families tending to save more and consume less of their total income than families with lower incomes. Nonetheless, an increase in an individual family's overall wealth tends to raise their consumption expenditures because their need for additional savings to meet their savings target is reduced. This is referred to as the **wealth effect,** and it was particularly strong during the stock market and housing booms of the late 1990s, when the personal saving rate went negative as households were consuming more than their income!

**wealth effect**

Although income and wealth probably dominate saving decisions, interest rates also play an important role. Interest rates affect an individual's choice between current consumption and saving for future consumption. The classical theory of interest assumes that individuals have a definite *time preference* for current over future consumption. A rational individual, it is assumed, will always prefer current enjoyment of goods and services over future enjoyment. Therefore, the only way to encourage an individual or family to consume less now and save more is to offer a higher rate of interest on current savings. If more were saved in the current period at a higher rate of return, future consumption would be increased. For example, if the current rate of interest is 10 percent and a household saves $100 instead of spending it on current consumption, it will be able to consume $110 in goods and services a year from now.

The classical theory considers the payment of interest a reward for *waiting*—the postponement of current consumption in favor of greater future consumption. Higher interest rates increase the attractiveness of saving relative to consumption spending, encouraging more individuals to substitute current saving (and future consumption) for some amount of current consumption. This so-called **substitution effect** calls for a *positive* relationship between interest rates and the volume of savings. Higher interest rates bring forth a greater volume of current savings. For example, if the rate of interest in the financial markets rises from 5 to 10 percent, the volume of current savings by households might increase from $100 billion to $200 billion.

**substitution effect**

## Saving by Business Firms

Households are not the only savers in the economy. Businesses also save. Most businesses hold savings balances in the form of retained earnings (as reflected in their equity or net worth accounts). In fact, the increase in retained earnings reported by businesses each year is a key measure of the volume of current business saving, which supplies most of the money for annual investment spending by business firms.

The critical element in determining the amount of business savings is the level of business *profits*. If profits are expected to rise, businesses will be able to draw more heavily on earnings retained in the firm and less heavily on the money and capital markets for funds. The result is a reduction in the demand for credit and a tendency toward lower interest rates. On the other hand, when profits fall but firms do not cut back on their investment plans, they will be forced to make heavier use of the money and capital markets for investment funds. The demand for credit will rise, and interest rates may rise as well.

Although the principal determinant of business saving is profits, interest rates also play a role in the decision of what proportion of current operating costs and long-term investment expenditures should be financed internally from retained earnings and what proportion should be financed externally from borrowing in the money and capital markets. Higher interest rates typically encourage firms to use internally generated funds more heavily in financing their projects. Conversely, lower interest rates encourage greater use of external funds from the money and capital markets.

## Saving by Government

Governments also save, though usually less frequently than households and businesses. In fact, most government saving (i.e., a budget surplus) appears to be unintended saving that arises when government receipts unexpectedly exceed expenditures. Income flows in the economy (out of which government tax revenues arise) and the passage of government spending programs are the dominant factors affecting government savings. However, interest rates can play a role in that higher interest rates raise interest payments owed on the government's debt. These higher expenditures tend to increase government deficits (or reduce budget surpluses) and, thereby, reduce government savings.

## The Demand for Investment Funds

Business, household, and government savings are important determinants of interest rates according to the classical theory of interest, but they are not the only ones. The other critical rate-determining factor is *investment spending,* most of it carried out by business firms.

Certainly, businesses, as the leading investment sector in the economy, require huge amounts of funds each year to purchase equipment, machinery, and inventories, and to support the construction of physical facilities. The majority of business expenditures for these purposes consists of *replacement investment;* that is, expenditures to replace equipment and facilities that are wearing out or are technologically obsolete. A smaller but more dynamic form of business capital spending is labeled *net investment:* expenditures to acquire new equipment and facilities in order to increase output. The sum of replacement investment plus net investment equals *gross investment.*

Replacement investment usually is more predictable and grows at a more even rate than net investment. This is due to the fact that such expenditures are financed almost exclusively from inside the firm and frequently follow a routine pattern based on depreciation formulas. Expenditures for new equipment and facilities (net investment), on the other hand, depend on the business community's outlook for future sales, changes in technology, industrial capacity, and the cost of raising funds. Because these factors are subject to frequent changes, it is not surprising that net investment is highly volatile and a driving force in the economy. Changes in net investment are closely linked to fluctuations in the nation's output of goods and services, employment, and prices.

### The Investment Decision-Making Process

The process of investment decision making by business firms is complex and depends on a host of qualitative and quantitative factors. The firm must compare its current level of production with the capacity of its existing facilities and decide whether it has sufficient capacity to handle anticipated demand for its product. If expected future demand will strain the firm's existing facilities, it will consider expanding its operating capacity through net investment.

Most business firms have several investment projects under consideration at any one time. Although the investment decision-making process varies from firm to firm, each business generally makes some estimate of net cash flows (i.e., revenues minus all expenses, including taxes) that each project will generate over its useful life. From this information, plus knowledge of each investment project's acquisition cost, management can calculate its expected net rate of return and compare with the anticipated returns from alternative projects, as well as with market rates of interest.

One common method for performing this calculation is the *internal rate of return (IRR) method,* which equates the total cost of an investment project with the future net cash flows (NCF) expected from that project discounted back to their present values. Thus,

$$\text{Cost of project} = \frac{NCF_1}{(1+r)^1} + \frac{NCF_2}{(1+r)^2} + \cdots + \frac{NCF_n}{(1+r)^n} \qquad (5.1)$$

where each NCF represents the expected annual net cash flow from the project and $r$ is its expected internal rate of return. The internal rate of return method performs two functions: (1) it measures the annual yield the firm expects from an investment project, and (2) it reduces the value of all future cash flows expected over the economic life of the project down to their present value. In general, if the firm must choose among several investment projects, it will choose the one with the *highest* expected internal rate of return.

Although the internal rate of return provides a yardstick for selecting potentially profitable investment projects, how does a business decide how much to spend on investment at any point in time? How many projects should be chosen? It is here that the money and capital markets play a key role in the investment decision-making process.

Suppose a business firm is considering the following projects with their associated expected internal rates of return:

| Project | Expected Internal Rate of Return (annualized) |
|---|---|
| A | 15% |
| B | 12 |
| C | 10 |
| D | 9 |
| E | 8 |

How many of these projects will be adopted? The firm must compare each project's expected internal return with the cost of raising capital—the interest rate—in the money and capital markets to finance the project.

Assume that funds must be borrowed in the financial marketplace to complete any of the above projects and that the current cost of borrowing—the rate of interest—is 10 percent. Which projects are acceptable from an economic standpoint? As shown in Exhibit 5.1, projects A and B clearly are acceptable because their expected returns exceed the current cost of borrowing (10 percent) to finance them. The firm would be indifferent about project C because its expected return is no more than the cost of borrowed funds. Projects D and E, on the other hand, are unprofitable at this time.

It is through changes in the cost of raising funds that the financial markets can exert a powerful influence on the investment decisions of business firms. As credit becomes more expensive, the cost of borrowed capital rises, eliminating some investment projects from consideration. For example, if the cost of borrowed funds rises from 10 to 13 percent, only project A in our earlier example would appear to be economically viable. On the other hand, if credit becomes more abundant and less costly, the cost of capital for the individual firm will tend to decline and more projects will become profitable. In our example, a decline in the cost of borrowed funds from 10 to 8½ percent would make all but project E economically viable.

**The Cost of Capital and the Business Investment Decision**

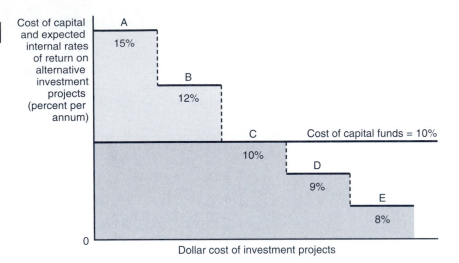

*Investment Demand and the Rate of Interest*   This reasoning explains, in part, why the demand for investment capital by business firms was regarded by the classical economists as *negatively* related to the rate of interest. At low rates of interest, more investment projects become economically viable and firms require more funds to finance a longer list of projects. On the other hand, as the rate of interest rises, fewer investment projects will be pursued and fewer funds will be required from the financial markets. For example, at a 12 percent rate of interest, only $100 billion in funds for investment spending might be demanded by business firms. If the rate of interest drops to 10 percent, however, the volume of desired investment might rise to $200 billion.

## The Equilibrium Rate of Interest in the Classical Theory of Interest

The classical economists believed that interest rates in the financial markets were determined by the interplay of the supply of saving and the demand for investment. Specifically, the equilibrium rate of interest is determined at the point where the quantity of savings supplied to the market is exactly equal to the quantity of funds demanded for investment. In Exhibit 5.2, the volume of saving in the economy is shown to increase with the rate of interest (S-curve), and the demand for investment is shown to fall as the rate of interest rises (I-curve). Equilibrium occurs at point *E,* where the equilibrium rate of interest is $i_E$ and the equilibrium quantity of capital funds traded in the financial markets is $Q_E$.

To illustrate, suppose the total volume of savings supplied by businesses, households, and governments at an interest rate of 10 percent is $200 billion (S-curve). Moreover, at this same 10 percent rate, businesses would demand $200 billion in funds for investment purposes (I-curve). Then 10 percent must be the equilibrium rate of interest, and $200 billion the equilibrium quantity of funds traded in the money and capital markets.

The market rate of interest moves toward its equilibrium level. However, supply and demand forces change so fast that the interest rate rarely has an opportunity to settle in at a specific equilibrium level. At any given time, the interest rate is probably above or below its true equilibrium level but moving *toward* that equilibrium. If the market rate is temporarily above equilibrium, the volume of savings exceeds the demand for investment capital, creating an excess supply of savings. Savers will

**Key URLs:**
Data on interest rates may be found at a wide variety of sites on the World Wide Web such as **bankrate.com** and **investinginbonds.com**

**The Equilibrium Rate of Interest in the Classical Theory**

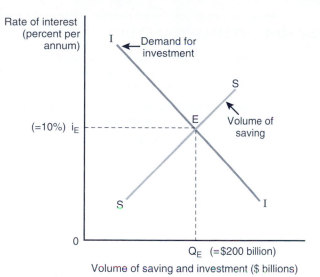

offer their funds at lower and lower rates until the market interest rate approaches equilibrium. Similarly, if the market interest rate lies temporarily below equilibrium, investment demand exceeds the quantity of savings available. Business firms will bid up the interest rate until it approaches the level at which the quantity saved equals the quantity of funds demanded for investment purposes.

The classical theory of interest rates helps us understand some of the *long-term forces* driving interest rates. For example, some analysts argue that, in the future, interest rates on average could be relatively low compared to historic norms—a forecast that so far has turned out to be correct since the turn of the new century. These analysts point out that the populations of the United States and most other nations are aging, shifting heavily toward those age groups in which individuals spend less of their current income and save more (in part to prepare for retirement), pushing interest rates down. This viewpoint assumes that people's consumption and savings habits tend to follow a predictable *life cycle,* with younger workers borrowing heavily in anticipation of higher incomes in the future and older workers, who may have reached their maximum annual earnings, saving heavily in anticipation of lower incomes in the future. The money and capital markets make a vital contribution to this process, directing the savings of older individuals into the hands of younger people who desire to improve their standard of living by borrowing.

## Limitations of the Classical Theory of Interest

The classical theory of interest has limitations. The central problem is that the theory ignores factors other than saving and investment that affect interest rates. For example, many financial institutions have the power to create money today by making loans to the public. When borrowers repay their loans, money is destroyed. The volume of money created or destroyed affects the total amount of credit available in the financial system and, therefore, must be considered in any explanation of interest rates. In addition, the classical theory assumes that interest rates are the principal determinant of the quantity of savings available. Today economists recognize that *income* and *wealth* are probably more important in determining the volume of saving. Finally, the classical theory contends that the demand for borrowed funds comes principally from the business sector. Today, however, both consumers and governments are also important

**QUESTIONS TO HELP YOU STUDY**

1. What are the functions or roles played by the rate of interest in the economy and financial system? Can you explain why each function is important to the well-being of individuals, businesses, and governments?

2. Explain the meaning of the term *pure* or *risk-free rate of interest*. Why is this interest rate important and what is its relationship to other interest rates?

3. If we could identify the forces shaping the risk-free or pure rate of interest, what advantage could this give us in explaining the many different interest rates we see every day in the real world?

4. In the classical theory of interest rates, what forces determine the market rate of interest? What assumptions does the classical theory of interest rest upon?

5. Explain why the supply curve in the classical theory of interest rates has a positive slope. Why does the demand curve in the classical theory have a negative slope?

borrowers. As we will see in the rest of this chapter, more recent theories about interest rates address a number of these limitations of the classical theory.

## 5.4   The Liquidity Preference or Cash Balances Theory of Interest Rates

The classical theory of interest has been called a *long-term* explanation of interest rates because it focuses on the public's thrift habits—a factor that tends to change slowly. During the 1930s, British economist John Maynard Keynes [4] developed a theory of the rate of interest that, he argued, was more relevant for policymakers and for explaining near-term changes in interest rates. This theory is known as the **liquidity preference** (or *cash balances*) **theory of interest rates.**

**liquidity preference theory of interest rates**

### The Demand for Liquidity

Liquidity preference theory contends that the rate of interest is a payment for the use of a scarce resource—*money* (cash balances). Businesses and individuals prefer to hold money for carrying out daily transactions and also as a precaution against future cash needs even though money's yield (or rate of return) is usually low or even nonexistent. Investors in fixed-income securities, such as government bonds, frequently desire to hold money or cash balances as a haven against declining asset prices. Interest rates, therefore, are the price that must be paid to induce money holders to surrender a perfectly liquid asset (cash balances) and hold other assets that carry more risk. At times the preference for liquidity grows very strong. Unless the money supply is expanded, interest rates will rise.

In the theory of liquidity preference, only two outlets for investor funds are considered: *bonds* and *money* or *cash balances* (including bank deposits). Money provides perfect liquidity (instant spending power). Bonds pay interest but cannot be spent until converted into cash. If interest rates rise, the market value of bonds paying a fixed rate of interest falls; the investor would suffer a capital loss if those bonds were converted into cash. On the other hand, a fall in interest rates results in higher bond prices; the bondholder will experience a capital gain if his bonds are sold for cash. To classical theorists, it was irrational to hold money because it provided little or no return. To

Our discussion of how interest rates affect business investment decisions focused upon the internal rate of return (IRR) method for comparing interest rates with the expected return on an investment project. Actually, the IRR method for evaluating investments is less widely used today than another method of investment analysis—the *net present value* (NPV) approach.

For example, suppose that we operate a business that is considering an investment project costing $1,000 and generating expected net cash flows (cash revenues less cash expenses) of:

| Year | Net Cash Flow |
|------|---------------|
| 1 | $100 |
| 2 | 200 |
| 3 | 300 |
| 4 | 400 |
| 5 | 500 |
| 6 | 600 |

after which the project becomes worthless. Thus, its internal rate of return (IRR) can be found from the formula:

$$\$1,000 = \frac{\$100}{(1+r)^1} + \frac{\$200}{(1+r)^2} + \frac{\$300}{(1+r)^3}$$
$$+ \frac{\$400}{(1+r)^4} + \frac{\$500}{(1+r)^5} + \frac{\$600}{(1+r)^6}$$

where the internal rate of return ($r$) turns out to be about 10 percent. If the going market rate on borrowed funds in the money and capital markets is 8 percent, this project is clearly acceptable because its expected internal rate of return exceeds the cost of borrowed funds.

Now suppose the firm believes its stockholders demand a minimum required after-tax return of 12 percent. Then the proposed project's net present value must be:

$$NPV = -\$1,000 + \frac{\$100}{(1+.12)^1} + \frac{\$200}{(1+.12)^2}$$
$$+ \frac{\$300}{(1+.12)^3} + \frac{\$400}{(1+.12)^4} + \frac{\$500}{(1+.12)^5}$$
$$+ \frac{\$600}{(1+.12)^6} \approx \$304$$

This proposed investment project is acceptable because its NPV is *positive* (NPV > 0) at about +$304.

With IRR, the implied reinvestment rate of return for each project's cash flows is equal to the calculated internal rate of return and, therefore, is likely to be different for each proposed project. However, under the NPV method, the implied reinvestment rate is the *same* for *all* projects—investors' required rate of return (i.e., the minimum necessary return on investment opportunities to keep a business's stock price unchanged). Thus, NPV measures the true opportunity cost of a project for an investor whose goal is *value maximization* (i.e., maximizing the value of each business firm's stock).

As interest rates rise, offering investors higher returns on other investment alternatives of comparable risk, then investors will tend to raise the required return they demand from an investment project. Fewer projects will be acceptable. Conversely, when interest rates fall, investors' required rates of return will tend to decline. Investment spending will tend to rise. Clearly, interest rates in the money and capital markets play a vital role in determining the volume of investment and in attracting savings to make investment possible.

proponents of liquidity preference, however, the holding of money (cash balances) could be a perfectly rational act if interest rates were expected to rise, because rising rates can result in substantial losses for investors in bonds.

*Motives for Holding Money (Cash Balances)* According to liquidity preference theory, the public demands money for three different purposes (motives). The *transactions motive* represents the demand for money (cash balances) to purchase goods and services. Because inflows and outflows of money (that is, income and expenditures) are not perfectly synchronized in either timing or amount and because it is costly to shift back and forth between money and other assets, businesses, households, and governments must keep some cash in the till or in demand accounts simply to meet daily expenses.

In the earliest versions of the theory, the transactions demand for money was assumed to be dependent on the level of national income, business sales, and prices. Reflecting money's role as a medium of exchange, higher levels of income, sales, or prices increase the need for cash balances to carry out transactions.

There is also a *precautionary motive* for holding money, which arises because we live in an uncertain world and cannot predict exactly what our expenditures, or perhaps even our income, will be in the future. For example, an unanticipated medical expense may arise, or a salesperson may find his income from sales commissions is unexpectedly low. In both cases, the household could meet its greater need for liquidity (cash balances) if it had held back some of its wealth in the form of reserves, or idle cash balances. This precautionary demand for money, therefore, increases in times of greater economic uncertainty.

While neither the transactions nor precautionary demands for money were believed to be very sensitive to interest rates, the demand for money could nonetheless affect short-term changes in interest rates as a result of the third motive for holding cash—the *speculative motive*—that stems from uncertainty about the future prices of bonds.

To illustrate, suppose an investor has recently purchased a corporate bond for $1,000. The company issuing the bond promises to pay $100 a year in interest income. To simplify matters, assume the bond is a *perpetual security.* This means the investor will receive $100 a year for as long as the security is held. The annual rate of return (or yield) on the bond, then, is 10 percent ($100/$1,000). Suppose now that the interest rate on bonds of similar quality rises to 12 percent. What happens to the price of the 10 percent bond? Its price in the marketplace will *fall* because its annual promised yield at a price of $1,000 is *less* than 12 percent. The 10 percent bond's price will approach $833 because at this price the bond's $100 annual interest payment gives the investor an approximate annual yield of 12 percent ($100/$833). In the reverse situation, if interest rates were to decline—say, to 9 percent—the 10 percent bond would experience a rise in its market price.

Therefore, at those times when there is greater uncertainty about future bond prices, the risk of a capital loss resulting from falling bond prices, as described above, will cause many investors to demand money or near-money assets (such as deposits in a bank, credit union, or money market mutual fund) instead of bonds. However, there is an opportunity cost, or loss of interest income, that results from holding idle cash balances. Therefore, high interest rates encourage investors to reduce their speculative demand for money at the risk of capital losses, while low interest rates encourage investors to reduce the risk of capital losses by increasing their money holdings. We may represent this speculative demand for money by a line or curve that slopes downward and to the right, as shown in Exhibit 5.3, reflecting a *negative* relationship between the speculative demand for money and the level of interest rates.

### Total Demand for Money (Cash Balances)

The total demand for money or cash balances in the economy is simply the sum of transactions, precautionary, and speculative demands. Because the principal determinant of transactions demand is income, and of precautionary demand is income uncertainty, not interest rates, these money demands are fixed at a certain level of national income. Let this demand be

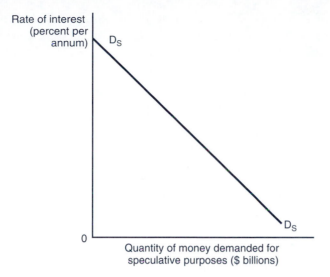

represented by the quantity $0K$ shown along the horizontal axis in Exhibit 5.4. Then, any amount of cash demanded in excess of $0K$ represents speculative demand. The total demand for money is represented along curve $D_T$. Therefore, if the rate of interest lies at the moment at $i_E$, Exhibit 5.4 shows that the speculative demand for money will be $KJ$ and the total demand for money will be $0J$.

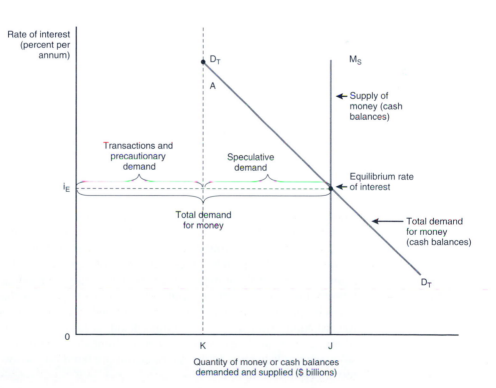

One way government policy attempts to stimulate a weak economy—a period of slow or no growth and high unemployment—is to lower short-term interest rates. The usual impact of this policy action is to stimulate investment demand by businesses, which spurs production, leading producers to hire additional workers. As a result, output (real gross domestic product, or GDP) tends to rise and unemployment declines.

During the Great Depression of the 1930s, when economic activity fell sharply, this policy appeared to be ineffective in many countries around the world. The problem was that lower interest rates did not stimulate demand for goods and services, no matter how low the government reduced interest rates. This condition came to be known as the *liquidity trap*. An economic condition that is generally believed to be necessary for a liquidity trap to occur is falling prices (*deflation*).

Since the time of the Great Depression there has been little evidence of a liquidity trap anywhere in the world—that is, until very recently in Japan. Beginning in the early 1990s, the Japanese economy—the world's second largest, after the United States—began to stagnate after decades of impressive growth. With falling prices, attempts to stimulate the Japanese economy by lowering short-term interest rates were not particularly successful. Economic stagnation and deflation continued for more than a decade, even though short-term interest rates had been driven essentially to *zero*, finally showing signs of leveling out early in the current century.

The recent Japanese experience has led to a revival of interest in the liquidity trap. Government policymakers around the globe have become more concerned about the possibility their economies also might begin to experience deflation. Given the experience of the Japanese economy, policymakers elsewhere are now cognizant of the fact that new ways to stimulate a weak economy may be needed, if similar circumstances in their economies cause interest rates to become an ineffective policy tool.

## The Supply of Money (Cash Balances)

The other major element determining interest rates in liquidity preference theory is the supply of money. In modern economies, the money supply is controlled, or at least closely regulated, by government. Because government decisions concerning the size of the money supply presumably are guided by the public welfare, not by the level of interest rates, we assume that the supply of cash balances is *inelastic* with respect to the rate of interest. Such a money supply curve is represented in Exhibit 5.4 by the vertical line $M_S$.

## The Equilibrium Rate of Interest in Liquidity Preference Theory

The interplay of the total demand for and the supply of money or cash balances determines the equilibrium rate of interest in the short run. As shown in Exhibit 5.4, the equilibrium rate is found at point $i_E$, where the total quantity of money demanded by the public ($D_T$) equals the quantity of money supplied ($M_S$). Above this equilibrium rate, the supply of money exceeds the quantity demanded, and some businesses, households, and units of government will try to dispose of their unwanted cash balances by purchasing bonds. The prices of bonds will rise, driving interest rates down toward equilibrium at $i_E$. On the other hand, at rates below equilibrium, the quantity of money demanded exceeds the supply. Some decision makers in the economy will sell their bonds to raise additional cash, driving bond prices down and interest rates up toward equilibrium.

Liquidity preference theory provides useful insights into investor behavior and the influence of government policy on the economy. For example, the theory suggests that it is rational at certain times for the public to hoard money (cash balances) and at other times to "dishoard" (spend away) unwanted cash. If the public disposes of some of its cash by purchasing securities, this action increases the volume of credit available in the money and capital markets. Other things equal, interest rates will fall. On the other hand, if the public tries to "hoard" more money (expanding its cash balances by selling securities), less money will be available for loans. Interest rates will rise, other factors held constant.

Liquidity preference theory illustrates how central banks, such as the Federal Reserve System and the European Central Bank (ECB), can influence interest rates, at least in the short term. For example, if higher interest rates are desired, the central bank can contract the size of the money supply and interest rates will tend to rise (assuming the demand for money is unchanged). If the demand for money is increasing, the central bank may be able to bring about higher interest rates by ensuring the money supply grows more slowly than money demand. In contrast, if the central bank expands the money supply, interest rates may decline in the short term (provided the demand for money does not increase).

## *Limitations of the Liquidity Preference Theory*

**Key URLs:**
For further information about the European Central Bank and the Federal Reserve, see ecb.int and federalreserve.gov

Like the classical theory of interest, liquidity preference theory has limitations. It is a short-term approach to interest rate determination that fails to capture the fact that over the longer term, interest rates are affected by changes in the level of income and by inflationary expectations. Indeed, it is impossible to have a stable equilibrium interest rate without also reaching an equilibrium level of income, saving, and investment in the economy. Also, liquidity preference considers only the supply and demand for the stock of money, whereas business, consumer, and government demands for credit clearly have an impact on the cost of credit. A more comprehensive view of interest rates is needed that considers the important roles played by *all* actors in the financial system: businesses, households, and governments.

### QUESTIONS TO HELP YOU STUDY

6. What are the origins of the *liquidity preference theory of interest?* What assumptions underlie this important idea about what determines market rates of interest?

7. The demand for money is a critical element in the *liquidity preference theory of interest*. What are the three main components of the demand for money?

8. What factors appear to determine the *transactions demand* for money? How about the *precautionary motive* for demanding and holding money? The *speculative motive?*

9. What makes up the *total demand* for money? What is the shape of the relationship between the total demand for money and the market rate of interest?

10. What determines the equilibrium interest rate under the liquidity preference theory of interest? What forces cause the equilibrium interest rate to move?

11. What are the principal limitations of the liquidity preference theory of interest?

## 5.5 The Loanable Funds Theory of Interest

A view that overcomes many of the limitations of earlier theories is the **loanable funds theory of interest rates.** It is the most popular interest-rate theory among practitioners and those who follow interest rates "on the street." The loanable funds view argues that the risk-free interest rate is determined by the interplay of two forces: the demand for and supply of *credit* (loanable funds). The demand for loanable funds consists of credit demands from domestic businesses, consumers, and governments, and also borrowing in the domestic market by foreigners. The supply of loanable funds stems from domestic savings, dishoarding of money balances, money creation by the banking system, and lending in the domestic market by foreign individuals and institutions.

### *The Demand for Loanable Funds*

*Consumer (Household) Demand for Loanable Funds*    Domestic consumers demand loanable funds to purchase a wide variety of goods and services on credit. Recent research indicates that consumers (households) are not particularly responsive to the rate of interest when they seek credit but focus instead principally on the nonprice terms of a loan, such as the down payment, maturity, and size of installment payments. This implies that consumer demand for credit is relatively *inelastic* with respect to the rate of interest. Certainly a rise in interest rates leads to some reduction in the quantity of consumer demand for loanable funds, whereas a decline in interest rates stimulates some additional consumer borrowing. However, along the consumer's relatively inelastic demand schedule, a substantial change in the rate of interest must occur before the quantity of consumer demand for funds changes significantly.

*Domestic Business Demand for Loanable Funds*    The credit demands of domestic businesses generally are more responsive to changes in the rate of interest than is consumer borrowing. Most business credit is for such investment purposes as the purchase of inventories and new plant and equipment. A high interest rate eliminates some business investment projects from consideration because their expected rate of return is lower than the cost of borrowed funds, rendering those projects unprofitable. On the other hand, at lower rates of interest many investment projects look profitable, with their expected returns exceeding the cost of funds. Therefore, the quantity of loanable funds demanded by the business sector increases as the rate of interest falls.

*Government Demand for Loanable Funds*    Government demand for loanable funds is a growing factor in the financial markets but does not depend significantly upon the level of interest rates. This is especially true of borrowing by the federal government. Federal decisions on spending and borrowing are made by Congress in response to social needs and the public welfare, not the rate of interest. Moreover, the federal government has the power both to tax and create money to pay its debts. State and local government demand, on the other hand, is slightly interest elastic because many local governments are limited in their borrowing activities by legal ceilings. When open market rates rise above these ceilings, some state and local governments are prevented from borrowing money from the public.

*Foreign Demand for Loanable Funds*    In recent years foreign banks and corporations, as well as foreign governments, have increasingly entered the huge U.S. financial marketplace to borrow billions of dollars. Foreign credit demands are sensitive to the spread between domestic lending rates and interest rates in foreign markets. If U.S. interest rates decline relative to foreign rates, foreign borrowers will be inclined to borrow more in the United States and less abroad. At the same time, with higher foreign interest rates, U.S. lending institutions will increase their foreign lending and reduce the availability of loanable funds to domestic borrowers. The net result, then, is a *negative* or *inverse relationship* between foreign borrowing and domestic interest rates relative to foreign interest rates.

## Total Demand for Loanable Funds

The total demand for loanable funds is the sum of domestic consumer, business, and government credit demands plus foreign credit demands. This demand curve slopes downward and to the right with respect to the rate of interest (see Exhibit 5.5 on page 135). Higher rates of interest lead some businesses, consumers, and governments to curtail their borrowing plans, while lower rates bring forth more credit demand. However, the demand for loanable funds does not determine the rate of interest by itself. The supply of loanable funds must be added to complete the picture.

## The Supply of Loanable Funds

Loanable funds flow into the money and capital markets from at least four different sources: (1) domestic saving by businesses, consumers, and governments; (2) dishoarding (spending down) of excess money balances held by the public; (3) creation of money by the domestic banking system; and (4) lending to domestic borrowers by foreigners. We consider each of these sources of funds in turn.

*Domestic Saving*   The supply of domestic savings is often the principal source of loanable funds. As noted earlier, most saving is done by households and is simply the difference between current income and current consumption. Businesses, however, also save by retaining a portion of current earnings and by adding to their depreciation reserves. Government saving, while relatively rare, occurs when current revenues exceed current expenditures.

There is evidence that some business and household saving may be goal oriented: the so-called **income effect.** For example, suppose an individual wishes to accumulate $100,000 in anticipation of retirement. Interest rates subsequently rise from 5 to 10 percent. Will this individual save more out of each period's income or less? Probably *less* because higher interest rates will enable the saver to reach the $100,000 goal with less sacrifice of current income. At higher interest rates, savings accumulate faster. On the other hand, a lower interest rate might lead to a greater volume of saving because a business firm or household then must accumulate savings at a faster rate to achieve its savings goal.

Clearly, then, the income effect would have the opposite result for the volume of saving than the substitution effect described earlier in our discussion of the classical theory of interest. The substitution effect argues for a *positive* relationship between the rate of interest and the volume of savings, while the income effect suggests a *negative* relationship between interest rates and savings volume. Thus, these two effects pull aggregate saving in opposite directions as interest rates change. It should not be surprising, therefore, that the annual volume of saving in the economy is difficult to forecast.

Recent research using econometric models has suggested the importance of another factor—the wealth effect—in influencing savings decisions. Individuals accumulate

**income effect**

**Key URL:**
For a discussion of savings goals and how to achieve them, consult such sources as the National Endowment for Financial Education (NEFE) at nefe.org

wealth in many different forms: real assets (e.g., automobiles, houses, land) and financial assets (e.g., stocks, bonds). What happens to the value of financial assets as interest rates change? If rates rise, for example, the market value of many financial assets will fall until their yield approaches market-determined levels. Therefore, a rise in interest rates will result in decreases in the value of wealth held in some financial assets, forcing the individual to save more to protect his or her wealth position. Conversely, a decrease in interest rates will increase the value of many financial assets, increasing wealth and necessitating a lower volume of current saving.

For businesses and individuals heavily in debt, however, the *opposite* effects may ensue. When interest rates rise, debt that was contracted in earlier periods when interest rates were lower seems less of a burden. For example, a home mortgage taken by a family when interest rates in the mortgage market were 5 percent seems a less burdensome drain on income when rates on new mortgages have risen to 10 percent. Therefore, a rise in interest rates tends to make those economic units carrying a large volume of debt relative to their financial assets feel better off. They may tend to save *less* as a result. A decrease in interest rates, on the other hand, may result in *more* saving due to the wealth effect.

The *net* effect of the income, substitution, and wealth effects leads to a relatively *interest-inelastic* supply of savings curve. Substantial changes in interest rates usually are required to bring about significant changes in the volume of aggregate saving in the economy.

*Dishoarding of Money Balances*   Still another source of loanable funds is centered on the public's demand for money relative to the available supply of money. As noted earlier, the public's demand for money (cash balances) varies with interest rates and income levels. The supply of money, on the other hand, is closely controlled by the government. Clearly the two—money demand and money supply—need not be the same. The difference between the public's total demand for money and the money supply is known as *hoarding.* When the public's demand for cash balances exceeds the supply, *positive hoarding* of money takes place as some individuals and businesses attempt to increase their cash balances at the expense of others. Hoarding *reduces* the volume of loanable funds available in the financial markets. On the other hand, when the public's demand for money is less than the supply available, *negative hoarding (dishoarding)* occurs. Some individuals and businesses will dispose of their excess cash holdings, *increasing* the supply of loanable funds available to others in the financial system.

*Creation of Credit by the Domestic Banking System*   Commercial banks and thrift institutions offering payments accounts have the unique ability to create credit by lending and investing their excess reserves (a process described in Chapters 12, 13, and 14). Credit created by the domestic banking system represents an additional source of loanable funds, which must be added to the amount of savings and the dishoarding of money balances (or minus the amount of hoarding demand) to derive the total supply of loanable funds in the economy.

*Foreign Lending to the Domestic Funds Market*   Finally, foreign lenders provide large amounts of credit to domestic borrowers in the United States. These inflowing loanable funds are particularly sensitive to the difference between U.S. interest rates and interest rates overseas. If domestic rates rise relative to interest rates offered abroad, the supply of foreign funds to domestic markets will tend to rise. Foreign lenders will find it more attractive to make loans to domestic borrowers. At the same

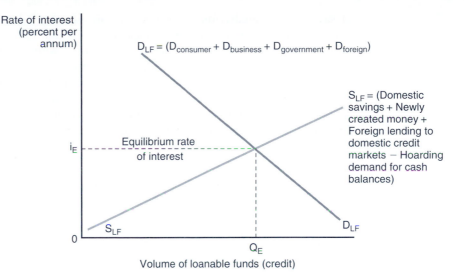

**EXHIBIT 5.5**

**Total Demand and Total Supply of Loanable Funds and the Equilibrium Rate of Interest in the Loanable Funds (Credit) Theory**

Rate of interest (percent per annum)

$D_{LF} = (D_{consumer} + D_{business} + D_{government} + D_{foreign})$

$S_{LF} = ($Domestic savings + Newly created money + Foreign lending to domestic credit markets $-$ Hoarding demand for cash balances$)$

$i_E$

Equilibrium rate of interest

$S_{LF}$

$D_{LF}$

0

$Q_E$

Volume of loanable funds (credit)

time, domestic borrowers will turn more to foreign markets for loanable funds as domestic interest rates climb relative to foreign rates. The combined result is to make the net foreign supply of loanable funds to the domestic credit market *positively* related to the spread between domestic and foreign rates of interest.

## Total Supply of Loanable Funds

The total supply of loanable funds, including domestic saving, foreign lending, dishoarding of money, and new credit created by the domestic banking system, is depicted in Exhibit 5.5. The curve rises with higher rates of interest, indicating that a greater supply of loanable funds will flow into the money and capital markets when the returns from lending increase.

## The Equilibrium Rate of Interest in the Loanable Funds Theory

The two forces of supply and demand for loanable funds determine not only the volume of lending and borrowing but also the rate of interest. *The interest rate tends toward the equilibrium point at which the total supply of loanable funds equals the total demand for loanable funds.* This point of equilibrium is shown in Exhibit 5.5 at $i_E$.

If the interest rate is temporarily *above* equilibrium, the quantity of loanable funds supplied by domestic savers and foreign lenders, by the banking system, and from the dishoarding of money (or minus hoarding demand) exceeds the total demand for loanable funds, and the rate of interest will be bid down. On the other hand, if the interest rate is temporarily *below* equilibrium, loanable funds demand will exceed the supply. The interest rate will be bid up by borrowers until it settles at equilibrium once again.

The equilibrium depicted in Exhibit 5.5 is only a *partial* equilibrium position, however. This is due to the fact that interest rates are affected by conditions in *both* domestic and world economies. For the economy to be in equilibrium, planned saving must equal planned investment across the whole economic system. For example, if planned investment exceeds planned saving at the equilibrium interest rate shown in Exhibit 5.5, investment demands will push interest rates higher in the short term. However, as additional investment spending occurs, incomes will rise, generating a greater volume of savings. Eventually, interest rates will fall. Similarly, if exchange rates between dollars, yen, and other world currencies are not in equilibrium with each other, there will be further opportunities for profit available to foreign and domestic lenders by moving loanable funds from one country to another.

Only when the economy (including the markets for goods and services and the labor market), the money market, the loanable funds market, and foreign currency markets are *simultaneously* in equilibrium will interest rates remain stable. Thus, a completely *stable* equilibrium interest rate over the long run will be characterized by the following set of circumstances:

1. Planned saving = Planned investment (including business, household, and government investment) across the whole economic system (i.e., equilibrium in the economy, including the markets for goods and services and for labor).

2. Money supply = Money demand (i.e., equilibrium in the money market).

3. Quantity of loanable funds supplied = Quantity of loanable funds demanded (i.e., equilibrium in the loanable funds market).

4. The difference between foreign demand for loanable funds and the volume of loanable funds supplied by foreigners to the domestic economy = The difference between current exports from and imports into the domestic economy (i.e., equilibrium in the balance of payments and foreign currency markets).

This simple demand-supply framework is useful for analyzing broad movements in interest rates. For example, if the total supply of loanable funds is increasing and the total demand for loanable funds remains unchanged or rises more slowly, the volume of credit extended in the money and capital markets must increase. Interest rates will fall. This is illustrated in Exhibit 5.6A, which shows the supply schedule sliding outward and to the right when $S_{LF}$ increases to $S'_{LF}$, resulting in a decline in the equilibrium rate of interest from $i_1$ to $i_2$. The equilibrium quantity of loanable funds traded in the financial system increases from $C_1$ to $C_2$.

What happens when the demand for loanable funds increases with no change in the total supply of funds available? In this instance, the volume of credit extended will increase, but loans will be made at higher interest rates. Exhibit 5.6B illustrates this. The loanable funds demand curve rises from $D_{LF}$, to $D'_{LF}$, driving the interest rate upward from $i_1$ to $i_2$.

---

### QUESTIONS TO HELP YOU STUDY

12. What are *loanable funds?* Why is this term important?

13. What factors make up the total *demand* for loanable funds? The total *supply* of loanable funds? List and define each of these demand and supply factors.

14. Explain how the equilibrium loanable funds interest rate is determined. Draw a graph to illustrate what the equilibrium rate of interest might look like.

15. Suppose the demand for loanable funds increases relative to the supply. What happens to the equilibrium rate of interest? Suppose, on the other hand, the supply of loanable funds expands with loanable funds demand unchanged. What does the equilibrium loanable funds interest rate look like under these circumstances?

16. What does it take to have a *permanently stable equilibrium interest rate* under the loanable funds theory of interest? How does this differ from a *temporary* or *partial* equilibrium loanable funds rate?

**EXHIBIT 5.6**

**Changes in the Demand for and Supply of Loanable Funds**

A. Effects of increased supply of loanable funds with demand unchanged

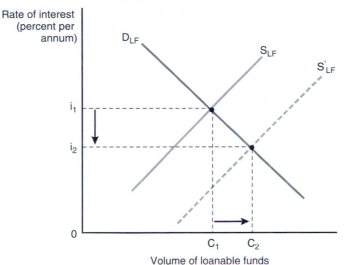

Volume of loanable funds

B. Effects of increased demand for loanable funds with supply unchanged

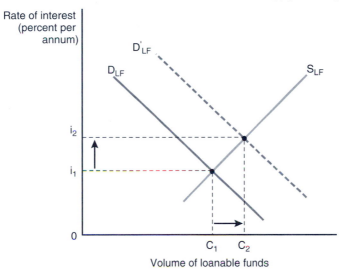

Volume of loanable funds

## 5.6 The Rational Expectations Theory of Interest

**rational expectations theory of interest rates**

In recent years, a fourth major theory about the forces determining interest rates has appeared: the **rational expectations theory of interest rates.** This theory builds on a growing body of research evidence that the money and capital markets are efficient institutions in digesting *new information* affecting interest rates and security prices.

For example, when new information appears about investment, saving, or the money supply, investors begin immediately to translate that new information into decisions to borrow or lend funds. So rapid is this process of the market digesting new information that asset prices and interest rates presumably incorporate the new data from virtually the moment they appear. As we saw in Chapter 3, in a perfectly efficient market, it is impossible to win excess returns consistently by trading on publicly available information.

This expectations theory assumes that businesses and individuals are *rational agents* who attempt to make optimal use of the resources at their disposal in order to maximize their returns. Moreover, a rational agent will tend to make *unbiased* forecasts of future asset prices, interest rates, and other variables. That is, he will make no systematic forecasting errors and will easily spot past patterns in forecast errors and correct them quickly.

If the money and capital markets are highly efficient in the way we have described, this implies interest rates will always be very near their equilibrium levels. Any deviation from the equilibrium interest rate dictated by demand and supply forces will be almost instantly eliminated. Security traders who hope to *consistently* earn windfall profits from correctly guessing whether interest rates are "too high" (and therefore will probably fall) or "too low" (and therefore will probably rise) are unlikely to be successful in the long term. Interest rate fluctuations around equilibrium are likely to be random and rapid. Moreover, knowledge of *past* interest rates—for example, those that prevailed yesterday or last month—will *not* be a reliable forecast of where those rates are likely to be in the future. Indeed, the rational expectations theory suggests that, in the absence of new information, the *optimal forecast* of next period's interest rate would probably be equal to the current period's interest rate because there is no particular reason for next period's interest rate to be either higher or lower than today's interest rate until new information causes market participants to revise their expectations.

Old news will *not* affect today's interest rates because those rates already have impounded the old news. Interest rates will change only if entirely *new and unexpected* information appears. For example, if the federal government announces for several weeks running that it must borrow an additional $10 billion next month, interest rates probably reacted to that information the first time it appeared. In fact, interest rates probably *increased* at that time, because many investors would view the government's additional need for credit as adding to other demands for credit in the economy and, with the supply of funds unchanged, interest rates would be expected to rise. However, if the government merely repeated that same announcement again, interest rates probably would *not* change a second time; it would be old information already reflected in today's interest rates.

Imagine a new scenario, however. The government suddenly reveals that, contrary to expectations, tax revenues are now being collected in greater amounts than first forecast and therefore no new borrowing will be needed. Interest rates probably will fall immediately as market participants are forced to revise their borrowing and lending plans to deal with a new situation. How do we know which *direction* rates will move? Clearly, the path interest rates take depends on *what market participants expected to begin with.* Thus, if market participants were expecting increased demand for credit (with supply unchanged), an unexpected announcement of reduced credit demand implies lower interest rates in the future. Similarly, a market expectation of less credit demand in the future (supply unchanged) when confronted with an unexpected announcement of higher credit demand implies that interest rates will rise.

We can illustrate the foregoing points by modifying the loanable funds theory of interest so that its demand and supply schedules reflect not just actual demand and supply but also the *expected* demand for and supply of loanable funds. For example, referring to Exhibit 5.7, suppose $D_0$ and $S_0$ reflect the *actual* supply and demand for loanable funds in the current period, while $D_F$ reflects the *actual* demand for loanable funds that will prevail in the next (future) time period. The supply of loanable funds is assumed to be the same in both time periods ($S_0 = S_F$).

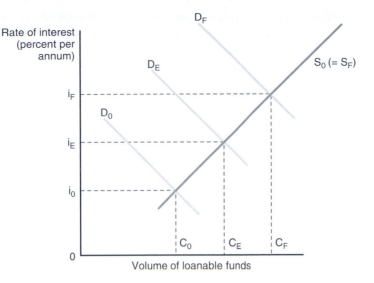

**EXHIBIT 5.7**

**Expected Demand for and Supply of Loanable Funds under the Rational Expectations Theory**

Now imagine that during the current period, the government makes an unexpected announcement of its increased need to borrow more money in future period $F$ due to an unusually large budget deficit. The result is a new expected demand for loanable funds curve $D_E$, projected to prevail in the next (future) period $F$ but as viewed by borrowers and lenders today in time period $0$. In this case, the equilibrium interest rate in the current period will not be $i_0$, but rather $i_E$, where the expected demand curve ($D_E$) intersects the actual supply curve $S_0$. The equilibrium quantity of loanable funds traded in the current period then will be $C_E$ not $C_0$. This is because, according to the rational expectations theory, borrowers and lenders will act as rational agents, using all the information they possess (including expected events, such as the government announcing it will need to borrow more money in a future period) to price assets *today*. When the future period arrives, the equilibrium interest rate will rise to rate $i_F$ and the quantity of loanable funds traded then will be $C_F$. The equilibrium rate moves upward because the demand for loanable funds in period $F$ is more than the expected future loanable funds demand as seen by market participants in period $0$.

Suppose, on the other hand, that actual loanable funds demand in period $F$ moves upward and beyond $D_0$ but by a smaller amount than was anticipated by investors in the market in period $0$. Demand schedule $D_F$ would then fall somewhere between $D_0$ and $D_E$. The equilibrium interest rate (with the supply curve unchanged) would be *lower* than $i_E$, lying somewhere between $i_0$ and $i_E$.

But this is a startling conclusion! Actual demand *increased* (above $D_0$, but not to $D_E$) in the next period with supply held constant. Still, the equilibrium interest rate *fell*! How could this be? Clearly, it makes sense only when we assume that the real world works the way the rational expectations theory says it should. *To know which way interest rates will go, we must know what the market expects to begin with.* In this example, demand for loanable funds rose but not as high as the market expected. Therefore, interest rates will *decline*, other factors held constant.

The rational expectations view argues that forecasting interest rates requires knowledge of the public's *current set of expectations*. If new information is sufficient to alter those expectations, interest rates and asset prices *must* change. If correct, this portion of the rational expectations theory creates significant problems for government policymakers. It implies that policymakers cannot cause interest rates to move in any particular direction without knowing what the public already expects to happen and, indeed, cannot change interest rates and asset prices at all unless government officials can convince the public that a new set of expectations is warranted. Moreover, because guessing what the public's expectations are is treacherous at best, rational expectations theorists suggest that *rate hedging*—using various tools to reduce the risk of loss from changing interest rates—*is preferable to rate forecasting*. Indeed, to be a consistently correct forecaster under the rational expectations theory you must know (1) what market participants expect to happen and (2) what new information will arrive in the market before that information actually arrives. That's a tall order!

A growing number of studies today imply that at least some elements of the rational expectations/efficient markets view *do* show up in actual market behavior. For example, studies by Mishkin [6] and others find that past interest-rate movements are *not* significantly related to current rates of return on bonds or stock—validating at least one of the theory's predictions. Other studies [7] have found that past information on economic conditions and money supply movements also appears to bear little correlation to today's interest rate levels or to observed changes in current interest rates. However, *unanticipated* growth in the money supply, income, and the price level *do* appear to be correlated with some bond and stock returns, especially with short-term interest rates. Moreover, adjustments in interest rates and asset prices to *new* information appear to be very rapid.

Nevertheless, the rational expectations view is still in the development stage. One key problem is that we do not know very much about how the public forms its expectations—what data are used, what weights are applied to individual bits of data, and how fast people learn from their mistakes. Moreover, several characteristics of real-world markets seem at odds with the assumptions of the expectations theory. For example, the cost of gathering and analyzing information relevant to the pricing of assets is not always negligible, as assumed by the theory, tempting many lenders and borrowers to form their expectations by rules of thumb (trading rules) that are *not* fully rational. Although rationally formed expectations appear to exist in large auction markets (such as the markets for government securities or for listed common stock), it is not clear that such is the case for other financial markets, such as those for consumer loans. Thus, not all interest rates and security prices appear to display the kind of behavior implied by the rational expectations theory.

## QUESTIONS TO HELP YOU STUDY

17. Can you explain what is meant by *rational expectations*?

18. What, then, is the *rational expectations theory of interest rates*? How does it differ from the other interest-rate determination theories, discussed in this chapter?

19. What *assumptions* underlie the rational expectations view of interest?

20. What are the implications of the rational expectations theory for those who try to *forecast* changes in market rates of interest? Based on this view of interest rates what would you recommend to interest-rate forecasters?

# Summary of the Chapter's Main Points

This important chapter focuses on the leading ideas today of what determines the level of and changes in market interest rates and asset prices. Its specific target is the *pure* or *risk-free rate of interest* (such as the interest rate attached to a government bond). Each theory of interest attempts to account for changes we see every day in this pure or risk-free market interest rate.

- The chapter explores the critical roles played by interest rates in the functioning of the money and capital markets and the economy. These fundamental interest rate roles include: (a) generating an adequate volume of savings in order to fund investment and growth in the economy; (b) directing the flow of credit in the economy toward those investment projects carrying the highest expected returns; (c) bringing the supply of money (cash balances) into alignment with the demand for money; and (d) serving as a tool of government economic policy so that the nation can better achieve its broad economic goals of full employment and avoidance of inflation.

- The *classical theory* of interest rates emphasizes the roles of savings and investment demand in determining market rates. The supply of savings is assumed to be positively related to the market interest rate, while the demand for investment is negatively related to the level of interest rates. The equilibrium interest rate in this interest rate model is established at the point where the supply of savings and investment demand are in balance with each other.

- The *liquidity preference theory of interest* looks at the demand and supply for money (cash balances), fixing the equilibrium interest rate in the money market at the point where the quantity of money in supply matches the demand for money. Demand for money consists of demands for cash balances for transactions purposes, precautionary savings, and speculation about the future course of interest rates and asset prices. The supply of money is heavily influenced by actions of the government, principally the central bank.

- The popular *loanable funds theory of interest* brings together elements of *both* the classical and liquidity preference theories, focusing upon the demand for credit (loanable funds) and the supply of credit (loanable funds). The aggregate demand for loanable funds includes credit demands from *all* sectors of the economy—businesses, consumers, and governments. The aggregate supply of loanable funds includes domestic and foreign savings, the creation of money by the banking system, and the hoarding or dishoarding of cash balances by the public. The equilibrium loanable funds interest rate tends to settle at the point where total demand for credit matches total credit supply.

- The *rational expectations theory of interest* focuses on the *expected* supply of credit relative to the *expected* demand for credit. This view of interest rates and asset prices assumes the money and capital markets are highly efficient in the use of information in determining the public's expectations regarding future changes in interest rates and asset prices. Interest rates and asset prices incorporate all relevant information quickly and change only when relevant *new* information appears. Forecasting market interest rates is presumed to be virtually impossible on a consistent basis because forecasters must know what new information is likely to arrive before that information appears and must assess how that new information will influence interest rates and asset prices when it does arrive.

- Collectively, the different views discussed in this chapter help guide us toward those fundamental forces that shape the level of and changes in market rates of interest, as well as the prices of assets. These include such critical forces as domestic and foreign savings, the demand for investment, the money supply, the demand for cash balances, and government economic policy (including the workings of central banks around the world). This chapter sets the stage for future chapters in Part Two of this text, where we attempt to discover what factors cause one interest rate to differ from another (including inflation, the term or length of a loan, credit or default risk, and several other important causal elements).

## Key Terms Appearing in This Chapter

rate of interest, 119
price of credit, 119
risk-free rate of interest, 120
classical theory of interest
    rates, 120
wealth effect, 121
substitution effect, 121

liquidity preference theory of interest
    rates, 126
loanable funds theory of interest
    rates, 132
income effect, 133
rational expectations theory of interest
    rates, 137

## Problems and Issues

1. The economy moves through business cycles, with periodic *expansions,* when economic activity is higher than average, and economic slowdowns, which, if severe enough, can lead to a *recession.* During expansion periods the volume of loanable funds available from the financial system tends to increase and real interest rates tend to rise. With this information in mind, explain the following:

    **a.** Why does the *demand* for loanable funds tend to increase during expansions?

    **b.** Why does the *supply* of loanable funds tend to increase during expansions?

    **c.** Does the supply of loanable funds tend to increase by *more* or *less* than the demand for loanable funds during economic expansions? How do you know?

2. Construct a supply of savings schedule (with all schedules and axes correctly labeled) that illustrates the *income effect.* Do the same to illustrate the *wealth* and *substitution effects.* Explain the differences you observe.

3. Suppose the going market rate of interest on high-quality corporate bonds is 12 percent. FORTRAN Corporation is considering an investment project that will last 10 years and requires an initial cash outlay of $1.5 million but will generate estimated revenues of $500,000 per year for 10 years. Would you recommend that this project be adopted? Explain why.

4. The statements listed below were gathered from recent issues of financial news sheets. Read each statement carefully and then (*a*) identify which theory or theories of interest rate determination are implicit in each statement and (*b*) indicate which *direction* interest rates should move if the statement is a correct analysis of the current market situation. Use appropriate supply-demand diagrams, where possible, to show the reasoning behind your answers to part (*b*).

   a. The factor which is likely to dominate interest rate changes in the weeks ahead is a tighter credit policy at the Federal Reserve.

   b. The White House unexpectedly disclosed today that budget negotiations with Capitol Hill have broken down. Market analysts are fearful of the effects on the bond and stock markets when trading begins tomorrow morning.

   c. Corporate profits have declined significantly in the quarter just concluded, following a year of substantial growth. Financial experts expect this negative trend to continue for at least the next six months.

   d. Personal consumption expenditures are rising rapidly, fueled by an unprecedented level of borrowing. Personal savings are up in real dollar terms, but the national savings rate dropped significantly this past year and further declines are expected. Economists believe this recent change in the savings rate explains the current trend in interest rates.

5. Suppose that total savings and business investment demand in the economy behave as shown in the table that follows (dollars are in billions):

| Total Investment Demand for Funds | Volume of Total Savings Expected | Alternative Market Interest Rates |
|---|---|---|
| $170 | $ 80 | 5% |
| 155 | 96 | 6 |
| 142 | 103 | 7 |
| 135 | 135 | 8 |
| 128 | 178 | 9 |
| 111 | 207 | 10 |
| 92 | 249 | 11 |
| 86 | 285 | 12 |

   According to the classical theory of interest, what equilibrium interest rate will prevail given the above schedules of planned saving and investment? What could cause the equilibrium rate to change?

6. Suppose the total demand for money is described by the following equation:
$$MD = 30 - 2i$$

   where *i* is the prevailing market interest rate. The total supply of money is described by the following equation:
$$MS = 3 + 7i$$

   According to liquidity preference, what is the equilibrium interest rate?

7. A firm is considering the adoption of a project that is expected to generate revenues for 10 years. These expected revenues (in dollars) are:

| Year 1: $200,000 | Year 6: $270,000 |
|---|---|
| Year 2:  250,000 | Year 7:  255,000 |
| Year 3:  300,000 | Year 8:  240,000 |
| Year 4:  300,000 | Year 9:  150,000 |
| Year 5:  280,000 | Year 10:  75,000 |

The total cost of the project, to be paid immediately upon adoption, is $1.6 million. Use a spreadsheet to compute the net present value of the project if:

   **a.** The firm's cost of capital is 6 percent. Should the project be adopted?

   **b.** The firm's cost of capital is 8 percent. Should the project be adopted?

   Suppose the firm has a second project that requires an initial outlay of $800,000 and is expected to generate revenues for only five years, and those revenues are of the same amounts as given above for years 1 to 5. Use the same spreadsheet to compute the net present value of this project if:

   **c.** The firm's cost of capital is 6 percent. Is this project one that the firm would like to adopt?

   If these are the only two projects that the firm is contemplating, what should the firm do if:

   **d.** Its capital budget is $1 million and its cost of capital is 6 percent?

   **e.** Its capital budget is $3 million and its cost of capital is 6 percent?

## Web-Based Problems

1. Why do explanations of interest rate movements differ among investment professionals? Examine at least two of the most popular accounts of daily interest rate changes. (Examples include **cnnfn.com** and **bondsonline.com.**) How does each source explain the most recent movements in market rates? Why are there differences among "experts" about why interest rates are changing?

2. Financial institutions are the principal source of loanable funds in the U.S. economy, with commercial banks accounting for the single largest share of credit (loanable funds) creation in the financial system. This exercise asks you to examine the amount of credit contributed to the economy by all commercial banks.

   Go to the Web site of the Federal Reserve: **www.federalreserve.gov** and click on the listing on their home page, "All Statistical Releases." Locate the current H.8 Release entitled: "Assets and Liabilities of Commercial Banks in the U.S." The first page of this release is the consolidated balance sheet for U.S. banks. Identify the amount of credit (loanable funds) created in the most recent year, referred to as "Bank Credit." How much credit is being created by U.S. banks on a per capita basis? (It is easy to find the total U.S. population on the Internet.) What percentage of these banks' total assets is represented by bank credit? What are the major uses of this credit by bank borrowers?

3. One source of credit in any economy is money created by the central bank. This credit is often referred to as the "monetary base" or "outside money," referring to the fact it is created outside the private financial system. This exercise asks you to compare the amount of credit created as outside money by two of the world's leading central banks: the Federal Reserve and the Bank of England in the United Kingdom.

Go to the each of the central bank Web sites: **www.federalreserve.gov** and **www.bankofengland.co.uk** and find the values of the monetary base. For the United States this can be found in the H.3 Statistical Release. For the U.K. go to:

**http://www.bankofengland.co.uk/statistics/ms/current/index.htm#a**

and look under Table A1.1.1, page 2. The monetary base is the sum of "Notes and coin in circulation outside the Bank of England" and "Reserve balances." Convert this sum to U.S. dollars using the current dollar/pound exchange rate (which is easily found on the Internet). Other information that you will need includes: (i) The gross domestic product (GDP) of the U.S. and U.K. (convert the British GDP into dollars), and (ii) The population of the U.S. and U.K. (This information is very easy to find on the Internet.)

To compare how much outside money is being provided in the two countries, you need to compare the numbers with respect to the size of these two economies. First, simply divide the outside money in dollars by population to determine the per capita amount in circulation. Which is larger? A second useful comparison is to construct a measure called *velocity* which is GDP divided by the monetary base. This gives some sense of how many times each dollar of outside money (on average) turns over through expenditures on goods and services in a year's time.

Find the velocity of the monetary base for both the U.S. and U.K. Which is larger? Is this consistent with the per capita supplies of outside money in the two countries? Could the fact that a larger portion of U.S. currency is held overseas versus U.K. currency held outside of the U.K. help to account for these differences? Please explain.

## Selected References to Explore

1. Dynan, Karen E., and Dean M. Maki. "Does Stock Market Wealth Matter for Consumption?" *Financial and Economic Discussion Series* 2001–23, Board of Governors of the Federal Reserve System, 2001.

2. Fisher, Irving. *The Theory of Interest,* New York: Macmillan, 1930.

3. Guo, Hui. "A Rational Pricing Explanation for the Failure of the CAPM," *Review,* Federal Reserve Bank of St. Louis, May/June 2004, pp. 23–33.

4. Keynes, John M. *The General Theory of Employment, Interest and Money,* New York: Harcourt Brace Jovanovich, 1936.

5. Marquis, Milt. "What's Behind the Low U.S. Personal Saving Rate?" *FRBSF Economic Letter,* Federal Reserve Bank of San Francisco, March 2002, pp. 1–3.
6. Mishkin, Frederick. "Efficient-Markets Theory: Implications for Monetary Policy," *Brookings Paper on Economic Activity 3* (1978), pp. 707–52.
7. Rozeff, Michael S. "Money and Stock Prices: Market Efficiency and the Lag in Effect of Monetary Policy," *Journal of Financial Economics* 1 (September 1974), pp. 245–302.
8. Sierminska, Eva, and Yelena Takhtamanova. "Disentangling the Wealth Effect: Some International Evidence," *FRBSF Economic Letter,* Federal Reserve Bank of San Francisco, January 19, 2007.

# Chapter 6

# Measuring and Calculating Interest Rates and Financial Asset Prices

## What's in This Chapter?
## Key Topics Outline

**Measures of Interest Rates on Wholesale Money Market Assets**

**Measures of Interest Rates and Prices on Stocks and Bonds**

**The Yield to Maturity and Holding-Period Yields**

**The Relationship between Interest Rates and Asset Prices**

**Interest Rates Quoted by Institutional Lenders: Simple Interest, Add-on Rate, Discount Method, the APR**

**Home Mortgage Loan Rates**

**Compounding Interest**

**The APY on Deposits**

## Learning Objectives

## in This Chapter

- You will learn how money market interest rates are determined, and how those interest rates are used by dealers when trading money market assets.

- You will explore the important relationships between the interest rates on bonds and other financial instruments and their market value or price.

- You will be introduced to the many different ways lending institutions may calculate the interest rates they charge borrowers for loans.

- You will be able to determine how interest rates or yields on deposits in banks, credit unions, and other depository institutions are figured.

## 6.1   Introduction to Interest Rates and Asset Prices

In the preceding chapter we discussed several theories regarding what determines the rate of interest. While these theories help us understand the forces that cause market interest rates to change over time, they provide little or no information about how interest rates should be *measured* in the real world. As a result, many different interest-rate measures have been developed for the different types of financial assets, leading to considerable confusion, especially for small borrowers and savers. In this chapter, we examine the methods most frequently used to measure interest rates and the prices of financial assets in the money and capital markets. We also take up the relationship between the prices of financial assets and market interest rates and how they impact each other.

## 6.2   Units of Measurement for Interest Rates

### Calculating and Quoting Interest Rates

**interest rate**

The **interest rate** is the price charged a borrower for the loan of money. This price is unique because it is really a *ratio* of two quantities: the total required fee a borrower must pay a lender to obtain the use of credit for a stipulated time period divided by the total amount of credit made available to the borrower. By convention, the interest rate is usually expressed in *percent per annum.* Thus,

$$\begin{array}{c}\text{Annual} \\ \text{rate of} \\ \text{interest on} \\ \text{loanable} \\ \text{funds (in} \\ \text{percent)}\end{array} = \dfrac{\begin{array}{c}\text{Fee required by the} \\ \text{lender for the} \\ \text{borrower to obtain credit}\end{array}}{\begin{array}{c}\text{Amount of credit made} \\ \text{available to the} \\ \text{borrower}\end{array}} \times 100 \qquad (6.1)$$

For example, an interest rate of 10 percent per annum on a $1,000, one-year loan to purchase a computer implies that the lender of funds has received a borrower's promise to pay a fee of $100 (10 percent of $1,000) in return for the use of $1,000 in credit for a year. The promised fee of $100 is in addition to the repayment of the loan principal ($1,000), which must occur sometime during the year.

Interest rates are usually expressed as *annualized percentages,* even for financial assets with maturities shorter than a year. For example, in the federal funds market, banks frequently loan reserves to each other overnight, with the loan being repaid the next day. Even in this market the interest rate quoted daily by lenders is expressed in percent per annum, as though the loan were for a year's time. However, various types of loans and securities display important differences in how interest fees and amounts borrowed are valued or accounted for, leading to several different methods for determining interest rates. Some interest rate measures use a 360-day year, while others use a 365-day year. Some employ compound rates of return, with interest income earned on accumulated interest, and some do not use compounding.

### Basis Points

Interest rates on securities traded in the open market rarely are quoted in whole percentage points, such as 5 percent or 8 percent. The typical case is a rate expressed in hundredths of a percent: for example, 5.36 percent or 7.62 percent. Moreover, most interest rates change by only fractions of a whole percentage point in a single day or

**basis point**

week. To deal with this situation, the concept of the basis point was developed. A **basis point** equals 1/100 of a percentage point. Thus, an interest rate of 10.5 percent may be expressed as 10 percent plus 50 basis points, or 1,050 basis points. Similarly, an increase in a loan or security rate from 5.25 percent to 5.30 percent represents an increase of 5 basis points.

## 6.3   Interest Rates in the Wholesale Money Markets

There is a vast array of financial markets where large sums of money are lent for short periods of time, say, up to one year. The markets in which these funds are traded are referred to as wholesale money markets. The details of these important financial markets—including what economic functions they perform, who the participants are, and why there are so many of them—will be described in Chapters 10 and 11. What we wish to discuss in this chapter is how interest rates are computed on these assets and how they are reported in the financial news.

### Computing Interest Rates on Money Market Assets That Are Sold at a Discount

Most money market assets are short-term assets on which the investor receives no income until the asset matures. The amount that the investor receives upon maturity is referred to as the asset's *par value* or *face value*. For example, one such asset is a 3-month (90-day) U.S. Treasury bill (T-bill) with a par value of $100,000. The price the investor pays for this asset will obviously be less than par value, or $100,000 in the example; otherwise the investor will not receive any return on his or her investment. This asset is therefore said to be *sold at a discount* to its par value.

**investment rate**

But how much is the investor willing to pay for this claim against the U.S. Government that he or she will be able to redeem in 90 days? The answer depends in large part on the rate of return the investor demands. On the street, this rate of return is often referred to as the *coupon-equivalent, bond-equivalent,* or **investment rate** of return, and is often designated IR. To compute the IR, three pieces of information are required. Two of them are provided by the issuer, or the U.S. Government in this example: the Par value and the number of Days to maturity. The third piece of information is the Purchase price, or how much the investor has invested. The formula then computes the actual rate of return for the investor, and then annualizes the return, as if the investment lasted one full year, or 365 days.

$$\text{IR} = \frac{(\text{Par value} - \text{Purchase price})}{\text{Purchase price}} \times \frac{365}{\text{Days to maturity}} \qquad (6.2)$$

Suppose that you are the investor and decide to purchase this Treasury bill for $99,000 and hold it until maturity. The annualized interest rate you would receive on this investment is:

$$\text{IR} = \frac{100,000 - 99,000}{99,000} \times \frac{365}{90} = 0.0410 \text{ or } 4.10\%$$

**bank discount rate**

If you were working as a dealer in the money markets and wished to purchase this T-bill, you would not be quoted a purchase price, but rather an interest rate. That interest rate is referred to as the **bank discount rate,** or simply the *discount rate,* denoted DR. The DR is *not* the *actual* annualized rate of return on the investment. It is used only for trading purposes and is usually easier to compute than the IR. The formula for the bank discount rate is:

$$DR = \frac{(\text{Par value} - \text{Purchase price})}{\text{Par value}} \times \frac{360}{\text{Days to maturity}} \quad \textbf{(6.3)}$$

Note that there are two differences between formulas (6.2) and (6.3). Rather than using the actual amount invested, or the purchase price, as the *investment base* in computing the DR, the par value is used. This simplifies the calculations because the par value is usually in round numbers, such as $100,000 in the example. The second simplification is to compute the DR on the basis of a 360-day year.

In the example, the DR that corresponds to IR of 4.10 percent is:

$$DR = \frac{100,000 - 99,000}{100,000} \times \frac{360}{90} = 0.040 \text{ or } 4.00\%$$

Notice that the DR is less than the IR. This is *always* the case. One reason is that the DR calculation uses a 360-day year, which reduces the numerator in the calculation. The second reason is that the investment base used in calculating the DR is *more than* the actual amount of the investment which is used in calculating the IR, while the actual interest earned, or the Par value − Purchase price, is the same in both calculations.

## *Holding-Period Yield on Money Market Assets Sold at a Discount*

An important feature of financial assets sold at a discount is that their price tends to rise over time and is exactly equal to par value upon maturity. However, the asset price will not rise in a steady, uniform manner, but will be influenced by continuous changes in market interest rates that take place throughout the day. This phenomenon is important to investors who may choose, in our example, to sell the T-bill before it matures. What is the annualized rate of return that investor would receive on this investment? This rate of return is referred to as the *holding-period yield,* and can be simply computed for assets sold at a discount by using the DR formula:

$$\begin{matrix} \text{Holding-Period yield on} \\ \text{assets sold at a discount} \end{matrix} = \text{DR when purchased} \pm \begin{matrix} \text{Change in DR over} \\ \text{the holding period} \end{matrix} \quad \textbf{(6.4)}$$

where:

$$\begin{matrix} \text{Change in DR over} \\ \text{the holding period} \end{matrix} = \frac{\begin{matrix}(\text{Days to maturity when} \\ \text{purchased} - \text{Days held})\end{matrix}}{\text{Days held}} \times \begin{matrix} \text{Difference in DR on date} \\ \text{purchased and date sold} \end{matrix} \quad \textbf{(6.5)}$$

In our example, suppose the investor sold the T-bill after 30 days for a price of $99,500. Formula (6.3) indicates the DR on the date the T-bill is sold is 3.00 percent. Then, the holding-period yield for the investor is:

$$\text{Holding-Period yield} = 4.00\% + \frac{90 - 30}{30} \times (4.00\% - 3.00\%) = 6.00\%$$

In this case, the decline in interest rates (reflected in the fall in the discount rate) caused the investor's rate of return on her investment during these 30 days to be higher than she had expected when the T-bill was first purchased. What would happen to the DR and the holding-period yield if the investor was only able to sell the T-bill for

| EXHIBIT 6.1 | Interest Rate Quotations on U.S. Treasury Bills | | | | |
|---|---|---|---|---|---|
| Maturity Date | Days to Maturity | Bid Rate (DR) | Ask Rate (DR) | Change in Ask Rate | Ask Yield (IR) |
| Nov 30 06 | 85 | 4.86 | 4.85 | −0.03 | 4.97 |
| Mar 01 07 | 176 | 4.92 | 4.91 | 0.01 | 5.10 |

Source: *The Wall Street Journal,* September 6, 2006.

$99,250 after 30 days, in which case she would have earned only $250 rather than $500 in interest income? Verify that the investor's holding-period yield would only have been 3 percent.

## Interest Rate Quotations on U.S. Treasury Bills

U.S. Treasury bills (T-bills) are money market assets that may have maturities upon issue of four weeks, three months, or six months. The information that concerns potential investors or owners of T-bills is the maturity date, the investment rate (IR), and the discount rates at which a T-bill may be bought or sold. Investors may also wish to know what happened to the value of the asset over the course of one trading day. All of this information is usually contained in the daily report of trading activity in the financial news. An example of this information is given in Exhibit 6.1.

This exhibit depicts the information on two U.S. T-bills that are being traded in the market. One has approximately 3 months to maturity and the other approximately 6 months to maturity. The *Bid Rate* and *Ask Rate* are the discount rates quoted by dealers who manage portfolios of T-bills. The Bid Rate is the discount rate that the dealer requires if he is to purchase the T-bill and add it to his portfolio, and the Ask Rate is the discount rate an investor would lock in (assuming he held the T-bill to maturity) if he purchased the T-bill from a dealer. Note that the Ask Rate is less than the Bid Rate. The difference between them, or the *Bid-Ask Spread*, represents the margin that enables a dealer to make a profit by creating this market. The *Ask Yield* is the investment rate (IR) that corresponds to the Ask Rate (DR). Note that the Ask Yield is higher than the Ask Rate. The Ask Yield represents the actual rate of return that the investor would receive if he bought the asset from the dealer and held it until maturity.

### QUESTIONS TO HELP YOU STUDY

1. Interest rates are often called the most important "price" within the financial markets. Why do you think this is so?

2. What is different about interest rates, or the *price of credit*, from other prices in the economy?

3. What exactly is a *basis point*? Why is it an important interest rate measure?

4. What is meant by the *par value* of an asset, and what does it mean when an asset is said to be sold *at a discount* to its par value?

5. What is the difference between an *investment rate* and a *bank discount rate*? As an investor in a money market asset, which one represents your actual rate of return on your investment?

6. What is the difference between the *bid rate* and the *ask rate*? Which one should always be higher? Why?

7. How does the *holding-period yield* differ from the *ask yield*?

## 6.4 Interest Rates on Bonds and Other Long-Term Debt Securities

Many financial assets are debt securities that have maturities exceeding one year and that obligate the issuer to make future payments to the asset holder. Unlike money market assets that are sold at a discount, most debt securities, such as U.S. Treasury notes or corporate bonds, represent a stream of future payments rather than a single lump-sum payment received upon maturity. Both the promised amount of those payments and the promised dates on which they are to be made are usually specified when the debt security is issued and do not vary over the life of the asset. Therefore, an investor must decide how much she is willing to pay for the entire stream of payments, while recognizing there is some risk borrowers may default on some or all of the promised payments.

### Yield to Maturity (YTM)

**yield to maturity (YTM)**

We begin with a concept that should become second nature to every investor: **yield to maturity (YTM).** As the name implies, the yield to maturity represents the rate of return an investor would receive if she bought the asset and chose to hold—not sell—the asset for its entire life. Even if the investor does not plan to hold the asset until it matures, its YTM is still extremely important. It represents the rate of interest the market is prepared to pay for a financial asset in order to exchange present dollars for future dollars—and this rate changes continuously with market conditions. Therefore, the yield to maturity establishes the market value of the asset that will determine how much an investor can sell the asset for should she decide to sell before maturity.

The stream of payments associated with a bond normally consists of a number of identical periodic coupon payments plus the par value of the bond received at maturity. A newly issued bond will typically have the following information stipulated: the par value (M), the dates of the coupon payments, and the **coupon rate.** The coupon rate is used to determine the amount of the annual interest income received by the investor in the form of coupon payments (C).

**coupon rate**

$$\text{Coupon} = \text{Coupon rate} \times \text{Par value} \qquad (6.6)$$

The market price of the bond (P) is then given by the present value of the stream of coupon payments and the par value.

$$P = \frac{C}{(1 + y)^1} + \frac{C}{(1 + y)^2} + \frac{C}{(1 + y)^3} + \cdots + \frac{C}{(1 + y)^n} + \frac{M}{(1 + y)^n} \quad (6.7)$$

where $y$ is the yield to maturity and $n$ is the number of periods (usually several years).

Formula (6.7) can be used to price a bond or any debt security with constant annual payments to the investor over the life of the asset. In this case, $y$ is the *annualized yield to maturity.*

What about financial instruments that make periodic payments to the investor more frequently than once a year? For example, most bonds pay interest semiannually, and other financial instruments may pay out quarterly or monthly. In this instance the bond-price, or yield-to-maturity, formula (6.7) needs to be modified to include the parameter $k$—a measure of the number of times during the year that interest income is paid to the holder of the asset. The asset price is then given by:

$$P = \frac{C/k}{(1 + y/k)^1} + \frac{C/k}{(1 + y/k)^2} + \frac{C/k}{(1 + y/k)^3} + \cdots + \frac{C/k}{(1 + y/k)^{nk}} + \frac{M}{(1 + y/k)^{nk}} \quad (6.8)$$

Suppose we have a 20-year government bond paying \$50 interest twice each year, then $k$ must equal 2 and there would be 40 periods ($n \times k = 20 \times 2$) in which the investor would expect to receive \$50 in interest income. As the above formula shows, we would have to divide the annualized yield to maturity ($y$) by $k$ and discount the expected payments over $n \times k$, rather than $n$, time periods.

To illustrate the use of this formula, assume an investor is considering the purchase of a bond due to mature in 20 years (with 40 semiannual interest-crediting periods) and carrying a 10 percent annual coupon rate, or 5 percent every six months. This asset is available for purchase at a current market price of \$850. If the bond has a par value of \$1,000, which will be paid to the investor when the asset reaches maturity, the bond's yield to maturity may be found by solving the equation:

$$\$850 = \frac{\$50}{(1 + y/2)^1} + \frac{\$50}{(1 + y/2)^2} + \cdots$$
$$+ \frac{\$50}{(1 + y/2)^{40}} + \frac{\$1,000}{(1 + y/2)^{40}} \quad (6.9)$$

In this instance, $y$ is close to 12 percent—a rate higher than its 10 percent annual coupon rate because the bond is currently selling at a *discount* from par.

Suppose this same \$1,000, 10 percent annual coupon bond were selling at a *premium* over par. For example, if this 20-year debt instrument has a current market price of \$1,200 and pays interest twice each year its yield to maturity could be found from the following equation:

$$\$1,200 = \frac{\$50}{(1 + y/2)^1} + \cdots + \frac{\$50}{(1 + y/2)^{40}} + \frac{\$1,000}{(1 + y/2)^{40}} \quad (6.10)$$

In this case, $y$ equals almost 8 percent. Because the investor must pay a higher current market price than par value (the amount the investor will receive back when the bond matures) this bond's yield to maturity must be *less* than its coupon rate.

**Key URL:**
To calculate yield to maturity and other yield measures on bonds and other financial instruments see, for example, **investopedia.com/ calculator**

From these two examples, we can answer the following question: How does the yield to maturity ($y$) compare with the coupon rate ($C/M$)? If the bond price is equal to the par value of the bond, or $P = M$, the bond is said to be *selling at par*, and the coupon rate is equal to the yield to maturity, or $y = (C/M)$. However, this is rarely the case. The market price of the bond and the bond's yield to maturity change continuously with market conditions, while the par value and the coupon rate remain fixed. Whenever the bond is *selling below par*, or $P < M$, the yield to maturity must have risen above the coupon rate, or $y > (C/M)$. Conversely, whenever the bond is selling *above par*, or $P > M$, then the yield to maturity must have fallen below the coupon rate, or $y < (C/M)$.

## *Holding-Period Yield on Bonds and Other Long-Term Debt Securities*

A slight modification of the bond-pricing or yield-to-maturity formula (6.7) results in a return measure for those situations in which an investor holds a bond or long-term

**holding-period yield**

debt security for a time and then sells it to another investor in advance of the asset's maturity. This so-called **holding-period yield,** denoted $h$, solves the following equation:

$$P = \frac{C}{(1 + h)^1} + \frac{C}{(1 + h)^2} + \frac{C}{(1 + h)^3} + \cdots + \frac{C}{(1 + h)^m} + \frac{P_m}{(1 + h)^m} \quad (6.11)$$

where $C$ is the annual payment received by the investor, $P$ is the original purchase price, and $P_m$ is the selling price after $m$ periods. Therefore, the annualized holding period yield ($h$) is simply the rate of discount equalizing the market price of the debt security with all annual payments between the time the asset was purchased and it is sold (including the sale price). If the asset is held to maturity, its holding-period yield equals its yield to maturity.

If income from an asset comes in more frequently than once per year, we would have to modify formula (6.7). Suppose that payments are received by the investor $k$ times during each year of the investor's holding period. In this case, we would divide each of the expected annual payments to the investor ($C$) and the annualized holding-period yield ($h$) by $k$. In addition, the number of time periods ($m$) that make up the investor's holding period must be multiplied by $k$ in order to help us find the correct annual holding-period yield ($h$).

## Understanding the Concepts of Yield to Maturity and Holding-Period Yield

It is often helpful in understanding the concepts of yield to maturity and holding-period yield to look at an example of how we determine and interpret these two rate of return measures. Suppose, for example, that an investor is thinking about the purchase of a corporate bond, $1,000 in face or par value, with a promised annual (coupon) rate of return of 10 percent. Assume the bond pays interest of $50 every six months. Currently the bond is selling for $900. Assume that this is a five-year bond that the investor plans to hold until it matures, when it is redeemed at par by the issuer of the bond. We have

$$\$900 = \frac{\$50}{(1 + y/2)^1} + \frac{\$50}{(1 + y/2)^2} + \frac{\$50}{(1 + y/2)^3} + \cdots$$

$$+ \frac{\$50}{(1 + y/2)^9} + \frac{\$50}{(1 + y/2)^{10}} + \frac{\$1,000}{(1 + y/2)^{10}} \quad (6.12)$$

**present value**

It is useful at this point to consider what each term in equation 6.12 means. Both the yield-to-maturity and holding-period-yield formulas are based on the concept of **present value:** Funds to be received in the future are worth *less* than funds received today. Present dollars may be used to purchase and enjoy goods and services today, but future dollars are only *promises* to pay and force us to postpone consumption until the funds actually are received. Equation 6.12 indicates that a bond promising to pay $50 every six months for a five-year period in the future plus a lump sum of $1,000 at maturity is worth only $900 in present value dollars. The yield, $y/2$, serves as a rate of discount reducing each payment of future dollars back to its present value in today's market. The further into the future the payment is to be made, the larger the discount factor, $(1 + y/2)^n$, becomes.

Turning the concept around, the purchase of a financial asset in today's market represents the investment of present dollars in the expectation of a higher return in the form of future dollars. The familiar *compound interest formula* (discussed later in this chapter) applies here. This formula

$$FV = P(1 + y)^t \tag{6.13}$$

indicates that the amount of funds accumulated $t$ years from now (FV or future value) depends on the principal originally invested ($P$), the investor's expected rate of return or yield ($y$), and the number of years the principal is invested ($t$). Thus, a principal of $1,000 invested today at a 10 percent annual rate will amount to $1,100 a year from now [i.e., $1,000 × $(1 + 0.10)^1$]. Rearrangement of the compound interest formula gives

$$P = \frac{FV}{(1 + y)^t} \tag{6.14}$$

Equation 6.14 states that the present value of FV dollars to be received in the future is $P$ if the promised interest rate is $y$. If we expect to receive $1,100 one year from now and the promised interest rate is 10 percent, the present value of that $1,100 must be $1,000.

Each term on the right-hand side of the yield-to-maturity and holding-period-yield formulas is a form of equation 6.14. Solving equation 6.12 for the yield to maturity of a bond simply means finding a value for $y$ which brings both right- and left-hand sides of the yield formula into balance, equating the current price ($P$) of a financial asset with the stream of future dollars it will generate for the investor. When all expected cash flows are not the same in amount, an electronic calculator or computer software may be used to find the solution. Fortunately, in the case of the bond represented in equation 6.12, the solution is not complicated. Rewrite equation 6.12 in the following form:

$$\$900 = \$50 \left[ \frac{1}{(1 + y/2)^1} + \frac{1}{(1 + y/2)^2} + \cdots + \frac{1}{(1 + y/2)^{10}} \right]$$
$$+ \$1,000 \left[ \frac{1}{(1 + y/2)^{10}} \right] \tag{6.15}$$

This indicates the bond will pay an annuity of $1 per year (multiplied in this case by $50) for five years (10 six-month periods) plus a lump sum of $1 (multiplied here by $1,000) at the end of the fifth year. Using a programmable calculator and entering the price (present value or PV) of the instrument (which is $900 in this case), the expected periodic interest payments (PMT = $50 semiannually), and the final value or payment ($1,000 in this example) tells us that $y$, the yield-to-maturity measure, is 12.83 percent. The investor interested in maximizing return would compare this yield to maturity with the yields to maturity available on other assets of comparable risk and liquidity.

Note that if the bond in this example had been a 10-year bond, but identical in every other way, then the investor with a five-year time horizon for his or her investment would receive a holding-period yield, $h$, of precisely the same 12.83 percent annualized yield-to-maturity, *if* he or she were able to sell the bond at precisely its par value. This result can be verified by setting $P_m = \$1,000$ in equation 6.11 and solving for $h$.

### *Price Quotations on U.S. Treasury Notes and Bonds*

U.S. Treasury notes (T-notes) and U.S. Treasury bonds (T-bonds) are debt securities with original maturities ranging from 2 to 30 years. In addition to a fixed maturity,

| EXHIBIT 6.2 | Price Quotations on U.S. Treasury Notes and Bonds | | | | |
|---|---|---|---|---|---|
| Coupon Rate | Maturity (month/year) | Bid Price ($100 par) | Asked Price ($100 par) | Change in Asked Price | Asked Yield (YTM) |
| 4.875 | Aug 08n | 100:03 | 100:04 | −3 | 4.79 |
| 4.625 | Aug 11n | 99:17 | 99:18 | −6 | 4.72 |
| 4.875 | Aug 16n | 100:23 | 100:24 | −14 | 4.78 |
| 4.500 | Feb 36 | 93:09 | 93:10 | −28 | 4.93 |

Source: *The Wall Street Journal*, September 6, 2006.

most of these securities make fixed coupon payments to their owners, usually semi-annually. An investor in a T-note or T-bond needs to know not only the price and maturity date of the security, but he must also know the date on which he would receive coupon payments, and he must be able to compute the amount of those coupon payments. In addition, he needs to know the security's current yield to maturity. This information is generally provided in the financial news, reporting daily trading activity in the market. An example is given in Exhibit 6.2.

In order for investors to be able to compare Treasury securities, the price quotes are based on each $100 of par value, and they are quoted in 32nds of a dollar (100:01 = $100.0313 or 100:16 = $100.50). The coupon rate quoted is an annualized rate, despite the fact that coupons are paid semiannually. For example, a coupon rate of 2.000 would imply that the Treasury Department will pay a $1.00 coupon every 6 months for each $100 in par value until the maturity date. Dealers in T-notes and T-bonds manage portfolios of those Treasury securities and stand ready to buy the T-note or T-bond at its announced Bid Price for each $100 in par value, and stand ready to sell the Treasuries at the Asked Price for each $100 in par value. Note that the Asked Price is greater than the Bid Price, with the difference representing the profit margin the dealer receives for making the market. How much the Asked Price has changed over the course of the previous day's trading is quoted in 32nds. The Asked Yield is the yield to maturity an investor purchasing the Treasury from the dealer would receive if he bought the security and held it to maturity. Note that if the dealer is willing to sell the T-note or T-bond at less than par (below 100), then the yield to maturity is above the coupon rate. For those T-notes and T-bonds selling above par (above 100), the yield to maturity is below the coupon rate.

## Price Quotations on Corporate Bonds

Investors in corporate bonds require exactly the same information as investors in Treasury bonds, but they are also interested in how much additional return they would be promised for taking the risk that, unlike the federal government, the corporation may not honor its obligations to make coupon payments and return the principal (par value) in full on the promised date. This additional information is usually provided in the daily price quotations in the financial news. An example is given in Exhibit 6.3.

The Coupon Rate and the Last Price are both based on a par value of $100. The Last Price and Last Yield represent the price paid per $100 of par value and the yield to maturity that the purchaser of the last recorded trade of the day realized. To compute the additional risk premium the investor expects to receive the Estimated Yield Spread represents the yield to maturity on that corporate bond minus the yield to maturity on

| EXHIBIT 6.3 | | Price Quotations on Corporate Bonds | | | | | |
|---|---|---|---|---|---|---|---|
| Company | Coupon Rate | Maturity (mo/day/yr) | Last Price ($100 par) | Last Yield (YTM) | Est. Yield Spread | Comparable US Treasury (yrs to mat) | $ Volume (000s) |
| AT&T | 6.250 | Mar 15, 2011 | 102.787 | 5.544 | 83 | 5 | 52,540 |
| Bell South | 5.200 | Sep 15, 2014 | 95.411 | 5.927 | 115 | 10 | 43,596 |

Source: *The Wall Street Journal,* September 6, 2006.

a comparable U.S. Treasury security at the time the corporate bond was purchased. The numerical value is in basis points.

The Comparable U.S. Treasury column gives the number of years to maturity on the most recently issued security of that maturity class. For example, if the Comparable U.S. Treasury has a maturity of 10 years, the yield on the corporate bond would be compared with the yield on the most recently issued 10-year U.S. T-note. In this case, 10 years would represent the maturity class of U.S. Treasuries with the number of years to maturity that most closely match the number of years left until the maturity of the corporate bond. The $ Volume column indicates how much trading took place over the course of the previous trading day. Note that, just as with U.S. T-notes and T-bonds, if the corporate bond is selling above par (Last Price exceeds 100), then its yield to maturity is below the coupon rate, and if the corporate bond is selling below par, then its yield is higher than the coupon rate.

## 6.5 Interest Rates and the Prices of Debt Securities

The foregoing yield or rate of return formulas illustrate a number of important relationships between the prices of financial assets and yields or interest rates that prevail in our financial system. One of these important relationships is expressed as follows:

> The price of a financial asset (especially for a bond or other debt security) and its yield or rate of return are *inversely related*—a rise in yield implies a decline in price; conversely, a fall in yield is associated with a rise in the financial asset's price.

To reinforce this fundamental principle, we should remind ourselves that investing in financial assets can be viewed from two different perspectives—the borrowing and lending of money or the buying and selling of financial assets. As noted in Chapter 5, the equilibrium rate of interest from the lending of funds can be determined by interaction of the supply of loanable funds with the demand for loanable funds. Demanders of loanable funds (borrowers) supply financial assets in the form of debt securities to the financial marketplace, and suppliers of loanable funds (lenders) demand debt securities and other financial instruments as an investment that will generate future income. Therefore, the equilibrium rate of return or yield on a debt security or similar financial instrument and its equilibrium price are determined at one and the same instant. In fact, they are simply different aspects of the same phenomenon—the borrowing and lending of loanable funds.

This point is depicted in Exhibit 6.4, which shows demand and supply curves for both the rate of interest (yield) and the price of financial assets (such as the price of bonds or similar financial instruments evidencing a loan of money). The supply of loanable funds curve (representing lending) in the interest rate diagram (Exhibit 6.4A) is analogous to the demand for financial assets curve (also representing lending) in the

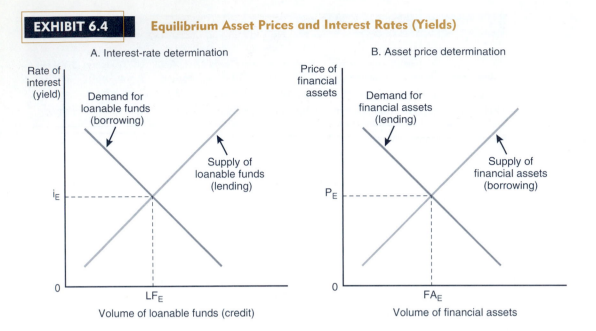

**EXHIBIT 6.4**        Equilibrium Asset Prices and Interest Rates (Yields)

A. Interest-rate determination

B. Asset price determination

price of financial assets diagram (Exhibit 6.4B). Similarly, the demand for loanable funds curve (representing borrowing) in the interest rate diagram (Exhibit 6.4A) is analogous to the supply of financial assets (also representing borrowing) in the price of financial assets diagram (Exhibit 6.4B).

We note that in Exhibit 6.4B borrowers are inclined to issue a larger volume of financial assets (such as bonds and other debt securities) at higher asset prices, while lenders are inclined to demand more financial assets at lower prices. In Exhibit 6.4A, on the other hand, borrowers are inclined to demand a smaller quantity of loanable funds at higher interest rates, while lenders are inclined to supply fewer loanable funds at lower interest rates. The *equilibrium interest rate* (or yield) in Exhibit 6.4A is determined at point $i_E$, where the demand for loanable funds equals the supply of loanable funds. Similarly, in Exhibit 6.4B, the equilibrium price for financial assets lies at point $P_E$, where the demand for and supply of financial assets are equal. Only at the equilibrium interest rate and equilibrium asset price will *both* borrowers and lenders be content with the volume of lending and borrowing taking place within the financial system.

The *inverse* relationship between interest rates and financial-asset prices can be seen even more clearly when we allow the demand and supply curves depicted in Exhibit 6.4 to move. This movement is illustrated in Exhibit 6.5. For example, suppose that, in the face of continuing inflation, business firms and households accelerate their borrowings, increasing the demand for loanable funds. As shown in the upper left-hand portion of Exhibit 6.5, the demand for loanable funds curve slides upward and to the right with the supply of loanable funds curve unchanged. This increasing demand for loanable funds also means that the supply of financial assets (principally in the form of bonds and other debt securities) must expand, as shown in the upper right-hand portion of Exhibit 6.5 by a shift in the supply curve from $S$ to $S'$. Both a new *lower* equilibrium price for financial assets and a *higher* equilibrium interest rate for loanable funds result.

| EXHIBIT 6.5 | **Effects of Changing Supply and Demand on Asset Rates (Yields) and Prices** |

A. Effects of an increase in the demand for loanable funds (credit): higher interest rates and lower asset prices

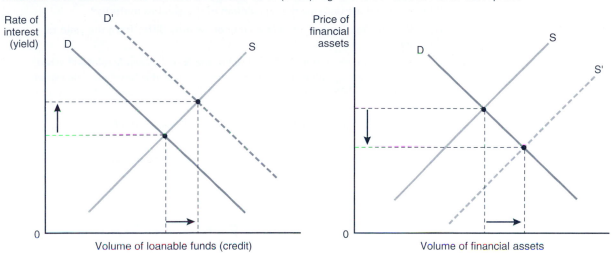

B. Effects of an increase in the supply of loanable funds (credit): lower interest rates and higher asset prices

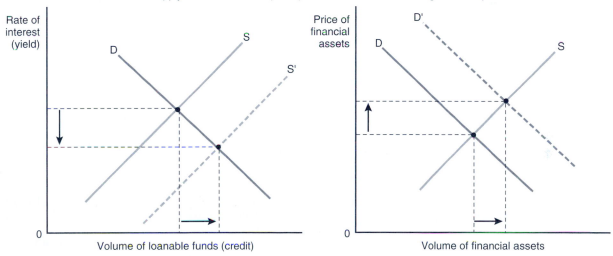

Conversely, suppose businesses and households decide to save more, expanding the supply of loanable funds. As shown in the lower left-hand portion of Exhibit 6.5, the supply of loanable funds curve slides downward and to the right from $S$ to $S'$. But with more savings available, the demand for financial assets curve must rise, as businesses and households look for more financial assets to buy as investments with their savings. Therefore, as shown in the lower right-hand portion of Exhibit 6.5, the asset demand curve slides upward and to the right, from $D$ to $D'$. The result is a *rise* in the equilibrium price of financial assets (especially the prices of debt securities) and a *decline* in the equilibrium interest rate.

**QUESTIONS TO HELP YOU STUDY**

8. Explain the meaning of the interest rate measure known as the *yield to maturity*.
9. What assumptions underlie the calculation of the yield to maturity?
10. How does the *holding-period yield* on a debt security differ from the yield to maturity?
11. Carefully explain why bond yields and bond prices are *inversely* related? What does this relationship tell you about the market value of a bond on a day when interest rates rise? Would you want to be managing a portfolio of bonds on that day? Why or why not?
12. When dealing in bonds, what are the differences between the *bid price*, the *ask price*, the *coupon rate*, and the *ask yield*?
13. What is meant by the statement that a bond is selling *above par*? *Below par*?

## 6.6    Rates of Return on a Perpetual Financial Instrument

Unlike the short-term money market assets and the longer-term debt securities we have discussed so far in this chapter, there are some financial assets that never mature and are referred to as *perpetual financial instruments*. These assets may be either fixed-income securities, which promise to make periodic payments of a known amount on preassigned dates, or variable-return assets, such as corporate stock, where future payments such as dividends may change over time.

### The Rate of Return on Fixed-Income Perpetuities

One example of a fixed-income perpetual financial instrument is the British *consol*—a perpetual bond issued by the British government that promises its holder a fixed coupon payment every year *ad infinitum*. The annual rate of return on this bond is known as a **perpetuity rate** and is simply computed as:

**perpetuity rate**

$$\frac{\text{Annual rate of return}}{\text{on a perpetual bond}} = \frac{\text{Annual cash flow promised}}{\text{Current price or present value}} \tag{6.16}$$

For example, if this bond promises interest payments of \$100 per year and currently sells for \$1,000 (its price or present value), its annual rate of return must be:

$$\frac{\textbf{Annual rate of return}}{\textbf{on a perpetual bond}} = \$100/\$1,000 = 0.10 \text{ or } 10\%$$

Conversely, the simple formula (6.16) can be rearranged to read:

$$\frac{\text{Present value (Current price)}}{\text{of a perpetual bond}} = \frac{\text{Annual cash flow promised}}{\text{Annual rate of return}} \tag{6.17}$$

Thus, with a \$100 promised annual coupon payment and an expected 10 percent annual rate of return, the current price (present value) of this instrument must be \$100/0.10 or \$1,000.

The formula for a perpetual financial instrument reminds us of several key points regarding value and the rate of return for financial assets (especially bonds and similar debt securities). First, an infinite stream of fixed payments does have a *finite value,* measured by a financial asset's current price (or present value). Second, there is an *inverse (or negative)* relationship between the current price and the rate of return or yield on a financial asset, especially for bonds and debt instruments.

## Interest Rates and Stock Prices

The most common type of perpetual financial instrument is *corporate stock,* which represents partial ownership of a business firm that is expected to exist forever, unless it goes bankrupt! As with bonds and other debt securities, there tends to be an inverse relationship between interest rates and corporate stock (equity) prices as well. However, this relationship is weaker than it is for bonds and does not always hold.

For example, if interest rates rise, debt instruments now offering higher yields become more attractive relative to stocks, resulting in increased stock sales and declining equity prices (all other factors held equal). Conversely, a period of falling interest rates often leads investors to dump their lower-yielding bonds and switch to equities, driving stock prices upward. Then, too, lower market interest rates tend to lower the overall cost of capital for businesses issuing stock, resulting in a rise in stock prices (provided expected corporate dividends do not fall).

What actually happens to stock prices when market interest rates change can often be understood by tracking changes in two fundamental factors that appear to influence *all* stock prices—the stream of shareholder dividends a company is expected to pay in current and future time periods [$E(D)$] and the minimum rate of return required by a company's shareholders ($r$). This minimum required rate of return is used to discount the infinite stream of expected dividends to determine their present values, the sum of which is the market price of the stock ($SP$). Assuming the dividend in the current period, $D_0$, is known, the stock price formula becomes:

$$SP = D_0 + \frac{ED_1}{(1 + r)^1} + \frac{ED_2}{(1 + r)^2} + \cdots = \sum_{t=0}^{\infty} \frac{E(D_t)}{(1 + r)^t} \qquad (6.18)$$

Clearly, a rise in expected dividends [$E(D)$] or a fall in the required risk-adjusted rate of return for the company's stockholders ($r$) leads to higher stock prices per share ($SP$), other factors held equal. However, there are *no* guarantees surrounding the stock price–interest rate relationship we have just described because *both* expected dividends and the required risk-adjusted rate of return ($r$) may change at the same time, offsetting one another and leaving stock prices unchanged or causing them to move in an unexpected direction.

The formula stated above for determining the price of a company's stock is a general formula that takes into account the possibility that the dividends paid by a corporation to its shareholders may vary in timing and amount as the months and years go by. However, for many companies in recent years dividends have tended to grow at a relatively constant rate from period to period, often shaped by corporate management to convey the image of company stability. If corporate dividends do grow at a constant rate, the formula for corporate stock prices becomes simpler and easier to follow:

$$SP = D_0(1 + r)/(r - g) \qquad (6.19)$$

where $D_0$ represents the current dividend and $g$ is expected constant annual growth rate of dividends in the future. As before, $r$ is the required rate of return for investors, or the rate of discount of future expected dividends, which reflects the perceived risk of investing in the company's stock, and also coincides with the cost of capital to the firm.

To illustrate the use of the above formula, suppose a company expects to pay a dividend of $2.50 per share in the initial period and to increase the amount of its future annual dividend payments by 5 percent each year. If the discount rate associated with the company's stock is 12 percent, then its current stock price will approach:

$$SP = \$2.50(1 + 0.12) / (0.12 - 0.05) = \$40.00 \text{ per share}$$

Clearly, it is easier to estimate the equity value for those companies—often the largest firms today—that pay a steady and predictable dividend rate.

## Calculating the Holding-Period Yield on Stock

The reasoning we used earlier to determine the yield to maturity and the holding-period yield on debt securities can also be applied to calculate the holding-period yield on corporate stocks (equities). To illustrate, suppose an investor is considering the purchase of shares of common stock issued by General Electric Corporation, currently selling for $40 per share. He plans to hold the stock for two years and then sell out at an expected price of $50 per share. If he expects to receive $2 per share in dividends at the end of each year (with no payments until the end of year 1), what holding-period yield ($h$) does the investor expect to earn? Modify formula (6.18) to reflect the fact that the stock will be sold two years from today at an expected price of $SP_2$:

$$SP = D_0 + \frac{ED_1}{(1 + h)^1} + \frac{ED_2}{(1 + h)^2} + \frac{SP_2}{(1 + h)^2}$$

or,

$$\$40 = \$0 + \frac{\$2}{(1 + h)^1} + \frac{\$2}{(1 + h)^2} + \frac{\$50}{(1 + h)^2}$$

A computer or calculator programmed to determine holding-period yields tells us that the expected annualized holding-period yield on GE's stock is 16.5 percent.

## Price Quotations in Corporate Stock

To make knowledgeable investments in the stock market requires the processing of a great deal of information. Fortunately, an army of financial analysts spend full time "on the street" gathering information and making the outcome of their analyses available to all. One way in which these analyses become available to investors is simply by traders' buying and selling equity shares in publicly traded firms. As described in Chapter 3, this trading activity renders the market fair game for small investors by efficiently incorporating information relevant to the value of a corporation as reflected in its stock price. Small investors are then able to examine the outcome of trading for any given day in a variety of news sources. One example of the information on stock prices reported regularly in the financial news is given in Exhibit 6.6.

Investors can readily obtain information on the price of a stock at the close of trading the previous day, or the Closing Price, how actively traded it was in terms of the dollar Volume (000s) of shares traded, and see whether the share price traded up or down from the previous day's close and by how much from the column headed Net Change. The closing price can also be compared with the stock's highest and lowest value over the

| EXHIBIT 6.6 | Price Quotations on Corporate Stocks | | | | | | |
|---|---|---|---|---|---|---|---|
| | 52-Week | | Dividend | | PE | Volume (000s) | Closing Price | Net Change |
| Stock | Hi | Low | ($/yr) Yield (%) | | | | | |
| IBM | 89.94 | 72.73 | 1.20 | 1.5 | 15 | 38,469 | 80.85 | −0.56 |
| Google | 475.11 | 285.28 | none | — | 56 | 40,418 | 384.36 | 5.76 |
| EKodak | 30.91 | 18.93 | 0.50 | 2.4 | * | 20,693 | 21.08 | −0.39 |

*Earnings were negative for the previous 12 months.
Source: *The Wall Street Journal,* September 6, 2006.

previous year, (i.e., its 52-Week Hi and 52-Week Low). The investor can also determine whether the stock is paying a dividend and, if so, what that dividend payment is per year, or Dividend ($/yr), and what that represents in terms of an investment yield based on the closing price, known as the Dividend Yield (%) or Dividend($/yr)/Closing Price.

Note that not all firms pay dividends on their stock. Those firms with good investment opportunities their management feels would expand earnings in the future may choose to retain their current earnings and reinvest in the company. This strategy has been pursued by "high tech" firms due to the extraordinary growth of that industry. As a result, the stock price of those firms has generally risen more rapidly than the market as a whole. Firms in more mature industries may choose to pay out their earnings as dividends to investors rather than retain them to finance future expansion because their growth opportunities may be more limited. Investors interested primarily in a stable stream of regular income would likely prefer to receive dividends. However, those investors who are willing to wait for the returns on their investment may choose to purchase shares of companies that are aggressively reinvesting their earnings in order to experience rapid growth. Presumably this growth would eventually translate into a higher share price.

Another piece of information reported in Exhibit 6.6 is the firm's price/earnings or PE ratio. This ratio is constructed by dividing the Closing Price by the earnings reported by the firm for the prior four quarters. An average PE ratio for the stock market as a whole is around 15. Firms expected to experience rapid growth in earnings in the future will tend to have high stock prices in relation to their prior year's earnings, and hence a high PE. Note that in the exhibit at least one firm had losses, or negative earnings, for the previous year, so its PE ratio is not reported.

### QUESTIONS TO HELP YOU STUDY

14. What is meant by a *perpetual financial instrument?* Give an example.

15. Why is it more difficult to determine the value of the payments received from holding a stock (i.e., dividends) than the payments received from a perpetual bond?

16. Can you explain the logic behind the stock price formula (6.18)? Does it still offer a way to assess the value of a share of stock for an investor, even if that investor does not plan to hold the stock for more than a year?

17. Why is the *dividend yield* not the full return that an investor in a stock would expect to receive?

18. What is the PE ratio? What could it signal about the market's expectations of future earnings for an individual firm?

## 6.7   Interest Rates Charged by Institutional Lenders

In this chapter, we have examined several different measures of the rate of return, or yield, on financial assets. Our list is not complete, however, for institutional lenders of funds—banks, credit unions, insurance companies, and finance companies, to name the most important—often employ very different methods to calculate the rate of interest charged on their loans.

### The Simple Interest Method

**simple interest method**

The widely used **simple interest method** assesses interest charges on a loan for only the period of time the borrower actually has use of borrowed funds. The total interest bill *decreases* the more frequently a borrower must make payments on a loan because the borrower has less money to work with each time the repayment of part of a loan is made to the lender. This definition of a *simple interest loan* follows the U.S. government's Truth-in-Lending law passed originally in 1968.

For example, suppose you borrow $1,000 for a year at simple interest. If the interest rate is 10 percent, your interest bill will be $100 for the year. This figure is derived from the formula

$$I = P \times r \times t \tag{6.20}$$

where $I$ represents the interest charge (in dollars), $P$ is the principal amount of the loan, $r$ is the annual rate of interest, and $t$ is the term (maturity) of the loan expressed in years or fractions of a year. (In this example, $\$1,000 \times 0.10 \times 1 = \$100$.)

If the $1,000 loan is repaid in one lump sum at the end of the year,

| Principal + Interest | = Total payment |
|---|---|
| $1,000 + $100 | = $1,100 |

Suppose, however, that this loan principal is paid off in two equal installments of $500 each, every six months. Then you will pay

| | Principal + Interest | = Total payment |
|---|---|---|
| First installment : | $500 + $50 (i.e., 6 months' interest on $1,000 at 10%) | = $  550 |
| Second installment : | $500 + $25 (i.e., 6 months' interest on $500 at 10%) | = $  525 |
| | | = $1,075 |

Clearly, you pay a lower interest bill ($75 versus $100) with two installment payments instead of one. This happens because with two installment payments you effectively have use of the full $1,000 for only six months. For the remaining six months of the year you have use of only $500.

A shorthand formula for determining the total payment (interest plus principal) on a simple interest loan with a single lump-sum payment at maturity is

$$\text{Total payment due} = P + P \times r \times t = P(1 + r \times t) \tag{6.21}$$

For example, borrowing $1,000 for six months at a 10 percent loan rate means the borrower owes:

$$\text{Total payment due} = \$1,000 + \$1,000 \times 0.10 \times 6/12 = \$1,050$$

The simple interest method is still popular today with many credit unions and banks.

### Add-On Rate of Interest

**add-on rate**

A method for calculating loan interest rates often used by finance companies and banks is the **add-on rate** approach. In this instance, interest is calculated on the full principal of the loan, and the sum of interest and principal payments is divided by the number of payments to determine the dollar amount of each payment. For example, suppose you borrow $1,000 for one year at an interest rate of 10 percent. You agree to make two equal installment payments six months apart. The total amount to be repaid is $1,100 ($1,000 principal + $100 interest). At the end of the first six months, you will pay half ($550), and the remaining half ($550) will be paid at the end of the year.

If money is borrowed and repaid in one lump sum (a single payment loan), the simple interest and add-on methods give the same interest rate. However, as the number of installment payments increases, the borrower pays a higher effective interest rate under the add-on method. This happens because the average amount of money borrowed declines with greater frequency of installment payments, yet the borrower pays the *same* total interest bill. In fact, the effective rate of interest nearly doubles when monthly installment payments are required. For example, if you borrow $1,000 for a year at 10 percent simple interest but repay the loan in 12 equal monthly installments, you have only about $500 available for use, on average, over the year. Because the total interest bill is still $100, the interest rate exceeds 18 percent.

### Discount Loan Method

**discount loan method**

Many commercial loans, especially those used to raise working capital, are extended on a discount basis. This so-called **discount loan method** for calculating loan rates determines the total interest charge to the customer on the basis of the amount to be repaid. However, the borrower receives as proceeds of the loan only the *difference* between the total amount owed and the interest bill. For example, suppose you borrow $1,000 for one year at 10 percent, for a total interest bill of $100. Using the discount method, you actually receive for your use only $900 (i.e., $1,000 − $100) in net loan proceeds. The effective interest rate, then, is

$$\frac{\text{Interest paid}}{\text{Net loan proceeds}} = \frac{\$100}{\$900} \times 100 = 11.11\% \qquad (6.22)$$

Some lenders grant the borrower the full amount of money required but add the amount of discount to the face amount of the borrower's note. For example, if you need the full $1,000, the lender under this method will multiply the effective interest rate (11.11 percent) times $1,000 to derive a total interest bill of $111.11. The face value of the borrower's note and, therefore, the amount that must be repaid becomes $1,111.11. However, the borrower receives only $1,000 for use during the year. Most discount loans are for terms of one year or less and usually do not require installment payments. Instead, these loans generally are settled in a lump sum when the note comes due.

### Home Mortgage Interest Rate

One of the most confusing of all rates charged by lenders is the interest rate on a home mortgage loan. Many home buyers have heard that under the terms of most mortgage loans, their monthly payments early in the life of the loan go almost entirely to pay the interest on the loan. Only later is a substantial part of each monthly payment devoted to reducing the principal amount of a home loan. Is this true?

Yes, and we can illustrate it quite easily. Suppose that you find a new home you want to buy and borrow $100,000 to close the deal. The mortgage lender quotes you an annual **home mortgage interest rate** of 12 percent. If we divide this annual interest rate by 12 months, we derive a monthly mortgage loan rate of 1 percent. The lender tells you your monthly payment will be $1,100 each month (to cover property taxes, insurance, interest, and principal on the loan). This means the first month's payment of $1,100 will be divided by the lender as follows: (1) $1,000 for the interest payment (or 1% per month × $100,000); and (2) $100 to be applied to the principal of the loan, insurance premiums, taxes, and so forth. For simplicity, let's assume the $100 left over after the $1,000 interest payment goes entirely to help repay the $100,000 loan principal. This means that next month your loan now totals just $99,900 (or $100,000 − $100). When you send in that next monthly payment of $1,100, the interest payment will drop to $999, and, therefore, $101 will now be left over to help reduce the loan principal. Gradually, the monthly interest payment will fall and the amount left over to help retire the loan's principal will rise. After several years, as the mortgage loan's maturity date gets near, each monthly payment will consist mostly of repaying loan principal.

How do mortgage lenders figure the amount of the monthly payment new home buyers must make on their home loan? The usual formula is

$$\text{Total amount borrowed} \times \frac{\left[\dfrac{\text{Loan interest rate}}{12}\right] \times \left[1 + \dfrac{\text{Loan interest rate}}{12}\right]^{t \times 12}}{\left[1 + \left(\dfrac{\text{Loan interest rate}}{12}\right)\right]^{t \times 12} - 1} \tag{6.23}$$

where $t$ stands for the number of years the money is borrowed, and the annual interest rate charged on the mortgage loan is divided by 12 to restate that interest rate on a monthly basis.

To see how this formula works, suppose a family takes out a $50,000 loan for 25 years at an interest rate of 12 percent to buy its new home. In this case, the required payment on the home mortgage loan each month would be

$$\$50,000 \times \frac{\left[\dfrac{0.12}{12}\right] \times \left[1 + \dfrac{0.12}{12}\right]^{25 \times 12}}{\left[1 + \dfrac{0.12}{12}\right]^{25 \times 12} - 1} = \frac{\$9,894.23}{18.7885} = \$526.62$$

Actually, the easiest way to calculate required home mortgage payments is by using an electronic calculator or computer software. Typically, just three pieces of data are needed—the number of payments to be made, the annual interest rate on the loan, and the amount the home buyer plans to borrow.

## *Annual Percentage Rate (APR)*

The wide diversity of rates quoted by lenders is often confusing and discourages shopping around for credit. With this in mind, the U.S. Congress passed the Consumer Credit Protection Act in 1968. More popularly known as *Truth in Lending,* this law requires institutions regularly extending credit to consumers to tell the borrower what interest rate he or she is actually paying and to use a prescribed method for calculating that rate.[1] Specifically, banks, credit unions, and other lending institutions are required to calculate an **annual percentage rate (APR)** and inform the loan customer what this rate is *before* the loan contract is signed. The APR, which measures the yearly cost of credit, includes not only interest costs but also any transaction fees or service charges imposed by the lender. The APR for loans is equivalent to the yield to maturity for bonds.

Today, financial calculators and financial functions in spreadsheet programs (such as Excel) allow loan officers and their customers to easily determine the APR attached to their loans. To illustrate how the APR is determined, suppose you borrow $1,000 at 10 percent simple interest but must repay your loan in 12 equal monthly installments. The amount of each required monthly payment (PMT) can be figured as follows:

$$\begin{aligned} \frac{\text{Required monthly}}{\text{loan payment}} &= \frac{\text{Interest owed } + \text{ Loan principal}}{\text{Number of payment periods}} \\ &= \frac{\$100 + \$1,000}{12} = \$91.67 \end{aligned} \tag{6.24}$$

We can enter in the calculator the number of payment periods, N (in this case, 12); the amount or present value (PV) that the lender is granting to you, the borrower, for the term of the loan (in this case, PV = −$1,000 the day the loan begins); the amount to be repaid each month (in this case, PMT = $91.67 as determined above); and the future value (FV) of the loan (which at the end of the loan's term is $0 because you are expected to completely pay back what you borrowed). The calculator tells us that the APR (the annual percentage rate or I/Y) is very close to 18 percent in this example.

Congress hoped that introduction of the APR would encourage consumers to exercise greater care in the use of credit and to shop around to obtain the best terms on a loan. It is not at all clear that either goal has been realized completely, however. Many consumers appear to give primary weight to the size of installment payments in deciding how much, when, and where to borrow. If their budget can afford principal and interest charges on a loan, many consumers seem little influenced by the reported size of the APR and are often not inclined to ask other lenders for their rates on the same loan. Consumer education is vital to intelligent financial decision making, but progress in that direction has been slow. However, there is some evidence that with growing use of the Internet a greater proportion of borrowers are shopping around for credit today.

**annual percentage rate (APR)**

**Key URL:**
Competition among home mortgage lenders has intensified with the growing use of the Internet by borrowers. At some sites—for example, **lenderscompete.com** —several different lenders may bid for a borrowing customer's loan.

**Key URL:**
For further information about the APR see Consumer Credit and Credit Protection Laws at **federalreserve.gov**

---

[1] See Chapter 21 for a discussion of consumer credit laws.

## Compound Interest

compound interest

Some lenders and loan situations require the borrower to pay **compound interest** on a loan. In addition, most interest-bearing deposits at banks, credit unions, and money market funds pay compound interest on the balance in the account as of a certain date. The compounding of interest simply means that the lender or depositor earns interest income on *both* the principal amount and on any accumulated interest. Thus, the longer the period over which interest earnings are compounded, the more rapidly does interest earned on interest and interest earned on principal grow.

The conventional formula for calculating the future value of a financial asset earning compound interest is simply

$$FV = P(1 + r)^t \tag{6.25}$$

**Key URL:**
Many different Web site sources discuss compounding of interest—for example, see **finaid.org**

where FV is the sum of principal plus all accumulated interest over the life of the loan or deposit, $P$ is the asset's principal value, $r$ is the annual rate of interest, and $t$ is the time expressed in years. For example, suppose \$1,000 is borrowed for three years at 10 percent a year, compounded annually. Using an electronic calculator to find the compounding factor, $(1 + r)^t$, gives

$$FV = \$1,000(1 + 0.10)^3 = \$1,000(1.331) = \$1,331$$

which is the lump-sum amount the borrower must pay back at the end of three years. The amount of accumulated compound interest on this loan must be

$$\text{Compound interest} = FV - P = \$1,331 - \$1,000 = \$331 \tag{6.26}$$

**Key URL:**
The World Wide Web has made it possible to search wide geographic areas for the best deposit and loan rates available in the marketplace. See, for example, **money.cnn.com/pf/banking/**

Increased competition in the financial institutions' sector has encouraged most deposit-type institutions to offer their depositors interest compounded more frequently than annually, as assumed in the formula above. To determine the future value of accumulated interest from such a deposit, two changes must be made in the formula: (1) the quoted annual interest rate ($r$) must be divided by the number of periods during the year for which interest is compounded, and (2) the number of years involved ($t$) must be multiplied by the number of compounding periods within a year. For example, suppose you hold a \$1,000 deposit, earning a 12 percent annual rate of interest, with interest compounded monthly, and you plan to hold the deposit for three years. At the end of three years, you will receive back the lump sum of

$$FV = P(1 + r/12)^{t \times 12} = \$1,000(1 + 0.12/12)^{3 \times 12}$$
$$= \$1,000(1.431) = \$1,431 \tag{6.27}$$

Total interest earned will be \$1,431 − \$1,000, or \$431. Compounding on a more frequent basis increases the depositor's accumulated interest and, therefore, the deposit's future value.[2]

---

[2]Many financial institutions quote deposit rates compounded *daily*. In this case, the annual interest rate ($r$) is divided by 360 for simplicity and the number of years ($t$) in the formula is multiplied by 365. Thus, the formula for *daily* interest rate compounding is

$$FV = P(1 + r/360)^{t \times 365}$$

## *The Annual Percentage Yield (APY) on Deposits*

**annual percentage yield (APY)**

**Key URL:**
The annual percentage yield (APY) is discussed on the Web at  **federalreserve.gov** under the Truth in Savings Act.

In 1991 the U.S. Congress passed the Truth in Savings Act in response to customer complaints about the way some depository institutions were calculating their customers' interest returns on deposits. Instead of giving customers credit for the average balance in their deposit accounts, some depository institutions were figuring a customer's interest return on the *lowest* balance in their account. The U.S. Congress responded to this practice by requiring depository institutions to calculate the *daily average* balance in a customer's deposit over each interest-crediting period and to use that daily average balance to determine the customer's **annual percentage yield (APY).**

For example, suppose a customer deposits $2,000 in a one-year savings account for six months (180 days) but then withdraws $1,000 to help meet personal expenses, leaving $1,000 for the remainder of the year (185 days). Then the customer's daily average balance would be:

$$\text{Daily average balance} = \frac{\$2{,}000 \times 180 \text{ days} + \$1{,}000 \times 185 \text{ days}}{365 \text{ days}} = \$1{,}493.15$$

Suppose the bank credits the customer's account with $100 in interest. If the account has a term of 365 days (a full year) or has no stated maturity, then the customer's annual percentage yield can be calculated from the simple formula:

$$\text{APY} = 100 \, [\text{Annual interest earned/Daily average balance}] \qquad (6.28)$$

In this case,

$$\text{APY} = 100 \, [\$100/\$1{,}493.15] = 6.70 \text{ percent}$$

On the other hand, if the deposit account runs for *less than* a year, a depository institution subject to the provisions of the Truth in Savings Act must use the formula:

$$\text{APY} = 100 \left[ \left( 1 + \frac{\text{Amount of interest earned/Daily average balance}}{} \right)^{365/\text{days in term}} - 1 \right] \qquad (6.29)$$

**Key URL:**
For data on credit card plans and the interest rates and other terms they impose on customers, see the credit card analyzer at  **moneycentral.msn .com/banking/services/ creditcard.asp**

For example, suppose a customer opens a savings account with a maturity of 182 days (six months) and leaves $1,000 in the account for the whole period. Suppose too that at the end of the deposit's term the bank credits the customer with $30.37 in interest earned. Then, the annual percentage yield (APY) that must be reported to the customer under the Truth in Savings Act would be

$$\text{APY} = 100[(1 + \$30.37/\$1{,}000)^{365/182} - 1] \approx 6.18 \text{ percent.}$$

Whenever a customer opens a new deposit account in the United States, he or she must be informed about how interest will be computed on his or her account, what fees will be charged that could reduce the customer's interest earnings, and what must be done to earn the full APY promised on the deposit.

**QUESTIONS TO HELP YOU STUDY**

19. Explain the meaning of the following terms and, where a formula is involved, explain the components of each formula:

    a. Simple interest

    b. Add-on interest

    c. Discount loan method

    d. APR

    e. Compound interest

    f. APY

20. How is the monthly payment that a home mortgage borrower must meet determined? Why is it that payments made early in the life of a typical home mortgage go largely to pay interest rather than repay principal?

## Summary of the Chapter's Main Points

Interest rates and asset prices are among the most important ingredients needed to help make sound financial decisions. Over the years, a number of methods have been developed to aid in the measurement and calculation of interest rates and asset prices within the financial system.

- Dealers in the wholesale money markets quote one another *bid* and *ask* bank discount rates on money market assets they are trading. These bank discount rates differ from actual rates of return, or investment rates, that investments yield to investors.

- Debt securities, such as government or corporate bonds, provide the investor with a fixed stream of returns. However, the market price of debt securities will vary inversely with market interest rates. The higher the rate of return the market demands for a fixed stream of income, the less it will pay, and the lower will be the asset's price.

- The *yield to maturity* is the expected rate of return of an asset if it is held until maturity. It effectively determines the asset's market value. If an investor chooses to sell an asset before maturity, the rate of return the investor receives, or the asset's *holding-period yield,* could be above, equal to, or below the asset's yield to maturity on date of sale, depending upon whether market interest rates have fallen, remained unchanged, or risen since the investor purchased the asset.

- Corporate stocks represent ownership in a firm and claims to a share of the firm's earnings. The price of the stock is given by the present value of its expected future stream of dividend payments. The rate at which these future dividends are discounted back to the present incorporates the risk the investor takes that the firm will not meet the dividend payments expected by the market. The greater this risk, the higher is the rate of discount on future expected dividends, and the lower tends to be the stock price.

- Often we observe stock prices falling during periods of rising interest rates. However, unlike bonds and other fixed-income securities, stock prices are sensitive to other factors besides interest rates (such as the condition of the economy, business profits, and dividend payouts to stockholders), so that the relationship between stock prices and interest rates is less predictable than in the case of debt securities.

- Lending institutions often calculate the loan rates they quote borrowers according to different interest rate measures. Examples include the *simple interest rate* (where interest owed is adjusted for repayments of the principal of a loan) and the *add-on interest rate* (where interest owed is added to the principal of a loan and divided by the number of payments called for in a loan agreement). Other loan-rate measures include the *discount loan method* (where interest is deducted at the beginning of a loan) and the *APR* (or annual percentage rate), which adjusts interest owed for repayments of loan principal. The *APR* is subject to regulation so that lenders must calculate it the same way and borrowers can more meaningfully compare one loan agreement against another in order to find the best deal.

- Interest rates or yields on deposits today are increasingly quoted as the *annual percentage yield* or *APY*. Regulations require that depositors receive APY information when taking out a new deposit or renewing an existing deposit in order to make an informed financial decision.

- Most depository institutions today pay *compound interest* on their deposits— that is, interest is earned on accumulated interest as well as on the principal invested in a deposit. Increasingly deposits accrue compound interest on a daily or other, more frequent basis than in the past.

- One of the more complicated interest rate and loan payment methods is the procedure used to figure loan rates and payment amounts on *home mortgage loans.* Under most home mortgage contracts, payments made early in the life of such a loan go largely to pay interest; only after several years are substantial portions of home mortgage payments directed to help repay loan principal.

## Key Terms Appearing in This Chapter

www.mhhe.com.rose10e

## Problems and Issues

1. Suppose a 10-year bond is issued with an annual coupon rate of 8 percent when the market rate of interest is also 8 percent. If the market rate rises to 9 percent, what happens to the price of this bond? What happens to the bond's price if the market rate falls to 6 percent? Explain why.

2. Preferred stock for XYZ corporation is issued at par for $50 per share. If stockholders are promised an 8 percent annual dividend, what was the stock's dividend yield at time of issue? If the stock's market price has risen to $60 per share, what is its new dividend yield?

3. You plan to borrow $2,000 to take a vacation and want to repay the loan in a year. The banker offers you a simple interest rate of 12 percent with repayment of principal in two equal installments, 6 months and 12 months from now. What is your total interest bill? What is the APR? Would you prefer an add-on interest rate with one payment at the end of the year? If the bank applied the discount method to your loan, what are the net proceeds of the loan? What is your effective rate of interest?

4. An investor is interested in purchasing a new 20-year government bond carrying a 10 percent annual coupon rate with interest paid twice a year. The bond's current market price is $875 for a $1,000 par value instrument. If the investor buys the bond at the going price and holds to maturity, what will be his or her yield to maturity? Suppose the investor sells the bond at the end of 10 years for $950. What is the investor's holding-period yield?

5. Calculate the bank discount rate of return (DR) and the YTM-equivalent return for the following money market instruments:

   **a.** Purchase price, $96; par value, $100; maturity, 90 days.

   **b.** Purchase price, $97.50; par value, $100; maturity, 270 days.

6. You have just placed $1,500 in a bank savings deposit and plan to hold that deposit for eight years, earning 5½ percent per annum. If the bank compounds interest daily, what will be the total value of the deposit in eight years? How does your answer change if the bank switches to monthly compounding? Quarterly compounding?

7. You decide to take out a 30-year mortgage loan to buy the home of your dreams. The home's purchase price is $120,000. You manage to scrape together a $20,000 down payment and plan to borrow the balance of the purchase price. Hardy Savings and Loan Association quotes you a fixed annual loan rate of 12 percent. What will your monthly payment be? How much total interest will you have paid at the end of 30 years?

8. A depositor places $5,000 in a credit union deposit account for a full year but then withdraws $1,000 after 270 days. At the end of the year, the credit union pays her $300 in interest. What is this depositor's daily average balance and APY?

9. A commercial loan extended to CIBER-LAND Corporation for $2.5 million assesses an interest charge of $350,000 up front. Using the discount loan method of calculating loan rates, what is the effective interest rate on this loan? Suppose that instead of deducting the interest owed up front, the company's lender agrees to extend the full $2.5 million and add the amount of interest owed to the face amount of CIBER's note. What, then, is the loan's effective interest rate?

**10.** Bill Evans won a cash prize of $100,000 in a charity fund-raising event. He decided to invest the money for the next five years to help pay for his son's college education. His financial advisor gave him two options for investing. Option A is to invest all the money in a stock mutual fund tied to the S&P 500. Option B is to buy a speculative stock, Advent-2, that has paid no dividends, with 50 percent of Bill's winnings and a 10-year T-note—a zero-coupon security— with the remainder. The advisor gave Bill three potential scenarios that could affect the value of these two investment portfolios.

**a.** Scenario 1: The S&P 500 will appreciate 10 percent in each of the first two years, and then grow at a 3 percent rate in the last three years, during which time the price of Advent-2 is expected to double in the first year and remain flat in the last four years, while the yield on the T-note falls from its current 4 percent to 2 percent.

**b.** Scenario 2: The S&P 500 will appreciate 10 percent in each of the upcoming five years, Advent-2 will increase by 20 percent each year, and the yield on the T-note will remain unchanged at 4 percent.

**c.** Scenario 3: The S&P 500 will appreciate 3 percent in the first two years and 5 percent in the subsequent three years, while the price of Advent-2 will fall by 10 percent in each of the first two years and then remain flat thereafter, as the yield on the T-note rises from 4 to 7 percent.

Use a spreadsheet to compute the future value after five years of the $100,000 investment under Option A and Option B for each of the three scenarios above. Can you say whether Option A or Option B is the better investment strategy?

## Web-Based Problems

**1.** The expression for computing the per-share stock price for a firm that is expected to have a constant dividend growth rate is given in Equation 6.19 in the text. This equation can be useful in understanding how the financial markets arrive at stock values for well-established firms operating in different markets. For example, consider IBM and American Electric Power (AEP)—both leaders in their industries and expected to experience relatively stable growth. We can use Equation 6.19 and data from the market to compute the market's expectation of earnings growth, which will be reflected in dividend growth, for these two companies.

**a.** Assume the markets demand a 6 percent return for investing in either IBM or AEP. Go to the appropriate Web sites for these two companies, such as **www.yahoo.com,** and find their current stock price and dividend. Use Equation 6.19 to compute the market's expectation of dividend (earnings) growth for these two firms. Which is larger? See if you can explain why by discussing the nature of the businesses these two companies are engaged in.

**b.** Equation 6.19 is derived from the more general expression for stock prices given by Equation 6.18 in the text. While Equation 6.19 can provide a useful guideline for market pricing of equities issued by large, well-established firms like IBM and AEP, it often runs into trouble when used to estimate stock values for new start-up firms or for established companies changing their business plan. To see this, try to repeat the process you followed in part (a) for Amazon.com (AMZN) and eBay (EBAY). What seems to be wrong? Can you explain why this equation fails to provide a reasonable estimate of the expected growth for these firms?

2. Go to the Treasury's Web site and locate the results of its most recent auction of 13-week (3-month) T-bills and of 10-year T-notes. One route for locating this information is: **http://www.treasurydirect.gov/RT/RTGateway?page=instit Home** then click on the "Auction Results" for the "13-wk" T-bill and the "10-yr" T-note.

   a. For the 3-month T-bill, obtain information on the Discount rate. From that information, along with the number of days to maturity, use formula (6.3) to solve for the market price of the T-bill. (Compare this number with what is reported.)

   b. Using the market price for the T-bill that you obtained in part (a), use formula (6.2) to find the investment rate. (Compare this number with what is reported.)

   c. From the information on the auction of the 10-yr T-note, did it sell above, at, or below par?

## Selected References to Explore

1. Sundaresan, Suresh. *Fixed Income Markets and Their Derivatives,* New York: International Thomson, 1997.
2. Trainer, Richard D. C. *The Arithmetic of Interest Rates,* New York: Federal Reserve Bank of New York, 1980.

# Chapter 7

# Inflation, Yield Curves, and Duration: Impact on Interest Rates and Asset Prices

## What's in This Chapter?
## Key Topics Outline

Inflation: What Is It? How Does It Affect Interest Rates?

The Fisher Effect

Alternative Views: Inflation, Changes in the Economy, and Interest Rates

Inflation and Stock Prices: What Are the Links?

TIPS and Other Inflation-Indexed Instruments

The Expectations Hypothesis and Other Views about Yield Curves

Uses for Yield Curves

Duration, Price Elasticity, Convexity, and Portfolio Immunization

## Learning Objectives

### in This Chapter

• You will discover what *inflation* is all about and how inflation can impact interest rates and the prices of financial assets.

• You will see how *yield curves* arise and view the controversy over what determines the shape of the yield curve.

• You will discover how yield curves can be a useful tool for those interested in investing their money and in tracking the health of the economy.

• You will explore the concept of *duration*—a measure of the maturity of a financial instrument—and see how it can be used to assist in making investment choices and in protecting against the risk of changes in interest rates.

## 7.1  Introduction

In Chapter 5 we examined the supply and demand forces believed to determine the rate of interest on a financial asset. We know, however, that there is not just one interest rate in the financial system, but thousands. We also know that these rates may differ substantially from one another, and the differences between various interest rates can change dramatically over time. For example, in 2004 the annualized interest rate on the six-month Treasury bill was just over 1 percent, while the 10-year Treasury note rate was 5.40 percent, and the yield on high-quality corporate bonds averaged almost 7 percent. Two years later, interest rates on these same securities had changed significantly. The 3-month T-bill rate was 5.25 percent, the 10-year T-note rate was 4.88 percent, and the high-grade corporate bond rate was 5.68 percent. Over this same period, the average loan rates that major banks were quoting to their most financially sound (prime) customers rose from near 4 percent in 2004 to 8.25 percent in 2006, while investors in state and local government (municipal) bonds saw the rate of return that they were being promised fall from close to 5 percent to 4.39 percent.

Why are all these rates so different from one another, and why do the relationships between them change so dramatically? Are these rate differences purely random, or can we attribute them to a limited number of factors that can be studied and perhaps predicted? Understanding the factors that cause interest rates to differ among themselves is an indispensable aid to the investor and saver in choosing financial assets for a portfolio. It is not always advisable, for example, to reach for the highest yield available in the financial marketplace. The investor who does so may assume an unacceptable level of risk, have his or her securities called in by the issuer in advance of maturity, pay an unacceptably high tax bill, accept a rate of return whose value is seriously eroded by inflation, or suffer other undesirable consequences. Without question, the intelligent saver and investor must have a working knowledge of the factors affecting interest rates and be able to anticipate possible future changes in those factors. In this chapter and the next we address these important issues.

## 7.2  Inflation and Interest Rates

**inflation**

One of the most serious problems that economies around the globe have had to confront is **inflation.** Inflation is defined as *the percentage increase in the average level of prices for all goods and services.* Some prices of individual goods and services are always rising while others are declining. However, inflation occurs when the *average* level of all prices in the economy rises.[1] Interest rates represent the "price" of credit. Are they also affected by inflation? The answer is *yes,* though there is considerable debate as to exactly *how* and by *how much* inflation affects interest rates.

### *The Correlation between Inflation and Interest Rates*

To be sure, the correlation in recent years between the rate of inflation in the United States and both long-term and short-term interest rates appears to be fairly strong. Exhibit 7.1, which reports two popular measures of the inflation rate—the Consumer Price Index (CPI) and the GDP deflator—and an important money market interest

---

[1]See Chapter 13 for a discussion of the nature, causes, and recent public policy responses to inflation.

| EXHIBIT 7.1 | Inflation and Interest Rates (Annual Rates, Percent) | | |
|---|---|---|---|
| | Rate of Inflation Measured by Percentage Change in | | Interest Rate on Negotiable Certificates of Deposit (six-month maturities) |
| Year | Consumer Price Index | GDP Deflator | |
| 1970 | 5.9 | 5.4 | 7.64 |
| 1980 | 13.5 | 8.8 | 12.94 |
| 1990 | 6.2 | 4.0 | 8.17 |
| 2000 | 3.4 | 2.1 | 6.59 |
| 2003 | 2.3 | 1.7 | 1.17 |
| 2006* | 5.0 | 4.1 | 4.97 |

Source: U.S. Department of Commerce (Bureau of Economic Analysis), Department of Labor (Bureau of Labor Statistics), and Board of Governors of the Federal Reserve System.
* 2006 data are for second quarter.

rate—the rate of return on a six-month, negotiable CD—suggests a close association between inflation and interest rates. For example, in 1980 inflation was historically at a high level for the U.S. economy. At the same time, the CD interest rate reached its high of nearly 13 percent. Afterward, the inflation rate fell to around the 2 percent mark by 2003, and the CD rate declined to a very low value of just over 1 percent. In subsequent years both the inflation rate and the CD rate have crept back up.

In summary, then, interest rates and inflation appear to be at least moderately correlated with one another. But is there really a *causal* connection between them?

## Nominal and Real Interest Rates

**nominal interest rate**

**real interest rate**

**inflation premium**

To explore the possible relationship between inflation and interest rates several key terms must be defined. First, we must distinguish between nominal and real interest rates. The **nominal interest rate** is the published or quoted interest rate on a financial asset. For example, an announcement in the financial press that major banks have raised their prime lending rate to 10 percent per annum indicates what nominal interest rate is now being quoted by banks to some of their best loan customers. In contrast, the **real interest rate** is the return to the lender or investor measured in terms of its actual purchasing power. In a period of inflation, of course, the real rate will be lower than the nominal rate. Another important concept is the **inflation premium,** which measures the rate of inflation *expected* by lenders and investors in the marketplace during the life of a particular financial instrument.

These three concepts *are* related. Obviously, a lender is most interested in the *real rate of return* on a loan; that is, the purchasing power of any interest earned. For example, suppose you loan $1,000 to a business firm for a year and expect the prices of goods and services to rise 10 percent during the year. If you charge a nominal interest rate of 12 percent on the loan, your *real* rate of return on the $1,000 loan is only 2 percent, or $20. However, if the actual rate of inflation during the period of the loan turns out to be 13 percent, you have actually suffered a real decline in the purchasing power of the monies loaned. In general, lenders will attempt to charge nominal rates of interest that give them desired *real* rates of return on their loanable funds based upon their expectations regarding inflation.

## The Fisher Effect

**Key URLs:**
Among the more interesting Web sites linking interest rates and inflation are
**globalfindata.com** and **economist.com**

In a classic article written just before the end of the nineteenth century, economist Irving Fisher [8] argued that the nominal interest rate was related to the real interest rate by the following equation:

$$\begin{matrix}\text{Expected} \\ \text{nominal} \\ \text{interest rate}\end{matrix} = \begin{matrix}\text{Expected} \\ \text{real} \\ \text{rate}\end{matrix} + \begin{matrix}\text{Inflation} \\ \text{premium}\end{matrix} + \begin{matrix}\text{Expected} \\ \text{real} \\ \text{rate}\end{matrix} \times \begin{matrix}\text{Inflation} \\ \text{premium}\end{matrix} \quad (7.1)$$

Clearly, if the expected real interest rate is held fixed, changes in expected nominal rates will reflect shifting inflation premiums (i.e., changes in the public's views on expected inflation). The cross-product term in the above equation (Expected real rate × Inflation premium) is often eliminated because it is usually quite small except in countries experiencing severe inflation.[2]

Does equation 7.1 suggest that an increase in expected inflation *automatically* increases expected nominal interest rates? Not necessarily. There are several different views on the matter. Fisher argued that the expected real rate of return tends to be relatively stable over time because it depends on such long-term factors as the productivity of capital and the volume of savings in the economy. Therefore, changes in the expected nominal interest rate are most likely to reflect changes in the inflation premium, not the expected real rate, at least in the short run. The expected nominal rate will rise by close to the full amount of the expected increase in the rate of inflation. For example, suppose the expected real rate is 3 percent and the expected rate of inflation is 10 percent. Then the expected nominal rate would be close to

$$\text{Expected nominal interest rate} = 3\% + 10\% = 13\% \quad (7.2)$$

According to Fisher's hypothesis, if the expected rate of inflation now rises to 12 percent, the expected real rate will remain essentially unchanged at 3 percent, but the expected nominal rate will rise to 15 percent.

**Fisher effect**

If this view, known today as the **Fisher effect,** is correct, it suggests a method of judging at least the *direction* of future interest rate changes. To the extent that a rise in the actual rate of inflation causes investors to expect greater inflation in the future, higher nominal interest rates will soon result. Conversely, a decline in the actual inflation rate may cause investors to revise downward their expectations of future inflation, leading eventually to lower nominal rates. This will happen because, in an efficient market, lenders will seek full compensation for the expected changes in the purchasing power of their money.

## Alternative Views about Inflation and Interest Rates

While the Fisher effect is among the most popular explanations of the link between inflation and interest rates, several alternative views of the inflation–interest rate connection have emerged over the years.

### The Harrod-Keynes Effect of Inflation
The Fisher effect conflicts directly with a view of the inflation–interest rate phenomenon developed originally by British economist Sir Roy Harrod. It is based upon the Keynesian liquidity preference theory

---

[2] For example, if inflation is running 5 percent a year and the real rate of interest is 3 percent, the cross-product term in equation 7.1 is only 0.05 × 0.03, or 0.0015. Equation 7.1 is derived from the relationship (1 + Nominal rate) = (1 + Real rate) × (1 + Inflation premium).

of interest rates discussed in Chapter 5. Harrod argues that the *real* rate *will* be affected by inflation but the nominal interest rate may not be. According to the liquidity preference theory, the nominal interest rate is determined by the demand for and supply of money. Therefore, unless inflation affects either the demand for or supply of money, the expected nominal interest rate must remain unchanged regardless of what happens to inflationary expectations.

What, then, is the link between inflation and interest rates according to this view? Harrod argues that a rise in inflationary expectations will lower the *real* rate of interest. In liquidity preference theory the real rate measures the inflation-adjusted return on bonds. However, conventional bonds, like money, are *not* a hedge against inflation because their rate of return is usually fixed by contract. Therefore, a rise in the expected rate of inflation lowers investors' expected real return from holding bonds. If the nominal rate of return on bonds remains unchanged, the expected real rate *must* be squeezed when there are expectations of more rapidly rising prices. Of course, this is only true for the existing bondholders. If they attempted to sell their bonds in the open market they would find that the price of those bonds had fallen, thereby restoring, at least in part, the original expected rate of return on the bonds to new investors.

**Harrod-Keynes effect**  This so-called **Harrod-Keynes effect** does not stop with bonds, however. There are two other groups of assets in the economy that, unlike bonds, may provide a hedge against inflation: *common stocks* and *real estate*. Inflationary expectations often lead to rising prices for homes, farmland, and commercial structures and occasionally to rallies in the stock market. Proponents of the Harrod-Keynes view argue that an increase in the rate of inflation causes the demand for these inflation-hedged assets to increase. Real estate and stock prices rise, while bond prices are falling. This process continues until an equilibrium among the returns on bonds, real estate, and other assets is achieved. This may result in lower expected rates of return on each of these assets. Thus, the Fisher and Harrod-Keynes effects have different predictions regarding the effect of inflation on interest rates.

### Anticipated versus Unanticipated Inflation

One of the most obvious weaknesses of the Fisher effect was its failure to distinguish between *anticipated* (or expected) and *unanticipated* (or unexpected) inflation. Fisher assumed that inflation is *fully anticipated*. As an example, suppose that both borrowers and lenders of funds expect an inflation rate for the next year of 10 percent and the real interest rate is 3 percent. We can illustrate this using Exhibit 7.2, which shows two sets of demand and supply curves for loanable funds: a set of *real* demand and supply curves intersecting at a 3 percent real interest rate, and a set of *nominal* demand and supply curves intersecting at a point just high enough to fully reflect the expected inflation rate (in this example, 10 percentage points higher than the real rate). The nominal supply and demand curves for loanable funds both shift upward just enough to ensure that the going nominal interest rate on a one-year loan is 3 percent plus 10 percent, or 13 percent. Lenders will be unwilling to lend money at any rate lower than 13 percent because they expect the prices of the goods and services they plan to purchase to increase by 10 percent during the life span of the loan.

Suppose, however, that all or a portion of the increase in inflation is *unanticipated*. In this case, there is no way to be certain about what the equilibrium nominal interest rate will be for the nominal rate may not fully reflect the amount of inflation expected. The simple one-for-one change in the expected nominal rate in response to changing inflationary expectations may not be exactly correct. However, if unanticipated inflation—once it is observed—is expected to persist, then the nominal interest rate should adjust accordingly.

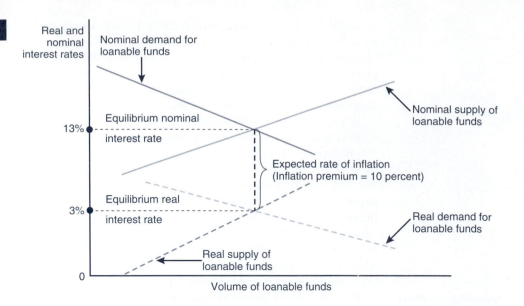

## The Inflation-Risk Premium

Recent research has also suggested that the Fisher effect may have left out a key term in the inflation–interest rate equation. The correct formula may look more like this:

$$\text{Nominal interest rate} = \text{Real interest rate} + \text{Expected inflation rate} + \text{Inflation-risk premium} \quad (7.3)$$

**inflation-risk premium**

The newly added term—the **inflation-risk premium**—represents compensation paid to a lender for that component of inflation that is *not expected*. Thus, the last term in the above equation represents uncertainty about what the actual inflation rate will turn out to be during the life of any particular financial instrument. For example, suppose the real rate is currently 3 percent, the expected rate of inflation is about 4 percent, and lenders are demanding an inflation-risk premium of 1 percent to compensate them should inflation rise faster than anticipated. The nominal interest rate must therefore be close to 8 percent.

The inflation-risk premium generally rises with the maturity of a nominal financial instrument because the longer the period until final payment of a loan, the greater the likelihood of unexpected inflation occurring. It is more difficult to forecast inflation over a lengthier period of time. Moreover, the longer the period before the final payment on a loan, the greater the cost of any inflation forecasting error a lender might make. Thus, the inflation-risk premium on a one-year loan might be half of a percentage point, but it might be closer to 1 percent on a 10-year bond. Recent research by Shen [15] for the United Kingdom suggests that the inflation-risk premium can be sizeable—a percentage point or more added to the nominal rate of return on inflation-risk-exposed assets.

## The Inflation-Caused Income Tax Effect

Finally, one factor affecting the link between inflation and interest rates that neither Fisher nor any of his contemporaries figured in was *income taxes*. As the old saying goes, nothing is more certain in life than death and taxes! And, surprisingly, something called the **inflation-caused income tax effect** may actually widen movements in nominal interest rates, resulting in nominal rates increasing by *more* than any given change in expected inflation.

**inflation-caused
income tax effect**

The heart of this argument is that lenders and investors not exempt from income taxes make lending and investing decisions on the basis of their expected real rate of return *after taxes.* If an investor desires to protect his or her expected real after-tax rate of return, then the expected nominal rate has to increase by a *greater* amount than any rise in the expected inflation rate because otherwise real after-tax returns will decline when expected inflation increases.

To see the validity of this argument, we observe that

$$
\begin{array}{c}
\text{Expected after-tax} \\
\text{real rate of return} \\
\text{earned by a} \\
\text{taxpaying} \\
\text{investor}
\end{array}
=
\begin{array}{c}
\text{Expected} \\
\text{nominal} \\
\text{rate}
\end{array}
-
\left[
\begin{array}{c}
\text{Expected} \\
\text{nominal} \\
\text{rate}
\end{array}
\times
\begin{array}{c}
\text{Taxpayer's} \\
\text{income tax} \\
\text{bracket rate}
\end{array}
\right]
-
\begin{array}{c}
\text{Inflation} \\
\text{premium}
\end{array}
\quad (7.4)
$$

Suppose an investor is in the 28 percent income tax bracket, so that a little more than a quarter of any additional income he or she earns is taxed. Moreover, suppose the current expected nominal interest rate on a one-year taxable financial asset this investor is interested in buying is 12 percent and the inflation premium (expected inflation rate) over the coming year is 5 percent. Then this investor's expected real after-tax return from the asset must be

$$
\begin{array}{c}
\text{Expected after-tax real} \\
\text{rate of return earned by} \\
\text{a taxpaying investor}
\end{array}
= 12\% - [12\%\,(0.28)] - 5\% = 3.64\% \quad (7.5)
$$

Now suppose the expected rate of inflation rises from 5 to 6 percent. By how much must the *expected nominal rate* on the taxable financial asset rise to yield this investor the *same* expected real return after taxes? The nominal rate must rise to 13.39 percent, for

$$
\begin{array}{c}
\text{Expected after-tax} \\
\text{real rate of return} \\
\text{earned by a} \\
\text{taxpaying investor}
\end{array}
= 13.39\% - [13.39\%\,(0.28)] - 6\% = 3.64\% \quad (7.6)
$$

Thus, a change of 1 percent in expected inflation requires a 1.39 percent change in the expected nominal rate to leave this taxed investor in the same place in terms of a real (purchasing-power) return.

The arithmetic shown above works both ways: a *reduction* in expected inflation by 1 percent requires a 1.39 percent *decline* in the nominal rate to leave the expected real after-tax return where it is. While investors in lower tax brackets would not require as numerically large a change in expected nominal rates to leave after-tax real returns unaltered, inflation tends to force most investors into higher and higher tax brackets as both prices and nominal incomes rise (unless government tax schedules are indexed to change with inflation).

### Conclusions from Recent Research on Inflation and Interest Rates

With all of the foregoing *possible* effects from inflation, what actually happens to nominal interest rates when the expected rate of inflation changes? As Fisher [8] originally suggested, the inflation-nominal interest rate relationship appears to be *positive: Higher rates of inflation ultimately lead to higher nominal interest rates in most cases.* However, on average, nominal interest rates appear to rise by somewhat *less* than any given increase in the expected inflation rate and decline by somewhat *less* than any given decrease in the expected inflation rate. This happens probably because inflation not only affects interest rates but also the wealth and incomes of businesses and households, among other things, setting in motion a host of changes in the economy and financial system. However, most of the change in expected inflation (perhaps 60 to 90 percent) appears to find its way into the nominal interest rate, suggesting that *the Fisher effect frequently tends to dominate other forces affecting the link between expected inflation and nominal interest rates.*

**Key URLs:**
The relationship between interest rates and inflation is discussed in numerous Web sites, including **interestratecalculator. com** and **finpipe.com**

Still, we should retain a healthy skepticism about research in this field. The topic of inflation and interest rates is plagued by numerous *measurement problems.* For example, there are no direct, widely accepted measures of the two key actors in the drama—the expected real rate and the expected rate of inflation. Because the underlying theory speaks of *expected* inflation and the *expected* real interest rate, there is the obvious problem of measuring people's expectations. We cannot, as a practical matter, survey all investors, and the results of such a survey would soon be irrelevant anyway because expectations can change fast. Note, too, that we cannot automatically derive the expected real interest rate merely by subtracting the current inflation rate from the current nominal rate; this gives us a measure of the actual (ex post) real rate at a single point in time, not necessarily the *expected* (ex ante) real rate.

## 7.3    Inflation and Stock Prices

The discussion so far has centered on the public's expectations about the prices of goods and services and their possible impact on interest rates attached to bonds and other debt securities. However, another interesting question centers on the relationship between expectations of inflation and *stock prices.* Does greater inflation cause the prices of corporate stock (equities) to rise? Common stock, for example, is widely viewed as a powerful hedge against inflation—a place to park your money if you want to preserve the purchasing power of your savings over the long haul.

Unfortunately, the facts often contradict what everybody "knows." For example, the stock market rose to unprecedented highs in the mid-1980s and again in the late 1990s, suggesting inflation was also on the rise. Yet, the U.S. inflation rate actually *fell* during these periods. One useful way to view this issue is to decide what factors determine the prices of corporate stock and see if those factors are likely to be affected by inflation.

In basic terms, the stock price per share of any corporation is positively related to the *dividends* investors expect the company to pay to shareholders in future periods and is negatively related to the *risk* attached to that stream of expected dividends, as we saw in Chapter 6. That is,

$$\text{Price per share of corporate stock} = \sum_{t=0}^{\infty} \frac{E(D_t)}{(1+r)^t} \tag{7.7}$$

where $E(D_t)$ are expected dividend payments in each period $t$, and $r$ is the rate of discount applied to those expected dividends to express them in terms of their present value. The riskier the corporation's dividend stream, the higher the required rate of discount, $r$, because investors demand a higher rate of return to compensate them for the added risk of holding stock (which promises no specific rate of return).

Clearly, if a rise in expected inflation raises stock prices, it must increase the amount of dividends shareholders expect each company to pay them [$E(D)$], or lower the perceived risk of holding stock ($r$), or both. On the other hand, stock prices will tend to fall if more inflation causes investors to lower their dividend expectations, increases

*Nominal contracts* are formal agreements that fix the terms in current (nominal) dollars under which a business firm will compensate its employees, creditors, and other suppliers of productive resources and the prices at which it will deliver its product or service to customers. Examples include business contracts with labor unions that fix wage rates, the issue of bonds at a fixed interest cost, or the valuing of business inventories and the depreciation of capital equipment using prespecified formulas. A business firm can be hurt by inflation, experiencing a fall in its stock price, if actual inflation turns out to be different from what it expected when it agreed to a nominal contract. However, some nominal contracts can benefit a firm experiencing inflation, particularly if the company correctly anticipated future price changes or, by using well-structured nominal contracts, managed to hold down its expenses or enhance its revenues. For example:

| If a business firm enters into nominal contracts that: | Then, if inflation turns out to be *greater than expected*: | However, suppose inflation turns out to be *less than expected*. Then: |
|---|---|---|
| A. Fix its expenses at a constant level or constant rate of growth (e.g., borrowing money at a fixed rate or paying employees a guaranteed wage) based on its current expectations for inflation. | Business revenues may grow faster than expenses, increasing profits; the firm's stock price may *rise*. | Business expenses may increase faster than revenues, reducing profits; the firm's stock price may *fall*. |
| B. Fix its revenues at a constant level or constant rate of growth (e.g., selling to customers at a guaranteed price for the coming year) based on its current inflationary expectations. | Business expenses may grow faster than revenues, reducing profits; the firm's stock price may *fall*. | Business revenues may grow faster than expenses, increasing profits; the firm's stock price may *rise*. |

the perceived risk to stockholders, or both. Is there any research evidence on which way the inflation-stock price relationship goes?

There are several conflicting views. One line of argument says that if inflation is fully expected by all investors, nominal (published) stock prices may rise but *real* stock prices may not change at all. This is because corporate revenues and expenses may grow equally fast and the size of each firm's net income and dividend payments may *not* be affected at all (assuming the company's board of directors does not change the dividend rate). On the other hand, if the rate of inflation is only partly expected but is expected to persist, then the amount of unexpected inflation may be captured by company stockholders, as opposed to debt holders, in the form of an unexpected increase in earnings that could cause real stock prices to rise until expectations had fully adjusted. Conversely, if the company's depreciation expenses on worn-out equipment are inadequate to offset the rising cost of new equipment in a period of inflation current before-tax corporate income will be overstated, resulting in higher taxes against the firm, lowering its after-tax income and reducing stockholder dividend payments. In this instance more rapid inflation would tend to *lower* stock prices. For example, a study by Ammer [1] finds a *negative* relationship between stock prices and inflation for several countries.

**nominal contracts**     Recently the concept of **nominal contracts** has emerged to help explain the inflation-stock price connection. Nominal contracts are agreements between parties, such as a company and its workers or customers, that fix prices or costs in terms of current dollar (nominal) values for a stipulated time period. For example, corporations and labor unions may agree to increase wages 10 percent a year until current labor-management contracts expire or pledge to deliver their products to customers at a fixed price during the coming year. Corporate rules for valuing inventories or calculating depreciation expenses are other examples of nominal contracts. If inflation subsequently rises faster or slower than a company expected when it entered into its nominal contracts, its profits may be squeezed or enhanced and its stock price may decrease or increase depending upon the circumstances. Thus, *the impact of inflation on stock prices may vary from firm to firm and from industry to industry, depending upon the actual rate of inflation and the terms of existing nominal contracts.*

An alternative view—called the *proxy effect*—argues for a *negative* relationship between inflation and stock prices but claims that relationship is *spurious,* not real. For example, changes in expected inflation are inversely related to fluctuations in expected output in the economy. If the public comes to believe that living costs will rise and the nation's economic output will decline, then real stock prices may fall due to a more pessimistic outlook for business profits. However, it is the expected decrease in the economy's output, not the expected change in living costs (inflation), that leads to a decline in stock prices. Research evidence on these newer views is decidedly mixed. The issue of stock prices and inflation awaits further research to find the right answers.

## 7.4 The Development of Inflation-Adjusted Securities

**TIPS**

In 1997 the U.S. Treasury offered a possible way for investors buying government securities—considered one of the safest of all conventional debt obligations—to gain protection against inflation. The Treasury began to issue inflation-indexed bonds called **TIPS** (Treasury Inflation Protection Securities), following the lead of such nations as Brazil and Great Britain, who experimented with inflation-indexed securities in earlier years.

Five- and 10-year TIPS were sold initially in the Treasury's experiment with these newly designed instruments. The Treasury also sells "I bonds" that are inflation-adjusted as part of its savings bond program. Investors buying these innovative bonds can literally separate out inflation risk exposure from interest rate risk exposure because TIPS adjust the payment of income to the investor to the actual amount of inflation experienced during the life of the bonds.

The inflation measure used to adjust the investor's return from TIPS is the Consumer Price Index (CPI), published by the U.S. Bureau of Labor Statistics and designed to reflect changes in the cost of living each month for a typical urban family. Thus, the real value of interest payments from a TIPS will be constant in purchasing power for those goods and services included in the CPI. This happens because the bond's nominal (face) value will increase at the same rate as the actual CPI inflation rate.

For example, suppose the rate of inflation in the CPI is zero right now and the U.S. Treasury issues a new TIPS that has a nominal (face) value of $1,000 and promises a real annual coupon rate of 3.5 percent for five years. If inflation remains at zero, this bond will pay $35 a year in real interest income and, at maturity, when it is redeemed by the U.S. Treasury, its nominal value will remain at $1,000. Suppose, however, that inflation suddenly increases to 4 percent (annual rate) the day after the bond is issued

**Key URL:**
Information regarding
the nature of and
the advantages
and disadvantages
attached to inflation-
adjusted securities
may be found at
the U.S. Treasury
site, **savingsbond.com**

and remains at that level for all five years of the bond's life. Then, the Treasury will calculate the bond's nominal value from the following formula:

$$\begin{matrix} \text{TIPS} \\ \text{inflation-adjusted} \\ \text{nominal value at maturity} \end{matrix} = \begin{matrix} \text{Original} \\ \text{face} \\ \text{value} \end{matrix} \left[ 1 + \begin{matrix} \text{Annual} \\ \text{rate of} \\ \text{inflation} \end{matrix} \right]^{\overset{\text{Time to maturity}}{\text{in years}}} \qquad (7.8)$$

In this example, the TIPS bond would have an inflation-adjusted nominal value at the end of its first year of:

**TIPS**
**inflation-adjusted nominal value** $= \$1,000 \ (1 + .04)^{1 \text{ year}} = \$1,040.00$
**at the end of the first year**

If the inflation rate remains at 4 percent over the next four years until the above bond reaches maturity, this TIPS would have a nominal value at the end of five years of:

**TIPS**
**inflation-adjusted nominal value** $= \$1,000 \ (1 + .04)^{5 \text{ years}} = \$1,216.65$
**at the end of 5 years**

The TIPS bond holder's annual nominal interest payment can be found from the simple formula:

$$\begin{matrix} \text{TIPS} \\ \text{inflation-adjusted} \\ \text{nominal value} \end{matrix} \times \begin{matrix} \text{Promised} \\ \text{coupon} \\ \text{rate} \end{matrix} = \begin{matrix} \text{Annual nominal} \\ \text{interest payment} \\ \text{from a TIPS} \end{matrix} \qquad (7.9)$$

If the bond's promised (coupon) rate is 3.5 percent, as in the example above, by the end of the bond's first year the amount of nominal interest earned by an investor would be:

$$\$1,040 \times .035 = \$36.40$$

instead of just $1,000 × 0.035, or $35, for a conventional bond whose principal is *not* adjusted for inflation. By the fifth year, when the TIPS described above reaches maturity, it will pay in annual nominal interest:

$$\$1,216.65 \times .035 = \$42.58$$

In summary, with an annual inflation rate of 4 percent a year, the inflation-adjusted bond just described would have increased its nominal principal and interest payments each year as follows:

| Period | Actual Annual Rate of Inflation (%) | TIPS's Principal Nominal Value at the End of Each Year | Nominal Interest Payment to the TIPS Bond's Holder at Year-End | Nominal Interest Payment from a Conventional (Noninflation-Adjusted) Bond |
|---|---|---|---|---|
| First year | 4% | $1,040.00 | $36.40 | $35 |
| Second year | 4 | 1,081.60 | 37.86 | 35 |
| Third year | 4 | 1,124.86 | 39.37 | 35 |
| Fourth year | 4 | 1,169.86 | 40.95 | 35 |
| Fifth year | 4 | 1,216.65 | 42.58 | 35 |

We must hasten to add, however, that even though the foregoing gains look impressive, the TIPS investor's real rate of return (that is, what he or she can actually buy with the earnings received) has *not* changed. The investor's *real* interest return must be:

$$
\begin{array}{c}
\text{Actual real rate} \\
\text{of return on} \\
\text{the TIPS}
\end{array}
=
\begin{array}{c}
\text{Nominal rate} \\
\text{of return on} \\
\text{the TIPS}
\end{array}
-
\begin{array}{c}
\text{Actual} \\
\text{annual CPI} \\
\text{inflation rate}
\end{array}
\qquad (7.10)
$$

Or, in the example above:

**Actual annual real rate of return on the 5-year TIPS bond = 7.5% − 4% = 3.5%**

The nominal return on the TIPS rises to 7.5 percent if inflation persists for five years at a 4 percent annual rate because *both* the face value of the bond and its interest earnings are adjusted upward. In contrast, if the markets fully anticipated this 4 percent inflation rate, then a conventional bond would have to fall in value to about

$$
\begin{array}{c}
\text{Adjusted real value} \\
\text{of a conventional} \\
\text{bond under inflation}
\end{array}
=
\dfrac{\text{Face value of conventional bond}}{\left[ 1 + \dfrac{\text{Actual}}{\text{annual rate of inflation}} \right]^{\text{Years to maturity}}}
\qquad (7.11)
$$

$$
= \frac{\$1,000}{(1 + .04)^5} = \$821.93
$$

in order to remain competitive in the market with TIPS and other inflation-adjusted assets available for purchase. The result for the conventional bond is an inflation-caused capital loss of $178.07 (or $1,000 − $821.93) if the investor sells the conventional bond prior to its maturity. Moreover, by the fifth year the investor's *real* annual interest income from the conventional bond would have dropped to only $28.77 [or $35/(1 + .04)^5] with inflation running at 4 percent a year. In contrast, as we saw in the table above, by holding a TIPS instead, this investor would receive a principal payment of $1,216.65 at the end of five years, gaining an additional $216.65 in nominal principal over a five-year period, or an average gain in principal of $43.33 per year. (Remember, however, that the investor's real principal value of the bond held at the end of five years would still be just $1,000, assuming a 4 percent annual inflation rate.) The TIPS's nominal price gain of $216.65 (or $1,216.65 − $1,000) plus its additional nominal interest revenues (which over five years will result in a total of $22.16 in additional interest income) would result in a nominal yield of about 7.5 percent.

Thus, Treasury inflation-index bonds (TIPS) are a relatively safe type of asset whose remaining risks include the danger that the real interest rate prevailing in the market will change (i.e., exposure to real interest rate risk). For example, real interest rates may rise and erode the real value of any bond; however, these new inflation-adjusted bonds make the management of risk more efficient by at least limiting an investor's overall risk exposure. The coupon (interest) income and the principal payment from these indexed bonds are both fixed in terms of purchasing power.

We should note, however, that not all inflation risk is eliminated by TIPS because rising inflation can drive an investor into a higher tax bracket, resulting in an after-tax rate of return that may be significantly less than the full inflation-adjusted real interest income from these special bonds. Moreover, TIPS are subject to market risk if an investor wishes to sell them ahead of their maturity date. However, Shen [15] has demonstrated that the overall market risk for inflation-indexed bonds appears to be smaller than that for conventional bonds. Still, most investors in the financial markets have been lukewarm in their response to TIPS, possibly because these innovative instruments appeared during a period when inflation was relatively low inside the United States.

Exhibit 7.3 illustrates the interesting relationship over time between the yields on inflation-adjusted versus noninflation-adjusted Treasury securities and the public's

**EXHIBIT 7.3**

**Relationship between Inflation and Yield Spreads for Inflation-Adjusted versus Unadjusted Securities**

Source: Federal Reserve Bank of Cleveland, Research Department, *Economic Trends,* November 2006.

Note: Inflationary expectations are based upon the monthly University of Michigan Household Survey.

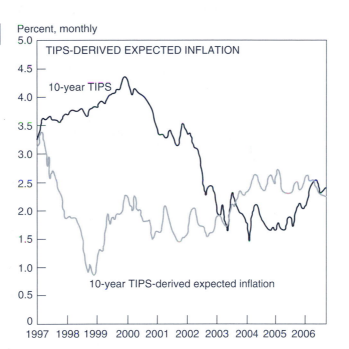

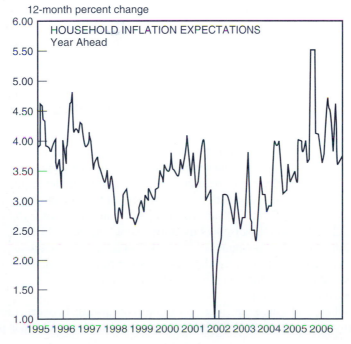

expectations regarding future inflation. The difference between the nominal market yield on TIPS and the nominal market yield on non-inflation-adjusted Treasury securities of the same maturity gives us an approximate financial market forecast of future inflation. Theory suggests that when the public comes to expect faster inflation, TIPS and other inflation-adjusted financial assets will become more valuable. Their prices will rise and their yields will fall relative to the yields on ordinary financial assets not bearing an inflation-adjustment mechanism.

---

### QUESTIONS TO HELP YOU STUDY

1. What is *inflation*? Why is it important?

2. Explain how inflation affects interest rates. What is the *Fisher effect*? What does it assume?

3. Explain how nominal contracts may cause inflation to affect the stock prices of some firms differently than it affects the stock prices of other firms.

4. In what ways might inflation cause the prices of corporate stock to rise or fall? How might the *proxy effect* appear to create an inflation-stock-price link?

5. What are *TIPS*? What advantages do they offer investors? Any disadvantages?

---

## 7.5   The Maturity of a Loan

**maturity**

One of the most important factors causing interest rates to differ from one another is the **maturity** (or term) of securities and loans. Financial assets traded today in the world's financial markets have a wide variety of maturities. In the federal funds and U.S. government securities markets, for example, some loans are overnight or over-the-weekend transactions, with the borrower repaying the loan in a matter of hours. At the other end of the spectrum, bonds and mortgages used to finance the purchase of new homes often stretch out 25 to 30 years, and some large corporations have recently issued 100-year bonds. Between these extremes lie thousands of financial assets issued by large and small borrowers with a tremendous variety of maturities.

### *The Yield Curve and the Term Structure of Interest Rates*

**yield curve**

The relationship between the rate of return (yield) on financial instruments and their maturity is called the *term structure of interest rates.* This term structure may be represented visually by drawing a **yield curve** for all financial assets having the same credit quality. Examples of the yield curve for U.S. government securities as it appeared during a period when the relationship between short-term and long-term interest rates was changing significantly is shown in the left-hand panel of Exhibit 7.4. The right-hand panel of Exhibit 7.4 displays the movements of the yield curve in more recent times when changes in the shapes of the yield curve were more moderate. We note that yield to maturity (measured by the annual percentage rate of return) is plotted along the vertical axis, and the horizontal scale shows the length of time (term) to final maturity (measured in years).

The yield curve considers only the relationship between the maturity or term of a financial asset and its yield at one moment in time (all other potentially influential

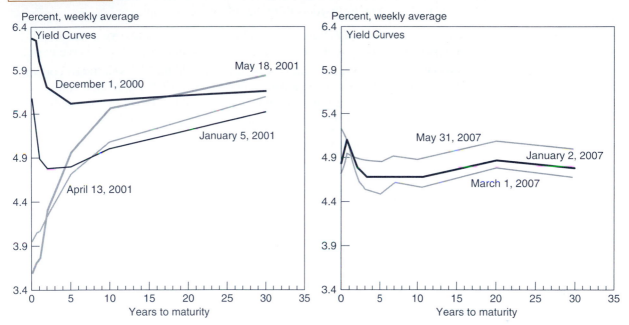

**A Variety of Yield Curves for U.S. Treasury Securities**

Source: U.S. Treasury Department and Federal Reserve Bank of Cleveland, *Economic Trends,* June 2001 and June 2007.

factors held constant). For example, we cannot draw a yield curve for assets bearing different degrees of credit risk or subject to different tax laws because both risk and tax laws affect relative yields along with maturity. We may, however, draw a yield curve for U.S. government securities of varying maturity, for example, because they all have minimal credit risk, the same tax status, and so on. Similarly, yield curves could be constructed for all corporate bonds or for all municipal bonds having the same credit rating.

## Types of Yield Curves

**Key URL:**
To follow the daily yield curve, see **investinginbonds.com**

Several different types of yield curves have been observed, but most may be described as upward sloping, downward sloping, or horizontal (flat). An upward-sloping yield curve indicates that borrowers must pay higher interest rates for longer-term loans than for shorter-term loans. A downward-sloping yield curve means that longer-term financial assets presently carry lower interest rates than shorter-term assets. Each of these different shapes that the yield curve may assume has important implications for lenders, borrowers, and the financial institutions that serve them.

## The Unbiased Expectations Hypothesis

**unbiased expectations hypothesis**

What determines the shape or slope of the yield curve? We can begin to answer this question by appealing to the **unbiased expectations hypothesis** of the term structure of interest rates. This theory emphasizes the importance of investor expectations regarding changes in shorter-term interest rates as the primary determinant of the shape of the yield curve. Let's look at an example to illustrate the basic proposition in this theory.

Suppose you are planning to invest $1,000 in U.S. government securities for the next two years, at the end of which time you will need those funds for purchases you anticipate making. You limit yourself to the following two options:

1. Adopt a *buy-and-hold* strategy, whereby you purchase a two-year (zero-coupon) bond today that is carrying a yield-to-maturity of $R_1 = 7$ percent; or

2. Adopt a *roll-over* strategy, under which you would buy a 1-year (zero-coupon) bond today yielding $r_1 = 5$ percent, and upon maturity of that bond at the end of the first year of your investment, you would roll over the proceeds (principal + interest) into an identical 1-year (zero-coupon) bond.

Under investment strategy 1, the total return after two years is:

$$\text{Total return, Strategy 1} = \$1{,}000\,(1 + R_1)^2 = \$1{,}000\,(1.07)^2 = \$1{,}144.90$$

Now consider investment strategy 2. In this case, the investor knows what the yield on his investment will be in the first year, but not in the second, since interest rates vary over time and are not completely predictable. Therefore, the best that he can do is make a forecast of what the future (forward) one-year interest rate will be and use this forecast to compute an *expected total return* for this investment strategy. Let this expected forward rate be denoted by $Er_2$. Then:

$$\text{Expected total return, Strategy 2} = \$1{,}000\,(1 + r_1)\,(1 + Er_2)$$
$$= \$1{,}000\,(1.05)\,(1 + Er_2) = \$1{,}050.00\,(1 + Er_2)$$

The unbiased expectations hypothesis states that any two investment strategies that are available in the market, and that involve assets which differ *only* by their terms to maturity, should yield the same holding period return to the investor. Therefore,

$$\text{Total return, Strategy 1} = \text{Expected total return, Strategy 2}$$

or,

$$\$1{,}144.90 = \$1{,}050.00\,(1 + Er_2) \quad \text{and} \quad Er_2 = 0.0904 \text{ or } 9.04\,\%$$

These results imply that if the investor were to adopt the roll-over strategy by investing in the short-term bond, he must be compensated in the second year with a higher rate of return to offset the low rate of return the first year. Otherwise, he would never buy the short-term asset. Since *all* potential investors have this same option available to them in the marketplace, funds would begin moving from short-term assets into longer-term assets. This would cause the price of the short-term assets to fall and their yield to rise, while the price of long-term assets would rise and their yields would fall. Such arbitrage activity would continue until the expected holding-period returns were once again brought back into equality. This would correspond to an equilibrium set of market interest rates for which investors would not seek to move funds across maturities in search of higher expected returns.

What can we conclude from this exercise? Whenever the current short-term interest rate is below the current long-term interest rate, or $r_1 < R_1$, then the short rate is expected to rise in the future, or $Er_2 > r_1$. The reverse is also predicted. Whenever the current short-term interest rate is above the current long-term interest rate, or $r_1 > R_1$, the short rate is expected to fall in the future, or $Er_2 < r_1$.

This basic conclusion can be extended to assets of any two maturities provided that their term to maturity is the only difference between them. In general, the unbiased

**Key URLs:**
The construction of yield curves is explored at such Web sites as **mathematicalfinance .com and at pvlinton .com/securiti .htm**

expectations hypothesis predicts that the current yields on a one-period asset, $r_1$, versus an $n$-period asset, $R_1$, will have the following relationship:

$$(1 + R_1)^n = (1 + r_1)(1 + Er_2)(1 + Er_3) \cdots (1 + Er_n) \tag{7.12}$$

where the left-hand side of equation (7.12) is the known total return per dollar from investing in the $n$-period asset and holding it until maturity, and the right-hand side is the expected total return per dollar from investing in the one-period asset and rolling it over for $n$ periods.

Note that equation (7.12) could be applied repeatedly to the yield curve, first by comparing a one-period asset with a two-period asset to compute the future expected one-period interest rate, $Er_2$, then again by comparing the one-period and three-period assets, to compute the next future expected one-period interest rate, $Er_3$, and so on, until the entire sequence of expected short-term interest rates is mapped out. This process gives a prediction of the relationship between the shape of the yield curve and future expected short-term interest rates.

*When the yield curve is upward-sloping, short-term interest rates are expected to rise. When the yield curve is downward-sloping, short-term interest rates are expected to fall. When the yield curve is flat (with a zero slope), short-term interest rates are not expected to change.*

### Assumptions of the Expectations Hypothesis

The unbiased expectations hypothesis assumes that investors act as *profit maximizers* over their planned holding periods and have no maturity preferences. All financial assets in a given risk class, regardless of maturity, are perfect substitutes for each other in the minds of investors. Under this theory all investors are *risk neutral*. That is, they do not care about the character of the distribution of possible returns from an asset, only about its expected (mean) return. Each investor will seek those individual assets or combinations of assets offering the highest expected (mean) rates of return. For example, it is immaterial to investors with a planned 10-year investment horizon whether they buy a 10-year bond, two 5-year bonds, or a series of 1-year bonds until their 10-year holding period terminates. Each investor will pursue the investment strategy that offers the highest expected rate of return or yield over the length of his or her planned holding period. Profit-maximizing behavior on the part of thousands of investors interacting in the marketplace ensures that holding-period yields on all financial assets move toward equality.

Once equilibrium is achieved, and assuming no transactions costs, the investor should earn the *same* yield from buying a long-term asset as from purchasing a series of short-term assets whose combined maturities equal that of the long-term asset. If the rate of return on long-term financial assets rises above or falls below the return the investor expects to receive from buying and selling a series of short-term assets, forces are quickly set in motion to restore equilibrium. Investors at the margin will practice *arbitrage* (moving funds from one market to another) until long-term yields once again are brought into balance with short-term yields.

## Policy Implications of the Unbiased Expectations Hypothesis

The unbiased expectations hypothesis has important implications for *public policy*. The theory implies that changes in the relative quantities of long-term versus short-term financial assets do *not* influence the shape of the yield curve *unless* investor expectations also are affected. For example, suppose the U.S. Treasury decided to refinance $100 billion of its maturing short-term IOUs by issuing $100 billion in long-term bonds. Would this government action affect the shape of the yield curve? Certainly the supply of long-term bonds would be increased, while the supply of short-term assets would be reduced. However, according to the expectations theory, the yield curve itself would not be changed *unless* investors altered their expectations about the future course of short-term interest rates.

To cite one more example, the Federal Reserve System buys and sells government securities frequently in the money and capital markets to promote the economic goals of the United States. Can the Fed (or, for that matter, any other central bank around the world) influence the shape of the yield curve by buying one maturity of financial assets and selling another? Once again, the answer is "no" *unless* the central bank can influence the interest-rate expectations of investors. Why? The reason lies in the underlying assumption of the unbiased expectations hypothesis: *Investors regard all financial assets, whatever their maturity, as perfect substitutes.* Therefore, the relative amounts of long-term assets versus short-term assets simply should *not* matter.

## The Liquidity Premium View of the Yield Curve

The strong assumptions underlying the unbiased expectations hypothesis coupled with the real-world behavior of investors have caused many financial analysts to question that theory's veracity. Securities dealers who trade actively in the financial markets frequently argue that other factors besides interest rate expectations also exert a significant impact on the character and shape of the yield curve.

For example, in recent years, most yield curves have sloped *upward.* This fact appears to be inconsistent with the unbiased expectations hypothesis since it requires investors to be expecting short-term interest rates to be rising most of the time, which they do not. Therefore, financial analysts have asked: Is there a *built-in bias* toward positively sloped yield curves due to factors other than interest rate expectations? The *liquidity premium view* of the yield curve suggests that such a *bias* exists.

Long-term financial assets tend to have more volatile market prices than short-term assets. Therefore, the investor faces greater risk of capital loss when buying long-term financial instruments. This greater risk of loss will be important to an investor who is *risk averse* (not risk neutral as in the expectations theory). To overcome the risk of capital loss, investors must be paid an extra return in the form of an interest rate (term) premium to encourage them to purchase long-term financial instruments. This additional rate or yield premium for surrendering liquidity—known as the **liquidity premium**—would tend to give yield curves a bias towards a *positive slope.*

**liquidity premium**

The liquidity premium can be incorporated into the unbiased expectations hypothesis by estimating the extent to which risk aversion biases upward long-term interest rates over short-term interest rates. In comparing the rates of return on a one-period and an *n*-period asset, equation (7.12) can be rewritten, with the liquidity premium denoted by $\lambda$, as:

$$(1 + R_1)^n = (1 + r_1)(1 + Er_2)(1 + Er_3)\ldots(1 + Er_n) + \lambda \qquad (7.13)$$

It is noteworthy that the size of the liquidity premium, $\lambda$, varies over time, but is always positive. Why then do some yield curves slope downward? In such instances, expectations of declining short-term interest rates simply overwhelm the liquidity premium effect.

Another important feature of the liquidity premium is that the size of this premium may not be the same when comparing, for example, yields on the 30-year T-bond versus the 3-month T-bill rather than, say, the yields on the 3-year T-note versus the 3-month T-bill. This feature of the liquidity premium may help explain why yield curves tend to *flatten out* at the longest maturities. (Note that this flattening out at the long-term end of the maturity spectrum is characteristic of all the yield curves shown in Exhibit 7.4.) There are obvious differences in liquidity between a 1-year and a 10-year bond, but it is not clear that major differences in liquidity exist between a 10-year bond and a 20-year bond, for example. Therefore, the size of the required liquidity (or term) premium may decrease for securities bearing longer maturities.

## 7.6 The Segmented-Markets and Preferred Habitat Arguments

### The Possible Impact of Segmented Markets on the Yield Curve

**market segmentation argument**

A strong challenge to the expectations and liquidity premium explanations of the yield curve appeared several years ago in the form of the **market segmentation argument,** or *hedging pressure theory.* The underlying assumption is that all financial assets are *not* perfect substitutes in the minds of investors. *Maturity preferences* exist among some investor groups, and those investors will not stray from their desired maturity range unless induced to do so by higher yields or other favorable terms on longer- or shorter-term assets.

Why might some investors prefer one asset maturity over another? Market segmentationists find the answer in a fundamental assumption concerning investor behavior, especially the investment behavior of financial intermediaries, such as mutual funds, pension funds, and banks. These investor groups, it is argued, often act as *risk minimizers* rather than profit maximizers as assumed under the expectations hypothesis. They prefer to *hedge* against the risk of fluctuations in the prices and yields of financial assets by balancing the maturity structure of their assets with the maturity structure of their liabilities.

For example, pension funds tend to have stable and predictable long-term liabilities. Therefore, these intermediaries prefer to invest in bonds, stocks, and other long-term financial assets. Banks, on the other hand, have volatile money market liabilities and thus prefer to confine the majority of their investments to shorter-term assets. These investor groups often employ the *hedging principle* of portfolio management: correlating the maturities of their liabilities with the maturities of their assets to ensure the ready availability of liquid funds when those funds are needed. This portfolio strategy reduces the risks of fluctuating income and loss of principal.

The existence of maturity preferences among investor groups implies that the financial markets are *not* one large pool of loanable funds but rather are segmented by maturity into a series of submarkets. Thus, the market for financial assets of medium maturity (for example, 5- to 10-year bonds) attracts different investor groups than the market for long-term (over 10-year) assets. Demand and supply curves within each maturity range are held to be the dominant factors shaping the level and structure of interest rates within that maturity range. However, interest rates prevailing in one maturity range are little influenced by demand and supply forces at work in other maturity ranges.

The segmented-markets or hedging-pressure theory does *not* rule out the possible influence of expectations in shaping the term structure of interest rates, but it argues that other factors related to maturity-specific demand and supply forces are also important.

## Policy Implications of the Segmented-Markets Theory

The segmented-markets theory, like the expectations theory, has significant implications for public policy. *If* markets along the maturity spectrum are relatively isolated from each other due to investor maturity preferences, government policymakers can alter the shape of the yield curve merely by influencing supply and demand in one or more market segments.

For example, if a positively sloped yield curve were desired, the government could flood the market with long-term bonds. Simultaneously, the government could purchase large quantities of short-term securities. The expanded supply of bonds would drive long-term interest rates higher, while government purchases of short-term securities would push short-term interest rates down, other factors held equal. Therefore, the government could alter the shape of the yield curve merely by shifting the supplies available of different maturities of financial assets relative to the demand for those assets. This conclusion directly contradicts the unbiased expectations hypothesis.

## The Preferred Habitat or Composite Theory of the Yield Curve

**preferred habitat**

During the 1960s and 1970s, an expanded model of the determinants of the yield curve appeared that attempted to combine the expectations, liquidity premium, and market segmentation arguments into a single theory. This composite view argues that investors seek out their **preferred habitat** along the scale of varying maturities of financial assets that matches their risk preferences, tax exposure, liquidity needs, regulatory requirements, and planned holding periods. Normally, an investor will not stray from his or her preferred habitat unless rates of return on longer- or shorter-term assets are high enough to overcome each investor's preferences. The result is that markets for financial assets are divided into distinct submarkets by these multifaceted investor preferences. Thus, according to the preferred habitat theory, factors other than expectations alone play a role in shaping the character of the yield curve.

Proponents of preferred habitat argue that investors derive their expectations about future interest rates on the basis of *historical experience*—the recent trend of interest rates and what history suggests is a "normal" range for rates. In the short term, the majority of investors expect current interest-rate trends to persist into the future; thus, rising interest rates in recent weeks often lead to the expectation that rates will continue to rise in the near term. However, investors generally expect that, given sufficient time (months or years), interest rates will return to their historical averages. An important implication here is that more recent movements in interest rates are linked to *past* interest rate behavior—a conclusion that tends to contradict the expectations and efficient markets theories of how the financial markets operate.

## Research Evidence on the Yield Curve

Which view of the yield curve is correct? A number of research studies (e.g., Campbell, [3]) seem to reject the unbiased expectations hypothesis and find that the yield curve

In recent years, the Federal Reserve has pursued a monetary policy of influencing short-term interest rates in the economy in order to achieve its macroeconomic goals of high and sustainable economic growth and employment in an environment of low inflation. Therefore, when economic activity slows, the Federal Reserve attempts to boost investment spending, in particular by lowering short-term interest rates, expecting a concomitant decline in longer-term interest rates, which reflect the cost of capital to firms wishing to make capital investments. Conversely, when the Federal Reserve begins to see inflation heating up, it will raise short-term interest rates in anticipation of higher long-term rates that will slow demand for investment goods and mitigate inflation.

This relationship between short-term and long-term interest rates is, therefore, an important one for the purposes of monetary policy. Historically, this relationship is positive, and the long-term interest rate appears to be largely composed of a weighted average of current and future expected short-term interest rates (holding risk and liquidity fixed). In a speech by then–Federal Reserve Chairman Alan Greenspan in Beijing, China in June 2005, the chairman noted a central fact that has puzzled policymakers recently. The Federal Reserve raised the key short-term interest rate on federal funds 200 basis points between mid-2004 and early 2006, only to see long-term bond yields *fall by 80 basis points*. In testimony before Congress in July, 2005, Mr. Greenspan stated that "such a pattern is clearly without precedent in our recent experience." He characterized this phenomenon as a "conundrum"—we simply don't know why it occurred.

In subsequent Congressional testimony, Mr. Greenspan summarized some of the research that staff economists at the Federal Reserve have conducted on this question.

He first observed that over the past decade long-term interest rates have fallen *worldwide* to low levels that are truly "remarkable." This suggested to him that this "conundrum" had its source in the continuing process of *globalization* of goods, services, and the financial markets.

With the breakup of the Soviet Union and the extraordinary emergence of many less-developed countries, most notably India and China, there has been an increasing flow of the worldwide pool of savings across political boundaries to finance the world's "low-cost productive capacity." This increase in global productive capacity has had the beneficial effect of keeping inflation and inflation risk low and has thereby been an important contributing factor to the decade-long downward trend in both real and nominal long-term interest rates.

In his concluding remarks in Beijing, Mr. Greenspan acknowledged our lack of understanding of all implications of globalization. However, he pointed to the increasing sophistication and interconnectedness of global financial markets and of their growing ability to respond flexibly to major shocks and to remain resilient in their aftermath, as occurred after 9/11. He concluded with the suggestion that policymakers find ways to enhance the ability of the markets to absorb shocks, and thereby reduce their reliance on officials' uncertain forecasting capabilities.

Note: Mr. Greenspan's speech at the international monetary conference in Beijing in June 2005 can be downloaded from the Federal Reserve Board's Web site at **http://www.federalreserve.gov/boarddocs/speeches/2005/20050606/default.htm**. His testimony before Congress in July 2005 can be found at **http://www.federalreserve.gov/boarddocs/hh/2005/july/testimony.htm#f6**.

does *not* have significant predictive power in forecasting interest rates. However, these findings are contradicted by other research studies (e.g., Longstaff [12]) that find evidence consistent with the unbiased expectations hypothesis. Some of these studies find significant forecasting power from the yield curve in predicting changes in interest rates, inflation, and the economy.

For example, Fama and Bliss [5] found that one-year forward interest rates could forecast changes in the one-year interest rate two to four years in advance. Moreover, there is some evidence that yield curves can provide useful forecasts of inflation over periods of one year or longer.

This longer-term forecasting power of the yield curve may be due to the tendency of interest rates to move back toward their historic mean levels over a sufficiently long period of time (known as *mean reversion*). Although all investors clearly do not regard all maturities of financial assets as perfect substitutes, there are sufficient numbers of traders in the financial marketplace who do *not* have specific maturity preferences. These investors are guided principally by the relative expected returns on different assets. Their beliefs and actions may bring about the results predicted by the expectations theory.

Nevertheless, there is evidence that nonexpectational factors, especially the demand for liquidity, do affect the shape of the yield curve. Studies by Van Horne [17] and others point to the existence of a liquidity premium attached to the yields on longer-term securities, compensating investors for added risk. Moreover, liquidity premiums appear to get smaller as we move toward longer asset maturities, and these premiums are also sensitive to the business cycle, rising in recessions and falling in business expansions. Also, term premiums do *not* appear to increase or decrease *uniformly* as maturity increases or decreases.

Recent research has delved more deeply into the issue of what kinds of events cause the yield curve's overall shape to change. Statistically, yield curves may change along any of at least three different dimensions: *level, slope,* or *curvature*.[3] As Exhibit 7.5A suggests, a change in the *level* of the yield curve means that interest rates all along the curve move roughly in parallel, shifting the whole curve up or down. Macroeconomic forces, such as increased inflation, a weaker economy, or significant technological change, may have their greatest impact on a yield curve's level.

In contrast, the curve's *slope* or steepness changes when shorter-term interest rates rise or fall by greater amounts than longer-term interest rates. One measure of the slope of a yield curve is the longest-term interest rate ($r_l$) minus the shortest-term interest rate ($r_s$) contained in the curve divided by the difference in their terms to maturity. When this interest rate (or yield) spread is positive, the yield curve is generally upward sloping. Statistical evidence from U.S. data suggests that shifts in Federal Reserve monetary policy are one of the major influences on the curve's slope. This effect is captured in Exhibit 7.5B which depicts the central bank tightening money and

---

[3] See especially Dai and Singleton [4] and Wu [19].

---

**EXHIBIT 7.5**    **The Level, Slope, and Curvature of Yield Curves**

A. Shifts in the *level* of the yield curve

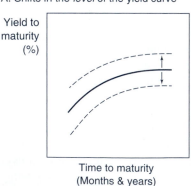

Yield to maturity (%)

Time to maturity (Months & years)

B. Changes in the *slope* of the yield curve

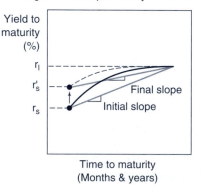

Yield to maturity (%)

$r_l$

$r_s'$    Final slope

$r_s$    Initial slope

Time to maturity (Months & years)

C. Changes in the yield curve's *curvature*

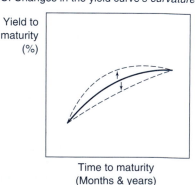

Yield to maturity (%)

Time to maturity (Months & years)

credit conditions by raising short-term interest rates from $r_s$ to $r_s'$. If long-term interest rates initially do not change (as shown) or change by a lesser amount than short rates (as is usually the case), then the average slope of the curve declines. In this example, the initial slope is seen to be steeper than the final slope.

Finally, as Exhibit 7.5C depicts, the *curvature* of a yield curve may change when interest rates in the middle of the maturity spectrum are impacted, such as by a shift in economic conditions of moderate length. This development would tend to give the yield curve a greater or lesser "hump" along its midsection. These various dimensions of a yield curve—its level, slope, and curvature—suggest that these curves are far more complex and more intimately connected with the economy and government policy than was once thought.

## 7.7  Uses of the Yield Curve

The controversy surrounding the determinants of the yield curve should not obscure the fact that this curve can be an extremely useful tool for borrowers and lenders.

*Forecasting Interest Rates*    If the expectations hypothesis is correct, the yield curve gives the investor a clue concerning the future course of interest rates. If the curve has an upward slope, for example, the investor may be well advised to look for opportunities to move away from long-term financial assets into investments whose market price is less sensitive to interest rate changes. A downward-sloping yield curve, on the other hand, suggests the likelihood of near-term declines in interest rates and/or a rally in bond prices if the market's forecast of lower rates turns out to be true.

One version of the yield curve—the so-called *yield spread* between long-term and short-term government securities—has been found in the United States to aid in the prediction of real growth in the economy and to seemingly forecast coming recessions in economic activity. According to several researchers a flattening of the yield curve conveys a strong signal that the economy is weakening, and this could foreshadow a looming recession. For example, a study by Stojanovic and Vaughan [16] finds that an inverted yield curve—where short-term interest rates are higher than long-term interest rates—has preceded U.S. economic recessions since 1960 and has generally out predicted other widely used forecasting data series, such as common stock prices and the U.S. Commerce Department's Index of Leading Economic Indicators. In general, the *smaller* the interest rate spread between long- and short-term interest rates, the *greater* the probability of a recession in the United States over the next four quarters. Moreover, recent studies (e.g., Bonser-Neal and Morley [2]) of Australia, Canada, Japan, the United States, and the nations of Western Europe suggest the yield spread seems to predict growth in GDP (gross domestic product) for these nations over the next year or so with greater accuracy than other popular economic indicators.

*Uses for Financial Intermediaries*    The slope of the yield curve is critical for financial intermediaries, especially depository institutions. A steepening yield curve is generally favorable for these institutions because they borrow most of their funds by selling short-term deposits and lend a significant portion of those funds long term. The more steeply the yield curve slopes upward, the wider the spread between borrowing and lending rates and the greater the potential profit for a financial intermediary. However, if the yield curve begins to flatten out or slope downward, this should serve as a warning signal to managers of these institutions.

A flattening or downward-sloping yield curve squeezes the earnings of financial intermediaries and calls for an entirely different portfolio management strategy than an upward-sloping curve. For example, if an upward-sloping yield curve starts to flatten out, portfolio managers of financial institutions might try to lock in relatively cheap sources of funds by getting long-term commitments from funds-supplying customers. Borrowers, on the other hand, might be encouraged to take out long-term loans at fixed rates of interest. Of course, the institution's customers also may be aware of impending changes in the yield curve and resist accepting loans or deposits with terms heavily favoring financial intermediaries.

### Detecting Overpriced and Underpriced Financial Assets

Yield curves can be used as an aid to investors in deciding which assets are temporarily overpriced or underpriced. This use of the yield curve derives from the fact that, in equilibrium, the yields on all financial assets of comparable risk should come to rest along the yield curve at their appropriate maturity levels. In an efficient market, however, any deviations of individual assets from the yield curve will be short-lived, so the investor must act quickly.

If a financial asset's rate of return lies *above* the yield curve for financial assets of comparable risk, this sends a signal to investors: The asset is temporarily *underpriced* relative to other assets bearing the same maturity. Other things equal, this is a *buy* signal some investors will take advantage of, driving the price of the purchased asset upward and its yield back down toward the curve. On the other hand, if an asset's rate of return is temporarily *below* the yield curve, this indicates a temporarily *overpriced* financial instrument, because its yield is below that of financial assets bearing the same maturity. Some investors holding this asset will *sell,* pushing its price down and its yield back up toward the curve. Exploiting these market imperfections can lead to large profits. As a consequence, the competition among well-placed investors to capture these extraordinary profits causes the mispricing of these assets to be relatively short-lived.

### Indicating Trade-Offs between Maturity and Yield

Still another use of the yield curve is to indicate the current trade-off between maturity and yield confronting the investor. If an investor wishes to alter the maturity of her portfolio, the yield curve indicates what gain or loss in rate of return may be expected for each change in the portfolio's average maturity.

With an upward-sloping yield curve, for example, an investor may be able to increase a bond portfolio's expected annual yield from 7 percent to 9 percent by extending the portfolio's average maturity from 1 to 10 years. However, the prices of longer-term bonds are more volatile, creating greater risk of capital loss. Longer-term assets tend to be less liquid than short-term assets. Therefore, the investor must weigh the gain in yield from extending the maturity of his or her portfolio against added price and liquidity risk. Because yield curves tend to flatten out for the longest maturities, the investor bent on lengthening the maturity of a portfolio eventually discovers that gains in yield get smaller for each additional unit of maturity. At some point along the yield curve it no longer pays, in terms of extra yield, to further extend the maturity of an investor's asset portfolio.

### Riding the Yield Curve

Finally, some active investors, especially dealers in government securities, have learned to "ride" the yield curve for profit. If the curve is positively sloped, with a slope steep enough to offset transactions costs, the investor may gain by timely portfolio switching.

For example, suppose that 3-month T-bills are currently carrying a discount rate of 4 percent, and 6-month T-bills have a 6 percent discount rate. Further suppose that a security dealer believes that these rates will persist into the future. He could "ride" the yield curve to higher profits by purchasing, say, a $10,000 U.S. T-bill with six months left to maturity, then sell it after three months. From the discount rate formula (6.3) in Chapter 6, we could compute the capital gain. He would purchase the T-bill for $9,700 and sell it for $9,800, yielding a capital gain of $100. Had he simply purchased a $10,000, 3-month T-bill initially, he would have paid $9,900 and received $10,000 upon maturity. In both cases, the dealer would receive interest income of $100 after three months; however, in the latter case of buying the shorter maturity 3-month T-bill, he would have had to make a higher investment ($9,900 versus $9,800), and the $100 interest income would have represented a lower rate of return. The proceeds from the sale of the 6-month T-bill at the end of three months could then be reinvested in additional 6-month T-bills, which could once again be sold after three months to raise the dealer's overall rate of return on his investments.

However, riding the yield curve can be risky because yield curves are constantly changing their shape. If the curve suddenly gets flatter or turns down, a potential gain can be turned into a realized loss. In this case, riding the yield curve may be less profitable than a simple "buy and hold" strategy. Experience and good judgment are indispensable in using the yield curve for profitable investment decision making.

---

### QUESTIONS TO HELP YOU STUDY

6. Explain the meaning of the phrase *term structure of interest rates*. What is a *yield curve*? What *assumptions* are necessary to construct a yield curve?

7. Explain the difference between the *expectations, market segmentation, preferred habitat,* and *liquidity premium* views of the yield curve. What does each theory assume?

8. What are the implications for investors and for public policy of each of the yield curve ideas mentioned in the preceding question?

9. What *uses* does the yield curve have? Why is each possible use of potential value to borrowers and lenders of funds?

10. What conclusions can you draw from recent research regarding the determinants of the yield curve? Which theory of the yield curve appears to be most supported by recent research studies?

---

## 7.8   Duration: A Different Approach to Maturity

### *The Price Elasticity of a Bond or Other Debt Security*

Theories of the yield curve remind us that longer-maturity financial assets tend to be more volatile in price. For example, for the same change in interest rates, the price of a longer-term bond generally changes more than the price of a shorter-term bond. A popular measure of how responsive a bond or other debt security's price is to changes in interest rates is its **price elasticity.** Thus:

**price elasticity**

$$
\begin{array}{c}
\text{Price elasticity of} \\
\text{a debt security} \\
(E)
\end{array}
=
\dfrac{\begin{array}{c}\text{Percentage change} \\ \text{over time in a} \\ \text{security's price}\end{array}}{\begin{array}{c}\text{Percentage change} \\ \text{over time in a} \\ \text{security's yield}\end{array}}
=
\dfrac{\dfrac{P_1 - P_0}{P_0}}{\dfrac{y_1 - y_0}{y_0}}
\qquad (7.14)
$$

where $P_0$ and $y_0$ represent a debt security's price and yield at some initial point in time, while $P_1$ and $y_1$ represent the security's price and yield at a subsequent point in time. Price elasticity is generally measured from a debt security's par-value coupon rate (that is, by setting $P_0$ in equation (7.14) equal to the par value and $y_0$ equal to the coupon rate). This results in larger downward price movements than upward price movements for a given percentage change in yield.[4] The price elasticity attached to a bond or other debt security must be negative, because rising interest rates (yields) result in falling debt security prices, and conversely.

For example, suppose we are interested in purchasing a 10-year bond, par value of $1,000, promising its holder a 10 percent coupon rate. Assume the bond pays interest of $100 once each year. Our discussion of the principles of bond pricing in Chapter 6 reminds us that if interest rates on comparable securities are currently at 10 percent, this bond will sell for exactly $1,000. If interest rates fall to 5 percent, this 10 percent bond will carry a price of about $1,389.70, and if rates climb to 15 percent, the bond's price will drop close to $745.10. What is the price elasticity of this bond, measured from par? From equation 7.14, we have for the *downward* movement in interest rates from 10 to 5 percent:

$$\text{Price elasticity of 10 percent bond (E)} = \frac{\dfrac{(\$1,389.70 - \$1,000)}{\$1,000}}{\dfrac{5\% - 10\%}{10\%}} = \frac{0.3897}{-0.5} = -0.779 \quad \textbf{(7.15)}$$

On the other hand, for an upward movement in interest rates from 10 to 15 percent, this bond's elasticity is $-0.510$. Clearly, $E$ is greater in absolute terms for a downward movement in interest rates (from 5 to 10 percent) than it is for a rise in interest rates (from 10 to 15 percent).

Higher price elasticity means that an asset goes through a greater price change for a given change in market rates of interest. And, as we noted above, longer-term debt securities generally carry greater price risk (their price elasticity, $E$, is larger) than shorter-term debt securities. However, this relationship between maturity and price elasticity is *not* linear (i.e., not strictly proportional). It is *not* true, for example, that 10-year bonds are twice as price elastic (and price volatile) as 5-year bonds. One important reason for this nonlinear relationship is that the price volatility and elasticity of a debt security depend upon the size of its *coupon rate*—the annual rate of return promised by the borrower—as well as upon its maturity.

### The Impact of Varying Coupon Rates

The lower a debt security's annual coupon (promised) rate, the more volatile (and elastic) its price tends to be. Investors buying lower coupon securities generally take on greater risk of price fluctuations. In effect, a debt security promising lower annual coupon payments behaves as though it has a longer maturity even if it is due to mature on the same date as a security carrying a higher coupon rate. With a low coupon (promised) rate the investor must wait longer for a substantial return on her funds because a greater proportion of the low-coupon security's total dollar return lies in the final payment at maturity when the bond's face value is returned to the investor. And the further in the future cash payments are to be received, the more sensitive is the present value of that stream of payments to changes in interest rates.

[4] That is, for the same change in yield, capital gains generally are larger than capital losses on the same financial asset.

**coupon effect**

The relationship we have been describing is called the **coupon effect.** It says simply that the prices of low-coupon securities tend to rise *faster* than the prices of high-coupon securities when market interest rates decline. Similarly, a period of rising interest rates will cause the prices of low-coupon securities to fall *faster* than the prices of high-coupon securities. Thus, the potential for capital gains and capital losses is greater for low-coupon than for high-coupon securities.

We can illustrate this coupon effect with a simple example. Consider two bonds with a par value of $1,000 each and both with two years left to maturity. One bond is a zero-coupon bond selling at a discount and yielding 6 percent. The other bond pays annual $60 coupons and is also yielding 6 percent. From equation (6.7) in Chapter 6 the market prices of these two bonds can be computed as:

$$P \text{ (zero-coupon bond)} = \frac{\$1,000}{(1.06)^2} = \$890.00$$

$$P \text{ (6\% coupon bond)} = \frac{\$60}{1.06} + \frac{\$60}{(1.06)^2} + \frac{\$1,000}{(1.06)^2} = \$1,000.00$$

Now suppose that interest rates instantly fell to 3 percent. Recomputing the two bond prices will give $P$ (zero-coupon bond) = $942.60 for a capital gain of $52.60 or 5.91 percent, while $P$ (6% coupon bond) = $1,038.27 for a capital gain of $38.27 or 3.83 percent. Thus, the capital gain was substantially higher for the zero-coupon bond.

## *An Alternative Maturity Index for a Financial Asset: Duration*

Knowledge of the impact of varying coupon (promised) rates on security price volatility and elasticity resulted in the search for a new index of maturity other than straight calendar time (years and months)—the maturity measure used in conventional yield curves. What was needed was a measure of the term of a bond that would allow financial analysts to construct a *linear* (strictly proportional) relationship between maturity and price volatility or elasticity, regardless of differing coupon rates. Such a measure would have the property, for example, that a doubling of maturity would mean a doubling of price elasticity, thereby giving us a very useful, direct measure of the price risk faced by an investor. This maturity measure is known as **duration** and has the very practical interpretation in its simplest terms as *the average expected length of time required for the investor in the financial asset to recover her initial investment.*

**duration**

Note that for a zero-coupon bond, no payments are received on the bond until it matures. Therefore, the duration of the bond equals its term to maturity. For a bond that pays coupons, its duration is *always* less than its term to maturity. A financial asset's duration ($D$) is computed as follows:

$$D = \frac{\begin{array}{c}\text{Present value of interest and} \\ \text{principal payments from a} \\ \text{security weighted by the} \\ \text{timing of those payments}\end{array}}{\begin{array}{c}\text{Present value of the security's} \\ \text{promised stream of interest} \\ \text{and principal payments}\end{array}} = \frac{\sum\limits_{t=1}^{n} \dfrac{I_t(t)}{(1+y)^t}}{\sum\limits_{t=1}^{n} \dfrac{I_t}{(1+y)^t}} \qquad (7.16)$$

In the duration formula above, $I$ represents each expected payment of principal and interest from the asset and $t$ represents the time period in which each payment is to be received. The discount factor, $y$, is the yield to maturity, with final asset maturity reached at the end of $n$ periods. Duration reflects the price elasticity of a financial instrument with respect to changes in the instrument's yield to maturity. As the formula indicates, $D$ is a *weighted-average* measure of maturity in which each payment of interest and principal is multiplied by the time period in which it is expected to be received.

We can explain the use of duration through an example. Let us imagine that an investor is interested in purchasing a $1,000 par-value bond that has a term to maturity of 10 years, a 10 percent annual coupon rate (with interest paid once a year), and a 12 percent yield to maturity based on its current price of $887.10. Then its duration must be

$$\text{Duration } (D) = \frac{\dfrac{\$100(1)}{(1.12)^1} + \dfrac{\$100(2)}{(1.12)^2} + \cdots + \dfrac{\$100(10)}{(1.12)^{10}} + \dfrac{\$1,000(10)}{(1.12)^{10}}}{\dfrac{\$100}{(1.12)^1} + \dfrac{\$100}{(1.12)^2} + \cdots + \dfrac{\$100}{(1.12)^{10}} + \dfrac{\$1,000}{(1.12)^{10}}} \qquad (7.17)$$

or

$$D = \frac{\$5,810.90}{\$887.10} = 6.55 \text{ years}$$

There is a simple way to calculate $D$ that has the added value of making it easy to check your figures. Using the example above of the 10-year bond with a 12 percent yield to maturity, we can set up the following table:

**Key URL:**
To learn more about calculating and using duration see, for example,
**investopedia.com/calculator**

| Period | Expected Cash Flows from Security | Present Values of Expected Cash Flows (at 12% Rate of Discount) | Time Period Cash Is to Be Received (t) | Present Value of Expected Cash Flows × t |
|---|---|---|---|---|
| 1 | $ 100 | $ 89.30 | 1 | $ 89.30 |
| 2 | 100 | 79.70 | 2 | 159.40 |
| 3 | 100 | 71.20 | 3 | 213.60 |
| 4 | 100 | 63.60 | 4 | 254.40 |
| 5 | 100 | 56.70 | 5 | 283.50 |
| 6 | 100 | 50.70 | 6 | 304.20 |
| 7 | 100 | 45.20 | 7 | 316.40 |
| 8 | 100 | 40.40 | 8 | 323.20 |
| 9 | 100 | 36.10 | 9 | 324.90 |
| 10 | 100 | 32.20 | 10 | 322.00 |
| 10 | 1,000 | 322.00 | 10 | 3,220.00 |
| | | $ 887.10 | | $5,810.90 |

Then, as above, the duration of this bond must be

$$D = \frac{\text{Sum of present values of (cash flow} \times t)}{\text{Sum of present values of cash flows}} = \frac{\$5,810.90}{\$887.10} = 6.55 \text{ years}$$

Note that the denominator of the ratio above ($887.10) is the same value as the bond's current price.

A number of duration's features are evident from this example. For example, duration is always *less* than the time to maturity for a coupon-paying security.[5] Duration increases with a longer stream of future payments, but the rate of increase in $D$ decreases as time to maturity increases. The larger an asset's yield to maturity, $y$, the lower its duration.

Duration reflects the amount and timing of *all* payments expected during the life of a financial asset, unlike the conventional measure of maturity—calendar time—which shows only the length of time until the final cash payment. As described earlier, duration can be thought of as an index of the average amount of time required for the investor to recover the original cash outlay used to buy the asset. Assets bearing higher values of $D$ are more volatile in price and, therefore, carry increased price risk. Low-coupon bonds, for example, have longer durations and, therefore, display more price risk than high-coupon bonds.

## The Convexity Factor

When pricing a financial asset, the elasticity of the asset's price with respect to its yield is an extremely important feature that helps characterize the asset's level of price risk. If an investor believes that interest rates could swing, say, as much as two percentage points during the anticipated holding period, then the asset's price elasticity informs him of the maximum capital loss (and gain) he could expect. However, for any asset, this elasticity is not constant across the range of possible interest rates that might prevail during the life of the asset and, hence, during the investor's holding period. That is, price elasticity is a function of the *level* of the asset's yield. In general, an asset's price elasticity is higher (in absolute terms) at lower interest rates. This relationship between price risk and yield can be quantified by a measure called **convexity,** which measures the rate of change of the elasticity of prices with respect to yield, or how rapidly the investor's risk diminishes as interest rates rise.

convexity

Convexity can be illustrated by computing price elasticities with the aid of graphs that display an asset's price versus its yield. For example, Exhibit 7.6 shows the relationship between the price and yield of two different bonds that have different convexity properties. Suppose an investor purchases Asset 1 at $100 when its yield is 2 percent, identified as point A on the graph. Consider how much the yield would have to increase in order for him to realize a capital loss of 10 percent. As shown in the graph, the price decline to $90 would require a rise of one percentage point in the yield to 3 percent, the point marked A*. Using the price elasticity formula (7.14), we obtain $E_A = -0.20$.

Consider the same asset when it was selling at $50 and yielding 6 percent (point B). A 10 percent capital loss would lower the price to $48.33, and the graph suggests this would also correspond to a rise in yield of one percentage point, from 6 to 7 percent, and a price elasticity of $E_B = -0.20$. In this example, the price elasticity of the bond did not change.

Now consider Asset 2. If the asset were purchased at $100 with a yield of 2 percent (point C), a capital loss of 10 percent would correspond to a fall in the asset's price to $90 (point C*). This price decline would require a rise in yield of two percentage

---

[5] See Chapter 6 for a discussion of yield to maturity and calculating discounted present values such as required in the above duration formula. Any security carrying installment payments of principal and/or interest will have a duration shorter than its calendar maturity. Only for zero-coupon bonds or for any loan in which principal and accumulated interest are paid in a lump sum at maturity will duration and maturity be the same.

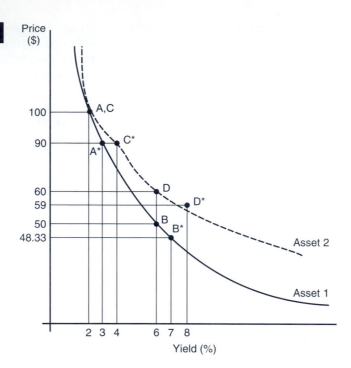

$$E_A \approx \frac{(90 - 100)/100}{(3 - 2)/2} = -0.200$$

$$E_B \approx \frac{(48.33 - 50)/50}{(7 - 6)/6} = -0.200$$

$$E_C \approx \frac{(90 - 100)/100}{(4 - 2)/2} = -0.100$$

$$E_D \approx \frac{(59 - 60)/60}{(8 - 6)/6} = -0.050$$

points from 2 to 4 percent, and the price elasticity would compute to $E_C = -0.10$. Suppose this same asset was yielding 6 percent and was priced at $60 (point D). How much of a capital loss would this investor experience if this asset's yield rose by two percentage points? In this case, the price would only fall to $59 (point D*), a capital loss of $1 or only 1.67 percent! This lower capital loss is reflected in the price elasticity, which is computed to be $E_D = -0.05$. In this case, the price elasticity of the bond *fell* as the yield *rose*. Research indicates that most fixed-income securities have precisely this property. The convexity measure for this asset would give the investor a precise relationship between changes in price elasticity and yield and could assist him in choosing fixed-income securities he may wish to incorporate into his investment portfolio.

## Uses of Duration

***Estimating Asset Price Changes***     Because duration is directly related to price volatility, there is a useful approximate relationship between changes in market interest rates and percentage changes in asset prices. This relationship may be written:

$$\begin{array}{c} \text{Percent change in} \\ \text{the price of an} \\ \text{asset (such as a} \\ \text{debt security)} \end{array} \approx -D\left[\frac{\Delta r}{1 + r}\right] \times 100 \qquad (7.18)$$

where $D$ is duration and $\Delta r$ is the change in interest rates. For example, consider the bond in the example above, whose duration was calculated to be 6.55 years. The bond's price at the coupon rate of 10 percent is $1,000, and at an $r$ of 12 percent, its price is $887.10. Thus, if the interest rate changes from 10 to 12 percent, the bond's approximate percentage decline in price would be

$$\text{Percent change in bond's price} \approx -6.55 \times \left[\frac{.02}{1 + 0.10}\right] \times 100 = -11.91\% \quad (7.19)$$

In this instance, if interest rates rise by two percentage points, the bond's price declines by almost 12 percent (measured from the bond's par value and coupon rate). An investor who expects interest rates to rise would find this information helpful in deciding whether to continue holding this bond. In general, investors concerned about the risk of loss due to rising interest rates tend to move toward financial assets of shorter duration, while falling interest rates usually lead investors toward assets of longer duration.

*Portfolio Immunization* Today, duration has aroused great interest among portfolio managers. The reason is its possible usefulness as a device to insulate (or, in the terminology of finance, *immunize*) asset portfolios against both market risk and/or reinvestment risk that can result from changing market interest rates. In theory, **portfolio immunization** can be achieved by simply acquiring a portfolio of assets whose average duration equals the length of the investor's desired holding period. If this is done, the effect is to hold the investor's total return *constant* regardless of whether interest rates rise or fall. In the absence of borrower default, the investor's realized return can be no less than the return he has been promised by the borrower. Only if the future course of interest rates were known for certain would portfolio immunization be a less than optimal strategy.

**portfolio immunization**

While the actual implementation of immunization strategies can be difficult and require close management of a financial asset portfolio, the basic concept of portfolio management using duration can be illustrated with a simple example. Suppose we are interested in purchasing a bond with a $1,000 par value that will mature in two years. The bond has a coupon rate of 8 percent, paying $80 in interest at the end of each year. Interest rates on comparable bonds also are currently at 8 percent but may fall to as low as 6 percent or rise as high as 10 percent. The buyer knows he or she will receive $1,000 at maturity, but in the meantime this buyer must face the uncertainty of having to reinvest the annual $80 in interest earnings from this bond at 6 percent, 8 percent, or 10 percent, depending on whether interest rates rise or fall.

Suppose interest rates decline to 6 percent. This bond will earn $80 in interest payments for year one, $80 for year two, but only $4.80 (or $80 × 0.06) when the $80 interest income received the first year is reinvested at 6 percent during year 2. With interest rates falling to 6 percent, the investor will earn only $1,164.80 in total over the two-year period:

| First year's interest earnings $\dfrac{}{\$80}$ | $+$ | Second year's interest earnings $\dfrac{}{\$80}$ | $+$ | Interest earned reinvesting the first year's interest earnings at a 6 percent interest rate $\dfrac{}{\$4.80}$ | $+$ | Par value of security returned to investor at maturity $\dfrac{}{\$1,000}$ | $=$ | Total return $\dfrac{}{\$1,164.80}$ |
|---|---|---|---|---|---|---|---|---|

$$(7.20)$$

On the other hand, what if interest rates rise to 10 percent after the first year? Again, the investor holding this bond earns $80 interest in each of the next two years but will also earn $8 in interest when he reinvests the $80 in interest income received at the end of the first year at the new rate of 10 percent ($80 × .10). In this case, the investor's total return from the bond will be $1,168 after two years:

| First year's interest earnings $\dfrac{}{\$80}$ | $+$ | Second year's interest earnings $\dfrac{}{\$80}$ | $+$ | Interest earned reinvesting the first year's interest earnings at a 10 percent interest rate $\dfrac{}{\$8.00}$ | $+$ | Par value of security returned to investor at maturity $\dfrac{}{\$1,000}$ | $=$ | Total return $\dfrac{}{\$1,168.00}$ |
|---|---|---|---|---|---|---|---|---|

Clearly, the bond buyer's earnings could drop as low as $1,164.80 (with a 6 percent interest rate) or rise as high as $1,168 (with a 10 percent interest rate). Is there a way to avoid this kind of fluctuation in earnings and stabilize the total return received? Yes, if the buyer finds a bond whose *duration matches his or her planned holding period.* For example, suppose the buyer finds a $1,000 bond that also carries an 8 percent coupon rate whose maturity exceeds two years but whose duration is exactly two years, matching the buyer's planned holding period. This means that, at the end of two years, the buyer will have to *sell* the bond at the price then prevailing in the market because it will not have reached maturity yet.

What will happen to the buyer's total earnings with a bond whose duration is exactly two years? First, if interest rates fall to 6 percent, the bond will earn $80 interest at the end of year 1 and another $80 at the end of year 2, but as before only $4.80 will be earned when the first year's interest income is invested during the second year at the low rate of 6 percent ($80 × 0.06). However, the bond's market price will *rise* to $1,001.60 due to the drop in interest rates. Therefore, the investor will receive in two years a total of $1,166.40 in cash:

| First year's interest earnings $\dfrac{}{\$80}$ | $+$ | Second year's interest earnings $\dfrac{}{\$80}$ | $+$ | Interest earned reinvesting the first year's interest earnings at a 6 percent interest rate $\dfrac{}{\$4.80}$ | $+$ | Market price received when selling bond at the end of the investor's planned holding period $\dfrac{}{\$1,001.60}$ | $=$ | Total return $\dfrac{}{\$1,166.40}$ |
|---|---|---|---|---|---|---|---|---|

$$(7.21)$$

Suppose instead that interest rates rise to 10 percent. Clearly, interest earnings will go up, but the bond's market price will be lower because of the rise in interest rates. In this case, the investor also receives a total return of $1,166.40:

| First year's interest earnings | | Second year's interest earnings | | Interest earned reinvesting the first year's interest earnings at a 10 percent interest rate | | Market price received when selling bond at the end of the investor's planned holding period | | Total return |
|:---:|:---:|:---:|:---:|:---:|:---:|:---:|:---:|:---:|
| $80 | + | $80 | + | $8.00 | + | $998.40 | = | $1,166.40 |

In the foregoing example, *the buyer earns identical total earnings whether inter-est rates go up or down!* This happens because, with duration set equal to the buyer's planned holding period, a fall in the reinvestment rate (in this case, down to 6 percent) is completely offset by an increase in the bond's price (in this instance, the bond's market value climbs from $1,000 to $1,001.60). Conversely, a rise in the reinvestment rate (up to 10 percent in the second case) is counterbalanced by a fall in the bond's market price (down to $998.40). The bond buyer's total return is fully protected regardless of the future path followed by interest rates.

Of course, there is a price to be paid for reducing risk exposure. Duration, like any interest-rate hedging tool, is *not* free. Suppose in the example above that the bond buyer had chosen not to worry about duration and just purchased a bond with a cal-endar maturity of two years. Suppose also that interest rates rose to 10 percent during the second year. Clearly, this investor would have earned a larger total return ($1,168) without using portfolio immunization. *The cost of immunization is a lower, but more stable, expected return.*

## Limitations of Duration

All this sounds easy: *To protect the return from a portfolio of assets against changes in interest rates, merely select a portfolio whose duration equals the time remaining in your planned holding period.* In practice, it does not work out quite this easily. For ex-ample, it is often difficult to find a collection of assets whose average portfolio duration exactly matches the investor's planned holding period. As time passes, the investor's planned holding period grows shorter, as does the average duration of the investor's portfolio. However, these two items—the remaining holding period and the duration of the investor's portfolio—are not likely to decline at the same speed. Therefore, an investor must constantly make portfolio adjustments to ensure that duration still equals the remaining length of the investor's planned holding period. And because many bonds are callable in advance of their maturity, bondholders may find themselves with a sudden and unexpected change in their portfolio's average duration.

Another problem with duration matching arises if the slope of the yield curve changes during the investor's planned holding period. In general, different patterns of interest rate movements require somewhat different measures of duration—a complex problem. Because the future path of interest rates cannot be perfectly forecast, immu-nization with duration cannot be perfect without developing a complicated model that takes into account a wide range of factors. Thus, there is always some risk associated with the use of conventional measures of duration due to uncertainty about future interest-rate movements. This type of risk is often called *stochastic process risk.*

Immunization using duration seems to work well because the largest single element seen in most interest rate movements is a parallel change in *all* interest rates (a factor that explains about 80 percent of the variability we see in interest rate movements over time). Thus, the assumption of duration models that interest rates tend to move in parallel (i.e., the slope and curvature of the yield curve do not change significantly over time) is not exactly true, but it represents a reasonably close approximation of what we often see in real-world markets. Thus, there is evidence that investors can achieve reasonably effective immunization by *approximately* matching the duration of their portfolios with their planned holding periods. The duration model, in other words, seems to be robust under a variety of market conditions.

---

### QUESTIONS TO HELP YOU STUDY

11. What is the *price elasticity* of a financial asset, and what useful information can it provide to an investor or portfolio manager?

12. What is the *coupon effect*? How would it figure into the assessment of selecting financial assets for an investment portfolio?

13. What is meant by the term *convexity* as it relates to the price of a financial asset? In what way could it be useful information to an investor?

14. Explain the meaning and importance of the concept of *duration*.

15. What is *portfolio immunization*? How does it work?

16. What are the *limitations* of duration and the portfolio immunization technique?

---

## Summary of the Chapter's Main Points

While theories of how interest rates are determined usually focus upon a single interest rate in the economy, there are in fact thousands of different interest rates confronting savers and borrowers every day. This chapter has focused our attention upon two major factors that cause interest rates to differ from security to security and loan to loan: (a) *inflationary expectations;* and (b) the *maturity, term,* or *duration* of a financial instrument.

- One key factor affecting interest rates is *expectations about inflation.* If lenders expect a higher rate of inflation to prevail during the life of a financial instrument they will demand a higher nominal return before making a loan. The *Fisher effect* argues that the expected nominal interest rate attached to a loan or security is the sum of its expected real rate plus the inflation premium (or expected rate of inflation). Fisher believed that the real rate would be relatively stable; therefore, changes in the nominal interest rate were due largely to changes in inflationary expectations.

- More recent research suggests that the relationship between inflation and interest rates may not be quite as simple as implied by the Fisher effect. For example, the *Harrod-Keynes effect* suggests that changes in the expected inflation rate may result, not in changes to the nominal rate, but in changes to the real rate of return instead. Moreover, the economy, the structure of tax rates investors face, and the public's spending and investment habits may significantly impact the linkages between inflation and interest rates. For example, the *taxation* of interest income may force the expected nominal interest rate to increase by more than expected inflation so that savers can protect their after-tax return.

- There is great controversy today surrounding the possible linkages between *inflation* and *stock prices.* Rising inflation doesn't necessarily lead to rising stock prices. The stock-price impact from inflation may depend on *nominal contracts*—that is, whether the revenues and expenses of a stock-issuing corporation are favorably or unfavorably affected by inflation as a result of agreements the company has entered into concerning the wages and salaries paid to its workforce, the goods sold to its customers, and borrowing costs. Inflation doesn't affect all stocks the same way because different businesses and individuals are involved in different nominal contracts.

- This chapter explores the usefulness of the *yield curve* in explaining interest rate movements. The yield curve visually captures the relationship between the annual rate of return on financial instruments (that differ only by maturity) and their term to maturity. Yield curves have sloped upward most frequently in recent years, with long-term interest rates higher than short-term rates. However, yield curves can slope downward or become relatively flat (horizontal).

- Why does the yield curve change its shape? The *unbiased expectations hypothesis* contends that yield curves reflect predominantly interest rate expectations. A rising yield curve suggests that short-term market interest rates are expected to rise, while a declining yield curve points to lower expected short rates in the future.

- Other viewpoints on the yield curve stem from the *liquidity premium, market segmentation,* and *preferred habitat* theories. For example, the *liquidity premium view* supplements the unbiased expectations hypothesis by suggesting that the greater risk associated with longer-term financial instruments results in these longer-maturity assets bearing higher average returns, giving an upward bias to the slope of yield curves.

- The *market segmentation* and *preferred habitat* views of the yield curve suggest that the supply of financial assets of different maturities can affect the yield curve's shape. For example, a sudden increase in the supply of longer-term financial instruments may cause long-term asset prices to fall and their yields to rise, tipping the yield curve toward an upward slope.

- Regardless of which view may be valid, yield curves can play a key role in the management of financial institutions, which borrow a substantial portion of their funds at the short end of the maturity spectrum and lend heavily at longer maturities. Yield curves can provide an indication of the marketplace's overall forecast of future interest rates, with upward-sloping curves implying rising interest rates and downward-sloping curves implying falling interest rates in the future.

- Yield curves may help identify underpriced or overpriced assets whose yields will lie above or below the curve at any moment in time. Moreover, some security traders "ride the yield curve," taking advantage of opportunities to sell short-term securities bearing the lowest yields and purchasing longer-maturity securities bearing higher interest rates.

- In recent years financial analysts have become somewhat dissatisfied with one of the two key factors making up the yield-curve relationship—the *term to maturity* or number of months and years until a financial asset is due to be retired. An alternative measure of maturity—*duration*—has become popular in recent years because it is a weighted average measure of the maturity of a financial instrument, capturing both the size and the timing of all cash payments from an income-generating asset or portfolio. Duration has grown in popularity among portfolio managers because it can be used to help *immunize* a single asset or a portfolio against possible losses due to changing interest rates.

- Duration also is linked to asset price volatility (or *price elasticity*) in a directly proportional way. Duration connects the percentage change in price of a financial asset to the change in its interest rate or yield. Longer-term assets tend to have longer durations and, therefore, greater price instability.

## Key Terms Appearing in This Chapter

**inflation,** 176

**nominal interest rate,** 177

**real interest rate,** 177

**inflation premium,** 177

**Fisher effect,** 178

**Harrod-Keynes effect,** 179

**inflation-risk premium,** 180

**inflation-caused income tax effect,** 180

**nominal contracts,** 183

**TIPS,** 184

**maturity,** 188

**yield curve,** 188

**unbiased expectations hypothesis,** 189

**liquidity premium,** 192

**market segmentation argument,** 193

**preferred habitat,** 194

**price elasticity,** 199

**coupon effect,** 201

**duration,** 201

**convexity,** 203

**portfolio immunization,** 205

## Problems and Issues

1.  According to the Fisher effect, if the real interest rate is 3 percent and the nominal interest rate is 8 percent, what rate of inflation is the financial marketplace expecting? Explain the reasoning behind your answer. If the nominal rate rises to 11 percent and follows the Fisher effect, what would you conclude about the expected inflation rate? The real rate?

2.  Mark wants a 3 percent real rate of return to invest in stock XYZ, and a 5 percent real rate of return to invest in stock ABC. Heidi believes that both stocks are less risky than Mark does and is willing to accept real rates of return of 2 percent on XYZ and 4 percent on ABC. Mark expects the inflation rate to be 3 percent and Heidi expects the inflation rate to be 5 percent. If the current yield on both XYZ and ABC is 6 percent, then which of these situations would follow?

    **a.** Mark would be willing to invest in XYZ, but not in ABC, while Heidi would not want to invest in either.

   **b.** Mark would invest in both XYZ and ABC, while Heidi would not invest in either.

   **c.** Both Mark and Heidi would be willing to invest in XYZ, but not in ABC

   **d.** Both Mark and Heidi would be willing to invest in both XYZ and ABC.

3. An investor buys a U.S. Treasury bond whose current yield to maturity is 10 percent. The investor is subject to a 33 percent federal income tax rate on any new income received. His real after-tax return from this bond is 2 percent. What is the expected inflation rate in the financial marketplace?

4. Indicate which applies. The liquidity premium:

   **a.** is negative *only* during an economic recession.

   **b.** is the result of greater price volatility for longer-term assets.

   **c.** biases the slope of the yield curve downward.

   **d.** causes long rates to always exceed short rates.

5. Suppose that the *actual* U.S. Treasury yield curve is approximately flat. This yield curve would suggest that the markets are expecting:

   **a.** short rates to remain essentially unchanged in the future.

   **b.** long rates to fall in the future.

   **c.** long rates to increase in the future.

   **d.** short rates to fall in the future.

6. Indicate which is true. The unbiased expectations hypothesis of the term structure of interest rates:

   **a.** applies only to assets that have the same maturity.

   **b.** applies only to assets that have the same default risk.

   **c.** ignores maturity of assets.

   **d.** ignores the market risk of assets.

7. An investor wishes to ride the yield curve to higher profits on an investment of $1,000. He observes in the market a zero-coupon T-note with one year left to maturity yielding 5 percent and another zero-coupon T-note yielding 7 percent with two years to maturity. What investment strategy should he pursue? Show how this investment strategy would be superior to a simple buy-and-hold strategy. Under what conditions will this strategy succeed? When will it fail?

8. Repeat problem 7, but where the market interest rates are: 7 percent for the 1-year, zero-coupon bond and 5 percent for the 2-year, zero-coupon bond.

9. Calculate the price elasticity of a 15-year bond around its $1,000 par value and 10 percent coupon rate if market interest rates on comparable bonds drop to 6 percent. The market price of the bond at a 6 percent yield to maturity is $1,392. Suppose now that the yield to maturity climbs to 14 percent. If the bond's price falls to $751.80, what is the bond's price elasticity?

10. Calculate the value of duration for a four-year, $1,000 par value U.S. government bond purchased today at a yield to maturity of 15 percent. The bond's coupon rate is 12 percent, and it pays interest at year's end. Now suppose the market interest rate on comparable bonds falls to 14 percent. What percentage change in this bond's price will result?

11. A bank buying bonds is concerned about possible fluctuations in earnings due to changes in interest rates. Currently the bank's investment officer is looking at a $1,000 par-value bond that matures in four years and carries a coupon rate of 12 percent. Market interest rates are also at 12 percent, but the bank's officer believes there is a significant probability interest rates could drop to 10 percent or rise to 14 percent during the first year and stay there until the bond matures. What would be this bond's total earnings over the next four years if interest rates rise to 14 percent? Fall to 10 percent? Remain at 12 percent? What will happen to total earnings if the investment officer finds another bond whose maturity is reached in five years but whose duration is four years—the same as the bank's planned holding period?

12. The 10-year Treasury bond rate is trading at 6.08 percent, while the one-year bond rate carries a yield to maturity of 5.35 percent. What is the yield spread between these instruments? What is this yield spread forecasting for the economy in the period ahead? Explain.

    Suppose the 10-year T-bond rate falls to 5.57 percent, while the one-year T-bond yield rises to 6.04 percent. What change in yield spread has occurred? What is the expected outlook for economic conditions following this particular change in the yield spread? Can you explain why?

13. Synchron Corporation borrowed long-term capital at an interest rate of 8.5 percent under the expectation that the annual inflation rate over the life of this borrowing was likely to be 5 percent. However, shortly after the loan contract was signed, the actual inflation rate climbed to 5.5 percent, where it is expected to remain until Synchron's loan reaches maturity. What is likely to happen to the market value per share of Synchron's common stock? Explain your reasoning.

14. A four-year TIPS bond promises a real annual coupon return of 4 percent and its face value is $1,000. While the annual inflation rate was approximately zero when the bond was first issued, the inflation rate suddenly accelerated to 3 percent and is expected to remain at that level for the bond's four-year term. What will be the amount of interest paid in nominal dollars each year of the bond's life? What will be the face (nominal) value of the bond at the end of each year of its life?

15. Jon wishes to invest $10,000 in U.S. Treasury securities for 10 years. He is considering the following investment strategies: (i) Buy a 10-year T-Note and hold it to maturity; (ii) Buy a 5-year T-Note and upon maturity roll over the principal and interest into a second 5-year T-Note; (iii) Buy a Treasury with one year to maturity, and continuously roll over the investment in 1-year Treasuries for 10 years. The current yields are: 2 percent on the 1-year Treasury; 4.25 percent on the 5-year T-Note; and 4.5 percent on the 10-year T-note. Jon's financial analysis indicates that market expectations are for the 1-year Treasury yield to rise by 50 basis points every year for the first five years and then remain unchanged for the next five years, and for the 5-year T-Note to be the same in five years as it is today. Using a spreadsheet, display the total return (including the initial investment) that Jon would have from his investment in each of the 10 years under each of the three investment strategies. (Hint: Let column 1 display the value of the investment (i) after one year in the first row, after two years in the second row, and so on, then repeat for investment (ii) in column 2, and for investment (iii) in column 3. Use additional columns for questions (d), (e), and (f),).

    **a.** What is today's liquidity premium in the 10-year yield versus the 1-year yield?

    **b.** What is today's liquidity premium in the 5-year yield versus the 1-year yield?

    **c.** What is today's liquidity premium in the 10-year yield versus the 5-year yield?

    **d.** Suppose that the actual short rate remained unchanged during the entire 10 years, how would that affect the 10-year rate of return on investment (3)?

    **e.** What would happen to the investment's 10-year rate of return if the one-year rate continued to rise at 50 basis points per year for years 5 through 10?

    **f.** If the 5-year T-note yield fell 50 basis points after five years, how much would this reduce the 10-year rate of return on investment (ii)?

    **g.** If the 5-year T-note yield rose 50 basis points after five years, how much would this reduce the 10-year rate of return on investment (ii)?

    **h.** Do exercises (d), (e), (f), and (g) illustrate why the liquidity premium is positive? Please explain.

## Web-Based Problems

**1.** Yield curves can be constructed for assets drawn from similar risk classes. Traditionally there are three types of yield curves that are typically followed in the financial markets. The dominant one is for U.S. Treasury securities. It is a plot of the yields for "on-the-run" (or most frequently issued) Treasuries for maturities: 3 months, 6 months, 2 years, 3 years, 5 years, 10 years, and 30 years. It is a simple matter to find this information from a wide variety of Internet sites, such as the U.S. Treasury Department, the Federal Reserve, and so on. This question asks you to search the Internet for the information you need to construct the other two yield curves that often follow in the financial press. One is for the highest quality debt of major U.S. corporations, which would range from 30-day commercial paper rates to 30-year corporate bonds. The second is similarly rated municipal bonds. These debt instruments of state and local governments have a much higher volume at longer maturities than shorter maturities, but see how much of the maturity spectrum from three months to 30 years you can find. Once you have gathered these data plot all three yield curves on the *same* graph. You should see similar patterns in all three. Why? However, you should also see that the corporate yield curve lies everywhere above the Treasury yield curve. Why? And the Treasury yield curve should lie everywhere above the municipal yield curve. Why?

**2.** During the late 1970s the inflation rate in the United States was in double digits. In response, the Federal Reserve decided to raise short-term interest rates dramatically to bring it down.

    **a.** What would you expect the yield curve to look like after this policy change?

    **b.** Visit the Fed's Web site at **federalreserve.gov** and click on the "Economic Research and Data" tab; then click on the "Statistics: Releases and Historical Data" tab and obtain historical data on "Selected Interest Rates" from the

H.15 release. From these data construct a Treasury yield curve for April 1980 and for the most recent month you can find.

**c.** Search the Internet for data on the current inflation rate (measured by the CPI) in the United States and the U.S. inflation rate in 1980. Does this information help to explain the shapes of the yield curves for these two time periods?

## Selected References to Explore

1. Ammer, John. "Inflation, Inflation Risk, and Stock Returns," *International Finance Discussion Paper 464,* Board of Governors of the Federal Reserve System, April 1994.

2. Bonser-Neal, Catherine, and Timothy R. Morley. "Does the Yield Spread Predict Real Economic Activity? A Multi-Country Analysis," *Economic Review,* Federal Reserve Bank of Kansas City, Third Quarter 1997, pp. 37–53.

3. Campbell, J. Y. "A Defense of Traditional Hypotheses about the Term Structure of Interest Rates," *Journal of Finance* 41 (1986), pp. 183–93.

4. Dai, Q., and K. Singleton. "Specification Analysis of Affine Term Structure Models," *Journal of Finance* 55 (October 2000), pp. 1943–78.

5. Fama, Eugene F., and R. R. Bliss. "The Information in Long Maturity Forward Rates," *American Economic Review* 72 (1987), pp. 680–92.

6. Fernald, John, and Bharat Trehan. "Is a Recession Imminant?" *FRBSF Economic Letter,* Federal Reserve Bank of San Francisco, November 24, 2006.

7. Feroli, Michael. "Monetary Policy and the Information Content of the Yield Spread," *Finance and Economics Discussion Series,* Z.11, Federal Reserve Board, Washington, DC, 2004.

8. Fisher, Irving. "Appreciation and Interest," *Publication of the American Economics Association,* August 1896.

9. Fuhrer, Jeffrey, and Geoffrey M. B. Tootell. "What Is the Cost of Deflation?" *Regional Review,* Federal Reserve Bank of Boston, Fourth Quarter 2003, pp. 2–5.

10. Gurkaynak, Refet S., Brian Sack, and Jonathan H. Wright. "The U.S. Treasury Yield Curve: 1961 to the Present," *Financial and Economic Discussion Papers, no. 2006–28,* Federal Reserve Board, 2006.

11. Haubrich, Joseph G. "Interest Rates, Yield Curves, and the Monetary Regime," *Economic Commentary,* Federal Reserve Bank of Cleveland, June 2004.

12. Longstaff, Francis A. "Time Varying Premia and Traditional Hypotheses about the Term Structure," *Journal of Finance* 41, no. 4 (September 1990), pp. 1307–14.

13. Poole, William. "Understanding the Term Structure of Interest Rates," *Review,* Federal Reserve Bank of St. Louis, September/October 2005, pp. 589–595.

14. Sack, Brian, and Robert Elsasser. "Treasury Inflation-Indexed Debt: A Review of the U.S. Experience," *FRBNY Economic Policy Review,* May 2004, pp. 47–63.

15. Shen, Pu. "How Important Is the Inflation Risk Premium?" *Economic Review,* Federal Reserve Bank of Kansas City, Fourth Quarter 1998, pp. 35–47.

www.mhhe.com/rose10e

16. Stojanovic, Dusan, and Mark D. Vaughn. "Yielding Clues about Recessions: The Yield Curve as a Forecasting Tool," *Economic Review,* Federal Reserve Bank of Boston, 1997, pp. 10–21.

17. Van Horn, James. "Interest-Rate Risk and the Term Structure of Interest Rates," *Journal of Political Economy,* August 1965, pp. 344–51.

18. Williams, John C. "Inflation Persistence in an Era of Well-Anchored Inflation Expectations," *FRBSF Economic Letter,* Federal Reserve Bank of San Francisco, October 13, 2006.

19. Wu, Tao. "What Makes the Yield Curve Move?" *FRBSF Economic Letter,* Federal Reserve Bank of San Francisco, no. 2003-15 (June 6, 2003).

www.mhhe.com/rose10e

# The Risk Structure of Interest Rates: Defaults, Prepayments, Taxes, and Other Rate-Determining Factors

## Learning Objectives in This Chapter

- You will see the effect of several different features of financial assets—such as their marketability, liquidity, default risk, call privileges, prepayment risk, convertibility, and taxability—on their interest rates and prices.

- You will learn why we have thousands of different interest rates within the global economy.

- You will discover how the "structure of interest rates" is built and why that rate structure is constantly changing.

- You will see why it is so difficult to accurately forecast interest rates and financial asset prices.

## What's in This Chapter? Key Topics Outline

Marketability and Liquidity

Default-Risk Premiums Attached to Interest Rates

Credit Ratings, Bankruptcies, and Junk Bonds

Credit Rating Agencies

Credit Derivatives

Call Privileges and Call Risk

Prepayment and Event Risk

Taxation of Asset Returns and Tax-Exempt Assets

Convertibility

The Structure of Interest Rates

## 8.1 Introduction

In the preceding chapter we examined two factors that cause the value of financial assets and, therefore, the interest rate or yield on one financial asset to be different from the interest rate or yield on another. These factors included the maturity or term of a loan or security and expected inflation. In this chapter we focus on a different set of elements influencing relative asset prices and interest rates: (1) marketability, (2) liquidity, (3) default risk, (4) call privileges, (5) taxation of security income, (6) prepayment risk, and (7) convertibility. The impact of each of these factors is analyzed separately, but it should be noted that yields on financial assets and their prices are influenced by several factors acting *simultaneously*. For example, the market yield on a 20-year corporate bond may be 8 percent, while the yield on a 10-year municipal bond may be 6 percent. The difference in yield and value between these two assets reflects not only the difference in their maturities but also any differences in their degree of default risk, marketability, callability, and tax status. To analyze differentials in yield and price between various financial assets, therefore, we must understand thoroughly *all* of the factors that shape interest rates and asset values in the global money and capital markets.

## 8.2 Marketability

**marketability**

An important consideration for an investor is *whether a market exists for those assets he or she would like to acquire.* Can an asset be sold quickly, or must the investor wait some time before suitable buyers can be found? This is the question of **marketability,** and financial instruments traded around the world vary widely in terms of the ease and speed with which buyers can be found.

For example, Treasury bills, notes, and bonds have one of the most active and deepest markets in the world. Large lots of marketable Treasury securities in multiples of a million dollars are bought and sold daily, with the trades taking place in a matter of minutes. Small lots (under $1 million) of these same securities are more difficult to sell. However, there is usually no difficulty in marketing even a handful of Treasury securities. Similarly, common stock actively traded on the New York, London, Frankfurt, or Tokyo exchanges typically can be moved in minutes, depending on the number of shares being sold. In active markets like these negotiations are usually conducted by telephone or e-mail and confirmed by wire. Frequently, payment for any securities purchased is made the same day by wire or within one or two days by check or draft.

For thousands of lesser-known financial assets not actively traded each day, however, marketability can be a problem. Stocks and bonds issued by smaller companies usually have a narrow, or "thin," market, often confined to the local community or region. Trades occur infrequently and it is often difficult to establish a consistent market price. A seller may have to wait months to secure a desired price or, if the security must be sold immediately, its price may have to be discounted substantially.

Marketability is positively related to the *size* (total sales or total assets) and *reputation* of the institution issuing the securities and to the number of similar securities outstanding. Not surprisingly, stocks and bonds issued in large blocks by the largest corporations and governmental units tend to find acceptance more readily in the global financial markets. With a larger number of similar assets available, buy-sell transactions are more frequent and a consistent market price can be established.

Marketability is a decided advantage to the asset purchaser (lender of funds). In contrast, the issuer of assets is not particularly concerned about any difficulties the purchaser may encounter in the resale (secondary) market unless lack of marketability significantly influences asset sales in the primary market. And where marketability is a problem it does influence the yield the issuer must pay in the primary market. In fact, there is a *negative* relationship between marketability and yield. More marketable assets generally carry *lower* expected returns than less marketable assets, other things held equal. Purchasers of assets that can be sold in the secondary market only with difficulty must be compensated for this inconvenience by a higher promised rate of return.

## 8.3 Liquidity

**liquidity**

Marketability is an important component of another feature of financial assets that influences their interest rate or yield: their degree of **liquidity.** A liquid financial asset is *readily marketable.* In addition, its price tends to be *stable* over time and it is *reversible,* meaning the holder of the asset can usually recover her funds upon resale with little risk of loss. Because the liquidity feature of financial assets tends to lower their risk, liquid assets carry lower interest rates than illiquid assets. Investors strongly interested in maximum profitability try to minimize their holdings of liquid assets. Examples of highly liquid assets, bearing relatively low rates of return, include most bank deposits, shares in money market funds, and marketable U.S. Treasury securities.

As noted recently by Fleming [4], measuring the liquidity of assets is a challenging task and research on that issue is continuing. One of the more popular measures of liquidity today is the *bid-ask spread*—the difference between the offer (bid) price at which an asset will be purchased and the price for which it is to be sold. For example, a security dealer like Goldman Sachs or Merrill Lynch may offer to buy (bid) $1,000 par-value Treasury bonds at a price of $952.50 ($95–8/32 per $100 in par value) and pledge to sell them (ask) for $952.81 ($95–9/32 per $100 in par value). In general, the narrower the bid-ask spread—in this case, 1/32 of a dollar, or 3.1 cents, per $100 in par value—the more liquid the asset in question tends to be because one of the dominant characteristics of a liquid market is low transactions cost. Other commonly used measures of liquidity include trading volume, frequency of trades, and average trade size, with more liquid instruments generally registering higher in trading volume, trading frequency, and average daily trade size.

## 8.4 Default Risk and Interest Rates

One of the most important factors causing one interest rate to differ from another in the global marketplace is the degree of default risk carried by individual assets. Investors in financial assets face many different kinds of risk, but one of the most important is

**default risk**

**default risk**—the risk a borrower will not make all promised payments at the agreed-upon times. All debt except some government securities is subject to varying degrees of default risk. If you purchase a 10-year corporate bond with a $1,000 par value and a coupon rate of 9 percent, the issuing company promises in the indenture (bond contract) to pay you $90 a year (or more commonly, $45 every six months) for 10 years plus $1,000 at the end of the 10-year period. Failure to meet *any* of these promised payments on time puts the borrower in default, and the lender may have to go to court to recover monies owed.

## *The Premium for Default Risk*

The promised yield on a risky asset is positively related to the risk of borrower default as perceived by investors. Specifically, the promised yield on a risky asset is composed of at least two elements:

$$\text{Promised yield on a risky asset} = \text{Risk-free interest rate} + \text{Default-risk premium} \tag{8.1}$$

or

$$\text{Default-risk premium} = \text{Promised yield on a risky asset} - \text{Risk-free interest rate} \tag{8.2}$$

The *promised yield* on a risky debt security is the yield to maturity that will be earned by the investor if the borrower makes all promised payments when they are due. As Exhibit 8.1 illustrates, the higher the degree of default risk associated with a risky debt security, the higher the default-risk premium on that security and the greater the required rate of return (yield) that must be attached to that asset as demanded by investors in the global financial marketplace. Any adverse development that makes a borrower appear riskier, such as a downturn in the economy or serious financial difficulties, will lead the market to assign a higher default-risk premium to his debt security. And if the risk-free rate remains unchanged, the financial asset's promised risky yield must rise and its price must decline.

## *The Expected Rate of Return or Yield on a Risky Asset*

Increasingly in recent years some of the largest business firms on the planet have been forced into default and subsequently declared bankruptcy. Among the largest corporate bankruptcy filers in modern history are:

WorldCom, Inc. (2002), with $103.9 billion in assets.

Enron Corp. (2001), with $63.4 billion in assets.

Conseco, Inc. (2002), with $61.4 billion in assets.

Texaco, Inc. (1987), with $35.9 billion in assets.

Refco Inc. (2005), with $33.3 billion in assets.

**EXHIBIT 8.1**

**The Relationship between Default Risk and the Promised Yield on Risky Assets**

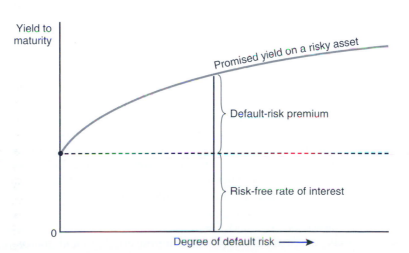

Global Crossing Ltd. (2002), with $30.2 billion in assets.

Pacific Gas and Electric Co. (2001), with $29.8 billion in assets.

UAL Corp. (2002), with $25.2 billion in assets.

Delta Air Lines, Inc. (2005), with $21.8 billion in assets.

Delphi Corporation (2005), with $16.6 billion in assets.

Not even governments have been exempt from default and ultimate bankruptcy, including Argentina, Russia, and Orange County, California. Volatile changes in business and consumer spending, interest rates, and commodity prices frequently have led to serious miscalculations by both large and small businesses and governments with sometimes fatal results. For this reason, many investors around the globe today have learned to look at the *expected* rate of return, or yield, on a risky asset as well as its *promised* yield.

**expected yield**    The **expected yield** is the weighted average of all possible yields to maturity from a risky asset. Each possible yield is weighted by the probability it will occur. Thus, if there are $m$ possible yields from a risky asset:

$$\text{Expected yield} = \sum_{i=1}^{m} p_i y_i \qquad (8.3)$$

where $y_i$ represents the $i$th possible yield on a risky asset and $p_i$ is the probability the $i$th possible risky yield will be obtained. Assessing these possible outcomes (yields) and the likelihood of their occurrence (probabilities) is the job of the financial analyst.

Let's take a simple example to illustrate how the expected yield on a risky asset might be determined. Suppose a corporate bond traded in today's market appears to have possible yields of 6 percent, 8 percent, and 10 percent, with probabilities of 50 percent, 30 percent, and 20 percent, respectively. Then, its *expected yield* would be:

**Expected yield on a bond** = 6% (0.50) + 8% (0.30) + 10% (0.20) = 7.40%

While this bond's current *expected* yield is 7.40 percent, the yield *promised* by its issuer may be quite different.

## Anticipated Loss and Default-Risk Premiums

For a risk-free asset held to maturity, the expected yield equals the promised yield. However, in the case of a risky asset, the promised yield may be greater than the expected yield and the yield spread between them is usually labeled the *anticipated default loss*. That is,

$$\text{Anticipated default loss on a risky asset} = \text{Promised yield} - \text{Expected yield} \qquad (8.4)$$

The concept of *anticipated default loss* is important because it represents each investor's view of what the appropriate default-risk premium on a risky asset should be. Let's suppose an investor carries out a careful financial analysis of a company in preparation for purchasing its bonds and decides the firm is a less risky borrower default-wise than perceived by the market as a whole. Perhaps the market has assigned the firm's bonds a default-risk premium of 4 percent; the investor believes, however, the true anticipated loss due to default is only 3 percent. Because the market's default-risk premium exceeds this investor's anticipated default loss, she would be inclined to *buy* the company's bonds. As she sees it, the risky asset's promised yield (including its market-assigned default-risk premium) is too high and, therefore, its price is too low.

To this investor, the company's bonds appear to be a bargain—a temporarily under-priced financial asset.

Consider the opposite case. An investor calculates the anticipated default loss on bonds issued by a government toll road project. He concludes that a default-risk premium of 5 percent is justified because of a significant number of uncertainties associated with the future success of the project. However, the current promised yield on the risky asset is only 10 percent and the risk-free interest rate is 6 percent. Because the market has assigned only a 4 percent default-risk premium, and the investor prefers a 5 percent default-risk premium, it is unlikely he will purchase the bond. As the investor views this bond, its promised risky yield is too low and, therefore, its price is too high.

Major financial institutions, especially insurance companies, banks, hedge funds, private equity firms, and pension funds, employ a large number of credit analysts for the express purpose of assessing the anticipated default loss on a wide range of assets they might like to acquire. These institutions believe they have a definite advantage over the average investor in assessing the true degree of default risk associated with any particular asset. This high level of technical expertise may permit major institutional investors to take advantage of underpriced assets where, in their judgment, the market has overestimated the true level of default risk.

**Key URLs:**
Among the more interesting credit rating agencies with Web sites to explore are **fitchratings.com**; **dufflc.com**; **jcr.co.jp/english/** and **bankwatch.org**

## Factors Influencing Default-Risk Premiums

What factors help to determine the default-risk premiums assigned by the market to different assets? For many years, privately owned rating agencies have exercised a dominant influence on investor perceptions of the default risk of individual security issues. The number of these credit-rating agencies has changed over the past several years through a combination of new entrants and consolidations. However, today Moody's Investors Services Inc. and Standard & Poor's Company (a subsidiary of McGraw-Hill Companies, Inc.) have about 80 percent of the market. Both companies rate individual security issuers according to their perceived probability of default (based on the borrower's financial condition and business prospects) and publish the ratings as letter grades. A summary of the grades used by these companies for rating corporate and municipal bonds is shown in Exhibit 8.2.

**Key URLs:**
Good sources for interpreting credit ratings are:
**personal.fidelity.com** and **beginnersinvest.about.com**

| **EXHIBIT 8.2** | **Bond-Rating Categories Employed by Moody's Investors Service and Standard & Poor's Corporation** | | |
|---|---|---|---|
| **Quality Level of Bonds** | **Moody's Rating Categories** | **Standard & Poor's Rating Categories** | **Default-Risk Premium** |
| High-quality or high-grade bonds | Aaa<br>Aa<br>A | AAA<br>AA<br>A | Lowest |
| Medium-quality or medium-grade bonds | Baa<br>Ba<br>B | BBB<br>BB<br>B | |
| Lowest grade, speculative, or poor-quality bonds | Caa<br>Ca<br>C | CCC<br>CC<br>C | |
| Defaulted bonds and bonds issued by bankrupt companies | —<br>—<br>— | DDD<br>DD<br>D | Highest |

**EXHIBIT 8.3**

**The Behavior of Interest Rates Attached to Risky versus Riskless Capital Market Securities**

Source: Federal Reserve Bank of St. Louis, *Monetary Trends,* February 2007.

**Long-Term Interest Rates**

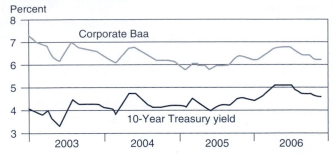

Moody's investment ratings range from Aaa, for the highest-quality securities with negligible default risk, to C, for those securities deemed to be speculative and carrying a significant prospect of borrower default. Quality ratings assigned by Standard & Poor's range from AAA, for high-grade ("gilt-edged") securities, to those financial instruments actually in default (D) or issued by bankrupt firms. Bonds falling in the four top rating categories—Aaa to Baa for Moody's and AAA to BBB for Standard & Poor's—are called *investment-grade issues.* Laws and regulations frequently require banks, insurance companies, and other financial institutions to purchase only those securities rated in these four categories. Lower-rated securities are referred to as *speculative issues.* The subset of speculative issues rated Ba to C by Moody's and BB to C by S&P are referred to as **junk bonds,** reflecting the likelihood of full repayment of these long-term debt securities as being significantly below that for bonds rated investment quality.

Exhibit 8.3 illustrates how the yields on bonds bearing different degrees of default risk (for example: 10-year U.S. Treasury notes versus Baa corporate securities) change relative to each other with the progression of time, fluctuations in the economy, and other factors. Exhibit 8.4 compares market yields on long-term U.S. Treasury bonds

**junk bonds**

| **EXHIBIT 8.4** | **Market Yield on Rated Corporate Bonds and Long-Term U.S. Treasury Bonds, 1992–2006** | | | | | | | |
|---|---|---|---|---|---|---|---|---|
| | **Average Yields (Percent per Annum)** | | | | | | | |
| **Type of Bond** | **1992** | **1994** | **1996** | **1998** | **2000** | **2002** | **2004** | **2006†** |
| Long-term U.S. Treasury bonds | 7.52% | 7.41% | 6.80% | 5.69% | 6.03% | 5.41% | 4.64% | 5.08% |
| Aaa corporate bonds* | 8.14 | 7.97 | 7.37 | 6.53 | 7.62 | 6.49 | 5.23 | 5.68 |
| Aa corporate bonds* | 8.46 | 8.15 | 7.55 | 6.80 | 7.83 | 6.93 | 5.37 | 5.91 |
| A corporate bonds* | 8.62 | 8.28 | 7.69 | 6.93 | 8.11 | 7.18 | 5.59 | 6.19 |
| Baa corporate bonds* | 8.98 | 8.63 | 8.05 | 7.22 | 8.36 | 7.80 | 6.06 | 6.59 |

*Corporate bond ratings are from Moody's Investors Service.

†2006 interest rates are averages for the month of August.

Source: Board of Governors of the Federal Reserve System, *Federal Reserve Bulletin,* selected issues.

with those on corporate bonds in the four top rating categories, Aaa to Baa. It is interesting to note that these yield relationships are all in the direction theory would lead us to expect. For example, the yield on Aaa corporate bonds—the least risky securities rated by Moody's and Standard & Poor's—is consistently lower than the yield attached to lower-rated (Baa) bonds. This suggests that investors in the marketplace tend to rank securities roughly in the same relative default risk order as the credit rating agencies do. This seems to be an appropriate strategy because there appears to be a high (though by no means perfect) correlation between the ratings assigned by the credit agencies and the actual default record of corporate bonds.

Recent research has found a pronounced association between market-assigned default-risk premiums and fluctuations (cycles) in business activity (recessions versus expansions or boom periods). For example, the yield spread between Aaa-and Baa-rated securities rises during economic recessions and decreases during periods of economic expansion. The correlation is not perfect, though. Fluctuations in output and income do not always influence the default-risk premium on one security versus another in the same way or to the same degree. However, when economic and financial conditions suggest to investors that uncertainty has increased and business prospects are less robust, the market generally translates these opinions into higher default-risk premiums.

Several studies in recent years have addressed the question of what factors influence default-risk premiums on securities and what factors rating firms use to evaluate default risk. Among the factors identified for corporate securities are variability in company earnings, the period of time a firm has been in operation, and the amount of leverage employed (i.e., volume of debt relative to equity capital).[1]

A company with volatile earnings runs a greater risk of experiencing periods when losses will exceed the firm's ability to raise funds. The longer a firm has been operating without default, the more investors come to expect continued successful performance. Greater use of financial leverage in the capital structure of a firm offers the potential for greater earnings per share of stock, because debt is a relatively cheap source of funds (especially when measured on an after-tax basis). However, financial leverage is a two-edged sword. As the proportion of borrowed funds rises relative to equity, the risk of significant declines in net earnings increases.

## Inflation and Default-Risk Premiums

Earlier, in Chapter 7 we discovered that inflation can cause interest rates to rise as investors in the financial markets demand to be compensated with higher nominal returns when expected inflation or uncertainty about future inflation goes up. However, *inflation also appears to affect the size of default-risk premiums on risky securities.* Default-risk premiums (often called "quality spreads") tend to be higher and more volatile when inflation is high and volatile. Greater uncertainty about inflation tends

---

[1]We do not know for sure what factors credit rating agencies use to assign default-risk ratings, but we do know they consider at least three levels of factors: (1) condition of the economy, (2) industry conditions, and (3) borrower-specific factors, including coverage ratios (earnings before interest and taxes to interest and principal payments owed), leverage ratios (debt-to-equity ratios), liquidity indicators (such as the ratio of current assets to current liabilities) and profitability measures (such as return on assets and return on equity). Studies of corporate bankruptcy have found some of these factors—especially liquidity, earnings, debt exposure, and stock prices—to be effective discriminators between corporations eventually declaring bankruptcy and healthy firms. Moreover, when a credit rating agency downgrades a firm's credit rating, the affected company's stock returns tend to fall immediately following the announcement.

to produce a "flight to quality" in the financial markets, and investors simply become more cautious about buying default-risk-exposed financial instruments. This is one of the many ways in which high and volatile price inflation can disrupt the efficient functioning of a market-oriented economy.

## Yield Curves for Risky Securities

As we saw in Chapter 7, yield curves on low-default-risk securities (such as U.S. government and high-grade corporate bonds) have a tendency to display a positive slope—they *rise* with advancing maturity. In contrast, there is some evidence that yield curves on high-default-risk instruments often have a downward (negative) slope or may have a significant bow or hump in them as maturity increases. If so, this unusual yield-curve shape *may* be traceable to the fact that bonds issued by poorer-quality borrowers are generally at their riskiest when first issued and appear to improve in quality (i.e., decline in default risk) the longer the issuer survives and manages to make the required payments. In other words, each required payment that is successfully made seems to lower the risk that subsequent payments will be missed.

While some studies tend to support this version of financial theory, recent work by Helwege and Turner [7] tends to find the opposite—that the yield curve for most speculative-grade bond issues *rises* with advancing maturity just as it does for debt issued by low-risk borrowers. This is one area where additional research is needed to help us identify the true yield-curve, default-risk relationship.

## The Volatile History of Junk Bonds

**Key URLS:**
To discover how credit ratings are assigned and how buyers of financial assets can find out about changes in companies' credit ratings, see Moody's Investors Service at **moodys.com/** and Standard & Poor's Corporation at **standardpoor.com**

The decades of the 1980s and 1990s ushered in the rapid growth and development of *junk bonds*—long-term debt securities whose full repayment is judged to be significantly less certain than is true for bonds rated investment quality. The term *junk bonds* arose years ago when several companies that were trapped in serious financial problems with low credit ratings ("fallen angels") were forced to issue inferior-quality bonds to stay alive. More recently, new companies and small established companies also have been able to reach the bond market, which previously was closed to them, by issuing these speculative-grade securities. Junk bonds also have been issued to facilitate mergers and, in the opposite situation, to prevent corporate takeovers. Some junk bonds are "zeros," which pay no interest, and others are "pics" that pay interest not in cash but in the form of new bonds—both ideal for companies with low or uncertain earning power. Such low-rated bonds may trade at interest yields of three or four percentage points or more over yields on comparable government securities.

**Key URLS:**
Developments in the "junk bond" market may be followed through such sources as **encyclopedia.com**; **www.finpipe.com/bndjunk.htm**; and **speculativebubble.com**

The number of individual investors and financial institutions interested in purchasing junk bonds grew rapidly during the 1980s due to few actual defaults on these bonds. At the same time, a leading investment banking firm, Drexel Burnham Lambert, Inc., pioneered new techniques to sell junk bonds that rapidly expanded the scope of the market. Many investors discovered that a well-diversified portfolio of junk bonds (e.g., about 12 different issues) appeared to lower overall portfolio risk to a level comparable to many higher-rated bonds. Thus, the yields offered on junk bonds appeared to be higher than their actual degree of default risk. Moreover, the development of an active market for junk bonds gave many small and new firms access to another source of financing besides borrowing from banks and finance companies. Certainly, the tax deductibility of interest expenses on corporate debt, the more recent development of sophisticated hedging instruments (such as swaps, credit derivatives, financial futures, and options) to combat market risk, and historically low borrowing

The credit-rating industry is highly concentrated with a small number of large firms dominating the business. The reason for this high concentration has to do with economies of scale in collecting credit information. Presumably, large rating agencies can do credit evaluations more economically and conveniently than can small investors who lack the necessary data and market contacts. Allegedly, large credit-rating companies have lower agency costs (because investors have developed confidence in the rating agencies' independence and competence at assessing the degree of risk exposure investors may face with any particular bond issue).

While theory might lead us to suspect that all credit agencies assign about the same ratings along equivalent credit risk scales, research by Cantor and Packer [2] suggests this is not always true. Even the same level of rating at two different credit agencies does not necessarily imply the same level of perceived default-risk exposure. Moreover, Moody's and Standard & Poor's tend to assign lower credit ratings, on average, than do other less well-known agencies. One explanation may be that Moody's and S&P have tougher credit standards, or it may be that those bond issuers requesting credit ratings expect to get a higher rating from a third or fourth credit reviewer and, thereby, save on their borrowing costs. When ratings are different, either the highest rating or the second-highest rating is often generally recognized in the market as the correct risk level, no matter which agency happens to assign the one rating chosen as "representative." Larger debt issuers also tend to get third or even fourth ratings because they face lower percentage rating costs.

Due to the importance of these credit ratings for establishing borrowing costs of issuers of debt, Congress has recently authorized the Securities and Exchange Commission (SEC) to regulate the industry. As part of its regulatory oversight, the SEC has selected five credit-rating agencies which it designates as nationally recognized statistical rating organizations (NRSROs). In addition to Moody's and Standard & Poor's, the remaining NRSROs are: A.M. Best Company, Dominion Bond Rating Service Limited, and Fitch, Inc.

The criteria for receiving this NRSRO designation by the SEC is that the rating agency must: (1) issue publicly available credit ratings that reflect current assessments of creditworthiness; (2) be generally accepted in the financial markets as an issuer of credible and reliable ratings by the predominant users of securities ratings; and (3) use "systematic procedures" for establishing ratings, managing potential conflicts of interest, and preventing misuse of nonpublic information. The systematic procedures used to establish credit ratings are proprietary to the individual rating agencies, but are based in part on past and probable future cash flows of the issuer, the volume and composition of outstanding debt, and the stability of the issuer's cash flows over time, along with the value of assets pledged as collateral and the securities' priority of claim against the issuer's assets in the event of default. In addition to relying on firm-specific information when carrying out these assessments of default risk, the overall condition of the economy, as well as factors affecting the industry of which the issuing firm is a part, play important roles in establishing credit ratings.

costs encouraged private corporations to make greater use of junk securities in order to raise new capital.

On the negative side, however, the continuing growth of junk bonds has aroused concern among government policymakers over possible future declines in the credit quality of corporate debt. For example, insurance company regulators from New York state acted to limit junk bond investments by insurance firms selling policies in that state, a move eventually followed by other insurance regulators across the United States. The use of junk bonds to finance hostile takeovers and the failure of hundreds of depository institutions that had purchased junk securities finally captured the attention of the U.S. Congress. Passage of the Financial Institutions Reform, Recovery, and Enforcement Act of 1989 outlawed further purchases of junk bonds by federally supervised depository institutions. In 1990, Drexel Burnham Lambert—at one time the king of junk bond dealers—declared bankruptcy.

Moreover, a recession in the U.S. economy in 1991 resulted in a wave of defaults by firms that had previously issued junk bonds, climbing up to a default rate as high as 11 percent, though by 1994 the mean default rate on junk bonds had dropped back to less than 2 percent. However, in 2001 a recession in the economy sent junk bond interest rates and business bankruptcies rising again, only to have them fall back again later in the new century. Research by Fons [5] and Helwege and Kleiman [6] suggests that junk bond default rates vary over time due to (1) the strength of the economy (with default rates dropping when the economy is strong); (2) the proportion of lower-rated bonds issued each year (with more lower-rated issues tending to increase the average default rate); and (3) an "aging effect" (with defaults more likely within the first three years of a junk bond issue).

Higher relative yields available on junk bonds coupled with a reduced supply of these securities sparked a market rally in junk bond prices and an upward surge in new offerings as the new century began. Much of the price gain appeared to be due to the emergence of junk bond mutual funds that often buy half or more of available new junk issues, along with historically low borrowing costs, comparatively low corporate default rates, high bankrupt-company recovery rates, and debt-driven corporate mergers, spinoffs, and buyouts. The rise in new junk bond offerings can also be traced to more borrowing companies bypassing rigid and expensive bank loans as a source of credit. In addition, the formation of the European Union (EU) has recently acted as a spur to international junk bond offerings as firms move to expand and take advantage of a huge new common market, using a common currency with sharply reduced trade barriers.

## The Junk-Bond Spread and the Economy

The behavior of yields on junk bonds has attracted the attention of economists trying to forecast changes in the strength or weakness of the economy. They have recently begun to focus on the so-called *junk-bond spread:*

$$\text{Junk-bond spread} = \text{Junk-bond yields} \\ - \text{Average yield on Aaa-rated coporate bonds} \qquad \text{(8.5)}$$

The basic argument concerning this measure of economic conditions is that a rise in the junk-bond spread indicates a growing fear among bond market investors that marginal-quality corporate borrowers are more likely to default on their debts. Thus, greater risk among corporate borrowers signals a weakening economy. In contrast, a decline in the junk-bond spread suggests fewer corporate bond defaults and, therefore, an improving economy.

There is some anecdotal evidence favoring the junk-bond-spread concept. For example, during the year 1999—a period of economic expansion in the United States—the yield spread between Ba corporate bonds—the highest quality junk bond issues—and Aaa (top-quality) corporate bonds was only about three-quarters of a percentage point (75 basis points). Capital market investors were pricing the risk of corporate business failures fairly low. In contrast, by August of 2001—when the U.S. economy was in a recession—this junk-bond-yield spread was more than a full percentage point (100 basis points) as capital market investors began to express concern that a weakening economy might sink a number of weaker companies. More research is needed on this

The buyers of bonds and other financial instruments must be ever watchful of *default risk*—failure to pay interest owed or to pay back the principal of a loan—which can occur in unexpected places and raise critical ethical issues involving corporate stockholders, managers, employees, and the public. A dramatic example of the dangers of lending funds to risky borrowers occurred when Enron Corporation became one of the largest corporate bankruptcies in U.S. history in 2001.

In the case of Enron—holding about $60 billion in assets—the ship went down fast with a jolting effect on the financial markets and on many individual investors. Enron was one of the largest energy companies in the United States, involved not only in the marketing and distribution of natural gas and other energy resources around the globe but also in trading derivatives that allowed producers and consumers to reduce the risk of energy price fluctuations. For years Enron scored one market success after another, generating excess returns for its shareholders, many of whom were employees and officers of the company.

Unfortunately, a combination of events threw Enron into bankruptcy court. The company had begun borrowing heavily to support its trading activities and the pile-up of corporate debt, coupled with the sell-off of many of its most valuable assets, made Enron vulnerable to adverse movements in energy prices. Slumping energy prices in the recession of 2001 wreaked havoc with Enron's revenues and asset values and, as the marketplace became aware of its growing financial troubles, the firm's borrowing costs soared. At the same time, investors in the market became aware of questionable accounting practices at the company which tended to inflate the value of its assets and overestimate its gains from market trading activities. Enron's bankruptcy threatened huge losses for many of its employees who had invested their personal savings and pension monies in the firm's stock. Remarkably, Enron's credit rating remained at investment grade until five days before it filed a federal bankruptcy petition, suggesting its problems were concealed from the public until the last moment.

so-called "economic forecaster," however, before we can confidently accept its predictions about business conditions and the strength of the economy.

## 8.5 New Ways of Dealing with Default Risk: Credit Derivatives

**credit derivatives**

Concern over defaults and business bankruptcies has led to new techniques for protecting lenders against default risk. Among the most popular default-risk hedging tools today are **credit derivatives**—financial contracts designed to offset at least a portion of any default losses that may occur from owning troubled loans or other credit assets. Credit derivatives transfer risk (but not credit assets themselves) from a lender to another individual or institution willing to bear that risk in return for a fee.

**Key URL:**
A good source of information on credit derivatives is: **credit-deriv.com**

These default-risk protection instruments include *credit swaps*, in which two or more investors in risky credit contracts agree to exchange at least some of the expected payments due from their borrowing customers. For example, a swap dealer may draw up an agreement involving two different lending institutions, located in different regions, who pledge to deliver all or part of a $50 million stream of loan payments expected from their customers. Because the contracting lenders serve different market areas, each lender, in effect, is no longer completely dependent on his or her own local loan market for revenue.

Alternatively, we may face a situation in which a credit swap is negotiated between lenders who specialize in different types of risky loans. For example, a major

**Diagram for a Credit Swap Arrangement**

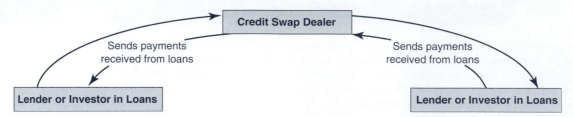

bank may devote a substantial portion of its asset portfolio to oil and gas loans, while another lending institution aggressively pursues loans to support commercial real estate projects, such as the construction of shopping malls and warehouses. Neither knows much about the other's loan specialties. However, by agreeing to exchange a portion of their specialized loan revenues, each lender is no longer so heavily dependent on a particular source of loan revenue. As illustrated in the diagram above, each lender has diversified its sources of revenue to a greater extent than before, so that, hopefully, each lending institution's revenue flows will be more stable over time.

Another example of a credit derivative is the *total return swap*. Under this arrangement a swap dealer may provide assurance that parties to this swap receive a minimum rate of return on the credit they have extended to borrowers. For example, the dealer may guarantee a lender a rate of return on its loans at least 2 percentage points higher than the prevailing market yield on long-term Treasury bonds. There is still risk here due to fluctuating interest rates, but the lender's credit risk attached to its loans has been reduced (unless, of course, the guarantor fails).

Under a *credit option,* an investor in risky assets may protect itself against such risks as rising borrowing costs or a decline in value of the risky assets it holds. For example, a risk-exposed lender may contact a swap dealer about an option contract that pays off if a loan begins to lose value. If the covered loan pays out as expected, however, the option becomes worthless and the lender loses the option fee he or she paid. Alternatively, a financial institution about to borrow a large amount of funds and fearing a drop in its credit rating may seek an option contract that reimburses the institution if its borrowing cost rises above some maximum amount (often determined by a maximum "base rate spread" of the risky loan rate over the prevailing riskless rate on government bonds).

Credit derivatives help to reduce default risk by shifting that risk to someone else willing to accept it in return for a fee. They have opened up the money and capital markets to a wider range of risky borrowers. However, this is a comparatively young financial marketplace that remains largely untested. Standardization of credit derivative contracts is under way, but many legal issues are open to controversy. To be sure, credit derivatives have been among the most rapidly growing financial contracts on the planet, approaching $35 trillion in notional (face) value in 2006 (approximately doubling in a year's time). But no one can yet be sure the credit-derivatives market could withstand a major downturn in the world economy when thousands of credit contracts might turn sour. Nevertheless, these derivatives are spreading rapidly around the globe. While still centered predominantly in the U.S. and U.K., rapid expansion in both Europe and Asia is anticipated. For example, the Bank of India has recently begun to create rules for the operation of a domestic credit derivatives market to help balance the rapid expansion of lending by India's banks.

## A Summary of the Default Risk–Interest Rate Relationship

In summary, careful study of the relationship between default risk and interest rates points to a fundamental principle in the field of finance: *default risk and expected return are positively related.* The investor seeking higher expected returns must also be willing to accept higher risk of ruin. Default risk is correlated with both *internal* (borrower-specific) factors associated with a loan and *external* factors (especially the state of the economy and changing demands for industry products and services).

---

### QUESTIONS TO HELP YOU STUDY

1. What does the term *marketability* refer to? How does it differ from *liquidity?* Why is it important to the saver and the issuer of a loan or security?
2. What is the relationship between marketability and yield on a financial instrument?
3. Explain the meaning of the term *default risk.* What factors appear to have the most influence upon the degree of default risk displayed by a financial asset?
4. In what ways are security *ratings* designed to reflect default risk?
5. Exactly what are *junk bonds?* Why are they issued? How does their actual yield compare to their degree of default risk? Why do you think this is so?
6. What are *credit derivatives?* What are their principal advantages and disadvantages?

---

## 8.6 Call Privileges and Call Risk

**call privilege**

Some corporate bonds, mortgages, municipal revenue bonds, and federal government bonds carry a **call privilege.** This provision of a bond contract (indenture) grants the borrower the option to retire all or a portion of a bond issue by buying back the bonds in advance of their maturity. Bondholders usually are informed of a call through a notice in a newspaper of general circulation, while holders of record of registered bonds are notified directly. Normally, when the call privilege is exercised, the security issuer will pay the investor the *call price,* which equals the securitie's face value plus a call penalty. The size of the *call penalty* is set forth in the indenture (contract) and generally varies inversely with the number of years remaining to maturity and the length of the call deferment period. In the case of a bond, one year's worth of coupon income is often the minimum call penalty required.

### Calculating the Yields on Called Financial Assets

Bonds and selected other financial assets may be callable immediately or the privilege may be deferred (postponed) for a time. In the corporate sector, bonds usually are not eligible for call for a period of 5 to 10 years after issue (known as a call *deferment period*) to give investors at least some protection against early redemption. Of course, calling a callable asset in advance of its final maturity can have a significant impact on the investor's effective yield, resulting in substantial *call risk.*

To demonstrate this, we recall from Chapter 6 that the yield to maturity of any financial asset is that discount rate, $y$, which equates the security's price, $P$, with the present value of all its future cash flows, $I_t$. In symbols:

$$P = \frac{I_1}{(1+y)^1} + \frac{I_2}{(1+y)^2} + \cdots + \frac{I_n}{(1+y)^n} \tag{8.6}$$

where $n$ is the number of periods until maturity. Suppose that after $k$ periods (with $k < n$), the borrower exercises the call option and redeems the called asset. The investor will receive the call price ($C$) for the asset, which can be reinvested at the current market interest rate, $i$. If the investor's planned holding period ends in time period $n$, the expected holding-period yield ($h$) can be calculated using the formula:

$$P = \frac{I_1}{(1+h)^1} + \frac{I_2}{(1+h)^2} + \cdots + \frac{I_k}{(1+h)^k} + \frac{i \times C_{k+1}}{(1+h)^{k+1}}$$
$$+ \frac{i \times C_{k+2}}{(1+h)^{k+2}} + \cdots + \frac{i \times C_n}{(1+h)^n} + \frac{C}{(1+h)^n} \tag{8.7}$$

Using summation signs, this reduces to

$$P = \sum_{t=1}^{k} \frac{I_t}{(1+h)^t} + \sum_{t=k+1}^{n} \frac{i \times C_t}{(1+h)^t} + \frac{C}{(1+h)^n} \tag{8.8}$$

The first term in equation 8.8 gives the present value of all expected cash flows ($I$) from a callable instrument until it is actually called in time period $k$. The second term captures the present value of income received by the investor after he or she reinvests at interest rate $i$ the call price ($C$) received from the security issuer. The third and final term in the equation shows the current discounted value of the call price the investor expects to receive when the holding period ends in time period $n$.

As an example, let's suppose that a corporate bond, originally offering investors an 8 percent coupon rate for 10 years and issued at $1,000 par, is called five years after its issue date when going market interest rates on investments of comparable risk are 6 percent. What is this bond's 10-year holding-period yield ($h$) if its call price equals par ($1,000) plus one year's worth of coupon income ($80)? We have:

$$1,000 = \sum_{t=1}^{5} \frac{\$80}{(1+h)^t} + \sum_{t=6}^{10} \frac{\$1,080 \times .06}{(1+h)^t} + \frac{\$1,080}{(1+h)^{10}} \tag{8.9}$$

The reader, using an electronic calculator, should verify that $h$, the 10-year holding-period yield, is 7.94 percent in this example. Thus, the investor holding this bond would receive 0.06 percent *less* in yield than if the bond had *not* been called but had instead been held to maturity.

Equations 8.8 and 8.9 show clearly that the investor in callable assets encounters two major uncertainties:

1. The investor does not know if or when the callable assets might be called (i.e., the value of $k$).
2. The investor does not know the market yield (reinvestment rate, $i$) that might prevail at the time the asset is called.

Therefore, how aggressively the investor chooses to bid for a callable instrument will depend upon:

1. The investor's expectations regarding future changes in interest rates, especially decreases in rates, during the term of the callable instrument.
2. The length of the deferment period before the asset is eligible to be called.
3. The call price (par value plus call penalty) the issuer is willing to pay to redeem the callable instrument.

## Advantages and Disadvantages of the Call Privilege

Clearly, the call privilege (which is a type of *option*) is an advantage to the security issuer because it grants greater financial flexibility and the potential for reducing future interest costs in the event that interest rates decline. On the other hand, the call privilege is a distinct disadvantage to the security buyer, who may suffer a reduction in expected holding-period yield if the security is called. The issuer will call in a security if the market rate of interest falls far enough so that savings from issuing a new security at lower interest rates more than offset the call penalty plus flotation costs of a new security issue. This means, however, that the investor who is paid off will be forced to reinvest the call price in lower-yielding assets.

Another disadvantage for the investor is that call privileges limit the potential increase in a financial asset's market price. In general, the market price of an asset will not rise significantly above its call price. The reason is that the issuer can call in an asset at its call price, presenting the investor with a loss equal to the difference between the prevailing market price and the call price. Thus, callable securities tend to have more limited potential for capital gains than noncallable securities.

## The Call Premium and Interest Rate Expectations

For all these reasons, financial assets that carry a call privilege generally sell at lower prices and higher interest rates than noncallable assets. Moreover, there is an inverse relationship between the length of the call deferment period and the required rate of interest on callable instruments. The longer the period of deferment and, therefore, the longer the investor is protected against early redemption and possible loss of yield, the lower the interest rate the borrower must pay. Issuers of callable assets must pay a *call premium* in the form of a higher rate of interest for the option of early redemption and for a shorter deferment period.

The key determinant of the size of the call premium is the *interest rate expectations* of investors in the marketplace. If interest rates are expected to rise, the risk a callable asset will actually be called is low. Borrowers are unlikely to call in their securities and issue new ones at a higher interest rate. As a result, the yield differential between callable and noncallable instruments normally will be minimal. The same conclusions apply even if interest rates are expected to decline moderately but not enough to entice borrowers to call in already-issued financial assets and issue new ones.

Securities are most likely to be called when interest rates are expected to fall substantially. In this instance, security issuers can save large amounts of money—more than enough to cover the call penalty plus flotation costs of issuing new instruments—by exercising the call privilege. Thus, the call premium is likely to be significant as investors demand a higher yield on callable issues to compensate them for increased *call risk*. For example, the yield spreads between callable bonds with long call deferments and those with short or no call deferments widen during such periods as investors come to value more highly the call deferment feature.

## Research Evidence on Call Privileges and Call Risk

Is there evidence of an expected *inverse* relationship between interest rate expectations and the value of the call privilege? Research studies generally answer in the affirmative. For example, when interest rates are high, the call premium rises, because investors expect interest rates to fall in the future, resulting in more callable assets being called in. Call provisions also influence yield spreads between corporate bonds, some of which have the call privilege attached, and government bonds, which generally are *not* subject to call. For example, when interest rates are expected to fall, the spread between corporate and government bond rates tends to widen. Moreover, bonds carrying a call deferment have lower rates of return than bonds that are callable immediately.

Research also suggests that calling in bonds to save on interest costs may be a "zero sum game" between bondholders and stockholders of a company issuing callable bonds. Gains by stockholders (due to higher earnings from savings on interest costs) may be offset by losses for bondholders (in the form of a lower effective holding-period yield). Generally, a call will occur when owners of the issuing firm believe they will benefit at the expense of the firm's creditors. In an efficient market, with all participants possessing identical interest rate expectations, callable assets will sell at a price and yield just sufficient to compensate buyers for call risk. Therefore, in theory at least, management of the issuing firm should be indifferent between issuing callable or noncallable bonds. Under some circumstances, however, call provisions may be beneficial to the callable security issuer where management believes it has greater knowledge of the future course of interest rates than does the market as a whole, where a call provision prevents security holders from blocking beneficial investments that a security-issuing entity might make, or where a call privilege lowers the sensitivity of a callable asset's market value to changes in interest rates. Additional research is needed to clarify more precisely who the winners and losers are likely to be from transactions involving callable instruments.

In recent years the proportion of corporate bonds issued with call privileges attached has declined significantly. One reason is the large number of shorter bond maturities, which means that issuing companies have less need to call in their outstanding bonds before they reach maturity. Then, too, there has been a virtual explosion in new financial instruments to hedge bond issues against interest rate risk, including financial futures, options, and swaps, reducing the need for the interest rate protection afforded by the call privilege. Finally, the yield premium associated with issuing callable bonds, rather than noncallable bonds, appears to have increased from time to time, discouraging many corporations from issuing bonds bearing a call feature. However, some institutions, such as the giant mortgage companies Fannie Mae (FNMA) and Freddie Mac (FHLMC), have issued large amounts of long-term callable debt to protect their income when market interest rates fall.

## 8.7  Prepayment Risk and the Yields on Loan-Backed Securities

A newer form of risk affecting the relative interest rates confronting modern investors arises when they acquire *loan-backed securities,* such as mortgage passthroughs, collateralized mortgage obligations (CMOs), auto-loan-backed securities, and credit-card-backed securities. These instruments are usually created when a lending institution removes a group of similar loans from its balance sheet and places them with a trustee (such as a security dealer) who, using the loans as collateral, sells securities to raise new capital for the lending institution. Each of these securities derives its value from the income-earning potential of the pool of loans that backs the securities. As loans in the pool generate interest and principal payments, these payments flow to holders of the loan-backed instruments.

Unlike ordinary bonds, which usually pay nothing but interest until they finally reach maturity, loan-backed financial instruments pay their purchasers a stream of income that includes *both* repayments of loan principal and interest. In this case, the purchaser may receive higher-than-expected repayments of principal early in the life of the pooled loans, possibly lowering his or her expected return from loan-backed securities. Investors in those loan-backed instruments that carry substantial

**prepayment risk**

**prepayment risk** will demand higher yields to compensate them for the risk associated with early prepayment of the loans backing the securities they hold.

Prepayment risk is especially troublesome for investors purchasing securities that are backed by pools of home mortgage loans. The pool of loans serving as collateral for these instruments generally consists of 25- and 30-year loans to purchase new homes. Many of these home loans will be retired early due to: (1) *refinancing of loans,* as homeowners try to get new, cheaper mortgage loans in order to lower their monthly mortgage payments as market interest rates fall; and (2) *home-owner turnover,* as families move and need to sell their homes or simply default on their loans.

**Key URLs:**
For further infoemation about prepayment risk see, for example, **investopedia.com/ terms/p/prepayment risk.asp** and **en.wikipedia.org/ wiki/prepayment**

The investor interested in purchasing loan-backed financial instruments needs to make certain assumptions about the likely prepayment behavior of the loans in the pool in order to decide what the true value of the loan-backed assets must be. Each package of pooled loans would have somewhat different characteristics due to variations in loan quality and location, the condition of the economy, and other factors. The current value of a loan-backed security can be determined from:

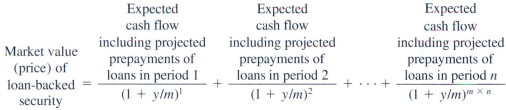

$$
\begin{aligned}
\text{Market value} \\
\text{(price) of} \\
\text{loan-backed} \\
\text{security}
\end{aligned}
=
\frac{
\begin{array}{c}\text{Expected}\\\text{cash flow}\\\text{including projected}\\\text{prepayments of}\\\text{loans in period 1}\end{array}
}{(1 + y/m)^1}
+
\frac{
\begin{array}{c}\text{Expected}\\\text{cash flow}\\\text{including projected}\\\text{prepayments of}\\\text{loans in period 2}\end{array}
}{(1 + y/m)^2}
+ \cdots +
\frac{
\begin{array}{c}\text{Expected}\\\text{cash flow}\\\text{including projected}\\\text{prepayments of}\\\text{loans in period } n\end{array}
}{(1 + y/m)^{m \times n}}
$$

(8.10)

where $y$ is the financial asset's yield to maturity, $m$ is the number of times during a year that interest and principal payments occur, and $n$ is the total number of years covered by the pooled loans. Note that each expected cash flow from a loan-backed instrument must be adjusted to reflect the risk that some loans will pay out early, increasing cash flows to an investor in these securities in the early years and, thus, reducing an investor's expected cash flow in later years. The greater the prepayment risk, the higher the yield tends to rise and the lower the loan-backed security's price tends to go.[2]

One of the most popular devices today used to reduce prepayment risk from loan-backed instruments is to divide the loan-backed security issue into classes or *tranches* bearing different degrees of estimated prepayment risk. Each tranche promises a different rate of return based on a different maturity and risk profile. The shortest maturity tranches (usually designated Tranche A) receive principal payments from prepaid loans *first* until all Tranche A securities are paid off. Then loan prepayments flow to investors in Tranche B, who are willing to accept somewhat higher prepayment risk, until this second group is also paid off. The process of directed repayments continues until the entire loan-backed security issue is retired.

In short, the upper (shorter-maturity) tranches carry lower prepayment risk and, therefore, promise a lower rate of return, while the lower (longer-maturity) tranches

---

[2]Actually, the relationship between the value of a loan-backed instrument and changes in market interest rates is quite complicated. For example, when interest rates fall, investors in loan-backed instruments will experience quicker recovery of their invested funds, as more borrowers repay their loans early and the lower interest rates increase the present value of the loan-backed instruments' cash flow. On the other hand, with more loans paid off early, the investor loses future interest payments that will never be received, and the funds received by the investor will have to be reinvested at lower market interest rates, reducing future earnings from the instrument. Generally, a loan-backed asset will fall in value when lost interest payments and reduced reinvestment income offset the benefits from quicker recovery of principal and a lower discount rate applied to future cash flows.

Research in recent years has revealed another risk factor that often affects the market value of debt and equity securities issued by corporations and other units raising funds in the money and capital markets.

**event risk**  This **event risk** factor consists of news announcements that reflect decisions by the management of a corporation or other fund-raising unit. Examples include announcements of new stock or bond offerings, changes in corporate dividend payments, stock splits, mergers, replacement of management, new product offerings, and so on.

Financial research suggests that announcements of events like these tend to have fairly predictable impacts on asset values and borrowing costs. For example,

| Event | Expected Market Response |
|---|---|
| Announcement of a new security issue | The issuer's security prices usually fall, at least temporarily. |
| Announcement of an increased stock dividend | The issuer's security prices usually rise, at least temporarily. |
| Announcement of a stock split | The issuer's security prices usually rise, at least temporarily. |
| Debt-equity swap (a company's bonds are replaced by stock) | The company's stock price usually falls, at least temporarily. |

Many financial analysts believe that events such as the foregoing trigger changes in asset prices and interest rates for the affected institutions because they convey *new information* about the possible future performance of these institutions. For example, the management of a business firm possesses inside (asymmetric) information on the firm's true financial condition. Presumably, management draws on this inside information when it elects to go ahead with a new security offering, a change in dividends paid to stockholders, launching a new product, etc. Investors in the marketplace regard announcements of such "events" as a revelation of how management views the firm's future prospects. The result is a reevaluation by investors of the value of a security issuer's stocks and bonds. Market prices and yields of those securities, therefore, will change with the appearance of new information.

**Sources:** See, for example, Driessen [3] and Norton and Pettengill [9].

reflect higher prepayment risk but promise a greater expected return. Different groups of investors prefer different tranches of loan repayments based on their portfolio characteristics, risk exposures, and regulations. For example, banks that face more

## QUESTIONS TO HELP YOU STUDY

7. What is a *call privilege?* Why is this privilege an advantage to a security issuer and a disadvantage to a buyer of financial instruments?

8. What types of *risk* are encountered by purchasers of callable *financial instruments?*

9. What is *prepayment risk?* What factors lead to an increase in prepayment risk?

10. How can a buyer of loan-backed assets reduce prepayment risk?

11. What is meant by the term *event risk* (see the nearby Financial Developments feature)? What factors appear to contribute to an increase in a corporation's stock price? A decrease in its stock price?

volatile, short-term claims against them tend to prefer investing in shorter tranches, while insurance companies and pension funds with longer-term liabilities tend to seek out loan-backed securities in longer-maturity tranches.

## 8.8   Taxation of Returns on Financial Assets

Key URLS:
For information about tax policy and filling out U.S. tax forms, see especially **federal taxreturn.com** and **irs.gov**

Taxes imposed by federal, state, and local governments have a profound effect on the returns earned by investors on financial assets. The income from most securities—interest or dividends and capital gains—is subject to taxation at the federal level and by many state and local governments as well. Government uses its taxing power, in part, to encourage the purchase of certain financial assets and, thereby, redirect the flow of savings and investment toward areas of critical social need. These perceived needs may change over time and are often reflected in changes to the tax code.

Over the past 20 years the federal tax code, in particular, has experienced many fundamental revisions. The consequences are that tax rates in general have risen in some years and fallen in others, while the mix of tax rates on various sources of income have undergone substantial changes. Some assets have become tax-exempt, some have achieved a tax-deferred status, and others have become more or less heavily taxed. It is important for investors to understand the implications that government tax policies have on the value of their investments, because every investor's situation is unique. However, there are some basics that every investor needs to be aware of.

Key URLS:
For further discussion of the latest U.S. tax laws see, for example, such sources as **smartmoney.com/tax** and **taxes.about.com**

### Tax-Exempt Securities

tax-exempt securities

One of the most controversial tax rules affecting securities is the tax-exemption privilege granted investors in state and local government (municipal) bonds. The interest income earned on municipal bonds is exempt from federal income taxes.[3] **Tax-exempt securities** represent a subsidy to induce investors to support local government by financing the construction of schools, highways, airports, and other needed public projects. The exemption privilege shifts the burden of federal taxation from buyers of municipal bonds to other taxpayers.

What investors benefit from buying municipals? The critical factor here is the marginal tax rate (tax bracket) of the investor—the tax rate he or she must pay on the last dollar of income received during the tax year. For individual investors, these marginal tax rates range from zero for nontaxpayers to as high as about 35 percent for the highest income-earning taxpayers. (See Exhibit 8.5 for an example of recent tax rates for individuals and corporations.) The marginal tax rate for corporations is 15 percent on the first $50,000 in taxable profits up to as high as 39 percent on net income above $100,000 to $335,000 and up to 38 percent for corporations earning $15 million to about $18$^{1}/_{3}$ million annually. In recent years, marginal tax rates of approximately 20 to 30 percent have represented a break-even level for investors interested in municipal bonds. Investors carrying marginal tax rates above this range often receive higher after-tax yields from buying tax-exempt securities instead of taxable securities. Below this range, taxable securities often yield a better after-tax return.

---

[3]Although the interest income from municipals is federal income tax exempt, capital gains on municipals are generally taxable as ordinary income. In addition, most states do not tax income from their own bonds or from the bonds issued by local governments within their borders. Income from U.S. government securities is usually exempt from state and local taxes but not from federal taxes.

| EXHIBIT 8.5 | Examples of Recent Marginal Federal Income Tax Rates (individual and corporate tax brackets shown) |

| INCOME TAX BRACKETS AND TAX RATES FOR SINGLE AND MARRIED TAXPAYERS (2006) | | | INCOME TAX BRACKETS AND TAX RATES FOR CORPORATIONS PAYING TAXES (2002–2007) | | |
|---|---|---|---|---|---|
| Single Taxpayers' Taxable Income | Married Taxpayers' Taxable Incomes* | Marginal Tax Brackets (%) | Taxable Incomes Bracket | Base Amount Owed | Marginal Tax Rate Applied to Excess over Base |
| $0–$7,550 | $0–$15,000 | 10% | Less than $50,000 | $    0 | 15% |
| $7,550–$30,650 | $15,000–$61,300 | 15 | $50,000–$75,000 | 7,500 | 25 |
| $30,650–$74,200 | $61,300–$123,700 | 25 | $75,000–$100,000 | 13,750 | 34 |
| $74,200–$154,800 | $123,700–$188,950 | 28 | $100,000–$335,000 | 22,250 | 39 |
| $154,800–$336,550 | $188,450–$336,550 | 33 | $335,000–$10 million | 113,900 | 34 |
| $336,550 and over | $336,550 and over | 35 | $10 million–$15 million | 3.4 million | 35 |
|  |  |  | $15 million–$18.33$\frac{1}{3}$ million | 5.15 million | 38 |
|  |  |  | Over $18.33$\frac{1}{3}$ million | 6.416$\frac{2}{3}$ million | 35 |

*Married taxpayers are assumed to be filing jointly.

Source: U.S. Treasury Department.

How would an individual figure his or her income tax? Suppose you are single and have taxable annual income (that is, gross income receipts less all exemptions and deductions allowable under tax law) of $25,000. Then you would owe:

Base amount owed + Excess income above preceding tax bracket × Marginal tax rate

| $755 | + | ($25,000 − $7,550) × 0.15, or |
|---|---|---|
| $755 | + | $2,617.50 |
|  | = | $3,372.50 in total federal income taxes owed |

What about a corporation? Suppose the company had annual net income (earnings) before taxes of $250,000. Then the company would owe federal taxes in the amount of:

Base amount owed + Excess earnings above preceding tax bracket × Marginal tax rate

| $22,250 | + | ($250,000 − $100,000) × 0.39, or |
|---|---|---|
| $22,250 | + | $19,500 |
|  | = | $41,750 in taxes owed |

Note: The taxable individual income brackets shown change each year as the inflation rate moves because the federal tax structure in the United States is indexed to inflation in order to at least partially prevent taxpayers from paying higher and higher taxes due solely to rising prices for goods and services. The above marginal tax rates do not reflect the Social Security Program's tax structure, which stands at 6.2 percent for up to $97,500 of annual earned income or 12.4 percent for a self-employed individual in 2007. There is also a 1.45 percent Medicare payroll tax levy against all of a person's annual earned income and, if you are self-employed, this Medicare tax rate jumps to 2.9 percent of annual earned income.

### The Effect of Marginal Tax Rates on After-Tax Yields

To illustrate the importance of knowing the investor's marginal tax rate in deciding whether to purchase tax-exempt assets, consider the following example. Assume the current yield to maturity on taxable corporate bonds is 12 percent, while the current tax-exempt yield on municipal bonds of comparable quality and rating is 9 percent. The after-tax yield on these two securities can be compared using the following formula:

$$\text{Before-tax yield} (1 - \text{Investor's marginal tax rate}) = \text{After-tax yield} \quad \text{(8.11)}$$

For example, for an investor in the 28 percent tax bracket (see Exhibit 8.5), the after-tax yields on these bonds are as follows:

| Taxable Corporate Bond | Tax-Exempt Municipal Bond |
|---|---|
| 12%  (1− 0.28) = 8.64% | 9% before and after taxes |

On the basis of yield alone, the investor in the 28 percent tax bracket would prefer the tax-exempt municipal bond.[4]

At what rate would an investor be *indifferent* as to whether securities are taxable or tax exempt? In other words, what is the break-even point between these two types of financial assets?

This point is easily calculated from the formula

$$\text{Tax-exempt yield} = (1 - t) \times \text{Taxable yield} \qquad (8.12)$$

where $t$ is the investor's marginal tax rate. Solving for the break-even tax rate gives

$$t = 1 - \frac{\text{Tax-exempt yield}}{\text{Taxable yield}} \qquad (8.13)$$

Clearly, if the current yield is 8 percent on tax-exempt securities and 10 percent on taxable issues, the break-even tax rate is $1 - 0.80$, or 20 percent. An investor in a marginal tax bracket *above* 20 percent would prefer the yield on a tax-exempt security to a taxable one at these prevailing interest rates, other factors held equal.

*Comparing Taxable and Tax-Exempt Securities*   The existence of both taxable and tax-exempt securities complicates the investor's task in trying to choose a suitable portfolio to buy and hold. To make valid comparisons between taxable and tax-exempt issues, the taxed investor must convert all expected yields to an *after-tax basis*.

In the case of the yield to maturity on a security this can be done by using the following formula:

$$P_0 = \sum_{i=1}^{n} \frac{I_i(1 - t)}{(1 + a)^i} + \frac{(P_n - P_0)(1 - t_{cg})}{(1 + a)^n} + \frac{P_0}{(1 + a)^n} \qquad (8.14)$$

which equates the current market value ($P_0$) of the security to the present value of all after-tax returns promised in the future. If the security is to be held for $n$ years, $I_i$ is the amount of interest or other income expected each year, and $t$ is the marginal income tax rate of the investor. If we assume the security will be sold or redeemed for price $P_n$ at maturity, then $(P_n - P_0)$ measures the expected capital gain on the instrument, which will be taxed at a rate, $t_{cg}$, which equals the taxpayer's ordinary income tax rate—up to a maximum of 15 percent under the most recent U.S. tax laws. Provided investors know their marginal income tax rate, the current price of the security, and the expected distribution of future income from the security, they can easily calculate discount rate $a$—the after-tax yield to maturity.

**Key URL:**
The Bond Market Association provides a free online calculator to aid investors in comparing tax-exempt bond yields with yields on taxable securities at **investinginbonds.com**

---

[4]The particular tax brackets favoring the purchase of municipals versus taxable securities change over time due to changes in tax laws and variations in the yield spread between taxable and tax-exempt securities.

For example, consider the case of a $1,000 corporate bond selling for $900 (with par value of $1,000), maturing in 10 years, with a 10 percent coupon rate. If an investor in the 33 percent federal income tax bracket buys and holds the bond to maturity, her after-tax yield, $a$, could be found from evaluating the following:

$$\$900 = \sum_{i=1}^{10} \frac{\$100(1 - 0.33)}{(1 + a)^i} + \frac{(\$1,000 - \$900)(1 - 0.15)}{(1 + a)^{10}} + \frac{\$900}{(1 + a)^{10}}$$

In this instance, the reader should verify that the after-tax yield, $a$, is close to 8.10 percent, assuming a 15 percent capital gains tax rate ($t_{cg}$).

Certainly, the tax-exempt privilege has lowered the interest rates at which municipals can be sold in the open market relative to taxable bonds and, therefore, the amount of interest costs borne by local taxpayers. For example, in January 2007, top-quality 10-year municipal bonds carried an average yield to maturity of about 4.00 percent, compared to 5.57 percent on comparable quality (taxable) 10-year corporate bonds—a yield spread of more than $1\frac{1}{2}$ percentage points or 157 basis points. However, the primary beneficiaries of the exemption privilege are investors who can profitably purchase municipals and escape some portion of the federal tax burden. Other taxpayers must pay higher federal taxes in order to make up for those lost tax revenues. By limiting the municipal market to these high tax-bracket investors, the tax-exempt feature has probably increased the volatility of municipal bond interest rates and made the job of fiscal management for state and local governments somewhat more difficult.

### Treatment of Capital Losses and Capital Gains

Net losses on investments made in financial assets are deductible for tax purposes within well-defined limits. For the individual taxpayer, a net capital loss is deductible up to the amount of the capital loss, the size of ordinary income, or $3,000, whichever is smaller. For example, suppose an investor experiences a net loss on securities held and then sold of $8,000. Suppose this person receives other taxable income of $20,000. How much of the capital loss can be deducted? What is this taxpayer's total taxable income? The maximum loss deduction in this case is $3,000 and, therefore, the taxpayer's net taxable income is $17,000 ($20,000 minus the $3,000 in deductible losses). Current federal law allows the taxpayer to carry forward into subsequent years the remaining portion of the loss ($5,000 in this example) until all of the loss has been deducted from ordinary income, but the loss cannot be carried backward.

Even more important, the U.S. Congress recently passed the Jobs and Growth Tax Relief Reconciliation Act of 2004 in an effort to accelerate private investment and promote economic development through lower taxes. For example, taxes on capital gains derived from investment assets and dividends received from corporate stock were lowered to only a 15 percent maximum, well below the tax rate on ordinary income. However, this easing of capital gains and dividend tax rates was subjected to a sunset provision that requires Congress to either extend the lower tax rates or allow these tax rates to snap back to their older, higher levels.

### 8.9  Convertible Securities

**convertibility**    Another factor that affects relative rates of return among different financial assets is **convertibility.** Convertible financial instruments consist of special issues of corporate bonds or preferred stock that entitle the holder to exchange these assets for a specific number of shares of the issuing firm's common stock. For example, Internet giant Amazon.com issued more than a billion dollars in 10-year convertible bonds in 1999, promising an annual interest return of 4.75 percent. Buyers were given the option, to be exercised at any time after issue, of exchanging each $1,000 bond for just slightly more than 6.4 shares of Amazon's common stock.

Convertibles are frequently called *hybrid securities* because they offer the investor the prospect of stable income in the form of interest or dividends plus capital gains on common stock once conversion occurs. While the timing of a conversion is most often at the option of the investor, an issuing firm often can "force" conversion of its securities by either calling them in or encouraging a rise in the price of its common stock (such as by announcing a merger offer) because conversion is most likely in a rising market.

Investors generally pay a premium for convertible securities over nonconvertible securities in the form of a higher price (and, in the case of convertible bonds, a lower promised rate of interest). Thus, convertibles usually carry a lower rate of return than other securities of comparable quality and maturity issued by the same company. This typically occurs because the investor in convertibles is granted a hedge against future market risk. If security prices fall, the investor still earns a fixed rate of return in the form of interest income from a convertible bond or dividend income from convertible preferred stock. On the other hand, if stock prices rise, the investor can exercise his or her option and share in any capital gains earned on the company's common stock.

**Key URL:**
Recent growth of convertible securities has led to the appearance of many new Web sites discussing convertibles. One example is **investopedia. com/terms/c/ convertiblebond.asp**

*Advantages for the Convertible Bond Issuer* Convertible bonds offer several significant advantages to the company that decides to issue them. Their most powerful issuer advantage is a *significantly lower interest cost* because, unlike conventional bonds, convertibles give the buyer potential access to capital gains and dividends from the stock that may replace the convertibles in the future. An interesting illustration of this substantial interest-cost advantage appeared in the corporate bond market early in 2007. The promised (coupon) rate on the 10 most actively traded convertible corporate bonds ranged from 0.375 percent (AMGEN) to 4.25 percent (Ford Motor Co.). In contrast, the 10 most actively traded investment-grade corporate bonds had promised (coupon) rates ranging from 5.45 percent (Morgan Stanley) to 7.375 percent (NEXTEL Communications), while junk bonds carried promised (coupon) rates as high as 11.00 percent (Movie Gallery). Convertibles experienced a dramatic rise as the new century progressed due to increased demand for these financial assets on the part of hedge funds, the emergence of new types of convertibles that allow issuers to make redemption in cash rather than in stock, the expansion of investment-grade convertibles, and increased arbitraging activity between issuers' convertibles and their nonconvertible securities.

A second powerful advantage to issuers of convertible bonds is the ability to *avoid issuing more common stock.* For a time, convertibles allow a firm to delay selling new stock. This may be desirable because the added shares may dilute the equity interests of current stockholders and reduce their earnings per share.

Finally, a third important advantage is *tax savings.* Interest on convertible bonds is a tax-deductible expense in the United States and many other countries. Dividends on stock, on the other hand, are not deductible from federal income taxes, though recent tax legislation in the United States has reduced the tax burden associated with stock dividends.

*Advantages for the Investor in Convertible Bonds*   Key advantages for an investor buying convertible bonds include, as seen above, the receipt of at least some interest income, even when the value of the common stock of the issuing company is on the decline. Moreover, if the issuer's common stock is rising in price, the same company's convertibles also tend to increase in value.

Moreover, there is a floor under the price of a convertible bond—known as its *investment value*—below which its price normally will not fall. This is the price that would produce a yield on the convertible equal to the yield on nonconvertible bonds of the same quality. However, investors are often counseled by financial analysts not to buy convertibles unless they would be happy holding the issuing company's stock, because the issuer may call in the securities early, forcing conversion. This particular situation may present the investor with a substantially reduced return.

## 8.10   The Structure of Interest Rates in the Financial System

As we conclude this chapter, it is important to gain some perspective on the fundamental purpose of this section of the book. In reality, Chapters 5, 6, 7, and 8 should be viewed as a unit, tied together by a common subject: what determines the level of and changes in interest rates and asset yields. In Chapter 5 we argued that there is *one* interest rate that underlies all interest rates and is a component of all rates. This is the *risk-free* (or pure) rate of interest, which is a measure of the opportunity cost of holding cash and a measure of the reward for saving rather than spending all of our income on consumption. All other interest rates are scaled upward by varying degrees from the risk-free rate, depending on such factors as inflation, the term (maturity) of a loan, the risk of borrower default, the risk of prepayment, and the marketability, liquidity, convertibility, and tax status of the financial assets to which those rates apply.

**interest rate structure**   There is, then, a *structure* to interest rates whose foundation is the risk-free rate (as determined by the demand and supply for loanable funds described in Chapter 5). Perhaps one picture of that **interest rate structure** is worth a thousand words. Recently, the yield to maturity on long-term U.S. Treasury bonds was reported as close to 4.94 percent, while corporate Baa bonds were quoted at an average yield of about 6.42 percent. As Exhibit 8.6 indicates, each of these rates, like *all* interest rates, is a summation of rewards (premiums) paid to lenders of funds to get those investors to hold a particular financial asset. Each reward or premium is merely compensation for bearing some kind of *risk,* for example: (1) the risk of giving up liquidity and accepting greater market risk from buying a longer maturity asset, (2) the risk of inflation (loss of purchasing power) over the term of an asset, (3) the risk the borrower will default on some or all of his promised payments, (4) the risk some assets can be called in before they mature and the investor may have to reinvest her money at a lower interest rate, and (5) the risk of accepting an asset with a weak resale market (low marketability). Each interest rate or yield we see in today's market is the *sum* of all of these risk premium factors plus the real risk-free interest rate. And when interest rates change, that change may be due to a change in the risk-free rate or to a change in any of the risk premium factors cited above.

Truly, interest rates are a complex phenomenon, affected by many factors. We need to keep this complexity in mind as we proceed to the next chapter and take on the

| EXHIBIT 8.6 | An Example of the Structure of Interest Rates in the Financial System |
|---|---|

During the month of October 2006: The long-term U.S. Treasury bond rate averaged 4.94% + 1.48% = 6.42%

while the Corporate Baa bond rate averaged:

**Estimated components of the rate on long-term U.S. Treasury bonds**

| | | |
|---|---|---|
| Rate premium for buying a long-term financial asset rather than a short-term financial asset | Liquidity premium | +0.44% |
| Rate premium for inflation risk | Expected inflation | +2.00% |
| Rate premium for forgoing consumption and saving money | Risk-free real rate of interest | +2.50% |
| | Total | 4.94% |

**Estimated components of the rate or yield spread between corporate Baa bond rate and long-term Treasury bond rate**

| | | |
|---|---|---|
| Rate premium for accepting a less market-able financial asset | Premium for lower marketability | +0.23% |
| Rate premium for accepting risk financial asset might be called | Call risk premium | +0.25% |
| Rate premium for accepting risk of borrower default | Default-risk premium | +1.00% |
| | Total | 1.48% |

Source: Bond rates derived from *Statistical Supplement to the Federal Reserve Bulletin,* January 2007, Table 1.35; interest-rate components estimated by the authors.

difficult task of trying to anticipate and forecast interest rate changes and discover how to hedge against possible losses due to interest rate movements.

## QUESTIONS TO HELP YOU STUDY

12. What types of financial instruments are most favored by tax laws?

13. What portion of the income generated by municipal bonds is considered tax-exempt and what portion is taxable income? Why do you think United States' laws are structured in this way?

14. Explain the relationship between a taxpayer's marginal tax rate and after-tax returns on corporate and municipal bonds. Would municipals be a worthwhile investment for you today? Explain why or why not.

15. What does *convertibility* refer to? Why are convertibles called *hybrid securities?*

16. Convertibles typically carry lower yields than nonconvertibles of the same maturity and risk class. Can you explain why?

17. What does *interest rate structure* refer to? What does the structure of interest rates tell us about the difficulties involved in forecasting interest rates?

# Summary of the Chapter's Main Points

This chapter has focused our attention upon multiple factors other than maturity and inflation that cause interest rates and prices to differ between one type of financial asset and another, including marketability, liquidity, default risk, call privileges, taxation, prepayment risk, and convertibility. Among the principal conclusions of the chapter are the following:

- *Marketability,* or the capacity to be sold readily, is positively related to an asset's price and negatively related to its rate of return or yield. More marketable financial instruments generally carry lower yields.

- *Liquid* financial instruments also tend to carry lower yields, but possess the advantages of ready marketability, stable price, and reversibility (i.e., the capacity to fully recover the funds originally invested).

- *Default risk*—the danger a borrower will not make all promised payments at agreed-upon times—results in the promised yields of risky assets rising above the yields on riskless financial instruments. Potential buyers of these instruments compare their estimated (subjective) probability of loss from a risky asset to the market's assigned default-risk premium.

- Default-risk premiums attached by the financial marketplace to the promised yields on risky assets tend to be heavily influenced by the *credit ratings* assigned by various credit rating agencies (such as Moody's Investors Service or Standard & Poor's Corporation) and by the condition of the economy. An expanding economy tends to result in lower default-risk premiums, while an economy trapped in a recession with rising business bankruptcies tends to generate higher default-risk premiums on risky assets.

- Many lower-rated companies with questionable credit ratings have issued speculative or *junk bonds* in large quantities in recent years. The rise of junk bonds has broadened the market for corporate debt, offering participating investors substantially higher yields than were previously available.

- Debt securities with *call privileges* attached tend to carry higher promised rates of return than financial instruments not bearing a call privilege. The right of a security issuer to call away the security he or she has previously issued and retire it in return for paying a prespecified price gives borrowers greater flexibility in adapting their capital structure to changing market conditions. Recently call privileges have been declining in use as corporate borrowers have discovered other ways of protecting themselves against risk.

- The rapid growth of *loan-backed securities* (such as mortgage-backed instruments) has given rise to *prepayment risk*—the danger loans used to back loan-backed securities may be paid back early, lowering an investor's expected yield from loan-backed instruments. Issuers of these instruments have sought to make them more attractive to buyers by creating different maturity classes (*tranches*) so that buyers can select how much prepayment risk they are willing to take on.

- *Event risk* has long been a significant factor in the pricing of corporate stock and debt securities. *Events* that appear to have an especially significant impact upon asset values include announcements of new security issues, stock dividends, stock splits, and management changes within a particular business firm.

- Financial assets generate interest or dividend payments and capital gains or losses—any or all of which may be subject to *taxation* at federal and state levels. Investors must be cognizant of continuing changes in tax laws and regulations. It is also important to be able to calculate tax-exempt yields versus taxable returns because some assets (such as municipal bonds) generate tax-exempt income and some investing institutions (such as credit unions and pension funds) are tax-exempt.

- Some corporate debt and stock instruments carry a *convertibility* feature that allows them to be exchanged for a certain number of shares of stock. Convertibles are often called "hybrid securities" because they offer not only relatively stable income (interest payments or fixed dividends) but also the prospect of substantial capital gains when converted into stock. Assets with convertibility features tend to sell at a higher price and a lower promised yield due to their potential for exceptional gains upon conversion.

- The chapter closes with an overview of the *interest rate structure* model, which aids us in understanding why there are so many different interest rates in the real world. Each different interest rate or yield is viewed in this model as the sum of the risk-free interest rate plus a series of risk premiums dependent on varying degrees of risk exposure. Among the risk premiums included in this model are liquidity and term (or maturity) risk, inflation risk, default risk, call risk, prepayment risk, and exposure to tax risk. Because these risk premiums can change at any time, interest rates themselves may change at any time and the causes of any particular interest rate movement can be very complex.

## Key Terms Appearing in This Chapter

**marketability,**  217

**liquidity,**  218

**default risk,**  218

**expected yield,**  220

**junk bonds,**  222

**credit derivatives,**  227

**call privilege,**  229

**prepayment risk,**  232

**event risk,**  234

**tax-exempt securities,**  235

**convertibility,**  238

**interest rate structure,**  240

## Problems and Issues

1.  A popular investment strategy for individuals about to retire is to pursue "laddered Treasuries." One example would be to purchase a fixed amount (perhaps $20,000) in 10-year U.S. Treasury notes each year for 10 years. Whenever a note matures, the investor "rolls over" that investment into another 10-year note of comparable size. In answering the following questions think about marketability, default risk, call provisions, and liquidity in addition to expected rates of return.

    a. Explain why this investment strategy would tend to provide a steady income. What could cause that income to vary over time?

**b.** Why is this investment strategy preferable to investing in "laddered high-grade corporate bonds"? Do corporate bonds have any advantages over the Treasuries?

**c.** What could you say about the preferences of an individual who chooses laddered corporates over Treasuries?

**d.** Under what conditions would the laddered-corporates portfolio be the better choice?

2. The market yield to maturity on a risky bond is currently listed at 14.50 percent. The risk-free interest rate is estimated to be 9.25 percent. What is the default-risk premium, all other factors removed? The promised yield on this bond is 15 percent. A certain investor looking at this bond estimates there is a 25 percent probability the bond will pay 15 percent at maturity, a 50 percent probability it will pay a 10 percent return, and a 25 percent probability it will yield only 5 percent. What is the bond's expected yield? What is this investor's anticipated default loss? Will the investor buy this bond?

3. A 10-year corporate bond was issued on January 1, 2004, with call privilege attached. The bond was sold to investors at $1,000 par value with a 10 percent coupon rate. The bond was called on January 1, 2007, at a call price paid to holders of par plus one year's coupon income. At the time, the prevailing market interest rate on securities of comparable quality was 8 percent. If a holder of this bond reinvested the call price at 8 percent for seven years, calculate this investor's holding-period yield for the entire period of 10 years. How much yield did the investor lose as a result of the call?

4. Aaa-rated municipal bonds are carrying a market yield today of 5.25 percent, while Aaa-rated corporate bonds have current market yields of 11.50 percent. What is the break-even tax rate that would make a taxable investor indifferent between these two types of bonds?

5. An investor purchases a 10-year U.S. government bond for $800. The bond's coupon rate is 10 percent and, at time of purchase, it still had five years remaining until maturity. If the investor holds the bond until it matures and collects the $1,000 par value from the Treasury and his marginal tax rate is 28 percent, what will his after-tax yield to maturity be?

6. If the following *events* happen to Alvernon Way Corporation, what is likely to happen to the company's stock price, all other factors held constant? Why?

**a.** Alvernon retires a bond issue with the issuance of new preferred stock.

**b.** Alvernon announces a dividend payment to holders of its common stock of $2.36 per share; security analysts had expected a dividend of $2.45 per share.

**c.** Alvernon is selling 270,000 new shares of common stock today.

**d.** Alvernon Class A common stock shares, currently priced at $140 per share, are splitting 2 for 1 next week.

**e.** Alvernon announces the development and marketing of a new medical device that promises significant relief for persons suffering from severe arthritis and stiffness of the joints.

**f.** Six weeks after receiving her largest salary bonus in history, Alvernon's chief operating officer announced early retirement today due to family and medical problems.

**g.** Alvernon has just been sued in federal court by the U.S. Department of Justice for alleged price fixing and antitrust violations.

 **7.** A pool of credit-card loans is expected to pay the following stream of cash flows for each quarter of the year as indicated in the table below. Key these numbers into the first two columns of a spreadsheet: time period in column one and cash flow in column two.

| Time Period | Expected Net Cash Flow Including Projected Prepayments |
|---|---|
| Year 1, Quarter 1 | $ 82 million |
| Year 1, Quarter 2 | 80 million |
| Year 1, Quarter 3 | 72 million |
| Year 1, Quarter 4 | 60 million |
| Year 2, Quarter 1 | 48 million |
| Year 2, Quarter 2 | 36 million |
| Year 2, Quarter 3 | 27 million |
| Year 2, Quarter 4 | 18 million |
| Year 3, Quarter 1 | 6 million |
| Year 3, Quarter 2 | 1 million |
| | $430 million |

**a.** If the yield to maturity on comparable quality instruments is 14 percent, what should be the total market value (price) of the securities issued against this particular pool of credit-card loans? (Hint: Use column 3 in the spreadsheet to compute the present value of each expected cash flow, then add the column.)

**b.** Suppose a firm issued one million fixed-coupon bonds with a maturity of 2½ years, and a coupon rate of 14 percent in order to purchase the pool of credit-card loans. If these bonds sold at par, what is the par value and what is their coupon (in dollars)? (Hint: Use column 4 in the spreadsheet to compute the present value of each dollar to be paid out in coupons, then the sum is the present value of each dollar paid over the 10 quarters.)

**c.** Repeat parts (a) and (b) with a yield to maturity of 10 percent. How do your results change?

## Web-Based Problems

**1.** As in most other industries, bank profits tend to fall during downturns in the economy. However, other factors also affect bank profitability, such as regulation and competition, as well as the portfolio decisions bank managers make. Certain financial ratios crudely measure the amount of financial risk facing any particular bank. Among these ratios are: (i) Loans/Deposits, which measures the liquidity of the bank's assets, with a high number indicating more liquidity risk; (ii) Nonperforming assets/Assets, which is the fraction of the bank's assets for which loan payments are delinquent, with a high number indicating more credit risk; and (iii) Equity/Assets, which indicates how much stockholder wealth (owner's equity) relative to the funds obtained from depositors and other creditors is backing the bank's assets, with a low number indicating greater default risk.

  **a.** Select 4 large commercial banks that are familiar to you.

  **b.** Go to the Bank Rate Monitor's Web site: **www.bankrate.com/brm/ safesound/ss_home.asp** and look up the banks that you listed in part (a). At the bottom of the discussion about the rating for each bank you can click into a page that contains financial information, including the above financial ratios (i)–(iii). Obtain these numbers.

  **c.** Search the Web and find the Moody's or S&P's bond rating for these banks. Compare these ratings with the financial ratio information that you obtained in part (b). Discuss any differences you observe.

2. The short-term market for corporate debt (commercial paper) is very sensitive to risk. Whenever the economy weakens, the issuance of commercial paper falls and the "price" of that risk increases as measured by the spread between the 90-day commercial paper rate and the three-month U.S. Treasury bill rate.

  **a.** Visit the Federal Reserve's Web site at **federalreserve.gov** and, after clicking on "Economic Research and Data," find "Selected Interest Rates." Construct the "risk spread" for the 90-day commercial paper rate minus the three-month T-bill rate and make a plot of the graph of this spread for the past 10 years using the G.13 monthly statistical release.

  **b.** Now locate the volume of "Nonfinancial Commercial Paper Outstanding" on the Fed's Web site. Plot this information for the same time period.

  **c.** Visit the National Bureau of Economic Research (NBER) Web site at **nber. com/cycles/cyclesmain.html** and locate the onset and end dates for any economic recessions that occurred in the U.S. economy over the past 10 years. Mark these dates on your graphs from parts (a) and (b) above.

  **d.** What are your conclusions regarding how the corporate debt (commercial paper) market responds to economic recessions?

## Selected References to Explore

1. Anson, Mark J.P.; Frank J. Fabozzi; Moorad Choudhry; and Ren-Raw Chen. *Credit Derivatives: Instruments, Applications, and Pricing,* New York: Wiley Press, Faboozi Series, January 2004.

2. Cantor, Richard, and Frank Packer. "Municipal Ratings and Credit Standards: Differences of Opinion in the Credit Rating Industry," *Staff Report No. 12,* Federal Reserve Bank of New York, April 1996.

3. Driessen, Joost. " Is Default Event Risk Priced in Corporate Bonds? " *Review of Financial Studies,* November 2004.

4. Fleming, Michael J. "Measuring Treasury Market Liquidity," *Economic Policy Review,* Federal Reserve Bank of New York, September 2003, pp. 83–108.

5. Fons, Jerome S. "Using Default Rates to Model the Term Structure of Credit Risk," *Financial Analysts Journal,* L (1994), pp. 25–32.

6. Helwege, Jean, and Paul Kleiman, "Understanding Aggregate Default Rates of High-Yield Bonds," *Current Issues in Economics and Finance,* Federal Reserve Bank of New York, May 1996, pp. 1–6.

7. Helwege, Jean, and Christopher M. Turner. "The Slope of the Credit Yield Curve for Speculative Grade Issues," *Research Paper No. 9725,* Federal Reserve Bank of New York, August 1997.

8. Krainer, John. "What Determines the Credit Spread?" *FRBSF Economic Letter,* Federal Reserve Bank of San Francisco, December 10, 2004, pp. 1–3.

9. Norton, Edgar, and Glenn N. Pettengill. "Event Risk Covenant Rating Announcements and Stock Returns," *Journal of Financial and Strategic Decisions,* 11, No. 2 (Fall 1998),

10. Viard. Alan D. "The Looming Challenge of the Alternative Minimum Tax," *Economic Letter,* Federal Reserve Bank of Dallas, Vol. I, No. 8 (August 2006), pp. 1–8.

# Chapter 9

# Interest Rate Forecasting and Hedging: Swaps, Financial Futures, and Options

## Learning Objectives

### in This Chapter

- You will discover why financial analysts today usually choose hedging (protecting) against losses from changing interest rates and asset prices rather than attempting to forecast interest rates or the prices of financial assets (such as stocks and bonds).

- You will explore several of the most popular tools currently in use to protect borrowers and lenders from losses due to movements in market interest rates and asset prices, including interest rate swaps, financial futures, and option contracts.

## What's in This Chapter?
## Key Topics Outline

Implied Interest Rate Forecasts and Asset Prices

Hedging against Loss with Swaps: Features and Examples

Financial Futures Contracts: Types, Trading Hedges, and Their Effects

Option Contracts: Types and Possible Payoffs

Accounting for Derivatives: Their Costs and Risks

## 9.1   Introduction

Thus far in Part 2 we have looked at several of the most important factors that cause interest rates and asset prices to change over time. Included in our survey have been such powerful rate- and price-determining factors as savings, investment demand, inflation, default risk, taxes, call features, convertibility, and marketability. Yet even this impressive list of influential factors does not account for all of the changes in interest rates and asset prices we observe daily in the real world. Political developments at home and abroad, changes in government policy, changes in corporate earnings and business conditions, announcements of new security offerings, and thousands of other bits of information flood the money and capital markets daily and bring about fluctuations in interest rates and asset prices. In fact, for actively traded assets, demand and supply forces are continually shifting, minute by minute, so that investors interested in these assets must constantly stay abreast of the latest developments in the financial marketplace. Failure to do so, for example, can place an investor's entire financial portfolio at risk. This chapter focuses on how investors can *hedge* against (reduce) risk associated with the unfavorable fluctuations in interest rates and asset prices that are ever-present threats to the value of their investments.

## 9.2   Implicit Interest Rate Forecasts and Asset Prices

As we described in previous chapters, asset prices normally fall when interest rates are rising, and vice versa. This inverse relationship between asset prices and interest rates is particularly pronounced with fixed-income securities, but is also reflected in the valuation of equities. Therefore, investors must keep a close eye on factors that may cause interest rates to rise or fall in the future because the value of their asset portfolios is at stake.

**business cycle**

Interest rates are notoriously difficult to predict. They do tend to follow the "ups and downs" of the **business cycle,** with market interest rates tending to rise during an economic expansion (when business profits are generally rising) and tending to fall during economic contractions (when business profits are low or even negative). This cyclical pattern of interest rates is more pronounced for short-term than for long-term interest rates, and is a well-established feature of the business cycle that is reflected in current interest rate expectations and, therefore, in asset prices. We have already seen, for example, how interest rate expectations are embedded in the term structure of interest rates (Chapter 7). Extracting the interest rate expectations of the market from the prices of various financial assets provides some of the most accurate predictions of future interest rate movements. These predictions are referred to as **implied market forecasts.**

**implicit market forecasts**

However, many factors affect interest rates and forecasts change continually as new information reaches the market. In fact, research has increasingly pointed toward time patterns in market interest rates that come close to a *random walk* — that is, changes in interest rates may be well described as random and, therefore, unpredictable on a consistent basis. Over the very long run, interest rates do appear to exhibit *long-run mean reversion,* implying that there is some long-run average to which they will eventually return. Nonetheless, the tendency of interest rates to "revert to the mean" in the long run appears to be swamped by short-run changes and not to provide very useful information for guiding short- or medium-term investments or market trading.

**Key URL:**
To understand how
business cycles
are defined in the
United States see the
National Bureau of
Economic Research
at **nber.org/**

**Key URL:**
To examine
fluctuations over
time in the economy
and interest rates
see the extensive
collection of economic
and financial
data series at the
Federal Reserve's
site, **economagic.com/
fedbog.htm**

In this chapter we will examine certain financial assets — financial derivatives—that were created in large measure to capture implicit market forecasts of future interest rates and asset prices. Because these forecasts are among the best available to investors, these financial derivatives have become valuable tools for portfolio managers trying to minimize their exposure to interest-rate risk through the principle of *hedging*. The popularity of these derivatives is demonstrated by their dramatic growth. The International Swaps and Derivatives Association estimated the outstanding value of these (interest rate, equity, and credit) derivatives worldwide in 2006 at more than a staggering 280 trillion dollars! This figure is 50 percent higher than it had been just two years earlier, and the growth of these markets shows no signs of abating.

Before examining these assets, we note here that although several hedging methods have been developed, there is a "price" for employing this form of insurance against losses due to changes in asset values or interest rates. *Hedging tends to lower interest rate and asset-price risk but also tends to reduce the profit potential that could be recovered from correctly forecasting the direction and magnitude of future interest rate and asset-price changes.* In short, hedging tools tend to even out the hills and valleys in an investor's returns from investing in financial assets, but they also tend to limit possible gains as well as possible losses. Therefore, they are useful primarily to investors who are *risk averse* (more concerned with avoiding unexpected losses than with preserving a chance for surprisingly large gains).

In the sections that follow we look at the most popular methods used today for controlling interest rate and asset-price risk: *interest rate swaps, financial futures,* and *option contracts.*

## 9.3 Interest Rate Swaps

### What Are Swaps?

interest rate swap

Early in the 1980s a new interest-rate and value hedging tool—the **interest rate swap**—became popular. In an interest rate swap, two participating business firms independently borrow from two different lenders and then exchange interest payments with each other for a stipulated period of time. In effect, each company helps pay off a portion of the interest cost owed by the other firm. The result is usually *lower* interest expense for both firms and a better *balance* between cash inflows and outflows for both firms. (See, for example, Exhibit 9.1.) Swaps give a borrowing company a powerful tool in managing its liabilities, helping to offset any maturity mismatches that may exist between its assets and liabilities.

Swaps were first used by multinational banks (such as JPMorgan Chase and Deutsche Bank) in the Eurocurrency markets beginning in 1982. These huge banks generally possess excellent credit ratings. This means that, if they wish to, multinational banks can borrow at low, fixed long-term interest rates. However, these international lending institutions may decide to "sell" their ability to borrow long term at low cost in exchange for what they want most: access to low-cost, short-term funds carrying floating interest rates in order to match their short-term, floating-rate assets. The development of interest rate swaps has made maturity matchups like this possible. The first domestic U.S. interest rate swap occurred when the Student Loan Marketing Association, a government-sponsored agency that guarantees college student loans, and ITT Corporation exchanged interest rate payments on some of their debt.

Most swaps today range from $25 million to $100 million in dollar volume (usually called the *notional* amount of the swap because this dollar amount never changes

**Key URL:**
The LIBOR rate that is
the reference interest
rate for most swaps is
set daily by the British
Bankers Association
following a survey
of leading banks.
See **bba.org.uk/**

**EXHIBIT 9.1**

**Using Interest Rate Swaps to Hedge against Fluctuating Interest Rates**

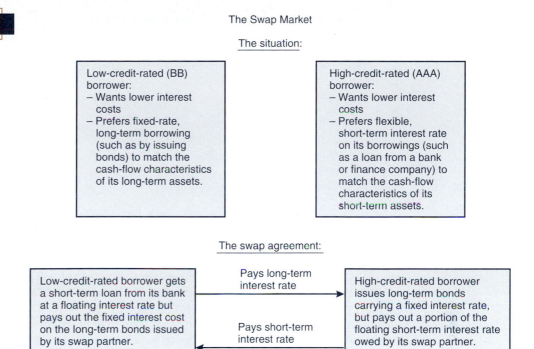

The Swap Market

The situation:

| Low-credit-rated (BB) borrower: <br>– Wants lower interest costs <br>– Prefers fixed-rate, long-term borrowing (such as by issuing bonds) to match the cash-flow characteristics of its long-term assets. | High-credit-rated (AAA) borrower: <br>– Wants lower interest costs <br>– Prefers flexible, short-term interest rate on its borrowings (such as a loan from a bank or finance company) to match the cash-flow characteristics of its short-term assets. |

The swap agreement:

Low-credit-rated borrower gets a short-term loan from its bank at a floating interest rate but pays out the fixed interest cost on the long-term bonds issued by its swap partner.

Pays long-term interest rate →

Pays short-term interest rate ←

High-credit-rated borrower issues long-term bonds carrying a fixed interest rate, but pays out a portion of the floating short-term interest rate owed by its swap partner.

<u>Result</u>: Both companies save on interest costs and better match the maturity structure of their assets and their liabilities. In reality, the two parties to the swap exchange only the *net difference* in their borrowing rates, with the party owing the highest interest rate in the market on the payment date paying the other party the interest-rate difference.

hands). They usually cover periods ranging from about 3 years to 10 years and involve both fixed- and floating-rate loans, with the floating rate often tied to the London Interbank Offer Rate on Eurodollar deposits (LIBOR), the prime rate, or the market yield on Treasury securities.

## How Swaps Work

Swaps work because the interest rate spreads related to default risk (called *quality spreads*) are generally greater in the long-term capital market than they are in the short-term money market. To see how swaps can simultaneously fulfill two goals— lower interest costs and better matching of the maturities of a firm's assets with the maturities of its liabilities—consider the following example. A top-rated corporation with a AAA credit rating can borrow in the long-term bond market at a 10 percent interest rate. However, this company prefers to borrow short-term money at a floating interest rate because it holds mainly short-term assets that roll over into cash just about the time its short-term borrowings come due. Because of the firm's top credit rating, it can borrow short-term funds at prime. Currently, the prime rate is 10 percent, but prime can rise or fall at any time.

A second company is interested in being the first company's swap partner, but this second firm has a credit rating no better than average. This firm has been told by its investment banker that it could issue long-term bonds at an interest rate of 11 percent. Alternatively, this lower-credit-rated firm could borrow short-term funds at prime plus

0.50 percent (making a current short-term loan cost of 10% + 0.50%, or 10.50%). However, the lower-rated firm would prefer to issue long-term bonds because it holds primarily long-term assets.

In summary, these two companies face the following situation:

| The Two Parties to the Swap: | Could Borrow in the Long-Term Bond Market at | Could Borrow in the Short-Term Loan Market at |
|---|---|---|
| Low-credit-rated borrower | 11% | Prime rate + 0.50% |
| High-credit-rated borrower | 10 | Prime rate |
| Quality spread | 1% | 0.50% |

(9.1)

In this case, *both* firms can save on interest costs if each company borrows in that financial market—long term or short term—in which it has the *greatest comparative interest cost advantage.*

A bank or securities dealer might aid these two firms by helping the top-rated firm sell long-term bonds in the open market at 10 percent, while the lower-rated company agrees to make the top-rated firm's bond interest payments. In the meantime, the lower-rated firm takes out a floating-rate bank loan in the same amount at an interest rate of prime plus 0.50 percent. The top-rated company agrees to pay this second firm a rate of prime *less one-quarter of a percentage point* (25 basis points), which would cover most of the lower-rated company's interest cost. If the prime rate remains at its current level of 10 percent, each firm would owe its swap partner the following:

- Low-credit-rated borrower pays the high-rated borrower the fixed 10 percent interest rate it owes on its long-term bonds.
- High-credit-rated borrower pays the low-rated borrower prime minus one-quarter point, that is, 10 percent – 0.25 percent or 9.75 percent to cover the short-term loan rate.
- Low-credit-rated borrower saves 11 – 10, or 1 percent in long-term interest cost less 0.75 (that is, 10.50 – 9.75) percent additional cost on the prime rate loan, for a net savings of 0.25 percent.
- High-credit-rated borrower saves 0.25 percent in interest cost (prime less 0.25 percent).

Today, borrowers often negotiate swap agreements with lenders at the same time they reach an agreement on a loan. For example, if a borrower is granted a floating-rate loan based on the prime rate but fears that interest rates are going up, he or she can convert that floating-rate loan into a *synthetic fixed-rate loan* through a swap agreement. Although the swap and the loan are usually separate contracts, together they have the net effect of giving the borrower a fixed borrowing cost. As the diagram in Exhibit 9.2 shows, when the borrower pays a floating rate to the lender, the borrower also pays a fixed interest rate to the lender under a swap agreement. Simultaneously under the swap agreement, the lender sends the borrower a floating-rate payment. Therefore, the floating-rate payment from the borrower under the loan agreement is offset by the lender's floating-rate payment to the borrower under the swap agreement. What's left over is the borrower's fixed-rate payment to the lender under the swap.

**EXHIBIT 9.2**

**The Synthetic Fixed-Rate Loan**

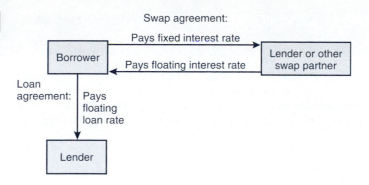

Thus, a floating-rate loan agreement has been transformed by a swap into a fixed-rate loan, even though the borrower remains legally committed to make all the scheduled floating interest rate payments called for by the loan agreement.

Recently the International Swaps and Derivatives Association (ISDA) began to survey daily the fixed interest rates on swaps of varying maturity traded in the global marketplace. Not surprisingly, this new data source reveals that *the longer the term of a swap agreement, the higher the interest rate attached.* Thus, like most other financial instruments, swaps generally display an upward-sloping yield curve. Interest-rate risk increases with longer-term swap contracts and swap partners have had to find ways of dealing effectively with this form of risk exposure.

Interest rate swaps have become much easier to arrange in recent years with the appearance of swap *brokers.* These financial firms—most often investment banks or commercial banks—usually charge a finder's fee of about ¼ of 1 percent of the principal (notional) amount of the swap to bring the two parties together under the swap agreement. Swap brokers charge more than this if they also are asked to administer the swap—that is, calculate the amount of interest owed by each party to the agreement, collect the monies owed, and distribute the required payments. The swap broker or another financial intermediary may also be asked to issue a *guarantee* in case either party to the swap cannot meet its obligation. These guarantees may cost from 1 to 15 basis points of the notional amount of the swap or more, depending on the credit record of each swap partner. In recent years, swap dealers have developed inventories of "unmatched" swaps—requests from customers who are willing to enter into swap agreements but need a counterparty to make the swap complete.

## The Risks of Swapping

Swaps are never without risk. Either party to the agreement may go bankrupt or even steal the funds owed to its counterparty, leaving its swap partner exposed to interest-rate risk. Swaps help to cover interest-rate risk but do not necessarily reduce *credit (default) risk.* A few swaps call for one or both parties to post collateral, but this is usually not done. Unfortunately, without collateral requirements, it is easy for a swap partner to overdo the use of swaps and get itself into trouble. One dramatic example of this occurred during the 1990s, when several municipalities in Great Britain took on far more swaps than their revenues could accommodate. In fact, one local government near London faced a swap interest bill so huge that, had a British court not intervened and negated its swap agreements, it would have had to tax each of its citizens thousands of pounds merely to pay off the interest owed on all of its

As we have seen, the parties to an interest rate swap merely exchange interest payments. A swap partner that pays out a floating (variable) interest rate is said to be in a *short position*, sending a variable interest rate to its swap partner and receiving a fixed interest rate in return. In contrast, the swap partner that pays out a fixed interest rate and receives, in return, a floating interest rate is said to be in a *long position* in the swap market.

Financial intermediaries frequently occupy a *hedged position* between the counterparties to a swap, meaning that the hedged institution pays and receives both floating and fixed interest rates. In this case, the intermediary is often a swap dealer, aiding its customers with their interest rate risk exposure. The dealer can make money on this hedged position in several different ways. A fee is often charged to bring these two counterparties together. Moreover, there may be a difference in the fixed interest rate or floating interest rate payments that the dealer receives and pays out. For example, this swap intermediary may collect an annual fixed interest rate of 8 percent from the counterparty in the long position and pay out only a fixed interest rate of 7.75 percent to the counterparty in the short position. The hedged institution may pocket the 0.25 percent difference in interest rates received and paid out.

*London Interbank Offer Rate on short-term dollar deposits traded by international banks.

swaps! However, because the notional amount of a swap is not at risk, typically a swap is less risky than a bond.

Swaps are themselves subject to *interest-rate risk* due to the fact that shifts in market interest rates can alter the value of existing swap agreements and, therefore, affect a swap's replacement cost. *Rising* market interest rates result in greater risk of default on a swap than do stable interest rates. For example, Procter & Gamble Co. lost close to $160 million during the 1990s on interest rate swaps entered into on the premise interest rates would fall, but they rose instead. A swap can be hedged against interest rate risk by entering into another swap agreement that is the mirror image of the first (a *matched pair*). Some companies use futures contracts or other hedging tools to counter interest rate risk from their swaps rather than proliferating still more swaps.

One notable advantage of swaps is the largely unregulated character of the market. Swaps are private agreements with minimal government interference. There is no regulatory commission to restrict the use of this hedging tool. Some firms do not report the amount of swaps they have outstanding. This means that investors interested in buying their bonds or their stock may not know how much risk exposure these companies carry in the form of swap obligations. However, recently the Financial Accounting Standards Board (FASB) tightened up on its rules applying to swaps and other derivatives, asking corporations to report the fair-market value of derivatives on their balance sheets, thus enhancing the disclosure by companies of their commitments under swaps and other derivative obligations.

**Key URL:**
Information on swaps and other derivative instruments may be found at such sites as **finpipe.com/derivglossary.htm**

## QUESTIONS TO HELP YOU STUDY

1. Why are interest rates and asset prices so difficult to forecast accurately?
2. Suppose you could forecast market interest rates and asset prices correctly on a consistent basis. What obvious advantages would this give you?
3. How do long- and short-term interest rates behave over the course of the economic business cycle? Why do you think they behave this way?
4. What is an *implied forecast?* Give an example.
5. What is *interest rate hedging?* What is its *goal?*
6. What are *interest rate swaps?* Why were these instruments developed?
7. What *risks* are associated with swap contracts? Can any of these risks be reduced?
8. When is a partner to a swap in *long position? A short position?* To what kinds of risk is each exposed?

## 9.4   Financial Futures Contracts

**financial futures contracts**

Among the most innovative markets to be developed in recent years are the markets for **financial futures contracts.** In the financial futures markets, the risk of future changes in market prices or yields attached to various assets is transferred to someone else—an individual or an institution—willing to bear that risk. Financial futures are used in both the short-term money market and the long-term capital market to protect both borrowers and lenders against changing interest rates and shifting asset prices.

**Key URL:**
For a review of the history of futures and options see **cbot.com**

### The Nature of Futures Trading

**hedging**

In the futures market, buyers and sellers enter into contracts for the delivery of assets at a specific location and time and at a price that is set when the contract is made. The principal reason for the existence of the futures market is **hedging**—the act of coordinating the buying and selling of a financial claim or other asset in order to protect it against the risk of future price fluctuations. For example, investors interested in hedging may buy a futures contract in order to lock in a price on a specific asset at a future date, and thus avoid loss in the event of a decline in the asset's price. In contrast, sellers of the futures contract are speculators, hoping to profit from a fall in the asset's price by the contract delivery date, so they could buy the asset in the spot market on that date and receive the higher contract price upon delivery. Note that hedging in futures markets does *not* reduce the overall risk in the market. Rather, it is a low-cost method of *transferring* the risk of unanticipated changes in asset prices or interest rates from one investor or institution (the hedger) to another (the speculator). Ultimately, some investor must bear the risk of fluctuations in the prices and yields of financial assets.

### Examples of Daily Price Quotations for U.S. Treasury Futures

While the complexity and fast pace of trading in the futures market can be daunting for the average investor, the essence of *all* futures markets is a prediction of the price or yield of an asset at a future date. An important example of such a market is the futures market for U.S. Treasury bonds. It is one of the most active markets for the forward delivery of an asset to be found anywhere in the world. Treasury bonds are a popular investment medium for individuals and financial institutions because of their safety and liquidity. Nevertheless, there is substantial market risk involved with longer-term Treasury bonds and notes due to their lengthy maturities and relatively thin market. Because the market for U.S. Treasury bonds is thinner than for Treasury bills (which must mature within a year) and Treasury bond durations are longer, T-bond prices are more volatile, creating greater uncertainty for investors. Not surprisingly, then, U.S. Treasury bonds were among the first financial instruments for which a futures market was developed for hedging risk. Today there are parallel markets for contracts covering foreign government bonds centered on exchanges in London, Tokyo, and elsewhere around the globe.

All U.S. Treasury bonds delivered under a given futures contract must come from the same issue. The basic trading unit is a $100,000 bond (measured at par) with a minimum maturity of 15 years and a coupon rate of 6 percent. Bonds with coupon rates above or below 6 percent are deliverable at a premium or discount from par in the months of March, June, September, and December. Delivery of Treasury bonds is accomplished by book entry, and accrued interest is prorated. Price quotes in the market are often expressed as a percentage of par value. The minimum price change that is recorded on published lists or in dealer quotations is $1/_{32}$ of a point, or $31.25 per $100,000 face-value contract.[1]

Sample data on financial futures prices for U.S. Treasury bond contracts appear in many financial news sheets and on computer screens all over the world. As shown in Exhibit 9.3, the first column indicates the months when each futures contract matures. The next four columns show the opening price for the September and December T-bond contracts when trading began in yesterday's market. The September contract, for example, opened at a price of 122–08 (or $122 and $8/_{32}$ on a $100 par value T-bond, or about $122,250 for a T-bond with a $100,000 face value). The September T-bond's futures price fluctuated during yesterday's trading from a high of $122,500 (or 122 and $16/_{32}$) to a low of $122,000 (or 122 and $0/_{32}$). Trading in the September bond contract closed (settled) at a price of 122 and $12/_{32}$ (or $122,375 for a $100,000 par-value bond) at the end of the day. This settlement price was $4/_{32}$ (or $125) higher than the previous trading day. The final data column, labeled "Volume of Open Interest," reveals the number of outstanding September futures contracts—in this case, more than 950,000—of T-bonds scheduled for delivery when the contract matures. At the bottom of the table information is often provided to interested investors on the volume of trading (number of contracts) for the most recent day and the preceding day.

## Why Hedging with Futures Can Be Effective

Because futures contracts of the type illustrated above essentially involve the transference of risk, the obvious question is: How much risk is being transferred? Obviously, the more risk the hedger transfers to the speculator, the more the hedger will have to pay to transfer that risk. What is needed is a measure of that risk.

A key feature of the futures market that allows the hedging process to transfer risk effectively is the fact that prices in the spot (cash) market are generally correlated with

---

[1]See Chapter 6 on asset prices and interest rates for the meaning of 32nds and points and how bonds and other financial asset prices and yields are measured.

| EXHIBIT 9.3 | Examples of Daily Price Quotations on Financial Futures Exchanges | | | | | |
|---|---|---|---|---|---|---|
| **U.S. Treasury Bond Financial Futures Contracts (in Denominations of $100,000; Prices in 32nds of 100 Percent)** | | | | | | |
| Month When Maturity Is Reached | Opening Price | High Trading Price | Low Trading Price | Settlement Price | Change from Previous Trading Day | Volume of Open Interest |
| September | 122–08 | 122–16 | 122–0 | 122–12 | +4 | 950,655 |
| December | 122–04 | 122–10 | 121–31 | 122–04 | 0 | 120,448 |

Estimated most recent trading volume: 320,000.

Previous day's trading volume: 366,580.

prices in the futures (or forward) market. Indeed, the price of a futures contract in today's market represents an estimate of what the spot (cash) market price will be on the contract's delivery date (less any storage, insurance, and financing costs). *Therefore, hedging essentially involves adopting equal and opposite positions in the spot and futures markets for the same assets. The risk that is being transferred must be related to how closely current and future spot prices or yields are related to one another.*

**basis**

The relationship between the price or yield of a financial asset in the cash or spot market and its price or yield in the futures market is captured in the concept of **basis.** Specifically, in terms of prices:

$$\begin{matrix} \text{Basis for a} \\ \text{futures contract} \end{matrix} = \begin{matrix} \text{Spread between the cash (spot) price of a commodity} \\ \text{or financial asset and the futures (forward) price for that} \\ \text{same commodity or asset at the same point in time.} \end{matrix} \quad (9.2)$$

For example, if long-term Treasury bonds are selling in today's cash market for immediate delivery at a price of $98 per bond (assuming a $100 par value) but are selling in the futures market today for forward delivery in three months at $88 per bond, the basis for this T-bond futures contract purchased today is $98 − $88, or $10. We can also define basis in terms of interest rates; it is the difference between the interest rate attached to an asset in the cash market and the interest rate on that same asset in the futures market.

One important principle of futures trading is the *principle of convergence.* As the delivery date specified in a futures contract draws nearer, the gap (basis) between the futures and spot prices for the same asset narrows. At the moment of delivery, the futures price and spot price on the same asset must be identical (except for transactions costs), so that the basis of the futures contract becomes zero. Whether a futures trade ultimately turns out to be profitable depends on what happens to its basis now and when the contract ends. *It is changes in basis that create risk in the trading of futures contracts.*

*Hedging through futures converts price or interest rate risk into basis risk.* One useful measure of basis risk in financial futures is the *volatility ratio:*

$$\begin{matrix} \text{Volatility ratio} \\ \text{for a} \\ \text{futures contract} \\ \text{(basis risk measure)} \end{matrix} = \frac{\begin{matrix} \text{Percentage change in cash (spot)} \\ \text{price of an asset} \end{matrix}}{\begin{matrix} \text{Percentage change in price of the futures} \\ \text{instrument used for hedging the asset} \end{matrix}} \quad (9.3)$$

The more stable the basis associated with a given futures trade–that is, the closer the volatility ratio is to one—the greater the reduction of risk achieved by the futures trader.

Financial futures and option contracts as well as swaps belong to a broad class of financial instruments called *derivatives*. These unique instruments depend for their value on one or more underlying securities or variables, such as stock prices, interest rates, or commodity prices. Recent experience has shown that derivatives pose their own special brand of risk for both buyers and sellers.

For one thing, derivatives involve at least two parties and either party may fail to deliver, exposing the other party to loss (*counterparty risk*). Other forms of risk associated with derivatives include *price risk* (as their market values change), *settlement risk* (when assets are delivered before payment is received), *operating risk* (due to faulty internal controls on trading activity), *legal risk* (if customers sue to recover their losses), and *regulatory risk* (when government rules are changed or violated). Derivatives can become so complex that it's easy for a trader to become entangled in multiple contracts and lose track of his or her true position and exposure to loss.

**Key URL:**
To learn more about the nature of financial futures, options, swaps and other derivatives, see such Web sources as **encyclopedia.com**

When cash and futures prices or interest rates move in parallel, the volatility ratio is one, and basis risk is zero. The futures markets "work" to offset risk, because the risk of changes in basis is generally less than the risk of changes in the price or yield from an asset. A hedger trading in futures to combat risk strives to find a futures contract whose price volatility most closely tracks the price behavior of the cash-market instrument that needs to be protected, pushing the volatility ratio as close to one as possible.

## Types of Hedges in Futures

Basically *three* types of hedges are used in the financial futures market today: the *long hedge*, the *short hedge*, and the *cross hedge*. Each type of hedge meets the unique trading needs of a particular group of investors.

**long hedge**

*The Long (or Buying) Hedge*    A **long hedge** involves the *purchase* of futures contracts today before the investor must buy the actual asset (such as Treasury bonds) desired at a later date. The purpose of the long hedge is to guarantee (lock in) a desired yield in case interest rates decline before assets are actually purchased in the cash market.

As an example of a typical long hedge transaction, suppose that an institutional investor anticipates receiving $1 million 90 days from today. Assume today is April 1 and funds are expected on July 2. The current yield to maturity on assets the investor hopes to purchase in July is 12.26 percent. We might imagine these assets are long-term U.S. Treasury bonds, which appeal to this investor because of their high liquidity and zero default risk. Suppose, however, that interest rates are expected to decline over the next three months. If the investor waits until the $1 million in cash is actually available 90 days from now, the yield on Treasury bonds may well be lower than 12.26 percent. Is there a way to lock in the higher yield available now even though funds will not be available for another three months?

Yes, if a suitable long hedge can be negotiated with another trader. In this case, the investor can *purchase* ("go long") 10 September Treasury bond futures contracts at their current market price. The number of bond futures contracts required may be figured as follows:

$$\frac{\text{Value of securities to be hedged}}{\substack{\text{Denomination of the} \\ \text{appropriate futures contract}}} = \frac{\$1 \text{ million}}{\$100,000} = 10 \text{ contracts} \qquad (9.4)$$

Cash payment on these contracts will not be due until September.

In many practical situations, the asset to be hedged and the time for risk protection will not exactly match available exchange-traded futures contracts. These differences introduce uncertainty into the process of determining exactly *how many* futures contracts will be needed. A formula that takes some of these problems into account is the following:

$$
\begin{array}{c}
\text{Number of} \\
\text{futures} \\
\text{contracts} \\
\text{needed}
\end{array}
=
\begin{array}{c}
\text{Value of} \\
\text{securities or} \\
\text{loans to be} \\
\text{hedged} \\
\overline{\text{Denomination}} \\
\text{of futures} \\
\text{contracts}
\end{array}
\times
\begin{array}{c}
\text{Volatility ratio} \\
\text{of price} \\
\text{movements in} \\
\text{the cash (spot) asset} \\
\text{relative to the} \\
\text{price of} \\
\text{the futures} \\
\text{contract}
\end{array}
\times
\begin{array}{c}
\text{Days exposed to} \\
\text{risk in the cash} \\
\text{(spot) market} \\
\overline{\text{Term of futures}} \\
\text{contracts}
\end{array}
\qquad (9.5)
$$

where the volatility ratio is the percentage change in market price of the cash (spot) asset relative to the percentage change in price of the desired futures contract over the most recent period. For example, if we wish to hedge $1 million in corporate bonds for 60 days with $100,000-denominated Treasury bond futures contracts covering 90 days and recent price movements of corporate bonds and T-bond futures have displayed a volatility ratio of 0.75, then

$$
\text{Number of futures contracts needed} = \frac{\$1 \text{ million}}{\$100,000} \times 0.75 \times \frac{60}{90} \approx 5 \text{ contracts}
$$
$$(9.6)$$

Suppose the price of T-bond futures contracts currently is 68–10, which is 68 and $^{10}/_{32}$, or $68,312.50 on a $100,000 face-value contract. Assume too that, as expected, bond prices rise and interest rates fall. At some later point, the investor may be able to sell these futures contracts at a profit, because their prices tend to rise along with rising bond prices in the cash market. Selling bond futures at a profit will help this investor offset the lower yields on Treasury bonds that will prevail in the cash market once the $1 million actually becomes available for investing on July 2.

The details of this long hedge transaction are given in Exhibit 9.4. We note that on July 2, the investor goes into the spot market and buys $1 million in 8¼ percent, 20-year U.S. Treasury bonds at a price of 82–13. At the same time, the investor sells 10 September Treasury bond futures at 80–07. Due to higher bond prices (lower yields) in July, the investor loses $139,687.50, because the market price of Treasury bonds has risen from 68–14 to 82–13. This represents an opportunity loss because the $1 million in investable funds was not available in April when interest rates were high and bond prices low. However, this loss is at least partially offset by a gain in the futures market of $119,062.50, because the 10 September bond futures purchased on April 1 were sold at a profit on July 2. Over this period, bond futures rose in price from 68–10 to 80–07. In effect, this investor will pay only $705,000 for the Treasury bonds purchased in the cash market on July 2. The market price of these bonds will be $824,062.50 (or 82 and $^{13}/_{32}$) per bond, but the investor's net cost is lower by $119,062.50 due to a gain in the futures market.

**The Short (or Selling) Hedge** A financial device designed to deal with rising interest rates is the **short hedge.** This hedge involves the immediate *sale* of financial futures until the actual assets must be sold in the cash market at some later point. Short

**short hedge**

| EXHIBIT 9.4 | An Example of a Long Futures Hedge Using U.S. Treasury Bonds | |
|---|---|---|
| **Spot (or Cash) Market Transactions** | | **Futures (or Forward) Market Transactions** |
| **April 1:** | | **April 1:** |
| A portfolio manager for a financial institution wished to "lock in" a yield of 12.26 percent on $1 million of 20-year, 8¼ percent U.S. Treasury bonds at 68–14. | | The portfolio manager purchases 10 September Treasury bond futures contracts at 68–10. |
| **July 2:** | | **July 2:** |
| The portfolio manager purchases $1 million of 20-year, 8¼ percent U.S. Treasury bonds at 82–13 for a yield of 10.14 percent. | | The portfolio manager sells 10 September Treasury bond futures contracts at 80–07. |
| **Results:** | | **Results:** |
| Opportunity loss of $139,687.50 due to lower Treasury bond yields and higher bond prices. | | Gain of $119,062.50 on futures trading (less brokerage commissions, interest cost on funds tied up in required cash margin, and taxes). |

Source: Based on an example developed by the Chicago Board of Trade in an *Introduction to Financial Futures.* Reprinted by permission of the Chicago Board of Trade.

hedges are especially useful to investors who may hold a large portfolio of assets they plan to sell in the future but, in the meantime, must be protected against the risk of declining prices. We examine a typical situation in which a securities dealer might employ the short hedge.

Suppose the dealer holds $1 million in U.S. Treasury bonds carrying an 8¾ percent coupon and a maturity of 20 years. The current price of these bonds is 94–26 (or 94 and $^{26}/_{32}$ which is $948.125 per $1,000 par value), which amounts to a yield of 9.25 percent. However, the dealer is concerned that interest rates may rise. Any increase in interest rates would bring about lower bond prices and therefore reduce the value of the dealer's portfolio. A possible remedy in this case is to *sell* bond futures to counteract the anticipated decline in bond prices. For example, suppose the dealer decides to sell 10 Treasury bond futures at 86–28 and 30 days later is able to sell $1 million of 20-year, 8¾ percent Treasury bonds at a price of 86 and $^{16}/_{32}$ for a yield of 10.29 percent. At the same time, the dealer goes into the futures market and *buys* 10 Treasury bond contracts at 79–26 to offset the previous forward sale of bond futures.

The financial consequences of these combined trades in spot and futures markets are offsetting, as shown in Exhibit 9.5. The dealer has lost $83,125 in the cash market due to the price decline in bonds. However, a gain of $70,625 (less brokerage commissions, interest on cash margins held, and any tax liability) has resulted from the fall in the futures price. This dealer has helped insulate the value of his asset portfolio from the risk of price fluctuations through a short hedge.

**cross hedge**

*Cross Hedging*    Another approach to minimizing risk is the **cross hedge**—a combined transaction between the spot market and the futures market using *different types of assets in each market.* This device rests on the assumption that the prices of most financial instruments tend to move in the same direction and by roughly the same proportion. Because this is only approximately true in the real world, profits or losses in the cash market will not exactly offset losses or profits in the futures market because

| EXHIBIT 9.5 | An Example of a Short Futures Hedge Using U.S. Treasury Bonds | |
|---|---|---|
| **Spot (or Cash) Market Transactions** | **Futures (or Forward) Market Transactions** | |
| **October 1:** | **October 1:** | |
| A securities dealer owns $1 million of 20-year, 8¾ percent U.S. Treasury bonds priced at 94–26 to yield 9.25%. | The dealer sells 10 Treasury bond futures contracts at 86–28. | |
| **October 31:** | **October 31:** | |
| The dealer sells $1 million of 20-year, 8¾ percent U.S. Treasury bonds at 86–16 to yield 10.29%. | The dealer purchases 10 Treasury bond futures contracts at 79–26. | |
| **Results:** | **Results:** | |
| Loss of $83,125 in spot (cash) market. | Gain of $70,625 on futures trading (less brokerage commissions, interest cost on cash margin maintained, and tax obligation). | |

Source: Based on an example developed by the Chicago Board of Trade in an *Introduction to Financial Futures.* Reprinted by permission of the Chicago Board of Trade.

*basis risk is greater with a cross hedge.* Nevertheless, if the investor's goal is to minimize risk, cross hedging is usually preferable to a completely unhedged position.

As an example, consider the case of a bank that holds corporate bonds carrying a face value of $5 million and an average maturity of 20 years. The bank's portfolio manager anticipates a rise in interest rates, which will reduce the value of the bonds. Unfortunately, there is only a limited futures market for corporate bonds, and the portfolio manager fears she cannot construct an effective hedge for these assets. However, futures contracts exist for U.S. Treasury bonds, providing a *short cross hedge* against the risk of a decline in the value of the corporate bonds.

## Executing a Trade, the Cash Margin, and the Settlement of the Contract

Most trading in financial futures contracts takes place through a broker or dealer who may find another party interested in participating in the trade or, more commonly, will contact a trader affiliated with an organized futures exchange. The floor trader will attempt to place the customer's order, either *electronically* or via *open outcry* on the floor of the exchange, seeking a counterparty interested in the terms being offered. If a trade is successful the customer will be asked to post a *cash margin* (equal to a specified percentage of the value of the contracts traded) with his or her broker.

What is the purpose of the *cash margin* each investor must post? It protects customers, brokers, and traders against market risk. At the end of each trading day, the exchange clearinghouse is required to *mark to market* (value) each contract outstanding based on its closing price that day. The cash margin covers the loss when a futures contract falls in price. If the price decline is more than a specified percentage of the margin, the investor may get a *margin call* to post additional cash or securities for protection.

When the delivery date arrives, the security's seller can do one of three things: (1) make delivery of the asset if he or she holds it; (2) buy the asset in the spot (cash) market and deliver it as called for in the futures contract; or (3) purchase a futures contract for the same asset with a delivery date exactly matching the first contract. This last

**Key URLs:**
Information on the trading and pricing of financial futures contracts appears in many places on the Web, including the National Futures Association at **nfa.futures.org** and the Commodity Futures Trading Commission at **CFTC.com**

option would result in a buy-and-sell order maturing on the same day, canceling each other out (zeroing out) and eliminating the necessity for making delivery. In reality, settlement of contracts generally occurs in the futures market by using offsetting buy-and-sell orders rather than making actual delivery.

## Payoff Diagrams for Long and Short Futures Contracts

We can represent losses or gains from trading in futures and from taking long or short hedging positions by using payoff diagrams of the type shown in Exhibit 9.6. In these diagrams, the different possible prices of futures ($F_t$) are shown along the horizontal axis. The vertical axis records any profits or losses (not including taxes and transactions costs) that result when futures prices move up or down.

A 45° line is drawn through the original purchase price ($F_B$) of the contract marked on both horizontal and vertical axes. Because the line through $F_B$ has an angle of 45°, this means that, along this line, a change of $1 in the futures price, up or down, also results in a $1 profit or loss to the holder of the contract. Note, too, that there is no profit or loss when the futures contract price equals its original, or base, purchase price, $F_B$.

As the left-hand diagram in Exhibit 9.6 illustrates, the buyer of a long hedge in futures scores a profit if the price of the underlying asset and the value of the associated futures contract rise. This happens if interest rates fall, causing subsequent futures prices to climb above their base price ($F_t > F_B$). On the other hand, suppose that futures prices fall below the original purchase price, so that $F_t < F_B$ because interest rates have risen. Then the holder of a long hedge will suffer a loss.

The right-hand diagram in Exhibit 9.6 shows that the holder of a short futures position suffers losses when interest rates decline. In this case, the prices of the futures contract and of the assets named in that contract increase, forcing the holder of a short hedge to buy assets or futures at a higher price ($F_t > F_B$) to make delivery or to cancel out the short position. On the other hand, if interest rates rise, then the prices of futures (and the associated assets) eventually may drop below their original purchase price ($F_t < F_B$), handing the short hedger a profit.

## Futures Contracts Offered on Exchanges Today

The number of different futures markets and the variety of futures contracts regularly traded have been expanding in recent years. Beginning in 1975 only one type

**EXHIBIT 9.6**          **Payoffs for Long and Short Futures Positions**

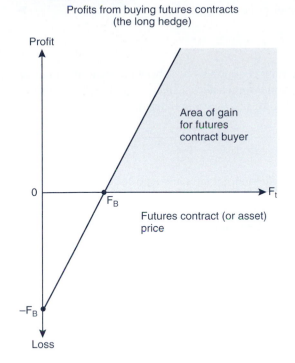

Profits from buying futures contracts
(the long hedge)

Profit

Area of gain
for futures
contract buyer

0                 $F_B$                                    $F_t$

Futures contract (or asset)
price

$-F_B$

Loss

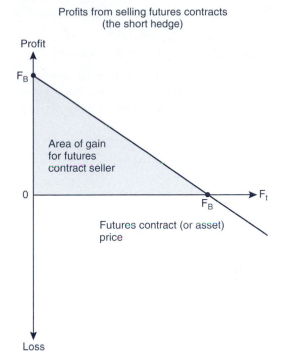

Profits from selling futures contracts
(the short hedge)

Profit

$F_B$

Area of gain
for futures
contract seller

0                        $F_B$              $F_t$

Futures contract (or asset)
price

Loss

of exchange-traded financial futures contract (attached to a GNMA mortgage-backed security) was traded in the United States. However, more than three decades later a wide variety of futures contracts were being traded on exchanges all over the world, including:

- Domestic and foreign government bonds and notes.
- Eurodollar and other Eurocurrency bank deposits.
- Federal funds loans, Treasury bills, and LIBOR-priced deposits.
- Common stock indexes (such as contracts tied to the Standard & Poor's 500 Stock Index, the Dow Jones Industrial Average, the Russell 2000 Index, and the New York Stock Exchange Composite Stock Index).
- Foreign currencies (such as the euro, the Mexican peso, the Swiss franc, the Japanese yen, the British pound, and the Canadian dollar).
- Interest rate swaps (with contracts covering 2-, 5-, and 10-year swaps).

In 2002 exchange-traded economic futures contracts began trading. These contracts essentially allow hedgers to cover exposure they may have in the form of assets whose value is particularly sensitive to certain economic news, such as the monthly U.S. employment report (i.e., nonfarm payroll numbers). The early success of these contracts has caused them to proliferate. Today, news items for which these contracts exist include:

- U.S. nonfarm payrolls.
- U.S. retail sales.

**Key URL:**
For further discussion of both old and new futures and option contracts available on today's international marketplaces see especially **info@cme .com**

- U.S. surveys of business confidence.
- U.S. initial unemployment claims.
- Euro-area "harmonized" consumer price index (CPI).
- U.S. GDP.
- U.S. trade balance.

Early research on the pricing of these futures contracts has shown them to be superior forecasting tools to surveys of professional forecasters. This research adds support to the usefulness of these newer futures markets as hedging instruments.

---

### QUESTIONS TO HELP YOU STUDY

9.  Define and explain the use of the following: (a) long hedge; (b) short hedge; and (c) cross hedge.

10. Which type of hedge named above works best in an environment of rising interest rates? Of falling interest rates? Illustrate both cases using a payoff diagram.

11. What is the basic purpose of futures trading in securities? Where is most futures trading carried out?

12. How do the spot (cash) markets differ from futures (forward) markets?

13. What is *basis*? Explain how the basis for a futures contract relates to trading risk.

14. For what specific kinds of securities is there now an active futures market? Who issues these securities?

15. What are economic futures contracts? Please give an example.

16. How can investors hedge possible changes in U.S. monetary policy?

---

## 9.5    Option Contracts

**option contract**

Another popular financial instrument used to manage risk is the **option contract.** An option contract is an agreement between a buyer and seller to grant the holder of the contract the right, but not the obligation, to buy or sell a futures contract or asset at a specified price on or before the day the contract expires. Options on farm commodities and on selected common stock have been traded for decades. There was an explosion of new options products in the 1980s, led by options on $100,000 Treasury bond futures introduced in October 1982. Then, in 1985, the International Monetary Market (IMM), a division of the Chicago Mercantile Exchange (CME), began trading option contracts on financial futures for Eurodollar deposits. As more investors began to take an interest in options trading, major exchanges around the world began developing many new option contracts on stock, foreign currencies, and financial futures contracts.

### *Basic Types of Option Contracts and Price Quotations*

**call options**

**strike price**

There are two basic types of option contracts. **Call options** give the contract buyer the right, but not the obligation, to buy ("call away") futures contracts or assets at a set price known as the **strike price.** The seller of the contract is called the *option writer.*

Under the terms of American options, the buyer may exercise the option and purchase the futures or assets specified from the writer at any time on or before the expiration date of the option. European options, on the other hand, can be exercised only on their expiration date. An option not used by its expiration date becomes worthless.

**put options**

**Put options** grant the contract purchaser the right, but not the obligation, to sell ("put," or deliver) futures contracts or securities to the option writer at a set (strike) price on or before the option's expiration date. Buyers of both call and put options

**option premium**

must pay an **option premium** for the privilege of being able to buy or sell futures or securities at a guaranteed price. By fixing the price of a financial transaction for a stipulated period, options provide an alternative way of hedging against market risk. Their principal advantage over futures contracts is that hedging with futures limits the hedger's profits. Options, in contrast, can be used to limit losses while preserving the opportunity to make unlimited profits.

**Key URL:**
Recently more options and other securities have been traded electronically for greater speed and efficiency. A prominent example was the International Securities Exchange at **iseoptions.com**, which began trading options beginning in 2000.

Most options on financial instruments are traded today on organized exchanges such as the Chicago Mercantile Exchange (CME) or the Chicago Board Options Exchange (CBOE). Exchange-traded options are standardized contracts with uniform terms that enhance the marketability of options. The exchange sets rules for trading and pricing. The exchange clearinghouse keeps a record of all trades and guarantees performance on all exchange-traded options. In effect, the clearinghouse becomes the ultimate seller to all option buyers and the ultimate buyer from all option sellers.

Many option contracts are liquidated before they expire by each trader making an offsetting purchase or sale. For example, the buyer of a call option can "erase" his or her contract by selling a call option involving the same security with the same expiration date and strike price. Put options are liquidated in the same fashion with the buyer (seller) of the put selling (buying) a comparable put on or before the expiration date.

## Examples of Price Quotes on Options Contracts

One of the best-known exchange-traded options is the Treasury bond option contract, traded on the Chicago Board of Trade's Options Exchange in units of $100,000. The T-bond option contract's current price is quoted in points ($1 on a base of $100) and 64ths of a point. An example of the data most investors usually see on exchange traded options on their computers and in financial newspapers is shown in Exhibit 9.7.

Note, for example, that the option to *call* $100,000 U.S. Treasury bond futures contracts between now and their maturity date in September that carry a strike price of

| EXHIBIT 9.7 | Examples of Daily Price Quotations on Option Contracts | | | |
|---|---|---|---|---|
| **U.S. Treasury Bond Futures Options**<br>**(in denominations of $100,000; prices in 64ths of 100 percent)** | | | | |
| Strike<br>(Exercise)<br>Price | Call Options<br>Settlement Prices<br>September | December | Put Options<br>Settlement Prices<br>September | December |
| 120 | 1–60 | 2–01 | 0–16 | 0–42 |
| 121 | 1–32 | 1–58 | 0–32 | 0–60 |
| 122 | 1–16 | 1–48 | 0–48 | 1–12 |

Estimated volume of trading: 120,000 contracts.

Open interest volume in call options: 485,776.

Open interest volume in put options: 250,715.

120 (that is, $120,000 for a $100,000 futures contract) was trading at a market price of 1–60 (that is, 1 and $^{60}/_{64}$ for a $100 par value option, or $1,937.50 on a $100,000 face value call option contract). The prices of put options on T-bonds expiring in September and December appear in a companion table to the right of the table of call options. Trading volume and the volume of uncanceled (open interest) options appear as a final item on many option price tables in the financial press.

As Exhibit 9.7 makes clear, the higher an option's strike price, the lower the call option's price (premium) tends to be, because there is less likelihood the call will be exercised. Moreover, call options expiring at a later date sell for higher premiums than those expiring sooner because there is more time in the case of the former options for security prices to change in a way that favors their exercise by the option buyer.

## Uses of Options

Options have many uses. Their two most common ones involve (1) protecting a future investment's yield against falling interest rates by using call options and (2) protecting against rising interest rates by using put options.

**Key URL:**
To learn more about options pricing and trading consider such sources as In the Money at **in-the-money.com**

### *Protecting against Declining Investment Yields*   A major concern of

most asset buyers is how to protect against falling yields and rising prices on assets that will be purchased in the future. Options offer a way to prepare for a future investment, even if the investor doesn't yet have sufficient cash to make the investment, by carrying out a temporary transaction that helps guarantee future yields. An option contract enables an investor to set a maximum price for assets targeted for future purchase.

For example, suppose a security dealer plans to buy $100 million in U.S. Treasury bonds in a few days and hopes to earn an interest yield of at least 7 percent. However, fearful of a substantial drop in interest rates before the dealer is ready to buy, he executes a call option on T-bond futures at a strike price of 120. If T-bond futures rise in value above 120 (i.e., fall below 7 percent in yield), the dealer probably will exercise the option because it is now "in the money." When the market price of a futures contract or, other asset rises above the strike price in the associated option contract, the buyer of the call option is said to be "in the money," because he or she can buy the futures contract or asset from the option writer at the strike price (in this case, at 120) and sell at a higher price (perhaps at 121) in futures or cash markets. The resulting profit (after paying the option's premium, taxes, and transactions costs) offsets the loss in yield on the planned investment due to a decline in market interest rates.

If interest rates go against the dealer's forecast, however, and rise instead, the call option will be "out of the money." Its strike price will be above the market's current price for the assets or futures covered by the option. In this case, the call will *not* be exercised, and the dealer will lose the premium he or she paid for the option. However, the fact that interest rates rose (and, therefore, Treasury bond prices fell) means the dealer can now purchase Treasury bonds at a cheaper price and a more desirable yield.

The profit on an exercised *call option* can be found from:

$$\text{Profit} = F - S - Pr - T \qquad \textbf{(9.7)}$$

where $F$ is the current futures or asset price, $S$ the strike price agreed upon in the option contract, $Pr$ the premium paid by the call option buyer, and $T$ any taxes owed as a result of the transaction. If the futures or other asset price, $F$, rises high enough, the buyer can call away futures contracts or other assets from the option writer at price

*S* and still have some profit left over after paying the premium (*Pr*) and any taxes incurred (*T*). However, if the futures price, *F*, declines, the option will go unexercised and the buyer's loss will equal −*Pr*. The seller of the unexercised call will then reap a profit of +*Pr*.

**Protecting against Rising Interest Rates**   In contrast to lenders, who often worry about falling yields, borrowers' concerns usually are to keep borrowing costs from rising. Consider a bank, for example, that must borrow millions of dollars daily and fears rising money market interest rates. Perhaps market rates on deposits are currently at 8 percent and the bank fears a substantial rise in deposit interest costs to 9 percent. Accordingly, the bank's deposit manager purchases a put option on Eurodollar futures at a strike price of 92. If these futures fall below 92 in price due to rising interest rates, the bank's liability manager may decide to exercise the put option and sell Eurodollar futures to the option writer at the strike price. The manager will then liquidate the bank's futures position by buying equivalent futures contracts at the now lower market price and profit from the spread between the strike price of 92 and the current lower market price. This profit will at least partially offset the bank's higher borrowing costs.

On the other hand, if interest rates do not rise, the bank's deposit manager will not exercise the put option. This will mean losing the full amount of the option premium, but the bank's borrowing costs will stay low. In this instance, it paid a premium for interest rate insurance that turned out not to be needed.

The profit to the buyer of a *put option* can be calculated from:

$$\text{Profit} = S - F - Pr - T \qquad \qquad (9.8)$$

where *S* is the strike price, *F* the market price of the futures or assets named in the option, *Pr* the premium paid for the option, and *T* taxes owed. If the futures or asset price, *F*, falls far enough below the strike price *S*, the put buyer will show a profit. On the other hand, if the futures or asset price rises, the put will go unexercised, and the buyer's loss will be measured by −*Pr*. The seller of the unexercised put will then experience a corresponding profit of +*Pr*.

## Payoff Diagrams for Valuing Options

We can diagram how options are valued by looking first at the value of a put option to the investor who holds it (the option buyer) on the date or dates the option can be exercised. Exhibit 9.8 illustrates the relationship between a put option's value and the value of the underlying futures contract or asset named in the option. Point *S* marked on the horizontal axis in Exhibit 9.8 represents the strike price, the price at which the futures contract or asset can be sold by the option's holder.

Suppose the option contract is on an asset currently selling for price $F_1$, which is more than its strike price, *S* (i.e., $F_1 > S$). In this case, the option has a current value of zero (actually less than zero because the option buyer had to pay premium *Pr*, which is lost if the option goes unexercised). The holder of the option would prefer to sell the asset she holds at current market price $F_1$ rather than deliver it to the option writer for a price of only *S*. If current price $F_1$ is significantly larger than *S*, however, the option buyer may still reap a substantial gain despite losing the option premium.

In contrast, suppose that the asset has a current price of $F_2$, where $F_2 < S$. In this instance, with a market price lower than the strike price, exercise of the option results in a profit for its buyer. The option buyer will deliver the asset to the option writer and

**EXHIBIT 9.8**

**Payoffs to the Option Buyer from Put Options**

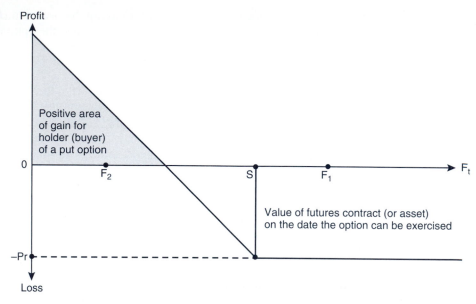

Profit

Positive area of gain for holder (buyer) of a put option

0

$F_2$      S      $F_1$      $F_t$

Value of futures contract (or asset) on the date the option can be exercised

−Pr

Loss

receive strike price $S$ for a net profit per contract of $S - F_2 - Pr - T$. Clearly for the holder of a put option, when $S > F_t$, the option will normally be exercised for a profit and be "in the money" as long as $S - F_t$ exceeds the option premium, taxes, and transactions costs. When $S < F_t$, the option will expire unexercised; the profit will be zero or negative and clearly will be "out of the money." Only within the triangle in the upper left-hand corner of Exhibit 9.8 will the holder of a put option reap positive gains.

From the standpoint of the writer (seller) of a *put option*, the writer benefits if the option is *not* exercised. This happens if the market value of the asset remains higher than the option's strike price, as at $F_1 > S$. Exhibit 9.9 shows the area of gain for the writer of a put option lies around and to the right of strike price $S$. In this region, the option currently is "out of the money" from the buyer's standpoint, and the writer pockets the premium paid by the option holder.

In the case of *call options,* the writer agrees to sell securities to the buyer of the option at a stipulated strike price. If, as shown in Exhibit 9.10, the market price of the

**EXHIBIT 9.9**

**Payoffs for Put Options to the Option Writer**

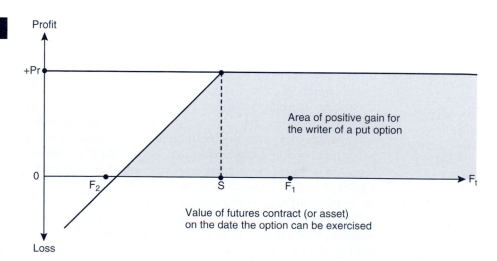

Profit

+Pr

Area of positive gain for the writer of a put option

0

$F_2$      S      $F_1$      $F_t$

Value of futures contract (or asset) on the date the option can be exercised

Loss

**EXHIBIT 9.10**

**Payoffs to the Option Buyer from Call Options**

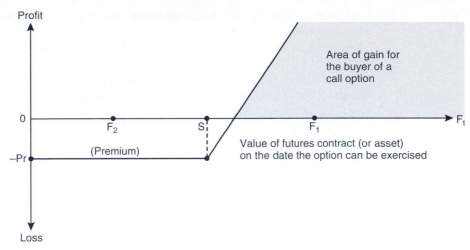

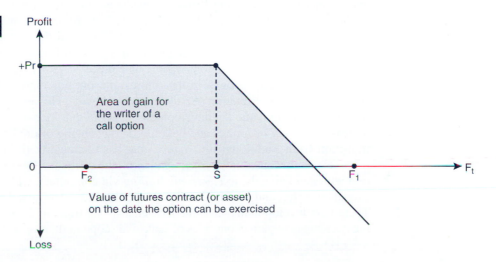

underlying asset rises above the strike price to $F_1$, the holder of the call option will exercise that option and call away the asset from the option writer at strike price $S$. Exercise of this now "in the money" call option will enable the option buyer to resell each of the newly acquired assets for a profit of $F_1 - S - Pr - T$. If, on the other hand, the market value of the assets falls *below* the option's strike price, as at $F_2$, the option holder would be better off purchasing the assets in the open market rather than exercising his or her option to buy at price $S$. The call will expire unused ("out of the money"), and the option buyer will suffer a loss due to the premium ($Pr$) he or she has paid. Thus, the area of positive gain to the holder of a call option generally lies to the right of the strike price in Exhibit 9.10 and in the upper right-hand portion of that diagram.

The writer of a call option, on the other hand, gains when the market value of the asset falls below the strike price, as at $F_2 < S$ in Exhibit 9.11. At this price and at all prices below $S$, the call option is "out of the money" for the option buyer and will go unexercised, allowing the option writer to earn the option premium, $Pr$. However, if the futures' or asset's market value climbs above $S$, as at price $F_1$ in Exhibit 9.11, the

**EXHIBIT 9.11**

**Payoffs to the Option Writer from Call Options**

writer must sell off from his portfolio of currently higher-valued assets to the option buyer at the low contract price $S$, taking a loss equal to $F_1 - S$. The call option clearly has become "in the money" for the option buyer. As shown in Exhibit 9.11, the region of positive gain for the writer of a call option lies in the upper left-hand portion of the price diagram (including price $F_2$). In contrast, futures or asset prices increasingly to the right of point $S$ result in decreasing profits or increasing losses for the option writer.

### Options Offered on Exchanges Today

Just like financial futures contracts, there are numerous options calling for the delivery of equities, debt instruments, or financial futures. Exchange-traded put and call options have grown especially rapidly in recent years and are focused on instruments such as 30-day federal funds futures, Eurodollar and Eurodeposit futures, euro-denominated deposit futures, U.S. Treasury bills, notes, and bonds, and selected currency futures (including contracts for the delivery of Japanese yen, the British pound, the Swiss franc, and the euro). There are also exchange-traded options on futures covering selected stock market indexes, such as the Dow Jones Industrial Average and the S&P Stock Index, the S&P and NASDAQ 100 stock indexes, and the New York Stock Exchange Composite Index.

Innovation is frequent in the options market; the exchanges are receptive to new instruments on a frequent basis. Recent examples include options on ETFs (which hold selected stock portfolios), LEAPs (which cover up to three years and are linked to any of about 450 stocks and 10 different stock indexes), and FLEX options (which permit professional investors to shape selected option contracts to match more closely their unique risk-management needs).

### 9.6 Exchanges Where Futures and Options Contracts Are Traded

Each exchange where futures and options are traded controls which contracts may be offered for sale, delivery dates and delivery methods, and the posting of prices. Furthermore, each exchange stands behind the transactions conducted through its facilities, paying off when the party to a contract fails to do so. Qualifications of traders and standards for admitting firms into exchange membership are monitored by each exchange's governing board. Overseeing the U.S. futures exchange industry are the Commodity Futures Trading Commission (CFTC) and the Securities and Exchange Commission (SEC). Similar regulatory bodies exist in European and Asian countries where active futures and options trading take place.

The extraordinary growth in the futures and options markets was for a time accompanied by a proliferation of exchanges worldwide. However, in recent years there have been two fundamental developments shaping that industry. The first is the ever-increasing variety of futures and options contracts being offered, and the second is the transition from traditional *pit trading,* that has characterized the older, more established exchanges, in which brokers gather on the exchange floor and convey information with hand signals, to *electronic trading* via computers, which many new smaller exchanges offer, and which promises greater accuracy and speed in facilitating trades. These two developments have encouraged a strong trend in the industry toward merging exchanges to gain economies of scale and scope in their operations that will permit an expansion in the menu of services and products offered, while reducing operating costs and accommodating the rapid rise in trading volume.

Most recently, merger activity among exchanges worldwide has heated up. The creation of Euronext out of mergers of equities and derivatives exchanges from the Netherlands, Brussels, and Paris in 2000 was followed in 2002 by the Euronext acquisition of the London International Financial Futures Exchange (LIFFE), one of the largest futures and options exchanges in Europe. EUREX, an electronic trading platform of financial derivatives operated jointly by the German stock exchange Deutsch Borse AG and the SWX Swiss Exchange, has been aggressively pursuing international markets with links to the Irish Stock Exchange and the Frankfort Stock Exchange. More recently EUREX has been making product offerings in a wide range of derivatives that have long been the province of the two U.S. giant stalwarts, the Chicago Board of Trade (CBOT) and the Chicago Mercantile Exchange (CME). In response, the CBOT and the CME announced a merger in 2006, which involves a consolidation of their "pit trading" floors (at the CBOT) and a merger of expanding electronic platforms. In late 2006, the Intercontinental Exchange (ICE), an Atlanta-based exchange specializing in energy-related derivatives products, announced plans for a merger with the New York Board of Trade (NYBOT), where contracts in many agricultural, currency, and index futures and options are traded. The ICE-NYBOT combination further links up international futures and options markets with the ICE's London-based subsidiary ICE Futures, which has offices in Calgary, Singapore, Houston, and Chicago, while the NYBOT operates a trading floor in Dublin. As these unfolding mergers suggest, the growing internationalization of financial markets is rapidly changing the landscape for market participants, and these changes are more pronounced in the most rapidly expanding segment of the financial-services industry: futures and options.

## 9.7  Risks, Costs, and Rules for Trading in Derivatives

### Risks and Costs Associated with Futures and Options

Futures and options trading is not without its own special risks and costs. The risk of price and yield fluctuations can be reduced by negotiating these contracts, but the investor faces the risk of changing interest rates and asset prices between futures and spot markets (*basis risk*). It is rare that gains and losses from simultaneous trading in spot, futures, or options markets exactly offset each other, resulting in a perfect hedge. There is the risk of broker cash margin calls due to adverse price movements (*margin risk*), as well as possible problems in liquidating an open position in futures or options (*liquidity risk*). Moreover, there are substantial brokerage fees for executing trades and required minimum deposits in margin accounts that tie up cash in non-interest-bearing assets. The decision to trade financial futures and options contracts is, like everything else in life, a cost versus benefit issue.

### Accounting Rules for Transactions Involving Derivatives

The rapid expansion of trading has led to new accounting rules to promote fuller disclosure of risk exposures and to permit management and outsiders to judge the effectiveness of hedging techniques. Late in the 1990s, the Financial Accounting Standards Board (FASB) issued FASB 133, followed subsequently by FASB 137 and 138.

These new rules stipulate that the derivative positions of publicly traded companies should be reflected in the values of assets and liabilities shown on their balance sheets. Derivatives must be reported at their *fair value,* as determined by an instrument's discounted cash flows (as explained in Chapter 6). Any shift in the fair value of a derivative or in the value of the underlying asset or liability being hedged must be captured on the hedging institution's income statement.

FASB also addressed the accounting consequences of *cash-flow hedges,* which are designed to protect the investor against liabilities associated with such things as interest income expected from loans and interest costs associated with taking on liabilities. The portion of a cash-flow hedge that is *effective* should be reflected in a hedging institution's equity capital. The ineffective part of any cash-flow hedge, on the other hand, must be recorded on the hedger's income statement.

---

### QUESTIONS TO HELP YOU STUDY

17. What risks and costs are inherent in financial futures and options trading?
18. What is FASB 133 and how does it relate to the value and impact of derivatives on publicly traded companies?

---

## Summary of the Chapter's Main Points

This chapter is devoted to forecasting (predicting) and hedging (risk protection activities) associated with changing interest rates and changes in the prices of financial assets. Among its most important conclusions are:

- Interest rates appear to bear a close relationship to the *economy,* and especially to the *business cycle,* tending to rise in periods of economic expansion and fall in recessions.

- Short-term interest rates tend to change more rapidly than long-term interest rates, moving over a much wider range than long-term interest rates as economic conditions change.

- Most interest rate forecasting approaches today are *implicit forecasts* that rely upon linkages between the economy and financial system, and upon tracking changing expectations of borrowers and lenders in the financial marketplace as reflected in such indicators as the prices and yields attached to financial futures contracts.

- The great difficulties inherent in forecasting interest rates have led many borrowers and lenders to practice *hedging,* insulating themselves at least partially from the ravages of fluctuating interest rates and asset prices in the financial marketplace.

- In recent years one of the most popular of all interest rate and asset-price hedging tools has been the *interest rate swap,* in which borrowing institutions exchange interest payments with each other. The net effect of a well-drawn swap agreement is to achieve a better balance between interest revenues and interest costs. Such transactions may also lower interest costs for participants in a swap agreement.

- During the 1970s and 1980s *financial futures* and *options contracts* on a variety of debt securities, stocks, and stock indexes began trading in the United States at the Chicago Board of Trade (CBOT) and the Chicago Mercantile Exchange (CME) and, subsequently, spread around the world on multiple exchanges, such as the London International Financial Futures and Options Exchange (LIFFE) and EUREX, operated jointly by the Deutsche Borse and the SWX Swiss Exchange. In recent years, the industry has been characterized by a proliferation of product offerings, an acceleration of the shift away from *pit trading* and toward *electronic trading,* and a trend toward growing merger activity—such as the CBOT–CME merger in the United States—to capture economies of scale and scope by lowering operating costs while accommodating ever-expanding trading volume.

- Both futures and options are contracts calling for the future delivery of assets or cash at an agreed-upon price in an effort to set the price or yield on a future trade and, thereby, lessen the risk associated with future asset price and interest rate fluctuations.

- Hedging with financial futures and option contracts transfers risk from one investor to another willing to bear that risk. The hedger contracts away all or a portion of the risk of asset-price and interest rate fluctuations in order to lock in a targeted rate of return or asset value. This is accomplished by taking equal and opposite positions in the spot (cash) market and in the forward (or futures) market or by purchasing put or call options to deliver or take delivery of designated assets at a stipulated price on or before a specific date.

- If interest rates are expected to *fall* and an investor desires to lock in a current high yield on an asset, he or she would buy a contract calling for the future delivery of the security (or other financial asset) at a set price (i.e., take on a *long hedge*) or purchase a *call option* contract. An opposite set of buy-sell transactions in the futures market (i.e., a *short hedge*) or in the options market (i.e., a *put option*) would generally be used if interest rates were expected to *rise*.

## Key Terms Appearing in This Chapter

www.mhhe.com.rose10e

## Problems and Issues

1. In an interest rate swap transaction, a large corporation can borrow in the bond market at a current fixed rate of 9 percent and also obtain a floating-rate loan in the short-term market at the prime bank rate. However, this firm wishes to borrow short term because it has a large block of assets that roll over into cash each month. The other party to the swap is a company with a lower credit rating that can borrow in the bond market at a long-term interest rate of 11.5 percent and in the short-term market at prime plus 1.50 percent. This lower-rated company has long-term predictable cash inflows, however. The higher-credit-rated company wishes to pay for its part in the swap an interest rate of prime less 50 basis points. The lower-rated company is willing to pay the underwriting cost associated with the higher-rated company's security issue, estimated to be 25 basis points. The swap transaction is valued at $100 million. What kind of interest rate swap can be arranged here? Which company will borrow short term and which long term? If the prime bank rate is currently 10 percent, who will pay what interest cost to whom? Explain what the benefit is to each party in this swap.

2. Suppose a top-quality firm with an A-1 or AAA credit rating can borrow at a fixed coupon rate attached to its bonds of 12 percent. Moreover, this firm's bank is willing to extend it a LIBOR-based loan at a rate of 9.5 percent that will change weekly as LIBOR moves. Working through its principal banker, this top-rated company makes contact with a firm whose credit rating is considerably lower (rated only BB). The lower-rated firm has been informed by its investment banker that it probably could sell bonds at a 14 percent coupon rate, and the finance company from which it receives short-term money has promised a LIBOR-based floating-rate loan of 11.25 percent. Could these two firms benefit from a swap under the interest rates given above? Which firm would save the most and under what circumstances? Will the company with the lower credit rating have to offer the top-credit-quality firm an added inducement to participate in a rate swap? What inducements could be used to equalize the interest savings for both parties?

3. A large money center bank plans to offer money market CDs in substantial volume (at least $100 million) in six months due to a projected upsurge in credit deals from some of its most valued corporate customers. Unfortunately, the bank's economist has just predicted that money market interest rates should rise over the next year (with perhaps a full 1.5 percentage point increase within the next six months). Explain why the bank's management would be concerned about this development. Suppose management expects its corporate loan customers to resist any loan terms that would automatically result in loan rates being immediately adjusted upward to reflect rate increases in the money market. What futures market transaction would you recommend? What is the best options contract alternative for the bank?

4. An investment banking firm discovers that 90 days from today it is due to receive a cash payment from one of its corporate clients of $972,500. The firm's portfolio manager is instructed to plan to invest this new cash for a horizon of three months, after which it will be liquidated. Interest rates are attractive today

at 10 percent, but a steep decline is forecast due to a developing recession. The portfolio manager decides to try to guarantee a 9 percent rate of return today on this planned three-month investment of cash.

  **a.** Describe what the manager should do today in the financial futures market. Then, indicate how he will close out the futures position eventually.

  **b.** What are the appropriate (buy-sell) steps for the manager if options on financial futures are to be used?

5. During the month just concluded, the prices of U.S. Treasury bonds fluctuated between a price of $95 (based on a $100 par value) and a price of $93. Treasury bond futures over the same period fluctuated between $92 and $88 (based on a $100 par value). How did the *basis* for T-bond futures contracts change over this period? What was the *volatility ratio* for T-bond futures for the month just ended? Now assume you wish to hedge for the next 30 days $25 million in Treasury bonds that you currently hold with $100,000 denomination T-bond futures contracts maturing in 90 days. Using the volatility ratio you calculated above, how many T-bond futures contracts will you need to buy to fully cover the $25 million in securities at risk?

 6. An investor buys a U.S. Treasury Bond on February 5, 2007. Afterward, its price fluctuates with prices given in the following table:

| DATE | Price per $100 Par Value (in 32nds) | DATE | Price per $100 Par Value (in 32nds) |
|---|---|---|---|
| February 5 | 100:00 | February 16 | 100:57 |
| February 6 | 100:03 | February 19 | 100:64 |
| February 7 | 100:05 | February 20 | 100:75 |
| February 8 | 100:04 | February 21 | 101:02 |
| February 9 | 100:07 | February 22 | 102:00 |
| February 12 | 100:08 | February 23 | 99:30 |
| February 13 | 100:11 | February 26 | 99:38 |
| February 14 | 100:15 | February 27 | 99:27 |
| February 15 | 100:55 | February 28 | 99:00 |

  **a.** Input the data from the above table into the first two columns of a spreadsheet.

  **b.** In columns (3) through (5), compute the value of call options with strike prices of 100:08 (column 3), 100:16 (column 4), and 101:00 (column 5). For each option contract with these strike prices determine the initial date on which the call option was "in the money," and the date on which the call option was the most valuable, assuming the premium paid on the option is 1 percent of the par value of the asset (and the investor pays no taxes).

  **c.** In columns 6 through 8, compute the value of put options with strike prices of 99:24 (column 6), 99:16 (column 7), and 99:00 (column 8). For each put option contract with these strike prices determine the initial date on which the put option was "in the money," and the date on which the put option was the most valuable, assuming that the premium paid on the option is 1 percent of the par value of the asset (and the investor pays no taxes).

## Web-Based Problems

1. Interest rate swap contracts carry market interest rates that vary with the maturity of each swap and its degree of risk exposure. There is also a swap yield curve that is constructed each day and is carefully followed by thousands of institutions and individuals. This version of the yield curve reports the interest rates that a fixed-rate swap partner would pay based on representative swap rates and maturities as collected by survey each day. Consulting information sources such as the International Swaps and Derivatives Association at **isda.org/index.html,** the Chicago Board of Trade at **cbot.com,** and the Federal Reserve System at **federalreserve.gov,** see if you can construct a recent swap yield curve. How does it compare with a Treasury yield curve (as found in *The Wall Street Journal* at **wsj.com,** for example) covering the same range of maturities? What might explain any differences you observe?

2. Visit the Web sites of the leading financial futures and options exchanges in recent years, such as the Chicago Board of Trade at ***cbot.com,*** the Chicago Mercantile Exchange at ***cme.com*** and the London Futures and Options Exchange now at the post-merger site **euronext.com/derivatives.** Make a list of the principal financial futures and options contracts (measured by trading volume) traded on these exchanges. Which contracts appear to be the most popular and why? What kinds of risk exposure does each contract deal with? What types of institutions would most benefit from these particular contracts? Were there any new futures or options contracts under development at the time you examined the Web sites?

## Selected References to Explore

1. Black, Fisher, and Myron Scholes. "The Pricing of Options and Corporate Liabilities," *Journal of Political Economy,* 81 (May–June 1973), pp. 637–654.

2. Gunther, Jeffrey W., and Thomas F. Siems. "Debunking Derivatives Delirium," *Southwest Economy,* Federal Reserve Bank of Dallas, March/April 2003, pp. 1, 5–9.

3. Gurkayak, Refet, and Justin Wolfers. "Macroeconomic Derivatives: An Initial Analysis of Market-based Forecasts, Uncertainty, and Risk," *NBER International Seminars on Macroeconomics 2005,* National Bureau of Economic Research, Cambridge, MA: MIT Press.

4. Haubrich, Joseph G. "Swaps and the Swaps Yield Curve," *Economic Commentary,* Federal Reserve Bank of Cleveland, December 2001, pp. 1–4.

www.mhhe.com.rose10e

5. Lopez, Jose A. "Supervising Interest Rate Risk Management," *FRBSF Economic Letter,* Federal Reserve Bank of San Francisco, No. 2004-26, September 17, 2004.

6. Nosal, Ed, and Tan Wang. "Arbitrage: The Key to Pricing Options," *Economic Commentary,* Federal Reserve Bank of Cleveland, January 1, 2004.

7. Sundaresan, Suresh. *Fixed-Income Markets and Their Derivatives,* Cincinnati: Southwestern Publishing, 1997.

# Appendix 9A: The Black-Scholes Model for Valuing Options

With the rapid growth of options around the world, analysts and investors began to take great interest in the question of how options should be valued or priced. However, establishing the true value of an option proved to be a daunting task that went unresolved for many years because options are so unusual. For example, unlike most bonds and stocks, many options turn out to be completely valueless due to adverse movements in the price of the asset to which they apply.

Suppose you hold a *call option* allowing you to purchase General Electric (GE) stock at $40 per share from the option writer but GE's stock remains *below* $40 in the market for the entire term of your option. Then you won't exercise it because you can buy GE stock more cheaply in the open market. On the other hand, if GE stock climbs above $40, say to $45 per share, you *will* exercise the call option and earn $5 for every GE share you acquire. Should the stock's market value continue rising, your profit will grow. But you don't know which outcome—profit or no value at all—will surface during the term of your option.

Discounting an option's possible future cash flows in order to find its true value is hard to do because so much depends upon whether the underlying asset will rise or fall in price. If, in the example above, GE stock rises above $40 per share, there *will* be future cash flows after exercising the option. On the other hand, if GE stock declines below $40, there not only will be *no* positive cash flow at all, but cash flow will actually be *negative* because the investor must pay out a premium to acquire the option to begin with.

How is it possible to correctly price an option bearing such skewed and uncertain cash flows? A major breakthrough occurred when researchers Fisher Black and Myron Scholes [1] developed a model to explain the price of a call option (*C*) using continuous-time mathematics. They discovered that the value of an option depends upon five key variables:

*Rf* = The *risk-free rate of interest* (such as that attached to default-free government securities), which is positively related to option prices.

*P* = The *current market value* (price) of the asset that is the subject of the option, which is positively related to the option's price.

*σ* = The *degree of volatility* in the value of the underlying asset, measured by the variance ($\sigma^2$) or standard deviation ($\sigma$) of its rate of return, which is also positively related to the price of the option.

*S* = The *strike price* specified in the option contract, which is negatively related to the price of the option.

*t* = The *length of time* between now and when the option expires, also positively related to the option's price.

The model that Black and Scholes developed to explain the price of a call option (*C*) states that the call option's price can be found by using the following equation:

$$C = P \times Nr\ (Y_A) - Se^{-Rft} \times Nr\ (Y_B) \quad \textbf{(9A.1)}$$

where

$$Y_A = [\ln(P/S) + Rft + \sigma^2 t/2]\sigma t^{1/2} \quad \textbf{(9A.2)}$$

and

$$Y_B = [\ln(P/S) + Rft - \sigma^2 t/2]\sigma t^{1/2} \quad \textbf{(9A.3)}$$

In the above formula, *ln* represents the log of a quantity relative to the base *e,* and *Nr* stands for the normal cumulative probability density function, measuring the probability that a normally distributed random variable will be equal to or less than *Y.* Many traders operating today on Wall Street use computer programs that calculate the expected value of an option as figured from formulas similar to those above and then buy or sell options or securities until option prices approach their expected levels. (See the accompanying box for an example of using the Black-Scholes formula to calculate an option's expected value.)

Reduced to nonmathematical terms, the preceding equations suggest that option prices depend on the expected value of the underlying asset named in the option and the expected value of the strike price on the day the option expires, both expressed in present value terms. The discount rate used is the risk-free interest rate because, Black and Scholes assumed, there are enough informed and technically sophisticated investors to effectively reduce risk close to the risk-free rate of return by constructing an adequately hedged investment portfolio. In such a portfolio, movements in the value of options, futures, and other assets will offset each other, leaving the value of the investor's total portfolio better protected against adverse price and rate movements (though there always remains some unhedgeable volatility risk). Subsequent testing of the Black-Scholes model suggests that it performs reasonably well at calculating the true value of European options (which can be exercised only on a single day), making significant errors only when the underlying assets have especially large or small variability in rates of return or, in the case of options on stock, when a stock's dividend payments are substantial.[1]

---

## Pricing Options: An Example

To illustrate how to price an option using the Black-Scholes model, let's suppose the current price of the asset in which we are interested is $100 with a standard deviation around its expected rate of return of 0.50, or 50 percent; that the option on this asset has a strike price of $95; and the risk-free interest rate is currently 10 percent. If the option will expire in three months (0.25 years), what is its expected price?

The expected current price of a *call option* (C) on this asset can be found from:

$$\text{Expected call option price } (C) = P \times Nr(Y_A) - Se^{-Rf \times t} \times Nr(Y_B)$$

where $P$ is the current market price, $S$ the strike price, $Rf$ the risk-free rate, and $t$ the option's time to maturity. The terms $Nr(Y_A)$ and $Nr(Y_B)$ measure the probability the option will have value to the buyer (i.e., the probability the option will eventually be exercised because it is "in the money"). The higher the probability an option will be "in the money," the higher must be its price to the option buyer. $Nr$ represents the normal distribution; the asset's return is assumed to be normally distributed.

We can calculate the probability this option will pay off from:

$$Y_A = [\ln(P/S) + Rf \times t + \sigma^2 t/2]/\sigma t^{1/2}$$

Substituting in the figures from our example,

$$Y_A = (\ln[100/95] + [0.10 \times 0.25] + 0.25 \times (0.50)^2/2)/0.50 \times (.25)^{1/2} = 0.43$$

*(continued)*

---

[1]The Black-Scholes formula in Equation 9A.1 measures the expected value of a *call option* (C). We can find the expected value of the corresponding *put* option having the same strike price and time to maturity by solving:

$$\text{Expected value of put} = C + Se^{-Rf \times t} - P$$

where $P$ is the price of the underlying security or futures contract and $S$, $Rf$, and $t$ are the same as defined for equation 9A.1.

The Black-Scholes option pricing model rests on some strong assumptions. It assumes there are no transactions costs or taxes, that the underlying asset does not pay out income during the life of an option, that the standard deviation of return is constant, that asset prices follow a continuous random process, that homogenous expectations exist among investors, and that the risk-free interest rate is constant over time and the same regardless of maturity. However, repeated testing suggests that even if these assumptions are violated, the option value estimates generated by the Black-Scholes model usually are fairly close to real-world values.

*(concluded)*

We derive the second probability estimate in the equation, $Y_B$, from:

$$Y_B = Y_A - \sigma t^{1/2} = (0.43) - (0.50) \times (0.25)^{1/2} = 0.18$$

Next, we find the corresponding values from the assumed normal distribution of asset prices, represented by $Nr(Y_A)$ and $Nr(Y_B)$. These we can look up in a table for the cumulative normal distribution or by using appropriate software. A portion of such a table is given below:

**Cumulative Normal Distribution Table**

| Y | Nr(Y) | Y | Nr(Y) | Y | Nr(Y) | Y | Nr(Y) |
|---|-------|---|-------|---|-------|---|-------|
| −0.50 | .3085 | −0.20 | .4207 | 0.12 | .5478 | 0.20 | .5793 |
| −0.40 | .3446 | −0.10 | .4602 | 0.14 | .5557 | 0.30 | .6179 |
| −0.30 | .3821 | 0.00 | .5000 | 0.16 | .5636 | 0.40 | .6554 |
| −0.25 | .4013 | 0.10 | .5398 | 0.18 | .5714 | 0.50 | .6915 |

Checking the above table and interpolating if necessary for normal probabilities associated with $Y_A$ and $Y_B$ gives:

$$Nr(0.43) = .6664$$
$$Nr(0.18) = .5714$$

Then, the expected value of the call option must be:

$$\text{Expected call option price } (C) = \$100 \times (.6664) - \$95 \times e^{-10 \times 0.25} \times (.5714) = \$13.70$$

Could we also find the value of a put option for this same asset? Assuming the same option strike price and maturity, the expected value of the corresponding put option would be:

$$\text{Expected put option price} = C + Se^{-Rf \times t} - P$$

Substituting in the calculated call option price ($C$) of $13.70, the asset's price ($P$) of $100, the strike price ($S$) of $95, the risk-free interest rate ($Rf$) of 10 percent, and 0.25 years time to maturity ($t$) from the example above, we get an expected put option price of:

$$\text{Expected put option price} = \$13.70 + \$95e^{(-.10 \times 0.25)} - 100$$

Checking the value of $e^{(-10 \times 0.25)}$ on a calculator gives:

$$\text{Expected put option price} = \$13.7 + \$95(0.9753) - \$100 = \$6.35$$

# Part 3

# The Money Market and Central Banking

When you think of "money" what comes to mind? Ferraris? Movie stars on opening night? South Beach? Those images suggest what money can *buy!* But where *is* the money that bought the Ferrari, the movie star's evening gown, or the time needed to get that South Beach tan? Typically, the actual dollars exchanged to acquire these symbols of wealth would continue to change hands long after those transactions were complete. For example, the car dealer who sold the Ferrari may have deposited the payment he received in his bank account. In turn, his bank may have purchased a Treasury bill with those funds and then issued a repurchase agreement against the T-bill to raise more money in order to cover a cash withdrawal by the movie star who purchased the evening gown. The salon that sold the gown may have deposited the proceeds of that sale in its money market fund, which in turn might have purchased a certificate of deposit (CD) from a bank that needed funds in order to make a vacation loan so the lady next door could lie contentedly in the white sand tanning her body at South Beach!

What makes all of this economic activity possible? It's not just money, but rather the institution we call "the money market." It's really not a single market, but rather a *collection* of markets. In the sequence of transactions discussed above there were exchanges of money for goods and services, but there were also exchanges of money for short-term financial instruments—the Treasury bill, the money market fund account, the bank CD, and the repurchase agreement—and for each of these financial instruments there are markets that are absolutely crucial to a smoothly functioning, vibrant economy. In Part 3 we want to think about "money," not in terms of the goods and services it buys, but in terms of the markets that make so many of these purchases possible because of their great speed and efficiency. Speed, dexterity, and innovation are hallmarks of the money market. Its sole purpose is to bring together those individuals or institutions with temporary cash surpluses—that could be earning interest—with those who demand cash in order to make purchases or pay debts. The needs of individuals and institutions demanding and supplying cash are varied and the rich array of short-term financial instruments created to accommodate those needs lies at the heart of the money market. Our first goal in Part 3, which we pursue in Chapters 10 and 11, is to understand each of the more important financial instruments that comprise the money market.

Our second goal in Part 3 is to examine a very important governmental institution in the money market—the *central bank*. The activities of the central bank are closely monitored and anticipated by the financial marketplace because of its ability to impact short-term interest rates. In Chapters 12 and 13 we examine the organization and activities of central banks, with particular emphasis on the U.S. central bank—the Federal Reserve System. Here we will gain an understanding of *how* the central bank can exercise its considerable influence over money market interest rates by altering the supply of money in the economy. The central bank's decision to change interest rates is actually made by just a handful of people. We will learn who these people are, how they are chosen, and, most importantly, why these policymakers may choose to alter short-term interest rates in order to affect the overall performance of the economy.

# Chapter 10

# Introduction to the Money Market and the Roles Played by Governments and Security Dealers

## What's in This Chapter?
## Key Topics Outline

Nature and Characteristics of the Money Market

Key Borrowers and Lenders and the Structure of the Money Market

Money Market Investor Goals and Investment Risks

Government Involvement in the Money Market

Treasury Bills: Growth, Types, and Yields

Primary Security Dealers

Repurchase Agreements (RPs)

## Learning Objectives

## in This Chapter

- You will understand the many roles and functions performed by the money market in order to aid the financial system and the economy.
- You will also be able to determine who the key actors—individuals and institutions—are in the workings of the money market.
- You will examine the roles that governments and security dealers play in the functioning of the money market.
- You will discover how Treasury bills and repurchase agreements (RPs) arise through borrowing and lending in the money market.

## 10.1 Introduction: The Market for Short-Term Credit

To the casual observer, the financial markets appear to be one vast cauldron of borrowing and lending activity in which some individuals and institutions are seeking credit while others supply the funds needed to make lending possible. All transactions carried out in the financial markets seem to be basically the same: Borrowers issue securities (financial assets) that lenders purchase. When the loan is repaid, the borrower retrieves the securities and returns borrowed funds to the lender. Closer examination of our financial system reveals, however, that beyond the simple act of exchanging financial assets and funds, there are major differences between one financial transaction and another.

For example, an individual may borrow $100,000 for 30 years to purchase a new home, whereas another's financing need may be for a six-month loan of $3,000 to cover an income tax obligation. A corporation may enter the financial markets this week to offer a new issue of 20-year bonds to finance the construction of an office building, and next week it may find itself in need of funds for just 60 days to purchase raw materials so that production can continue.

Clearly, then, the purposes for which money is borrowed within the financial system vary greatly among individuals and institutions and from transaction to transaction. And the different purposes for which money is borrowed result in the creation of different kinds of financial assets, having different maturities, risks, and other features. In this chapter and the others in Part Three, we will be focusing on a collection of financial markets that share a common purpose in their trading activity and deal in financial instruments with similar features. Our particular focus is on the *money market*—the market for short-term credit.

*In the money market nearly all loans have an original maturity of one year or less.* Money market loans are used to help corporations and governments pay the wages and salaries of their workers, make repairs, purchase inventories, pay dividends and taxes, and satisfy other short-term, working capital needs. In this respect, the money market stands in sharp contrast to the capital market. The capital market deals in long-term credit—that is, loans and securities over a year to maturity, typically used to finance long-term investment projects. There are important similarities between the money and capital markets, as we will see in subsequent chapters, but there are also important differences that make these two markets unique.

## 10.2 Characteristics of the Money Market

### What the Money Market Does

The money market, like all financial markets, provides a channel for the exchange of financial assets for money. However, it differs from other parts of the financial system in its emphasis on loans to meet purely short-term cash needs (i.e., current account, rather than capital account, transactions). The **money market** is the mechanism through which *holders of temporary cash surpluses meet holders of temporary cash deficits.* It is designed, on the one hand, to meet the short-term cash requirements of corporations, financial institutions, and governments, providing a mechanism for granting loans as short as overnight and as long as one year to maturity. At the same time, the money market provides an investment outlet for those spending units (also principally corporations, financial institutions, and governments) that hold surplus cash for short periods of time and wish to earn at least some return on temporarily idle funds. The essential function of the money market is to bring these two groups into contact with each other in order to make borrowing and lending possible.

**money market**

## The Need for a Money Market

Why is such a market needed? There are several reasons. First, for most individuals and institutions, inflows and outflows of cash are rarely in perfect harmony with each other. Governments, for example, collect taxes from the public only at certain times of the year, such as in April in the United States, when personal and corporate income tax payments are due. Disbursements of cash must be made throughout the year, however, to cover the wages and salaries of government employees, office supplies, repairs, and fuel costs, as well as unexpected expenses. When taxes are collected, governments usually are flush with funds that far exceed their immediate cash needs. At these times, they frequently enter the money market as lenders and purchase Treasury bills, certificates of deposit (CDs), and other attractive financial assets. Later, however, as cash runs low relative to current expenditures, these same governmental units must once again enter the money market as borrowers of funds, issuing short-term notes attractive to money market investors.

Business firms, too, collect sales revenues from customers at one point in time and dispense cash at other points in time to cover wages and salaries, make repairs, and meet other operating expenses. The checking account of an active business firm fluctuates daily between large cash surpluses and low or nonexistent cash balances. A surplus cash position frequently brings such a firm into the money market as a net lender of funds, investing idle funds in the hope of earning at least a modest rate of return. Cash deficits force it onto the borrowing side of the money market, however, seeking other institutions with temporary cash surpluses. Clearly, then, the money market serves to bridge the gap between receipts and expenditures of funds, covering cash deficits with short-term borrowing when current expenditures exceed receipts and providing an investment outlet to earn interest income for units whose current receipts exceed their current expenditures.

**Key URL:**
To help find answers to issues raised as you read this chapter, you may enjoy checking out **investopedia.com**

To fully appreciate the workings of the money market, we must remember that *money* is one of the most perishable of all commodities. The holding of idle surplus cash is expensive, because cash balances earn little or no income for their owners. When idle cash is not invested, the holder incurs an opportunity cost in the form of interest income that is forgone. Moreover, each day that idle funds are not invested is a day's income lost forever. When large amounts of funds are involved, the income lost from not profitably investing idle funds for even 24 hours can be substantial. For example, interest income from a loan of $10 million for one day at a 10 percent annual rate of interest amounts to nearly $2,740 (or $10,000,00 \times 0.10/365$). In a week's time, $19,178 in interest would be lost from not investing $10 million in idle funds. Many students of the financial system find it hard to believe that investment outlets exist for loans as short as one day or even less. However, billions of dollars in credit are extended in the money market overnight or for only a few daylight hours to securities dealers, banks, and nonfinancial corporations to cover temporary shortfalls of cash. As we will see in the next chapter, one important money market instrument—the federal funds loan—is designed mainly for extending credit within a day or less or over a weekend.

## Key Borrowers and Lenders in the Money Market

Who are the principal lenders of funds in the money market? Who are the principal borrowers? (See Exhibit 10.1 for an overview of the structure of the money market.) These questions are difficult to answer, because the same institutions frequently

**EXHIBIT 10.1** The Money Market Landscape: Structure and Organization of the Short-Term Funds Market

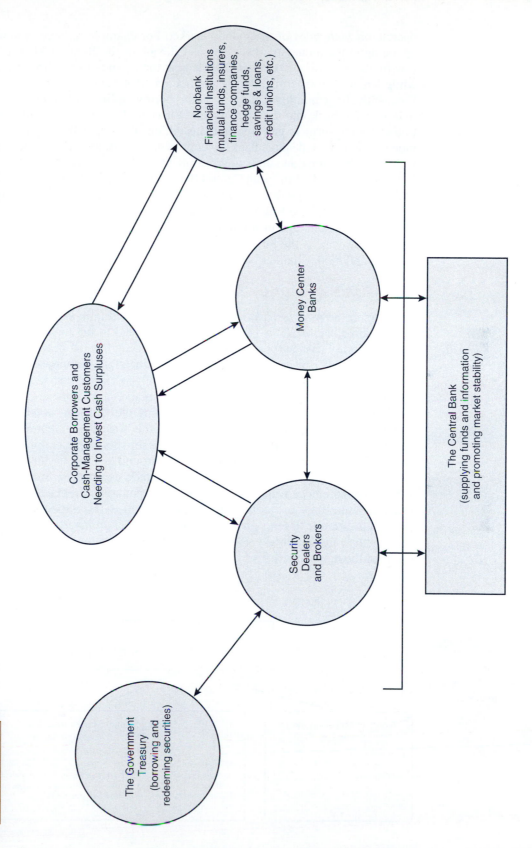

operate on *both* sides of the money market. For example, a large commercial bank operating in the money market (such as Citibank or the Bank of Montreal) will borrow funds aggressively through CDs, federal funds, and other short-term instruments while lending short-term funds to corporations that have temporary cash shortages. Frequently, large nonfinancial corporations borrow millions of dollars on a single day, only to come back into the money market later in the week as a lender of funds due to a sudden upsurge in cash receipts. Institutions that typically play *both sides* of the money market include large banks, securities dealers, finance companies, major nonfinancial corporations, and units of government. Even central banks, such as the Federal Reserve System, the European Central Bank (ECB), the Bank of England, or the Bank of Japan, may be aggressive suppliers of funds to the money market on one day and reverse themselves the following day, demanding funds through the sale of securities in the open market. One institution that is virtually always on the demand side of the market, however, is the government. The U.S. Treasury, for example, is among the largest of all money market borrowers.

## The Goals of Money Market Investors

Investors in the money market seek mainly *safety* and *liquidity,* plus the opportunity to earn some income. This is because funds invested in the money market represent only temporary cash surpluses and are usually needed in the near future to meet tax obligations, cover wage and salary costs, pay stockholder dividends, and so on. For this reason, money market investors are especially *sensitive to risk.*

The strong *aversion to risk* among money market investors is especially evident when there is even a hint of trouble concerning the financial condition of a major money market borrower. For example, when the huge Penn Central Transportation Company collapsed in 1970 and defaulted on its short-term commercial notes, the short-term commercial paper market virtually ground to a halt because many investors refused to buy even the notes offered by top-grade companies. Similarly, during the 1980s, when the huge Continental Illinois Bank had to be propped up by government loans, the rates on short-term certificates of deposit (CDs) issued by other big banks surged upward due to fears on the part of money market investors that *all* large-bank CDs had become more risky. (See Exhibit 10.2 for a summary of the goals and instruments of the money market.)

**EXHIBIT 10.2**

**The Goals and Instruments of the Money Market**

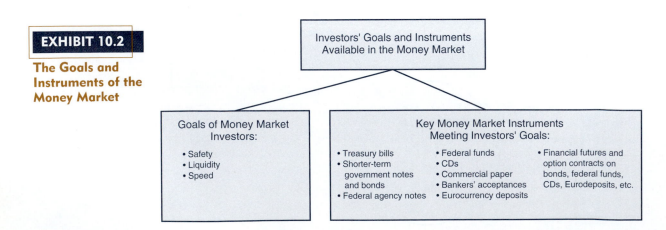

## Types of Investment Risk That Investors Face

What kinds of risk do investors face in the financial markets? And how do money market instruments rank in terms of these different kinds of risk?

**market risk**

First, all securities, including money market instruments, carry **market risk** (sometimes called *interest rate risk*), which refers to the danger that their prices will fall (and interest rates rise), subjecting the holder to a capital loss. Even Treasury notes and bonds decline in price when interest rates rise. However, most money market assets are debt instruments that carry a fixed rate of return if the asset is held to maturity. Therefore, market risk is only a problem if the investor's time horizon for his or her investment is shorter than the maturity of the asset.

**reinvestment risk**

Not only can security prices fall, but so can interest rates. This latter development increases an investor's **reinvestment risk**—the risk that earnings from a financial asset will have to be reinvested in lower-yielding assets at some point in the future. Even government securities carry reinvestment risk.

**default risk**

Securities issued by private firms and state and local governments carry **default risk.** For such securities, there is always some positive probability the borrower will fail to meet some or all of his or her promised principal and/or interest payments (as happened to Orange County, California, in 1995, and to Enron Corporation and Argentina in 2001, for example, as discussed earlier in Chapter 8).

**inflation risk**

Lenders of funds face the possibility that increases in the average level of prices for all goods and services will reduce the purchasing power of their income. This is known as **inflation risk** (sometimes called *purchasing power risk*). Lenders usually attempt to offset anticipated inflation by demanding higher contract rates on their loans.

**currency risk**

International investors also face **currency risk:** possible loss due to unfavorable changes in the value of foreign currencies. For example, if a U.S. investor purchases British Treasury bills on the London money market, the return from these bills may be severely reduced if the value of the British pound falls relative to the dollar during the life of the investment.

**political risk**

Finally, **political risk** refers to the possibility that changes in government laws or regulations will result in a diminished rate of return to the investor or, in the extreme case, a total loss of invested capital. For example, the windfall profits tax on U.S. petroleum companies levied by Congress during the 1980s generally reduced the earnings of petroleum stockholders. Investors in industries that are closely regulated, such as banking and public utilities, continually run the risk that new price controls, output quotas, or other restrictions will be imposed, reducing their earnings potential. In some foreign countries, facilities and equipment owned by U.S. corporations have been expropriated by national governments, resulting in total loss for the investors involved. A summary of each of the foregoing kinds of risk is shown in Exhibit 10.3.

Money market instruments generally offer more protection against such risks than most other investments. The prices of money market securities tend to be remarkably stable over time compared to the prices of bonds, stocks, real estate, and commodities such as wheat, oil, and gold. Money market instruments generally do not offer the prospect of significant capital gains for the investor, but neither do they normally raise the specter of substantial capital losses. Similarly, default risk is expected to be minimal in the money market. In fact, money market borrowers must be well-established institutions with impeccable credit ratings before their securities can be offered for sale in this market.

**liquidity**

Few investments today adequately protect the investor against inflation risk. Money market securities are no exception. However, they do offer superior **liquidity,** allowing

| EXHIBIT 10.3 | Types of Risk Confronting Investors in the Money and Capital Markets |
|---|---|
| **Type of Risk** | **Definition** |
| Market risk | The risk to investors whose investment horizon is shorter than the maturity of a financial asset that the market price (value) of that asset will decline, resulting in a capital loss when sold. Sometimes referred to as *interest rate risk*. |
| Reinvestment risk | The risk to investors whose investment horizon exceeds the maturity of a financial asset that they will be forced to place earnings from that maturing asset into a lower-yielding investment because interest rates have fallen. |
| Default risk | The probability a borrower will fail to meet one or more promised principal or interest payments on a loan or security. |
| Inflation risk | The risk that increases in the general price level will reduce the purchasing power of earnings from a loan, security, or other investment. |
| Currency risk | The risk that adverse movements in the price of one national currency vis-à-vis another will reduce the net rate of return from a foreign investment. Sometimes referred to as *exchange rate risk*. |
| Political risk | The probability changes in government laws or regulations will reduce an investor's expected return from an investment. |

the investor to cash them in quickly, with little risk of loss of principal when a promising inflation-hedged investment opportunity comes along.

Currency risk concerns the international investor who frequently must convert one currency into another. That risk has increased dramatically in recent years due to the increase in foreign exchange rates that float with market conditions. Investors who purchase securities in foreign markets cannot completely escape currency risk, but they are probably less prone to such losses when buying money market instruments due to the short-term nature of money market assets. These assets also provide some hedge against political risk because they are short-term investments and fewer dramatic changes in government policy are likely over brief intervals of time. Moreover, the appearance of the euro in the European money market has helped to reduce some forms of currency risk in one of the world's largest international markets for goods and services.

## QUESTIONS TO HELP YOU STUDY

1. What exactly do we mean by the term *money market?*
2. Explain why there is a critical need within the financial system to have money market instruments available to anyone who can afford them.
3. What are the principal *goals* usually pursued by money market investors?
4. Who are the principal borrowers and lenders in the money market?
5. Define the following types of *risk:* (a) market risk; (b) default risk; (c) inflation risk; (d) currency risk; and (e) political risk. Which of these risks are *minimized* by purchasing money market instruments? Does investing in the money market avoid *all* of the foregoing risks?

## Money Market Maturities

Despite the fact that money market investments cover a relatively narrow range of maturities—one year or less—there are maturities available within this range to meet just about every short-term investment need. We must distinguish here between original maturity and actual maturity, however. The interval of time between the issue date of a security and the date on which the borrower promises to redeem it is the security's **original maturity. Actual maturity,** on the other hand, refers to the number of days, months, or years between today and the date the security is actually retired.

original maturity
actual maturity

Original maturities on money market instruments range from as short as one day or a few hours on many loans to banks and security dealers to a full year on some bank deposits and Treasury bills. Obviously, once a money market instrument is issued, it grows shorter in actual maturity every day. Because there are thousands of money market assets outstanding, some of which reach maturity each day, investors have a wide menu from which to select the precise length of time they need to invest their cash.

## Depth and Breadth of the Money Market

The money market is extremely *broad* and *deep,* meaning it can absorb a large volume of transactions with only small effects on security prices and interest rates. Investors can easily sell most money market instruments on short notice, often in a matter of minutes. This is one of the most efficient markets in the world, containing a vast network of securities dealers, money-center banks, and funds brokers in constant touch with one another and alert to any bargains. The slightest hint that a financial instrument is underpriced (i.e., carries an exceptionally high yield) usually brings a flood of buy orders, but money market traders are quick to dump or avoid overpriced financial assets. This market is dominated by active traders who constantly search their video display screens for opportunities to arbitrage funds; that is, they move money from one corner of the market with relatively low yields to another where investments offer the highest returns available. Overseeing the whole market are central banks (such as the European Central Bank, the Bank of Japan, the People's Bank of China, and the Federal Reserve System) around the globe, who try to ensure that trading is orderly and that asset prices are reasonably stable.

There is no centralized trading arena in the money market as there is on a stock exchange, for example. The money market is a telephone and computer market, in which participants arrange trades over the phone or through computer networks and usually confirm by wire. Speed is of the essence in this market because, as we observed earlier, money is a highly perishable commodity. Each day that passes means millions of dollars in lost interest income if newly received funds are not immediately invested. Most business between traders, therefore, is conducted in seconds or minutes, and payment is made almost instantaneously.

## The Speed of Money Market Payments: Federal Funds versus Clearinghouse Funds

How can funds move so fast in the money market? The reason is that money market traders usually deal in **federal funds.** These funds are mainly deposit balances of banks and thrift institutions held at the regional Federal Reserve banks and at larger correspondent banks. For example, when a securities dealer that manages a portfolio of financial assets buys securities from an investor, it immediately contacts its bank and requests that funds be transferred from its account to the investor's account at

federal funds

Money markets around the world share several common characteristics. They reconcile cash imbalances for public and private individuals and institutions and do so at low levels of risk for both borrowers and lenders. Money markets transmit government economic policies, aiding governments in financing their deficits (fiscal policy) and in managing the growth of money and credit (monetary policy).

Each nation has its own money market, though some are poorly developed and others reach far beyond national boundaries to involve traders on many continents. There is an *international money market* that arches over domestic money markets all over the globe and ties them together. The heart of the international money market is the *Eurocurrency market,* where large-bank deposits are traded outside the boundaries of the country where a particular currency is issued. No nation's money market today is unaffected by movements in interest rates and security prices in the international money market.

National money markets around the globe tend to fall into one of two types—those (such as the United States and Great Britain) that are *securities market dominated,* where most borrowing and lending is through open-market trading of financial instruments, and those that are *bank dominated,* where bank borrowing and lending is at the center of most transactions (as in Japan and China). However, worldwide deregulation of many financial institutions is under way, with the probable outcome that more money markets of the future are likely to become more security trading oriented and less dominated by a few large financial institutions.

In developing countries, money markets are typically dominated by large banks because their securities markets usually are not well developed. Bank-dominated money markets have a potential weakness, however, as economic problems experienced in Asia during the late 1990s suggest. They can yield more easily to government pressure, resulting in many bad loans, and they may slow the development of long-term capital markets, which promote greater economic stability. Central banks, such as the Federal Reserve and the European Central Bank, are usually the single most important institution in money markets, regardless of whether they are security dominated or bank dominated.

another banking firm. Many of these transactions move via a public or private wire network (such as the Federal Reserve's electronic wire transfer network in the United States). In this case, the central bank or funds transfer firm removes funds from the reserve account of the buyer's bank and transfers these reserves to the seller's bank. The transaction is so quick the seller of securities has funds available to make new investments, pay bills, or to use for other purposes the same day a trade is carried out or a loan is made. Federal funds are often called *immediately available* funds because of the speed with which money moves from one bank's reserve account to that of another.

Contrast this method of payment with that generally used in the capital market and by most businesses and households. When most of us purchase goods and services a check, credit card, or debit card is often the most desirable means of paying the bill.

**clearinghouse funds**   Funds transferred by check are known as **clearinghouse funds,** because, once the buyer writes a check, it goes to the seller's depository institution, which forwards that check to the deposit-type institution upon which it was drawn. If the two depositories are in the same community, they exchange bundles of checks drawn against each other every day through the local clearinghouse—an agreed-upon location where checks and other cash items are delivered and passed from one depository institution to another.

Clearinghouse funds are an acceptable means of payment for most purposes, but not in the money market, where *speed* is of the essence. It takes at least a day to clear many local checks and perhaps two to three days for checks moving between distant cities. For money market transactions, this is far too slow, because no interest can be earned until the check is collected. Clearinghouse funds also have an element of *risk,* because a check may be returned as fraudulent or for insufficient funds. Similar risks accompany credit and debit cards. Federal funds transactions, however, are both speedy and safe.

## A Market for Large Borrowers and Lenders

The money market is dominated by a relatively small number of very large financial institutions. No more than a hundred banks in New York, London, Tokyo, Singapore, and a handful of other money centers are at the heart of this marketplace. Many money market transactions are carried out by these very large institutions which account for the bulk of federal funds trading. In addition, financial assets move readily from sellers to buyers through the market-making activities of major securities dealers and brokers. And, of course, governments and central banks around the world play major roles in this market as the largest borrowers and as regulators, setting the rules of the game. For example, the Federal Reserve System, operating principally through the trading desk at the Federal Reserve Bank of New York, is in the market frequently, either supplying funds to banks and security dealers or absorbing funds through security sales.

Individual transactions in the money market involve huge amounts of funds. *Most trading occurs in multiples of a million dollars.* For this reason, the money market is often referred to as a *wholesale market* for funds, as opposed to the *retail market* where most households and small businesses borrow and save their money.

---

### QUESTIONS TO HELP YOU STUDY

6. What is the difference between the *actual maturity* and the *original maturity* of a financial asset? Why is this difference important in the money market?

7. How do money markets around the world differ from one another?

8. What are *federal funds* and how do they differ from *clearinghouse funds?*

9. Which of these two types of funds—federal funds versus clearinghouse funds—are most important in the money market and why is this so?

10. Is the money market predominantly a wholesale or retail marketplace? How do you know?

11. What are the principal financial instruments traded in the money market? What common characteristics do these instruments possess?

---

## 10.3   Government Involvement in the Money Market

Thus far, this chapter has presented an overview of the characteristics of the money market. For the remainder of the chapter and in the other chapters in Part Three we will focus on key institutions that literally make the money market "go"—governments, security dealers, commercial banks, corporations, federal agencies, and central banks.

### The Roles That Governments Play in the Money Market

Of all the institutions that trade for funds in the vast money market it is difficult to find one institution that is more important, directly or indirectly, to the proper functioning of the money market than the *governments* around the world. Governments set the rules of the money market "game" through regulation, and they consistently rank among the top issuers of money market debt. Moreover, working through central banks (like the European Central Bank and the Federal Reserve System)—institutions chartered by government—governments help to shape money market conditions and set the tone for daily borrowing and lending activities.

## Selling Treasury Bills to Money Market Investors: The Anchor of the Money Market

Government is usually the most visible in the money market when it *borrows money*. Indeed, many money markets around the world have come into existence for the principal reason of giving governmental authorities a place to raise new cash quickly (other than resorting to taxes on their citizens). One of the largest of all borrowers in the money market is the U.S. Treasury Department, which enters the market every week to sell one of the world's most popular financial instruments—*Treasury bills*. Nor is the United States alone. Governments around the globe issue Treasury bills or their equivalent to raise short-term funds and meet their expenses.

**U.S. Treasury bills**

**U.S. Treasury bills** are direct obligations of the United States government, indicating that tax revenues or any other source of government funds can be used to repay holders of these financial instruments. By law, Treasury bills must have an original maturity of one year or less. T-bills were first issued by the U.S. Treasury in 1929 to cover the federal government's frequent short-term cash deficits.

In the United States the federal government's fiscal year runs from October 1 to September 30. However, individual income taxes—the largest single source of federal revenue—are not fully collected until April of each year. Therefore, even in those rare years when a sizable budget surplus is expected, the government is likely to be short of cash during the fall and winter months and often in the summer as well. During the spring, personal and corporate tax collections are usually at high levels, and the resulting inflow of funds can be used to retire some portion of the securities issued earlier in the fiscal year. T-bills are suited to this seasonal ebb and flow of government cash because their maturities are short, they find a ready market among investors, and their prices adjust readily to changing market conditions.

### Volume of Bills Outstanding

The volume of U.S. Treasury bills outstanding, as shown in Exhibit 10.4, grew rapidly during periods of escalating public debt, with a more than tenfold increase from 1970 to 2006. However, as a share of the total marketable debt of the U.S. government, T-bills have been on the decline from more than one-third to just over one-fifth of the total, as the U.S. Treasury has shifted its borrowing vehicles more heavily toward longer-term debt issues. Nonetheless, the market for Treasury bills remains one of the most liquid and most active markets in the world. Indeed, its growth has come at a time of rapid global economic expansion during which the volume of global transactions has been accelerating and has aided banks and other investors in the increasingly challenging task of efficiently managing their cash positions.

### Types of Treasury Bills

There are several different types of Treasury bills. *Regular-series bills* are issued routinely every week or month in competitive auctions. Bills issued in regular series carry original maturities of one month (4 weeks), three months (13 weeks), and six months (26 weeks). Today regular-series bills are auctioned weekly. The six-month bill provides the largest amount of revenue for the U.S. Treasury.

| EXHIBIT 10.4 | U.S. Treasury Bills: Total Amount Outstanding and Their Proportion of the Marketable Public Debt of the United States, 1960–2006 | | |
|---|---|---|---|
| End of Year | Total Volume of Bills Outstanding ($ Billions) | Marketable Public Debt of the United States ($ Billions) | T-bills as a Percent of the Total Marketable Public Debt |
| 1960 | $ 39.4 | $ 189.0 | 20.8% |
| 1970 | 87.9 | 247.7 | 35.5 |
| 1980 | 216.1 | 623.2 | 34.7 |
| 1990 | 527.4 | 2,195.8 | 24.0 |
| 2000 | 646.9 | 2,966.9 | 21.8 |
| 2006* | 911.5 | 4,354.0 | 20.9 |

*2006 figures are for the third quarter.

Source: Board of Governors of the Federal Reserve System, *Federal Reserve Bulletin,* selected issues.

On the other hand, *irregular-series bills* are issued when the Treasury has an emergency need for cash. These instruments include strip bills and cash management bills. A package offering of bills requiring investors to bid for an entire series of different bill maturities is known as a *strip bill.* Investors who bid successfully must accept bills at their bid price each week for several weeks running. *Cash management bills,* on the other hand, usually consist simply of reopened issues of bills that were sold in prior weeks and, therefore, carry the actual maturity of the original issue.

**auction**

*How Bills Are Sold*    Treasury bills are sold using the **auction** technique. The marketplace, not the Treasury, sets bill prices and yields. A new regular bill issue is usually announced by the U.S. Treasury on Thursday of each week (except for holidays) with bids from investors due the following Monday before 1 PM New York time. Interested investors complete a form tendering an offer to the Treasury for a specific bill issue at a specific price. These forms must be filed by the Monday deadline with one of the regional Federal Reserve banks or branches or with the Treasury's Bureau of the Public Debt. The interested investor can appear in person at a Federal Reserve bank or branch to fill out a tender form, submit it by mail, or place an order in person or electronically through a security broker or depository institution. T-bills are now also traded online and are usually issued the Thursday following Monday's auction.

The Treasury entertains both competitive and noncompetitive tenders for bills, other than cash management bills, for which only competitive tenders are accepted. *Competitive* tenders typically are submitted by large investors, including banks and securities dealers, who bid for millions of dollars' worth at one time. Although anyone can submit a bid for his or her own account, depository institutions and registered government security brokers and dealers may also bid on behalf of their customers. Institutions submitting competitive tenders bid aggressively for bills, trying to offer the Treasury a "price"—expressed as a discount rate of interest (DR)—high enough to win an allotment of bills. In contrast, *noncompetitive* tenders (normally less than about $1 million each) are submitted by small investors who agree to accept the price determined by the auction. Generally, the Treasury fills all noncompetitive orders for bills. The Federal Reserve, acting as the fiscal agent for the Treasury, conducts the auctions.

In the typical bill auction, Federal Reserve officials array all the bids received from the highest price bid to the lowest price. All competitive bids must be expressed as a DR or discount rate—a measure of a bill's rate of return. (See chapter 6.) For example, a typical series of bids in a Treasury auction might appear as follows:

| Hypothetical Prices and Discount Rates Bid for Three-Month U.S. Treasury Bills | |
| --- | --- |
| **Treasury Bill Prices** | **Treasury Bill Discount Rates Bid** |
| $99,115 | 3.540% |
| 99,114 | 3.545 |
| 99,113 | 3.550 |
| 99,111 | 3.555 |
| 99,110 | 3.560 |
| 99,109 | 3.565 |
| 99,108 | 3.570 |

**Key URL:**
For information on current and past Treasury auctions, see **TreasuryDirect .gov**

Note in the table above that the column measuring possible T-bill prices expresses each bill's price as though it had a $100 par (face) value. In fact, the minimum denomination for U.S. Treasury bills is $1,000 and they are issued in multiples of $1,000 above that minimum. Once the volume of noncompetitive tenders is subtracted from the total amount of T-bills being auctioned, the highest competitive bidder receives bills and those who bid successively lower prices also receive bills until all available securities have been awarded. The lowest successful price bid, known as the "stop-out"(or market-clearing) price, becomes the common price that all successful bidders actually pay to the Treasury.

Many successful bidders choose to sell their bills immediately in the secondary market, giving unsuccessful bidders a chance to add to their own T-bill portfolios. Payments for bills won in the auction must be made in federal funds, cash, cashier's check, certified personal check, by redeeming maturing Treasury securities or coupon payments, or, when permitted by the Treasury, through crediting Treasury tax and loan accounts at banks.[1]

All bills today are issued only in *book-entry form*—a computerized record of ownership maintained at the Federal Reserve banks, through private depository institutions, and at the U.S. Treasury Department. The Federal Reserve manages the National Book-Entry System (NBES), which keeps records of Treasury security purchases for depository institutions, and depository institutions, in turn, keep records on their customers' purchases. Alternatively, a purchaser of Treasuries can keep an electronic account with the U.S. Treasury Department's *Treasury Direct* system, showing all the buyer's holdings of Treasury obligations. Settlement of transactions involving purchases and sales of new bills or other Treasury securities takes place mainly through depository institutions, led by a few large clearing banks that process a large volume

---

[1]These so-called T&L accounts are Treasury deposits kept in thousands of the nation's depository institutions. The purpose of these accounts is to minimize the impact on the financial system of Treasury tax collections and debt-financing operations. As taxes are collected or securities are sold, the Treasury deposits the funds received in these T&L accounts and withdraws money from them as needed into its checking accounts held at the Federal Reserve banks.

| EXHIBIT 10.5 | An Example of the Outcome of an Auction of U.S. Treasury Bills* | |
| --- | --- | --- |
| | 13 Week or 91-Day Bills | 26 Week or 182-Day Bills |
| Volume of bills requested | $47.3 billion | $38.3 billion |
| Volume of bids accepted by the U.S. Treasury Department | $16.6 billion | $12.8 billion |
| Noncompetitive tender offers accepted by the U.S. Treasury Department | $ 2.2 billion | $ 1.9 billion |
| The bill price established in this auction | 98.730 | 97.490 |
| | (on a $ 100 basis) | (on a $ 100 basis) |
| The discount yield established in this auction (DR) | 5.025% | 4.965% |
| Percentage of bids at the market's yield or rate of return | 50% | 50% |
| Investment or coupon-equivalent rate of return (IR) | 5.160% | 5.164% |

*All successful Treasury bill bids are filled at a single price as determined by the bill yield that clears the market. A competitive bidder whose bid rate or yield is the highest rate or yield (lowest price) accepted may not receive the full amount of bills he or she requested. Competitive bidders who bid too low a price (i.e., filed too high a yield bid) may have their bids rejected depending upon the market-determined outcome of each Treasury auction.

of transactions daily. One advantage of using Treasury Direct is that the U.S. Treasury charges no fees for purchases or reinvestments, but does charge a fee of $45 for each Treasury security sold before its maturity date.

## Results of a Recent Bill Auction

Key URLs:
Key references for learning more about money market instruments and rules include: U.S. Treasury Department
publicdebt.treas.gov;

Federal Reserve Bank of New York ny.frb.org;

Board of Governors of the Federal Reserve System
federalreserve.gov; and

Federal Deposit Insurance Corporation
fdic.gov

A summary of the results from each T-bill auction is published in financial news sheets all over the world. The results of a recent U.S. Treasury bill auction are illustrated in Exhibit 10.5. In this particular example, two maturities of bills—13 and 26 weeks—were offered to the public, and both issues were heavily oversubscribed. More than $47 billion in 13-week bills and over $38 billion of 26-week bills were requested by the public; however, the Treasury only awarded $16.6 billion of the shorter-term bills and $12.8 billion of the 26-week bills.

Noncompetitive tenders in the amount of $2.2 billion for the 13-week issue and about $1.9 billion for the 26-week issue received their bills. The market-clearing auction price for the 13-week bill was $98.730 per $100 par value. The 26-week issue sold for an auction price of $97.490 for a $100-denominated instrument. This works out to a 5.025 percent discount rate of return (DR) on the 13-week bill and a 4.965 percent discount rate of return (DR) on the 26-week issue. On a yield-to-maturity (investment return [IR]) basis—a rate of return measure for bills we discussed in chapter 6—the 13-week bill carried a market-clearing investment return of 5.160 percent, while the 26-week bill posted an investment (IR) yield of 5.164 percent.

## Market Interest Rates on Treasury Bills

Due to the absence of default risk and because of the superior marketability of T-bills, the yields on these popular financial instruments are typically among the lowest in the money market. And because of the tremendous size of the bill market, conditions there tend to set the tone in other segments of the money market. A rise in T-bill rates, for example, often is quickly translated into increases in interest rates attached to other money market instruments.

U.S. Treasury bills and other U.S. government securities are traded 24 hours a day around the globe. But many people are not aware that governments in Europe, Asia, and the Americas also issue their own T-bills. For example, the Bank of Canada, acting as agent for the Canadian government, auctions bills to a select list of banks and dealers authorized to bid for themselves and their customers. In addition, Canada's provinces borrow through Provincial Bills, normally issued in denominations up to $100,000 (expressed in Canadian dollars).

In Europe, Treasury bills are issued by several governments and widely traded. Bills issued by the United Kingdom rank among the most popular in Western Europe. Leading central banks in Europe regularly trade in the bill market and monitor T-bill rates as a barometer of credit market conditions.

Treasury bills are a relatively recent government financing instrument in Japan, first appearing in 1986, but they are now sold regularly. Japan also issues Financing Bills to cover the emergency cash needs of the Japanese government. Similarly, in Korea the government issues Treasury bills irregularly, and thus, the secondary market for this money market instrument is not yet fully developed.

The Treasury bill market is one of the most important for the development of an efficient and fluid financial system in any nation. The bill market is a natural channel for government economic policy and can aid in the development of a strong central banking and financial market system.

Although the prices of Treasury bills tend to be relatively stable, yields on bills fluctuate widely in response to changes in economic conditions, government policy, and a host of other factors. This can be seen clearly in Exhibit 10.6, which gives annual averages for the secondary market yields on 3- and 6-month bills. T-bill rates typically fall during periods of recession and sluggish economic activity as borrowing

**EXHIBIT 10.6**

**Market Interest Rates on U.S. Treasury Bills, Three- and Six-month Maturities (Annual Percentage Rates)**

Source: Board of Governers of the Federal Reserve System; *Federal Reserve Bulletin,* Selected monthly issues.

*Figures are averages for October 2006.

| Year | 3-Month | 6-Month |
|------|---------|---------|
| 1990 | 7.50 | 7.46 |
| 1991 | 5.38 | 5.44 |
| 1992 | 3.43 | 3.54 |
| 1993 | 2.95 | 3.05 |
| 1994 | 4.25 | 4.64 |
| 1995 | 5.49 | 5.56 |
| 1996 | 5.01 | 5.08 |
| 1997 | 5.06 | 5.18 |
| 1998 | 4.78 | 4.83 |
| 1999 | 4.64 | 4.75 |
| 2000 | 5.82 | 5.90 |
| 2001 | 3.40 | 3.45 |
| 2002 | 1.61 | 1.75 |
| 2003 | 1.01 | 1.05 |
| 2004 | 1.37 | 1.58 |
| 2005 | 3.15 | 3.39 |
| 2006* | 4.92 | 4.92 |

and spending sag. Note, for example, the decline in bill yields in 1991–1992 and 2001–2003. These years were periods in which the economy reached the peak of a boom period and then dropped into a recession. During periods of economic expansion, on the other hand, T-bill rates frequently surge upward, as happened, for example, between 1993 and 1997.

It is interesting to examine the shape of the *yield curve* for bills. As Exhibit 10.6 suggests, that curve usually *slopes upward,* with six-month bill maturities generally carrying the highest yields, and three-month bill maturities among the lowest yields. This is not always the case, however, as 1990 and 2006 illustrate. Sometimes the bill yield curve seems to signal the onset of a recession by sloping downward or lying relatively flat.

### Investors in Treasury Bills

**Key URLs:**

While the Federal Reserve System regulates economic conditions largely through trading in T-bills, other central banks often use other tools. For example, the European Central Bank (ECB) auctions off liquid funds weekly, offering loans to banks through its Marginal Lending Facility and operating a Deposit Facility where banks in the European system can deposit excess liquidity at a predetermined deposit interest rate. See especially **www.ecb. int/press/key** and **www .ecb.eu/home/glossary/ html**

Principal holders of Treasury bills include commercial banks, nonfinancial corporations, state and local governments, and the Federal Reserve banks. Commercial banks and private corporations hold large quantities of bills as a reserve of liquidity until cash is needed. The most attractive feature of bills for these institutions is their ready marketability and stable price. The Federal Reserve banks conduct many of their open market operations in T-bills (or in repurchase agreements collateralized with T-bills) because of the depth and volume of activity in this market. The Fed purchases and sells bills in an effort to influence other money market interest rates, alter the volume and growth of bank credit, and ultimately affect the volume of investment spending and borrowing in the economy.

---

**QUESTIONS TO HELP YOU STUDY**

12. What has been the principal cause of periods of rapid growth in the volume of Treasury bills? Identify one such period and explain.

13. Explain why Treasury bills are so popular with investors (savers) all over the world.

14. Why have governments found Treasury bills such an effective instrument for raising new funds?

15. What are the various types of Treasury bills? How do they differ?

16. Explain how a Treasury auction works in the United States. Can you find some advantages stemming from this type of sale?

17. What is the "normal" or "typical" shape of the yield curve for T-bills? What other shapes have been observed and why do you think these occur?

18. Who are the principal *buyers* of Treasury bills today? Make a list of the key factors that you believe motivate these investors to buy bills.

---

## 10.4   Primary Dealers in Government Securities

**primary dealers**

The money market depends heavily on the buying and selling activities of securities dealers to move funds from cash-rich units to those with cash shortages. Today, close to two dozen **primary dealers** in government securities trade in both new and previously issued Treasury bills as well as Treasury bonds and notes. As shown in the primary dealer list on page 299, these firms include such market leaders as

Due in part to competition and the nature of auction methods used by the U.S. Treasury Department prior to November 1998 to sell T-bills and other government securities, primary dealers had a significant incentive to "corner" the government securities market and to "collude" so that all dealers received some share of all new securities issued and made a profit. In such a huge market, dealers could easily overbid, eliminating potential profits by either posting bid prices that were too high or by underbidding, receiving no securities from the government to meet their obligations to their customers. Thus, dealers had a strong incentive to *share information* with each other on the size of the orders they planned to place with the government and on the prices they hoped to bid. In 1991 rumors swept through the financial markets that collusion was rampant. After several weeks of investigation, officials at the Federal Reserve and the Securities and Exchange Commission alleged they had evidence of improper trading practices on the part of the old-line primary dealer, Salomon Brothers (now part of Citigroup Global Markets, Inc.).

It was alleged that Salomon cornered a $12-billion-plus auction of U.S. Treasury notes in May 1991, inflating the amount of its bid to the Treasury well beyond the 35 percent maximum share of a new issue normally allowed. When Salomon wound up with nearly 90 percent of the new Treasury notes, other dealers filed complaints that they were being "squeezed"—forced to pay exorbitant prices to purchase the new notes in order to fill their own customers' orders. Subsequently, government investigators found evidence of manipulation of at least seven other government auctions. Moreover, the government wound up paying higher borrowing costs as a result of market manipulation.

In the wake of the Salomon scandal, the U.S. Treasury and the Federal Reserve Bank of New York set up new rules by which government securities would be auctioned in the future. For one thing, customers purchasing large amounts of government securities through dealers were thereafter required to *verify in writing* the amounts they bid before they could receive any new securities. Any security dealer or broker registered with the SEC, not just primary dealers, could file bids on behalf of its customers without putting up a deposit or guarantee. The U.S. Treasury promised it would move swiftly to automate the bidding process for government securities rather than relying on traditional handwritten bids. These steps were reinforced by the U.S. Congress when it enacted the Government Securities Act Amendments of 1993, broadening the U.S. Treasury's authority to regulate the government securities market.

In 1997 the Treasury Department set up large position-reporting rules and, from time to time, has conducted "test calls" in which dealers whose net position in a particular Treasury instrument exceeds $2 billion have been required to report the extent of their holdings. The goal has been to discourage market manipulation and prevent one or a few dealers from putting a "squeeze" on other traders.

Perhaps the most important outcome of the Salomon scandal was a fundamental change in the way the Treasury auctions new securities. At the time of the scandal the auction method in use was called a *first-price sealed-bid auction*, or English auction. Although it possessed the advantage of allowing the market to set the prices, the English auction had definite weaknesses. It encouraged dealers to bid high to increase their probability of winning some of the auctioned securities. However, the higher the price bid, the lower the expected profit when any Treasury securities won in the auction were sold in the secondary market, because the highest bidders had to follow through on their commitment and pay the Treasury what they had bid even though other successful bidders were paying a lower amount for the same securities. Moreover, the high bidders could sell their securities for no more later in the resale market than those who bid less. In effect, dealers bidding the highest prices faced a real "winner's curse," because they incurred greater probability of loss when they attempted to resell the securities won in the auction to their customers. The first-price sealed-bid auction probably reduced the aggressiveness of competitive bidding by dealers and resulted in the Treasury getting a lower price for its securities.

Several experts suggested changes in the design of Treasury auctions. The winning recommendation was to set up a *Dutch* or *uniform-price auction*, in which bids are arrayed by price from highest to lowest but all the securities in the auction are sold for just *one price*— the highest bid just sufficient to sell out the whole issue, sometimes referred to as the "market clearing" or "stop-out" price. Thus, the price paid by every successful participant in a Dutch auction is identical and usually comes fairly close to the market consensus price, meaning less of a winner's curse. Dutch auctions tend to incite more aggressive bidding and to encourage more individuals and institutions to participate in Treasury auctions.

Merrill Lynch, Goldman Sachs, Morgan Stanley, and Bear Stearns. Just over half are banks or securities affiliates of banks.

| List of Primary Dealers Authorized to Trade with the Federal Reserve Bank of New York | |
|---|---|
| BNP Paribus Securities Corp. | Goldman, Sachs & Co. |
| Banc of America Securities LLC | Greenwich Capital Markets Inc. |
| Barclays Capital Inc. | HSBC Securities (USA) Inc. |
| Bear Sterns & Co., Inc. | J. P. Morgan Securities Inc. |
| Cantor, Fitzgerald & Co. | Lehman Brothers Inc. |
| Citigroup Global Markets, Inc. | Merrill Lynch Government Securities Inc. |
| Countrywide Securities Corp. | Mizuho Securities USA Inc. |
| Credit Suisse First Boston LLC | Morgan Stanley & Co., Incorporated |
| Daiwa Securities America Inc. | Nomura Securities International, Inc. |
| Deutsche Bank Securities Inc. | UBS Securities LLC |
| Dresner Kleinwort Wasserstein Securities LLC | |

Source: Primary Dealer List—Federal Reserve Bank of New York, February 8, 2007.

**Key URL:**

The role of government security dealers in supporting the market for government securities is discussed in the publications of the Federal Reserve Bank of New York. See especially Primary Dealer Lists—Federal Reserve Bank of New York at **newyorkfed .org/markets/ pridealers-listing.htm**

The term *primary dealer* simply means that a dealer firm is qualified to trade securities directly with the Federal Reserve Bank of New York in order to assist the U.S. central bank in achieving its monetary policy objectives. To join the Fed's primary dealer list, the firm must agree to be available to trade securities at all times and to post adequate capital. Close to half of all primary dealer firms are controlled by corporations located outside the United States, including dealers with roots in Canada, Japan, France, Germany, and Great Britain. Many customers prefer to trade only with primary dealers. Moreover, achieving primary dealership status gives foreign dealers a solid foothold in U.S. markets. The primary dealers agree to "meaningfully participate" in trading with the Federal Reserve at any time the Fed wishes, to make "realistic" bids, and to trade continuously in the full range of government securities.

## 10.5 Dealer Borrowing and Lending Activities in the Money Market

Government security dealers supply a huge volume of T-bills and other securities daily to the financial marketplace. To do so, these dealers depend heavily on the *money market* for borrowed funds. Most dealer houses invest little of their own equity in the business. The bulk of operating capital is obtained through borrowings from banks and other institutions. A major dealer firm carries hundreds of millions of dollars in securities in its trading portfolio, with 95 percent or more of that portfolio supported by short-term loans, some carrying only 24-hour maturities.

### *Demand Loans for Dealers*

Among the most frequently used sources of dealer funds are demand loans from the largest banks and repurchase agreements (RPs) with banks and other lenders. Every day major banks post interest rates at which they are willing to make short-term loans to dealers. Generally, one rate is quoted on new loans and a second (lower) rate is **demand loan** posted for renewals of existing loans. A **demand loan** may be called in at any time if the banks need cash in a hurry. Such loans are virtually riskless, however, because they usually are collateralized by U.S. government securities, which may be transferred temporarily to the lending bank or to its agent.

| EXHIBIT 10.7 | Example of a Typical RP Loan Transaction | | | |
|---|---|---|---|---|
| | **Security Dealer** | | **Manufacturing Company** | |
| | Assets | Liabilities | Assets | Liabilities |
| a. Lender of funds—a manufacturing company—has a $1 million surplus in its cash account. | | | Deposit at bank +$1 million | |
| b. A security dealer and the company settle on an RP with the dealer using the borrowed funds to buy securities. | Securities held +$1 million | RP borrowing from manufacturer +$1 million | Deposit at bank −$1 million  RP loan to security dealer + $1 million | |
| c. The RP agreement is concluded and the funds returned (plus interest). | Dealer's cash account −$1 million | RP borrowing from manufacturer −$1 million | Deposit at bank +$1 million  RP loan to security dealer − $1 million | |

## Repurchase Agreements (RPs) for Dealers and Other Money Market Participants

**repurchase agreement (RP)**

A popular alternative to the demand loan is the **repurchase agreement (RP).** Under this agreement, the dealer sells securities to a lender but makes a commitment to buy back the securities at a later date at a fixed price plus interest. Thus, *RPs are simply a temporary extension of credit collateralized by marketable securities.* Some RPs are for a set length of time (*overnight* or *term RPs*), while others, known as *continuing contracts,* carry no explicit maturity date but may be terminated by either party on short notice. Larger banks provide both demand loans and RPs to dealers, and larger banks, in turn, borrow from dealers and other nonbank institutions through RPs in order to avoid deposit reserve requirements and prohibitions against their paying interest on demand deposit accounts. Moreover, nonfinancial corporations have provided a growing volume of funds to dealers through RPs in recent years. Other lenders active in the RP market include state and local governments, insurance companies, and foreign financial institutions who find the market a convenient, relatively low-risk way to invest temporary cash surpluses that may be retrieved quickly when the need arises.

The typical RP loan transaction can be described easily through the use of T accounts (which display changes to a balance sheet) for a dealer and for the lender of funds. Exhibit 10.7 presents a typical example of such a loan. In this case, we assume a manufacturing company has a temporary $1 million cash surplus. The company is eager to loan its temporary cash surplus right away to avoid losing even a single day's interest, while the dealer wishes to borrow at the low-cost RP loan rate in order to purchase interest-bearing securities. The borrowing dealer and the lending company agree on a $1 million RP loan—the minimum loan usually made in this market—collateralized by Treasury bills, with the dealer agreeing to buy back the bills within a few days and to pay the interest on the loan. Normally, securities that form the collateral for the RP are placed in a custodial account held by a third party. When the loan is repaid, the dealer's RP liability is automatically canceled and the securities are returned to the dealer.

There is evidence that this safety device of placing securities involved in an RP agreement into a separate custodial account has not always been scrupulously followed in the past. Moreover, because the majority of outstanding RP loans are simply recorded as book entries at the Federal Reserve banks, verification of what has been done with the pledged securities can be difficult. The result is that if a dealer goes out of business, a customer lending money under an RP to that dealer may have difficulty recovering the securities pledged as collateral behind the loan. Following the collapse of several dealer firms and the failure of several savings and loan associations that lost millions of dollars from inadequately collateralized security loans to those same dealers, federal authorities imposed stricter reporting requirements on the dealers. The Government Securities Act, passed in 1986, granted the U.S. Treasury additional oversight authority to protect the public from "unscrupulous" dealers. Under the act, new rules require written contracts between dealers and investors lending them money that describe where the securities in the RP are held. These written contracts also must specify whether other securities can be substituted for those held as loan collateral, and note that RPs are not protected by federal deposit insurance. The Securities and Exchange Commission and the federal banking agencies must enforce any rules for the government securities market that the Treasury Department writes.

Until recently, RPs were principally overnight transactions or expired in a few days. Today, however, there is a substantial volume of one- to three-month agreements, and some carry even longer maturities. The interest rate on RPs is the return that a dealer must pay a lender for the temporary use of money and is closely related to other money market interest rates. The RP (or repo) rate is based on the differences between the underlying security's current price and the agreed-upon future repurchase price. Usually, the securities pledged behind an RP are valued at their current market prices plus accrued interest (on coupon-bearing securities) less a small "haircut" (discount) to reduce the lender's exposure to market risk. The longer the term and the riskier and less liquid the securities pledged behind an RP, the larger the "haircut" will be to protect the lender in case security prices fall. Periodically, RPs are "marked to market," and if the price of the pledged securities has dropped, the borrower may have to pledge additional collateral.

Interest income from repurchase agreements is determined from the formula:

$$\frac{\text{RP interest}}{\text{income}} = \frac{\text{Amount}}{\text{of loan}} \times \frac{\text{Current}}{\text{RP rate}} \times \frac{\text{Number of days loaned}}{360 \text{ days}} \qquad (10.1)$$

For example, an overnight loan of $100 million to a dealer at a 7 percent RP rate would yield interest income of $19,444.44. That is,

$$\text{RP interest income} = \$100{,}000{,}000 \times .07 \times \frac{1}{360} = \$19{,}444.44$$

**Key URL:**

The interest rates on repurchase agreements (RPs) and other developments in the RP market may be traced through such Web sites as the Federal Reserve Bank of New York at **ny.frb .org**

Under a continuing contract RP, the interest rate changes daily, so the calculation above would be made for each day the funds were loaned, and the total interest owed would be paid to the lender when the contract is ended by either party. The current RP rate is usually close to the federal funds interest rate (which we will discuss in Chapter 11) as well as the prevailing Treasury bill rate.

## A New Type of RP: The GCF Repo

As we have seen, repurchase agreements are very important in the operations of the primary dealers. Today RPs finance more than $3 trillion of dealers' security holdings annually. However, traditional RPs are somewhat inflexible and more costly than they need to be. In 1998, as described by Fleming and Garbade [4], the Fixed Income Clearing Corporation (FICC) and two dealer-clearing banking firms—J. P. Morgan

The terrorist attacks of September 2001 affected many areas of the financial system, not the least of which was the market for RPs. In the immediate wake of the attacks in New York and Washington, DC, thousands of investors rushed to buy government securities as a "safe haven" for their funds. This action resulted in a serious shortage of Treasury notes in the dealer market, because the dealers needed these instruments to serve as collateral for their borrowings carried out through RPs.

The RP market soon began to experience "failed" trades. Dealers who had promised to return government securities that they had borrowed could not do so. Many investors holding government securities simply declined to lend them to anyone, including dealers.

The result was a form of "systemic risk"—similar to the game of dominoes. When one dealer couldn't deliver the securities it had promised to provide another dealer, the second dealer couldn't honor its own delivery commitments, and so on.

The U.S. Treasury quickly responded to this problem in the $600 billion-a-day Treasury security market with a rarely used move—it borrowed money when it didn't need to! The Treasury simply held emergency auctions and sold notes. The result was an expansion in the supply of available T-notes, making it easier for dealers to cover their positions and raise funds. Simultaneously, the Federal Reserve began lending T-notes out of its own portfolio to the primary dealers it works with on a regular basis. A potentially serious financial crisis was avoided.

Chase and the Bank of New York—stepped in to create a General Collateral Finance (GCF) Repo which subsequently has grown rapidly.

Prior to the appearance of GCF Repos, each RP transaction involving a particular dealer was settled independently of all other RP transactions, trade by trade. A dealer with multiple RPs outstanding could not settle the *net* amount owed to and received from all other parties in the market. Moreover, dealers had less flexibility in choosing the collateral they must pledge behind an RP (usually having to specify by 11 AM which securities they planned to deliver and post later that same afternoon). Significant changes in collateral pledged often resulted in the costly renegotiation of existing RP agreements. However, with the new GCF Repos, dealers working through a central clearinghouse—the FICC—are allowed to make changes in the securities they will ultimately deliver as collateral until late in the day (usually until 4:30 PM), thus giving the borrowing institution greater control over its collateral. Moreover, each dealer can *net* out the amount of its RP lending and borrowing activity with the FICC, resulting in a smaller volume of payments, fewer instruments actually changing hands, and reduced transactions costs and trading risks.

## Sources of Dealer Income

The primary dealers take substantial risks to make a market for new Treasury bills and other financial instruments. To be sure, the securities they deal in are among the highest-quality instruments available in the financial marketplace. However, the prices of even top-quality securities can experience rapid declines if interest rates rise. Moreover, established dealer houses cannot run and hide but are obliged to stand ready at all times to buy and sell on customer demand, regardless of the condition of the market. In contrast to securities brokers, who merely bring buyers and sellers together, dealers take a *position of risk,* which means that they act as principals in the buying and selling of securities, adding any securities purchased to their own portfolios.

Dealers stand ready to buy specified types of securities at an announced *bid* price and to sell them at an announced *asked* price. This is called *making a market* in a particular financial instrument. The dealer hopes to earn a profit from such market-making activities in part from the positive spread between bid and asked prices for the same security. This spread varies with market activity and the outlook for interest rates but is narrow on bills (often about $50 per $1 million or less). Spreads range higher on longer-term securities, on small transactions, and on securities not actively traded due to greater risk and greater cost.

As we have seen, the dealers' holdings of securities are financed by borrowing, so their portfolio positions are extremely sensitive to fluctuations in interest rates. For this reason, dealers frequently shift from long positions to short positions, depending on the outlook for interest rates. A **long position** means that the dealers have purchased securities outright, taken title to them, and will hold them in their portfolios until a customer comes along. Long positions typically increase in a period of falling interest rates. A **short position,** on the other hand, means that dealers have sold securities they do not presently own to a customer. In doing so, they hope the prices of those securities will fall (and interest rates rise) before they must acquire the securities and make delivery. Obviously, if interest rates fall (and security prices rise), the dealer will experience capital gains on a long position but losses on a short position. On the other hand, if interest rates rise (resulting in a drop in security prices), the dealer's long position will experience capital losses, and the short position will post a gain.

**long position**

**short position**

In periods when interest rates are expected to rise, dealers typically reduce their long positions and go short. Conversely, expectations of falling rates lead dealers to increase their long positions and avoid short sales. By correctly anticipating interest rate movements, the dealer can earn sizable *position profits.* Dealers also receive **carry income,** the difference between interest earned on securities they hold and their cost of borrowing funds. Generally, dealers earn higher rates of return on the securities they hold than the interest rates they pay for loans, but this is not always so. Because most dealer borrowings are short term, they normally are better off if the yield curve is positively sloped.

**carry income**

To help reduce exposure to risk, security dealers have recently diversified the revenue-generating services they offer. Some dealer firms now trade in foreign currencies, commodities (such as oil), security options, futures contracts, and swap contracts. Leading dealers—for example, Merrill Lynch & Co. and Citigroup Global Markets—offer cash management services in which they hold the funds of customers and invest them in securities, earning cash management fees from those same customers. Dealers have also tried to stabilize their income by acting much like banks and other financial intermediaries, simultaneously borrowing and lending money through a technique known as *matched book,* in which funds are borrowed through low-cost short-term RPs and then are loaned out through longer-term, higher-yielding RPs. (See, for example, Exhibit 10.8.) The yield spread between these "matched" RPs gives the dealer a net profit unless, of course, the slope of the yield curve suddenly changes and the dealer is forced to borrow short-term money at significantly higher interest rates.

## *Dealer Positions in Securities*

Dealer holdings of U.S. government and other securities are both huge and subject to erratic fluctuations. For example, in 1991 the dealers held a massive net long position in U.S. government securities of nearly $20 billion before falling to a sizable net short position of −$3.3 billion early in 1992. Late in 2006 government security dealers once

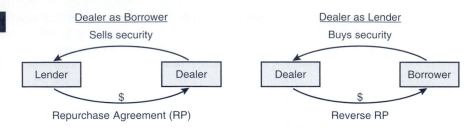

**EXHIBIT 10.8**

**Repurchase Agreements (RPs) as a Vehicle for Dealers in Securities and Other Financial Institutions to Borrow and Lend Money**

again held a substantial net short position in U.S. Treasury bills, notes, and bonds, but revealed a massive long position in federal agency securities, corporate bonds, and mortgage-backed securities.

Why is there often a tremendous difference in the size and direction of dealer portfolios from year to year? Interest rate movements and interest rate expectations explain a substantial proportion of the changes we observe in dealer positions. For example, in 1991–92 an economic recession drove short-term interest rates sharply lower, holding out the lure of much higher profits if the dealers could shift their holdings into a long position. In contrast, as the new twenty-first century unfolded many dealers feared inflation might rise, pushing market interest rates higher and leading to big losses on dealers' long positions. Other dealers, however, held a contrary opinion, suggesting that inflation might soon be brought under control, allowing the Federal Reserve and perhaps other central banks around the world to push interest rates lower, permitting savvy dealers eventually to profit from any long positions they might hold in corporate, mortgage-backed, and federal agency bonds. Only time would tell which view of market outlook would turn out to be right.

Dealers make heavy use of interest rate hedging tools today to further protect their portfolios from losses due to changes in interest rates. They are active participants in the *financial futures* markets and also are making increased use of *forward commitments,* in which a dealer sells securities but does not deliver to the customer until later. A dealer often does not hold the securities to be delivered under the forward commitment but waits to acquire them near the promised delivery date. This strategy minimizes risk of loss due to interest rate changes because the dealer is exposed to risk for only a brief period before delivery is made.

## Dealer Transactions and Government Security Brokers

Trading among dealers and between dealers and their customers amounts to billions of dollars each day. Indeed, so large is the government securities market that the volume of trading often exceeds the total volume of trading on many of the world's stock exchanges. Government securities dealers trade among themselves usually through *brokers.* Government security brokers do not take investment positions themselves but try to match bids and offers placed with them by dealers and other investors. Each broker operates a closed-circuit TV network showing dealer prices and quantities available. These half-dozen interdealer brokers make price and trade information efficiently available and allow the dealers to remain anonymous in their trading.

Intense competition generally exists among government-security brokers. During the 1990s, for example, a "price war" broke out among leading brokerage houses in which commissions were cut by 50 percent or more and volume discounts were offered to the largest dealers. In some cases, dealers were told that if they placed a specified minimum volume of orders each month, any subsequent trades during that same month would be handled free of charge by the advertising broker. The principal motivation for the sudden appearance of "bargain" brokerage rates was a sharp decline in trading volume, related to a slowdown in the economy.

Dealerships are a cutthroat business in which each dealer is out to maximize its returns from trading, even if gains must be made at the expense of competing dealers. Indeed, market analysts housed within each dealer firm study the daily price quotations of competitors. If one dealer temporarily underprices securities (offering excessively generous yields), other dealers are likely to rush in before the offering firm has a chance to correct its mistake. It is a business with little room for the inexperienced or slow-moving trader and fraught with low margins and unstable earnings. For example, in 1982 two major firms—Drysdale Government Securities, Inc., and Lombard-Wall, Inc.—collapsed. These closings were soon followed by four more dealer failures: Lion Capital Group, RTD Securities, E.S.M. Government Securities, and Bevill, Bresler & Schulman Asset Management Corporation. In 1989 and 1990, several foreign-owned dealers, including Britain's National Westminster Bank PLC, Lloyds Bank PLC, Midland Bank PLC, and L.F. Rothchilds & Co., as well as Australia's Westpac Banking Corporaton, withdrew from the Fed's primary dealer list due to falling trading volume and declining profit margins. U.S. primary dealer Drexel Burnham Lambert also withdrew from that list in 1990 and filed for protection under the federal bankruptcy code. With soaring competition both at home and abroad, several primary dealers have posted substantial net losses in recent years. Government security prices and interest rates appeared to become somewhat less volatile as the twenty-first century began. Unfortunately for the dealers, it is generally in periods of high price and rate volatility that these firms generate the most revenue, because the volume of security trading rises and there is more demand for interest rate risk protection at that time.

One of the most remarkable features of the dealer's business is how rapidly market conditions and the dealer's financial position can deteriorate. Large losses in tens of millions of dollars can be recorded in a few hours. Moreover, dealers may buy large quantities of bonds that are not yet issued (*when-issued securities*) without any money down and payment not due until delivery later on, only to discover that within minutes the market values of these securities have dropped like a stone. Yet the dealers are *essential* to the smooth functioning of the financial markets, to the successful placement of billions of dollars in securities issued each year, and to the successful pursuit of monetary policy by central banks.

## QUESTIONS TO HELP YOU STUDY

19. Explain why security dealers are essential to the smooth functioning of the securities markets and especially the money market.

20. What is a *demand loan*? How does it help security dealers obtain the financing they need?

21. What is a *repurchase agreement* (RP)? Explain what an RP's role is in financing the operations of security dealers.

22. In what different ways do security dealers generate *income* and make a profit?

23. To what types of *risk* is each form or source of dealer income subject? How might a dealer handle these different forms of risk exposure?

24. What causes the positions that dealers hold in securities to change over time?

## Summary of the Chapter's Main Points

This chapter has presented a broad overview of one of the most important components of any financial system, the *money market*. The chapter then explores the roles played by governments and security dealers in keeping the money market functioning efficiently.

- *Money markets* are defined as the collection of institutions and trading relationships that move short-term funds from lenders to borrowers. All money market loans have an original maturity of *one year or less*. Thus, money market transactions typically consist of credit flows from lenders and borrowers that last for only hours, days, weeks, or months, unlike the *capital markets,* where credit transactions may cover many years.

- Most loans extended in the money market are designed to provide short-term working capital to businesses and governments so they can purchase inventories, pay dividends and taxes, and deal with other immediate needs for cash. Their short-term cash needs arise from the fact that inflows and outflows of cash are *not* perfectly synchronized. In the real world, even with the best planning available, temporary cash deficits and temporary cash surpluses are more often the rule rather than the exception.

- Money market investors are typically conservative when it comes to placing their savings in financial instruments. They usually will accept little or no risk of borrower default, prefer financial instruments whose prices are stable, and usually require an investment from which their funds can be recaptured quickly (i.e., they prefer assets with high liquidity and marketability). The market's great sensitivity to risk helps explain why money market interest rates are among the lowest interest rates in the financial system.

- One of the most important of all institutions active in the money market is *government,* which sets the rules by which the money market operates and typically is among the largest of all money market borrowers. Indeed, the market for government securities sets the tone for the whole financial system in terms of interest rates, security prices, and the availability of credit to both governments and private borrowers. It is an indispensable tool for the government to finance its large volume of debt, and interest rates on government securities serve as reference rates for thousands of private loan contracts.

- Moreover, money market investors all over the globe rely upon government securities as a safe haven for their cash reserves. This is especially true of *Treasury bills,* which are direct government debt obligations with an original maturity of a year or less. And it is in this same market today that most government economic policy changes begin.

- At the heart of the government security market are *security dealers* that actively make markets for a broad range of government and private security issues. These dealers actively raise funds to support purchases of securities from their customers. Among their most important funds sources are *demand loans* from lenders and *repurchase agreements* negotiated with financial and nonfinancial corporations. Demand loans can be canceled at any time by the borrower or the lender and carry daily posted interest rates. Repurchase agreements are collateralized loans, using high-quality securities (especially government IOUs) as collateral.

## Key Terms Appearing in This Chapter

money market,  283
market or interest rate risk,  287
reinvestment risk,  287
default risk,  287
inflation (or purchasing power)
  risk,  287
currency risk,  287
political risk,  287
liquidity,  287
original maturity,  289
actual maturity,  289

federal funds,  289
clearinghouse funds,  290
U.S. Treasury bills,  292
auction,  293
primary dealers,  297
demand loan,  299
repurchase agreement (RP),  300
long position,  303
short position,  303
carry income,  303

## Problems and Issues

1.  Determine which of the following statements are *true* and which are *false*. For those that are *false,* identify and correct what makes them false.

    **a.** Government securities dealers rely principally on demand loans from banks for financing their purchase of RPs.

    **b.** Government securities dealers use collateral for the backing of RPs that they do not usually obtain until after they purchase the RP.

    **c.** Government securities brokers often trade government securities with dealers but do not incur interest rate risk in the process.

    **d.** Government securities brokers usually take short positions in government securities when interest rates are expected to be rising, and long positions when interest rates are expected to be falling.

2.  Adam is returning to college in the fall and has $5,000 saved for his tuition, with $2,500 to be paid at the beginning of September and $2,500 to be paid at the beginning of next January. He is considering the purchase of a new 3-month T-bill with $2,500, and upon maturity placing the proceeds in an interest-bearing checking account in order to earn some interest income until he needs those funds for his January tuition. This investment strategy exposes Adam to:

    **a.** reinvestment risk that interest rates will rise after he makes the investment.

    **b.** reinvestment risk that interest rates will fall after he makes the investment.

    **c.** market risk that interest rates will rise after he makes the investment.

    **d.** market risk that interest rates will fall after he makes the investment.

3.  How much interest would be earned (on a simple interest basis) from a three-day money market loan for $1 million at an interest rate of 12 percent (annual rate)? Suppose the loan was extended on the third day for an additional day at the going market rate of 11 percent. How much total interest income would the money market lender receive?

4.  A government securities dealer is currently borrowing $25 million from a money center bank using repurchase agreements based on Treasury bills. If today's RP

rate is 6.25 percent, how much in interest will the dealer owe the bank for a 24-hour loan?

5. Suppose that a dealer borrows cash through a $40 million RP from a manufacturing corporation for one day. If the dealer will have to pay $3,500 in interest on this loan, what is the current RP loan rate?

6. An automobile company, NISSAN, has a temporary cash surplus and lends its funds overnight through a repurchase agreement to a government securities dealer, earning $55,600 in interest income when the RP loan rate stood at 5.70 percent. What was the size of the loan that NISSAN granted to the securities dealer?

7. Ninety-one-day Treasury bills carry an investment return (IR) of 6.25 percent. What is their purchase price? What is their discount rate (DR)?

 8. A dealer in government securities is considering buying $875 million in 10-year Treasury notes and $1,425 million dollars in 6-month Treasury bills. Current yields on the T-notes average 7.15 percent, while 6-month T-bill yields average 3.28 percent. The dealer can currently borrow $2,300 million through one-week repurchase agreements at an interest rate of 3.20 percent. Compute the dealer's expected carry income in each of the following scenarios. (Hint: A spreadsheet can be most useful here. Perform the succession of calculations for the T-note in row 1; the succession of calculations for the T-bill in row 2; and the expenses from the RP in the row 3. Then, compute the carry income from the appropriate columns where income and expenses have been computed for each scenario.)

a. The dealer purchases the T-notes and T-bills and finances them with the RP under the terms listed above.

b. Same as part (a) above except that interest rates change to 7.30 percent on the T-notes, 5.40 percent on the T-bills and 5.55 percent on the RP, and the dealer must refinance the T-note and T-bill purchases at the new RP rate.

c. Same as part (b) above except the dealer had not purchased the T-notes and T-bills until *after* interest rates changed.

d. Repeat part (b) in the case where rates changed to 7 percent on the T-notes, 5.10 percent on the T-bills, and 4.5 percent on the RP.

e. Repeat part (b) except the dealer had not purchased the T-notes and T-bills until *after* the interest rates changed.

f. Based on the above results, is it always good for the dealer when interest rates rise? How about when they fall? Please explain.

g. Could the dealer have benefited by a short position in case (b) or (d) above? Please explain.

## Web-Based Problems

1. Visit one of today's sources of financial news (such as *The Wall Street Journal*) where you can find a complete listing of all U.S. Treasury securities along with the trading activity from the previous day. Identify the T-bills with 14, 91, and 182 days to maturity (or as close to these terms as you can find).

a. Which of these U.S. Treasury securities have the lowest yield to maturity?

b. Based on the information from part (a) how would you describe the slope of the yield curve over the maturity range covered by T-bills?

c. Does your answer to part (b) suggest anything about how the slope of the yield curve in the less-than-one-year maturity range changed as a result of the previous day's trading activity?

d. If there was a change reported in part (c) and if this change would have been due exclusively to a changed perception of future inflation by the financial markets, would the markets have raised or lowered their expectations for inflation?

2. Some of the largest government securities dealers are called "primary dealers" because they are authorized to deal directly with the Federal Reserve. However, these dealers also engage in many other types of transactions involving the purchase and sale of U.S. Treasury securities, federal agency securities, mortgage-backed securities, and corporate securities. (You will learn about each of these instruments in the chapters that follow.) The purpose of this exercise is to understand how important these dealers are to the market for Treasuries—the principal market through which the Federal Reserve conducts monetary policy. In answering the following questions, you will consider both their outright purchases and sales from their portfolios and their RP transactions.

a. Visit the Web site for the Federal Reserve Bank of New York at ny.frb.org, pull down the menu for "Markets," and click on "Primary Dealers."

b. Go to the section on the "Weekly Release of Primary Dealer Transactions" and compute the ratio of total outright transactions in U.S. government securities to the total of all transactions listed for this group of dealers. What do you conclude about the relative importance of trading in U.S. Treasuries for primary dealers?

c. Compute the ratio of outright transactions in Treasuries with nondealers ("other") to the total transactions of primary dealers with nondealers. How does this alter your view of the relative importance of trading in U.S. securities for primary dealers?

d. Compute the ratio of total transactions within the primary dealer group to total transactions. What do you conclude about the need for dealers to trade with each other in order for the group as a whole to perform its particular role as financial intermediary more efficiently?

## Selected References to Explore

1. Adrian, Tobias, and Michael J. Fleming. "What Financing Data Reveal about Dealer Leverage?" *Current Issues in Economics and Finance,* Federal Reserve Bank of New York, Vol. 11, No. 3 (March 2005), pp. 1–7.

2. Bartzsch, Nikolaus; Ben Craig; and Falko Fecht. "The Eurosystem Money Market Auctions: A Banking Perspective," *Working Paper 05/06,* Federal Reserve Bank of Cleveland, May 2005.

3. Dupoint, Dominique, and Brian Sack. "The Treasury Securities Market: Overview and Recent Developments," *Federal Reserve Bulletin,* December 1999, pp. 785–806.

4. Fleming, Michael J., and Kenneth D. Garbade. "The Repurchase Agreement Refined: The GCF Repo," *Current Issues in Economics and Finance,* Federal Reserve Bank of New York, June 2003, pp. 1–7.

5. Fleming, Michael J. "Repurchase Agreements with Negative Interest Rates," *Current Issues in Economics and Finance,* Federal Reserve Bank of New York, Vol. 10, No. 5 (April 2004), pp. 1–7.

6. Fleming, Michael J., and Kenneth D. Garbade. "Who Buys Treasury Securities at Auction?" *Current Issues in Economics and Finance,* Federal Reserve Bank of New York, Vol. 13, No. 1 (January 2007), pp. 1–7.

7. Garbade, Kenneth D., and Jeffrey F. Ingber. "The Treasury Auction Process: Objectives, Structure, and Recent Adaptations," *Current Issues in Economics and Finance,* Federal Reserve Bank of New York, Vol. 11, No. 2 (February 2005), pp. 1–11.

# Chapter 11

# Commercial Banks, Major Corporations, and Federal Credit Agencies in the Money Market

## Learning Objectives

### in This Chapter

- You will discover several of the most important ways that *banks* and other depository institutions borrow and lend funds and supply other critical services needed in the money market.

- You will explore the nature and characteristics of one of the oldest of all money market instruments—*commercial paper*—and discover the important roles played by large corporations in both borrowing and lending funds in the money market.

- You will learn how *federal credit agencies,* by borrowing funds from the money market, provide financial aid to several sectors of the economy (including agriculture, home buyers, and small businesses).

- You will see *internationalization* at work in the money market, which efficiently allocates scarce capital almost everywhere on the planet.

## What's in This Chapter?
## Key Topics Outline

The Key Roles Banks Play in the Money Market

The Federal Funds Market: Source of Bank Funding and a Vehicle for Public Policy

Negotiable CDs Sold by Banks: Origins, Growth, and Innovations

Creating Eurocurrency Deposits in International Banking

The Growth and Decline of Bankers' Acceptances

Major Corporations in the Money Market: Commercial Paper

The Rapid Expansion of Federal Credit Agencies

## 11.1   Introduction

In the previous chapter we examined the central characteristics of money market instruments and described the critical roles played by governments and securities dealers in the daily functioning of the money market. We learned of the importance of two key markets—for Treasury bills and repurchase agreements—that take center stage in many money market transactions. In this chapter we explore the contributions to the global money market made by *commercial banks, major corporations,* and *government-sponsored credit agencies.* We will focus on the key money market instruments that originate with these institutions, including federal funds, negotiable CDs, Eurocurrency deposits, bankers' acceptances, commercial paper, and agency securities. As you will see, these institutions frequently work on both sides of the money market—often lending and borrowing short-term money at the same time. They are also among the most innovative and interesting of the thousands of participants trading in the money market every day.

## 11.2   The Roles Played by Banks in the Money Market

The single most important privately owned institution in most money markets is the *commercial bank.* Large money center banks, such as those headquartered in New York City, London, Paris, Tokyo, and a handful of other major cities around the globe, provide billions of dollars in funds daily through the money market to governments and corporations in need of cash. As we saw in the previous chapter, bank loans and repurchase agreements are a principal source of financing for dealers in

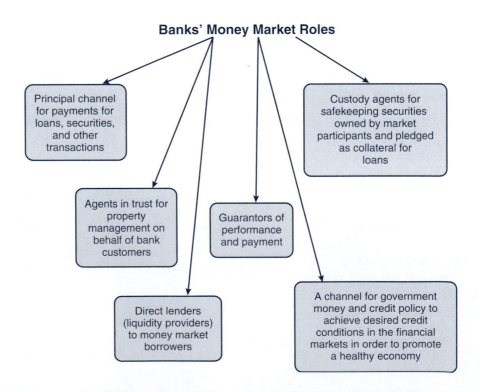

**Banks' Money Market Roles**

- Principal channel for payments for loans, securities, and other transactions
- Agents in trust for property management on behalf of bank customers
- Direct lenders (liquidity providers) to money market borrowers
- Guarantors of performance and payment
- A channel for government money and credit policy to achieve desired credit conditions in the financial markets in order to promote a healthy economy
- Custody agents for safekeeping securities owned by market participants and pledged as collateral for loans

securities, while banks also make large purchases of Treasury bills and other money market securities. Banks support private corporations borrowing in the money market, both by purchasing their securities and by granting lines of credit to backstop a new security issue. Banks supply credit to support the movement of goods in domestic and international trade. And both large and small banks today readily lend their cash reserves to other financial institutions and to industrial corporations to cover short-term liquidity needs.

For banks to lend huge amounts of funds daily in the money market, they must also borrow heavily in that market. The owners (stockholders) supply only a minor portion of a commercial bank's total resources; the bulk of bank funds must be *borrowed.* The majority of bank borrowings come from *deposits,* but a growing portion of the industry's financing needs is supplied directly by the *money market.* However, bank managers today are often cautious in their use of money market borrowings. Such funds can be expensive to use at times, and their interest cost is more volatile than for most kinds of deposits. Many banks follow the strategy of maintaining a roughly equal balance between their lending and borrowing activities in the money market. The volume of short-term bank debt is counterbalanced by a nearly equal volume of short-term bank assets.[1]

In this chapter, we examine three of the most important money market sources of funds for banks and other deposit-type financial institutions: *federal funds, negotiable certificates of deposit (CDs),* and *Eurocurrency deposits.* We will also discuss a device sometimes used by international banks to fund the expansion of global trade—the *bankers' acceptance.*

## 11.3 Federal Funds Provided by the Banking System

**federal funds**

As we saw in the introductory chapter to the money market (Chapter 10), **federal funds** are among the most important of all money market instruments for one key reason: *Fed funds are the principal means of making payments in the money market.* By definition, federal funds are any monies available for immediate payment ("same-day money"). They are generally transferred from one depository institution to another by simple bookkeeping entries requested by online computer, by wire, or by telephone after a purchase of securities is made or a loan is granted or repaid.

### The Nature of Federal Funds and Their Uses

The name *federal funds* came about because, early in the development of the market, the principal source of immediately available money was the reserve balance each member bank of the Federal Reserve System had to keep at the Federal Reserve bank in its region of the United States. If one bank needed to transfer funds to another, it needed only contact the Federal Reserve bank in its district, and funds were readily transferred into the appropriate reserve account—a transaction accomplished in seconds by telephone, telegraph, or, more recently, by computer.

---

[1]The idea of maintaining a roughly *equal* balance between borrowing and lending in the money market follows one of the oldest concepts in the field of finance: the *hedging principle.* As discussed in Chapter 7, in a world of uncertainty, borrowers of funds can reduce their liquidity risk by matching the maturity of their assets and liabilities. This approach reduces the risk of borrowing when funds are not needed and lowers the risk of not having sufficient cash when bills come due.

Today, however, the Fed funds market is far broader in scope than just reserves on deposit with the Federal Reserve banks. For example, virtually all depository institutions keep funds with large correspondent banks in central cities; these deposits may be transferred readily by telephone, by computer, or by wire from the account of one bank to that of another. They also may be borrowed by the institution that holds the correspondent deposit, simply by transferring funds from the correspondent deposit to an account titled "Federal funds purchased" and reversing these entries when the loan matures. Savings associations and credit unions maintain deposits with commercial banks or with the Federal Reserve banks that also are available for immediate transfer to a customer or to another financial institution. Business corporations and state and local governments can lend federal funds by executing repurchase agreements with securities dealers, banks, and other funds traders. Securities dealers who have received payment for securities sold can turn around and make their funds immediately available to borrowers through the federal funds market. Without question, however, the most important of all borrowers in the Fed funds market are *commercial banks.*

## Use of the Federal Funds Market to Meet Reserve Requirements

**legal reserve requirement**

Banks and other depository institutions *must* hold in a special legal reserve account liquid assets equal to a fraction of the funds deposited with them by the public. Banks are aided in this endeavor by the fact that their **legal reserve requirement** is calculated on a daily average basis over a two-week period, known as the *reserve computation period.* For example, the reserve computation period for *transaction deposits* (e.g., checking accounts) stretches from a Tuesday through a Monday two weeks later. The Federal Reserve calculates the daily average level of transaction deposits held by each depository institution over this two-week period and then multiplies that average by the required reserve percentage (3 percent for smaller banks and 10 percent for larger banks, for example) to determine the amount of legal reserves that must be held by each institution. These legal reserves must average the required amount over a two-week period known as the *reserve maintenance period.*

The manager of each depository institution's *money desk*—the department responsible for keeping track of the depository's legal reserve position—must adjust each institution's reserve balance at the district Federal Reserve bank to the right level over the two-week reserve maintenance period. The federal funds market is an indispensable tool for this kind of daily reserve management, especially for the largest and most aggressive banks that hold few reserves of their own. Indeed, many large banks today borrow virtually all of the legal reserves behind their deposits from the federal funds market.

## Mechanics of Federal Funds Trading

The mechanics of federal funds trading vary depending on the locations of buying (borrowing) and selling (lending) institutions. For example, suppose two banks involved in a federal funds transaction are located in the heart of the New York money market. These banks could simply exchange checks. The borrowing bank could be handed a check drawn on the lending bank's reserve account at the Federal Reserve Bank of New York. This check is payable immediately ("same-day money"), and therefore Fed funds would be transferred to the borrower's reserve account before the close of business that same day. The lender, on the other hand, may be given a check drawn on

The federal funds market in the United States is not the only market for interbank loans. Banks in many other countries have established a market for making loans of reserves to each other. While the U.S. Fed funds market works well, sometimes foreign interbank markets run into trouble with serious consequences for the rest of the economy. A dramatic example of how troubles in interbank lending can send tremors through a country's financial system occurred in Russia during the 1990s.

Newspaper stories and rumors spread through Russia's banking system to the effect that several Russian banks were not sound. Accordingly, many of Russia's more than 2,500 banks then in operation simply stopped extending loans to one another. Many Russian bankers indicated they could not get enough information on other banks to decide whether these banks were solvent enough to pay back their interbank

loans. The overnight market for ruble-denominated deposits ground to a halt, and some banks offered interest rates as high as 1,000 percent in an effort to get a loan! Moreover, with bankers not trusting each other, the Russian public began to mistrust their banks, resulting in scores of depositors demanding to retrieve their funds.

Many observers were concerned that the Russian banking system might collapse. One possible solution was to have Russia's central bank grant loans to banks in trouble. Only a few days into the crisis, the central bank began buying publicly held government bonds in order to flood the system with liquidity. However, over the longer term, reform of the Russian banking system to clarify regulations, install risk-management systems, and require banks to release more information about their true financial condition was needed.

---

the borrower. This last check is "one-day money" (payable the following day) because it must pass through the New York clearinghouse for settlement. Thus, funds flow instantly to the borrowing bank's reserve account and are automatically returned to the lending bank's reserve account the next day or whenever the loan agreement terminates. In the past decade this process has been streamlined by computers connected online. For example, the lending bank can simply contact the Federal Reserve Bank of New York's computer and ask it to electronically move funds from the lender's reserve account to the borrower's reserve account immediately, with the transaction usually reversed the next day. Interest on the Fed funds loan may be included when the funds are returned, paid by separate check, or settled by debiting and crediting the appropriate correspondent balances.

If the transacting institutions are not both located within the same Federal Reserve district, the loan transaction proceeds in much the same way except that *two* Federal Reserve banks are involved. Once borrower and lender agree on the terms of a loan, the lending institution directly, or indirectly through a correspondent bank, contacts the Federal Reserve bank in its district, requesting an electronic transfer of federal funds. The Reserve bank then transfers reserves through the Fed's wire network (FEDWIRE) to the Federal Reserve bank serving the region where the borrowing institution is located. Funds travel the reverse route when the loan is terminated.

How do Fed funds borrowers and lenders contact each other to find out who has surplus funds to lend and who is short of funds? Computer networks and the telephone are the most common media for communicating between institutions in need of funds and those with surplus funds. In addition, a handful of *Fed funds brokers* active in the money market bring buying and selling institutions together, indicating via telephone and their computer network what funds are available and at what interest rate. In brief, there are three principal segments of the Fed funds market among banks today; (1) brokered funds; (2) nonbrokered direct loans among major banks; and

(3) correspondent rebookings, where smaller banks loan their excess reserves through the deposits they hold at large correspondent banks in money centers.

## Volume of Borrowings in the Funds Market

Banks borrow billions of dollars each day in the federal funds market. The large banks in New York City, by virtue of their strategic location at the heart of the domestic money market, still account for a disproportionate share of all Fed funds transactions. However, the market has broadened considerably in recent years to include both domestic and foreign banks in Atlanta, Chicago, San Francisco, and other major U.S. cities, as well as thousands of smaller banks in outlying areas.

Most federal funds loans are *overnight* (one-day) transactions or *continuing contracts* that have no specific maturity and can be terminated without advance notice by either party. One-day loans carry a fixed rate of interest, but continuing contracts often do not. There is a growing volume of loans lasting beyond one day. These longer-maturity interbank loans are usually called *term* federal funds and are being supplied increasingly by foreign banks, savings and loan associations, insurance companies, pension funds, and finance companies as a safe and profitable way to warehouse funds until they are needed for longer-term commitments.

## Interest Rates on Federal Funds

The federal funds interest rate is highly volatile from day to day, although on an annual basis, it tends to move roughly in line with other money market interest rates. The short-term volatility of the funds rate arises from substantial variations in the volume of funds made available by lenders each day and the size of daily cash deficits experienced by banks and other money market participants. The funds rate tends to be most volatile toward the close of the reserve maintenance period, depending on whether larger banks are flush with or short of reserves. There are also seasonal patterns, with the funds rate tending to rise around holiday periods when loan demand and deposit withdrawals are often heavy.

## Federal Funds and Government Economic Policy

**Key URLs:**
Key sources on the Web for following developments in the federal funds market include **ny.frb.org** and **frbatlanta.org/publica**

The federal funds market is an easy and riskless way to invest excess reserves for short periods and still earn some interest income. It is essential to the daily management of bank reserves, because credit can be obtained in a matter of minutes to cover emergency situations. Fed funds are also critical to the whole money market, because these funds serve as the principal means of payment for securities and loans. Moreover, the funds market transmits the effects of Federal Reserve monetary policy quickly throughout the banking system because the Fed routinely sets target levels for the federal funds interest rate and raises or lowers these targets, depending on whether the Fed wishes to slow down borrowing and spending in the economy or speed it up. Using daily open market operations—buying and selling securities—the Fed is able to push the funds rate in the desired direction on any given day. There appears to be a particularly close relationship between the federal funds interest rate target and the Federal Reserve's inflation target. The U.S. central bank tends to raise the federal funds rate when inflation in the prices of goods and services rises to a level the Fed finds unacceptable and tends to lower the funds rate when inflation declines.

Money market investors follow policy announcements of the Federal Reserve, as well as public statements made by Federal Reserve officials in speeches or in Congressional testimony, for clues as to which direction Federal Reserve monetary policy may be

## The Federal Funds Rate and the Rise of Sweep Accounts

Recently, the volume of legal reserves U.S. banks hold at the Federal Reserve banks has decreased substantially. Many banks have discovered a way to reduce their required reserve balances by rapidly switching funds out of customers' demand deposit accounts, which currently carry legal reserve requirements, into time and saving deposits, which carry *no* reserve requirements, often returning the funds to demand deposits the next day. These switching arrangements—known as *sweep accounts*—not only reduce a bank's required legal reserves but also allow some customers to earn interest on checking account balances. More than $200 billion in sweep account arrangements were in place by the beginning of the twenty-first century, and, partly as a result, legal reserve balances fell by more than half.

Unfortunately, one consequence of the decline in legal reserves was an apparent increase in the volatility of the federal funds interest rate because there were fewer reserves to be traded in the federal funds market. This increased volatility was of special concern because the federal funds rate is the Federal Reserve's prime instrumental target for achieving the goals of monetary policy. If the funds rate becomes too difficult to control, the Fed might have greater difficulty hitting its desired interest rate targets. The financial markets and the economy might become more difficult to control, and the public could become more confused about the central bank's true goals for money and credit.

It should be noted, however, that the apparent increased volatility of the federal funds interest rate has been modest and bank managers seem to have adjusted well to the changing funds rate environment. In part, this is due to the improved technology of communications between the Fed and the banks that keep reserve balances at the Federal Reserve's regional banks. For example, the Fed now makes it possible for bankers to monitor on their computer screens, on a real-time basis, debits and credits to individual legal reserve accounts so that managers can see more clearly how their reserve position stands and can better anticipate surpluses and deficits. Moreover, as we will see in Chapter 13, recent changes in the Fed's policy for administering its discount (loan) window will likely put a ceiling on future movements in the Fed funds rate and, thereby, lower the volatility of the Fed funds rate by eliminating "spikes" that would otherwise occur during periods when the demand for liquidity is particularly acute.

**Key URL:**
The key role of the federal funds market in aiding the central bank of the United States, the Federal Reserve System, in the conduct of monetary policy is discussed on several Web sites, especially the Intended Federal Funds Rate at **federalreserve. gov/fomc**

### QUESTIONS TO HELP YOU STUDY

1. Define the term *federal funds*. Why are federal funds so important to the functioning of the money market?

2. Who are the principal *borrowers* active in the federal funds market? Why are they attracted to this market for the funds they require?

3. Who are the principal *lenders* active in the federal funds market? Why do they find this market a good place to lend money?

4. Describe the process of legal reserve position adjustment that depository institutions go through. What role does the federal funds market play in helping depository institutions manage their so-called *money* or *legal reserve position*?

5. Why has the federal funds market become so important to the United States' central bank, the Federal Reserve System, in carrying out the government's *monetary policy* operations?

moving—toward tighter credit conditions and a higher federal funds rate or toward looser credit conditions with a lower federal funds rate. As we saw earlier in Chapter 9, investors are now able to hedge against unexpected or adverse changes in the federal funds rate through two relatively new instruments traded at the Chicago Board of Trade: a federal funds futures contract and an options contract on Fed funds futures. The prices and interest rates attached to these two contracts are sensitive to changing market expectations regarding future changes in the Federal Reserve's target for the Fed funds rate. Money market investors can "lock in" a particular interest rate on short-term borrowings or loans and obtain a glimpse of the market's forecast for future funds rate movements.

## 11.4 Negotiable Certificates of Deposit (CDs) Issued by Banks

**negotiable certificate of deposit (CD)**

One of the largest of all money market instruments, measured by dollar volume, is the **negotiable certificate of deposit (CD).** A CD is an interest-bearing receipt for funds left with a depository institution for a set period of time.[2] Banks and other deposit-type institutions issue many types of CDs, but true money market CDs are negotiable instruments that may be sold any number of times before reaching maturity and carry a minimum denomination of $100,000. The usual round-lot trading unit for money market CDs is $1 million.

The interest rate on a large negotiable CD is set by negotiation between the issuing institution and its customer and generally reflects prevailing market conditions. Therefore, like interest rates on other money market securities, CD interest rates rise in periods of tight money, when loanable funds are scarce, and fall in periods of easy money, when loanable funds are more abundant.

The negotiable CD is one of the youngest of all U.S. money market instruments. It dates from 1961, when First National City Bank of New York (later Citibank) began offering the instrument to its largest corporate customers. Simultaneously, a small group of dealers agreed to make a secondary (resale) market for CDs of $100,000 or more. Other money center banks soon entered the competition for corporate funds and began to offer their own CDs.

The decision to sell this new money market instrument was an agonizing one for banks because CDs tended to increase the average cost and volatility of bank funds. However, banks had little choice but to offer the new instrument or face the loss of billions of dollars in interest-sensitive deposits. The cash management departments of major corporations have become increasingly aware of the many profitable ways available to invest their short-term funds. Prior to the introduction of the negotiable CD, many bankers found their biggest corporate customers were reducing their deposits and buying Treasury bills and other money market instruments. The CD was developed to attract those lost deposits back into the banking system.

Negotiable CDs are a real success story for most banks. In 2007, large ($100,000+) time deposits outstanding at banks and thrifts operating in the United States totaled more than $1.7 trillion. This compares with only about $100 billion in large CDs roughly two decades earlier.

### *Terms Attached to CDs and Who Buys Them*

Negotiable CDs may be *registered* on the books of the issuing depository institution or issued in *bearer form* to the purchasing investor. CDs issued in bearer form are

---

[2]The minimum maturity permitted for CDs under federal regulation is seven days. There is no legal upper limit on CD maturities, however. Unlike T-bills, CDs must be issued at par and trade on an interest-bearing basis. Payment is made in federal funds on the day each CD matures.

more convenient for resale in the secondary market because they are in the hands of the investors who own them. Denominations range from $25,000 to $10 million, although CDs actively traded in the money market carry a minimum denomination of $100,000. Maturities range upward to around 18 months, depending on the customer's needs. However, most negotiable CDs have maturities of six months or less. CDs with maturities beyond one year are called *term* CDs.

Interest rates on newly issued CDs are computed as a yield to maturity but are quoted on a 360-day basis. The general formula to use is:

$$\text{Funds owed the depositor} = D + \frac{n}{360} \times D \times i \qquad (11.1)$$

**Key URL:**
Current yields available on negotiable CDs and the latest developments in the CD market can be followed daily via such Web sites as **bankrate.com**

where $D$ is the original deposit principal; $i$ is the promised yield to maturity based upon a 360-day year; and $n$ is the number of days that interest is earned. For example, if a business firm purchases a $100,000 negotiable CD for six months at an interest rate of 7.50 percent, it would receive back at the end of 180 days:

$$\$100,000 \times \left(1 + \frac{180}{360} \times 0.075\right) = \$103,750$$

To convert the yield on newly issued CDs to a true coupon-equivalent yield for a full 365-day year, that is, to determine the CD's true yield to maturity (YTM), we must multiply the 360-day-based yield ($i$) that is quoted by the issuing bank by the ratio 365:360. That is,

$$\text{YTM}_{\text{CDs}} = i \times \frac{365}{360} \qquad (11.2)$$

For example, a 360-day yield ($i$) of 6.25 percent for a CD would mean a coupon-equivalent return (YTM) for that same CD of:

$$\text{YTM} = 6.25 \text{ percent} \times \frac{365}{360} = 6.33 \text{ percent}$$

In the secondary (resale) market, yields on negotiable CDs are figured by the bank discount rate (DR) method that we described in Chapter 6. For example, a 6-month $100,000 CD bearing a 7.50 percent promised interest rate at maturity but sold three months (90 days) early for $98,200 would carry a discount yield (DR) of:

$$\text{DR}_{\text{CD}} = \frac{\$100,000 - \$98,200}{\$100,000} \times \frac{360}{90} = 7.20 \text{ percent}$$

As Exhibit 11.1 suggests, the yield on CDs normally is slightly above the Treasury bill rate due to greater default risk, a thinner resale market, and a state and local government tax exemption on earnings from Treasury bills. Because investors can easily *arbitrage* between short-term markets, moving funds toward the highest yields, the CD interest rate hovers close to the average of current and future federal funds interest rates expected by investors to prevail over the life of the CD and is also close to the Eurodollar deposit rates (discussed later in this chapter) posted in London each day. Of course, as Exhibit 11.1 also reminds us, the yield spread between CDs and other

| EXHIBIT 11.1 | **Key Money Market Interest Rates over Time—Average Annual Interest Rates Attached to U.S. Treasury Bills, Money Market CDs ($100,000 or more), Federal Funds, Commercial Paper, Eurodollar Deposits, and Prime Bank Loans** | | | | | | |
|---|---|---|---|---|---|---|---|
| | **Annual Period** | | | | | | |
| **Instrument** | **1985** | **1990** | **1995** | **2000** | **2002** | **2004** | **2006** |
| U.S. Treasury bills: | | | | | | | |
| Three-month | 7.47% | 7.50% | 5.49% | 5.82% | 1.61% | 1.37% | 4.73% |
| Six-month | 7.65 | 7.46 | 5.56 | 5.90 | 1.68 | 1.58 | 4.81 |
| Federal funds | 8.10 | 8.10 | 5.83 | 6.24 | 1.67 | 1.35 | 4.97 |
| Bank certificates of deposit: | | | | | | | |
| Three-month | 8.04 | 8.15 | 5.92 | 6.46 | 1.73 | 1.57 | 5.16 |
| Six-month | 8.24 | 8.17 | 5.98 | 6.59 | 1.81 | 1.74 | 5.24 |
| Eurodollar deposits, three-month | 8.27 | 8.16 | 5.93 | 6.45 | 1.73 | 1.55 | 5.19 |
| Nonfinancial commercial paper, three-month | 7.95 | 8.06 | 5.93 | 6.31 | 1.69 | 1.41 | 5.10 |
| Prime bank loan rate | 9.93 | 10.01 | 8.83 | 9.23 | 4.68 | 4.34 | 7.96 |

Source: Federal Reserve Board's Web site at **federalreserve.gov.**

Note: Bank CD rates are based upon weekly average rates quoted by five dealers. Treasury bill yields are those quoted in the secondary (resale) market on a bank discount basis extracted from daily closing bids. Commercial paper rates are quotes from leading dealer houses.

money market instruments varies over time, depending on investor preferences, the supply of CDs and other money market instruments, and the financial condition of issuing banks.

One of the most interesting developments in recent years has been the appearance of a *multitiered* (segmented) market for CDs. Investors have grouped issuing banks into different risk categories, and yields in the market are scaled accordingly. This development is a legacy of the collapse of such banking giants as Franklin National Bank of New York in 1974 and Continental Illinois Bank of Chicago in 1984. Faced with the spector of major bank failures, banks viewed as less stable by investors are usually compelled to issue their CDs at higher interest rates.

CDs from the largest and most financially sound banks are rated *prime;* smaller banks or those viewed as less stable issue *nonprime* CDs at higher interest rates. As is true for any depositor in a U.S. insured bank, the holder of a regular-type CD is covered against loss by the Federal Deposit Insurance Corporation up to $100,000 if the issuing bank fails. Unfortunately, this insurance is of limited value to a corporation holding a million-dollar or larger CD. However, holders of large CDs do help to discipline their banks from taking on excessive risk by threatening to withdraw their funds if the banks with which they trade become too risky.

## *Buyers of CDs*

The principal buyers of negotiable CDs include corporations, state and local governments, foreign central banks and governments, wealthy individuals, and a wide variety of financial institutions. The latter include insurance companies, pension funds, investment companies, savings banks, credit unions, and money market funds. Large CDs appeal to these investors because they are readily marketable at low risk, may be issued in any desired maturity, and carry a somewhat higher yield than that on Treasury bills. However, the investor gives up some marketability in comparison with T-bills because the resale market for CDs operates well below the average daily volume of trading in bills.

Most buyers hold CDs until they mature. However, prime-rate CDs issued by billion-dollar banks are actively traded in the secondary market. The purpose of the secondary market is principally to accommodate corporations that need cash quickly or see profitable opportunities from the sale of their deposits. Also, buyers of CDs who want shorter maturities or higher yields than are available on *new* CDs will enter the secondary market or redeem them in advance of maturity.

### New Types of CDs

Bankers have become increasingly innovative in packaging CDs to meet the needs of customers as the years have gone by. One notable innovation in CD history occurred in 1975, when the *variable-rate CD* was introduced. Variable, or floating-rate, CDs generally carry maturities out to five years, with an interest rate adjusted every 30, 90, or 180 days (known as a *leg* or *roll* period). The floating interest rate is usually tied to movements in the secondary-market yield on fixed-rate CDs, the prevailing federal funds interest rate, the prime bank rate, or the going market interest rate on Eurodollar deposits. A variable-rate CD may give the investor a higher return than normally would be obtained by continually renewing short-term CDs and is a popular investment for money market mutual funds.

Another innovation soon followed when Morgan Guaranty Trust (now part of JPMorgan Chase) in New York City introduced the *rollover* or *roly-poly CD*. Because 6-month CDs are the maximum maturity usually traded in the secondary market, Morgan offered its customers longer term CDs with higher rates, but in packages composed of a series of 6-month CDs extending for at least two years. Thus, the roly-poly CD promised higher returns plus the ability to market some CDs in the package early to meet emergency cash needs. However, the bank's customer was still obligated to purchase the remaining certificates on each six-month anniversary date until the contract expired.

Recent years have ushered in still more CD innovations: for example, *jumbo CDs, Yankee CDs, brokered CDs, bear and bull CDs, installment CDs, rising-rate CDs, adjustable-rate CDs,* and *foreign-index CDs. Jumbo CDs* are large ($100,000+), negotiable CDs issued by thrift institutions, such as savings and loan associations and savings banks. *Yankee CDs* are issued in the United States by foreign banks (mainly Japanese, Canadian, and European institutions) that usually have offices in U.S. cities. *Brokered CDs* consist of CDs sold through brokers or dealers in maximum $100,000 denominations to qualify for federal insurance. *Bear and bull CDs,* whose rates of return are linked to stock market performance, first appeared in the mid-1980s. *Installment CDs,* in contrast, allow customers to make a small initial deposit and then gradually build up the balance in the account to some target level. *Rising-rate CDs* are usually longer-term deposits whose promised yield increases over time with penalty-free withdrawals permitted on selected anniversary dates. *Adjustable-rate CDs* may extend up to 36 months in maturity and allow the investor to renegotiate the interest rate (obtain the current CD rate) once during the life of the CD in the event money market rates rise. Further innovations in CDs are likely in the future as banks struggle to adjust their fund-raising efforts in the face of increasingly stiff competition for funds.

---

## QUESTIONS TO HELP YOU STUDY

6. What is a large *negotiable* CD?

7. When were CDs first offered in the money market? Why were CDs developed?

8. What factors appear to influence the interest rate offered on CDs issued by a depository institution?

9. What is meant by the term *multitiered* market?

10. What is the difference between a *prime-* and a *nonprime-rated* CD? Which carries the higher interest rate? Why?

11. What is a variable-rate CD? A brokered CD? Is it likely that depository institutions will continue to develop and bring forward new types of CDs in the future? Why?

---

## 11.5   Eurocurrency Deposits in International Banks

**Eurocurrency Market**

Comparable to the domestic CD market, a chain of international money markets trading in deposits denominated in the world's most convertible currencies stretches around the globe. This so-called **Eurocurrency market** has arisen because of a tremendous need worldwide for funds denominated in dollars, euros, pounds, yen, and other relatively stable currencies. For example, as U.S. corporations have expanded their operations in Europe, Asia, and the Middle East, they have needed huge amounts of U.S. dollars to purchase machinery and other goods and to pay taxes. The same companies have also required large volumes of other national currencies to carry out transactions in the countries where they are represented. To meet these needs international banks headquartered in the world's key financial centers began during the 1950s to accept deposits from businesses, individuals, and governments denominated in currencies other than that of the host country and to make loans denominated in those same currencies.

**Key URLs:**
The nature and origins of the Eurocurrency markets are discussed in a wide range of publications prepared by the staff of the Federal Reserve Bank of New York at **ny. frb.org**, and for the Federal Reserve System as a whole at **federalreserve.gov**

One of the earliest sources of Eurocurrency deposits was the former Soviet Union, which, in the 1950s, moved huge amounts of dollar-denominated assets out of the United States in order to avoid sequestration (capture) of its funds by U.S. authorities. Anti-Soviet sentiment was then running high in the United States, and a number of highly publicized spy trials and Congressional hearings aroused the interest of the American public. A short time later, several large American banks themselves moved some of their dollar deposits abroad (especially to their Caribbean branch offices) to avoid restrictive U.S. regulations. Thus, the Eurocurrency market was born.

### What Is a Eurodollar?

**Eurodollars**

Because the dollar remains the chief international currency today, the market for Eurodollars is the leading component of the Eurocurrency markets. What are **Eurodollars?** They are deposits of U.S. dollars in banks located outside the United States. The banks in question record the deposits on their books in U.S. dollars, not in their home currency. The majority of Eurodollar (and other Eurocurrency) deposits are held in Europe and in Caribbean branch offices, but these deposits have spread worldwide.

Frequently, banks accepting Eurodollar deposits are foreign branches of U.S. banks. For example, in London—still the center of the Eurocurrency market today—branches of U.S. banks outnumber British banks and bid aggressively for deposits denominated in U.S. dollars. Many of these funds are loaned to the banks' home offices in the United States to meet reserve requirements and other liquidity needs. The remaining funds are loaned to private corporations and governments abroad. No one knows exactly how large the Eurodollar market is or how big the overall marketplace is for *all* Eurocurrency deposits. One reason is that the market is unregulated. Many banks refuse to disclose publicly their deposit balances in various currencies. Another reason for the relative lack of information on market activity is that Eurocurrencies are merely bookkeeping entries on a bank's ledger and not currencies. You cannot put Eurocurrency deposits in your pocket like bank notes or coins.

Eurocurrency deposits are continually on the move in the form of loans. They are employed to finance the import and export of goods, to supplement government tax revenues, to provide working capital for the foreign operations of multinational corporations, and to provide liquid reserves for the largest banks. In total, the Eurocurrency markets represent the largest of all money markets worldwide, with total funds probably exceeding $5 trillion.

Some experts believe Eurodollar growth eventually may slow or the volume of Eurodollar deposits may even decline as the European Union matures and the euro continues to grow in international prominence, creating a strong rival to U.S. dollars and dollar deposits. European central banks, for example, may have less need for U.S. dollar reserves as the European Community expands and may begin to dump some of their huge holdings of dollar-denominated assets, reducing the value of the U.S. dollar and U.S.-issued securities in international markets.

## The Creation of Eurocurrency Deposits

To illustrate how Eurocurrency deposits arise, we trace through a typical example. Our discussion is in terms of Eurodollars, but the reader should be aware that the process being described applies to *any* type of Eurocurrency deposit.

Suppose a French exporter of fine wines ships cases of champagne to a New York importer, accompanied by a bill for $1 million. The importing firm pays for the champagne by issuing a check denominated in dollars and deposits it right away in a U.S. bank—First American Bank—where the French firm maintains a checking account. After this check clears, the results of the transaction are as follows:

| French Exporter | | First American Bank | |
|---|---|---|---|
| **Assets** | **Liabilities** | **Assets** | **Liabilities** |
| Demand deposit in U.S. bank +$1 million | | | Demand deposit owed French exporter +$1 million |

Is the deposit shown above a Eurodollar deposit? *No,* because the deposit of dollars occurred in the United States, where the dollar is the official monetary unit. Suppose, however, the French exporter is offered an attractive rate of return on its dollar deposit by its own local bank in Paris and decides to move the dollar deposit there. The Paris bank wants to loan these dollars to other customers who need to pay bills or make purchases in the United States. After the wine exporter and its Paris bank have negotiated the terms of the deposit and the funds are transferred, the French exporter receives a receipt for a dollar-denominated time deposit in its Paris bank. That bank, in return, now holds claim to the original dollar deposit in the United States. The Paris bank has at least one U.S. correspondent bank and asks to have the original dollar deposit transferred there. We show these transactions as follows:

| French Exporter | |
|---|---|
| *Assets* | *Liabilities* |
| Demand deposit in U.S.bank −$1 million | |
| Time deposit in Paris bank +$1 million | |

| First American Bank | |
|---|---|
| *Assets* | *Liabilities* |
| Reserves transferred to U.S. correspondent bank −$1 million | Demand deposit owed French exporter −$1 million |

| U.S.Correspondent Bank | |
|---|---|
| *Assets* | *Liabilities* |
| Reserve received from First American Bank +$1 million | Demand deposit owed Paris bank +$1 million |

| Paris Bank | |
|---|---|
| *Assets* | *Liabilities* |
| Deposit in U.S correspondent bank +$1 million | Time deposit owed French exporter +$1 million |

Do we now have a Eurodollar deposit? *Yes,* in the form of a $1 million time deposit in a Paris bank. The wine exporter's deposit has been accepted and recorded on the Paris bank's books in U.S. dollars, even though the official monetary unit in France is the euro. Let's follow this Eurodollar deposit through one more step. Assume now that the Paris bank makes a loan of $1 million to an oil company based in Manchester, England. The British company needs dollars to pay for a shipment of petroleum drilling equipment from Houston, Texas. By securing a dollar credit from the Paris bank, the British oil firm, in effect, receives a claim against dollars deposited in U.S. banks. The appropriate entries would be as follows:

| Paris Bank | |
|---|---|
| *Assets* | *Liabilities* |
| Loan to British oil company +$1 million | |
| Deposit in U.S. correspondent bank −$1 million | |

| British Oil Company | |
|---|---|
| *Assets* | *Liabilities* |
| Demand deposit in U.S. correspondent bank +$1 million | Loan owed to Paris bank +$1 million |

| U.S. Correspondent Bank | |
|---|---|
| *Assets* | *Liabilities* |
| | Deposit owed to Paris Bank −$1 million |
| | Deposit owed to British oil company +$1 million |

Note that we have assumed the British oil company holds a deposit account in the same U.S. bank where the Paris bank held its deposits. This may not always be the case, but it was done here to reduce the number of accounting entries. If another U.S. bank were involved, we would simply transfer deposits and reserves to it from the U.S. correspondent bank that held the account of the Paris bank. The result would be exactly the same as in our example.

We must notice that, regardless of all the different transactions that took place, *the total amount of dollar deposits and bank reserves remained unchanged.* Funds were merely passed from bank to bank (especially through their overseas branches) as loans were extended and deposits made in the Eurodollar market. Thus, Eurodollar activity does *not* alter the total reserves of the banking system. In fact, the workings of the Eurocurrency markets remind us of a fundamental principle of international finance: *Money itself usually does not leave the country where it originates; only the ownership of money is transferred across international boundaries.*

The chain of Eurocurrency loans and deposits in our example above will go on unbroken as long as such loans are in demand and the funds are continually redeposited somewhere within the international banking system. Some economists believe that Eurobanks, like domestic U.S. banks, can create a multiple volume of deposits and loans for each Eurocurrency deposit they receive. However, this view has been disputed by a number of analysts who point out that major Eurobanks in their borrowing and lending activities are closer to nonbank financial institutions than to banks. Eurobanks appear to closely match the maturities of their assets (principally loans) with the maturities of their liabilities (principally Eurocurrency deposits and money market borrowings); thus, funds raised in the Eurocurrency markets tend to flow through Eurobanks back into those same markets. Rather than creating money, Eurobanks appear to function more as "efficient distributors of liquidity." If there is any actual credit or money creation in the Eurosystem, leading to a multiplication of deposits, the deposit multiplier must be close to one.[3]

Just as Eurocurrency deposits are created by making loans, they are also destroyed as loans are repaid. In our example, suppose the British oil company trades pounds for dollars with a foreign currency dealer and uses the dollars purchased to repay its loan from the Paris bank. At about the same time, the dollar time deposit held by the French exporter matures, and the exporter spends those dollars in the United States. As far as U.S. banks are concerned, total deposits and reserves remain unchanged. However, as a result of these transactions, all dollar deposits would now be held in the United States and, therefore, would have ceased to be Eurocurrency deposits.

[3]See Chapters 12, 13, and 14 for discussions of various aspects of the deposit multiplier. The granting of a Eurocurrency loan to a borrower does not give the borrower "money" in a strict sense. Eurocurrency deposits are not generally acceptable as a medium of exchange to pay for goods and services. They are more like regular time deposits (that is, bank CDs). The holder of a Eurocurrency deposit must convert that deposit into some national currency unit (such as euros or dollars) before using it for spending. Thus, Eurocurrency deposits are not negotiable instruments. The Eurocurrency system does not create money in the traditional sense. A lender of Eurocurrency who needs liquid funds before a deposit matures must go back into the market and negotiate a separate loan.

Interest usually is paid only at maturity unless the Eurodeposit has a term of more than one year. Most deposit interest rates are tied to the London Interbank Offer Rate (LIBOR)—the rate at which major international banks offer term Eurocurrency deposits to each other. The rate is usually fixed for the life of the deposit, though floating rates tied to changes in LIBOR are not uncommon on longer-term deposits, with promised interest rates reset every three to six months at a spread over LIBOR.

## *Eurocurrency Maturities and Risks*

Eurocurrency deposits are short-term time deposits (ranging from overnight to call money loaned for a few days out to one year) and therefore are true money market instruments. However, a small percentage are long-term time deposits, extending in some instances to about five years. Many Eurocurrency deposits carry one-month maturities to coincide with payments for shipments of goods. Other common maturities are 2, 3, 6, and 12 months.[4] The majority are interbank liabilities that pay a fixed interest rate.

Funds move rapidly in the Eurocurrency market from bank to bank in response to demands for short-term liquidity from corporations, governments, and Eurobanks themselves. Traders thousands of miles distant may conduct negotiations by satellite, computer networks, or telephone, with written confirmation coming later. Funds normally are transferred on the second business day after an agreement is reached through correspondent banks.

Eurocurrency deposits are known to be volatile and highly sensitive to fluctuations in interest rates and currency prices. A slight difference in interest rates or currency values between two countries can cause a massive flow of Eurocurrencies across national boundaries. One of the most famous examples of this phenomenon occurred in Germany during the 1970s when speculation that the German mark would be upvalued brought an inflow into Germany of billions in dollar deposits within hours, forcing the German government to cut its currency from its official exchange value and allow that currency to float upward.

Eurocurrency deposits are not without risk. There is *political risk* because governments may restrict or prohibit the movement of funds across national borders, as the United States did for a time during the Iranian crisis and more recently following the terrorist attacks on September 11th of 2001. There may be disputes between nations over the legal jurisdiction and control of deposits. *Default risk* may also be a factor because banks in the Eurobank system may fail; Eurocurrency deposits may be uninsured, or, because of their large size, only partially insured. This problem is compounded by the fact that it is usually more costly to secure information on the financial condition of foreign banks than on domestic banks. However, on the positive side, Eurobanks are among the largest and most stable banking institutions in the world. Moreover, most foreign nations have tried to encourage the growth of Eurocurrency markets through relatively lenient regulation and taxation.

## *The Supply of Eurocurrency Deposits*

Where do Eurocurrency deposits come from? The sources of Eurodollar deposits provide a good example of how and why this market continues to grow. For example, a major factor in the Eurodollar market's growth has been the enormous balance-of-payments deficits the United States has run in nearly every year since the 1950s.[5] U.S. firms building factories and purchasing goods and services abroad have transferred ownership of dollar deposits to foreign institutions. Domestic shortages of oil and natural gas have forced the United States to import the majority of its petroleum needs,

---

[4]Banks active in the Eurocurrency market for liquidity-adjustment purposes use *short-date* deposits. Comparable to federal funds in the domestic U.S. money market, short dates represent deposits available for as long as 14 days, though generally they are weekend or two-day money, with some seven-day maturities as well. Short dates may carry fixed maturities or simply be payable on demand with minimal notice (such as 24 or 48 hours).

[5]See Chapter 23 for a discussion of the causes and effects of U.S. balance-of-payment deficits.

generating enormous outflows of dollars to oil-producing nations. The OPEC countries, for example, accept dollars in payment for crude oil and use the dollar as a standard for valuing most of the oil they sell. U.S. tourists visiting China, Europe, Japan, and other foreign destinations frequently use dollar-denominated traveler's checks or take U.S. currency with them and convert it into local currency overseas. Dollar loans made by U.S. corporations and foreign-based firms have added to the vast Eurodollar pool. Many of these dollar deposits have gravitated to foreign central banks, such as the Bank of England and the European Central Bank, as these institutions have attempted to support the dollar and their own currencies in international markets.

## Eurodollars in U.S. Domestic Bank Operations

U.S. banks draw heavily on overnight Eurodollar deposits as a means of adjusting their domestic reserve positions. Thus, the manager of the money desk at a large U.S. bank, knowing the bank needs extra cash reserves today, can contact foreign banks holding dollar deposits and arrange a loan. The manager can also contact other U.S. banks with branches abroad and borrow Eurodollars from them. Alternatively, if the money manager's own bank operates foreign branches accepting dollar deposits, these can be placed at the disposal of the home office.

Eurodollar borrowing has been especially heavy during periods of rapidly rising interest rates in the United States. Such borrowings are extremely interest rate sensitive, however. When U.S. money market rates fell precipitously from record highs during the 1980s and 1990s and domestic sources of reserves became much less expensive, American banks repaid their Eurodollar borrowings nearly as fast as they borrowed these international deposits in earlier periods when market interest rates were at record highs.

Eurodollars often carry slightly *higher* reported interest rates than many other sources of bank reserves, such as domestic certificates of deposit, due to perceptions of higher risk, although this is not always the case. However, there are fewer legal restrictions on the borrowing of Eurodollars and other Eurocurrency deposits. For example, Eurodollar deposits have no reserve requirements or insurance fees today. In contrast, U.S. banks at times may have to pay assessments to the Federal Deposit Insurance Corporation on domestic deposits to cover the costs of insurance.

**Key URL:**
For further discussion of the London Interbank Offer Rate (LIBOR), see the British Bankers Association at **bba.org.uk/**

In addition to meeting their own reserve needs from the Eurocurrency market, banks have aided their corporate customers in acquiring Eurocurrency deposits. Direct loans in Eurocurrencies are made by banks, and these banks will readily swap Eurocurrencies at the customer's request. Although most Eurocurrency loans to nonbank customers are short-term credits to provide working capital, a sizable percentage consists of medium-term (one- to five-year) loans for equipment purchases, frequently set up under revolving credit agreements. Both borrowers and lenders in the Eurocurrency market can more effectively hedge against interest rate risk on these international loans today due to the expansion of Eurocurrency interest rate futures markets centered in London, Chicago, and other leading international financial centers.

**London Interbank Offer Rate (LIBOR)**

Eurodollar loan rates extended by major international lenders have two components: (1) the cost of acquiring Eurocurrency deposits (usually measured by the **London Interbank Offer Rate (LIBOR)** on three- or six-month Eurodeposits) and (2) a profit margin ("spread") based on the riskiness of the loan and the intensity of competition. Profit margins are low on Eurocurrency loans (often well below a single percentage point) because the market is highly competitive, lending costs are low, and the risk is normally low as well. Borrowers are generally well-known institutions with substantial net worth and solid credit standing. Loan transactions are usually carried out in large denominations, ranging up to $100 million or more.

## Recent Innovations in the Eurocurrency Markets

Beginning in the 1980s, the Eurocurrency market witnessed rapid growth in medium-term credit arrangements between international banks and their corporate and governmental customers. These so-called *note issuance facilities* (NIFs) often span several years and allow the customer to borrow by selling short-term IOUs (typically maturing in three to six months) to investors. The underwriting banks backstop this customer paper either by purchasing any paper that remains unsold or by providing standby credit at an interest rate spread over LIBOR. The notes issued are often denominated in U.S. dollars with par values of $100,000 or higher. With bank support, NIFs are roughly equivalent to Eurocurrency CDs and compete with them for investor funds.

## Benefits and Costs of the Eurocurrency Markets

For the most part, the development of Eurocurrency trading has resulted in substantial benefits to the international community, especially to multinational corporations. The market ensures a high degree of funds mobility between international capital markets and provides a true international market for liquidity adjustments. It has provided a mechanism for absorbing huge amounts of U.S. dollars flowing overseas and lessened international pressure to forsake the dollar for gold and other currencies. The market reduces the cost of international trade by providing an efficient method of economizing on transactions balances. Moreover, it acts as a check on domestic monetary and fiscal policies and encourages *international cooperation* in economic policies, because interest-sensitive traders in the market will quickly spot interest rates that are out of line and move funds from one point on the globe to another. Central banks, such as the Bank of England and the European Central Bank, monitor the Eurocurrency markets continuously in order to moderate inflows or outflows of funds that may damage their domestic economies.

The capacity of Eurocurrency markets to mobilize massive amounts of funds has occasionally brought severe criticism from regulators in Europe, the United States, and Asia. They sometimes see the market as contributing to instability in currency values. Moreover, the market can wreak havoc with any particular nation's monetary and fiscal policies designed to cure its domestic economic problems, especially if the nation is experiencing severe inflation and massive inflows of Eurocurrency occur at the same time. The net effect of Eurocurrency expansion, other things being equal, is to push domestic interest rates down, stimulate credit expansion, and accelerate inflation (which may ultimately result in higher market interest rates). The ability of local authorities to deal with inflationary problems might be overwhelmed by a Eurocurrency glut. This danger is really the price of freedom, for an unregulated market will not always conform to the plans of government policymakers.

## 11.6  Bankers' Acceptances

As the Eurocurrency markets remind us, the money market today is not confined within the boundaries of a single nation or even a single continent. As world trade has expanded in recent years, the need for financing instruments associated with the expansion of international commerce has also grown. Historically, one of the oldest and most respected short-term financing instruments designed to facilitate international trade is the *banker's acceptance.*

### How Bankers' Acceptances Are Used in International Trade

banker's acceptance

A **banker's acceptance** is a *time draft* drawn on a bank by an exporter or an importer to help pay for merchandise or to purchase foreign currencies. Its purpose is to shift default risk for the lender in a credit transaction from the borrower to the more creditworthy bank.

The role of acceptances is most easily understood from an example. A primary use of a banker's acceptance is to finance the purchase of internationally traded goods while those goods are in transit. Suppose, for example, a U.S. importer receives coffee from a Brazilian grower and the exporter requires payment for the coffee before it leaves Brazil. However, the U.S. importer may wish to borrow cash to finance this purchase and then repay the borrowings from the resale of coffee once it reaches the United States. The Brazilian grower may be reluctant to grant the importer a loan due to credit risk. In this circumstance, a viable option for the importer is to acquire a banker's acceptance from a well-regarded bank and use this claim against the bank to support the purchase.

There may be several options available to an importer once he possesses the acceptance. He may simply sell it in the secondary market for cash that can be sent to the exporter. He may use the claim itself to purchase the commodities if the exporter is willing to acquire this claim on the bank in exchange for the goods; or he may have his bank arrange to shift funds to the exporter through the exporter's Brazilian bank, with the Brazilian bank retaining the acceptance. Note that the ultimate lender to the importer is not the U.S. bank, but rather the party that ultimately acquires the acceptance. That party could be an investor in the secondary market—such as a money market mutual fund, the exporter himself, or the exporter's Brazilian bank. In any case, the credit risk associated with this loan lies with the U.S. bank, not with the coffee importer.

In order for the U.S. importer to acquire the banker's acceptance from his bank, he must negotiate an agreement that effectively requires him to send money to the bank before the acceptance comes due. If all works smoothly, the coffee importer will receive the coffee, sell it, and use a portion of the proceeds to retire its obligation to the bank in time for the bank to have those funds available to redeem the acceptance from whoever owns it on its maturity date. The difficulty lies in the credit risk of the importer. If he defaults on the loan, it is the U.S. bank that must make good on the acceptance and absorb the loss. Therefore, acceptance financing does not necessarily reduce credit risk; it *shifts* the exposure to the importer's default risk from the lender to the bank. The only credit risk the exporter faces is the risk the issuing bank will default on the acceptance when it matures. As we will see below, this risk is generally minimal. The reason for such an arrangement is that the issuing bank is in the business of evaluating credit risk and, therefore, is better suited to price that risk in its agreement with the U.S. coffee importer than the Brazilian coffee grower would be. To protect itself, the issuing bank will generally have the acceptance collateralized by the merchandise being shipped (the coffee in this example). As part of these arrangements, the merchandise itself is nearly always insured to protect against loss of collateral during shipment or warehousing.

## Bankers' Acceptances as Investment Instruments

Acceptances generally carry maturities ranging from 30 to 270 days (with 90 days the most common) and are considered prime-quality instruments comparable to prime negotiable bank CDs, U.S. Treasury bills, and prime commercial paper, although their trading volume is much smaller. They are traded among banks, money market mutual funds, industrial corporations, local governments, federal agencies, insurance companies, and securities dealers as a high-quality investment and source of ready cash. They do not carry a fixed rate of interest but are sold at a discount in the open market like Treasury bills (see Chapters 6 and 10). The prime borrower under an acceptance is charged a commitment fee which is about 1 1/2 percent (1/8 of 1 percent per month) for top-quality customers. U.S. banks are normally limited in the dollar amount of acceptances they can create to 150 percent of their core capital (capital paid-in plus surplus), but may receive special permission from the Federal Reserve to expand their issuances to 200 percent of their core capital.

If the bank wishes to sell an acceptance in advance of its maturity, the rate of discount it must pay is determined by the current bid rate on acceptances of similar maturity in the open market. The yield on acceptances is usually only slightly higher than on Treasury bills because banks that issue them generally have solid international reputations. Acceptance rates hover close to negotiable CD rates offered by major banks because both acceptances and CDs are unconditional obligations of the issuing bank to pay. Adding to the stature of acceptances, depository institutions are permitted to borrow reserves from the Fed's discount window using certain types of acceptances as collateral. The U.S. Treasury also permits banks to use them as collateral to back Treasury tax and loan accounts (cash reserves) held in a majority of the nation's banks.

## The Decline in Bankers' Acceptances

Acceptance financing expanded rapidly during the 1970s and early 1980s. However, after peaking at about $80 billion in 1984, it has been in steady decline, falling to only $700 million in 2006. The decline in acceptances is primarily due to: (1) greater utilization of foreign currencies in international transactions, such as the yen and the euro;

### QUESTIONS TO HELP YOU STUDY

12. What is the *Eurocurrency market* and why is it needed?

13. Define the term *Eurodollar*. Can a U.S. bank create Eurodollars? How?

14. Describe the process by which Eurocurrency deposits are created. What happens to the total volume of domestic bank reserves and deposits in the process of creating Eurocurrency deposits?

15. Can Eurocurrency deposits be *destroyed?* How can this happen?

16. What are the principal *sources* of Eurocurrency deposits? Make a list.

17. What role do Eurodollar deposits play in *reserve management operations* of U.S. banking firms? What are the advantages of Eurodollar borrowings over other sources of reserves for banks? The disadvantages?

18. Evaluate the Eurocurrency markets from a social point of view. What are their major benefits and costs to the public and to market participants? In your opinion, should these markets be more closely regulated or should they remain relatively free of regulation?

19. What exactly is a *banker's acceptance?*

20. Explain why acceptances historically have been attractive to exporters and importers of goods moving between different countries. Why has the volume of acceptances declined in recent years?

21. What are the advantages and disadvantages of the banker's acceptance as an investment instrument?

(2) greater reliance on direct bank loans by major exporters and importers; and (3) a shift by many international corporations away from banks and toward the open market to meet their financing needs, principally through the issuance of bonds and commercial paper. How these factors led to erosion in the volume of acceptances outstanding is a striking example of the impact of technology, financial innovation, the integration of world economies, and the globalization of the financial marketplace that continues to shape the landscape of international finance.

## 11.7 Evaluating the Money Market Costs of Funds Needed by Bankers

It is useful to conclude our discussion about banks' borrowing funds in domestic and foreign money markets by illustrating how a banker evaluates the choices among such sources as federal funds, negotiable CDs, and Eurocurrency deposits. Among other key factors, a banker must keep in close touch with money market developments each day, paying particular attention both to current money market interest rates and to forecasts about future interest rates.

Consider an example. Suppose that this past year federal funds were trading at an annual interest rate of about 4 percent and the average interest rate that major money-center banks were paying to bring in deposits of large ($100,000) negotiable CDs from their customers was about 4.25 percent on three-month maturities. Similarly, international banks were selling three-month Eurodollar deposits at 4.30 percent.

Even though legal reserve requirements on domestic CDs had been set at zero several years earlier by the Federal Reserve Board, a bank raising money by issuing domestic CDs still might have been compelled to pay deposit insurance fees to the Federal Deposit Insurance Corporation (FDIC) equal to the full amount of the CD (not just the $100,000 portion covered by insurance). The U.S. deposit insurance fee has frequently been set at zero for the majority of insured banks in recent years, but let's assume for purposes of illustration that the FDIC's current insurance fee on domestic deposits issued by financially sound money-center banks is 0.0004 cents per dollar (or 4 cents per $100) on any deposits received from the public.

Suppose a money-center bank needed to borrow $1 million for at least a day. Its daily cost of funds derived from each of these three sources would be:

Federal funds:

$$\$1 \text{ million} \times 0.0400 \times \frac{1}{360} = \$111.11 \tag{11.3}$$

Domestic negotiable CDs:

$$\underbrace{\$1 \text{ million} \times 0.0425 \times \frac{1}{360}}_{\text{Deposit interest cost}} + \underbrace{\$1 \text{ million} \times 0.0004 \times \frac{1}{360}}_{\text{Deposit insurance cost}} = \$119.17 \tag{11.4}$$

Eurodollar deposits from the international money market:

$$\$1 \text{ million} \times 0.0430 \times \frac{1}{360} = \$119.44 \tag{11.5}$$

On this particular day in the money market, the cheapest funds source was *borrowing in the federal funds market*. However, because the domestic CD and Eurodollar deposit interest rates were fixed for three months in this instance (in contrast with the federal funds interest rate, which changes every day), if the Fed funds rate was expected to rise significantly, this borrowing bank might well decide to borrow at the currently more expensive CD or Eurodollar rates. Clearly, a banker borrowing in the money market must consider not only the level of current money market interest rates but also expected *future* interest rates and government regulations when choosing a source of funding.

## 11.8 Concluding Comment on Bank Activity in the Money Market

The money market has not always been as important a source of funds for banks as it is today. In past history even many of the largest money-center banks regarded borrowings from the money market as only a secondary source of funds. Bankers were aware that heavy dependence on money market borrowing would make their earnings more sensitive to fluctuations in interest rates. However, the force of competition soon intervened. Major corporations began to seek out alternative investments for their short-term funds rather than holding most of their money in bank deposits. Bankers were forced to turn to the money market for additional funds.

As we have seen in this chapter, the banking community approached the problem in several different ways. One was to offer a new financial instrument—the negotiable certificate of deposit—to compete directly for short-term corporate funds. Another approach was to draw more intensively on existing sources of money market funds, especially the federal funds market. Thousands of small depository institutions in towns and rural areas across the United States began supplying their excess legal reserves to larger banks in the central cities, hoping to boost their earnings. In turn, the greater supply of Federal funds encouraged the largest banks to rely even more heavily on the money market and less on customer deposits as a source of reserves.

The rapid expansion of the CD and federal funds markets was just the beginning of banking's *money market strategy*. When the Federal Reserve became concerned over the rapid growth of CDs and federal funds and clamped down with tight-money policies, innovative financial managers were forced to find new sources of reserves or face a real cutback in their lending activities. Many turned to the Eurocurrency market, borrowing deposits from abroad, or to repurchase agreements backed by government securities to raise new funds.

**liability management**

All of these clever maneuvers form part of a technique called **liability management.** Bankers quickly came to realize that simply by varying the daily interest rates they were willing to offer on CDs, Eurocurrency deposits, and other funds sources, they could gain a measure of control over their liabilities. If more funds were needed to accommodate customer loan demand, a bank active in the money market would simply offer a higher yield on the particular money market instrument it desired to use. If a smaller volume of funds was required at another time, the institution could lower its offer rate on money market borrowings.

**Key URLs:**
To learn more about modern liability management see, for example, such Web sites as **almprofessional.com** and **contingency-analysis.com**

What is especially fascinating about liability management strategies is that they have had precisely the effects many analysts predicted from the start. The earnings of financial institutions *have* become more sensitive to fluctuations in interest rates; and in periods of rapidly escalating market interest rates, profit margins have often been squeezed. Whether this adverse impact on the earnings of banks and other money market participants will continue into the future remains to be seen due to changing technology and the growing use of risk-management tools. The great innovative abilities of these institutions, freed in recent years by deregulation, will do much to shape their earnings performance in the years ahead. But whatever the future holds, bankers have transformed the money market into a far larger and more dynamic institution than at any other time in history.

---

**QUESTIONS TO HELP YOU STUDY**

22. What factors influence a banker's choice among negotiable CDs, Eurocurrency deposits, and federal funds as important sources of borrowed reserves for banking institutions?

23. What exactly is meant by the term *liability management?* What changes has it brought to the depository institutions' industry?

---

## 11.9 Major Corporations in the Money Market: Commercial Paper

Each year leading corporations, such as Verizon, General Motors, Marriott Corp., General Electric, and Philip Morris, borrow billions of dollars in the money market through the sale of unsecured promissory notes, known as *commercial paper.* Not long ago a survey of this short-term corporate debt market by the Federal Reserve System counted more than a thousand corporations in the United States (and a growing number of companies overseas) regularly selling their commercial notes to money market investors.

### The Nature of Commercial Paper

**commercial paper**

**Commercial paper** is one of the oldest of all money market instruments, dating back to the eighteenth century in the United States. By definition, commercial paper consists of short-term, unsecured promissory notes issued by well-known companies that are financially strong and carry high credit ratings. The funds raised from a paper issue normally are used for *current transactions*—to purchase inventories, pay taxes, meet payrolls, and cover other short-term obligations—rather than for *capital transactions* (long-term investments). However, a substantial number of paper issues today are used to provide "bridge financing" for such long-term projects as building pipelines and office buildings and manufacturing assembly lines. In these instances issuing companies usually plan to convert their short-term paper into more permanent financing when the capital market looks more favorable.

Commercial paper is generally issued in denominations designed to meet the needs of the buyer (such as multiples of $1,000). It is traded mainly in the primary market. Opportunities for resale in the secondary market are more limited, although some dealers today assist their customers by redeeming a portion of the notes they sell. Because of the limited resale possibilities, investors are usually careful to purchase those paper issues whose maturity matches their planned holding periods, though resale opportunities (liquidity) have increased in recent years. The most common maturities are 7, 15, 30, 60, and 90 days and about 99 percent is issued in electronic not paper form.

### Types of Commercial Paper

**direct paper**

There are two major types of commercial paper—direct paper and dealer paper. The main issuers of **direct paper** are large finance companies and bank holding companies that deal directly with the investor rather than using a securities dealer as an intermediary. These companies, which regularly extend installment credit to consumers and large working capital loans and leases to business firms, announce the interest rates they are currently paying on various maturities of their paper. Investors select their preferred maturities and buy the securities directly from the issuer. Interest rates may be adjusted during the day the paper is being sold to regulate the inflow of investor funds so that borrowing companies achieve their funding goals.

Leading finance company borrowers in the direct paper market include General Motors Acceptance Corporation (GMAC), General Electric Capital Corporation (GE Capital), CIT Financial Corporation, and Commercial Credit Corporation. The leading U.S. bank holding companies that issue commercial paper are centered around the largest banks in New York, Chicago, San Francisco, and other major U.S. cities.[6] Today, about 50 financially oriented U.S. companies account for nearly all directly placed paper, with finance companies issuing the most in total. All of these firms have an ongoing need for huge amounts of short-term money, possess top credit ratings and have established working relationships with major institutional investors in order to place new paper rapidly.

Directly placed paper must be sold in large volume to cover the substantial costs of distribution and marketing. On average, each direct issuer will borrow at least $1 billion per month. Issuers of direct paper do not have to pay dealers' commissions, but these companies operate a marketing division to maintain contact with active investors. Selected issuers, like New York's Citigroup, sell commercial paper in weekly auctions in which buyers bid and the issuing company accepts the highest price (lowest yield) bid. Sometimes direct issuers sell their paper even when they have no need for funds in order to maintain a good working relationship with active investors. These companies also cannot escape paying fees to banks for supporting lines of credit, to credit rating agencies that rate their paper, and to agents (such as trust companies) that dispense required payments and collect funds.

**dealer paper**

The other major variety of commercial paper is **dealer paper,** issued by security dealers on behalf of their corporate customers. Also known as *industrial paper,* dealer paper is issued mainly by nonfinancial companies (including public utilities, manufacturers, retailers, and transportation companies), as well as by smaller bank holding companies and finance companies, all of which tend to borrow less frequently than firms issuing direct paper.

Industrial paper is used primarily to fund accounts receivable and inventory for the issuing companies and is usually closely connected to fluctuations in business inventory levels. The issuing company may sell the paper directly to the dealer, who buys it less discount and commission and then attempts to resell it at the highest possible price in the market. Alternatively, the issuing company may carry all the risk, with the dealer agreeing only to sell the issue at the best price available less commission, referred to as a *best efforts basis.* Finally, the open-rate method may be used in which the borrowing company receives some money in advance but the balance depends on how well the issue sells in the open market.

While we might expect the interest rates attached to direct (or finance company) paper to be *lower* than interest rates on dealer (mainly nonfinancial) paper, because the latter is generally issued by smaller firms with somewhat greater risk exposure, the reverse—direct paper rates being slightly higher than dealer paper rates—has often been true in

---

[6]Bank holding companies issue *both* direct and dealer paper, with the largest companies going the direct placement route. Much of this bank-related paper comes from finance company subsidiaries of large bank holding companies. Frequently, a holding company will issue paper through a nonbank subsidiary and then funnel the proceeds to one or more of its subsidiary banks by purchasing some of the banks' assets. This gives the affiliated banks additional funds to lend and may be especially helpful when a bank is having trouble raising new funds.

| EXHIBIT 11.2 | Volume of Commercial Paper Outstanding ($ billions, end of period) | | | | | | |
|---|---|---|---|---|---|---|---|
| Instrument | 1985 | 1990 | 1995 | 2000 | 2002 | 2004 | 2006* |
| Domestic issues: | | | | | | | |
| Financial | $187.8 | $365.6 | $464.2 | $1,206.7 | $1,128.8 | $1,131.6 | $1,541.9 |
| Nonfinancial | 72.2 | 116.9 | 157.4 | 278.4 | 119.9 | 101.6 | 114.2 |
| Foreign issues: | | | | | | | |
| Financial | 26.0 | 54.8 | 35.6 | 83.3 | 235.1 | 316.6 | 409.7 |
| Nonfinancial | 8.0 | 20.6 | 20.6 | 37.6 | 19.2 | 13.3 | 23.9 |
| All issues | 293.9 | 557.8 | 677.7 | 1,606.1 | 1,503.0 | 1,563.1 | 2,089.7 |

*2006 data are for the third quarter.

Source: Board of Governors of the Federal Reserve System, *Flow of Funds Accounts.*

recent years. A key reason centers on the relative growth of the two types of commercial paper. Direct or finance-company paper has maintained a relatively high volume of new issues, while nonfinancial or dealer paper has recently declined in the volume of new offerings.

## The Recent Track Record of Commercial Paper

As Exhibit 11.2 indicates, the total volume of commercial paper nearly tripled between 1990 and 2000. Indeed, as Exhibit 11.3 indicates, commercial paper issues have doubled, tripled, or quadrupled in volume in nearly every decade since 1960. By 2006, more than 1,700 companies had over $2 trillion in commercial notes outstanding. Much of the market's growth was due to financial paper issued by finance companies and bank holding companies.

What factors explain the growth of commercial paper? One factor is the relative cost of other sources of credit compared to interest rates prevailing on commercial paper. For the largest, best-known corporations, commercial paper has often been a cost-effective substitute for bank loans and other forms of borrowing. This is especially true for nonfinancial companies issuing paper through dealers. These firms usually come to the paper market when it is significantly cheaper to borrow there than to tap bank lines of credit. Also, many companies use the paper market today to participate in interest rate swaps, which are designed to hedge against losses from fluctuating interest rates.[7]

**EXHIBIT 11.3**

**Growth of Commercial Paper Issues in the United States**

| Year | Outstanding Volume of Paper in Billions of Dollars |
|---|---|
| 1960 | $   4.5 |
| 1970 | 33.1 |
| 1980 | 121.6 |
| 1990 | 557.8 |
| 2000 | 1,606.1 |
| 2006* | 2,089.7 |

Source: Board of Governors of the Federal Reserve System, *Flow of Funds Accounts.*

*2006 data is for the third quarter.

[7]Chapter 9 contains an explanation of interest rate swaps.

Another reason for the market's growth is the high quality of most commercial paper obligations. Many investors regard this instrument as a close substitute for Treasury bills and other money market instruments. As a result, market yields on commercial paper tend to move in the same direction and by similar amounts as the yields on other money market securities. This fact is shown clearly in Exhibit 11.1 earlier in this chapter, which compares market yields on commercial paper, Treasury bills, negotiable CDs, Eurodollar deposits, and federal funds and indicates that these interest rates tend to stay relatively close to each other. We note that commercial paper yields are usually higher than market rates on comparable maturity Treasury bills due to the greater risk and lower marketability of paper and the fact that Treasury bills are exempt from state and local taxation.

Investors in commercial paper demand high quality and are typically very sensitive to risk. As a consequence, even corporations with the highest credit ratings are nearly always required to secure a line of credit at a bank for a small fee or hold a compensating deposit at their bank to help backstop their paper. However, this line of credit is not always sufficient for the paper issuer to find a receptive market when it attempts to place its paper in the hands of investors. One reason is that the line of credit cannot be used to directly guarantee payment if the company goes bankrupt. Moreover, the lender may renege on the credit line if the borrowing company has had a "material adverse change" in its financial condition. Consequently, this line of credit is not always sufficient for a firm to have access to financing in the commercial paper market and, in times of an economic downturn, the volume of commercial paper outstanding can shrink dramatically.

**credit enhancements**

Overcoming this strong aversion to risk that investors in commercial paper exhibit, while providing a basis for the market's recent growth is the expanding use of **credit enhancements**—standby letters of credit, indemnity bonds, and other irrevocable payment guarantees. For example, a lending institution may issue a certificate that promises repayment of principal and/or interest on a customer's paper if the borrowing company fails to do so. The result is that such paper, often called *documented notes,* usually carries the higher credit rating of the guarantor rather than the lower credit rating of the issuing firm. Through these guarantees, mortgage companies, utilities, and small manufacturers in large numbers have been attracted into a market that otherwise would be closed to them, still saving on interest costs even after paying a guarantor's fee.

Other groups recently entering the market include foreign banks and industrial companies, international financial conglomerates, and state and local governments (which offer *tax-exempt* commercial paper). Paper issued in the United States by foreign firms is called *Yankee paper* and frequently can be sold at lower interest costs in the United States than abroad. However, foreign borrowers in the U.S. market generally must pay higher interest costs than U.S. companies of comparable credit rating to compensate U.S. buyers for the added difficulty of gathering information on foreign borrowers and, in many cases, the lack of name recognition. Nonetheless, foreign issues of commercial paper in the United States have grown substantially in recent years, as indicated in Exhibit 11.2.

## *Commercial Paper as Investment Instruments*

The high quality of commercial paper results in comparatively low investment yields. However, relative to other wholesale money market assets, commercial paper often has higher yields resulting from slightly higher risk and lower liquidity.

The commercial paper market in the United States has been copied abroad for many years now, though other countries have added their own special features. Among the leading national paper markets today are those of Japan, France, Canada, and Sweden.

One of the most dramatic developments in the history of commercial paper markets has been the relatively recent development of the Japanese yen-denominated paper market. Yen-denominated paper was first allowed to be offered in domestic Japanese markets by the Ministry of Finance in 1987. Many Japanese companies had threatened to move their short-term borrowing abroad unless the Japanese government relaxed its rules. A year later, foreign businesses were given permission to sell "Samurai paper" inside Japan.

With so many U.S. companies operating in Canada and many Canadian firms having money market access inside the United States, the Canadian paper market has relatively modest dimensions. Like U.S. paper, Canadian paper must be backed by a bank line of credit to catch the attention of money market investors. It has a broader range of maturities (usually from demand notes, cashable in 24 hours, out to about one year) than in the United States and also tends to be issued in larger denominations (usually $100,000 or more).

During the mid-1980s the *Europaper market* emerged, soaring in volume because borrowing companies were able to tap a larger reservoir of foreign cash. Many U.S. corporations having difficulty borrowing in the domestic market, often because of declining credit quality, turned to the Euromarket, which appeared to be less quality-conscious. The heaviest investors in Europaper are international banks, private corporations, and central banks. The bulk of Europaper is sold through dealers with interest rates linked to Eurobank deposit rates.

Maturities of U.S. commercial paper range from three days ("weekend paper") to nine months. Most commercial notes carry an original maturity of 60 days or less, with an average maturity ranging from 20 to 45 days. U.S. paper is generally not issued for maturities longer than 270 days because, under the provisions of the Securities Act of 1933, any security sold in U.S. markets for a longer term must be registered with the Securities and Exchange Commission. Yields to the investor are calculated by the *bank discount method,* just like Treasury *bills* as illustrated in Chapter 6. Like T-bills, most commercial paper is issued at a discount from par. The investor's yield arises from the price appreciation of the security between its purchase date and maturity date.

The minimum denomination of commercial paper issues is usually $25,000, although among institutional investors who dominate the market, the usual minimum denomination is $1 million. Payment is made at maturity on presentation to the particular bank listed as agent on the note. Settlement in federal funds is usually made the same day the note is presented for payment by its holder.

## QUESTIONS TO HELP YOU STUDY

24. What do we mean by the term *commercial paper?*

25. Why is commercial paper attractive to such money market investors as banks, insurance companies, money market funds, and industrial companies?

26. Describe the functions that *dealers* perform in the functioning of the commercial paper market. In what market segment are they most active? Least active?

27. Why do some investors find commercial paper unsatisfactory for their needs?

| EXHIBIT 11.4 | Spread between the Average Prime Rate Quoted by Major U.S. Banks and the Three-Month Commercial Paper Rate, Selected Years | | |
|---|---|---|---|
| Year | Bank Prime Lending Rate | Three-Month Commercial Paper Rate | Rate Spread in Percentage Points |
| 1998 | 8.35% | 5.34% | 3.01% |
| 2000 | 9.23 | 6.31 | 2.92 |
| 2002 | 4.67 | 1.69 | 2.98 |
| 2004 | 4.34 | 1.41 | 2.93 |
| 2006 | 7.96 | 5.10 | 2.86 |
| 2007* | 8.25 | 5.17 | 3.08 |

Source: Federal Reserve's Web site: *federalreserve.gov.*

Note: The prime rate is the average of rates posted by major U.S. banks. The three-month commercial paper rate is the unweighted average of offer rates quoted by at least five dealers. The prime rate is averaged for each year.

*2007 Figures for January.

## Advantages of Issuing Commercial Paper

There are several financial advantages to a company able to tap the paper market for funds. Generally, interest rates on paper are lower than the interest rates on corporate loans extended by banks. For example, in recent years the bank prime rate has averaged several percentage points higher than the rate on three-month dealer paper has. (See Exhibit 11.4.)

Moreover, the effective rate on many commercial loans granted by banks is even higher than the quoted prime rate, due to the fact that corporate borrowers may be required to keep a percentage of their loans in a bank deposit. This *compensating balance* requirement may be 15 to 20 percent of the amount of the loan. Suppose a corporation borrows $100,000 at a prime interest rate of 8.50 percent but must keep 20 percent of this amount ($20,000) on deposit with the bank granting the loan. Then the effective annual loan rate is 10.625 percent [or $8,500/($100,000 − $20,000)].

Another advantage of borrowing in the paper market is that interest rates there are often more flexible than bank and finance company loan rates. A company in need of funds can raise money quickly through either dealer or direct paper. Dealers maintain close contact with the market and generally know where cash may be found. Frequently, notes can be issued and funds raised the same day.

Generally, larger amounts of funds may be borrowed more conveniently through the paper market than from other sources, particularly bank loans. This situation arises due to federal and state regulations that limit the amount of money a bank can lend to a single borrower. Corporate credit needs frequently exceed an individual bank's loan limit, and a group of banks (consortium) has to be assembled to make the loan. However, this takes time and may require lengthy negotiations. The paper market is generally faster than trying to hammer out a loan agreement among several parties, though some experts believe that the current consolidation of the banking and finance industry worldwide, creating fewer, but much larger, lending institutions, could limit the growth of the paper market in future years.

The ability to issue commercial paper gives a corporation considerable leverage when negotiating with banks and other lenders. For example, a banker who knows that a customer can draw on the paper market for funds is more likely to offer advantageous terms on a loan and be more receptive to future customer credit needs.

## Possible Disadvantages from Issuing Commercial Paper

Despite the advantages, there are some risks for corporations that choose to borrow frequently in the paper market. One of these is the risk of alienating banks and other institutional lenders whose loans might be needed when a real emergency develops. The paper market is sensitive to financial and economic problems. This fact was demonstrated convincingly in 1980 when Chrysler Financial, the finance company subsidiary of Chrysler Corporation, was forced to cut back its borrowings in the paper market due to the widely publicized troubles of its parent company, which sought and eventually received government assistance. However, the paper market appears to have strengthened and become so broad in recent years that it may be more tolerant of defaults and corporate failures. For example, in January and February 1997 when auto lender Mercury Finance Company defaulted on more than $300 million in paper, there was little effect outside the automobile industry on the paper market as a whole, though Enron's collapse in 2001 did depress this market for a time.

At times, it is difficult even for companies in sound financial condition to raise funds in the paper market at reasonable rates of interest. It helps to have a friendly banker available to supply emergency credit when this market turns sour. Another problem lies in the fact that paper cannot usually be paid off at the issuer's discretion, but generally must remain outstanding until maturity. In contrast, many bank loans permit early retirement without penalty. In addition, yields on commercial paper are open market rates that tend to fluctuate with the daily ebb and flow of supply and demand forces in the marketplace. In the wide swings between easy and tight money and between depressed and resurgent economic activity, commercial paper rates have fluctuated between extreme highs and lows. Indeed, the paper market is highly volatile and difficult to predict. This is why many corporations eligible to borrow there still maintain close working relationships with institutional lenders and employ interest rate hedging techniques (such as financial futures contracts).

## Who Buys Commercial Paper?

The most important investors in the commercial paper market include nonfinancial corporations, money market mutual funds, bank trust departments, small banks, pension funds, insurance companies, and state and local governments. In effect, this is a market in which corporations borrow from other corporations. These investor groups generally regard paper as a low-risk outlet for their surplus funds, although recent financial problems and a few defaults among paper issuers have caused some investor groups, such as money market funds, to sharply cut back their purchases of lower-quality paper.

As the 1990s began, the U.S. Securities and Exchange Commission (SEC) became particularly concerned about the safety of money market funds and the risk to the savings of thousands of investors who, by that time, had placed nearly $500 billion with the money market fund industry. More than half the industry's assets had been invested in commercial paper, with an increasing proportion of these investments in lower-quality issues bearing higher but riskier yields. These lower-quality commercial notes are often acquired by more aggressive money fund managers interested in attracting more savings deposits by offering higher returns. Following several paper defaults, the SEC ruled that money market funds could hold no more than 5 percent of their total assets in less than top-quality (not prime-rated) commercial paper, nor could they place any more than 1 percent of their assets in the paper of any one non-prime-rated corporate issuer. Money funds must inform investors that their shares are not insured or guaranteed by the U.S. government. The new rules appear to enhance the safety of savings held with money market funds, which now hold over a quarter of all paper outstanding, but they may also have placed a future restraint on the growth of the commercial paper market, making it more difficult for many companies, especially those with less-than-top credit ratings, to sell their paper.

### *Continuing Innovations in the Paper Market*

master note

One important innovation in the direct paper market is the **master note,** most frequently issued to bank trust departments and other permanent money market investors by finance companies. Under a master note agreement, the investing firm agrees to take some paper each day up to an agreed-upon maximum amount. Interest owed is figured on the average daily volume of paper taken on by the investor during the current month. The prevailing interest rate on six-month commercial paper is generally used to determine the appropriate rate of return.

An extension of the paper market has appeared in the form of *medium-term notes* (MTNs). These 9-month to 10-year notes are issued by investment-grade corporations, normally carry a fixed interest rate, and are generally noncallable, unsecured obligations marketed through dealers. They are particularly suited to companies with substantial quantities of medium-term assets who wish to balance these assets with IOUs longer than the short maturities attached to conventional commercial paper. First sold by automobile finance companies in the 1970s, the MTN market has attracted industrial and utility companies and a secondary market has developed with several investment banking firms trading these medium-length instruments.

Beginning in the 1980s, a new form of paper began to appear—*asset-backed commercial paper*—in which loans or credit receivables are pooled into packages and paper is then issued as claims against that pool (that is, the credit receivables are *securitized*). The loans or receivables are removed from the issuing company's balance sheet and placed in a *special-purpose entity* (SPE), which issues the paper and uses the proceeds to purchase the receivables. Among the most popular assets pooled to back these unique paper issues are credit-card receivables, installment sales contracts, and lease receivables. Participants in these programs include banks, finance companies, and retail dealers. Banks find them a handy vehicle for assisting their corporate customers to obtain financing without having to loan them money and incur credit costs. A bank can earn fees for advising the paper-issuing customer, reviewing the quality of assets to be pooled, and supplying credit enhancements (usually in the form of letters of credit, surety bonds, etc.) and liquidity enhancements (to help retire maturing paper in case of temporary cash shortfalls) for outstanding paper issues.

Asset-backed paper gives issuing corporations a low and stable cost of financing often far cheaper than either direct financing through a bank or finance company or *factoring,* in which a company sells its accounts receivable to a lender at a sizable discount from face value. For those asset-backed paper issues backed by credit and liquidity guarantees, any change of fortune at the customer's business should not appreciably affect the firm's actual funding costs. The SPE normally issues enough paper to cover the discounted purchase price of the company's receivables and uses the proceeds from the paper issue to purchase the firm's receivables. The issuing customer usually services the underlying receivables, collecting interest and principal payments and passing the funds along to the SPE, or a bank chosen by the customer may service the receivables supporting the paper issue. The fact that paper is issued for less than the full nondiscounted value of the receivables generates a margin of value to protect investors.

## Commercial Paper Ratings and Dealer Operations

Commercial paper is rated *prime, desirable,* or *satisfactory,* depending on the credit standing of the issuing company. Firms desiring to issue paper generally will seek a credit rating from one or more of several rating services, including such firms as Moody's Investors Service; Standard & Poor's Corporation; Fitch Investors Service; Duff & Phelps; Canadian Bond Rating Service; Japanese Bond Rating Institute; Dominion Bond Rating Service; and IBCA, Ltd.—with the first two rating companies especially prominent. Moody's assigns a rating of Prime-1 (P-1) for the highest-quality paper, with lower-quality issues designated as Prime-2 (P-2) or Prime-3 (P-3). Standard & Poor's assigns ratings of A-1 + or A-1, A-2, and A-3; Fitch uses F-1, F-2, or F-3. Any issue rated below P-2, A-2, or F-2 usually sells poorly or not at all.

Generally, commercial notes bearing credit ratings from at least two rating agencies are preferred by investors. The rating assigned to an issue often depends heavily on the liquidity position and the amount of backup lines of credit held by the issuing company. Moreover, there is evidence—for example, Crabbe and Post [3]—that when a paper issuer's credit rating is lowered, large reductions occur in its volume of paper outstanding within a few weeks, reflecting declining demand for the downgraded issues. Eloyan, Maris, and Young [5] found that a company's stock price tends to fall if its commercial paper is downgraded in quality or if its paper is placed on credit watch lists because of financial problems.

## Dealers in Paper

The market is concentrated among a handful of dealers that account for the bulk of all trading activity. Top commercial paper dealers today include Citicorp (or Citigroup), the Credit-Suisse-First Boston Corporation, Morgan Stanley Dean Witter, and Merrill Lynch. Dealer firms charge varying fees to borrowing companies, depending on the size of an issue and how much paper the company has issued through the dealer recently. The dealer market has become more intensely competitive in recent years as many new foreign dealers have emerged. And dealer activities have further increased in the wake of passage of the Gramm-Leach-Bliley Act in 1999 that allowed U.S. financial holding companies to underwrite more securities through their affiliated securities firms. Dealers maintain inventories of unsold issues and repurchased paper, but they usually expect to turn over most of a new issue within 24 hours.

### QUESTIONS TO HELP YOU STUDY

28. What are the principal *advantages* accruing to a company large enough to tap the commercial paper market for funds? Make a list of these advantages.

29. What are the principal *disadvantages* of commercial paper to an issuer? To buyers?

30. Who are the *principal investors* in commercial paper? Why do the types of investors you have named find commercial paper attractive?

31. How is commercial paper *rated?* Why does its rating matter?

32. Explain what *credit enhancements* are. What is *asset-backed* commercial paper? How have these devices aided growth of the paper market?

## 11.10   Credit Agencies in the Money Market

For nearly a century now, the federal government has attempted to aid certain sectors of the economy that appear to have an unusually difficult time raising funds in the money and capital markets. These "disadvantaged sectors" include agriculture, housing, small businesses, and college students. Dominated by smaller, less creditworthy borrowers, these sectors allegedly are pushed aside in the race for scarce funds by large corporations and governments, especially in periods of tight money.

Beginning in 1916, the federal government began to create special agencies or departments to make direct loans to or guarantee private loans extended to these disadvantaged borrowers. As the decades went by, such institutions as the Farm Credit System, the Small Business Administration, the Federal Home Loan Mortgage Corporation, and the Federal National Mortgage Association became familiar names to active investors worldwide who purchased these agencies' certificates, notes, and bonds. In turn, several of these agencies would buy selected assets from private lenders (creating a secondary market), giving these lenders additional capital for making new loans to disadvantaged borrowers. (See Exhibit 11.5.) Today, federal credit agencies are large enough and, with the government's blessing, financially strong enough to compete successfully for funds in the open market and channel those funds to areas of pressing social need.

### *Types of Federal Credit Agencies*

**government-sponsored agencies**

There are two types of federal credit agencies: government-sponsored agencies and true federal agencies. **Government-sponsored agencies** are *not* officially a part of the federal government's structure but are quasi-private institutions. They are federally chartered but privately owned. In some instances, their stock is traded on major securities exchanges. The borrowing and lending activities of government-sponsored agencies are *not* reflected in the federal government's budget. This has aroused the ire of many fiscal conservatives who regard the credit-granting operations of government-sponsored agencies as a disguised form of government spending. Some critics contend the agencies have been used to get around limits on federal spending. Because these agencies are omitted from the federal government's books, annual federal deficits look smaller and conceal the full extent of federal deficit financing.[8]

**EXHIBIT 11.5**

**Government Agencies: Performing the Roles of a Financial Intermediary**

Borrowing funds from the open market and from other government agencies → Federal and government-sponsored credit agencies → Granting loans to disadvantaged sectors / Guaranteeing loans made by other lenders / Buying loans from the secondary market

[8]Public concern over the growth of federal agency activities has increased in recent years. To the extent that agency borrowing and lending increase the total amount of credit available in the economy and add to aggregate spending for goods and services, they may add to inflationary pressures. Agency borrowing is not generally limited by restrictions that apply to direct debt obligations of the U.S. government. Moreover, there is a tendency to create a new agency each time a new problem rears its head, increasing the cost of government activities. For example, in 1987, the Financing Corporation (FICO) was established to bail out the failing Federal Savings and Loan Insurance Corporation (FSLIC), and in 1989, the Resolution Funding Corporation (REFCO) was created to support the liquidation of hundreds of failing savings and loans that the FSLIC could no longer handle. The creation of these and many other special agencies has raised a number of significant issues concerning government involvement in the private sector of the economy. How many other firms should the federal government guarantee against failure in the future? Upon what basis are such guarantees to be made? What happens to the efficiency of the market system when some firms are not allowed to fail?

| EXHIBIT 11.6 | Principal Borrowers in the Federal Agency Market |
|---|---|

**Agencies of the Federal Government**

| | |
|---|---|
| Export-Import Bank (EXIM) | Postal Service (PS) |
| U.S. Railway Association | Tennessee Valley Authority (TVA) |
| Farmers Home Administration (FMHA) | Federal Deposit Insurance Corporation (FDIC) |
| General Services Administration (GSA) | |
| Government National Mortgage Association (GNMA, or Ginnie Mae) | |

**Government-Sponsored Agencies**

| | |
|---|---|
| Banks for Cooperatives (BC) | Federal Land Banks (FLB) |
| College Construction Loan Insurance Association (CCLIA, or Connie Lee) | Federal National Mortgage Association (FNMA, or Fannie Mae) |
| Federal Farm Credit Banks (FFCB) Federal Home Loan Banks (FHLB) | Student Loan Marketing Association (SLMA, or Sallie Mae) |
| Federal Home Loan Mortgage Corporation (FHLMC, or Freddie Mac) | Financing Corporation (FICO) Financing Assistance Corporation (FAC) |
| Federal Intermediate Credit Banks (FICB) | Resolution Funding Corporation (REFCO) |
| Federal Agricultural Mortgage Corporation (FAMC, or Farmer Mac) | |

**federal agencies**

In contrast, true **federal agencies** are legally a part of the government's structure. They are owned and operated by the United States government. Their borrowing and lending activities are included in the federal budget. The more these federally owned agencies borrow, the larger the government's budget deficit tends to become or, during any years that budget surpluses occur, those budget surpluses tend to decrease as federal agency borrowing grows. The principal government-sponsored and federal agencies that borrow regularly in the money and capital markets are shown in Exhibit 11.6.

**financial intermediaries**

In their borrowing and lending activities, federal and government-sponsored agencies act as true **financial intermediaries.** They issue attractively packaged notes and bonds to capture funds from savers, and they direct the resulting flow of funds into loans and loan guarantees to farmers, small business owners, home mortgage borrowers, and other sectors. The securities issued by government-sponsored agencies are usually *not* guaranteed by the federal government, but many investors believe the government is "only a step away" in the event any agency gets into serious trouble.

## Growth of the Agency Security Market

Armed with this implied government support, the agency market has soared in recent years, with the volume of outstanding securities climbing from about $2 billion during the 1950s to nearly $2.7 trillion today. (See Exhibit 11.7.) On an average day, the leading federal agency borrowers (especially the federal mortgage-market agencies) borrow at an interest cost that is at least a third of a percentage point cheaper than for the largest and best-known private borrowers, due primarily to the federal government's implied financial support. Moreover, the government-sponsored agencies consistently have been profitable in recent years, though they do face credit (default) risk and interest rate risk on the loans they issue or buy and the debt they sell.

Government-sponsored agencies are permitted to draw on the U.S. Treasury for funds up to a specified limit with Treasury approval. However, neither principal nor interest on the debt of government-sponsored agencies is guaranteed by the federal government, although the issuing agency guarantees its own securities. In contrast, securities of agencies owned by the federal government are fully guaranteed by the credit of the U.S. government. The government-sponsored agencies generally have capitalization requirements that limit the rate of growth of their debt, but sponsored agencies tend to operate with considerably less capital per dollar of debt than do most private lending institutions, giving them a distinct advantage in the money and capital markets over most private borrowers.

The lower capitalization of government-sponsored agencies aroused concern in the early 2000s due to their heavier use of financial derivatives and apparent increases in risk exposure. The financial condition of the two top government-sponsored home mortgage agencies—FNMA (Fannie Mae) and FHLMC (Freddie Mac)—came under heavy scrutiny in the financial press as new regulations required greater disclosure of their current financial positions. At about the same time, allegations of internal accounting irregularities,

operating inefficiencies, and the charging of excessive fees for their services added to the pressures placed on these particular agencies by federal rulemakers and the financial marketplace. Some mortgage agencies suffered substantial investment losses as thousands of home buyers refinanced their mortgage loans when market interest rates fell to historic lows, thereby reducing the expected yield from mortgage-backed securities—the principal investments held by some of the most prominent federal agencies.

Ultimately, OFHEO (the Office of Federal Housing Enterprise Oversight), chief regulator of Fannie Mae and Freddie Mac, reached an agreement with these two agencies, requiring Fannie and Freddie to increase their capital in order to control their risk exposure and possibly slow their growth. Under further scrutiny from OFHEO, Fannie and Freddie's accounting practices have been revised, particularly in how they value their assets (especially their mortgage-loan-related assets) and how they compensate management.

**Key URLs:**
For on overview of the activities of the Federal National Mortgage Association and the Federal Home Loan Mortgage Corporation, see **fanniemae .com,** and **.freddiemac.com**

**Federal Financing Bank (FFB)**

The agency market is dominated by the government-sponsored agencies, which have limited access to government coffers and must rely mainly on the open market to raise money. In contrast, the federal agencies, which are part of the federal government, are financed through the **Federal Financing Bank (FFB),** which borrows money from the Treasury. The FFB is closely supervised by the Treasury Department and, in fact, is staffed by Treasury employees.[9] All FFB debt is fully guaranteed by the United States government.

Money market borrowing is usually done by issuing discount notes, which, like Treasury bills and commercial paper, have no promised interest rate but are sold at a price below their par value. Dealers sell the notes for a small fee, with banks, mutual funds, insurance companies, thrifts, and pension funds purchasing most of them. The sponsored agencies also issue short-term coupon securities and variable-rate notes. Long-term borrowing in the capital market is usually accomplished by issuing debentures, either on a monthly basis or irregularly as the need for funds arises.

---

[9]The U. S. Treasury has to add a certain amount to its regular borrowings each year to cover any Federal Financing Bank (FFB) drawings. The FFB was created by Congress in 1973. Up to that time each federal agency did its own borrowing. As a result, the number of different agency issues was proliferating at a rapid rate, creating confusion among investors. Centralization of borrowing in one agency, it was hoped, would increase efficiency in the funding process, improve the marketability of agency securities, and give the U.S. Congress a more adequate measure of the growth of agency activities.

| EXHIBIT 11.7 | Total Debt Outstanding of Federal and Government-Sponsored Agencies, 2006* ($ Billions) |
|---|---|
| **Agency** | **Total Debt Outstanding** |
| Federal agencies: | |
|    Export-Import Bank | $   NA |
|    Federal Housing Administration | 0.3 |
|    Postal Service[†] | — |
|    Tennessee Valley Authority | 25.4 |
|    Other agencies | 0.1 |
| Total federal agency debt[‡] | $   25.8 |
| Government-sponsored agencies: | |
|    Federal Home Loan Banks | 745.2 |
|    Federal Home Loan Mortgage Corporation | 744.8 |
|    Federal National Mortgage Association | 961.7 |
|    Farm Credit Banks[§] | 92.1 |
|    Student Loan Marketing Association | 58.5 |
|    Resolution Funding Corporation[§] | 30.0 |
|    Other agencies | 9.3 |
| Total government-sponsored debt[‡] | $2,645.7 |
| Total agency debt outstanding | $2,671.5 |

Source: Board of Governors of the Federal Reserve System, *Federal Reserve Bulletin,* January 2007, Table 1.44.
*Data as of December 2006. NA means data not currently available.

[†]Off-budget agency.

[‡]Figures may not reflect column totals due to rounding and unavailability of some data.

[§]In January 1979, the Farm Credit Banks began issuing consolidated bonds to replace those securities previously issued by the Federal Land Banks, the Federal Intermediate Credit Banks, and the Banks for Cooperatives. The Resolution Funding Corporation was established by the Financial Institutions Reform, Recovery, and Enforcement Act of 1989.

Longer-term agency securities are available in denominations as small as $1,000, while the shorter-term notes traded in the money market generally come in minimum denominations of $50,000 or more. They are subject to federal income taxes, but many are exempt from state and local taxes. However, state and local government estate, gift, and inheritance taxes do generally apply to agency obligations. Depository institutions may use agency securities as collateral for loans from the Federal Reserve's discount window and as collateral pledged to secure government deposits at banks and other depositories.

The heaviest agency borrowers in recent years, as indicated in Exhibit 11.7, have been the Federal National Mortgage Association (FNMA), the Federal Home Loan Banks (FHLB), the Federal Home Loan Mortgage Corporation (FHLMC), the Student Loan Marketing Association, and the Farm Credit Banks. These agencies account for well over three-quarters of the outstanding debt issued by all federal and government-sponsored agencies, and an active secondary market exists for the short-term debt of these agencies. Most agency borrowing goes to support, directly or indirectly, the housing market and agriculture.

The securities of all government-sponsored agencies are regarded as highly similar by investors. Comparable maturities tend to have about the same yield, regardless of the issuing agency. Each agency is able to borrow at interest rates below the average yield on its asset portfolio due to government support but pays a slightly higher interest

**Key URL:**
One of the most controversial of the federal credit agencies in recent years is the Student Loan Marketing Association. For an overview of its operations see **salliemae.com**

rate than the U.S. Treasury. Most of this small difference in interest cost is due to the fact that agency securities are less marketable than Treasury IOUs. The Treasury issues a security homogeneous in quality and other characteristics, but the agency market is splintered into many pieces. The yields on agency securities are lower than yields on private debt issues, however, due to their actual or implied government support.

## Characteristics and Marketing of Agency Securities

Agency securities are generally short to medium term in maturity (running out to about 10 years). However among the most rapidly growing segment is the money market segment—agency securities under one year to maturity. Among the most active buyers of agency securities are banks, state and local governments, government trust funds, and the Federal Reserve System. The Federal Reserve has been authorized to conduct open market operations in agency IOUs since 1966. Fed buying and selling of these securities has helped improve their marketability and stature among private investors. Major securities dealers who handle U.S. government securities also generally trade in agency issues.

Government-sponsored agencies have become innovative borrowers in recent years. For example, FNMA and SLMA have sold securities in foreign markets, some of these denominated in foreign currencies or sold in "dual currency" form in which interest is paid in a foreign currency and the principal is repaid at maturity in U.S. dollars. These agencies have also used interest rate swaps and currency swaps to protect themselves against the risk of fluctuating interest rates and currency prices.

---

### QUESTIONS TO HELP YOU STUDY

33. Federal agencies active in the financial markets were usually set up to aid so-called *disadvantaged sectors* of the economy. Identify these sectors and give some examples.

34. What is the difference between a *government-sponsored agency* and a *federal agency?*

35. What are the principal investment characteristics of federal agency securities? Which groups of investors are attracted to them and why?

---

## Summary of the Chapter's Main Points

In this chapter we have examined some of the most important money market institutions, including banks, major corporations, and federal credit agencies. Among the key points were the following:

- *Banks* are among the most important financial institutions in the money market, providing credit to security dealers, industrial firms, and other money market participants. They are the principal channel for making payments in the money market, acting as guarantors of payments and as custodians for the safekeeping of financial instruments. Finally, banks serve as a key channel for government economic policy, particularly in regulating the supply and cost of money and credit.

- Two of the most important domestic sources of funds in the money market that support the activities of banks are federal funds and negotiable CDs (certificates of deposit). *Federal funds* represent "immediately available" money in the form of large-denomination deposits that can be wired the same day from lenders to borrowers and then back again. *Negotiable CDs* are savings deposits with fixed or variable interest rates that are issued in denominations of $100,000 or more.

- Other important sources of money market funding for banks are *Eurocurrency deposits,* which consist of time deposits denominated in a currency other than the currency of the country where the bank accepting these deposits is located. (Thus, a deposit of U.S. dollars in Great Britain is a Eurodollar deposit.) They are not immediately spendable funds but constitute a reservoir of liquidity that can be used as a basis for expanding the volume of credit available within the international financial system.

- Among the most important sources of Eurocurrency deposits are tourist travel abroad, balance-of-payments deficits with other nations, and investments made overseas. Banks also use Eurocurrency deposits to help supply liquid reserves to support bank lending and investing activities.

- One of the best-known and oldest of bank-issued money market instruments is the *banker's acceptance,* which constitutes a time draft drawn against a bank. The accepting bank pledges payment upon a specific date in the future. Widely used for many years to fund exports and imports of goods in international markets, the volume of acceptances has recently been declining as other financial instruments have moved in to take over the same role. Moreover, information flows between countries are more complete today, reducing some of the risk of foreign trade that acceptances were designed originally to deal with.

- Eurocurrency deposits, federal funds, and negotiable CDs help banks meet the *legal reserve requirements* that the central bank (in the United States, the Federal Reserve System) imposes upon their deposit holdings. Bankers must continually compare the cost and availability of federal funds, CDs, Eurocurrency deposits, and other sources of bank funds in order to secure the reserves they require.

- Major corporations are active as both borrowers and lenders in the money market. One of the best known of their borrowing instruments is *commercial paper.* The paper market has grown over the years as major industrial corporations and financial-service companies, facing growing demands for their products and services, have turned increasingly to the open market for capital. The commercial paper market has provided a relatively low cost, flexible vehicle for raising short-term cash.

- Commercial paper has offered several distinct *advantages* over other sources of corporate funds, including ready access to new funds, lower interest rates than on most other sources of capital, and leverage to use against other lenders of funds when seeking new financing. A borrowing company with a high credit rating may be able to tap the paper market for funding and can always threaten to go to that market if a lending institution refuses to make a loan on reasonable terms. However, the paper market also has some *disadvantages,* being highly volatile at times with a scarce supply of available credit.

- One of the most rapidly growing of all money market segments involves trading in the IOUs issued by *federal agencies,* such as the Federal National Mortgage Association or the Farm Credit System. These agencies were set up to provide credit or help develop a market for loans to disadvantaged sectors of the economy, such as farms and ranches, new home buyers, and small businesses.
- Federal and government-sponsored agencies act like financial intermediaries, borrowing and lending funds at the same time. They rely upon the government's implied or expressed guarantee to give them an advantage in the competition for funds, lowering their cost of financing. With the government's implicit or explicit backing, these agencies issue securities almost as attractive as U.S. Treasury securities to most investors, but with slightly higher yields than are available on direct government obligations.

## Key Terms Appearing in This Chapter

**federal funds,**  313

**legal reserve requirement,**  314

**negotiable certificate of
   deposit (CD),**  318

**Eurocurrency market,**  322

**Eurodollars,**  322

**London Interbank Offer Rate
   (LIBOR),**  327

**banker's acceptance,**  328

**liability management,**  332

**commercial paper,**  333

**direct paper,**  333

**dealer paper,**  334

**credit enhancements,**  336

**master note,**  340

**government-sponsored agencies,**  342

**federal agencies,**  343

**financial intermediaries,**  343

**Federal Financing Bank (FFB),**  344

## Problems and Issues

1. A money-center bank is trying to decide which source of funding to rely upon to cover loans being made today. It needs to borrow $10 million in either the federal funds market or in the negotiable CD market. Funds are needed for at least a week, but the bank's money desk manager is most concerned about the next 24 hours. Federal funds are currently trading at 4.80 percent; rates on new negotiable CDs posted by leading banks have reached 4.70 percent. FDIC insurance fees are currently 27 cents per $100.

   Calculate the cost to the bank for each of these funds sources. If you were a banker, which source would you prefer to use?

2. Glenwood National Bank is short of required legal reserves. The bank's money manager estimates it will need to raise an additional $50 million in funds to cover its reserve requirement over the next three days. Federal funds are trading today at 5.90 percent, and the bank's economist has forecast a federal funds rate of 6.15 percent tomorrow and 6.20 percent the next day. Negotiable CDs in minimum maturities of seven days have been trading this morning at 5.85 percent, with a forecast of 5.90 percent tomorrow and 5.98 percent the next day. The FDIC charges 30 cents per $100 for insurance coverage.

Calculate the lowest-cost source of funding for Glenwood National Bank and the next cheapest source for borrowing over the next three days (today, tomorrow, and the next day). What are the relative advantages and disadvantages of each of these funding sources?

3. If Sterling Corporation purchases a $5 million bank CD that matures in 90 days and promises an interest return of 6.25 percent, how much in total will Sterling receive back when this CD matures?

4. What is the coupon-equivalent yield to maturity (YTM) on a 30-day negotiable CD promising an annualized interest return (*i*) of 5.95 percent?

5. Calculate the bank discount rate (DR) attached to a 60-day, $1 million CD selling in the secondary market for $990,000.

6. JP Morgan Chase Bank is short cash reserves in the amount of $225 million—a condition expected to last for the next five business days—and is weighing (a) securing a loan in the domestic federal funds market, where the interest rate prevailing today is 5.45 percent; (b) issuing 7-day domestic negotiable CDs at a current market rate of 5.50 percent; or (c) tapping its foreign branch offices for 30-day Eurodollars at a market rate of 5.58 percent. The estimated noninterest cost of all of these various funding sources is approximately the same, except that the domestic CDs currently carry an annual FDIC insurance fee of $0.04 per every $100 in deposits received from the public. Which source of funds would you recommend the bank make use of? What factors should the bank's funds management division weigh in making this borrowing decision?

7. A new issue of 90-day commercial paper is available from a dealer in New York City at a price of $97.60 on a $100 basis. What is the bank discount yield on this note if held to maturity?

8. A note traded in the commercial paper market will mature in 15 days. The dealer will sell it to you at $98.35 on a $100 basis. What is the note's discount rate of return?

9. Commercial paper was purchased in the secondary market 30 days from maturity at a bank discount yield of 9 percent. Ten days later, it was sold to a dealer at an 8 percent discount rate. What was the investor's holding-period yield?

10. What is the difference in basis points between the discount rate of return (DR) and the investment rate of return (IR) on a $10 million commercial paper note purchased at a price of $9.85 million and scheduled to mature in 25 days?

11. A commercial paper note with $1 million par value and maturing in 60 days has an expected discount return (DR) at maturity of 6 percent. What was its purchase price? What is this note's expected coupon-equivalent (investment return) yield (IR)?

12. Alamo Corporation requests a $20 million, 90-day loan from its bank, which proposes to make the requested loan at an interest rate of 6 percent and a compensating balance requirement of 10 percent of the amount of the loan. What will Alamo's effective loan rate be under these terms? Suppose 90-day commercial paper sold by dealers is currently trading at an interest rate of 6.0 percent. What is the interest rate spread between the effective loan rate quoted by the bank and the current commercial paper rate? Does the bank's proposed loan carry any advantages that borrowing through the commercial paper market won't necessarily provide Alamo Corporation?

13. What price would attach today to Europaper issued at par (100) with a maturity of 180 days and carrying a discount rate of 7 percent?

14. What is the appropriate discount rate for a 270-day Europaper issue priced at par (100) and expected to sell today at a discounted price of 96?

15. A bank is willing to issue a line of credit to fully back a $25 million issue of commercial paper for a fee of 1 percent. If any portion of the line is used, an interest rate of 8 percent will be assessed. The compensating balance requirement for the line of credit is 5 percent, while the portion of the line that is used carries a 20 percent compensating balance requirement. How much will the borrowing company pay for the full unused line? Suppose $1.5 million is actually drawn upon for unexpected expenses and the balance of the credit line is used merely to back the paper issue. How much will the borrowing firm pay in total bank charges?

16. What is the discount rate (DR) and the investment return (IR) on the following commercial notes?

|    | Face Value | Purchase Price | Maturity in Days |
| --- | --- | --- | --- |
| a. | $10,000,000 | $ 9,750,000 | 60 |
| b. | $22,500,000 | $21,350,000 | 45 |
| c. | $48,750,000 | $46,975,000 | 30 |
| d. | $60,175,000 | $48,850,985 | 15 |

17. A German manufacturer of furniture sells a large order of home furnishings to an outlet store in Houston. The Houston firm pays for the shipment by wiring funds from its local bank through Fedwire to the German firm's account at JP Morgan Chase Bank in New York City. Subsequently, the German manufacturer decides to invest half of the funds received in a dollar deposit offered by Barclays Bank in London, where interest rates are particularly attractive. No sooner are the funds deposited in London than a Japanese auto company, shipping cars to the U.S. and Europe, asks the London bank for a loan to purchase raw materials in the United States.

   Later, when the loan falls due, the Japanese firm will go into the currency market to purchase dollars in order to retire its Eurodollar loan at Barclays Bank, receiving a dollar deposit at a U.S. bank. When the loan is repaid, Barclays gains the dollar deposit in the United States and uses the deposit to pay off the German firm when its time deposit matures. The German firm chooses to deposit the funds received from Barclays in its demand deposit account at JP Morgan Chase Bank in New York City because it now needs to buy goods and services in the United States.

   Construct T accounts that reflect the foregoing transactions. In particular, show the proper entries for: (1) payment by the Houston firm to the German furniture company; (2) deposit of the funds in London; (3) the loan to the Japanese automaker; (4) repayment of the loan; and (5) return of funds to the United States. Indicate which deposit is a Eurodollar deposit and if any Eurodollars are destroyed at any particular stage.

18. A company known as Standard Quality Importing ships DVD players made in Japan to retail dealers in the United States and Europe. It decides to place an order with its Japanese supplier for 10,000 DVD players at $200 each after

securing a line of credit from Guaranty Security Bank in Los Angeles. Guaranty issues a credit letter to the Japanese supplier promising payment in U.S. dollars 90 days hence. However, the Japanese firm needs the promised funds within seven days from receipt of the credit letter to make purchases of technical components from an electronics firm in Phoenix, Arizona. Explain and illustrate with T accounts and diagrams how a banker's acceptance would arise from the foregoing transactions, how the Japanese supplier could receive the dollars she needs in timely fashion, and what would happen to the acceptance at the end of the 90-day period. Use T account entries to show the movement of funds from the importer to the Japanese supplier, to the electronics firm, and to money market investors.

19. Instel Corporation has been offered a $100 million, 3-month loan at a fixed rate of 90-day LIBOR plus ⅜% margin or at the prevailing federal funds rate plus ½% margin with the loan rate adjusted every 24 hours to the federal funds rate prevailing at the close of business each day. These rates, along with prevailing yields on U.S. Treasury bills, are posted in London and New York as follows:

| 90-Day LIBOR rate on Eurodollar deposits | 4.275% | 3-month U.S. Treasury bill rate | 4.12% |
|---|---|---|---|
| Federal funds rate | 4.08 | 6-month U.S. Treasury bill rate | 4.20 |
| One-month (30 day) U.S. Treasury bills | 4.05 | 1-year U.S. Treasury bill rate | 4.30 |

Which set of loan terms would you recommend to Instel's treasurer? Why?

20. A British investor withdraws her million-dollar deposit from Citicorp Bank, N.A., and converts the deposit into a dollar-denominated, 30-day CD in a Belgian commercial bank at the going market rate (LIBOR) of 5.85 percent. Almost immediately, the Belgian bank makes a loan of $750,000 to an aluminum frames manufacturer at LIBOR plus 30 basis points for 21 days. When the CD matures and the deposit is returned to Citicorp, how much in interest income will the depositor receive? How much will the aluminum frame manufacturer pay in total interest expense for its 21-day bank loan? Show the proper accounting entries for all of the foregoing transactions (including the return of funds to the original depositor).

## Web-Based Problems

1. The negotiable CD market represents an important source of short-term funds for many banks. Among the important assets of banks are Treasury bills and business loans extended to "blue chip" companies with excellent credit ratings.

   a. Go to the FRED II database maintained by the Federal Reserve Bank of St. Louis at **research.stlouisfed.org/fred2** and download historical data for the interest rates paid on six-month CDs and six-month T-bills as well as the information needed to construct a series for the prime bank lending rate (i.e., the rate banks charge their best corporate clients).

    **b.** On a single graph plot *two* interest-rate spreads: (i) the 6-month T-bill rate minus the 6-month CD rate and (ii) the prime lending rate minus the 6-month CD rate.

    **c.** Do your results from part (b) indicate why a bank could not operate by raising money in the CD market and investing all of it in Treasuries?

    **d.** Is corporate lending profitable for banks when they rely on the CD market to raise funds? Why or why not?

**2.** The Eurodollar market has become an important vehicle for larger banks to raise short-term funds in the money market. Using a spreadsheet program to make the required computations easily:

    **a.** Visit the Federal Reserve's Web site at **federalreserve.gov/releases/h6/hist** and obtain a monthly time series covering the last 20 years for the volume of Eurodollars held by domestically chartered U.S. commercial banks.

    **b.** Go to **federalreserve.gov/releases/h8/data.htm** and obtain monthly data covering the same time period as in part (a) for seasonally adjusted Total Liabilities of all domestically chartered U.S. commercial banks.

    **c.** Form a ratio of Eurodollar deposits (from part [a]) to total liabilities (from part [b]) and graph the results.

    **d.** How has bank reliance on Eurodollars as a funds source changed in each of the past two decades? Can you suggest plausible reasons for the changes?

## Selected References to Explore

**1.** Bartolini, Leonardo; Svenja Gudell; Spence Hilton; and Krista Schwarz. "Intraday Trading in the Overnight Federal Funds Market," *Current Issues in Economics and Finance,* Federal Reserve Bank of New York, Vol. 11, No. 11 (November 2005), pp. 1–7.

**2.** Bratzsch, Nikolaus; Ben Craig; and Falko Fecht. "The Eurosystem Money Market Auctions: A Banking Perspective," *Working Paper 05-06,* Federal Reserve Bank of Cleveland, May 2005.

**3.** Crabbe, Leland, and Mitchell A. Post. "The Effect of SEC Amendments to Rule 2A-7 on the Commercial Paper Market," *Finance and Economics Discussion Series 199,* Board of Governors of the Federal Reserve System, May 1992.

**4.** Downing, Chris, and Stephen Oliner. "The Term Structure of Commercial Paper Rates," *Finance and Economics Discussion Series* (Z.11), #2004-18, Board of Governors of the Federal Reserve System, April 2004.

**5.** Eloyan, Fayez A.; Bryan A. Maris; and Philip J. Young. "The Effects of Commercial Paper Rating Changes and Credit-Watch Placement on Common Stock Prices," *The Financial Review,* Vol. 31, No. 1 (February 1996), pp. 149–67.

**6.** Hilton, Spence. "Trends in Federal Funds Rate Volatility," *Current Issues in Economics and Finance,* Federal Reserve Bank of New York, Vol. 11, No. 7 (July 2005), pp. 1–7.

7. McAndrews, James J. "Alternative Arrangements for the Distribution of Intraday Liquidity," *Current Issues in Economics and Finance,* Federal Reserve Bank of New York, Vol. 12, No. 3 (April 2006), pp. 1–11.

8. Poole, William. "The GSEs: Where Do We Stand," *Review,* Federal Reserve Bank of St. Louis, May/June 2007, pp. 143–151.

9. Shen, Pu. "Why Has the Nonfinancial Commercial Paper Market Shrunk Recently?" *Economic Review,* Federal Reserve Bank of Kansas City, First Quarter 2003, pp. 55–76.

# Chapter 12

# Roles and Services of the Federal Reserve and Other Central Banks around the World

## Learning Objectives in This Chapter

- You will explore the many different roles played and functions performed by *central banks* around the world.

- You will see how and why the *Federal Reserve System* came to be established as the U.S. central bank and how the Fed is organized to carry out the many tasks it must perform, not only domestically but also as part of the global financial system.

- You will discover the importance of *central bank independence* from the dictates of governments and the importance of *transparency* in making policymakers' intentions clear.

- You will understand the concept of *legal reserves* and how actions taken by the central bank influence the level and growth of legal reserves and, ultimately, deposits and loans.

## What's in This Chapter?
## Key Topics Outline

Roles and Functions of Central Banking

Goals Pursued by Central Banks around the World

Channels of Central Banking: Their Influence on the Economy and Financial Markets

The Fed and the European Central Bank: How Do They Compare?

History and Structure of the Federal Reserve System

Central Bank Independence and Transparency: Their Importance Today

Bank Reserves and Deposit and Money Multipliers

## 12.1   Introduction to Central Banking

**central bank**

One of the most important financial institutions in any modern economy is the **central bank.** Basically, a central bank is an agency of government that has important public policy functions in monitoring the operation of the financial system, controlling the growth of a nation's money supply, and enhancing the performance of its economy. Central banks ordinarily do not deal directly with the public; rather, they are "bankers' banks," communicating with banks and securities dealers in carrying out their essential policymaking functions. (For a list of the world's leading central banks and their Web site addresses, see the Financial Developments box on page 358.) The central bank of the United States is the **Federal Reserve System,** a creation of the U.S. Congress charged with issuing currency, regulating the banking system, and taking measures to protect the purchasing power of the dollar and promote full employment. In this and the following chapter, we examine in detail the nature and impact of central bank operations and the major problems faced by central bank managers today.

**Federal Reserve System**

## 12.2   The Roles of Central Banks in the Economy and Financial System

### Control of the Money Supply to Avoid Severe Inflation

Central banks, including the Federal Reserve System, perform several important functions in a modern economy. (See Exhibit 12.1.) One of their most important functions is *control of the money supply in order to avoid severe inflation.*

What is money? Money is a financial asset that serves as a *medium of exchange* in the purchase of goods, services, and other financial assets. Based on the medium of exchange value of money, the nation's money supply could be defined as the sum of all currency and coin held by the public, plus the value of all publicly held checking accounts and other deposits against which drafts may be made (such as NOWs and money market accounts). However, money has another important function—serving as a *highly liquid store of value* that enables its owner to carry purchasing power through time in a form that is readily accessible and can be relied upon to carry out transactions whenever needed. Recognizing this feature of money leads to a broader definition of the nation's money supply to include time and savings accounts at banks and nonbank financial intermediaries (such as money market mutual funds).

However we define money, the power to regulate its quantity and value in the United States was delegated by the U.S. Congress early in the twentieth century to the Federal Reserve System. The Fed has become not only the principal source of currency used by the U.S. public but also a key government agency helping the U.S. Treasury stabilize the value of the dollar and protect its integrity in international markets. Why is control of the money supply so important? One reason is that changes in

**EXHIBIT 12.1**

**Roles Usually Played by Central Banks in the Financial System**

- Control of the money supply to avoid severe inflation
- Market stabilization
- Lender of last resort
- Supervisor of the banking system
- Protecting and improving the flow of payments

the money supply seem to be closely linked to changes in economic activity. In other words, there appears to be a statistically significant relationship between current and lagged changes in the money supply and changes in nominal gross domestic product (GDP).[1] The implication of these studies is that, if the central bank can control the growth rate of money, it can influence the nominal growth rate of the economy as a whole.

Another important reason for controlling the money supply is that, in the absence of effective controls, money in the form of paper notes, computer entries, and bank deposits could expand virtually without limit. The marginal cost of creating additional units of money is essentially *zero*. It costs no more to print a $100 bill than to print a $1 bill. (Which is why you are unlikely to hear of very many counterfeit $1 bills floating around!) Therefore, the banking system or the government or both are capable of increasing the money supply well beyond the economy's capacity to produce goods and services. Such a situation has often been described as "too much money chasing too few goods" and leads to severe price inflation that can slow overall economic activity eventually.

It is not surprising that modern governments have come to rely so heavily on central banks as guardians of the quantity and value of their currencies. For example, the Federal Reserve System and other central banks enter the financial markets frequently in an attempt to control domestic price inflation in order to protect the purchasing power of the home currency. It is generally believed that by accomplishing this task, central banks make their most important contribution toward promoting growth in the economy's output and employment. Thus, it is often argued today that price level stability *must* be the principal long-run goal of central bank policy and, therefore, that central banks *must* pay close attention to how fast money and credit are allowed to expand in order to avoid severe inflation.

## Stabilizing the Money and Capital Markets

**Key URL:**
For a review of the structure, laws, and performance of central banks around the world, see the Web site of the Center for the Study of Central Banks at **law.nyu.edu/ centralbankscenter**

A second vital function of central banking is *stabilization of the money and capital markets.* The financial system must transmit savings to those who require funds for investment so the economy can grow. If the system of money and capital markets is to work efficiently, however, the public must have confidence in financial institutions and be willing to commit its savings to them. If the financial markets are unruly, with volatile fluctuations in interest rates and security prices, or if financial institutions are prone to frequent collapse, public confidence in the financial system might well be damaged. The flow of investment capital may dry up, resulting in a drastic slowing in the rate of economic growth and a rise in unemployment.

All central banks play a role in fostering the mature development of financial markets and in ensuring a stable flow of funds through those markets. Pursuing this objective, a central bank may, from time to time, provide funds to major securities dealers and/or depository institutions when they have difficulty financing their portfolios or providing an adequate supply of credit so that buyers and sellers may easily acquire or sell securities and borrowers interested in making investments can find adequate funding. When the money supply and interest rates rise or fall more rapidly than seems consistent with economic goals and the desired volume of saving and investment in the economy, a central bank may intervene in the financial marketplace.

---

[1]For example, see the references at the end of the chapter for the Federal Reserve Bank of San Francisco [4] and Marquis [7].

## Lender of Last Resort and Supervisor of the Banking System

Another essential function of many central banks is to supervise and monitor the condition of the banking system and serve as a *lender of last resort*. This latter function involves providing liquid funds to those financial institutions in need, especially when alternative sources of funds have dried up. For example, through its discount window, the Federal Reserve will provide funds to selected deposit-type financial institutions to cover their short-term cash deficiencies. The central bank's discount window can supply large amounts of emergency funds very quickly, as occurred, for example, in the wake of the September 11, 2001, terrorist attacks when the Federal Reserve moved rapidly to supply liquidity to the struggling U.S. economy. As we will see, before the Federal Reserve System was created, one of the weaknesses in the financial system of the United States was the absence of a lender of last resort to aid financial institutions squeezed by severe liquidity pressures. More recently, the European Central Bank (ECB) began providing funds to the banking system through weekly money market auctions.

## Maintaining and Improving the Payments Mechanism

Finally, central banks have a role to play in *maintaining and improving the payments mechanism.* This may involve the central bank helping to clear checks, providing an adequate supply of currency and coin, wiring funds from one account to another, and preserving confidence in the value of the fundamental monetary unit. A smoothly functioning and efficient payments mechanism is vital for business and commerce. If checks or electronic payments cannot be cleared in timely fashion (as happened in the immediate wake of the terrorist crisis in September 2001) or if the public cannot get the currency and coin it needs to carry out transactions, business activity will be severely curtailed. The result might well be large-scale unemployment and a decline in the nation's rate of economic growth.

**Key URLs:**
To explore the concept of "lender of last resort" see, in particular, **answers. com/topic/ lender-of-last-resort** and **investopedia.com/ terms/l/lenderof lastresort.asp**

## 12.3   The Goals and Channels of Central Banking

### Central Banks' Goals

Central banking is *goal oriented*. Since World War II, the United States and other industrialized nations have accepted the premise that government is responsible to its citizens for maintaining high levels of employment, combating inflation, and promoting sustained growth in the economy so that living standards rise and jobs are available for all who want to work.

Specifically, central banking in the United States and in most other nations today is directed toward:

1. *Achieving maximum sustainable output and employment,* and

2. *Promoting stable prices.*

Of these two key monetary-policy objectives, more and more central banks around the globe are directing their primary effort toward the *promotion of stable prices*—that is, their focus is on *avoiding severe inflation.* They recognize that monetary policy can have a very significant *long-run* impact on inflation, and that inflation can be very dangerous because it can reduce economic growth by introducing mistakes in

Bank of England (bankofengland.gov)
Bank of Japan (boj.ur.jp)
Swiss National Bank (snb.ch)
Bank of Canada (bankofcanada.ca/en)
Banque Nationale de Belgique (Belgium) (bnb.be/)
European Central Bank (ECB) (ecb.int)
Deutsche Bundesbank (Germany) (bundesbank.de/)
Banca D'Italia (bancaditalia.it)

Reserve Bank of Australia (rba.gov.au/)
Banco Central do Brasil (bcb.gov.br/)
Federal Reserve System (federalreserve.gov)
Banque de France (banque-france.fr/)
Reserve Bank of New Zealand (rbnz.govt.nz/)
De Nederlandsche Bank NV (The Netherlands) (dnb.n/)
The People's Bank of China (pbc.gov.cn/english/)

business and consumer planning, by misallocating the economy's scarce resources and redistributing its wealth (primarily from lenders to borrowers), and by increasing interest rates (especially long-term interest rates).

So strong has been the recent emphasis on *long-run price stability* as the principal target of central bank monetary policy that a growing number of nations have set *inflation-rate targets* or *target ranges*. By attaching specific numbers to their goal of promoting stable prices, many central banks now have a way to measure their progress in the fight against inflation. Examples of central banks and nations adopting specific inflation-rate targets or target ranges include Australia, Brazil, Canada, the countries that are members of the European Monetary Union, Hungary, Israel, South Korea, New Zealand, Poland, Sweden, Switzerland, and the United Kingdom. The majority of these nations have established a *target range* for inflation that typically lies in the 1 to 3 percent annual rate range.

Notice that the United States is not on the inflation targeting list of countries discussed above. Neither the U.S. Congress nor the Federal Reserve has yet spelled out a specific numerical inflation target beyond the generic phrase "promoting stable prices." This does not mean that the Fed does not pay close attention to the U.S. inflation rate, but that, due to the lack of specific numerical guidelines, it is up to the judgment of Federal Reserve policymakers to determine what the term "stable prices" really means. To paraphrase a famous statement by former Federal Reserve Chairman Alan Greenspan, *"Price stability exists when inflation is so low that it does not materially affect important economic decisions [such as savings and investment]."*

Moreover, it is important to note that, given recent experience in Japan, central banks also must be prepared to deal with *deflation*. If the inflation rate turns negative and average prices fall (as happened in Japan for much of the 1990s), central bankers must deal with a new set of economic problems. Deflation tends to redistribute wealth from borrowers to lenders, make credit more difficult to obtain, push stock and real estate prices lower, and slow productive investment and job growth. In summary, both inflation and deflation present potential pitfalls to the successful management of national and global economies by central banks.

## Challenges in Achieving Central Bank Goals

Through their influence over interest rates and the growth of the money supply, central banks are able to influence the economy's progress toward the above goals. Achievement of all central bank goals simultaneously has proven to be difficult,

**Key URL:**
Articles and speeches by central banking officials around the world are compiled by the Bank for International Settlements at **bis.org/review**

however. One reason is that the goals often *conflict*. Pursuit of price stability, for example, may require higher interest rates and restricted credit availability—policies that tend to increase unemployment and slow economic growth. Central bank policymaking is often a matter of accepting *trade-offs* (compromises) among multiple goals.

Central banking in most major nations today operates principally through the *marketplace*. Modern central banks operate as a balance wheel in promoting and stabilizing the flow of savings from surplus-spending units to deficit-spending units. They try to ensure a smooth and orderly flow of funds through the money and capital markets so that adequate financing is available for worthwhile investment projects. This means, among other things, avoiding panics due to sudden shortages of available credit or sharp declines in the values of financial assets. However, most of the actions taken by the central bank to promote a smooth flow of funds are carried out through the marketplace rather than by government order. For example, the central bank may encourage interest rates to rise in order to reduce borrowing and spending and combat inflation, but it does not usually allocate credit to particular borrowers. The private sector, working through supply and demand forces in the marketplace, is left to make its own decisions about how much borrowing and spending will take place and who is to receive credit.

## The Channels through Which Central Banks Work

It is useful at this point to give a brief overview of the channels through which modern central banks influence conditions in the economy and financial system. Central bank policy affects the economy as a whole by making the following adjustments:

- Changes in the cost and availability of credit to businesses, consumers, and governments.
- Changes in the volume and rate of growth of the money supply.
- Changes in the financial wealth of investors as reflected in the market value of their stocks, bonds, and other security holdings.
- Changes in the relative prices of domestic and foreign currencies (currency exchange rates).
- Changes in the public's expectations regarding future money and credit conditions and currency values (see Exhibit 12.2).

The central bank has a number of policy tools at its command to influence the cost of credit (interest rates); the value (prices) of financial assets; money supply volume and growth; the relative prices (exchange rates) of world currencies; and the public's expectations regarding future interest rates, currency prices, and credit conditions. In the United States, the principal policy tools used by the central bank are open market operations, changes in required reserves held by depository institutions, and changes in the discount rate on central bank loans. Many of these same tools are used by other central banks around the world, with a growing reliance upon open market operations, which appear to be the most popular monetary tool in nations around the globe.

Changes in interest rates, security prices, and bank reserves that result from the use of the central bank's policy tools influence, first of all, the cost and availability of credit. If borrowers find that credit is less available and more expensive to obtain, they are likely to restrain their borrowing and spending for both capital and

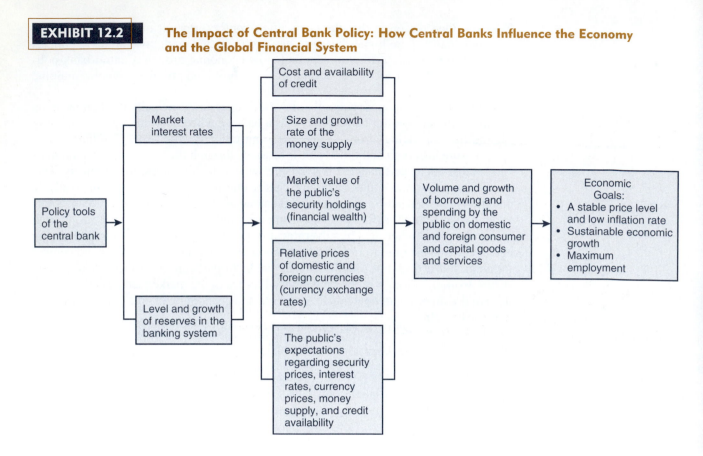

**EXHIBIT 12.2**

**The Impact of Central Bank Policy: How Central Banks Influence the Economy and the Global Financial System**

consumer goods at home and abroad. This results in a slowing in the economy's rate of growth and perhaps a reduction in inflationary pressures. Second, if the central bank can reduce the rate of growth of the money supply, this policy may eventually slow the growth of income and production in the economy due to a reduction in the public's demand for goods and services.

Third, if the central bank raises interest rates and thereby lowers security prices, this will tend to reduce the market value of the public's holdings of stocks, bonds, and other securities. The result would be a decline in the value of investors' financial wealth, altering the public's borrowing and spending plans and, ultimately, influencing employment, prices, and the economy's rate of growth. Fourth, the central bank can make changes in domestic interest rates relative to foreign interest rates, which will affect the exchange ratios (relative prices) in world markets between domestic and foreign currencies. If the price of the home currency falls relative to foreign currency prices, the home country's exports will become cheaper and more sought after abroad, stimulating domestic production and creating more jobs.

In recent years, economic research has suggested a fifth channel for central bank policy to affect the economy: *its impact on the public's expectations* regarding future credit costs, money supply growth, the value of loans and securities, and relative currency values. If central bank operations result in shifting public expectations, businesses and consumers will alter their borrowing, spending, and investing plans (unfortunately, not always in the direction the central bank wishes), which can

In 1998 a new central bank—the ECB, or European Central Bank—joined the world's financial institutions devoted to pursuing monetary policy and stabilizing economies. Formed as part of the European Union (EU), the new central bank, headquartered in Frankfurt, Germany and representing all member nations of the EU as well as affecting the economic lives of more than 300 million European citizens, is reshaping the structure of interest rates on the European continent and assisting in the expansion of a common EU currency, the euro that has been adopted by most of the EU's member states. It has been aided in this task by the central banks of all participating EU countries, representing the new European System of Central Banks (ESCB). The principal goal of the ECB, as defined by the Masstricht Treaty, is to pursue *price stability*. The ECB is also assisting the European Monetary Institute and the central banks of EU member nations in developing a new electronic payments network comparable to the Federal Reserve's FEDWIRE, called TARGET—the Trans-European Automated Real-Time Gross Settlement Express Transfer—allowing cross-border payments to be processed in Europe's new currency.

The ECB faced multiple challenges when it first began operations in the twenty-first century. It had to finalize the design and the powers of its organizational structure and governing council, learn how to use its policy tools effectively, establish credibility with international investors as well as its own citizens, and figure out how to maintain a uniform monetary policy for multiple European nations, each with a different mix of industries and varying social and political systems. It seeks to achieve uniform interest rates throughout its territory, though the central banks of EU member states retain the right to set their own nations' interest rate levels.

Each member state, regardless of its size, has only one vote on the ECB's Governing Council, which contains the governors of the member countries' central banks and is chaired by the ECB's president—a position comparable to the Chairman of the Board of Governors of the Federal Reserve System. The ECB is not as clearly dominated by its president as is the Fed with its Board chairman and, therefore, the ECB may be somewhat slower to respond to crises than is the Federal Reserve System. The ECB's Executive Board, which runs its daily operations, is appointed by the European Council of Ministers and confirmed by the European Parliament. In principle at least, the European central banking system could be one of the most independent central banks in the world, as its charter can be modified only by *unanimous* consent of all member nations.

have profound effects on the economy's rate of growth and the creation of jobs. We will have more to say about these important channels of central bank policy in Chapter 13.

## QUESTIONS TO HELP YOU STUDY

1. What *functions* do central banks perform in a market-oriented economy? Explain why each function is important in the functioning of a market-oriented economic system.

2. What are the principal *goals* central banks pursue in order to carry out monetary policy?

3. To what extent are the principal goals of central bank monetary policy consistent or inconsistent with each other? What does a central bank do when the goals it wishes to pursue directly conflict with each other?

4. What are the principal *channels* through which central banks, including the Federal Reserve System, work to influence the economy and achieve their goals?

## 12.4   History of the Federal Reserve System— Central Bank of the United States

The United States was one of the last major nations in the Western world to permanently charter a central bank, after two early attempts in 1791 and 1816 that ultimately failed. The Bank of England was established in 1694; the Bank of France and the central banks of Switzerland and Italy were founded during the eighteenth century. Most major industrialized nations early in their histories recognized the need for an institution that would provide a measure of stability and control over the growth of money and credit. Public officials in the United States were hesitant to permanently charter a central bank, for fear that it would possess great financial power and restrict the availability of credit to a growing nation. However, a series of economic and financial crises in the late nineteenth and early twentieth centuries forced the U.S. Congress to act, resulting in the creation of the Federal Reserve System.

### Problems in the Early U.S. Banking System

To understand fully why the Federal Reserve System was created, we must understand the problems that plagued the U.S. financial system throughout much of this nation's early history. Many of these problems were born in the years prior to the Civil War, when the states, not the federal government, controlled the banking system. Unfortunately, with a few notable exceptions, the states generally did a poor job. Charters for new banks frequently were awarded by state legislatures, subject to political lobbying and influence peddling. If a new bank's organizers had the right political connections, a charter could be obtained by individuals with little banking experience and with minimal capital invested in the business.

Deposit banking was not as popular then as it is today. Most people preferred hard money (currency and coin) to deposits. As a result, banks made loans simply by printing and issuing their own paper notes, which circulated as currency. Because few controls existed, there was a tendency to issue these notes well beyond the financial strength of the bank making the loans. Frequently, charters were granted to "wildcat banks" that would issue a large quantity of notes and then disappear. Some banks, promising to redeem their notes in gold or silver coin, set up "redemption centers" in locations nearly impossible for the public to reach, such as in the middle of a swamp. Needless to say, there was a high failure rate among these poorly capitalized, ill-managed institutions, resulting in substantial losses to unlucky depositors.

Responding to these problems and also to the tremendous financial strain imposed by the Civil War, Congress passed the National Banking Act of 1863. This act authorized the establishment of federally licensed commercial banks, subject to regulations imposed by a newly created office, the Comptroller of the Currency, a part of the U.S. Treasury Department. Any group of businesspeople could organize a *national bank,* provided they could show that the new bank would be profitable within a reasonable period of time (usually within three years), meet minimum equity capital requirements imposed by the Comptroller's office, and not endanger the viability of banks already operating in the local area. Under the provisions of the National Banking Act, the chartering of commercial banks was, in the main, removed from the political sphere and made subject to carefully spelled-out rules. At the same time, Congress attempted to drive state-chartered banks into the national banking system by imposing a 10 percent tax on state bank notes. It was argued that most bankers would prefer the more liberal state regulations and avoid applying for national bank charters unless they were forced to do so.

To help finance the Civil War, Congress authorized national banks to issue their own notes as circulating currency. However, these notes had to be collateralized by U.S. government securities. Under terms of the National Banking Act, federally chartered banks could issue notes up to 90 percent of the value of Treasury securities they deposited with the Comptroller of the Currency. The result was to create a money medium under federal control to help pay for the Civil War by creating a demand from banks for U.S. government securities. Even more important, the National Banking Act created a *dual banking system,* with both federal and state authorities having important regulatory powers over banks. Unfortunately, these authorities were given overlapping powers. In recent years competition between federal and state regulatory agencies has sometimes resulted in actions detrimental to the public interest.

## Creation of the Federal Reserve System

Several festering problems resulted in the creation of the Federal Reserve System. For one thing, new national bank notes authorized by the National Banking Act proved to be unresponsive to the nation's growing need for a money or cash medium. The need for money and credit grew rapidly as the United States became more heavily industrialized and the Midwest and Far West opened up to immigration. Farmers and ranchers in these areas demanded an "elastic" supply of money and credit—adequate to their needs at relatively low cost. As we will soon see, the new Federal Reserve System would attempt to deal with this problem by issuing a currency of its own and by exercising closer control over the growth of money and credit.

As deposit banking and the writing of checks became increasingly popular, another serious problem appeared. The process of clearing and collecting checks was too slow and expensive. Then, as now, most checks written by the public were local in character, moving funds from the account of one local customer to that of another. These checks normally are cleared routinely through the local clearinghouse, which is simply a location where representatives of local banks meet daily to exchange checks drawn on each other's banks. For checks sent outside the local area, however, the collection process proved to be more complicated, with some checks passing through several banks before reaching their final destination.

**Key URLs:**
To learn more about the history of the Federal Reserve System, see such Web sites as Fed101 at **kc.frb.org/fed101** and the Federal Reserve Bank of Minneapolis at **mpls.frb.org**

Before the Federal Reserve System was created, many banks charged a fee (*exchange charge*) for the clearing and redemption of checks. This fee was usually calculated as a percentage of the par (or face) value of each check. Banks levying the fee were called *no-par* banks because they refused to honor checks at their full face value. To avoid exchange fees, bankers would try to route the checks they received only through banks accepting and redeeming them at par. Often this meant routing a check through scores of banks in distant cities until days or weeks had elapsed before the check was finally cleared. Such a delay was not just annoying, but also served as an impediment to business transactions. Exchange charges resulted in needless inefficiency and increased the true cost of business transactions far above their nominal cost. A new national check-clearing system was needed that honored checks at par and moved them swiftly between payee and payer. This responsibility too was given to the Federal Reserve System, which insisted that all checks cleared through its system be honored at full face (par) value.

A third problem with the banking and financial system of that time was recurring liquidity crises. Then, as now, money and bank reserves tended to concentrate in leading financial centers, such as New York City or San Francisco, where the greatest need for loanable funds existed. Bank reserves flowed into the major cities as smaller banks in outlying areas deposited their reserves with larger banking institutions to earn greater returns. However, when the pressures for agricultural credit increased in rural areas, many country banks had to sell securities and call in their loans to city banks in the nation's financial centers to come up with the necessary funds. Thus, when the reserve demands of country banks were larger than expected, security prices in leading financial centers plummeted due to massive sell-offs of bank-held securities. Panic selling by other investors soon followed, leading to chaos in the marketplace.

The banking system clearly needed a lender of ready cash to provide liquidity to those banks with heavy cash drains and to protect the stability of the financial system. A serious financial panic in 1907 finally led to the creation of the Federal Reserve System. In 1908, Congress created the National Monetary Commission to study the financial needs of the nation. The commission's recommendations were forwarded to Congress and ultimately resulted in passage of the Federal Reserve Act, signed into law by President Woodrow Wilson in December 1913.

## The Early Structure of the Federal Reserve

The first Federal Reserve System was quite different from the Fed of today. The original Federal Reserve Act reflected a mix of diverse viewpoints: an effort to reconcile competing political and economic interests. There was great fear the Fed would have too much control over financial affairs and operate against the best interests of important segments of society. For example, small businesses, consumer groups, and farmers were concerned the Fed might pursue restrictive credit policies, leading to high interest rates. In addition, it was recognized that the Federal Reserve would become a major financial institution wherever it was located. Any city that housed a Federal Reserve bank was likely to become a major financial center.

Responding to these various needs and interest groups, Congress created a truly "decentralized" central bank. Not 1 but 12 Federal Reserve banks were chartered, stretching across the continental United States. Each Reserve bank (which opened in November, 1914) was assigned its own district, over which it possessed important regulatory powers. A supervisory board of seven members was set up in Washington, D.C., to provide oversight of the actions taken by the 12 District banks. In practice, this supervisory board was ineffectual. The Federal Reserve District banks retained all of the essential decision-making authority within the early Fed's system and operated independently.

## Goals and Policy Tools of the Fed

To deal with the financial problems of that day, the Federal Reserve Act permitted each regional Reserve bank to open a *discount window* where eligible banks could borrow reserves for short periods of time. However, borrowing banks were required to present high-quality, short-term business loans (commercial paper) to secure the loans they needed. The Fed's chief policy tool of the day was the *discount rate* charged on these loans, with each Reserve bank having the authority to set its own rate. By varying this rate, the Reserve banks could encourage or discourage banks' propensity to discount commercial paper and borrow reserves. Central bankers could promote easy or tight credit conditions and influence the overall volume of deposits and loans.

The Federal Reserve banks were given authority to issue their own paper notes to serve as a circulating currency, but these notes had to be 100 percent backed by Fed holdings of commercial paper plus a 40 percent gold reserve. Almost as an afterthought, Congress authorized the Reserve banks to trade U.S. government securities in the open market, known as *open market operations,* in order to give the Reserve banks a source of revenue to cover their operating costs. (Today these open market operations are the Fed's principal monetary policy tool.) Reserve requirements were imposed on deposits held by member banks of the system, but the Fed could not readily change these requirements.

Slowly but surely, economic, financial, and political forces combined to amend the original Federal Reserve Act and remake the character and methods of the central bank. The leading causes of change were war, economic recessions, and more recently, inflation. For example, to combat economic recession, fight wars, and pursue desired programs, the U.S. government issued billions of dollars in debt. As the debt began to grow, it seemed only "logical" to permit greater use of U.S. government securities in the Federal Reserve's operations. Banks were authorized to use government securities as backing for loans from the Fed's discount window. The Fed itself was called on to play a major role in stabilizing the market for U.S. government securities to ensure that the Treasury would have little difficulty in refinancing its maturing debt. Government securities were made eligible as collateral for the issue of new Federal Reserve bank notes.

More than any other historical event, however, it was the Great Depression of the 1930s that changed the character of the Federal Reserve. Faced with the collapse of the banking system and unprecedented unemployment—roughly a quarter of the U.S. labor force was thrown out of work during the 1930s—Congress entrusted the Fed with sweeping monetary powers as a result of the passage of the Banking Acts of 1933 and 1935. Significant changes also were made in the central bank's operating structure and lines of authority.

The seven-member Board of Governors in Washington, D.C., became the central administrative and policymaking group. Thereafter, any changes in discount rates charged by the Reserve banks had to be approved in advance by the Board of Governors. The Board was granted authority to set minimum reserve requirements on deposits and maximum interest rates that banks could pay on those deposits. To control speculative buying of stocks, the Reserve Board was empowered to set margin requirements specifying what proportion of a security's market value the investor could borrow to buy that security. Recognizing that open market operations in U.S. government securities were rapidly becoming the Fed's main policy tool, a powerful policymaking body—the Federal Open Market Committee—was created in 1935 to oversee the conduct of open market operations. In summary, the Great Depression brought about a *concentration of power* within the Federal Reserve System so the Fed could pursue unified policies and speak with one voice concerning monetary affairs.

## 12.5 How the Fed Is Organized Today

**Board of Governors**

The Federal Reserve System today has an organizational structure that resembles a *pyramid.* As Exhibit 12.3 shows, the apex of the pyramid is the **Board of Governors,** the Federal Reserve's chief policymaking and administrative group. At the middle level of the pyramid are the Federal Reserve District banks, which carry out system policy and provide essential services to depository financial institutions in their particular district and the Federal Open Market Committee. The bottom of the pyramid contains the member banks of the system, which the Fed supervises and regulates, and the manager of the System Open Market Account, who is responsible for buying and selling securities to achieve the goals of Fed monetary policy.

**EXHIBIT 12.3**

**How the Federal Reserve System Is Organized**

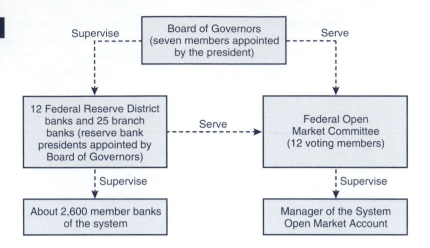

## The Board of Governors

**Key URL:**
See Board of Governors at **federalreserve. gov** for additional information about the Federal Reserve Board.

The key administrative body within the Federal Reserve System is the Board of Governors. The board consists of seven persons appointed by the president of the United States and confirmed by the Senate for maximum 14-year terms. Terms of office are staggered, with one board member's appointment ending every even-numbered year. Over a 14-year period the whole board will rotate its membership. When a member of the Federal Reserve Board resigns or dies, the president may appoint a new person to complete the remainder of the unexpired term, and that member may be reappointed to a subsequent full term. However, no member who completes a full term can be reappointed to the Board of Governors. The president designates one member of the board as its chairperson and another as vice chairperson, and both serve four-year terms in those positions. In selecting new board members, the president is required to seek a fair representation of the financial, agricultural, industrial, and commercial interests and geographical divisions of the country and may not choose more than one member from any one Federal Reserve district.

**Key URL:**
To examine the sources of income and expenses for the Federal Reserve Banks explore **federalreserve. gov/Boarddocs/ press/other/ 2007/200701092/ default.htm**

The powers of the Federal Reserve Board are extensive. The board sets reserve requirements on deposits held by depository institutions subject to its rules; reviews and determines the discount rate charged on loans to depository institutions; sets margin requirements on the public's purchases of securities; and provides leadership in the conduct of open market operations through the Federal Open Market Committee. Besides its monetary policy functions, the Board supervises the activities of the 12 Reserve District banks and has supervisory and regulatory control over member banks of the system. It regulates financial holding companies, foreign banks entering the United States, and the overseas activities of U.S. banks.

In principle, the Board is independent of both legislative and executive branches of the federal government. This independence is supported by terms of office much longer than the president's (up to 14 years) and by the fact that the Fed does not depend on the U.S. Congress for operating funds. The Federal Reserve supports itself from revenue generated by selling its services (such as clearing checks), making loans through the discount window, and earning interest on its considerable holdings of U.S. government securities. (In February 2007, the Fed held approximately 9 percent of the $8.7 trillion in U.S. government debt.) These monies are not retained by the Fed, because it is operated in the public interest and not for profit. All monies left over after expenses, dividends paid to member banks, and minimal allocations to equity reserves are transferred to the U.S. Treasury to help reduce tax collections from the private sector. For example, recently the Fed reported the following information about its sources of income and expense:

| Income and Expenses Statement for the Federal Reserve Banks ($ billions) | |
| --- | --- |
| Total income of the Federal Reserve Banks in 2006 | $37.838 |
| Principal sources of the Fed's income | |
| Interest income from securities held in the Fed's portfolio | 36.415 |
| Fees charged for Fed services (check clearing, wire transfers, etc.) | 0.909 |
| Miscellaneous income from loans and other sources | 0.427 |
| Operating expenses | 2.420 |
| Transferred to Treasury | $34.189 |

**Source:** Federal Reserve Press Release January 9, 2007.

## The Federal Open Market Committee

**Federal Open Market Committee (FOMC)**

Aside from the Federal Reserve Board, the other key policymaking group within the system is the **Federal Open Market Committee (FOMC).** It has been called the most important committee of individuals in the United States because its decisions concerning the conduct of monetary policy and the cost and availability of credit affect the lives of millions of people. Membership on the FOMC consists of the seven members of the Federal Reserve Board and the presidents or first vice presidents of the Reserve banks. Only the seven members of the Board and five of the Reserve bank presidents or their representatives may vote when a final decision is reached on the future conduct of monetary policy, however. The president of the Federal Reserve Bank of New York is a permanent voting member of the FOMC, the presidents of the Chicago and Cleveland Federal Reserve banks alternate in filling one other voting seat, and the remaining three voting positions on the FOMC are rotated annually among the presidents of the nine remaining Federal Reserve banks. Each Reserve bank representative occupying a rotating seat serves a voting term of one year.

**Key URLs:**
The Federal Open Market Committee— known as the FOMC—is widely followed by active investors around the globe. Greater understanding on why the FOMC is so important to interest rates and credit conditions may be found in such Web sites as **federal reserve.gov/fomc** and through the publications of the Federal Reserve Bank of New York at **ny.frb.org**

By tradition, the chairperson of the Federal Reserve Board and the president of the New York Federal Reserve bank serve as chairperson and vice chairperson of the FOMC. The law stipulates that the FOMC will meet in Washington, D.C., at least four times a year. In practice, however, the committee meets about eight times a year and more frequently if emergencies develop. Between regularly scheduled meetings, telephone conferences may occur, and the members of the FOMC may be asked to cast votes by telephone or telegram. FOMC meetings are *not* open to the public because confidential financial information frequently is discussed and also because the Fed wants to avoid sending false signals to the financial marketplace. Only Federal Reserve Board members, selected board staff, the Reserve bank presidents and their aides, and the manager and deputy manager of the System Open Market Account are permitted to attend FOMC meetings. A brief summary of the policy decisions taken at these meetings is immediately available to the public and minutes of FOMC meetings are released with a lag of approximately two months after a meeting is held.

The name Federal Open Market Committee implies that this committee's sole concern is with the conduct of Federal Reserve open market operations in securities. In fact, the FOMC reviews current economic and financial conditions and considers *all* aspects of monetary policy at its meetings. It also cooperates with the U.S. Treasury in protecting the dollar in foreign exchange markets. Once a consensus is reached concerning the appropriate future course for monetary policy, a directive is given to the manager of the System Open Market Account (SOMA), who is a vice president of the Federal Reserve Bank of New York. The SOMA manager is told in general terms how open market operations should be conducted in the weeks ahead and what the FOMC's targets are, especially for the federal funds interest rate attached to overnight loans of reserves between banks. Decisions made by the FOMC and actions of the SOMA manager at the securities trading desk in New York are binding on the entire Federal Reserve System.

## *The Federal Reserve Banks*

**Federal Reserve bank**

When the Federal Reserve System was created in 1913, the nation was divided into 12 districts, with one **Federal Reserve bank** in each district responsible for supervising and providing services to the member banks located there. Reserve banks were established in the cities of Atlanta, Boston, Chicago, Cleveland, Dallas, Kansas City, Minneapolis, New York, Philadelphia, Richmond, San Francisco, and St. Louis. In addition, 24 branches (later expanded to 25) were created to serve particular regions within the 12 districts.

Using computers and high-speed sorting machines, the regional Reserve banks route checks and other cash items drawn on financial institutions in one city and deposited in another city back to the institutions on which they were drawn for proper crediting of the amounts involved. Although the Fed processes only about 40 percent of all checks written in the United States, it still handles billions of checks and other paper items that reflect billions of transactions carried out by businesses and individuals each year. Recently, the volume of paper checks and other paper cash items handled by the Fed has been declining, however, as the public has been gradually switching to electronic means of payment and electronic *images* of checks now travel between many depository institutions rather than paper checks themselves.

The Federal Reserve maintains an electronic network (known as FEDWIRE), which transfers millions of dollars daily in money and securities among banking institutions in the United States that maintain reserves or clearing accounts with the Fed. Approximately 30 automated clearinghouses (ACHs) are operated by the Reserve banks and their branches to handle the direct deposit of payrolls, mortgage payments, and other funds transfer requests electronically. The Reserve banks fulfill requests from depository institutions to ship currency and coin to them at those times when the public needs more pocket money and store excess currency and coin when less pocket money is needed.

The Reserve banks serve as the federal government's *fiscal agent.* This involves keeping the financial accounts of the U.S. Treasury, delivering and redeeming U.S. government securities, and conducting auctions of newly issued U.S. government debt (centered in the Federal Reserve Bank of New York). The Reserve banks also accept deposits for federal income, excise, and unemployment taxes. In addition to serving as the federal government's fiscal agents, the Reserve banks closely supervise the activities of member banks within their districts. They conduct field examinations of all state-chartered member banks and supervise bank holding companies headquartered in their region.

The Reserve banks play a significant role in the conduct of money and credit policy. Each Reserve bank houses a research division to study regional economic and financial developments and conveys this information to the Board of Governors and the Federal Open Market Committee. Only 5 of the 12 Reserve banks have voting seats on the FOMC, but all 12 Reserve bank presidents or first vice presidents attend FOMC meetings to report on conditions in their districts and give their views on the appropriate course for monetary policy. Thus, collectively, the voting and nonvoting Reserve bank presidents (or their representatives), along with the Federal Reserve Board's own staff, provide the FOMC with a comprehensive and fairly timely picture of the entire nation's economic health. The Reserve banks also administer the discount windows where loans are made to financial institutions in their district.

Each Federal Reserve bank is a corporation chartered by Congress. Officially, the Reserve banks are owned by the member banks of their districts, which select a majority of each bank's board of directors. Each Reserve bank president is nominated by that Reserve bank's board of directors, and the appointment is confirmed or denied by the Federal Reserve Board. Under federal law, the board of directors of each Federal Reserve bank must consist of nine directors, six elected by bankers in the district (with three of these directors representing bankers and three the general public or nonbank interests in the same district) and three directors selected by the Federal Reserve Board. The regional Reserve banks are closely controlled by the Federal Reserve Board, which not only reviews officer appointments but also may remove any officer or director of a Federal Reserve bank and examine, reorganize, or even liquidate a Reserve bank if this appears to be necessary to serve the public interest.

Although under the terms of the original Federal Reserve Act the Reserve banks could set the discount rate on loans to depository institutions, these rate changes must now be approved by the Federal Reserve Board in Washington. The regional banks are required to participate in all open market transactions on behalf of the system. These purchases and sales are carried out through the FOMC at the Federal Reserve Bank of New York, but the Reserve banks must provide the securities needed for open market sales and must also take their *pro rata* share of any security purchases the Federal Reserve System makes. As Exhibit 12.4 reveals, the Federal Reserve banks

| EXHIBIT 12.4 | The Balance Sheet of the Federal Reserve System |
|---|---|

The Federal Reserve System's Consolidated Assets and Liabilities, February 21, 2007* ($ billions)

| Assets | | Liabilities and Capital Accounts | |
|---|---|---|---|
| Gold and special drawing rights certificates | $ 13.2 | Liabilities: Federal Reserve notes | $ 771.2 |
| Coins | 1.0 | Reverse repurchase agreements | 38.1 |
| Loans to depository institutions | < 0.1 | Deposits from banks & thrifts | 14.2 |
| U.S. government and federal agency securities held | 812.9 | U.S. Treasury account | 5.3 |
| | | Foreign and other accounts | 0.3 |
| Cash items in process of collection | 9.7 | Deferred availability cash items | 7.5 |
| | | Other liabilities | 5.6 |
| Other assets | 37.8 | Capital: | 31.7 |
| Total assets | $874.6 | Total liabilities and capital | $ 874.6 |

Source: Board of Governors of the Federal Reserve System, Release H.4.1(a), February 22, 2007.

Note: End-of-month estimates; slight inaccuracies may exist because of rounding.

*Consolidated for all 12 regional Federal Reserve Banks.

The issue of central bank independence from government has become a center of controversy in recent years. Several studies (e.g., Alesina [1] and Bade and Parkin [2]) have found a significant *negative* correlation between the inflation rate experienced by leading industrial countries and the degree of independence from the political process enjoyed by their central banks. Some researchers have concluded that economies generally perform better when central banks enjoy greater independence from government because there is a strong political temptation to overissue money (thereby igniting inflation) in order to fund extravagant government programs.

The independence from government control enjoyed by central banks varies widely around the world, however. In the European Central Bank, for example, board members have eight-year terms, but the ECB has the additional protection that its charter cannot be changed without the unanimous vote of all member nations. In the United States, members of the Federal Reserve's Board of Governors can serve for up to 14 years, which limits the power of Congress or the president to alter Fed policy in the short run. Moreover, the Federal Reserve does not depend upon Congress for income—it generates its own revenues through security trading and service fees.

Several bills have been introduced in the U.S. Congress in recent years to restrict the freedom of action of the Fed. One proposal would expand the authority of the Government Accounting Office (GAO) to audit *all* phases of Federal Reserve operations. Another proposal would require congressional approval of anyone who wishes to serve as president of a Federal Reserve Bank.

Still another proposed change calls for denying Federal Reserve bank presidents any voting seats on the Federal Open Market Committee (FOMC), the Fed's chief policymaking body. There has even been a call for videotaping FOMC meetings as is now done for many congressional sessions and court trials. Recent presidential administrations have proposed stripping the Fed of its bank examination functions in order to allow it to concentrate on money and credit policy. For its part, the Fed has argued that these changes would render monetary policy less effective.

Some experts have argued that the whole structure of the Fed needs revamping in an age of electronics with the banking system increasingly dominated by a few huge banks. They argue that some of the Federal Reserve banks are no longer needed and should be closed. The current geographic distribution of the Federal Reserve banks does not fully reflect the vast population shifts that have occurred in the United States since the Fed was founded. In an era of computers and satellite communications, the Fed's vast network of banks and branches *may* be an increasingly inefficient system. However, the Fed argues that many of its regional offices will likely always be needed to provide convenient services to local areas and to monitor regional conditions.

collectively held almost $813 billion in securities—their principal asset—and had issued $771 billion in Federal Reserve notes—the principal circulating currency of the United States and the principal liability of the Federal Reserve banks—in 2007.

## The Member Banks of the Federal Reserve System

**member banks**

The **member banks** of the Federal Reserve System consist of national banks, which are required to join the system, and state-chartered banks that agree to conform to the Fed's rules. Today, Federal Reserve member banks constitute a minority of all U.S. banks, a little over one-third of the total. There are about 1,700 national banks and about 900 state-chartered banks registered as members of the Federal Reserve System, compared to approximately 4,800 nonmember banks.

Member banks must subscribe to the stock of the Reserve bank in their district in an amount equal to 6 percent of their paid-in capital and surplus accounts. However, only half of this amount must actually be paid, with the rest payable on call. Member banks are bound by Federal Reserve rules regarding capital, deposits, loans, branch

**Key URL:**
The structure of the Federal Reserve System is also discussed at some length at **banx.com**

Former Federal Reserve Board Chairman Alan Greenspan is once reported to have said, "Since I became a central banker, I have learned to mumble with great coherence."

In recent years, the Federal Reserve (along with selected other central banks around the world) has attempted to achieve greater **transparency** in its monetary policy deliberations and in policy decisions that it makes. The Fed's aim is to make monetary policymakers' intentions about current and future policy clear ("transparent") to the public. The central bank believes that greater openness about what it is doing and why will help minimize the waste of resources caused by market players' decisions that may be misguided or may result from people trying to protect themselves against uncertain future monetary policies that they do not understand and cannot predict. In brief, if money and credit policy is truly "transparent," borrowers and lenders should be informed enough that they come to expect the *same* policy actions as the policymaker does.

To achieve greater transparency, the Federal Reserve releases a brief statement to the press at the close of each of its FOMC meetings (which is immediately made available on the Web site of the Board of Governors of the Federal Reserve System at **federalreserve.gov**). The Fed's press release summarizes the decisions of the FOMC and the major issues of concern that could affect future policy decisions. These statements are *always* released, even if there is no change in the current stance of monetary policy. A transcript of the actual minutes of FOMC meetings is then made available with a lag of about two months following each meeting.

The Federal Reserve's move toward greater transparency has been mirrored by many other central banks around the world, including the Bank of England, the ECB, and especially the Bank of Japan (BOJ). The BOJ has adopted a very detailed approach to transparency since the Japanese government granted the bank greater independence just a few years ago. The Bank of Japan Law, passed in 1997, states that "after each Board meeting for monetary control matters, the chairman shall, without delay, prepare a document which contains an outline of the discussion at the meeting in accordance with the decisions made by the Board, and publish the document upon its approval at another Board meeting for monetary control matters." The Bank of Japan has pledged to release the minutes of its policy meetings, to announce to the public its key policy decisions right after each meeting, to publish reports on the Japanese economy each month, and to release schedules for its future policy meetings at least six months in advance. The BOJ's Web site at **boj.or.jp** provides daily reports of its account balances. Collectively, these recent changes suggest the BOJ has become one of the most transparent central banks in the world.

**transparency**

operations, formation of holding companies, and policies regarding the conduct of officers and boards of directors. These banks are subject to supervision and examination by the Federal Reserve at any time. Moreover, member banks must hold reserves behind their deposits at levels specified by the Federal Reserve Board.

A number of important privileges are granted to member banks. Legally, they are "owners" of the Federal Reserve banks because they hold the stock of these institutions and elect six of their nine directors. A 6 percent annual dividend is paid to member banks on their holdings of Federal Reserve bank stock. Member banks may borrow reserves through the discount window of the Reserve bank in their district and use the Fed's check-clearing system to process checks and other cash items coming from distant cities. However, this is not an exclusive privilege, because nonmember banks and thrifts may also use the Fed's check-clearing facilities, provided they agree to maintain a clearing account with the Reserve bank in the region. An intangible benefit of membership is the prestige that comes from belonging to the Federal Reserve System. Many bankers believe membership in the system attracts large business deposits and correspondent accounts from smaller banks that otherwise might go elsewhere.

## QUESTIONS TO HELP YOU STUDY

5. What major problems in the late nineteenth and early twentieth century led to the creation of the Federal Reserve System? How did the creation of the Fed help solve these problems?

6. In what ways did the early Federal Reserve System differ from the Federal Reserve we see today?

7. What are the principal responsibilities assigned to the *Board of Governors of the Federal Reserve System?* To the *Federal Open Market Committee?*

8. What are the *Federal Reserve banks* expected to do in serving the public and the banking system?

9. What duties are assigned to the *manager of the System Open Market Account?*

10. What is meant by *monetary policy transparency?*

## 12.6   Roles of the Federal Reserve System Today

In the course of this chapter we have talked about the many roles the Federal Reserve plays in the financial system and how these roles have changed over time. In this section we pull together all of the Fed's responsibilities and roles to give a more complete view of how the central bank interfaces with the financial markets and the banking system.

### The Clearing and Collection of Checks and Other Payments Media

As we saw earlier in this chapter, one of the earliest tasks of the Federal Reserve System was to establish a nationwide system for clearing and collecting checks and other cash items. When a depository institution receives a check or other draft drawn on another institution in a distant city, it can route this cash item through the Federal Reserve banks. The Fed credits an account called Deferred Availability Items on behalf of the institution sending in the check or other draft and routes that cash item or its electronic image to the institution on which it was drawn for eventual collection. At the end of a specified period, the depository institution sending in the check or draft will receive credit in its legal reserve account for the amount of the cash item. Eventually, the check or its image reaches the institution on which it was drawn and is deducted from that institution's reserve account.

Fed check-processing volume and Fed revenues from check-clearing services have been on the decline since the middle to late 1990s. Electronic means of payment (such as debit cards and point-of-sale terminals) have been growing even as check writing has declined and the Federal Reserve has begun closing some of its check-clearing facilities around the United States. Today, in the wake of The Check Clearing for the 21$^{st}$ Century Act (more popularly known as Check 21), the Fed is investing in electronic imaging equipment. The Check 21 law, which became effective in October 2004, permits the creation of new negotiable instruments—*substitute checks* that are reproductions of original checks through digital imaging and are the legal equivalents of traditional paper checks—that will further speed the modern payments process.

## Issuing Currency and Coin and Related Services

The Fed helps to promote an efficient payments mechanism not just through the clearing of checks and other payments drafts but also by issuing its own currency in response to public need. Today, nearly all of the paper money in circulation consists of Federal Reserve notes, issued by all 12 of the Reserve banks and backed mainly by Federal Reserve holdings of government securities. These notes are liabilities of the Federal Reserve bank issuing them. In fact, Federal Reserve notes are a lien against the assets of the Fed, payable to the holder in the event the Reserve banks are ever liquidated. When the public demands more currency, financial institutions request a shipment of new currency and coin from the Federal Reserve bank in the region, which maintains an ample supply in its vault. Payment for the shipment is made simply by charging the legal reserve account of the institution requesting the shipment. In the opposite situation, when depository institutions receive deposits of currency and coin from the public beyond what they wish to hold in their vaults, the surplus is shipped back to the Reserve banks. Depository institutions receive credit for these return shipments through an increase in their legal reserve accounts at the Reserve bank.

Prior to 1981, most Federal Reserve services, including the clearing of checks and shipments of currency and coin, were provided free of charge. However, the Depository Institutions Deregulation and Monetary Control Act (DIDMCA) of 1980 required the Fed to assess fees for such services as transportation of currency and coin, check clearing, wire transfer of funds, the use of Federal Reserve automated clearinghouse facilities, and the safekeeping and redemption of government securities. All fees set by the Fed are to be reviewed annually and set at levels that, over the long term, recover the total costs of providing each service. A primary reason for requiring fees for Fed services was to enable private firms offering similar services to compete with the Fed on a more even footing.

## Maintaining a Sound Banking and Financial System

Another important function of the Federal Reserve System today is to maintain a sound banking and financial system. It contributes to this goal by serving as a lender of last resort—providing loans of reserves to depository institutions that hold their legal reserve accounts with the Fed through the discount window of each Reserve bank. The window represents a source of funds that can be drawn on without taking reserves away from other banks, and it helps to avoid a liquidity squeeze brought about by sudden changes in economic and financial conditions (as occurred following the terrorist attacks in New York and Washington, D.C., on September 11, 2001). The Fed also promotes a sound banking system by supervising and monitoring member banks and bank holding company organizations, reviewing the quality and quantity of their assets and capital and making sure that federal and state laws are followed. The strategy of bank supervision has shifted in recent years to take advantage of modern technology to conduct continuous risk assessments of individual banking organizations and combine both on-site and off-site examinations.

## Serving as the Federal Government's Fiscal Agent

**fiscal agent**

The Fed serves as the government's chief **fiscal agent.** In this role, it holds the Treasury's payments account and clears any checks or other drafts presented against that account. The Fed supervises the thousands of Treasury Tax and Loan Accounts (TT&L) maintained in banks across the United States, which hold the bulk of the

Treasury's cash balances until it needs these monies for spending. The Fed also makes recurring payments (for example, salary checks for government employees) for the federal government through its electronic network of automated clearinghouses. The Federal Reserve banks receive bids when new Treasury securities are offered and provide securities to the purchasers. They redeem maturing U.S. government securities as well. In general, the Fed is responsible for maintaining reasonable stability in the government securities market so that any new Treasury offerings sell quickly and the government raises the amount of money it needs.

### *Providing Information to the Public*

**Key URL:**
For in-depth information on publications currently available from the Federal Reserve see especially **federal reserve.gov.**

Another critical function that the Federal Reserve has performed particularly well in recent years is to provide *information* to the public. Each Reserve bank has its own research staff, and the Board of Governors maintains a large staff of economists who follow current economic and financial developments and recommend changes in policy. The Fed makes available on a daily, weekly, and monthly basis an impressive volume of statistical releases, special reports, and studies concerning the financial markets and the condition of the economy. This information function is one of the more important contributions of the central bank.

### *Carrying Out Monetary Policy*

**monetary policy**

The most critical job of the Federal Reserve (and for most other central banks around the world) is to carry out **monetary policy.** Monetary policy may be defined as the use of various tools by the central bank to control the availability of loanable funds in an effort to achieve national economic goals, such as full employment and reasonable price stability. The policy tools reserved for the Federal Reserve include deposit reserve requirements, discount rates, open market operations, and margin requirements on purchases of securities. We will examine the Fed's policy tools in detail in Chapter 13.

---

> **QUESTIONS TO HELP YOU STUDY**
>
> 11. List the principal *functions* of the Federal Reserve System today and explain why each of these functions is important.
> 12. What is the Federal Reserve's *primary job* (that is, its principal role or function)?
> 13. When we use the term *ECB*, what is meant?
> 14. How is the ECB *similar* to the Federal Reserve and in what ways is it *different* from the Fed?
> 15. Explain why the ECB is likely to be one of the world's most important central banks.

---

## 12.7 The Key Focus of Central Bank Monetary Policy: Interest Rates, Reserves, and Money

If the Federal Reserve's most critical job is *monetary policy*—regulating money and credit conditions in an effort to strengthen the economy—what target or targets does the Fed pursue in order to impact the money and capital markets and, ultimately, the economy as a whole?

Today the principal target of most central banks around the globe is *market interest rates,* pushing them higher in order to slow borrowing and spending in the economy and pushing them lower if the economy needs to grow faster. However, to impact market interest rates the Federal Reserve and other central banks must have a "lever" to pull—a device or tool to use over which the central bank has relatively close control.

The central bank's "lever"—its principal immediate monetary policy target—is usually *the volume of legal reserves available to the banking system.* In the United States, these consist mainly of deposits held at the Federal Reserve banks plus currency and coin held in bank vaults. These reserves are the raw material out of which depository institutions create credit and cause the money supply to grow. And because growth of the money supply appears to be closely linked to changes in income, production, prices, and employment, most central banks pay close attention to fluctuations in the quantity of reserves that depository institutions have at their disposal. The total supply of reserves can be changed directly by open market operations—the Federal Reserve's principal policy tool and a growing central bank tool worldwide—and by making loans to depository institutions through the central bank's credit or discount window. Central banks also can exert a powerful effect on the growth of money and credit by changing legal reserve requirements applicable to deposits held by depository institutions.

Central banks like the Fed can nudge market interest rates in any desired direction by manipulating the legal reserve balances with which depository institutions work. When the supply of reserves is reduced relative to the demand for reserves, interest rates tend to rise as scarce funds are rationed among competing financial institutions. Conversely, an expansion in the supply of reserves usually leads to lower interest rates because of the increased availability of loanable funds. Why do these changes occur? What are the specific links between bank reserves and the money supply?

## 12.8 Reserve Composition and the Deposit and Money Multipliers

To answer the preceding questions, we need to look closely at what makes up the supply of reserves at depository institutions. All U.S. depository institutions offering selected kinds of deposits are required to hold a small percentage of those deposits in an asset account known as **legal reserves.** Legal reserves in the United States consist of the amount of deposits each institution keeps with the Federal Reserve bank in its district plus the amount of currency and coin held in its vault. (Other central banks often include other types of assets in their definitions of legal reserves—for example, government securities.)

**legal reserves**

Legal reserves may be divided into two parts: *required reserves* and *excess reserves.* In particular,

$$\text{Total legal reserves} = \text{Required reserves} + \text{Excess reserves} \qquad \textbf{(12.1)}$$

In the United States,

$$\text{Total legal reserves} = \begin{array}{c}\text{Deposits at the}\\\text{Federal Reserve}\\\text{banks}\end{array} + \begin{array}{c}\text{Vault cash held on the}\\\text{premises of depository}\\\text{institutions}\end{array} \qquad \textbf{(12.2)}$$

**required reserves**
**excess reserves**

**Required reserves** are those holdings of cash and deposits at the Fed that a depository institution *must* hold to back the public's deposits. **Excess reserves** are the amount of reserves left over after we deduct required reserves from total legal reserves. Excess reserves may be used to make loans, purchase securities, or for other purposes. Because legal reserve assets earn no interest income, most depository institutions try to keep their excess reserves close to zero. For example, the largest banks today frequently run reserve deficits and must borrow additional legal reserves in the money market to avoid costly penalties. The actual composition of legal reserves—that is, the exact proportion of deposits at the Federal Reserve versus vault cash—is left up to individual depository institutions to decide. Unlike larger depository institutions, the majority of small depositories meet their reserve requirements entirely with vault cash.

## The Deposit Multiplier

The distinction between excess and required reserves is important because it plays a key role in the growth of money and credit in the economy. Depository institutions offering checkable (transaction) deposits have the unique ability to create and destroy deposits—which are the bulk of the money supply—at the stroke of a pen or, in today's world, the press of a computer key. Although an individual depository institution cannot create more deposit money than the volume of excess reserves it holds, the banking system as a whole can create a multiple amount of deposit money from any given injection of reserves by using its excess reserves to make loans and purchase securities.

The dollar volume of deposits (and loans) that the banking system can create for each new dollar of excess legal reserves injected into the banking system is known as **deposit multiplier** the **deposit multiplier.**

The size of the deposit multiplier depends in part on the quantity of required reserves banks must hold. The Federal Reserve establishes reserve requirements as a percentage of banks' total transaction deposits, or the volume of checking account balances currently on deposit. This requirement gives us a simple expression to determine banks' required reserves:

$$\frac{\text{Required}}{\text{reserves}} = RR_D \times \frac{\text{Transaction}}{\text{deposits}} \qquad \textbf{(12.3)}$$

**reserve requirement** where $RR_{DD}$ is the Federal Reserve's **reserve requirement ratio** on transaction **ratio** deposits.[2]

Banks may also choose to hold some excess reserves rather than lend out all of their excess funds in order to maintain a protective "cushion" to meet unexpected withdrawals without falling below their required reserve holdings. These *desired excess reserves* tend to grow in proportion to the volume of transactions deposits. Therefore, the volume of these desired excess reserves can be expressed as:

---

[2]Today, only transaction deposits carry legal reserve requirements imposed by the Federal Reserve Board in the United States. Time and savings deposits at banks and other depository institutions carry zero reserve requirements, although the Federal Reserve Board retains authority to reimpose reserve requirements on nonpersonal (business) time deposits at any time that conditions seem to warrant that change. Such a reimposition of legal reserve requirements on time accounts seems unlikely, however, because the Fed decided some time ago that legal reserve requirements represented a heavy "tax" on bank reserves that, in some instances, threatened the competitiveness of deposits compared to other forms of liquid assets sold to the public. In 2006 Congress passed the Financial Services Regulatory Relief Act authorizing the Federal Reserve to begin paying interest on reserves and to reduce or eliminate reserve requirements. The Fed has begun a systematic review of how to implement provisions of this new act, which are to take effect October 1, 2011.

$$\frac{\text{Excess}}{\text{reserves}} = EXR \times \frac{\text{Transaction}}{\text{deposits}} \tag{12.4}$$

where *EXR* is referred to as the *excess reserves ratio,* and represents the amount of excess reserves that banks wish to hold for each dollar of transaction accounts.

From equations (12.1), (12.3), and (12.4), we can find the relationship between total reserves in the banking system and the volume of transaction deposits they support.

$$\frac{\text{Total}}{\text{reserves}} = RR_D \times \frac{\text{Transaction}}{\text{deposits}} + EXR \times \frac{\text{Transaction}}{\text{deposits}}$$

$$= (RR_D + EXR) \times \frac{\text{Transaction}}{\text{deposits}} \tag{12.5}$$

This expression (12.5) indicates that one dollar of reserves in the banking system supports $\dfrac{1}{RR_D + EXR}$ dollars in transaction deposits.

To see that this is exactly the deposit multiplier we sought, consider an example. Suppose that the Federal Reserve set the reserve requirement ratio at $RR_D = 0.10$, and banks wish to maintain one dollar in excess reserves for every \$1,000 in transaction deposits, or $EXR = 0.001$. If banks suddenly found themselves with \$1 million in excess reserves beyond what they desired to hold, they would begin to extend loans in order to earn interest on those reserves. However, these loans would show up as deposits, perhaps at other banks and therefore, both required reserves and desired excess reserves would increase, but not by the full amount of the \$1 million in initial undesired excess reserves. Therefore, additional loans would be made with these new deposit funds and the process would continue. Eventually, as loans and deposits grew, all of the \$1 million in undesired excess reserves would be absorbed by the banking system in a combination of additional required reserves and additional desired excess reserves in accordance with reserve requirements and the banks' management decisions on how many excess reserves they wish to maintain. When this process ends, the total amount of deposits (and loans) created by the banking system in the process of absorbing new excess reserves can be determined by the deposit multiplier.

$$\frac{\text{Maximum}}{\text{volume of}}_{\text{new deposits and loans}} = \frac{\text{Deposit}}{\text{multiplier}} \times \frac{\text{New}}{\text{excess reserves}} \tag{12.6}$$

or, $\dfrac{\$1,000,000}{0.10 + 0.0001} = \$9,990,009.99$ in new transaction deposits.

These calculations assume that total reserves in the banking system remains \$1 million higher after the initial increase. The \$1 million was converted from undesired excess reserves into required reserves and desired excess reserves due to the expansion of loans and deposits as banks sought to transform their undesired excess reserves into earning assets.

This process also works in the opposite direction. That is, a *withdrawal* of reserves from depository institutions can destroy deposits and loans. For example, a withdrawal of deposits by the public that causes depository institutions to have a \$1 million deficiency in their required and desired excess reserves would eventually lead to a \$9,990,009.99 decline in existing transaction deposits.

## *The Money Multiplier*

Although the concept of a deposit multiplier is useful for some purposes, central bankers are usually more interested in a related concept known as the **money multiplier.** It defines the relationship between a measure of the money supply that is closely related to spending and income in the economy to the total reserve base available to depository institutions. The most important measure of the money supply is M2, which includes transaction deposits, currency and coin, and other liquid assets principally held by households (such as savings and time deposits and shares in money market funds).

An important point to note about currency and coin is that fluctuations in the volume held by the public have a direct bearing on the reserves held by depository institutions, affecting both the size and rate of growth of transaction accounts and reserves. If the public desires to hold less pocket money, the excess currency and coin typically is redeposited in transaction accounts, increasing both reserves and demand deposits. Recognizing this important link between currency and bank reserves, economists have developed the concept of the **monetary base,** which is simply the sum of legal reserves plus the amount of currency and coin held by the public:

$$\text{Monetary base} = \text{Legal bank reserves} + \text{Currency in the hands of the public} \qquad (12.7)$$

Why is the monetary base important? Its components represent most of the liabilities of the central bank (in the United States, the Federal Reserve System). Therefore, the total dollar volume of the monetary base, often referred to as **high-powered money,** can be closely controlled by the Fed using open market operations and its other policy tools that are discussed at length in the next chapter. The link between the quantity of high-powered money that the Fed controls and the M2 measure of the money supply, which is an important factor in determining the rate at which nominal GDP grows, is characterized by the money multiplier.

$$\text{Money multiplier} \times \text{Monetary base} = \text{Money supply M2} \qquad (12.8)$$

To derive an expression for the money multiplier, we note that the monetary base can be expressed as:

$$\text{Monetary base} = (RR_D + EXR) \times \text{Transaction deposits} + CD \times \text{Transaction deposits}$$

$$= (RR_D + EXR + CD) \times \text{Transaction deposits} \qquad (12.9)$$

where *CD* is referred to as the **currency-deposit ratio.** It reflects the desire of households to maintain a desired balance between the two media of exchange: currency and checking accounts. For example, if $CD = 1.20$, then households would wish to maintain $1.20 in cash for every $1.00 they maintain in checking accounts.

A relationship between M2 and transactions deposits can also be derived in a similar manner. Using the definition of M2, we can write:

$$\text{Money supply M2} = \text{Transaction deposits} + \text{Currency in the hands of the public} + \text{Other household liquid assets} \qquad (12.10)$$

$$= \frac{\text{Transaction}}{\text{deposits}} + CD \times \frac{\text{Transaction}}{\text{deposits}} + LA \times \frac{\text{Transaction}}{\text{deposits}}$$

$$= (1 + CD + LA) \times \frac{\text{Transaction}}{\text{deposits}} \qquad \textbf{(12.11)}$$

where $LA$ is the desired ratio of liquid savings assets (consisting of savings accounts, small CDs, and money market funds) to transaction deposits (checking accounts) that households wish to maintain. For example, if $LA = 9.25$, then households are choosing to hold approximately \$9.25 in liquid savings assets for every \$1.00 in their checking accounts.

From equations (12.8), (12.9), and (12.11), we can obtain the following expression for the money multiplier:

$$\frac{\text{Money}}{\text{multiplier}} = \frac{1 + CD + LA}{RR_D + EXR + CD} \qquad \textbf{(12.12)}$$

This expression tells us how much the M2 money supply will increase for each \$1 increase in the monetary base. For example, using the numbers from above, the money multiplier equals $\dfrac{1 + 1.20 + 9.25}{0.10 + 0.0001 + 1.20}$, or 8.81. Therefore, when the Fed engineers an increase in the monetary base of \$1 billion, M2 will increase by \$8.81 billion.

The monetary base–money multiplier relationship identifies the most important factors that explain changes in the money supply, and it also helps us understand how a central bank like the Federal Reserve System can influence the money and credit creation process. In the United States, the Fed is one of the principal determinants of the size of the monetary base, along with the public and the U.S. Treasury, since the monetary base includes most of the liabilities of the Fed. It can increase or decrease the total supply of reserves to change the size of that base. Alternatively, the Fed may choose merely to offset actions taken by the public or the Treasury to keep the size of the monetary base unchanged. Finally, the central bank can change the required reserve ratios behind deposits, which will affect the magnitude of the money multiplier. Occasionally, when the central bank wishes to exert a potent impact on economic and financial conditions, it makes changes in *both* the monetary base and the money multiplier. In the next chapter, we take a close look at the tools the Federal Reserve System uses to influence the size of the monetary base, the money multiplier, and, ultimately, the nation's supply and cost of money and credit.

## QUESTIONS TO HELP YOU STUDY

16. What is/are the principal target(s) of monetary policy?

17. What are *legal reserves? Required reserves? Excess reserves?* Why are these concepts important?

18. Why are deposit-type intermediaries able to create money? What factors increase the deposits the banking system can create with any given injection of new reserves?

19. What factors *reduce* the *money-creating abilities* of the banking system?

20. In what ways can a central bank influence the *money and credit creation process?*

21. Why should a central bank like the Federal Reserve worry about money and credit growth?

## Summary of the Chapter's Main Points

In this chapter we examined the important roles played by *central banks* in the global financial system and the economy.

- Central banks function to control the money and credit supply, maintain stable conditions in the financial markets, serve as a lender of last resort to aid financial institutions in trouble, and maintain and improve the mechanism for making payments for purchases of goods and services.

- In most industrialized countries central banking is *goal-oriented,* aimed principally at the economic goals of reasonable stability in the prices of goods and services (i.e., the avoidance of significant inflation) and sustainable economic growth. In the Western world, central banks operate to achieve the foregoing goals principally by working in the *private financial marketplace,* influencing credit conditions but leaving to private borrowers and lenders the basic decision of whether to create credit, borrow, or spend.

- Central banks appear to influence the spending, saving, and borrowing decisions of millions of individuals and businesses through at least five interrelated *channels*—the cost and availability of credit, the volume and rate of growth of the money supply, the market value of assets held by the public, the relative prices of global currencies, and the public's expectations regarding domestic and international economic conditions.

- The central bank of the United States is the *Federal Reserve System.* Its chief administrative body is the *Board of Governors,* which controls such important policy tools as deposit reserve requirements, margin requirements on purchasing stocks and other securities, and changes in the discount rate on loans made by the Fed to depository institutions.

- Another important policymaking unit within the Federal Reserve System is the *Federal Open Market Committee (FOMC),* composed of the seven members of the Federal Reserve Board and the presidents of the 12 Federal Reserve banks, which oversees the use of the Fed's chief monetary policy tool—*open market operations.*

- The 12 *Federal Reserve District banks* represent the Fed's regional presence across the United States. These banks supervise private banks and financial holding companies within their individual districts, decide which depository institutions can borrow reserves from the Fed, and provide such services as clearing and collecting checks, shipping currency and coin, wiring funds to effect payments, and the safekeeping of securities.

- Each Federal Reserve bank also serves as a *fiscal agent* for the U.S. government and performs such services as dispensing and collecting the government's funds and selling and redeeming government securities.

- The Federal Reserve's most critical task (and the most important job of other central banks around the globe) today is the conduct of *monetary policy* in order to achieve the nation's economic goals. Today the Fed primarily targets market interest rates by manipulating the volume of reserves available to the banking system, which, in turn, affect the supply of deposits and money through the *deposit* and *money multipliers.* By creating or absorbing excess reserves available to depository institutions, the central bank can impact the growth and cost of money and credit and, ultimately, the economy as a whole.

## Key Terms Appearing in This Chapter

## Problems and Issues

1. As discussed in this chapter, the Federal Reserve has two policymaking groups: the Board of Governors and the Federal Open Market Committee (FOMC). Describe the composition of each of these groups, how their members are appointed, and the length of each member's term. What are the particular policy decisions these two important groups are responsible for?

2. What special status is awarded to the president of the Federal Reserve Bank of New York (FRBNY) in the determination of U.S. monetary policy? Why is this so?

3. In the text it was stated that the FOMC meets at least eight times each year on preannounced dates in order to set monetary policy. What would happen if an emergency situation developed in the financial markets? Would the Federal Reserve have to wait until the next scheduled FOMC meeting?

4. Suppose that households wished to maintain $1.00 in pocket money (currency and coin) and $10.00 in liquid savings assets (small CDs, money funds, and savings accounts) for every $1.00 in their checking accounts (transaction deposits). If banks choose their desired reserves to be ten cents for every dollar of transaction deposits, what are the *reserve multiplier* and the *money (M2) multiplier* if the Federal Reserve's reserve requirement ratio is: **(a)** 8 percent; **(b)** 10 percent; and **(c)** 12 percent?

5. If households' currency-deposit ratio is 1.25, and they desire to maintain $9.25 in liquid savings assets for each dollar in their checking accounts, what must the banks' excess reserves ratio be if the money multiplier is 10? If the banks changed their excess reserves ratio to one dollar for every $1,000 of transaction deposits, compute the effect this would have on the money multiplier.

6. Suppose the Federal Reserve uses data to estimate the currency-deposit ratio to be 0.90, the ratio of liquid savings assets to transaction deposits to be 8.00, and the excess reserves ratio to be 0.001.

   **a.** If it wished to increase M2 by $10 billion, how much would it have to raise the monetary base?

**b.** How far off would the Federal Reserve have been if it conducted policy as you describe in (a), but the currency-deposit ratio turned out to be 1?

**c.** How far off would the Federal Reserve have been if it conducted policy as you describe in (a), but the liquid asset to transaction deposits ratio turned out to be 10?

**d.** How far off would the Federal Reserve have been if it conducted policy as you describe in (a), but the excess reserves ratio turned out to be 0.003?

## Web-Based Problems

1. As we discovered in this chapter, monetary policy operates through the banking system by altering the volume of bank reserves, and, thereby, influencing the total quantity of money and credit in the economy, thereby affecting short-term interest rates. The Federal Reserve does not have perfect control over the money supply due to changes in the behavior of banks and households. Changes in bank regulations can also affect the ability of the Federal Reserve to create money. The purpose of this exercise is to examine how the changes in these factors have altered the money multiplier over time. Use a spreadsheet to answer this question.

   **a.** Visit the Federal Reserve's Web site, **federalreserve.gov/releases,** and look up the following historical data for the past 20 years (using monthly data) and enter them into columns in your spreadsheet: From the H.6: (i) currency (in the hands of the public); (ii) transaction deposits (equal to the sum of demand deposits and other checkable deposits); and (iii) liquid assets in M2 (non-M1 components of M2, including savings deposits, small time deposits, and retail money funds). From the H.3: (i) required reserves; (ii) excess reserves; (iii) total reserves; and (iv) the monetary base.

   **b.** In each of the next three columns of your spreadsheet, compute: (i) the currency-deposit ratio; (ii) the ratio of liquid savings assets (non-M1 M2) to transaction deposits; and (iii) the excess reserves ratio.

   **c.** In each of the next two columns of your spreadsheet, compute: (i) the deposit multiplier, and (ii) the money (M2) multiplier.

   **d.** Produce graphs of the series that you computed in (b) and in (c). By comparing these graphs can you tell what caused the deposit and money multipliers to change?

2. Traditionally, the most important measure of the U.S. money supply (for the purpose of providing information to the Federal Reserve on how it ought to conduct monetary policy) has been M2. The rationale is that M2 bears the closest long-term relationship with overall economic activity measured by nominal GDP (i.e., total expenditures on goods and services produced inside the United States). The ratio of nominal GDP to M2 is referred to as the "velocity" of M2 to capture how many times each dollar is spent ("turns over") on average during the year.

   **a.** Visit the U.S. Commerce Department's Web site for its Bureau of Economic Analysis at **bea.gov/bea/dn/gpdlev.xls** and extract the annual data for "GDP in billions of current dollars" for the past 20 years.

    **b.** Go to the Federal Reserve's Web site at **federalreserve.gov/releases** and extract the data for M2 for the last month of each of the past 20 years from Table 1 of the H.6 release.

    **c.** Using the data from parts (a) and (b) construct a time series for the "velocity" of M2 over the past 20 years and produce a graph of M2 velocity versus time. Does this ratio appear to have a constant long-run trend that might provide a reliable indicator of economic activity that the Federal Reserve could use? If not, when does it appear to have been reliable and when does it appear to have gone awry? Can you explain why?

**3.** A directory of central banks around the world is available from the Center for the Study of Central Banks at **law.nyu.edu/centralbankscenter.** Which of the central banks listed maintain the most comprehensive Web sites (i.e., provide the most detailed information regarding their operations and organizational structure and the performance of their national economies)? What types of information do you believe a central bank's Web site should make available to the public? Why?

## Selected References to Explore

**1.** Alesina, Alberto. "Macroeconomics and Politics," in *NBER Macroeconomic Annual,* MIT Press, Cambridge, MA, 1988.

**2.** Bade, Robin, and Michael Parkin. "Central Bank Laws and Monetary Policy," Unpublished Mimeograph, Department of Economics, University of Western Ontario, 1987.

**3.** Carlston, Charles T., and Timothy S. Fuerst. "Central Bank Independence: The Key to Price Stability?" *Economic Review,* Federal Reserve Bank of Cleveland, September 1, 2006, pp. 1–3.

**4.** Federal Reserve Bank of San Francisco. "U.S. Monetary Policy: An Introduction," *FRBSF Economic Letter,* Parts 1–4, January-February 2004.

**5.** Gavin, William T., and William Poole. "What Should a Central Bank Look Like?" *The Regional Economist,* Federal Reserve Bank of St. Louis, July 2003, pp. 5–9.

**6.** Jordan, Jerry L. "Money and Monetary Policy for the Twenty-First Century," *Review,* Federal Reserve Bank of St. Louis, November/December 2006, pp. 485–510.

**7.** Marquis, Milton. "Setting the Interest Rate," *FRBSF Economic Letter,* Federal Reserve Bank of San Francisco," No. 2002-30 (October 11, 2002), pp. 1–3.

**8.** Walsh, Carl E. "Transparency in Monetary Policy," *FRBSF Economic Letter,* Federal Reserve Bank of San Francisco, No. 2001-26 (September 7, 2001), pp. 1–3.

**9.** Yellen, Janet L. "Enhancing Fed Credibility," *FRBSF Economic Letter,* Federal Reserve Bank of San Francisco, No. 2006-05 (March 17, 2006), pp. 1–7.

**10.** Yellen, Janet L. "Monetary Policy in a Global Environment," *FRBSF Economic Letter,* Federal Reserve Bank of San Francisco, No. 2006-12/13 (June 2, 2006), pp. 1–7.

www.mhhe.com/rose10e

# Chapter 13

# The Tools and Goals of Central Bank Monetary Policy

## What's in This Chapter?
## Key Topics Outline

The Tools of Central Banking around the World

Open Market Operations: Nature, Types, and Impact

Reserve Requirements and the Discount Rate: Effects and Limitations

Interest Rate Targeting and the Federal Funds Rate

Economic Goals of the Fed and Other Central Banks

Central Bank Inflation Targeting

Conflicting Goals and Policy Limitations

## Learning Objectives

### in This Chapter

- You will understand how the policy tools available to central banks around the world really work in carrying out money and credit policies and in affecting the cost and availability of loanable funds.

- You will discover how the Federal Reserve System controls credit and interest rate levels inside the United States.

- You will see the various ways in which central bank policy actions affect a nation's economic goals, including control over inflation and sustaining adequate economic growth and maximum employment.

- You will learn about the difficulties that central banks face in achieving their policy goals.

## 13.1   Introduction to the Tools and Goals of Monetary Policy

As we discussed in the preceding chapter, central banks like the Federal Reserve System have been given the task of regulating the money and credit system in order to achieve economic goals. Prominent among these goals are the achievement of maximum employment, a stable price level, and sustainable economic growth. As recent experience has demonstrated, these objectives are not easy to achieve and frequently conflict, at least in the short run. Still, the central bank has powerful policy tools at its disposal with which to pursue these economic goals. Our purpose in this chapter is to examine the policy tools available to the Federal Reserve, and many other central banks as well, in carrying out its task of controlling the supply of credit and affecting the cost of borrowed funds in order to achieve the nation's economic goals.

## 13.2   General versus Selective Credit Controls

To change the volume of reserves available to depository institutions for lending and investing and to influence interest rates in the economy, the Federal Reserve System, along with other central banks, uses a variety of policy tools. Some of these tools are **general credit controls,** which affect the entire banking and financial system. Included in this list are open market operations, the discount rate, and reserve requirements. A second set of policy tools may be labeled **selective credit controls** because they affect specific groups or sectors of the financial system. Moral suasion and margin requirements on the purchase of listed securities are examples of selective credit controls.

**general credit controls**

**selective credit controls**

## 13.3   General Credit Controls in Central Banking

### *Open Market Operations*

The principal policy tool of the Federal Reserve (and many other central banks as well) is **open market operations.** By definition, open market operations in the United States consist of buying and selling U.S. government and other securities by the Federal Reserve System to affect the quantity and growth of legal reserves and, ultimately, general credit conditions. Open market operations are the most flexible policy tool available to the Fed, suitable for fine-tuning short-term interest rates and the availability of credit in the financial markets when this is necessary. Other central banks around the world may use different types of securities to buy or sell in conducting their open market operations, especially if they lack a "deep" market for their government's debt. Among the more common financial instruments traded by many central banks today are bank deposits, derivative securities, and central bank debt. Open market operations are rapidly becoming the most popular tool of leading central banks around the globe. An important example is the new European Central Bank (ECB) that was granted the open market tool; it selects which financial instruments can be used and under what terms and conditions, but the ECB's operations must be carried out through the central banks of its member countries.

**open market operations**

*Effects of Open Market Operations on Interest Rates*   The open market tool has two major effects on the banking system and credit conditions. First, it has an *interest rate effect.* For example, in the United States, the Fed typically buys or sells a large quantity (often exceeding a billion dollars worth) of government securities in the financial marketplace at any one time. If the Fed is *purchasing* securities, this adds additional demand for these securities in the market, which tends to increase their prices and lower their yields. In this case, interest rates decline. If the Federal Reserve is *selling* securities from its portfolio, this action increases the supply of securities available in the market, tending to depress their prices and raise their yields. In this case, interest rates tend to rise.

### Effects of Open Market Operations on Reserves

The principal day-to-day effect of central bank open market operations is to change the level and growth of *legal reserves.* For example, a Federal Reserve *purchase* of government securities *increases* the reserves of the banking system and expands its ability to make loans and create deposits, increasing the growth of money and credit. In contrast, a *sale* of securities by the Federal Reserve *decreases* the level and growth of reserves and ultimately reduces the growth of money and credit. The impact of Federal Reserve open market operations on the reserve positions of depository institutions with accounts in the United States is illustrated in Exhibit 13.1.

**Fed Purchases** In the top portion of Exhibit 13.1, we assume the Fed is making *purchases* of U.S. government securities in the open market from either depository institutions, which keep their reserve accounts at the Federal Reserve banks, or from other institutions and individuals. If purchases are made from depository institutions, the Federal Reserve System would record the acquisition of securities in the System's asset account—U.S. securities—and pay for the securities acquired by increasing the reserve accounts of the selling institutions. Thus, reserves of depository institutions at the Fed *rise,* while institutional holdings of securities fall by the same amount. Note that *both* total and excess reserves rise in the wake of a Fed purchase, assuming that depository institutions have no reserve deficiencies to begin with. With these extra reserves, additional loans can be made and deposits created that will have an expansionary impact on the availability of credit in the economy.

An expansionary effect would also take place were the Federal Reserve to buy securities from an institution or individual other than a depository institution. Legal reserves would increase, but total deposits—a component of the money supply—would increase as well. Deposits would rise because the central bank would issue a check to pay for the securities it purchased and that check would be deposited in some financial institution, which would, in turn, present the check to the Federal Reserve for crediting to the institution's legal reserve account. Excess reserves would then have risen, making possible an expansion of deposits and loans on the part of depository institutions. Note, however, that the rise in excess reserves is *less* in this case than would occur if the Fed bought securities only from depository institutions that maintain reserve accounts with the Federal Reserve banks. This is due to the fact that some of the new legal reserves created by the Fed purchase must be pledged as required reserves behind the newly created deposits. Therefore, Federal Reserve open market purchases of securities have *less* of an effect on total credit and deposit expansion if the Fed's transaction involves only nondeposit financial institutions and individuals.

**Fed Sales** Central bank *sales* of securities *reduce* the growth of reserves, deposits, and loans. For example, as shown in the bottom half of Exhibit 13.1, when the Federal Reserve sells U.S. government securities from its portfolio to a depository institution or to a dealer with an account at a depository institution, that institution must pay for those securities by letting the Fed deduct the amount of the purchase from its reserve

| EXHIBIT 13.1 | Central Bank Open Market Operations |
|---|---|

### The Federal Reserve Buys Securities

**Open Market Purchase from a Bank or Other Deposit-Type Financial Institution:**

| Depository Financial Institution | | Federal Reserve Bank | | Effects |
|---|---|---|---|---|
| Assets | Liabilities | Assets | Liabilities | |
| U.S. securities 1,000 <br> Reserves at Fed + 1,000 | | U.S. securities + 1,000 | Reserves + 1,000 | Total and excess legal reserves increase. |

**Open Market Purchase Not from a Depository Financial Institution:**

| Depository Financial Institution | | Federal Reserve Bank | | Effects |
|---|---|---|---|---|
| Assets | Liabilities | Assets | Liabilities | |
| Reserves at Fed + 1,000 | Deposits + 1,000 | U.S. securities + 1,000 | Reserves + 1,000 | Total and excess legal reserves increase; deposits increase. |

### The Federal Reserve Sells Securities

**Open Market Sale to a Bank or Other Deposit-Type Financial Institution:**

| Depository Financial Institution | | Federal Reserve Bank | | Effects |
|---|---|---|---|---|
| Assets | Liabilities | Assets | Liabilities | |
| U.S. securities + 1,000 <br> Reserves at Fed − 1,000 | | U.S. securities − 1,000 | Reserves − 1,000 | Total and excess legal reserves decrease. |

**Open Market Sale Not to a Depository Financial Institution:**

| Depository Financial Institution | | Federal Reserve Bank | | Effects |
|---|---|---|---|---|
| Assets | Liabilities | Assets | Liabilities | |
| Reserves at Fed − 1,000 | Deposits − 1,000 | U.S. securities − 1,000 | Reserves − 1,000 | Total and excess legal reserves decrease; deposits decrease. |

account. Both total reserves and excess reserves *fall*. If depository institutions were fully loaned up with no excess reserves available, the open market sale would result in a reserve deficiency. Some institutions would be forced to sell loans and securities or borrow funds in order to bring in additional reserves, thereby reducing the availability of credit.

Suppose the central bank were to sell securities to an individual or a nondeposit institution. As Exhibit 13.1 reveals, in this instance, *both* reserves and deposits fall. Credit becomes less available and usually more expensive.

### How Open Market Operations Are Conducted in the United States

All trading in securities by the Federal Reserve System is carried out through the System's Trading Desk, located at the Federal Reserve Bank of New York. The

Trading Desk is supervised by the manager of the System Open Market Account (SOMA), a vice president of the New York Fed. The SOMA manager's activities are, in turn, supervised and directed by the Federal Open Market Committee. In reality, the Fed does not trade with the public; rather all Fed security purchases and sales are made through a select list of primary U.S. government securities dealers who agree to buy or sell in amounts called for by the Trading Desk at the time the Fed wishes to trade. Many of these dealers are banks that have securities departments. The rest are exclusively dealers in U.S. government and selected private securities.

Federal Reserve purchases and sales of Treasury bills, repurchase agreements, and other financial instruments normally are huge in volume. For example, during the month of October 2006, Fed purchases of repurchase agreements (RPs) exceeded $175 billion and its rollover of reverse RPs were nearly $650 billion. By the end of that month the Fed held securities in its own portfolio amounting to more than $772 billion (at face value), of which more than $277 billion were U.S. Treasury bills and better than $495 billion were Treasury notes and bonds. It also held in custody on behalf of foreign governments and official institutions nearly $1.7 trillion in marketable securities. Most of its portfolio is short in maturity, rolling over within a year, keeping Fed traders in New York busy much of the time.

**The Policy Directive**   How does the SOMA manager decide whether or not to buy or sell securities in the open market on a given day? The manager is guided, first of all, by a *policy directive* issued to the Federal Reserve Bank of New York following the conclusion of each meeting of the Federal Open Market Committee (FOMC). The SOMA manager attends each FOMC meeting and participates in its policy discussions. He or she listens to the views of each member of the Federal Reserve Board and the Reserve bank presidents, who describe economic conditions in their region of the country. The manager also receives the benefit of a presentation by staff economists of the Federal Reserve Board who analyze current economic and financial developments.

In recent years, with the issuance of a policy directive to the SOMA manager at the Fed's Trading Desk in New York, the FOMC has been releasing to the public a *Federal Open Market Committee Statement* regarding its planned course of action after each committee meeting (normally by 2:15 PM. EST on the last day of an FOMC meeting). These policy statements reflect the central bank's efforts to be more *transparent* (i.e., to make more public disclosures) and to be more *accountable* to the public for what it does. An example of a recent policy statement is shown in Exhibit 13.2. This statement summarizes the Federal Reserve's view of current economic developments, particularly those that pertain to the growth of output in the economy and to movements in prices and employment. The FOMC specifies a target level for a key money market interest rate—the *effective federal funds rate.*[1]

We note that the FOMC policy statement is extremely general in nature and recognizes the need for flexibility as market conditions change. Many factors other than Federal Reserve operations affect interest rates and credit availability. Consequently, the Federal Open Market Committee must be flexible and trust the SOMA manager's judgment in responding to daily conditions in the money market, which subsequently may be quite different from those anticipated when the FOMC held its last meeting.

---

[1] See Chapter 11 for a discussion of the federal funds market and the determinants of the effective federal funds interest rate.

| EXHIBIT 13.2 | Federal Open Market Committee Statement |
|---|---|

The Federal Open Market Committee decided today to keep its target for the federal funds rate at 5 1/4 percent.

Recent indicators have suggested somewhat firmer economic growth, and some tentative signs of stabilization have appeared in the housing market. Overall, the economy seems likely to expand at a moderate pace over coming quarters.

Readings on core inflation have improved modestly in recent months, and inflation pressures seem likely to moderate over time. However, the high level of resource utilization has the potential to sustain inflation pressures.

The Committee judges that some inflation risks remain. The extent and timing of any additional firming that may be needed to address these risks will depend on the evolution of the outlook for both inflation and economic growth as implied by incoming information.

Voting for the FOMC monetary policy action were: Ben S. Bernanke, Chairman; Timothy F. Geithner, Vice Chairman; Susan S. Bies; Thomas M. Hoenig; Donald L. Kohn; Randall S. Kroszner; Cathy E. Minehan; Frederic S. Mishkin; Michael H. Moskow; William Poole; and Kevin M. Warsh.

Source: Board of Governors of the Federal Reserve System Web site, **www.federalreserve.gov,** January 31, 2007.

**Key URL:**
For a more complete overview of the structure and operations of the Federal Open Market Committee (FOMC) and the SOMA manager, see especially **federalreserve.gov/ fomc**

**The Conference Call**   As an added check on the decisions of the SOMA manager, a conference call between staff economists at the Federal Reserve Board, a member of the FOMC, and the SOMA manager is often held each day before trading occurs. The SOMA manager updates those sitting in on the conference call on current conditions in the money market and then makes a recommendation on the type and volume of securities to be bought or sold that day. At this point, the conference call participants may make alternative recommendations. Usually, however, the SOMA manager's recommendation is taken and trading proceeds.

*Types of Open Market Operations*   There are four basic types of Federal Reserve open market operations. (See Exhibit 13.3.) The so-called *straight,* or *outright, transaction* refers to the sale or purchase of securities in which outright title passes to the buyer on a permanent basis. In this case, a permanent change occurs in the level of legal reserves, up or down. Thus, when the Federal Reserve wants to bring about a *once-and-for-all* change in reserves, it tends to use the *straight* or *outright* type of transaction—something that normally takes place only a few times during the year. One reason the Fed wishes to make occasional permanent additions to its portfolio of government securities is to account for the secular growth in the liquidity demands of a growing economy.

In contrast, when the Fed wishes to have a *temporary* effect on bank reserves, correcting temporary mismatches between the demand for and supply of reserves, it employs a *repurchase agreement* with a securities dealer. Under a repurchase agreement (RP)—today the most popular type of open-market operation—the Fed buys securities from dealers but agrees to sell them back within a short period of time, usually the following day.[2] The result is a temporary increase in legal reserves that will be reversed when the Fed sells the securities back to the dealers. Such RPs frequently are used during holiday periods or when factors are at work that have resulted in a temporary shortfall in reserves.

---

[2]See Chapter 10 for an explanation of how these repurchase agreements are used as a source of funds for securities dealers.

## Outright or Straight Open Market Transaction
(permanent change in the level of reserves held by depository institutions)

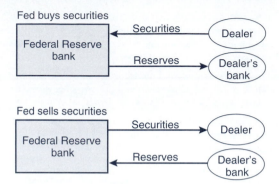

Fed buys securities

Fed sells securities

## RP or Reverse RP Transaction
(temporary change in the level of reserves held by depository institutions)

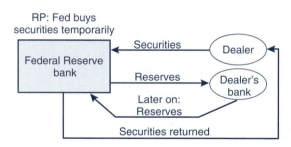

RP: Fed buys
securities temporarily

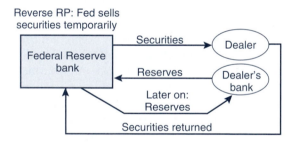

Reverse RP: Fed sells
securities temporarily

## Runoff Transaction
(permanent reduction in the level of reserves held by depository institutions)

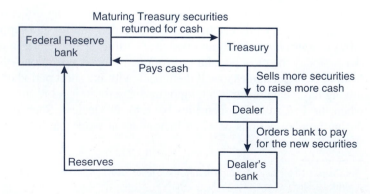

**Agency Transaction**
(may or may not affect the level of reserves held by depository institutions depending on the type of transaction)

A. First Type of Agency Transaction

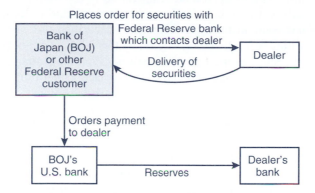

Net Effect: *No* change in total reserves held by depository institutions as reserves merely shift from one depository institution to another; Fed acts only as a broker, contacting a dealer to complete the security transaction.

B. Second Type of Agency Transaction

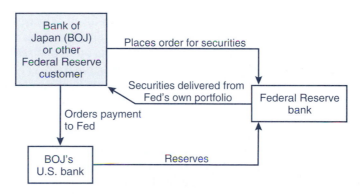

Net Effect: Total reserves of depository institutions fall in this particular transaction as payment for the securities acquired is made to the Fed; Fed acts as a security dealer.

A good example of how the RP can be used to deal with temporary emergencies appeared in September 2001 when, in the wake of a terror attack on the United States, the Fed injected about $80 billion in additional liquidity into the U.S. financial system using repurchase agreements with primary security dealers. A week later, as market conditions stabilized, the Fed withdrew most of these extra funds.

The Fed can also deal with a temporary excess quantity of reserves by using a matched-sale purchase (MSP) transaction, commonly called a *reverse RP*. In this instance, the Fed agrees to sell securities to dealers for a brief period and then to buy them back. Frequently, when deliveries are slowed by weather or strikes, the result is a sharp increase in the volume of uncollected checks (float), giving depository institutions millions of dollars in excess reserves until the unpaid items are cleared. The Fed can absorb these excess reserves using reverse RPs until the situation returns to normal. Incidentally, reverse RPs are used for the types of problems just described because the Fed is not allowed by law to use a simpler and less costly approach to the problem—borrowing from the public—in order to reduce the volume of reserves available to the banking system.

The third type of open market operation is the *runoff.* The Federal Reserve may deal directly with the U.S. Treasury in acquiring and redeeming securities. Suppose the Fed has some maturing U.S. Treasury securities and wishes to replace them with new securities currently being offered by the Treasury in its latest public auction. The amount of securities the Fed takes will *not* then be available to the public, reducing the quantity of securities sold in the marketplace. Other things being equal, this would tend to raise security prices and lower interest rates.[3]

On the other hand, the Fed may decide *not* to acquire new securities from the Treasury to replace those that are maturing. This would mean the Treasury would be forced to sell an increased volume of securities in the open market to raise cash in order to pay off the Fed. At the same time, the Treasury would draw funds from its deposits held at private banks, reducing bank reserves, to redeem the Fed's maturing securities. Other things equal, security prices would fall and interest rates rise. Credit market conditions would tighten up. Moreover, the Federal Reserve saves on transaction costs (in the form of dealer fees) by dealing directly with the Treasury and not conducting a regular open market transaction through private security dealers.

Finally, the Fed also conducts purchases and sales of securities on behalf of foreign central banks and other official agencies and institutions that hold accounts with the New York Federal Reserve Bank, known as *agency operations.* The Fed may buy or sell securities from its own portfolio to accommodate these foreign accounts or merely act as an intermediary between the foreign accounts and security dealers.

For example, suppose that the Federal Reserve Bank in New York has just received a request from the Bank of Japan to purchase U.S. government securities. That central bank has probably built up too much cash in its U.S. accounts and has decided to earn some interest on that cash by buying some U.S. Treasury bonds. To pay for the securities, the Bank of Japan transfers a portion of its deposit at a U.S. bank to its deposit account at the New York Fed. The Fed's Trading Desk may contact private dealers and make the purchase on behalf of the Bank of Japan, crediting the dealers' banks for the purchase price of the securities and reducing the Bank of Japan's deposits at the Fed. In this case, total reserves of the U.S. banking system *do not change,* falling initially but then rising back to their original level.

However, the Fed may decide to sell the Bank of Japan securities from its *own* portfolio (that is "from System account"). In this case, bank reserves fall initially, as the Bank of Japan pays for its purchase, but do not rise again. The money received from this Fed sale is "locked up" within the Federal Reserve System and does not flow out to private banks. In general, sales of Federal Reserve-held securities to foreign accounts reduce U.S. bank reserves; purchases of securities from foreign accounts that go into the Fed's own security account increase U.S. bank reserves.

### *Goals of Open Market Operations: Defensive and Dynamic*    In the use of any of its policy tools, the Federal Reserve, like other central banks, always has in mind the basic economic goals of maximum employment, a stable price level, and

---

[3]The Fed is prohibited by law from purchasing government securities directly from the Treasury Department out of concern that such transactions could lead to government abuse of Federal Reserve credit and result in serious inflation in the economy.

Different central banks around the world often emphasize different policy tools. For example, the Bank of England (BOE) relies primarily upon purchases of British Treasury and commercial bills to affect interest rates and the availability of credit. The BOE also may make changes in the basic lending rate it charges borrowing banks and securities houses.

The Bank of Canada (BOC) focuses its energies mainly on the buying and selling of short-term Treasury bills and repurchase agreements. The Canadian central bank also impacts reserves in the banking system by moving government deposits between the BOC and private banks within the Canadian system. Canada's central bank phased out its use of legal reserve requirements in 1994.

The European Central Bank (the ECB) may use a variety of open market instruments (including repurchase agreements, outright purchases and sales of securities, currency swaps, and the issuance of debt). The ECB also has the power to loan funds to financial institutions in need of liquidity and impose reserve requirements on short-term deposits and other forms of short-term debt. However, the use of the ECB's open market policy tool is somewhat dispersed because the central banks of the European Community's member states actually carry out open market operations.

The Bank of Japan (BOJ) uses security trading, primarily in commercial bills but also increasingly in Japanese government securities, to influence domestic credit conditions. The BOJ makes loans to banks through its discount window. In several other Asian countries—Indonesia, Korea, Taiwan, Hong Kong, and the Philippines—central banks issue and trade in their own IOUs in order to influence economic conditions.

Central banks do not change policy tools very often. However, with deregulation of financial markets and financial institutions becoming more alike all over the world, more central banks are choosing to work through the *private marketplace* to accomplish their goals, increasingly emphasizing the buying and selling of government and corporate financial instruments to change or maintain existing credit conditions. Such arbitrary, non-market-determined tools as interest rate and credit ceilings, currency (exchange-rate) controls, reserve requirements, and central bank loan or discount rates are increasingly being phased out or deemphasized. The discount (loan) windows of leading central banks today are more often used to relieve temporary stresses faced by individual financial institutions rather than to achieve broad policy goals—one of the reasons the Federal Reserve made major changes in its discount window policies, as discussed later in this chapter.

sustainable economic growth. However, only a portion of the Federal Reserve's daily open market activity is directed toward those particular goals. The Fed is also responsible on a day-to-day basis for stabilizing the money and capital markets and keeping the financial markets functioning smoothly. These technical adjustments in market conditions are often referred to as *defensive* open market operations. Their basic purpose is to preserve the *status quo* and to keep the present pattern of interest rates and credit availability about where it is.

For example, suppose the Fed believes the current level of reserves held by the banking system—about $42 billion—is just right to hold interest rates and credit conditions where they are. However, due to changes in other factors affecting bank reserves (such as the public demanding more currency and coin from banks to spend over the holidays), total reserves in the system are expected to fall to $41 billion. The Fed is likely to buy about $1 billion in securities so that total reserves remain at $42 billion—a *defensive operation*.

In contrast, when the Federal Reserve is interested in the pursuit of broader economic goals, it engages in *dynamic* open market operations. These operations are designed to upset the status quo and to change interest rates and credit conditions to a level the Fed believes more consistent with its economic goals. For example, if the Fed believes the economy needs to grow faster to create more jobs, it may come to the conclusion that total reserves in the banking system must increase from $42 billion to $44 billion. In this case, the Fed's Trading Desk is likely to launch an aggressive program of buying securities until reserve levels reach $44 billion. Open market operations have now become *dynamic,* not merely defensive.

The fact that open market operations are carried out for a wide variety of purposes makes it difficult to follow a central bank's daily transactions in the marketplace and to draw firm conclusions about the direction of monetary policy. On any given day, the central bank may be buying or selling securities defensively merely to stabilize market conditions without any longer-term objectives in mind. The central bank is really a balance wheel in the financial system, supplying or subtracting reserves as needed to eliminate demand-supply mismatches on any given day. Although experienced central bank watchers find the daily pattern of open market operations meaningful, unless the investor possesses inside information on the motivation of central bank actions, it is exceedingly difficult to "read" daily open market operations. A longer-term view is usually needed, supplied in part by the FOMC's policy statement, to see the direction in which the central bank is trying to move the financial system.

## QUESTIONS TO HELP YOU STUDY

1. Why are *open market operations* increasingly the most popular monetary policy tool? What are the principal effects of open market operations on the financial system?

2. Describe the relationship between the SOMA manager and the FOMC. What is a *policy directive* and what is a *policy statement?* What policy target does the Federal Reserve use?

3. Explain the difference between an *RP* and a *straight* (or outright) open market transaction. Why is each used? What is a *runoff?* An *agency* operation?

4. Explain the difference between *defensive* and *dynamic* open market operations.

## Changes in the Federal Reserve's Discount Rate

**discount rate**

One of the oldest of all monetary policy tools is the **discount rate**—the interest rate the Federal Reserve banks (and many other central banks as well) charge on loans they grant to other institutions (principally banks and security dealers). In the United States, any depository institution that accepts transaction (payments) accounts or non-personal time deposits (mainly business CDs) and holds a legal reserve account at the Fed may request a loan from the discount window maintained by the Federal Reserve bank in its region. For the most part, these loans are regarded as *temporary credit* and a *backup source of funds* to the money market, where credit is usually cheaper and easier to find.

**Key URL:**
For further discussion of recent changes in the Fed's discount rate policy, see especially
federalreserve.gov/pubs/bulletin/2002/02index.htm

On January 9, 2003, the Federal Reserve redesigned the discount windows of the Federal Reserve banks in an effort to streamline the Fed lending process, reduce administrative costs, lower the historic reluctance of depository institutions to seek Federal Reserve credit, and stabilize conditions in the marketplace for reserves (principally the federal funds market). The Fed also created two new types of loans, labeled *primary credit* and *secondary credit,* to replace older loan categories that used to be called "adjustment" and "extended" credit. A third loan category—known as *seasonal credit*—was retained.

*Primary credit* today is extended only to *sound* depository institutions—that is, those with adequate capital and supervisory ratings in the top safety and soundness categories. A borrowing institution seeking primary credit no longer has to demonstrate, as it did in the past, that it has sought funds from other sources *before* coming to the Fed. These loans may be used for *any* lawful purpose, including the expansion of a depository institution's assets and to help finance the sale of federal funds to other institutions.

*Secondary credit,* on the other hand, is intended for borrowing institutions that do *not* qualify for primary credit. Moreover, the secondary-credit borrower may *not* employ the money it receives to expand its assets. For example, a depository institution requesting secondary credit cannot *arbitrage* funds, borrowing from the Fed at a cheaper interest rate and lending those funds to another borrower at a higher interest rate.

*Seasonal credit* is usually available only to relatively small depositories that show a clear pattern of seasonal (intrayear) fluctuations in their deposits and loans. For example, *farm banks* experience their greatest need for liquidity around planting and harvesting times in their local communities, and are typically smaller banks with less ready access to the capital markets.

The Fed's discount rate on the loans described above is expressed in annual percentage terms. The board of directors of each Federal Reserve bank decides whether the discount rate in their district needs to be changed. However, the Federal Reserve Board in Washington, D.C., must approve any discount rate change in any of the 12 Federal Reserve districts. This procedure serves to prevent the existence of different discount rates from region to region of the nation for lengthy periods of time.

The most significant policy change recently made by the Fed involved setting the discount rate on primary and secondary credit *above* the target interest rate on federal funds. For example, in 2007 the Fed's Federal Open Market Committee (FOMC) set its target for the federal funds rate at 5 1/4 percent. Accordingly, the discount rate on primary credit was initially set at 1 percentage point (or 100 basis points) *above* the target federal funds rate and the rate on secondary credit was set at 1 1/2 percentage points (or 150 basis points) *above* the Fed funds rate target. Seasonal credit loan rates are usually much lower than either primary or secondary loan rates, however, and are usually based on prevailing market interest rates. (For a summary of recent discount-window loan rates, see Exhibit 13.4.)

**Key URL:**
For a review of different types of Federal Reserve discount rates see, for example, **money-rates. com/fed.htm**

In earlier times the discount rate was nearly always *less* than the federal funds rate, creating a great temptation for depository institutions to garner funds from the Reserve banks and relend those monies in the Fed funds market. To prevent this maneuver the Fed was forced to become a vigilant "watch dog." However, its actions tended to discourage many institutions from seeking *any* form of Federal Reserve credit and borrowings at the discount window nearly ceased. With the changes instituted during 2003 the Fed hopes that depository institutions will be less reluctant to seek out discount-window loans, though borrowers will, in effect, be paying a penalty rate for the credit they receive. As illustrated in Exhibit 13.5, discount-window borrowing still remains small in volume—usually less than 1 percent of total legal reserves in the banking system—and seasonal credit tends to be the largest loan type by dollar volume, followed by primary credit.

The Fed's decision to create the new loan categories of primary and secondary credit and raise the discount rate *above* most other money market rates was motivated by several factors. One was the 9/11 terrorist crisis, during which time several leading banks and primary security dealers found themselves in desperate need of liquid

| EXHIBIT 13.4 | The Discount Rates Charged by the Federal Reserve Banks on Loans to Depository Institutions (percent per annum), February 2007 | | |
|---|---|---|---|
| **Discount Rates at the Federal Reserve Banks by District** | **Types of Loans Available from the Discount Window** | | |
| | **Primary Credit** | **Secondary Credit** | **Seasonal Credit** |
| Boston, New York, Philadelphia, Cleveland, Richmond, Atlanta, Chicago, St. Louis, Minneapolis, Kansas City, Dallas, and San Francisco | 6.25% | 6.75% | 5.30% |

Source: Board of Governors of the Federal Reserve System, *Federal Reserve Bulletin*, February 2007, Table 1.14.

Notes: Primary credit loans are available from the Federal Reserve banks for very short terms as a backup source of liquidity to those depository institutions that are in generally sound financial condition in the judgment of the Federal Reserve bank granting the loan. Secondary credit may be extended to depository institutions not qualifying for primary credit, while seasonal credit is available to relatively small depositories with regular seasonal funds needs that cannot be satisfied through other lenders.

funds and conventional funds sources dried up. The new discount-window policy ensures a "no hassle" supply of primary credit to sound depository institutions facing emergencies. Moreover, the fixed, positive spread between the discount rate and the federal funds rate target is expected to lower the volatility of the federal funds market rate, making it somewhat easier for the central bank to achieve its interest rate targets and reduce the interest rate risk for borrowers in the federal funds market. Indeed, under the newly revised policy, the primary credit rate is expected to serve as a *cap* for the prevailing market rate on federal funds because an attempt by the funds rate to rise above the discount rate would likely direct more borrowers to the Fed's discount window.

### Borrowing and Repaying Discount Window Loans

Depository institutions that borrow regularly at the discount window keep a signed loan authorization form at the Federal Reserve bank in their district and keep U.S. government securities or other acceptable collateral on deposit there. When a loan is needed, the officer responsible for managing the borrowing institution's legal reserve position contacts the district Federal Reserve bank and requests that the necessary funds be deposited in that institution's reserve account.

In Exhibit 13.6, we illustrate the borrowing process by supposing that a depository institution has requested a loan of $1 million and the Fed has agreed to make the loan. The borrowing bank receives an increase in its account, Reserves Held at Federal Reserve Bank, of $1 million. At the same time, the bank's liability account, Bills Payable, increases by $1 million. On the Federal Reserve bank's balance sheet,

**Key URL:**
For a review of the discount rate policies of the Federal Reserve over time and of various other central banks see, in particular **research. stlouisfed.org/wp/ more/1996-001/**

| EXHIBIT 13.5 | Types of Discount Window Loans Granted by the Federal Reserve Banks, November 2006 (in millions of dollars) | | |
|---|---|---|---|
| **Primary Credit** | **Secondary Credit** | **Seasonal Credit** | **Total Discount-Window Loans** |
| $48 | $0 | $112 | $160 |

Source: Board of Governors of the Federal Reserve System, *Federal Reserve Bulletin*, February 2007, Table 1.12.

| EXHIBIT 13.6 | Borrowing and Repaying Loans from the Central Bank |
|---|---|

**Borrowing from a Federal Reserve Bank:**

| Federal Reserve | | | | Commercial Bank or Other Depository Institution | | | |
|---|---|---|---|---|---|---|---|
| *Assets* | | *Liabilities* | | *Assets* | | *Liabilities* | |
| Discounts and advances | +$1 million | Bank reserves | +$1 million | Reserves held at Federal Reserve bank | +$1 million | Bills payable | +$1 million |

**Repayment of Borrowings from the Fed:**

| Federal Reserve | | | | Commercial Bank or Other Depository Institution | | | |
|---|---|---|---|---|---|---|---|
| *Assets* | | *Liabilities* | | *Assets* | | *Liabilities* | |
| Discounts and advances | −$1 million | Bank reserves | −$1 million | Reserves held at Federal Reserve bank | −$1 million | Bills payable | −$1 million |

the loan is entered as an increase in Bank Reserves of $1 million—a liability of the Federal Reserve System—and also as an increase in a Fed asset account, Discounts and Advances. When the loan is repaid, the transaction is reversed.

Quite clearly, borrowings from the Fed's discount window *increase* total reserves available to the banking system. Repayments of those borrowings cause total reserves to *fall*.

### Effects of a Discount Rate Change

Most observers today believe that at least *three* effects follow from a change in the lending rates of most central banks. One is the *cost effect.* An increase in the discount rate may mean it is more costly to borrow reserves from the central bank than to use some other source of funds. Other things being equal, loans from the discount window and the total volume of borrowed reserves may decline. Conversely, a lower discount rate may result in an acceleration of borrowing and more reserves flowing into the banking system. Of course, the strength of the cost effect depends on the prevailing spread between the discount rate and other money market interest rates.

Key URL:
For a more detailed overview of the discount windows and discount rates of the Federal Reserve banks see especially frbdiscountwindow.org

A second consequence of changes in the discount rate is the *substitution effect.* A change in the discount rate may cause other interest rates to change as well. This is due to the fact that the central bank is one source of borrowed reserves, but certainly not the only source. An increase in the discount rate, for example, makes borrowing less attractive, but borrowing from other sources, such as the Eurodollar market, may become relatively more attractive. Borrowers may shift their attention to other markets, causing interest rates there to rise as well. A lowering of the central bank's discount rate, on the other hand, may cause a downward movement in other interest rates.

The final possible effect of a discount rate change is the *announcement effect.* The discount rate may have a psychological impact on the financial markets because the central bank's lending rate is widely regarded as an indicator of monetary policy. If, for example, the Federal Reserve raises its discount rate, some observers may regard this as a signal the Fed is pushing for tighter credit conditions. Market participants may respond by reducing their borrowings and curtailing their spending plans.

Unfortunately, the psychological impact of the discount rate may work *against* the central bank as well as *for* it. It is possible, for example, that if the Federal Reserve raises its discount rate, borrowers will respond by accelerating their borrowings in an effort to secure the credit they need before interest rates move even higher. Such an action would tend to thwart the Fed's objective of slowing the growth of borrowing and spending.

Beginning in 1999, the Fed's discount rate was set up to follow the federal funds interest rate (discussed earlier in Chapter 11). Each time the target federal funds rate—the Federal Reserve's principal policy target today—was changed by the Federal Open Market Committee, the discount rate was moved in parallel fashion. As we noted earlier in this chapter, this policy was reinforced in 2003 when the spread between the discount rate on primary credit and the Fed's current target for the Fed funds rate was set at one percentage point (100 basis points). The result of this new policy has been to turn the discount rate and the discount window into a relatively passive tool in the conduct of U.S. monetary policy. This new minimal role for the discount rate (plus the very small amount of borrowing actually taking place through the discount window) has led to proposals to eliminate this policy tool. Yet, as the terrorist attacks in September 2001 demonstrated, access to the discount window can help stabilize the economy in times of crisis and provide badly needed liquidity in a hurry. History teaches us that policy tools that may have little importance today can suddenly become important again.

## *Reserve Requirements*

Since the 1930s in the United States, the Federal Reserve Board has had the power to vary the amount of required legal reserves member banks must hold behind the deposits they receive from the public, as we saw earlier in Chapters 11 and 12. With passage of the Depository Institutions Deregulation and Monetary Control Act (DIDMCA) in 1980, nonmember banks and other depository financial institutions (including credit unions and savings and loan associations) were required to conform to the deposit

**reserve requirements**

**reserve requirements** set by the Fed.

Early in the Fed's history, it was believed that the primary purpose of reserve requirements was to safeguard the public's deposits. Most recently, we have come to realize that their principal use is to give the central bank a powerful tool for affecting the supply of money and credit in the economy, particularly if emergency situations arise in the financial markets. Indeed, reserve requirements are probably the most potent policy tool the Federal Reserve System has at its disposal today. However, changes in reserve requirements are a little-used policy tool in the United States, and their role is likely to diminish in the future. In 2006 Congress passed legislation—scheduled to take effect on October 1, 2011—that (1) would authorize the Federal Reserve to pay interest on reserve balances member banks hold with the Federal Reserve (if the Federal Reserve so chooses), and (2) would allow the Federal Reserve to adjust reserve requirements downward, even to the point of eliminating them completely. (See the accompanying Financial Developments box.) In recent years, these actions have been taken by many other nations, including Canada, New Zealand, and the United Kingdom. In the meantime, reserve requirements will remain in force as a tool that

**FINANCIAL DEVELOPMENTS**

The Financial Services Regulatory Relief Act of 2006: Is There a Future for Reserve Requirements?

In 1980 the United States Congress embarked on what has proven to be a very long, methodical road to undo many of the Depression-era regulations of the banking system. The financial markets and institutions in the United States during that period were subjected to severe strain as thousands of firms went out of business and individuals were seeing their personal wealth along with their jobs vanish, as unemployment climbed to over 20 percent. At that time Congress, concluding that the financial system in the United States bore much of the blame for the Great Depression of the 1930s, instituted a series of new laws and regulations and created a number of regulatory bodies, such as the Securities and Exchange Commission and the Federal Deposit Insurance Corporation among others, whose charge was to oversee activities within the financial marketplace.

In its zeal to ensure stability and fair play in the financial markets, Congress enacted many pieces of legislation that have not withstood the test of time, and it has gradually lifted many of the restrictions on competition these earlier laws instituted, while simultaneously strengthening legislation from that earlier era that proved successful. One of the latest legislative acts of Congress along these lines was the Financial Services Regulatory Relief Act of 2006. Its principal purpose was to recognize the fact that depository institutions engaging in investment activities as brokers and dealers were not uniformly regulated, effectively overburdening some institutions with regulatory filings, and so on. As part of the process of addressing this inequity, two other pieces of regulatory reform long sought by the Federal Reserve were enacted. One gave the Federal Reserve statutory authority to pay interest on the reserve balances depository institutions maintain with the Federal Reserve (provided the interest rate set is in line with prevailing short-term interest rates). The Federal Reserve had long argued that the prohibition on paying interest on these reserves was an unnecessary tax that was passed along to households in the form of lower interest on their bank deposits and represented an economic inefficiency that should be eliminated. The second provision allowed the Fed to choose to reduce or even eliminate reserve requirements on financial institutions if they felt this action would serve the public interest.

The fact that both of these provisions were enacted simultaneously, although they do not take effect until 2011, is relevant. The effectiveness of the Federal Reserve's open market operations is dependent upon strong demand by banks for reserves. The elimination of reserve requirements reduces the artificial demand that regulation created and could reduce the control the Fed has over the rate of growth of money and credit in the economy. However, the ability of the Federal Reserve to pay a market rate of interest on the deposits banks maintain in their Federal Reserve reserve accounts increases the demand for reserves and enhances the Fed's monetary control. Exactly how the balance of these offsetting forces on the banks' overall demands for reserves and, hence, on the Fed's ability to conduct monetary policy effectively is currently under study. Ultimately, the Fed must decide on the appropriate balance between the interest rate they pay on bank reserve balances and on whether and if so, how much, reserve requirements should be imposed on banks in order to balance their objectives of high economic efficiency and sufficient monetary control.

the Federal Reserve may have recourse to utilize if it perceives that conditions in the financial markets and the macroeconomy require it.

*Effects of a Change in Deposit Reserve Requirements*  A change in deposit reserve requirements—which acts like a "tax" on deposits—has at least *three* different effects on the financial system. First, it *changes the deposit multiplier* (or coefficient of expansion), which affects the amount of new deposits and loans the banking system can create for any given injection of new reserves. A change in reserve requirements also *affects the size of the money multiplier,* influencing the rate of increase in the money supply. If the Fed increases reserve requirements, the deposit multiplier and the money multiplier are *reduced,* slowing the growth of money, deposits, and loans. On the other hand, a decrease in reserve requirements increases the size of both the deposit multiplier and the money multiplier. In this instance, each dollar of additional reserves will lead to accelerated growth in money, deposits, and loans.

Second, a change in reserve requirements affects the *mix between excess and required legal reserves.* If reserve requirements are *reduced,* a portion of what were required reserves now becomes excess reserves. Depository institutions will soon convert all or a portion of these newly created excess reserves into loans and investments, expanding the money supply. Similarly, an *increase* in reserve requirements will mean that some depository institutions will be short required legal reserves. These institutions will be forced to sell securities, cut back on loans, and borrow reserves from other financial institutions to meet their reserve requirements. The money supply will grow more slowly and may even contract.

Third, *interest rates* also respond to a change in reserve requirements. A move by the central bank toward higher reserve requirements may soon lead to higher interest rates, particularly in the money market, as depository institutions scramble to cover any reserve deficiencies. Credit becomes less available and more costly. In contrast, a lowering of reserve requirements tends to bring interest rates down and increase investment spending and income.

*An Illustration*   Exhibit 13.7 illustrates the effects of changes in reserve requirements. Suppose depository institutions are required to keep 10 percent of their deposits in legal reserves: $100 of legal reserves will then be needed to support each $1,000 in deposits. If there is sufficient demand for loanable funds, institutions will probably loan or invest the remaining $900. Suppose that the Federal Reserve increases reserve requirements from 10 percent to 15 percent. As a result, more legal reserves are necessary to support the same volume of deposits, and institutions have a $50 reserve deficit for each $1,000 of deposits. This deficit may be covered by selling financial assets, borrowing funds, or reducing deposits.

On the other hand, suppose required reserves are lowered from 10 percent to 8 percent. There are now $20 in excess reserves for each $1,000 in deposits, and that excess can be loaned or invested, creating new deposits. We should note that *total* legal reserves available to the banking system are *not* affected by changes in reserve requirements. A shift in reserve requirements affects only the *mix* of legal reserves between required and excess.

*Current Levels of Reserve Requirements*   In the United States, reserve requirements are imposed by the Federal Reserve Board on all depository institutions eligible for federal deposit insurance. Three types of deposits are, potentially at least, subject to legal reserve requirements:

1. *Transaction accounts,* which are deposits used to make payments by negotiable or transferable instruments and include regular checking accounts, NOW accounts, and any account subject to automatic transfer of funds.

2. *Nonpersonal time deposits,* which are interest-bearing time deposits—including savings deposits and money market deposit accounts (MMDAs)—held by businesses and governmental units, but not by individuals.

3. *Eurocurrency liabilities,* which are borrowings of deposits from banks and bank branches located outside the United States.

As shown in Exhibit 13.8, the reserve requirements for 2006 transaction deposits—checkable or draftable accounts for making payments—are zero for banks holding

| EXHIBIT 13.7 | Effects of Changes in Reserve Requirements on Deposits, Loans, and Investments |
| --- | --- |

With a 10 percent reserve requirement, $100 of reserves is needed to support each $1,000 of deposits.

| Depository Institution | | | |
| --- | --- | --- | --- |
| **Assets** | | **Liabilities** | |
| Legal reserves | 100 | Deposits | $1,000 |
| Required | 100 | | |
| Excess | 0 | | |
| Loans and investments | $ 900 | | |
| | $1,000 | | $1,000 |

**Increase in reserve requirements:**

If required reserves are increased from 10 percent to 15 percent, more reserves are needed against the same volume of deposits. Any deficiencies (negative excess reserves) must be covered by liquidating loans and investments or by borrowing.

| Depository Institution | | | |
| --- | --- | --- | --- |
| **Assets** | | **Liabilities** | |
| Legal reserves | $ 100 | Deposits | $1,000 |
| Required | 150 | | |
| Excess | −50 | | |
| Loans and investments | 900 | | |
| | $1,000 | | $1,000 |

**Decrease in reserve requirements:**

If required reserves are reduced from 10 percent to 8 percent, excess reserves are created which can be loaned to the public or invested in other types of financial assets.

| Depository Institution | | | |
| --- | --- | --- | --- |
| **Assets** | | **Liabilities** | |
| Legal reserves | $ 100 | Deposits | $1,000 |
| Required | 80 | | |
| Excess | 20 | | |
| Loans and investments | 900 | | |
| | $1,000 | | $1,000 |

total transaction deposits totaling $8.5 million or less (known as the *reserve requirement exemption amount*) and 3 percent for depository institutions with transaction accounts exceeding $8.5 million and up to $45.8 million. Transaction deposits exceeding $45.8 million are assessed a 10 percent reserve requirement.[4] Time and

[4]The Federal Reserve Board is empowered to vary reserve requirements on transaction accounts over $45.4 million between 8 and 14 percent. The $45.8 million dividing line (known as the *low reserve tranche*) is indexed and changes each calendar year by 80 percent of the percentage change in total transaction accounts of all depository institutions during the previous year ended June 30. In addition, the Garn-St Germain Depository Institutions Act of 1982 stipulated that some minimum amount of reservable liabilities (transaction accounts, nonpersonal time deposits, and eurocurrency liabilities) of each depository institution be subject to a zero reserve requirement, adjusted by the Federal Reserve Board each year by 80 percent of the percentage increase in total reservable liabilities. By 2006, this zero reserve requirement base had been expanded to $8.5 million.

| EXHIBIT 13.8 | Reserve Requirement Ratios for All Banking Firms in the United States | | |
| --- | --- | --- | --- |
| Type of Deposit and Deposit Interval | Percentage Reserve Requirement | | Permissible Statutory Range % |
| Net transaction accounts: | | | |
| $0–$8.5 million | 0% of amount | | — |
| Over $8.5 million and up to $45.8 million | 3% of amount | | 3% |
| Over $45.8 million | $1,119,000, plus 10% of amount over $45.8 million | | 8–14 |
| Nonpersonal time deposits | 0% of amount | | 0–9 |
| Eurocurrency liabilities | 0% of amount | | None |

Source: National Archives and Records Administration Web site for the *Electronic Code of Federal Regulations,* www.ecfr.gpoaccess.gov, May 2, 2007.

Notes: Required reserves must be held in deposits with the Federal Reserve banks or in vault cash. Nonmember depository institutions may maintain their reserve balances with a Federal Reserve bank indirectly on a pass-through basis with certain approved depository institutions. Depository institutions subject to reserve requirements include banks, savings and loan associations, credit unions, agencies and branch offices of foreign banks, and Edge Act and Agreement corporations that offer checkable deposits or business time deposits. Edge Act and Agreement corporations are affiliates of banks and bank holding companies that deal mainly with international (off-shore) accounts.

savings deposits and eurocurrency liabilities currently carry zero reserve requirements, although the Federal Reserve Board could impose new reserve requirements on these deposits at any time. Average reserve requirements usually are higher on transaction accounts than on time and savings accounts because transaction balances are considered to be less stable than time and savings deposits.

Clearly, the largest *depository institutions* carry the heaviest reserve requirements. This is due to the fact that larger financial institutions hold the deposits of thousands of smaller deposit intermediaries. The failure of a large depository institution can send shock waves through the entire financial system and threaten the economic viability of many other institutions as well.

Changes in reserve requirements can be used to carry out major shifts in government economic policy. The reserve requirement tool is exceedingly powerful, so that even a small change affects hundreds of millions of dollars in legal reserves. Moreover, it is an inflexible tool. Required reserve ratios cannot be changed frequently because this would disrupt the banking system. Not surprisingly, changes in reserve requirement ratios do not occur often, having averaged no more than once every three to five years since World War II. In fact, the Federal Reserve has not changed reserve requirement ratios since 1992.

Today in the United States, legal reserves apply only to checkable-type deposits and are gradually fading in their impact on the banking system. Depository institutions have found innovative new ways (such as "sweep accounts" that temporarily move customer funds out of a deposit account subject to reserve requirements) to lower their required reserve levels. Indeed, most depositories now meet their reserve requirements by holding vault cash rather than keeping large balances at the Federal Reserve banks. By way of comparison, the new European Central Bank (ECB) imposed a 2 percent reserve requirement on the short-term deposits and debt of financial institutions subject to its authority. Unlike the Federal Reserve, however, the ECB pays interest on required reserve balances.

## 13.4 Selective Credit Controls Used in Central Banking

Open market operations, the discount rate, and reserve requirements are often called *general credit controls* because each has an impact on the whole financial system. Another set of policy tools available to the Federal Reserve and other central banks, however, is more *selective* in its impact, focusing on particular sectors of the economy. Nevertheless, use of some of these selective tools can contribute toward the overall objectives of the central bank to achieve maximum employment, stabilize prices, and sustain economic growth.

### Moral Suasion by Central Bank Officials

**moral suasion**

**Key URLs:**
For a discussion of the nature and role of moral suasion in central bank policy, see **investopedia.com/terms/m/moralsuasion.asp** and **investerwords.com/3119/moral_suasion.html**

A widely used selective policy tool is known as **moral suasion.** This refers to the use of "arm-twisting" or "jawboning" by central bank officials to encourage banks and other lending institutions to conform with the spirit of its policies. For example, if the Federal Reserve wishes to tighten credit controls and slow the growth of credit, Fed officials issue letters and public statements urging financial institutions operating in the United States to use more restraint in granting loans. These public statements may be supplemented by personal phone calls from top Federal Reserve officials to individual lending institutions, stressing the need for more conservative policies. Some central banks, such as the Bank of Japan, use the moral suasion tool as an important supplement to their other policy tools.

### Margin Requirements

**margin requirements**

**Key URLs:**
To learn more about security margin requirements, see such sources as **nyse.com, speculativebubble.com,** and **nasdr.com**

A selective credit control still under the exclusive control of the Federal Reserve Board is the use of **margin requirements** on the purchase and short sales of stocks and convertible bonds. Margin requirements were enacted into law with passage of the Securities Exchange Act of 1934. This federal law limited the amount of credit that could be used as collateral for a loan. Regulations G, T, and U of the Federal Reserve Board prescribe a maximum loan value for marginable stocks, convertible bonds, and short sales. That maximum loan value is expressed as a specified percentage of the market value of the securities at the time they are used as loan collateral. The margin requirement on a regulated security, then, is simply the difference between its market value (100 percent) and the maximum loan value of that security.

For example, as shown in Exhibit 13.9, the current margin requirement on stock is 50 percent. This means that common and preferred stock can be purchased on credit with the stock itself used as collateral. However, the purchaser can borrow only up to a maximum of 50 percent of the stock's current market value. He or she must put up the remainder of the stock's purchase price in cash money.

**Key URL:**
For a further review of the Federal Reserve's credit controls and policymaking, see **kc.frb.org/fed101**

As Exhibit 13.9 suggests, margin requirements are not often changed. In fact, the current U.S. margin requirements on stocks, convertible bonds, and short sales have remained unchanged since January 1974. Most observers of the financial markets believe the imposition of margin requirements was unnecessary. These requirements arose out of the turmoil of the Great Depression of the 1930s, when many believed speculative buying and selling of stocks had contributed to the U.S. economy's sudden collapse. This was probably *not* the case, but margin requirements do ensure that a substantial amount of cash will be contributed by the buyer of securities, keeping borrowing against these securities within reasonable limits. One serious limitation of this selective tool is that it does *not* cover purchases of *all* types of stocks and bonds. For this reason, its future use as a tool of monetary policy is likely to remain very limited.

| EXHIBIT 13.9 | Federal Reserve Margin Requirements on Stocks, Convertible Bonds, and Short Sales (percent of market value and effective date) | | | | | |
|---|---|---|---|---|---|---|
| Security | March 11, 1968 | June 8, 1968 | May 6, 1970 | Dec. 6, 1971 | Nov. 24, 1972 | Jan. 3, 1974 |
| Margin stocks | 70% | 80% | 65% | 55% | 65% | 50% |
| Convertible bonds | 50 | 60 | 50 | 50 | 50 | 50 |
| Short sales | 70 | 80 | 65 | 55 | 65 | 50 |

Source: Board of Governors of the Federal Reserve System, *Federal Reserve Bulletin,* February 2007, Table 1.36.

Note: Regulations G, T, and U published by the Board of Governors of the Federal Reserve System, in accordance with the Securities Exchange Act of 1934, limit the amount of credit to purchase or carry margin stocks when the securities to be purchased are used as collateral. Margin requirements specify the maximum loan value of the securities expressed as a percentage of their market value at the time a loan is made.

## QUESTIONS TO HELP YOU STUDY

5. How and why does a depository institution borrow from the central bank? Explain what may happen when a central bank changes its *discount* or *lending rate*. What are the principal advantages and disadvantages of the discount rate tool?

6. How does the *reserve requirement* tool affect the ability of deposit-type financial institutions to create money? What are the principal advantages and disadvantages of the reserve requirement tool?

7. Why do you think reserve requirements and discount rates are not widely used policy tools at many central banks around the world? Are reserve requirements and the discount rate a general credit control or a selective credit control? Why?

8. What is *moral suasion*? Do you belive this tool can be effective?

9. Explain how *margin requirements* affect the financial system. Why is this policy tool not frequently used?

## 13.5   Interest Rate Targeting

The Federal Reserve and other central banks around the world have given increasing weight in recent years to targeting *the cost and availability of credit in the money market.* One reason is that central banks are charged with the responsibility of stabilizing conditions in the financial markets to assure a smooth flow of funds from savers (lenders) to borrowers. In addition, central banks must ensure the government securities market functions smoothly so that adequate supplies of credit are available to security dealers and the federal government can market its billions of dollars in debt securities without serious difficulty. But to what aspects of the money market does a central bank like the Federal Reserve pay the most attention today?

### The Federal Funds Rate

As we saw earlier in Chapter 11, the money market indicator that usually feels the first impact from Federal Reserve policy moves is the *effective federal funds rate.*

Beginning in 1989 the Fed adopted a *federal funds interest rate targeting procedure*—the monetary policy approach it uses today. When the Fed sells securities, the supply of reserves available to depository institutions is reduced and, other things held equal, the Fed funds rate—the interest rate charged on overnight borrowings of reserves in the banking system—tends to rise. On the other hand, a Federal Reserve purchase of securities increases available reserves to depository institutions, which tends to push the Fed funds rate down.

Beginning in 1994, the Federal Reserve adopted a new policy of "openness" or "transparency" when it comes to announcing its target for the federal funds interest rate, letting the public know right away what the current funds rate target is and explaining its reasoning to the public if it is moving the funds rate target. However, history has shown that when the Fed begins to adjust interest rates either upward or downward it does so incrementally and over an extended period of time that could extend for a year or more. This gradual process by which the funds rate target is adjusted in a series of 25 or 50 basis point moves all in the same direction (either up or down) has come to be known as **policy inertia.** This policy inertia is evident in Exhibit 13.10, which displays how the federal funds rate target has changed in the recent past, and how closely the federal funds rate tracks the Fed's chosen target.

As Exhibit 13.10 illustrates, once the Fed begins to raise or lower interest rates, the process could persist for months, and market participants have to gauge how long this process will last in order to gain perspective on how much the federal funds rate will ultimately be increased or decreased by the time the current round of rate adjustments is completed. In keeping with the Fed's policy of increased transparency, announcements following the meetings of the FOMC that describe the new funds rate target have often included a hint—in a little more than a sentence—as to whether the FOMC believes it is more likely in the future to be raising, lowering, or leaving the target unchanged. This hint is referred to as the **bias,** and is often the most intensely scrutinized wording within the FOMC's announcement.

**policy inertia**

**Key URL:**
For greater understanding of the causes and effects of policy inertia, see, for example **frbsf.org/publications/economics/letter/2007/el2007-03.html**

**bias**

**EXHIBIT 13.10**

**FOMC's Target for the Federal Funds Interest Rate**

Source: Federal Reserve Bank of St. Louis Web site: www.research.stlouisfed.org.

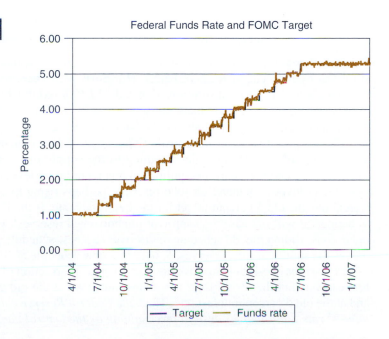

**EXHIBIT 13.11** | **The Federal Reserve's Impact on the Federal Funds Interest Rate**

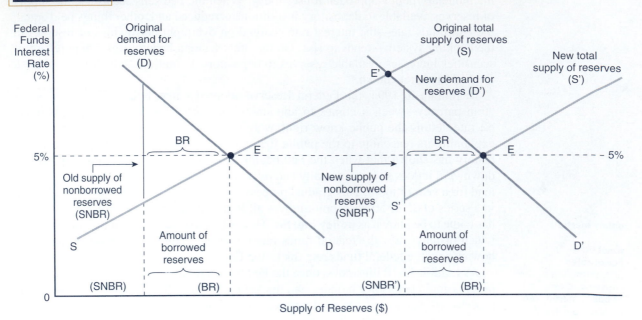

How is the Federal Reserve's Trading Desk able to maintain the federal funds rate so close to its announced rate target? Exhibit 13.11 provides us with an illustration of the process. Suppose the Fed has targeted a Fed funds rate of 5 percent and the funds rate currently sits at the 5 percent level, where the total demand for reserves by depository institutions (represented by schedule *D* in Exhibit 13.11) intersects the supply of total reserves (represented by schedule *S*), achieving an equilibrium rate of interest at *E*.

We note that the supply of total reserves consists of the sum of borrowed and nonborrowed reserves:

**Total reserves = Borrowed reserves + Nonborrowed reserves**

**borrowed reserves**

**nonborrowed reserves**

**Borrowed reserves** (labeled *BR* in Exhibit 13.11) are loans made to depository institutions by the Federal Reserve banks. **Nonborrowed reserves** are legal reserves that belong to depository institutions (labeled *SNBR* in Exhibit 13.11). Through open market operations the central bank impacts primarily nonborrowed reserves which, in turn, affect total reserves available to the banking system.

Now, suppose that depository institutions increase their demand for total reserves to *D'*. If the Federal Reserve does nothing to the supply of reserves, the Fed funds rate must rise above its current equilibrium 5 percent target level to accommodate the new higher level of demand for total reserves, perhaps rising to equilibrium level *E'*, well above the old 5 percent target for the Fed funds rate. If the Fed doesn't want this to happen, it will increase the supply of nonborrowed reserves by using open market operations, sliding the old schedule *SNBR* over to a new schedule, *SNBR'*. This action moves the supply of total reserves, *S*, over to a new schedule *S'*. If the amount of borrowed reserves doesn't change, we now have a *new* intersection of supply and demand for reserves, but the level of the Fed funds rate stays at the old equilibrium point *E*, and at the old 5 percent interest rate. Thus, *the Federal Reserve can keep the Fed funds interest rate at or near its desired level so long as the central bank is willing to offset*

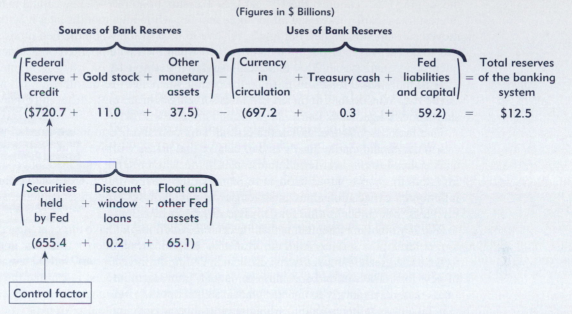

(Figures in $ Billions)

*An example:* The Fed's current target might be to keep total reserves around $12.5 billion in order to stabilize interest rates.

*The problem:* Currency in circulation in the public's hands is expected to increase by $1 billion over the next two-week period, all other factors held constant. Bank reserves will fall and interest rates are likely to rise as the public

withdraws this pocket money from banks unless the Federal Reserve acts.

*Possible solution:* Use open market operations to purchase $1 billion in U.S. government securities (the Fed's open-market control factor) through the Trading Desk of the New York Federal Reserve Bank.

**Key URLs:**
One way to follow interest rate targeting in the United States is to check frequently with such Web sites as **federalreserve.gov/ fomc** and **economagic. com**

changes in the demand for total reserves and in the demand for borrowed reserves by making appropriate adjustments in the supply of nonborrowed reserves through open market operations.

Of course, the central bank cannot maintain the Fed funds rate exactly at its target level every hour of every day. This is because depository institutions are constantly changing their demands for reserves and their attitudes about borrowing reserves from the Federal Reserve banks. Moreover, interest rates are impacted by the public's expectations regarding inflation and by the total demand for and supply of credit within the financial system. The Fed's Trading Desk manager, acting on behalf of the FOMC, tries to project what the banking system's demand for reserves is likely to be in order to supply enough reserves through open market operations to keep the federal funds rate at or close to its target level. Similarly, the Trading Desk manager must make further corrections through open market operations when his or her forecasts are off the mark.

## Fed Funds Targeting and Long-Term Interest Rates

Finally, one more important point about targeting the federal funds rate should be noted. Just because the Fed can manipulate the federal funds rate—a key money market interest rate—does not mean that long-term capital market interest rates will also respond in the same way to the Fed's activities. For example, when the Federal Reserve nudged the Fed funds rate *downward* in November of 2002 in order to bolster the sagging U.S. economy, the 10-year U.S. Treasury bond rate—a key capital market interest rate—hardly moved at all for three months, while nine months later it actually moved substantially higher, not lower, relative to its position when the Fed funds rate was lowered. A similar phenomenon occurred when the Fed embarked on a series of interest rate increases in 2004 that are illustrated in Exhibit 13.10. Long-term interest rates actually fell throughout most of the period when short-term interest rates were on the rise. Why do long-term interest rates sometimes move quite differently than the short-term federal funds rate?

One factor is *inflation.* When the central bank cuts short-term interest rates investors in the capital market may come to believe that prices will rise. Thus, easier monetary policy lowers short-term interest rates in the near term, but may lead longer-term investors to expect higher short-term interest rates in the future. Ultimately, higher inflationary expectations may push long-term interest rates upward as capital market investors seek compensation for their fear of greater inflation.

The key point to remember is that the central bank does *not* have direct control over longer-term interest rates. And, unfortunately, it is long-term interest rates that appear to have the greatest impact on investment spending in the economy and the creation of new jobs. The central bank must be patient. Short-term interest rates, like the Fed funds rate, react quickly to changes in central bank policy, but long-term interest rates may take months to respond to what the central bank is trying to do. Monetary policy often operates with long and variable time lags.

## 13.6   The Federal Reserve and Economic Goals

For many years, the Federal Reserve System, along with other central banks around the world, has played an active role in the stabilization of the economy and the pursuit of economic goals. These goals include controlling inflation, maximizing employment, and promoting sustainable economic growth. In recent years, these goals have proven to be extremely difficult to achieve in practice. Nevertheless, the Fed and other central banks remain committed to them, with an increasing emphasis on maintaining long-run price stability.

### *The Goal of Controlling Inflation*

*Inflation*—a rise in the general price level of all goods and services produced in the economy—has been among the more serious economic problems of the world during the past half century, with many nations experiencing far higher annual rates of inflation than those currently prevailing in the United States. Moreover, inflation is *not* new; price levels have been generally rising since the beginning of the Industrial Revolution in Europe nearly 300 years ago. There is also evidence of outbreaks of rampant inflation during the Middle Ages and in both ancient and more recent times.

What are the *causes* of inflation? During the 1960s and 1970s, war and government spending were certainly contributing factors. Soaring energy and food costs, higher home mortgage rates, and rapid increases in labor and medical care costs also played key roles until the 1980s brought a turnaround, as Exhibit 13.12 reveals. Another contributing factor was the decline in the value of the U.S. dollar in international markets. The dollar's weakness relative to other major currencies, such as the Japanese yen,

## The Federal Funds Futures Market— An Aid to Market Participants Trying to Guess Which Way the Central Bank Is Headed

Since early in 1994 the Federal Reserve has been setting target levels for the daily average federal funds interest rate. Moreover, when the Fed publicly announces a new target level for the effective federal funds rate, usually following a meeting of its Federal Open Market Committee (FOMC), the effective Fed funds rate moves quickly toward the new target level. This procedure of setting clear and explicit interest rate targets and doing it right away has helped make it easier for investors to "tune in" on what the central bank is trying to do.

In October 1988 the Chicago Board of Trade (CBOT) began public trading of a federal funds futures contract in the amount of $5 million for 30 days and priced on the basis of 100 less the overnight federal funds rate for the delivery month. For example, if the prevailing federal funds interest rate is 5 percent, the contract's value is 100 - 5, or 95 (on a $100 basis). These futures contracts are usually traded for the current month out to about six or seven months ahead. The federal funds interest rate on these contracts may be found any time during the trading day through radio, television, or the Internet.

The futures contracts' funds rate is a *forecast* by the market of what the Federal Reserve is likely to do with its *target federal funds rate* in the near future. Thus, investors can put together a forecast of the decisions likely to be made by the FOMC at little cost. The creation of the new futures contract and the Fed's willingness to be more open with its plans for the funds rate and with how it views the economy's condition has made monetary policy more *transparent* and more helpful to active market investors.

During 2003, CBOT opened daily trading on an *option contract* to buy or sell Fed funds futures. This put or call option for federal funds futures may well improve the accuracy of future market forecasts of the funds rate. Unlike the trading going on in Fed funds futures, which gives us some idea of the "average" Fed funds rate the market as a whole currently expects, the newer options contract tells us something about the *range of opinion* in the financial marketplace regarding where the funds rate might be headed.

Recent research suggests that CBOT's various contracts for federal funds are a generally unbiased forecaster of what the actual funds rate is likely to do. The marketplace's prediction of the effective funds rate seems particularly accurate right before the next scheduled meeting of the FOMC. (See especially Nosal [9] and Carlson, Melock, and Sahinoz [1].)

| EXHIBIT 13.12 | Measures of the Average Annualized Rate of Inflation in the United States |

| | Period | | | | | | | | | | |
|---|---|---|---|---|---|---|---|---|---|---|---|
| | 1961–65 | 1966–70 | 1971–75 | 1976–80 | 1981–85 | 1986–90 | 1991–95 | 1996–2000 | 2002 | 2004 | 2006 |
| Consumer price index (CPI) | 1.4% | 4.5% | 7.9% | 11.1% | 7.1% | 4.5% | 3.6% | 2.9% | 2.5% | 3.3% | 2.5% |
| Producer price index, finished goods (PPI) | 0.9 | 2.9 | 9.1 | 10.5 | 4.6 | 2.9 | 1.9 | 2.3 | 1.9 | 4.9 | 0.7 |
| Implicit price deflator for gross domestic product | 1.4 | 4.7 | 7.9 | 8.8 | 5.1 | 3.5 | 2.4 | 1.7 | 1.7 | 3.2 | 2.5 |

Source: Federal Reserve Bank of St. Louis.

raised the prices of imports into the United States and lessened the impact of foreign competition on domestic producers until the dollar strengthened significantly during the 1990s.

With the opening of the twenty-first century, inflationary pressures continued to be muted, owing principally to the continued resurgence of productivity growth in the United States that had begun during the 1990s. This greater productivity allowed businesses to increase the supply of goods and services without employing additional labor or capital in their production, thus keeping a lid on price increases. Later, when the economy dipped into recession in 2001, the demand for goods and services fell, and, for a brief period, the Fed switched its concern from inflation to deflation, which appeared to be a real threat for the first time since the Great Depression of the 1930s. However, once the economy regained its momentum, deflationary fears subsided and the Fed has once again become concerned about a resurgence of inflation. Nonetheless, this episode provided an important lesson for the Fed. It became aware that the conduct of monetary policy during deflationary times, when the economy is weak, may be very difficult, especially if the target federal funds rate has already been lowered close to zero.

Still another causal factor is *inflationary expectations:* the anticipation of continued inflation by businesses and households. Once underway, inflation may develop a momentum of its own, as consumers spend more and borrow more freely to stay ahead of rising prices, sending prices still higher. Businesses and labor unions begin to build inflation into their price and wage decisions, passing higher costs along in the form of higher prices for goods and services. This process may for a time result in a wage-price spiral in which each plateau of increased costs is used as a basis for justifying further price increases.

Inflation creates distortions in the allocation of scarce resources and hurts certain groups. For example, it tends to discourage saving and encourages consumption at a faster rate to stay ahead of rising prices. Moreover, the decline in the savings rate tends to discourage capital investment. Unfortunately, this means the economy's growth in productivity (output per worker-hour) tends to slow, so the supply of new goods and services cannot keep pace with rising demands, putting further upward pressure on prices. At the same time, workers often seek cost-of-living adjustments in wages and salaries, leading to an increase in labor costs. Some workers represented by strong unions or in growth industries may be able to keep pace with inflation, but other groups, including retired persons and government employees, whose income is fixed or rises slowly, often experience a decline in their real standard of living when inflation is on the rise.

**Key URLs:**
For Further exploration of inflation targeting procedures among central banks see, for example, **nber.org/papers/w9577**; **frbsf.org/econrsrch/wklylyltr/wklylyltr98/el98-18.html**; and **en.wikipedia.org/wiki/Inflation-targeting**

*Central Bank Targeting of Inflation*     Beginning in the 1990s several central banks around the world began setting *target inflation rates* to shoot at with their policy weapons. New Zealand was the first nation to establish a formal inflation-targeting regime. Canada followed in 1991, Great Britain in 1992, and Australia and Sweden in 1993. Before they joined the European Community, Spain and Finland adopted an inflation-targeting approach and the European Central Bank (ECB) soon declared that price stability was its primary goal. Other prominent nations with inflation targets include Brazil, the Czech Republic, Hungary, Israel, South Korea, Poland, and Switzerland—overall at least 21 countries in total. In contrast, the United States (along with Japan) has set no explicit inflation rate target, though it seeks to drive inflation so low that it doesn't affect business and consumer decisions.

Inflation targets vary among the nations that have set them—some are *point targets* and others are *inflation rate target ranges.* For example, New Zealand's central bank has expressed its determination to keep inflation within a 0 to 3 percent annual rate range. (The New Zealand central bank's governor can be fired if he or she misses the target range!) Most other countries seek to hold inflation near 2 percent annually and the target inflation-rate range is normally somewhere close to 1 to 3 percent. The key inflation measure most widely used is usually some index of consumer prices, such as the Consumer Price Index (CPI). If the target or target range is missed, some nations give their central banks a specific time period to get the inflation rate back on track—for example, 18 months to two years.

The jury is still out on the success or failure of central bank inflation targeting. Certainly the central bank is the most likely institution to pursue inflation targets successfully. But some central bankers are hesitant to set specific numerical inflation-rate targets, fearing a loss of flexibility and possible adverse consequences if the public becomes aware the announced target has been missed. For example, might a missed inflation target lead to even greater inflation? More evidence is needed on the actual benefits and costs of inflation targeting.[5]

**deflation**

*Deflation*   Price stability can be disrupted by falling prices, or **deflation,** as well as by rising prices, or *inflation.* Deflation plagued Japan for more than a decade in the 1990s and early 2000s, during which time its economy—once the star performer among industrialized economies—experienced an average annual growth rate of close to *zero* percent! In an effort to reinvigorate its economy, the Bank of Japan took monetary policy to its limits by driving interest rates to zero and then continuing to inject reserves into the banking system at a rapid pace—a policy that came to be known as *quantitative easing.* This policy has met with only limited success. Because it represents one of the few experiences over the past century of developed economies attempting to grapple with deflation, it is not surprising that this policy has caught the attention of central bankers around the world who, for so long, have been struggling to reduce inflation rates down to the low single digits.

**hyperinflation**

*Hyperinflation*   At the other extreme of deflation is **hyperinflation,** when the inflation rate exceeds 100 percent per year. Inflation rates of this magnitude may seem too unusual to residents in the United States or Europe, for example, where inflation rates have never approached these figures since World War II more than half a century ago. However, many economies around the world have had bouts of hyperinflation relatively recently, some of which have lasted for decades—Brazil, Argentina, and Israel are three examples of these economies, where in some cases the inflation rate exceeded 1,000 percent per year! Living in such an environment can be difficult for businesses, consumers, and governments. Prices of goods and services may have to be changed daily! And currency may be losing value so rapidly that everyone has to go to extraordinary lengths to protect their wealth. Economies suffering from hyperinflation have generally performed poorly, and the measures taken by governments to rid their economies of hyperinflation have proven to be costly in terms of economic growth

---

[5]Recent research (Federal Reserve Bank of St. Louis, [5]) suggests that inflation targeting has been most successful in those nations that previously had relatively high levels of inflation. To be successful, *credibility* with the public seems to be critical, along with a strong commitment on the part of a central bank to be honest and transparent in the goals it seeks and in its outlook for the economy. Moreover, inflation targeting tends to reduce the correlation between current and past inflation.

and employment in the short run. However, in the long run, eliminating hyperinflation has brought greater economic growth and more rapid job creation.

## The Goals of Full Employment and Stable Economic Growth

For the past half century, the Federal Reserve has also been committed to achieving the highest level of employment consistent with sustainable long-run economic growth. However, translating these lofty goals into practical policy objectives has proven difficult. To achieve these goals, the Fed has attempted to pursue policies that promote a smoothly functioning economy in which the economy's resources of capital, labor, and entrepreneurial talent are efficiently deployed in the production of goods and services to provide for the greatest standard of living for the country's citizens.

But how do policymakers know when the economy's resources are efficiently deployed? What does this mean in terms of employment? Does full employment mean zero unemployment? If not, then what is the maximum sustainable level of employment, and to what level of unemployment does this correspond? Can they look only at the current level of economic growth without regard to the future? Shouldn't the rate of investment in expanding the economy's resources be an important criterion? These are difficult questions with which the policymakers must grapple and the answers they arrive at are subject to change over time, due to new technology, demographic shifts, changes in the economy's international competitiveness, and other factors.

*The Natural Rate of Unemployment*　Some unemployment is inevitable in a market-oriented economy, where the workforce is constantly changing in size and composition and where workers are free to change jobs and businesspeople are free to hire and fire workers. There is a minimum level of unemployment, which the government attempts to measure, referred to as *frictional unemployment,* which arises from the temporary unemployment of job seekers, who are either new to the workforce or who are in transition from one job to another, perhaps in search of higher pay or better working conditions. This frictional unemployment is often referred to as the *full employment level of unemployment,* or the **natural rate of unemployment.** The economy's actual unemployment rate is measured as the percentage of the workforce actively seeking employment. When the unemployment rate equals the natural rate, then the economy's labor resources are thought to be fully employed. But what is the natural rate of unemployment?

**natural rate of unemployment**

As Exhibit 13.13 illustrates, the average unemployment rate in the United States during the 1950s and 1960s suggested to economists the economy's natural rate of unemployment was around 5 to 5 1/4 percent. However, during the 1970s and early 1980s, as the unemployment rate seemed to ratchet upward to higher levels with each succeeding recession and stubbornly refused to fall, economists began to raise their estimates of the natural rate of unemployment up to around 6 to 6 1/4 percent. Two key factors leading to this secular rise in unemployment were the post-World War II baby boom generation reaching working age and the rapid increase in the number of adult women seeking jobs. The upward surge in the participation rate of women in the workforce may have been due to a decline in fertility rates, more varied jobs available to women, and the erosion of family incomes due to inflation. Both the entries of baby boomers and more women into the workforce raised the supply of labor faster than the economy could create new jobs to absorb all of these new workers.

**U.S. Civilian Unemployment Rate**

Source: U.S. Department of Labor: Bureau of Labor Statistics.

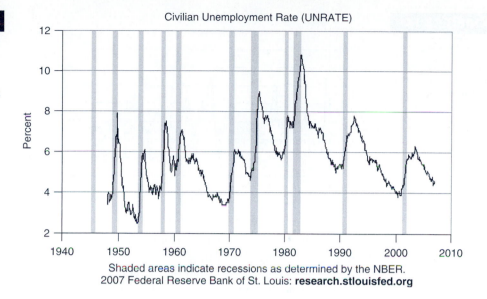

Civilian Unemployment Rate (UNRATE)

Shaded areas indicate recessions as determined by the NBER.
2007 Federal Reserve Bank of St. Louis: **research.stlouisfed.org**

**Key URLs:**
For a deeper understanding of the GDP gap measure of an economy's performance and a target for central bank policy, see especially, **answers. com/topic/gdp-gap-/** and **financial-dictionary.the free dictionary.com/ GDPtGap**

**potential GDP**

**GDP gap**

Sometime during the 1980s, this trend began to reverse. After the unemployment rate peaked at more than 10 percent during the deep recession in the early 1980s—which was its highest level since the Great Depression—the unemployment rate began to ratchet down, with lower peaks in each recession preceding sustained declines during the historically long periods of economic expansion that followed. Today, economists believe the surges in the labor supply have been largely absorbed by the economy and the natural rate of unemployment is back down to its historic pattern of close to 5 percent.

These historical changes in the natural rate of unemployment are better understood today than they were at the time they were taking place. The Federal Reserve did not have the benefit of hindsight. Indeed, it not only had the problem of understanding what the current natural rate was, but had to project what the natural rate of unemployment would be in the future. Exhibit 13.13 suggests just how difficult this process has become. New questions are being posed today with which policymakers will have to concern themselves. As one example, technology has significantly altered the demands of the workplace with an increased emphasis on high-skilled workers. Just how well the economy's system of education and technical training responds to these demands will have a significant impact on employment decisions of firms and consequently on the natural rate of unemployment.

*The Output Gap*    The difficulties with identifying changes in the natural rate of unemployment have caused the Federal Reserve to focus on additional indicators of the economy's long-run sustainable growth path. Using statistical methods, the Fed creates a measure of what the level of real GDP would be if the economy were fully utilizing its economic resources of capital, labor, and entrepreneurial talent in an efficient manner. This measure is called **potential GDP.** When real GDP is equal to potential GDP, the economy is thought to be on its long-run growth path, with the unemployment rate equal to the natural rate. To gauge how far away the economy is from this desired growth path, the Federal Reserve tracks a measure referred to as the **GDP gap,** which is the difference between actual GDP and

**EXHIBIT 13.14**

**The GDP Gap**

Source: Federal Reserve
Bank of St. Louis, **www.
research.stlouisfed.org.**

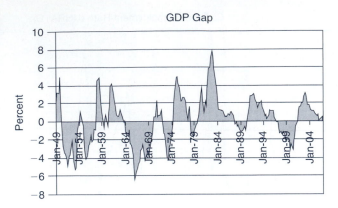

GDP Gap

potential GDP as a percentage of potential GDP. Exhibit 13.14 displays how this GDP gap has changed over time.[6]

A *negative* GDP gap is a sign the economy is underperforming relative to its capability, producing less output in the form of goods and services, generating lower incomes, and creating fewer jobs. The Federal Reserve takes that condition as one signal that corrective policy action may be in order, whereby it would lower interest rates and stimulate investment and job growth. Conversely, the Fed interprets a *positive* GDP gap as a sign the economy may be in for a bout of higher inflation with the demand for goods and services outpacing the ability of the economy to increase production in the short run, thus resulting in higher prices. A positive GDP gap is one sign the Fed should raise interest rates to slow the demand for goods and services until the economy has increased its production capacity sufficiently to bring supply and demand back into balance without rapid increases in the inflation rate.

## 13.7   The Conflicting Goals and the Limitations of Monetary Policy

As we have seen in this chapter, central banks can have a difficult time assessing how well the economy is performing relative to its long-run potential to generate income and jobs and continually improve economic standards of living. Trying to understand what the optimal rate of inflation should be or what the natural rate of unemployment and potential GDP are at any point in time are not simple matters. Conditions are always changing. Former Fed Chairman Alan Greenspan used to refer to "imbalances" that he would see in the economy, such as an overvalued stock market, a housing boom, an excessive rise in employment costs that businesses were experiencing, inadequate concern about risk among investors, and so forth. To complicate matters, our monetary policy cannot address just these *current* imbalances, but must project what the economic consequences are likely to be in the *future* as these imbalances are resolved. For example, how extensive the fallout will be to a stock market correction, a slowdown in the housing sector, a rise in retail prices needed to restore business profits to normal levels following a sharp rise in labor costs, or an increase in loan default

---

[6]The GDP gap in Exhibit 13.14 is based on the estimate of potential GDP made by the Congressional Budget Office. It may differ from the one used by the Federal Reserve, whose estimates are not available to the public.

rates and a contraction of credit, if investors become more risk-averse and cautious in their lending activity? None of these issues are easy to assess, much less respond to confidently with a monetary policy designed to mitigate their adverse consequences for the economy.

The inherent difficulties in projecting the future evolution of the economy is perhaps the principal reason why we observe monetary policy inertia, described earlier in this chapter. Given the uncertainties policymakers face and the fact that confirming information (data) arrives only incrementally, a methodical, go-slow approach may provide the best strategy for implementing policy in order to minimize the implications of mistakes that could be made in assessing the economy's future. (See Rudebusch [11].) Another source of uncertainty is the ever-changing structure of a dynamic healthy economy, where the best policy response to a given situation may not be the same today as it was yesterday. One current strand of research into the design of monetary policy [3] recognizes that policymakers face uncertainties with regard to the underlying structure of the economy, and the research attempts to offer a criterion for selecting actions that will minimize the consequences of policy mistakes over the varying views of how the economy would respond to policy changes.

Recognition of these problems has interjected a great deal of caution among central bankers in their attempts to "fine-tune" the evolution of economies over time. Underscoring the need for caution is the fact that policy goals can sometimes conflict with one another. Attempts to reduce unemployment may increase inflation, and vice versa; attempts to reduce inflation could unduly slow the overall rate of economic growth. Because of the potentially conflicting nature of policy goals and the inherent difficulty in fine tuning, and in response to the ravages of high inflation that were inflicted on many economies around the world during the 1970s and 1980s, many governments recently have chosen to direct their central banks to focus principally, if not exclusively, on controlling inflation over the medium to long term (on average, over a one- to two-year period). It is generally agreed that monetary policy can be successful in achieving this inflation-fighting goal. Nonetheless, many central banks continue to focus on fine-tuning objectives, at least to some degree. Research [2] suggests that a compromise between these objectives may be best thought of as choosing the *trade-off* between variability in inflation versus variability in output and employment. Policymakers must choose which of these choices would have the greatest impact on the welfare of the population they serve.

In addition to dealing with the problems cited above, central banks like the Federal Reserve cannot completely control financial conditions with the view that those changes would subsequently affect the overall economy as desired. Changes in the structure of the economy due to deregulation, financial innovations, increasing global integration of money and capital markets, and the breathtaking speed of new technological developments feed back into the supply of credit and the structure of interest rates, and even into how monetary policy itself impacts the financial markets. It becomes exceedingly difficult, especially on a weekly or monthly basis, to sort out the effects of monetary policy from the impact of broader economic forces. As a result, international markets have come to exert a greater impact on the domestic economy and on central bank policymaking, while changes in domestic interest rates may not be as potent a factor affecting the economy as they were even a decade ago. Central bankers must learn how to deal with these changes in fundamental economic relationships and operate within the limitations they impose.

## QUESTIONS TO HELP YOU STUDY

10. What is *interest-rate targeting?* Which interest rate does the Federal Reserve focus upon in its conduct of monetary policy?

11. If the Federal Reserve wishes to put *upward* pressure on market interest rates, what would it be most likely to do? How would it proceed to push the federal funds rate in an upward direction? How would it *lower* the funds rate?

12. What are the principal economic *goals* of the Federal Reserve System? How do they relate to the *natural rate of unemployment* and the *GDP gap?*

13. How could the Fed cause changes in the rate of inflation? In unemployment and economic growth?

14. Describe the *trade-offs* that appear to exist among key economic goals. How do these trade-offs appear to influence the central bank's ability to achieve economic goals?

15. What is meant by *policy inertia?* What is the rationale behind the policies that produce it? What are the principal *limitations* of monetary policy?

## Summary of the Chapter's Main Points

The policy tools used by central banks, such as the Federal Reserve System, impact the quantity and growth of legal reserves in the banking system and, in turn, the cost and availability of credit.

- The principal immediate target of Federal Reserve policy today is the *federal funds interest rate,* which, in turn, affects interest rates in both the money market and the capital market and, ultimately, the strength of the economy as a whole.

- The main policy tool used by the Federal Reserve to influence the cost and availability of credit is *open market operations*—the buying and selling of securities through the Trading Desk of the Federal Reserve Bank of New York. Open market *sales* tend to raise interest rates and restrict the supply of credit available, while open market *purchases* tend to lower interest rates and expand the supply of credit.

- The Fed, like many other central banks around the globe, has other policy tools at its disposal in the form of *deposit reserve requirements* and the *discount (loan) rates* of the individual Federal Reserve banks. An increase in reserve requirements or in the discount rate tends to tighten money and credit policy, slowing borrowing and spending, while a reduction in reserve requirements and discount rates tends to ease monetary policy, leading to an expansion of credit at lower cost.

- While open market operations, reserve requirements, and discount rates represent *general credit controls,* many central banks also have *selective credit controls* that impact specific groups or sectors of the financial system and the economy. The Federal Reserve's selective controls include moral suasion (or psychological pressure applied by central bank officials) and margin requirements (which restrict purchases of selected securities on credit).

- As open market operations have become the central tool of many central banks around the globe, different varieties of this important central bank tool have been developed. Examples include straight or outright open market operations (where actual title to security ownership changes hands), repurchase agreements (where only temporary transfer of security ownership occurs), runoff transactions (where the central bank demands cash for maturing securities it holds), and agency transactions (where the central bank acts to buy or sell securities on behalf of a central bank customer, such as a foreign government or foreign central bank).

- Besides central bank monetary policy, actions of the public (such as demanding additional supplies of currency and coin) and operations of the government's treasury (such as collecting taxes) also impact interest rates and reserves in the financial system. The central bank must often act *defensively* to counteract these other sources of change in the financial marketplace, using its policy tools as a counterweight to the actions of the public and government.

- When the Federal Reserve decides to change the desired level of the federal funds interest rate, it uses open market operations to change the quantity of *nonborrowed reserves* held by depository institutions. Nonborrowed reserves plus borrowed reserves (loaned to depository institutions by the Federal Reserve banks) make up the supply of total reserves at the disposal of the banking system.

- The principal goals pursued by most central banks include the *control of inflation,* achieving *maximum employment,* and attaining *sustainable economic growth,* where the last of these coincides with the optimal use of the economy's resources of capital, labor, and entrepreneurial talent.

- To identify when the economy is utilizing its resources to maximum benefit, the Federal Reserve monitors the deviation of unemployment from a statistical estimate of the *natural rate of unemployment* and the GDP gap, both of which are measures of how far the economy is from optimally utilizing its resources of capital, labor, and entrepreneurial talent.

- The natural rate of unemployment and *potential GDP* vary over time due to changes in the structure of the economy and are difficult to identify. This is one problem the Fed and other central banks confront when attempting to fine-tune the economy by smoothing out business cycle fluctuations. This problem, along with the experience of high inflation in recent decades, has contributed to a greater emphasis of central banks around the world on medium- to long-term anti-inflation objectives.

- Conflicts in achieving the policy goals of central banks may force them to seek compromises, sometimes only achieving a portion of the goals they are seeking.

- Structural change in the economy, new financial innovations, and the increasing integration of international money and capital markets have altered the manner in which the financial markets respond to central bank policy and have changed the relationship between the financial markets and the rest of the economy. Both of these factors have complicated the design and implementation of central bank monetary policy.

## Key Terms Appearing in This Chapter

**general credit controls,** 385

**selective credit controls,** 385

**open market operations,** 385

**discount rate,** 394

**reserve requirements,** 398

**moral suasion,** 403

**margin requirements,** 403

**policy inertia,** 405

**bias,** 405

**borrowed reserves,** 406

**nonborrowed reserves,** 406

**deflation,** 411

**hyperinflation,** 411

**natural rate of unemployment,** 412

**potential GDP,** 413

**GDP gap,** 413

## Problems and Issues

1.  Describe what is likely to happen to interest rates, deposits, and total bank reserves as a result of the transactions listed below:

    **a.** The Federal Reserve sells $50 million in securities outright to a bank.

    **b.** The Federal Reserve buys $85 million in securities outright from a bank.

    **c.** The Federal Reserve sells $93 million in securities outright to a nonbank security dealer.

    **d.** The Federal Reserve buys $42 million in securities outright from a nonbank security dealer.

    **e.** The Federal Reserve sells $21 million in securities from its own portfolio to a foreign central bank.

    **f.** The Federal Reserve buys $37 million in securities for its own portfolio that are being offered for sale by a foreign central bank.

    **c.** The Federal Reserve declines the U.S. Treasury's offer to roll over $150 million in Treasury notes that are maturing in the Fed's own portfolio in exchange for new Treasury notes; instead the Federal Reserve demands cash from the Treasury.

2.  Suppose the banking system's nonborrowed reserves total $48.3 billion, with total legal reserves standing at $51.2 billion. What must borrowed reserves be? This morning the Federal Reserve decided to undertake the sale of $500 million in government securities through open market operations. What will be the new level of nonborrowed reserves? If interest rates do not change, what will be the new level of total reserves? What must you assume to make this calculation? If interest rates do change, which way are they likely to move?

3.  If the total supply of nonborrowed reserves equals $500 million and borrowed reserves are $50 million at the current equilibrium federal funds rate (FFR), and if the supply of total reserves is described by the following equation:

$$S = \$530 \text{ million} + 4\,\text{FFR}$$

    What is the equilibrium federal funds rate (FFR)? What could the central bank do to increase the federal funds rate above its current equilibrium level? How could it reduce the funds rate below its current equilibrium level?

4. First National Bank of Elderidge borrowed $550,000 from the Federal Reserve Bank of St. Louis last Friday. The bank received short-term adjustment credit for three days and plans to repay its loan at the close of business Monday. Show the proper accounting (T-account) entries for this transaction when the loan was taken out on Friday and when it is repaid Monday afternoon. How much did total bank reserves rise when this loan was made? Are reserve requirements a factor here?

5. Discuss the validity of the following statements in both the short run and long run:

   **a.** If the Federal Reserve achieves its goal for GDP, it will achieve its goal for employment, and vice versa.

   **b.** If the Federal Reserve achieves its goal for price stability, it will achieve its goal for employment, and vice versa.

## Web-Based Problems

1. Under current interest rate targeting procedures used by the Trading Desk at the Federal Reserve Bank of New York, the only money market interest rate that is officially targeted is the federal funds rate. How closely do other money market interest rates follow the targeted Fed funds rate? Using either the interest rate databank provided at **economagic.com** or through the Federal Reserve Board's H.15 release at **federalreserve.gov/releases/h15/update/,** determine how closely untargeted money market interest rates followed the targeted Fed funds rate on a weekly and a monthly basis over the past year. Answer this question by entering the data into a spreadsheet, and then (**a**) prepare graphs comparing the funds rate and alternative money market rates (such as the CD, Eurodollar, and T-bill rates), and (**b**) calculate the correlations between these market rates.

2. The Federal Open Market Committee (FOMC) is sometimes called the single most important committee in America because of all the people and businesses who are affected by its decisions. Using the Web site **federalreserve.gov/fomc,** prepare a brief description of the makeup of this committee (i.e., who serves), what its principal tasks are, and the time schedule the committee maintains. Explain why you believe the FOMC is so important to many individuals, businesses, and governments.

3. How do the general and selective credit controls employed by the Bank of Canada at **bankofcanada.ca/en,** the Bank of England at **bankofengland.gov,** the Bank of Japan at **boj.or.jp/en,** and the European Central Bank at **ecb.int** differ from those employed by the Federal Reserve System? Which credit control tool appears to be most important and most widely used among these prominent central banks?

## Selected References to Explore

1. Carlson, John B.; William R. Melock; and Erkin Y. Sahinoz. "An Option for Anticipating Fed Action," *Economic Commentary,* Federal Reserve Bank of Cleveland, September 1, 2003, pp. 1–4.

2. Chatterjee, Satyajit. "The Taylor Curve and the Unemployment-Inflation Trade-off," *Business Review,* Federal Reserve Bank of Philadelphia, Third Quarter 2002, pp. 26–33.

3. Dennis, Richard. "Uncertainty and Monetary Policy," *FRBSF Economic Letter,* Federal Reserve Bank of San Francisco, No. 2007-03 (January 26, 2007).

4. Emmons, William R.; Aeimit K. Lakdawala; and Christopher J. Neeley. "What Are the Odds? Option-Based Forecasts of FOMC Target Changes," *Review,* Federal Reserve Bank of St. Louis, November/December 2006, pp. 543–61.

5. Federal Reserve Bank of St. Louis. "Inflation Targeting: Prospects and Problems," *Review,* July-August 2004.

6. Feinman, Joshua. "Reserve Requirements: History, Current Practice and Potential Reform," *Federal Reserve Bulletin,* June 1993, pp. 569–89.

7. Jordan, Jerry L. "Money and Monetary Policy for the Twenty-First Century," *Review,* Federal Reserve Bank of St. Louis, November/December 2006, pp. 485–510.

8. Meyer, Laurence H. "Inflation Targets and Inflation Targeting," *Review,* Federal Reserve Bank of St. Louis, November/December 2001, pp. 1–13.

9. Nosal, Ed. "How Well Does the Federal Funds Futures Rate Predict the Future Federal Funds Rate?" *Economic Commentary,* Federal Reserve Bank of Cleveland, October 2001.

10. Poole, William. "Inflation Targeting," *Review,* Federal Reserve Bank of St. Louis, May/June 2006, pp. 155–63.

11. Rudebusch, Glenn D. "Monetary Policy Inertia and Recent Fed Actions," *FRBSF Economic Letter,* Federal Reserve Bank of San Francisco, No. 2007-03 (June 26, 2007).

12. Stevens, Ed. "The New Discount Window," *Economic Commentary,* Federal Reserve Bank of Cleveland, May 15, 2003, pp. 1–4.

13. Swanson, Eric. "Would an Inflation Target Anchor U.S. Inflation Expectations?" *FRBSF Economic Letter,* Federal Reserve Bank of San Francisco, No. 2006-20 (August 11, 2006), pp. 1–3.

14. Thornton, Daniel L. "The Lower and Upper Bounds of the Federal Open Market Committee's Long-Run Inflation Objective," *Review,* Federal Reserve Bank of St. Louis, May/June 2007, pp. 183–193.

www.mhhe.com/rose10e

# Part 4

# Financial Institutions: Organization, Activities, and Regulation

Banking has sometimes been called a "confidence game." You place your money in a "demand deposit" account—perhaps earning a modest rate of interest—with the assurance that you can withdraw any of it at any time. The bank then turns around and loans the money out at a higher interest rate to households, businesses, and governments, who in turn agree to repay their loans in the future.

Suppose *all* of the banks' depositors wanted to withdraw *all* of their money and close their accounts. How would the bank pay up? The answer is that banks and similar depository institutions are counting on this event never happening! They expect *new* deposits to replace withdrawals, with only short periods of time during which withdrawals exceed deposits. During those brief intervals they use up their cash reserves or borrow or sell some of their marketable assets. On balance, however, the public's confidence that banks will be there tomorrow to honor their commitments to depositors is the essence of a *sound* banking system, and a sound banking system is essential to a vibrant, smoothly functioning economy.

In Part 4 we will look at the inner workings of the major financial-service institutions in the global economy. We begin in Chapter 14 with *commercial banks,* which lie at the heart of the financial systems of most modern economies. The largest of these institutions now possess well over a trillion dollars in assets and have operations that literally encircle the globe. However, banks are not alone in providing financial services. Nonbank financial institutions, including *savings and loans, credit unions, savings banks, money market funds, pension funds, insurance companies, finance companies,* and *mutual funds,* perform many of the same functions as commercial banks and are able to compete successfully (under somewhat different sets of rules) by specializing in terms of customer base or product offerings. The activities of nonbank financial institutions in the marketplace are described in Chapters 15 and 16.

Regulation of financial institutions has proven challenging. Inadequate regulation can create financial panic, while excessive regulation can induce significant losses for society by inhibiting economic activity. Chapter 17 describes how regulators have grappled with this trade-off most recently and how they have come to increasingly rely on the *marketplace itself* to structure rules that assure customers that the "confidence game" they are playing with their financial institutions is worth playing.

# Chapter 14

# The Commercial Banking Industry: Structure, Products, and Management

## What's in This Chapter?
## Key Topics Outline

The Organizational Structure of Modern Commercial Banking

Economies of Scale, Consolidation, and Convergence within the Banking Industry

Branch, Holding Company, and International Banking

Financial-Service Convergence and the Gramm-Leach-Bliley Act

Automation and the Changing Technology of Banking

Bank Balance Sheets and Income Statements

Money Creation and Destruction by Banks and Bank Accounting

## Learning Objectives

## in This Chapter

- You will understand how important commercial banks are to the functioning of a modern economy and financial system.

- You will explore the structure of the United States' banking industry—one of the most important in the world.

- You will examine the content of bank financial statements and learn how to read them.

- You will see how banks create and destroy money and credit and why this activity is vital to the operation of both the economy and the financial system.

## 14.1  Introduction to Banking

The dominant privately owned financial institution in the economies of most countries is the *commercial bank*. This institution offers the public both deposit and credit services, as well as a growing list of newer and more innovative services, such as investment advice, security underwriting, insurance, and financial planning. The name *commercial* implies that these banks devote most of their resources to meeting the financial needs of business firms. In recent decades, however, commercial banks have significantly expanded their offerings of financial services to individuals and families and to units of government around the world. The result is the emergence of a financial institution that has been called a *financial department store* because it satisfies the broadest range of financial service needs in the global economy.

The importance of banks may be measured in a number of ways. They hold close to a quarter of the total assets of all financial institutions headquartered in the United States, as well as a major (often larger) share of financial assets abroad. Banks are still the principal means of making payments, through the checking accounts (demand deposits), credit and debit cards, and electronic transfer services they offer. And banks are important because of their ability to create money from excess reserves made available from the public's deposits. The banking system can take a given volume of excess cash reserves and, by making loans and investments, generate a multiple amount of credit—a process explored later in this chapter.

Banks today are the principal channel for government policy. In the United States, the Federal Reserve System implements policies to affect interest rates and the availability of credit in the economy mainly through altering the level and growth of reserves held by banks and other depository institutions. The same is true in Canada, Great Britain, the European Community, China, Japan, and many other nations. Today, commercial banks are the most important source of consumer credit (i.e., loans to individuals and families) and one of the major sources of loans to small businesses. Banks are major buyers of debt securities issued by federal, state, and local governments. For all of these reasons, commercial banks play a dominant role in the money and capital markets and are worthy of detailed study if we are to understand more fully how the financial system works.

## 14.2  The Structure of U.S. Commercial Banking

**banking structure**

The structure of U.S. banking is unique in comparison with other banking systems around the globe. The term **banking structure** focuses on the number and different sizes of commercial banks operating in thousands of local communities across the nation. Although the banking systems of most other nations consist of a few large banking organizations operating hundreds or thousands of branch offices, the U.S. system is dominated numerically by thousands of small banks. For example, in 2006 nearly 7,500 commercial banking institutions were operating in the United States, compared to less than a dozen domestically chartered banks in Canada and less than three dozen domestically owned banks in the United Kingdom and Mexico.

Not surprisingly, most American banks are modest in size compared to banks in other countries. Close to half of all U.S. commercial banks hold assets of under $100 million each; only about 6 percent hold assets of a billion dollars or more and actively compete in global markets for loans and deposits. Smaller banks predominate in numbers, but larger banks hold a disproportionate share of the industry's assets. For example, the small handful of all U.S. banks with $1 billion or more in assets hold more

| EXHIBIT 14.1 | Number of Operating Insured Commercial Banks and Branch Offices in the United States, Year-End 2006 | |
|---|---|---|
| Type of Bank | Number of Banks | Number of Branch Offices |
| National banks | 1,776 | 39,664 |
| State-chartered member banks | 896 | 14,274 |
| Total member banks of the Federal Reserve System | 2,672 | 53,938 |
| Nonmember state-chartered banks | 4,781 | 21,945 |
| Total of all U.S.-insured commercial banks | 7,453 | 75,883 |

Source: Board of Governors of the Federal Reserve System, *Annual Report 2006.*

than four-fifths of all assets in the industry. Yet by 2004 only three U.S. banking organizations out of more than 7,000 held a trillion dollars or more in assets—Citigroup, Bank of America, and JPMorgan Chase.

Most banks in the United States are chartered by the states rather than by the federal government. As shown in Exhibit 14.1, of the roughly 7,500 U.S. commercial banks in operation in the year 2006 over three-quarters were **state-chartered banks.** The remaining banks, classified as **national banks,** were chartered by the federal government. National banks, on average, are larger and include nearly all of the nation's billion-dollar banking institutions. All national banks must be insured by the Federal Deposit Insurance Corporation (FDIC) and must also be members of the Federal Reserve System ("the Fed"). State-chartered banks may elect to become members of the Fed if they are willing to conform to Federal Reserve rules. Moreover, most states require newly chartered banks to secure FDIC deposit insurance protection for their customers' accounts. The vast majority of U.S. banks (more than 98 percent) are FDIC insured, but only a minority have elected to join the Fed. Nevertheless, Fed member banks hold at least three-quarters of all bank deposits in the United States. (We will have more to say about the roles of the Federal Reserve, the FDIC, and other bank regulatory agencies in Chapter 17.)

**state-chartered banks**
**national banks**

## A Trend toward Consolidation

**consolidation**

A number of structural changes have affected the banking industry in recent years. One of the most important is the drive toward **consolidation** of industry assets into fewer, but much larger, banking organizations.

## Falling Industry Numbers As Small Banks Are Taken Over by Larger Ones

The United States is still a nation heavily populated with small banks. But great pressures are operating to form much larger banking organizations in order to make more efficient use of industry resources. During the past quarter century the number of U.S. commercial banks has dropped from about 14,000 to less than 7,500. Consequently, the average U.S. bank is substantially larger today than in the past.

Moreover, as noted in a recent study by Gunther and Moore [3], the largest U.S. banks have been gaining market share rapidly at the expense of small and medium-size banks. Adjusting for inflation, these Federal Reserve researchers found that the share of the U.S. banking industry's assets accounted for by the smallest banks (each with less than a billion dollars in assets) fell from about 23 percent to about 12 percent between 1984 and 2006, while the largest banks (each with more than $25 billion in assets) saw their industry share soar from about 40 percent to more than 76 percent over the same time period. In numbers, the smallest banks declined from about 11,000 in 1984 to just over 7,000 in 2006. Almost simultaneously, the average profitability of the largest banks grew to outstrip the profitability of the industry's smallest banks—an outcome traceable to increased competition from bank and nonbank financial firms, new technology that reduced the advantage of banks having a local presence, and the development of services that could be offered over wider geographic areas.

### A Countertrend: Both Small and Large Banks May Survive

While consolidation of smaller into larger banks continues today, there are indications the consolidation trend may be slowing down inside the United States (see especially Jones and Critchfield [5]). The total number of banking organizations may be approaching a point of stability. Perhaps the number of worthwhile bank targets to acquire is leveling out. This suggests that today in the United States, mergers in the industry are roughly counterbalanced by the creation of new banks. Contrary to many earlier predictions, the industry may be settling into a *divided* organizational structure—a small number of global money-center banks coexisting alongside thousands of community banks serving smaller cities and suburban areas. As long as smaller banks are willing to compete, remain efficient, and keep their production costs low they need not be driven from the financial-services industry.

### Economies of Scale Support a Consolidating Industry

**Key URLs:**
Economic growth has a powerful effect in increasing bank size and, through consolidation, lowering bank costs, leading to higher profitability. Powerful examples include the recent rapid growth of three of China's leading banks, including Industrial and Commercial Bank of China at **icbc .com.cn/e-index.jsp**; the Bank of China Ltd at **bochk .com/**; and China Construction Bank at **ccbhk.com/**

Research studies over the years suggest that as banks grow in size, their costs often tend to increase more slowly than their output, resulting in some cost savings. For example, a 100 percent rise in customer accounts may result in only a 92 percent increase in the cost of bank operations, at least up to a certain moderate firm size. When automated bookkeeping and computer processing of accounts are used, substantial economies of scale appear to characterize bank lending and the offering of checking accounts. Under pressure from a cost squeeze and increased competition from other financial institutions, many U.S. bankers view the strategy of growing into larger-sized organizations as a strong competitive response. However, scale economies resulting from bank growth appear to be modest. Once a bank reaches $1 billion or so in assets, its cost-of-production per unit of service appears to roughly level out. One reason is that as banks become larger, they tend to multiply their service offerings and, thereby, increase costs. For some large banks, this factor may outweigh the benefits of low fund-raising costs and risk reduction that they frequently achieve by diversifing across a wide array of markets and services.

### Branch Banking

**branch banking**

The drive toward consolidation of banks into larger organizations is most evident in the long-term historical shift toward **branch banking.** Until the 1940s and 1950s, the United States was a nation of *unit banks,* each housed in only a single office. For example, in 1900 there were 12,427 banks, but only 87 of these had any branches. Today, however, the majority of banks are branch banking organizations. Moreover, the number of branch offices has increased dramatically in recent years. In 1950 there

FINANCIAL DEVELOPMENTS

Leading Bank Holding Companies (BHCs)
Registered in the United States and Measured
by Their Asset Size in $ Billions
(ranked as of March 31, 2005)

| Top Bank Holding Companies | Total Assets | Top Bank Holding Companies | Total Assets |
|---|---|---|---|
| Citigroup Inc., NY | $1,490 | Taunus Corp., NY | $362 |
| Bank of America Corp., NC | 1,214 | HSBC North America, IL | 351 |
| JPMorgan Chase & Co., NY | 1,178 | U.S. Bancorp., MN | 199 |
| Wachovia Corp., NC | 507 | SunTrust Banks, Inc., GA | 165 |
| Wells Fargo & Company, CA | 435 | Citizens Financial Group, RI | 142 |

Source: Board of Governors of the Federal Reserve System, **www.federalreserve.gov.**

were approximately 4,700 branch banking offices in operation; by 2006, the number of total U.S. full-service branches had climbed to more than 75,000, as shown in Exhibit 14.1.

The growth of branching has been aided by the liberalization of many state and federal laws to permit greater use of branch offices as a means for growth. As we will see more fully in Chapter 17, interstate bank expansion inside the United States continues to grow due, in part, to the passage of the Riegle-Neal Interstate Banking bill by the U.S. Congress in 1994, allowing nationwide branching. The spread of branching across the United States has also been aided by a massive population shift to suburban and rural areas and to the sunbelt states. Many of the largest banks have followed their customers to distant markets through branching and mergers to protect their sources of funds and their earnings. Recent research suggests that the development of interstate banking has had a *stabilizing* impact on the banking industry with somewhat less volatile revenues and earnings than in the past.

Banks have also pursued greater geographic expansion through branch offices because of the strong competitive challenge they face from a host of nonbank financial-service firms, including security dealers, mutual funds, insurance companies, credit unions, and dozens of other financial institutions. Many of these nonbank institutions (especially credit unions, mutual funds, and pension plans) appear to have gained market share at the expense of banks, often by offering better returns and more flexible services. The rise of this outside competition has brought strong protests from the banking community for faster government deregulation of the industry and for permission to offer many new services through thousands of neighborhood branches.

## Bank Holding Companies (BHCs)

**Key URL:**
The principal trade association representing the U.S. banking industry is the American Bankers Association, which has a useful Web site about the industry at **aba.com**

**bank holding company**

Paralleling the rapid growth of branch banking has been the growth of bank holding companies, which originated in the nineteenth century. A **bank holding company (BHC)** is a corporation organized to acquire and hold the stock of one or more banks. The company may also hold stock in nonbank business ventures. Holding companies have become popular as vehicles to avoid laws prohibiting the extension of branch banking and as a way to offer services that banks themselves cannot offer.

Bank holding companies have grown rapidly in the United States. In 1960 there were just 47 registered holding company organizations, controlling only about 8 percent of the total assets of U.S.-insured banks. By the twenty-first century U.S.–registered holding companies numbered close to 6,000 and held about 96 percent of U.S. bank assets. In

**Key URL:**
The size, acquisitions, and recent performance of leading U.S. bank holding companies may be traced through the National Information Center of the Federal Financial Institutions Examination Council at **ffiec.gov/nic**

the international markets as well, holding companies have become the predominant bank organizational form because of their advantages in raising capital, spreading out their risk exposure, and allowing entry into new business opportunities, such as insurance agencies, finance companies, mortgage companies, and consulting firms. These ventures represent an attempt to diversify banking operations to reduce risk and gain access to a broader market. Unfortunately, many bankers have found that, often, they cannot manage effectively a highly diverse set of nonbank businesses. In recent years several large holding companies (e.g., Citigroup and Travelers) have sold off some of their nonbank business ventures in an effort to cut costs and raise more capital.

## Financial Holding Companies (FHCs)

A new type of financial-services holding company (FHC) was created in 1999 as a result of passage of the Gramm-Leach-Bliley (GLB) Act. Provided these entities hold strong capital positions and possess sound management, they are permitted to bring together under the same corporate umbrella, commercial banks, investment banks, insurance companies, and selected other affiliated companies that are "financial in nature" and "compatible" with banking. Thus, FHCs come closest to mirroring the organizational structures and service menus of leading European banks, such as Deutsche Bank AG of Frankfurt and HSBC Holdings based in London, by offering the broadest array of services of any financial-services provider. Moreover, with joint approval of the U.S. Treasury Department and the Federal Reserve Board the menu of services FHCs can offer may be expanded in the future.

As the twenty-first century unfolded almost 650 holding companies selling services in the United States, including both domestic and foreign-based firms, had qualified as FHCs. While their numbers represent less than 10 percent of all bank holding companies registered in the United States, the banking affiliates of FHCs account for more than 90 percent of the total assets of the U.S. banking industry.

## International Banking

The growth of banking organizations at home has been paralleled by their growth abroad. This expansion overseas has not been confined to the largest institutions in such established money centers as New York, Chicago, and San Francisco but also includes leading banks in regional financial centers such as Atlanta, Charlotte, and Miami. However, worldwide, London and New York dominate the international banking marketplace. Several of the largest banks receive half or more of their net income from foreign sources, although several U.S. banks have reduced their overseas activity recently due to poorly performing international loans and high operating costs.

While branch banks and holding companies have dominated the recent expansion of banking inside the United States, bank expansion into many international markets has taken place through an even wider variety of unique organizational forms. *Representative offices,* the simplest form, represent the "eyes and ears" of a bank in foreign markets, helping to market each bank's services to both old and new customers, but these limited-service facilities cannot take deposits or book loans. In contrast, a *branch office* offers all or most of the services the home office provides, including the taking of deposits and the booking of loans. International banks sometimes find it less expensive to acquire an existing bank overseas with an established clientele than to set up their own branch office. The acquired institution becomes a *subsidiary* of the international bank, retaining its own charter and capital stock. Alternatively, a bank may establish a *joint venture* with a foreign firm, sharing expenses but gaining access to the expertise and customer contacts already made by the foreign company.

Banks today penetrate overseas markets for a wide variety of reasons. In many cases, their corporate customers expanding abroad demand access to multinational banking facilities. The huge eurocurrency market, which spans the globe, also offers an attractive source of bank funds when domestic funding sources are less available or more costly. Foreign markets frequently offer fewer regulatory barriers and less competition than may be found at home, but they also entail more risk.

Foreign banks have grown rapidly in the United States, with many of the largest Canadian, European, and Asian banks viewing the 50 states as a huge economically and politically stable common market. Most notable of late has been the expansion of Chinese banking inside the United States, led by the Bank of China and China's Bank of Communications that operate U.S. branch offices. (See Exhibit 14.2 for a list of some of the world's largest banks and their principal financial-service competitors.)

**Key URLs:**
Mergers are reshaping the global banking industry, especially in Europe where several leading banks are pursuing their former rivals across national boundaries. Prominent examples are Unicredit of Italy and Société Générale of France, as well as Barclays Bank of the United Kingdom, Royal Bank of Scotland, and ABN Amro of the Netherlands. See especially, **unicreditgroup.eu**; **socgen.com**; **abnamro.com**; and **barclays.co.uk**.

| EXHIBIT 14.2 | Some of the Largest Banks around the Globe | |
|---|---|---|
| Citigroup, United States | Barclays Bank, United Kingdom |
| Mitsubishi UFJ Financial Group, Japan | Credit Agricole Group, France |
| Mizuho Financial Group, Japan | Dresdner Bank, Germany |
| Mitsui Trust Holdings, Japan | BNP Paribus, France |
| Industrial and Commercial Bank of China | Hong Kong Bank |
| HSBC Holdings PLC, United Kingdom | Royal Bank of Canada |
| Union Bank of Switzerland (UBS) | Canadian Imperial Bank |
| Deutsche Bank, Germany | Wells Fargo, United States |
| JPMorgan Chase Bank, United States | Toronto–Dominion Bank, Canada |
| Wachovia Corp., United States | Royal Bank of Scotland Goup |
| Banco Santander, Spain | UniCredit, Italy |
| ABN Amro Hldg., Netherlands | Banca Intesa S.p.A., Italy |
| Société Générale, France | Credit Suisse, Switzerland |
| China Merchants Bank | Banco Bilbao V.A., Spain |
| Bank of China | China Construction Bank |
| Bank of America, United States | |

Sources: Board of Governors of the Federal Reserve System and various central banks.

Moreover, foreign banks were able to offer some services, such as underwriting corporate securities or selling insurance, that U.S. banking organizations were restrained from offering until the Financial Services Modernization (Gramm-Leach-Bliley) Act was passed in 1999. Congress initially responded to the foreign bank invasion by passing the International Banking Act in 1978, bringing foreign banks under federal regulation for the first time. Passage of the FDIC Improvement Act in 1991 also ushered in even greater regulatory control over foreign bank activity inside the United States, granting the Federal Reserve authority to close the U.S. offices of foreign banks if they are operated in an unsafe manner or are violating U.S. laws.

## 14.3 The Convergence Trend in Banking

Perhaps the most common characteristic of all international banks today is their striving to offer a full line of services to all customers. Thus, *commercial banks,* which specialize predominantly in lending and deposit taking, are combining with *investment banks,* which deal in securities issued by their customers and *insurance companies,* that provide risk-management services. Several banks in Canada, Great Britain, and Western Europe long ago took an additional step to become *universal* and *merchant banks.* Universal banks, like Germany's Deutsche Bank and Britain's Barclays Bank, provide not only deposit, loan, and security underwriting services but also consulting, insurance, real estate sales, and hundreds of other services. Merchant banks make private equity investments in businesses, investing some of their owners' capital in their customers' projects, thus becoming principals as well as creditors in business investment projects. As a result, merchant and universal banks tend to make longer-term investments than traditional banks and are active in both the money market and the capital market simultaneously.

**convergence**

One of the most important structural changes occurring in banking today is **convergence.** This means that banking organizations are looking more and more like other financial-service providers, offering many of the same services as security firms, insurance companies, and other service suppliers. In turn, the public is finding it much tougher today to distinguish banks from other financial-service businesses. Competition between bank and nonbank service companies is intensifying, forcing many bank and nonbank companies to consolidate into fewer, but much larger multiservice organizations.

### Bank Failures

**Key URL**
Information about U.S. bank failures each year can be found at **fdic.gov/bank**

The rapid expansion of services has not protected some banks from getting into serious trouble, however, due to declining economies and falling real estate and stock prices coupled with excessive government control over who does and does not receive loans. For example, recently banks in Japan, Korea, and Russia were forced to grapple with financial crises, with many banks collapsing or being swept up into mergers to add vitally needed capital and more experienced management. In contrast, for most of the history of the United States, the American banking industry has experienced a relatively low failure rate (less than 1 percent of the U.S. banking population failing each year, on average). This comparatively low volume of bank failures in the United States is due to extensive regulatory supervision, a relatively strong economy, and conservative management on the part of most banks. For example, in 2004, only four banks (out of an industry population of almost 7,700) were closed, with the Federal Deposit Insurance Corporation taking control of their assets as receiver. The insured deposits and selected assets of these four failed U.S. banks were sold to other FDIC-insured banking firms. When 2005 and 2006 rolled around no FDIC-insured bank failures were reported.

The reasons behind most bank failures are numerous. Some bankers are willing to accept greater risk in their operations, in part because of intensified competition and government insurance of deposits. Moreover, a worldwide movement toward banking **deregulation** (which we will discuss more fully in Chapter 17) has given banks greater opportunities to market new services and expand geographically without such strict government controls, but it has also increased their opportunities for failure. Some analysts argue that even more important is the *volatility of economic and financial conditions*—especially the prices of many foreign currencies and commodities, which fluctuate with market conditions. Increased economic volatility can make bank earnings and stock prices more unstable and force bankers to devote more time to the control and management of risk. An additional factor in bank failure is crime—fraud, embezzlement, and outright theft—which banks and bank regulators are working to combat with stronger security measures.

As Walter [9] observes, bank failures are often more difficult to resolve than the failures of other businesses and typically require some form of regulation over the failure process in order to avoid misallocation of resources. Deposit insurance, designed mainly to head off depositor runs against healthy banks, reduces the incentive of most depositors to demand that a troubled bank pay off its creditors and pay higher interest rates on its deposits. A troubled bank can continue to raise funds by selling government-insured deposits, no matter how bad its financial situation might be, thus increasing its reliance on the government's deposit guarantees and increasing the amount the government must pay insured depositors when the bank's doors are finally closed.

Thus, the marketplace frequently does *not* set in motion the timely closure of problem banks and lets many uninsured depositors escape before failure occurs. This was one of the reasons the U.S. government enacted the Federal Deposit Insurance Corporation Improvement Act of 1991. Under the terms of this law, the FDIC was given broad new powers to resolve problem-bank situations, taking control even before a bank becomes insolvent. The Improvement Act restricts the ability of regulatory agencies to prop up a troubled bank with government loans when it really should be closed. Current rules require that problem banks either raise more capital from their stockholders or be turned over to a receiver (usually the FDIC) to sell off their assets.

## Changing Technology

Banking today is passing through a technological revolution. Computer terminals and high-speed information processing are transforming the industry, stressing convenience and speed in handling such routine transactions as making deposits, extending loans, and paying for purchases of goods and services. Most of the new technology is designed to reduce labor and paper costs, making the banking industry less labor intensive and more capital intensive.

Among the most important pieces of technology in the industry are automated teller machines (ATMs). These machines accept deposits, dispense cash, and accept payments on loans and other bills owed by customers. For many banking transactions they perform as well as human tellers do, with the added advantage of 24-hour availability. Initially, ATMs were placed on bank premises, but their growth has expanded to shopping centers, gasoline stations, airports, and subway terminals. In these locations, they are known as *remote service units* (RSUs). As the twenty-first century began there

**deregulation**

**Key URLs:**
A substantial number of brick-and-mortar banks as well as electronic banks have created a full menu of online services. Internet banks, in particular, tend to offer some of the highest yields available on savings and money market accounts. Examples include such institutions as Capital One FSB at **capitalone.com**; ING Direct at **ingdirect .com**; and Met Life Bank at **metlifebank .com**. To compare the different interest rates offered by different banks, customers can check such online sources as **www.bankrate.com** and **www.consumer-action.org/English/ PressReleases.**

were more than 350,000 ATMs in the United States alone, though their growth soon began to level out as newer and more convenient technologies caught on.

Related to ATMs are point-of-sale (POS) terminals located in retail stores, gas stations, and other commercial establishments. Connected online to the bank's computer, POS terminals accept plastic credit and debit cards, permitting the customer to pay instantly for a purchase without the necessity of cashing a check or driving to an ATM.

Another important piece of electronic machinery is the automated clearinghouse (ACH). An ACH transfers information from one financial institution to another and from account to account via computer tape. The majority of financial-service institutions offering payments services are members of about three dozen ACHs serving the United States. They are used principally for handling business payrolls and processing government transactions. Check truncation systems are being used alongside ACHs, transmitting images of checks ("substitute checks") electronically from one financial institution to another, eliminating the need to transport paper, as authorized by the recently enacted Check 21 Act.

Finally, banking over the *Internet* through home and office computers continues to expand rapidly, allowing customers to quickly enter their requests for financial information and conduct remote financial transactions. A growing portion of bank Web sites are offering 24-hour transactional services, such as bill paying, transferring funds, applying for new loans, and security trading. Several Internet-only ("virtual") banks have been started recently, seeking to take advantage of low overhead and greater customer convenience. Unfortunately, this banking model has not been highly successful despite the savings on brick and mortar over conventional banks. Reasons for the comparatively weak performance of Internet-only banking institutions include their lack of volume and restricted range of services. However, virtual banks may become competitive in the future as more and more customers go online with their transactions and as the cost of conventional banking transactions continues to rise.

One problem that must be overcome in offering future banking services online, however, is the increasing incidence of *identity theft,* where unauthorized users attempt to gain access to customer accounts, stealing funds or fraudulently taking out loans in a legitimate customer's name. At least 5 percent of Internet users claim they have given up on online banking recently due to its security problems and lack of protection for their savings and good credit reputation. A growing number of banks today pledge to replace any customer funds lost to identity thieves; however, the cost of providing these customer-support programs can be very high.

New regulations effective in the United States on December 31, 2006 require bankers to develop more sophisticated account-access procedures in order to protect their online customers. Examples include randomly asking a customer one or more personal questions (such as the customer's former address), the use of tokens to randomize account passwords, or the use of a customer's physical characteristics (such as a handprint or retinal scan) to provide positive identification before giving the customer access to a bank account.

Recent technological changes have profound implications for bank costs, employment, and profitability. In the future, customers will have less and less need to enter a bank building. Their future banking needs will be met mainly by electronically transferring information rather than by requiring people to move from one location to another. The banker's principal function will be one of providing the necessary channels and letting customers conduct their own transactions. This development implies fewer but more highly skilled employees and more capital equipment. Heavy investment in computers and money machines will result in substantial fixed costs, requiring a large

**Key URLs:**
Numerous banks, such as Key Bank of Cleveland, have begun to develop "contact centers" to offer services and develop relationships with customers in order to sell more services. To explore this development in the industry, see especially **banktech.com** and **key.com/**

**Key URL:**
For further information about protecting customer privacy and security online, see the brochure "What You Should Know about Internet Banking" at **chicagofed.org/consumer-information**

**Key URL:**
To learn about possible careers in banking see especially **aba.careersite.com**

volume of transactions and favoring the largest banking organizations. New technologies should further intensify pressures for consolidation and convergence into banks smaller in number but much larger in size and scope of services. In the long run, technology should lower overall operating costs and save the industry billions of dollars.

---

**QUESTIONS TO HELP YOU STUDY**

1. In what ways are commercial banks of special importance to the money and capital markets and the economy?
2. Four dominant movements in the structure of U.S. banking in recent years have been:
   a. The spread of branch banking.
   b. The growth of holding companies.
   c. The rise of interstate banking.
   d. The convergence of bank and nonbank firms.
   Explain what has happened in these four areas and why.
3. What is *consolidation* in banking? What appears to be driving this trend?
4. How numerous are bank failures and what seem to be their most important causes? Why are bank failures different from the failures of other businesses and how are they resolved today?
5. What changes are under way in bank technology? With what effects?

---

## 14.4  Portfolio Characteristics of Commercial Banks

Commercial banks are the "department stores" of the financial system. They tend to offer a wider array of financial services than any other financial institution, meeting the credit, payments, and savings needs of individuals, businesses, and governments. This characteristic of financial diversity is reflected in the basic financial statements of the industry—the balance sheet (or report of condition) and the income and expense statement (or report of income). Exhibit 14.3 provides a list of the principal uses of funds (assets) and the major sources of funds (liabilities and equity capital) for all FDIC-insured U.S. commercial banks as they appeared on a recent industry balance sheet (report of condition).

### *Balance Sheet Items*

*Cash and Due from Banks (Primary Reserves)*    All commercial banks

**primary reserves**    hold a substantial part of their assets in **primary reserves,** consisting of cash and deposits held with other banks. These reserves are the banker's first line of defense against withdrawals by depositors and customer demand for loans. Banks generally hold no more cash than absolutely required to meet short-term contingencies, however, because the yield on cash assets is minimal. The deposits held with ("due from") other banks provide an implicit return, however, because they are a means of "paying" for correspondent banking services. In return for the deposits of smaller banks, larger U.S. correspondent banks provide such important services as clearing checks

| EXHIBIT 14.3 | Bank Report of Condition (Balance Sheet): Assets, Liabilities, and Capital of Insured Commercial Banks in the United States ($ billions, year-end figures) |

| | 1980 | | 1990 | | 2000 | | 2006[†] | |
|---|---|---|---|---|---|---|---|---|
| | Billions of Dollars | Percent of Total Assets | Billions of Dollars | Percent of Total Assets | Billions of Dollars | Percent of Total Assets | Billions of Dollars | Percent of Total Assets |
| **Assets:** | | | | | | | | |
| Cash and deposits due from banks | $ 331.9 | 17.9% | $ 318.0 | 9.4% | $ 369.8 | 5.9% | $ 397.6 | 4.1% |
| Investment securities: | | | | | | | | |
| U.S. Treasury securities | 104.5 | 5.6 | 150.8 | 4.4 | 75.7 | 1.2 | 44.7 | 0.5 |
| Federal agency securities | 59.1 | 3.2 | 275.6 | 8.2 | 634.7 | 10.2 | 1054.7 | 11.0 |
| State and local govt. securities | 146.3 | 7.9 | 83.5 | 2.5 | 92.6 | 1.5 | 125.3 | 1.3 |
| Corporate bonds | 13.4 | 0.7 | 85.9 | 2.5 | 233.5 | 3.7 | 409.8 | 4.3 |
| Corporate stock | 1.8 | 0.1 | 8.8 | 0.3 | 41.1 | 0.7 | 14.2 | 0.1 |
| Investment totals | $ 325.0 | 17.5% | $ 604.6 | 17.8% | $1,077.6 | 17.3% | $ 1648.7 | 17.2% |
| Total loans and leases, gross | 1,016.5 | 54.8 | 2,110.2 | 62.3 | 3,819.1 | 61.2 | 5660.7 | 59.0 |
| Real estate loans | 269.1 | 14.5 | 829.8 | 24.5 | 1,670.3 | 26.8 | 3,161.7 | 32.9 |
| Commercial and industrial loans | 391.0 | 21.1 | 615.0 | 18.1 | 1,048.2 | 16.8 | 1,096.7 | 11.4 |
| Loans to individuals | 187.4 | 10.1 | 403.5 | 11.9 | 609.7 | 9.8 | 827.1 | 8.6 |
| Agricultural loans | 32.3 | 3.2 | 33.3 | 1.0 | 48.1 | 0.8 | 52.6 | 0.5 |
| Loans to depository institutions | 81.2 | 8.1 | 51.2 | 1.5 | 120.5 | 1.9 | 164.6 | 1.7 |
| All other loans and leases | 55.5 | 5.5 | 177.4 | 5.2 | 322.3 | 5.2 | 358.0 | 3.7 |
| Less: Unearned income | −21.0 | −2.1 | −13.7 | −0.4 | −3.0 | −0.1 | −2.3 | −0.0* |
| Allowance for loan and lease losses | −10.1 | −0.5 | −55.5 | −1.6 | −64.1 | −1.0 | −69.7 | −0.7 |
| Net loans and leases | 1,006.4 | 54.2 | 2,054.6 | 60.6 | 3,752.1 | 60.4 | 5,589.3 | 58.2 |
| Bank premises and equipment | 26.7 | 1.4 | 51.4 | 1.5 | 75.7 | 1.2 | 93.9 | 1.0 |
| Other real estate owned | 2.2 | 0.1 | 21.6 | 0.6 | 3.2 | 0.1 | 4.9 | 0.1 |
| Intangible assets | NA | NA | 10.6 | 0.3 | 102.7 | 1.6 | 345.6 | 3.8 |
| All other assets | 163.4 | 8.8 | 328.5 | 9.7 | 857.6 | 13.5 | 1522.3 | 15.9 |
| Total assets | $1,855.7 | 100.0% | $3,389.5 | 100.0% | $6,238.7 | 100.0% | $9,602.3 | 100.0% |
| **Liabilities:** | | | | | | | | |
| Total deposits | $1,481.2 | 79.8% | $2,650.1 | 78.2% | $4,176.6 | 66.9% | $6,383.0 | 66.5% |
| Demand deposits | 431.5 | 23.3 | 463.9 | 13.7 | 679.3 | 10.9 | 530.6 | 5.5 |
| Savings deposits | 200.9 | 10.8 | 798.1 | 23.5 | 1,567.0 | 25.1 | 2,770.0 | 28.8 |
| Time deposits | 554.7 | 29.9 | 1,094.7 | 32.3 | 1,371.5 | 22.0 | 1,816.5 | 18.9 |
| Other deposits | 294.1 | 15.8 | 293.4 | 8.7 | 558.8 | 9.0 | 1,265.9 | 13.2 |
| Borrowings in the money market | 177.7 | 9.6 | 385.3 | 11.4 | 1,256.2 | 20.1 | 1,821.6 | 19.0 |
| Subordinated capital notes and debentures | 6.5 | 0.4 | 23.9 | 0.7 | 87.0 | 1.4 | 132.7 | 1.4 |
| Other liabilities | 82.7 | 4.5 | 111.5 | 3.3 | 189.4 | 3.0 | 293.3 | 3.1 |
| Total liabilities | $1,748.1 | 94.2% | $3,170.8 | 93.5% | $5,709.1 | 91.5% | $8,630.5 | 89.9% |
| **Equity capital:** | | | | | | | | |
| Perpetual preferred stock | $ 0.1 | 0.0* | $ 1.7 | 0.1 | $ 3.4 | 0.1 | $ 5.3 | 0.1 |
| Common stock | 21.7 | 1.2 | 30.9 | 0.9 | 31.2 | 0.5 | 33.3 | 0.3 |
| Surplus | 37.8 | 2.0 | 92.4 | 2.7 | 259.4 | 4.2 | 582.3 | 6.1 |
| Undivided profits | 48.0 | 2.6 | 93.7 | 2.8 | 236.9 | 3.8 | 350.8 | 3.7 |
| Total equity capital | 107.6 | 5.8 | 218.6 | 6.4 | 529.6 | 8.5 | 971.7 | 10.1 |
| Total liabilities and capital | $1,855.7 | 100.0% | $3,389.5 | 100.0% | $6,238.7 | 100.0% | $9,602.3 | 100.0% |

*Less than $50 million.

[†]2006 figures are as of June 30, 2006.

Source: Federal Deposit Insurance Corporation, *Historical Statistics on Banking, 1934–1992; Statistics on Banking,* selected years; and **fdic.gov**.

and processing records by computer. Thousands of smaller banks invest their excess cash reserves in loans to other banks (called *federal funds*) with the help of their larger correspondents.

### Investment Security Holdings and Secondary Reserves

Commercial banks hold securities acquired in the open market as a long-term investment and as a secondary reserve to help meet short-term cash needs. Some banks still hold sizable quantities of *municipal securities*—bonds and notes issued by state, city, and other local governments—because their interest income is tax exempt, although recent tax reform legislation has substantially limited the tax advantages of municipal notes and bonds for many banks. However, holdings of *U.S. Treasury obligations* and especially *debt obligations issued or guaranteed by federal agencies* (such as the Federal National Mortgage Association ["Fannie Mae"] or the Farm Credit System) are much larger in volume today than any other type of securities in U.S. bank investment portfolios. Banks generally favor shorter-term government securities because these securities can be marketed readily to cover short-term cash needs and are free of default risk. In the most recent period banks have been shifting more heavily toward federal agency securities due to their higher yields and strong credit quality.

A related type of security purchased in large volume by banks are loan-backed securities, each representing an interest in a pool of previously made loans, which pay interest and principal to investors as the loans are paid out. Most loan-backed securities held by banks are backed by government-guaranteed real estate mortgages or credit-card receivables. By the turn of the century mortgage-backed securities accounted for more than half of all investment securities held by U.S. banks.

Banks also hold small amounts of corporate bonds and notes, although they generally prefer to make direct loans to businesses as opposed to purchasing their securities in the open market. Under existing regulations, many banks around the globe are forbidden to purchase most types of corporate stock. However, banks do hold corporate stock as collateral for some of their loans and are allowed to invest in selected equities, such as the stock of small business investment companies, community development corporations, and the Federal Reserve banks.

Recently, American banks have been under strong regulatory pressure to value their security holdings and selected other assets and liabilities at current or fair market value rather than at book value on the day they were acquired. The long-range goal is to make bank balance sheets reflect more accurately the true condition of each bank so that capital-market investors and depositors can make a more informed judgment about the bank's true financial standing. Unfortunately, this step has done little, thus far, to improve the quality of information coming from bank financial reports.

### Loans

The principal business of banks is to make *loans* to qualified borrowers (or at least make it easier for their customers to find credit from some source with a bank perhaps agreeing to underwrite a customer's security issue or guarantee a loan from a third-party lender). Loans are among the highest yielding assets a bank can add to its portfolio, and they often provide the largest portion of traditional banks' operating revenue.

Banks make loans of reserves to other banks through the *federal funds market* and to securities dealers through *repurchase agreements*. Far more important in dollar volume, however, are direct loans to businesses and individuals. These loans arise from negotiation between the bank and its customer and result in a written agreement designed to meet the specific credit needs of the customer and the requirements of the bank for adequate security and income.

As shown in Exhibit 14.3, a substantial portion of total bank credit is extended to commercial and industrial business customers in the form of direct loans. Historically, commercial banks have preferred to make *short-term loans* to businesses, principally to support purchases of inventory. Recently, however, banks have lengthened the maturity of their business loans to include *term loans* (which have maturities over one year) to finance the purchase of buildings, machinery, and equipment. Moreover, longer-term loans to business firms have been supplemented in recent years by equipment leasing plans. These leases are the functional equivalent of a loan—that is, the customer not only makes the required lease payments while using the equipment but is also responsible for repairs and maintenance and for any taxes due. Lease financing carries not only significant cost and tax advantages for the customer but also substantial tax advantages for a bank, because it can depreciate leased equipment.

Banks are also important lenders in the real estate field, supporting the construction of residential and commercial structures. In fact, real estate loans are, by volume, the most important bank loan category. Major types of loans in the real estate category include farm and real estate credit, conventional and government-guaranteed (FHA and VA) single-family residential home loans, conventional and government-guaranteed loans on multifamily residences (such as apartments), and mortgage loans on nonfarm commercial properties. Today banks are the most important source of construction financing in the economy.

**Key URLs:**
To learn more about trends in bank balance sheets (reports of condition) and other financial reports for the banking industry as a whole see **fdic. gov/bank** and for individual banking firms see **fdic.gov/ bank/index.thml**

One of the most dynamic areas in bank lending today is the making of installment loans to individuals and families, particularly loans secured by a property owner's equity in his or her home (i.e., *home equity loans,* the interest costs of which may be tax-deductible to the borrower). Home equity loans can be used to finance a college education, start a new business, or cover a variety of other financial needs not related to housing. While banks began making home equity loans equal to a fraction of a home owner's equity, intense competition among lenders has resulted in some home equity loans and lines of credit today exceeding the value of the home owner's equity investment in a home, increasing lenders' risk. Banks also finance the purchase of automobiles, home furnishings, and appliances and provide funds to modernize homes and other properties and to pay for education and travel.

There is a growing concern today that consumer loans, particularly of the credit-card variety, have become more risky for banks due to higher default rates. Many banks and credit-card companies have increased their issue of new credit cards explosively, democratizing debt in order to reach millions of new customers, many of whom represent serious risks for lenders. Intense competition has encouraged many banks to give credit cards to customers who may have little or no credit history, some of whom turn out to be poor credit risks.

## Loan Loss Allowances and Loan Risk

Recently bankers have faced the necessity of closely examining the *quality,* not just the quantity, of their loans, especially in the wake of the terrorist attacks of 9/11. Recent events have demonstrated the great sensitivity of bank loan performance to changes in the economy. Problem loans reduce bank revenues, raise operating expenses, and force bankers to reexamine their relationships with customers and redesign the terms they are offering on loan contracts.

In order to capture each bank's loan risk exposure, bank balance sheets today frequently include both *gross loans and leases,* or the sum of the face amount of all loans and lease contracts currently outstanding, and *net loans and leases,* which equal gross loans less *unearned income* and *allowance for loan losses.* Unearned income represents any payments received from borrowing customers that have not yet been earned under the accrual accounting methods employed in modern banking—for example, if a customer pays loan interest up front before that interest income is actually earned by the bank. As loan income *is* earned it is gradually converted from the unearned income account to interest income.

The allowance for loan and lease losses (ALL), on the other hand, is a loss reserve or contra-asset account. The ALL is built up over time by annual deductions from a bank's current income based on its recent loan loss experience (usually referred to as the annual "provision for loan losses" expense account). As some loans turn uncollectible, they will usually be charged off, not against current bank earnings, but against the ALL account on the balance sheet, reducing a bank's *net* loans and leases account.

*Deposits*    To carry out their extensive lending and investing operations, banks draw on a wide variety of deposit and nondeposit sources of funds. Most bank funds—about two-thirds of the total—come from *deposits.* There are three main types of deposits: demand, savings, and time. *Demand deposits,* more commonly known as *checking accounts,* are an important means of making payments because they are safer than cash and are widely accepted (although recently smart cards, credit and debit cards, and other transfers by electronic means have generally outstripped demand deposits as payments media). *Savings deposits* generally are in small dollar amounts; they bear a relatively low interest rate but may be withdrawn by the depositor with no notice. *Time deposits* carry a fixed maturity, a penalty for early withdrawal, and usually offer the highest interest rates a bank will pay. Time deposits may be divided into nonnegotiable certificates of deposit (CDs), which are usually small, consumer-type accounts, and negotiable CDs that may be traded in the open market in million-dollar amounts and are purchased mainly by corporations all over the world.

**transaction accounts**

In recent decades, new forms of checkable (demand) deposits have appeared, combining the essential features of both demand and savings deposits. These **transaction accounts** include negotiable orders of withdrawal (NOWs) and automatic transfer services (ATS). NOW accounts may be drafted to pay bills but also earn interest, while ATS is a preauthorized payment service in which the bank transfers funds from an interest-bearing savings account to a checking account as necessary to cover checks written by the customer. Two newer types of transaction accounts—money market deposit accounts (MMDAs) and Super NOWs—are designed to compete directly with the high-yielding share accounts offered by money market funds. They carry prevailing market rates on short-term funds and can be drafted via check, automatic withdrawal, or telephone transfer.

In recent years banks have experienced a shift in their deposits toward more costly interest-bearing accounts, such as MMDAs. These newer deposits are generally *market-linked accounts,* the returns of which are tied to movements in market interest rates and security prices, reflecting prevailing credit conditions in the financial system. This shift toward more expensive, market-responsive deposits reflects the growing sophistication of bank customers, who have adopted efficient cash management practices and insist on competitive returns on their funds.

Moreover, the cost of attracting customer funds has been further increased by the tendency of bankers to expand their services in an effort to offer their customers "one-stop" financial convenience. Thus, to retain old customers and attract new ones, many banks have developed or are working through franchise agreements to offer (1) security brokerage services so that customers can purchase stocks, bonds, and shares in mutual funds and pay by charging their deposit accounts; (2) insurance counters to make life, health, and property-casualty insurance coverage available (often through joint ventures with affiliated or cooperating nonbank firms); (3) account relocation services and real estate brokerage of homes and other properties for customers who move; (4) financial planning centers to aid customers with important personal and business decisions; and (5) merchant banking services that aid major corporations with their long-term equity financing requirements. These newer service options have opened up new markets for banks, but they have also created new risks for bank management and demanded greater efficiency in bank operations.

**nondeposit funds**

### Nondeposit Sources of Funds

One of the most significant trends in banking in recent years is greater use of **nondeposit funds** (borrowings), especially as competition for deposits has increased. Principal nondeposit sources of funds for banks today include purchases of reserves (federal funds) from other banks, security repurchase agreements (when securities are sold temporarily to raise money and then bought back later), and the issuance of capital notes. Capital notes are of particular interest because many of these securities may be counted under current regulations as "capital" for purposes of determining how much a bank can lend (i.e., its *loan limit*). Both state

**EXHIBIT 14.4**

**Securitizations of Bank Loans to Raise New Funds**

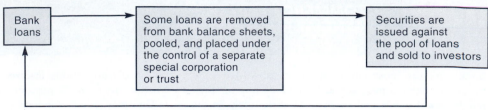

Securitizations of Bank Loans to Raise New Funds

| Bank loans | → | Some loans are removed from bank balance sheets, pooled, and placed under the control of a separate special corporation or trust | → | Securities are issued against the pool of loans and sold to investors |

Proceeds of security sales flow back to the bank as a new source of funds

and federal laws limit the amount of money a bank can lend to any one borrower to a fraction of the bank's capital. To be counted as capital, however, capital notes must be subordinated to deposits, so that if a bank is liquidated, the depositors have first claim to its assets.

Recently banks have turned to new nondeposit funds sources, including floating-rate CDs and notes sold in international markets, sales of loans, securitizations of selected assets, and standby credit guarantees. The floating-rate securities tend to be longer-term borrowings of funds, stretching out beyond one year, with an interest rate adjusted periodically to reflect changing conditions in international markets. Larger banks (such as JP Morgan Chase and Citibank) have expanded their sales of short-term business loans from their books, usually selling these credits in million-dollar blocks to raise new funds. Better-quality loans have been packaged into asset pools and *securitized*—that is, used as collateral for bank security issues that are sold to investors through a security dealer. (See Exhibit 14.4.) The bank secures additional funds to **securitized assets** make new loans and investments from these **securitized assets,** which include packages of auto, credit-card, home mortgage, and other loan types. The packaged loans generate interest and principal payments, which are passed through to investors who purchased the securities backed by these loans.

**standby letter of credit** Finally, many large banks today frequently issue a **standby letter of credit** on behalf of their customers who borrow from another lender or sell securities in the open market. As illustrated in Exhibit 14.5, standbys contain the bank's pledge to pay (guarantee) if its customer cannot pay a third party. They generate fee income for the bank without using up scarce funds or booking more assets that would require a bank to pledge more capital behind them.

**EXHIBIT 14.5**

**Bank Standby Letter of Credit Issued on Behalf of One of Their Customers**

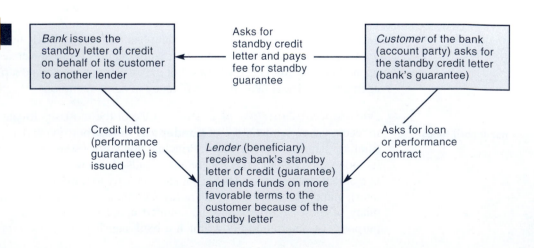

Bank Standby Letter of Credit Issued on Behalf of One of Their Customers

*Bank* issues the standby letter of credit on behalf of its customer to another lender

Asks for standby credit letter and pays fee for standby guarantee

*Customer* of the bank (account party) asks for the standby credit letter (bank's guarantee)

Credit letter (performance guarantee) is issued

*Lender* (beneficiary) receives bank's standby letter of credit (guarantee) and lends funds on more favorable terms to the customer because of the standby letter

Asks for loan or performance contract

Many of these activities are *off-balance-sheet transactions*—not recorded on a bank's balance sheet and using up little or no bank capital. However, securitizations, standby credits, and other off-balance-sheet activities help banks provide services to their customers and earn *fee* (noninterest) *income*—the fastest growing form of bank revenue. The result is an expansion in net earnings without booking additional assets on the bank's balance sheet.

## Equity Capital

**Key URLs:**
To more fully understand the many facets of the banking industry, see the Web sites of several leading banks, including Citibank at **citibank.com**; JP-Morgan Chase at **jpmorganchase .com**; Wells Fargo Bank at **wellsfargo .com**; and Capital One at **capitalone.com**

*Equity capital* (or net worth) supplied by a bank's stockholders provides only a minor portion (only about 10 percent, on average) of total funds for most banks today. In fact, while the ratio of equity capital to bank loans and deposits has risen recently, it previously had been in decline for several decades due to falling profit margins, inflation, and efforts by bank managers to employ greater financial leverage. This concerned many financial experts because one of the most important functions of equity capital is to keep a bank open in the face of operating losses until management can correct its problems. Recently, federal law has mandated minimum capital-to-asset ratios for banks, and many banks have expanded their equity capital positions. There is also a set of cooperative international capital regulations for major banks in the United States, Great Britain, Japan, and the nations of Western Europe, imposing minimum capital requirements on all banks in leading industrialized countries based on the degree of risk exposure each of these banks faces.[1]

## Income Statement Items

*Revenues and Expenses*  The majority of bank revenues come from interest and fees on loans and investment securities, as shown by the industry's income and expense statement or report of income. Other, less important sources of income include earnings from trust (fiduciary) activities and service charges on deposit accounts, although the latter have been growing rapidly of late.

Bank expenses have risen significantly in recent years, threatening to squeeze the industry's operating income. Greater competition from bank and nonbank financial institutions has resulted in increases in the real cost of raising funds, and the expense of upgrading computers and automated equipment has placed an added drain on bank revenues. Interest expense on deposits and other borrowed funds is the principal expense item for many banks, along with the salaries and wages of their employees.

Recently, interest expenses on deposits and other bank borrowings have declined in percentage terms due, in part, to lower average market interest rates. In addition, major banks have been shifting more and more of their activities off their balance sheets. Indeed, as Poposka, Vaughan, and Yeager [6] observe, the largest banks are evolving from traditional deposit-taking and loan-making institutions into complex banking companies carrying on such off-balance-sheet activities as selling risk protection to their customers and controlling their own risk exposure by selling many of their risky assets to investors in the money and capital markets. Examples of these increasingly complex banking organizations include Citigroup, JPMorgan Chase, and Bank of America in the United States and Barclays Bank in Great Britain.

---

[1]See Chapter 17 for a fuller discussion of the Basel Agreement on bank capital requirements.

| EXHIBIT 14.6 | Bank Report of Income (Earnings and Expense Statement): Income and Expenses of Insured Commercial Banks in the United States, 1980, 1990, 2000, and 2006 |
| --- | --- |

| | 1980 | | 1990 | | 2000 | | 2006[‡] | |
| --- | --- | --- | --- | --- | --- | --- | --- | --- |
| | Billions of Dollars | Percent of Total Operating Income | Billions of Dollars | Percent of Total Operating Income | Billions of Dollars | Percent of Total Operating Income | Billions of Dollars | Percent of Total Operating Income |
| Total interest income | $176.4 | 92.5% | $320.5 | 85.4% | $428.0 | 73.7% | $260.4 | 70.1% |
| Total interest expense | $120.1 | 63.0% | $205.0 | 54.6% | $224.2 | 38.6% | $117.9 | 31.7% |
|   Net interest income | $ 56.3 | 29.5% | $715.5 | 30.8% | $203.8 | 35.1% | $142.4 | 38.3% |
| Total noninterest income: | 14.3 | 7.5 | 54.9 | 14.6 | 152.8 | 26.3 | 111.2 | 29.9 |
|   Service charges on deposits | 3.2 | 1.7 | 11.4 | 3.0 | 23.8 | 4.1 | 17.6 | 4.7 |
|   Other noninterest income | 11.2 | 5.9 | 43.4 | 11.6 | 129.0 | 22.2 | 93.6 | 25.2 |
| Total noninterest expense: | 46.7 | 24.5 | 115.8 | 30.8 | 215.8 | 37.2 | 146.4 | 39.4 |
|   Employee salary and benefits | 24.7 | 13.0 | 51.8 | 13.8 | 88.5 | 15.2 | 67.2 | 18.1 |
|   Occupancy expenses | 7.4 | 3.9 | 17.4 | 4.6 | 26.8 | 4.6 | 17.7 | 4.5 |
|   All other noninterest expenses | 14.6 | 7.7 | 46.6 | 12.4 | 100.5 | 17.3 | 61.4 | 16.5 |
| Net noninterest income | −32.4 | −17.0 | −60.9 | −16.2 | −63.0 | −10.8 | −35.2 | −9.5 |
| Provision for loan and lease losses | 4.5 | 2.4 | −32.1 | 8.6 | 29.3 | 5.0 | 10.9 | 2.9 |
| Pretax net operating income | 19.5 | 10.2 | 22.6 | 6.0 | 111.5 | 19.2 | 96.3 | 25.9 |
| Securities gains (or losses) | −0.9 | −0.5 | 0.5 | 0.1 | −2.3 | −0.4 | −0.8 | −0.2 |
| Applicable income taxes | 4.7 | 2.5 | 7.7 | 2.1 | 38.0 | 6.5 | 31.4 | 8.4 |
| Net extraordinary items | 0.0* | 0.0[†] | 0.6 | 0.2 | −0.3 | 0.1 | 0.4 | 0.1 |
|   Net income after taxes | $ 14.0 | 7.3% | $ 16.0 | 4.3% | $ 71.2 | 12.3% | $64.7 | 17.4% |

*Less than $50 million.

[†]Less than 0.50 percent.

[‡]2006 figures are for the year ended June 30.

*Notes:* NA means "not available." Columns may not add to totals due to rounding error.

Source: Federal Deposit Insurance Corporation.

**Key URL:**
You can track recent trends in U.S. bank earnings and expenses through *FYI* and *Bank Trends*, two publications appearing on the Federal Deposit Insurance Corporation's Web site at **fdic.gov**

*Interest and Noninterest Margins*　A careful perusal of the statement of earnings and expenses (Report of Income) for all U.S. insured banks in Exhibit 14.6 shows an interesting arrangement of revenue and expense accounts. First, bankers record all of their interest income. Then the total interest paid out on all borrowed funds is subtracted to derive each bank's net interest income or *interest margin.* The interest margin measures how efficiently a bank is performing its most basic function of borrowing and lending funds. For many banks this margin is the principal determinant of their profitability.

Of increasing importance in the industry, however, is the *noninterest margin,* which is the difference between total noninterest income (such as service fees on deposits) and noninterest expenses (such as employee salaries and benefits). The noninterest margin is growing in importance as a determinant of bank profits because banks are developing new services that generate noninterest fees, such as security underwriting services, guaranteeing the loan a customer has gotten from another lender, managing pension plans for corporations, and so forth. Because bankers face stiff competition for funding, they have little influence over the interest expenses on their borrowed funds. Accordingly, they work especially hard to minimize their *noninterest expenses,* particularly employee costs, by substituting automated equipment for labor.

## QUESTIONS TO HELP YOU STUDY

6. What are the principal *uses* of commercial bank funds? Major *sources* of funds?
7. What new sources and uses of funds have been developed in banking recently?
8. Explain how *securitization* of loans helps a bank raise new funds.
9. What benefits do *standby credit letters* provide for banks and their customers?
10. What are a bank's principal *revenue* and *expense* items?
11. What is the *net interest margin?* The *noninterest margin?* Why are they important?

## 14.5 Managing Commercial Bank Performance Today

As preceding pages of this chapter suggest, bank management is one of the toughest challenges in the financial-services marketplace today. Banks are buffeted by powerful forces—competition, regulation, technological change, and shifting economic conditions—and these forces sometimes overwhelm their defenses, causing them to fail. In response, bank managers have developed several fundamental principles to guide their decision making.

### Managing Bank Assets, Liabilities, Revenues, and Expenses

One of the greatest challenges bank managers face is making new loans and properly monitoring those loans already on the books. This challenge is a stiff one because loans are usually a bank's number-one asset and number-one revenue generator. Moreover, most of a bank's risk exposure is usually concentrated in its loan portfolio. Top-performing banks today routinely prepare *written loan policies,* designed to guide loan decisions and shape the whole loan portfolio the way management and the stockholders prefer. Written loan policies help to train new loan officers and assist management in determining how well its policies are being followed.

In addition to making loans, banks also extend credit to their customers by purchasing a customer's securities (principally stocks and bonds), which bankers place in their *investment portfolio.* Bank investment portfolios provide a source of income that supplements loan income and stabilizes overall revenue and earnings. Because risk is normally heaviest in the loan portfolio, bank investments are generally positioned in safer assets to help offset loan risk. Moreover, investments in marketable securities can be drawn upon for cash when the bank faces significant liquidity pressures. An investments officer must consider several different factors when deciding which securities to add to a bank's investment portfolio, including their expected after-tax rate of return, how that expected return correlates with returns from other assets the bank holds, the credit rating of the securities under review, and the projected liquidity (cash) needs of the institution.

Perhaps more than any other business, banks are challenged by continuing *liquidity (cash) requirements.* They must raise cash at a reasonable cost at precisely those times cash is needed, often in huge volume. Banks are "liquidity sensitive" because many of their deposits are payable immediately upon customer demand. A bank's liquidity manager must invest surplus cash right away to avoid loss of income and cover cash deficits as soon as they arise.

**Key URL:**
Beginning in 2003, the FDIC made it easier to understand the important linkages between local economic conditions and bank performance through its FDIC State Profiles databank at **fdic.gov**

In order to meet a bank's liquidity needs, two different strategies are usually employed: asset conversion or liability management. With *asset conversion,* assets from the bank's portfolio of loans and securities are *sold* to raise new cash. Most banks hold sizeable quantities of Treasury bills and other easily cashable assets to cover possible liquidity deficits. However, this strategy has shortcomings. It requires banks to surrender income when assets are sold and forces them to "store" liquidity in low-yielding assets that tend to reduce earnings.

In contrast to the asset conversion strategy, with *liability management* the necessary amount of liquidity is *borrowed.* Borrowing only occurs when there is an actual need for cash and the amount borrowed can be varied simply by changing the terms offered to those institutions with surplus cash. However, borrowing liquidity can be costly and that cost is often volatile. Therefore, most banks use a combination of asset conversion and liability management.

Recent research by Bradley and Shibut [1] shows that the sources of liquid funds banks borrow daily to support the growth of their assets are proliferating rapidly, creating new challenges for bank management. Bankers today must rely less upon traditional deposits to raise the cash they need and more on innovative, interest-sensitive sources of liquidity. Examples include federal funds (overnight loans of reserves between depository institutions); repurchase agreements (short-term borrowings using holdings of investment securities as collateral); brokered deposits (deposit accounts divided into smaller amounts fully protected by federal insurance and placed by brokers with banks offering the highest yields); cash advances from government agencies (such as the Federal Home Loan Banks); and sweep accounts (those permitting bankers to move customers' deposits back and forth between conventional and target accounts, promising higher returns, and lowering the legal reserves banks must hold behind their deposits).

Finally, the bank's liquidity management team must pay special attention to the largest depositors and to those customers with large outstanding credit lines. The cash needs of these particular customers must be carefully monitored because they are likely to have the greatest impact upon the bank's cash position. By discovering ahead of time when a large deposit will be withdrawn or when a credit line will be tapped for money, bank managers can make good decisions on when and where to raise new cash.

## Monitoring the Performance of a Bank

**Key URL:**
For interesting discussions about how to understand and analyze bank performance, see especially the FDIC's FYI at **fdic.gov/bank/analytical/fyi**

Today, banks are closely watched by their customers, by regulators, and by investors in the money and capital markets. Their performance is evaluated not only relative to each institution's own goals but also relative to the performance of the bank's competitors. Four dimensions of bank performance tend to be most closely followed in the industry:

1. The market value or stock price of a banking institution.
2. The rate of return or profitability ratios of a bank.
3. The bank's risk exposure along several different dimensions.
4. The operating efficiency of the institution.

The principles of financial management teach that a bank's *stock price* is usually the single best indicator of how well the firm is performing because its shareholders must be satisfied they are earning a competitive return on their capital. However, many banks around the world either do not have stockholders or have stock so infrequently traded that a realistic value cannot be determined. This is why many banks pay close attention to measures of *profitability,* such as the *return on assets* (ROA) and the *return on equity capital* (ROE)—the ratios of net after-tax income divided by total assets or equity capital.

Other important performance indicators include the *net interest margin,* which reflects the "spread" between interest revenue from loans and investments and interest expense associated with deposits and other borrowings divided by bank size. Another key indicator is the *ratio of equity capital* (or *net worth*) *to total assets.* If the risky assets a bank holds decline in value by more than the volume of its owners' equity (net worth), the institution may become insolvent. Similarly, the banker must monitor the proportion of all loans outstanding that are judged to be *noncurrent* and, therefore, not paying out as promised and determine how adequately noncurrent loans are *covered* by loan-loss reserves set aside by management. If these *loan-loss* measures deteriorate, management must respond quickly to strengthen the bank's equity capital and improve its loan quality.

To aid bankers in monitoring their institutions' performance, several government and private agencies provide comprehensive data on bank performance and construct peer groups so that a banker can compare the performance of his institution to the performance of similar banks. Among the most popular of these sources are the UBPRs (Uniform Bank Performance Reports) compiled by the Federal Financial Institutions Examination Council (FFIEC) inside the United States. This information is supplemented by numerous credit-rating agencies that monitor the riskiness of banks around the world.

**Key URLs:**
In the U.S., several rating agencies assess the safety and soundness of banks and selected other financial institutions and their customers, such as IDC Financial Publishing (**idcfp.com**), Sheshunoff Information Services (**sheshunoff.com**); and Veribank (**veribank.com**).

Exhibit 14.7 provides an example of peer-group average performance ratios for all U.S.-insured banks as prepared by the FDIC and the FFIEC. Notice, for example, that, early in 2006 the banking industry's average return on assets (ROA) was 1.35 percent and its average return on equity (ROE) stood at 13.07 percent. The average net interest margin was 3.46 percent and the ratio of equity capital to total assets averaged just over 10 percent. A bank manager would want to compare her institution against these and other group performance measures to see if her bank lies above or below industry standards. How well has the industry been doing lately? Quite well in terms of ROA and ROE—both of which are substantially above historical averages—while net worth (equity) relative to total assets has held fairly steady in the 9 to 10 percent range. Moreover, for most categories of banks the quality of assets (especially loans) was relatively strong early in 2006. For example, as shown in Exhibit 14.7, assets that were *noncurrent* (particularly loans whose promised payments were past due more than 90 days) represented only about half of 1 percent of the industry's total assets. Reserves the industry set aside to cover potential loan losses exceeded noncurrent loans by nearly 160 percent for the industry as a whole, indicating bankers were relatively well prepared should loan losses begin to rise as, in fact, happened in several subsequent quarters.

**Key URL:**
To compare the performance of banks against peer groups of banking firms see especially the Uniform Bank Perfomance Reports (UBPRs) available through **ffiec. gov**

Another important dimension of bank performance centers on *efficiency,* often measured by the ratio of operating efficiency to operating revenues, which recently has hovered below 60 percent (especially among larger banks), giving the industry an impressive edge of operating income over operating costs. Industry analysts have also focused increasingly on the relationship between noninterest income and noninterest expenses, both of which banks appear to have better control over than they do their interest revenues and expenses. Noninterest expenses are generally larger than noninterest income for most banks and, therefore, the industry's *net noninterest margin* (i.e., noninterest income less noninterest expenses) is generally negative. However,

**EXHIBIT 14.7** Key Performance Measures for FDIC-Insured Commercial Banks in the United States, 2006* (Average Level of Performance for Peer Groups of Banking Institutions)

| Dollar Amounts in Billions First Quarter 2006 | Asset Concentration Group | | | | | | | | | |
|---|---|---|---|---|---|---|---|---|---|---|
| | Commercial Banks | International Banks | Agricultural Banks | Credit Card Lenders | Commercial Lenders | Mortgage Lenders | Consumer Lenders | Other Specialized <$1 Billion | All Other <$1 Billion | All Other >$1 Billion |
| Number of FDIC-insured | 7,491 | 4 | 1,641 | 28 | 4,194 | 195 | 88 | 388 | 907 | 46 |
| Total assets | $ 9,333 | $ 1,972 | $ 140 | $ 356 | $ 3,436 | $ 413 | $ 52 | $ 40 | $ 109 | $ 2,816 |
| Total deposits | 6,218 | 1,193 | 114 | 104 | 3537 | 257 | 31 | 30 | 90 | 1,863 |
| Net income | 32.06 | 5.56 | 0.49 | 4.09 | 11.71 | 1.03 | 0.29 | 0.13 | 0.30 | 8.51 |
| Percent profitable | 93.4% | 100.0% | 96.7% | 93.3% | 93.0% | 91.8% | 96.6% | 81.7% | 95.8% | 98.3% |
| Average return on assets (ROA) | 1.35 | 1.16 | 1.26 | 4.58 | 1.36 | 1.05 | 2.19 | 1.74 | 1.07 | 1.22 |
| Average return on equity (ROE) | 13.07 | 14.33 | 11.82 | 18.75 | 13.22 | 9.61 | 22.54 | 9.23 | 9.63 | 12.72 |
| Net interest margin | 3.46 | 2.56 | 4.05 | 9.05 | 3.92 | 2.82 | 4.56 | 3.01 | 3.76 | 3.08 |
| Equity to assets | 10.38 | 7.95 | 10.81 | 27.22 | 10.28 | 10.81 | 9.63 | 18.77 | 11.09 | 9.57 |
| Noncurrent assets plus other real estate owned to total assets† | 0.48 | 0.42 | 0.67 | 1.17 | 0.49 | 0.55 | 0.51 | 0.24 | 0.54 | 0.37 |
| Loan-loss coverage ratio‡ | 159.84 | 151.39 | 157.58 | 262.0 | 190.04 | 69.48 | 227.78 | 201.90 | 163.96 | 144.90 |
| Efficiency ratio (%) | 56.92 | 62.22 | 61.28 | 45.70 | 56.56 | 57.46 | 47.23 | 72.55 | 66.98 | 57.98 |
| Noninterest Income to total assets | 2.22 | 3.13 | 0.64 | 11.13 | 1.45 | 1.17 | 2.58 | 8.21 | 0.91 | 2.14 |
| Noninterest Expenses to total assets | 3.06 | 3.35 | 2.69 | 9.04 | 2.86 | 2.19 | 3.19 | 8.09 | 2.93 | 2.82 |

*Figures as of first quarter 2006.

†Nonaccruing loans and loans past due 90+ days.

‡Loss reserves as a percentage of noncurrent loans.

Source: Federal Deposit Insurance Corporation.

this margin recently has become less and less negative as bankers have raised service fees, developed new sources of fee income, and worked hard to reduce their noninterest expenses through increased operating efficiency.

Finally, notice that bank performance depends heavily upon the *type of bank* we are talking about. The right-hand side of Exhibit 14.7 groups U.S. banks according to their *asset concentration*—that is, those product lines that most characterize what each bank does. What is remarkable is how different in performance the different types of banks tend to be. For example, *credit-card-oriented banks* tended to achieve the highest profitability ratios—well above the industry average. However, credit-card banks also reported the biggest loan-loss problems and were compelled to hold more equity capital relative to their assets to deal with greater risk exposure. In contrast, banks devoted primarily to commercial and mortgage lending posted much lower profitability ratios, but they also enjoyed fewer loan losses and less risk exposure. Performance measurement must always take into account differences in bank size, location, and especially the product-line focus each bank adopts as its principal service mission.

---

### QUESTIONS TO HELP YOU STUDY

12. How do banks control *risk* in their loans and in their investment portfolios?

13. Why are banks so sensitive to *liquidity risk?* How do they raise cash to meet liquidity needs?

14. What are the most popular measures of *bank performance?* What do they measure?

---

## 14.6 Money Creation and Destruction by Banks and Bank Accounting Methods

Commercial banks differ from many other financial institutions in one critical respect: *Banks have the power to create money in the form of new checkable deposits, credit-card lines, debit cards, and other immediately spendable funds.* The banking system creates and destroys billions of dollars in money each day.

**money creation**

**Money creation** by banks is made possible because the public readily accepts claims on bank deposits (mainly checks, credit and debit cards, and computer entries) in payment for goods and services. In addition, the law requires individual banks to hold only a fraction of the amount of deposits received from the public as cash reserves, thus freeing up a majority of incoming funds for making loans and purchasing investment securities.

**legal reserves**

As we saw previously in Chapters 12 and 13, vault cash and deposits at the Fed constitute a U.S. bank's holdings of **legal reserves**—those assets acceptable for meeting legal reserve requirements behind the public's deposits. In turn, each bank's legal reserves may be divided into required reserves and excess reserves. *Required reserves* are equal to the legal reserve requirement percentage ratio times the volume of deposits subject to reserve requirements. For example, if a bank holds $50 million in checkable (transaction) deposits and the law requires it to hold 3 percent of its transaction accounts in legal reserves, the reserve requirement for this bank would be $50 million $\times$ 3%, or $1.5 million.

**excess reserves**

On the other hand, **excess reserves** equal the difference between the total legal reserves actually held by a bank and the amount of its required reserves. For example, if a bank is required to hold legal reserves equal to $1.5 million but finds on a given date that it has $500,000 in cash on the premises and $1.5 million on deposit with the Federal Reserve bank in its region, this bank holds $500,000 in excess reserves.

## The Creation of Money and Credit

The distinction between excess and required reserves is important because it plays a key role in the growth of bank loans and the creation of money by the banking system. To understand why, we need to make certain assumptions concerning how banks account for their transactions with customers and the regulations they face. To simplify the arithmetic, assume that one of the banking system's key regulators, the Federal Reserve, has set a basic legal reserve requirement of 20 percent behind the public's deposits. Therefore, for every dollar that the public deposits in the banking system, each bank must put aside in either vault cash or deposits at the Federal Reserve 20 cents as required reserves. Assume also that, initially, the banking system is "loaned up"—that is, bankers have loaned out all excess reserves available to them. In addition, assume all bankers are profit maximizers and attempt to loan out immediately any excess funds available to earn the most income possible.

Suppose that a deposit of $1,000 is made from some source outside the banking system. For example, the public may decide to convert a portion of its currency and coin holdings ("pocket money") into bank deposits for greater convenience and safety. Suppose a deposit of $1,000 appears at Bank A as shown in Exhibit 14.8. This exhibit contains an abbreviated balance sheet (T account) for Bank A with changes in its assets shown on the left-hand side and changes in its liabilities and net worth shown on the right-hand side.

Under the assumed Federal Reserve regulations, Bank A is required to place $200 aside as required legal reserves (i.e., 20 percent of the $1,000 deposit), leaving excess reserves of $800. Because the $800 in cash earns little or no interest income, the banker will immediately try to loan out these excess reserves. Banks make loans today by simple accounting entries. The borrower signs a note indicating how much is borrowed, at what rate of interest, and when the note will come due. In return, the banker creates a checking (transaction) account in the borrower's name. In our example, assume that Bank A has received a loan request from one of its customers and decides to grant the customer a loan of $800—exactly the amount of excess reserves it holds.

Banks find that, when they make loans, the borrowed funds are withdrawn rapidly as borrowers spend the proceeds of their loans. Moreover, it is likely that most of the borrowed funds will wind up as deposits in other banks as borrowing customers draw money from their loan balances. For this reason, Bank A will not loan out more than the $800 in excess reserves it currently holds. This way, when a borrower spends his or her funds and the money flows to other banks, Bank A will have sufficient funds in reserve to cover the cash letters demanding payment that it will receive from other banks.

Assume that the $800 loaned by Bank A eventually winds up as a deposit in Bank B. As indicated in Exhibit 14.8, Bank B must place $160 (20 percent) of this deposit in required reserves; it then has excess reserves of $640, which are quickly loaned out. As the new borrowers spend their funds, the $640 in loans will find its way into deposits at Bank C. After setting aside required reserves of $128, Bank C has excess reserves of $512. It too will move rapidly to loan out these funds if suitable borrowers can be found.

Powerful trends are reshaping banking around the globe:

1. *Deregulation* of banking in the United States, Japan, and in many other nations, permitting private markets to determine bank prices and services instead of governments.

2. Increased *penetration of foreign markets* by major banks and other financial institutions, so that financial services are increasingly becoming a global industry with few territorial boundaries.

3. Growing *proliferation of services* (i.e., financial innovation) as bankers respond to increased competition, including the spread of securities underwriting, insurance services, and real estate development.

4. A spreading *technological revolution* with more transactions carried out via teller machines, satellites, "smart" cards, fax machines, the World Wide Web, and other innovative devices instead of through human labor, transforming banking into an increasingly automated, capital-intensive industry.

5. *Changing sources and uses of funds* as banking's customer base changes toward more financially sophisticated, more interest-sensitive depositors. Banks are doing more "off-balance-sheet" support of their customers' service needs, providing credit guarantees, financial advice, and consulting. These support services earn fee income for banks.

6. Growing *international cooperation* between regulatory agencies in different countries to promote uniform regulation and uniform supervision of banks.

## EXHIBIT 14.8

**The Creation of Credit and Deposits by the Banking System**

### 1. Bank A Receives New Deposit

| Assets | | Liabilities | |
|---|---|---|---|
| Required | | Deposits | 1,000 |
| reserves | 200 | | |
| Cash | 800 | | |

### 2. Loan Made by Bank A

| Assets | | Liabilities | |
|---|---|---|---|
| Required | | Deposits | 1,000 |
| reserves | 200 | | |
| Loans | 800 | | |

### 3. Deposit of Loan Funds in Bank B

| Assets | | Liabilities | |
|---|---|---|---|
| Required | | Deposits | |
| reserves | 160 | from Bank A | 800 |
| Cash | 640 | | |

### 4. Loan Made by Bank B

| Assets | | Liabilities | |
|---|---|---|---|
| Required | | Deposits | 800 |
| reserves | 160 | | |
| Loans | 640 | | |

### 5. Deposit of Loan Funds in Bank C

| Assets | | Liabilities | |
|---|---|---|---|
| Required | | Deposits | |
| reserves | 128 | from Bank B | 640 |
| Cash | 512 | | |

### 6. Loan Made by Bank C

| Assets | | Liabilities | |
|---|---|---|---|
| Required | | Deposits | 640 |
| reserves | 128 | | |
| Loans | 512 | | |

By making loans whenever there are excess reserves, the banking system can generate a volume of deposits larger than the amount of the initial deposit received by Bank A.

**EXHIBIT 14.8**

(continued)

| | Transactions within the Banking System | | |
|---|---|---|---|
| Name of Bank | Deposits Received | Loans Made | Required Reserves |
| A | $1,000 | $ 800 | $ 200 |
| B | 800 | 640 | 160 |
| C | 640 | 512 | 128 |
| D | 512 | 410 | 102 |
| — | — | — | — |
| — | — | — | — |
| Final amounts for all banks in the system | $5,000 | $4,000 | $1,000 |

The pattern of these changes in deposits, loans, and reserves should now be clear. The results are summarized in the bottom portion of Exhibit 14.8. Note that the total volume of bank deposits has been considerably expanded by the time it reaches the third or fourth bank. Similarly, the total volume of new loans grows rapidly as funds flow from bank to bank within the system. By making loans whenever excess reserves appear, the banking system eventually creates money in the form of deposits and loans in amounts larger than the original volume of new funds received.

## Destruction of Deposits and Reserves

Not only can banks expand deposits and money, but they can also destroy deposits and money. This is illustrated in Exhibit 14.9, in which a depositor has withdrawn $1,000 from a transaction account at Bank A and has decided not to place the money on deposit in another bank. Recall that behind the $1,000 deposit, Bank A holds only $200 in required reserves. This means that when the deposit is withdrawn, that bank will have a net deficiency of $800. If Bank A is loaned up and has used all of its cash to make loans and investments, it will have to raise the necessary funds through the sale of securities or through borrowing.

Suppose that Bank A decides to sell securities in the amount of $800. As indicated in Exhibit 14.9, the sale of securities increases Bank A's legal reserves by the necessary amount. However, the individuals and institutions that purchase those securities pay for them by electronic transfers of funds or by writing checks against their deposits in other banks, reducing the legal reserves of those institutions.

For example, assume that Bank B loses deposits of $800 and required legal reserves of $800 as Bank A gains these funds. Considering Bank A and Bank B together, total deposits have fallen by $1,800. This deposit contraction has freed up $360 ($200 + $160) in required reserves. However, if Bank B is also loaned up and has a net reserve deficiency of $640, further contraction of deposits will occur as Bank B attempts to cover its reserve deficiency by drawing reserves from other banks. Ultimately, deposits will contract by a larger amount as banks try to cover their reserve deficits by raising funds at the expense of other banks.

## Implications of Money Creation and Destruction

This capacity of banks to create and destroy money and deposits has a number of important implications for the financial system and the economy. Creation of money by

**EXHIBIT 14.9**

**Deposit and Credit Destruction in the Banking System**

**Depositor withdraws funds:**

| Federal Reserve Bank | | | Bank A | | |
|---|---|---|---|---|---|
| **Assets** | **Liabilities** | | **Assets** | **Liabilities** | |
| | Member bank reserves | −1,000 | Required reserves   −1,000 | Deposits | −1,000 |

If Bank A was loaned up when the withdrawal occurred, it will now have a reserve deficiency of $800 as indicated below:

| | |
|---|---|
| Total reserves lost at Bank A when depositor withdrew funds | $1,000 |
| Required reserves no longer needed due to deposit withdrawals | −200 |
| Net reserve deficit at Bank A | $ 800 |

| Bank A | | Bank B | | |
|---|---|---|---|---|
| **Assets** | **Liabilities** | **Assets** | **Liabilities** | |
| Securities   −800 | | Required reserves   −800 | Deposits | −800 |
| Required reserves from Bank B   +800 | | | | |

The sale of securities in the amount of $800 enables Bank A to cover its reserve deficit. However, assume that customers of Bank B bought those securities and that bank was already loaned up. Bank B now has a reserve deficiency of $640. Thus:

| | |
|---|---|
| Total reserves lost at Bank B after deposit withdrawals to purchase Bank A's securities | $800 |
| Required reserves no longer needed due to deposit withdrawal | −160 |
| Net reserve deficit at Bank B | $640 |

banks is one of the most important sources of credit funds in the global economy—an important supplement to the supply of savings in providing funds for investment so the economy can grow faster. Money created by banks is instantly available for spending and, therefore, unless carefully controlled by government action, can fuel inflation. As we saw earlier in Chapters 12 and 13, that is why the Federal Reserve System and other central banks around the globe regulate interest rates and the growth of credit principally by influencing the growth of bank reserves and deposits.

## QUESTIONS TO HELP YOU STUDY

15. How are banks able to *create money?*
16. Is the ability of banks to create money of significance for the economy and the creation of jobs?
17. What are the dangers of money creation by banks?
18. How do banks *destroy money?*
19. Why is money creation and destruction of importance in the pursuit of public policy?

## Summary of the Chapter's Main Points

The banking industry has undergone significant financial and structural changes in recent years as well as expanding the number of services banks offer the public.

- One key trend reshaping the global banking industry is *consolidation* into fewer, but larger, banks serving geographically broader markets. Banking is one of the leading industries in mergers and acquisitions each year.

- Inside the United States the growing importance of larger banks has been accomplished through the rapid expansion of branch banks, holding companies, and interstate banking firms. In Europe and Asia banking units are spreading, crossing national boundaries and also investing in banking facilities inside the United States.

- Leading banks around the globe have reached out to become *universal banks,* offering not only traditional services (including checking and savings deposits and loans) but also securities underwriting, insurance policy sales and underwriting, real estate services, and longer-term corporate equity funding, generating new sources of revenue but also new risks for the banking community. Larger banks increasingly are experiencing *convergence,* offering many of the same services as other financial industries, such as insurance companies and security firms. The result is the appearance of more complex, multiservice conglomerates and financial holding companies (FHCs).

- *Cost pressures* have encouraged banks not only to grow larger, but to automate many of their services. This has enabled many banks to reduce the number of their employees and close many full-service branch offices, reducing the costs of financial-service production and delivery.

- A growing list of bank services are now being offered through automated teller machines (ATMs), computer networks and the Internet, and via telephones, satellites, and cable television systems. In short, banking is becoming a more heavily *fixed-cost industry* (based on greater volumes of capital equipment), with a smaller proportion of variable costs (especially labor time).

- The industry's financial statements are also undergoing changes. More of a bank's resources today typically are devoted to loans and to fee-generating services (such as assisting customers with financial planning). At the same time, nondeposit borrowings and stockholders' equity capital have grown as sources of funds while deposits—the traditional main source of bank funding—have become somewhat less important as a key money source.

- There is greater interest today than ever before in measuring and tracking *bank performance.* The techniques bank managers use to control their institution's risk exposure and operating costs while achieving competitive rates of return for their stockholders are increasingly of interest as well. Bank managers are especially sensitive to changes in the condition of their institution's loan portfolio, investment security portfolio, and liquidity (or cash) position, as well as the cost of raising new funds and the preservation of net worth to prevent the bank from becoming insolvent.

- Among the many different measures of bank performance in use today are return on assets (ROA), return on equity capital (ROE), the net interest margin, operating efficiency ratios, the net noninterest margin, the ratio of equity capital to total assets as a measure of solvency risk, and the proportion of all loans that are delinquent or judged to be worthless.

- The performance of banks today is heavily influenced by their *asset concentration*—that is, by the product lines they offer to the public. Among the most profitable banks today are credit-card banks, while banks that concentrate their assets in quality commercial and mortgage loans tend to have somewhat lower returns but also less exposure to loan losses, fraud, and other risks common in the credit-card field.

- Finally, banks are still the most important institution in most financial systems around the globe. They remain the leading financial institution in creating money. Banks create money both by offering transaction deposits and by granting loans (credit). However, more and more nonbank financial institutions are competing with banks in money and credit creation.

## Key Terms Appearing in This Chapter

banking structure,  423

state-chartered banks,  424

national banks,  424

consolidation,  424

branch banking,  425

bank holding company,  426

convergence,  429

deregulation,  430

primary reserves,  432

transaction accounts,  436

nondeposit funds,  437

securitized assets,  438

standby letter of credit,  438

money creation,  445

legal reserves,  445

excess reserves,  446

## Problems and Issues

1. Given the following information on the revenues and expenses of First National Bank, determine the bank's net income after taxes for the year just concluded:

| | | | |
|---|---|---|---|
| Salaries and employee benefits | $ 80,000 | Applicable income taxes | $ 50,000 |
| Interest on deposits | 170,000 | Occupancy costs | 11,000 |
| Interest on loans | 320,000 | Provision for loan losses | 22,000 |
| Income from U.S. Treasury securities | 75,000 | Miscellaneous expenses | 8,000 |
| Extraordinary items, net | -0- | Interest on municipal securities | 86,000 |
| Interest on nondeposit borrowings | 30,000 | Service charges on deposits | 10,000 |
| Net securities gains | -0- | Miscellaneous operating revenues | 13,000 |

2. Construct the report of condition (balance sheet) for First National Bank for December 31 of the year just ended from the following information:

| Equity capital | $ 50 million | Real estate loans | $ 60 million |
| Demand deposits | 100 million | U.S. Treasury securities | 25 million |
| Savings deposits | 150 million | Commercial and | |
| Time deposits | 200 million | industrial loans | 300 million |
| Federal funds borrowings | 12 million | Other liabilities | 38 million |
| Cash and due from banks | 20 million | Municipal securities | 55 million |
| Other assets | 50 million | Loans to individuals | 40 million |

3. See if you can fill in correctly the missing items from the balance sheet (report of condition) and the statement of earnings and expenses (report of income) of the bank whose financial accounts are listed below:

| **Balance Sheet** | | **Statement of Earnings and Expenses** | |
|---|---|---|---|
| Cash and interbank deposits | $ 11 | Revenue sources: | |
| Investment securities | ? | Domestic loan interest and fees | $ ? |
| Federal funds sold | 8 | Foreign loan interest and fees | 6 |
| Loans, gross | 81 | Income from security investments | 4 |
| Allowance for loan losses | (6) | Miscellaneous revenues | 1 |
| Unearned discount on loans | (1) | Total revenues | ? |
| Net loans | ? | | |
| Premises and fixed assets | 2 | Expenses: | |
| Miscellaneous assets | 5 | Interest on deposits | ? |
| Total assets | $110 | Interest on nondeposit borrowings | 1 |
| Demand deposits | ? | Salaries and wages | 2 |
| Savings deposits | 20 | Occupancy costs | 1 |
| Time deposits | 65 | Provision for loan losses | 1 |
| Nondeposit borrowings | 12 | Miscellaneous expenses | 2 |
| Total liabilities | ? | Total expenses | 15 |
| Stockholder's equity capital | 4 | Net operating income | 3 |
| | | Income taxes | ? |
| | | Net income (or loss) after taxes | 1 |

4. Suppose you have been given the financial information below for a commercial bank:

| Income taxes owed | $ 13 | Interest on nondeposit borrowings | $ 8 |
| Noninterest revenues from service fees | 70 | Salaries and wages | |
| Interest revenues from loans | 129 | of bank employees | 27 |
| Interest and dividends from | | Overhead costs | 3 |
| investments in securities | 26 | Loan-loss provision | 2 |
| Dividends paid to stockholders | 4 | Securities gains (or losses) | 0 |
| Interest paid to depositors | 64 | | |

a. Calculate this bank's net interest income, net noninterest income, pretax net operating income, net income after taxes, undivided profits (or retained earnings), total revenues, and total expenses.

b. Suppose the above bank's return on assets (ROA)—the ratio of its net income after taxes to total assets—is 0.85 percent. What is the total of the bank's assets in dollars?

c. Suppose this bank's return on stockholders' equity capital (ROE)—the ratio of its net income after taxes to total equity capital—is 12 percent. What is the bank's total equity capital in dollars?

d. Suppose the above bank's total deposits equal 75 percent of its total liabilities. How many deposits in total dollar volume does the bank hold?

## Web-Based Problems

1. As one of the chief regulators of the banking system, the Federal Reserve must monitor the lending activities of commercial banks. The bank loan category typically carrying the greatest default risk is Commercial and Industrial (C&I) Loans. The Fed monitors these particular loans through a survey of Senior Loan Officers. The following will help you get an idea about the types of information this periodic survey provides.

a. Visit the Fed's Web site at **federalreserve.gov** and click on "Surveys and Reports." Then click on "Senior Loan Officer Opinion Survey on Bank Lending Practices" and find the most current survey. Download the "Charts" (pdf) at the bottom of the report.

b. Have banks tightened lending standards on C&I loans since the previous survey?

c. Have banks raised interest rates on C&I loans since the previous survey?

d. Referring to the graphs that you considered in parts (b) and (c), can you identify any patterns that suggest what happens to business lending during recessions?

2. The profits of large, diversified banks do not always mirror those of other industries. Therefore, the market value of their stocks will not necessarily move in lockstep with the stock market as a whole. The purpose of this exercise is to see how well the stocks of the largest of these banks have performed in recent years relative to a broad measure of stock market value—the S&P 500 Stock Index.

a. Go online to a Web site such as that of *The Wall Street Journal*, **online.wsj.com,** and obtain the closing stock prices for the last trading day of each month for the past five years for each of the top four bank holding companies (measured by total assets) listed in the Financial Developments box on page 426. Also, obtain the value of the S&P 500 on those days. Enter these data into a spreadsheet.

b. Assume a hypothetical investment of $100,000 that could have been invested on the first month for which you have collected data in one of two portfolios: (i) $25,000 in each of the banks; or (ii) $100,000 in an index fund based on the S&P 500. Compute the monthly value of your investment for each of these two investment portfolios. How well do they track one another? Were there times when investment (i) was superior to (ii), and vice versa?

c. Compute an annualized rate of return on the two investments you can follow each month. Plot these rates of return. How well do they appear to track one another?

d. One factor that could explain some of the differences you observe is the dividend policy of banks versus that of the "typical" firm. Check on the Web site to discover what the dividend payout (yield) is for banks versus the "typical" firm. Which one is higher? How would this affect the appreciation of banks' stocks versus the market as a whole?

3. As the text explains, the sources of bank revenue have been changing significantly over the past several years and all banks are not making the same choices. For example, some banks have focused more intently on developing their credit-card business, while others have moved into a variety of financial service offerings, while still others have continued to rely upon traditional business and consumer loans to generate revenues. This exercise asks you to compare some of the financial ratios of several of the largest U.S. banks.

a. Please go to a Web site such as *The Wall Street Journal*'s **online.wsj.com** and look up the financial information for each of the banking companies listed in the Financial Developments box on page 426. Obtain their profit margin, return on equity, and return on assets for the past 12 months.

b. According to these measures how did these banking companies perform relative to each other? Relative to the industry average?

c. Can you identify any reasons for significant discrepancies between the financial ratios among these large banking companies?

## Selected References to Explore

1. Bradley, Christine M., and Lynn Shibut. "The Liability Structure of FDIC-Insured Institutions: Changes and Implications," *FDIC Banking Review,* Vol. 18, No. 2 (2006), pp. 1–37.

2. Gowrisankaran, Gautam. "Bank ATMs and ATM Surcharges," *FRBSF Economic Letter,* No. 2005-36, Federal Reserve Bank of San Francisco, December 16, 2005, pp 1–3.

3. Gunther, Jeffrey W., and Robert R. Moore. "Small Banks' Competitors Loom Large," *Southwest Economy,* Federal Reserve Bank of Dallas, January/February 2004, pp. 1, 9–18.

4. Hanc, George. "The Future of Banking in America," *FDIC Banking Review,* Vol. 16, No. 1, Federal Deposit Insurance Corporation, 2004, pp. 1–28.

www.mhhe.com.rose10e

5. Jones, Kenneth D., and Tim Critchfield. "The Declining Number of U.S. Banking Organizations: Will the Trend Continue?" *Future of Banking Study,* Federal Deposit Insurance Corporation, 2004.

6. Poposka, Klimentina; Mark D. Vaughan; and Timothy J. Yeager. "The Two Faces of Banking: Traditional Loans and Deposits vs. Complex Brokerage and Derivative Securities," *The Regional Economist,* Federal Reserve Bank of St. Louis, October 2004, pp. 10–11.

7. Santomero, Anthony M. "Banking in the 21 st Century," *Business Review,* Federal Reserve Bank of Philadelphia, Third Quarter 2004, pp. 1–4.

8. Strahan, Philip E. "Bank Diversification, Economic Diversification?" *FRBSF Economic Letter,* Federal Reserve Bank of San Francisco, No. 2006–10 (May 12, 2006), pp. 1–3.

9. Walter, John R. "Closing Troubled Banks: How the Process Works," *Economic Quarterly,* Federal Reserve Bank of Richmond, Winter 2004, pp. 51–68.

10. Yom, Chiwon. "Limited-Purpose Banks: Their Specialties, Performance, and Prospects," *FDIC Banking Review,* Vol. 17, No. 1, Federal Deposit Insurance Corporation, 2005, pp. 19–36.

# Chapter 15

# Nonbank Thrift Institutions: Savings and Loans, Savings Banks, Credit Unions, and Money Market Funds

## Learning Objectives

### in This Chapter

- You will see how significant *thrift institutions* are in the functioning of a modern economy and financial system.
- You will discover what types of *services* thrift institutions offer to the public and who their principal competitors are.
- You will come to understand the principal differences between major types of thrift institutions as well as their principal similarities and why these differences and similarities are important.

## What's in This Chapter?
## Key Topics Outline

The Savings and Loan and Savings Bank Industries: Origins and Characteristics

Mutuals versus Stock Companies

Deregulation and Sources and Uses of Thrifts' Funds

Maturity Mismatch and Other Thrift Industry Problems

Possible Remedies for Thrift Industry Problems

Credit Unions: Their Uniqueness in Services, Size, and Membership

Credit Union Industry Advantages and Future Challenges

Money Market Mutual Funds: Origins and Competitive Advantages

Money Fund Asset Profiles and Safety Concerns

## 15.1   Introduction to Thrift Institutions

There is a tendency in discussions of the financial system to minimize the role of nonbank financial institutions and to emphasize the part played by commercial banks in the flow of money and credit. For many years, financial experts did not consider the liabilities of nonbank financial institutions—including deposits in savings and loan associations, savings banks, money market funds, and credit unions—as really close substitutes for bank deposits. It was argued that interindustry competition between banks and other financial institutions was slight and, for all practical purposes, could be ignored. Today, however, an entirely different view prevails concerning the relative importance of nonbank financial institutions. We now recognize that these institutions play a vital role in the flow of money and credit within the financial system and are particularly important in selected markets, such as the home mortgage market and the market for personal savings.

In truth, many nonbank financial institutions are becoming increasingly like commercial banks and are competing for many of the same customers. Moreover, banks themselves are offering many of the services traditionally offered by nonbank financial firms, such as brokering securities and selling insurance (often through joint ventures with nonbank firms). Thus, *both* bank and nonbank institutions are rushing toward each other in the services they offer and markets they serve—a phenomenon called *convergence.* This is why financial analysts today stress the importance of studying the *whole* financial institutions' sector to understand how the financial system works. In this chapter and the next, we examine the major types of nonbank financial institutions that channel the public's savings into loans and investments.

## 15.2   Savings and Loan Associations (S&Ls)

**savings and loan associations**

**Savings and loan associations** (S&Ls) are among the largest of all thrift institutions, accepting deposits and extending loans and other services primarily to *household customers.* S&Ls emphasize longer-term loans to individuals and families in contrast to the shorter-term lending focus of many other deposit-type financial institutions. In particular, in the United States savings and loans are a major source of mortgage loans to finance the purchase of single-family homes and multifamily dwellings (such as apartments and duplexes). At the same time, savings and loans today are developing many new financial services to attract customers and boost their earnings.

The history of S&Ls looks much like a roller-coaster ride—periods of prosperity punctuated by periods of financial disaster. For example, hundreds of S&Ls failed during the 1980s and early 1990s, and many have since converted into commercial bank and savings bank charters, some becoming branch offices of other depository institutions. We will discuss the causes of the industry's periodic problems in the sections that follow.

### Origins of S&Ls

The first savings and loans originated in the eighteenth century as British building societies founded on the principle of "neighbors helping neighbors." Many were called *building and loan societies,* in which money was solicited from individuals and families so that certain members of the contributing group could finance the building of their homes. Sometimes the association simply drew names out of a hat to determine who was to receive the next loan. Frequently these building associations were disbanded after all their members had received loans to begin construction of their dwellings. The first U.S. savings and loan appeared in the Philadelphia area in 1831.

The early S&Ls were managed and directed by their depositors with larger depositors often having greater influence in directing the activities of the association. Also, the same individuals and families who provided funds for lending generally were also borrowers from the savings and loan. Gradually over time, however, as S&Ls grew to become major players in the financial marketplace, savers and borrowers were frequently different groups, professional managers were hired to conduct daily operations, and investors in the money and capital markets provided a major share of many associations' funding bases.

As discussed above, S&Ls began essentially as a *single-product industry,* accepting savings deposits from individuals and families and lending those funds to home buyers. More recently, however, competition from banks, credit unions, and mutual funds, coupled with deregulation and many failures, has forced savings and loans to diversify their operations and aggressively solicit new customers.

**mutuals**

Many savings and loans are **mutuals** and, therefore, have *no stockholders.* Technically, they are owned by their depositors. However, many associations are converting or have converted to stock form. *Stockholder-owned S&Ls* can issue capital stock to increase their net worth—a privilege that is particularly important when a savings and loan is growing rapidly and needs an additional source of long-term capital. Stockholder-owned associations, on average, are much larger in size than mutuals.

## How Funds Are Raised and Allocated

Savings and loans, like credit unions, are gradually broadening their role, with many choosing to offer a full line of financial services for individuals and families. Other S&Ls are branching out into business credit and commercial real estate lending.

*Asset Portfolios*    Residential mortgage loans dominate the asset side of the savings and loan business. Exhibit 15.1 shows the combined financial assets and liabilities of both savings and loans and savings banks (which we will discuss next in this chapter).

As revealed in the exhibit, direct mortgage credit (predominantly loans to purchase new homes) accounts for nearly two-thirds of all industry assets. But the current era has brought rapid growth in other housing-related investments, such as mortgage-backed securities, mobile home loans, and home equity loans. Mortgage-backed securities include pass-throughs issued by the Government National Mortgage Association, participation certificates (PCs) issued by the Federal Home Loan Mortgage Corporation, and collateralized mortgage obligations (CMOs). Pass-throughs, PCs, and CMOs are investor shares in the earnings generated by pools of mortgage loans, backed by the issuing government agency or put together by a private lender. As discussed earlier in Chapter 14, these forms of *loan securitizations* allow thrifts to package many of their housing-related loans, remove them from their balance sheets, and generate new sources of fee income. CMOs are a little more flexible than other types of loan-backed securities because they can be found in short, medium, and long maturities, helping S&Ls minimize their risk exposure from changing market interest rates and from mortgage loans being paid off early.

As we will see in Chapter 17, the savings and loan industry was first deregulated in the early 1980s and given broad new service powers, including checking accounts, credit cards and other consumer lending services, commercial real estate loans, trust

| EXHIBIT 15.1 | Combined Financial Balance Sheet of Savings and Loans and Savings Banks, 2006* ($ billions) |
| --- | --- |

| Balance Sheet Item | Amount | Percentage of Total Assets |
| --- | --- | --- |
| Assets: | | |
| Checkable deposits and currency | $  20.7 | 1.1% |
| Reserves held at the Federal Reserve banks | 2.8 | 0.3 |
| Time and savings deposits | 3.4 | 0.2 |
| Federal funds and security RPs | 13.9 | 0.8 |
| Corporate equities | 26.2 | 1.4 |
| U.S. government and federal agency securities | 200.5 | 11.0 |
| State and local government (tax-exempt) securities | 9.4 | 0.5 |
| Corporate and foreign bonds | 86.1 | 4.7 |
| Mortgage loans | 1192.3 | 65.2 |
| Consumer credit | 98.1 | 5.4 |
| Loans to business firms and others | 62.5 | 3.4 |
| Miscellaneous assets | 112.9 | 5.0 |
| Total financial assets | $1,828.8 | 100.0% |
| Liabilities: | | |
| Checkable deposits | $  86.2 | 5.1% |
| Small time and savings deposits | 637.2 | 36.7 |
| Large ($100,000 +) time deposits | 375.8 | 21.6 |
| Borrowings through security repurchase agreements | 77.0 | 4.4 |
| Borrowings from the Federal Home Loan banks and other loans and advances | 318.5 | 18.3 |
| Corporate bonds | 8.5 | 0.5 |
| Investments by parent companies | 12.1 | 0.7 |
| Miscellaneous liabilities | 220.9 | 12.5 |
| Total liabilities | $1,736.8 | 100.0% |

*Figures are for first quarter of 2006. *Note:* Columns need not add to totals because of rounding errors.
Source: Board of Governors of the Federal Reserve System.

services, investments in mutual funds, and the power to invest in riskier corporate and government bonds. Predictably, many S&Ls went overboard, bought too many "junk" bonds, and launched into new services with little preparation, while market interest rate changes added to their losses. Hundreds collapsed, so that by the 1990s, new legislation pushed S&Ls back toward the home mortgage market, where they have the majority of their loans today.

*Liabilities of S&Ls*   Savings deposits provide the bulk of funds available to the savings and loan industry. However, there has been a significant shift in deposit mix in recent years from those savings accounts earning the lowest interest rate to deposits earning higher and more flexible returns. Particularly important among the newer higher-yield savings deposit plans offered by the industry are money market deposit accounts, CDs, NOW and Super NOW accounts, and Keogh and IRA retirement accounts. **Money market deposit accounts (MMDAs)** and Super NOWs were authorized for banks and S&Ls in 1982. Both of these deposit accounts are draftable by

**money market deposit accounts (MMDAs)**

check and carry interest rates that change with market conditions. One unfortunate side effect of these newer deposits is that savings and loans today are faced with a costlier and, at times, a more volatile deposit base.

Savings and loans also rely on several nondeposit sources of funds to support their loans and investments. One of the most important consists of advances (loans) from the Federal Home Loan Bank (FHLB) System, which provides extra liquidity in periods when deposit withdrawals are heavy or when loan demand exceeds incoming deposits. As we saw above, another rapidly growing source of funds is securitized assets, when S&L loans are packaged together into a pool of loans (often backed by the guarantee of a government agency), and debt securities are issued against these pooled assets and sold to investors to raise longer-term funds. Thrift institutions continue to make widening use of *securitized assets,* issued against a growing list of home mortgage and consumer installment loans, to supplement their deposit flows and keep funding costs down. The ability of a loan-securitizing institution to remove securitized assets from its balance sheet tends to lower its total assets and improves its ratio of capital to assets, possibly lessening regulatory pressure on the institution to raise more capital.

Another popular nondeposit funds source is *loan sales*—sales of existing loans to investors in the secondary (resale) market. These sales of S&L assets tend to be heaviest during periods when loan demand is high and deposit growth is sluggish, and they give savings and loans the opportunity to invest in new, higher-yielding loans. They also help S&Ls better diversify their assets and avoid an increased regulatory burden (such as government demands for raising more owners' capital). One danger, however, is that lending institutions may sell their best-quality loans, leaving them with a riskier loan portfolio overall.

Equity capital or net worth (i.e., the retained earnings and reserves held by individual savings and loans) presently makes up only about 5 percent of total S&L funds sources but is important to the public. The net worth account absorbs losses and keeps the doors open until management can correct problems. In the early 1990s the federal government of the United States was empowered by Congress to close those banks and thrifts whose net worth had fallen close to zero. Since then, the S&L industry's net worth position has improved substantially.

## Trends in Revenues and Costs

**Federal Deposit Insurance Corporation (FDIC)**

During the mid-1980s and early 1990s, savings and loans experienced one of the darkest periods in their history. Many savings associations were unprofitable or had little net worth. Dozens of ailing associations were helped into mergers by the **Federal Deposit Insurance Corporation (FDIC),** which purchased sizable amounts of questionable industry assets. The industry's former deposit insurance agency (the FSLIC) went bankrupt during the 1980s, to be replaced at the beginning of the 1990s by the Savings Association Insurance Fund (SAIF), managed by the FDIC. SAIF protected S&L deposits up to $100,000 (though qualified retirement deposits are now covered by federal insurance up to $250,000). At the same time, Congress moved to authorize agency-assisted mergers in which troubled S&Ls could be merged with stronger associations or with other depository institutions (such as a commercial bank through its holding company).

One indication of the industry's recent roller-coaster ride from disaster to success is the track record of its assets, deposits, and net earnings in recent years:

| | Trends in Assets, Deposits, and Net Income after Taxes of U.S. Thrifts: Savings and Loans and Savings Banks | | |
|---|---|---|---|
| Year | Total Financial Assets of Savings and Loans and Savings Banks Reported at Year-End ($ Billions) | Total Deposits of Savings and Loans and Savings Banks Reported at Year-End ($ Billions) | Net Income after Taxes of U.S. Savings and Loans and Savings Banks ($ Millions) |
| 1980 | $ 792 | $ 665 | $ 781 |
| 1988 | 1,641 | 1,605 | −12,057 |
| 1994 | 1,009 | 734 | 4,200 |
| 1996 | 1,032 | 721 | 6,802 |
| 2000 | 1,219 | 727 | 8,014 |
| 2003 | 1,474 | 925 | 18,050 |
| 2005 | 1,837 | 1,068 | 16,416 |
| 2006* | 1,829 | 1,100 | NA |

*2006 figures are for first quarter only.

Source: Board of Governors of the Federal Reserve System, *Flow of Funds Accounts;* Federal Deposit Insurance Corporation; and Office of Thrift Supervision.

**Key URL:**
Trends in the performance of the savings and loan industry may be followed in several Web sites, such as **ots.treas.gov**

As the preceding figures suggest, the industry's overall assets and deposits peaked in 1988 and then began to fall until near the end of the twentieth century—the result of large numbers of failures and the conversions of some S&Ls into other kinds of financial intermediaries (most notably, commercial and savings banks). By the mid-1990s, industry profitability began to improve, however, achieving a return on assets (ROA) of 1.15 percent in 2005, just slightly below the ROA for the commercial banking industry that same year. More than 90 percent of savings and loans reported positive profits, with significantly fewer troubled loans on the books and increased core capital to protect against unexpected losses. Bank holding companies have helped to strengthen the S&L industry by purchasing large numbers of thrifts, converting many to bank charters or turning them into branch offices of existing banks.

Recent industry earnings might have been even higher except for mandates from the U.S. government that thrifts help recapitalize the Savings Association Insurance Fund (SAIF) in order to bring its deposit insurance reserves up to the levels required by the U.S. Congress. Nevertheless, S&Ls continue to gather strength in the new century and are becoming quite innovative, developing many new fee-based income-generating services (including servicing outstanding home mortgage loans, selling loans in the secondary market, and offering credit card plans). Many S&Ls are directing their lending into newer areas—such as construction loans, commercial real estate loans, and consumer loans used for purposes other than buying a new home (including financing college educations, starting new businesses, or purchasing new or used automobiles). Moreover, these thrift institutions have turned increasingly to the Federal Home Loan Banks (FHLBs)—federal agencies designed to help the thrift industry—and to new security issues to fund their operations when their deposits have grown too slowly.

What factors got the savings and loan industry into such serious trouble during the 1980s and 1990s? Might these same factors reappear and cause trouble again in the future? Why did the industry nearly collapse and so many S&Ls sink beneath the

**Key URLs:**
One of the innovative ways some leading savings associations chose to reduce the gap between their interest-sensitive assets and liabilities has been to offer *adjustable-rate mortgages* (ARMs) whose rate of return changes with market interest rates. A few, such as Golden West Financial, went a step further in offering *option ARMs*, permitting home buyers to vary what they pay monthly down to some minimum amount. However, when home buyers pay less than the full amount due, the unpaid amounts are added to the customer's loan balance, resulting in "negative amortization." If interest rates rise, ARMs result in a heavier burden for individuals and families carrying home mortgage debt. For examples, see **golden westfinance.com** which was acquired in 2006 by **wachovia.com**.

waves during this earlier period of crisis? One primary cause was the fact that savings and loans, historically, have issued mortgage loans carrying mostly fixed interest rates while selling deposits to the public whose interest rates closely mirror changing market conditions. In short, many S&L assets were interest rate *insensitive* in earlier years (and many still are), while most of their liabilities have been (and still are) highly interest rate *sensitive*. During periods of rapidly rising market interest rates, the industry's net interest margin—the difference between interest earnings on assets and interest costs on borrowed funds—has often been severely squeezed. Indeed, in several recent periods, short-term interest rates paid on deposits exceeded interest rates earned on long-term loans, and the industry's net interest margin turned *negative* for a time.

Other recent trends also have kept average S&L profitably below that of commercial banks. The individuals and families whose savings provide the bulk of association funds have become more financially sophisticated, withdrawing deposits whenever high returns are available elsewhere or whenever there is even a hint of trouble in the industry. Unquestionably, the savings and loan industry has been damaged to some extent by the growth of money market funds—aggressive institutions that offer small savers higher and more flexible yields—and, more recently, by the public's keen interest in stock and bond mutual funds. At the same time, government rules have prevented S&Ls from introducing more flexibility into their investments so their revenues can grow as fast as their operating costs.

The pressures of competition and technological change have caused many savings and loans to merge or be absorbed by larger institutions. As a result, the number of independently owned associations in the United States has been declining for more than four decades. The S&L population decreased from about 6,300 in 1960 to only about 1,200 by the beginning of the new century. By 2005 FDIC-insured savings associations (including both savings and loans and savings banks) numbered only about 1,300 institutions or less than one-sixth of the number of commercial banks operating in the United States. More savings and loans are likely to be absorbed into larger financial institutions (especially bank holding companies) in the future, and many current savings associations are likely to have their thrift charters converted into bank charters in order to be able to offer a wider range of financial services. Among the leading S&Ls and savings banks headquartered in the United States today include Washington Mutual, Seattle, at **wamu.com;** Golden West Financial Corp., Oakland, at **worldsavings.com;** Sovereign Bancorp, Philadelphia, at **sovereignbank.com;** Astoria Financial Corp, Lake Success, at **astoriafederal.com;** ING Bank, St. Cloud, Minnesota, at **www.ing.com;** E*Trade Bank in New York City at **bank.etrade.com;** and Indy Mac Bancorp, Inc., Pasedena, California, at **myindymacbank.com.**

## *Possible Ways to Strengthen the S&L Industry in the Future*

If savings and loans are to continue to be competitive and remain successful thrift institutions in the future, they will need help from several sources: (1) sound decision making by management to further diversify their activities by geographic area and services offered; (2) careful management of the loan portfolio to put good loans on the books and minimize future loan losses; (3) better use of risk-management tools (such as financial futures, swaps, and options) to reduce interest rate risk exposure and minimize damage from maturity mismatches; and (4) further relaxation of government regulations to permit the offering of new services and the merging of smaller associations into larger financial-service companies.

Savings and loan associations, savings banks, and credit unions face a common problem that, at several times in the past, has caused many of them to fail. *The maturities* (and, therefore, the expected streams of future cash payments) *of many of their assets and their liabilities do not match*. In particular, asset maturities are usually longer than the maturities attached to their liabilities. For example, the majority of savings and loan and savings bank assets are home mortgage loans, which usually take years to pay out, while the bulk of their liabilities are savings deposits and checking accounts that are often turned into cash in a matter of hours, days, or weeks. This means that thrifts must be prepared to pay out large amounts of cash on short notice. Moreover, the interest costs on their borrowed funds (including interest owed on deposits) tend to change faster, up or down, than the interest revenues from their assets.

Suppose their volume of *interest-rate-sensitive liabilities (ISL)* (consisting largely of short-term savings and checkable deposits) exceeds their volume of *interest-rate-sensitive assets (ISA)* (such as floating-rate loans or short-term loans about to mature). That is, for most thrift institutions, ISA < ISL. A liability or an asset is interest sensitive if its rate of return changes with market conditions. This difference in the thrifts'

volume of interest-rate-sensitive assets and liabilities is called the GAP:

$$GAP = ISA - ISL$$

If rate-sensitive liabilities are larger than rate-sensitive assets, the GAP is *negative*, which is the situation for many thrift institutions.

The GAP concept tells us that a thrift with a negative GAP will lose interest income if interest rates rise. Interest costs attached to the thrift's rate-sensitive liabilities will move upward by greater volume than the revenues from rate-sensitive assets. The thrift's net interest income (i.e., interest revenues less interest expenses) will tend to fall.

We can visualize this classic maturity mismatch faced by many thrift institutions by viewing the diagram below. Deposit rates, like most other short-term interest rates, change rapidly and move over a wide range, rising as the economy expands and inflation increases and falling as the economy slows down or inflation weakens. In contrast, the average rate of return on a thrift's long-term assets tends to change more slowly. Losses build up when short-term interest rates exceed long-term interest rates. We recall from Chapter 7 that this situation coincides with an "inverted yield curve"—often a harbinger of a slowdown in the economy.

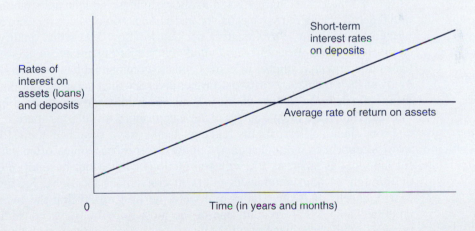

Aggressive S&Ls today are branching out in several different directions. Some have followed a *real estate model*, literally becoming mortgage banking firms. These savings associations are selling off their long-term mortgages and converting into real estate service organizations, managing and developing property and brokering mortgages. Others have become *family financial centers*, offering a full range of retail financial services to the consumer. Home mortgages continue to dominate their asset portfolios, but most S&Ls today offer adjustable-rate mortgages (ARMs), whose yields adjust more readily to changing market conditions, as well as fixed-rate mortgages (FRMs) and a wide variety of other consumer-oriented loans. Other S&Ls have adopted a *diversified model,* becoming holding company organizations with ownership of retail-oriented consumer banks, mortgage banking firms, commercial credit affiliates, and other businesses. Only time will tell which of these models will continue to be successful amid the changing character of the financial marketplace. One hopeful sign has been the return to profitability of many S&Ls that survived the terrible debacle of the 1980s and 1990s and managed to direct their assets into better-quality investments and achieve greater operating efficiency.

## 15.3   Savings Banks (SBs)

**savings banks**

**Savings banks** were first established in 1810 by Reverend Henry Duncan, minister of Ruthwell Church in Dumfriesshire, Scotland, where the Savings Bank Museum now resides. These customer-owned institutions were originally set up to combat poverty and grant low-income savers and borrowers access to the financial system. Up to that time small savers and borrowers were virtually shut out of the markets for credit and thrift services.

The idea behind savings banking spread rapidly around the globe, especially in Europe and along the East Coast of the United States. The first savings bank in the United States, the Philadelphia Savings Fund Society, appeared in 1816. Through much of their history savings banks concentrated upon the sale of two key services—savings accounts and residential (home) mortgage loans. Today, however, they have expanded far beyond their original service menu, trading corporate and government bonds and stock; offering credit and debit cards; granting installment loans to purchase autos, appliances, and other household items; and granting loans for commercial construction.

In 1982 the U.S. Congress voted to allow savings and loan associations to convert into federally chartered savings banks, and savings banks to convert into S&Ls if they wished to do so. In 1989 Congress decided to allow S&Ls that qualify to become commercial banks. Recently, substantial numbers of S&Ls have converted to savings banks (along with a number of conversions to commercial bank charters) in an effort to lower their regulatory costs and further diversify their services. For this reason, the distinction between savings and loans, savings banks, and commercial banks is very blurred. The public often cannot tell these depository institutions apart.

From their earliest origins, savings banks have designed their financial services to appeal to individuals and families. Deposit accounts often can be opened for amounts as small as $1, with transactions carried out by mail, electronically, or through 24-hour automated tellers in convenient locations. Savings banks in Massachusetts and New Hampshire were the first to develop the interest-bearing and checkable NOW account, one of the most important new consumer financial services of the past generation. Many savings banks advertise the availability of family financial counseling services, home equity loans, and a wide variety of home mortgages and personal savings instruments.

### Number and Distribution of Savings Banks and Regulatory Supervision

The number of savings banks operating today is relatively small. The combined total of FDIC-insured savings and loans and savings banks fell from 3,626 in 1985 to only

**Key URLs:**
To learn more about the history and recent problems of the savings bank industry see, for example, **answers .com/savings9020banks** or **savingsbankmuseum .co.uk/savings-banks-history.html**

**Key URL:**
The key federal regulator of savings associations is the Office of Thrift Supervision at **ots. treas.gov**

**Key URL:**
For additional information about the performance measures frequently used to assess the behavior of savings and loans and savings banks each year see, in particular, **financial servicesfacts.org/ financial2/banking/ thriftinstitutions**

about 1,300 by 2005. The U.S. Congress authorized the chartering of federal savings banks (FSBs) in 1978, which led to an increase for a time in the savings bank population. Unfortunately, many of these institutions failed in the economic dislocations of the late 1980s and early 1990s, along with hundreds of savings and loan associations. Savings banks today are scattered throughout the United States. Massachusetts leads the list, followed by New York. Other states in which savings banks are important include California, Connecticut, Maine, New Hampshire, New Jersey, Pennsylvania, Texas, and Wisconsin.

At the level of the federal government, as opposed to the states, the Office of Thrift Supervision (OTS) is the primary federal rulemaker and enforcer for federally chartered and state-chartered savings associations—both savings and loans and savings banks. Established inside the U.S. Treasury Department in 1989, the OTS has offices in Washington D.C., Atlanta, Dallas, Jersey City, and San Francisco. Its supervisory activities are supported financially by assessments and fees charged thrift institutions.

## How Funds Are Raised and Allocated

Technically, savings banks are owned by their depositors. All earnings available after funds are set aside to provide adequate reserves must be paid to the depositors as owners' dividends. The industry's role in the financial system can be seen by looking at its financial balance sheet, which is shown for both savings and loans and savings banks combined in Exhibit 15.1. On the asset side, the key instruments are mortgage loans and mortgage-related instruments, which account for the majority of industry assets.

Most of the mortgage total represents direct mortgage loans to build single-family homes, apartments, shopping centers, and other commercial and residential structures. The remainder of the mortgage asset total is devoted primarily to mortgage-backed securities, such as Government National Mortgage Association (GNMA) pass-through securities (also known as Ginnie Maes), and similar mortgage-related securities backed by pools of mortgages.[1]

A distant second in importance to mortgages are savings bank investments in non-mortgage loans (mainly consumer installment credit to finance purchases of furniture and appliances, autos, educational and medical services, and other household cash needs), corporate bonds, corporate stock, and government bonds. Also, many states have recently liberalized their regulations to allow savings banks to make increased purchases of common and preferred stock. Because most of their stock dividend income is exempt from federal taxation or carries a very low tax rate, savings banks recently have taken greater interest in the stock market, though law and tradition limit the growth of savings bank investments in the stock market.

The principal source of funds for savings banks is *deposits.* Savings deposits have no specific maturity but may be withdrawn at any time by the customer, and they generally carry among the lowest rates of interest. Time deposits, on the other hand, have fixed maturities, and savings banks tend to pay higher interest rates on these deposit accounts, depending on their maturity date.

The larger savings banks have established extensive branch office systems and have been highly innovative in offering new services. Nearly all savings banks today offer checkable NOW accounts, money orders, loans against savings accounts, and home equity and home improvement loans. Many savings banks also offer life insurance policies to their customers where permitted by law.

---

[1] See Chapter 22 for a discussion of GNMA pass-throughs and other mortgage-related securities.

One of the more alarming developments in the financial institutions' sector as the twenty-first century began to unfold was the rapid rise of *subprime lending* by banks and thrift institutions. This form of credit consists mainly of consumer and small business loans extended to poor credit risks at lofty interest rates.

Subprime lending rests on the principle that if you as a lender price a low-quality loan correctly to account for its added risk, you can still make money from such a loan despite the risks involved. The higher the degree of risk exposure (i.e., the lower the borrower's credit rating), the more the lender charges to compensate for risk exposure—sometimes well above a 20 percent interest rate. Some authorities refer to the highest-cost subprime loans as "predatory lending" because borrowers are more likely to default on such loans.

Unfortunately for some financial institutions over the past decade, loan losses outstripped revenue growth as loan defaults soared. Moreover, many high-risk borrowers were able to get their high-rate loans refinanced, paying off their subprime lenders sooner than expected. Subprime lending proved to be highly sensitive to economic conditions; a weaker economy generated a large volume of defaults among subprime loans and failures among lenders who granted them.

An added cause of problems in this field are "loan residuals" in which certain loans are packaged together and securities representing claims against the pool of loans are sold to investors in the capital market. Because the loan package is, on the whole, less risky than individual loans would be, the lender is able to borrow more cheaply using securitized loans as collateral and profit from a more favorable interest-rate spread. This spread or "residual" is usually recorded on the lender's balance sheet as an asset, though it can be a volatile one. Higher interest rates often cause these "residual" assets to plunge in value.

Some of the largest depository institutions ran into trouble as a result of subprime lending, such as First Union Corp.'s Money Store, which was closed in 1998. These events suggest that a prolonged economic slump can create serious losses on subprime loans. For this reason, bank and thrift regulators have been discouraging highly risky subprime lending.

**Key URLs:**
For a more in-depth look at the savings bank industry, you may wish to visit the Web sites of such popular institutions as American Federal Savings Bank at **americanfsb.com** and Washington Mutual Savings Bank at **washingtonmutual .com**

Like savings and loan associations, savings banks have discovered that the customers they serve have become more financially sophisticated in recent years. Higher-yielding deposit accounts have grown faster than lower-yielding savings plans. The most pronounced shift has been from regular passbook savings accounts to fixed-maturity time deposits and money market accounts that carry contract interest rates that float with market conditions. The net result of all of these changes has been to push up overall interest expenses, put pressure on earnings, and, at times, increase the volatility of savings bank funds flows. Savings banks today must also be more concerned with changing electronic technology, which is forcing them to automate more of their routine services and make customer access to their facilities and services more convenient than ever before.

## Current Trends and Future Problems

**Key URLs:**
To learn more about savings banking in Europe, where the industry began, see especially **savings-banks.org/** and **scotbanks.org. uk/banking-history.php**

The savings bank industry faces a number of problems that will significantly affect its future as a conduit for savings and investment. One factor is increasing competition with savings and loan associations, credit unions, and commercial banks offering similar services. Because of the heavy concentration of savings bank assets in mortgage-related investments, savings banks are less flexible than commercial banks in adjusting to changing financial conditions and to the changing service needs of their customers. Some have earnings problems due to inflexible asset structures and bad loans, coupled with higher fund-raising costs. On the other hand, many savings banks have countered this relative inflexibility in their asset structures with aggressive competition for funds and innovative new services. The future growth of this industry, like that of most other financial institutions, will depend heavily on its ability to gain the necessary changes in government regulations in order to respond to changing financial market conditions.

---

**QUESTIONS TO HELP YOU STUDY**

1. How did *savings and loans* get started? How does the history of savings and loans compare with the history of *savings banks?* Which is the oldest institution?

2. What exactly are *mutuals?* How do these institutions differ from stockholder-owned depository institutions?

3. Why did the savings and loan industry and some savings banks get into serious trouble during the 1980s and 1990s?

4. What solutions have been developed to deal with the savings and loan and savings bank industries' problems and to strengthen their performance in the twenty-first century?

---

## 15.4 Credit Unions (CUs)

**credit unions**

The characteristics and operations of **credit unions**—among the most numerous of thrift institutions—have been a largely neglected area of research in the financial system. Recently, however, there has been a revival of interest in credit union behavior. One reason has been the rapid growth of this financial intermediary. For example, credit union assets have more than tripled since 1990 (see Exhibit 15.2), though a combination of failures and mergers among smaller CUs has recently slowed credit union growth somewhat. U.S. credit unions are the third-largest institutional supplier of nonmortgage installment credit to individuals and families,

| EXHIBIT 15.2 | Credit Unions in the United States and around the Globe | | |
|---|---|---|---|
| Year | Number of Credit Unions in the United States | Number of Credit Union Members in the United States | U.S. Credit Union Assets ($ Millions) |
| 1950 | 10,586 | 4,617,086 | $ 1,005 |
| 1960 | 20,094 | 12,025,393 | 5,651 |
| 1970 | 23,687 | 22,775,511 | 17,872 |
| 1980 | 21,465 | 43,930,569 | 68,974 |
| 1990 | 14,549 | 61,610,957 | 221,759 |
| 2000 | 10,684 | 79,751,853 | 449,799 |
| 2005 | 8,695 | 84,810,000 | 678,697 |

**Credit Unions around the Globe:**

Number of credit unions belonging to the World Council of Credit Unions, 2005: 42,705 CUs

Worldwide membership, 2005: 157,103,072 people

Worldwide assets (in U.S. dollars): $894.5 billion

Sources: Credit Union National Association, *Credit Union Report 2005;* World Council of Credit Unions, Inc., *2005 Statistical Report;* and Board of Governors of the Federal Reserve System, *Flow of Funds Accounts.*

trailing only commercial banks and finance companies and outstripping installment credit extended by savings and loans and savings banks more than two-to-one. These institutions are household-oriented intermediaries, offering deposit and credit services to individuals and families. Their long-run survival stems mainly from being able to offer low loan rates and high deposit interest rates to their customers and from their relatively low operating costs associated with the help of volunteers and simple organizational structures.

Credit unions are cooperative, self-help associations of individuals rather than profit-motivated financial institutions. Savings deposits and loans are offered only to members of each association and not to the general public. The members of a CU are technically the *owners,* receiving dividends and sharing in any losses that occur. Each member gets one vote regardless of the size of his or her account.

Credit unions began in nineteenth-century Germany in order to serve low-income individuals and families, working primarily in industrial jobs and on farms, by providing them with inexpensive credit and a ready outlet for their savings. The CU movement began as a response to "loan sharking," where poorer households were charged extremely high interest rates (*usury*) for small cash loans. They came to the United States (beginning in the state of New Hampshire) in 1909. Early growth was modest until the 1950s, when these institutions broadened their appeal to middle-income individuals by offering many new financial services.

The credit union sector remains small compared to other major financial institutions, accounting for only about 10 percent of all consumer savings in the United States. However, worldwide, the industry's potential for future growth appears promising due to its innovative character and solid public acceptance. The CU has become an aggressive competitor of banks and savings associations for both savings accounts and consumer installment loans. Beginning in 1978, credit unions were authorized to offer money market certificates, which can carry the same terms as the money market deposit plans sold by banks. In addition, many CUs offer payroll savings plans through which employees can automatically set aside a portion of their salary in a savings account.

Credit union loans have kept pace with the growth of their deposits and today account for about 10 percent of all consumer installment loans in the United States and a substantial portion of these loans worldwide. Consumer loan rates charged by CUs are fully competitive with (and often lower than) loan rates charged by most other major consumer lenders. Moreover, CUs frequently grant their borrowing members interest refunds of up to 20 percent of the amount of a loan. Some credit unions provide life insurance free to their borrowing customers, a service charged for by most other lending institutions. Thus, CUs often accept a smaller spread between their loan and deposit interest rates. This is possible because their operating costs are among the lowest of all financial-service firms. Frequently, the sponsoring employer or association provides free office facilities, and credit union members elect officers and directors who frequently serve with no compensation at all.

Interestingly enough, CUs often report one of the lowest default and delinquency rates on their loans of any lending institution in the financial system. Why? One reason is that they make fewer business loans than many competing financial institutions (especially banks), which, particularly during downturns in the economy, can become very risky credits. Another factor is something we are about to discuss—the common bond between credit union members which seems to encourage most borrowing members to repay their loans in a timely fashion.

**Key URLs:**
To learn more about credit unions, you may enjoy viewing their Web sites—for example, take a look at the site of the American Credit Union of Milwaukee at **americancu.org** and the Chicago Post Office Employees Credit Union at **mycreditunion.com**

## Credit Union Membership

CUs are organized around a common affiliation or *common bond* among their members. Most members work for the same employer or for one of a group of related employers. Moreover, if one family member belongs to a credit union, other family members usually are eligible as well. Occupation-related CUs account for about two-thirds of all U.S. credit unions. About one-fifth are organized around nonprofit associations, such as a labor union, a church, or a fraternal or social organization. Common area of residence, such as a city or state, and age (e.g., an association for retired persons) have also been used to get CUs started. The Federal Credit Union Act permits these types of credit unions: (1) common bond (members from a single group); (2) community (members from a single area); and (3) multiple bond (members from several groups).

In recent years, CUs have been allowed to define their members' common bond so liberally that millions of people have become eligible for credit union membership, and the industry in the United States has recently come under attack in the courts by bankers' groups for its lenient membership rules and special tax advantages. During its 1998 term, the U.S. Supreme Court voted to limit membership in federally chartered CUs to members working for a single employer or to individuals residing in the same community—that is, individuals must share a single common bond. Recent legislation introduced in Congress has now overridden key parts of that Supreme Court ruling, however, allowing most credit unions to keep their existing membership base and to merge multiple (unrelated) fields of membership.

## Size of Credit Unions

There is a strong shift today toward fewer, but larger CUs. For example, the number of associations reached an all-time high in 1969 at almost 24,000 but now totals fewer than 9,000 in the United States, with the decline due primarily to mergers, failures, and a structural shift in the U.S. economy away from manufacturing industries (where credit unions have concentrated historically) toward more service industries (where CU activity tends to be more subdued). With fewer credit unions but continued industry growth, the average-size CU has risen substantially in recent years.

For example, although only about one-sixth of credit unions held more than $1 million in assets in 1970, today the median-size credit union falls in the $2 to $5 million asset size range. This suggests that *size* does matter in today's credit union business. There is evidence (e.g., in Wilcox [5,6]) of substantial economies of scale in the credit union industry, whereas such economies are more modest in banking. The biggest CUs have a significant cost advantage over smaller ones as evidenced by the fact that between 1980 and 2004 the asset size of the average credit union increased about tenfold.

Bigger CUs have outperformed smaller ones, reporting lower noninterest expenses and higher net incomes. Larger credit unions, accordingly, are able to pay higher interest rates to their deposit customers. These performance advantages for larger credit unions should put pressure on the CU industry to continue consolidating into fewer, but larger institutions for years to come.

Accompanying these changes in the average size of a CU worldwide, total membership has not stopped its upward climb either. Around the globe more than 150 million people belong to one or more of over 42,000 credit unions scattered across nearly 100 countries. Inside the United States alone, CU members grew from fewer than 5 million people in 1950 to nearly 85 million early in this new century.

Financial institutions do battle not only within their market areas, fighting each other for the attention of customers, but also in courts and legislative bodies over differences in the rules and regulations they face. For example, when the set of rules applying to banks becomes more restrictive than the set of rules applying to credit unions, a phenomenon called "regulatory arbitrage" may occur. CUs may grow faster than banks. Bankers may fight back, both in the marketplace and through the legal process.

U.S. bankers fought back in the courts, and by February 1998 had won a considerable victory in the U.S. Supreme Court, forcing future credit union membership to be limited more closely to traditional common-bond boundaries. However, U.S. CUs appealed this court decision to their supporters in Congress and overturned much of it via new legislation—the Credit Union Membership Access Act. This bill (H. R. 1151), signed into law by President Clinton in August 1998, divides CUs into several different groups:

1. Single-common-bond credit unions whose members share a common occupation or association.

2. Multiple-common-bond credit unions with members arising from more than one group having a common bond.

3. Community credit union members, living in or joining an organization that is part of a well-defined local area or neighborhood.

This latest credit union law limits multiple-common-bond CUs to 3,000 members except in cases where the National Credit Union Administration (NCUA) finds that achieving efficiency or safety and soundness requires a larger organization. Moreover, NCUA can approve larger multiple-common-bond CUs if a particular area seems to be underserved. Existing credit union memberships are grandfathered under this most recent law, thereby allowing previously diverse CUs to continue operating with their current members.

Credit unions can expand their membership if they are adequately capitalized, are capable of serving larger numbers of people, provide affordable services, are operating in safety, and would not harm existing credit unions. However, as they expand, CUs must conform to capitalization (net worth) rules similar to those faced by banks and other thrift institutions, and the largest CUs must have annual independent audits. Finally, credit unions were granted an avenue of escape from their industry if they so desire—they can convert themselves into banks and other types of depository institutions, enjoying more lenient capital requirements, broader business lending services, and issuing shares of stock, though they will then face taxes.

Note: For more on credit unions, see especially No.s 96–843, 96–847, 1185.ct.927, and Emmons and Schmid [2].

## New Services Offered

**share drafts**

Credit unions are expanding the number of services they offer. Some sell life insurance. Others act as brokers for group insurance plans where state law permits. Many CUs are active in offering 24-hour automated or telephone and Internet services, travelers checks, financial planning services, retirement savings, credit cards, home equity and first-mortgage loans, and money orders. Larger credit unions compete directly with banks for transaction accounts by offering **share drafts**—interest-bearing checkbook deposits. A substantial proportion of U.S. CUs also offer credit cards and automated teller machines (many of which are linked nationwide through an electronic exchange network in order to accommodate members who travel). Several recently began to take loan applications via fax and personal computers and offer preauthorized drafts, telephone, or electronic bill paying.

U.S. credit unions are under intense pressure to develop new services and penetrate new markets due to increasing competition from other financial institutions and a decline in the demand for their historically most important credit service—automobile loans—where they face fierce competition from banks and finance companies (such as GMAC and Ford Motor Credit). In addition, because a larger proportion of family income today is spent on food, fuel, education, and other necessities, CUs have been shifting many of their loans into these areas. First-mortgage loans to purchase new homes and second-mortgage loans to repair or improve existing homes, as well as home equity credit to fund a wide variety of household purchases, have grown rapidly and now account for roughly a third of all credit union assets. (See Exhibit 15.3.) Finally, loans to small businesses have recently been added to many CU service menus, along with auto and equipment leases. As the new century unfolded, credit unions' most rapidly growing loans included fixed- and adjustable-rate first home mortgages, second home mortgage loans, and home equity loans and lines of credit.

Like banks, credit unions have a dual (federal and state) regulatory structure. First chartered only by the states, the federal government entered the picture in 1934 with passage of the Federal Credit Union Act, which created the National Credit Union Administration. The NCUA issues charters of incorporation for federally supervised CUs. A second layer exists in the industry today in the form of corporate credit unions (CCUs), that make loans to CUs in need of financial help, process their checks, and professionally invest credit union funds.

Under current rules in the United States, credit unions are permitted to make unsecured loans to members (including credit-card loans) not exceeding five years to maturity and to grant secured loans out to 30 years. In 2006 the Financial-Services Regulatory Relief Act allowed federal credit unions to extend loans out to 15 years and to offer check-cashing and money transfer services to anyone in their field of membership. Their permissible investments in securities are limited to a list prescribed by either state or federal regulations. In the main, CUs are permitted to acquire

**Key URLs:**
Up-to-date news about developments in the credit union industry may be found in **cujournal.com** and in the Credit Union Times at **cutimes.com**

| EXHIBIT 15.3 | Financial Assets and Liabilities Held by U.S. Credit Unions, 1980–2006 ($ billions) | | | |
|---|---|---|---|---|
| Item | 1980 | 1990 | 2000 | 2006* |
| **Financial Assets:** | | | | |
| Checkable deposits and currency | $ 1.2 | $ 4.8 | $ 26.7 | $ 47.3 |
| Time and savings deposits | 7.1 | 21.7 | 15.5 | 20.8 |
| Federal funds loans and security RPs | 0.7 | 14.6 | 4.0 | 9.2 |
| U.S. government and federal agency securities | 4.3 | 23.0 | 69.1 | 121.7 |
| Home mortgage and equity loans | 4.7 | 48.2 | 124.9 | 249.2 |
| Consumer installment loans | 44.0 | 93.1 | 184.4 | 228.8 |
| Miscellaneous assets | 5.7 | 9.3 | 16.3 | 25.6 |
| Total financial assets | $67.7 | $214.7 | $440.9 | $702.6 |
| **Liabilities:** | | | | |
| Checkable deposits/shares | $ 3.3 | $ 22.2 | $ 51.3 | $ 78.2 |
| Small time and savings deposits/shares | 57.9 | 175.3 | 312.7 | 462.6 |
| Large ($100,000+) deposits/shares | 0.5 | 3.3 | 25.1 | 63.8 |
| Loans from the Federal Home Loan banks and other advances | — | — | 3.4 | 14.6 |
| Miscellaneous liabilities | 3.1 | 3.9 | 5.6 | 19.7 |
| Total liabilities | $64.8 | $204.7 | $398.1 | $638.9 |

*Figures for 2006 are as of the first quarter.

Source: Board of Governors of the Federal Reserve System, *Flow of Funds Accounts,* selected issues.

U.S. government securities; to hold savings deposits at banks, savings and loan associations, and federally insured credit unions; and to purchase selected federal agency securities. They rely heavily on U.S. government securities and on savings deposits to provide liquidity to meet deposit withdrawals and accommodate member credit needs. CUs pay dividends to their members, but they are considered *nonprofit associations,* doing business only with their owners, and, therefore, are classified as *tax-exempt mutual organizations.* Among the largest credit unions in the United States are the Navy Federal Credit Union, Virginia, at **navyfcu.org;** the State Employees' Credit Union at **www.secu.org;** the Pentagon Credit Union at **www.pennfed.org;** the Boeing Employees Credit Union at **www.becu.org;** and the Orange County Teachers Credit Union at **www.octfeu.org.**

## A Strong Competitive Force

Credit unions represent stiff competition for commercial banks, savings banks, and other financial institutions serving consumers. Today, roughly one of every four Americans belongs to a credit union—roughly double the proportion of a decade earlier. True, the total number of CUs is down in some areas, such as in the United States, where a consolidation movement is under way. However, this industry has repeatedly demonstrated its capacity for service innovation and its ability to compete successfully for both consumer loans and savings accounts against some of the largest financial-service competitors in the world.

The American Bankers Association (ABA) has strongly objected to the many advantages under law that credit unions appear to possess compared to commercial banks. These advantages include an exemption from federal income taxes, while banks pay a substantial portion of their earnings (roughly a third in recent years) in federal taxes. Moreover, with the help of their trade associations (such as the Credit Union National Association) and their regulators (such as the National Credit Union Administration), CUs appear to many bankers to have reached far beyond their original charters which called for providing small cash loans at reasonable interest rates and a safe outlet for family savings. Instead, credit unions today appear to be aggressive multiservice financial intermediaries, active in such diverse fields as small business loans, home mortgage and home equity loans, and recreational vehicle lending, as well as providing such services as selling insurance and brokering stocks and bonds. Then, too, bankers must support their local communities with development loans and other services under the terms of the Community Reinvestment Act (CRA). In contrast, CUs are generally exempt from this kind of direct community support. The ABA and other banking groups have filed lawsuits to limit the services credit unions can offer, restrict how far they can reach to attract new members, or make them follow the same rules for taxation and community support as bankers face. To date, CUs have successfully defended themselves against most of these challenges.

## 15.5  Money Market Funds (MMFs)

A fourth major nonbank thrift institution appeared on the scene as recently as 1974. In that year, the first **money market mutual fund**—a financial intermediary pooling the savings of thousands of individuals and businesses and investing those monies in short-term, high-quality money market instruments—opened for business. Taking advantage of the fact that interest rates on most deposits offered by commercial and savings banks were then restrained by government regulation, the money fund offered share accounts

**Key URL:**
To learn more about the American Bankers Association's position on credit unions, see especially **aba. com/Industry+Issues/ Issues_CU_menu.htm**

**Key URLs:**
To compare credit unions with banks and other thrift institutions, recent studies prepared by the U.S. Treasury Department may be helpful. Visit **treasury. gov/press/releases/ report3070.htm** and **treasury. gov/press/releases/ report3071.htm**

**money market mutual fund**

whose yields were free to reflect prevailing interest rates in the money marketplace. Thus, the money fund represents the classic case of profit-seeking entrepreneurs finding a loophole around ill-conceived government regulations (many of which have since been repealed or eased). Leading money market funds today include such institutions as Merrill Lynch CMA Money Fund at **askmerrill.ml.com;** Fidelity Cash Reserves at **fidelityinvestor.com;** Touchstone Money Market Fund at **touchstonefunds.com;** and Vanguard MMR Prime Portfolio at **Vanguard.Fasttrack.Net.**

**Key URL:**
The most frequently asked questions about money market funds are answered by The Investment Company Institute at **ici.org/aboutfunds**

The growth of money market funds was explosive. As of year-end 1973, there were only 15 in existence, with assets totaling just $100 million. Money funds appeared to peak in 1982, when more than 200 of them held about $200 billion in assets (see Exhibit 15.4). Beginning in late 1982 and 1983, a decline in their assets set in as depository institutions fought back with Super NOWs and money market deposit accounts (MMDAs), both authorized by the U.S. government in 1982 to carry unregulated interest rates. Subsequently, however, money market funds resumed their rapid growth, making sharp gains during the late 1980s, the 1990s, and into the twenty-first century. In fact, 2001 was the best year ever in money market fund history, with assets spiraling upward to a record of nearly $2.3 trillion late in that year before sliding back to about $2 trillion held in 989 money funds in 2006.

This recent growth pattern probably reflects several factors, including increased public concern about saving and preparing for the retirement years and the public's concerns about risks in the economy, particularly after the recession and the terrorist attacks of 2001. Another factor boosting money funds is the comparatively light regulations tying the industry down. There are no legal interest rate ceilings limiting what a money fund can pay to its shareholders and, unless a money fund happens to impose them, no penalties for early withdrawal of funds, as is required of customers by many commercial banks and thrift institutions.

**Key URLs:**
If you are interested in further exploring the operation of money market funds, see, for example, Scudder Tax-Free Funds at **scudder.com** and the Franklin Tax-Exempt Money Fund at **franklintempleton.com**

However, money market funds are not without their limitations. For example, during the 1980s a number of these thrifts reached out for riskier, but higher yielding, issues of commercial paper (i.e., short-term corporate notes) so they could offer

| EXHIBIT 15.4 | Money Market Funds: Assets Held and Total Shares Outstanding, 1980–2006* ($ billions) | | | |
|---|---|---|---|---|
| Item | 1980 | 1990 | 2000 | 2006* |
| Financial Assets: | | | | |
| Checkable deposits and currency | $ 0.2 | $ 11.4 | $ 2.2 | $ −4.3 |
| Time and savings deposits | 21.0 | 21.0 | 142.4 | 183.5 |
| Loans made through security RPs | 5.6 | 59.0 | 183.0 | 341.4 |
| Foreign deposits | 6.8 | 27.1 | 91.1 | 97.3 |
| U.S. government and federal agency securities | 8.2 | 82.4 | 275.6 | 238.1 |
| State and local government (tax-exempt) securities | 1.9 | 83.6 | 244.7 | 347.5 |
| Open-market paper | 31.6 | 206.7 | 608.6 | 489.8 |
| Miscellaneous assets | 1.2 | 7.3 | 264.5 | 316.5 |
| Total assets | $76.4 | $498.4 | $1,812.1 | $2,014.1 |

*2006 figures are for first quarter of the year.

*Note:* Columns may not add to totals because of rounding.

Source: Board of Governors of the Federal Reserve System, *Flow of Funds Accounts; Financial Assets and Liabilities,* selected issues.

higher returns to savers. Unfortunately, massive losses soon occurred for some money funds. These losses on investments in commercial paper led the U.S. Securities and Exchange Commission (SEC) to impose limits on money market fund investments in less than top-quality securities, restricting their investments in lower-quality financial instruments to no more than 5 percent of their total assets. No more than 1 percent of a money fund's assets may be placed in securities coming from a single corporate issuer.

Moreover, future money market fund investments were restricted by the SEC to securities that are rated in one of the two highest rating categories by at least two nationally recognized credit-rating companies (such as Moody's and Standard & Poor's). In the same year, the SEC allowed money funds to reach for somewhat longer-maturity financial instruments, allowing them to buy securities with maturities up to 13 months compared to a 12-month maximum under previous rules. However, the Commission reduced the permissible average maturity of a money fund's investment portfolio from a maximum of 120 days to a maximum of only 90 days. In 1996 the SEC tightened restrictions on money funds investing in risky derivative securities (such as futures or options) in order to reduce the risk that changing interest rates might threaten a money fund's stability and solvency. These new restrictions were accompanied by widely publicized reminders to the general public that savings left with money market funds are *not* protected by federal insurance.

**Key URL:**
Trends in the money market funds industry can be followed via iMoneyNet at **imoneynet.com**

On the whole, however, money market funds hold high-quality assets—primarily U.S. Treasury bills, repurchase agreements (RPs), bank CDs, and commercial paper—which helps explain why money market funds remain so popular with millions of investors. The interest-bearing securities they acquire generally carry low risk of borrower default and limited fluctuations in price. Contributing to the low-risk character of money fund investments is their short average maturity of only a few weeks or months. The short maturity of fund investments results in a highly liquid security portfolio that can be adjusted quickly to changing market conditions. Many funds declare dividends on a daily basis, crediting their earnings to customer accounts and often notifying the customer by mail monthly of any additional shares purchased with the dividends earned. Most are "no load" funds that do not charge their customers commissions for opening an account, purchasing additional shares, or redeeming shares for cash.

Another advantage of money funds for many investors is the ease with which their accounts can be accessed. Most funds allow the customer to write checks to redeem shares, provided the amount of each check exceeds a designated minimum ($100 or $500 is common). The customer is issued a book of checks and can write and deposit checks in his or her local bank account, often receiving credit for a deposited check from the local bank the same day, even though it may take several days for the check to be collected. Meantime, interest is still being earned on the monies waiting in the customer's share account. Most money funds also offer customers the option of purchasing or redeeming shares by wire or by telephone. Today, money funds serve as: (1) cash-management vehicles where market rates of return can be earned on funds used for daily transactions; (2) tax-sheltering vehicles for those investors who choose shares in tax-exempt money market funds; (3) a temporary repository for liquid funds waiting for a major purchase or waiting for the appearance of higher-return investments expected to appear later in the marketplace; and (4) a haven of safety for savings when the rest of the financial marketplace appears to be too volatile and risky for a conservative saver to commit his or her funds immediately.

Many local newspapers and financial newssheets, as well as brokers' screens, report the current rates of return (yields) posted by the largest money market funds, as well as the volume of assets currently held by each of these funds. An illustration of a typical daily newspaper report on a couple of money market funds appears in Exhibit 15.5. Most money funds manage their assets with the goal of keeping their NAV (i.e., net asset value, or selling price) fixed at $1 per share. They carry no extra sales charge (that is, are not front-end loaded) and must stand ready to redeem the saver's shares for cash each business day. Shareholder dividends are earned every day in proportion to the number of shares each saver owns in the fund. All money market funds must register with the Securities and Exchange Commission and abide by its rules in offering shares to the public.

Despite their numerous advantages for customers interested in professional management of short-term funds, money market funds today possess some competitive disadvantages that must be overcome if their rapid growth is to continue. For one thing, their toughest competitors—commercial banks—today face fewer regulations than before, can invest in longer-term, higher-yielding assets than money funds, and

| EXHIBIT 15.5 | An Example of Typical Money Market Fund Information Reported Daily by Security Brokers and Dealers, and in Daily Newspapers | | |
|---|---|---|---|
| Name or Abbreviation of Money Market Fund | Average Maturity of Fund's Portfolio in Days | Weekly Average Annualized Yield on the Fund's Assets | Millions of Dollars in Assets Held by the Fund (on the date indicated) |
| KPR Municipal Money Market Fund (KPRM) | 54 | 2.97% | $ 878 |
| Z.Row Money Market Assets (ZRMA) | 43 | 4.68 | 1,651 |

have a broader customer base. Moreover, money fund share accounts are *not* government insured, although many of the funds have attempted to deal with this problem by arranging for private insurance or by creating funds invested solely in default-free government securities. Moreover, the yield differential between posted yields on money market fund share accounts and money market deposits at banks has narrowed in recent years. The money fund industry has recently shown itself to be vulnerable to *low* market interest rates, finding it difficult to pay shareholders a positive interest rate on their savings. With money market interest rates near zero early in the new century, operating expenses at many funds began to eat up interest from investments, resulting in significant losses. A handful of money funds closed early in the twenty-first century, while others raised their fees or cut operating expenses in order to survive.

Certainly the money market funds are not likely to go away. They are a potent competitor for both small individual savings accounts and businesses' liquid funds. However, barring further restrictive federal regulation of bank and thrift deposits, all bank and thrift institutions, including money funds, will continue to compete for savings and transaction accounts on relatively equal terms, leading to intense competition and occasional failures among competing financial institutions.

## QUESTIONS TO HELP YOU STUDY

5. *Credit unions* are one of the fastest-growing financial intermediaries in the United States and in many other parts of the world as well. What explains this rapid growth?

6. What *services* do credit unions offer that compete with the services offered by banks and other thrift institutions? Why are bankers' groups in particular concerned about the expansion of credit unions?

7. What advantages do credit unions have over banks? What disadvantages?

8. How and why did *money market funds* begin to appear during the 1970s? What factors have contributed to their recent growth?

9. Exactly how are money funds different from banks and credit unions in their behavior and the assets they hold?

10. If you are a small saver, what advantages do money funds appear to offer you relative to banks and credit unions? What are their disadvantages?

## Summary of the Chapter's Main Points

*Thrift institutions*—savings and loan associations, savings banks, credit unions, and money market funds—are among the most popular financial institutions within the financial system. They are especially well known to individuals and families (households)—their principal customer base. Among the key points in this chapter are:

- Thrift institutions began their history primarily to reach small savers (principally individuals and families) and help this group of customers achieve home ownership, a better education, satisfactory preparation for retirement, and other personal financial goals. Over time, however, thrifts have diversified their services and attempted to reach out to a broader customer base, including both households and business enterprises.

- Some thrift institutions (particularly money market funds) have experienced fairly steady growth, while others (especially savings and loan associations) have experienced more volatile and somewhat more uncertain growth. Many of the more troubled thrift institutions have been merged into larger and healthier financial-service providers (including banks and financial holding companies) or have simply closed their doors.

- Nevertheless, thrift institutions have continued to be tough competitors, often outbidding bankers for their customers' checking accounts, savings, home mortgages, and personal installment loans. Unlike many other financial intermediaries they are primarily *local* service providers, though some have grown to become nationally and internationally known institutions.

- Like the banking industry (discussed in the previous chapter), the thrift industry is experiencing rapidly changing technology as it seeks to provide more electronic financial services in order to lower overhead and personnel costs and improve service.

- Thrifts have paralleled banks in the trend toward *consolidation,* contracting into smaller numbers of institutions. However, the average thrift institution has increased substantially in overall size. In turn, these larger thrifts have broadened their service menus and are reaching out to expand their beachfront within the global financial marketplace.

## Key Terms Appearing in This Chapter

**savings and loan associations (S&Ls),** 457

**mutuals,** 458

**money market deposit accounts (MMDAs),** 459

**Federal Deposit Insurance Corporation (FDIC),** 460

**savings banks (SBs),** 464

**credit unions (CUs),** 467

**share drafts,** 470

**money market mutual fund (MMFs),** 472

## Problems and Issues

1. Stronghold Money Fund is a relatively new *money market fund* with about $400 million in total financial assets and shares outstanding (each maintained at a value of $1.00 per share). Most of the fund's accounts represent the savings of high-income, interest-sensitive investors. Stronghold's current distribution of financial assets is as follows:

| | |
|---|---|
| U.S. Treasury securities | $170 million |
| Federal agency securities | 115 million |
| Prime bank CDs | 85 million |
| Prime commercial paper issues | 30 million |

Interest rates are expected to rise substantially in the money market over the next several weeks or months and Stronghold's management is concerned that its relatively low current yield (a seven-day average of 4.05 percent, one of the lowest yields among existing funds) may result in the loss of many of its more interest-sensitive share accounts. The fund's average maturity is currently 34 days, which is also substantially less than the industry's current average maturity of about 45 days.

What steps would you recommend to help Stronghold Money Fund prepare for an apparent impending change in money market conditions?

2. Identify the terms and concepts defined or described below as discussed in this chapter.

  **a.** Investment company investing only in short-term financial instruments.

  **b.** Interest-bearing checking accounts offered by a credit union.

  **c.** Nonprofit associations providing financial services only to their members.

  **d.** Depository institutions owned by their depositors.

  **e.** Insures deposits placed in U.S. banks and savings and loan associations.

  **f.** Deposits bearing market-sensitive interest rates and subject to withdrawal by check.

  **g.** A leading home mortgage lender in the United States.

## Web-Based Problems

**1.** As part of the ongoing process of consolidation among depository institutions in recent decades, many savings and loans have converted their charters to a bank charter and/or have been merged with large commercial banking companies.

  **a.** Visit the Web site of the Office of Thrift Supervision at **ots.treasury.gov.** Click the tab "Data and Research" and then click "Thrift Industry Charts" and open the most recent set of charts (pdf-file). Go to the chart "Number and Assets."

  **b.** What appears to have happened to the total number of institutions in the industry over the past four years?

  **c.** What appears to have happened to the industry's size (as measured by total assets) over the past four years?

  **d.** What do your answers to parts (b) and (c) have to say about the average size of firms in the industry?

 **2.** Historically, credit unions have been much smaller in size than most commercial banks or savings and loans and have focused their client base on consumer loans. However, as described in the text, the role of CUs among depositories has been changing. The purpose of this exercise is to examine a few key features of the structure of federal credit unions and compare them with commercial banks.

  **a.** Visit the Web site of the National Credit Union Administration at **ncua.gov** and click on "Credit Union Data" under the tab "Data and Services." Then click "5300 Quarterly Data" and obtain the most recent consolidated balance sheet.

    **b.** Download the spreadsheet "Cbsfcu.xls."

    **c.** Under the heading "Consumer Loans," lump together the following assets on the consolidated balance sheet: (i) unsecured credit card loans; (ii) all other unsecured loans; (iii) new auto loans; and (iv) used auto loans. What share of total assets does this represent?

    **d.** Turn back to Exhibit 14.3 and compare the percentage that you computed in part (c) to the share of loans made by commercial banks listed as "loans to individuals." What do you conclude about the composition of credit unions' clients (and why they borrow from the credit union) versus those who are served by commercial banks? Is the difference suggested by the numbers pronounced or do the two institutions appear to be similar?

**3.** The differences between commercial banks and thrifts have been dwindling in recent years as *convergence* among depository institutions has continued to take place. However, some differences remain as reflected on their balance sheets.

    **a.** Refer to the aggregate balance sheet for commercial banks in the United States (Exhibit 14.3) and the aggregate balance sheet of savings and loans and savings banks in the United States (Exhibit 15.1). Discuss any differences you observe and relate those differences to the "mission" of these financial institutions with respect to the principal markets they serve.

    **b.** Refer to the aggregate balance sheet of credit unions (Exhibit 15.3) and describe differences you observe compared to the balance sheet of commercial banks (Exhibit 14.3). Discuss those differences with respect to the markets CUs serve versus those served by commercial banks?

    **c.** Make a similar comparison as in part (a) above between CUs versus S&Ls and savings banks.

**4.** Money market mutual funds (MMFs) accept deposits in a manner similar to commercial banks and thrift institutions (S&Ls, savings banks, and CUs).

    **a.** Deposits in money market funds, commercial banks, S&Ls, savings banks, and CUs represent assets to depositors. With respect to the characteristics of these assets, what is different about deposits (shares) in MMFs versus deposits in other depository institutions?

    **b.** In what ways do MMFs utilize their deposited funds (share accounts) that differ from commercial banks, S&Ls, savings banks, and CUs?

## Selected References to Explore

**1.** Duca, John V. "How Low Interest Rates Impact Financial Institutions," *Southwest Economy,* Federal Reserve Bank of Dallas, November/December 2003, pp. 1, 8–12.

**2.** Emmons, William R., and Frank A. Schmid. "Credit Unions Make Friends— But Not with Bankers," *The Regional Economist,* Federal Reserve Bank of St. Louis, October 2003, pp. 4–9.

**3.** Insurance Information Institute, *Financial Services Facts, Thrift Institutions and Credit Unions,* **www.financialservicesfacts.org.,** 2006.

4. Walter, John R. "Not Your Father's Credit Union," *Economic Quarterly,* Federal Reserve Bank of Richmond, Vol. 92/4, Fall 2006, pp. 353–77.

5. Wilcox, James A. "Economies of Scale and Continuing Consolidation of Credit Unions," *FRBSF Economic Letter,* Federal Reserve Bank of San Francisco, No. 2005-29 (November 4, 2005).

6. _____. "Performance Divergence of Large and Small Credit Unions," *FRBSF Economic Letter,* Federal Reserve Bank of San Francisco, No. 2006-19 (August 4, 2006).

7. Willis, Jonathan L. "What Impact Will E-Commerce Have on the U.S. Economy?" *Economic Review,* Federal Reserve Bank of Kansas City, Quarter II (2004), pp. 53–71.

8. World Council of Credit Unions. *Statistical Report 2005,* Madison, WI, 2006.

# Chapter 16

# Mutual Funds, Insurance Companies, Investment Banks, and Other Financial Firms

## Learning Objectives

### in This Chapter

- You will explore the many roles played by a variety of financial institutions ranging from mutual funds, insurance companies, and investment banks to finance companies, mortgage banks, and security dealers.

- You will discover the different *services* each of these institutions offers to the public.

- You will examine the principal *sources and uses of funds* that these financial firms draw upon to carry out their daily activities.

- You will be able to understand more fully many of the problems faced by financial institutions operating in today's money and capital markets.

## What's in This Chapter?
## Key Topics Outline

Mutual Funds: Advantages for the Small Investor

New Types of Mutual Funds

Goals, Earnings, and Tax Status of Mutual Funds

Pension Funds: Objectives and Types of Retirement Plans

Pensions' Investment Strategies and Rules

Life and Property-Casualty Insurers: Old and New Services Provided

Investment Policies and Insurable Risks

Finance Companies: Types of Companies, Asset Portfolios, and Funding Sources

New Consumer Options: Pawn, Title, and Check-Cashing Credit Providers

Investment Bankers, Mortgage Banks, REITs, Venture Capital and Leasing Companies

Trends Affecting All Financial Institutions

## 16.1  Introduction

We now turn to a highly diverse group of financial institutions that attract savings mainly from individuals and families and, for the most part, make long-term loans in the capital market. Included in this group are *mutual funds* (sometimes called investment companies), *pension funds* (or, as they are sometimes called, retirement plans), and *life* and *property-casualty insurers,* which today are among the leading institutional buyers of bonds and stocks. *Finance companies,* another member of this group of financial institutions, are active lenders to both business firms and consumers (households) and borrow heavily in the money market. Also included in this chapter is an overview of the *investment banking industry,* which underwrites new security offerings for corporations and governments around the world. As we will see, these institutions provide important services to participants in virtually every corner of the money and capital markets.

## 16.2  Mutual Funds (or Investment Companies)

**mutual fund**
**investment companies**

One of the most rapidly growing of all financial institutions over the past two decades is the **mutual fund** or, as it is more properly called, the investment company. **Investment companies** provide an outlet for the savings of thousands of individual investors, directing their funds into bonds, stocks, and money market securities. These companies are especially attractive to the small investor, to whom they offer continuous management services for a large and varied security portfolio. By purchasing shares offered by an investment company, the small saver gains greater diversification, risk sharing, lower transaction costs, opportunities for capital gains, and indirect access to higher-yielding securities that can be purchased only in large blocks. In addition, most investment company stock is highly liquid, because these companies stand ready at all times to repurchase their outstanding shares at current market prices. The majority of mutual fund shares are held by individuals and families rather than by institutional investors. Close to half of all American households own shares in mutual funds today.

### *The Background of Investment Companies*

Investment companies, first developed in Great Britain during the nineteenth century, made their initial appearance in the United States in the city of Boston in 1924, serving as a vehicle for buying and monitoring subsidiary corporations. Many were unsuccessful in the early years, and the Great Depression of the 1930s forced scores of these firms into bankruptcy. New life was breathed into the industry after World War II, however, when investment companies appealed to a rapidly growing middle class of savers. They were also buoyed by rising stock prices that attracted millions of investors, most of whom had modest amounts to invest and little knowledge of how the financial markets work. The industry launched an aggressive advertising campaign that attracted more than 40 million shareholders during the 1960s alone.

Then the roof fell in as the long postwar bull market in stocks collapsed in the late 1960s and 1970s. Small investors began to pull out of the stock market in droves. Many investment companies disappeared in this shakeout period, most of them consolidated into larger firms.

*Bonds and Money Market Funds*  The future of the industry seemed in doubt until a new element appeared: *innovation.* Managers began to develop new types of investment companies designed to appeal to groups of investors with specialized financial needs. By tradition, investment companies had stressed investments in common stock, offering investors capital appreciation with rising stock prices as well as current dividend income. With the stock market performing poorly, these firms turned their focus increasingly to bonds and money market instruments. New *bond funds* directed the majority of the funds into corporate debt obligations or tax-exempt municipal bonds. Their principal objectives in recent years have been to generate current income and, in the case of the municipal bond fund, a higher after-tax rate of return for the investor. Capital appreciation is normally a secondary consideration to bond funds.

*Money market funds,* discussed in Chapter 15, emerged in 1974 with the announced intent of holding money market securities, mainly commercial paper and government bills. They were created in response to record-high interest rates and the desire of the small investor to skirt around federal interest rate ceilings on savings deposits offered by banks and thrift institutions. In addition, the money funds have offered investors professional management of their liquid funds.

*Stock Funds* The traditional stock-investing mutual funds began to grow rapidly again during the 1980s and 1990s. Although money market funds rescued the investment companies during the turbulent 1970s, equity-oriented mutual funds have outpaced the money market funds more recently, with money flowing in from individuals and institutions primarily for retirement purposes and from investors eager to take advantage of higher expected long-term yields on selected stocks versus the relatively low yields available on bank deposits and other short-term investment instruments. Moreover, several stock funds have outperformed the market as a whole by purchasing stocks from smaller, rapidly growing firms dealing in high-tech products, health care, and other specialty areas.

By the fall of 2000, at the height of the technology-driven "bubble" in the stock market, the assets of mutual funds of all types approached $5 trillion, compared to little more than $1 trillion in 1990. Nevertheless, many stock funds did *not* outperform the market and, when the stock market bubble burst, scores of funds plummeted in value. Their plight was further exacerbated by the onset of a recession in the U.S. economy and the relatively slow recovery that followed. Thousands of investors were discouraged from placing their savings in the stock market and, therefore, turned away from many mutual funds. By mid-2002 mutual fund assets had fallen below $3.7 trillion. However, the market soon rebounded, reaching almost $6.5 trillion in 2006.

*Index and Exchange-Traded Funds* The increased volatility evident in the stock market as the new century unfolded—particularly in high-tech stocks—helped boost the popularity of *index funds*. These innovative investment companies invest in a portfolio of stocks and other instruments that reflect the whole market or a large segment of that market. For example, some of these funds hold a basket of stocks that closely track the S&P 500 Stock Index, the Russell 2000 Index, or the Wilshire 5000 Index. Thus, index fund values tend to move synchronously with the overall market and minimize the investor's risk exposure from holding individual stocks. Index funds are also comparatively low-cost funds (i.e., a larger percentage of earnings generated tend to wind up in the hands of investors).[1]

---

[1] *Index funds* are based on the theory of efficient markets, which argues that in the long run, few money managers can beat the market as a whole. Thus, index funds tend to hold their investments longer and charge lower brokerage and service fees than do investment companies that turn over their security portfolios more rapidly. (See Chapters 3 and 20 for further discussion of market efficiency.)

Investment companies—among the fastest-growing major financial institutions in recent years—have also been a source of controversy among regulators and the public. These mutual funds provide savers with multiple benefits—easy access to the financial marketplace, professional asset management services, greater liquidity, and ready marketability.

While benefits such as these are appreciated by most investors, there is growing research evidence that many mutual fund investors *may* pay too much for the services they receive: One of the most significant fees paid by customers are *advisory fees*, which range between 0.50 and 0.60 percent of the "typical" mutual fund's net assets. Advisory fees compensate professional managers for the research and investment decisions they carry out on behalf of the fund that hires them.

Of course, advisory fees are not the only charges fund investors often wind up paying. Many funds charge a *front-end* or *back-end load*, comparable to a brokerage fee or sales commission, which may range upwards of 5 to 8 percent of funds contributed. And there may be *administrative costs* and *share distribution fees* among others, which in total, may range from 0.3 or 0.4 percent of net assets into the 1 or 2 percent of net assets range and sometimes more. These expenses investors must pay are subtracted from a fund's investment revenues to determine the net earnings flowing to shareholders (with the majority of earnings usually reinvested in additional shares rather than removed from the fund). The funds' total liabilities (which are usually fairly small) are subtracted from a mutual fund's total assets to determine its net asset value (NAV) per share—the price at which a fund usually trades.

It appears that operating costs decline as a mutual fund grows so that investors may benefit more from investing in larger mutual funds—one reason industry mergers are soaring. In any event, knowing what fees and expenses a mutual fund charges or experiences is one of the wisest things an investor can do.

**Key URLs:**
To learn more about exchange-traded funds see such examples as iShares Russell 3000 Index ETF at **iShares.com;** S&P 500 Proshares at **proshares.com;** and Vanguard Total Stock Market ETF at **https://flagship. vanguard.com/VGApp/ hnw/FundsSnapshot.**

The growing popularity of index funds subsequently led to the appearance of *exchange-traded funds* (ETFs)—baskets of stocks that trade much like individual stocks and less like conventional mutual funds. Each ETF is linked to a particular stock index (such as the S&P 500 Stock Index), upon which its value is based, and trades *continuously* during normal trading hours. This means the price of an ETF changes frequently on any given day, unlike traditional mutual funds that usually trade at a single price established at the market's close each day. The current center of ETF trades is the AMEX— the American Stock Exchange at **amex.com.** The fact that ETFs trade continuously on an exchange makes them more attractive to active day traders and less susceptible to illegal trading practices like those experienced by regular mutual funds. By 2007 there were close to 500 ETFs, holding nearly $500 billion in assets, compared to only about 30 ETFs and less than $13 billion in assets as the new century began.

**Key URLs:**
To explore more fully the nature of investment companies (mutual funds) view the Web sites of two of the very largest families of funds at Fidelity **(fidelity.com)** and Vanguard **(vanguard.com)**

### Global and Vulture Funds

The past three decades have been marked by the rapid growth of *global funds.* These are stock and bond funds whose income-earning securities come from all over the world. These funds have access to security trading 24 hours a day through active exchanges in London, Tokyo, Singapore, Hong Kong, and other financial centers around the globe. Managers of these funds believe higher returns are attainable with a balanced international portfolio, as opposed to a portfolio of domestic securities alone. Unfortunately, the risk attached to these global funds has often proven to be higher than expected (as in Asia and Japan, for example). Another innovative investment company developed recently is the *vulture fund,* which purchases securities from firms in trouble in the hope of scoring exceptional returns should these firms recover or when their more valuable assets are liquidated.

*Small-Cap to Large-Cap Funds*   A group of funds experiencing considerable popularity in recent years are the *small-cap, mid-cap,* and *large-cap* investment companies. These funds specialize in the stocks of companies that occupy different size groups. For example, the smallest-size firms in terms of total capitalization (i.e., the total market value of the firms' outstanding shares of stock) are called "small caps" while the largest companies are referred to as "large caps." There has been some evidence in recent years that small- and mid-cap firms represent riskier investments but often provide higher average returns than do large-cap companies. In contrast, the large-cap funds frequently claim they offer more stable long-run returns than small-cap and mid-cap funds.

*Life-Cycle Funds*   Among the most rapidly growing investment companies of late are *life-cycle funds* that seem to be gradually replacing more traditional pension plans. These funds invest heavily in stocks (perhaps 80 or 90 percent or more) in the early years of an investor's account and then reallocate the investor's money into more conservative investments (such as bonds) as retirement approaches. Passage of the Pension Protection Act of 2006 has stimulated the growth of these funds because it encourages businesses to set up employee pension programs even for those employees not wishing to accumulate long-term savings.

*Hedge Funds*   During the 1990s and early into the new century *hedge funds* became prominent and by 2006 held well over a trillion dollars in industry assets. These funds are really private partnerships that sell shares to a limited number of wealthy ("accredited") investors in the hope of reaping large returns from high-risk investments. While most mutual funds require a minimum opening investment of around $1,000, hedge funds often ask for a minimal investment of at least a million dollars or more. In this case the word "hedge" refers to a promise by the fund of generating relatively stable returns by diversifying their trading over a broad range of assets (including stocks, bonds, commodities, and real estate) and making heavy use of leverage.

Hedge funds are essentially unregulated investment companies that almost anyone can start, even from the privacy of their home, and can accept literally any kind of risk exposure. (For a more detailed look at hedge-fund risk see Adrian [1].) Some of the larger hedge funds have moved aggressively to pool huge amounts of private equity and fuel corporate takeovers, while others have taken on large volumes of complex derivative contracts (such as futures, options, and swaps) in an effort to exceed or stay abreast of broad market indicators such as the S&P 500 or the Russell 2000 Indexes. Recent trends in the aggressive management of some hedge funds have led to calls for more extensive regulation of the industry, especially as these funds have begun to pursue smaller, more vulnerable investors.

Finally, the hedge fund industry continues to grow rapidly and concentrate a growing portion of its assets under management in the largest funds—for example, the 100 largest hedge funds account for close to 70 percent of industry resources. In many cases larger hedge funds are able to offer stronger risk-management services, post lower trading and financing costs, and score higher average returns (including trading gains generally known as "carry"). Nevertheless, pressures on the hedge fund sector have increased recently, placing several of these institutions in trouble and shutting some of them down.

## Tax and Regulatory Status of the Industry

Investment companies have a favorable tax situation. As long as they conform to certain rules to qualify as an investment company (such as those spelled out in the Investment Company Act of 1940), they pay *no* federal taxes on income generated by

**Key URLs:**
Examples of the most prominent hedge funds in the industry include Fortress Investment Group LLC at **fortressinv.com/**; Farallon Capital Management LLC at **faralloncapital.com**; Citadel Investment Group LLC at **citadelgroup.com**; and Tudor Investment Corpat at **tudorfunds.com/**

**Key URL:**
One of the most famous hedge fund failures was Long-Term Capital Management (LTCM) LLP that closed in 2000 after several billion dollars in losses. See especially answers.com/topic/long-term-capital-management, for additional information on this troubled hedge fund.

**Key URL:**
A useful discussion of the nature and risks of hedge funds appears in a Securities and Exchange Commission brochure entitled "Hedging Your Bets: A Heads Up on Hedge Funds and Funds of Hedge Funds," at **sec.gov/answers/hedge.htm**

their security holdings. However, no less than half of their resources must be devoted to securities and cash assets. Investment companies must maintain a highly diversified portfolio: A maximum of one-quarter of their total resources can be devoted to securities issued by any one business firm. Only a small portion of net income (no more than 10 percent) can be retained in the company. The rest must be distributed to shareholders. Investment companies and the securities they issue must be registered with the Securities and Exchange Commission (SEC).

## Open-End and Closed-End Investment Companies

There are two basic kinds of investment companies. *Open-end investment companies*— often called *mutual funds*—buy back (redeem) their shares any time the customer wishes, and sell shares in any quantity demanded. Thus, the amount of their outstanding shares changes continually in response to public demand. The price of each open end company share is equal to the *net asset value* of the fund—that is, the difference between the values of its assets and liabilities divided by the volume of shares issued.

Open-end companies may be either *load* or *no-load* funds. Load funds offer shares to the public at net asset value plus a commission to brokers marketing their shares. No-load funds sell shares purely at their net asset value. The investor must contact the no-load company or its representative directly, however. Whether load or no-load, open-end investment companies are heavily invested in common stock, with corporate bonds running a distant second. As Exhibit 16.1 shows, corporate stock represents more than two-thirds of the mutual-fund industry's assets, with government and corporate bonds accounting for most of the remaining assets.

| **EXHIBIT 16.1** | **Number of Mutual Funds and the Financial Assets Held by Mutual Funds (Open-End Investment Companies)** | |
|---|---|---|
| **Types of Mutual Funds** | **No. of Funds** | **Percent of Total** |
| Equity (stock) funds | 4,586 | 57% |
| Bond funds | 2,015 | 25 |
| Hybrid(mixed) funds | 505 | 6 |
| Money market funds | 871 | 11 |
| Total | 7,977 | 100% |
| **Asset Holdings** | **Amount in 2006\* ($ Billions)** | **Percent of Total Assets** |
| Security repurchase agreements | $ 125.3 | 1.9% |
| Corporate stock (equities) | 4,529.2 | 70.0 |
| U.S. Treasury and federal agency securities | 648.3 | 10.0 |
| State and local government (municipal) securities | 321.9 | 5.0 |
| Corporate and foreign bonds | 729.6 | 11.3 |
| Open-market paper | 107.0 | 1.7 |
| Miscellaneous assets | 11.6 | 0.2 |
| Total financial assets held | $6,472.9 | 100.0% |

Sources: Board of Governors of the Federal Reserve System, *Flow of Funds Accounts*, and Insurance Information Institute.

Note: Columns may not add to totals due to rounding error.

\*Figures through the first quarter of 2006.

Considering the mutual fund industry's heavy investment in stocks, it is not surprising to learn that more than half of the industry's population of nearly 8,000 funds were stock (equity) funds. A quarter of all funds were bond-oriented and about 6 percent were hybrids (that is, combined stock and bond funds). Finally, about 870 funds (about 11 percent of the industry) were money market funds, of which nearly 600 were taxable and about 275 were tax-exempt money funds.

*Closed-end investment companies* sell only a specific number of ownership shares, which usually trade on an exchange. An investor wanting to acquire closed-end shares must find another investor who wishes to sell; the investment company itself does not take part in the transaction. These funds often attract investors by offering "double discounts," which consist of discounted prices on the stocks they hold and discounted share prices to buy into the fund itself. Closed-end companies issue a variety of securities to raise funds, including preferred stock, regular and convertible bonds, and stock warrants. In contrast, open-end companies rely almost entirely on the sale of equity shares to the public in order to raise the funds they need.

## Changing Investment Strategies

The investment strategies of both open- and closed-end mutual funds appear to be undergoing substantial changes. One of the most prominent changes is greater use of *derivatives,* including financial futures, options, and both credit and interest rate swap contracts (discussed earlier in Chapters 8 and 9). These instruments seem to offer funds' managers the opportunity to boost their returns relative to competing investments, more closely track market indexes, and achieve greater diversification, though the complexity of these instruments has raised regulators' concerns about funds' risk exposure.

## Goals and Earnings of Investment Companies

Investment companies adopt many different goals. *Growth funds* are interested primarily in long-term capital appreciation and tend to invest mainly in common stocks offering strong growth potential. *Income funds s*tress current income in their portfolio choices rather than growth of capital, and they typically purchase stocks and bonds paying high dividends and interest. *Balanced funds* attempt to bridge the gap between growth and income, acquiring bonds, preferred stock, and common stock that offer both capital gains (growth) and current income.

The majority of investment companies give priority to capital growth over current income, although funds stressing income, such as bond and dividend funds, money market funds, and option funds (which issue options against a portfolio of common stocks) have become more important in recent years. While most investment companies hold a highly diversified portfolio of securities, a few specialize in stocks and bonds from a single industry or sector (such as precious metals or oil and natural gas).

Policies and goals for investing funds are determined by an investment company's board of directors, which is elected by its shareholders. Its assets, however, are managed by an *investment advisory service* in return for an annual fee (usually less than 2 percent of a fund's assets). The contract between investment adviser and mutual fund must generally be approved by the fund's stockholders. Most funds have very few employees; the majority of their services (such as recordkeeping and investment advice) are "outsourced" to other firms. A mutual fund's price per share (or net asset value [NAV]) is often published in daily newspapers. As illustrated below, newspapers usually print the abbreviated name of the fund, its price or net asset value per

**Key URLs:**
Keeping track of daily developments in the mutual fund industry can be done by following such Web sites as the Mutual Fund Investor's Center at **mfea.com**, and the Mutual Fund Investing Newsletter at **funds-newsletter.com** To explore the investments made by mutual funds on a quarterly basis, see especially **sec.gov/edgar.shtml**

share the preceding business day, the net change in price from the day before, the year-to-date return, and the trailing three-year annualized return. Thus:

| Name | NAV per Share | Net Chg | % YTD return | 3-Year % RET |
|------|---------------|---------|--------------|--------------|
| Balanced Equity Fund (BalEq) | $15.60 | +0.08 | 4.3 | 10.0 |

It is not at all clear that mutual funds hold a significant advantage over other investors in seeking the highest returns available in the financial marketplace. Moreover, there is evidence that, with the possible exception of index funds, many of these companies roll over their portfolios too rapidly, which runs up the cost of managing the fund and tends to reduce investor earnings. Less frequent trading activity on the part of investment companies might well result in greater long-term benefits for savers. As we saw earlier in Chapter 3, research evidence has been mounting for a number of years that security markets are relatively efficient. Overvaluation or undervaluation of securities is, at most, a temporary phenomenon. In this kind of environment, it is doubtful that investment companies are of significant benefit to the largest investors, though they may aid small investors in reducing information and transaction costs and opening up investment opportunities not otherwise available.

As the new century began, many investment companies began to raise their account fees and require customers to put up larger minimum investments, thereby increasing the burden on the small investor. The industry has cited declining investment volume and higher operating costs as a result of these adjustments. And, indeed, recent research evidence suggests that there are significant economies of scale in the investment company industry, with larger funds reporting substantially lower operating costs per dollar of net assets (NAV) held.

**Key URLs:**
To learn more about calculating mutual funds' operating expenses and how they may affect investors' returns see, for example, the SEC's Mutual Fund Cost Calculator at **sec.gov** or NASD's Mutual Fund Expense analyzer at **nsad.com**

To keep track of industry performance, an investor service—*Morningstar* at **www.morningstar.com**—provides online, up-to-date ratings of individual mutual funds in the form of a "reward-to-risk" ratio that allows investors to readily compare one fund against another. Among the largest mutual fund companies, in terms of total assets, are Fidelity Investments at **www.fidelity.com;** The Vanguard Group at **www.vanguard.com;** Franklin Templeton Investments at **www.franklintempleton.com;** JP Morgan Chase at **www.jpmorganchase.com;** and Morgan Stanley at **www.morganstanley.com.**

## Scandal Envelops the Mutual Fund Industry

As the twenty-first century began, the mutual fund industry—which in the U.S. alone has attracted close to 100 million investors—found itself confronted with a major public relations problem and possible loss of thousands of customers. There was mounting evidence that managers of several prominent funds had engaged in actions that were either illegal under federal and state law or represented a violation of several funds' own internal rules, reducing potential returns to millions of investors.

Manager and trader transgressions included allegations of "late trading" and "market timing." Under the apparently widespread practice of *late trading,* some favored investors were permitted to buy and sell funds' shares at a price established hours earlier when the market closed. This procedure made it easy for these privileged investors to reap substantial trading profits, given that they already knew the per-share value of their transactions. In turn, some of the favored investors pledged to make substantial investments in those mutual funds that granted them late-trading privileges.

Other investment companies apparently permitted day traders to engage in *market timing* of their shares—a practice prohibited by most funds because it drives up fund expenses and, other factors held equal, lowers potential shareholder returns. Market timers rapidly turn over their holdings of mutual fund shares and other financial instruments, hoping to take instant advantage of daily rises and falls in market prices. They may buy and sell shares several times a day, depending upon market movements and the appearance of new information. In some cases, the "market timers" were affiliated with the funds whose shares they traded, giving them access to inside information.

These highly questionable and often illegal practices led to widespread calls for new legislation and for tighter regulation of the behavior of the mutual fund industry, including new rules calling for greater disclosure of:

1. All the fees borne by shareholders in each fund.
2. How the compensation of a fund's managers is determined.
3. How rapidly each fund's asset portfolio turns over and what this implies for an investor in the fund.
4. The fund's written policies and practices regarding late trading and market timing.
5. How broker-dealer commissions are determined and whether brokers and dealers are paid any incentives to promote the sale of the fund's shares among their customers.
6. The makeup of each mutual fund's board of directors (including information concerning which directors are independent of the fund itself).

In addition, the Securities and Exchange Commission (SEC) required banks, broker-dealers, and administrators of retirement plans to submit trading orders to mutual funds before 4 PM in the afternoon in order for their customers to receive that day's price. Any trading orders received after 4 PM EST would receive the next day's price. At this point in time, no one knows for sure how many criminal indictments and new rules will eventually emerge from this latest scandal on Wall Street. However, it seems clear that, for many investors, their long-standing trust in the management of mutual funds has been seriously damaged.

## 16.3 Pension Funds

**pension funds**

**Pension funds** protect individuals and families against loss of income in their retirement years by allowing workers to set aside and invest a portion of their current income. A pension plan places current savings in a portfolio of stocks, bonds, and other assets in the expectation of building an even larger pool of funds in the future. In this way, the pension plan member can balance planned consumption after retirement with the amount of savings set aside today.

### Types of Pension Funds

Two main types of pension plans exist today. *Defined benefit* plans promise a specific monthly or annual payment to workers when they retire based upon a specific benefits formula that typically takes into account the size of their salary during the working years and their length of employment. In contrast, *defined contribution* plans (such as an IRA or 401(k) plan) specify how much must be contributed each year in the name of each worker but the amount to be received when retirement is reached will vary depending upon the amount saved and returns earned on accumulated savings.

### Defined-Benefit and Contribution Plans

Defined-benefit pension programs have the advantage of guaranteed income if the employee remains with a particular employer for a relatively long period, but an employee who leaves early or is dismissed before retirement may get little or nothing. Under the defined contribution approach, however, the funds saved belong to the employee and are portable, provided the employee stays on the job long enough (usually one to two years) for the savings to be "vested" in his or her name. Defined benefit plans are declining as a percentage of all pension programs, while defined contribution plans are rising and now account for the majority of private pension programs. Leading pension funds include the California Public Employees' Retirement System at **calpers.ca.gov;** British Columbia Municipal Superannuation Fund at **pensionsbc.ca;** New York City Police Pension Fund at **nyc.gov/nycppf;** and TIAA-CREF Pension Plan at **tiaa-cref.org.**

### Cash-Balance Pension Funds

In an effort to reduce sponsoring employers' costs and provide added flexibility a highly controversial form of pension plan—a *cash-balance plan*—has appeared recently, especially at some of the largest companies (such as IBM, AT&T, Xerox, Cigna, and Delta Airlines). Cash-balance plans tend to favor young workers, while they may actually reduce older workers' benefits. With such a plan, employers typically make a hypothetical contribution to an employee's retirement account equal to a percentage of that employee's annual salary and credit the employee's pension account with annual interest earnings based upon a reference interest rate (such as the U.S. Treasury bond rate).

For example, suppose an employee enrolled in a cash-balance plan is promised a 5 percent pay credit each year with interest on all accumulated credits based on the 30-year U.S. Treasury bond rate. If this employee receives a salary of $50,000 a year, then $2,500 will be credited to his or her hypothetical pension account which will accrue interest until benefit payments begin. At retirement the participating employee may receive periodic payments based on his or her accumulated credits (though, as a matter of practice, many employees take a lump-sum payment when they retire).

Under many cash-balance plans you have to be a plan participant for at least five years in order to receive benefits. When converting from a traditional pension plan to a cash-balance plan, the employer determines the accumulated value held in the old pension under each employee's name and may transfer all or only a portion of that accumulated value into the employee's new account. In short, employers have considerable discretion over how much built-up credit each employee receives upon conversion to a cash-balance plan. Older workers seem most vulnerable and may have to work additional years to catch up to where they were when their employer converted to a cash-balance pension program.

In 2006 a new federal law, the Pension Protection Act, clarified the rules for setting up and managing cash-balance pensions. The Protection Act reduced the potential for lawsuits claiming that these plans discriminated against older workers, clearing the way for more businesses to adopt cash-balance pension programs. Most cash-balance plans were required to adopt a 3-year (accelerated) vesting schedule so that employees could qualify sooner for at least some pension benefits.

Clearly, the prime beneficiary of the cash balance plan is the *employer,* as the ultimate purpose is usually to hold business costs down. Fortunately, for most U.S. employees with employer-sponsored pension programs federal law entitles covered employees to be informed each year about the funding status of their pension program and to request a periodic statement of vested benefits accrued. Such a request may be made once each year in writing and the employer must reply within 30 days.

| EXHIBIT 16.2 | Total Assets of Private and Public Pension Funds, Selected Years ($ billions) | | | | | | | |
|---|---|---|---|---|---|---|---|---|
| Type of Pension Plan or Program | 1940 | 1950 | 1960 | 1970 | 1980 | 1990 | 2000 | 2006* |
| Private pension programs: | $2.0 | $12.1 | $ 52.0 | $138.2 | $422.7 | $2,324.8 | $4,576.4 | $4,875.7 |
| Insured plans | 0.6 | 5.6 | 18.8 | 41.2 | 165.8 | 695.7 | 1,456.1 | — |
| Noninsured plans | 1.4 | 6.5 | 33.2 | 97.0 | 286.8 | 1,629.1 | 3,120.3 | — |
| Government pension programs: | $4.3 | $25.8 | $ 56.1 | $125.9 | $289.8 | $1,203.5 | $3,288.2 | — |
| State/local retirement systems | 1.6 | 5.3 | 19.3 | 60.3 | 185.2 | 720.8 | 2,293.1 | 2,790.9 |
| Federal civilian systems | 0.6 | 4.2 | 10.5 | 23.1 | 75.8 | 247.5 | 796.7 | 1,068.7 |
| Railroad retirement program | 0.1 | 2.6 | 3.7 | 4.4 | 2.1 | 9.9 | 14.9† | — |
| Social security program (OASDI) | 2.0 | 13.7 | 22.6 | 38.1 | 26.5 | 225.3 | 567.0† | — |
| Total assets of all funds | $6.3 | $37.9 | $108.2 | $262.0 | $712.3 | $3,528.3 | $7,864.6 | — |

*2006 figures are based on first quarter.

†Indicated figures are for 1996.

Note: Columns may not add to totals due to rounding error.

Source: Securities and Exchange Commission; Railroad Retirement Board; U.S. Department of Health and Human Services; the American Council of Life Insurance; and the Federal Reserve Board.

## Growth of Pension Funds

Pension funds have been among the most rapidly growing of all financial intermediaries. Between 1980 and 2006, the assets of all private and public pension funds multiplied more than 10 times over, reaching close to $9 trillion in the United States alone. (See Exhibit 16.2.) Approximately half of all full-time workers in private businesses and three-quarters of all civilian government employees are protected by pension plans other than the U.S. Social Security program (OASDI). About 200 million persons are insured by or are direct or indirect beneficiaries of the Social Security program, which pays cash benefits to more than 50 million Americans each year.

Pension fund growth in the past has been spurred on by the relatively few retirees drawing pensions compared to the number of people working and contributing to a pension program. That situation is changing rapidly, however; individuals over 65 years of age now represent one of the fastest growing segments of the world's population. The growing proportion of retired individuals will threaten the solvency of many private pension funds and has already created significant future funding problems for various government programs (such as the U.S. Medicare and Medicaid programs) designed primarily to aid the elderly.[2]

Competition among employers for skilled management personnel has also spurred pension fund growth, as firms have tried to attract top-notch employees by offering attractive fringe benefits. This growth factor is likely to persist into the future due to a possible shortage of skilled entry-level workers as the population ages. Some experts foresee a real problem in this area, stemming from recent difficulties pension plans have had in keeping up with inflation and with the increasing number of retirees. Workers in the future are likely to demand better performance from their retirement plans and greater control over how their long-term savings are invested.

**Key URL:**
You can keep track of ongoing developments in the pension fund industry through such Web sites as that established by the International Foundation for Employee Benefit Plans at **ifebp.org**

[2]The present ratio of working adults to retired persons in the U.S. population is about 3:1. This ratio is projected to shrink to about 2:1 within little more than a generation. When the U.S. Social Security Act was passed in 1935, there were 11 working adults for each retired individual.

Pension funds set aside current savings in a pool of earning assets in the hope of accumulating a larger amount of savings that will provide a stream of income during retirement years. For example, suppose an employee is scheduled to retire in five years and has $2,500 deposited in her retirement account this year. If the pension plan promises her a 6 percent annual yield on each dollar set aside for retirement, the $2,500 she sets aside today will be worth:

$$\begin{array}{l} \text{Value of funds} \\ \text{contributed today} \\ \text{at retirement} \end{array} = \begin{array}{l} \text{Amount set} \\ \text{aside today} \end{array} \left( 1 + \begin{array}{l} \text{Promised} \\ \text{rate of return} \end{array} \right)^{\text{Years invested}}$$

$$= \$2,500(1 + .06)^5 = \$3,345.57$$

Suppose this same employee who plans to retire in five years has $2,500 contributed every year between now and retirement and earns 6 percent on each dollar saved. Then her total savings pool at retirement will be:

$$\begin{array}{l} \text{Total funds} \\ \text{available at} \\ \text{retirement} \end{array} = \begin{array}{l} \text{Amount of savings} \\ \text{contributed} \\ \text{each year} \end{array} \times \begin{array}{l} \text{Sum of compound interest factors} \\ \text{for savings contributed each year} \\ \text{up to retirement at interest rate } i \end{array}$$

$$= \$2,500[(1 + .06)^5 + (1 + .06)^4 + \cdots + (1.06)^1]$$

$$= \$14,937.50$$

How much annual income can this employee look forward to in retirement? The answer depends on the annual annuity rate promised and whether the employee has access to (i.e., is vested with) all funds contributed in her name. Suppose this employee is *vested* with the full amount shown above (i.e., a vesting ratio of 1.00) and is promised an annual annuity (income) rate of 5.5 percent based on her life expectancy. Then her expected annual retirement income from this one pension plan will be:

$$\begin{array}{l} \text{Expected annual} \\ \text{retirement} \\ \text{income} \end{array} = \begin{array}{l} \text{Annual} \\ \text{annuity} \\ \text{rate} \end{array} \times \begin{array}{l} \text{Total funds available} \\ \text{to employee at} \\ \text{retirement} \end{array} \times \text{Vesting ratio}$$

$$= 0.055 \times \$14,937.50 \times 1.0 = \$821.56$$

## Investment Strategies of Pension Funds

Pension funds are long-term investors with limited need for liquidity. Their incoming cash receipts are known with considerable accuracy because a fixed percentage of each employee's salary is usually contributed to the fund. At the same time, cash outflows are not difficult to forecast, because the formula for figuring benefit payments is stipulated in the contract between the fund and its members. This situation encourages pensions to purchase common stock, long-term bonds, and real estate and to hold these assets on a permanent basis. Indeed, pension plans represent the single largest group of investors in the stock market. In addition, interest income and capital gains from investments are exempt from federal income taxes, and pension plan members are not taxed on their contributions unless benefits are actually paid out.

Although favorable taxation and predictable cash flows favor longer-term, somewhat riskier investments, the pension fund industry is closely regulated in many of its investment activities. The Employee Retirement Income Security Act (ERISA) requires all U.S. defined-benefit private plans to be *fully funded,* which means that any assets held plus investment income must be adequate to cover all promised benefits. ERISA also requires that investments must be made in a "prudent" manner, which is usually interpreted to mean that they be invested in highly diversified holdings of high-grade common stock, corporate bonds, and government securities along with some real estate investments.

Although existing regulations emphasize conservatism in pension-fund investments, private pensions have been under intense pressure in recent years by management and employees of sponsoring companies to be more liberal in their investment policies. The sponsoring employer has a strong incentive to encourage its affiliated pension plan to reduce operating expenses and earn the highest possible returns on its investments. This permits the company to minimize its contributions to the plan. However, the Financial Accounting Standards Board has issued SFAS 87, which requires *defined-benefit pension plans* to disclose their funding status more fully, asking businesses to make projections of their future pension obligations, publish estimates of how much in benefits employees will receive, and report any *unfunded* portion of pension benefits on each business's balance sheet as a liability. These accounting requirements have made some businesses offering pension plans look weaker and, along with strict government regulations, have caused many firms to abandon their pension programs, leaving it to their employees to develop and manage their own retirement plans.

## Pension Fund Assets

The particular assets held as investments by pension funds depend heavily on whether the fund is government controlled or a private venture. As shown in Exhibit 16.3, private funds currently devote the largest percentage of their investments to corporate stock, which represented about 45 percent of their assets in 2006. Shares in mutual funds, which represent indirect holdings of corporate stocks and bonds, ranked second, accounting for about 27 percent of all private pensions' assets. With few liquidity needs, private pension funds held relatively small amounts of cash and bank deposits, although their holdings of U.S. government and federal agency securities have remained substantial (about 7 percent of their total assets) due to the relatively high yields and safety of these financial instruments. Many of the largest pension plans also hold substantial real estate investments for asset diversification and as a hedge against inflation.

Corporate stock recently has become more important in the portfolios of government pensions than among many private pension plans. As Exhibit 16.3 shows, state and local government pension programs held almost 65 percent of their assets in corporate stock. Government pension plans also maintained significant holdings of corporate bonds and U.S. government and federal agency securities, representing about 7 and 15 percent of their assets, respectively. The pressure of regulation falls more heavily upon government (public) pensions than upon private plans. As a result, the investments of government pensions tend to be somewhat more conservative, with heavier concentrations in higher-grade assets.

Nevertheless, all pensions, public and private, have come under intense pressure recently as market fluctuations and growing business operating costs have tended to widen the gap between what many pensions have promised to pay their members (which is their principal liability) and the market value of their current asset holdings. Partly as a result, pension accounting standards are changing. In Europe (especially in the United Kingdom) many pension plans are required to record their assets at current

| EXHIBIT 16.3 | Financial Assets Held by Private Pension Funds and State and Local Government Employee Retirement Funds | |
|---|---|---|
| **Assets Held by Private Pension Plans** | **Amount in 2006\*** **($ billions)** | **Percent of** **Total Assets** |
| Checkable deposits and currency | $ 10.8 | 0.2% |
| Time and savings deposits | 65.5 | 1.3 |
| Money market fund shares | 87.6 | 1.8 |
| Security repurchase agreements | 23.9 | 0.5 |
| Open market paper | 34.2 | 0.7 |
| U.S. Treasury and federal agency securities | 344.6 | 7.1 |
| Corporate and foreign bonds | 268.0 | 5.5 |
| Mortgage loans | 9.8 | 0.2 |
| Corporate stock (equities) | 2,220.6 | 45.5 |
| Shares in mutual funds | 1,341.5 | 27.5 |
| Miscellaneous assets | 469.2 | 9.6 |
| Total financial assets held | $ 4875.7 | 100.0% |
| **Assets Held by State and** **Local Government Pension Plans** | **Amount in 2006\*** **($ billions)** | **Percent of** **Total Assets** |
| Checkable deposits and currency | $ 18.3 | 0.7% |
| Time and savings deposits | 2.1 | 0.1 |
| Money market fund shares | 12.5 | 0.4 |
| Security repurchase agreements | 21.3 | 0.8 |
| Open market paper | 28.9 | 1.0 |
| U.S. Treasury and federal agency securities | 421.9 | 15.1 |
| State and local government (tax-exempt) securities | 1.2 | 0.0† |
| Corporate and foreign bonds | 202.1 | 7.2 |
| Mortgage loans | 20.7 | 0.7 |
| Corporate stock (equities) | 1,811.8 | 64.9 |
| Miscellaneous assets | 250.1 | 9.0 |
| Total financial assets held | $2,790.9 | 100.0% |

\*Figures are for the end of the first quarter of 2006.
†Less than 0.25 percent.
Note: Columns may not add to totals due to rounding error.
Source: Board of Governors of the Federal Reserve System, *Flow of Funds Accounts.*

market value. Similar proposals have appeared in the United States, leading to passage of new pension legislation—specifically, the Pension Protection Act of 2006.

This new law simplified the rules for funding defined-benefit pension plans and accelerated the funding of these plans, allowed workers to make larger tax-favored contributions to their pension accounts, encouraged more education for workers regarding their pension options, and promoted automatic enrollment in defined-contribution pension programs (such as IRAs and Keoghs). Pension plans were required to calculate annually the ratio of the fair market value of their assets to the present value of their liabilities, requiring most plans to move toward a ratio value of one within seven years. Annual installment payments are required to "fix" underfunded plans, which must develop and implement a funding improvement plan.

The startling collapse of Enron Corporation of Houston—one of the largest bankruptcy filings in U.S. history—in 2001 and 2002 aroused a storm of controversy about how employee retirement plans are set up and managed. The Enron case led some authorities to conclude that pension law in the United States may be too heavily tilted toward favoring employers rather than employees.

When the Employee Retirement Income Security Act (ERISA) was passed by the U.S. Congress in 1974 it permitted companies to contribute their own stock to their employees' retirement plan with few limitations. This loophole soon led to many businesses placing 50 percent or more of their employees' retirement account in company stock. Clearly, employees in these situations receive little or no risk-reducing benefits from asset portfolio diversification.

Why were firms like Enron tempted to put so much of their own stock in their employee retirement plans? These "inside" stock sales created more demand for the company's stock and drove its price higher. Moreover, contributing stock instead of cash helped conserve the employer's cash reserves.

Even more controversial, pension law allowed these corporate retirement plans to block employee sales of company stock until an employee reached a certain age. In Enron's case, this was 50 years of age. Thus, many Enron employees watched helplessly as the company's stock declined drastically in value but were unable to "unlock" their holdings. These awkward restrictions on retirement portfolio diversification and on early stock sales have led to some changes in pension rules, including stricter limits on investing workers' pensions in their employer's stock and greater disclosure of insider transactions.

In 2005 federal reform legislation required employers to fully fund their plans within 7 years (though companies in bankruptcy proceedings were given 10 years to meet their pension-plan funding obligations).

## Factors Affecting the Future Growth of Pension Funds

Most experts believe that pension fund growth may continue to be rapid in the future, particularly due to uncertainty surrounding the U.S. Social Security program. With government and business playing a smaller role, individual workers will be compelled to rely more heavily upon their own resources to finance their retirement years. Still, there appear to be serious problems ahead for both the growth and stability of pension plans. One concern is the rising proportion of pension beneficiaries to working contributors, related to the aging of the population. At the same time, the cost of maintaining pension programs has increased dramatically. The full funding of a defined benefit plan to cover all promised benefits may place extreme pressure on corporate profits, particularly if declining security markets diminish investment returns.

Even more important is the rising cost of government regulation, which has imposed costly reporting requirements on the industry, granted employees the right to join pension programs soon after they are hired, and allowed pension plan members to acquire ownership and control more quickly of monies contributed on their behalf. These government regulations have forced many private pension plans to close. The control of others has been turned over to a financial institution—typically a bank trust department or life insurance company—that is better able to deal with the current rules. Many defined-benefit private pension plans are in weak financial condition, especially those connected to corporations that are in trouble or have failed. In addition, some of the best pension plans have been terminated because their sponsoring employers wished to recapture their assets, the value of which had risen over the years.

Worse still, the pension insurance agency created by the U.S. Congress in 1974—the Pension Benefit Guaranty Corporation (known as PBGC or, more popularly, as "Penny

**Key URL:**
For further
information on
the activities of
Penny Benny, see
especially **pbgc.gov**

Benny")—has recently reported sharply rising budget deficits. Penny Benny was set up to guarantee the pension benefits of employees with defined-benefit pension plans. Unfortunately, more and more corporations have sought financial relief from the courts by abandoning their costly pension programs and dumping them in Penny Benny's lap. Among the largest companies jettisoning their underfunded pension plans have been United Airlines, who gave up its $6.6 billion pension program in 2005—the largest pension plan in American history to fail, and Bethlehem Steel, which posted a $3.7 billion pension shortfall in 2002, covering just under 100,000 current and former employees.

Currently, Penny Benny insures the retirement plans of more than 40 million American workers and retirees. As Penny Benny has been compelled to take over more troubled companies' pension programs, especially in the declining manufacturing sector, the gap between what it has promised to pay out to pension plan members and its available assets has widened significantly, exceeding a $23 billion deficit in 2005. Unless the PBGC significantly reduces member benefits or charges companies with pension plans higher insurance fees, it may be compelled to turn to the U.S. Congress (and, ultimately, U.S. taxpayers) for a costly rescue. In the meantime the Financial Accounting Standards Board (FASB) ruled in 2006 that companies must include on their balance sheets the size of the overall surplus or deficit in their retirement plans. For businesses with large pension plan deficits their net worth may decline significantly and even turn negative.

In short, the pension fund sector faces problems that will require creative solutions in the future, including a redefining of the role of public and private institutions in assuring an equitable and adequate distribution of retirement monies to those who have earned them.

---

## QUESTIONS TO HELP YOU STUDY

1. What advantages do *investment companies* (mutual funds) offer the small saver? Why has their growth been so erratic in recent years?

2. Define the following terms:

   | | | |
   |---|---|---|
   | *a. Open-end company* | *d. Money market fund* | *g. Global funds* |
   | *b. Closed-end company* | *e. Growth funds* | *h. Index funds* |
   | *c. Bond fund* | *f. Balanced funds* | *i. Hedge funds* |

3. What is the principal function of *pension funds?* Explain why these institutions have been among the most rapidly growing financial institutions in recent years. Do you expect their growth to be faster or slower in the future? Why? What is the difference between a defined-benefit and a defined-contribution pension plan?

4. What are the principal assets acquired by pension funds? What factors guide their selection of assets to hold? What problems has the pension industry run into in recent years?

---

## 16.4 Life Insurance Companies

**life insurance company**

The recent rapid growth of mutual funds and pension funds contrasts sharply with the somewhat more moderate growth of one of the oldest financial-service firms—the **life insurance company.** Life insurers have been operating for centuries in Europe, and the life insurance company was one of the first financial institutions founded in the

American colonies. The Corporation for Relief of Poor and Distressed Presbyterian Ministers and of the Poor and Distressed Widows and Children of Presbyterian Ministers, established in 1759, was the first U.S.-based life insurer.

Today life insurers have branched out to include not only traditional life insurance policies in their service menus, but also *health insurance* and *annuity plans*. Health insurance programs cover a portion of their policyholders' medical and dental bills, while annuity plans aid clients in building their long-term savings for college educations, new home purchases, and especially for retirement. Many of the largest life carriers have now branched far afield from their origins, insuring damage to personal and business property, which places them in the territory of another insurance industry—*property-casualty insurers*—which we discuss in section 16.5.

Life insurance companies offer their customers a hedge against the risk of financial loss that often follows death, disability, ill health, or retirement. Policyholders receive risk protection in return for the payment of policy premiums that are set high enough to cover estimated benefit claims against the company, all operating expenses, and a target profit margin. Additional funds to cover claims and expenses are provided by the earnings from investments made by life insurance companies in bonds, stocks, and

| EXHIBIT 16.4 | The Principal Kinds of Insurance Policies and Annuity Plans Sold by Many Life Insurance Companies |
|---|---|
| Ordinary or whole life insurance | Insurance protection that covers the entire lifetime of the policyholder. Premiums build up cash values that may be borrowed by the policyholder. |
| Term life insurance | Insurance coverage for a certain number of years so that the policyholder's beneficiaries receive benefit payments only if death occurs within the period of coverage. |
| Endowment policy | A policy with benefits payable to the living policyholder on a specified future date or to the policyholder's beneficiaries if death occurs before the date specified in the policy. |
| Group life insurance | Master insurance policy covering a group of people, usually all working for the same employer or members of the same organization. |
| Industrial life insurance | Small-denomination life policies with premium payments collected monthly or weekly by a company agent. |
| Universal life insurance | Insurance protection with premium payments whose amount and timing can be changed by the policyholder and including a savings account with a flexible rate of return. |
| Variable life insurance | Insurance protection whose benefits vary in amount with the value of assets pledged behind the policy contract. |
| Adjustable life insurance | A flexible form of insurance protection that permits the policyholder to alter some of the policy's terms, period of coverage, or face value. |
| Credit life insurance | A policy pledged to pay off a loan in the event the borrower dies or becomes disabled. |
| Health insurance | Coverage of medical bills, the cost of hospitalization, and possible loss of income arising from accidents and disease. |
| Fixed annuities | Pools of savings built up over time and expected to pay out a fixed stream of income payments beginning on a future date. |
| Variable annuities | Savings plans invested in assets that may appreciate in value over time and pay out an income stream whose size depends on the changing market value of invested savings. |

Source: American Council of Life Insurance.

other assets approved by law and government regulation. The principal kinds of life insurance policies sold by life insurers are listed in Exhibit 16.4.

## The Insurance Principle

**Key URL:**
For a summary of recent developments in sales of life insurance policies and annuities, see especially **financial servicesfacts.org/ financial2/insurance**

The insurance business is founded upon the *law of large numbers.* This mathematical principle states that a risk not predictable for one person can be forecast with reasonable accuracy for a sufficiently large group of people with similar characteristics. For example no insurance company can accurately forecast when any one person will die, but its actuarial estimates of the total number of policyholders who will die in any given year are usually quite accurate.

Life insurance companies today insure policyholders against three basic kinds of risk: *premature death,* the *danger of living too long and outlasting one's accumulated assets,* and *serious illness or accident.* Many policies combine financial protection against death, disability, and retirement with savings plans to help the policyholder prepare for some important future financial need, such as purchase of a home or meeting the costs of a college education. Actually, most benefit payments are made to living, rather than deceased, policyholders, who receive annuity payments or health insurance benefits of various kinds.

Life insurance companies are among the leading sources of retirement (pension) benefit payments for older citizens, and today more than 60 million U.S. citizens are enrolled in pension programs managed by life insurers, including more than $500 billion in tax-deferred retirement savings plans known as IRAs and Keogh plans. Many life-insurer-managed pension plans consist of *fixed annuity accounts* or *variable annuity accounts.* The fixed annuities pay out a stable stream of income to the customer, based upon the amount saved, the expected rate of return on those savings, and the withdrawal rate agreed to between the annuitant and the insurance company. Variable annuities, in contrast, pay out a variable stream of income to the customer that changes over time as the value of accumulated savings in the annuitant's account fluctuates with market conditions.

## Investments of Life Insurance Companies

Life insurers invest the bulk of their funds in long-term securities such as bonds, stocks, and mortgages, thus helping to fund real capital investment by businesses and governments. They are inclined to commit their funds long term due to the high predictability of their cash inflows and outflows. This predictability normally would permit a life insurance company to accept considerable risk in the securities it acquires. However, both law and tradition require a life insurer to act as a "prudent person." This restriction is imposed to ensure sufficient funds are available to meet all legitimate claims from insurance policyholders or their beneficiaries at precisely the time those claims come due.

**Key URLs:**
The life insurance industry and the current trends reshaping that industry can be followed through such Web sites as the U.S. Business Reporter at **activemedia-guide.com** and through the site *of Risk and Insurance Magazine* at **riskandinsurance.com**

Life insurance companies generally pursue *income certainty* and *safety of principal* in their investments. The majority of corporate securities they purchase are in the top four credit-rating categories.[3] Life insurers frequently follow a "buy and hold" strategy, acting as long-term holders of securities rather than rapidly turning over their portfolios. This investment approach reduces the risk of fluctuations in income and avoids having to rely as heavily on forecasting interest rates. We should note, however, that many life insurers have become more active traders in securities. Emphasizing performance more than permanence in their investments, larger life insurance companies

---

[3]See Chapter 8 for an explanation of security ratings.

| EXHIBIT 16.5 | Financial Assets and Liabilities of Life Insurers | |
|---|---|---|
| Asset and Liability Items Outstanding | Amount in 2006[*] ($ Billions) | Percent of Total Assets |
| Assets held: | | |
| Checkable deposits and currency | $ 48.8 | 1.1% |
| Money market fund shares | 126.9 | 2.8 |
| Open market paper | 39.7 | 0.9 |
| U.S. Treasury and federal agency securities | 464.2 | 10.4 |
| State and local government (municipal) securities | 33.8 | 0.8 |
| Corporate and foreign bonds | 1,874.2 | 41.8 |
| Loans to policyholders | 106.6 | 2.4 |
| Mortgage loans | 287.5 | 6.4 |
| Corporate stock (equities) | 1,214.7 | 27.1 |
| Mutual funds shares | 137.8 | 3.1 |
| Miscellaneous assets | 144.5 | 3.2 |
| Total financial assets held | $4,478.7 | 100.0% |
| Liabilities outstanding: | | |
| Loans and advances | $ 12.2 | 0.3% |
| Life insurance reserves | 1,054.1 | 25.1 |
| Pension fund reserves | 2,286.6 | 54.5 |
| Miscellaneous liabilities | 845.1 | 20.1 |
| Total liabilities outstanding | $4,198.0 | 100.0% |

[*]Figures are for the end of the first quarter of 2006.
Note: Columns may not add to total due to rounding error.
Source: Board of Governors of the Federal Reserve System, *Flow of Funds Accounts.*

**Key URLs:**
To understand the life insurance industry more fully, you can look in on a couple of the world's largest life insurers: Prudential Insurance at **prudential.com** and Metropolitan Life Insurance at **metlife .com**

have set up trading rooms to more closely monitor the performance of their investment holdings, selling out and reinvesting in higher-yielding alternatives when circumstances warrant. Because this active investment strategy creates additional risk, many larger insurers use financial futures, options, and other risk-hedging tools and more closely match asset and liability maturities to protect themselves against losses from fluctuating interest rates.[4]

Exhibit 16.5 shows the kinds of investments held by U.S. life insurance companies. The primary investment is in *corporate bonds* issued by both domestic and foreign companies. Several companies ran into trouble recently from heavy purchases of high-risk ("junk") corporate bonds as well as from poorly performing real estate investments, forcing state regulations to take over and liquidate their assets. Industry regulators have recently restricted further purchases of junk bonds. Holdings of common and preferred stock, although smaller, have become significant in recent years at just over a quarter of industry assets. Life insurance companies have shown renewed interest in corporate stock due to the growing importance of variable annuity and variable life insurance policies in their sales programs.

Another important asset held by life insurance companies is *mortgage loans* on farm, residential, and commercial properties, amounting to about 6 percent of industry assets.

---

[4]See Chapter 9 for a detailed discussion of various interest rate hedging methods, including financial futures, options, swaps, and other risk-protection tools.

Substantial changes have occurred in life insurer mortgage investments in recent years. The industry has frequently reduced its holdings of farm and residential mortgages on one-to four-family homes and increased its holdings of commercial mortgages, including loans on retail stores, shopping centers, office buildings, apartments, hospitals, and factories. The higher yields and shorter maturities of the latter loans explain much of the recent growth of commercial mortgage lending by the life insurance industry. However, life insurers continue to provide substantial indirect support to the residential mortgage market by making heavy purchases of federal agency securities, most of which come from government agencies aiding the home mortgage loan market.

Government securities play a secondary but still important role in the portfolios of life insurance companies, representing about 10 percent of life insurers' asset holdings. These securities serve the important function of providing a reservoir of *liquidity* because they may be sold with little difficulty when cash is required. U.S. life insurers buy mostly federal government securities rather than state and local government obligations. The industry has only a limited need for the tax-exempt income provided by state and local bonds because its effective tax rate is relatively low.

One asset whose importance increased dramatically in earlier years, though it has slowed recently, is *loans to policyholders*. The holder of an ordinary (whole life) insurance policy can borrow against the accumulated cash value of that policy, which increases each year. The interest rate on policy loans is stated in the policy contract and in some (especially older policies) may be quite low. Policy loans tend to follow the business cycle, rising in periods when economic activity and interest rates are increasing, and declining when the economy or interest rates are headed down. Because of this cyclical characteristic, policy loans represent a volatile claim on the industry's resources. When policy loan demand is high, life insurance companies may be forced to reduce their purchases of bonds and stocks. In recent years, however, most new whole life policies have had floating loan rates tied to an index of corporate bond yields, and policyholder borrowing has settled into a relatively small percentage of industry assets.

## Sources of Life Insurance Company Funds

The primary funding source for life insurers comes from *premium receipts* from sales of various kinds of annuites and insurance policies. Premiums from sales of annuity plans and health insurance policies have actually grown faster than sales of traditional life insurance policies in recent years. Annual net income from investments in bonds, stocks, and other assets averages only about a third of premium receipts. The industry's net earnings after expenses roughly equal its net investment income each year, because most premiums from the sale of policies are ultimately returned to policyholders or their beneficiaries. This means that, on balance, the industry hopes to roughly break even from its insurance underwriting operations (with premiums flowing in approximately equal to benefits paid out) while earning the majority of its profits from its investment income.

This normal expectation of greater insurance- and annuity-related income than insurance industry claims and expenses sometimes goes awry when tragic events occur. A dramatic example of such an "exogenous shock" to the life insurance industry struck on September 11, 2001, when terrorist attacks on the United States resulted in great loss of life as well as huge property damage. Actually, life insurers often have built-in protections against such costly events should they decide to use them. For example, many life insurance policies exclude the payment of insurance claims resulting from acts of war unless, as happened frequently following the events of September

**Key URLs:**
To discover more about "XXX bonds" or death bonds see, for example, financial-dictionary.thefree dictionary.com/death-backed bonds or ft.com/cms

When insurance companies agree to provide risk protection to their customers, how do they decide how much to charge?

Consider an example. Suppose a life insurer has 100,000 policyholders, each 40 years of age with a $1 million life insurance policy. The company must set an annual premium so it will have sufficient cash to pay the beneficiaries of any policyholders who die this year.

The first thing the insurer must do is determine the expected number of deaths. Actuarial science has produced mortality tables that predict how many individuals of any age are expected to die each year out of every 1,000 persons. If the expected death rate for 40-year-olds is 4 per 1,000, the expected number of deaths in the coming year from this group of 100,000 policyholders is:

$$\begin{aligned} \text{Expected} \atop \text{deaths} &= {\text{Number of} \atop \text{policyholders}} \atop {\text{in age group}} \times {\text{Expected} \atop \text{mortality} \atop \text{rate}} \\ &= \frac{100}{\text{thousand}} \times \frac{4 \text{ per}}{\text{thousand}} = \frac{400 \text{ deaths}}{\text{expected}} \end{aligned}$$

If each policyholder has a $1 million policy, the insurance company must prepare for expected claims of:

$$\begin{aligned} {\text{Expected} \atop \text{claims}} &= {\text{Expected} \atop \text{deaths}} \times {\text{Policy} \atop \text{amounts} \atop \text{promised}} \\ &= 400 \times \$1 \text{million} = \$400 \text{ million} \end{aligned}$$

How much should the insurance company charge each policyholder in premiums? Suppose the 400 deaths expected will occur toward the end of this year. We want to determine how much to charge *all* policyholders at the beginning of this year to be ready for $400 million in claims at year's end. We need to estimate how much the insurance company will earn when it invests the premiums paid by its policyholders in stocks, bonds, and other financial assets. Let's suppose the company estimates it will earn an average of 8 percent on its asset portfolio in the coming year. Thus, to have $400 million available at year's end, the company needs the following amount from its policyholders at the beginning of the year: $400 million/$(1 + .08)^1$ = $370.4 million, or $3,704 per policyholder.

However, this calculation does not include operating costs (e.g., salaries of sales personnel), including the need to earn a normal profit for the company's stockholders. Suppose it will cost $2.6 million to service the insurance needs of policyholders this year. This operating cost is called the *loading*, which must be added to the net premium to drive the *gross premium* charged policyholders:

$$\begin{aligned} {\text{Gross} \atop \text{premium}} &= \frac{\$370.4 \text{ million} + \$2.6 \text{ million}}{100,000 \text{ policyholders}} \\ &= \$3,730 \text{ per policyholder} \end{aligned}$$

Insurance premium rates are also shaped by *competition*, which tends to hold premium rates down and encourages insurers to be more efficient. One powerful demographic factor pushing life insurance premium rates down recently has been the fact that people are living longer, on average. This trend tends to lengthen the stream of premiums policyholders must pay and delays the filing of claims.

2001, the companies involved waive such exclusions. Finally, life insurers recently have been selling "XXX" bonds to raise funds that are linked to life expectancy and mortality statistics that pay off when people die.

## Structure and Growth of the Life Insurance Industry

The majority of the approximately 1,500 U.S. life insurance companies are corporations owned by their stockholders. The rest are *mutuals,* which issue ownership shares to their policyholders. However, mutuals are bigger, on average, and typically were established much earlier than stockholder-owned companies. Most new insurance companies in recent years have been *stockholder owned,* and a substantial number of mutuals have converted to *stock* companies (such as Prudential Insurance) to gain greater financial flexibility and open up new sources of capital. Recently, several big life insurers have converted to stockholder form by creating mutual holding companies, attracting new stockholder capital and issuing stock options to their employees.

The U.S. life insurance industry's population reached a high of almost 2,350 in 1988 and has been falling ever since. Most recently, many of the biggest life insurers worldwide are merging with banks and securities firms, diversifying their services and reaching across continents. Thus, the largest life insurers today are *converging* with other financial-service industries to form huge multiproduct businesses. The world's leading life/health insurance companies include AXA, France at **axa-france.fr;** Nippon Life Insurance, Japan at **nissay.co.jp;** Aviva, United Kingdom at **aviva.com**:. The Prudential, United Kingdom at **prudential.com**: and MetLife Insurance, United States at **metlife.com**.

**Key URL:**
Health insurance companies are often part of or closely related to life insurers. You can follow developments in the health insurance industry via such Web sites as the Healthcare Insurers at **plunkettresearch.com**

## New Services

Life insurers are under increasing pressure to develop *new services* due to a long-term decline in their share of household savings and pressure on their earnings caused by new high-cost, more-automated service delivery systems. Many analysts argue that life insurance is becoming less attractive a product as the population ages, while retirement planning and retirement savings instruments (such as annuities) are likely to grow in importance. Increasing competition from other financial intermediaries, especially mutual funds, has also played a major role in encouraging the development of new services. Among recent developments are the offering of such innovative services as universal and adjustable life insurance, level-premium term insurance, variable premium and variable life insurance, mutual funds, tax shelters, venture capital loans, corporate cash management systems, and deferred annuities.

*Universal life insurance* allows the customer to change the face amount of his or her policy and the size and timing of premium payments, as well as earn higher investment returns from any premiums paid in. Premium payments on universal life insurance usually are invested in a money market fund. Another example of the more flexible life insurance products emerging in recent years is *adjustable life insurance,* which permits the policyholder to change periodically from a whole life policy to term insurance (which offers protection only for a designated period) and back again to deal with changing circumstances. Adjustable policies allow the policyholder to increase or decrease the face value of a policy, the period of insurance protection, and the size of premium payments within limits spelled out in the policy contract. A variation of this idea is *variable premium life insurance,* which grants the policyholder lower premium payments when investments made by the life insurer earn a greater return. *Variable life insurance* pays benefits according to the value of assets pledged behind the policy rather than paying a fixed amount of money. There is normally a guaranteed minimum benefit for the policyholder's beneficiary, however—a form of inflation-hedged life insurance. Finally, *level-premium term insurance bearing guaranteed premiums* continues to grow because it is cheaper with expanding life expectancies and easier to purchase online, by telephone, or through other electronic channels.

Life insurers have also been active in *venture capital loans* to help start new businesses and in offering professional funds management services to many businesses that have neither the time nor the experience to manage their own cash accounts. Life insurers have also found success in attracting *deferred annuity* accounts in which an individual will deposit funds with the insurer under an agreement to receive a future stream of income flowing from those deposited funds beginning on a future date. The insurer agrees to invest the funds in earning assets that will grow over time and escape taxation until the customer actually begins receiving income.

In recent years, insurance companies have found a way to supplement their cash inflows from insurance premiums by selling *guaranteed investment contracts* (GICs) to large institutional investors such as pension funds and state and local governments. Similar to deposits, GICs promise investors a fixed rate of return for a stipulated period. Many corporations and governmental units that have sold bonds in the open market have in turn purchased GICs with the proceeds of those bond issues. GICs have increased insurance company risk somewhat, however, because of their relatively high fixed cost.

One area of growing need is insurance coverage for small businesses. New businesses are being formed today in large numbers, with more than 30 million uninsured persons currently working for them in the United States alone. The provision of life and health insurance for owners and employees of small firms has become a promising service area for those insurers able to correctly price the coverages they provide. Another area of need for the future is health and life insurance for individuals, such as retired citizens, who are no longer members of group insurance plans but have longer life expectancies.

Without question, the new services offered by life insurers in future years will depend heavily upon favorable changes in government laws and regulations. One prominent example is expanded entry into Japan and China, two of the largest insurance and pension plan markets in the world, but this opportunity is dependent upon the willingness of the Japanese and Chinese governments to let more foreign financial firms come in. Life insurers must also continue to lower the cost of marketing and delivering their services, such as through increased use of telephone, television, and Internet sales as well as automation and joint-venture sales of policies through banks and stockbrokers. Correspondingly, the industry has made cuts in its traditional vehicle for the delivery of services—local insurance agencies.

## 16.5  Property-Casualty Insurance Companies

**property-casualty insurers**

**Property-casualty (P/C) insurers** offer protection against fire, theft, bad weather, negligence, and other acts and events that result in injury to persons or property. So broad is the range of risk for which these companies provide protection that P/C insurers are referred to as *insurance supermarkets*. In addition to their traditional insurance lines—automobile, fire, marine, personal liability, and property coverage—many of these firms have branched into the health and medical insurance fields, clashing head-on with life insurers offering the same services. Others have merged with whole new industries and, thereby, reached out to large numbers of potential new customers with an expanded menu of services.

### Makeup of the Property-Casualty (P/C) Insurance Industry

The property-casualty insurance business has grown rapidly in recent years due to the effects of inflation, rising crime rates, and an increasing number of lawsuits arising from product liability and professional negligence claims. There were about 3,000 P/C companies in the United States as the twentieth century drew to a close, holding more than $900 billion in total assets. Stockholder-owned companies are dominant, holding about three-fourths of the industry's total resources. Mutual companies—owned by their policyholders—command roughly one-fourth of all industry resources.

The leading P/C insurers in the world today include Allianz, Germany at **allianz.com;** American International Group, United States at **aig.com;** Munich Re Group, Germany at **marclife.com/links/mrgroup.html;** State Farm Insurance Companies, United States at **statefarm.com;** Berkshire Hathaway, United States at **berkshire-hathaway.com;** Zurich Financial Services at **zurich.com;** Allstate Insurance Company, United States at **allstate.com;** and Swiss Reinsurance, Switzerland at **swissre.com.**

Property-casualty insurers are also grouped by whether they are *agency companies* or *direct writers.* Agency firms sell policies primarily through local agents who earn commissions on their sales from many different insurance companies. Direct writers sell directly to the public (often via telephone, the Web, or television) or have their own dedicated agents to promote their products. In recent years direct writers have captured a rapidly growing share of the insurance industry.

## *Changing Risk Patterns in Property/Liability Coverage*

Property-casualty insurance is a riskier business than life insurance. The risk of policyholder claims arising from crime, fire, personal negligence, and similar causes is less predictable than is the risk of death. Moreover, inflation has had a potent impact on the cost of property and services for which this form of insurance pays. For example, the cost of medical care and repair of automobiles has increased at a more rapid pace than the overall cost of living in recent years.

Equally important, basic changes now seem to be under way in the risk patterns of many large insurance programs, creating problems in forecasting policyholder claims and in setting new premium rates. Examples include a rapid rise in medical malpractice suits; a virtual explosion in product liability claims against manufacturers of automobiles, home appliances, medicines, and other goods; a recent rise in civilian fire deaths and losses due to airplane crashes and weather damage; a rapid increase in terrorist-related losses; and the emergence of billions of dollars in claims from *toxic torts,* arising from individuals suffering from illness or injury caused by exposure to asbestos, lead, nuclear radiation, and other hazardous substances.

**Key URL:**
For an overview of disaster risks and key underwriters of disaster risk, see in particular, **disaster information.org/stats .htm**

Natural disasters have also proven to be exceptionally difficult for P/C insurers that are providing catastrophic insurance for floods, droughts, earthquakes, and hurricanes. One particular event that led to a major reassessment of the industry's exposure to such risks was Hurricane Andrew that devastated South Florida in 1992, becoming one of the largest natural disasters in history with an estimated $20 billion in insured property losses. These losses exceeded the "worst case scenarios" of potential losses inflicted by a single storm and forced a number of P/C insurers into bankruptcy. Many other insurers began pulling out until Florida's legislature intervened and forced a moratorium on insurance companies attempting to cancel existing policies. This action set in motion a series of legislative reforms designed to assure that catastrophic hurricane insurance would continue to be provided to homeowners and businesses at affordable rates. They included establishing the Florida Hurricane Catastrophe Fund (FHCF) to relieve financial stress on insurers in the aftermath of future hurricane disasters. The FHCF is financed by the insurance industry, but maintains a borrowing capacity based on low (tax-free) municipal bond interest rates to supplement the fund in extreme cases.

The terrorist attacks in September 2001 subjected insurance companies to one of the most panicky episodes in their history. The attacks on the New York City World Trade Center and the Pentagon cost more than 3,000 lives and millions of dollars in property damage. Fear of possible collapse ran through the insurance industry (with the stock prices of leading insurers falling precipitously) in the wake of these tragedies.

Because the terrorist attacks came from outside the normal purview of the financial system, this huge external shock to the insurance industry was completely unexpected. Insurance companies had no time to adjust the premiums they charge to cover the claims they faced. Many insurers feared they would have inadequate reserves to pay off a flood of policyholder claims.

Proposals were made to the U.S. government to backstop the industry and become an "insurer of last resort."

A number of insurers indicated that they had little choice but to include new *terror-exclusion clauses* in policies sold to the public. Reason: A number of leading *reinsurers*—companies that accept some of the risks taken on by primary insurance providers—declared they would no longer underwrite terrorist-related risks. At the same time, several insurers debated whether or not to enforce a standard exclusion that has been included in many policies for years—denial of any claims arising from "acts of war." Regardless, some companies have recently begun to offer anti-terror coverage and the insurance industry appears to have weathered the financial storm that the 9/11 tragedy created.

In addition, the Florida legislature passed stricter building codes to minimize structural damage from winds and tides, provided for funding to improve hurricane risk assessment models to better inform regulators about proper insurance rates, and set about to improve coordination of state and national emergency relief agencies to minimize post-hurricane damage due to flooding and tornadoes and the eventual loss of life. Nonetheless, with predictions of hurricane forecasters that the Atlantic basin is currently in a period of heightened hurricane activity, the risk of future catastrophic insurance losses looms large. The extraordinary hurricane season of 2004 that saw *four* hurricanes (Charley, Frances, Ivan, and Jeanne) make landfall in the state of Florida and, more recently, the sweeping invasion of the U.S. GulfCoast by Hurricane Katrina which did unprecedented damage to New Orleans, is evidence that these concerns are probably warranted.

To reduce risk, more P/C insurers have become *multiple-line companies,* diversifying into many different lines of insurance. Another risk-reducing device of growing importance is the *reinsurance* market, in which an insurer contracts with other companies to share some of the risks of its insurance underwriting in return for a share of the insurer's premium. The leading reinsurance firms today include Munich RE Group, Swiss RE Group, Berkshire Hathaway RE Group, and GE Insurance Solutions.

One consequence of Hurricane Andrew, the devastating Northridge earthquake (in the Los Angeles area) in 1994, and more recent disasters has been the creation of *monoline* reinsurance companies that specialize in property damage associated exclusively with wind and earthquake damage but that operate worldwide. In addition to these structural changes taking place within the industry, there have been a number of financial innovations, such as weather derivatives and catastrophe bonds.

Catastrophe bonds are issued through special purpose vehicles (SPVs) or through reinsurers in an effort to raise new funds and spread insurance risks over larger numbers of capital-market investors. Buyers of these bonds get their money back plus a preset rate of return if damaging casualties fail to occur above a certain threshold

**Key URL:**
For a more in-depth discussion of the reinsurance market and reinsurance contracts, see especially **iii.org/media/hot topics insurance/finite**

level. Weather derivatives, on the other hand, pay an agreed-upon amount if unusual weather conditions emerge (including extreme fluctuations in snowfall, rain, or temperatures) that result in damage to businesses, households, and other institutions.

It is interesting to compare the distribution of assets held by life insurance companies to those assets held by P/C companies. The net cash flows of the two industries—their annual premium incomes—are roughly comparable. Yet life insurers hold about three and one-half times the assets of P/C insurers. Much of the difference is explained by the fact that life insurance is a highly predictable business, whereas property and personal injury risks are not. Most life insurance policies are long-term contracts, and claims against the insurer are not normally expected for several years. In contrast, P/C claims are payable from the day a policy is written because an accident or injury may occur at any time. Therefore, although life insurers can stay almost fully invested, P/C insurers must be ready at all times to meet claims from their policyholders. In addition claims against P/C companies are directly affected by inflation, which drives up repair costs. Most life insurance policies, in contrast, pay the beneficiary a fixed sum of money or an amount based upon the market value of investments that back the policies.

## Investments by Property-Casualty (P/C) Companies

The majority of funds received by P/C companies are invested in corporate and foreign bonds, state and local government bonds, and common stock. P/C insurers, unlike many financial institutions, are subject to the full corporate income tax (except that policyholder dividends are tax-deductible for the issuing company). Faced with a potentially heavy tax burden, these companies find tax-exempt state and local government bonds an attractive investment, but they also like the high yields and steady income promised by corporate bonds. As shown in Exhibit 16.6, industry holdings of

**Key URL:**
Will my insurance company be around when I need it? One way to answer that question is to check with the company that provides quality ratings for insurance companies, A. M. Best Company, at **bestweek.com**

| EXHIBIT 16.6 | Financial Assets and Liabilities of Property-Casualty Insurers | |
|---|---|---|
| Asset and Liability Items Outstanding | Amount in 2006* ($ billions) | Percent of Total Assets |
| Assets held: | | |
| Checkable deposits and currency | $   19.3 | 1.5% |
| Security repurchase agreements | 72.1 | 5.6 |
| U.S. Treasury and federal agency securities | 189.0 | 14.8 |
| State and local government (municipal) securities | 306.9 | 24.0 |
| Corporate and foreign bonds | 283.4 | 22.1 |
| Commercial mortgage loans | 2.8 | 0.2 |
| Corporate stock (equities) | 214.9 | 16.8 |
| Miscellaneous assets | 191.3 | 14.9 |
| Total financial assets outstanding | $1,279.7 | 100.0% |
| Liabilities outstanding: | | |
| Taxes payable | 39.4 | 4.8% |
| Miscellaneous liabilities | 780.8 | 95.2 |
| Total liabilities outstanding | $ 820.2 | 100.0% |

*Figures are for the end of the first quarter of 2006.
Note: Columns may not add to totals due to rounding errors.
Source: Board of Governors of the Federal Reserve System, *Flow of Funds Accounts*.

state and local bonds represented nearly a quarter of its total financial assets, with corporate and foreign bonds representing a slightly smaller proportion of industry assets at 22 percent.

Another important asset—corporate stock, representing close to a sixth of all industry assets—is intended to protect industry earnings and net worth against inflation. Other significant investments include U.S. government securities and federal agency securities, due primarily to their greater safety and liquidity.

## Sources of Income

**Key URLs:**
In order to learn more about the problems and issues in the property/casualty insurance industry, see the Web sites of two of the largest P/C firms: State Farm Insurance Companies at **statefarm.com** and Allstate Insurance at **allstate.com**

Like life insurance firms, P/C insurers plan to roughly break even on their insurance product lines and earn most of their net return from their investments. Achieving the break-even point in casualty insurance underwriting can be difficult, however, due to rising costs, intense competition, increased litigation, the frequent reluctance of state insurance commissions to boost policy premiums, and new forms of risk such as terror, product liability, and global warming. In fact, property-casualty insurers have experienced billions of dollars in underwriting losses in selected years, though their profits soared after the first of the new century as the number of hurricanes making landfall subsided, home prices softened, and more effective risk-management tools appeared.

## Business Cycles, Inflation, and Competition

Property-casualty insurance is an industry whose earnings and sales revenue reflect the ups and downs of the business cycle. This cyclical sensitivity, coupled with the vulnerability of P/C insurers to inflation, has created a difficult environment for insurance managers. Inflation pushes up the cost of claims, while intense competition holds premium rates down. Among U.S. P/C companies a key challenge today is the rapid growth of foreign insurance underwriters who have entered the United States in large numbers, including such companies as Allianz, Munich Re Group and Zurich Financial Services. Moreover, many U.S. corporations have started their own *captive* insurance companies. To improve their situation for the future, P/C insurers must become more innovative in developing new services and more determined to eliminate those services that result in underwriting losses, and they must reduce their operating costs. This will not be easy due to extensive regulations and public pressure for lower insurance rates.

---

### QUESTIONS TO HELP YOU STUDY

5. Against what kinds of *risk* do life insurance companies protect their policyholders? What about property-casualty insurers?

6. Compare and contrast the asset portfolios of life insurance companies with the asset portfolios of property-casualty insurers. Explain any differences you observe.

7. What factors influence the *premiums* insurers charge their policyholders?

8. What is happening to the mix of services offered by life insurers and property-casualty insurance companies? Why?

One of the best examples of the struggles insurance companies have faced in recent years to preserve their profitability and capital is Lloyds of London (**lloyds .com**)—the three-centuries-old insurance market in which individual investors (called "names") underwrite the risks taken on by its clients in return for premiums and investment income. Lloyds has insured some unusual risks, including actress Elizabeth Taylor's eyes, while also underwriting the reward for corralling the Loch Ness monster! What is equally unusual about Lloyds is that its "names" (underwriters) pledge their entire net worth, if necessary, to cover their share of any losses that occur.

From time to time the risks associated with a volatile economy, political upheaval, weather fluctuations, environmental damage, and other sources of loss, have resulted in burgeoning claims that have threatened Lloyds's resources. One point in Lloyds's favor is that it requires full (100 percent) setting aside of reserves behind any possible claims, whereas most regular insurers set aside fewer reserves and count on other income (mainly investment earnings) to help cover claims received. Moreover, Lloyds has imposed special levies on its members and, for the first time in its history, recently allowed corporate capital to come in. The venerable insurer has also turned more heavily to the reinsurance market (where policies are written to back up any excess risk presented by conventional insurance contracts). These recent steps by Lloyds illustrate how creative the managers of insurance companies must be to deal with the risks and intense global competition that confront the industry today.

## 16.6 Finance Companies

**finance companies**

**Finance companies** are sometimes called *department stores of consumer and business credit.* These institutions grant credit to businesses and consumers for a wide variety of purposes, including the purchase of business equipment, automobiles, vacations, and home appliances. Most authorities divide firms in the industry into one of three groups—consumer finance companies, sales finance companies, and commercial finance companies.

### Different Finance Companies for Different Purposes

*Consumer finance companies* make personal cash loans to individuals and issue consumer credit cards. The majority of their loans are home equity loans; loans to support the purchase of passenger cars, recreational vehicles, home appliances, and mobile homes; and credit to cover medical and hospital expenses, educational costs, and travel. Loans made by consumer finance companies are considered to be riskier than other consumer installment loans and, therefore, generally carry steeper finance charges than those assessed by many other lending institutions (such as banks and credit unions). Among the leaders in consumer finance are Household International at **household.com** and Beneficial Finance Corp. at **beneficial.com.**

*Sales finance companies* make indirect loans to consumers by purchasing installment paper from dealers selling automobiles and other consumer durables. Many of these firms are "captive" finance companies controlled by a dealer or manufacturer, whose principal function is to promote sales of the sponsoring firm's products. Generally, sales finance companies specify in advance to retail dealers the terms of installment contracts they are willing to accept. Frequently they will give the retail dealer sample contract forms, which the dealer fills out when a sale is made. The contract is then sold to the finance company. Among the leading "captive" finance companies are Ford Motor Credit Co. at **fordcredit.com** and GMAC Financial Services at **gmacfs.com.**

**Key URL:**
For a useful overview of recent developments in the finance company industry, see especially **financialservicefacts.org/ financial2/finance/ overview/**

*Commercial finance companies* focus principally on extending credit to business firms. Most of these companies provide accounts receivable financing or factoring services to small- or medium-sized manufacturers and wholesalers. With accounts receivable financing, the commercial finance company may extend credit against the borrower's receivables in the form of a direct cash loan. Alternatively, a factoring arrangement may be used in which the finance company acquires the borrowing firm's credit accounts at an appropriate discount rate to cover the risk of loss. Most commercial finance companies today do not confine their credit-granting activities to the financing of receivables but also make loans secured by business inventories and fixed assets. In addition, they offer lease financing for the purchase of capital equipment and rolling stock (such as airplanes and railroad cars) and make short-term unsecured cash loans. Among the principal commercial finance companies today are GE Capital Corporation at **gecapital.com** and Morgan Stanley Dean Witter Credit Corp. at **morganstanley.com.**

We should not overdramatize the differences among these three types of finance companies. Larger companies are active in all three areas. In addition, most finance companies today are extremely diversified in their credit-granting activities, offering a wide range of installment and working capital loans, credit-card loans, leasing plans, and long-term credit to support capital investment. Exhibit 16.7 shows that business loans are the most important assets held by finance companies, accounting for nearly 40 percent of the industry's assets, followed by loans to individuals, accounting for slightly more than a quarter of all assets. However, returns on the equity capital of consumer-oriented finance companies average about double the equity-capital returns of commercial-oriented companies, though the former tend to experience the most

| EXHIBIT 16.7 | Financial Assets and Liabilities Held by Finance Companies | | |
|---|---|---|---|
| **Asset and Liability Items Outstanding** | | **Amount in 2006\*** **($ Billions)** | **Percent of Total Assets** |
| Assets held: | | | |
| Checkable deposits and currency | | $ 45.2 | 3.5% |
| Mortgage loans | | 294.5 | 22.7 |
| Consumer credit | | 346.5 | 26.7 |
| Business loans and advances | | 507.2 | 39.0 |
| Miscellaneous assets | | 106.1 | 8.2 |
| Total financial assets held[†] | | $1,299.5 | 100.0% |
| Liabilities outstanding: | | | |
| Open market paper | | $ 139.8 | 9.1% |
| Corporate bonds | | 823.5 | 53.8 |
| Bank loans (not elsewhere classified) | | 66.7 | 4.4 |
| Miscellaneous liabilities (including foreign direct investment in the United States and investments by parent companies) | | 499.5 | 32.7 |
| Total liabilities outstanding | | $1,529.5 | 100.0% |

\*Figures shown are for end of first quarter of 2006.

[†]Financial assets held do not include receivables from operating leases granted by finance companies, such as consumer auto loans that are booked to operating income. The leased equipment is *not* a financial asset.

Note: Columns may not add to totals due to rounding error.

Source: Board of Governors of the Federal Reserve System.

volatile returns. Real estate mortgage loans have also become a significant portion of industry assets, representing one of the fastest-growing finance company assets in recent years. Smaller amounts of funds are held in cash to provide immediate liquidity.

## Growth of Finance Companies

Finance companies have been profoundly affected by recent changes in the character of competition among all financial intermediaries. The lack of an extensive network of branch offices has put many finance companies at a disadvantage in reaching the household borrower who values convenience. As a result, both banks and thrifts have been able to capture a larger share of the consumer loan market at the expense of finance companies. For example, data compiled by the Federal Reserve Board show that finance companies held about 45 percent of nonresidential consumer loans extended by financial institutions in 1950 but only about 16 percent as the twenty-first century opened, although captive finance companies of automobile manufacturers (such as Ford Motor Credit) have done well vis-à-vis their competitors by offering discount-rate loans. By way of comparison, over the same time interval, credit unions have more than tripled their share of the consumer loan market. Despite the struggle of most finance companies to maintain their share of the financial-services marketplace, some of these companies have grown tremendously, largely by merger. For example, GE Capital, which recently has made extensive acquisitions of consumer finance companies in Europe, ranks today as the largest nonbank financial firm in the world, with assets in excess of $600 billion.

Many experts now believe that the fastest growing market for finance companies in future years will be in business-oriented, not consumer-oriented, financial services. Revolving credit, working capital loans, merger and acquisition loans, and equipment leasing are among the fastest growing forms of credit extended by finance companies today. Recently, finance companies have expanded their lending programs to include small- and medium-sized businesses, making loans to and accepting some of the stock of these firms. However, home equity lending to consumers has also grown rapidly in recent years.

## Methods of Industry Financing

**Key URL:**
For a virtual tour of GE Capital, the world's largest finance company, see especially **gecapital.com**

Finance companies are heavy users of *debt* in financing their operations. Principal sources of borrowed funds include bank loans, short-term notes (commercial paper), and debentures (bonds) sold primarily to banks, insurance companies, nonfinancial corporations, and parent companies. (See Exhibit 16.7.) The source of funds that these companies emphasize most heavily at any given time depends on the structure of interest rates. When long-term rates are high, these companies tend to emphasize commercial paper and short-term bank loans as sources of funds; when long-term rates are relatively low, longer-term bonds have been drawn on more heavily.

## Recent Changes in the Character of the Finance Company Industry

*Consolidation in the Industry*    The structure of the finance industry has changed markedly in recent years. As in the case of banks, credit unions, and savings and loans, the number of finance companies has been trending *downward*, although the average size of such companies has grown considerably. A survey by the Federal

Reserve Board revealed that about 50 years ago there were more than 6,000 finance companies operating in the United States, but by the beginning of the twenty-first century, less than a thousand finance companies could be found, many of these operating as finance company subsidiaries belonging to bank holding companies or large manufacturing companies. The industry is concentrated; the 20 top firms holding three-quarters or more of all industry receivables.

This long-term downtrend in the industry's population reflects a number of powerful economic forces at work. Rising cost pressures, the broadening of markets, the need to innovate, and intensified competition have encouraged finance companies to strive for larger size and greater operating efficiency. Many smaller companies have sold out to larger conglomerates. Despite their declining numbers, however, finance companies continue to be a potent force in the markets for business and consumer credit.

**Key URLs:**
To learn more about small loan companies, see such sites as **paydayloaninfo.org/states.cfm**, **responsiblelending.org/pdfs**, and **ftc.gov**

*New Types of Finance Companies* Relatively new forms of consumer-oriented finance companies have been emerging recently in the form of *pawnshop, rent-to-own, title loan,* and *check-cashing companies*—sometimes referred to as "fringe banks." These small finance companies invite customers to pledge their personal assets (such as an automobile, home, television set, or future paycheck) in return for a loan at a relatively high rate of interest (often the loan rates far exceed 100 percent). These businesses open up the financial system to a whole new tier of customers (mainly lower-income individuals and families) who are short of immediate cash and often have poor credit histories. The result is that pawnshop, rent-to-own, title loan, and check-cashing companies most frequently seem to serve those customers who have few other places from which they can borrow money.

## 16.7 Investment Banks

**investment bank**

**Key URL:**
If you are interested in a career in investment banking check out the site **careers-in-finance.com**

One of the most important institutions in the financial system (and also one of the riskiest) is the **investment bank.** These financial firms are not deposit-takers like the commercial and savings banks we discussed in the preceding two chapters. Rather, investment banks raise funds for and provide financial advice to corporations and government agencies around the world. The principal function of investment banks is to help market large volumes of *new* stocks, bonds, and other financial instruments issued by their corporate and governmental customers in order to raise new money, acting as "wholesalers" in attracting and distributing capital.

### The Underwriting Function of Investment Banks

These specialized "banks" are especially prominent in the offering of new corporate debt and equity securities, state and local (municipal) bonds and notes, and securities issued by various units of the federal government, including Treasury debt and agency securities issued by such institutions as Fannie Mae (the Federal National Mortgage Association), Freddie Mac (the Federal Home Loan Mortgage Corporation), and the Farm Credit Administration. They *underwrite* new offerings of these financial instruments, purchasing them from the original issuer and placing them in the hands of buyers, hopefully at a higher price than the price paid the issuer.

Security underwriting places investment banks at substantial *risk* because the market value of the securities being underwritten may fall, presenting the underwriter with substantial losses on resale. To mitigate these risks, often several investment bankers will band together to form a *syndicate* in order to bid for and market a new security issue, thereby spreading risk exposure among multiple underwriters.

## Other Investment Banking Services

Investment banks also deal with risk by offering a long menu of diverse services so their revenue flows are not dependent on security underwriting alone. For example, they give advice on the best terms and times to engage in corporate mergers and acquisitions (including leveraged buyouts of companies) and when and where to venture into new markets, at home and abroad. Several are active traders in commodities and foreign currencies as well as debt and equity instruments. They manage assets for their customers (which include pension funds and major corporations) and set up hedge funds and other investment companies to attract their clients' investable funds.

## Leading Investment Banks and the Convergence of Commercial and Investment Banking

Investment banking firms include some of the best-known names in the financial world—for example, Morgan Stanley at **morganstanley.com,** Goldman Sachs Group at **gs.com,** Merrill Lynch Capital Markets at **ml.com,** Credit Suisse Group at **credit-suisse.com/en/home.html,** Lehman Brothers at **lehman.com,** and Bear Stearns at **bearstearns.com.** Competition between these financial firms has become intense as markets have become global in their scope. In the wake of the repeal of the Glass-Steagall Act of 1933—which, for nearly 60 years, legally separated commercial and investment banking—many investment banks have been absorbed in recent years by commercial banking companies. Under the terms of the Gramm-Leach-Bliley (GLB) Act of 1999, investment banks may be acquired by holding companies centered around a commercial bank, be set up as subsidiary corporations of banks themselves, or acquire or start their own commercial banking affiliates.

The amalgamation of commercial and investment banking opens up a wider menu of services that bankers can sell to their major corporate customers. For example, the clientele of a combined commercial and investment banking firm may be offered conventional bank loans, if this traditional form of credit best meets a customer's financing needs or, alternatively, may be guided into the open market to seek out cheaper and more abundant funds through the sale of stocks, bonds, and other securities. Clearly, firms that operate simultaneously as both commercial and investment banks have a distinct advantage over their competitors in today's financial-services marketplace.

## 16.8   Other Important Financial Institutions

**security brokers and dealers**

**Key URL:**
For up-to-date facts on the security broker-dealer industry, see in particular **financial servicefacts.org/financial2/securities/overview/**

In addition to the financial firms we have discussed thus far, a number of other financial-service institutions have developed over the years to meet the specialized needs of their customers. For example, **security brokers and dealers** provide a conduit for buyers and sellers of stocks, bonds, and other marketable financial instruments to adjust their holdings of these assets. For their part, *security dealers* stand ready to buy private and government securities from their clients and sell those same instruments to other clients who need to make adjustments in their investment portfolios. By standing ready to buy and sell particular assets, dealers literally "make a market" for the assets they trade. In contrast, *security brokers* do not "take a position of risk" as dealers do when they buy and hold assets from their customers. Rather, brokers merely bring buyers and sellers together and facilitate the exchange of assets.

Brokers and dealers reduce information costs for buyers and sellers of financial instruments and help increase the liquidity of the instruments they trade. Brokerage commissions and dealer fees are charged to compensate these financial firms for the services they provide, although intense competition in this field (especially with the appearance of discount brokers) and the development of efficient computer software to support online trading have led to downward pressure on brokerage commissions and dealer fees and encouraged security brokers and dealers to develop and offer their customers an expanded menu of services (including securities' research, cash management, and financial planning services). The leaders in this industry include such familiar names as Merrill Lynch at **ml.com;** Fidelity at **fidelity.com;** Paine Webber at **painewebber.com;** Charles Schwab at **charlesschwab.com;** and A. G. Edwards & Company at **agedwards.com.**

**venture capital firms**

A rising but highly volatile financial-service industry today consists of **venture capital firms.** These businesses gather funds from private investors and other sources and then look for promising new businesses or rapidly emerging companies in which to invest. They often fund the development of innovative new products or services, such as new computer software or medicines, in the hope of earning exceptional returns if these new products or services succeed. Many large banks, insurance companies, and other traditional financial intermediaries have set up affiliated venture-capital companies to make these risky investments and hold the high-risk stocks or bonds of promising new or rapidly growing businesses.

**Key URL:**
To learn more about venture capital firms, see the Web site of the National Venture Capital Association at **nvca.org**

**mortgage bank**

A key financial firm supporting the mortgage loan market is the **mortgage bank.** Mortgage bankers commit themselves to take on new mortgage loans used to fund the construction of homes, office buildings, and other structures. They carry these loans for a short time until the mortgages can be sold to a long-term (permanent) lender such as an insurance company or thrift institution. As in the case with other dealer operations, the financial risks to the mortgage banker are substantial. A rise in interest rates sharply reduces the market value of existing fixed-rate mortgage loans, presenting the mortgage banker with a loss when it sells loans out of its portfolio. The risk of rising interest rates and falling mortgage prices encourages mortgage banks to turn over their portfolios rapidly and to arrange lines of credit from lending institutions to backstop their operations. These firms also service the mortgage loans they sell to other lenders, collecting loan payments and inspecting mortgaged property. Among the leading privately owned mortgage bank and mortgage finance companies today are Wells Fargo Home Mortgage Inc. at **wellsfargo-mn.com;** Chase Manhattan Mortgage Corp. at **chase.com;** National City Mortgage Company at **nationalcitymortgage.com;** Countrywide Financial Corp. at **countrywide.com;** General Motors Acceptance Corp. at **gmacfs.com;** and Washington Mutual Bank at **wamu.com.**

**Key URL:**
Additional information about the mortgage banking industry is available from the Web site of the Mortgage Bankers Association at **mbaa.org**

**government-sponsored enterprises (GSEs)**

The most prominent mortgage banking operations today are centered around **government-sponsored enterprises (GSEs),** created originally by the U.S. Congress in order to improve the flow of mortgage credit from lenders to homeowners, farmers, and other groups in need of lower-cost, more abundant long-term loans. Leading the GSE group are the Federal National Mortgage Association (FNMA or Fannie Mae), the Federal Home Loan Mortgage Corporation (FHLMC or Freddie Mac), and the Federal Home Loan Banks (FHLBs), responsible today for more than three-quarters of the residential mortgage loans in the United States. The GSEs claim they have played a major role in expanding home ownership so that more than two-thirds of all American households now live in their own dwelling—one of the highest home-ownership rates in the world.

**real estate investment trusts (REITs)**

Authorized by federal law in 1960, **real estate investment trusts (REITs)** are publicly held, tax-exempt corporations that must receive at least three-quarters of their gross income from real estate transactions (such as rental income, mortgage interest, and sales of property). They also must devote at least three-quarters of their assets to real estate property loans, cash, and government securities. REITs raise funds by selling stock and debt securities and invest most of their available funds in mortgage loans to finance the building of apartments, housing tracts, office buildings, shopping centers, and other commercial ventures.

**leasing companies**

**Key URLs:**
You can learn more about REITs from the National Association of Real Estate Investment Trusts at *nareit.com*
To explore trends in the leasing company industry, see such sites as The Association for Equipment Leasing and Finance at *elaonline.com*

**Leasing companies** represent still another kind of specialized financial institution that provides customers with access to productive assets, such as airplanes, automobiles, and equipment through the writing of leases. These leases allow a business or household to rent assets often at a lower cost than borrowing money and owning those same assets. The leasing company, on the other hand, benefits from the stream of lease payments and gains substantial tax benefits from depreciating the leased assets. Competition is intense in this industry because of the entry of scores of banks and bank holding companies, insurance and finance companies, and manufacturing firms that have either opened leasing departments or formed subsidiary leasing companies.

## 16.9  Trends Affecting All Financial Institutions Today

There are several major trends affecting virtually all financial institutions today. One of these trends is *increasing cost pressures* resulting from expenses associated with raising funds for lending and investing and burgeoning land, labor, and equipment costs that have narrowed profit margins. Another trend is *consolidation,* in which each financial institution tries to expand its size to improve efficiency and ease its cost burdens. A key result of the consolidation movement is declining numbers of independent financial institutions, while the remaining institutions average much larger in size and organizational complexity.

Still a third trend is *service diversification,* as all major financial institutions have invaded each other's traditional markets with new services in an effort to offset rising costs and expand profit margins. Service diversification has led to a blurring of functions among different financial institutions to such an extent that it is becoming increasingly difficult to distinguish between different financial firms—a phenomenon known as *homogenization.*

Service diversification has led to *convergence* as banks, insurance companies, security firms, and other types of financial institutions rush toward one another and, increasingly, merge with each other to become large financial conglomerates. This convergence trend has been aided considerably by passage of the Financial Services Modernization (Gramm-Leach-Bliley or GLB) Act passed in the United States in 1999. GLB permits banks, insurers, and securities firms (as well as selected other financial firms) to reach across industry boundaries and link up with each other.

An added dimension of convergence and service diversification has been provided recently by large nonfinancial businesses, such as Wal-Mart, that have begun to offer check-cashing services and sales of debit cards and money orders to their customers, many of whom are "unbanked" (i.e., have no formal connection to the banking system). Some of these nonfinancial businesses (such as GM and Target) have managed to secure special corporate charters, including thrift and industrial loan charters, to give them a foothold inside the banking system.

The offering of many new services over wider market areas has been made possible by another trend in the financial institutions' sector: a *technological revolution,* particularly in the growing adoption of automated electronic equipment for transferring financial information. Increasingly, there is less and less need to walk into the offices of a financial institution, because many transactions can be handled more efficiently via home and office computers linked online to each financial firm's computer network.

The technological revolution has made possible a global financial system and unleashed a trend toward *global competition* in which all financial institutions find themselves increasingly in a common market, competing for many of the same customers. Distance and geography no longer shelter financial institutions from the forces of demand and supply in the financial system as they often did in the past. Accompanying the rise of global competition is a drive toward *regulatory cooperation,* so that financial institutions headquartered in different countries face essentially the *same* regulatory rules. There is a trend toward harmonizing laws and regulations so that no one country's financial institutions operate at a competitive disadvantage vis-à-vis those of another country.

Many of the new services and technological innovations and the development of global competition have come into existence because of a trend toward *deregulation,* in which the content and prices of financial services increasingly are being determined by the marketplace rather than by government rules. Most of the deregulation movement, thus far, has centered upon depository institutions and security dealers and brokers in Canada, the United States, Japan, Great Britain, Australia, and Western Europe. However, as depository institutions and securities firms continue to receive new service powers and expand their markets, it is quite likely that the whole panoply of financial institutions will seek to further loosen the regulatory rules that bind them today. It is hoped the public will be the ultimate beneficiary in terms of more and better financial services at lower cost.

## QUESTIONS TO HELP YOU STUDY

9.  What role do *finance companies* play in supplying funds to the financial marketplace? How many different kinds of finance companies are there?

10. A growing sector within the general finance company industry consists of *small-loan companies,* which include *pawnshops, rent-to-own stores, title loan firms,* and *check-cashing companies?* What do these firms do? What kinds of customers do they serve?

11. What are *investment banks?* Why are they important to the economic and financial system? What risks do they face?

12. What is a *REIT?* A *mortgage bank?* A *leasing company?* Why do you think these specialized lenders came into being? Have they faced any serious problems of late?

13. What functions do security brokers and dealers perform within the financial system? Why are these security companies so important to the money and capital markets?

14. In the concluding section of this chapter, several major trends affecting all financial institutions today were discussed. Identify these trends. Which ones do you see as long-term trends likely to continue indefinitely into the future? Which may be short-lived (if any)? Explain your answer.

## Summary of the Chapter's Main Points

This chapter examined the services offered by and the portfolio characteristics of a wide variety of different financial institutions, including mutual funds or investment companies, pension funds, life and property-casualty insurance companies, finance companies, security firms, mortgage banks, real estate investment trusts, leasing companies, venture capital firms, and financial conglomerates of various types.

- Several of the financial institutions discussed in this chapter—particularly *pension funds* and *insurance companies*—provide risk protection for their customers against death, ill health, negligence, loss of property, and the danger of outliving one's savings in retirement. In addition, pension funds, insurance companies, and most of the other financial-service institutions examined in this chapter make loans in the money and capital markets to businesses, individuals, and governments. They are predominantly *capital market institutions,* focused mainly upon providing long-term credit.

- Among the most rapidly growing financial institutions of the past decade have been *investment companies*—most often referred to as *mutual funds.* Investment companies sell shares to the public and use the proceeds of those sales to buy various types of stocks, bonds, and other securities. Shareholders in a mutual fund receive earnings based on the performance of the securities held by the company. Mutual funds have grown rapidly in recent years, in part because they offer small savers better access to the financial marketplace, provide professional funds management and portfolio diversification, and supply liquidity if a customer needs to quickly convert his or her investments into cash.

- Among the more rapidly growing sectors in this financial-services field are *finance companies,* which provide credit to businesses and households. Finance companies too are merging into fewer but larger firms with a growing menu of loans and other financial services. However, this financial-service industry is also developing numerous small-loan companies (in the form of pawnshops, title loan companies, rent-to-own stores, and check-cashing facilities) that cater to individuals and families, particularly those customers presenting greater risk of loan default.

- One of the most exciting and potentially rewarding financial-service industries is *investment banking.* Investment bankers assist corporations and governments in raising new capital by purchasing their clients' stocks, bonds, and other securities and reselling those same securities to other investors. In addition to security underwriting services, investment bankers supply technical advice to businesses interested in pursuing mergers and acquisitions or entering into new product lines or new market areas.

- The chapter concludes its survey of major financial institutions with an overview of such key industries as *real estate investment trusts* (*REITs*) and *mortgage banks,* which serve the home loan industry and also provide funds for commercial building projects. Another key sector is *security brokers and dealers* who make it possible for the public to buy and sell securities to adjust the quality and yield on their investment portfolios. Finally, financial support for many businesses today comes from *leasing companies,* who rent facilities and equipment to expanding firms and *venture capital companies,* who inject capital and management expertise into new firms or into rapidly growing enterprises that have limited sources of funding available to them.

- All of the financial institutions discussed in this chapter are undergoing major changes in the form of *consolidation* of smaller financial-service firms into larger financial-service providers. Not only are financial firms in the same industry growing larger, but many are reaching across industries and combining different service providers under one corporate umbrella—a phenomenon known as *convergence.* This convergence trend has been helped along by new government legislation (such as the Financial Services Modernization [Gramm-Leach-Bliley] Act passed in the United States in 1999).

- In an effort to lower production costs and reduce risk exposure, most financial institutions are diversifying their services—developing and adding new services in order to reduce the overall risk exposure to their revenues and net earnings. One result of this *service diversification* trend is to make more and more financial companies look alike (*homogenization*) because they are offering many of the same services as their neighbors. Even nonfinancial businesses, such as Wal-Mart and GM, have joined the service diversification and convergence trends, offering credit and debit cards that compete with similar services offered by conventional financial firms.

- Changes in the *technology of information gathering and distribution* have had a greater impact on financial institutions than most other industries, permitting these institutions to serve their customers with greater accuracy and speed over wider geographic areas. New computer-based technology has allowed financial-service firms to reduce their personnel expenses and become less labor-intensive but more capital-intensive in their service production and distribution activities.

- More financial-service institutions have become *international* in their focus, reaching across national borders with their services. This trend toward *globalization* has contributed to *the emergence* of much larger financial firms and broader financial service menus. Globalization has also encouraged government regulatory agencies in various countries to reach out to each other and cooperate in their oversight of the activities and performance of the financial-services sector.

## Key Terms Appearing in This Chapter

www.mhhe.com.rose10e

## Problems and Issues

1. The manager of a life insurance company is trying to decide what annual premium to charge a group of policyholders, each of whom has just reached his or her 40th birthday. A check of mortality tables indicates that, for every million persons born 40 years ago, 3 percent die, on average, sometime during their 40th year. If the company has 10,000 policyholders in this age bracket and each has taken out a $50,000 life insurance policy, estimate the probable amount of death benefit claims against the company. How much must be charged in premiums from each policyholder just to cover these expected claims? Suppose the company has operating expenses (plus a target profit) on sales to these policyholders of $500,000. What annual premium must be charged each policyholder to recover expenses and meet expected benefit claims?

2. A pension fund has accumulated $1 million in a retirement plan for James B. Smith, who retires this month at age 65. If Mr. Smith has a life expectancy of 75 years, what is the minimum size of the annual annuity check the pension plan will be able to send him each year (assuming that the value of the pension fund's investments remains stable)? Should he insist on receiving that size payment each year? Why or why not? What other kinds of information would be helpful in analyzing Mr. Smith's financial situation at retirement?

3. An employee has just joined SONY Corporation and a pension plan is set up in her name under which the company will contribute $5,000 per year and the employee herself will contribute $1,000 per year. How much will this year's contributed funds be worth in 10 years if the pension plan pledges a 7 percent annual return on each dollar saved? Suppose the employee plans to retire in 10 years. How much will be available in total at retirement if the company and the employee contribute the amounts noted above each year for the next 10 years and this employee owns (is vested with) the full amount of savings contributed to the pension plan? If the pension promises an annual annuity rate of 6 percent, given this employee's life expectancy, what annual retirement income can she expect?

4. Delbert Ray is planning to retire this year and draw upon the accumulated savings in his pension plan, which amount to $205,800. Mr. Ray is vested with 80 percent of the accumulated funds and, based on his life expectancy, has been promised an annual annuity (income) rate of 3.5 percent. What is Delbert Ray's expected annual retirement income from his pension plan?

5. What is the difference between the markets served by a property-casualty insurer, a life insurer, and a reinsurance firm? Which of them has the potential for the greatest risk exposure?

6. Some economists and financial analysts argue that "captive" finance companies, such as General Motors Acceptance Corporation (GMAC), have advantages over their principal regulated competitors—banks and thrift institutions—because the captives are not regulated as heavily. Others argue that because of their ties with parent companies, the captives have superior information about the value of the collateral for many of the loans they make. Explain the logic behind these arguments. Provide as much detail as you can in explaining how these two factors could enhance the competitive advantage of captive finance companies in the markets they serve.

## Web-Based Problems

1. Auto loans represent an important share of all loans made by finance companies. This category includes loans for both new and used autos. The purpose of this exercise is to compare the average loan contracts for new and used autos that these companies offer. Complete the following:

   a. Visit the Federal Reserve's Web site at **federalreserve.gov** and click on "Economic Research and Data." On the next page, go to "Statistics: Releases and Historical Data" and find the most recent G.20 Finance Companies release.

   b. For each of the five years listed, compute the interest rate spread between the interest rate on used car loans and the interest rate on new car loans. Are you surprised at the size of this rate spread? What does your finding suggest about the relative risk associated with new car loans and used car loans? Has this spread changed much over the five years shown? Can you suggest reasons why?

   c. Is there much of a difference between new and used car loans in terms of: (i) maturity; (ii) the down payments; and/or (iii) the size of the loan? What might account for these differences?

2. Stock market mutual funds have become major investment vehicles for households over the past few decades. One advantage of these funds is the reduction in the level of risk that an investor can achieve through portfolio diversification (i.e., by not having "all of your eggs in one basket"). Some mutual funds allow you to "buy the market" by investing in a portfolio of stocks that reflects a broad market index such as the S&P 500. To assess the possible advantages offered by some mutual funds over investing in individual stocks, choose a particular stock from the Dow Jones Industrial Average Index (such as IBM or Microsoft). Visit a Web site, such as **finance.yahoo.com** that provides historical stock market data and gather into a spreadsheet the information needed to answer the following questions:

   a. Find the current price of the individual stock you have chosen (the closing price from the previous day) and the number of shares outstanding. Compute the total market value of the company in question (its share price times number of shares outstanding, often called its "market capitalization").

   b. Find monthly data over the past three years for the (closing) company share price and (closing) value of the S&P 500 Stock Index. For the individual stock you picked, find the six-month period over the past three years for which your stock experienced *the greatest price appreciation* and compute the percentage increase.

   c. Compare the gain you found in (b) to the percentage increase in the S&P 500 index over the same period. Would you have been better off owning the single stock you chose or picking a mutual fund that let you "buy the market" (in this case, the S&P 500 index)?

   d. Now repeat the process you just went through for the six-month period that would have yielded *the smallest price appreciation or largest price decline* for the single stock you chose. Would you have been better off investing in the single stock you chose or in a market-tracking mutual fund (such as a fund mirroring the performance of the S&P 500 index)?

3. The property-casualty insurance industry has had its ups and downs in recent years with claims resulting from terrorism and natural disasters. The purpose of this exercise is to examine how these factors affect the stock prices of property-casualty insurers by focusing on one of the largest U.S. firms in the insurance industry: Allstate Corporation.

   a. Please go to **finance.yahoo.com** and download into a spreadsheet the monthly stock price data for Allstate Corporation (symbol ALL) and for the S&P 500 Index for the past 10 years.

   b. For each month compute percentage changes in ALL and the S&P 500 Index from the same month of the previous year. For example, calculate the year-over-year percentage change in the ALL for January 2007 using the formula 100 percent times [(the ALL stock price for January 2007) − (the ALL stock price for January 2006)]/(the ALL stock price for January 2006).

   c. Plot the year-over-year percentage changes in ALL's stock price and in the S&P 500 on the same graph.

   d. Examine the graph in part (c). Can you identify the effects of the terrorist attacks on 9/11 and of Hurricane Katrina on ALL's stock price and on the S&P 500? What about the entire 2004 hurricane season? Why do you have to compare ALL's stock values with the S&P 500 to identify the impact of these events on ALL?

---

## Selected References to Explore

1. Adrian, Tobias. "Measuring Risk in the Hedge Fund Sector," *Current Issues in Economics and Finance,* Federal Reserve Bank of New York, March/April 2007, pp. 1–7.

2. Berlin, Mitchell. "That Thing Venture Capitalists Do," *Business Review,* Federal Reserve Bank of Philadelphia, January/February 1998, pp. 15–26.

3. Cummins, J. David. "Should the Government Provide Insurance for Catastrophes?" *Review,* Federal Reserve Bank of St. Louis, Vol. 88, No. 4 (July/August 2006), pp. 337–79.

4. Dynan, Karen R.; Kathleen W. Johnson; and Samuel Slowinski. "Survey of Finance Companies," *Federal Reserve Bulletin,* January 2002, pp.1–14.

5. Engen, Eric M., and Andrew Lehnert. "Mutual Funds and the U.S. Equity Market," *Federal Reserve Bulletin,* December 2000, pp. 797–812.

6. Friedberg, Leora, and Michael T. Owyang. "Not Your Father's Pension Plan: The Rise of 401k and Other Defined Contribution Plans," *Review,* Federal Reserve Bank of St. Louis, January-February 2002, pp. 23–34.

7. Harshman, Ellen, Fred C. Yeager, and Timothy J. Yeager. "The Door Is Open, but Banks Are Slow to Enter Insurance and Investment Arenas," *The Regional Economist,* Federal Reserve Bank of St. Louis, October, 2005, pp 5–9.

8. Hube, Karen. "The New Rules of Retirement Saving," *Smart Money,* November 2006, Insert, pp. 1–11.

9. Kumar, Amil. "Who Doesn't Have Health Insurance and Why?" *Southwest Economy,* Federal Reserve Bank of Dallas, November/December 2004, pp 1–4.

10. Kwan, Simon. "Underfunding of Private Pension Plans," *FRBSF Economic Letter,* Federal Reserve Bank of San Francisco, No. 2003-16, June 13, 2003.

# Chapter 17

# Regulation of the Financial Institutions Sector

## Learning Objectives

## in This Chapter

- You will explore the reasons why financial institutions represent one of the most regulated sectors in the modern world.
- You will discover the many types of *regulation* (government rule-making) affecting the behavior and performance of financial institutions.
- You will understand how regulation has influenced and shaped the structure of financial-service industries.

## What's in This Chapter?
## Key Topics Outline

Why Financial Institutions Are Regulated

Do Regulations Help or Harm Financial Institutions?

The Structure of Banking Regulation in the United States

Changing the Rules on Interstate Banking and Investment Banking: The Riegle-Neal and Gramm-Leach-Bliley Acts

Basel I and II: Controlling Bank Capital

Market Discipline as a Regulator of Financial Institutions

Regulating Thrift Institutions: Federal and State Agencies

Insurance and Pension Fund Regulation

The Regulation of Finance Companies and other Financial Firms

Trends in the Regulation of Financial-Service Firms

## 17.1 Introduction to Financial Institutions Regulation

Financial institutions are one of the most heavily regulated of all businesses in the modern world. Around the globe, these financial-service firms face stringent government rules limiting the services they can offer; the territories they can enter; the makeup of their portfolios of assets, liabilities, and capital; and even how they price and deliver services to the public. As we will see in this chapter, a variety of reasons have been offered for heavy government intrusion into the financial institutions' sector, including protecting the public's savings, fighting inflation, ensuring that consumers receive an adequate quantity and quality of reasonably priced financial services, and protecting the privacy of the public's financial records.

**regulation**

Many economists, financial analysts, and financial institutions have argued over the years that **regulation** has done more harm than good for both financial institutions themselves and for the public they serve. In particular, government restrictions allegedly have allowed less-regulated financial-service firms to invade the marketplace and capture many of the customers of highly regulated financial institutions, who are not sufficiently free to compete effectively. Moreover, regulations are often backward-looking, addressing problems that have long since disappeared, and they may compound this problem of "relevancy" by changing more slowly than the free marketplace, inhibiting the ability of regulated financial firms to stay abreast of new technologies and changing customer tastes. Other observers, however, argue that government regulations have achieved positive results in the financial institutions' sector, reducing the number of failed financial firms, promoting more stable financial markets, and reducing the incidence of racial, religious, age, and sex discrimination in the public's access to financial services.

In this chapter we explore these and other issues as we examine the variety of government regulations and regulatory agencies that oversee financial firms today, assess the reasons for and the effectiveness of existing regulations, and explore recent efforts to deregulate the financial institutions' sector.

## 17.2 The Reasons behind the Regulation of Financial Institutions

Government rules controlling what financial institutions can and cannot do have been developed for many reasons. One reason is a concern about the *safety of the public's funds,* especially the safety of the savings owned by millions of individuals and families. The reckless management and ultimate loss of personal savings can have devastating consequences for a family's future economic well-being and lifestyle, particularly at retirement. While savers have a responsibility to carefully evaluate the quality and stability of a financial institution before committing their savings to it, governments have long expressed a special concern for small savers who may lack the financial expertise and access to quality information necessary to be able to judge the true condition of a financial institution. Moreover, many of the reasons that cause financial firms to fail—such as fraud, embezzlement, deteriorating loans, or manipulation of the books by insiders—are often concealed from the public.

Related to the desire for safety is a government's goal of *promoting public confidence* in the financial system. Unless the public is confident enough in the safety and security of their funds placed under the management of financial institutions, they will withdraw their savings and thereby reduce the volume of funds available for productive investment to construct new buildings, purchase new equipment, set up new businesses, and create new jobs. The economy's growth will slow and, over time, the public's standard of living will fall.

Government rules are also aimed at ensuring *equal opportunity and fairness in the public's access to financial services.* For example, in an earlier era, many groups of customers—women, members of racial minority groups, the elderly, and those of foreign birth—found that their ability to borrow money on competitive terms was often severely restricted. Consumers of financial services were not well organized then, and the discriminatory policies of lending institutions seemed to change very slowly, particularly in markets where competition was subdued. While many economists believed that the potent force of competition generated by both domestic and foreign service suppliers would eventually kill off the vestiges of discrimination, other observers argued that such an event might take a very long time, particularly in those markets where financial firms colluded with each other and agreed not to compete.

Many regulations in the financial institutions' sector spring from the ability of some financial institutions to *create money* in the form of credit and debit cards, checkable deposits, and other accounts that can be used to make payments for purchases of goods and services. History has shown that the creation of money is closely associated with *inflation.* If uncontrolled money growth outstrips growth in the economy's production of goods and services, prices will begin to rise, damaging especially those consumers on fixed incomes, as their money balances can buy fewer and fewer goods and services. Thus, the regulation of *money creation* has become a key objective of government activity in the financial sector.

Regulation is often justified as the most direct way to aid so-called *disadvantaged sectors* in the economy—those groups that appear to need special help in the competition for scarce funds. Examples include new home buyers, farmers, small businesses, college students, and low-income families. Governments often place high social value on subsidizing or guaranteeing loans made to—and supporting financial institutions that lend money to—these particular sectors of the economy.

Finally, the enforcement of government rules for financial institutions has arisen because *governments themselves depend upon financial institutions for many important services.* Governments borrow money and depend upon financial institutions to buy a substantial proportion of government IOUs. Financial firms also aid governments in the collection and dispersal of tax revenues and in the pursuit of economic policy through the manipulation of interest rates and the money supply. Thus, governments frequently regulate financial institutions simply to ensure these important financial services will continue to be provided at reasonable cost and in a reliable manner.

What are we to make of these reasons so often posed for the extensive government regulations applied to many financial institutions? Few of them can go unchallenged. For example, while safety is important for many savers, no government can completely remove risk for savers. Indeed, in the long run, it may be more efficient and far less costly for governments to promote full disclosure of the financial condition of individual financial institutions and let competition in a free marketplace discipline poorly managed, excessively risky financial-service firms. Similarly, there is no question that discrimination on the basis of sex, race, religious affiliation, or other irrelevant factors is repugnant, but can we be more effective in eliminating discrimination by some method other than by struggling to enforce complicated rule books and by requiring endless compliance reports? Perhaps the same ends could be achieved by lowering the regulatory barriers to competition and by making it easier for customers hurt by discrimination to recover their damages in court.

Certainly the ability of financial institutions to create money needs to be monitored carefully, because excessive money growth can easily generate inflation and weaken the economy. But aren't there already enough tools available to control money growth? For example, when money grows too fast, a central bank like the Federal Reserve System can use its powerful tools to slow money growth. And wouldn't it be more efficient to pay direct money subsidies to disadvantaged groups (such as new home buyers) rather than to reach these groups indirectly by regulating financial institutions and interfering with the free operation of the financial-services marketplace? As for providing a reliable stream of financial services to governments, wouldn't profit-motivated financial institutions be likely to provide these services whenever it was profitable to do so?

In brief, there are no absolutely irrefutable arguments justifying the regulation of financial institutions. Much depends on your personal political philosophy regarding society's goals and whether those goals are more likely to be achieved by an unfettered marketplace or by collective action through government laws and regulations. As we shall see shortly, there is a trend today toward gradually allowing private markets to discipline risk taking by financial institutions and to minimize the role of government. **deregulation** Progress toward **deregulation** of the financial sector is slow, however, and can easily be derailed if financial institutions abuse the new liberties that come their way.

## Does Regulation Benefit or Harm Financial Institutions?

For many years a controversy has been brewing as to whether government regulations help or hurt financial institutions. One of the earliest arguments on the positive side was propounded by economist George Stigler [11], who suggested that regulated industries, far from dreading regulation, actually *invite* government intrusion, expecting to benefit from it. In the early history of the United States, for example, the railroads often prospered because government subsidized their growth and protected them from competition. Because regulators may prevent or restrict entry into an industry, the firms involved may earn excess profits ("monopoly rents") due to the absence of strong competitors. Therefore, the lifting of regulatory rules (deregulation) may bring about decreased profits for some financial institutions.

A more balanced view of the benefits and costs of regulation has been offered by Edward Kane [7]. He suggests that regulation tends to increase public confidence in the regulated industry. Thus, customers may trust their banks' stability and reliability more because they are regulated, increasing customer loyalty to regulated firms and helping to shelter them from risk. Moreover, regulation may lead to a curious form of "innovation," which Kane labels the *regulatory dialectic*. He believes that regulated firms are constantly searching for ways around government rules in order to increase the market value of their business. Once they find a regulatory loophole that attracts regulators' attention, new rules are imposed to close the gap. But this leads to still more "innovation" by regulated businesses in order to escape the new restrictions. The result is a continuing chain reaction: Regulations spawn innovative escapes that, in turn, give rise to new rules in a never-ending struggle between the regulators and the regulated.

Notice, too, that the so-called "innovation" brought on by the regulatory dialectic is not the most productive form of innovation from society's point of view. Instead of developing ways to lower costs and deliver financial services more efficiently, financial institutions are spending their time and energy looking for regulatory loopholes—something they wouldn't do if the regulations weren't there in the first place. This

The growing specter of terrorism and the use of money-laundering techniques around the globe have given rise to new legislation and new regulations affecting banks, savings and loans, credit unions, check-cashing and money-order businesses, security and currency dealers, and thousands of other firms selling transaction-related services.

For example, the *Bank Secrecy Act*, passed by the U.S. Congress in October 1970, grants the Treasury Department authority to demand that financial-service institutions covered by the law keep records of their customers' transactions. Any *suspicious* financial activity is to be recorded in a Suspicious Activity Report (SAR) and forwarded to the Treasury's Financial Crimes Enforcement Network. Banks and other institutions mentioned in the law must maintain files on transactions that may "have a high degree of usefulness in criminal, tax, and regulatory investigations and proceedings."

A law with similar purposes and scope appeared following the terrorist attacks of 9/11 in the form of the *USA Patriot Act*, passed in the Fall of 2001 and amended in 2006. Banks and selected other financial firms must "know their customers" much better than in the past. They are required to verify the *identity* of customers opening a new account. Bank personnel now routinely check drivers' licenses, Social Security numbers,

birth dates, taxpayer IDs, and other personal customer information and compare these against a list of known or suspected terrorists supplied by the U.S. government. Any suspicious items that emerge are to be reported to the U.S. Treasury Department.

These laws and their accompanying regulations have stirred up considerable controversy in both the United States and in Europe, where similar laws have appeared. Law enforcement agencies argue that these newer, tougher rules are needed to keep up with criminal elements who engage in illegal transactions and use the financial system as a vehicle to support drug trafficking, terrorism, and other illegal acts. The most likely targets today are those individuals and businesses gathering funds inside Europe and the United States and moving those funds abroad to escape detection.

Opponents often object to the fact that information gathered under these rules can be used without a customer's permission or knowledge and without a court order. Those bearing the heaviest burdens from these government rules appear to be financial-service institutions who, in some cases, must develop extensive recordkeeping and monitoring systems. Debate over the wisdom and effectiveness of these laws and regulations is likely to continue well into the future.

**Key URL:**
To explore more fully the controversies surrounding the Bank Secrecy and Patriot Acts see, for example, **privacilla.org/government/banksecrecyact.html**

"wasted" time and energy, Kane believes, places regulated firms at a disadvantage vis-à-vis their unregulated competitors. Other factors held equal, the market share of regulated firms begins to fall. Many economists believe this has happened to banks and other depository institutions in recent decades, as security brokers and dealers, finance companies, and mutual funds, facing fewer regulations, have captured many of the banking industry's biggest and most profitable customers, reducing the share of the financial-service marketplace controlled by depository institutions.

Thus, regulations are costly and can reduce the competitiveness of regulated financial firms relative to nonregulated or lesser-regulated businesses. For example, a recent study of the banking industry by Ellihousen [4] estimates that regulatory costs for this particular financial-service industry amounted to between 12 and 13 percent of all banks' noninterest costs, or about $15 to $16 billion per year. Moreover, some regulations, such as compliance with the disclosure rules regarding suspicious customer transactions under the Bank Secrecy and Patriot Acts, are particularly costly. Regulatory costs are labor intensive, particularly the costs of making sure each institution is in compliance with all the rules. Financial managers devote great amounts of time to regulatory compliance activities. However, there do appear to be economies of scale associated with regulatory compliance costs, so financial institutions tend to save somewhat on these costs as they grow larger. This cost factor may limit the entry of new institutions into the financial-services field, discourage the development of new services, and encourage consolidation of smaller financial-service companies into bigger ones. Regulators should be especially cautious about making frequent minor changes in regulatory rules, which appears to be a more costly practice than making major, but infrequent, rule changes.

On balance, then, regulation of financial institutions may be a "tale of two cities," delivering both the best of times and the worst of times. Regulation may increase regulated firms' profitability and shelter them from risk, resulting in fewer failures, but perhaps at the price of less efficient financial firms. In return for greater stability and public confidence in financial institutions, customers may be less well served in terms of prices charged and quality of services delivered.

## 17.3   The Regulation of Commercial Banks

Due to their importance in the financial system, *commercial banks* are typically the most regulated of all financial institutions. Moreover, in the United States, banking is often more heavily regulated than in most other industrialized countries. From the banking system's earliest history there has been a fear of concentrated power in banking because bank credit and other banking services are so vital to the well-being of businesses and households.

Responsibility for regulating banks operating in the United States today is divided among three federal banking agencies and the 50 state governments. These regulatory agencies have overlapping responsibilities, so most banks are subject to multiple jurisdictions. The regulatory agencies responsible for enforcing most of banking's ground rules include the Federal Reserve System, the Comptroller of the Currency, and the Federal Deposit Insurance Corporation—all at the federal level—and the state banking commissions of the 50 states. Exhibit 17.1 provides a summary of the principal regulatory powers exercised by these federal and state agencies in the United States.

### The Federal Reserve System (The Fed)

**Federal Reserve System**

The **Federal Reserve System** is responsible for examining and supervising the activities of all its member banks. When a member bank wishes to merge with another bank or establish a branch office, it must notify the Fed. The Fed must review and approve the acquisition of bank and nonbank businesses by bank holding companies operating inside the United States. The Federal Reserve is responsible for supervising U.S.-based international banking corporations, for overseeing the operations of member banks in foreign countries, and for regulating the activities of foreign banks inside the United States. The Fed also sets reserve requirements on deposits for all depository institutions.

### Office of the Comptroller of the Currency (The OCC)

**Comptroller of the Currency**

The **Comptroller of the Currency**—also known as the Administrator of National Banks—is a division of the U.S. Treasury established under the National Banking Act of 1863. The Comptroller is the oldest federal regulatory agency in the United States and has the power to issue federal charters for the creation of *new national banks*. These banks, once chartered, are subject to an impressive array of regulations, most of which pertain to the kinds of loans and investments that may be made and the amount and types of capital each bank must hold. All national banks are examined periodically by the Comptroller's staff and may be liquidated or consolidated with another financial institution if deemed to be in the public interest.

**EXHIBIT 17.1** Principal U.S. Bank Regulatory Agencies

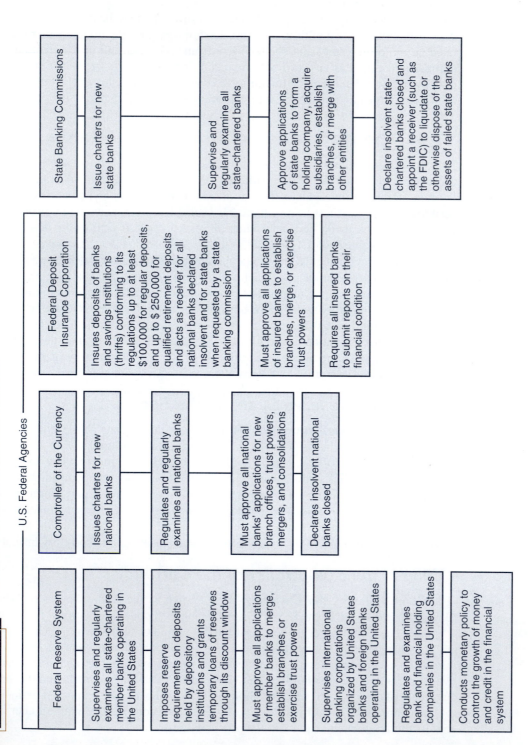

U.S. Federal Agencies

**Federal Reserve System**

- Supervises and regularly examines all state-chartered member banks operating in the United States
- Imposes reserve requirements on deposits held by depository institutions and grants temporary loans of reserves through its discount window
- Must approve all applications of member banks to merge, establish branches, or exercise trust powers
- Supervises international banking corporations organized by United States banks and foreign banks operating in the United States
- Regulates and examines bank and financial holding companies in the United States
- Conducts monetary policy to control the growth of money and credit in the financial system

**Comptroller of the Currency**

- Issues charters for new national banks
- Regulates and regularly examines all national banks
- Must approve all national banks' applications for new branch offices, trust powers, mergers, and consolidations
- Declares insolvent national banks closed

**Federal Deposit Insurance Corporation**

- Insures deposits of banks and savings institutions (thrifts) conforming to its regulations up to at least $100,000 for regular deposits, and up to $250,000 for qualified retirement deposits and acts as receiver for all national banks declared insolvent and for state banks when requested by a state banking commission
- Must approve all applications of insured banks to establish branches, merge, or exercise trust powers
- Requires all insured banks to submit reports on their financial condition

**State Banking Commissions**

- Issue charters for new state banks
- Supervise and regularly examine all state-chartered banks
- Approve applications of state banks to form a holding company, acquire subsidiaries, establish branches, or merge with other entities
- Declare insolvent state-chartered banks closed and appoint a receiver (such as the FDIC) to liquidate or otherwise dispose of the assets of failed state banks

## *Federal Deposit Insurance Corporation (FDIC)*

The **Federal Deposit Insurance Corporation** insures deposits of commercial banks, savings banks, and savings and loans that meet its regulations. As a result of passage of the Financial Institutions Reform, Recovery, and Enforcement Act of 1989, the FDIC's insurance reserves were divided between the Bank Insurance Fund (BIF), backing commercial bank deposits; and the Savings Association Insurance Fund (SAIF), securing the deposits of savings and loans and savings banks. With passage of the Depository Institutions Deregulation and Monetary Control Act of 1980, each depositor was limited to a maximum of $100,000 in insurance coverage should a bank or savings institution fail. Under the terms of the FDIC Improvement Act of 1991, each participating bank was assessed a fee equal to a fraction of its eligible deposits to build and maintain the national insurance fund.[1]

One of the most important functions of the FDIC is to act as a check on state banking commissions, because few banks today—even those with state charters—open their doors without FDIC deposit insurance. The FDIC reviews the adequacy of capital, earnings prospects, character of management, and public convenience and needs aspects of each application before granting deposit insurance. This agency is also charged with examining insured banks *not* members of the Federal Reserve System. The FDIC acts as receiver for all failed national banks and for failed state-chartered banks when requested by a state banking commission. In most cases, an insolvent bank will be merged with or absorbed by a healthy one. If no suitable buyer can be found, the failed bank will be closed and the depositors paid off.

The savings and loan debacle of the 1980s, coupled with the failure of hundreds of banks during the late 1980s and early 1990s, eventually led to the realization that the federal deposit insurance system as originally created was flawed. Until the mid-1990s, each bank, no matter how risky, paid the *same* insurance premium per dollar of the public's deposits. Moreover, until passage of the Financial Institutions Reform, Recovery, and Enforcement Act (FIRREA) of 1989, there was lax enforcement of federal bank capital standards, which led to excessive risk exposure to the federal insurance fund. The result was the appearance of a "moral hazard" problem in which banks and savings and loans could attract low-cost deposits (due to the benefit of cheap insurance coverage) and then invest in highly risky assets, knowing the government would, in effect, underwrite their gamble. Because the FDIC's reserves began declining in the 1980s, numerous proposals were brought forward to strengthen the deposit insurance system. Finally, with the deposit insurance fund almost drained away, the FDIC Improvement Act of 1991 put Congress on record in favor of risk-adjusted deposit insurance premiums. The FDIC was ordered to charge riskier banks higher

---

[1] Under the terms of the Financial Institutions Reform, Recovery, and Enforcement Act in 1989 the FDIC's insurance fund, which is invested in government securities, was required to hold assets that amount to a minimum of 1.25 percent of the amount of all insured deposits. When the Federal Deposit Insurance Reform Act of 2005 was passed the FDIC was allowed to set the deposit insurance reserve ratio (usually called the Designated Reserve Ratio or DRR) between 1.15 and 1.50 percent. If insurance reserves fall below 1.15 percent of all insured deposits, the FDIC is empowered to levy assessments against insured depository institutions to bring reserves back into the acceptable range within five years. Should insurance reserve holdings rise above 1.35 percent the FDIC can begin reimbursing depository institutions in the form of dividend payments to bring the reserve ratio back down toward the desired range. Over 90 percent of all U.S. banks and thrifts have paid zero insurance fees for several years running because the FDIC's reserves have generally exceeded the amount required. Only a few banks and thrifts have paid significant FDIC insurance fees recently because of their weak capital positions and poor examination ratings. However, the FDIC's board of directors was granted the power, under the terms of the Federal Deposit Insurance Reform Act of 2005, to price deposit insurance according to risk for all insured depository institutions regardless of the level of the reserve ratio (DRR).

deposit insurance fees. Moreover, the FDIC was given authority to borrow additional funds through the U.S. Treasury Department.

Recently several bankers' associations and government policymakers have proposed raising the U.S. deposit insurance limit well above the current $100,000 level. Supporting arguments include concern over inflation because the present insurance limit on regular deposits of $100,000 was set back in 1980 and, on nonretirement deposits at least, has not been increased since that time. Moreover, there is concern that in the eyes of the public, banking risk may have increased with banks being allowed to affiliate more aggressively now with nonbank businesses.

Opponents argued, on the other hand, that raising the insurance limit would not benefit small savers—the group it is principally designed to help—and might well increase the "moral hazard" problem, making depositors even less inclined to monitor the risky behavior of their banks. Among the biggest banks there was concern that deposit insurance fees might be raised, adding substantially to operating costs. There was also a serious disagreement among bankers and managers of thrift institutions over the government maintaining *two* separate insurance funds—the Bank Insurance Fund (BIF) and the Savings Association Insurance Fund (SAIF), with different costs and rules.

Finally, the Federal Deposit Insurance Reform Act of 2005 resolved at least some of the foregoing issues. For example, beginning in 2011 the boards of the FDIC and the National Credit Union Administration (NCUA) were empowered to adjust deposit insurance coverage for inflation every five years, rounding to the nearest $10,000, if warranted.

Moreover, the maximum insurance limit on qualified retirement deposits was raised from $100,000 to $250,0000. Thus, the recent reform measures mean that each depositor is insured to *at least* $100,000. Riskier depository institutions are expected to pay higher insurance premiums, though depositories that participated in building up the federal insurance fund in prior years became eligible to receive credits, reducing their future insurance burden and allowing them to receive dividend payments if the insurance fund rises above certain stipulated levels. Lastly, the BIF and SAIF insurance funds were merged into one entity—the Deposit Insurance Fund (DIF)—subject to a single set of operating rules and fees for all covered depository institutions.

## State Banking Commissions

**state banking commissions**

The regulatory powers of the federal banking agencies overlap with those of the **state banking commissions** that regularly examine all state-chartered banks within their borders. The states also set rules prescribing the minimum amount of equity capital for individual state-chartered banks, issue charters for new state banks, and review and approve applications of state-chartered banks for establishing new branch offices and for mergers and acquisitions. Indeed, state regulatory authorities have played an important role in a number of the great issues surrounding banking in the United States over the past century and more, most notably in the rules that apply to the geographic expansion of banks across state lines.

## Opening Competition across Political Boundaries

**Key URLs:**
State regulation of banks and other financial institutions is traceable through Web sites maintained by all state regulatory agencies—for example, **banking. state.tx.us** for the state of Texas and **azbanking.com** for the Arizona Banking Department.

In the mid-nineteenth century and until recently, banks operating in the United States were restricted by federal and state law against competing across different geographic markets, which were generally defined by political boundaries. It was believed that "too much competition" could lead to excess volatility in bank profits and introduce instability into the nation's banking system, thereby endangering the savings of depositors. As the twentieth century unfolded, the composition of depositors increasingly shifted from businesses to households and concerns over deposit safety mounted following a series of financial panics around the turn of the century and during the Great Depression of the 1930s. Many states passed laws effectively limiting the chartering of new banks, outlawing bank branching across city or county boundaries, and forbidding banking firms from branching across state borders.

Unfortunately, these geographic restrictions on bank expansion proved costly, with customers experiencing a reduction in the availability of loans and the variety of services offered, as well as an increase in loan rates and service fees as banks exploited their *monopoly power* provided by the limited number of charters that restricted competition in their local markets. These geographic rules also became increasingly ineffective as innovative bankers spotted loopholes they could climb through and gradually cover larger and larger geographic markets. For example, many large banks formed *holding companies*—corporations controlling the stock of one or more banks—which acquired networks of smaller banks and nonbank businesses that offered banklike services but were not subject to legally imposed geographic barriers.

Over time the geographic barriers to bank expansion have been gradually lifted through federal and state legislation (especially during the 1980s and 1990s). (See especially Exhibit 17.2.) The public's fear of bank instability has been dealt with more efficiently through alternative regulatory measures—for example, providing increased security for depositors through deposit insurance, pursuing closer regulation of bank loan and investment activity, and requiring bank stockholders to bear greater risk of loss should their banks get into trouble. In addition, advances in communications technology and financial innovation have rendered many old restrictions obsolete.

To be sure, the process of deregulating the banking industry by allowing banks to compete more aggressively across wider geographic markets was a slow one, proceeding state by state. However, the federal government finally stepped into the process in 1994, passing the Riegle-Neal Interstate Banking and Branching Efficiency Act (see Exhibit 17.3). This sweeping law granted bankers the freedom to open branch offices across state lines and permitted banking organizations in any state to be acquired by holding companies. Nearly all states chose to allow interstate banking subject to a variety of special conditions (such as protection from acquisition for newly chartered banks in a few states).

**Key URLs:** Information and data on bank mergers appears at multiple Web sites, such as clevelandfed.org/ research and at fdic.gov

One of the consequences of geographic deregulation has been sharply increased *consolidation* within the banking and thrift industries, including many megamergers that have created the first trillion-dollar banking organizations in U.S. history (such as Citigroup, Bank of America, and JPMorgan Chase). To be sure, the federal government moved to impose tighter controls over these mergers through passage of the Bank Merger Act of 1960 and its recent amendments, requiring regulatory approval of any proposed merger and allowing the U.S. Department of Justice to block mergers in the courts if competition, bank safety, or the availability of services to the public are being threatened. Nevertheless, in the wake of thousands of mergers and acquisitions, the U.S. banking industry is more concentrated today than ever before, with the 20 largest banking organizations controlling at least 60 percent of all assets in the U.S. banking system. In more than two-thirds of the 50 states, in excess of 15 percent of branch offices now belong to out-of-state depository institutions. (Bank of America alone has 5,700 branches in at least 29 states and holds almost 10 percent of nationwide deposits.) More than 500 U.S. banks operate out-of-state branch offices.

| EXHIBIT 17.2 | Key Federal Laws That Have Affected the Structure and Regulation of the U.S. Banking Industry and Foreign Banks Operating in the United States over the Years |
|---|---|
| National Bank Act (1863–1964) | Authorized federal chartering and supervision of banks by the Comptroller of the Currency. |
| Federal Reserve Act (1913) | Created the Federal Reserve System as central bank and guarantor of the banking system's liquidity. |
| Banking Act of 1933 | Created the FDIC to insure the public's deposits and denied banks the power to underwrite corporate securities, separating commercial banking from investment banking. |
| Bank Holding Company Act (1956) | Required holding companies controlling two or more banks to register with the Federal Reserve Board; prohibited control by out-of-state holding companies of banks within a given state without that state's permission. |
| Bank Merger Act (1960) | Required mergers involving federally supervised banks to have the approval of their principal federal regulatory agency. |
| Bank Holding Company Act Amendments (1970) | Made holding companies controlling only one bank subject to Federal Reserve regulation; confined nonbank business ventures of bank holding companies to offering bank-related services. |
| International Banking Act (1978) | Brought foreign banks operating in the United States under federal regulation for the first time. |
| Depository Institutions Deregulation and Monetary Control Act (1980) | Granted nonbank thrift institutions broader deposit and credit powers like those possessed by banks, began the phaseout of federal deposit rate ceilings, imposed uniform deposit reserve requirements on banks and thrifts, and increased deposit insurance coverage up to $100,000 per depositor. |
| Garn-St Germain Depository Institutions Act (1982) | Authorized banks and thrifts to offer money market deposit accounts and granted thrifts additional commercial and consumer lending powers. |
| Financial Institutions Reform, Recovery, and Enforcement Act (1989) | Restructured the federal supervisory agencies responsible for monitoring savings and loan associations, allowed bank holding companies to acquire savings and loans, and created two deposit insurance funds—one for banks (BIF) and the other for savings and loans (SAIF) under the FDIC. |
| Federal Deposit Insurance Corporation Improvement Act (1991) | Provided additional funding and borrowing authority for the FDIC; gave federal regulatory agencies the power to close an undercapitalized bank or thrift; required the FDIC to set deposit insurance fees based on a bank's risk exposure; and imposed new rules on foreign bank expansion inside the United States. |
| Riegle-Neal Interstate Banking and Branching Efficiency Act (1994) | Allowed holding companies to acquire banks in any state and banks to branch across state lines. |
| Financial Services Modernization (Gramm-Leach-Bliley) Act (1999) | Permitted financial-service providers to form financial holding companies (FHCs) offering banking, insurance, securities, and other services under one controlling corporation and regulated the sharing of private consumer information. |
| Federal Deposit Insurance Reform Act of 2005 | Deposit insurance coverage on qualified retirement accounts was increased to $250,000, the BIF and SAIF insurance funds were combined into the Deposit Insurance Fund (DIF), and federal insurance agencies empowered to increase insurance coverage to combat inflation every five years beginning in 2010 if this step appears warranted. |
| Financial Services Regulatory Relief Act of 2006 | Attempted to eliminate unnecessary and overly burdensome regulations applying to depository institutions, including new service powers for selected thrift institutions and authorized the Federal Reserve to pay interest on legal reserve balances and to lower the required reserve ratio on transaction accounts to zero if warranted, effective October 2011. |

| **EXHIBIT 17.3** | **The Riegle-Neal Interstate Banking and Branching Efficiency Act of 1994** |
|---|---|

President Bill Clinton signed this nationwide bank holding company and interstate branching law on September 29, 1994. This sweeping banking law included the following provisions:

1. Holding companies can acquire banks in any state even if state law prohibits such acquisitions.

2. However, no one banking organization can control more than 10 percent of nationwide deposits or more than 30 percent of the deposits in a single state unless a state chooses to waive this latter limit.

3. A banking organization can merge with banks in other states and convert those acquired banks into branch offices unless the state or states involved elect to "opt out" of interstate branching.

4. Branch offices established by national banks must conform to local laws requiring consumer protection, fair lending, and investments in local communities. Federal regulatory agencies must consider the views of local community organizations prior to closing an interstate banking organization's branch office situated in a low-income neighborhood.

5. Foreign-owned banks with subsidiary corporations based in the United States can acquire banks and branches across state lines to the same extent as domestic banks.

In an effort to guard against excessive concentration in the industry, the Riegle-Neal law held that no one banking organization would be allowed to control more than 10 percent of nationwide deposits or more than 30 percent of all deposits in a single state (unless the state involved chooses to waive this upper limit). Finally, to prevent large interstate banking organizations from draining most of the deposits out of local markets, banks that expand across state lines are required to commit a substantial percentage of their incoming funds to locally based loans, so that branch offices controlled by interstate banks have loan-to-deposit ratios comparable to the average loan-to-deposit ratios in the states they enter.

## Regulation of the Services Banks Can Offer

Even as banks have sought greater freedom to expand geographically, they have also fought for new service powers in order to retain their existing customers and attract new ones. Unfortunately, regulations have been tight and sometimes unyielding in this area out of concern for bank safety (as service innovation can be highly risky) and because of a desire to protect certain nonbank financial institutions, such as credit unions and savings and loans, from tough bank competition.

**Glass-Steagall Act**

Probably the most influential law in American history in defining bank service powers was the **Glass-Steagall Act** (or Banking Act) of 1933. This sweeping law confined bank service powers essentially to the making of loans and the taking of deposits, while insurance services were largely relegated to insurance companies and home lending was centered in savings and loan associations and savings banks. U.S. bankers also lost an important service power they possessed in the decades before Glass-Steagall—the power to assist their largest corporate customers by purchasing corporate stock and then reselling it in the open market. Foreign banks continued to offer corporate bond and stock *underwriting services* to American companies, and U.S. banks were active in the security underwriting business overseas through a variety of affiliated organizations, but until recently they lost customers to security dealers and foreign banks (principally from Canada and Western Europe) in domestic securities' underwriting, except where limited exceptions were granted from federal restrictions. Bankers avidly sought security underwriting powers because this business can be highly profitable and it complements traditional lending services.

Beginning in the late 1980s, the Federal Reserve Board began to permit individual banking organizations on a case-by-case basis to underwrite selected types of securities through separate subsidiaries. For example, individual institutions such as Bankers Trust of New York (now part of Deutsche Bank), Citicorp (now Citigroup), and Security Pacific Corporation (now part of Bank of America) were granted authority to underwrite certain loan-backed securities and some forms of corporate debt. In September 1990, J. P. Morgan (now JPMorgan Chase) was extended the power to underwrite new issues of corporate stock and was soon joined by half a dozen other American banks in selling their business customers' stock. However, tight restrictions were imposed upon all participating banks. For example, the underwriting of previously forbidden types of securities had to be carried out through a special subsidiary, not by the bank itself, and any revenue generated could represent only a minor portion of total revenues.

Despite such restrictions, however, U.S. banks' share of all corporate security underwriting activities grew rapidly and many bankers continued to ask for further expansion of their security underwriting powers. However, any proposed changes in the law faced stiff opposition from trade groups, representing those industries banks most wanted to enter. There was also concern among regulators that bank affiliation with nonbank industries would stretch the "federal safety net" (e.g., the protection provided by deposit insurance from the FDIC and low-interest loans from the Federal Reserve) to the breaking point.

### The Gramm-Leach-Bliley (GLB) Act

**Financial Services Modernization (Gramm-Leach-Bliley) Act**

**financial holding companies (FHCs)**

Finally, in November 1999, the **Financial Services Modernization (Gramm-Leach-Bliley or GLB) Act** was passed, permitting banks to affiliate with security underwriting firms, insurance companies, and selected other types of businesses. This could be done by creating **financial holding companies (FHCs)** that own shares in all of the above businesses or through a subsidiary structure in which a bank or other financial firm operates securities firms and other subsidiaries. This law opened up the United States for the first time in more than half a century to *universal* or *multidimensional* banking.

Surprisingly few financial-service providers rushed out to form FHCs right away—less than a fifth of the largest bank holding companies and a few securities houses, insurance companies, and smaller banking organizations—though 19 of the 20 largest U.S. banks currently belong to an FHC. Most financial institutions seem content with the organizational structures they already operate and many are waiting to see what the final rules for operating an FHC are going to look like in the future.

As we saw in Chapter 4, each business affiliated with an FHC is regulated and supervised by its *traditional functional regulator.* For example, the insurance company affiliate of an FHC would be regulated by a state insurance commission, while the securities affiliate would be supervised by the Securities and Exchange Commission (SEC). If the FHC contains a national bank, that bank's primary regulatory supervisor would be the Comptroller of the Currency. Supervision of the FHC as a whole, however, is the responsibility of the Federal Reserve. Any banks belonging to an FHC must be "well-capitalized" and "well-managed."

The long-standing debate over U.S. banks being allowed to offer security underwriting services is a reminder of the difficulties the banking industry has always faced when it tries to develop and offer new services. Bankers have argued that new services will add little to or even could *reduce* bank risk because earnings generated by these new services may have a low positive, or even a negative, correlation with the earnings from traditional bank services. For example, during periods of rising short-term interest rates, when long-term interest rates are usually increasing at a slower pace, banks' borrowing costs are often rising more rapidly than their interest income on loans, thus squeezing their profit margins. However, at this same time, earnings from securities underwriting services or the sale of insurance services could be on the rise, reducing the overall volatility in bank earnings.

Moreover, bankers contend, unless their institutions can keep up with shifting public demand for financial services, they are in danger of becoming irrelevant to the workings of the financial system. Regulators, however, generally adopt a "go slow" approach in order to assess the risks involved for depositor safety. Bankers who wish to retain federal deposit insurance coverage must expect that regulations are likely to continue to be a significant hurdle to service innovation for the foreseeable future.

## The Rise of Disclosure and Privacy Laws in Banking

One of the most rapidly expanding areas of banking regulation today centers around *disclosure rules*—regulations requiring financial institutions to reveal certain information to customers (in an effort to encourage shopping around and avoid deception) and to regulators (to improve supervision of the industry). Among the most prominent examples are the Truth in Lending Act (1968) and the Truth in Savings Act (1991), which require disclosure of all interest rates and fees associated with selling loans and deposits to individuals. Similarly, the Home Mortgage Disclosure Act (1975) requires banks to report to the public and to regulators the locations of both their approved and rejected applications for loans to purchase or improve homes as a check on possible discrimination in home lending. The FDIC Improvement Act (1991) requires depository institutions to notify their customers and regulators in advance when branch offices are to be closed. Finally, the Community Reinvestment Act (1977) stipulates that bankers must make an affirmative effort to serve *all* segments of their trade territory, including low-income neighborhoods, and to disclose to the public their community service performance ratings. Regulators must review a bank's community service record before approving its request to offer new services, merge with or acquire other businesses, or set up new facilities.

**Key URL:**
For a review of the new rules on customer privacy and the sharing of personal information, see the Web site maintained by the Federal Trade Commission (FTC) at **ftc.gov**

A "reverse disclosure" law appeared in the United States in 1999 under the label of the Financial Services Modernization (GLB) Act. This new set of government rules permits customers of selected financial-service providers to stop the sharing of at least some of their *nonpublic personal information* with other businesses, except that customers must first contact their financial institutions and indicate they do not wish their personal data to be conveyed to others (such as to telemarketing firms). Otherwise, information sharing is generally permitted. However, each covered financial-service provider must publish at least once a year a *privacy policy statement* and offer its customers the right to "opt out" of at least some personal information sharing. The firm issuing this statement can even decide not to share its customers' personal data with affiliates of the same company if it wishes to do so, thereby placing tougher privacy-protection rules on itself than the law requires.[2]

---

[2] With passage of the 2006 Financial Services Regulatory Relief Act, federal banking agencies were ordered to design model privacy notices to serve as guides for bankers providing their own privacy notices to their customers. These model notices must be succinct, comprehensible to consumers, and permit consumers to compare the privacy practices of different financial-service providers.

Corporate scandals by the dozen rocked publicly owned companies around the world as the twenty-first century opened. Suddenly, investors in the financial marketplace realized that some of the information they were receiving from financial and nonfinancial companies was being deliberately distorted to benefit the few at the expense of the many. The U.S. Congress responded in 2002 with passage of the *Sarbanes-Oxley Act*. This law covers corporate audits, financial reporting, public disclosures, corporate governance, and possible conflicts of interest in the corporate world.

While most of the attention was focused on companies outside the financial sector (such as Enron and WorldCom), the public soon came to realize that the new accounting and financial reporting rules also apply to publicly held financial firms. Indeed, any financial-service entity that sells securities registered under Section 12 of the Securities Exchange Act of 1934 or

that files periodic reports under section 15(d) of that same law is subject to the new regulations.

Publicly held companies must create audit committees, composed of independent members of their boards of directors, who are responsible for choosing the firm's auditors and determining their compensation. Auditors must remain independent from the companies being audited and cannot provide their customers with certain kinds of consulting advice (including legal and investment advice). The CEOs and CFOs of public companies must certify the accuracy of financial reports filed with the Securities and Exchange Commission (SEC). These reports must "fairly represent" their companies' true condition without "misleading" or "material misstatements." Unlike earlier regulations, these latest rules stress openness and transparency, financial honesty, and the intention to do what is right for the investing public and for employees, no matter how damaging the truth might be.

These and other disclosure and privacy rules have aroused a storm of controversy. For most such rules, it is not clear that the benefits of greater disclosure outweigh the costs involved. For example, the U.S. Office of Management and Budget has estimated that U.S. bankers commit an average of at least 7.5 million hours each year just to comply with the Truth in Lending Act mentioned above. Nor is it clear that the public pays much attention to these disclosure requirements, though the public does appear to pay an increasing amount of attention today to protecting its privacy, particularly when it comes to privacy protection for its personal financial and medical information.

## The Growing Importance of Capital Regulation in Banking

In addition to the spread of interstate banking and the explosion in bank branching activity, another major trend today reshaping the regulation of financial institutions centers upon their *capital*—the long-term funds invested in a financial institution, mainly by its owners. For example, when stockholders buy ownership shares in a bank, they have a claim against the bank's earnings and assets. However, the stockholders bear all the risks of ownership. If the bank fails to generate sufficient earnings, the stockholders may receive no dividend income, and if the bank fails, they could lose everything.

Beginning in the 1980s, regulators in leading industrialized countries came to the conclusion that regulatory control over risk taking by banks is best centered upon a bank's *owners*. When a bank chooses to take on more risk, its owners should be asked to increase their financial commitment by supplying more capital. Because stockholder capital is expensive to raise and could be lost completely if the bank fails, the owners are likely to monitor its risk taking more closely, pressuring management to be more prudent.

*Basel I*   This concept of making owners more responsible for the consequences of risk taking by their banks led in June 1988 to the adoption of *minimum capital*

**Basel I Agreement**

**Key URL:**
Additional information
regarding the terms of
the Basel I Agreement
on bank capital and
its importance for the
banking industry may
be found at **bis.org**

*standards* for banks in Western Europe, Canada, Japan, and the United States. The so-called **Basel I Agreement** (named for Basel, Switzerland, where it was first adopted) stipulated that banks in all participating nations must have a minimum ratio of total capital to risk-weighted assets of 8 percent. Risk-weighted assets are determined by classifying each of a bank's assets into categories based on each asset's degree of risk exposure and then multiplying the volume of assets in each category by a risk weight ranging from 0 for cash and government securities to 1.00 for commercial and consumer loans and to 2.00 for highest-risk and below-investment-grade assets. Thus:

$$
\begin{aligned}
\text{Total risk-weighted} \\
\text{assets on a bank's} \\
\text{balance sheet}
\end{aligned}
=
\begin{aligned}
&0 \times (\text{Cash and U.S. government securities}) + 0.20 \times (\text{Other} \\
&\text{types of government securities and interbank deposits}) + \\
&0.50 \times (\text{Residential mortgage loans, government revenue} \\
&\text{bonds, and selected types of mortgage-backed securities}) + \\
&1.00 \times (\text{Commercial and consumer loans}) + 2.00 \times (\text{Assets} \\
&\text{of the highest risk exposure})
\end{aligned}
$$

The Basel I Agreement was unique in also including off-balance-sheet commitments that banks often make to their largest customers and use to hedge themselves against risk, including credit commitments to grant future loans and futures, options, and swap contracts. The amount of each off-balance-sheet item is multiplied by a fractional amount known as its "credit-equivalent" value, which is, in turn, multiplied by a risk weight. The volume of risk-weighted off-balance-sheet items is then added to a bank's risk-weighted on-balance-sheet assets. Thus:

$$
\begin{aligned}
\text{Total risk-weighted} \\
\text{on- and off-balance-} \\
\text{sheet items}
\end{aligned}
=
\begin{aligned}
\text{Total risk-weighted} \\
\text{assets on a bank's} \\
\text{balance sheet}
\end{aligned}
+
\begin{aligned}
\text{Total risk-weighted} \\
\text{off-balance-sheet} \\
\text{items}
\end{aligned}
$$

To determine a bank's total capital, its longer-maturity liabilities and its equity (owners') capital are classified into two broad categories:

$$
\begin{aligned}
\text{Tier-one or} \\
\text{permanent (core)} \\
\text{capital}
\end{aligned}
=
\begin{aligned}
&\text{Tangible equity (including common stock)} + \text{Perpetual} \\
&\text{preferred stock} + \text{Surplus} + \text{Retained earnings} + \\
&\text{Capital reserves} - \text{Intangibles}
\end{aligned}
$$

$$
\begin{aligned}
\text{Tier-two or} \\
\text{supplemental} \\
\text{capital}
\end{aligned}
=
\begin{aligned}
&\text{Subordinated capital notes and debentures over} \\
&5 \text{ years to maturity} + \text{Limited-life preferred} \\
&\text{stock} + \text{Loan-loss reserves}
\end{aligned}
$$

The Basel I Agreement required each bank in all participating countries to hold the following *capital minimums:*

$$
\frac{\text{Tier-one capital}}{\begin{array}{c}\text{Total risk-weighted on- and} \\ \text{off-balance-sheet items}\end{array}} = \text{At least } 0.04, \text{ or } 4 \text{ percent}
$$

$$
\frac{\text{Tier-one plus Tier-two capital}}{\begin{array}{c}\text{Total risk-weighted on- and off-} \\ \text{balance-sheet items}\end{array}} = \text{No less than } 0.08, \text{ or } 8 \text{ percent}
$$

Thus, a bank with a 4 percent tier-one capital ratio and a 5 percent tier-two capital ratio would have a ratio of total capital to risk-weighted on- and off-balance-sheet items of 9 percent, 1 percent above the minimum required. However, if a bank had only a 3 percent tier-one capital ratio and a tier-two capital ratio of 5 percent, it would actually fall *below* the minimum required capital ratio. This is because it would need to have at least a 4 percent tier-one capital ratio and could count toward meeting the Basel I capital requirements only an amount of tier-two capital up to the amount of its tier-one capital. Thus, this bank would be short 1 percent in tier-one capital and would have to work out a plan with its principal regulatory agency to raise additional tier-one capital.

A bank holding more than the required minimum amount of capital is allowed to expand its services and facilities with few or no regulatory restrictions imposed. However, if bank capital drops below the minimum percentage of risk-exposed assets, regulatory rules become increasingly strict, restraining the bank's growth and subjecting its operations to greater supervision. This regulatory policy, called *prompt corrective action,* was adopted in the United States with passage of the FDIC Improvement Act of 1991. In addition, as we saw earlier, U.S. rules require riskier, inadequately capitalized banks to pay higher fees for deposit insurance.

*Basel II*    It wasn't long before Basel I began to show signs of weakness as a vehicle for promoting safety and soundness. Regulators soon realized Basel I's capital rules were failing on at least two grounds: (1) They failed to pick up important differences in risk exposure from bank to bank; and (2) They couldn't keep up with the rapid pace of innovation occurring in the industry, which tends to make old regulations obsolete. A new regulatory system was required that would allow for adjustments in capital based on the relative amounts and types of risk each bank actually faced.

Moreover, clever bankers were discovering loopholes in Basel I and taking advantage of them. For example, as we saw in the preceding numerical example, bank assets were grouped into broad *risk categories*—so broad, in fact, that assets of significantly different risk often carried the *same* capital requirements. (For example, credit card loans and business loans generally carried the same risk weights under Basel I, despite significant differences in loss rates between these two types of loans.) Bankers quickly discovered they could boost returns by shifting from lower-risk assets to higher-risk assets bearing the same risk weight. Thus, banks were taking on additional risk without necessarily having to make additions to their capital in order to counter that added risk.

**Basel II Agreement**    Accordingly, the Basel Committee on International Bank Capital Standards set to work on a *new* set of guidelines known as the **Basel II Agreement.** This new approach, scheduled to take effect in 2008 or later, focuses primarily upon the largest banks in the world. Banks that qualify (most likely, about 20 of the largest international banks) will be allowed to develop their own internal models of risk assessment (known as the *internal-ratings-based* [IRB] approach) and use those models to calculate their own risk exposure and capital requirements. These models must be able to measure the "value at risk" (VAR) in each bank's portfolio, which in turn must be subjected to "stress tests" that project how well the value of that portfolio will hold up when confronted with a wide range of possible market conditions (such as a dramatic shift in the shape and slope of the yield curve).

Basel II recognizes that banks may have different capital requirements based upon their own unique services and risk exposures and that bankers themselves are best able to assess that risk. For example, banks of comparable size and location may post different service menus and hold widely varying types of risky assets. Of course, the

**Key URLs:**
For regulatory proposals to implement the Basel II Agreement see, for example, **www. Federalreserve.gov/ generalinfo/basel2/ DraftNPR**. Additional information about the proposed capital rules for smaller banks, known as Basel Ia, see especially *Federal Register*, Vol. 70, No. 202, pp. 61068-78

risk-assessment models developed by these banks and their calculation of minimum capital requirements are both subject to regulatory review to determine if the methods used are "reasonable."

Basel II considers a wider range of risks than did Basel I. While Basel I was primarily directed at measuring *credit* (default) *risk*, Basel II brings in refined estimates of *market risk* exposure and adds new capital requirements for *operational risk* (i.e., the risk of loss from such events as crime and destructive weather, the breakdown of internal information systems, workplace hazards, etc.). Bank capital must be sufficient to offset *all* of these potential risk exposures. Basel II also places greater emphasis on increased public disclosure of banks' true risk situation, allowing the *marketplace* to play a greater role in disciplining banks that engage in reckless behavior.

This is not to say that Basel II solves all of the problems of modern banking regulation. Quite to the contrary, it faces significant problems of its own. For one thing, Basel II will place great demands on regulators to become better trained in their understanding of bank risk and in using the sophisticated tools available to deal with that risk. Moreover, not all of the components of bank risk are satisfactorily measurable. This means a bank's total risk exposure will still remain something of a "hazy" estimate.

Moreover, the risk-determining models currently available cannot be satisfactorily applied inside the majority of banks—which are far smaller than the leading international money-center banks for which Basel II was originally developed. A compromise approach needs to be worked out for smaller banks, most likely including many of the elements of Basel I.

In fact, during 2005 U.S. banking agencies proposed a new set of capital rules for the great majority of modest-size banking firms, known as Basel Ia. Under this regulatory proposal more risk categories may be created to refine risk measurement and greater use may be made of *external* credit ratings. Overall, smaller banks may wind up holding more capital relative to their asset size than is true of the biggest banks, possibly putting smaller institutions at a competitive disadvantage.

## *The Unfinished Agenda for Banking Regulation*

The tremendous changes in regulation in recent years—including the adoption of nationwide banking, permitting universal banking with multiple financial services, and the spreading internationalization of regulation as evidenced by Basel I and II Agreements—might lead us to think there is little left to do in reshaping the future structure of bank regulation. Nothing could be further from the truth! Banking in most countries remains heavily burdened by constraining government rules. Slowly, and along something of a zig-zag path, banking is experiencing an era of *deregulation,* as legal constraints are being lifted on a variety of banking activities.

More and more regulators of financial institutions are handing over a larger share of the regulation and supervision of financial institutions and the financial system to the *private marketplace*—often referred to as *market discipline.* If a financial firm is viewed as too risky, the marketplace will make it pay for that added risk by increasing its funding costs. Moreover, financial institutions' regulation is focusing increasingly upon the quality and comprehensiveness of the financial firm's *risk management systems,* making sure each financial-service provider understands the risks it faces and has adequate internal controls to deal with those risks. As we saw in the preceding section on the Basel Agreements, a key element in managing risk is making sure each financial institution has *adequate capital* (particularly the capital supplied by its owners) to protect itself from large and unexpected losses.

It seems clear that *market data* will be used more heavily in the future to assess the condition and performance of financial-service providers. Market discipline will be used as a supplement to the work of regulatory supervisors in order to yield a more complete picture of each financial firm's risk exposure. Among the key market data items regulators will likely watch are:

1. A financial institution's stock price and stock price volatility (equity risk).
2. The market value and interest rate attached to senior debt instruments issued by a financial institution (such as subordinated notes and debentures).
3. The volume and interest cost attached to uninsured liabilities (such as deposits not covered by federal insurance).
4. Changes in the proportion of uninsured liabilities (such as uninsured deposits) relative to other sources of funding for a financial firm.

In brief, *market-based information* seems to offer for the future a low-cost method of evaluating the condition and riskiness of banks and other financial-service firms that will aid supervisory and regulatory agencies in doing their job better. *Supervision of financial institutions in the future will rest primarily upon three main pillars: government examinations, capital requirements, and the discipline provided by the private marketplace.*

---

### QUESTIONS TO HELP YOU STUDY

1. What are the principal *purposes* or *goals* of financial institutions' regulation?
2. What impact does *regulation* appear to have upon the availability and cost of financial services to the public? Upon financial institutions themselves?
3. What agencies are responsible for the regulation and supervision of commercial banks? What aspects of banking does each agency regulate and supervise?
4. How is the nature of government regulation of financial institutions changing today? What is the new focus of recent regulation? Why do you think this change is occurring?
5. What are the principal features of the Financial Services Modernization (Gramm-Leach-Bliley) Act? Why was it passed?
6. How will Gramm-Leach-Bliley likely affect the structure of the banking and financial-service industries? Why?
7. How will Gramm-Leach-Bliley affect the disclosure of financial information and the privacy rights of the customers of financial-service firms? Do you think additional legislation is needed in this field?
8. What are the *Basel I* and *Basel II* Agreements? What is their purpose?
9. What types of *market data* will be used more intensively in the future to aid the regulators of financial firms?

---

**Key URLs:**
Information about credit union regulations may be found at the federal level through the National Credit Union Administration site at **ncua.gov**. If you are interested in state regulatory agency information, call up the particular state in question. If you want to find out about financial institutions' regulation in foreign countries, you may want to call up their names—for example, in Canada look at the Department of Finance at **fin.gc.ca**

## 17.4 The Regulation of Thrift Institutions

As we saw in Chapter 15, nonbank thrift institutions include credit unions, savings and loan associations, savings banks, and money market mutual funds. Like commercial banks, each of these institutions also faces an impressive array of federal or state regulations, or both.

## *Credit Unions*

In the United States, credit unions are chartered and regulated at both the state and federal levels (see Exhibit 17.4). Today about three-fifths of all credit unions are chartered by the federal government; the remainder are chartered by the states. Federal credit unions have been regulated since 1970 by the **National Credit Union Administration (NCUA)**—an independent agency within the federal government. Most deposits are insured by the National Credit Union Share Insurance Fund (NCUSIF) up to at least $100,000 (except for qualified retirement deposits that now are protected up to $250,000). State-chartered credit unions may qualify for federal insurance if they conform to NCUA's regulations.

**National Credit Union Administration (NCUA)**

Credit unions, like banks, are closely regulated in the services they can offer the public, the investments they can make with their depositors' money, and the types of deposits they can sell. Fortunately for the industry, regulations have been liberalized in recent years through such federal deregulation laws as the **Depository Institutions Deregulation and Monetary Control Act (DIDMCA)** (1980), which gave U.S. credit unions the power to offer checkable deposits (share drafts) and home mortgage (real estate) loans in order to be able to compete effectively with banks, and the

**Depository Institutions Deregulation and Monetary Control Act (DIDMCA)**

| EXHIBIT 17.4 | Government Agencies That Regulate Nonbank Thrifts (U.S. Federal and State Agencies) | | | | |
|---|---|---|---|---|---|
| **Nonbank Thrift Institution** | **Chartering and Licensing of Thrifts** | **Setting Up New Branches** | **Mergers and Acquisitions** | **Deposit Insurance** | **Supervision and Examination** |
| Credit unions | National Credit Union Administration (NCUA)/state credit union departments | No approval required | NCUA/state credit union departments | NCUA Share Insurance Fund/state deposit insurance departments | NCUA/state credit union departments |
| Savings and loan associations | Office of Thrift Supervision/state savings and loan departments | Office of Thrift Supervision/ Federal Deposit Insurance Corporation (FDIC)/state banking or savings and loan departments | Office of Thrift Supervision/ FDIC/state savings and loan departments | FDIC/state insurance departments | Office of Thrift Supervision/ state savings and loan departments |
| Savings banks | Office of Thrift Supervision/ state banking departments | Office of Thrift Supervision/ state banking departments | Office of Thrift Supervision/ FDIC/state banking departments | FDIC/state insurance departments | FDIC/state banking departments |
| Money market funds | Securities and Exchange Commission (SEC) | No approval required | No approval required | No government insurance; some funds have private insurance | Securities and Exchange Commission (SEC) for selected activities |

Source: Federal Reserve Bank of New York, and the authors.

Financial Services
Regulatory Relief Act
(FSRRA)

**Financial Services Regulatory Relief Act (FSRRA),** 2006, which permitted federally chartered credit unions to offer money transfer instruments and loans with maturities of 15 years or more.

## Savings and Loans

**Key URL:**
For further
information on the
current regulation of
credit unions, see the
National Association
of State Credit Union
Supervisors at
**nascus.org**

*Savings and loan associations* are also regulated by and can receive their charter of incorporation from either state or federal government agencies. About 40 percent have charters from state authorities who also supervise their activities and regularly examine their books, while the remainder have federal charters. Federal savings and loans are insured (up to at least $100,000 per depositor, except for qualified retirement deposits covered up to $250,000) by the Federal Deposit Insurance Corporation (FDIC).

S&Ls chartered by the states also may qualify for insurance coverage from the FDIC. Both federally chartered and federally insured state associations are supervised and examined by the **Office of Thrift Supervision (OTS),** established as a bureau of the U.S. Treasury Department in 1989. Also armed with certain S&L supervisory powers, such as regulating the capital positions of these savings associations, is the FDIC. Moreover, qualified S&Ls can borrow emergency funds from the Federal Home Loan Banks and from the discount windows of the Federal Reserve banks.

Office of Thrift
Supervision (OTS)

Regulation of the savings and loan industry over the past two decades has resembled a roller coaster, with wide swings from deregulating the industry to imposing much tougher restrictions. For example, two major laws passed in the early 1980s— the Depository Institutions Deregulation and Monetary Control Act of 1980 and the **Garn–St Germain Depository Institutions Act** of 1982—granted federally supervised savings and loans major new service powers (such as credit cards and consumer installment loans) so they could compete directly with commercial banks. Then, after hundreds of S&Ls failed in the 1980s and early 1990s, in part because they sometimes moved too quickly to offer these new services, the federal government substantially tightened the rules surrounding savings and loan operations with passage of the **Financial Institutions Reform, Recovery, and Enforcement Act (FIRREA)** of 1989. No longer could S&Ls buy low-quality (junk) bonds, and the majority of their lending had to be focused on the housing industry. Designed to restore public confidence in savings and loans, this new law stipulated that to be a "qualified thrift lender" (QTL), eligible for special tax benefits and able to borrow funds at low cost from the Federal Home Loan Banks—a lender of last resort for the industry—S&Ls must hold a minimum of 70 percent of their total assets in mortgage loans, mortgage-backed securities, and other qualifying assets.

Garn–St Germain
Depository
Institutions Act

Financial Institutions
Reform, Recovery,
and Enforcement Act
(FIRREA)

This latter provision of the Financial Institutions Reform, Recovery, and Enforcement Act proved to be severely constraining on S&Ls that chose to remain in the thrift industry. Many converted to commercial or savings banks to enjoy more freedom and flexibility. In November 1991, these restrictive rules limiting S&L asset diversification were eased somewhat with passage of the FDIC Improvement Act, allowing savings associations to become qualified thrift lenders (QTLs) if a minimum of 65 percent of their portfolio assets were in mortgage-related investments or other qualified assets. Moreover, a portion of consumer loans and mortgage loans previously sold could be counted toward meeting the new requirements to qualify for special federal tax benefits as a QTL. (See Exhibit 17.5.)

**Key URL:**
S&Ls are among
the world's leading
institutions
in residential
mortgage lending,
which presents its
own regulatory
challenges. For
further information
on regulation in this
area, see the Web
site of the American
Association of
Residential Mortgage
Regulators at
**aarmr.org**

The savings and loan industry was further jolted by tough new *regulatory forbearance* rules when the Financial Institutions Reform, Recovery, and Enforcement Act was passed in 1989 and when the FDIC Improvement Act (FDICIA) appeared

| EXHIBIT 17.5 | Major Provisions of the Federal Deposit Insurance Corporation Improvement Act of 1991 Applying to Savings and Loan Associations, Savings Banks, Credit Unions, and Commercial Banks |
|---|---|

**Recapitalization of the FDIC and Protecting Federal Insurance Reserves**

1. The Federal Deposit Insurance Corporation (FDIC) is empowered to borrow an additional $30 billion from the U.S. Treasury to be repaid from future insurance premiums. The FDIC may also borrow using the assets of failed institutions as collateral.

2. Federal regulators may close an undercapitalized bank or thrift institution that is not yet insolvent. Critically undercapitalized institutions (with ratios of tangible equity capital to asset ratios below 2 percent) may be placed in receivership. Regulations become increasingly strict as a depository institution's capital position weakens and may include requiring a merger, restricting growth, and replacing management.

3. Riskier depository institutions will be assessed higher insurance fees. The FDIC must assess sufficient fees to bring federal insurance reserves up to at least 1.25 percent of all insured deposits. This so-called designated reserve ratio (DRR) was later modified by the FDIC Reform Act of 2005, allowing the FDIC to set this ratio between 1.15 and 1.50 percent of all insured deposits.

4. The FDIC may prohibit undercapitalized depository institutions or those with no more than average capital from accepting deposits placed with them by security brokers unless the FDIC finds this is not unsafe.

**New Rules on Services Offered and Foreign Banks**

1. Misleading advertising of deposits is prohibited and any adverse change in deposit terms must be communicated to depositors 30 days prior to the change. Moreover, any insured depository institution must notify its customers and its principal regulator at least 90 days before closing any branch office.

2. Savings and loans may qualify for special benefits (e.g., tax benefits and borrowing from the Federal Home Loan Banks at low cost) if at least 65 percent of their total assets are in mortgage-related assets or other qualified assets.

3. The Federal Reserve Board must approve new offices and service activities of foreign banks and can revoke a foreign bank's license to operate in the United States if it is pursuing unsafe or illegal activities or is not adequately supervised by regulators in its home country.

4. Federal savings associations can loan up to 35 percent of their total assets to individuals and families.

5. Savings associations and banks can merge with each other, subject to regulatory approval.

in 1991. Prior to these laws, regulatory agencies often allowed insolvent depository institutions to keep their doors open, and permitted them to pay higher and higher interest rates in an effort to keep the public's deposits invested in these troubled institutions. This form of regulatory forbearance drove up deposit costs for all depository institutions and, on occasion, drove some healthy banks and S&Ls to the point of failure. Moreover, if the regulators were eventually forced to close the insolvent institutions, the delay in taking action made it difficult to sell the failed institutions to healthy companies for enough money to recover all the costs involved. While regulatory forbearance was originally designed to save deposit insurance money, it often wound up costing the government's insurance fund more in the long run.

**FDIC Improvement Act (FDICIA)**

Congress put a stop to regulatory forbearance when the **FDIC Improvement Act (FDICIA)** was passed. Under this law, a bank or thrift can be closed if its ratio of tangible equity capital to total assets falls below 2 percent for more than 90 days. The troubled institution *must* be closed down or sold to a healthy firm if its undercapitalized condition lasts for more than 270 days. Thus, bank and thrift regulators do not have to wait until a depository institution has zero capital (i.e., is technically bankrupt) to close it, permitting the regulators to sell the troubled institution while it still retains enough value to interest potential buyers.

**Key URLs:**
To learn more about the regulation of savings associations, you may wish to examine the Web site of the Office of Thrift Supervision at **ots.treas.gov** at the federal level and, at the state level, the American Council of State Savings Supervisors at **acsss.org**

## Savings Banks

*Savings banks,* like savings and loans, can be chartered by either the states or the federal government. State and federal governments also share responsibility for insuring savings bank deposits (see again Exhibit 17.4). However, most savings banks have their deposits insured by the Federal Deposit Insurance Corporation up to $100,000 for regular accounts and up to $250,000 in the case of qualified retirement accounts. Regulations are designed to insure maximum safety of deposits, accomplished principally through close control over the types of assets a savings bank is permitted to acquire. For example, state law and the "prudent person" rule enforced by the courts generally limit savings bank investments to first-mortgage loans, U.S. government and federal agency securities, high-grade corporate bonds and stocks, and municipal bonds. Investment powers are restricted in this industry because it focuses upon small depositors who may not be able to evaluate the riskiness of these institutions. On the negative side, however, these strict regulations limit the flexibility of savings banks in responding to customer service needs.

One regulatory issue involving savings banks that has been publicly prominent in recent years concerns the trend toward converting mutuals into stockholder-owned savings associations. As we saw in Chapter 15, the purpose of these mutual-to-stock conversions is to infuse new capital into these organizations and force them to become more profit and cost conscious and act in the interest of their owners. These conversions have sometimes led to multimillion-dollar windfalls for the managements and directors of mutuals, with few gains for depositors—who, legally at least, own a mutual savings bank. Employees and trustees of these associations sometimes award themselves options to buy a major proportion of the converted savings banks' new stock. Management of the converting bank may pick an appraisal firm that underprices the initial stock offering. When trading begins in the new stock, its price often rises rapidly to its true market value and insiders may score substantial gains.

Recently, U.S. regulators began to clamp down on these mutual-to-stock conversions. In the case of savings banks, the FDIC requires the submission of a conversion plan, which that agency may approve or disapprove in an effort to make sure depositors are not cheated and "insiders" not "unjustly enriched."

## Money Market Funds

The final type of nonbank thrift is the *money market mutual fund.* Because this intermediary sells shares in pools of securities, it is primarily regulated by the U.S. Securities and Exchange Commission (SEC), which limits the majority of fund investments (95 percent or more) to top-quality securities and restricts the maximum and average maturity of money fund security holdings. The SEC requires money funds to issue a prospectus to any potential buyer of their shares detailing the objectives of the fund, describing its recent performance, and revealing in what assets the shareholders' money has been invested. Today, in an effort to protect the small saver, funds must remind their customers their shares are *not* government insured and, therefore, may not always be able to maintain their par (usually $1.00) value.

## 17.5   The Regulation of Insurance Companies

While not quite as heavily regulated as depository institutions, insurance companies face tough regulations, imposed primarily by state insurance commissions. The fundamental purpose of regulation is to ensure the public is not overcharged or poorly served and to guarantee adequate compensation to insurance companies themselves. A new insurance company must be chartered under the rules of a particular home state (with most selecting states that have the most lenient rules, such as Arizona or Delaware). Once chartered, each company must submit periodic reports to state commissions, its agents must be licensed by the states, and the terms of its policies (including the premium rates it charges policyholders) must be approved.

Both the courts and state commissions insist that any investments of incoming policyholder premiums must conform to the common law standard of a "prudent person." While speculative investments by insurance companies rose considerably during the century, recent periods have ushered in a somewhat more conservative standard, with state insurance commissions inside the United States and regulators in other countries putting pressure on insurance companies to increase the quality of their asset portfolios and maintain minimum levels of capital as protection against risk. Finally, federal law as the twenty-first century was dawning permitted banks and insurance companies to affiliate with each other inside the United States, similar to what other nations (especially those in Western Europe) have allowed for some time. To facilitate such mergers an increased number of insurers have recently converted from mutual to stockholder-owned companies.

## 17.6 The Regulation of Pension Funds

Because pension funds have risen rapidly to hold the bulk of retirement savings for millions of workers, they have been subject to heavier regulation by the courts and government agencies in recent years. Because employers—the principal creators and managers of pension plans—have an incentive to take on considerable risk in an effort to minimize the cost burden they carry, many pension plans today remain only *partially funded;* that is, the market value of their assets plus expected investment income does *not* fully cover all the benefits promised to pension plan members. While English common law requires pension plans to be "prudent" managers of their members' retirement savings, some pensions have branched out into riskier investments, including real estate projects and derivative securities contracts.

**Key URLs:**
To learn more about the challenges associated with the regulation of pension funds see the Pension Benefit Guarantee Corporation at **pbgc. gov/workers+retirees/ about-pbgc/content/ page/3176.html** and for a recent report of PBGC's risk exposure see **cbo.gov/ftpdocs/ 66xx/doc6646/09-15- PBGC.pdf**

Responding to concerns about pension safety and employee accessibility, the U.S. Congress during the 1970s passed the Employee Retirement Income Security Act (ERISA), which requires full funding of private pensions and prudent investment policies. ERISA granted employees the right to join a pension program, in most cases after only one year on the job. More rapid *vesting* of accumulated benefits was also required so that employees can recover a higher portion of their past contributions should they decide to retire early or move to another job. Trying to eliminate the danger pensions may not have adequate funds to pay future claims against them, Congress now requires employers eventually to cover any past liabilities not fully funded at present (normally within seven years). In addition, a federal agency, the Pension Benefit Guaranty Corporation (PBGC or "Penny Benny") was created to insure at least some vested employee benefits. Currently, Penny Benny insures the pension benefits of more than 40 million U.S. workers who belong to about 85,000 defined-benefit pension plans that promise a specific future level of retirement income. In contrast, Penny Benny does *not* insure defined-contribution plans which today have more than 60 million members but do not promise a specific amount of future income.

Under the terms of the Deficit Reduction Act of 2005 and the Pension Protection Act of 2006, Penny Benny (PBGC) can collect from the defined-benefit pension programs it insures both a flat-rate insurance premium of $30 per plan participant after 2005 (which became indexed for inflation after 2006) and a variable-rate insurance premium equal to 0.9 percent of any unfunded vested benefits. In addition, pension plan sponsors are subject to termination premiums of $1,250 per plan participant for up to 3 years if they literally "dump" their liabilities on PBGC but later recover from bankruptcy.

Despite this recently amended insurance premium schedule, Penny Benny still faces a "moral hazard" problem—under its current scheme riskier pension plans tend to be subsidized at the expense of safer plans. While its liabilities and fiscal deficit continue to rise, PBGC has only limited authority to regulate insured pensions and a relatively small line of credit available from the U.S. Treasury in case of financial emergencies.

However, Penny Benny recently has been brought under closer Congressional oversight and its executive director must now be confirmed by the United States Senate. Despite recent legislation, however, there is a further need for more comprehensive pension reform so that *all* pension plan members have reasonable assurance of receiving their benefits, even when sponsoring employers fail or, as in the case of Enron Corporation, break the law.[3]

## 17.7   The Regulation of Finance Companies

As we saw in Chapter 16, finance companies rank among the most important lenders to consumers and businesses. The bulk of regulation of this industry is at the state level and focuses principally upon the making of consumer loans. Several states impose maximum loan rates so that finance companies are limited in the amount of interest they can charge consumers, which tends to limit the volume of credit extended to riskier households. The states, trying to protect consumers, also usually spell out the rules for installment loan contracts and the conditions under which automobiles, home appliances, or other household assets can be repossessed for nonpayment of a loan extended by a finance company.

New forms of small finance companies (sometimes called "fringe banks") have, in recent years, rapidly spread across the United States, making the riskiest of consumer loans. These "payday loan companies," "title loan companies," "pawn shops," "rent to own" firms, and "check-cashing" outlets are regulated by state governments with some states placing ceilings on the loan rates they may charge and imposing minimum capital requirements on each small-loan company. Several other states have either outlawed these institutions or restricted their growth due to concerns they may take advantage of troubled borrowers who often have to surrender their property when they cannot meet the high interest rates (frequently over 100 percent) that these firms may charge. Today at least 35 states regulate this fastest-growing type of financial firm and more regulation at both federal and state levels *may* be on the way.

---

[3] Besides recent legislative and regulatory efforts to protect the accumulated pension benefits of thousands of active and retired employees the most recent relevant legislation—especially the Pension Protection Act (PPA) of 2006—attempts to encourage greater long-term savings by low- and moderate-income individuals and families. Employers can automatically enroll eligible employees in qualified defined-contribution, tax-deferred retirement accounts (especially 401(K) plans) unless an employee expressly chooses to "opt out" of their employer's pension program. Moreover, inflation-adjusted tax credits of up to 50 percent are available to lower-income families in an effort to stimulate more voluntary participation in retirement savings programs. Under the terms of PPA the lowest income earners are offered the biggest credits against the federal taxes they owe, percentage-wise, for contributions they make to their retirement savings.

## 17.8 The Regulation of Investment Companies (Mutual Funds)

Investment companies (or mutual funds), which invest primarily in pools of stocks or bonds on behalf of individuals and institutional customers, are regulated predominantly by the federal government in the United States. Among the most important controlling federal laws are the Investment Company Act and Investment Advisers Act, passed by the U.S. Congress in 1940. Registration of investment company ownership shares and the submission of periodic reports to the Securities and Exchange Commission (SEC) are mandatory. The SEC requires mutual funds to provide their customers with a *prospectus* that describes each company's goals, performance, and financial condition. It is the SEC's duty to make sure the rights of shareholders are fully protected, including shareholders' right to elect at least two-thirds of an investment company's board of directors and the right to approve the choice of an investment advisory service that will manage the company's asset portfolio and make buy/sell decisions. In 2003 and 2004 the SEC crafted several new rules to promote fair dealing by mutual funds, including requiring that their boards be at least 75 percent independent and that these funds have regulatory compliance officers.

**Key URL:**
For additional information on the regulation of investment companies and other security-issuing and security-trading firms, see especially the Web site of the North American Association of Securities Administrators at **nasaa.org**

We should note that not all investment companies are closely regulated. The most rapidly growing investment company of the past decade—the *hedge fund*—is almost totally free of government controls, provided these funds restrict their customers to those with very high net worth. Because hedge funds can invest in the widest range of the riskiest assets, several have recently collapsed or gotten into serious trouble, including the huge Long-Term Capital Management fund that collapsed just before the turn of the century and, more recently, the Amaranth Fund which bet heavily on the future direction of natural gas prices. These and other problems encountered by many different kinds of investment companies have led to widespread calls for closer government regulation of this often trouble-plagued industry.

## 17.9 An Overview of Trends in the Regulation of Financial Institutions

In this chapter we have tried to convey a sense of the great complexity of regulations that surround the financial institutions' sector and the rationale for those regulations. We have seen that regulation is rooted in the belief financial institutions occupy a special place in the economy and the behavior and performance of financial institutions can profoundly affect the welfare of businesses and households. Thus, regulation seeks to promote their safety and stability in order to preserve public confidence and avoid institutional failures.

Unfortunately, the regulation of financial institutions has not proceeded at a measured pace over time. New rules often have been piled on top of old rules, in many cases set up to deal with problems no longer important in today's economy. Thus, regulations can become a costly burden that significantly increases financial institutions' operating costs and limits the cleansing effects of failure and competition. Research evidence suggests the ultimate impact of regulation is to restrict the entry of new competitors, raising financial service prices but also reducing the likelihood of institutional failures.

The thrust of regulation is changing. It is seeking a lower profile as more governments today seek to pull back from the financial marketplace and allow management and owners of financial institutions to face more fully competition in the marketplace and to respond directly to customers' demands rather than those of regulators' alone. Instead of seeking to wall off and protect one type of financial institution from another, there is growing recognition that the distinctions between financial institutions are blurring and that, eventually, all financial firms must learn how to compete with one another and how to be efficient enough to survive without government support.

Regulators are letting *markets* do more of the regulation of financial firms and they are also learning how to *cooperate* more because the financial-service companies they oversee are becoming more alike and acquiring each other. In short, regulators must share more information with each other in order to be effective in the future. Indeed, there is a trend in Europe toward creating just one regulator to supervise *all* financial-service providers.

As financial-service industries are gradually being deregulated, the focus of regulation is moving away from strict rules about services offered and geographic expansion to *controlling risk taking*. More regulatory attention has recently been focused

Shortly after the principal regulator of the securities industry, the Securities and Exchange Commission (SEC), was created, the U.S. Congress enacted the Maloney Act in 1939, giving the SEC power to *delegate* securities industry regulation to various professional organizations. National associations of security brokers and dealers were authorized to self-regulate their own member firms, subject to SEC review.

For example, under current rules any broker or dealer required by law to register with the Securities and Exchange Commission must also become a member of the National Association of Securities Dealers (NASD) unless the broker or dealer firm does its business only on a national exchange where it is a member. Professional self-regulatory groups like NASD must make sure their members are dealing fairly with customers, determine if members have sufficient capital and adequate procedures to protect against failure, look for violations of securities law, arbitrate disputes between securities businesses and their customers, and license professional traders. The major exchanges, such as the New York Stock Exchange and Chicago Board of Trade, are examples of other self-regulatory institutions aiding the SEC in regulating the securities business.

**Securities and Exchange Commission (SEC)**

upon the amount of *capital* contributed by a financial institution's owners relative to the amount of risk accepted in its assets and off-balance-sheet activities. Regulators increasingly are insisting that financial institutions have in place written plans describing their policies and procedures for managing exposure to a wide variety of risks, especially credit risk, interest rate risk, and currency and commodity risk.

At the same time, there is increasing regulatory interest in greater *public disclosure*—making sure the public is fully informed about prices, service fees, risk exposures, and possible penalties they may pay for loans, deposits, and other key financial services. The fundamental idea is that an informed consumer will make better decisions regarding the use of financial services. Fuller disclosure stimulates competition as informed consumers shop around for the best terms available.

This issue moved closer to the front of the current regulatory agenda in 2001 when Enron Corporation filed for bankruptcy—at that time, the largest such filing in U.S. history—amid allegations of deceptive accounting practices, illegal insider trading, and lax oversight of its activities in the commodities and securities markets. Regulators are paying closer attention to business accounting practices and corporations' use of off-balance-sheet transactions, especially such government agencies as the Securities and Exchange Commission (SEC) and the Commodities Futures Trading Commission (CFTC) in the United States.

For one of the few times in the past century, the future path of government regulation of the financial sector lies in doubt. We are beginning to evaluate more seriously the benefits and costs of letting governments set rules for financial institutions. We are asking more frequently: What purpose is served by both old and proposed new rules? Do the costs of both old and new regulations outweigh their benefits? How will market forces be distorted, and what will society gain or lose as a result of government interference with market forces? And, do we really need *multiple* regulatory agencies when financial-service firms are looking more similar to each other, offering many of the same services, and merging with each other in growing numbers? Shouldn't fewer numbers of financial institutions be matched by fewer regulators? On the other hand, does having multiple regulators actually bring some benefit, such as promoting

In recent years, nations around the globe have often copied each other's regulations—in effect, learning from one another's mistakes and successes. For example, when Mexico and the nations of Asia got into trouble with bad loans and extensive failures in their banking systems, these countries selected recovery models that seemed to bear a close relationship to the approach used by the United States to resolve its hundreds of bank and thrift institution failures during the 1980s and 1990s. Nevertheless, important differences still remain in how regulation of financial institutions takes place around the globe.

One key difference lies in providing the public with deposit insurance coverage. Many nations have no formal deposit insurance plans at all. Others (e.g., Switzerland) have no fund that accumulates over time to prepare for future failures (as happens in the United States with the FDIC, for example). Rather, when a failure occurs the remaining solvent banks are asked to contribute sufficient funds to reimburse any depositors that have to be paid off.

Many *common* trends in the structure of financial-service industries do show up around the world, however. For example, most financial systems are consolidating into fewer but larger financial firms, and some banks seem to be losing market share to nonbank firms (such as security dealers, mutual funds, and pension funds). Yet some nations' financial systems (such as Germany and Japan) remain dominated by banks, which hold the bulk of financial assets, while in other countries security brokers and dealers are very important (as in Great Britain and the United States). In the latter nations, securities regulation and supervision has become as important a government activity as bank regulation.

Just as important differences exist in financial institutions' regulation from country to country, there is a trend toward greater *international cooperation* and more common rules (e.g., the Basel Agreement on Capital Standards for banks in industrialized countries). Some experts believe this *coordination* and *homogenization* of rules across nations will grow and may result ultimately in true multinational regulatory agencies that "level the playing field" so that leading financial institutions around the world all play by the same rules of the game.

competition among them and, thereby, minimizing the prospect of overzealous enforcement by one dominating government agency? It is answers to these questions that will form the guideposts to the future of financial institutions' regulation in the twenty-first century.

### QUESTIONS TO HELP YOU STUDY

10. Which particular government agencies regulate the following financial institutions: credit unions, savings and loan associations, savings banks, insurance companies, finance companies, investment companies, pension funds, and security brokers and dealers?

11. What *trends* are reshaping financial institutions' regulation today? Why has *capital regulation* become so important?

12. What new *disclosure rules* have recently appeared? Do you think these disclosure requirements help or hurt financial institutions? Why or why not?

13. Why might there be a need for *fewer* regulatory agencies in the financial sector today?

14. Based on your reading of this chapter, how has *globalization* of the financial sector impacted the regulatory agencies that oversee financial institutions?

## Summary of the Chapter's Main Points

Because financial institutions provide essential services to the public and can have a potent impact on the economy, regulation of the financial sector is extensive around much of the globe. Government rules encompass nearly every aspect of the behavior and performance of financial institutions, including the services they offer, their management policies, their financial condition, and their ability to expand geographically.

- *Regulation* involves governments setting rules that bind financial institutions to obey laws and protect the public interest. These rules are enforced by agencies and commissions that often operate at local, regional, and national levels.

- *Deregulation* is becoming a reality for many financial institutions as more and more governments eliminate some rules to allow financial-service institutions to be governed more by the private marketplace and less by government dictation.

- Among the key bank regulatory agencies active in the United States are the Federal Reserve System, the Office of the Comptroller of the Currency, the Federal Deposit Insurance Corporation, and the 50 state banking commissions. The Federal Reserve oversees member banks of the Federal Reserve System and financial holding companies (FHCs). The Comptroller of the Currency is responsible for the oversight of national (i.e., federally chartered) banks. The Federal Deposit Insurance Corporation supervises nonmember banks and insures the deposits of more than 98 percent of all banks selling deposits inside the United States. The 50 state banking commissions supervise banks that have state charters of incorporation and often have regulatory responsibility for other types of financial institutions, such as state-chartered credit unions or savings and loan associations.

- Recent laws have dramatically changed the shape of financial-service industries. Examples include the Depository Institutions Deregulation and Monetary Control Act (1980), the Riegle-Neal Interstate Banking Act (1994), and the Financial Services Modernization (Gramm-Leach-Bliley) Act (1999). These laws have brought about such changes as giving more service powers to commercial banks and thrift institutions so they can compete more freely with each other, permitting banks to branch across state lines, and allowing banking firms to affiliate with insurance companies, security firms, and other businesses just as financial firms have done in Europe for decades.

- Key regulatory agencies for nonbank financial institutions include the Office of Thrift Supervision, which supervises savings and loan associations; the National Credit Union Administration, which oversees federally chartered credit unions and supervises the credit union deposit insurance fund (NCUSIF); the Securities and Exchange Commission, which focuses principally on the behavior of security brokers and dealers and on the activities of corporations borrowing money in the open market; and boards or commissions present in each of the 50 U.S. states, which often regulate insurance firms, finance companies, and certain security firms and trust companies.

- The nature of government regulation of the financial sector is changing today, with the *private marketplace* gradually substituting for government rules.

www.mhhe.com.rose10e

Today regulators are paying less attention to making and enforcing new rules and often find themselves pulling back to permit the discipline of the financial marketplace to play a greater role in controlling risk taking by financial firms. Regulators are also insisting that owners of financial institutions (principally their stockholders) supply more of the capital these firms need to serve the public. The result is some shifting of financial institutions' risk from the public to the private owners of these businesses.

## Key Terms Appearing in This Chapter

## Problems and Issues

1. A commercial bank has the following components in its capital account:

| | | | |
|---|---|---|---|
| Common stock | $110 | 10-year subordinated debt | $ 25 |
| Undivided profits | 160 | Loan-loss reserves | 280 |
| Perpetual preferred stock | 15 | Equity reserves | 50 |
| Surplus | 35 | Limited-life preferred stock | 5 |

How much tier-one (or core) capital does this bank have? Tier-two capital?

2. First National Bank of Wimbley reports tier-one capital of $60 million and tier-two capital of $70 million. First National has assets of $10 million with a risk weight of zero, assets of $350 million with a 0.2 risk weight, assets of $680 million with a 0.5 risk weight, and assets of $1,010 million with a risk weight

of 1.00. What is First National's total risk-weighted assets? Does the bank have enough tier-one capital under the terms of the Basel I Agreement? Enough total capital? Why or why not? Would this bank likely have to conform to the rules of the Basel II agreement when Basel II takes full effect?

3. Indicate what type of financial institution is being described by each of the following items:

   **a.** SEC regulations require that at least two-thirds of this financial institution's board of directors must be elected by its stockholders.

   **b.** Risk coverage is based upon the number of plan members.

   **c.** Regulated almost entirely by state boards or commissions.

   **d.** Most of the regulation of this financial institution focuses upon its policies and procedures for making consumer loans.

   **e.** Deposits are insured by NCUSIF.

   **f.** This financial institution's principal regulatory agency is the OTS.

   **g.** All of these financial-service firms were originally mutual in form, but many have recently become stockholder-owned, filing conversion plans with their principal federal regulatory agency.

   **h.** This financial institution must warn individual savers that their shares are not government insured and they may not always be able to maintain their fixed par value.

   **i.** This financial service organization receives its corporate charter (certificate of association) from the Comptroller of the Currency.

   **j.** This financial institution is chartered by the states but belongs to the Federal Reserve System.

## Web-Based Problems

1. As described in the text there is a shift under way in the regulation of financial institutions toward more market-based solutions to regulatory issues. One of the most important aspects of this shift has been an increased emphasis on capital adequacy standards, with improved methods of assessing the overall level of risk inherent in a financial institution's asset holdings. The purpose of this exercise is to examine how well capitalized some of the more well-known commercial banks are relative to the tier-one and tier-two capital requirements described in this chapter.

   **a.** Choose three commercial banks that differ by asset size. Go to the Federal Reserve Board's Web site: **ffiec.gov/nicpubweb/nicweb/nichome.aspx** and click on the "Institution Search" tab. For each bank enter the name of the commercial bank (for example, Citicorp) and begin the search. (Note: if more than one bank has the same name, be sure to choose the parent company.) This will direct you to a page where you can choose either: the Bank Holding Company Performance Report (BHCPR) or the Consolidated

Financial Statement for BHCs (FRY-97). The data you seek is contained in both reports. On the BHCPR you can find the information on the table entitled: "Risk-Based Capital." On the FRY-97 you can find it on "Schedule HC-R- Regulatory Capital." Using either report find: (i) Total assets; (ii) Total risk-weighted assets; (iii) the Tier 1 risk-based capital ratio; and (iv) the Total risk-based capital ratio. Load these data into a spreadsheet for each of the three banks over each of the past five years.

**b.** How well were these firms meeting the capital adequacy standards in the most recent year for which data are available?

**c.** How much did the risk adjustment to the assets lower their tier-1 and tier-2 capital ratios (i.e., what would those ratios have been without the risk adjustment)?

**d.** Which of these banks have become better capitalized and which have seen their capital adequacy position decrease recently? What might have caused these changes?

2. An early indicator of potential problems at a depository institution is the volume of "nonperforming loans" on which borrowers are delinquent in their payments. Depository institutions are required by regulators to keep close track of these loans. The purpose of this problem is to examine the current significance of nonperforming loans at thrift institutions.

**a.** Visit the Web site of the Office of Thrift Supervision at **ots.treasury.gov** and click the tab "Data and Research." Click on "Industry Performance" and then "Thrift Industry Charts" and open the most recent set of charts (pdf-file).

**b.** Look up the chart containing "Loans 30–89 Days Past Due—Five Quarters." For this group of thrifts as a whole, list the six categories of loans in order from those having the highest percentage of "nonperforming loans" to those having the lowest percentage of "nonperforming loans." Compared to businesses, do households appear to be more or less consistent in paying their debts to these financial institutions?

**c.** Which type of household loan has the best loan payoff record?

**d.** Do you see any trends in the "nonperforming loans" in any loan category over the past year?

3. Nearly every year banks "fail" and go into receivership. The Federal Deposit Insurance Corporation (FDIC) is the principal regulatory agency responsible for assuring minimal disruptions for borrowers, depositors, and local communities as a result of failed banks. The purpose of this exercise is to see how the FDIC goes about closing a failed bank.

**a.** Visit the FDIC's Web site at **fdic.gov** and click the tab "Industry Analysis." Next click on "Failed Banks" and then click on "Failed Bank Information." Choose one of the banks listed as having failed over the past few years and click on the report.

**b.** If you had deposits in that troubled institution, what would have happened to them?

**c.** If you had a loan with that bank, what would have happened to it?

**d.** If you had been a customer of the failed institution, do you think you would have had any major problems accessing your deposits or dealing with the repayment of your loan?

4. Credit unions must deal with delinquent or "nonperforming" loans that are held primarily by households. Many of these loans are "unsecured" (i.e., without specific collateral). However, a large proportion of the loans made by credit unions do have collateral in the form of new or used autos. Increasingly, credit unions are issuing mortgage loans secured by the borrower's home.

   a. Visit the Web site of the National Credit Union Administration (NCUA), which is the chief regulator of federally chartered credit unions, at **ncua.gov.** Click on "Credit Union Data" under the tab "Data and Services." Then click "5300 Quarterly Data" and obtain the most recent December consolidated balance sheet.

   b. Download the spreadsheet "Cbsfcu.xls."

   c. Go to the last page labeled on the tab "RATIOS."

   d. What is the percentage of total loans collectively held by federal credit unions that are labeled as "delinquent"?

   e. What is the percentage of total assets that the "delinquent" loans represent?

   f. One way to protect against the risk of loan delinquencies is to hold very safe assets. What is the largest category of "investment" assets held by federal credit unions? Are these generally safe assets? Please explain.

## Selected References to Explore

1. Bodie, Zvi. "On Asset-Liability Matching and Federal Deposit and Pension Insurance," *Review,* Federal Reserve Bank of St. Louis, July/August 2006, pp. 323–29.

2. Cummins, J. David. "Should the Government Provide Insurance for Catastrophes?" *Review,* Federal Reserve Bank of St. Louis, July/August 2006, pp.337–79.

3. Demyanyk, Yuliya; Charlotte Ostergaard; and Bent Sorensen. "Banking Deregulation Helps Small-Business Owners Stabilize Their Income," *The Regional Economist,* Federal Reserve Bank of St. Louis, April 2007, pp. 10–11.

4. Ellihousen, Gregory. The Cost of Banking Regulation: A Review of the Evidence, *Staff Study 171,* Board of Governors of the Federal Reserve System, April 1998.

5. Federal Deposit Insurance Corporation. *Annual Report 2006,* Washington DC, February 15, 2007.

6. Federal Reserve Bank of Philadelphia. "New Basel Capital Accord," *Banking Legislation and Policy,* 22, No. 3 (July-September 2003), pp. 4–5.

7. Kane, Edward J. "Accelerating Inflation, Technological Innovation and the Decreasing Effectiveness of Banking Regulation," *The Journal of Finance,* May 1981, pp. 355–67.

8. Killgo, Kory, and Kenneth J. Robinson. "Banking on Basel: An Alternative for Capital Requirements," *Southwest Economy,* Federal Reserve Bank of Dallas, July/August 2006, pp. 11–13, 16.

9. Kwan, Simon. "The Present and Future of Pension Insurance," *FRBSF Economic Letter,* Federal Reserve Bank of San Francisco, 2003-25, (August 29, 2003).

10. Lopez, Jose A. "U.S. Supervisory Standards for Operational Risk Management," *FRBSF Economic Letter,* Federal Reserve Bank of San Francisco, 2007-11 (May 4, 2007).

11. Stigler, George J. "The Theory of Oligopoly," *Journal of Political Economy,* February 1965, pp. 44–61.

12. Weinberg, John A. "Competition among Bank Regulators," *Economic Quarterly,* Federal Reserve Bank of Richmond, Fall 2002, pp. 19–36.

# Part 5

# Governments and Businesses in the Financial Markets

All parents wish for their children a better quality of life—better health, more wealth, and greater happiness—than they themselves have known. And history offers reasons to be optimistic that those wishes may come true. With each successive generation, people have led longer, healthier, and more prosperous lives than those who came before them. This track record is due, in part, to the continual striving of governments and businesses to efficiently transform new technology and new knowledge into a greater quantity and an increasing variety of higher quality goods and services than ever existed before. These efforts often involve planning, experimentation, and up-front expenditures that cannot be fully funded from the revenues that governments derive from taxes and user fees and from the profits that businesses receive from sales. In these instances, governments and businesses—with a wide array of financing requirements—turn to the money and capital markets for funds. Without those markets, we would see very little improvement over time in our own standard of living or the standard of living of our children.

Part 5 of this book examines the many creative ways in which governments and businesses obtain the financing they require. First, we look at governments and ask: How large is the U.S. government's budget and on what is the money spent? How much of this spending is covered by borrowing? When and how does the U.S. government deliberately engage in deficit spending in order to stimulate the economy, thereby increasing the national debt? How does it manage the national debt? What are the special funding needs of state and local governments and how have these needs grown? How do their credit ratings and access to the debt markets differ from those of the federal government?

Next, we shift our focus to the wide range of debt instruments and equity issues that businesses use to fund their projects. When should a firm issue bonds to raise money and when should it sell stock? Does the intended use of the funds affect the method of financing selected? How important are the firm's financial statements to the source and cost of funds? How do new issues of debt and equity get placed in the financial marketplace? How are existing issues traded, and how do you know their true value?

In answering these and other questions, we learn that the complexity of the financing requirements among governments and businesses demands the highly flexible and innovative financial markets that we observe today.

# Chapter 18

# Federal, State, and Local Governments Operating in the Financial Markets

## Learning Objectives

### in This Chapter

- You will examine the many important roles played by the government's Treasury Department in supporting government programs and in pursuing the government's goals and objectives.

- You will be able to identify how the government raises new funds and how it manages to spend the funds it raises.

- You will understand how the activities of the Treasury Department impact the money and capital markets and the economy.

- You will explore the various ways state, county, and city governments raise funds needed to supply services to the public.

- You will be able to describe the different instruments state and local governments use to attract money and why these instruments are attractive to many investors.

## What's in This Chapter?
## Key Topics Outline

Sources and Uses of Federal Government Funds

Effects of Government Borrowing, Taxing, and Spending: Fiscal Policy

Debt Management: A Tool of Economic Policy

Size and Composition of the Public Debt

Types of Debt Securities Issued by States and Local Governments

Key Characteristics of Municipal Debt

How State and Local Government Securities Are Marketed

## 18.1    Introduction to the Role of Governments in the Financial Marketplace

One of the most important institutions in any economy is the federal government's treasury or department of revenue. However, in the United States (and in most other nations as well) governments exist at several levels—federal or national, state, and local (e.g., cities and counties). And, the majority of these governmental units are legally entitled to enter the money and capital markets and borrow money. Moreover, the fund-raising activities of governments at all levels—borrowing money and raising revenue from taxes and fees—clearly impact the economy and affect market interest rates, asset prices, and overall credit conditions. In this chapter we look closely at two powerful sets of governmental institutions in the United States—the U.S. Treasury Department and the revenue departments of state and local governments.

## 18.2    Federal Government Activity in the Money and Capital Markets

### The Treasury Department in the Financial Marketplace

In the United States, the Treasury Department exerts a powerful impact on the financial system because of two activities it pursues on a continuing basis. One of these is **fiscal policy**, which refers to the taxing and spending programs of the government designed to promote high employment, sustainable economic growth, and other worthwhile economic goals. A second area in which the Treasury exerts an impact on financial conditions is **debt management policy**, which involves the financing and refunding of government debt in a way that may contribute to broad economic goals and minimize the burden of the debt upon the public and the economy. These Treasury policymaking activities may influence interest rates and the availability of credit for all sectors of the economy. In general, the Treasury pursues policies designed to achieve its economic goals without disturbing the functioning of the financial markets or unduly interfering with the operations of the Federal Reserve System, the nation's central bank.

**fiscal policy**

**debt management policy**

### The Fiscal Policy Activities of the U.S. Treasury

Congress dictates the amount of funds the U.S. government will spend each year for a variety of programs ranging from welfare to national defense. Congress also determines the federal tax rates that must be paid by individuals and businesses. Frequently, Congress votes for a higher amount of spending than can be supported by federal tax revenues. Alternatively, due to a slowdown in the economy, tax revenues may fall short of projections and not be sufficient to cover planned expenditures. Either way, the result is a **budget deficit**, requiring the U.S. Treasury to borrow additional funds in the financial markets. On the other hand, government revenues may exceed expenditures, resulting in a **budget surplus**, which the Treasury may use to build up its cash balances or to retire debt previously issued.

**budget deficit**

**budget surplus**

As shown in Exhibit 18.1, U.S. Treasury budget surpluses have been very infrequent. In fact, until 1999, the federal budget had been in surplus in only eight fiscal years since 1931. However, an agreement between the U.S. Congress and President Clinton led to more slowly growing federal expenditures, while a generally strong economy coupled with higher tax rates resulted in steadily advancing tax receipts.

| EXHIBIT 18.1 | Federal Government Revenues, Expenditures, and Net Budget Surplus or Deficit, Selected Fiscal Years, 1969–2007* | | |
|---|---|---|---|
| **Fiscal Years** | **Total Revenues** | **Total Expenditures** | **Net Budget Surplus or Deficit** |
| 1969 | $ 186.9 | $ 183.6 | $ +3.2 |
| 1970 | 192.8 | 195.6 | −2.8 |
| 1980 | 517.1 | 590.9 | −73.8 |
| 1990 | 1,032.1 | 1,253.1 | −221.0 |
| 2000 | 2,025.5 | 1,789.2 | +236.2 |
| 2006* | 2,285.5 | 2,708.7 | −423.2 |
| 2007* | 2,415.9 | 2,770.1 | −354.2 |

*Estimates by the U.S. Department of the Treasury and the Office of Management and Budget. Recent estimates by the Congressional Budget Office suggest budget deficits for 2006 and 2007 may be smaller than shown due to rising tax collections.

Note: Figures based on the unified budget for fiscal years. Before 1977, fiscal years ran from July 1 through June 30. Thereafter, the federal government's fiscal year covered the October 1–September 30 period.

Sources: The President's Council of Economic Advisers, *Economic Report of the President,* selected years; and Board of Governors of the Federal Reserve System, *Federal Reserve Bulletin,* selected monthly issues.

Federal budget deficits fell from a peak of close to $340 billion in 1992 to only about $30 billion in fiscal 1998. A federal budget surplus finally emerged late in the 1990s and into the opening fiscal year of the twenty-first century.

Subsequently, however, sizeable federal budget deficits reappeared as a more slowly growing economy and tax cuts lowered tax revenues. Moreover, as we move deeper into this century, sizeable federal budget deficits may continue due, in part, to the Iraq War, public pressure for increased homeland security, and the growing financial burden imposed on federal, state, and local governments by the Social Security, Medicare, and Medicaid programs for the elderly and disabled. These deficits will increase further if Congress and the president choose new federal spending programs in the future in an attempt to stimulate the economy.

Finally, it must be noted that, just like you and me, the government experiences periods of cash shortages in certain weeks and months, even during those fiscal years when the annual budget is in balance overall or even running a surplus. For example, during the 2000 fiscal year—a year in which the U.S. Treasury posted the largest budget surplus in its history—federal receipts during the month of October trailed expenditures by $11 billion, requiring the Treasury to borrow money to fill this temporary revenue gap. Subsequently, in December of the same year, federal receipts outstripped government spending by more than $30 billion, permitting the Treasury to pay back some of its earlier borrowings. In short, the Treasury will continue to need to borrow money every fiscal year in order to cover temporary cash shortages and refund outstanding debt, regardless of whether the annual federal budget is in surplus or running a deficit.

## Sources of Federal Government Funds

What are the sources of revenue the federal government draws upon to fund its activities? The principal sources of federal revenue and spending programs are presented in Exhibit 18.2. On the revenue side, the bulk of incoming funds is derived from taxes levied against individual and family incomes. In fiscal 2007, for example,

| EXHIBIT 18.2 | Federal Government Revenues, Expenditures, and Net Budget Surplus or Deficit, 2007* (estimates, $ billions) | |
|---|---|---|

| Budget Item | Amount | Percent of Total |
|---|---|---|
| On-and off-budget *receipts* by source: | | |
|   Individual income taxes | $1,096.4 | 45.4% |
|   Corporation income taxes | 260.6 | 10.8 |
|   Social insurance taxes and contributions | 884.1 | 36.6 |
|   Other sources of revenue | 174.8 | 7.2 |
|     Total revenues | $2,415.9 | 100.0% |
| On- and off-budget *expenditures* by function: | | |
|   National defense | 527.4 | 19.0% |
|   International affairs | 33.3 | 1.2 |
|   Health care | 280.9 | 10.1 |
|   Income security programs | 367.2 | 13.3 |
|   Social Security and Medicare | 977.9 | 35.3 |
|   Net interest payments on the federal debt | 247.3 | 8.9 |
|   Other expenditures[†] | 336.0 | 12.1 |
|     Total expenditures | $2,770.1 | 100.0% |
| Net surplus (+) or deficit (−) | −354.2 | |

*Estimates for Fiscal 2007.
[†]Includes veterans' benefits, science, space and technology, energy, natural resources, and agriculture.
Note: Columns may not add to totals due to rounding.
Sources: President's Council of Economic Advisers, *Economic Report of the President,* selected years; and Board of Governors of the Federal Reserve System, *Federal Reserve Bulletin,* selected monthly issues.

individuals were expected to pay just over $1 trillion in income taxes, representing about 45 percent of all federal revenues that year. Social Security taxes were forecast to supply nearly $900 billion—almost 37 percent of all federal revenues. Corporate income taxes were projected to contribute about 10 percent, and other taxes and fees for government services were expected to provide about 7 percent of all federal revenues.

During the past two decades personal income tax revenue has risen or held steady as a proportion of all government receipts, reflecting Congress's desire to shift a greater share of the tax burden onto more wealthy citizens. At the same time, payroll taxes for social insurance increased as Congress moved to rescue the Social Security system from deepening deficits. Corporate taxes were increased in an effort to offset declining personal tax rates and help to reduce budget deficits. As the twenty-first century began, however, a new presidential administration guided by George W. Bush sought to lower corporate and personal tax rates to stimulate the economy and increase saving and investment. Predictably, when the economy slowed and defense and homeland security spending rose, federal budget deficits soared.

These changes in tax rates suggest that the federal government has attempted in recent years to make the tax structure more responsive to the nation's economic and social problems. When the economy headed down into a recession, or inflation pushed individuals into higher tax brackets, Congress generally responded (though often with considerable lags) and made appropriate income tax adjustments.

## Federal Government Expenditures

The U.S. government today collects an enormous volume of revenue from its citizens. For example, federal revenues were projected to climb above $2.4 trillion in fiscal 2007. Where does the federal government spend this money?

**Key URL:**
The most recently compiled budget of the U.S. government is available from the Office of Management and Budget at
**gpo.gov/usbudget**

Exhibit 18.2 indicates that about two-thirds of all federal spending goes for national defense and various income security programs, including Social Security, Medicare, and unemployment compensation. The latter programs are designed to sustain the spending power of individuals who are retired, ill or disabled, or temporarily unemployed. During the 1990s, the collapse of the Warsaw Pact in Europe and economic and political problems inside the states of the former Soviet Union stimulated the U.S. government to begin cutting back on spending for national defense (as a "peace dividend" from the end of the Cold War) and to shift more resources toward social programs and environmental protection (including more funds for medical research, improved educational opportunities for children, an upgrading of public housing and rental assistance programs, stronger antidrug programs, safeguarding air travel, and more aggressive efforts to clean up the environment). As the twenty-first century opened, however, a more conservative presidential administration took control and spending priorities shifted toward national defense, guarding against terrorism at home and abroad, and educational programs, with fewer monies directed toward other spending categories.

In recent years, several changes in tax and spending laws have taken place in an effort to make the U.S. government's fiscal policy a more effective tool for achieving the nation's goals. However, the truth is that fiscal policy has significant limitations and often has proven ineffective. A major problem centers on *timing*. Fiscal policy often operates with long and variable lags. First, the legislature must agree on new tax and spending rules and then the Treasury and other government agencies must implement those rules. In the meantime, economic conditions may change, making the new tax and spending rules obsolete. Many authorities today suggest that fiscal policy should be aimed, not at short-run objectives like dampening the business cycle, but at longer-range goals, such as promoting greater economic efficiency and greater equity in the allocation of scarce resources.

---

### QUESTIONS TO HELP YOU STUDY

1. What exactly is *fiscal policy? Debt management policy?*

2. Explain how fiscal and debt management policy might be used to help fight inflation and unemployment. Can you see any weaknesses or potential problems with the use of these policy tools?

3. List (from largest to smallest) the principal sources of federal government revenue. What are the principal federal spending programs?

---

## Effects of Government Borrowing on the Financial System and the Economy

What are the effects of government borrowing on the economy and the financial markets? If the federal government runs a *small* budget deficit, it is possible for the Treasury to cover this small shortfall in revenues by drawing upon its accumulated

| EXHIBIT 18.3 | The Treasury Borrowing Money from the Public and Spending the Borrowed Funds | | | |
|---|---|---|---|---|
| | Federal Reserve Banks | | Depository Financial Institutions | |
| | Assets | Liabilities | Assets | Liabilities |
| The Sale of Securities by the Treasury to the Public | | Legal reserves of depository institutions −20 Government deposits +20 | Legal reserves of depository institutions −20 | Deposits of the public −20 |
| The Treasury Spends the Borrowed Funds by Issuing Checks to the Public | | Government deposits −20 Legal reserves of depository institutions +20 | Legal reserves of depository institutions +20 | Deposits of the public +20 |

cash balances held at the Federal Reserve banks. However, when government deficits are large, substantial amounts of new debt securities (IOUs) must be sold to close the budget gap. The mechanics of how the Treasury *borrows* money from the public in the open market and then *spends* the borrowed funds may be illustrated with the T-accounts shown in Exhibit 18.3.

Suppose, as illustrated in Exhibit 18.3, the Treasury needs to borrow $20 billion, which it raises by selling bonds to the public. As the public pays for these attractive interest-bearing, low-risk securities, it writes checks against its deposits held with depository institutions. When the Treasury cashes these checks at its bank—the Federal Reserve—the legal reserves of depository institutions *fall,* as do deposits held by the public (other factors held constant), and the government has new deposit money to spend. Subsequently, the government spends the newly acquired money, writing checks totaling, in our example, $20 billion against its accounts at the Federal Reserve banks and distributing those checks to members of the public to whom it owes money. In this second round, deposits held by the public *rise* by $20 billion and the legal reserves of depository institutions climb by the same amount.

The likely impact of this sequence of government borrowing and spending on the economy and the financial markets has been one of the most hotly debated issues in the history of economics and finance. The economy and the financial system are so complex, with so many changes going on at the same time, it is extremely difficult to make any dependable predictions about the ultimate outcome of government borrowing and spending.

For many years now, the conventional wisdom has been that new government borrowing, followed by the spending of those newly acquired government funds, may add to planned investment and consumption spending by businesses and households, tending to increase the economy's production and income levels, thus creating more jobs. However, it also has been argued that the additional borrowing and spending could eventually set in motion inflation, causing the prices of goods and services to increase and tending as well to force nominal interest rates upward. With higher interest rates, investment spending, production, and income might fall. We must be cautious here, however, because there is little solid evidence that government budget deficits cause

| EXHIBIT 18.4 | The Treasury Uses Its Surplus Funds to Pay Off and Retire Government Securities Held by the Public | | | |
|---|---|---|---|---|
| | **Federal Reserve Banks** | | **Depository Institutions** | |
| | Assets | Liabilities | Assets | Liabilities |
| The Treasury Collects a Net Surplus of Tax Revenues from the Public | | Legal reserves of depository institutions −20  Government deposits +20 | Legal reserves of depository institutions −20 | Deposits of the public −20 |
| The Treasury Buys Back Government Securities Held by the Public and Retires Them | | Government deposits −20 | Legal reserves of depository institutions +20 | Deposits of the public +20 |

inflation; indeed, current budget deficits appear to be more closely linked to past inflation rather than the other way around.[1]

Recent research into the impact of government borrowing and spending has introduced yet another argument: Interest rates and security prices in an *efficient market* simply may not respond to increased government borrowing and spending. This may happen, in part, because the government's borrowing and spending may have a "crowding out effect" on the private sector of the economy—that is, additional government borrowing and spending may discourage some private borrowing and spending. Thus, there may be little *net* gain in terms of economic activity or any significant changes in interest rates as a result of deficit spending by the government. With so many conflicting arguments about government borrowing and spending, this is an area where more research is needed.[2]

Incidentally, what happens when the government runs a budget surplus and uses a portion of that surplus to *retire debt*? Exhibit 18.4 summarizes the simple mechanics involved in such a debt-retirement transaction.

Suppose, as shown in Exhibit 18.4, that the Treasury collects $20 billion more in tax revenues than it spends, thus withdrawing a net $20 billion from the economy. The

---

[1]The T accounts in Exhibit 18.3 illustrate the Treasury borrowing from the public. There is an alternative route to securing new funds, but it is highly dangerous and, in the United States anyway, restricted by law. This alternative method involves direct borrowing by the Treasury from the central bank, the Federal Reserve System. The Treasury sells government securities to the Federal Reserve banks and receives money in its checking account at the Fed. Initially there is no change in the public's deposits or in legal reserves. When the newly borrowed funds are spent, however, the public's deposit balances rise, as do reserves in the banking system. Financially speaking, this is a highly inflationary way for the government to borrow money. It is the equivalent of simply *printing money* and distributing it to the public, most likely causing prices to rise if the economy is near full production and employment and the central bank does nothing to offset this "monetizing" of the government's debt.

[2]While most studies find little or no connection between market interest rates and budget deficits, a new study by Laubach [8] at the Federal Reserve finds a significant relationship. Specifically, this study found that an increase in the ratio of projected deficits to U.S. GDP by 1 percentage point produces a quarter point (i.e., 25-basis point) rise in long-term interest rates—some evidence for the "crowding out" effect.

Treasury might save this surplus to apply to future cash needs, but if the surplus is sizeable, it will more likely choose to reduce its debt either by reducing the amount of maturing debt that it "rolls over" (replacing it with new debt) or by holding "reverse auctions"—buying back some of its debt from those who hold it. Indeed, this is what the U.S. government did as the twentieth century drew to a close. (For example, in the year 2000, the U.S. government used reverse auctions and other means to reduce the marketable public debt of the United States by just over $300 billion.)

Does debt retirement have any predictable effects on the economy and financial system? Once again, this field is filled with controversy and disagreement. Some economists argue that running budget surpluses and retiring the government's debt tends to slow economic activity as funds are transferred from taxpayers (who may, on average, have a higher propensity to spend) to government security investors (who may have a higher propensity to save rather than spend), thereby slowing the economy. Others argue that retirement of government debt simply makes more room for private borrowing and spending. If markets are truly *efficient* and the government is transparent about what it is doing with the public debt, there may be little impact at all. Clearly, we need to know much more about this subject before drawing any rock-solid conclusions.

---

**QUESTIONS TO HELP YOU STUDY**

4. Describe the possible impacts of *government borrowing* upon the financial system and the economy.
5. Describe the possible effects of *retiring government securities* on the financial system and the economy.
6. What is meant by the term *crowding-out effect?* What does recent research suggest about the link between government deficits, interest rates, and inflation?

---

## Management of the Federal Debt

**public debt**

As we noted at the beginning of this chapter, one of the most important activities of any government's treasury is managing the nation's debt. In the United States, the Treasury Department in Washington, D.C. manages the huge **public debt.** The U.S. public debt is the largest single collection of securities available in the financial system today. Securities issued by the Treasury are regarded by investors as having zero *default risk* because the federal government possesses power both to tax and to create money. The government, unless overthrown by war or revolution, can always pay its bills by taxing its citizens.

Government securities do carry *market risk,* however, because their prices fluctuate with changes in demand and supply. In fact, the longer the term to maturity of a government security, the more market risk it tends to possess.

The principal role of government securities in the financial system is to provide *liquidity.* Corporations, banks, and other institutional investors rely heavily on government securities as a readily marketable reserve to be drawn upon when cash is needed quickly. Although private securities do carry higher explicit yields than government debt of comparable maturity, the greater liquidity of government securities represents an added (implicit) return to the investor.

## The Size and Growth of the Public Debt

How much money does the federal government owe? As shown in Exhibit 18.5, the gross public debt of the United States had reached more than $8 trillion in 2006. On a per capita basis, the public debt amounts to nearly $28,000 for every man, woman, and child living in the United States.

How did the federal debt become so large? Wars, economic recessions, and the rapid expansion of military expenditures and social programs have been among the principal causes. The federal government's debt began during the American Revolution as the United States needed money to fight for its independence. However, the central government's debt was relatively insignificant until the Great Depression of the 1930s when the administration of President Franklin D. Roosevelt chose to borrow heavily to fund government programs and provide more jobs. Even so, the public debt amounted to scarcely more than $50 billion at the beginning of World War II. The public debt multiplied five times over during the war years, approaching $260 billion by the end of World War II. Embroiled in the most destructive and costly war in history, the U.S. government borrowed resources from the private sector to build planes, ships, and other war materials in enormous quantities.

For a brief period following World War II, it appeared that much of the public debt might be repaid. However, the Korean War intervened during the 1950s, followed by a series of deep recessions when tax revenues declined. The advent of the Vietnam War, along with costly Great Society programs and rapid inflation during the 1960s and 1970s, sent the debt soaring (see Exhibit 18.6). Between 1970 and 1980, the public debt of the United States more than doubled; it then tripled to more than $3 trillion during the 1980–1990 period. Between 1990 and 2000, the federal government's debt expanded again, this time by more than $2 trillion. However, the total debt of the United States government began to decline in fiscal 2000 as budget surpluses emerged and some government debt could be repaid. Lower interest rates on the federal debt,

| EXHIBIT 18.5 | The Public Debt of the United States, 2006 ($ billions) | |
|---|---|---|
| **Type of Securities** | **Amounts** | **Percent of Gross Public Debt** |
| Interest-bearing public debt | $8,351.7 | 99.8% |
| Marketable debt: | 4,340.4 | 51.8 |
| Bills | 1,042.1 | 12.4 |
| Notes | 2,409.7 | 28.8 |
| Bonds | 526.7 | 6.3 |
| Inflation-indexed notes and bonds | 347.9 | 4.2 |
| Nonmarketable debt: | 4,030.8 | 48.2 |
| State and local government series | 234.8 | 2.8 |
| Foreign issues | 3.4 | 0.0* |
| Savings bonds and notes | 192.0 | 2.3 |
| Government account series | 3,551.2 | 42.4 |
| Non-interest-bearing debt | 19.5 | 0.2 |
| Total gross public debt | $8,371.2 | 100.0% |

*Figure is less than 0.05 percent.
Note: Columns may not add to totals due to rounding. Figures are for first quarter of 2006.
Sources: Board of Governors of the Federal Reserve and the U.S. Treasury Department.

| EXHIBIT 18.6 | The Public Debt of the United States in Selected Years, 1950–2007* ($ billions at year-end) | | |
|---|---|---|---|
| **Year** | **Total Gross Public Debt** | **Year** | **Total Gross Public Debt** |
| 1950 | $225.4 | 1990 | $3,364.8 |
| 1960 | 287.7 | 2000 | 5,662.2 |
| 1970 | 388.3 | 2006 | 8,680.2 |
| 1980 | 930.2 | 2007* | 8,849.7 |

*2007 figures are for first quarter.
Sources: Board of Governors of the Federal Reserve System and the U.S. Treasury Department.

the end of the Cold War, and a long-term economic boom extending through much of the 1990s made it possible for the federal budget to approach a surplus position as the new century began—a true federal budget surplus for the first time since 1969. However, the new budget surplus was soon threatened by a new economic recession in 2001, made worse by the terrorist attacks of 9/11, throwing the United States' federal budget back into substantial deficits as the twenty-first century began to unfold.

How much government debt is simply too much? Opinions vary greatly on the answer to that question. For example, James Madison, fourth president of the United States, once declared: "A public debt is a public curse." Much more recently economist Laurence Kotlikoff [7] of the National Bureau of Economic Research has written that the official and unofficial liabilities of the U.S. government are so massive that "financial implosion is just around the corner." In contrast, Alexander Hamilton, the first U.S. Treasury Secretary under the Constitution, once wrote: "A national debt, if it is not excessive, will be to us a national blessing." Who is right?

The answer depends, in part, on the standard used to gauge the size of the public debt. Measured against the national income (the earnings of individuals and businesses that can be taxed to repay the debt), the public debt is lower now than it was a generation ago. For example, in 2006, the gross public debt amounted to about 65 percent of the U.S. gross domestic product (GDP), compared to well over 100 percent at the end of World War II. Moreover, other forms of debt in the U.S. economy total as much or more than the public debt. For example, total mortgage debt outstanding in 2006 was more than $12 trillion and the combined debt of the private sector and state and local governments was more than double that of the federal government. It should be remembered that U.S. government securities are at one and the same time both debt obligations of the government and also highly desirable marketable, liquid assets to the millions of investors who hold them.

Another issue to keep in mind about today's federal debt and its possible burden on the economy and the financial marketplace concerns the difficulties we face in trying to accurately measure the true *size* of the debt. It turns out that the answer to the question—How big is the federal debt?—is not all that easy. For example, *inflation* increases the size of the debt because it tends to increase government deficits. In an inflationary period, the government typically must borrow more, but this does not necessarily mean the burden of the debt has increased: Government may not be exerting a greater impact on the economy. Moreover, the size of the public debt is typically measured in terms of the *par value* of government securities outstanding. But when interest rates rise, the *market value* of government debt falls. Thus, a significant rise in interest rates will cause the value of that portion of the government's debt held by private investors to decline.

Accurate measurement of the burden imposed by debt also means we must consider the value of *assets* held by government. Most national governments hold a reserve of gold and foreign currencies. We might also add the estimated value of government buildings, military hardware, highways, and airports. Thus, we may distinguish between *gross liabilities* of the federal government and its *net liabilities*—government debt minus government assets. Including all the government's assets at their fair market value would yield substantially smaller net government liabilities. Of course, to be fair, we also have to consider the amount of debt owed by off-budget federal agencies (such as the farm credit agencies or the federal mortgage agencies), which amounts to more than a third of the gross public debt. And *contingent liabilities* might be added to the government's debt total, such as deposit insurance like that offered by the FDIC to guarantee bank deposits or the Social Security Fund which must eventually pay retirement benefits to millions of citizens. Clearly, measuring the true size of the government's debt is a difficult job. For this reason, we must be careful before jumping to any hasty conclusions about how large or significant the public debt is or what its impact on the economy and financial markets might be.

### The Composition of the Public Debt

The U.S. public debt as traditionally measured consists of a wide variety of government IOUs with differing maturities, interest rates, and other features. A small amount—less than 1 percent—carries no interest rate at all. This *noninterest-bearing debt* consists of paper currency and coins issued by the U.S. Treasury Department. However, virtually all paper money in circulation today is in Federal Reserve notes, which are not officially a part of the public debt but are obligations of the Federal Reserve banks.

More than 99 percent of all federal debt securities are *interest bearing* and may be divided into two broad groups: marketable securities and nonmarketable securities. By definition, *marketable securities* may be traded any number of times before they reach maturity. In contrast, *nonmarketable securities* must be held by the original purchaser until they mature or are redeemed by the Treasury. It is marketable debt that has the greatest impact on the cost and availability of credit in the money and capital markets, and it is these securities over which the Treasury exercises the greatest control.

### Marketable Public Debt

The marketable public debt totaled about $4.3 trillion in 2006, representing just over half of all interest-bearing U.S. government obligations (as shown in Exhibit 18.5). The marketable public debt today is composed of just three types of securities: Treasury bills, notes, and bonds. By law, a U.S. Treasury bill must mature within one year. In contrast, U.S. Treasury notes range in original maturity from 1 to 10 years, and Treasury bonds may carry any maturity, although generally, when issued, they have a maturity of 10 or more years.[3] With their greater liquidity and marketability, Treasury bills, notes, and bonds have been attractive savings outlets to individual and institutional investors for many years.

---

[3]Both Treasury notes and bonds bear interest at a fixed interest rate payable semiannually, while bills do not carry a fixed interest rate but earn price gains instead as their market price rises over time. Treasury bonds may carry a call option, allowing the Treasury to redeem them early provided the Treasury gives at least four months' notice (though the U.S. government has issued only noncallable securities since 1985). Marketable notes and bonds have been issued in multiples of $1,000 and $5,000 depending upon maturity. Bills are available in multiples of $1,000. Payment for purchases of new Treasuries generally must be made in cash, immediately available (electronic) funds, the exchange of eligible securities, or by check to the Federal Reserve banks or the U.S. Treasury.

Among the most attractive marketable Treasury obligations in recent years have been Treasury Inflation-Protected Securities (TIPS) whose volume rose from zero in 1996 to just over $400 billion by the close of 2006, or to about 5 percent of the U.S. public debt. As discussed earlier in Chapter 7, TIPS have proven especially attractive to investors concerned about the damage inflation can do to the value of their assets and their investment earnings because TIPS' semiannual payments are indexed to changes in the consumer price index (specifically, the *U.S. City Average of All Items Consumer Price Index for Urban Consumers*, published by the Bureau of Labor Statistics).

*Nonmarketable Public Debt*   The nonmarketable public debt consists mainly of Government Account series securities issued by the Treasury to various government agencies and trust funds (see again Exhibit 18.5). These agencies and trust funds include the Social Security Administration, the Government National Mortgage Association, the Postal Service, and several smaller government agencies. As these governmental units accumulate funds, they turn them over to the Treasury in exchange for nonmarketable IOUs, thus reducing the federal government's borrowing activity in the open market. Another component of the nonmarketable debt is U.S. savings bonds sold to the general public in small denominations, which represent just over 2 percent of the public debt.

Holdings of U.S. dollars by foreign governments and foreign investors have remained at a high level in recent years due to oil imports and the flow of U.S. capital to Europe, Asia, and the Middle East. Because large foreign holdings of dollars represent a constant threat to the value of the U.S. dollar in international markets, the Treasury periodically issues fairly small amounts of nonmarketable dollar-denominated securities to attract these foreign funds. To increase U.S. government holdings of foreign currencies that can be used to settle international claims, the Treasury can sell foreign-currency-denominated securities to investors abroad as well. The Treasury also issues special securities to state and local governments. These securities provide a temporary investment outlet for the funds raised by local governments when they borrow in the open market.

*Investors in U.S. Government Securities*   Who *holds* the public debt of the United States? Each month, the Treasury makes estimates of the distribution of its securities among various groups of investors, drawing on data supplied by the Federal Reserve banks, government agencies, and private trade organizations. The results from a recent Treasury ownership survey are shown in Exhibit 18.7.

It is evident from the survey that a large portion of Treasury debt—almost half—is held by private individuals and institutions. Rather surprising to many observers, however, is the relatively large proportion of the federal government's debt—just over half—held by the government itself. For example, in 2006 U.S. government agencies and trust funds, including the Social Security Trust Fund and other federal departments, held about 40 percent of the total federal debt. In addition, the Federal Reserve banks held almost 10 percent of all public debt outstanding.

The sheer size of the government's holdings of its own debt is viewed with alarm by some analysts. A large volume of government debt held out of circulation in federal vaults tends to thin the market for government securities, reducing the volume of trading. Other factors held constant, interest rates and security prices become more volatile, discouraging some investment. This could be important because the market for government securities is currently the anchor of the financial system.

| EXHIBIT 18.7 | Investors in the U.S. Public Debt, 2006* ($ Billions at End of First Quarter) | | |
|---|---|---|---|
| **Investor Group** | | **Amount Held in 2006*** | **Percent of Total Ownership** |
| Federal government: | | | |
|   U.S. government agencies and trust funds | | $3,502.0 | |
|   Federal Reserve banks | | 758.5 | |
|     Total for federal government issues | | $4,260.5 | 50.9% |
| Private investors: | | | |
|   Depository institutions | | $115.0 | |
|   Mutual funds | | 250.8 | |
|   Insurance companies | | 176.8 | |
|   State and local government treasuries | | 462.8 | |
|   Individuals: | | | |
|     Savings bonds | | 205.9 | |
|   Pension funds: | | | |
|     Private pension funds | | 182.2 | |
|     State and local government pension funds | | 128.6 | |
|   Foreign and international investors | | 2,082.3 | |
|   Miscellaneous investors* | | 509.4 | |
|     Total for private investors | | $4,114.0 | 49.1% |
|     Total for all investor groups | | $8,374.5 | 100.0% |

*The miscellaneous investor group includes holdings of Treasury securities by individuals, government-sponsored enterprises, brokers and dealers, bank personal trusts and estates, corporate and noncorporate businesses, and other investors. N/A indicates not available. Figures are for the first quarter of 2006.
Sources: Board of Governors of the Federal Reserve System and the U.S. Treasury Department.

Among private holders of the federal government's debt, pension funds, mutual funds, state and local governments, and individuals are at or near the top of the list. In 2006, for example, individual investors held about 3 percent of the public debt—the majority of these holdings in U.S. savings bonds. Pension funds held almost 4 percent, while mutual funds held about 3 percent of all Treasury-issued securities.

The proportion of the U.S. public debt held by foreign investors, including foreign central banks, governments, and other international investors, has risen significantly in recent years to about one-quarter of all issues outstanding. The foreign contingent of investors is very important—they hold about $2.1 trillion dollars in U.S. Treasuries and represent the single largest investor group holding U.S. Treasury securities outside the federal government itself.

The bulk of foreign holdings of U.S. securities seems to be centered in China, Great Britain, and Japan. Foreign holdings of government securities result, in part, from a rise in U.S. imports that lead foreign investors to build up dollar deposits in banks abroad. These investors have converted many of their dollars into purchases of Treasury securities in the money and capital markets. Foreign holdings of U.S. Treasury securities have remained relatively high recently due to the development of active over-the-counter markets for longer-term Treasuries in London, Tokyo, and other financial centers. These overseas U.S. Treasury security markets have given Treasuries round-the-clock liquidity and are especially attractive to such investors as

According to a recent U.S. Treasury survey, foreign investors held more than $2 trillion in U.S. government securities of various kinds! Why are foreign investors such heavy buyers of United States government securities?

A key source of this trend favoring foreign investors has been U.S. trade deficits, with Americans paying for what they buy abroad by contributing dollar-denominated securities to foreign investors. Then, too, the United States appears to many foreigners to be a "safe haven" compared to many foreign markets. Many overseas territories are in turmoil with weaker economies and, in some cases, unstable governments. By way of contrast, American businesses, bank deposits, stocks, and bonds look like havens of safety as well as sources of profitability.

This story is not all positive, however. Some analysts fear that foreign investors may be more "fickle" than domestic buyers of government securities. Any sign of trouble inside the United States may send some foreign investors racing for the exits, dumping Treasuries along the way. The result could be a sharp decline in the value of the dollar in international markets and an upsurge in borrowing costs for businesses and individuals inside the United States. Then, too, there is fear among some domestic individuals and institutions that foreign investors may literally "take over" much of the country, controlling industries—such as steel, oil, transportation, and managing seaports and airfields—that may be vital to homeland security. Recently the U.S. Congress moved toward opposing some foreign interests from acquiring control of selected vital domestic assets.

multinational corporations and foreign governments who find U.S. trading hours inconvenient. In the interdealer market, trading in Treasury bills worldwide starts at a minimum size of about $5 million, while T-notes and bonds trade in units of a million dollars. Transactions between the U.S. Treasury and brokers, dealers, and other investors in *new* Treasury IOUs around the globe have totaled more than $3 trillion annually in recent years, fueled by 150 to 200 Treasury auctions per year.

## QUESTIONS TO HELP YOU STUDY

7. Describe the types of securities that make up the *public debt* of the United States. What portions of this debt can the U.S. Treasury Department most closely control?

8. What problems exist when you try to measure the true *size* of the government's debt? Do you have any suggestions on how to deal with this measurement problem?

9. List the principal *holders* of the United States' public debt. What trends seem to be under way in the ownership of federal securities?

## *Methods of Offering Treasury Securities*

Management of the public debt is a complicated task. Treasury debt managers are called on continually to make decisions about raising new money and refunding maturing securities. They must decide what kinds of securities to issue, which maturities will appeal to investors, and the form in which an offering of securities should be made.

**auction method**

**Key URL:**
A computer-generated summary of each Treasury auction's results through the Web site of the Bureau of Public Debt is available at **publicdebt.treas. gov/**

### The Auction Method

Today, the **auction method** is the principal means of selling Treasury notes, bonds, and bills. Although several different methods have been used over time, all such techniques have a number of features in common. Both competitive and noncompetitive tenders for new securities, whose dollar amount and maturity are announced about one week in advance, are invited from the public. Competitive bidders usually include money-center banks and securities houses. About 2000 security brokers and dealers are registered to trade in the U.S. government securities market. Noncompetitive bidders, including smaller financial institutions and individuals, average about 20,000 or more per Treasury auction. Noncompetitive bidders receive an allotment of securities at the average or prevailing auction price up to a maximum amount determined by the Treasury. As we have seen, federal agencies and trust funds purchase large amounts of Treasury issues. These agencies participate in virtually every auction but pay the price charged noncompetitive bidders. They receive a special allotment of securities in exchange for their maturing issues after the regular auction is concluded.

### Types of Treasury Auctions

The Treasury has used several different auction methods over the years. Today, however, the auction method used for new T-notes, bonds, and bills is known as a *yield auction.* The Treasury announces the amount of securities it plans to sell a few days in advance and calls for yield bids on the day of the auction accurate to 1/10 of 1 basis point for bonds and notes and accurate to ½ of one basis point for T-bill issues. Investors submitting competitive bids for Treasury bonds and notes must express their offers on a minimum annual percentage-yield basis at which they would buy these securities or on a minimum discount-rate (DR) basis at which they would buy T-bills. Thus, the Treasury does not set the interest (coupon or discount) rate, but leaves the determination of both interest rate and price to the auction process itself.[4]

Once the Treasury announces a forthcoming auction the securities to be auctioned immediately trade on a "when-issued" basis among dealers and other large, active market participants. This market for advance sales supplies participants with valuable data about the expected price and yield of a new Treasury security the day it will be formally auctioned off. Experts argue that the "when-issued" market promotes greater transparency, reduces bidding risk, and increases competition in the market for Treasury IOUs.

When the Treasury's auction does take place those investors bidding the lowest annual percentage yield or discount rate (i.e., the highest price) normally will be awarded new securities. Awards will continue to be made at successively higher yields or discount rates (i.e., lower and lower bid prices) until the new issue is completely exhausted. The U.S. Treasury today uses what is called a *uniform* or *single price auction.* This means that, even though bids vary in price and yield from bidder to bidder, all successful bidders wind up paying *the same price*—the lowest price that just clears the market of all available securities (known as the *stop-out price* or *stop*).

### Marketing Techniques

The Treasury places new securities *directly* with the investing public. New T-bills, notes, and bonds can be purchased directly from the U.S. Treasury Department's Bureau of the Public Debt or from the Treasury's agents—

---

[4]Sometimes the Treasury *reopens* a particular security offering and sells additional amounts of the outstanding issue. If a T-bond or note issue is "reopened" the interest (coupon) rate remains the same as when this security was first offered. See especially Garbade and Ingber [4].

the Federal Reserve Banks—either by mail, via telephone, or online. *Competitive tenders*—bids from the largest and most active market participants that will be priced competitively in the auction—are accepted from primary dealers and a few other bidders, such as government agencies, at the Federal Reserve banks until 1PM EST, the day new securities are sold. Smaller-volume investors (including individuals) can place *noncompetitive tenders*—submitted by bidders who don't bid a particular yield or price but agree to accept the single price established in the auction—up to a maximum amount of $5 million each, submitted before noon EST the day the auction is held. No single bidder can receive more than 35 percent of the total offering.

**book-entry form**

**Key URL:**
For a full
description of the
role and services
provided by the
TREASURYDIRECT
System,
see **treasurydirect.gov**

*Book Entry*　　The marketable public debt is issued today in **book-entry form.** This means investors do *not* receive an engraved certificate representing ownership of Treasury IOUs but instead receive a statement of account. The investor's name and amount of securities purchased are recorded in an Account Master Record in the automated book-entry TreasuryDirect System maintained by the Bureau of the Public Debt or in what is called the *commercial book-entry system* maintained by financial institutions and government security brokers and dealers on behalf of themselves and their customers. Depository institutions are permitted to hold security safekeeping accounts at the Federal Reserve Banks where their own security holdings and those of their customers are recorded. As interest is received or securities are sold or purchased, banks credit or debit these accounts and the TreasuryDirect System. Book entry is the safest form in which to hold any security because it significantly reduces the risk of theft. Dealers, on the other hand, generally receive delivery of newly auctioned securities through the Fixed Income Clearing Corporation (FICC), a clearing agency registered with the SEC.

*Other Services Offered Investors*　　To encourage greater participation in the government securities market and stimulate demand for new Treasury issues, both the Federal Reserve and the Treasury offer a number of other services to investors. For example, securities held in book-entry accounts at the Federal Reserve banks may be transferred by wire almost anywhere using the Fed's electronic wire transfer network. Interest and principal payments are electronically deposited on the due date into the deposit account each investor designates for that purpose. This device makes it easy to sell Treasury securities before maturity on a same-day basis.

*On-the-Run and Off-the-Run Treasury Securities*　　Treasury IOUs issued in the most recent auction are referred to as "on the run", while those issued in earlier auctions are labeled "off the run." Most secondary (resale) market transactions involve "on-the-run" securities as dealers work to unload their bloated inventories of new securities acquired from the latest Treasury auction. Thus, on-the-run Treasuries tend to be more liquid and trade at somewhat higher prices than off-the-run Treasury IOUs. Active market participants often try to profit from these pricing anomalies by trading between on-the-run and off-the-run instruments.

*Treasury Interest Rates as Global Benchmarks for Other Interest Rates*　　The market interest rates attached to Treasury bonds, notes, and bills serve as critical *benchmarks* for the fixed-income security market around the globe. Millions of loans granted to borrowers each year use Treasury market interest rates as *base rates*. For example, short-term (money market) interest rates on commercial loans are often tied to T-bill rates and may be set a few basis points higher than the prevailing T-bill rate. Longer-term loans, such as commercial and home mortgages, are frequently tied to Treasury note and bond rates, especially the prevailing market interest rates attached to 10-year and 30-year T-bonds. For example, 10-year T-bond rates hovered around 5 percent during the first part of 2006, while contract rates on mortgage loans to finance the purchase of newly built homes averaged close to 6.5 percent, or a spread of about 1.5 percentage points above the T-bond rate. Generally, as the T-bond rate is ratcheted upward or downward home mortgage loan rates are adjusted accordingly in order for lenders to maintain their desired profit margin from these loans.

## The Goals of Federal Debt Management

**Key URLs:**
Dealers trading government securities trade with each other through interdealer brokers, including such institutions as BrokerTec at **ICAP.com**; Cantor Fitzgerald at **cantor.com**; and Hilliard Farber at **hilliardfarber.com**

Over the years, the Treasury has pursued several different goals in the management of the public debt. These goals may be divided into two broad groups: (1) *housekeeping goals,* which pertain to the cost and composition of the public debt; and (2) *stabilization goals,* which have to do with the impact of the debt on the economy and the financial markets.

*Minimize Interest Costs*    The most important housekeeping goal is to keep the interest burden of the public debt as low as possible. The Treasury has not always been successful in the pursuit of this goal, however. Today, the interest burden of the public debt is the sixth largest category of federal expenditures after welfare payments, unemployment insurance, health care, Social Security payments, national defense, and miscellaneous federal spending. This interest burden on the U.S. taxpayer increases when interest rates rise or the volume of debt increases faster than the nation's income.

*Economic Stabilization*    A broader goal of debt management is to help stabilize the economy, promoting maximum employment and sustainable economic growth while avoiding rampant inflation. This may involve issuing *long-term* Treasury securities in a period of *economic expansion* and issuing *short-term* securities in a period of *recession.* The issuance of long-term securities may tend to increase long-term interest rates and therefore act as a brake on private investment spending, slowing the economy. On the other hand, issuing short-term securities during a recession may take pressure off long-term interest rates and avoid discouraging investment spending needed to provide jobs.

Unfortunately, the goal of economic stabilization often conflicts with other debt management goals, particularly the goal of minimizing the interest burden of the debt. If the Treasury sells short-term securities in a period of expansion when interest rates are high and then rolls over those short-term securities into long-term bonds during a recession when rates are low, this strategy tends to minimize the debt's average interest cost. The Treasury is able to lock in cheaper long-term rates. From a stabilization point of view, however, this may be the wrong thing to do. The short-term debt may fuel inflation during an economic expansion, while long-term debt issued during a recession may drive up interest rates and reduce private investment. Treasury debt managers are confronted with tough choices among conflicting goals.

## The Impact of Federal Debt Management on the Financial Markets and the Economy

What effect do Treasury debt management activities have on the financial markets and the economy? This is a subject of heated debate among financial analysts. Most experts agree that in the short run, the financial markets become more agitated and interest rates tend to rise when the Treasury is borrowing, especially when *new money* is involved. A mere exchange of new for old securities usually has minimal effects, however, unless the offering is very large.

The longer-run impact of Treasury debt management operations is less clear. Certainly the *liquidity* of the public's portfolio of securities changes. For example, suppose $10 billion in Treasury bonds are maturing next month. Treasury debt managers decide to offer investors $10 billion in 10-year notes in exchange for the maturing bonds. The bonds, regardless of what their original maturity might have been, are now short-term securities (with one-month maturities). If investors accept the new 10-year notes in exchange for the one-month bonds, the average maturity of the public's security holdings obviously has lengthened, all else being equal. Longer-term securities, as a rule, are less liquid than shorter-term securities.

Will this reduction in public liquidity affect spending habits and interest rates? The research evidence on this question is conflicting, with many studies finding little effect from debt management activities. However, there is some evidence that *lengthening debt maturities* may increase the public's demand for money and *raise interest rates.* In contrast, if the Treasury offers shorter-term securities, this tends to make the public's portfolio of securities more liquid and may reduce the demand for money. The result may be an increase in spending for goods and services and, for a time, *lower* interest rates.

Still another possible debt management impact is on the *shape of the yield curve. Lengthening* the average maturity of the debt tends to increase long-term interest rates relative to short-term rates. The yield curve may assume a *steeper positive slope,* favoring short-term investment over long-term investment. On the other hand, *shortening* the debt's maturity tends to reduce longer-term interest rates and raise short-term rates. The yield curve may *flatten out,* if positively sloped, or even turn down, favoring long-term investment over short-term investment. The net impact on total investment spending would depend on whether private investment is more responsive to short-term interest rates or long-term interest rates.

On balance, most authorities are convinced debt management activities of the Treasury do *not* have a major impact on economic conditions. The effects of debt management operations appear to be secondary compared to the more powerful impact of monetary and fiscal policy on the economy and financial markets. The optimal policy is probably one that makes Treasury refunding operations as unobtrusive as possible, especially when these operations might interfere with monetary policy activities of the central bank. Nevertheless, debt management represents a policy tool that might be used by government in the face of serious economic problems.

---

### QUESTIONS TO HELP YOU STUDY

10. Describe the current auction method for selling U.S. Treasury securities.

11. List the principal *goals* of Treasury debt management. What is the essential difference between housekeeping goals and stabilization goals? To what extent could these goals conflict with each other?

12. Explain how changes in the maturity structure of the public debt might affect interest rates, the yield curve, and spending and saving in the economy.

## 18.3   State and Local Governments in the Financial Markets

The Treasury is often joined in the marketplace by thousands of state and local governments also borrowing money. Indeed, the borrowing and spending activities of state and local governments have been one of the most dynamic, rapidly growing segments of the financial system in recent years. Pressured by rising populations and inflated costs, states, counties, cities, school districts, and other local units of government have been forced to borrow in growing numbers to meet increased demands for their services.

Despite the rapid growth in borrowing by state and local governments, many investors consider state and local debt obligations a highly desirable investment medium due to their overall high quality, ready marketability, and tax exemption feature. The interest income generated by state and local securities is exempt from federal income taxes. However, most states exempt their own securities from state income taxes, encouraging residents to buy their own states' bonds, while they typically tax interest from out-of-state bonds.[5] As a result, these high-quality debt obligations—known as **municipals**

**municipals**—appeal to heavily taxed investors such as top-income-bracket individuals and large corporations, especially in high-tax states like California and New York. In addition, an active secondary market permits the early resale of many higher-quality state and local government bonds.

### *Growth of State and Local Government Borrowing*

The rapid growth of state and local government borrowing is reflected in Exhibit 18.8, which shows the total volume of municipal securities outstanding between the years 1940 and 2006. State and local government indebtedness grew slowly until the 1950s, when it nearly tripled. The volume of municipal debt doubled again during the 1960s and more than doubled during the 1970s and 1980s. By 2006, state and local debt outstanding was approaching $2 trillion.

What factors account for this strong record of growth in municipal borrowing? *Rapid population* and *income growth* are two of the most important causes. The U.S.

| EXHIBIT 18.8 | Total Debt Issued by State and Local Governments in the United States, 1940–2006* ($ billions) | | |
|---|---|---|---|
| Year | Debt Outstanding at Year-End | Year | Debt Outstanding at Year-End |
| 1940 | $ 20.3 | 1980 | $ 302.8 |
| 1950 | 24.1 | 1990 | 848.6 |
| 1960 | 70.8 | 2000 | 1,183.6 |
| 1970 | 145.5 | 2006* | 1,994.9 |

Sources: U.S. Department of Commerce: Board of Governors of the Federal System, *Flow of Funds: Assets and Liabilities Outstanding;* and the *Federal Reserve Bulletin,* selected issues.

---

[5]In 2007 the U.S. Supreme Court agreed to eventually decide if it is unconstitutional for a state to tax state and local bonds issued by other states but exempt its own bonds from taxation. Most states that levy income taxes exempt their own state's securities from income taxation which means these particular securities are generally exempt from *any* federal, state, or local government tax levies.

population rose from less than 132 million in 1940 to an estimated 300 million by 2006—a gain of nearly 170 million people in a span of less than 70 years. Rapid population growth implies that many local government services, such as schools, highways, and fire protection, must also expand rapidly. Tax revenues cannot provide all of the monies needed to fund these facilities and services, so borrowing steps in.

Another factor pushing state and local borrowing higher is the *uneven distribution of population growth across the nation*. Beginning in the 1950s, a massive shift of the U.S. population out of the central cities into suburban areas began to take place. This demographic change was augmented during the 1970s, 1980s, and 1990s by a movement of population and industry into small towns and rural areas to escape the social and environmental problems of urban living, and toward the western and southern states in search of warmer climates and new business opportunities. Smaller outlying communities were transformed into cities with a corresponding need for new streets, schools, airports, and freeways to commute back to the central cities for work, recreation, and shopping. The result was an upsurge in borrowing by existing local units of government and the creation of thousands of *new* borrowing units in the form of sewer and lighting districts, power and water authorities, airport and toll-road boards, and public housing authorities. Today, the United States has more than 80,000 state, county, municipal, and other units of local government. And at least 50,000 of them have the authority to issue debt, although some have constitutional prohibitions against large budget deficits and most have limits on how much they can borrow. Almost 4.5 million investors are active in the municipal bond market.

Accompanying the growth and shift of the U.S. population has come an *upgrading of citizens' expectations* concerning the quality of government services. We expect much more from government today than we did a generation ago. Particularly noticeable is an increased demand for government services that directly affect the quality of life, such as better-designed schools, and improved health care facilities. Instead of gravel roads and narrow highways, local citizens demand paved streets and all-weather highways. Many municipal governments are active in providing cultural facilities, such as libraries and museums, and are expected to play leading roles in controlling environmental pollution. Indeed, according to economists Garrett and Rhine [5], state and local government expenditures per citizen have risen from less than $800 in 1948 to more than $4,300 in 2004, growing significantly faster than federal government spending per person.

All of these public demands have had to be financed in an era of rising construction and labor costs, exacerbating the money burdens of local governments. Moreover, in the early 1990s and again in the wake of 9/11, many local governments were faced with sluggish economic growth and the loss of some of their tax base upon which to build for the future, though later economic growth accelerated and many state and local governments subsequently racked up sizeable budget surpluses. These changes remind us what a powerful influence the economy has on the demand for local government services and on the volume of government borrowing.

State and local governments are expected to continue to borrow heavily in future years, in part because the federal government seems intent on reducing its contributions to local funding and because of expected lower interest rates. In fact, the so-called "new federalism" marks an ongoing trend toward turning more social services over to the states to fund and manage. The states, in turn, seem to be passing more program responsibilities on to counties, cities, and other local governmental units, putting additional financial stress on these smallest units of government.

## Sources of Revenue for State and Local Governments

Borrowing by state and local governments supplements their tax revenues and income from fees charged to users of government services. When tax and fee revenues fail to grow as fast as public demands, municipal borrowings rise. Moreover, when long-term capital projects are undertaken, long-term borrowing rather than taxation is often the preferred method of governmental finance.

As we study state and local governmental borrowing in the financial markets, it is useful to have in mind the principal sources and uses of state and local funds. Where do the majority of state and local government revenues come from? And where does most of the money go? Exhibits 18.9 and 18.10, drawn from a recent census of state and local units of government, provide some answers to these questions.

As expected, most state and local government *revenues* are derived from *local* sources of funds: the citizens these governments serve. About four-fifths of state and local government revenues normally are derived from local sources. However, intergovernmental transfers of funds, including state aid to local schools and federal aid to the states, also provide a significant share of total revenues. Local governments receive about a third of their revenues from state governments, on average.

**EXHIBIT 18.9** Sources of Revenue and Expenditures for State and Local Governments ($ billions for fiscal 2002–2003)

| General Revenue Sources | Amounts | Percentage of Total | General Expenditures by Function | Amounts | Percentage of Total |
|---|---|---|---|---|---|
| Property taxes | $ 296.7 | 16.8% | Education | $ 621.3 | 34.1% |
| Sales and gross receipts taxes | 337.8 | 19.2 | Highways | 117.7 | 6.5 |
| Individual income taxes | 199.4 | 11.3 | Public welfare spending | 310.8 | 17.1 |
| Corporate profits taxes | 31.4 | 1.8 | | | |
| Revenue from the federal government | 389.3 | 22.1 | | | |
| All other sources of revenue (including user fees and miscellaneous general revenues) | 508.7 | 28.9 | All other state and local government spending (including expenses for public safety, housing, parks and recreation, interest on debt, hospitals, transportation and terminals, environmental cleanup and pollution prevention, administration, interest on debt, and general and miscellaneous expenditures) | 772.1 | 42.4 |
| Total revenues | $1,763.2 | 100.0% | Total expenditures | $1,821.9 | 100.0% |

Note: Excludes revenues or expenditures of publicly owned utilities, liquor stores, and insurance trusts, as well as intergovernmental transactions between state and local governments. Columns may not add to totals due to rounding error.

Source: Economic Report of the President, 2006.

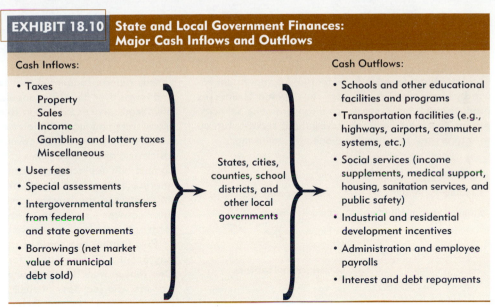

**EXHIBIT 18.10** | **State and Local Government Finances: Major Cash Inflows and Outflows**

**Cash Inflows:**

- Taxes
    Property
    Sales
    Income
    Gambling and lottery taxes
    Miscellaneous
- User fees
- Special assessments
- Intergovernmental transfers from federal and state governments
- Borrowings (net market value of municipal debt sold)

States, cities, counties, school districts, and other local governments

**Cash Outflows:**

- Schools and other educational facilities and programs
- Transportation facilities (e.g., highways, airports, commuter systems, etc.)
- Social services (income supplements, medical support, housing, sanitation services, and public safety)
- Industrial and residential development incentives
- Administration and employee payrolls
- Interest and debt repayments

Source: U.S. Bureau of the Census, and authors' adjustments.

Not surprisingly, *taxes* are the largest single revenue source for state and local governments. Property taxes are the mainstay of *local* government support, followed by sales taxes. *State* governments, in contrast, rely principally upon sales and income taxes. Selective sales taxes on alcoholic beverages, entertainment, gasoline, tobacco, and other specialized products and services are levied mostly at the state level and have increased significantly in recent years. User fees have also grown rapidly, with many cities and counties increasing their charges and fees for government services and for access to public facilities in recent years. Income taxes are imposed almost exclusively at the state level and are levied mainly against individuals rather than corporations. Most recently, property taxes have become more important as a source of local government funds, while income taxes have declined somewhat in the wake of a more slowly growing economy.

Not shown in Exhibit 18.9 is the growing use of lotteries and taxation of gambling that close to 40 states have either set in motion or are seriously considering. State lotteries often dedicate net revenues from ticket sales to support a specific government service such as education. Lotteries have become a popular alternative to higher taxes or to slicing government services because they are a voluntary form of taxation, but they incur high administrative costs and often contribute only a small portion of needed funds.

*State and Local Government Expenditures*    Where do state and local governments *spend* most of their funds? As Exhibit 18.9 suggests, *education* is the single largest item on the budgets of local governmental units and usually ranks number one or two on state budgets as well. *Social services,* including public welfare and medical care, occupies second place in local government spending but often ranks first in some state budgets. *Transportation services,* especially highway construction and maintenance, often ranks third in state spending, but generally ranks lower for local

**Key URL:**
Trends in state and local government spending for a single state can usually be dialed up by visiting an individual state's Web site—for example, for the state of Minnesota use **auditor.leg.state.mn.us**

The last three decades have featured a movement toward *privatization*—letting privately owned businesses produce and offer some local government services. Among the most common government services turned over to private suppliers have been the following:

| | |
|---|---|
| Hospitals | Natural gas |
| Landfills | Water supplies |
| Stadiums and auditoriums | Electric power |
| Airports | Fire protection |
| Public transportation | Libraries |
| Sewer systems | Correctional facilities |

By 1987, when the first census of U.S. governments to inquire about privatization took place, almost 40 percent of cities and towns with populations of at least 25,000 had contracted out to a private business at least one former government-provided service. Subsequent census reports suggested that the percentage of cities and towns over 25,000 in population with at least some privatized services had risen to about half of the total. Many state and local officials have seen privatization as a way to lower the cost of government, promote greater efficiency, and reduce taxes. The theory is that private competition replacing government monopolies should improve both service quality and cost. Some local governments see the private sourcing route as a way to offer services—stadiums or utilities, for example—the local area could not otherwise afford.

Privatization lost some of its steam as the new century opened. No one knows for sure why this occurred. One reason may be resistance from local government workers who fear loss of their jobs. Private production of government services seems to be seriously considered when a local community is facing a fiscal crisis and needs to stop providing some of its more costly services. However, when times improve, fewer governments seem interested in the privatization route.

governments. Overall, education, Medicare and general health care, public welfare, highway construction, sanitation, and correctional facilities represent close to two-thirds of state and local government spending today.

Some of the most important government services account for only a minor share of annual public budgets. For example, the cost of ensuring public safety—police and fire protection—generally accounts for less than 10 percent of local government expenditures. Sewer and sanitation services, protection of the environment, and housing programs to aid the poor normally represent about 10 percent of local government costs but often a much smaller share of state government spending.

State and local government expenditures have grown rapidly in recent years. In 1997, expenditures by state and local units topped the $1.25 trillion level. This figure was five times larger than the level of state and local government spending in 1980. By 2003, spending by these governmental units reached more than $1.7 trillion. Local tax revenues have simply been inadequate to handle this kind of growth in current (short-term) and capital (long-term) expenditures. Moreover, there is a growing perception that many municipal facilities need modernizing. Accordingly, borrowing in the money and capital markets against future government revenues in order to accommodate local needs for renovation, modernization, and expansion of facilities has soared. Moreover, as the new century dawned the federal government was passing a bigger share of welfare and social programs back to the states, adding to their borrowing needs.

The fiscal situation at the *local* level—cities, counties, and school districts—is often less "rosy" than for many states due to pressure from citizens for lower taxes and the prospect of further cutbacks in federal financial aid. Many local governments face rising populations of jail inmates, school-age children, and aging and indigent individuals

**Key URL:**
The economic condition of states, metropolitan areas, and counties may be traced through a new FDIC Web site called RECON at **fdic.gov**

**Key URL:**
Data revealing the fiscal condition of state and local governments in the United States are readily available through a key Web site of the U.S. Bureau of Economic Analysis at **bea.gov**

and families who need subsidized housing and health care. Added to these fiscal problems are many government employee retirement funds that are not yet fully funded, requiring governments to set aside more funds or even borrow using pension-obligation bonds to insure their employees receive pensions they have been promised.

## Motivations for State and Local Government Borrowing

State and local governments borrow money for several reasons. The first is to *satisfy short-term cash needs*—meet payrolls, make repairs, purchase supplies, cover fuel costs, and maintain adequate levels of working capital. Most state and local governments use tax-anticipation notes (to be discussed later) and other forms of short-term borrowing as a supplement to tax revenues to meet these immediate cash needs. Frequently, the construction phase of a building project is financed from short-term funds and then permanent financing is obtained by selling long-term bonds.

The second major reason for state and local government borrowing is to *finance long-term capital investment;* that is, to build schools, highways, and similar permanent facilities. Long-term projects of this sort account for the bulk of all municipal securities issued each year. Some governmental units try to anticipate future financial needs by borrowing when interest rates are low even though a project will not begin for a substantial period of time. Funds raised through anticipatory borrowing are then "warehoused" in various investments (such as Treasury bills and notes) until actual construction begins.

In recent years, local governments have occasionally employed *advance refunding* of securities. Advance refundings occur when a governmental unit has been granted a higher credit rating on its bonds by a rating agency, such as Moody's Investors Service or Standard & Poor's Corporation. Bonds issued previously with lower credit ratings (higher interest rates) may be called in and new securities issued at lower cost.

Any significant decline in market interest rates usually gives rise to more advance refunding activity by state and local governments—a practice that has sometimes led to alleged "pay to play" activities in which security underwriters have tried to persuade local government officials (sometimes by making contributions to local political campaigns) to refund outstanding debt and thereby generate more underwriting fees.

---

## QUESTIONS TO HELP YOU STUDY

13. The market for state and local government debt has been among the most rapidly growing financial markets over the past half century. Why has this growth occurred?

14. Can you foresee any serious problems on the horizon as state and local governments work to deal with the rapid growth of public demands on their budgets?

15. What are the principal sources of *revenue* for state and local governments today? Where do they spend the bulk of their incoming funds?

16. For what principal reasons do state and local governments borrow money?

17. Why is the condition of the *economy* of special importance to state and local governments in planning their revenues and expenditures?

---

## Types of Securities Issued by State and Local Governments

Many different types of securities are issued by state and local governments today. (See, for example, Exhibit 18.11.) One useful distinction is between short-term securities, which are generally issued to provide working capital, and long-term securities, used mainly to fund capital projects (such as the construction of new buildings or highways).

| EXHIBIT 18.11 | New Security Issues of Tax-Exempt State and Local Governments, 2005 ($ billions) | | |
|---|---|---|---|
| **Types of Issue and Issuer or Use of Funds** | **2005** | **Use of Funds** | **2005** |
| All issues | $409.7 | Use of proceeds from new capital issues: | |
| Type of issue: | | | |
| General obligation | 146.0 | Education | $71.0 |
| Revenue | 263.6 | Transportation | 25.3 |
| Type of issuer | | Utilities and conservation | 10.0 |
| State governments | 31.6 | Social welfare | NA |
| Special districts | 298.7 | Industrial aid | 18.7 |
| Municipalities, counties and townships | 79.4 | Other purposes | 60.7 |
| Issues for new capital, total | 223.8 | | |

Note: Issues represented in the table are to raise new capital and refund outstanding debt.
Source: Board of Governors of the Federal Reserve System, *Federal Reserve Bulletin*, selected issues.

*Short-Term Securities*   The most popular short-term securities issued by state and local governments are **tax-anticipation notes (TANs), revenue-anticipation notes (RANs),** and **bond-anticipation notes (BANs).**

**tax-anticipation notes (TANs)**

**revenue-anticipation notes (RANs)**

**bond-anticipation notes (BANs)**

**Tax-Anticipation and Revenue-Anticipation Notes**   These notes are used to attract funds in lieu of tax receipts or other revenues expected to be received in the near future. Governments, like businesses and households, have a daily need for cash to meet payrolls and purchase supplies. However, funds raised through taxes usually flow in only at certain times of the year. To satisfy their continuing need for cash between tax dates, state and local governments issue short-term notes with maturities ranging from a few days to a few months. Many of these short-term issues are acquired by local banks. When tax funds are received, the issuing government pays off the note holders.

**Bond-Anticipation Notes**   These short-term IOUs, also called *BANs,* are used to provide temporary financing of a long-term project until the time is right to sell long-term bonds. A school district, for example, may need to start construction on new school facilities due to pressure from rising enrollments. If market interest rates currently are too high to permit the issue of bonds, then construction can start from funds raised from bond-anticipation notes. Once the project is under way and interest rates decline to more modest levels, the school district then sells its long-term bonds and retires the bond-anticipation notes.

*Long-Term Securities*   The most common type of municipal borrowing is through long-term bonds. There are two main types of municipal bonds issued today—**general obligation bonds** and **revenue bonds.**

**general obligation bonds**

**revenue bonds**

**General Obligation Bonds**   These bonds, known as *GOs,* are the most secure form of municipal borrowing from the standpoint of the investor because they are backed by the "full faith and credit" of the issuing government and may be paid from *any* revenue source. State, county, and city governments, along with school districts, have the power to tax citizens to meet principal and interest payments on any debt issued. GOs are fully backed by this taxing power and often must be approved by public referendum before issue. The quality (level of risk) of GOs depends on the economic base (income and property values) of local communities and the total amount of debt issued.

**Revenue Bonds**   In contrast, *revenue bonds* are payable only from a specified source of revenue, such as a toll road or a sewer project, and usually do not require a public referendum before they can be issued. These securities are not guaranteed or backed by the taxing power of government. Instead, revenue bonds depend for their value on the revenue-generating capacity of the particular project they support.[6]

Both general obligation and revenue bonds have grown rapidly, especially among revenue bonds. Much of the growth of revenue issues is due to programs designed to

[6]Some municipal bonds display characteristics of *both* GO and revenue securities. For example, a *special tax bond* is payable from the revenues generated by a special tax, such as a tax on gasoline. Many special tax bonds are backed by the full faith, credit, and taxing power of the issuing governmental unit, giving them the character of GOs. *Special assessment bonds* are payable only from assessments against property constructed or purchased from the proceeds of the bonds issued and arise from sewer and street construction or similar projects. Special assessment issues may take on the character of GOs when backed by the taxing power of the issuer. *Authority bonds* are issued by special governmental units set up by states, cities, or counties to construct and manage certain facilities, such as airports. Authority bonds may be either GOs or revenue issues.

provide housing for low-income groups, improve medical facilities, provide student loans, and help local governments modernize their facilities.

### Types of Revenue Bonds

Among the best-known revenue issues are *student-loan revenue bonds* (SLRBs), which have been issued by some government agencies that lend money to college students. The federal government guarantees principal and interest payments from an SLRB, provided the issuing agency's loan-default ratio is low. If a high percentage of students default on their loans, federal guarantees are limited to only a certain portion of the principal and interest payments on the bonds.

In the housing field, several forms of state and local revenue bonds have been used. For example, *life-care bonds* may be issued by state and local development agencies to provide housing for the elderly. Investor funds may be secured by lease rentals and mortgages against the property.

Construction of hospital facilities may be supported by *hospital revenue bonds.* These bonds have been issued by state authorities to build hospitals for lease to public or private operating agencies. Hospital revenue bonds may have their principal and interest secured by lease rentals and a mortgage against hospital property.

A type of municipal security that serves both public and private interests is the *industrial development bond* (IDB). These securities originally were used to finance plant construction and the purchase of land, which is then leased to a private company. More recently, IDBs have financed the construction of industrial parks, electric-generating plants, pollution control equipment, and other capital items. Their purpose is to attract industry into a local area and increase jobs and tax revenues. However, the use of public funds raised through the tax-exempt borrowing privilege for private purposes soon disturbed members of Congress. The Deficit Reduction Act of 1984 listed several prohibited uses of IDB money, placed a ceiling on IDBs stemming from a single issuer, and restricted the total amount that could be issued from each state based upon its population. Accordingly, issuers of IDBs must plan farther in advance and work to get their new security issues approved and sold early in the new year before a local government's quota for IDB issues runs out.

Many local governments still borrow or use a portion of their current or expected future tax revenues to offer incentives for the development of new businesses in their area. Unfortunately, recent research suggests most businesses decide on which states and localities to enter based primarily upon such features as climate, energy costs, nearness to the firms' markets, and the availability of labor with the necessary skills—factors often beyond a local government's control—rather than being enticed by the financial incentives offered by many communities. (See, for example, Bradbury, Kodrzycki, and Tannenwald [2].)

### Innovations in Municipal Securities

The vast majority of state and local securities promise the investor a *fixed* rate of return. Unfortunately, this can reduce the attractiveness of GOs and revenue bonds in periods of rising interest rates and inflation. During such periods, new municipal instruments often appear. For example, some tax-exempt revenue bonds have been issued as *floaters.* In one case, U.S. Steel issued $48 million in government-sponsored pollution control bonds with a flexible (floating) interest rate to protect investors against future rate changes. Buyers were so attracted by this novel idea that an additional $500 million in floating-rate bonds soon came to market, promising a yield tied to changes in interest rates on Treasury bonds.

Still another innovation is the *option bond,* which bears a fixed rate of interest but can be sold back to the issuer or the agent at par after a specific period. One example was a $43 million issue of 9 percent, single-family mortgage bonds offered by Denton County, Texas. Although these bonds do not come due until 2013, a trustee guaranteed to buy back all eligible bonds. More recently, several municipal borrowers reduced the maturities of their bonds from 30 years to the 10- to 15-year range to improve their flexibility to the issuers and prospective buyers.

*Lottery bonds* have recently been offered in some states that have a strong demand for new capital. For example, Florida recently issued these bonds, backed by expected lottery revenues, to finance the building of new school facilities as the state's population continues to grow rapidly. Oregon and West Virginia also have offered bonds secured by lottery revenues in recent years.

Particularly interesting is the recent development of *securitized bonds,* which pledge future tax collections to retire a bond issue. New York City, for example, offered $650 million in municipal bonds tied to its anticipated tax receipts. A few states and cities had conducted similar financings before New York City's mega-issue of securitized bonds by bundling up delinquent property tax accounts, calling them "receivables," and using them as an asset to borrow against. While this device appears to open up significant new borrowing potential, it does raise the prospect of endangering a local government's credit rating if it runs into unexpected expenses or if a weaker economy results in an unexpected fall in tax collections.

### Key Features of Municipal Debt

*Tax Exemption* The unique feature of municipal securities is the **tax-exemption privilege.** Interest income from qualified municipal securities is exempt from federal income taxes; in addition, state law usually exempts municipals from income taxes levied by the state of issuance. This exemption feature was created so that federal, state, and local governments would not interfere with each other in raising funds and providing services to their citizens. It arises from a constitutional doctrine known as

**tax-exemption privilege**

---

**QUESTIONS TO HELP YOU STUDY**

18. Give a concise definition of each of the following state and local government securities, and explain how each is used:

| | |
|---|---|
| *Tax-anticipation notes* | *Revenue-anticipation notes* |
| *Bond-anticipation notes* | *General obligation (GO) bonds* |
| *Revenue bonds* | *Special tax bonds* |
| *Special assessment bonds* | *Authority bonds* |

19. *Revenue bonds* issued by state and local governments and public agencies have grown more rapidly than other types of state and local government securities in recent years. Several different kinds of revenue obligations are listed below. Explain the principal purpose or function of each of the following instruments:

| | |
|---|---|
| *SLRBs* | *Hospital revenue bonds* |
| *Life-care bonds* | *Industrial development bonds (IDBs)* |

20. What are the comparative risks faced by investors in choosing between *general obligation bonds* and *revenue bonds?* What advantage(s) do revenue issues offer the investor?

| | | | | |
|---|---|---|---|---|
| **EXHIBIT 18.12** | **The Impact of the Tax-Exemption Feature on the After-Tax Yields of Long-Term Corporate and Municipal Bonds** | | | |
| **Investor Group** | **Before-Tax Yield on Seasoned Aaa Corporate Bonds** | **Appropriate Federal Income Tax Bracket for Each Investor Group** | **After-Tax Yield on Seasoned Aaa Corporate Bonds** | **Before-Tax and After-Tax Yield on Aaa Municipal Bonds** |
| Individuals in the highest income bracket | 10% | 35% | 6.50% | 7.75% |
| Large corporate investors: | | | | |
| Manufacturing and industrial corporations | 10 | 35 | 6.50 | 7.75 |
| Property-casualty insurance companies | 10 | 35 | 6.50 | 7.75 |
| Commercial banks | 10 | 35 | 6.50 | 7.75 |
| Individuals in middle-income tax brackets | 10 | 28 | 7.20 | 7.75 |
| Individuals and institutions in the lowest income bracket | 10 | 10 | 9.00 | 7.75 |
| Tax-exempt investors (governments, pension funds, charities, foundations, and credit unions) | 10 | 0 | 10 | 7.75 |

**Key URLs:**
Not all states and local government securities are tax-exempt. *Public purpose bonds* carry the tax-exemption feature, while *private purpose bonds* are taxable unless specifically exempted. Under the terms of the Tax Reform Act of 1986 private purpose bonds are taxable if more than 10 percent of the proceeds benefit private interests or if the proceeds of the issue are secured by or payable from property employed for a business use. See, for example, **answers. com/topic/municipal_ bond; munios.com;** and **nsr/.org/msrbl/ glossary/view**

"reciprocity" in which various levels of government recognize each other's sovereignty over a variety of governmental functions.

Capital gains on municipal securities are *not* tax exempt, however, unless the security is issued at a discount from par. In that special case, any increase in price up to par value is considered part of the security's interest return and is tax exempt. However, if the security continues to rise in price, that portion of the gain above par is subject to taxation once the investor realizes the gain.

**An Interest Subsidy to High-Income Investors**   The tax-exempt feature has been controversial for many years. It is a government subsidy to high-tax-bracket investors. This is true because the value of the exemption increases with the investor's marginal income tax rate. Exhibit 18.12 illustrates the impact of the investor's marginal income tax rate (or tax bracket) on the relative attractiveness of municipals compared to taxable securities. This exhibit compares the approximate after-tax yield on high-grade corporate bonds, which are fully taxable, with the yield on comparable quality municipal bonds, assuming that Aaa-rated corporate bonds are trading currently at a 10 percent before-tax yield and Aaa municipal bonds are trading at 7.75 percent. Because the 10 percent corporate bond yield is a before-tax rate of return, we must adjust it using the investor's marginal income tax rate to derive the after-tax rate of return. The before-tax corporate yield is multiplied by $(1 - t)$, where $t$ is the investor's applicable federal tax rate.

Exhibit 18.12 illustrates the effect of this calculation with marginal tax rates ranging from 0 to 35 percent. For an investor in the top 35 percent tax bracket, the after-tax return on Aaa corporate bonds was 10 percent $\times$ $(1 - 0.35)$, or 6.50 percent. Clearly, an investor in this high-income group would prefer to purchase municipal bonds yielding 7.75 percent rather than corporate bonds returning just 6.50 percent after taxes, other factors being equal. The same conclusion holds true for larger corporations and banks confronted with the top 35 percent federal tax rate.[7] Even for middle-bracket investors facing a moderate income tax rate (such as 28 percent), municipals often are attractive in terms of their after-tax return.

Of course, the foregoing analysis focuses exclusively on after-tax rates of return, ignoring differences in liquidity and other features of taxable and tax-exempt securities. A corporation or an individual who needs to hold securities for liquidity purposes, for example, might well hold taxable issues, such as U.S. government securities, that can be converted into cash quickly with little risk of loss, even though their after-tax yields may be lower than yields on municipal bonds.

For income tax brackets below the top rung, taxable securities compare more favorably with municipals. For example, many small private investors whose applicable federal income tax rate may range from 10 to 15 percent find taxable securities more lucrative and purchase few municipals. In effect, the tax-exempt feature limits the demand for state and local government securities to so-called *retail investors*—high-income individuals and mutual funds that appeal to individuals as investors—as well as property-casualty insurers, large nonfinancial corporations, and other higher tax-bracket investors. This limitation may represent a serious problem in future years when many local governments must raise an enormous volume of new funds to accommodate rapidly expanding populations.

The tax exemption feature is an advantage to municipal governments because it keeps their interest cost low relative to interest rates paid by other borrowers. These savings can be passed on to local citizens in the form of lower taxes. Of course, the U.S. Treasury is able to collect less revenue from high-bracket investors as a result of the exemption privilege and must tax low-bracket taxpayers more heavily to make up the difference. Therefore, the *total* tax bill from all levels of government is probably little affected by the tax-exempt feature of municipals.

*Exemption Contributes to Market Volatility*   Because the market for municipal bonds is limited by the tax-exempt privilege to top-bracket investors, prices and interest rates on municipal bonds tend to be volatile. Prices of tax-exempt bonds tend to rise during periods when corporate and individual incomes are rising because top-bracket investors have greater need to shelter their earnings from taxation at those times. However, a fall in individual or corporate earnings often leads to sharp reductions in the demand for municipal bonds. Prices of tax-exempt issues may plummet, and interest costs confronting borrowing governments may rise during those periods when corporate profits are squeezed. This makes financial planning in the state and local government sector more difficult.

---

[7]Recent federal tax laws have sharply reduced the attractiveness of municipal securities to banks and other top tax-bracket investors. Successive tax laws have lowered the top corporate tax rate, forcing the after-tax yield on municipal bonds closer to the after-tax return on taxable securities. Federal tax reform, therefore, has made municipal bonds less attractive relative to all taxable securities. Many investors, especially individuals, still find municipals attractive, however, because they are one of only a few tax shelters left after federal tax reform. Banks, on the other hand, have significantly reduced their municipal holdings relative to taxable loans and U.S. government securities because federal laws have sharply reduced the tax deductibility of bank borrowing costs when banks purchase municipals. Now banks tend to concentrate their purchases in so-called "bank-qualified" municipal issues that are brought to market by smaller units of government but still promise tax benefits for the purchasing bank. Overall, these tax law changes have resulted in a shift in the municipal market toward higher-income individuals and mutual funds.

*Credit Ratings*    A feature of municipal securities that makes them especially attractive to investors is their high credit rating. About 10 percent of all municipal securities are AAA-rated by Moody's Investors Service and Standard & Poor's Corporation; about half are AA- or A-rated. A relatively small proportion of all state and local government securities are rated "speculative" (that is, rated below Baa by Moody's or BBB by Standard & Poor's) or carry no published rating. This means most municipal issues are considered to be of *investment quality* rather than speculative buys and the investment quality issues have a historical default rate of one percent or less.

Recently, Moody's Investors Service began to attach numerical modifiers to its standard A and B credit ratings for municipal securities. These newer Moody's bond ratings for state and local government debt include the following:

**Moody's State and Local Government Bond Rating Symbols**

| | |
|---|---|
| Aaa | Ba1 |
| Aa1 | Ba2 |
| Aa2 | Ba3 |
| Aa3 | B1 |
| A1 | B2 |
| A2 | B3 |
| A3 | Caa |
| Baa1 | Ca |
| Baa2 | C |
| Baa3 | |

In the above ratings, the modifier 1 means a new municipal bond issue ranks at the higher end of its rating category, 2 indicates a mid-range quality state and local security, and 3 implies the debt issue is judged to be at the low end of its credit-rating class. Notice that the lowest-grade speculative municipal issues have *no* numerical modifiers.

Moody's began to apply the numerical modifiers to the ratings for state and local government debt because of several recent trends affecting the municipal sector, including:

1. A shift in the primary investor groups holding state and local bonds, as banks, for example, largely withdrew from heavy municipal bond holdings due to reduced tax incentives, while tax-exempt mutual funds and money market funds became major buyers. These latter institutions need finer grading and more accurate valuation of municipal bonds because they are frequently forced to liquidate their holdings of municipals quickly.

2. Evidence of substantial credit risk and volatility in the state and local government sector as more local governments experience fiscal stress as the federal government transfers more responsibilities to local governments and many local taxpayers resist new programs and new taxes.

**Factors behind Setting Credit Ratings**    In assigning credit ratings to municipals, Moody's and other rating services consider the past repayment record of the borrowing unit of government, the quality and size of its tax base, the volume of debt outstanding, local economic conditions, and future prospects for growth. The fact that many municipal issues are backed by taxing authority or may draw on several different sources of revenue for repayment of principal and interest helps to keep the investment quality of tax-exempt municipal issues high. This is particularly important for regulated financial institutions that buy municipals. For example, regulations generally prohibit depository institutions from acquiring debt securities rated below Baa or BBB (so-called speculative issues). These restrictive rules encourage state and local governments to keep their credit ratings high in order to encourage more active participation by regulated financial institutions in bidding for new municipal securities.

**Recent Credit Quality Problems** Until recently, state and local governments possessed almost unblemished credit records. No major defaults on municipal securities had occurred for nearly half a century. However, the turbulent economic environment of recent decades has caused many investors to reassess the credit standing of municipals, especially the bonds issued by some of the largest cities and those associated with special local government projects, such as operating public utilities or building toll roads. Nonetheless, there have been relatively few actual defaults on municipal bonds in recent years (though about 6,000 local government defaults have occurred in U.S. history as a whole) and, when they have occurred, investors usually have received back the principal value of their bonds (with some loss of interest).

The recent problems in the municipal bond market first surfaced in the dramatic financial crisis experienced by New York City during the 1970s. Soaring costs for municipal services, excessive reliance on short-term debt, and high unemployment combined to threaten that city with record high interest costs and financial default. Then in 1978, Cleveland, Ohio, became the first major U.S. city to default on its debt since the Great Depression of the 1930s. This was followed by an even bigger debacle in 1983, to the tune of more than $2 billion, when a nuclear power consortium among several municipal governments—the Washington Public Power Supply System—fell into default under the weight of project delays and cost overruns.

The most widely publicized municipal default in modern times occurred in the summer of 1995 when Orange County, California, one of the largest urban areas in the United States, declared bankruptcy, with close to $800 million in unpaid obligations. The rapid growth in that county's population put its local government in a bind due to soaring demand for public services. However, Orange County voters rejected several proposals to raise taxes. County officials, in dire need of revenue, then adopted an aggressive investment policy, including heavy investments in derivatives, which lost about $2.5 billion when interest rates rose. Faced with numerous claims from creditors (including other local governments that had invested their funds with Orange County), county officials worked for nearly a year to hammer out a repayment plan to cover most of Orange County's debts.[8]

The Orange County debacle set the tone for credit quality issues as the twentieth century ended and the twenty-first century began. Following the lead of Orange County, a number of states, cities, and other local units of government have experienced a significant decline in their financial strength and stability. Not surprisingly, credit-rating agencies like Moody's and Standard & Poor's have put several municipal governments on their "credit watch" lists and some have recently had their credit ratings lowered. Many of these troubled governments are confronted with slow or no economic growth, a declining tax base, rising unemployment, aging populations, soaring health care costs for employees and citizens, and employee retirement

---

[8]See Chapter 8 for more discussion of the Orange County bankruptcy.

plans that have become substantially underfunded, posing a serious drain on future government revenues. Probably the most dramatic example is the city of Pittsburgh, Pennsylvania. In 2003, Standard & Poor's lowered Pittsburgh's credit rating five notches from investment grade to junk-bond status—affecting nearly $900 million of that city's outstanding debt. Nor was Pittsburgh alone—during the same year there were 10 downgrades of state government credit ratings scattered among six different states.

Orange County's financial collapse and Pittsburgh's credit downgrade reminded investors that local government failures are an ever-present possibility. Government bankruptcies are more likely in areas of economic decline or in localities where growth has outstripped the ability of cities and counties to provide government services. Moreover, many local governments have found in recent years that their citizens are unwilling to approve additional taxes or authorize the issuance of new debt.

Partly as a result of recent government financial problems, the Securities and Exchange Commission (SEC) has amended its Rule 15c2-12 to bar security dealers from marketing new municipal security issues unless the issuers agree to provide annual financial reports and continuing disclosure of "material events" (such as delinquencies, defaults, modification of security holders' rights, credit rating changes, or sale of property backing a security issue) to designated national databanks. The SEC approved a rule to severely limit the campaign ("pay to play") contributions that security dealers sometimes make to local government officials and to those running for public office. The idea is to protect investors in municipals from the adverse consequences of political corruption arising from state and local governments' borrowing money.

**Key URL:**
For an explanation of how municipal bond insurance works, see especially Municipal Bond Insurance at **munibondadvisor .com/BondInsurance .htm**

**Insurance for Municipal Bonds**   Investor concern over the quality of some municipal securities and the potential failure of some state and local government projects led to the creation of "sleep insurance" for selected municipal issues. First offered by Ambac Indemnity Corp. in the early 1970s and later by such companies as Municipal Bond Investors Assurance Corp. (MBIA), Financial Security Assurance, Inc., and Financial Guarantee Insurance Corporation, these insurance policies, which guarantee timely payment of principal and interest, now cover many top-rated state and local government bonds. Such insurance protection normally is requested and paid for by the bond issuer or the issuers' representative, not the investor purchasing the bonds. However, buyers of insured bonds usually receive lower yields compared to noninsured bonds. Therefore, issuers benefit from insurance because they can sell their bonds at lower interest cost. Rating agencies generally grant higher credit ratings to insured municipal securities. However, if the credit rating of the insurance company falls, interest rates on municipal bonds insured by that particular company also tend to rise. Bond insurance has become more important in recent years as retail customers (individuals and mutual funds) have come to capture a larger share of purchases of new municipal securities.

One additional form of municipal "insurance" that has recently grown in popularity is the rise of bank credit lines and standby guarantee letters. These credit back-up contracts help to increase the salability of municipals by reassuring potential investors that a bank will provide the necessary liquidity if the issuing government faces a cash shortage.

serialization

*Serialization*   Most municipal bonds are *serial* securities. **Serialization** refers to the splitting up of a single bond issue into several different maturities. Thus, an issue of $25 million in bonds to build a municipal stadium might include the following securities:

| Amount | Due in |
|---|---|
| $1 million | 1 year |
| $1 million | 2 years |
| $1 million | 3 years |
| • | • |
| • | • |
| • | • |
| $1 million | 25 years |

Splitting a single issue of municipals into multiple maturities contrasts with the practice employed by most corporate borrowers and the federal government. Corporations, for example, generally issue *term* bonds in which all securities in the same issue come due on the same date. In effect, serialization of municipal bonds is a way of *amortizing* state and local debt.

Why is serialization popular in the municipal field? Before serial bonds were widely adopted, state and local bonds were generally term securities. A sinking fund was created at time of issue, and annual contributions were made to the fund until sufficient monies were accumulated to pay off the bond at maturity. However, sinking funds proved irresistible to unscrupulous politicians and governments facing financial emergencies. Accumulated funds often disappeared, leaving virtually nothing to retire municipal debt when it came due. The serial feature seemed to offer a solution to this problem.

Unfortunately, serialization created as many problems as it solved. For one thing, splitting a security issue into different maturities reduces the liquidity and marketability of municipals. When a municipal issue is split into multiple maturities there may be only a small amount outstanding in any one maturity class. The volume of trading for particular maturities is, therefore, limited. Serialization also complicates offering new securities, because a number of different investor groups must be attracted into the bidding. For example, money market funds, banks, and individuals generally prefer the shorter-term (1-to-10-year) securities, while mutual funds and insurance companies often want only longer-term bonds.

## How Municipal Bonds Are Marketed

**Key URLs:**
Keeping up with municipal prices and interest rates is easier today due to such sites as CNN/Money at **cnnfm.com** and the Bond Market Association at **bondmarkets.com**

The selling of municipals is usually carried out through a syndicate of dealers. These institutions underwrite municipals by purchasing them from issuing units of government and reselling the securities in the open market at a higher price. Prices paid by underwriting firms may be determined either by competitive bidding among several syndicates or by negotiation with a single dealer or syndicate. Competitive bidding normally is employed in the marketing of general obligation bonds, while revenue bonds more frequently are placed through private negotiation.

In competitive bidding, syndicates (which may contain from two to upwards of a dozen or more underwriters) interested in a particular bond issue will estimate its potential reoffer price in the open market and what their desired underwriting commission must be. Each syndicate wants to bid a price high enough to win the bid but low enough so that the securities later can be sold in the open market at a price sufficient to protect the syndicate's commission. That is,

Bid price + Underwriting commission = Market reoffer price

The winning bid carries the lowest *net interest cost* (NIC) to the issuing unit of government. The NIC is simply the sum of all interest payments that will be owed on the new issue divided by its principal amount.

Bidding for new issues of municipal bonds is a treacherous business. Prices, interest rates, and market demand change rapidly. In fact, the tax-exempt market is one of the most volatile of all financial markets, due, in part, to the key role played by mutual funds, banks, insurance companies, and individual investors who tend to turn over their portfolios rapidly. Legal interest rate ceilings, which prohibit some local governments from borrowing when market interest rates climb above those ceilings, also play a significant role in the volatility of municipal trading. These combined factors render the tax-exempt market highly sensitive to the business cycle, monetary policy, and a host of other factors.

The specter of high interest rates often forces postponement of hundreds of millions of dollars in new security issues, and the onset of lower interest rates may unleash a flood of new security offerings. Still another problem is the unpredictability of federal tax reform legislation, which may reduce the volume and attractiveness of many municipal securities. The nature of this large debt market can suddenly change, with serious consequences for many of its players. Still, the rewards of municipal bond underwriting can be substantial, even though only a handful of dealers make a continuous market for these securities. For example, during 1998 one of the largest municipal bond underwritings in history involved almost $7 billion in bonds issued to fund New York's takeover of the Long Island Lighting Company. In this instance, the team of underwriters involved received about $40 million in underwriting fees.

**Key URLs:**
Among the leading dealers in the municipal bond market are Goldman Sachs at **gs.com**; Bear Stearns & Company at **bearstearns.com**; Lehman Brothers at **lehman.com**; and Merrill Lynch at **ml.com**

## Problems in the Municipal Market

The municipal market has been plagued by a number of problems over the years, some related to its unique tax-exempt character. Many observers question the social benefit of the tax-exemption privilege. Although state and local governments can borrow more cheaply as a result of tax exemption, the federal government must tax nonexempt groups more heavily to make up the lost revenue.

A number of proposals have been advanced over the years for improving the depth and stability of the municipal market by eliminating the tax-exempt feature. One interesting idea calls for reimbursing state and local governments for loss of the tax-exempt privilege by paying federal subsidies. A related idea calls for paying a subsidy directly to investors who choose to buy municipal securities. A federally sponsored *Urbank* was proposed a number of years ago that would issue its own bonds and direct the proceeds of bond sales to municipal governments. One criticism of this approach is the danger of increased federal controls over local government activities.

Even more challenging for the municipal market than the debate over tax exemption are spiraling needs for state and local funds—for example, growing demands for new housing, medical, and recreational facilities for the elderly; demands for more equitable funding of schools located in poorer communities versus those situated in richer communities; the rapidly unfolding costs associated with defenses against possible terrorist attacks; and a large prison population that will continue to require major expenditures for adequate correctional facilities. Added to these demands are expensive *infrastructure* problems—water and sewer systems that are wearing out; city streets and bridges worn down from adverse weather and heavy usage; deteriorating public buildings and highly expensive new building codes to deal with earthquakes and

In recent years the federal government has been passing more and more of its programs (such as welfare payments) along to the states, granting the states more power to implement federal programs and curtailing some of the old federal rules that limited what state and local governments could do. As a result, state and local government spending (net of federal aid) has recently risen to more than 10 percent of U.S. GDP. This trend is called "devolution" and seems consistent with the move toward greater deregulation, decentralization, and free enterprise happening around the globe.

There is concern among some state and local authorities that local governments are not well prepared to pick up the *financial burdens* inherent in this "new federalism". Many local governments already face a lack of financial resources and growing taxpayer resistance even before adding the burden of former federal programs tossed into their fiscal backyard. Some state and local governments may have to cut back on social services to their citizens that, in the past, used to help stabilize their economies. The result may be an overall shrinkage in government activity that may benefit some states (particularly local areas where individuals average higher private-sector incomes) but hurt other localities not as economically well off.

Overall, the quality of government service may eventually decline, though some researchers believe devolution is still desirable because it comes closer to what the original authors of the U.S. Constitution intended regarding federal powers versus local government powers. Some authorities believe the ultimate solution may be to take advantage of the federal government's superior ability to collect revenues while using state and local governments' superior knowledge of local service needs. This suggests that, from an efficiency point of view, the federal government should gather tax revenues and give state and local authorities greater discretion about how, where, and for whom those revenues are to be spent.

other potential disasters; and developing shortages of water and electrical-generating capacities.

Local government revenues will have to keep up with these demands for funds despite projected slower growth in the economy and the likelihood of less genous support from the federal government. More states will be under pressure to "pass the buck" to their local governments and force cities, counties, and school districts to deal with their own problems and find their own funding sources. Equally scary for many local government officials is the unwillingness among many taxpayers today to authorize new borrowing and new construction. They see government as too big and too costly. While more state and local government funds are needed as population continues to grow (reaching 300 million in the United States in 2006), it is not clear those needed funds can be raised at reasonable cost given the current structure and rules surrounding the market for municipals.

## QUESTIONS TO HELP YOU STUDY

21. What are the principal features of state and local government securities that have made them attractive to many groups of investors?

22. How has recent federal tax legislation impacted the market for municipals?

23. Describe how state and local government securities are marketed. What risks do bidders face in this marketplace?

24. What key problems do you believe state and local governments may face in the years ahead?

# Summary of the Chapter's Main Points

In this chapter we examined the roles played by governments in the financial markets when they borrow money, levy taxes, and spend the funds they raise. We explored the fiscal policy and debt management practices of governments at all levels— federal or national, state, and local. Among the key points made in the chapter are the following:

- The chief fiscal agency of the United States is the U.S. Treasury Department. Other governments around the world have similar departments that generally engage in two principal activities: (a) financing government expenditures through taxation, borrowing, and accessing other funds sources; and (b) managing the government's outstanding debt.

- The government most powerfully affects the financial system and the economy through its taxing and spending activities, or *fiscal policy.* The government also can set in motion changes in the economy through its *debt management policy.* This policy strategy involves changing the composition of the government's debt (e.g., changes in the ratio of short-term to long-term government securities outstanding).

- If a government's fiscal policy results in a *budget deficit,* with expenditures outstripping revenues, it will most likely be forced to borrow. Market interest rates may tend to rise, while total income and spending may tend to move higher unless the central bank offsets the government's *fiscal policy* action or private borrowing and spending decline.

- On the other hand, governments may run a *budget surplus,* with revenues outpacing expenditures, and therefore may need to borrow less money. If the budget surplus is large, a substantial portion of that surplus may be used to retire outstanding debt. Income and market interest rates may fall unless the central bank acts to offset the impact of the government's debt retirement program.

- The government may be able to use *debt management policy* to change conditions in the economy. For example, if the U.S. Treasury refunds maturing short-term securities by issuing new long-term securities, this action may reduce the liquidity of the public's security holdings as the average maturity of the public debt increases. Short-term interest rates may tend to rise, while income (spending and production) may fall. In contrast, a government policy that emphasizes short-term borrowing may lead to more rapid economic growth and less unemployment, but possibly at the cost of greater inflation.

- The United States government carries one of the largest public debts in the world and, recently, due to a sluggish economy, record defense spending to conduct war and fight terrorism, and costly social programs, that debt has been rising rapidly. With such a large and complex debt structure, Treasury debt managers must work to refund maturing government securities every week and quarter of the year. Their principal focus is on managing the *marketable* debt of the United States, represented by Treasury bills, notes, and bonds, which is sold to the public primarily through security dealers. Today U.S. government agencies, the Federal Reserve System, and foreign investors hold a majority of the public debt of the United States.

- In addition to heavy borrowing by the U.S. Treasury Department, state and local governments also borrow billions of dollars each year to fund the construction of public facilities and to supply themselves with working capital to cover daily costs associated with providing government services to their citizens.

- The borrowings of these localized units of government are specially privileged under the U.S. Constitution and U.S. Treasury Department regulations. Their interest earnings are exempt from federal income taxation and many states exempt the interest earnings on their own debt from state and local taxes. The tax-exemption feature makes these financial instruments (called *municipals*) uniquely attractive to investors occupying the highest tax brackets.

- Major factors driving state and local government borrowing have included rapid population and income growth, the upgrading of citizen expectations for publicly provided services, and a shifting of responsibility for funding many local services from federal to state and local units of government.

- Key revenue sources for state and local governments include sales and income taxes, property taxes, user fees, and funds transfers among governmental units. The largest categories of state and local government expenditures include education, social services, transportation services, health services, and construction spending.

- Many different types of securities are issued by local governments to borrow money. Short-term municipals include tax-anticipation notes (TANs), revenue-anticipation notes (RANs), and bond-anticipation notes (BANs). Each of these instruments is issued in the expectation that revenues to pay them off will subsequently appear.

- Long-term security issues include *general obligation (GO) bonds* and *revenue bonds.* The latter depend for their repayment on revenues generated by specific municipal projects, such as toll roads and toll bridges. There has been a tendency in recent years to develop many new types of state and local government securities such as securitized municipal bonds and lottery bonds.

- Among the many significant features of municipal securities are their *tax-exempt* feature and their *subsidization* of high-tax-bracket investors—both of which tend to create a relatively volatile market. State and local obligations also may be *serialized* or broken up into a range of maturities in order to appeal to a wider variety of potential buyers and minimize the risk of misusing public funds.

- Local government securities are generally of high credit quality with low perceived default risk. However, in recent years a few notable failures have appeared, causing investors to rapidly move their funds to investments of higher quality. Recent failures have spurred the expanded use of *municipal bond insurance.*

- Larger issues of municipals are generally marketed through security dealers under competitive bidding. However, there are some signs of taxpayer resistance to the continuing issuance of state and local debt obligations and the higher taxes that usually follow their sale in the money and capital markets.

## Key Terms Appearing in This Chapter

fiscal policy,  559

debt management policy,  559

budget deficit,  559

budget surplus,  559

public debt,  565

auction method,  572

book-entry form,  573

municipals,  576

tax-anticipation notes (TANs),  583

revenue-anticipation notes
  (RANs),  583

bond-anticipation notes (BANs),  583

general obligation bonds,  583

revenue bonds,  583

tax-exemption privilege,  585

serialization,  590

## Problems and Issues

1. The U.S. government can pay for an increase in its expenditures by one of three methods. It can raise taxes, issue debt, or print money. Explain what the Treasury Department would have to do to employ the last of these methods.

2. Many state governments have complained in recent years about the "unfunded mandates" of the federal government, whereby social programs that were previously funded by the federal government or new programs are passed down to the states. Explain what would happen if the federal government cuts taxes to stimulate the economy at a time when additional unfunded mandates were being pressed upon the states. Would federal tax cuts have the same beneficial effect on the economy as before?

3. Suppose that, due to an unexpected decline in federal income tax collections, the Treasury is compelled to borrow an extra $40 billion to cover planned expenditures in the current government budget. Based upon the discussion in this chapter, what would be some of the possible effects of this additional borrowing on the financial markets and the economy?

4. Suppose that, due to drastic cuts in federal spending and strong economic growth, it now appears that the federal government will experience a $100 billion budget surplus in its cash account at the Federal Reserve. It will use the balance to retire $100 billion in government securities. Based on the discussion in this chapter, what would be some of the possible effects of this debt retirement operation on the economy and the financial markets?

5. Suppose the federal government's revenue and expenditure accounts in this fiscal year display the amounts shown below (each item in billions of U.S. dollars):

| | | | |
|---|---|---|---|
| Social security benefits | $400 | Social insurance taxes | |
| Individual income tax collections | 850 | and contributions | 600 |
| National defense | 275 | International affairs | 20 |
| Net interest payments on the federal debt | 250 | Corporate income taxes | 200 |
| Miscellaneous revenue sources | 160 | Health care and Medicare | 350 |
| Income security programs | 260 | Miscellaneous expenditures | 220 |

What were the government's total revenues and expenditures in this most recent year? Was the budget in surplus or in deficit? All other factors held constant, what are some of the possible effects of this year's government budget position on the economy's level of income and interest rates? Explain your reasoning.

6. Suppose the public debt of the United States consisted of the following types of security issues (all figures in billions of dollars):

| | |
|---|---:|
| Treasury bills | $ 750 |
| Savings bonds and notes | 180 |
| Government account series | 1,500 |
| Federal government currency | 6 |
| Treasury bonds | 600 |
| Special notes issued to foreign investors | 45 |
| Treasury notes | 2,200 |
| Special bonds and notes sold to states and local governments | 165 |

Calculate the following: *total marketable debt, total nonmarketable debt, total interest-bearing debt,* and *gross public debt.*

7. Corporate bonds carrying an A rating are currently being priced to yield 8.62 percent. For an investor in the 28 percent income tax bracket, what yield must an A-rated municipal bond carry to make this investor *indifferent* as to the yield difference between the corporate and the municipal bond?

8. Sandoval County issued AA-rated bonds at a net interest cost of 6.85 percent. If annual interest payments promised on these bonds amount to $12.75 million, what was the principal amount of municipal bonds issued by Sandoval County?

9. Consider the case in which state and local governments across the United States collected or spent the following amounts classified as shown (all figures in billions of dollars for the most recent fiscal year):

| | | | |
|---|---:|---|---:|
| Property taxes | $175 | Individual income taxes | $70 |
| Education | 430 | Corporate income taxes | 15 |
| User fees | 25 | Governmental administration | 49 |
| Highways | 88 | Interest on debt | 104 |
| Sales and gross receipts taxes | 125 | Intergovernmental funds transfers | |
| Public safety | 80 | from the federal government | 150 |
| Environment and housing | 78 | General and miscellaneous | |
| Miscellaneous general revenue | 200 | expenditures | 75 |

What was the total revenue and total expenditures for state and local governments combined? Was the state and local government sector running an overall deficit or surplus in its combined budget? Will borrowing likely be necessary to finish out the current fiscal year?

10. Identify the name for each of the types of state and local government securities described below:

a. Long-term debt payable only from revenues generated by a toll road.

b. Debt issued to support the construction of new business facilities.

c. Short-term borrowing that will later be replaced by long-term state or local government bonds.

**d.** Long-term securities issued under the Federal Housing Act to support the provision of low-income residential dwellings.

**e.** State or local government debt repayable from any revenue source.

**f.** Short-term borrowing in lieu of expected local government tax receipts.

## Web-Based Problems

1. Depository institutions rely on both Treasury and federal agency securities as well as municipal bonds to balance out the level of risk in their asset portfolios (which regulatory agencies watch closely) and to add liquidity to their portfolios. The purpose of this exercise is to see how large, medium-size, and small banks differ in how heavily they rely on Treasuries and municipal bonds.

   **a.** Go to the Federal Deposit Insurance Corporation's (FDIC) Web site: **fdic.gov** and locate their "Statistics on depository institutions." Acquire and key into a spreadsheet the following balance sheet data for the end of each of the past 10 calendar years (ex. for 12/31/2006) for three categories of commercial banks: small (less than $100 million in total assets); medium (between $100 million and $1 billion in total assets); and large (over $1 billion in total assets): (i) Total *Assets;* (ii) Total *Securities;* (iii) Total municipal bonds, referred to as *Securities issued by states & political subdivisions.*

   **b.** For each category of bank, compute for each year: (i) the percentage of total *Securities* that are represented by municipal bonds, and (ii) the percentage of total *Assets* that are represented by municipal bonds.

   **c.** What differences emerge from (b) between large, medium-size, and small banks in their reliance placed on securities and on municipals?

   **d.** Have there been any significant changes in the use of securities and municipals by banks over the past ten years?

2. One of the more interesting sites on the World Wide Web is the Bureau of the Public Debt in the U.S. Treasury Department at **treas.publicdebt.gov** and the related site known as Treasury Direct at **treasurydirect.gov**. These sites contain a great deal of information about U.S. Treasury activities in the money and capital markets, about changes in the public debt of the United States, and about the government's revenue and expense budget. Using these two popular Web sites, research the following questions:

   **a.** What types of securities does the Treasury make available to investors? (Make a list.)

   **b.** In the latest Treasury auction, what was the volume of securities traded and what were their prices and yields?

   **c.** What are "strips" and how does the Treasury aid investors interested in these particular securities?

   **d.** What are Monthly Treasury Statements (MTS)?

   **e.** For the most recent month, how much revenue did the Treasury receive and how much did it spend?

www.mhhe.com.rose10e

3. Answer the following questions while referring to the Treasury's popular Web sites, **publicdebt.treas.gov** and **treasurydirect.gov:**

   a. What is the size of the public debt of the United States right now?

   b. How big is that debt on a per capita basis?

   c. How has the volume of the public debt changed over time since the nation's founding under the Constitution?

   d. What is the Monthly Statement of the Public Debt and what does it contain? Can you see how this information might be useful to active buyers of Treasury securities?

4. The leading dealers in the world assisting state and local governments in raising new funds include such well-known financial institutions as Goldman Sachs at **gs.com**, Merrill Lynch at **ml.com**, Bear Stearns at **bearsterns.com**, and Lehman Brothers at **lehman.com**. Check out the official Web sites of these leading municipal dealers, viewing each Web site from two perspectives: (a) the viewpoint of the financial manager of a state or local government interested in seeking advice about raising new funds, and (b) the viewpoint of an investor possibly interested in buying municipal bonds and notes. From these two different perspectives, which dealer has the most helpful and inviting Web site and why do you think so? What recommendations would you offer to Web site managers and designers working for Goldman Sachs, Merrill Lynch, Bear Stearns, and Lehman Brothers? Explain the basis for your recommendations.

## Selected References to Explore

1. Baxandall, Phineas. "Taxing Habits: The Economics of Sin Taxes," *Regional Review,* Federal Reserve Bank of Boston, First Quarter 2003, pp. 19–26.

2. Bradbury, Katherine L.; Yolanda Kodrzycki; and Robert Tannenwald. "The Effects of State and Local Public Policies on Economic Development: An Overview," *New England Economic Review,* Federal Reserve Bank of Boston, March/April 1997, pp. 1–47.

3. Fleming, Michael J. "Who Buys Treasury Securities at Auction?" *Current Issues in Economics and Finance,* Federal Reserve Bank of New York, Vol. 13, No. 1 (January 2007), pp. 1–7.

4. Garbade, Kenneth D., and Jeffrey F. Ingber. "The Treasury Auction Process: Objectives, Structure, and Recent Adaptations," *Current Issues in Economics and Finance,* Federal Reserve Bank of New York, Vol. 11, No. 2 (February 2005), pp. 1–11.

5. Garret, Thomas A., and Russell M. Rhine. "On the Size and Growth of Government," *Review,* Federal Reserve Bank of St. Louis, January/February 2006, pp. 13–30.

6. Jossi, Frank. "The Taxing Issue of E-Commerce," *Fedgazette,* Federal Reserve Bank of Minneapolis, November 2003, pp. 9–11.

7. Kotlikoff, Lawrence J. "Is the United States Bankrupt?" *Review,* Federal Reserve Bank of St. Louis, July/August 2006, pp. 235–57.

8. Laubach, Thomas. "New Evidence on the Interest Rate Effects of Budget Deficits and Debt," *Finance and Economics Discussion Series,* Paper No. 2003-12, Board of Governors of the Federal Reserve System, May 2003.
9. Leduc, Sylvian. "Deficit-Financed Tax Cuts and Interest Rates," *Business Review,* Federal Reserve Bank of Philadelphia, Second Quarter 2004, pp. 30–37.
10. Saving, Jason L. "Fiscal Fitness: The U.S. Budget Deficit's Uncertain Prospects," *Economic Letter,* Federal Reserve Bank of Dallas, April 2007, pp. 1–7.
11. Taylor, Lori. "The Sales Tax Crunch," *Southwest Economy,* Federal Reserve Bank of Dallas, May/June 2003, pp. 1–4.

# Chapter 19

# Business Borrowing: Corporate Bonds, Asset-Backed Securities, Bank Loans, and Other Forms of Business Debt

## Learning Objectives

### in This Chapter

- You will examine the different ways business firms issue debt securities and negotiate loans in order to borrow funds in the money and capital markets.

- You will learn about the key factors that cause businesses to increase or decrease the volume of debt funds they seek to raise within the financial markets.

- You will see the often powerful impact that business borrowing has upon market interest rates and credit conditions inside the financial system.

## What's in This Chapter?
## Key Topics Outline

## 19.1   Introduction to Business Borrowing

Business firms draw on a wide variety of sources of funds to finance their daily operations and to carry out long-term investment. In 2006, for example, nonfinancial business firms in the United States raised nearly $1.9 trillion in funds to carry out long-term investments, purchase inventories of goods and raw materials, and acquire financial assets. Of this total, approximately $516 billion (about 27 percent) was supplied from the financial markets through issues of bonds, stocks, notes, and other financial instruments. In this chapter, we look at sources of borrowed (debt) funds used by businesses today. In the next chapter, we consider the advantages and disadvantages of stock (equity) as a source of business funding.

## 19.2   Factors Affecting Business Activity in the Money and Capital Markets

The funding demands of businesses are fueled by their desire to acquire new assets and replace existing assets (such as plant and equipment) that are wearing out. Specifically, at any point in time,

> *Total funding demands of business firms*
>
>   = *Desired increases in short-term assets* (inventories of goods and
>   raw materials, credit (receivables) extended to customers, and
>   holdings of marketable securities and other short-term assets)
>   + *Desired increases in long-term assets* (plant and equipment,
>   construction of new homes and other facilities for sale, and the
>   start-up or acquisition of other business firms)                    (19.1)

These total funding demands from the business sector can be met from funds generated *inside* each firm (*internal financing*) in the form of undistributed profits and depreciation reserves and from funds generated from *outside* the individual firm (*external financing*) in the money and capital markets. Specifically,

> Total business funding demands − Undistributed profits and
>
>   depreciation reserves from inside each firm
>
>   = *Business demands for external financing from
>   the money and capital markets*                                     (19.2)

Many factors affect the extent to which business firms draw on the money and capital markets for external funds. One prominent factor is the *condition of the economy*. A booming economy generates rapidly growing sales, encouraging businesses to borrow in order to expand inventories and to issue stocks and bonds in order to purchase new plant and equipment. In contrast, a sagging economy normally is accompanied by declining sales and a reduction in inventory purchases and long-term investment. Other factors being equal, the need for external fund-raising declines when the economy grows more slowly or heads down into a recession. In contrast, rising demand for business goods and services is usually translated into rising demand for short- and long-term capital supplied from the financial marketplace.

   *Credit availability* and *interest rates* also have powerful effects on business fund-raising activity in the money and capital markets. Rising interest rates that typically accompany a period of economic prosperity eventually choke off business borrowing and spending plans due to the increasing cost of carrying inventories, floating new securities, and renewing credit lines. Falling interest rates, on the other hand, can stimulate business borrowing and spending, leading to a restocking of inventories and an expansion of long-term investment financed by bonds, stocks, and direct loans.

A third factor in influencing how heavily businesses draw on the money and capital markets for financial support is the *level and expected growth of internally generated funds* (earnings and cash flow) for each firm. The financial markets are largely a *supplemental funds source* for most businesses, drawn upon to backstop internal cash flows when credit availability and economic conditions are favorable and when internally generated cash is inadequate to cover all desired business investments. Because business firms' earnings and cash flows tend to be volatile, it should not surprise us to learn that business fund-raising activity in the financial system is also highly volatile. Heavy business borrowings in one year to fill the *funding gap* between desired business capital spending and internally generated funds often are followed by a dearth of new security offerings and significant paydowns of outstanding loans the next year, particularly if internal funds have risen or if business expectations about the state of the economy have soured.

These marked fluctuations in business fund-raising result in wide swings in interest rates and security prices. Much of the volatility in stock and bond prices reported in the daily financial press may be attributed to the on-again, off-again character of financial market activity by the business sector. The key actors in this rapidly changing drama are, of course, the largest industrial corporations, which have the financial stature to tap both the open market and the negotiated loan markets for debt and equity funds. Skillful analysts often can read which way the wind is blowing as far as interest rates and security prices are concerned by watching what is happening to the current earnings and investment plans of major business corporations.

## 19.3 Characteristics of Corporate Notes and Bonds

**corporate bond**
**corporate note**

If a corporation decides to use long-term funds to finance its growth, the most popular forms of long-term financing are the **corporate bond** and **corporate note.** This is especially true for the largest corporations whose credit standing is so strong they can avoid dealing directly with an institutional lender such as a bank, finance company, or insurance company and sell their IOUs in the open market. Small companies without the necessary standing in the eyes of investors usually must confine their long-term financing operations to negotiated loans with an institutional lender (such as a bank or finance company), an occasional stock issue, and heavy use of internally generated cash.

### Principal Features of Corporate Notes and Bonds

A distinction needs to be drawn here between notes and bonds. By convention, a *note* is a corporate debt contract whose original maturity is five years or less; a *bond* carries an original maturity of more than five years. Both securities promise the investor an amount equal to the security's par value at maturity plus interest payments at specified intervals. Because both securities have similar characteristics other than maturity, we will use the word *bond* to refer to both notes and bonds in the discussion that follows.

Corporate bonds are generally issued in units of $1,000 and earn income that, in most cases, is fully taxable to the investor. These securities are known as *registered bonds* because the owner of these instruments must register with the issuing company in indenture

**Key URLs:**
For an interesting and up-to-date look at the market for corporate bonds, see especially the Bond Market Association at **investinginbonds.com,** the CBS Market Watch at **cbsmarketwatch.com,** and Financial Pipeline at **finpipe.com**

order to collect interest. Each bond is accompanied by an **indenture,** listing rights and obligations of borrower and investor. Indentures usually contain *restrictive covenants* designed to protect bondholders against actions by a borrowing firm or its shareholders that might weaken the value of the bonds by diminishing the firm's ability to meet its obligations to bondholders, thus increasing the risk of default. For example, restrictive covenants in an indenture may prohibit increases in a borrowing corporation's dividend rate (which would reduce the ability of the firm to rely on internal financing), limit additional borrowing, restrict merger agreements, or limit sale of the borrower's assets. These and other terms in a bond indenture are enforced by a third party—the trustee (often a bank trust department)—that represents investors holding the bonds. More restrictive indentures tend to lower interest costs for a borrowing company.

## Recent Trends in Original Maturities of Corporate Bonds

The maturities attached to newly issued corporate bonds have fluctuated widely with changing economic conditions and shifts in expectations for interest rates and inflation. At the beginning of the twentieth century many railroads sold bonds with 100-year-plus maturities. During the 1950s and 1960s, corporations found a ready market for 20- to 30-year bonds, and telephone companies managed to sell 40-year bonds. Such long-term debt contracts are desirable from a borrowing company's point of view because they can lock in low interest costs for many years and make financial planning much simpler. However, the 1970s and 1980s ushered in a trend toward much shorter-maturity corporate debt issues (many in the 5- to 15-year range), due in part to rapid inflation and interest rates that soared to record levels. The development of sophisticated interest rate hedging tools (such as futures, options, and swaps) aided companies moving toward these shorter-maturity bonds because these tools help minimize damage from volatile shorter-term interest rates. Sharply lower interest rates and subdued inflation in the 1990s and into the twenty-first century, however, set in motion a swing back to longer maturity bonds. For example, two government agencies, the Resolution Trust Corporation (disbanded in 1996) and the Tennessee Valley Authority, issued 40- to 50-year bonds, while such companies as Walt Disney and Coca-Cola brought 100-year issues to market.

## Call Privileges Attached to Corporate Bonds

A considerable proportion of corporate bonds outstanding today carry *call privileges,* allowing early redemption (retirement) of the bonds if market conditions prove favorable. The call privilege represents a way to shorten the average maturity of corporate bonds and gives the firm greater flexibility in financing its operations. However, it can be expensive when interest rates are high and expected to fall. Investors realize the bond is likely to be called if interest rates fall and therefore demand a higher yield as compensation for the risk the bond will be retired. However, most corporate bonds are issued today *without* a call privilege attached due to the added interest cost involved and the availability of hedging instruments such as futures and options.

## Sinking Fund Provisions

Some corporate bonds are backed by *sinking funds* designed to ensure the issuing company will be able to pay off bonds when they come due. Periodic payments are made into the fund on a schedule usually related to the depreciation of any assets supported by the bonds. The trustee is charged with the responsibility of making sure the user places the right amount of money in the sinking fund each time a payment is due. Periodically, a portion of the bonds may be retired from monies accumulated in the sinking fund (often annually). The presence of sinking funds tends to reduce borrowing costs.

## Yields and Costs of Corporate Bonds

Yields on the highest-grade corporate bonds tend to move closely with yields on government bonds. In contrast, yields carried by lower-grade corporate bonds are more closely tied to conditions in the economy and to factors specifically affecting the risk position of each borrowing firm. Bonds issued by the largest U.S. companies are, with few exceptions, listed and traded on the New York or American stock exchanges, although the largest volume of corporate bond trading passes through dealers operating off the exchanges.

As we noted in Chapter 6, there are several different ways to measure the rate of return to the investor or the cost to the firm of issuing a debt security. From the point of view of the issuing company, one widely quoted measure of the cost of a bond is its *coupon rate*—the rate of interest the company promises to pay as printed on the face of the bond. However, the coupon rate may understate or overstate the true cost of a bond to the issuing company, depending on whether the bond was issued at a discount or at a premium from its par value. A better measure of the cost of issuing a bond is to compare the *net proceeds* from a bond sale available for the borrowing company's use to the present value of the stream of cash payments the firm must make to bondholders.

For example, suppose a corporation issues $1,000 par bonds, but flotation costs reduce the net proceeds to the company from each bond to $950.[1] If the bonds mature in 10 years and carry a 10 percent coupon rate, the before-tax cost, $k$, to the issuing company is figured as follows:

$$\text{Net proceeds per bond} = \frac{\text{Interest cost in year 1}}{(1 + k)^1} + \frac{\text{Interest cost in year 2}}{(1 + k)^2}$$

$$+ \cdots + \frac{\text{Interest cost in year 10}}{(1 + k)^{10}}$$

$$+ \frac{\text{Principal payments in year 10}}{(1 + k)^{10}} \tag{19.3}$$

In this example:

$$\$950 = \frac{\$100}{(1 + k)^1} + \frac{\$100}{(1 + k)^2} + \cdots + \frac{\$100}{(1 + k)^{10}} + \frac{\$1,000}{(1 + k)^{10}}$$

The use of a financial calculator or computer software indicates that $k$ in this example is 10.85 percent.

However, interest charges on debt are *tax deductible,* making the after-tax cost considerably less than the before-tax cost, especially for the largest and most profitable firms. For the largest corporations with annual earnings in the top tax bracket, the marginal federal income tax rate is 38 percent. Thus, a large company issuing the bond described above would incur an after-tax cost ($k'$) of

$$k' = k(1 - t) \tag{19.4}$$

---

[1]The major elements of flotation cost for a new bond issue are the underwriting spread of the securities dealer who agrees to sell the issue, registration fees, paper and printing charges, and legal fees.

where $k$ is the before-tax cost and $t$ is the firm's marginal tax rate. In this example,

$$k' = 10.85\%(1 - 0.38) = 6.73\%$$

Of course, if the firm were in a lower tax bracket, the after-tax cost of its debt would be higher. In the case of an unprofitable company (whose effective tax rate is zero), the after-tax cost of debt would equal its before-tax cost.

The before- and after-tax costs of debt vary not only with each firm's tax rate but also with conditions in the financial markets. During periods of economic expansion, when the supply of credit tends to become increasingly scarce relative to the demand for credit, the cost of borrowing may rise in order to allocate the available supply of credit among many competing uses (unless, of course, an expanding economy contributes to lower default-risk premiums on corporate loans). In buoyant times, bonds often must be marketed at lower prices and higher interest rates. Conversely, during periods when the economy contracts into a recession, the cost of borrowing may tend to decline as the demand for credit cools down (unless, of course, default-risk premiums on corporate loans rise significantly). In depressed times, the prices of corporate debt securities may rise and their interest returns may fall.

There are, however, exceptions to the foregoing pattern. For example, sometimes the volume of borrowing increases markedly during business recessions as companies attempt to lock in the relatively low interest rates that may be available at that time. This happened during the 2000–2003 period when the global economy was in a recession and inflation was subdued. Business borrowing rates in the financial markets fell to 40-year lows and the market for long-term corporate debt was, at times, flooded with new debt security issues.

## Signals Corporate Bond Issues May Send to the Financial Marketplace

Like the taking on of other types of debt or the issuing of new stock, firms choosing to sell corporate bonds to raise funds send "signals" to the financial markets that, in turn, can affect the value of their securities in the minds of investors. For example, the apparent *motivation* for a new bond issue can be critical. If a bond issue announcement appears to be driven by an unanticipated cash-flow shortage from the assets of the issuing company and the market is aware of this, bond and equity prices of the issuer may fall and its borrowing costs may rise. On the other hand, a new bond sold to expand and/or improve a firm's capitalization, to make a timely and well-considered acquisition, or for reasons other than unexpected cash deficits seems to send a *positive* signal to the market, and bondholders of the issuing firm may receive some positive abnormal returns. Where the financial markets cannot successfully discern the motivation for a new debt issue, equity and debt investors may experience *negative* abnormal returns due, perhaps, to the implication that the assets the issuing company holds may be of lower value than first thought.

## The Most Common Types of Corporate Bonds

*Debentures*    There are many different types of corporate bonds issued in the financial markets. Among the most common is the **debenture,** which is *not* secured by any specific asset owned by the issuing corporation. Instead, the holder of a debenture is a general creditor of the company and looks to the earning power and reputation of the borrower as the source of the bond's value.

**debenture**

### Subordinated Debentures

A related form of bond is the *subordinated debenture,* frequently called a *junior security.* If a company goes out of business and its assets are liquidated, holders of subordinated debentures are paid only after all nonsubordinated creditors receive monies owed them. Thus, there is greater risk with these instruments and a higher interest cost to the issuing firm.

### Mortgage Bonds

**mortgage bonds**

Debt securities representing a claim against specific assets (normally plant and equipment) owned by a corporation are known as **mortgage bonds.** For example, Ford Motor Company issued close to $15 billion in these secured bonds in 2006, using some of its factories and its Volvo brand as collateral.

Mortgage bonds may be either *closed end* or *open end.* Closed-end mortgage bonds do not permit the issuance of any additional debt against the assets already pledged under the mortgage. Open-end bonds, on the other hand, allow additional debt to be issued against pledged assets, which may dilute the claims of current bondholders. For this reason, open-end mortgage bonds typically carry higher yields than closed-end bonds. Sometimes several mortgage bonds with varying priorities of claim are issued against the same assets. For example, the initial issue of bonds against a corporation's fixed assets may be designated first mortgage bonds, and later second mortgage bonds may be issued against those same assets. If the company were liquidated, holders of second mortgage bonds would receive only those funds left over after holders of the first mortgage bonds were paid off.

### Income Bonds

Bonds often used in corporate reorganizations and in other situations when a company is in financial distress are known as *income bonds.* Interest on these bonds is paid only when income is actually earned, making an income bond similar to common stock. However, holders of income bonds do have a prior claim on earnings over both stockholders and holders of subordinated debentures. Some income bonds carry a cumulative feature under which unpaid interest accumulates and must be fully paid before stockholders receive any dividends.

### Equipment Trust Certificates

Resembling a lease in form, *equipment trust certificates* are used most frequently to acquire industrial equipment or rolling stock (such as railroad cars or airplanes). Title to the assets acquired is vested in a trustee (often a bank trust department), which leases these assets to the company issuing the certificates. Periodic lease payments are made to the trustee, who passes them along to certificate holders. Title to the assets passes to the borrowing company only after all lease payments are made. Both equipment trust certificates and mortgage bonds tend to post lower interest rates than other corporate bonds because they are backed by specific marketable assets.

### Industrial Development Bonds

**industrial development bond (IDB)**

For many years now, state and local governments have been active in helping private corporations meet their financial needs. One of the most controversial forms of government-aided, long-term business borrowing is the **industrial development bond (IDB).** These bonds are issued by a local government borrowing authority to provide buildings, land, or equipment to a business firm. Because governmental units can borrow more cheaply than most private companies, the lower debt costs may be passed along to the firm as an inducement to move to a new location, bringing jobs to the local economy. The business firm normally guarantees both interest and principal payments on the IDBs by renting the buildings, land, or equipment at a rental fee high enough to cover debt service costs.

## *Innovations in Corporate Debt*

Corporate bonds are traditionally called *fixed-income* securities because most pay a fixed amount of interest each year. This creates a problem for bondholders when interest rates rise, inflation increases, or both, because then the real market value of fixed-income securities falls. In recent years, repeated bouts with inflation or reduced quality ratings on corporate bonds have spurred companies to develop *new* types of bonds whose return to the investor is sensitive to changing inflation and changing bond values. New bonds have appeared with deferred interest payments and variable coupon (promised) rates of return to investors, in an attempt to help issuing companies with near-term cash shortages. Among the most interesting of these innovative securities are discount bonds, floating-rate bonds, commodity-backed bonds, and medium-term notes (MTNs).

*Discount bonds* are sold at a price below par and appreciate toward par as maturity approaches. Thus, the investor earns capital gains as well as interest, while the issuing corporation usually can issue discount bonds at a lower after-tax cost than conventional bonds. Some discount bonds, known as **zero coupon bonds,** pay no interest at all. First used by J.C. Penney in 1981, "zeros" pay a return based solely on their price appreciation as they approach maturity. However, the annual price increase (or "phantom interest") is taxable as ordinary income, not as capital gains, under current IRS regulations.

**zero coupon bonds**

*Floating-rate bonds* have their annual promised interest rate tied to changes in long-term or short-term interest rates. *Commodity-backed bonds* carry a face value tied to the market price of an internationally traded commodity, such as gold, silver, or oil. More recently, *inflation-linked corporate notes* have appeared. For example, shortly after the new century began, SLM Corporation—the student loan marketing company—issued a debt instrument promising investors an annual interest return 2.12 percent above the inflation rate, as measured by the annualized percentage change in the consumer price index (CPI). Other companies offering similar inflation-protected bonds included Merrill Lynch, Morgan Stanley, and Household International. Out of fear that inflation might eventually take off running, the issuers of these particular securities hedged themselves with derivatives to avoid the prospect of high future borrowing costs.

*Medium-term Notes (MTNs),* carrying maturities of 1 to 10 years, were used as far back as the 1970s, but literally exploded onto the corporate fund-raising scene in the past 25 years, emerging as a major funding tool. As Exhibit 19.1 shows, the gross new issuance of MTNs by U.S. corporations more than tripled between 1993 and 2005, from amounts of $86 billion to over $285 billion, while outstandings rose from $210 billion to nearly $713 billion. Financial corporations have issued the lion's share— almost 90 percent—of MTNs outstanding, and their reliance on them continues to grow. Nonfinancial businesses have reduced their issuance of MTNs somewhat in recent years, although outstandings remain far above the levels of the early 1980s.

One of the distinguishing hallmarks of U.S. corporate debt markets is their ability to provide funds to businesses at virtually every stage of their existence—from completely *new* ventures (where venture capital firms, pension plans, and even some banks provide start-up capital), to firms going public for the first time (i.e., initial public offerings, or IPOs, where venture capitalists and pension plans are often joined by insurance companies and wealthy individuals), to mature companies that have either routine long-term capital needs (often satisfied via the public sale of bonds to large

| EXHIBIT 19.1 | Medium-Term Notes ($ billions) | | | | |
|---|---|---|---|---|---|
| | 1993 | 1996 | 1999 | 2002 | 2005 |
| | Outstandings | | | | |
| All U.S. corporations | $210.9 | $287.3 | $420.6 | $515.9 | $712.9 |
| Financial corporations | 125.4 | 194.5 | 320.2 | 422.9 | 641.3 |
| Nonfinancial corporations | 85.5 | 92.8 | 100.4 | 93.0 | 71.6 |
| | Gross New Issuance | | | | |
| All U.S. corporations | $ 86.1 | $93.7 | $170.8 | $257.7 | $285.2 |
| Financial corporations | 57.8 | 82.0 | 149.3 | 237.4 | 277.8 |
| Nonfinancial corporations | 28.2 | 11.7 | 21.5 | 20.4 | 7.4 |

Note: Numbers may not add up due to rounding.
Source: Federal Reserve Board's Web site, **www.federalreserve.gov.**

numbers of investors and institutions), to companies with unusual financing needs (which may require the private sale of a new debt issue to a handful of sophisticated investing institutions). Most notable in recent years is the wider opening of corporate debt markets to small- and medium-size firms who can more easily sell lower-quality "junk" debt securities in the open (public) market than in the past, such as by getting *credit guarantees* from investment banks and other strong institutions in order to reduce the riskiness of the debt issues, and, thereby, broaden the group of investors interested in their new debt offerings.

**Key URL:**
For more information on the European corporate debt market, see especially the European Issues segment of the Securities Industry and Financial Markets Association's Web site at **sifma.org**

One of the most exciting developments in the corporate bond market today is the rapid growth and development of Europe's corporate bond market, spurred on by that continent's new unity into one economy and one financial system. Differences in bond yields issued from different European Community (EC) member nations have recently declined, so that European bond dealers are finding that traditional arbitrage profits— switching between the bonds of different European countries—are sharply reduced. With the decline in interest-rate spreads, European bond dealers are looking for new ways to make money, such as by increasing the size of the European junk bond market and getting bond-issuing firms more interested in asset-backed bonds. At the same time, significant volumes of euro-denominated bonds are appearing in global financial markets in order to take advantage of public interest in the new EC international currency, the euro. Some U.S. companies, like Citigroup, offer European investors asset-backed securities, discussed in the next section of this chapter, while U.S. investors are increasingly seeking out European junk bonds because American investors are more used to buying high-risk bonds than are many European investors and U.S. long-term interest rates in recent years have been among the lowest in modern history.

## 19.4 Asset-Backed Securities Issued by Corporations

**Key URLs:**
To further explore the features of asset-backed securities see, for example, **finpipe .com, key.com,** and **mortgage101.com**

During the 1970s and 1980s, as borrowing costs for corporations soared along with inflation, both financial and nonfinancial corporations began searching for *new* ways to raise capital, expand their operations, and reduce risk exposure. They received help from a major innovation in the home mortgage market, where housing lenders—in cooperation with federally sponsored mortgage agencies (including the Federal National

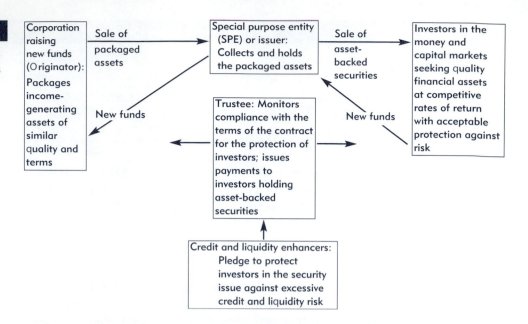

**EXHIBIT 19.2**

**Issuing Asset-Backed Securities to Raise New Funds for Corporations in Need of Capital**

Mortgage Association [FNMA], the Government National Mortgage Association [GNMA], and the Federal Home Loan Mortgage Corporation [FHLMC])—were successfully developing a new channel for corporate fund-raising called **asset-backed securities (ABS).**[2] Groups of home mortgage loans, usually supported by guarantees issued by federal agencies, were being packaged by lenders, removed from the lenders' balance sheets, and placed in a separate trust account. Then, with the help of an investment bank or other securities firm, new securities backed by the packaged loans were sold in the open market to raise new capital. (See Exhibit 19.2.)

asset-backed securities (ABS)

securitization

The process that gives rise to the creation of asset-backed securities, known as **securitization,** offers several potential *advantages* to those larger corporations able to use the device. For example, securitization may:

1. Reduce the cost of raising funds below the cost of issuing traditional bonds or borrowing from a bank or finance company.

2. Grant companies greater control over their balance sheets, including the ability to take on *new* assets that may bear higher returns or lower risk than assets that are being securitized and removed from a company's balance sheet.

3. Avoid the issuance of additional balance sheet debt until a company is prepared to do so.

4. Improve the financial strength of an issuing firm by increasing its ratio of equity capital relative to its total assets and liabilities.

5. Permit greater asset diversification, which may bring more stability to company earnings and reduce the overall cost of capital.

6. Provide a new source of company earnings in the form of servicing fees or residual income from the difference between the yield on securitized assets and the yield on securities issued against those assets.

---

[2]For a detailed discussion of the roles played by the FNMA, the GNMA, and the FHLMC in the residential mortgage market, see especially Chapters 11 and 22.

**Key URL:**
One of the leading weekly sources of information on the asset-backed securities market in the Asset Securitization Report (ASR) at **asreport.com**

**Key URL:**
To learn more about the structure, rules, and trading of asset-backed securities, see especially **en. wikipedia.org/wiki/ asset-backed-security**

Financial and nonfinancial companies not connected to the mortgage market soon discovered this asset-backed fund-raising tool was also available to them. Investment banks, such as Bear Stearns and Goldman Sachs, for example, agreed to provide advice on how and when to establish a trust (or "special purpose entity") that would hold the pool of assets removed from a company's balance sheet, as well as advice on when to sell securities against the pooled assets. Moreover, banks and other lenders (enhancers) agreed to make lines of credit available to backstop expected cash flows from the packaged assets, to help insure that investors in asset-backed securities receive the payments they are promised.

Over the past three decades corporations have intensively searched their balance sheets for income-generating assets that might be securitized to raise new money. To be attractive to most investors, the assets in question must be of high quality or adequately secured by credit guarantees, have a common purpose, and carry relatively uniform terms. The more popular non-mortgage-related assets that have surfaced in recent years to back security issues include accounts receivable, business equipment leases, small business loans, credit-card loans, consumer automobile loans and leases, computer and truck leases, mobile home loans, farm loans, and energy loans.

As Exhibit 19.3 suggests, the use of asset-backed securities by a wide variety of financial-service and nonfinancial corporations has risen significantly in recent years. Especially notable are recent increases in security issues backed by loans to large and small businesses, student loans, commercial and residential mortgages, and accounts

| EXHIBIT 19.3 | The Issue and Growth of Asset-Backed Securities (ABS) | | | | | | | |
|---|---|---|---|---|---|---|---|---|
| | **Year-End Volume in Billions of Dollars** | | | | | | | |
| **Assets Backing Issued Securities** | **1999** | **2000** | **2001** | **2002** | **2003** | **2004** | **2005** | **2006** |
| Loans to businesses and student loans | $83 | $90 | $108 | $105 | $104 | $105 | $89 | $90 |
| Residential (mortgage) loans* | 396 | 425 | 487 | 548 | 677 | 1087 | 1677 | 1937 |
| Commercial mortgages | 116 | 165 | 223 | 248 | 291 | 337 | 433 | 527 |
| Consumer loans | 457 | 528 | 598 | 633 | 597 | 572 | 605 | 671 |
| Consumer leases† | 10 | 7 | 7 | 6 | 6 | 5 | 4 | 4 |
| Accounts (trade) receivable | 67 | 83 | 88 | 83 | 77 | 76 | 96 | 122 |
| Real estate investment trust assets | 12 | 10 | 7 | 14 | 30 | 82 | 115 | 130 |
| **Percent of asset-backed securities issued as:** | | | | | | | | |
| Corporate bonds | 61% | 56% | 64% | 75% | 79% | 77% | 79% | 77% |
| Commercial paper | 39 | 44 | 36 | 25 | 21 | 23 | 21 | 23 |

*Residential (mortgage) loans include single-family homes and multifamily dwellings.
†Receivables from operating leases, such as consumer auto leases.
Note: Figures rounded to the nearest billion dollars.
Source: Board of Governors of the Federal Reserve System, *Flow of Funds Accounts,* Statistical Release Z.1, various quarterly issues.

receivable arising from credit sales of goods. Note also in Exhibit 19.3 that the majority of asset-backed securities are issued in the form of long-term corporate bonds, with the remainder issued in the form of commercial paper (i.e., short-term corporate IOUs nine months or less to maturity).

---

### QUESTIONS TO HELP YOU STUDY

1. Explain what is meant by the statement: "The financial markets are a supplemental funds source for business." What factors appear to affect the volume of business fund-raising from the money and capital markets?

2. What *advantages* does the issuance of debt have over other sources of funds that a business firm might pursue? How about *disadvantages*?

3. Define each of the following terms having to do with business borrowing:

   | | |
   |---|---|
   | *Indenture* | *Sinking fund* |
   | *Call privilege* | *Mortgage bond* |
   | *Subordinated debenture* | *Industrial development bond (IDB)* |
   | *Income bond* | *Debenture* |
   | *Trustee* | *Equipment trust certificate* |

4. Explain how the *true* cost of a corporate bond may be determined.

5. How are *asset-backed securities* created?

6. What advantages do asset-backed securities offer an issuing corporation?

---

## 19.5   Investors in Corporate Debt

**Key URLs:**
An increasingly popular source of working capital for small businesses are cash advances based on their credit-card sales. Examples of this form of credit-card factoring may be found at **business .com/directory/ financial-services; AmericanCapital Advance.com;** and **AmeriMerchant.com**

Today the investor market for corporate bonds, asset-backed securities, and other forms of corporate debt is dominated by insurance companies, mutual funds, and pension funds (see Exhibit 19.4). Pension funds prefer buying corporate debt in the open market; insurance companies, on the other hand, frequently purchase their corporate securities directly from the issuing company in an off-the-market transaction. The stability of cash flows experienced by pension funds and insurance companies permits them to pursue corporate debt securities with long maturities and to lock in their higher yields.

One of the more dynamic investor segments in U.S. corporate securities includes *foreign* institutions, particularly leading security dealers, banks, and insurance firms, such as Credit Suisse and Deutsche Bank. Many purchases of U.S.-issued corporate debt instruments have been associated with foreign takeovers of U.S. companies and the desire of foreign investors to pursue safer investments in the United States in order to escape political and economic turmoil abroad and to take advantage of strong U.S. economic conditions relative to other parts of the globe. Then, too, purchase of dollar-denominated assets such as corporate bonds gives foreign investors a way to store U.S. dollars at high yield until those dollars are needed either to buy U.S. goods or to purchase commodities sold in international markets that are denominated in dollars (such as oil).

Banks are *not* among the heaviest investors in corporate bonds, though their investments in asset-backed securities, especially those backed by pools of residential mortgages, have grown rapidly due to their safety and relatively high yields. Generally, bankers prefer to deal personally with a business customer and grant a loan specifically tailored to the borrower's needs rather than to enter the impersonal bond

| EXHIBIT 19.4 | Principal Investors in Corporate and Foreign Bonds, 2006* | |
|---|---|---|
| **Investor Group** | **Amount** | **Percent of Total Bond Holdings** |
| Households | $ 697.9 | 7.5% |
| Rest of the world (foreign investors) | 2,737.9 | 29.5 |
| Commercial banks | 780.6 | 8.4 |
| Savings institutions | 89.1 | 1.0 |
| Life insurance companies | 1,881.8 | 20.2 |
| Property-casualty insurance companies | 278.6 | 3.0 |
| Private pension funds | 284.8 | 3.1 |
| State/local government pension funds | 211.0 | 2.3 |
| Mutual funds and money market funds | 1,182.0 | 12.1 |
| Security brokers and dealers and other investors | 397.2 | 4.3 |
| Government-sponsored enterprises | 406.0 | 4.4 |
| Other investors | 351.1 | 3.8 |
| Totals | $9,298.0 | 100.0% |

*Figures are for the fourth quarter of the year at annualized rates.
Note: Columns may not add to totals due to rounding.
Source: Board of Governors of the Federal Reserve System, *Flow of Funds Accounts: Financial Assets and Liabilities,* Fourth Quarter 2006.

market. Increasingly in recent years, banks have become direct competitors with the corporate bond market through the granting of *term loans.* A term loan has a maturity of more than one year. Responding to inflation and the rising cost of business equipment, bankers have gradually extended the maturity of term loans, with many falling in the 5- to 10-year maturity range. Interest rates on such loans often exceed the interest cost on corporate debt sold in the open market, however, especially when banks also insist the borrowing firm keep funds on deposit with the bank.

One area of concern among investors in corporate debt in recent years has been an apparent decline in overall credit quality. For example, a substantial proportion of all corporate bonds issued over the past few decades in the United States has been "junk bonds." Significant numbers of industrial bond issuers have seen their credit ratings reduced. As the danger of default has risen, capital market investors have demanded higher promised rates of interest on newly issued corporate debt and/or special covenants, allowing investors to redeem their holdings of corporate debt instruments with the issuing companies at a fixed price if their credit rating is lowered or if the investors' position is weakened by restructuring the issuing firm's capital.

The rapid growth of bonds and other debt instruments in the United States in recent years has not been matched by a rise in bond holdings of U.S. residents. The discrepancy between the growth in supply and the increase in domestic demand has been filled by foreign investors. For example, between 1995 and 2006, the value of bonds outstanding issued by U.S. financial and nonfinancial companies more than tripled from $2.5 trillion to nearly $8.2 trillion. Over this same period, foreign investors (especially from Europe, Japan, the Asian mainland, Canada, and Latin America) have increased their holdings of U.S. corporate bonds by nearly fivefold, from $461 billion to more than $2.7 trillion. These numbers stand in contrast to the more modest 2 1/2-fold increase of foreign bond holdings by U.S. residents between 1995 and 2006, from $413 billion to a little over $1.1 trillion.

## 19.6   The Secondary Market for Corporate Debt

The resale (secondary) market for corporate bonds, asset-backed securities, and other corporate debt instruments is relatively limited compared to the larger resale markets for common stock, municipal bonds, and other long-term securities. Trading volume is generally thin, even for some debt instruments issued by the largest corporations. Part of the reason is the small number of individuals active as investors in this market. Individuals generally have limited investment time horizons (holding periods) and tend to turn over their portfolios rapidly when other attractive investments appear. In the past, the volume of secondary market trading in corporate debt instruments was also held back by the "buy and hold" strategies of many institutional investors, especially insurance companies and pension funds. Many of these firms purchased corporate debt instruments exclusively for interest income and were content to purchase the longest-term issues and simply hold them to maturity. However, under pressure of volatile interest rates and inflation, many institutions buying corporate debt have shifted into a more aggressive strategy labeled *total performance*. Portfolio managers are more sensitive today to changes in prices and look for near-term opportunities to sell corporate securities and reap capital gains. In fact, a number of insurance companies, pension funds, and mutual funds operate their own trading departments and keep constant tabs on developments in the corporate market.

Unlike the stock market, no one central exchange for the trading of bonds and other debt instruments dominates this debt market. Although corporate instruments are traded on all major exchanges, including the New York Stock Exchange (NYSE), most secondary market trading is conducted over the telephone and through electronic networks linking customers, brokers, and dealers. Dealers commit themselves to take on large blocks of securities, either from other dealers or from pension funds, insurance companies, and other clients. Dealers now try to close out positions taken in individual corporate debt instruments very quickly, frequently acting only as intermediaries in trades between buyers and sellers—without committing their own capital in order to avoid possible losses from changing market interest rates.

## 19.7   The Marketing of Corporate Debt

New corporate bonds, asset-backed securities, and other forms of corporate debt may be offered publicly in the open market to all interested buyers or sold privately to a limited number of investors. The first route, known as **public sales,** accounts for the largest portion of corporate security sales each year. Among smaller companies and those firms with unique financing requirements, however, a second route, known as **private or direct placements,** has often been popular.

**public sales**

**private or direct placements**

### *Public Sales*

**investment bankers**

Public sales in the open market are handled principally by **investment bankers,** including such well-known investment houses as Bear Stearns, Goldman Sachs, and Citigroup, Inc.[3] Investment banks underwrite new issues of corporate securities and give advice to corporations on their financing requirements. An investment banking firm may singly take on a new issue of corporate securities or band together with other underwriters to form a *syndicate*. Either way, the investment banker's game plan is to

---

[3]For a more extensive discussion of the services provided by investment bankers, see especially Chapter 16.

acquire new corporate securities at the lowest possible price and sell them as quickly as possible in order to turn a profit. An investment banker may purchase the securities from the issuing company directly or merely guarantee the issuer a specific price for his securities. With either approach, it is the investment banker who carries the risk of gains or losses when corporate securities are marked for sale in the open market.

The largest issues of corporate securities sold in the open market are usually bid upon by several groups of underwriters. Competition among these syndicates can be intense. Investment bankers hope to acquire a new corporate security issue at the lowest possible bid price and place the securities with investors at a higher retail price, maximizing the *spread,* or return on invested capital. Unfortunately, each new corporate bond issue is always somewhat different from those that have traded before and may involve hundreds of millions or even billions of dollars. Moreover, a decision on what price to bid for new corporate securities must be made *before* the bonds are released for public trading; in the interim, prices may change drastically. If the underwriter bids too high a price, the investment bank may not be able to resell the securities at a price high enough to recover the cost and secure an adequate spread. To cite an example, a number of years ago, IBM Corporation offered $1 billion in notes and debentures through a collection of Wall Street underwriters. Unfortunately, just as the IBM issue was coming to market, bond prices tumbled (due, in part, to an announcement by the Federal Reserve suggesting credit conditions might be tightened to deal with inflation). The underwriters suffered a massive loss on this particular corporate issue.

Competition in the bidding process tends to narrow the underwriter's spread between bid and asked price. If several investment banking houses band together in a syndicate, a consensus bid price must be hammered out among the participants. Disagreements frequently arise within a syndicate, often due to different perceptions about the probable future direction of interest rates. Because dozens of underwriters may be included in a single syndicate, the task of reaching a compromise and placing a unified bid for a new corporate security issue may prove impossible. The old syndicate may break apart, with those bidders still interested hurriedly piecing together a new bid.

A number of factors are considered in pricing a new corporate debt issue. Certainly the credit ratings assigned by Moody's, Standard & Poor's Corporation, Fitch Ratings, or other rating agencies are a key item, because many investors rely on such agencies for assessing the risk carried by a new corporate security.[4] Another factor is the "forward calendar" of corporate security offerings, which lists new issues expected to come to market during the next few weeks. Obviously, if a heavy volume of new offerings is anticipated in the near term, prices will decline unless additional demand appears. Changes in government policy must be anticipated because that policy can have profound effects on corporate security prices. Other factors considered by investment bankers include the size of the issue, how aggressive other bidders are likely to be, and the strength of the "book," which consists of indications of advance investor interest in the new corporate security being offered.

Once the securities are received from the issuing company, the underwriters advertise their availability at the price agreed on by all members of the syndicate. *Delay* in selling new securities is one of the investment banker's worst enemies, because

---

[4]Chapter 8 provides a full discussion of default risk premiums in bond rates, and how these premiums are affected by the credit ratings of major ratings agencies.

The market for corporate bonds is dominated by *giants*—leading companies borrowing money and leading investment banking houses assisting them in finding reliable funding at low cost. Most outstanding corporate bonds are not heavily traded—at least compared to the huge daily volume of trading for government securities and many mutual funds. Among the relatively few corporate debt securities that are actively traded in considerable volume every day are:

### Sample of the Leading Fixed-Rate Corporate Bonds Traded in Today's Financial Market

| Issuing Company | Coupon Rate | Year Matures | Current Yield |
|---|---|---|---|
| SLM Corp. | 5.375% | 2014 | 5.678% |
| Daimler Chrysler | 6.500 | 2013 | 5.605 |
| HSBC Finance Corp. | 5.500 | 2016 | 5.633 |
| Home Depot | 5.875 | 2036 | 6.010 |
| CIT Group, Inc. | 4.500 | 2008 | 6.292 |
| Alcoa | 5.950 | 2037 | 6.111 |

Sources: Web sites and financial reports of issuing companies.

Note the generally *positive* relationship between current yield and maturity, with longer-term bonds generally posting higher rates of return. Other key factors in shaping investor returns are the issuer's credit rating, the size of the issue, and the specific terms accompanying each bond contract (indenture). Corporate bond yields are most frequently compared to rates of return on government securities, with the latter regarded as essentially default-free financial instruments. Thus, a key indicator of the market's assessment of the current level of default risk on corporate bonds is the *yield spread* between corporate bonds and government securities that are comparable in maturity.

Note how the corporate–Treasury yield spread rises in periods of economic recession (e.g., 2001–2002), when more businesses may be prone to failure, but drops lower in more prosperous periods (e.g., 2005–2007). The decision to offer new bonds is usually made in consultation with an investment banker who may underwrite all or part of a new issue, thus accepting the market risk associated with purchasing and reselling the bonds. Leading underwriters of corporate debt instruments are listed below

### The Spread between the Market Yields on Aaa Corporate Bonds and 10-Year U.S. Treasury Notes

| | 2000 | 2001 | 2002 | 2003 | 2004 | 2005 | 2006 | 2007* |
|---|---|---|---|---|---|---|---|---|
| Aaa Corporate Bonds | 7.62% | 7.08% | 6.49% | 5.66% | 5.63% | 5.23% | 5.59% | 5.30% |
| 10-year U.S. Treasury note | 6.03 | 5.02 | 4.61 | 4.01 | 4.27 | 4.29 | 4.80 | 4.56 |
| Corporate Treasury yield spread | 1.59 | 2.06 | 1.88 | 1.65 | 1.36 | 0.94 | 0.79 | 0.74 |

*Yields posted in March 2007.

Source: Federal Reserve Board's Web site, **www.federalreserve.gov.**

### Leading Underwriters of Corporate Bonds and Notes around the Globe

| | | |
|---|---|---|
| Merrill Lynch & Co. | Citigroup, Inc. | Goldman Sachs Group |
| Lehman Brothers | Morgan Stanley | Credit Suisse Group |
| Deutsche Bank AG | JP Morgan Chase | Bear Stearns Group |

Sources: Annual reports of issuing companies; Standard & Poor's Corporation's Market Insight, Educational Version (**mhhe.com/edumarketinsight**); and Board of Governors of the Federal Reserve System.

Late in the 1990s an intense controversy with strong ethics overtones emerged concerning the pricing practices of dealers in the corporate market. Some dealer firms appeared to be marking up the prices of corporate bonds sold to their customers well above the prevailing open-market price—sometimes with markups of 5 to 10 percent or more. One factor that facilitated these large markups was the delay in getting up-to-date information on actual trading prices. While many stocks are traded on both organized exchanges and through dealers who post new prices almost instantaneously, debt instruments are more frequently traded over the counter, where some dealers can quote a range of prices because the buyer may not be able to easily compare the price being offered against recent trades involving the same or similar securities.

Dealers often defend markups by pointing to the risks they face when they purchase blocks of corporate securities; the value of their holdings may drop suddenly when interest rates rise. An added problem is market diversity. Some securities may go for several hours or days without a transaction taking place, leaving the dealer with no current price to use as a reference point for pricing a new sale. Still, many investors would like to have a sales receipt that details *all* of the costs they are paying (including dealer markups). Borrowers sometimes report a similar information problem—a security issuer may be unable to get precise quotes on securities sold in order to calculate the true cost of newly raised funds. Clearly, this information would be of great help to a business trying to decide whether to issue new debt or to explore other possible sources of funding.

additional financing must be obtained to carry unsold securities. Also, there is added risk of price declines as time increases. To speed the process of selling new corporate instruments, many investment banking firms today have relationships with retail brokerage companies that maintain working agreements with large buyers, such as insurance companies, pension funds, and mutual funds.

What happens to the market prices of securities sold by investment banking syndicates is the key determinant of the success or failure of the underwriting process. It takes only a small decline in retail price before the underwriter's profit is eliminated. Moreover, unfavorable price movements can damage the reputation of the investment banker with investors and the client companies that issue new securities. Clearly, investment banking is both risky and competitive.

## Private Placements

In recent years, private placements of corporate bonds, asset-backed securities, and other corporate instruments with one or a limited group of well-informed investors have represented a fairly small, but still important proportion of public sales. For example, in recent years, private placements have accounted for about 15 percent of public market sales of corporate bonds (though, by way of contrast, private placements of corporate stock recently have exceeded 50 percent of all public sales of stock). However, the ratio of private to public sales is sensitive to the changing composition of borrowing companies and economic conditions. Usually, periods of rising interest rates and reduced credit availability bring more borrowing companies into the public market, and falling interest rates often bring a rise in private placements. For the largest corporations, public sales and private placements are *substitutes.* When interest rates are high or credit is tight in one of these markets, the largest borrowers tend to shift to the other market. Although the size of the bond issue and the issuing firm's financial leverage are also important determinants of whether to borrow in the public

**617**

versus private markets, economies of scale in issuing bonds in the public market tend to encourage firms with large debt issues to turn to the public market, while a highly levered firm (one with a high debt-to-equity ratio) is more likely to borrow in the private market due to the structure of debt contracts in the private markets that more readily address potential agency costs that may be of greater concern to lenders. However, most borrowers in the private market are small- and medium-sized corporations whose access to public debt markets is more restricted.

Private placements were significantly aided by a ruling of the U.S. Securities and Exchange Commission (SEC) known as Rule 144A. The SEC eliminated restrictions on the secondary trading of private placements by large institutional investors (known as QIBs, or qualified investment buyers). This step, in effect, created a secondary market for privately placed corporate securities, overcoming one of the historic barriers confronting investors who otherwise might be interested in privately placed securities. Revisions in Rule 144A have brought investment banks into the private placement arena to underwrite and distribute these securities. Privately placed corporate debt has become more liquid, bringing major new investors, such as mutual funds, into this market. The private-placement market has also been aided by the increasing presence of foreign investors and foreign issuers of private securities in U.S. markets and by the growing number of corporate mergers and divestitures. Much of the divestiture activity reflects companies attempting to downsize their operations in order to trim operating costs or to raise scarce capital by selling marketable assets. Corporate mergers, in contrast, reflect broadening of markets and the search for economies of scale in production and marketing.

Who buys privately placed bonds? Life insurance companies, finance companies, and pension funds, historically, have been principal investors in this market. These institutions hope to secure higher yields and protection against call privileges by engaging in *direct negotiation* with borrowing corporations and by using due diligence and engaging in careful monitoring of any loans they grant. The avoidance of call privileges is of special benefit to life insurance companies and pension funds because these institutions prefer the stable income that comes from purchasing long-term debt instruments and holding them to maturity. In fact, institutional investors active in the private-placement market frequently impose extra fees in a sales contract containing an allowance for early retirement of a security by the issuing corporation. Investors other than life insurance companies and pension funds tend to play smaller roles in the private market due to their lack of expertise, small size, and the limited resale market for privately placed securities. In recent years, some life insurance companies have sharply curtailed their purchases of privately placed securities due to public pressure on insurers to strengthen their balance sheets and because many borrowers in the private-placement market have experienced lower credit ratings, presenting more risk to investors.

There are several advantages to the borrower from a private placement. One is the lower cost of distribution because there are no registration fees associated with the issuance of a prospectus as there would be with a public sale. Private placements are exempt from registration with the Securities and Exchange Commission (SEC). Generally, more rapid placement of corporate securities takes place in the private market because only a few buyers are involved and the loan is confidential. Special concessions can often be secured, such as a commitment for future borrowing. For example, a corporate borrower may negotiate a private sale of $50 million in traditional bonds to an insurance company but also may be granted a line of credit up to $2 million a year over the next five years. This kind of commitment is not usually possible in the impersonal public market, where the features of most corporate offerings are highly standardized. Moreover, lenders in the private market try to tailor the terms of a loan to match the specific cash flow needs of borrowers. This may involve a conventional fixed-rate credit contract at the prevailing interest rate, a floating-rate loan that can be retired early if cash flows permit, or even a participating loan in which the lender charges a lower interest rate in return for a share of income from the project financed.

There is limited evidence that private placements may be more effective than public-sale corporate bond issues in keeping "agency conflicts" between borrowers and lenders under control (see Chapter 3). Due in part to the superior debt monitoring ability of the typical private-placement market buyer and the greater possibility of renegotiation of terms under a private sale as the conditions surrounding borrowers and lenders change, the private-placement market may minimize agency conflicts between lenders and borrowers, helping to protect the interests of both buyers and sellers. The advantages of the private-placement market make it particularly appealing to smaller businesses, privately held companies, and many foreign firms. However, predictably, private-sale borrowers usually pay higher costs for their issues than those companies (particularly very large firms) that can easily move back and forth, if they wish, between public-sale and the private-sale markets.

One disadvantage is that interest costs generally are higher in private sales than in public sales. Moreover, private sale instruments are less liquid and often carry more risk of default. One indication of this is that privately placed debt issues tend to have more restrictive covenants in order to protect lenders. Still, the larger the size of a corporate issue, the smaller the cost differential between public and private placements tends to be.

## QUESTIONS TO HELP YOU STUDY

7. Who are the *principal buyers* of corporate notes and bonds and other private debt instruments? Why are these groups of investors especially interested in acquiring these instruments?

8. Describe the important role that *investment bankers* play in the functioning of the corporate security market.

9. What are the principal types of *risk* investment bankers take on? What factors must an investment banker consider in *pricing* a new corporate security issue?

10. Explain what is meant by a *private placement*. Who purchases privately placed corporate securities and why?

11. What are the principal *advantages* to a business borrower from offering debt in the private-placement market? Can you see any *disadvantages*?

## 19.8  The Volume of Borrowing by Corporations

The volume of borrowing through new issues of corporate bonds and other debt instruments has grown rapidly in recent years (see Exhibit 19.5). For example, annual offerings of new corporate debt securities approximately doubled in each decade of the 1970s and 1980s, and then increased more than eightfold between 1990 and 2000. In 2002 GE Capital brought to market the largest U.S. dollar-denominated corporate bond issue then recorded in history at $11 billion. During 2005, new bond issues of

**EXHIBIT 19.5**

**The Growth of Corporate Bonds and Notes Issued by Companies in the United States ($ millions)**

| Year | New Issues of Corporate Year Bonds and Notes |
|------|---------------------------------------------|
| 1950 | $    4,920 |
| 1960 | 8,081 |
| 1970 | 30,321 |
| 1980 | 53,199 |
| 1990 | 114,500 |
| 2000 | 944,810 |
| 2005 | 2,323,735 |

Note: All figures in the exhibit represent gross proceeds of issues maturing in more than one year and are the principal amount or number of units multiplied by the offering price. Figures exclude secondary offerings, employee stock plans, mutual funds, intracorporate transactions, and Yankee bonds (sold by foreign corporations inside U.S. territory). Before 1987, the figures included only those issues that were underwritten.
Source: U.S. Department of Commerce and Board of Governors of the Federal Reserve System.

American corporations totaled more than $2.3 trillion. Much of this growth in corporate borrowing could be traced to inflation in earlier years, which reduced the real cost of debt, the increased use of financial leverage to boost returns to corporate stockholders, the development of international capital markets, and relatively lower long-term interest rates that prevailed early in the twenty-first century. This track record suggests the corporate debt market is sensitive to economic conditions and to changes in the cost of long-term credit.

Another factor that has spurred the private security market's growth is a rash of corporate takeovers and merger proposals. Targets for these corporate raids have included such well-known companies as CBS, Firestone Tire, Fleet Boston Financial Corp., Hilton Hotels, Uniroyal, Pennzoil, AT&T, Gillette, and Paine Webber, to name just a few. Many of these mergers have been motivated by deregulation of key industries in recent years, including the airlines, banking, and telecommunications; by more liberal antitrust rules followed by the U.S. government; and by the desire of many foreign investors to establish operations inside U.S. territory.

**junk bonds**

Frequently, these proposed mergers include plans to offer millions of dollars in **junk bonds**—high interest-cost, low credit-rated (below investment grade) debt securities—as well as bank loans to finance the transaction. With the expanded use of debt, credit ratings of scores of corporations have been reduced in recent years and several major corporate failures have occurred, with bankruptcy declared by several well-known firms, including Enron, Kmart, Polaroid, United Airlines, and WorldCom. Nevertheless, the growth of the *junk bond market* has been spurred by corporations' desire to restructure their capital, replacing stock with debt or replacing short-term securities with longer-term financial instruments. In addition, skilled dealer houses, led by Credit Suisse, Citigroup, Deutsche Bank, and Goldman Sachs, resurrected the junk bond market in a dramatic way as the twenty-first century opened.

In fact, the volume of corporate stock retirements, replaced in many instances by debt, has been increasing for many years. Among larger corporations (those listed in the S&P 500), stock retirements due to mergers, acquisitions, and buybacks exceeded $400 billion for the 12 months ending in June 2006, up from around $130 billion in 2001. Mergers and acquisitions (M&As) have been on the increase in recent decades due, in part, to a more lenient antitrust policy adopted by federal regulators that has allowed more M&As to take place without government challenge. Another factor encouraging the replacement of retired stock with debt is that many companies not well known to investors have been able to approach the long-term debt markets for funds for the first time, as the rapid expansion of the market for junk bonds and the growing use of credit guarantees have permitted lower-quality borrowers to successfully tap the open market for funds.

A substantial proportion of recent corporate takeovers has been in the form of **leveraged buyouts,** in which a single investor or small group of investors (frequently including senior management of the target company) buys the publicly owned stock of a business firm by borrowing 80 to 90 percent or more of the purchase price from banks and the bond market. In many leveraged buyouts (LBOs), the assets of companies previously publicly owned (that is, their stock was widely dispersed among thousands of investors) are conveyed to closely held private companies and partnerships. In these instances, the takeover group is counting on faster growth and improved profitability of the target company or on selling some of its assets to pay off a huge volume of acquisition debt.

These debt-funded mergers have generated much proposed federal and state legislation over the years to prevent "corporate raiders" from taking over some companies. Some targeted firms have developed *shark repellents* or *poison pills,* such as favorable deals for outside investors not affiliated with a corporate raider, revisions in corporate charters that make it more difficult for outsiders to take over the firm, and the taking on of heavy debt which makes the company less attractive as a takeover target. Surprisingly, research evidence shows that stockholders of companies targeted for acquisition benefit from takeover activity, even when the planned takeover is unsuccessful. Investors apparently believe such takeovers will improve the efficiency and profitability of the target companies beyond what their existing management has been able to do and the stock of the target firm often rises in value, at least initially. Perhaps in recognition of this beneficial effect, along with efforts to clean up recent corporate scandals, fewer poison pills and other takeover defenses have been used in recent years. For example, familiar poison pill users like Circuit City and Goodyear Tire and Rubber have recently been dismantling some of their takeover defenses. The corporate market today appears to be more open to mergers and acquisitions than it has been in several years.

## 19.9  Bank Loans to Business Firms

### The Volume of Bank Credit Supplied to Businesses

Banks are direct competitors with the corporate debt security markets in making both long-term and short-term credit available to businesses. Unfortunately for many banks, growing numbers of corporations that once relied upon banking firms for the bulk of their funding have turned instead to selling securities in the open market, decreasing somewhat the relative importance of banks within the financial system. Still, the volume of bank credit made available to businesses remains enormous. For example, by March 2007 commercial and industrial loans extended by banks operating in the United States totaled nearly $1.2 trillion, or about 20 percent of all U.S. bank loans. Banks grant their loans to a wide variety of firms covering all major sectors of the business community. And bankers have come to play a key supporting role in the corporate debt market, issuing standby credit guarantees on behalf of borrowing companies to pay off their customers' debt if the borrowing companies cannot do so.

In recent years, the Federal Reserve Board has carried out periodic surveys of business lending practices by banks across the United States. These surveys indicate that

leveraged buyouts
**Key URLs:**
Investors like to keep close track of bond market conditions in order to look for favorable trades. Several good Web sites to follow the market include **cnnfn.com** and **bondmarkets.com**

bank loans to businesses tend to be relatively short in maturity, although they seem to have been lengthening somewhat in recent years. For example, the average maturity of commercial and industrial loans (weighted by loan amount) was 524 days in the February 2007 survey, with longer-term loans (or maturities exceeding one year) averaging 54 months. Usually, the longer-term loans carry higher interest rates than loans with shorter maturities, due to the greater default risk associated with longer maturity loans and the fact that the Treasury yield curve is normally upward sloping, calling for higher rates on long-term loans. Moreover, the larger and longer term a business loan is, the more likely its interest rate will *float* with market conditions. Clearly, banks become more determined to protect themselves against unexpected inflation and other adverse developments through floating interest rates as the maturity and size of a business loan increase.

## The Prime, or Base, Interest Rate on Business Loans

**prime bank rate**
**base rate**

One of the best-known and most widely followed interest rates in the financial system is the **prime bank rate,** sometimes called a **base rate,** or *reference rate.* The prime rate is an annual percentage rate banks may quote to their most creditworthy customers. Most prime loans are unsecured, but borrowers often are required to keep a deposit at the lending bank equal to a specified percentage of the loan. This *compensating balance* may be 15 to 20 percent of the amount loaned. Even for a prime borrower, therefore, the *true cost of a bank loan is often higher than the prime rate itself.* Most prime loans are short-term—one year or less—loans taken out to finance purchases of business inventory and other working capital needs or to support construction projects.

Each bank must set its own prime or base rate. Beginning in the 1930s, however, a uniform prime rate began to appear, with differences in loan rates from bank to bank quickly eliminated by competition. Split primes do occur for some periods of time, however. A bank strapped for loanable funds may keep its prime rate temporarily above rates posted by other banks in order to allocate its more limited supply of credit. Similarly, a bank with ample funds to lend may post a prime temporarily below market to encourage its customers to borrow more frequently and in larger amounts.

Traditionally, the prime rate was set by one or more of the nation's leading banks, and other banks followed the leader. However, a major innovation in the market for prime loans occurred in 1971 when Citibank of New York (now a part of Citigroup) announced it would *float* its prime. Citibank's basic lending rate was pegged on a weekly basis at half a percentage point above the yield on 90-day commercial paper. Other leading banks soon followed, pegging their prime rates to prevailing yields on Treasury bills and other money market instruments. Linking the prime to such active money market rates as those attached to Treasury bills and commercial paper resulted in a more flexible base lending rate. The prime has come to reflect more accurately the forces of shifting credit demands, fluctuations in government policy, and inflation. A more flexible prime has enabled banks to better protect their interest margins—the difference between the return on loans and the cost of borrowed funds—and to make credit more readily available to customers willing to pay the price.

Many business loans today are priced at *premiums* above the prime or other base rate because only the most financially sound customers qualify for prime or below-prime loans. Nevertheless, commercial loan rates typically are tied to the base rate through a carefully worked out formula. One popular approach, *prime plus,* adds on a rate premium for default risk and often an additional premium for longer maturities (term risk). Thus, the banker may quote a commercial customer "prime plus 2," with a

1 percent premium above the base rate for default risk and another 1 percent premium for term risk. Other banks may use the *times-prime* method, which multiplies the base rate by a risk factor. For example, the business customer may be quoted a loan at 1.5 times prime. If the current prime is 10 percent, this customer pays 15 percent. If the loan carries a floating rate, then the interest rate in future periods can always be calculated by multiplying the base rate by 1.5.

Which of these prime-rate formulas the banker uses may depend on his or her forecast of interest rates. In a period of falling rates, interest charges on floating-rate loans figured on a times-prime basis decline faster than those based on prime plus. When interest rates are on the rise, times-prime pricing results in more rapid increases in business loan rates. Therefore, times-prime financing is more sensitive to the changing cost of bank funds over the course of the business cycle.

### Other Examples of Base Rates for Business Loans

**Key URLs:**
To explore and keep abreast of LIBOR—the most widely used corporate base rate—see, in particular, **bba.org.uk/public/libor/** and **bankrate.com/tvm/ratehm.asp**

The prime bank rate is one example of a base rate for business loans, but it is by no means the only example in today's world. In fact, most commercial loan rates today are tied to base rates other than prime. This is frequently the case for large multinational corporations that have ready access to both domestic and international credit markets. For example, the *London Interbank Offer Rate (LIBOR)* on short-term Eurodollar deposits is often used as a base rate for the largest corporate loans. In some cases, the commercial paper rate, the federal funds interest rate, and the secondary market rate on bank CDs are also used as popular base rates.

Smaller numbers of borrowers today remain tied to the prime rate. Typically, borrowers in this category include less mobile customers with fewer alternative credit sources than many of the largest corporations. The largest businesses frequently can demand credit at interest rates significantly less than prime. These large loans are often made today at contract interest rates that are only a fraction of a percentage point (i.e., a few basis points) above a lender's actual cost of obtaining funds in the money market.

### 19.10  Commercial Mortgages

**commercial mortgage**

The construction of office buildings, shopping centers, and other commercial structures is generally financed with an instrument known as the **commercial mortgage.** Short-term mortgage loans are used to finance the construction of commercial projects, and longer-term mortgages are employed to pay off short-term construction loans, purchase land, and cover property development costs. The majority of long-term commercial mortgage loans are made by life insurance companies, thrift institutions, finance companies, and pension funds; in contrast, commercial banks are the predominant short-term commercial mortgage lender. Banks support the construction of office buildings and other commercial projects with loans secured by land and building materials. These short-term mortgage credits fall due when construction is completed, with permanent financing of the project then passing to insurance companies and other long-term lenders.

Substantial volatility exists in the commercial mortgage market, due to multiple causes. One causal factor is the sensitivity of commercial construction borrowing to changes in market interest rates. For example, during the the past decades commercial borrowing costs dropped to the lowest levels in many years and, partly in response, construction soared, led by the rapid expansion of retail store chains, multifamily dwellings (especially apartments and condos), and office space. Unfortunately, participants in this market have a tendency to overshoot with their investment plans, often frantically building up new facilities when market conditions appear promising, only to find themselves facing excess capacity and ruinously high vacancy rates (as occurred, for example, in some urban markets in 2003 and 2007).

In the past, most commercial real estate financing was provided through *fixed-rate mortgages.* Faced with inflation and a volatile economy, however, commercial mortgage lenders began searching for new financial instruments to protect their return. Many mortgage lenders today combine both debt and equity financing in the same credit package. The best-known example is the *equity kicker,* where the lending institution grants a fixed-rate mortgage but also receives a share of any net earnings from the project. For example, a life insurance company may agree to provide $50 million to finance the construction of an office building. It agrees to accept a 15-year mortgage loan bearing a 10 percent interest rate. However, as a hedge against inflation and higher interest rates, the insurance company may also insist on receiving 10 percent of any net earnings generated from office rentals over the 15-year period.

Another device used recently in commercial mortgage financing is *indexing.* In this case, the annual interest rate on a loan may be tied to prevailing yields on high-quality government or public utility bonds. Lender and borrower may agree to renegotiate the interest rate at certain intervals, such as every three to five years. There is also a trend toward shorter maturity commercial mortgage loans—many as short as five years—with the borrower paying off the debt or refinancing the unpaid principal with the same or another lending institution.

During the 1990s, asset-backed securitization entered the commercial mortgage market. Private mortgage lenders and federal mortgage agencies (such as the FNMA and the FHLMC) sought ways to free up their lending capacity by packaging large numbers of commercial real estate loans, taking them off the balance sheet, and then issuing securities against the packaged loans. Sellers of these securities (led by such well-known investment firms as Goldman Sachs and Prudential Insurance Company) frequently arranged guarantees from the security issuers, resulting in a growing portion of commercial mortgage-backed securities being rated "investment grade" and attracting major financial institutions (such as insurance companies and pension funds) as buyers. Nevertheless, securitized commercial mortgages have proven to be highly sensitive to changing economic conditions. For example, default rates on securitized loans, especially those connected to hotel, retail, and apartment mortgages, rose sharply in the 2003–2007 period following a global recession as the twenty-first century began.

## QUESTIONS TO HELP YOU STUDY

12. What is a *leveraged buyout?* A *junk bond?* What are the dangers associated with these financial devices and instruments?

13. Supply a definition for each of the following terms:

    Term loan              Prime rate

    Floating rate          Compensating balance

14. For what purposes are *commercial mortgages* issued? What changes have occurred recently in the terms attached to these mortgage instruments?

15. What is an *equity kicker?* What are its principal advantages over a straight commercial mortgage loan?

# Summary of the Chapter's Main Points

This chapter focused upon businesses raising funds by borrowing in the open market and by seeking loans extended by banks and other financial institutions.

- The majority of funds drawn upon by business firms to meet their working capital and other investment needs normally come, not from the financial marketplace, but from *inside* the individual business firm. In most periods more than half of business capital requirements are supplied by earnings and noncash depreciation expenses (i.e., *internal cash flow*).

- Nevertheless, each year a significant portion of business investment needs is met by selling securities or negotiating new loans in the financial markets. The financial system is a backstop for the operations of business firms for those periods when internally generated cash fails to increase fast enough to support the growth of sales.

- The financial markets provide both short-term working capital to meet current expenses and long-term funds to support the purchase of buildings and equipment. The principal external sources of working capital include trade credit (accounts payable), bank loans and acceptances, short-term credits from nonbank financial institutions (such as finance companies), and sales of commercial paper in the open market.

- For businesses in need of long-term funding, the principal funds sources are the sale of traditional corporate bonds and notes, asset-backed securities, term loans from banks, the issuance of common and preferred stock, and commercial mortgages.

- Traditional corporate *bonds* have original maturities of more than five years; *notes* carry maturities of five years or less. There is a trend toward shorter maturities of corporate securities, fueled in part by the explosive growth in *medium-term notes (MTNs).* Financial innovations have opened this market to a wider range of business borrowers. Indexing of corporate bond rates to broader movements in the economy has also become more common.

- A wide variety of different bond and note issues have been developed to provide investors with varying degrees of security and risk protection, including debentures, zero coupon bonds, equipment trust certificates, mortgage bonds, and industrial development bonds. Each type of bond is accompanied by an *indenture,* spelling out the rights and obligations of borrowers and investors.

- The most dynamic sector of the corporate debt market in recent years has centered on *asset-backed securities (ABS)*–interest-bearing debt instruments that arise from a process called *securitization.* Loans, accounts receivable (credit sales), and other income-generating assets are pooled by a company and removed from its balance sheet. The pooled assets are placed in a separate trust account (a special purpose entity, or SPE) and securities, representing claims against the pooled assets, are then sold to investors in the open market who are promised income generated by the assets in the pool. The issuing corporation gains new funds and an opportunity to change the makeup of its balance sheet, possibly making its financial position appear stronger.

- Corporate debt securities are purchased by a wide range of investors today, but the dominant buyers are insurance companies, pension funds, mutual funds, and banks. New corporate securities may be offered publicly in the *open market,* where competitive bidding takes place, or in a *private sale* to a limited group of investors. Public sales account for the largest portion of annual long-term borrowings, but the private market appeals to many smaller firms unable to tap the open market for funds and to companies with unique financing needs or lower credit ratings. Public sales offer the advantage of competition, as investment bankers bid against each other to underwrite a new security issue.

• The corporate bond and asset-backed security markets have faced competition in recent years from both domestic and foreign commercial banks making long-term business loans. These *term loans* are generally used to purchase equipment. Most such loans carry floating interest rates tied to the *prime lending rate* or some other base rate (such as LIBOR).

• Banks have always been a leading financial institution in extending both short-term and long-term loans to business firms. These loans support the construction of office buildings, shopping centers, and other commercial structures and provide working capital to support daily operations. Banks generally specialize in short-term mortgages that finance business construction, while long-term commercial mortgage financing is provided mainly by insurance companies, thrift institutions, and pension funds. Bankers' overall role in providing credit to the business sector has been declining somewhat in recent years as more firms turn to the open market to raise funds. However, banks have increasingly come to play a supporting role in guaranteeing and monitoring corporate debt.

## Key Terms Appearing in This Chapter

corporate bond, 603
corporate note, 603
indenture, 604
debenture, 606
mortgage bonds, 607
industrial development
 bond (IDB), 607
zero coupon bonds, 608
asset-backed securities (ABS), 610

securitization, 610
public sales, 614
private or direct placements, 614
investment bankers, 614
junk bonds, 620
leveraged buyouts, 621
prime bank rate, 622
base rate, 622
commercial mortgage, 623

## Problems and Issues

1. *None* of the following statements is correct. Identify what is wrong with the italicized portion of each statement and make appropriate corrections.

   a. Most businesses raise the majority of funds needed for their current operations and future growth by *issuing traditional corporate bonds, issuing corporate stock, or borrowing from banks.*

   b. Smaller businesses rely heavily on *commercial banks and publicly traded debt issues* to meet their borrowing needs.

   **c.** The explosive growth of medium-term notes (MTNs) in recent years is attributable in part to the fact that they allow the borrowing corporation to attain a better *maturity match between the firm's liabilities and the assets with which the MTNs are secured.*

2. Discuss access to the following sources of borrowings and the advantages and disadvantages of employing each for a large, publicly held corporation and a small, less established firm.

   **a.** Publicly placed traditional corporate bonds.

   **b.** Privately placed debt.

   **c.** Junk bonds.

   **d.** Securitization of accounts receivable.

   **e.** Bank loans.

3. What is the difference between *venture capital* and an *initial public offering (IPO)?* How would the groups of interested investors likely differ between the two?

4. A corporation sells $5,000 par-value bonds at par in the open market, bearing an 8 percent coupon rate. Costs of marketing the issue, including dealer's commission, amounted to $200 per bond. If the bonds are due to mature in 15 years, what is their before-tax cost to the corporation? If the issuing company is in the 35 percent tax bracket, what is the bonds' after-tax cost to the firm?

5. A corporation borrows $5 million from a bank at a 12 percent prime rate. If the bank requires the company to hold 15 percent of the amount of the loan on deposit as a compensating balance, what is the effective rate of interest on the loan?

 6. A small business is in need of a short-term (one-year) loan of $10,000. It solicits two banks, Bank of Friendship (BOF) and Bank of Honesty (BOH), to obtain the loan. Both banks agree and offer floating rate loans, but differ on the interest rate terms. BOF offers a loan based on a rate that is 2 percent above the current prime rate of 6 percent. BOH offers a loan based on a rate of $1\frac{1}{3}$ times the prime rate, with the principal to be paid at the time the loan matures. Note that the initial rate

| Month | Scenario (i) | Scenario (ii) | Scenario (iii) |
|---|---|---|---|
| 1 | 6.1% | 5.9% | 6.1% |
| 2 | 6.2 | 5.8 | 6.2 |
| 3 | 6.3 | 5.7 | 6.3 |
| 4 | 6.4 | 5.6 | 6.4 |
| 5 | 6.5 | 5.5 | 6.5 |
| 6 | 6.5 | 5.5 | 6.6 |
| 7 | 6.5 | 5.5 | 6.6 |
| 8 | 6.5 | 5.5 | 6.5 |
| 9 | 6.5 | 5.5 | 6.4 |
| 10 | 6.5 | 5.5 | 6.3 |
| 11 | 6.5 | 5.5 | 6.2 |
| 12 | 6.5 | 5.5 | 6.1 |

is 8 percent for both loans. To evaluate the loan proposals, the small business must forecast the prime rate. It sees three possible prime interest rate scenarios over the life of the loan as displayed in the table on the previous page.

**a.** Compute the total interest expense for each of the three scenarios. Which loan offer would be chosen for scenario (i)? Scenario (ii)? Scenario (iii)?

**b.** Assume the business attaches a one-third probability to each of the three scenarios. Which loan offer should it choose? Explain these results.

**c.** Assume the business attaches a probability of 25 percent for scenarios (i) and (iii) and a 50 percent probability for scenario (ii). Which loan offer would it choose? Why?

## Web-Based Problems

**1.** It was stated in this chapter that the major sources of funds for businesses needing to finance their ongoing operations and future growth are *internally generated funds*. For the most part, these funds come from earnings that the individual firm does not pay out as dividends to its shareholders. The *dividend policy* as well as the willingness of the firm to borrow varies from company to company, but also from industry to industry.

   **a.** Visit the Web site **finance.yahoo.com** and identify groups for Microsoft, Ford Motor Company, American Electric Power, and Dow Chemical by keying in their names or symbols. Note that information on the industries can then be acquired by clicking the "Industries" tab, and then clicking the industry group, such as "Electric Utilities" from the subsequent page.

   **b.** For each of the above firms, identify its dividend policy by determining its dividend payout ratio (i.e., its annualized dividend divided by its share price) and rank the companies from high to low.

   **c.** For each of the four industry groups these companies represent, find the average debt-to-equity ratio and rank the industries from high to low.

   **d.** From your results in parts (b) and (c) discuss how these industry groups vary in their reliance on internally generated funds and determine whether the selected firms within those industry groups appear to be representative of their industry as a whole.

**2.** One of the forms in which households maintain their wealth is corporate debt. This exercise asks you to determine what share of the *net worth* (total assets less total liabilities) of all U.S. households is represented by corporate debt and how this share has changed over time.

   **a.** Visit the Federal Reserve's Web site at **federalreserve.gov** and click on the tab "Research and Statistics." From there, go to "Historical Data and Current Releases" and find the historical data for the quarterly "Flow of Funds Accounts."

   **b.** Go to the appropriate table in the "Flow of Funds" collection of tables (usually, L.100) and determine the share of "corporate and foreign bonds" to "net worth" from the available data for each final quarter for the years 1960, 1970, 1980, 1990, 2000, and the most recent quarter available.

   c. Discuss the numbers in part (b). Do corporate bonds appear to be a relatively large or small share of households' wealth holdings? Has that share been stable over time? What possible explanations do you have for the changes that you observe in the data?

## Selected References to Explore

1. Ammer, John, and Nathanael Clinton. "Good News Is No News? The Impact of Credit Rating Changes on the Pricing of Asset-Backed Securities," *International Finance Discussion Papers,* No. 809 (July), Board of Governors of the Federal Reserve System, Washington, DC, 2004.

2. Bitler, Marianne P.; Alicia M. Robb; and John D. Wolken. "Financial Services Used by Small Businesses: Evidence from the 1998 Survey of Small Business Finances," *Federal Reserve Bulletin,* April 2001, pp. 183–205.

3. Culp, Christopher L., and Andrea M. P. Neves. "Financial Innovations in the Leveraged Commercial Loan Market," *Journal of Applied Corporate Finance,* XI (Summer 1998), pp. 94–105.

4. Ergungor, O. Emre. "Securitization," *Economic Commentary,* Federal Reserve Bank of Cleveland, August 15, 2003, pp. 1–4.

5. Kwan, Simon, and Willard T. Carleton. "Financial Contracting and the Choice Between Private Placement and Publicly Offered Bonds," *Working Paper No. 2004–20,* Federal Reserve Bank of San Francisco, 2004.

6. Laderman, Liz. "The Geographic Scope of Small Business Lending: Evidence from the San Francisco Market," *FRBSF Economic Letter,* No, 2006–36 (December 15), Federal Reserve Bank of San Francisco, 2006, pp. 1–3.

7. Lopez, Jose A. "Concentrations in Commercial Real Estate Lending," *FRBSF Economic Letter,* No. 2007–01 (January 5), Federal Reserve Bank of San Francisco, 2007, pp. 1–3.

8. Peristani, Stavros, and Gijoon Hong. "Pre-IPO Financial Performance and Aftermarket Survival," *Current Issues in Economics and Finance,* Vol. 10, No. 2 (February), Federal Reserve Bank of New York, 2004.

9. Prowse, Stephen D. "A Look at America's Corporate Finance Markets," *Southwest Economy,* Federal Reserve Bank of Dallas, September-October 1997, pp. 1–11.

www.mhhe.com.rose10e

# Chapter 20

# The Market for Corporate Stock

## Learning Objectives

### in This Chapter

- You will learn about the characteristics of common and preferred corporate stock.
- You will be able to identify the principal investors in corporate stock.
- You will understand the role that equities play in financing business investment.
- You will be able to compare and contrast the roles and functions of the organized stock exchanges and the over-the-counter market.
- You will explore the question of *market efficiency* and examine the evidence regarding stock market efficiency.

## What's in This Chapter?
## Key Topics Outline

**The Stock Market and the Economy**

**Features of Common and Preferred Stock**

**Leading Stock Market Investors**

**Equity as a Source of Finance**

**The Exchanges and the Over-the-Counter (OTC) Market**

**The Third Market and Private Equity Issues**

**National and International Market Developments**

**Stock Market Efficiency, and Technical and Fundamental Analysis**

## 20.1  Introduction to the Stock Market

In the preceding chapters, we focused almost exclusively on the markets for debt securities and the extension of credit and the role of corporate borrowing in financing the operations of the firm. In this chapter, we examine the markets for a unique security that is not debt but *equity*. It is a certificate representing *ownership* of a corporation. Unlike debt, corporate stock grants the investor no promise of return. Rather, it grants only the right to share in the firm's assets and earnings, if any.

Corporate stock is unique in one other important respect. All of the securities markets we have discussed to this point are intimately bound up with the process of moving funds from ultimate savers to ultimate borrowers in order to support investment and economic growth. In the stock market, however, the bulk of daily trading activity involves the buying and selling of securities already issued rather than the exchange of financial claims for new capital. For example, in 2005 corporations in the United States issued more than $115 billion in new shares of stock, but this volume of new shares was equal to only about 1 percent of the total amount of stock outstanding.[1]

Despite the relatively small volume of new stock issues compared to shares already issued, the stock market continues to have a significant impact on the *expectations* of businesses when planning future investments. Stock trading indirectly affects employment, growth, and the general health of the economy.[2] In this chapter, we take a close look at the basic characteristics of corporate stock, its role in financing the operations of the firm, and the markets where that stock is traded.

## 20.2  Characteristics of Corporate Stock

All corporate stock represents an ownership interest in a corporation, conferring on the holder a number of important rights as well as risks. In this section, we examine the two types of corporate stock issued today: common and preferred shares.

### *Common Stock*

**common stock**

The most important form of corporate stock is **common stock.** Like all forms of equity, common stock represents a *residual* claim against the assets of the issuing firm, entitling the owner to share in the net earnings of the firm when it is profitable and to share in the net market value (after all debts are paid) of the company's assets if it is liquidated. By owning common stock, the investor is subject to the full risks of ownership, which means the business may fail or its earnings may fall to unacceptable levels. However, the risks of equity ownership are limited, because the stockholder normally is liable only for the amount of his or her investment.

If a corporation with outstanding shares of common stock is liquidated, the debts of the firm must be paid first from any assets available. The preferred stockholders then receive their share of any remaining funds. Whatever is left accrues to common stockholders on a *pro rata* basis. Common stock is generally a *registered* instrument, with the holder's name recorded on the issuing company's books.

---

[1]These figures do not reflect stock buybacks, which are discussed later in the chapter.
[2]One broad index of stock market prices—Standard & Poor's Composite Index—is considered to be a *leading indicator* of subsequent changes in economic conditions, especially of future developments in industrial production, employment, and total spending (GDP). Thus, the stock market often turns in its greatest gains in the deepest part of a recession and turns down before a boom is over. The stock market seems to provide a forecast of business capital spending plans and output, perhaps reflecting the fact that it captures the expectations of the business community.

The volume of stock a corporation may issue is limited by the terms of its *charter of incorporation.* Additional shares beyond those authorized by the company's charter may be issued only by amending the charter with approval of the current stockholders. Some companies have issued large amounts of corporate shares, reflecting not only their need for large amounts of equity capital but also a desire to broaden their ownership base.

The *par value* of common stock is an arbitrarily assigned value, often printed on each stock certificate, though some stock has no specified par value. Where present, par value is usually set low relative to the stock's current market value. Originally, par was supposed to represent the owner's initial investment per share in the firm. The only real significance of par today is that the firm cannot pay any dividends to stockholders that would reduce the company's net worth per share below the par value of its stock.

Common stockholders are granted a number of rights. Stock ownership permits them to *elect the company's board of directors,* who, in turn, choose officers responsible for day-to-day management of the firm. Common shareholders have a *preemptive right* (unless specifically denied by the firm's charter) which gives current shareholders the right to purchase any new voting stock, convertible bonds, or preferred stock in order to maintain their current *pro rata* share of ownership. For example, if a stockholder holds 5 percent of all shares outstanding and 500 new shares are to be issued, this stockholder has the right to subscribe to 25 new shares.

Although most common stock grants each stockholder one vote per share, nonvoting common may also be issued. Some companies issue Class A common, which has voting rights, and Class B common, which carries a prior claim on earnings but no voting power. The major stock exchanges do not encourage publicly held firms to issue classified stock, but classified shares are used extensively by privately held firms whose stock is not traded on a major exchange.

A right normally granted all common stockholders is the *right of access* to the minutes of stockholder meetings and to lists of existing shareholders. This gives stockholders some power to reorganize the company if management or the board of directors is performing poorly. Common stockholders may vote on all matters that affect the firm's property as a whole, such as a merger, liquidation, or the issuance of additional equity shares.

Key URLs:
For further information about the characteristics of *common stock,* see especially stocks.about.com/od/understandingstocks/a/stock and thismatter.com/money/stocks/stocks.htm

## Preferred Stock

preferred stock

The other major form of stock issued today is **preferred stock.** Preferred carries a stated annual dividend expressed as a percent of the stock's par value. For example, if preferred shares carry a $100 par value with an 8 percent dividend rate, then each preferred shareholder is entitled to dividends of $8 per year on each share owned, provided the company declares a dividend. Common stockholders receive whatever dividends remain after preferred shareholders receive their annual dividend.

Preferred stock occupies middle ground between debt and equity securities, including advantages and disadvantages of both forms of raising long-term funds. Preferred stockholders have a *prior claim* over the firm's assets and earnings relative to claims of common stockholders. However, creditors must be paid before either preferred or common stockholders. Unlike creditors, preferred stockholders cannot press for bankruptcy proceedings against a company that fails to pay them dividends. Nevertheless, preferred stock is part of a firm's equity capital and strengthens its net worth, allowing it to issue more debt in the future. It also is a more flexible financing arrangement than debt because firms may choose not to pay dividends to their shareholders if corporate earnings are inadequate.

Generally, preferred stockholders have no voice in the selection of management unless the corporation fails to pay dividends for a stipulated period. A frequent provision in corporate charters gives preferred stockholders the right to elect some members of the board of directors if dividends are passed for a full year. Dividends on preferred stock, like those on common stock, are *not a* tax-deductible expense. This makes preferred shares more expensive to issue than debt, especially for companies in higher tax brackets. However, IRS regulations specify that 70 percent of stock dividends received by corporations from unaffiliated companies *are* tax deductible. This deductibility feature makes preferred stock attractive to companies seeking to acquire ownership shares in other firms and sometimes allows preferred shares to be issued at a lower net interest cost than debt securities. In fact, corporations themselves are the principal buyers of preferred stock.

Many preferred shares are *cumulative,* which means the passing of dividends results in an arrearage that must be paid in full before common stockholders receive anything. Some preferred shares are *participating,* allowing the holder to share in the residual earnings normally accruing entirely to common stockholders. To illustrate how the participating feature might work, assume an investor holds 8 percent participating preferred stock with a $100 par value. After the issuing company's board of directors votes to pay the stated annual dividend of $8 per share, the board also declares a $20 per share common stock dividend. If the formula for dividend participation calls for common and preferred shareholders to share *equally* in any net earnings, then each preferred shareholder will earn an additional $12 to bring her total dividend to $20 per share as well. Not all participating formulas are this generous, and most preferred issues are *nonparticipating,* because participation is detrimental to the interests of common stockholders.

Most corporations plan to retire their preferred stock, even though it usually carries no stated maturity. In fact, preferred shares usually carry *call provisions.* When interest rates decline, the issuing company may exercise the call privilege at the price stated in the formal agreement between a firm and its shareholders. Some preferred issues are *convertible* into shares of common stock at the investor's option. The company retires all converted preferred shares and may force conversion by simply exercising the stock's call privilege. New preferred issues are often accompanied by a sinking fund, whereby funds are accumulated for eventual retirement of preferred shares. A trustee is appointed to collect sinking fund payments from the company and periodically call in preferred shares or purchase them in the open market. Although sinking fund provisions allow the issuing firm to sell preferred stock with lower dividend rates, payments into the fund drain earnings and may reduce dividend payments to common stockholders.

**Key URL:**
To learn more about the nature and characteristics of *preferred stock,* see especially
**QuantumOnline.com**

In recent years, corporations have developed new types of *variable-rate preferred stock,* carrying a floating dividend rate that makes the stock a substitute for short-term debt. Many variable-rate preferred issues allow their dividend rate to be reset, which may be accomplished by a marketing agent or via special auction. Some companies have issued *Dutch-auction* preferred shares, a process by which stock buyers submit interest rate bids and the highest interest rate bid clears the auction. Frequently, the dividend rate has a ceiling rate based on a key reference rate (such as the market yield on commercial paper). Many preferred shares issued recently have had an exchange option attached, giving the issuing company the choice of exchanging preferred stock for debt securities. Not long ago another hybrid form of preferred stock, "MIPS" (monthly income preferred shares), appeared; MIPS are counted as equity but carry interest payments like debt. Thus, MIPS help to reduce the prominence of a company's debt and tend to lower its federal taxes. However, MIPS have recently come under attack in the wake of the failure of Enron Corporation, which made use of them.[3]

Yet another form of preferred equity that appeared in the 1990s is *convertible preferred,* sometimes called "toxic" or "death" spiral convertibles. Each share can eventually be exchanged for an unspecified number of common stock shares, with the number of new common shares depending upon the stock's market price when conversion occurs. If the issuing firm is in trouble and its common stock is plunging in value, preferred shareholders receive a growing share of the firm's ownership.

In summary, from the standpoint of the *investor,* preferred stock represents an intermediate investment between bonds and common stock. Preferred shares often provide more income than bonds (particularly in years of strong corporate earnings), but the investment is also usually at greater risk. Preferred prices tend to fluctuate more widely than bond prices for the same change in market interest rates. Compared to common stock, preferred shares generally carry a lower expected rate of return but are, in turn, often less risky. From the standpoint of *issuing corporations,* preferred shares also seem to lie between bonds and common stock, offering the advantages of equity (especially in the option to pay or not pay dividends and in strengthening the balance sheet), but also offering several advantages of debt (including limited life and fixed financing costs in many cases).

**Key URL:**
To assess the risks associated with preferred stock, many investors consult **FitchRatings.com**

### QUESTIONS TO HELP YOU STUDY

1. In what important ways does the stock market *differ* from other securities markets we have described in earlier parts of this book?
2. What major differences do you see between corporate stock and corporate debt obligations (discussed in the previous chapter)?
3. What are the essential characteristics of *common stock?*
4. What priority of *claim* do common stockholders have in the event a corporation is closed and liquidated? What limits the volume of shares a company may issue and have outstanding at any point in time?
5. Discuss the nature of *preferred stock.* In what ways are preferred shares similar to corporate debt and in what ways are they similar to common stock?

## 20.3 Stock Market Investors

Corporate stock is one of the most widely held financial assets in the world. Only one other financial asset—government securities—is held by as large and diverse a group of individuals and institutions as are common and preferred stock. One important source of information on stockholders in the United States is the Federal Reserve

[3]Regular preferred stock has become more attractive to investors in the United States lately because the dividend payments it generates are now subject to a low 15 percent tax rate (comparable to the low U.S. tax rate on capital gains). However, the majority of preferred shares currently traded in the U.S. are trust preferred shares that, for tax purposes, are treated as corporate debt, not stock. Thus, trust preferred shareholders receive interest, not dividend payments and are subject to ordinary income tax rates (which range as high as 35 percent).

| EXHIBIT 20.1 | Key Investors Buying Corporate Stock in the United States ($ billions at year-end; market values) | | | | | | | | |
|---|---|---|---|---|---|---|---|---|---|
| | **1980** | | **1990** | | **2000** | | **2006** | | |
| **Groups of Investors** | **Amount** | **Percent of Total** | **Amount** | **Percent of Total** | **Amount** | **Percent of Total** | **Amount** | **Percent of Total** | |
| Households (individuals and families) | $1,010 | 70.3% | $1,960 | 55.5% | $8,036 | 43.4% | $5,483 | 26.6% | |
| Rest of the world | 75 | 5.2 | 244 | 6.9 | 1,643 | 9.2 | 2,831 | 18.6 | |
| Commercial banks | * | — | 2 | 0.1 | 12 | 0.1 | 35 | 0.2 | |
| Savings banks | 4 | 0.3 | 9 | 0.3 | 24 | 0.1 | 25 | 0.1 | |
| Life insurers | 46 | 3.2 | 82 | 2.3 | 892 | 5.1 | 1,405 | 6.8 | |
| Property-casualty insurers | 32 | 2.2 | 80 | 2.3 | 194 | 1.1 | 233 | 1.1 | |
| Pension funds: Private | 232 | 16.2 | 606 | 17.2 | 1,971 | 11.1 | 2,668 | 13.0 | |
| Government | 44 | 3.1 | 285 | 8.1 | 1,355 | 7.9 | 2,098 | 10.2 | |
| Investment companies (mutual funds) | 42 | 2.9 | 233 | 6.6 | 3,227 | 18.3 | 5,018 | 24.4 | |
| Security brokers/dealers and other investors | 10 | 0.7 | 30 | 0.9 | 274 | 3.7 | 808 | 3.9 | |
| | $1,436 | 100.0% | $3,531 | 100.0% | $17,627 | 100.0% | $20,603 | 100.0% | |

*Less than $1 billion.

Note: Columns may not add to totals due to rounding.

Source: *Flow of Funds Accounts,* compiled quarterly by the Board of Governors of the Federal Reserve System.

Board's Flow of Funds Accounts.[4] Exhibit 20.1 gives the names of major investor groups and their total holdings of common and preferred stock for the years 1980, 1990, 2000, and 2006.

From Exhibit 20.1 we see that direct holdings of stock by *households*—individuals and families—represent the largest share of investors in corporate stock in the United States; however, their share is declining. In 2006, households held more than 26 percent of all corporate stock outstanding, down from around 70 percent in 1980. The principal reason for this decline in the household group's market share is the phenomenal growth of *pension funds*—private and governmental—and *mutual funds,* each holding about one-fourth of all shares outstanding. For the most part, these funds represent indirect investments of households in the stock market, managed on their behalf by *institutional investors.*

Unlike households, who tend to buy and hold stock for long periods, institutional investors actively trade shares of stock in an effort to keep their portfolios properly "balanced" based on their perception of the current economic climate. On any given day, the bulk of market transactions is conducted by institutional traders. The growth of pension funds reflects the great flexibility households today have in directing where their retirement savings are to be invested, along with their desire to take advantage of higher expected returns in the stock market. The growth of mutual funds points

---

[4]See Chapter 3 for an explanation of the method of construction and the types of information contained in the Flow of Funds Accounts provided by the Federal Reserve Board.

| EXHIBIT 20.2 | Recent Movements in Stock Prices and Yields |
|---|---|

| Years | New York Stock Exchange Composite (12/31/02 = 5000) | Dow Jones Industrial Average | Standard & Poor's Composite Index (1941–43 = 100) | NASDAQ Composite (2/05/71 = 100) | Common Stock Yields | |
|---|---|---|---|---|---|---|
| | | | | | Dividend-Price Ratio (D/P) | Earnings-Price Ratio (E/P) |
| 1960 | — | 618.04 | 55.85 | — | 3.47% | 5.90% |
| 1970 | 483.4 | 753.19 | 83.22 | — | 3.83 | 6.45 |
| 1980 | 720.2 | 891.41 | 118.78 | 168.61 | 5.26 | 12.66 |
| 1990 | 1,939.4 | 2,678.94 | 334.59 | 409.17 | 3.61 | 6.47 |
| 2000 | 6,805.9 | 10,734.90 | 1,427.22 | 3,783.67 | 1.15 | 3.63 |
| 2003 | 5,456.5 | 8,993.59 | 965.23 | 1,647.07 | 1.77 | 3.84 |
| 2007* | 9,827.9 | 13,362.87 | 1,512.58 | 2,576.34 | — | — |

*2007 figures are for the May 9 close.

Note: Index values reflect averages of daily closing prices. The NYSE figures include all stocks listed on that exchange. The Dow Jones Industrial Average sums the share prices of 30 leading companies, though the DJIA's composition has changed over time. Five hundred blue-chip stocks are included in the S&P Composite. Dividends are aggregate cash dividend payments (annual rate) divided by the aggregate market value of the underlying shares based upon Wednesday's closing prices. Earnings-price ratios are averages of quarterly earnings-to-price ratios.

Sources: Board of Governors of the Federal Reserve System; and President's Council of Economic Advisors, *Economic Report of the President,* various annual issues.

to increased interest among middle-income investors, who invest in relatively small installments, seek out low or no brokerage commissions, wish to take advantage of the services of professional fund managers, and hope to lower the risk of their stock investments by buying into a diversified portfolio.

Among the remaining major investor groups holding corporate stock acquired in the United States are *foreign investors,* whose portion of the U.S. equities market climbed above 18 percent in 2006. American markets appeared less vulnerable to economic and political disaster than many of the markets overseas. However it should be noted that the holdings of foreign equities by U.S. residents totaled about $3.9 trillion in 2006, which is approximately $1 trillion more than foreign investors' holdings of U.S. stocks. Finally, *deposit-type intermediaries*—commercial and savings banks— collectively held less than 1 percent of available shares in 2006. State and federal laws severely limit savings bank investments in corporate stock and prohibit the majority of commercial banks from investing in most stocks for their own portfolios.

The fact that stocks generally carry greater risk than debt instruments for investors is reflected in higher expected returns on stocks. Exhibit 20.2 illustrates the relatively high historical returns that many investors have realized in the form of stock price appreciation. For example, the broad market indexes of the NYSE Composite and the S&P 500 grew more than tenfold between 1980 and 2007, while the "blue chip" Dow Jones Industrial Average and the tech-heavy NASDAQ each experienced roughly a thirteenfold increase.

In the late 1990s, investors began to think: "Even an idiot can make a profit trading in stocks." Unfortunately for the unwary, stocks worldwide fell across a broad front in the year 2000, especially the shares of high-tech firms which dominated the NASDAQ Composite Index. The latter dropped about 60 percent between 2000 and 2003. Small investors by the millions headed for the exits as the new century opened and even major institutional investors sought shelter. Adding force to the decline was a global

**Key URLs:**
Keeping track of stock price movements on a daily basis has become easier due to the presence of several good Web sites, including WWQ Real Time Streaming Quotes at **quote.com** and the American Stock Exchange at **amex.com**

**Key URLs:**
For additional information on key stock indexes see, for example, **sec. gov/answers/indices. htm; money.cnn.com/ data/markets/;** and **quickmba.com/finance/ invest/indices.shtml**

economic recession—the first downturn in a decade. The market would not resume its upward climb until 2003, when a recovering economy and stronger corporate earnings helped push stock prices higher, reaching new record highs early in 2007. In this rebound, *small-cap stocks* (companies posting capitalization of less than $1.5 billion) led the way with a dramatic price rally.

In Chapter 6, we learned that the price of a share of stock reflects the present value of a firm's expected future dividends. Factors that cause investors to raise their expectations of a firm's ability to pay higher dividends in the future would cause its stock price to rise, while contrary information indicating weaker potential for dividend growth would tend to lower the stock price. Other factors that enter into the assessment of the value of a firm's share price include the general level of interest rates in the economy and greater perceived risk that projected dividends will actually be paid. These latter factors increase the rate at which future expected dividends are discounted back to the present, hence lowering the value placed on them today.

Changing expectations of investors and stock analysts can cause wild fluctuations in stock prices, even on a daily basis. A recent example occurred on February 27, 2007, when the Dow Jones Industrial Average lost 416 points, which corresponded to 3.3 percent of the value of the stock market in that single day's trading. However, within two months, the DJIA was hitting record highs once again. Despite this volatility, there have been very few decades over the past century in which stock prices did not rise.

As shown below, average stock yields have significantly outdistanced bond yields and substantially beaten average long-run returns on other popular investments.

| The Long-Run Return Premium Paid by Stocks over Other Investments | |
| --- | --- |
| Financial Instrument | Long-Run Average Annual Real Rate of Return for the 1925–2001 Period |
| Corporate stocks listed on the New York Stock Exchange | 7.42% |
| Corporate bonds | 2.64 |
| U.S. government notes and bonds | 1.85 |
| U.S. Treasury bills | 0.60 |

Source: New York Stock Exchange and Board of Governors of the Federal Reserve System.

Not only have corporate stocks responded positively to periods of strong economic growth and moderate inflation, but they have also increased in response to the growing urgency of millions of individuals preparing for their retirement years. Due to significant advances in medical technology and improved nutrition, people are living much longer today. As a result, they require greater growth in savings in order to sustain their income over a longer time span. For many investors, stocks may be an effective means of ensuring savings keep up with inflation and may provide a decent long-run standard of living.

One of the fascinating, yet unanswered questions about corporate stock is, what outside factors are stock prices most sensitive to from a statistical point of view? Two obvious candidates are *inflation* and *market interest rates.* Many investors have believed for a long time that stocks are among the best long-term hedges against inflation, though, as we saw in Chapter 7, that is not necessarily true, particularly for stocks issued by companies having contracts that cause their costs to rise faster than their revenues when inflation strikes. More rapid inflation can throw a company's stockholders into higher tax brackets and increase investors' capital gains taxes, thereby lowering their after-tax returns from stock and reducing stock prices. Stock prices would

According to some of the most popular stock-valuation models, stock prices depend upon two critical factors—the *expected stream of dividends* a share of stock will pay to its owner over time, and the *degree of risk* attached to that expected dividend stream. The expected dividend stream is *positively* related and the risk factor is *negatively* related to a stock's market value.

For the past 50 years, stock dividend yields have generally fallen (though most recently in the new century some recovery has set in). *A stock's dividend yield is determined by adding up its total per-share stockholder dividends for a year and then dividing by the current price of the stock.* Since reaching a peak at close to 9 percent during the 1950s, average dividend yields have generally fallen, dropping to about 1 percent as the twenty-first century dawned. Why? We are not sure, but higher stock prices (and the prospect of greater

capital gains), the increased use of stock options for employee compensation, until recently the relatively heavy taxation of dividends, and companies rushing to expand by retaining earnings have each played a role.

However, this trend may now be reversing as some dividend yields are rising. Recent corporate scandals (especially those involving excessive rewards for corporate insiders) and the poor choices made by many companies when reinvesting their earnings have recently combined to raise dividend yields. Another key factor is a new tax law passed in 2003 that lowers the maximum dividend tax rate for U.S. investors from 35 percent to 15 percent. Today the majority of S&P 500 companies are paying dividends and the number of dividend payers seems to be rising. Dividend-paying stocks have become more attractive to investors seeking a stable stream of future income.

also be expected, statistically, to be closely tied to movements in market interest rates because: (1) Interest-bearing debt securities compete with stocks for investors' money (so higher interest rates may pull money out of stocks and into bonds, for example); (2) Interest rate levels affect the discount rate applied to future stock dividend streams and, thereby, should be inversely related to the level of stock prices; and (3) Higher market interest rates make it more expensive for investors buying stock on margin to borrow funds and, therefore, tend to discourage the demand for those stocks not expected to be strong performers. However, a study by Golob and Bishop [1] suggests that stock prices seem to follow inflation more closely than they do market interest rates. The inflation rate measured by the consumer price index appeared to explain more of the observed changes in stock earnings-price ratios than did market rates of interest.[5]

## 20.4 Equity as a Source of Funding

To finance fixed investment in physical plant and equipment, inventories, and any financial assets a firm wishes to acquire, management can choose from three broad categories of funding. It can use its retained earnings—the portion of its net income not paid in dividends to its shareholders; it can borrow in the credit markets; or it can issue new shares of stock. There is a large body of research spanning many decades attempting to ascertain what the "optimal mix" of retained earnings, debt, and equity

---

[5]Recent research suggests that stock prices and the proportion of investors' portfolios devoted to stock are influenced by several additional factors than those discussed above. For example, there appears to be a "home bias" in stock acquisitions as domestic investors tend to overweight their portfolios with domestic stocks (and bonds as well) relative to foreign securities, contrary to what rational stock-value models would suggest. Accordingly, many foreign corporations in recent years have helped to offset the "home bias" of U.S. investors by cross-listing their stock on U.S. exchanges, increasing their financial disclosures, and committing to stronger corporate governance practices. See, for example, Sarker and Li [5].

should be. This research has identified a number of factors influencing the funding choice, and has concluded the best mix will vary across firms and over time.

Most corporations rely primarily on retained earnings to meet their funding needs. However, these earnings may not always be sufficient to match the investment expenditures a corporation would like to make. It may have the option of reducing dividends, but such a choice is seldom made. Once a firm has set a dividend, the market expects its earnings to remain high enough to support that dividend payout schedule. A cut in dividends is generally taken as a signal the firm's earnings potential has deteriorated and its stock price generally suffers. This consideration may force a firm with inadequate retained earnings to turn to the debt or equity markets.

An important factor in choosing between debt and equity is the differential tax treatment of corporate expenses. Interest expense on debt is tax deductible, while dividend payments and capital gains on a firm's stock are not. Therefore, a firm acting in the interests of its shareholders would tend to minimize the number of shares of stock outstanding and turn to the debt markets for funding. This choice would tend to increase the firm's earnings per share, which is a crude measure of the return on its stocks.

However, as a firm continues to grow, an overreliance on debt could begin to erode the willingness of the credit markets to purchase the firm's notes or bonds. Ever-rising interest expenses are likely to raise warning flags in the market that a sudden downturn in earnings could force a firm into bankruptcy for failure to meet its interest payments to creditors. A scenario of this type will be reflected in higher interest rates that the firm must pay to borrow. This added cost may more than offset the tax benefit of debt financing over equity financing and turn a firm toward the equity markets. Issuing new equity would likely begin to lower a firm's debt-to-equity ratio which the markets may interpret as a strengthened financial position. The additional risk premium the firm has to pay in order to borrow in the credit markets would begin to ease.

As a result, most firms rely upon a mix of retained earnings, debt, and equity to fund their ongoing capital investment program. This mix differs across firms that may be at a different point in the life cycle of their industry. For example, a high-tech start-up company with excellent growth prospects will likely experience a very high demand for its stock, as investors want to hold claims on the firm's future earnings stream. In this case, the firm can normally raise money more cheaply in the equity markets. Moreover, most businesses of this type will likely refrain from paying *any* dividends. This is exactly what an investor would want the firm to do if it perceives the firm's investment options to be attractive. There is a risk, however, of a firm relying too much on the equity markets. It may be sending a signal to investors that management believes its stock is overvalued by the market. If this interpretation is made by investors, then the stock will be punished, and they would tend to sell.

There are other times when corporations may seek to buy back their own stock in the open market. In fact, many U.S. corporations have been doing that in record numbers in the past several years. Among the more aggressive buybacks are: Microsoft, which announced a $20 billion buyback (approximately 8 percent of its outstanding shares) in 2006 with plans to purchase another $20 billion over the subsequent five years; ExxonMobil, which purchased $30 billion of its own shares in 2006, reducing its outstanding shares from 60 billion to 56 billion, followed by another $8 billion buyback during the first three months of 2007; and IBM, which bought 97 million of its own shares in 2006 to reduce the number of shares outstanding by 4.6 percent to 1.6 billion, with plans to continue additional purchases.

Why would a firm buy back its own stock? Many reasons have been offered. For example, a firm may believe its stock is undervalued by the market. If so, a stock buyback could be a good investment for the firm's shareholders, and has often been seen by the market as a signal of confident management. However, analysts focus on financial ratios that represent quick snapshots of the financial health of a firm. These include earnings per share (EPS), return on assets (ROA), and return on equity (ROE), among others. In the case of a buyback announcement, accompanied by a boost in the stock price (as frequently occurs), the normal expectation is for an improvement in each of these financial ratios. For example, by reducing the number of shares outstanding, the firm's earnings per share would rise provided it can maintain its current earnings. Shares of stock are recorded on a firm's balance sheet as assets and as equity. Therefore, reducing assets and equity could raise both ROA and ROE. All of these indicators could be positive signs that would benefit current shareholders.

Other positive factors that could influence this decision include: (1) the ability of the firm to place repurchased stock in what is referred to as *treasury shares,* which can be reissued without additional filing fees in the future, should the firm wish to tap the equity market for funds; (2) the desire to minimize *dilution* of earnings that often accompany employee stock option plans, whereby employees are able to make investments in the firm through systematic payroll deductions that frequently avoid brokerage fees and are often accompanied by employee contributions; and (3) tax benefits that accrue to shareholders by avoiding dividend taxation.

Is there a downside to stock buybacks? The answer is *yes,* especially if buybacks are used inappropriately. A stock buyback could be seen by investors not as a signal management believes its stock is undervalued, but as a sign management has run out of creative ideas for growing the company. Such a negative interpretation would likely hurt the firm's share price over time. Many buybacks are initiated through a Dutch auction, where the terms of the buyback are set competitively. However, tender offers made by the firm may result in an excessive repurchase price that would harm earnings growth in the future and be detrimental to existing shareholders. Finally, buybacks are sometimes viewed as *quick fixes* to temporarily make a firm appear to be in a stronger financial condition than it truly is. Over time, buybacks could contribute to deterioration in earnings growth and disappoint investors.

The potential costs and benefits of stock buybacks must be weighed by management. They must be seen as an option that allows management to achieve the proper balance in its mix of funding between retained earnings, debt, and equity, while at the same time ensuring that a firm has adequate funding to meet its investment needs.

## 20.5 The Process of Price Discovery in the Equity Markets

The process of "price discovery" in the equity markets is the means by which a value is placed on shares of stock. Ideally, trades take place in competitive markets and the price of an equity realized in the most recent trade should reflect the true market value of a stock. The information technology revolution of the past two decades, coupled with the drive to enhance the speed and accuracy of the price discovery process, has fundamentally altered and is continuing to transform the equity markets.

### *Organized Exchanges*

**organized exchanges**

There are two basic market structures under which equity prices are determined. One is the **organized exchanges,** which in the United States include the New York Stock Exchange (NYSE), the American Stock Exchange (AMEX), and numerous regional exchanges, such as Boston, Cincinnati, Pacific, and Philadelphia. Major money centers

| EXHIBIT 20.3 | International Focus: Leading Stock Exchanges Active around the World in Recent Years | |
|---|---|---|
| New York Stock Exchange | | Brussels Exchange |
| American Stock Exchange | | Sydney Exchange |
| Amsterdam Exchange | | Hong Kong Exchange |
| Tokyo Exchange | | Singapore Exchange |
| Osaka Exchange | | Copenhagen Exchange |
| London Exchange | | Shanghai Exchange |
| Frankfurt Exchange (DAX) | | Taipei Exchange |
| Paris Bourse (MATIF) | | Toronto Exchange |
| Mexico City Exchange | | Wellington Exchange |
| Montreal Exchange | | Swiss Stock Exchange |

around the globe including London, Frankfurt, Hong Kong, and Tokyo also host organized exchanges that operate under similar rules and regulatory systems to govern trade. (See Exhibit 20.3 for a more extensive list.) Traditionally, organized exchanges are "open outcry" auction markets, where buyers and sellers call out orders to a "specialist" on the floor of the exchange who acts as an intermediary for stocks listed on the exchange by matching up buy and sell orders in accordance with price and quantity requirements of buyers and sellers.

For example, the New York Stock Exchange has a trading floor of about 36,000 square feet with 20 trading posts, each staffed by a specialist. All trading must be carried out by member firms on that location, and each NYSE-listed stock is traded at one of these trading posts by a *single* specialist. The price of each successive trade is posted on monitors set up around the trading floor to continuously inform buyers and sellers what the last price was for each share traded. Surrounding the main floor are about 1,500 booths where brokers receive customer orders for shares electronically or via telephone, after which they seek out the specialist handling each stock requested. Exchanges like the NYSE permit the enforcement of trading rules in order to achieve the efficient and speedy allocation of equity shares at competitive prices.

Member firms trade listed securities on the exchange floor, either for their own accounts or for their customers. Most members own "seats" on the exchange, which they are allowed to sell or lease with approval of the exchange's governing board. The member firms fulfill a wide variety of roles on an exchange. Some act as *floor traders* that buy and sell only from their own accounts. Floor traders are really speculators whose portfolios turn over rapidly as they drift from post to post on the exchange floor looking for profitable trading opportunities. Other members serve as *commission brokers,* employed by member brokerage firms to represent the orders of their customers, or *floor brokers,* who are usually individual entrepreneurs carrying out buy and sell orders from other brokers not present on the exchange floor.

*Specialists* oversee trading in each stock. The specialist firms operating on the New York Stock Exchange act as *both* brokers and dealers, buying and selling for other brokers and for themselves when there is an imbalance between supply and demand for the stocks in which they specialize. For example, when sell orders pile up for the stocks for which a specialist firm is responsible, it moves in to buy some of the offered shares, creating a market and providing liquidity by trading for its own account. Specialists can help create orderly and continuous markets and stabilize prices by agreeing to cover unfilled customer orders and by posting bid and ask prices

**Key URLs:**
To learn more about the major stock exchanges, go to their principal Web sites—for example, **nyse.com** and **amex.com**

An interesting recent innovation on several stock exchanges are ETFs, or exchange-traded funds, which are similar to index mutual funds but can be traded like ordinary stocks. See, for example, Morningstar at **morningstar.com** and STREETTRACKS at **streettracks.com**

**Key URL:**
For a closer look at several foreign exchanges, see especially **fese.be**

to interested investors. However, recently specialists on the NYSE have come under close scrutiny for alleged rule violations and possible trading irregularities. Finally, a few *odd-lot traders,* representing large brokerage firms dealing with the public, are also active on the exchange floor. Odd lots are buy or sell orders involving fewer than 100 shares that come primarily from individuals. The odd-lot trader purchases 100 or more shares—a *round lot*—and retains any extra shares not needed by customers.

*Foreign Exchanges*    Stock exchanges have emerged in every region of the globe, especially in Asia, Europe, and the Americas. Around the Pacific Rim, exchanges in Australia, China, Hong Kong, India, Singapore, and South Korea have become established leaders in the market for stocks. In Europe, exchanges in Austria, Belgium, France, Germany, Great Britain, and Switzerland have attracted the interest of global investors, as have exchanges in Russia and South Africa. In the Americas, Argentina, Brazil, Chile, and Mexico have active exchanges that publish their daily trading statistics for investors around the world.

The second-largest economy in the world (behind the United States) is Japan. It has recently swung from more than a decade of economic stagnation and financial chaos into a more stable period of economic growth, and Japanese stock exchanges are receiving renewed interest from international investors. The largest Japanese exchange is the Tokyo Stock Exchange (TSE), which operates in two different sections. The First Section offers exchange services for shares of the largest corporations; the Second Section deals in the shares of smaller corporations. Most investors follow changes in Japanese stock prices by consulting the Nikkei Index, which tracks the average unweighted price of 225 shares traded each day on the TSE. A broader Japanese stock price indicator is the TOPIX, which reflects the current prices of all large-company stocks traded on the Tokyo Exchange. Rivaling the growth of the Tokyo exchange has been another exchange in Osaka, about 250 miles southwest of Tokyo. Osaka trades individual shares and futures contracts linked to the Nikkei index of 225 stocks.

*Contributions of Exchanges*    Stock exchanges are among the oldest financial institutions. The New York Stock Exchange, for example, was set up following an agreement among 24 Wall Street brokers in May 1792. Stock exchanges were opened in Tokyo and Osaka, Japan, in 1878. Exchanges provide a continuous market centered in an established location with rigid rules to ensure fairness in trading. By bringing together buyers and sellers, the exchanges appear to make stock a more liquid investment, promote efficient pricing of securities, and make possible the placement of huge amounts of financial capital.

## Over-the-Counter (OTC) Markets

over-the-counter (OTC) market

The second basic market structure used in trading equities is the **over-the-counter (OTC) market,** where trades take place through a decentralized computerized network of brokers and dealers, such as the National Association of Securities Dealers Automated Quotation (NASDAQ) system in the United States. Most trading of stocks throughout the world today takes place in an over-the-counter market. The customer places a buy or a sell order with a broker or dealer that is relayed via telephone, wire, or computer terminal to the dealer or broker with securities to sell or an order to buy. Prices are listed on a computerized trading system where all eligible brokers (for example, members of NASDAQ) can continuously observe the best price for their clients.

Many traders in the OTC market act as *principals* instead of brokers as on the organized exchanges. That is, they take "positions of risk" by buying securities outright for their own portfolios as well as for their customers. These dealer firms handle the same stock so customers can shop around. All prices are determined by negotiation with dealers acquiring securities at *bid* prices and selling them at *asked* prices.

The OTC market in the United States is regulated by a code of ethics developed by the National Association of Security Dealers (NASD)—a private organization that encourages ethical behavior among member firms and their employees. It registers and supervises more than 5,000 brokerage firms and more than 650,000 securities representatives. Traders who break NASD's rules may be fined, suspended, or thrown out of the organization. NASD regularly issues alerts to the public regarding schemes and scams in the securities market.

## *Evolving Trading Platforms*

These alternative market structures of organized exchanges versus OTC markets are often referred to as "trading platforms." For a firm to have its stock traded on an organized exchange, its stock must be listed. The requirements for a corporation to have its stock listed on an exchange vary across exchanges, and corporations have to choose the exchange for which they are eligible and whose trading platform most directly suits their needs for market liquidity, and other concerns.

The listing requirements of the NYSE are among the most comprehensive, serving to limit NYSE trading to stocks issued by the largest domestic and foreign companies. While the NYSE's listing requirements vary with the location of a firm (foreign or domestic) and other factors, the NYSE generally requires a parent company to have more than a million shares available for public trading, before-tax annual earnings of at least $2.5 million, and worldwide capitalization of at least $750 million dollars. The basic intent of listing rules is to ensure the listed firm has sufficient shares available to support an ongoing market for its stock and discloses sufficient data so investors can make informed decisions.

Even if a company meets all listing requirements, its stock must still be approved for admission by the exchange's board of directors, elected by firms with seats on the exchange. Corporations successful in listing their stock must disclose their financial condition, publish quarterly earnings reports, and help maintain an active public market for their shares. If trading interest in a particular firm's stock falls off significantly (as in the case of Enron Corporation in 2002), the firm may be *delisted*. Some companies may be granted "unlisted trading privileges" if their stock has been listed on another exchange. Recently, foreign firms have been admitted in large numbers to most major exchanges. Foreign companies with more than $5 million in assets and at least 500 shareholders whose stock is traded in the United States must register with the Securities and Exchange Commission, unless specifically exempted.

One of the most important advantages claimed for listing on an exchange is that it improves the *liquidity* of a corporation's stock. (A relatively large volume of shares can be sold without significantly depressing the price.) This feature is of special concern to large institutional investors (such as mutual funds and pension funds) that have come to dominate daily trading in the equities market, because these institutions trade in large blocks rather than a few shares at a time. Allegedly, a corporation can improve the market for its stock by becoming listed on a securities exchange.

In the past, listing on one exchange may have precluded trading on other exchanges. However, that is no longer the case, as there are many examples of multiple listings. Moreover, technology has changed the landscape for equity trading, driven in large measure by the rapid growth of electronic trading and exploiting the speed of the

Internet. Today new trading platforms are evolving rapidly, with electronic trading capturing an increasing share of the market. Innovators in the marketplace, such as Archipelago Exchange and Instinet, have led the way, demonstrating the demand for this new, highly efficient form of trading. Today, more than 50 percent of the trading of NASDAQ-listed stocks, nearly 75 percent of AMEX-listed stocks (which recently merged with NASDAQ), and approximately 20 percent of NYSE-listed stocks are now conducted on these "automated quote-driven market centers," often referred to as **electronic communication networks (ECNs).** These ECN systems allow trading to take place in stocks listed on virtually all major equity markets with trading "hours" each day substantially lengthened. The latter feature has become ever more important as technology continues to accelerate globalization of the equity markets, with trading in the major equities of the world soon to be possible at any time, any place.

Major exchanges have taken notice of these developments. NASDAQ has created its own automated electronic trading platform, called SuperMontage, and has acquired firms who were leaders in the development of this new technology, including acquisition of Instinet Group. The NYSE has recently merged with another major innovator, Archipelago Exchange, with plans to fully integrate the latter's electronic system into the NYSE's traditional open outcry auction system. As part of this merger, the new firm was called NYSE Group and for the first time in its history, this venerable institution, that had formerly been privately owned by its members, becomes a for-profit, publicly traded firm. In 2007 NYSE Group merged with Euronext—one of the largest exchange organizations in Europe, operating in France, the Netherlands, Belgium, and Portugal. The new firm is publicly traded as NYSE Euronext, with a market capitalization of over $21 billion.

These rapid changes in the marketplace have required continual updating of regulations by the Securities and Exchange Commission (SEC), whose responsibility is to ensure that an efficient and fair trading environment exists for all market participants. They are particularly attuned to the needs of small investors, and provide protection from fraud and insider or deceptive trading practices that may place the small investor at a competitive disadvantage.

## 20.6  The Third Market: Trading in Listed Securities off the Exchanges

The market for securities listed on a stock exchange but traded over the counter is known as the **third market.** Broker and dealer firms not members of an organized exchange are active in this market. The original purpose of the third market was to supply large numbers of shares to institutional investors. These investors engage mainly in *block trades,* defined as transactions involving 1,000 shares or more. Presumably, block traders possess the technical know-how to make informed investment decisions and carry out transactions without assistance from a stock exchange. By trading with third-market broker and dealer firms, who in effect, compete directly with specialists on the exchanges, a large institutional investor may be able to lower transaction costs and trade securities faster.

Historically, the third market has been a catalyst in reducing brokerage fees and promoting trading efficiency, stimulating the unbundling of commissions at many U.S. broker and dealer firms in order to more accurately reflect the true cost of each trade. Many brokerage firms offer customers an array of peripheral services, such as research on market trends, security credit, and accounting for purchases and sales. However, the customer may pay for these services whether or not he or she uses them,

---

**electronic communication networks (ECNs)**

**Key URLs:**
For a look at the over-the-counter market, explore such Web sites as **nasdaq.com** and **nasd.com**

**third market**

**Key URLs:**
For additional information about market microstructure theory and research, see especially **lemssup.it/WPLem/files/1999_19.pdf**; **sec.gov/news/speech/spch050605css.htm**; and **en.wikipedia.org/wiki/market-microstructure**

The financial markets have been one of the most rapidly growing segments of the economy in recent years, propelled by rapid expansion in new technologies, the consolidation of financial institutions, and the establishment of more liberal rules by governments working to lighten the burden of market regulations. As the financial marketplace has soared in volume and breadth, researchers have increasingly focused upon *how different trading mechanisms influence the price and volume of various financial assets*. For example, researchers today seek to determine the importance of what can be traded, who can trade, how orders can be submitted and matched, and who is informed about trades that occur, in different financial markets around the globe?

*Market microstructure* research is devoted to studying the functional organization of a particular marketplace—how do traders discover each other and settle on their terms of trade? This field of research is complex because there are often large amounts of data flowing by and many different types of market mechanisms at work daily in the real world, including dealer-dominated markets, auction markets, limit-order markets, hybrid markets (with auction, dealer and limit-order features present), electronic trading schemes, open outcry, and continuous trading. And all of these must be studied in an environment with ongoing consolidation of security exchanges and other market forces at work.

Microstructure research has pointed toward several important (albeit, tentative) conclusions about financial-market functioning—for example:

- The *timing of daily trading activity* seems to matter with early trades often having more price impact than trades of the same size occurring late in the day.

- Investors generally can trade at lower cost the *more liquid* a marketplace and the greater the number of market participants.

- Markets with *higher transactions costs* tend to damp trading activity and some trading may shift toward markets with lower transaction costs.

- *Bid-ask* (trading) *spreads* between selling and buying prices provide compensation for market makers (dealers) supplying liquidity and tend to be larger for assets with longer investment horizons where there are informational asymmetries and where greater market volatility prevails.

- Market makers, who provide immediacy to the carrying out of trades and who stand ready to buy or sell on demand, can suffer large losses when dealing with *informed investors* but may offset these losses by also trading with poorly informed investors.

- *Market transparency* refers to the ability of market participants to obtain relevant information concerning the trading process. Greater market transparency tends to reduce trading costs, leads to faster diffusion of information, more efficient pricing, less market power, higher trading volume, and greater liquidity.

- *Electronic trading markets* are often highly transparent, providing participants with more relevant and timely trading information, while dealer-dominated markets tend to be more opaque with limited information available to the public regarding bids and volume.

- A large volume of market microstructure research today points to the persistence of hard-to-explain *anomalies in stock returns*, including unusual returns that seem related to the day of the week (particularly Monday) and month of the year (especially January) when trading takes place.

- The results of microstructure research vary significantly with *type of financial instrument* and *type of market*—for example, stock, bond, and foreign-exchange markets are often quite different from one another in their functioning and transparency.

In brief, market microstructure theory contends that *price determination and liquidity* for a particular financial asset depend not only on conventional demand and supply forces, but also on the mechanisms through which price and trading information is disclosed and distributed, the presence or absence of market makers, varying order processes, the presence of different trading rules, and the degree of market transparency through which investors can see and understand what is happening in the marketplace.

Note: Among the many good references on research findings in the market microstructure field, see especially Hasbrouch [2], Naes and Skjetrop [4], Spatt [7], and Stoll [8].

As the new century began to unfold hundreds of companies were issuing *options* to buy shares of company stock for their managements and selected other employees. Each option issued gives a company executive or other employee the future right to buy an employer's stock at a specific "strike price." When the option "vests" in the receiving employee (usually after a year has passed) he or she contacts a company administrator who places a request with the firm's transfer agent to secure the necessary shares. Should the issuing company's stock subsequently rise in value, option recipients can reap significant gains in personal wealth by exercising their options, buying company stock at the low strike price, only to sell the shares subsequently at a higher current market price. Many companies view stock options as a powerful incentive for their employees to work hard and improve their firms' performance, ultimately raising the value of the company and benefiting their shareholders.

Normally, stock options are granted by a firm's board of directors or compensation committee and carry strike prices at or near the fair value of the company's stock on the date the options are issued. Recently, however, dozens of firms apparently have gone a step further and "backdated" their options, permitting conversion of options into shares of stock at a price that prevailed in an earlier period when stocks were much cheaper than on the day options were issued. These backdated deals usually grant employees immediate "paper profits" that *may* reduce their incentive to improve company performance. As evidence of extensive backdating activity emerged in 2006, the largest investigation of corporate fraud in at least a generation encompassing more than 100 companies, was set in motion.

Many of these deals took place in the wake of the 9/11 terrorist tragedy when stock prices plummeted for a time and several leading firms took advantage of the lower stock values to reward some of their employees. For example, about two weeks after 9/11, Merrill Lynch granted its president options to purchase more than 750,000 shares at a price about 15 percent below the pre-terrorist-attack price. Backdating practices seem to dovetail with the strategies pursued by many leading corporations aimed at bidding away the best managers from competing firms and holding onto them by offering lavish compensation packages.

Is backdating good or bad for the companies involved and their shareholders? It does seem somewhat unfair to investors who do not have access to these special deals, and it may increase a company's accounting and tax problems (including the possible necessity of restating earnings). Moreover, company executives receiving incorrectly dated options *may* have to pay a 20 percent surtax on their gains over and beyond ordinary income and capital gains taxes. However, backdating does *not* appear, as some have charged, to weaken incentives for employees to work hard in order to improve the performance of their companies. Moreover, the offering firm still retains control over how much added value it intends to extend to those it favors with stock options.

Some companies appear to have covered up their actions and filed inaccurate financial reports in the wake of these special deals, lowering returns to outside shareholders. In some cases, option recipients themselves got to choose the most favorable calendar dates for their new stock options, significantly enhancing their personal returns. Recently civil and criminal charges have been filed against some executives for allegedly manipulating the terms of stock options to benefit corporate insiders and then lying about what they did. Passage of the Sarbanes-Oxley Act in 2002 has made backdating somewhat harder due to the law's tougher reporting requirements.

and as the 1990s ended and the new century began, serious questions were being raised about the bias in broker/dealer market research services, which seemed to promote stocks security firms wished to unload. The largest institutional investors have little need for such services, however, and they seek brokers and dealers offering their services at minimum cost. Numerous "discount" brokerage houses have appeared, and commissions charged institutional investors have dropped substantially, leading many institutional customers to abandon that third market and return to more traditional channels for executing their security orders.

## 20.7 The Private Equity Market

Just as there is a public market for the most popular stocks, led by the organized exchanges and over-the-counter trading, so is there a *private equity market* where new businesses, privately held companies and partnerships, troubled firms, and even larger publicly traded companies can find financing and support for out-of-the-ordinary financial transactions.

Funding a company through a private sale of stock has several advantages. Privately conveyed shares are exempt from costly SEC registration requirements because the public does not become involved with these privately placed shares. Then, too, like the private placements in the corporate debt markets, firms in need of greater equity capitalization but unable to successfully reach the public market, due perhaps to their small size, questionable credit ratings, or complicated financing requirements, often find private equities a reasonable solution to their problems. An added factor is the recent expansion of a new type of financial-service firm almost tailor-made for the private equity markets—the *limited partnership*. Limited partnerships have recently grown as an important investment vehicle for wealthy individuals and institutional stock investors, and many of these partnerships have become skilled in arranging private equity deals that may return substantial rewards to their members. This form of partnership allows stock market investors to turn their long-term funds over to a professional funds manager who accepts most of the risks and makes portfolio decisions that must be decided along the way.

These innovative partnership agreements can often force stock-issuing firms to put the interests of the partnership's stockholders first, unlike many publicly traded companies who have thousands of stockholders and whose managements, not stockholders, often control the companies and may reap most of the benefits. Also, pension funds—among the very largest of all stock-buying institutions in today's global markets—have recently been allowed by regulation to take greater positions in privately held stock. That step has brought huge amounts of new capital into private equity markets. Certainly, the rise of the private equity market has boosted the growth of new businesses. Venture capitalists have given tens of thousands of new firms the necessary funds to get started and also allowed smaller companies to grow bigger by funding their buy-outs of other businesses.

## 20.8 Investment Banking and the Sale of New Stock

**investment bankers**

Whether offered in the private equity market or in the public market, the majority of new stock issues are sold today through **investment bankers.** These firms advise their corporate customers on the proper timing for issuing new stock and frequently purchase (underwrite) newly issued shares for resale to their investor clients (including pension and mutual funds, insurance companies, and wealthy individual investors). Among the leading stock underwriters in the global market today are Citigroup, Inc., UBS Warburg, Merrill Lynch & Co., Goldman Sachs Group, Morgan Stanley, and Lehman Brothers.

The *underwriting* of corporate stocks is among the riskiest of all ventures. Stock values are highly sensitive to fluctuations in economic conditions and to changes in government policy. An investment banker must estimate the resale value of the stock he or she has pledged to buy, but that price can change dramatically in minutes, posing substantial gains or losses that can never be fully anticipated.

**Key URLs:**
The subject of stock options (particularly employee stock options) has become highly controversial in the wake of recent corporate failures. See such Web sites as Employee Stock Options at **nceo.org,** and Accounting for Stock Options at **fed.org**

**IPOs**

One of the most dynamic services offered by investment bankers are **IPOs,** or *initial public offerings*—the issue of stock from companies that have never before sold ownership shares to the public. Many of these fledgling corporations start out as small single proprietorships, partnerships, or family-owned companies. Subsequently, these businesses, if successful, find that private sources of funding are inadequate to sustain their future growth. They turn to investment bankers to guide them into a larger funding arena. Other IPOs arise because a firm's private owners want to cash in on their firm's growth and financial success. A substantial number of IPOs in recent years have come from "high flyers"—principally high-technology customers with innovative new products or software. (The most famous of the recent "high flyers" was the IPO of Google Inc., cofounded by students at Stanford University. Stanford's holdings of Google shares at the time of this IPO were valued at nearly $180 million.) Investment banks often tout these new offerings as "unprecedented opportunities" for profit and, indeed, during the prosperous 1990s numerous IPOs shot upward in price from the moment they first appeared.

So large have been recent IPO profits for many investment houses and their clients that an investigation of the industry began under the leadership of the Securities and Exchange Commission—the principal U.S. regulator of investment banking activities. Regulators soon unearthed a number of questionable, if not illegal, activities surrounding the IPO market. For example, some investment banking houses allegedly received kickbacks from large, wealthy investors in order to gain early access to new IPOs coming to market. Some investors claimed they were pressured to purchase IPOs at inflated prices or to buy other securities the banker was selling in order to get access to new IPOs. Hundreds of lawsuits involving some of the largest investment banks on Wall Street were filed by clients who claimed large losses due to market manipulation and preferential treatment for the most favored clients.

Recent events in the investment banking business serve as stern reminders of how risky this financial-service business really is. There is usually high *market risk* due to the exceptional price volatility of many stocks (especially shares issued by smaller companies). Also, there is substantial *regulatory risk* as the industry's practices have come under increased scrutiny in response to clients—both those seeking underwriting services and investors looking for new securities to add to their portfolios—who have begun to complain about the fairness of the security underwriting process.

---

### QUESTIONS TO HELP YOU STUDY

6. What is meant by the *process of price discovery* as it relates to the equity markets? How does it relate to market efficiency?

7. What are the principal differences between trading in stocks *over the counter* and trading on an *organized exchange?* How would you rate these two markets in terms of their advantages for the small investor? the large investor?

8. Who are the principal investor groups active in the stock market? How might the investment motives of these groups differ?

9. What are the essential differences among the following segments of the market for corporate stock?

   | | |
   |---|---|
   | Organized exchanges | Over-the-counter market |
   | Third market | Private equity market |

10. What services do *investment bankers* provide to what groups of clients? What *risks* do investment bankers face and why?

## 20.9 The Development of a Unified International Market for Stock

### The National Market System

The foregoing discussion makes clear that the stock market is fractured into several different parts, each with its own unique collection of market makers and, in some cases, its own unique collection of customers. However, one of the most significant developments in recent decades has been a movement to weld all parts of the equities market together into a single market for all traders and investors. In 1975, the U.S. Congress passed the Securities Act Amendments, which instructed the Securities and Exchange Commission—chief regulatory agency for the capital markets—to "facilitate the establishment of a national market system for securities" in order to further the development of widespread trading in equities and bring greater competition to the stock market.

Although the 1975 amendments did not specify what the proposed *national market system* would eventually look like, the intent of Congress was to ensure that all investors would have ready access to information on security prices and could transact business at the best available price. Moreover, with greater mobility of funds from one exchange to another or between the exchanges and the over-the-counter market, the resulting increase in competition in stock trading might reduce the cost to corporations of raising new capital.

After the Securities Act Amendments became law, the New York Stock Exchange announced that it would begin reporting daily trades of NYSE-listed stocks as they occurred on the exchanges. This meant that up-to-the-minute information on the latest stock trades would be reported on a *consolidated* or *composite tape* regardless of which exchange handled the transaction. However, no information was provided on the best bid and asked prices available. The Securities and Exchange Commission responded to this need by asking each U.S. stock exchange to make its quotations available to brokers and dealers everywhere.

The first major step in that direction was the development of an Intermarket Trading System (ITS). Brokers and specialists could then compare bid and ask prices on all major U.S. exchanges for about 700 different stocks through a central computer system. In effect, ITS brought major U.S. equities markets into direct price competition with one another for trades in the most popular corporate stocks. Aiding the unified market's spread was a decision by the Securities and Exchange Commission, known as Rule 19c-3, which stated that new stock could be traded off the exchange by exchange member firms. Previously, a broker or securities dealer with membership on a particular exchange could not trade listed stocks anywhere but on the floor of that exchange. This decision brought the U.S. exchanges and OTC market into direct competition with each other for the trading of *new* stock.

### NASD and Automated Price Quotations

As the 1980s began, the National Association of Security Dealers (NASD) moved to promote a broader market system by further automating price quotations on over-the-counter stock. Computer terminals with expanded capacity were set up to include a wide array of information on bid and asked prices offered by traders who might be thousands of miles apart. At the same time, NASD and representatives of the ITS moved to link quotations and trading on the six major U.S. exchanges electronically with OTC quotations and trading through NASD's automated price quotation system (NASDAQ). NASDAQ today quotes prices for close to 5,000 financial instruments.

At about the same time, the Securities and Exchange Commission adopted new regulations aimed at improving the flow of stock price information to brokers and investors. Previously, the NASDAQ system for securities traded over the counter had carried only "representative" bid and asked prices. However, NASDAQ was soon required to display on its terminals the highest bid prices and the lowest asked prices present in the market. The new rule aided investors in determining what price brokers were actually paying to execute a customer purchase order or what the true sales price was when the customer placed his or her shares on the market. This new rule promoted competition among OTC brokers and made it easier for customers to negotiate low commission rates. Another SEC rule required that the consolidated tape carrying price quotations for stock listed on the major exchanges always include the *best* price available on *any* stock, regardless of which exchange is quoting that price.

Subsequently, NASD set up a National Market System to shuttle information to investors immediately on completion of stock sales. NASD also set in motion a program for automated settlement of security trades, called the System of Automated Linkages for Private Offerings, Resales, and Trading (PORTAL). This system made possible purchases and sales of unregistered domestic and foreign bonds and stocks. NASD's automated security price quotation system also set up computer telephone connections with the International Stock Exchange and the Singapore Stock Exchange, cross-listing and executing trades among a growing list of foreign securities. For example, a New York or London trader could instruct his Tokyo office to track stock prices while his home office was closed, and if prices reach a designated level, the overseas office would trade the securities involved according to guidelines received from the home office.

## The Advent of Shelf Registration

The trend toward deregulation of the U.S. financial sector really began to exert its most potent impact on stock purchases and sales during the 1980s. On March 5, 1982, the SEC put Rule 415—the Shelf Registration Rule—into operation, allowing many large firms selling *new* stocks and bonds to register an issue with the SEC and then sell securities from that issue at any time during the next two years. *Shelf registration* substantially reduced the cost of offering new stocks and bonds and gave offering companies greater flexibility in selecting when to enter the financial marketplace to sell new securities. Shelf registration increased competition in the underwriting of new issues.

## Global Trading in Equities

These developments in the United States leading toward a unified national market for corporate stock were joined during the 1990s and into the new century by movement toward a true international equities market in which the sun never sets on purchases and sales of stock somewhere. The trading of both U.S. corporate stock and shares of foreign companies on exchanges in Hong Kong, Singapore, Tokyo, Sydney and in other exchanges around the globe began to rival exchange trading in the United States and Western Europe. Electronic communications networks now girdle the globe, allowing traders in distant financial centers to search for the best prices wherever they might be. Trading firms can "pass the book" to their overseas branch offices as the sun moves west to keep abreast of the international stock and debt markets. Recent research suggests stock markets in Europe, Asia, and the United States are becoming *cointegrated,* sending shock waves to each other as price movements occur, sometimes in remote corners of the globe.

As the 1990s began, the New York Stock Exchange announced plans for after-hours trading sessions via computer without fees and with minimal disclosure rules. These announcements represented an effort by the NYSE to lure back from overseas substantial numbers of pension funds, investment companies, and other large institutional investors that were trading elsewhere. Institutional trading of large blocks of stock inside the United States was given a boost recently when the U.S. Securities and Exchange Commission created Rule 144a, allowing financial institutions to trade large blocks of privately placed stocks and bonds without having to go through complicated disclosure procedures. The SEC also approved the launching of a system that made possible the trading of exchange-listed stocks after U.S. exchanges closed.

At about the same time, the National Association of Securities Dealers announced plans to extend the hours of operation of its automated quotations network to cover hours when the London International Stock Exchange was open, supporting the growth of predawn stock trading inside the United States. Initially, NASDAQ International proposed to offer computer-screen trading of 400 to 500 stocks beginning at 3:30 AM EST in the United States. Not to be outdone, the American Stock Exchange, the Chicago Board Options Exchange, and Reuters Holdings PLC of Great Britain declared their intention to launch a system for night trading. The Chicago Mercantile Exchange and Reuters announced plans for the Globex after-hours electronic order-entry and trade-maturity trading system involving purchases and sales of financial futures contracts, setting in motion an international partnership among futures exchanges in the United States and Europe. The Chicago Mercantile Exchange and the Singapore International Monetary Exchange also established a trading link, making it possible for identical futures contracts to be traded and closed out on either exchange. One of the areas of most rapid growth in the internationalization of the stock market is the cross-listing of stocks. For example, a U.S. corporation can request to have its stock listed on exchanges in London, Frankfurt, Tokyo, and other exchanges around the globe.

Paralleling the expansion of cross-listing is global stock underwriting in which only a portion of new stock issues may be sold in their country of origin. Today many large stock issues have underwriters from multiple countries, helping a corporate customer reach the widest possible range of international buyers.

## *The Development of ADRs*

**American depository receipts (ADRs)**

Further evidence of the growing links between U.S. and foreign stock markets emerged in the 1980s and 1990s with the development of new international financial instruments. For example, U.S. exchanges began trading **American depository receipts (ADRs)**—dollar-denominated claims on foreign shares of stock that are kept in safekeeping by U.S. financial institutions (usually by commercial banks and investment banking houses). In effect, ADRs are negotiable warehouse receipts for deposits of foreign stock that U.S. investors can trade without having to assume the risks of trading in foreign currencies. Among the more popular foreign firms whose ADRs have been traded regularly in the United States are Cifra and Telefonos de Mexico, British Petroleum, and Reuters Holdings in the United Kingdom.

**Key URL:**
Detailed information on ADRs can be found at **adr.com**

ADRs present some special risks of their own, however. For one thing, their underlying value is sensitive to fluctuations in foreign currency prices. A sharp decline in the value of the home country's currency, for example, can result in a significant loss of return. Moreover, foreign stock prices tend to be more volatile than the prices of most actively traded U.S. equities. To be successful in the ADR market, U.S. investors must become more aware of foreign business developments—information that often is difficult and costly to obtain, though the development of the World Wide Web (along with 24-hour television news services like CNN and Bloomberg) has aided international investors in staying abreast of new developments around the globe. Many U.S. investors have come to prefer *sponsored* ADRs, for which the foreign firm issuing stock hires a U.S. company (such as a bank) to serve the interests of buyers and provide them with pertinent information about the stock and its issuing company.

## 20.10  Valuing Stocks: Alternative Approaches

There are literally thousands of professional portfolio managers and stock market analysts who spend their time searching through information they hope will help them pick the winners in the market. They do not all use the same approach to placing a value on individual stocks. Some focus on trends in prices that might point to whether a stock is rising or falling and when it is about to reach a short-term peak or trough. Others look carefully at the issuing firm's financial statements and study its likely success in the current economic and political environment. While most small investors cannot hope to compete successfully in achieving the depth of knowledge professional investors possess, the good news is that *competition among professional investors tends to lead to an efficient market*—one in which information that has value is quickly incorporated into stock prices through the trading activities of professional investors. Because this information arrives randomly in the market, stock prices themselves also tend to behave in a nearly random fashion.

**random walk**

In its purest form, this characteristic of stock prices is referred to as a **random walk**—that is, successive changes in stock prices are as unpredictable as a sequence of numbers created by a random-number generator. The end result is that even the best-informed financial analyst has no greater ability to predict the future direction of stocks than does the average small investor. Therefore, a small investor who maintains a sufficient amount of diversification in his or her stock portfolio can do nearly as well as a professional portfolio manager. This "leveling out" of the investor playing field is the result of the collective efforts of all professionals who strive to correctly process all of the information in the marketplace that is relevant to the stocks they are following. The ability to quickly and correctly perceive the importance of new information to stock prices is what makes professionals successful and what they strive to achieve each day.

### Technical and Fundamental Analysis

Professionals do not adhere strictly to the *random walk hypothesis* in conducting their trades—otherwise they would have nothing to do! Each trader performs his or her own analysis and no one trader looks at *everything*. Traders use the information that works for them in structuring their own trades or in making their stock recommendations.

One group tends to focus on patterns that emerge in *past* data. They draw charts reflecting prior upswings and downdrafts in stock prices and attempt to identify "resistance levels"—upper or lower barriers that stock prices have not been able to penetrate easily in the past. If a stock's price passes through one of these resistance levels, then these analysts are inclined to think it is likely to move further up, if it was an upper barrier, or down, if it was a lower barrier. They must then set new resistance levels and continue to monitor price movements in an effort to find the right time to buy or sell.

**technical analysis**

This approach to stock selection is known as **technical analysis** and its adherents are often referred to as "techies" or "chartists." The "charts" followed by technical analysts can become extraordinarily detailed, incorporating such factors as the volume of trading, where a high trading volume that occurs when the market is rising may be interpreted as "momentum" that will carry stock prices higher. Some technical analysts—known as "contrarians"—track investor sentiment and find that when *too many* professional investors are optimistic, the market is set for a *fall*. Usually, technical analysts follow their *own* collections of technical indicators they believe have helped them make successful stock choices in the past.

**Key URL:**
To learn about the principles of technical analysis see, for example, **tradersfloor .com**

**Key URL:**
To explore the nature of fundamental analysis in more detail see, in particular, **greekshares.com/ fundamental.asp**

**fundamental analysis**

A second group of investors focuses attention on the financial performance of individual companies and tries to understand how well these companies are likely to perform in the current environment. Their task is to identify firms with strong balance sheets, meaning assets of a firm have good market value and are not overly diluted by the firm's liability and capital structure. For example, they do not want to see a firm carrying too much debt or exposed to too much interest-rate (or other forms of) risk. This approach to stock selection is called **fundamental analysis.** In evaluating the "fundamentals" of a firm, these analysts concern themselves with more than a business's financials. They may ask: Are we headed into a recession? Is the industry this firm is a part of about to suffer a major setback or be enhanced by new technology? Is government considering tough new regulations for this industry? These factors can have major consequences for stock prices, but they are often not easy to factor into those prices.

## Private Information

Most studies examining how efficient the stock market is at incorporating relevant information have concluded it is very difficult to systematically exploit publicly available information for profit. There are some exceptions, however, referred to as *anomalies.*

For example, the observation that stock prices more often tend to rise, rather than fall, during the month of January is referred to as the "January effect." However, these anomalies are not completely reliable indicators. Otherwise, they would be akin to free money sitting on the table waiting for someone to pick it up!

Not all information important to the value of a stock is in the public domain. For example, corporate managers are often aware of decisions the firm may be making or they may have information regarding the firm's recent performance that has not yet been made public. Respected financial news reporters are aware of the content of the columns they write or what they will say in television interviews before their reports are publicly known. These individuals are most likely to know whether and how that information will affect individual stock prices. Until this *private information* is made public, those who possess it can trade profitably. Such "insider trading" is unethical and, in many cases, illegal. Once discovered, this type of trading activity is generally not tolerated because it creates an uneven playing field for investors that works to the disadvantage of *both* small investors and professionals who are not in possession of this private information.

---

**QUESTIONS TO HELP YOU STUDY**

11. What role do *circuit breakers* play in the equities market? What are their possible advantages and disadvantages?

12. What is the *national market system*? *Shelf registration*?

13. Why did *ADRs* develop? Why are they important?

14. What is the *random walk* hypothesis? Does research evidence tend to support or deny the validity of this hypothesis?

15. What is an *efficient market*? What are the consequences of market efficiency for the behavior of stock prices? Does recent research support the idea that the stock market is efficient?

16. What factors do *technical analysis* and *fundamental analysis* focus on in valuing stocks?

17. What advantages does private information give to the market participants who possess it?

---

## Summary of the Chapter's Main Points

The market for corporate stock is the most widely followed of all securities markets, with millions of shares changing hands each day. In this chapter, the following points were made:

- Most stock trades involve *not* the creation of new funds—the raising of new capital—but rather the exchange of existing shares for money. Thus, most stock trading takes place in the *secondary market,* not the primary (or new issue) market.

- Trading in equity shares reveals a close correlation with *economic conditions.* Advancing stock prices appear to be a leading indicator, forecasting the growth of the economy, in part because business investment spending appears to be influenced by what is expected to happen to stock prices.

- Corporate stock can be divided into two major types: common and preferred stock. *Common stock* represents a residual claim against the assets of the issuing firm, entitling the owner to share in the earnings of the firm when it is profitable and in the market value of the company's assets if it is liquidated. *Preferred stock* carries a stated annual dividend expressed as a percent of the stock's par value.

- *Households*—individuals and families—are the dominant holders of corporate stock, followed by *pension funds, mutual funds,* and *insurance companies.*

- The principal source of funding for business investment is *retained earnings.* When retained earnings are not sufficient to meet business funding needs, firms must turn to the debt and equity markets.

- The market for corporate equity shares normally is divided into two main parts—the *organized exchanges* and the *over-the-counter market.* Trading on the exchanges is governed by regulations and formal procedures to promote competition and to contribute toward improved liquidity of equity shares. The over-the-counter (OTC) market is less formal than the organized exchanges and generally involves broker-to-broker or dealer-to-dealer transactions on behalf of stock buyers and sellers.

- New *trading platforms* have emerged that exploit recent innovative information technology to enhance the speed and efficiency of the equity markets—a process that is likely to continue in the future.

- Additional and unique branches of the stock market have become important in recent years. These include a *third market,* in which exchange-listed stocks are traded over the counter; and a *private equity market,* where new businesses, privately held companies and partnerships, troubled firms, and even larger publicly traded companies can find financing for their long-term equity needs. The private equity market is involved in selling shares off the major exchanges, with trading taking place between stock issuers and limited partnerships, venture capital companies, and other specialized investors.

- The stock market has become *global* in scope, rising from a series of national markets due to advances in the technology of information and funds transfer.

- Competition for information among professional investors causes stock markets to be *efficient*—quickly incorporating new, publicly available information into the prices of stocks.

- Because new information arrives randomly, an informationally efficient stock market is characterized by stock prices that closely follow a *random walk.* Daily changes in stock prices appear to be essentially random and unforecastable.

- Some professional investors employ *technical analysis* when selecting stocks for their portfolios by charting patterns in the data; others rely on *fundamental analysis,* which calls for a detailed examination of a corporation's financial statements and other factors that could affect industry groups and the economy as a whole.

## Key Terms Appearing in This Chapter

## Problems and Issues

1. From the standpoint of the firm and the investor, explain how the exercise of a "call provision" in a firm's preferred stock differs from the repurchase of a firm's common stock. Is the firm or the investor the beneficiary of the "call provision"? Explain. How does the call provision affect the preferred stock price?

2. Preferred stock is often referred to as a "hybrid security" that shares features of both a corporate bond and common stock. Is this comparison true? Please explain. Compare preferred stock and corporate debt in terms of both default and market risk. Which should have the higher expected return?

3. Referring to Exhibit 20.1, explain the statement, "Institutional investors dominate share holdings." Do they dominate trading activity in the stock market? Explain.

4. Zeno Corporation had earnings per share for the quarter of 50 cents. It currently pays a dividend of 30 cents per share for each of its one million shares outstanding. It would like to make a $300,000 investment in the current quarter. Discuss the pros and cons of funding the investment with: (a) retained earnings; (b) debt; or (c) new equity issues.

5. A common stockholder of Milton Corporation is entitled to a *pro rata* share of any new stock issued by the company. If the firm plans to issue 500,000 new shares at a price of $3.50 per share and this particular stockholder currently holds 1.6 percent of all Milton's shares outstanding, how many new shares is this shareholder entitled to purchase? At what total cost?

6. Riter-Cal Corporation has preferred shares outstanding carrying a $35 par value and promising a 6 percent annual dividend rate. Daniel Smith holds 200 shares of R-C's preferred stock. What annual dividend can he expect to receive if the company's board of directors votes to pay the regular dividend? Suppose R-C's preferred stock consists of *participating* shares, with preferred shareholders participating equally in net earnings with the firm's common stockholders. If the company declares a $10 per share common stock dividend, how much in additional per-share dividends will each of its preferred shareholders receive?

## Web-Based Problems

1. The purpose of this exercise is to identify the shift that has taken place over the past decades in trading activity among two of the major stock markets in the United States with different trading platforms: the New York Stock Exchange (NYSE) and the National Association of Securities Dealers Automated Quotation (NASDAQ).

   a. Obtain and place in the first two columns of a spreadsheet historical data for the average daily volume of shares traded per month (e.g., the average daily volume for the month of August 2005, etc.) on the NYSE and on NASDAQ for the period covering January 1986 to the present. The NYSE data are available at **nyse.com/marketinfo.** Go to the menu "NYSE

Data Library" and click "NYSE Statistics Archive". The NASDAQ data are available at **finance.yahoo.com.** Click "Market Stats" under the "Investing" tab; select "US" under "Indices"; click the "NASDAQ" tab; and on the next window, locate NASDAQ Composite and click "More" under "Related Info"; on the next window click "Historical Prices", and select the sample period on the subsequent page.

    **b.** Graph the volume data for both NYSE and NASDAQ. What has happened to the overall volume of trading? What do these figures suggest about the need for efficiency in completing trades?

    **c.** In column 3 of your spreadsheet compute the ratio of volume at the NYSE to volume over NASDAQ. Graph this ratio. What does this graph suggest about the shift that is taking place in the trading activity on the two markets? Can you think of reasons why that might be true?

**2.** One of the significant controversies surrounding the use of stock options for employee compensation focuses upon how to value and account for these particular options. Using such key Web sites as Accounting for Stock Options at **fed.org,** Looks Smart at **lookssmart.com,** The Options Trader at **theoptionstrader.com,** and Employee Stock Options at **nceo.org,** explain why the employee stock option accounting issue has become so important. Also, discuss the merits and weaknesses of proposed solutions to this stock option valuation problem.

**3.** The Web site for CNN Money at **money.cnn.com/magazines/moneymag/ bestfunds/2007/actively.htm** publishes *Money Magazine*'s list of the top 100 mutual funds each year. Call up the latest list, known as The Money 100, and determine which fund has the highest one-year return, the highest three-year return, and the highest five-year return. Compare the expense ratio of these top performers to the average expense ratio for all other funds in The Money 100 list and for the class of funds (type or category assigned by *Money Magazine*) from which the top performers come. What makes up the expense ratio as reported in *Money Magazine?* Does there seem to be any relationship at all between the performance of mutual fund shares and each fund's expense ratio? Would you expect to find a performance relationship between a fund's rate of return and its expense ratio? Why or why not?

## Selected References to Explore

**1.** Golob, John E., and David G. Bishop. "Do Stock Prices Follow Interest Rates or Inflation?" *Research Working Paper 96-13,* Federal Reserve Bank of Kansas City, 1996, pp. 1–21.

**2.** Hasbrouch, Joel. *Empirical Market Microstructure: The Institutions, Economic, and Econometrics of Securities Trading,* Oxford University Press, 2007.

**3.** Haubrich, Joseph G. "Expensing Stock Options," *Economic Commentary,* Federal Reserve Bank of Cleveland, November 2003, pp. 1–4.

**4.** Naes, Randi, and Johannes Skjeltrop. "Is the Market Microstructure of Stock Markets Important?" *Economic Bulletin,* Vol. 77, March 2006, pp. 123–32.

5. Sarker, Asani, and Kai Li. "Should U.S. Investors Hold Foreign Stocks?" *Current Issues in Economics and Finance,* Federal Reserve Bank of New York, March 2002.

6. Shiller, Robert. *Market Volatility,* Cambridge, MA: MIT Press, 1989.

7. Spatt, Chester S. "Broad Themes in Market Microstructure," Presented by the Director of the Office of Economic Analysis, Securities and Exchange Commission, to the Market Microstructure Meeting of the National Bureau of Economic Research, Cambridge, MA, May 6, 2005.

8. Stoll, Hans R. "Market Microstructure," in *Handbook of the Economics of Finance,* Vol. 1, Part 1, Elsevier Publishers, 2003, pp. 553–604.

# Part 6

# Consumers in the Financial Markets

Regardless of our jobs or professions, our social status or lifestyles, we are all *consumers* of financial services supplied by the money and capital markets. In fact, individuals and families (households) are among the most important borrowers of funds in today's marketplace. As consumers, households can finance their purchases of goods and services using current income, but when their expenditures exceed their income they must either borrow from the money and capital markets or liquidate some of their accumulated savings.

While we tend to stress most heavily the role of consumers as *borrowers* in the money and capital markets, consumers are also among the leading *lenders* within the financial system. When the household sector's current income exceeds its expenditures, the surplus income contributes to the amount of funds that flow to businesses and governments seeking to borrow money.

In this segment of the text, we examine the household sector as *both* a lender and a borrower of funds. We discover which financial services are most important to consumers today and how consumer preferences for various financial instruments and services have changed over time. We explore the fundamental financial characteristics of consumers—how they lend funds and what alternative sources of borrowing are available to them. And we learn more about the important consumer protection laws that have sheltered individuals and families for many years now whenever they venture into the treacherous and often murky waters of the financial marketplace.

In Part 6, we also look at one of the largest of all financial markets—the market for residential mortgage loans—a marketplace that makes possible the "American dream" of home ownership. Purchasing a home is one of the most important and most difficult financial decisions that an individual will make during his or her lifetime. We will look into the factors that consumers should consider when borrowing to purchase a new home and the types of loans provided today by the residential mortgage market. We also will see how and why government has come to play such a major role in shaping who gains access to home mortgage credit and on what terms. Understanding the complexities of the mortgage market will enable you to become a wise consumer who avoids costly mistakes and reaps the substantial rewards of owning your own home.

# Chapter 21

# Consumer Lending and Borrowing

## Learning Objectives

### in This Chapter

- You will see the vital contributions made by *consumers*—households (individuals and families)—in supplying loanable funds to the money and capital markets through savings.

- You will learn about the important role consumers play as major *borrowers* of funds within the financial system and the laws that protect their rights.

- You will explore the principal characteristics and unique features of *consumer lending institutions*, including banks, credit unions, and finance companies.

## What's in This Chapter?

### Key Topics Outline

Consumers as Borrowers and Lenders of Funds

Growing Menu of Consumer-Oriented Financial Services

Credit and Debit Cards: Convenience and Risk

What Determines Consumer Borrowing?

Key Consumer Lending Institutions

Factors Lenders Consider in the Consumer Loan Decision

Credit Scoring Techniques

Financial Disclosure, Discrimination, and Identity Theft

Consumer Bankruptcy and a New Bankruptcy Law

## 21.1 Introduction to Consumer Lending and Borrowing

Among the most important of all financial markets are those providing savings instruments and credit to individuals and families (households). Many financial analysts have referred to the modern era as the *age of consumer finance* because individuals and families not only have become the principal source of loanable funds flowing into the financial markets today but also are one of the largest borrowing groups in the entire financial system. Moreover, the market for household financial services is the one market that *everyone,* regardless of profession or social status, will enter at various times during his or her lifetime. In this chapter, we examine the major characteristics of the consumer market for financial services, the principal lenders active in this market, and some important regulations applying to household borrowing and lending today.

## 21.2 Consumers as Lenders of Funds

Each of us is a consumer of goods and services every day of our lives. Scarcely a day passes that we do not enter the marketplace to purchase food, shelter, entertainment, and other essentials of modern living. We are also well aware, perhaps from personal experience, that consumers often borrow heavily in the financial marketplace to achieve their desired standard of living. U.S. households borrowed nearly $1.5 trillion in 2006, for example, and by the end of that year owed more than $12 trillion to various lending institutions.

What is not nearly so well known, however, is the fact that consumers as a group are also among the most important *lenders* of funds in the economy. Loanable funds are supplied by consumers when they purchase financial assets from other units in the economy. In 2006, gross savings by U.S. households reached almost $1.1 trillion, of which almost $900 billion flowed into bank deposits, bonds, stocks, and direct cash loans to others. The consuming public is among the chief sources of the raw material—loanable funds—exchanged in the money and capital markets.

### Financial Assets Purchased by Consumers

If consumers make loanable funds available to other units in the economy by purchasing financial assets, what kinds of financial assets do they buy? And what are the principal sources of borrowed funds for consumers? The Federal Reserve Board's *Flow of Funds Accounts* provide us with a wealth of information on the borrowing and lending habits of households. Exhibit 21.1 summarizes information contained in recent Flow of Funds reports on the kinds of financial assets acquired by U.S. households. One fact immediately evident is the wide diversity of financial assets purchased by individuals and families, ranging from those of very low risk and short maturity (such as bank deposits and government securities) to long-term, higher-risk investments (such as mortgages and corporate stock).

One of the most important household financial assets today is *corporate stock* (equities), led by a dramatic rise in holdings of shares in mutual funds (investment companies). The recent growth in households' common stock investments may reflect concern about a possible resumption of serious inflation. Then, too, many individuals and families are concerned that when they reach retirement, Social Security, Medicare, and other government retirement plans will simply be inadequate to cover living costs and health care expenses in their final years. Reflecting this same concern, *pension fund reserves* in total ranked at the top among all household assets, exceeding

**EXHIBIT 21.1**  Principal Financial Assets Held by U.S. Households, 1970, 1980, 1990, 2000, and 2006 ($ billions)

| Financial Assets Held | 1970 Amount | 1970 Percent | 1980 Amount | 1980 Percent | 1990 Amount | 1990 Percent | 2000 Amount | 2000 Percent | 2006* Amount | 2006* Percent |
|---|---|---|---|---|---|---|---|---|---|---|
| Demand deposits and currency | $ 112.5 | 4.4% | $ 219.5 | 3.3% | $ 412.4 | 2.8% | $ 225.3 | 0.7% | $ 338.5 | 0.9% |
| Time and savings accounts | 419.4 | 16.4 | 1,239.0 | 18.8 | 2,465.0 | 16.6 | 3,125.6 | 9.2 | 4,889.2 | 12.3 |
| Shares in money market mutual funds | — | — | 62.2 | 0.9 | 386.6 | 2.5 | 970.7 | 2.9 | 956.7 | 2.4 |
| U.S. government securities† | 77.5 | 3.0 | 160.0 | 2.4 | 471.2 | 3.2 | 594.6 | 1.8 | 1,155.4 | 2.9 |
| State and local government securities | 35.4 | 1.4 | 104.5 | 1.6 | 575.0 | 3.9 | 460.7 | 1.4 | 860.1 | 2.2 |
| Open market paper | 12.5 | 0.5 | 38.3 | 0.6 | 63.2 | 0.4 | 72.6 | 0.2 | 169.3 | 0.4 |
| Corporate and foreign bonds | 29.5 | 1.2 | 30.0 | 0.5 | 233.5 | 1.6 | 576.4 | 1.7 | 854.2 | 2.1 |
| Mortgages | 50.0 | 2.0 | 87.2 | 1.3 | 143.5 | 1.0 | 117.7 | 0.3 | 176.8 | 0.4 |
| Corporate stock | 572.5 | 22.4 | 875.4 | 13.3 | 1,781.4 | 12.0 | 7,650.1 | 22.5 | 5,684.5 | 14.3 |
| Investment companies (mutual funds) | 40.4 | 1.6 | 45.6 | 0.7 | 456.6 | 3.1 | 2,900.1 | 8.5 | 4,537.4 | 11.4 |
| Life insurance reserves | 130.7 | 5.1 | 220.6 | 3.3 | 391.7 | 2.6 | 819.1 | 2.4 | 1,096.8 | 2.8 |
| Pension fund reserves | 253.8 | 9.9 | 970.4 | 14.7 | 3,376.3 | 22.8 | 9,067.3 | 26.7 | 11,108.6 | 27.9 |
| Security credit and other assets | 823.3 | 32.2 | 2,549.5 | 38.6 | 4,089.3 | 27.6 | 7,361.8 | 21.7 | 7,978.8 | 20.0 |
| Total financial assets | $2,557.5 | 100.0% | $6,602.2 | 100.0% | $14,827.7 | 100.0% | $33,937.0 | 100.0% | 39,806.3 | 100.0% |

*Figures for 2006 are first quarter only (annualized).

†Figures include securities issued by federal agencies and government-sponsored enterprises (GSEs).

Note: Columns may not add to totals due to rounding.

Source: Board of Governors of the Federal Reserve System, *Flow of Funds Accounts.*

$11 trillion by the year 2006. Of course, many of the reserves held by pension plans are also invested in corporate stock, as are many *life insurance reserves.*

In third place among household holdings of financial assets are *deposits* in banks, savings and loan associations, credit unions, and other thrift institutions. These checkable demand deposits and time and savings deposits represented about 13 percent of the total financial asset holdings of U.S. consumers in 2006. Moreover, as Exhibit 21.1 reveals, the importance of deposits in consumer financial investments generally increased until the 1980s and early 1990s—when households became concerned about a rising tide of bank and thrift institution failures. At the same time, better yields appeared to be available from investments in *corporate stock* (including mutual funds) and *government and corporate bonds.*

There has also been a significant rise in household investments in small businesses, which are often owned and operated by an individual or a family. By 2006, household investments in the equity of unincorporated business firms (included under *Other assets* in Exhibit 21.1) totaled almost $7 trillion. When jobs become more difficult to find, more individuals and families organize their own businesses. At the same time, there is an ongoing trend toward early retirement and the launching of second careers by creating new businesses.

## *Recent Innovations in Consumer Savings Instruments*

One of the most important of all trends affecting consumer savings and lending today is a veritable explosion of *new financial instruments.* In today's world, banks, brokerage houses, credit unions, insurance companies, and other financial institutions compete aggressively for consumer savings, not only by offering higher returns where the law allows but also by proliferating new services. Like a Baskin-Robbins ice cream store, financial institutions offer household customers 31 or more flavors of savings and transaction accounts as well as credit plans to meet a wide variety of personal financial needs.

**NOW account**

This trend toward financial service proliferation began with the introduction of the **NOW account** in New England in 1970. NOWs are checkbook deposits that, like any checking account, can be used to pay for purchases of goods and services. But when NOWs were first developed they broke new ground by paying *interest* on checkbook deposits—which federal law prohibited for regular checking accounts. NOWs were permitted nationwide beginning in 1981 as a result of passage of the Depository Institutions Deregulation and Monetary Control Act (DIDMCA) of 1980. This law also called for the gradual phasing out of federal interest rate ceilings on bank and thrift institution deposits so that consumers could receive competitive, market-determined interest rates on their savings.

DIDMCA also authorized two services that compete directly with NOWs. One of these—automatic transfer services (ATS)—permits the consumer to preauthorize a bank to move funds from a savings account to a checking account to cover overdrafts. The net effect is to pay interest on transaction balances at the savings account rate. Credit unions are permitted to offer their own version of the NOW account, known as the *share draft.* These checkbook plans often pay among the highest interest rates on liquid funds.

During the 1970s, money market mutual funds first appeared, offering consumers *share accounts* with low denominations (most allowing accounts to be opened for a few hundred dollars). Like NOWs, share accounts were developed originally to get around federal deposit interest rate ceilings and give smaller savers access to competitive rates of return on their savings. Later, several prominent brokerage houses began offering *consumer cash management services,* in which funds could be held in an interest-bearing money market fund until transferred into stocks, bonds, or other securities, or accessed via check or credit card. Closely related to these services is the *wrap account,* for which a security broker assembles a suitable portfolio of stocks, bonds, and other assets for the consumer and actively manages that portfolio in return for an annual fee.

Life insurance firms soon began offering a related service known as *universal life insurance.* Savings contributed by the policyholder are placed in a money market fund, with the life insurer making periodic withdrawals to pay the premiums on the life insurance policy. The consumer is offered life insurance protection plus a higher return on his savings.

As the 1980s began, U.S. consumers were granted the right to make limited contributions each year, tax free, to an *individual retirement account (IRA)* offered by financial institutions or by employers with qualified pension plans. Similarly, *Keogh Plan accounts* were created to help self-employed persons prepare for retirement by building up their savings tax-free gradually over time. Tax-favored retirement accounts were supplemented further in the 1990s when new types of accounts—for example, *Roth* and *Education IRAs*—were created to give household investors new tax-sheltered savings vehicles to prepare for retirement and to help offset the spiraling cost of a college education. The Roth IRA proved to be particularly popular because not only could the consumer invest monies and generate tax-sheltered earnings but, for qualified accounts, withdrawals could be made tax-free (unlike the conventional IRAs and Keogh plans). Legislation early in the twenty-first century significantly expanded the amount of savings that could be placed in these tax-sheltered accounts and, as a result of the Federal Deposit Insurance Reform Act of 2005, qualified retirement deposits (such as IRA deposits) had their federal insurance coverage increased from $100,000 to $250,000 and were made eligible for an inflation adjustment every five years.

Beginning in the late 1970s flexible savings plans became popular as many consumers fought to stay ahead of inflation through savings instruments whose rates of return were sensitive to changes in the cost of living and changing market interest rates. *Money market certificates of deposit* were authorized by federal regulation with interest rates that change as market yields on U.S. government securities fluctuated. In 1982, the Garn-St Germain Depository Institutions Act allowed banks and thrift institutions to offer deposits competitive with shares offered by money market mutual funds, in the form of money market deposit accounts (MMDAs) and Super NOWs, each offering flexible interest rates but accessible via check to pay for purchases of goods and services. As the 1990s approached, several banks and savings associations, led by Chase Manhattan Bank (now JP Morgan Chase) of New York, introduced *market-index certificates of deposit* with returns linked to stock market performance.

Accompanying the development of more flexible-yield types of deposits, life insurance companies and pension programs began to offer new types of *annuity accounts* that build up cash value and promise either a future lump-sum payment or a stream of future income payments. The much older fixed-value annuity plans were supplanted in many markets by *variable-rate annuities* and *variable-rate insurance plans,* whose value depends on the market performance of the assets that make up these savings vehicles. With the right kinds of investments an individual or family can develop a sizeable reservoir of accumulated savings to protect their standard of living in the later stages of life.

More recently in the 1990s *corporate equities,* in the form of both individual corporate stocks and pools of shares held in *mutual funds,* exploded in popularity among household savers. Many individuals and families concluded their long-range savings were not growing fast enough for their future needs (especially in meeting the challenges of saving for retirement, inflation, and college costs), particularly if those savings were held in deposits at banks and thrift institutions where promised interest yields were often very low. Equities, on the other hand, seemed to offer the promise of much

**Key URL:**
To understand more about the Federal Deposit Insurance Reform Act and its impact on retirement savings instruments available to consumers see the Federal Deposit Insurance Corporation's 2006 annual Report at **fdic.gov**

larger long-term returns. Moreover, the pooling of equities in mutual funds appeared to lower the consumer's risk exposure to help offset the lack of federal insurance coverage. At the same time, the Securities and Exchange Commission (SEC) required mutual funds to clarify for the public their method of figuring their rates of return and required these funds to simplify their reports so that consumers could more easily understand what they were buying. The market for individual corporate stocks and shares in mutual funds sagged early in the twenty-first century under adverse economic pressures, but then surged toward record levels as the new century moved forward.

These recent innovations are designed to bring individuals and families into the financial markets as more active lenders of funds. The newest financial services offer the consumer greater *financial flexibility*—easier access to liquid funds for transaction purposes and the ability to move funds more easily from one type of savings instrument to another. The newest savings instruments offer the potential for higher rates of return more closely tied to changing interest rates and security prices in the open market.

One interesting feature of the consumer market worth remembering is that many households do *not* make a practice of purchasing *all* their financial services from one source. Instead, households tend to *bundle,* or *cluster,* their purchases of services from certain financial firms. One typical clustering centers around the purchase of a checking account. Usually, a specific depository institution will be chosen to hold a family's main checking account—in most cases, a bank, credit union, or savings and loan that is convenient. Savings accounts are often placed locally as well, although increasingly households have turned to distant financial firms, such as mutual funds, to help them invest their savings at the best yields. Credit services—home mortgages, credit cards, and installment loans—frequently are purchased from a separate financial firm, such as a finance company, savings association, or bank. The financial-service firms from which households purchase credit often are *local* firms, but frequently they will search both inside and outside the local area to find a loan on the best terms, particularly if the loan is large or the consumer is seeking a new credit card. Most households seem to regard checkable deposits (payments accounts), savings accounts, and credit as *separate* financial products for which they will seek out the best terms available.

**Key URLs:**
In recent years, a number of important groups and nonprofit associations have attempted to encourage individuals to save more and borrow less. See, for example, **governmentguide.com** and **nefe.org**

## QUESTIONS TO HELP YOU STUDY

1. Which sector of the economy usually provides the greatest amount of loanable funds for borrowers to draw upon? Does this sector primarily make direct loans or indirect loans to borrowers?

2. What is currently the most important *financial asset* held by U.S. households? Which financial asset is in second place in household (consumer) portfolios? Third place?

3. Define the following terms:

| | |
|---|---|
| NOWs | Mutual funds |
| MMDAs | Fixed and variable annuities |
| Roth IRAs | Share drafts |
| Home equity loans | Universal life insurance |
| ATS | Money market shares |
| IRAs | |

In what ways do the financial instruments and services listed above benefit consumers?

## 21.3   Consumers as Borrowers of Funds

We have noted that consumers provide most of the savings out of which financial assets are created in the money and capital markets. However, it is also true that consumers are among the most important borrowers in the financial system. Total credit market debt owed by U.S. households was just over $12 trillion in 2006. (See Exhibit 21.2). This was only slightly less than the total amount owed by the federal government, government-sponsored enterprises, and all state and local governments combined. In total, debt owed by households in America represents close to a third of all credit-market debt outstanding.

### *Is Consumer Borrowing Excessive?*

Are consumers too heavily in debt today? Certainly, the volume of household debt outstanding is huge in both absolute terms and relative to most other sectors of the economy. However, to judge whether consumer borrowing is really excessive, that debt should be compared to the financial assets consumers hold. These assets, presumably, can be drawn on to meet any interest and principal payments that come due on consumer borrowings. Exhibit 21.3 shows that, although the volume of consumer debt has increased rapidly in recent years, the volume of household financial assets has also grown very fast. For example, in 2006, financial assets held by U.S. households exceeded their estimated liabilities by nearly $28 trillion. Moreover, the absolute dollar size of that financial asset cushion has generally increased over the past half-century (as the third row of figures in Exhibit 21.3 demonstrates).

When we measure the *ratio of consumer liabilities to financial assets,* however, the picture is not quite so optimistic. As shown in Exhibit 21.3 this liability-to-asset ratio rose from just over 10 percent in 1950 to more than 30 percent in 2006. Whether the household liability–financial asset ratio stands at an "excessive" level depends, of course, on economic conditions and the educational level of consumers. If the average consumer today is better educated and more capable of managing a larger volume of debt, a higher ratio of liabilities to financial assets is probably not an alarming development. Moreover, the total wealth held by consumers includes not just their financial assets but also their real assets, such as homes, automobiles, furniture, and appliances. Recently the Federal Reserve estimated that U.S. households held nearly $25 trillion in owner-occupied housing and consumer durable goods. When combined with households' financial assets the total wealth of American households stood at $64 trillion—more than five times the volume of household debt.

The fact that households as a group hold more assets than liabilities does not mean that the recent buildup of consumer debt is completely innocuous, however. Recently, government policymakers have been especially concerned about a so-called *portfolio effect* that they believe might slow the future growth of the U.S. economy. Consumer borrowings rose rapidly during the 1980s, 1990s and into the twenty-first century. The ratio of household debt-service payments to personal disposable income climbed to the highest levels in history. To the extent that U.S. households feel excessively burdened with this large debt accumulation and fearful about losing their jobs, they may cut back on consumption spending. Because consumer spending is the largest component of the nation's GDP (production and income), a slowdown of household spending can lead directly to slower economic growth. This concept of a household portfolio effect argues that consumers may alter their level of spending until they once again feel comfortable with the balance between their income, assets, and liabilities.

## EXHIBIT 21.2 The Principal Debt Obligations (Liabilities) of U.S. Households, 1970, 1980, 1990, 2000, and 2006 ($ billions)

| Debt (Liabilities) Outstanding | 1970 Amount | 1970 Percent | 1980 Amount | 1980 Percent | 1990 Amount | 1990 Percent | 2000 Amount | 2000 Percent | 2006* Amount | 2006* Percent |
|---|---|---|---|---|---|---|---|---|---|---|
| Home and other mortgages | $299.6 | 62.6% | $ 946.8 | 65.2% | $2,586.6 | 69.5% | $4,958.1 | 67.0% | $ 8,943.6 | 73.3% |
| Consumer nonresidential credit | 133.7 | 27.9 | 374.7 | 25.7 | 911.0 | 24.5 | 1,862.0 | 25.1 | 2,336.9 | 19.2 |
| Bank loans n.e.c.[†] | 6.1 | 1.3 | 27.8 | 1.9 | 17.9 | 0.5 | 74.1 | 1.0 | 117.9 | 1.0 |
| Other loans | 20.9 | 4.4 | 52.1 | 3.6 | 81.7 | 2.2 | 119.8 | 1.6 | 119.5 | 1.0 |
| Security credit | 6.9 | 1.4 | 24.7 | 1.7 | 38.8 | 1.0 | 235.1 | 3.2 | 249.4 | 2.0 |
| Trade credit | 6.5 | 1.4 | 13.8 | 0.9 | 66.8 | 1.8 | 134.7 | 1.8 | 166.4 | 1.4 |
| Deferred and unpaid life insurance premiums | 5.1 | 1.1 | 12.9 | 0.9 | 16.5 | 0.4 | 19.6 | 0.3 | 22.5 | 0.2 |
| Other liabilities | 18.5 | 3.9 | 51.5 | 3.5 | 122.1 | 3.3 | 389.4 | 5.3 | 247.6 | 2.0 |
| Total liabilities | $478.7 | 100.0% | $1,453.0 | 100.0% | $3,719.3 | 100.0% | $7,403.5 | 100.0% | $12,198.8 | 100.0% |

*2006 figures are for first quarter only.

[†] Not elsewhere classified.

Note: Columns may not add to totals due to rounding. Includes nonprofit organizations.

Source: Board of Governors of the Federal Reserve System.

| EXHIBIT 21.3 | The Household Sector as a Net Lender of Funds to the Rest of the Economy | | | | | | |
|---|---|---|---|---|---|---|---|
| | Amounts Outstanding at Year-End ($ billions) | | | | | | |
| Item | 1950 | 1960 | 1970 | 1980 | 1990 | 2000 | 2006* |
| Total financial assets held by households | $735.2 | $1,348.6 | $2,557.5 | $6,602.2 | $14,827.7 | $33,937.0 | $39,806.3 |
| Total debts (financial liabilities) of households | 76.3 | 223.4 | 478.7 | 1,453.0 | 3,719.3 | 7,403.5 | 12,198.8 |
| Difference: | | | | | | | |
| Financial assets minus liabilities | $658.9 | $1,125.2 | $2,078.8 | $5,149.2 | $11,108.4 | $26,533.5 | $27,607.5 |
| Ratio of household liabilities to financial assets | 10.4% | 16.6% | 18.7% | 22.0% | 25.1% | 21.8% | 30.6% |

*2006 figures are as of the first quarter.

Source: Board of Governors of the Federal Reserve System.

Of course, pulling in the opposite direction from the portfolio effect discussed above may be the *wealth effect*. With the prices of many stocks, bonds, and other consumer-held assets rising at various times in recent years, household net worth increased substantially (approaching $54 trillion in 2006). This upsurge in consumer wealth caused many individuals and families to feel comfortable with heavier debt loads, believing they could sell off their higher-valued assets if trouble appeared on the horizon. Unfortunately, consumers may have overestimated the true value of their recent gains in wealth. If everyone tries to sell off their assets to repay debt, asset values will sink and many households will wind up feeling poorer.

## Categories of Consumer Borrowing

**Key URLs:**
Consumer borrowing and savings activities have captured great interest lately and are frequently discussed on the Web. Two Web sites to explore are The Consumer Information Center at **consumer.gov** and MSN at **msn.com**

**residential mortgage credit**

**installment credit**

**noninstallment credit**

The range of consumer borrowing needs is enormous. Loans to the household sector support a more diverse group of purchases than is true of any other sector of the economy. Consumers borrow *long term* to finance purchases of durable goods, such as single-family homes, automobiles, boats, and home appliances. They borrow *short term* to cover purchases of nondurable goods and services, such as medical care, vacations, food, and clothing. Financial analysts frequently divide consumer credit into three broad categories: (1) **residential mortgage credit**, used to support the purchase of new or existing homes; (2) **installment credit**, used primarily for long-term nonresidential purposes; and (3) **noninstallment credit**, generally used for short-term cash needs.

Which of these forms of consumer borrowing is most important? Exhibit 21.2 provides a clear answer. The dominant form of consumer borrowing is aimed at providing shelter for individuals and families through mortgage loans. Home mortgage indebtedness by U.S. households climbed above $10 trillion in 2006, representing about four-fifths of all household debt. Moreover, the volume of home mortgage credit flowing to households has grown rapidly in recent years with the attractiveness of home ownership as a tax shelter and with recent tax reforms that favor home-equity loans secured by the borrower's home (even though funds borrowed often go for nonhousing-related expenditures).

*Installment credit,* the second major component of consumer debt, consists of all consumer liabilities other than home mortgages that are retired in two or more consecutive payments, usually monthly or quarterly. Several major types of installment credit are extended by lenders in this field: automobile credit; revolving credit; mobile home loans; loans to purchase furniture, appliances, and medical care; debt consolidation loans, and other installment loans. As shown in Exhibit 21.2, consumer installment debt totaled more than $2 trillion in 2006, more than five times the amount in 1980.

The final major category of consumer debt is *noninstallment credit,* which is normally paid off in a lump sum. This form of consumer credit includes single-payment loans, charge accounts, and credit for services such as medical care and utilities. The total amount of noninstallment loans outstanding is difficult to estimate because many such loans are made by one individual to another or by department stores, oil and gas companies, and professional service firms that are not required to report their lending activities. Commercial banks, however, make a substantial volume of noninstallment loans to consumers and are considered the leading lender in this field.

## 21.4  Home Equity Loans

**home equity loan**

One new form of consumer borrowing closely related to residential mortgage credit is the **home equity loan.** Like traditional home mortgages, a home equity loan is secured by a borrower's home. However, unlike traditional home mortgages, many home equity loans consist of a prearranged revolving credit line the borrower can draw on for purchases of goods or services over the life of the credit line.

**Key URLs:**
For further exploration of the risks and other challenges of home equity loans see, for example, **ftc.gov/bcp/conline/pubs/homes/homeeqt.shtm** and **federalreserve.gov/pubs/Homeline/**

With a home equity line of credit, a consumer can literally write himself or herself a loan simply by writing a check or presenting a credit card for purchases made up to a stipulated maximum amount, known as the *borrowing base.* The borrowing base equals the difference between the appraised market value of the borrower's home and the unpaid amount of the mortgage against that home multiplied by a fraction (often 0.70, or 70 percent). Thus, a home currently valued at $100,000 with an outstanding mortgage loan against it of $40,000 would give the homeowner a base amount to borrow against of about ($100,000 − $40,000) × 0.70, or $42,000. Moreover, under current U.S. tax laws, the interest owed on a loan secured by the borrower's home that qualifies under all the rules laid down in the Internal Revenue Code represents a tax-deductible expense, encouraging consumers to substitute home equity loans for other types of credit whose interest cost is *not* tax deductible.[1]

Most home equity loan rates are linked to the bank prime interest rate (or other base interest rate, such as the U.S. government bond rate) plus an extra margin for risk (i.e., a floating loan rate). Federal law requires that a maximum (ceiling) interest rate be established for all such loans so that a home-equity borrower has some protection against extreme interest rate risk. Home equity loans cover 10 to 15 years in most cases, although a substantial proportion can be continued indefinitely. The Consumer Protection Act of 1988 prohibits a home equity lender from canceling a loan unless fraud, failure to pay, or other violations of the loan contract occur. Thus far, most home equity loans have been used to pay off other debts (especially credit-card loans), make home improvements, buy automobiles, or finance an education.

---

[1]U.S. tax laws state that the interest paid on home equity loans may still be tax deductible even if the home mortgage is taken out for reasons other than to buy or improve the borrower's principal residence. However, there are conditions that must be satisfied for tax deductibility, so homeowners should consult IRS regulations to make sure their home equity loan qualifies under current tax rules.

The rapidly rising cost of college tuition (averaging about 6 percent annually on average, or more than twice the yearly rise in the Consumer Price Index) has led to a soaring volume of education loans for students trying to get in and complete college degree programs. This highly competitive and expanding credit market has attracted scores of banks and other private lenders as well as government-sponsored loan programs.

Unfortunately, where there is strong demand for credit some lending institutions will find questionable ways to push aside competition and set up profitable "inside" arrangements. For example, some loan companies made cash or stock awards to colleges and universities and to officials of sponsoring agencies in order to get on "preferred lender" lists, directing students and their families to particular loan programs. Some lending institutions apparently managed to breach government databases (such as the National Student Loan Data System) containing personal information on thousands of college student borrowers.

Implicated in this unfolding scandal were admissions personnel at some schools, some staff members at government education agencies, and several leading private lending institutions, including SLM (better known as Sallie Mae) which packages and sells student loans to major lending institutions. The U.S. Department of Education, Congress, and several states soon launched investigations, looking for possibly illegal student loan marketing practices.

For further information on student lending institutions see, for example, such Web sites as the U.S. Department of Education's student financial aid information center at **studentaid.ed.gov,** the National Student Loan Data System at **nslds.ed.gov,** and the Student Loan Marketing Association at **salliemae.com.**

Home equity credit has proved to be especially attractive to consumer lending institutions. These loans tend to have a lower rate of default because borrowers feel more responsible when their home is pledged as collateral and that collateral tends to have a more stable value. Moreover, the cost of making home equity loans is usually lower than the cost of a series of short-term loans made to the same customer. In addition, these loans typically carry interest rates that adjust to the market, whereas many other consumer loans have fixed interest rates. Finally, home equity credits help the lender build a working relationship with a customer better than most other types of consumer loans, creating more opportunities to sell that customer additional services. However, if the borrower cannot make the loan payments, his or her home may be repossessed and sold to pay back the lender. This risk of repossession may have increased in some instances because of a recent decline in the proportion of their homes that Americans actually own (i.e., the equity in the home relative to the home's market value), which has declined from about 70 percent in 1983 to about 50 percent in 2006. Many financial experts recommend that consumers use home equity credit with caution, particularly when their employment prospects are uncertain.

## 21.5  Credit and Debit Cards

**credit card**

One of the most popular forms of installment credit available to consumers today comes through the **credit card.** Through this encoded piece of plastic, the consumer has instant access to credit for any purchase up to a prespecified limit. In the language of finance, credit extended by a credit card is referred to as *revolving credit* because the borrower can borrow up to a prespecified limit, repay, and borrow again. Thus, the credit card has removed the "liquidity" constraint that restricted the spending power of millions of consumers, democratizing access to credit and spending power.

**debit card**

More recently, another piece of plastic—the **debit card**—has made instant cash available, made check cashing much easier, and made possible rapid electronic payment for purchases of goods and services. The growth of credit and debit cards has been truly phenomenal. Current estimates suggest that there are well over a trillion credit and debit cards in use worldwide, and leading nonfinancial companies (such as General Motors and General Electric) have recently entered in large numbers as suppliers of credit-card services.

A wide array of new consumer financial services is being offered today through plastic credit- and debit-card programs, including revolving credit lines, preauthorized borrowing, the purchase of medical services and entertainment, and the payment of everyday household bills. In the future, customers will need to make fewer trips to their financial-service provider because transactions will be handled mainly over the telephone, through a conveniently located computer terminal, or through "smart cards" that have prepayment-encoded information (such as a credit line the cardholder can use for making purchases). The hometown financial institution will lose much of its convenience advantage for local customers. It will be nearly as convenient for the customer to maintain a checking, savings, or loan account in a city hundreds of miles away as to keep it in a local financial institution. In short, the ticket to many consumer financial services increasingly will be through a plastic credit or debit card and a computer, with the capability to process financial data across great distances. By 2010 current estimates suggest consumers will pay for over half their purchases with credit and debit cards rather than cash and checks.

## Credit Cards

Customers who use credit cards merely as a substitute for cash are referred to as *convenience users*. These people tend to be in upper-income brackets and do not necessarily seek stores accepting their cards. In contrast, customers who maintain large outstanding credit card balances are referred to as *installment users* because they pay only a portion of their outstanding balance each month. These individuals frequently are in lower-and middle-income brackets and tend to be the most profitable credit-card customers for card-issuing firms.

One recent trend in credit cards that has benefited consumers but hurt many issuers is the heavy over-issue of credit cards to consumers who are already heavily in debt or have flawed credit records, resulting in a substantial rise in the number of delinquent accounts. Moreover, to reach out for a bigger market share, many card issuers have recently cut their loan margins. Accordingly, thousands of borrowers have used their ability to borrow using cheaper-rate cards in order to pay off their accumulated debts run up earlier on higher-rate cards (known as "card surfing"). The net result has been to lower the profitability of many card programs. While, historically, credit-card loan rates have been among the "stickiest" interest rates in the financial system, these rates recently have become more flexible, and competition among card issuers has intensified. A "shakeout" appears to be under way, with smaller credit-card programs consolidating into larger ones.

For both convenience users and installment users, the principal advantage of credit cards is *convenience*. The installment loan feature is a major attraction because it functions as a revolving line of credit, granting loans at no cost for an average of about one month by taking advantage of interest-free grace periods. In addition, the card itself serves to identify the customer and makes pertinent information available when the privilege of using the card is exercised. Most merchants know that charge cardholders tend to have higher incomes and better payment records than the general population.

Recently, new cards have appeared that not only charge zero annual fees but also give customers rebates or discounts on purchases the more the card is used. A particularly popular feature is to grant "frequent flyer miles" with designated airlines based on the amount charged against the credit card which encourages customer usage. This feature permits the credit-card customer to obtain flyer miles at no cost, provided the balance on the card is paid off during the "grace period," thus avoiding interest expense.

Charge-offs (bad debts) from overusage of credit cards has recently been rising. Part of the explanation lies in the fact that many households (including lower-income households) now have several cards, and there has been an increase in the proportion of families actually borrowing against their cards. With heavier debt burdens, the average credit-card account is probably somewhat riskier, resulting in growing bad debt in the credit-card field.

## Debit Cards

Until recently, commercial banks were the only major financial institutions actively involved in the plastic card field. This situation changed rapidly during the 1970s and 1980s, however, as nonbank financial institutions (principally credit unions, savings banks, savings and loans, security brokers, finance and insurance companies) successfully invaded the plastic card market, frequently offering not only credit cards, but also *debit cards*. While a credit card permits the customer to buy now and pay later, debit cards are merely a convenient way of paying *now*. A debit card enables users to make deposits and withdrawals from an automated teller machine and also to pay for purchases by direct electronic transfer of funds from their own accounts to the merchant's account. Debit cards are also used for identification and check-clearing purposes and to access remote computer terminals for information or for moving funds.

**Key URL:**
To explore more fully the advantages and disadvantages of debit cards see especially ftc.gov

Closely related to the debit card are "smart cards," which are encoded with the customer's account number and balance available for spending. These are a substitute for immediately spendable cash. "Smart cards" have not done particularly well in the United States to date, due, in part, to the risks involved and the availability of other payments media. These stored-value cards have been successful in Europe, however, and are expected to become more important worldwide in the new century.

Debit cards appear to have gained on both credit cards and checks in recent years as the preferred method of paying for goods and services sold in stores. Many consumers seem to like the discipline that debit cards bring to their lives because the money is automatically taken out of their checking account, usually the same day a purchase is made. Users have less temptation to spend more money than they have. Moreover, with debit cards the consumer has fewer checks to write.

Debit cards have been profitable for many small banks in the United States, who earn a fee for each transaction. In contrast, credit cards are profitable mainly for the largest banks because this is a service characterized by strong economies of scale. Credit-card programs require high volume to overcome high operating costs, defaulted accounts, and credit-card fraud. Unfortunately, however, debit cards may have a legal drawback, possibly protecting the customer less if the card is lost or stolen. Federal law limits consumer losses on credit cards, but a debit card can be used to drain a customer's checking account before he or she realizes what's happening. However, some financial-service providers have indicated a willingness to cover all or a portion of any losses in those cases where fraud can be verified.

## 21.6  The Determinants of Consumer Borrowing

As we noted earlier, consumers represent one of the largest groups of borrowers in the financial system. Yet individual consumers differ widely in their use of credit and in their attitudes toward borrowing money. What factors appear to influence the volume of borrowing carried out by households?

Recent research points to a number of factors that bear on the consumer's decision of when and how much to borrow. Leading the list is the size of *individual or family income* and *accumulated household wealth.* Families with larger incomes and greater accumulated wealth tend to use greater amounts of debt, both in absolute amounts and relative to their income. In part, the debt-income relationship reflects the high correlation between income levels and education. Families whose principal breadwinners have made a significant investment in education are most often aware of the advantages (as well as the dangers) of using debt to supplement current income. Moreover, there appears to be a high positive correlation between education and the income-earning power of the principal breadwinners in a family.

The *stage in life* in which adult income-earning members of a family find themselves is also a major influence on household borrowing. The *life cycle hypothesis* contends that young families just starting out tend to be heavy users of debt. The purchase of a new home, automobile, appliances, and furniture follow soon after a new family is formed. As children come along, living costs rise and a larger home may be necessary, resulting in additional borrowing. Young families are willing to take on these additional debts because they expect a stream of future income throughout their working lives. Later, the family's income rises, children leave home, and saving increases, while borrowing falls relative to income because older families expect a shorter income stream before retirement arrives and, therefore, work to pay off their debts and build up their savings.

Consumer borrowing is correlated with the *business cycle.* During periods of economic expansion, the number of jobs increases, and households become more optimistic about the future. New borrowings usually outstrip repayments of outstanding loans, and the total volume of household debt rises. When an economic expansion ends and a recession begins, however, unemployment rises and many households become pessimistic about the future. Some, fearing a drop in income or loss of a job, build up savings and cut back on borrowing. Thus, both consumer saving and borrowing tend to follow the ups and downs of the business cycle. Households tend to use borrowing and saving as devices to *smooth out* consumer spending over the course of the business cycle.

In recent decades, *price expectations* have also influenced consumer borrowing, especially when the rate of inflation begins to accelerate. Postponing the purchase of an automobile, a new home, and so forth, often means these goods may simply cost more in the future. If family incomes are not increasing as fast as consumer prices, it often pays to "buy now" through borrowing rather than to postpone purchases.

Fluctuations in *interest rates* also play a role in shaping the volume and direction of consumer borrowing. Interest rates rise as the economy expands and gathers momentum. At first, the rising rates are not high enough to offset strong consumer optimism, and household borrowing continues to increase. As the period of economic expansion reaches a peak, however, the rise in interest rates may become so costly that consumer borrowing begins to decline. The drop in borrowing leads to a decline in consumer spending, which may worsen the impending recession. Of course, as we saw earlier, interest rates are not the sole determinant of consumer borrowing. The size of debt payments and consumer income, the fate of a consumer's investments and wealth position, age, employment outlook, and a host of other factors shape how much and when consumers choose to borrow money.

## 21.7   Consumer Lending Institutions

Financial intermediaries—banks, savings and loan associations, credit unions, and finance companies—account for most of the loans made to consumers in the economy. However, as Exhibit 21.4 indicates, a growing share of consumer loans are being sold off the balance sheets of traditional lenders and placed in loan pools (securitizations), often under the guidance of security dealers. While many traditional consumer lenders have lost ground in terms of their share of all consumer loans outstanding, the loan pools have significantly gained market share. At the same time, lenders pooling their loans and moving them off their balance sheets thereby gain new cash and the ability to make more loans.

Although each type of financial institution prefers to specialize in a few selected areas of consumer lending, there has been a tendency in recent years for institutions to

| EXHIBIT 21.4 | Leading Consumer Lending Institutions in the United States | | |
|---|---|---|---|
| **Total Nonmortgage Loans at Year-End ($ billions)** | | | |
| **Lending Institutions** | **1995** | **2000** | **2006\*** |
| Commercial banks | $ 502.0 | $ 541.5 | $ 713.2 |
| Finance companies | 152.1 | 220.5 | 498.7 |
| Credit unions | 131.9 | 184.4 | 233.0 |
| Savings institutions | 40.1 | 64.6 | 102.6 |
| Nonfinancial businesses | 85.1 | 82.7 | 56.6 |
| Pools of securitized assets (no longer on the balance sheets of the original lenders) and other lending institutions | 211.6 | 521.3 | 712.3 |
| Totals outstanding | $1,122.8 | $1,615.0 | $2,316.4 |

\*2006 figures are as of first quarter.
Source: Board of Governors of the Federal Reserve System.

diversify their lending operations across many different types of loans. One important result of this diversification has been to bring *all* major consumer lenders into direct competition with each other.

## Commercial Banks

The single most important consumer lending institution is the *commercial bank.* Commercial banks approach the consumer in at least three different ways: by direct lending, through purchases of installment paper from merchants, and by making loans to other consumer lending institutions. Roughly half of all bank loans to consumers (measured by dollar volume) consist of mortgages to support the purchase, construction, or improvement of residential dwellings; the rest consist of installment and non-installment credit to cover purchases of goods and services. In the mortgage field, commercial banks often prefer to provide short-term construction financing rather than to make long-term permanent loans for family housing, though most banks make both types of loans.

Banks make a wider variety of consumer loans than any other lending institution. They grant almost half of all auto loans extended by financial institutions to consumers each year. However, most bank credit in the auto field is indirect—installment paper purchased from auto dealers—rather than being extended directly to the auto-buying consumer. Moreover, banking's leadership in auto lending has been challenged in recent years by finance companies and credit unions. Indeed, in many forms of consumer installment credit today, the lead of commercial banks is threatened by challenges from aggressive nonbank lenders who see the consumer market as a key growth area for the future.

## Finance Companies

Finance companies have a long history of active lending in the consumer installment field, providing funds directly to the consumer through thousands of small loan offices and indirectly by purchasing installment paper from dealers. These active household lenders provide auto loans and credit for home improvements and for the purchase of appliances and furniture. Finance companies often face state-imposed legal limits on the interest rates they can charge for household loans and on loan size.

## Other Consumer Lenders: Credit Unions, Savings Associations, and Small Loan Companies

Other consumer installment lenders include credit unions, savings and loan associations, savings banks, and so-called "fringe banks" (such as check-cashing, payday, and title loan companies). *Credit unions* make a wide variety of loans for such diverse purposes as purchases of automobiles; vacations; home repair; and, more recently, mortgage credit for the purchase of new homes. Only the members of a credit union may borrow from that institution, however.

Also important in the consumer loan field are *savings and loans* and *savings banks.* Although these institutions have long been dominant in residential mortgage lending, they have moved aggressively to expand their portfolios of credit-card, education, home improvement, furniture, appliance, and mobile home loans in recent years. Much of the drive for expansion in the consumer credit field is due to recent federal deregulation of the services offered by savings institutions.

Finally, among the most rapidly growing consumer lenders in recent years have been *small loan companies*—often called "fringe banks"—that lend primarily to distressed borrowers. Included here are such high-rate lenders as "check-cashing" companies, "title loan" companies, "payday lenders," "pawn shops," and "rent to own" shops. *Check cashing firms* and *payday lenders* agree to accept a post-dated check from the borrowing customer which will be cashed later by the lender, in return for which the lender makes an immediate cash loan to the customer. *Title loan companies* agree to take control of the title to a valuable asset (such as a borrowing customer's automobile) as collateral for making a loan. If the customer fails to repay the loan the lender keeps title to the asset. *Pawn shops* accept assets that a customer may bring in, hold those assets, and extend the customer a loan based on a fraction of the assets' value. If the customer does not repay, the pawn shop retains the assets it has taken in and eventually sells them. Finally, *rent-to-own* stores provide customers with the use of furniture, home appliances, and other assets for rental fees that may subsequently be applied to the purchase price of those rented assets.

The loans made by these small-loan companies are normally short term, covering only a few days or weeks, and are designed primarily to tide families over until the next payday arrives. But the loan rates charged are among the highest assessed by the consumer credit industry and loan defaults are frequent.

## 21.8 Factors Considered in Making Consumer Loans

Consumer loans are considered one of the most profitable uses of funds for many financial institutions. There is evidence, however, that such loans usually carry greater risk than most other forms of credit, and they tend to be more costly to make per dollar of loan. On the other hand, the lender often can offset these costs by charging higher interest rates.

**Key URLs:**
To learn more about "fringe banking" see addall.com/detail/0871541955.html; outreach.missouri.edu/ceupdate/scripts/1999/06/fringebanking.htm; ftc.gov and thefreedictionary.com/small+loan+company

Making consumer loans is a challenging dimension of modern financial management. It requires not only a thorough knowledge of household credit reports and financial statements but also an ability to assess the character of the borrower. Over the years, many loan officers have developed decision "rules of thumb" as an aid to processing and evaluating consumer loan applications. For example, some consumer loan officers insist that household debt (exclusive of housing costs) should not exceed 20 to 30 percent of a family's gross income. For younger borrowers, without substantial assets to serve as collateral for a loan, a cosigner may be sought whose assets and financial standing represent more adequate security. The *duration of employment* of the borrower is often a critical factor, and many institutions deny a loan request if the customer has been employed at his present job for less than a year.

The *past payment record* of a customer usually is a key indicator of *character* and the likelihood the loan will be repaid in timely fashion. Many lenders refuse to make loans to consumers who evidence "pyramiding of debt"—frequent borrowing from one financial institution to pay another. Evidence of sloppy money handling, such as large balances carried on charge accounts or heavy installment payments, may be regarded as a negative factor in a loan application. Loan officers may be alert to evidence of a lack of *credit integrity* as reflected in frequent late payments or actual default on past loans. Regardless of the strength of the borrower's financial position, if the customer lacks the willingness to repay debt, the lender has made a bad loan.

Most lenders believe those who *own valuable property,* such as land or marketable securities, are a better risk than those who do not own such property. For example, homeowners are usually considered better risks than those who rent. Moreover, a borrower's chance of getting a loan often goes up if he or she does other business (such as maintain a deposit) with the lending institution. If more than one member of the family works, this may be viewed as a more favorable factor than if the family depends upon only a single breadwinner, who may become ill, die, or lose a job. Having a telephone at home is another positive factor in evaluating a loan application because the telephone gives the lender an inexpensive way to contact the borrower. One way to lower the cost of a loan is for the consumer to pledge a deposit or other liquid asset as security behind the loan. The disadvantage here is that such a pledge ties up the asset pledged until the loan is repaid.

## 21.9 Credit Scoring Techniques

The rapidly changing world of information technology has had a significant impact on the processes used for evaluating consumer loan applications. Today advanced statistical techniques are employed to assemble information about applicants for consumer loans, analyze the information gathered, and develop a *numerical score* for each would-be borrower that measures each borrower's default risk in a more precise way. Using that score, lenders can make a decision as to whether a borrower has scored high enough to qualify for a loan.

**credit scoring techniques**

Today **credit scoring techniques** are used for a wide variety of loans and other financial services, including deciding who should receive credit cards, what their credit limit should be, what families should receive mortgage loans to help purchase new homes, and even who should receive insurance coverage and at what price.

The most famous of the credit scoring systems in use today was developed by Fair Isaac Corporation (more widely known as FICO). Fair Isaac has developed sophisticated prediction techniques to prepare credit scores for thousands of consumers, distributing this information to credit bureaus, lenders, and even to consumers themselves who want to know their current credit score and how they might improve it. Indeed, consumers who can raise their credit score often save a great deal of money by qualifying for lower loan rates and insurance premiums.

**Key URLs:**
For more information about FICO and other credit scoring systems, see especially **myfico. fanniemae.com** and **hsh.com/ pamphlets/about+fico .html**

FICO and similar credit scoring systems base the scores they calculate on a credit applicant's *payment history* (i.e., how much has been borrowed in the past and when amounts owed were repaid), the current volume and type of debt each consumer has outstanding, and the type of credit currently being requested. FICO assigns scores that fall between 300 and 850, with the higher score indicating greater probability of repayment. However, under the FICO system each lending institution decides what minimum cut-off score applies. For example, some lenders say that a score below 550 is unacceptable, while others may insist on a minimum score of at least 650 before any loan can be granted.

Credit scoring systems have numerous advantages for lenders and consumers. They allow lenders to handle a large volume of credit requests at comparatively low cost and offer the customer quick turnaround in receiving a "yes" or "no" decision regarding loan approval. On the downside, however, credit scoring systems must frequently be reevaluated to make sure they are contributing to good credit decisions at a statistically significant level and are not discriminating against borrowers on the basis of race, religion, sex, or other irrelevant factors.

## QUESTIONS TO HELP YOU STUDY

9. Discuss the factors that influence the volume of borrowing by individuals and families. What role do you believe inflation plays in the borrowing and savings decisions of households today?

10. What factors do lending institutions usually consider when evaluating a consumer loan application? Why?

11. What are the principal types of *consumer lending institutions* in the financial system?

12. Many lenders contend that loans to individuals and families are among the riskiest loans made within the financial system. Do you believe this is true? What kinds of risk do consumer loans present to a lender? How can lenders help combat this risk exposure?

13. What is *credit scoring* and why is it used extensively today in evaluating consumer loan applications?

## 21.10   Financial Disclosure and Consumer Credit

Important new laws have appeared in recent years designed to protect the consumer in dealings with lending institutions. One area of emphasis is *financial disclosure:* making all relevant information available to the customer before a commitment is made. Moreover, if all important information is laid out before an agreement is reached, this may encourage the consumer to shop around to find the cheapest and most convenient terms available. However, there is considerable debate today on whether consumer protection legislation has really accomplished its goals as many consumers do not seem to care about information disclosures and do not appear to shop around, though the WorldWide Web may give a big boost to personal shopping behavior.

### *Truth in Lending*

**Truth in Lending**

In 1968, Congress passed a watershed piece of legislation in the consumer credit field—the Consumer Credit Protection Act, more widely known as **Truth in Lending.** Shortly after the act was passed, federal regulatory agencies prepared new rules to implement and enforce the principles of Truth in Lending, such as the Federal Reserve Board's Regulation Z.

Truth in Lending simply requires banks and other lenders to provide sufficient information about a credit contract, in easily understood terms, so that the consumer can make an intelligent decision about purchasing credit. The law does not tell creditors how much to charge or to whom they may lend money. At the same time, consumers were granted certain rights. For example, they have the right to cancel or rescind a credit agreement within three business days if their home is included as part of the collateral for a loan. This *right of rescission* applies to the repair or remodeling of a home or the taking out of a mortgage on an existing home, where the credit requested is intended for personal or agricultural purposes and results in a debt obligation repayable in more than four installments.

Under the terms of Truth in Lending a lender must tell the customer the annual percentage rate of interest (APR) charged on a loan. Lenders must disclose the total

**Key URLs:**
To learn more about the rules and regulations surrounding the Truth in Lending law see, for example, smartagreements.com/bltopics/BLTop 41.html and http://en.wikipedia.org/wiki/Truth-in-Lending-Act

dollar cost associated with granting a loan—known as the *finance charge*—the sum of all charges the customer must pay as a condition for securing the loan. These charges may include credit investigation fees, insurance to protect the lender, and points on a mortgage loan. Once the finance charge is determined, it must be converted into the APR by comparing it with the amount of the loan. The APR is really the ratio of the dollar finance charge to the unpaid balance of a loan, determined by the actuarial method. Because all lenders must quote the APR, computed by the same method, this makes it easier for the consumer to shop around and purchase credit from the cheapest source available.

The concept of Truth in Lending has been extended in a number of directions in recent years. One important dimension concerns *advertising*. A lender that advertises one attractive feature of a credit package to consumers must also disclose other relevant credit terms. For example, a car dealer that advertises low down payments must also disclose other aspects of the loan, such as how many payments are required, what the amount of each payment is, and how many months or years are involved before the loan is paid off.

## Fair Credit Billing Act

**Fair Credit Billing Act**

In 1974, Congress passed the **Fair Credit Billing Act** in response to a torrent of consumer complaints about billing errors, especially on credit cards. Many individuals found that they were being billed for items never purchased or received, that some merchants would not respond when contacted about billing errors, and that finance charges were frequently assessed even though the consumer claimed no responsibility for charges listed on the billing statement.

The Fair Credit Billing Act requires a creditor to respond to a customer's billing inquiry within 30 days. In most cases, the dispute must be resolved within 90 days. The customer may withhold payment of any amounts in dispute, although he or she must pay any portions of a bill not in dispute. However, no creditor can report a customer as "delinquent" over amounts of a bill that are the subject of disagreement until the disparity has been resolved. A creditor who fails to respond to the customer's inquiry or makes no effort to settle the dispute may forfeit the disputed sum up to $50.

**Fair Credit Reporting Act**

**Key URLs:**
To learn more about credit bureaus and credit ratings see especially equifax.com, experian.com, or transunion.com
Are financial-service firms subject to federal restrictions on telemarketing, including the Federal Trade Commission's famous "Do-Not-Call" rule? Banks and insurance companies are subject to this rule, according to an FTC ruling in 2003. See especially ftc.gov/donotcall

## Fair Credit Reporting Act

An extension of Truth in Lending occurred when the **Fair Credit Reporting Act** was passed by Congress in 1970. This law entitles consumers to have access to their credit files, kept by credit bureaus active in the United States and Canada. These credit bureaus supply subscribing lenders with vital information on amounts owed and the payment records and credit ratings of individuals and families. They aid greatly in reducing the risks inherent in consumer lending. However, because the information credit bureaus supply has a substantial impact on the availability of credit to individuals and families, their activities and especially the accuracy of information they provide have been brought under closer scrutiny in recent years.

Under the provisions of the Fair Credit Reporting Act, the consumer is entitled to review his or her credit file at any time. Moreover, he or she may challenge any items that appear in the file and demand an investigation. The credit bureau must respond, and if inaccuracies exist or if an item cannot be verified, it must be removed or the inaccuracies corrected. If the consumer determines that an item in the credit file is damaging and requires clarification, he or she may insert a statement of 100 words or less explaining the consumer's version of the matter. Data in the file are supposed to be shown only to properly identified individuals for approved purposes or on direct written request from the consumer. Information cannot be disclosed to anyone after a period of seven years unless the consumer is seeking a loan of $50,000 or more, purchasing life insurance, applying for a job paying $20,000 or more per year, or has declared personal bankruptcy. The consumer may sue if damaged by incorrect information in a credit file. Many financial analysts today recommend that consumers check their credit bureau report several months before applying for a major loan and, otherwise, at least once a year.

### Consumer Leasing Act

In 1976, Congress passed the *Consumer Leasing Act,* which requires disclosure by leasing companies of the essential terms of any lease involving personal property, such as an automobile. The customer must be told about all charges, any insurance required, the terms under which the lease may be canceled, any penalties for late payment, and any express warranties that go with the property.

### Competitive Banking Equality Act

In 1987 the *Competitive Banking Equality Act* was passed into law, requiring depository institutions to disclose more fully the terms on various *deposit services* they offer. One major change was the required disclosure of how many days a depositor must wait before a check deposited in an account becomes available for spending. Some depository institutions had previously delayed the granting of credit for some deposits for a week or even longer. The new law stipulated that no more than one business day usually can intervene between the day of deposit of a local check and the customer receiving credit for that deposit. Nonlocal checks must be credited to the customer's account in no more than four business days.

### Fair Credit and Charge Card Disclosure Act

Reflecting concern over the rapid expansion of credit-card debt, the *Fair Credit and Charge Card Disclosure Act* was passed in 1988. Credit-card issuers were required to notify consumers of the interest rates, fees, and other terms attached to these credit accounts, spelled out in easy-to-read format (known as the "Schumer Box" after its congressional sponsor). Card customers were to be supplied with a toll-free phone number and address to help get their credit-card questions answered.

### Truth in Savings Act

A further effort to make sure consumers are adequately informed about the deposit accounts they purchase was made in November 1991 when Congress passed the *Truth in Savings Act.* This law prohibits inaccurate or misleading advertising concerning deposit accounts. Each depository institution must maintain a publicly available schedule of information for each class of accounts offered and distribute that information to both new and established account holders. If depositors would be adversely affected by a change in the terms of a deposit, notice of that adverse change must be provided to the deposit holder at least 30 days before the change becomes effective. Moreover, the customer must receive interest on the *full* amount of the principal deposited in an account, not on just the amount that a depository institution claims is available for investing in earning assets.

## *The Financial Services Modernization (Gramm-Leach-Bliley) Act*

In an effort to protect a household's personal financial information, the U.S. Congress passed the **Financial Services Modernization Act** (known also as *GLB* after its sponsors) in the fall of 1999. This new law requires financial-service firms to tell household customers, at least once a year, what their policy is in the handling of personal, nonpublic data—known as a *privacy policy*. Consumers must be informed about any of their personal data that may be shared with other businesses (such as telemarketing firms, for example). Each consumer has to be offered the possibility to "opt out" of at least some information sharing. However, many consumer groups have recently complained that this law is too weak in protecting consumers' personal data and have demanded new privacy rules at federal and state levels.

## *Identity Theft*

**Key URL:**
Useful information about stopping identity theft is available from the Federal Trade Commission at **ftc.gov**

**identity theft**

To learn more about dealing with *identity theft*, see especially **ftc.gov**. For information about how to file an identity theft complaint, contact the Identity Theft Clearinghouse, Federal Trade Commission, 600 Pennsylvania Ave., NW, Washington, D.C., 20580.

Disclosure of information can be a great aid to consumers and lenders intent on making sound financial decisions. However, there are cases where disclosing too much information can be very damaging to consumers. Such is the case with the world's fastest growing crime today—**identity theft**—which has been fueled by the rapid expansion of the Internet.

The term "identity theft" refers to the stealing of someone's private information (such as his or her Social Security number, driver's license number, credit-card account number, etc.), usually for the purpose of representing oneself as the person whose information has been stolen. Identity thieves use illegally obtained private information to access an individual's checking account, charge-card accounts, and other personal items in an effort to drain away the victim's money and credit lines. For a person victimized by identity theft, it may take months or even years to straighten out the damage to one's personal credit accounts and reputation. Moreover, because many lenders today have pledged to absorb some or all of their customers' losses when a credit-card or deposit-account number is stolen, the cost to financial-service providers of offsetting the damages from identity theft approaches several billion dollars a year. This crime tends to drive up interest rates and results in higher financial-service fees for *all* consumers.

The Financial Services Modernization Act (discussed in the preceding section) was passed, in part, to create tougher laws to deal with identity theft. Stiffer criminal penalties were imposed to punish financial predators and various federal agencies (such as the Federal Trade Commission) were directed to increase public awareness of the dangers of identity theft and to instruct consumers on ways to protect their private information from thieves. Then, in 2003, the *Fair and Accurate Credit Transactions (FACT) Act* was passed, permitting consumers to initiate a "fraud alert" by contacting the national credit bureaus if identity theft is suspected and block the distribution of fraudulent information.

Among the remedies for identity theft recommended by financial planners today are periodically checking your credit bureau report (at least once a year) for any unexpected transactions, destroying unwanted credit or debit cards, asking mail and telephone marketers to remove your name from their contact lists, and avoiding giving out any personal data to people you don't know. None of these suggested steps completely removes the risk of having one's good name stolen, but they can reduce the *probability* of becoming a victim of identity theft.

## 21.11   Credit Discrimination Laws

The civil rights movement has had an impact on the granting of consumer loans. Among the most important civil rights laws involving consumer credit are the *Equal Credit Opportunity Act* of 1974 and its amendments in 1976, the *Fair Housing Act* of 1968, the *Home Mortgage Disclosure Act* of 1975, and the *Community Reinvestment Act* of 1977. The fundamental purpose of these laws is to *outlaw discrimination* in the granting of credit and other vital financial services. Today, lenders must be able to justify in terms of fairness and objectivity not only the loans that are made but also those that are not made.

### Community Reinvestment Act and Financial Institutions Reform, Recovery, and Enforcement Act

**Community Reinvestment Act**

One of the most important and controversial pieces of financial legislation is the **Community Reinvestment Act,** signed into law by President Jimmy Carter in 1977. Under its terms, financial institutions are required to make an "affirmative effort" to meet the credit needs of low- and middle-income customers. Each commercial and savings bank must define its own "trade territory" and describe the services it offers in that territory. Once a year, each institution must prepare an updated map that delineates the trade territory it will serve, without deliberately excluding low- or moderate-income neighborhoods. Customers are entitled to make written comments, which must be available for public inspection, concerning the lender's performance in meeting the credit needs of its designated trade area. The basic purpose of the Community Reinvestment Act (CRA) is to prevent gerrymandering out low-income neighborhoods and other areas that a lender may consider undesirable.

In 1989, the *Financial Institutions Reform, Recovery, and Enforcement Act* was passed, requiring public disclosure of a bank's performance rating (known as a CRA rating) in meeting the credit needs of its local community. Moreover, the *FDIC Improvement Act* of 1991 required greater disclosure of the reasons why a depository institution received the particular community service (CRA) rating that it did. The CRA ratings currently assigned to financial institutions are O (outstanding), S (satisfactory), N (needs to improve), and SN (substantial noncompliance).

### Equal Credit Opportunity Act

**Equal Credit Opportunity Act**

The **Equal Credit Opportunity Act** of 1974 forbids discrimination against credit applicants on the basis of age, sex, marital status, race, color, religion, national origin, receipt of public assistance, or good-faith exercise of rights under the federal consumer credit protection laws. Married women, for example, may receive credit under their own signature, based on their own personal credit record and earnings, without having their husband's joint signature. Credit applicants must be notified, in writing, of the approval or denial of a loan request within 30 days of filing a completed application. The lender may not request information on the borrower's race, color, religion, national origin, or sex, except in the case of residential mortgage loans (where the government can gather such information in order to detect illegal discrimination). Under the FDIC Improvement Act of 1991, the regulatory agencies must refer loan discrimination violators to the U.S. Justice Department for possible prosecution.

### Fair Housing and Home Mortgage Disclosure Acts

Two other important antidiscrimination laws are the Fair Housing Act, which forbids discrimination in lending for the purchase or renovation of residential property, and

**Bankruptcy Abuse Prevention and Consumer Protection Act**

the Home Mortgage Disclosure Act (HMDA). The latter requires financial institutions to disclose to the public the amount and location of their home mortgage and home improvement loans. HMDA was designed to eliminate *redlining,* in which some lenders would mark out areas of a community as unsuitable for home loans. Both HMDA and the Fair Housing Act require nondiscriminatory advertising by lenders. No longer can a consumer lending institution direct its advertisements solely to high-income neighborhoods to the exclusion of other potential customers. On written advertising, the Equal Housing symbol must be attached. Clearly, then, in advertising the availability of credit and in the actual granting of credit, the principles of civil rights and nondiscrimination apply.

Recent research evidence is mixed on the issue of whether discrimination in home mortgage lending or any other kind of financial service really exists. One study by Munnell, Tootell, Browne, and McEneany [11] suggested that minority applicants in the city of Boston, for example, were about 40 percent more likely than white applicants to be rejected for home mortgage loans. Other recent studies question this finding because of mitigating factors and point out that minority lending has been growing faster than other forms of credit in recent years.

## 21.12 Bankruptcy Law Changes

Since the founding of the United States under the Constitution, America's federal and state governments have set up processes for distressed household and business borrowers to obtain relief from their debts and make a fresh start. As we moved into the twenty-first century U.S. bankruptcy filings soared, in some years topping more than a million households annually. Part of this rapid increase was attributable to economic pressures, the lack of financial discipline, and the threat that future bankruptcy laws would be tougher and more costly. Interestingly enough, most studies of the bankruptcy phenomenon find the principal cause of bankruptcy filings to be the incidence of tragic events in people's lives (loss of a job, destruction of a home, medical expenses, divorce, etc.).

Tougher bankruptcy legislation *was* finally signed into law in April 2005. Labeled the **Bankruptcy Abuse Prevention and Consumer Protection Act,** the new legislation set in place significant hurdles for consumers to overcome in order to obtain relief from their debts. For example, applicants must fulfill the requirements of a U.S. Trustee–approved credit counseling program. This requirement is designed to get the troubled household to explore credit counseling as a possible alternative to the more dramatic step of petitioning for bankruptcy. However, if a household still seeks bankruptcy protection, it must then complete a U.S. Trustee–approved course of instruction in personal financial management. Moreover, substantially more personal financial information must be revealed under the new bankruptcy process, and the accuracy of that information must be attested to by an attorney or other qualified professional assisting the petitioner.

Eligibility for filing under the new bankruptcy code is subject to a *means test,* which calls for determining the applicant's monthly average income and comparing that figure to the median income level in his or her home state. Filers have a choice of applying under either Chapter 7 or Chapter 13. Generally, Chapter 7 filings are preferred by applicants because this chapter erases all or, at least, the majority of current household debts. In contrast, Chapter 13 filings require the petitioner to follow a bankruptcy court–sanctioned debt repayment plan. The new law requires filers whose average monthly income exceeds their home state's median income level to apply under the stricter Chapter 13, not the more lenient Chapter 7.

The Bankruptcy Abuse Prevention Act aroused a storm of controversy. Proponents argued that its tougher requirements would slow reckless borrowing and thereby limit the number of borrower defaults, lowering credit costs for all lenders and borrowers. Moreover, advocates believed the new code would alter the composition of household debt, encouraging consumers to rely more heavily upon housing-secured debt rather than credit-card borrowings and other nonresidential-based debt. Opponents, on the other hand, pointed out that most bankruptcy petitions were related to the incidence of serious family problems and that the new code would needlessly punish people when they are already down and out. The opposition predicted a rise in abandoned homes, debtor flight, plunging credit ratings, and more families living in poverty. Time will tell us more, hopefully, about the validity of these conflicting arguments.

---

### QUESTIONS TO HELP YOU STUDY

14. What is *Truth in Lending?* Describe the law's major provisions and explain why it was enacted in the first place.

15. What protections are offered to individual and family consumers under the *Fair Credit Billing Act? Consumer Leasing Act? Fair Credit Reporting Act? Fair Credit and Charge Card Disclosure Act? Financial Services Modernization Act?*

16. What are the principal purposes of the *Community Reinvestment Act? Equal Credit Opportunity Act? Fair Housing Act? Home Mortgage Disclosure Act?* Assess the benefits and costs of these laws.

17. What changes in consumer rights and required disclosure of information to the consumer occurred when the *Financial Institutions Reform, Recovery, and Enforcement Act* was passed? With passage of the *Truth in Savings Act? FDIC Improvement Act?*

18. Why have so many consumer *bankruptcies* occurred in recent years? How might these bankruptcies be prevented?

19. What are the principal provision of the *Bankruptcy Abuse Prevention and Consumer Protection Act?* What are the act's basic goals?

---

## Summary of the Chapter's Main Points

One of the most remarkable developments over the past century has been the awakening of the *consumer* as a leading borrower and lender of funds within the global financial system.

- *Households*—individuals and families—have become the principal sources of loanable funds in the money and capital markets in most years. They are also among the leading borrowing sectors in the financial system.

- Due to intense competition in the financial-services sector, new consumer-oriented services have appeared in profusion in recent years in an effort to attract and hold consumer accounts. Examples include NOWs, money market deposits, share accounts in money market mutual funds, universal life insurance policies, consumer cash management services, and home equity loans.

- While consumers are among the leading borrowing groups in the economy, overall their dollar holdings of financial assets far exceed their indebtedness, though their ratio of liabilities to financial asset holdings has risen in recent decades.

- Lenders to the household sector consider multiple factors in deciding whether or not to grant a loan, including the size and stability of a consumer's income, length and stability of residence, amount of installment debt outstanding, and any holdings of valuable assets (including stocks, bonds, and other assets of readily marketable value). Increasingly, *credit scoring* systems are being used to evaluate consumer loan requests, relying on computer processing and advanced statistical techniques to speed up and lower the cost of making consumer loan decisions.

- Important federal laws have been passed in the United States over the past four decades to accomplish two major objectives: (a) *disclose the terms* of loans and other financial services so the household customer can make an informed financial decision; and (b) *prevent discrimination* in gaining access to financial services (especially access to credit). The Truth in Lending, Fair Credit Billing, Fair Credit Reporting, and Truth in Savings Acts *promote greater disclosure* of the terms attached to loans, savings deposits, and other financial services, while the Equal Credit Opportunity Act and the Community Reinvestment Act focus mainly on *preventing discrimination* against consumers seeking access to financial services. Among the most recent laws passed are the Financial Services Modernization (Gramm-Leach-Bliley) Act and the Fair and Accurate Credit Transactions Act, which deal with protecting consumer *privacy* and stopping the rapid rise in *identity theft*.

- U.S. bankruptcy laws have been a center of controversy between consumers and lenders since the 1970s when a more liberal bankruptcy code was enacted and the numbers of household bankruptcies began to climb significantly. Fearing that debt relief rules for households might have become unbalanced in favor of the consumer, Congress passed the Bankruptcy Abuse Prevention and Consumer Protection Act of 2005 that raises the cost of applying for bankruptcy protection and demands that households seeking debt relief receive training in the hope of avoiding future financial problems.

## Key Terms Appearing in This Chapter

## Problems and Issues

1. Home equity loans to consumers are generally based on the *residual value* of a home (i.e., market value less the remaining balance on the outstanding home mortgage loan) and the fraction of that value (known as the *loan-to-value ratio*) that the lending institution is willing to lend. The customer's borrowing base is the product of these two entities. Calculate the customer's borrowing base in the situations described below:

| Appraised Value of Borrower's Home | Mortgage Loan Balance Outstanding | Lender's Required Loan-to-Value Ratio |
|---|---|---|
| a. $173,500 | $ 67,800 | 75% |
| b. $64,150 | $ 23,948 | 70% |
| c. $251,400 | $111,556 | 80% |
| d. $789,000 | $340,722 | 82% |

2. Indicate which consumer-oriented law or laws apply in each of the situations described below:

   a. Matthew Crey is discussing with a bank loan officer the terms on a loan he needs to buy a car for his family.

   b. Robert and Mary Nash believe they were discriminated against when their loan to purchase a new home was denied.

   c. Sally Ferrel was denied a loan because of an adverse report from her credit bureau, which she believes is in error.

   d. Herbert Coleman has just received his credit-card bill and finds several charges were made against his account that are not legitimate.

   e. Mary Eacher leased an automobile from a dealer for three years, but the lease was abruptly canceled even though Mary was making all required payments on time.

   f. First National Bank of Arden has just announced its latest CRA rating received from federal bank examiners.

   g. Earl and Susan Tolber believe they were denied a home improvement loan because their address is in a neighborhood where the local bank does not like to make such loans.

   h. Bill Gell decides to "opt out" of letting his bank and his insurance company share information about him with other businesses.

   i. Jean Shal has just been notified by her bank that it is going to reduce the interest rate on her certificate of deposit when it is renewed.

   j. John Saral is confused about the terms of a credit card and needs additional information from the card company.

   k. Bob and Rachel Hamm are unable to meet their monthly debt-service payments and are about to lose their home.

3. Construct a balance sheet and estimate the annual take-home income of the Williams family from the information presented on the next page:

| Checking account balance | $ 2,860 | Credit union deposit | $ 550 |
| Credit-card obligations | 7,400 | Bank loan | 13,800 |
| Department store debt | 1,875 | Estimated market value of | |
| U.S. savings bonds | 3,460 | Home | 81,000 |
| Unpaid life insurance premiums | 625 | Autos | 23,780 |
| Gas and oil credit-card balances | 289 | Furniture and appliances | 13,490 |
| Home mortgage | 68,500 | Cash surrender value | |
| Mutual fund shares | 15,430 | of life insurance | 3,770 |
| Pension plan assets | 47,995 | | |
| Annual take-home income— 0.28 of the family's total assets | | | |

Would you grant this family a loan of $10,000 to fund the purchase of new kitchen appliances and repairs to the family automobile? Why or why not?

## Web-Based Problems

1. Commercial banks are a principal provider of nonmortgage consumer credit. However, not all banks focus their business so exclusively on this type of lending, with some preferring to concentrate more on mortgage lending or business loans. This exercise asks you to select six of the largest U.S. banks and compare them with respect to the emphasis they place on consumer lending.

   a. Choose six commercial banks that differ by asset size. Go to the Federal Reserve Board's Web site, **ffiec.gov/nicpubweb/nicweb/nichome .aspx,** and click on the "Institution Search" tab. For each bank enter the name of the commercial bank (for example, Citicorp) and begin the search. (Note: if more than one bank has the same name, be sure to choose the parent company.) Choose the report "Consolidated Financial Statement for BHCs (FRY-97)." Page through this report to "Schedule HC.C–Loans and Lease Financing Receivables." For each bank, obtain the data for: (i) "Loans secured by real estate" (which are mortgages and home equity loans); (ii) "Commercial and industrial loans"; (iii) "Loans to individuals for household, family, and other personal expenditures" (which are consumer loans); and (iv) "Total" (at the bottom of the schedule, which is total loans and leases). Load these data into a spreadsheet for each of the six banks over each of the past five years.

   b. Compute the ratio of categories (i), (ii), and (iii) to (iv) for each bank for each year.

   c. Can you identify differences across banks in their reliance on consumer loans?

   d. Have consumer loans changed much in these portfolios over this time period? If so, what do you think might account for the change?

2. A significant recent development in the financing of consumer loans has been the growth in *securitization* of many forms of consumer debt. A major category

of consumer loans involves the purchase of new and used autos. Many lending institutions have found it profitable to be the originator of these loans, which they then package and sell as a single portfolio. The purpose of this exercise is to observe the growth in new and used auto loans carried by these firms. Use a spreadsheet to complete this exercise.

a. Visit the Federal Reserve's Web site at **federalreserve.gov/releases** and find the G.20 monthly release data on finance companies.

b. From there, identify the dollar value of new and used auto loans ultimately financed by finance companies over the past 20 years and plot these data. Hint: Look under "Auto Loans," "Amount Financed (dollars)." You will need to obtain several "releases" in order to put together a complete data set.

c. Now go to the U.S. Commerce Department's Bureau of Labor Statistics Web site at **bea.gov** and obtain data on the dollar value of all new autos sold in the United States in each of the past 20 years. There are various ways to navigate this informative Web site. One possibility is to click "National" on the Bureau's home page, then on successive pages click "Gross Domestic Product," "Interactive NIPA Tables," and "List of All NIPA Tables." From there, scroll down to Table 7.2.5B: "Motor Vehicle Output." From that table, look for the data regarding final sales of domestic product, personal consumption expenditures, and new motor vehicles.

d. Form the ratio of new car loans financed by finance companies to the dollar value of all new cars sold and plot this ratio. What do you observe?

3. Reliance on credit scoring systems to assess the creditworthiness of a loan applicant has become a routine practice among lending institutions. Use the Web sites **fico.com** and **freddiemac.com** to answer the questions below:

a. How do lending institutions benefit by using credit scoring systems?

b. How do consumers benefit from having their credit score easily available to lenders?

c. How might consumers be adversely affected by the credit scoring system?

d. Are you able to determine your own credit score?

e. Based on your current credit score, would you qualify for receiving a home mortgage loan? Explain.

f. What could you do to raise your credit score?

## Selected References to Explore

1. Akers, Douglas; Jay Golter; Brian Lamm; and Martha Solt. "Overview of Recent Developments in the Credit Card Industry," *FDIC Banking Review,* Vol. 13, No. 3 (2005), pp. 23–35.

2. Bauer, Paul W. "What You Should Know about Identity Theft," *Economic Commentary,* Federal Reserve Bank of Cleveland, September 15, 2002, pp. 1–3.

www.mhhe.com.rose10e

3. Borzekowski, Ron; Elizabeth K. Kiser; and Shaista Ahmed. "Consumers' Use of Debit Cards: Patterns, Preferences, and Price Response," *Finance and Economics Discussion Series No. 2006-16,* Z.11, Board of Governors of the Federal Reserve System, 2006.

4. Borzekowski, Ron, and Elizabeth K. Kiser. "The Choice at the Checkout: Quantifying Demand across Payment Instruments," *Finance and Economics Discussion Series No. 2006-17,* Z.11, Board of Governors of the Federal Reserve System, 2006.

5. Bucks, Brian K.; Arthur B. Kennickell; and Kevin B. Moore. "Recent Changes in U.S. Family Finances: Evidence from the 2001 and 2004 Survey of Consumer Finances," *Federal Reserve Bulletin,* 2006, pp. A1–A38.

6. Edmiston, Kelly D. "A New Perspective on Rising Nonbusiness Bankruptcy Filing Rates: Analyzing the Regional Factors," *Economic Review,* Federal Reserve Bank of Kansas City, Second Quarter 2006, pp. 55–83.

7. Gerdes, Geoffrey R.; Jack K. Walton; May X. Liu; and Darrel W. Parke. "Trends in the Use of Payments Instruments in the United States," *Federal Reserve Bulletin,* Spring 2005, pp. 180–201.

8. Hunt, Robert M. "A Century of Credit Reporting in America," Working Paper 05-13, Federal Reserve Bank of Philadelphia, June 2005.

9. Kliesen, Kevin L. "Do We Have a Saving Crisis?" *The Regional Economist,* Federal Reserve Bank of St. Louis, July 2005, pp. 4–9.

10. Mester, Loretta J. "What's the Point of Credit Scoring?" *Business Review,* Federal Reserve Bank of Philadelphia, September/October 1997, pp. 3–16.

11. Munnell, A., L.Browne, J. McEneaney, and G. Tootell. "Mortgage Lending in Boston: Interpreting HMDA Data," *American Economic Review,* Vol. 86 (March 1996), pp. 25–53.

12. Rose, Peter S. "The Performance of Outstanding CRA-Rated Banks," *Bankers Magazine,* September-October 1994, pp. 53–59.

13. Weinberg, John A. "Borrowing by U.S. Households," *Economic Quarterly,* Federal Reserve Bank of Richmond, Vol. 92, No.3 (Summer 2006), pp. 177–194.

www.mhhe.com.rose10e

# Chapter 22

# The Residential Mortgage Market

## Learning Objectives

### in This Chapter

- You will discover how the largest of all domestic financial markets in the United States—the *residential mortgage market*—functions in order to supply credit to build and buy homes, apartments, and other dwellings for individuals and families.

- You will come to understand the problems faced by lenders of residential mortgage money in designing new loan contracts that will protect them against inflation and other risks.

- You will discover what important jobs are performed by federal government agencies or by government-sponsored mortgage firms, such as Fannie Mae (FNMA) and Ginnie Mae (GNMA), in supporting the development of the market for home mortgage loans.

## What's in This Chapter?
## Key Topics Outline

Trends in Home Prices and Loan Terms

The Structure of the Mortgage Loan Market

Mortgage Lending Institutions and Their Preferred Market Segments

Government Reshapes the Mortgage Market: Lending, Guaranteeing, Making Markets

Mortgage-Linked Securities and Prepayment Risk

Innovations in Mortgage Instruments

Refinancing Existing Loans and Home Equity Borrowing

## 22.1 Introduction to the Residential Mortgage Market

One of the most important goals for many families is to own their own home. Besides the psychic benefits of privacy and a feeling of belonging to the local community, home ownership confers important financial and economic benefits on those families and individuals able and willing to make the investment. The market value of single-family residences has risen substantially faster than the rate of inflation over the long run, offering individuals and families of even modest means one of the few available hedges against inflation. Moreover, the interest cost on home mortgages is tax deductible in the United States, reducing significantly the *after-tax* interest rate levied on residential mortgage loans.

Unfortunately for families seeking home ownership, the residential mortgage market is often treacherous, swinging quickly from low interest rates and ample credit to high and rising rates with little credit available. In this volatile market, home ownership may become an impossible dream for many families, though a greater proportion of U.S. households than ever before own their own homes today. The wide swings characteristic of the residential mortgage market also send reverberations throughout the economy. In fact, today the housing market appears to be playing a powerful *counter-cyclical* role, providing funds to households when they refinance their homes and, thereby, boosting consumption spending and preventing downturns in the economy from becoming deeper than they otherwise might be.

## 22.2 Recent Trends in New Home Prices and the Terms of Mortgage Loans

**conventional home mortgage loan**

We can get a glimpse of the tremendous pressures buffeting the market for residential mortgages today by looking at recent trends in the prices of new homes and the cost of financing them. Exhibit 22.1 provides recent data on the average terms quoted on a **conventional home mortgage loan** in the United States. A conventional mortgage loan is *not* guaranteed by the government but is purely a private

| EXHIBIT 22.1 | Prices and Yields of Conventional Home Mortgage Loans | | | | |
|---|---|---|---|---|---|
| **Item** | **1974** | **1980** | **1990** | **2000** | **2006\*** |
| Primary market: Conventional mortgages on new homes | | | | | |
| Purchase price ($000) | $40.10 | $83.50 | $153.20 | $234.50 | $346.00 |
| Amount of loan ($000) | 29.80 | 59.30 | 112.40 | 177.00 | 253.20 |
| Loan/price ratio (percent) | 74.30 | 73.30 | 74.50 | 77.40 | 75.50 |
| Maturity (years) | 26.30 | 28.20 | 27.30 | 29.20 | 29.20 |
| Fees and charges ("points") | 1.30% | 2.10% | 1.93% | 0.70% | 0.67% |
| Contract interest rate (percent per year) | 8.71 | 12.25 | 9.68 | 7.41 | 6.71 |
| Yield on FHA mortgages (percent per year) | 9.22 | 13.95 | 10.17 | 7.74 | NA |

\*Figures for 2006 are averages for February.
Sources: Board of Governors of the Federal Reserve System, *Federal Reserve Bulletin* and *Statistical Supplement to the Federal Reserve Bulletin,* Table 1.53, various issues.

The dream of home ownership has been satisfied for more people today than at any other time in American history. Many people think this is a good trend, both psychologically and financially, giving families an asset that is likely to appreciate in value and providing a borrowing base for raising funds in order to start a new business, send children to college, etc.

However, homes can be costly to maintain and difficult to sell (illiquid). Home ownership can also make it hard for a family to adequately diversify its assets, because a home often represents an individual family's single largest investment. Moreover, homes fluctuate in value with the economy and with changes in their age and condition. Many families having low or moderate income have literally "sunk" most of their wealth in a single asset whose value may plummet due to factors beyond their control.

In the long run, however, home prices have tended to stay up with or even outstrip inflation. At times housing values have not performed quite as well as the stock market, even though interest payments on home mortgage debt and property taxes can help to reduce a family's taxable income. However, housing values appear to be somewhat more stable than stock prices (often moving in the opposite direction), helping a family to diversify its investment returns and lower its overall risk exposure.

**Key URLs:**
To examine recent data on the changing character of the mortgage market see, for example, HSH Associates Statistical Releases at **hsh.com** and Wholesale Access at **wholesaleaccess.com**

contract between the home buyer and the lending institution. In this case, the lender of funds bears the risk the home buyer will default on principal or interest payments associated with a mortgage loan, forcing foreclosure and resale of the home (although today most conventional loans are insured by private insurance companies). In contrast, mortgage loans issued through the Federal Housing Administration (FHA) or Veterans Administration (VA) are partially guaranteed as to principal and interest by the federal government and are primarily used to finance low and moderately priced housing.

As shown in Exhibit 22.1, the average purchase price of a conventional single-family residence in the United States has more than doubled over the past two decades. With housing prices and the demand for new homes fairly strong, sellers and lending institutions have worked to accommodate more borrowers by increasing the average percentage of a new home's purchase price they are willing to lend, to more than 75 percent in recent years. We note from Exhibit 22.1 that mortgage lenders are also willing to extend credit for longer periods. The average maturity of conventional home mortgage loans climbed above 29 years as the new century began to unfold. The average contract interest rate on conventional mortgage loans dipped to about 6.7 percent as the new century opened—the lowest in decades. These relatively low home-loan interest rates helped to boost U.S. home ownership so that about two-thirds of American households own their own dwelling.

Unfortunately, offsetting the relatively low home-mortgage loan rates of recent years have been high home prices. These high prices have shut out a large number of families from fulfilling a long-sought-after American dream—owning your own home. Several factors account for this dramatic long-term escalation in the price of home ownership. Certainly, inflation has played a key role in driving up building costs, and this increase has been passed on to the consumer. On the demand side, a substantial rise in the number of new family formations has occurred in recent years. Added to this has been a rapid increase in individuals living alone and in single-parent households. Therefore, although the U.S. birth rate has dropped to some of the lowest levels in history, the increase in new families and in single-adult households dramatically increased the demand for housing,

**EXHIBIT 22.2**

**Total Mortgage Debt Outstanding in the United States at Year-End ($ billions)**

| Year | Amount |
| --- | --- |
| 1950 | $ 72.8 |
| 1960 | 206.8 |
| 1970 | 451.7 |
| 1980 | 1,451.8 |
| 1990 | 3,807.3 |
| 2000 | 6,885.3 |
| 2006* | 12,329.3 |

*Figures through the first quarter of 2006.
Sources: Board of Governors of the Federal Reserve System, *Annual Statistical Digest,* 1971–1975, and *Federal Reserve Bulletin,* selected issues.

especially for low- and medium-priced homes. In many markets real home prices have risen faster than homeowner incomes, discouraging some potential home buyers.

## 22.3 The Structure of the Mortgage Market

### Volume of Mortgage Loans

**Key URL:**
A nice summary of unfolding trends in the home mortgage industry is available through the Web site of the Mortgage Bankers Association of America at **mbaa.org**

Mortgages are among the most important securities in the financial system. The total of all mortgages outstanding in the United States is now more than $12 trillion (see Exhibit 22.2), which makes the mortgage market the largest primary security market inside the United States.

### Residential versus Nonresidential Mortgage Loans

**residential mortgages**

**nonresidential mortgages**

The mortgage market can be divided into two major segments: (1) **residential mortgages,** which encompass all loans secured by single-family homes and other dwelling units, and (2) **nonresidential mortgages,** which include loans secured by business and farm properties. Which of these two sectors is more important? As Exhibit 22.3 shows, loans to finance the building and purchase of homes, apartments, and other residential units dominate the U.S. mortgage market, accounting for about

**EXHIBIT 22.3** **Mortgage Loans Outstanding, 2006* ($ Billions)**

| Type of Property | Amount | Percent of Total |
| --- | --- | --- |
| Residential properties (one-to four-family and multifamily structures)† | $10,116.0 | 82.3% |
| Nonresidential properties (commercial and farm) | 2,183.3 | 17.7 |
| All properties | $12,329.3 | 100.0% |

*Figures are as of the first quarter of 2006.
† Note that not all residential loans go to just households but may include businesses and other units in the economy.
Source: Board of Governors of the Federal Reserve System, *Federal Reserve Bulletin,* selected issues.

four-fifths of all mortgage loans outstanding. Mortgages on commercial and farm properties accounted for less than one-fifth of all mortgages issued. Because residential mortgages dominate the market, it should not be surprising that households are the leading mortgage borrowers, accounting for about four-fifths of outstanding mortgage debt. The next largest group of mortgage borrowers—business firms—runs a distant second.

---

### QUESTIONS TO HELP YOU STUDY

1. What has happened in recent years to new home prices? To interest rates and other terms on conventional home mortgage loans? What are the *causes* of these trends?

2. Residential mortgages may be classified in several different ways. Describe the structure of the mortgage market as it relates to each of the following dimensions:

   Type of mortgage contract—conventional versus government guaranteed.

   Residential versus nonresidential mortgages.

   Type of mortgage borrower.

3. What are the advantages and disadvantages of home ownership for the consumer?

4. How does the behavior of the home mortgage market reveal the problems that home buyers and mortgage lenders face as they operate in this huge financial marketplace?

---

## 22.4 Mortgage-Lending Institutions

In the years before World War II, mortgages were one of the most widely held securities in the financial system, comparable to stock in the great diversity of investors who chose to add these securities to their portfolios. Individuals were then the dominant mortgage investors, with financial institutions in second place. However, the rapid growth of commercial and savings banks, insurance companies, government agencies, and mortgage pools (where groups of loans are packaged together) as major mortgage lenders during the past half century has forced individual investors into the background.

Exhibit 22.4 shows the total amounts of mortgage loans held by various lender groups in 2006. Savings and loan associations, once the principal private mortgage-lending institution in the United States, have now dropped to less than 10 percent of all mortgage loans outstanding. Commercial banks now rank number one among private lending institutions, holding nearly one-quarter of all mortgage credit outstanding. In general, the relative share of the mortgage market accounted for by traditional private mortgage-lending institutions, such as savings and loans and insurance companies, has declined, while banks, pension funds, finance companies, and government agencies have accounted for a growing share of outstanding loans. Noteworthy in this regard has been the rapidly expanding role of *mortgage pools:* lender-packaged groups of high-quality residential mortgages insured or guaranteed by a government agency and in which investors hold shares, entitling them to a portion of any interest and principal payments generated by the pool. We will have more to say about mortgage pools

**Key URL:**
It is interesting to explore the nature and structure of the mortgage market in other countries. For example, for a look at the Canadian mortgage market, see **mortgagesincanada .com/residential**

| EXHIBIT 22.4 | Principal Lenders in the U.S. Mortgage Market, 2006* | |
|---|---|---|
| Lender Group | Volume of Mortgage Loans Held by Lender ($ Billions) | Percent of Total |
| Savings institutions (savings and loan associations and savings banks) | $ 1,192.3 | 9.7% |
| Commercial banks | 3,024.7 | 24.5 |
| Life insurance companies | 287.5 | 2.3 |
| Individuals and other private lenders | 1,243.4 | 10.1 |
| Mortgage pools or trusts: | 6,031.5 | 48.9 |
| Government National Mortgage Association | 403.4 | |
| Federal Home Loan Mortgage Corp. | 1,375.1 | |
| Federal National Mortgage Association | 1,972.8 | |
| Private mortgage conduits (including securitized loans) | 2,280.2 | |
| Federal and related agencies: | 549.8 | 4.5 |
| Government National Mortgage Association | 0.3 | |
| Federal Home Loan Mortgage Corporation | 62.9 | |
| Federal National Mortgage Association | 249.0 | |
| Farmers Home Administration | 73.6 | |
| Federal Land Banks | 55.2 | |
| Federal Housing and Veterans Administration | 4.6 | |
| Other agencies | 104.2 | |
| | $12,329.3 | 100.0% |

*2006 figures are for the first quarter of the year.
Note: Columns may not add to totals due to rounding.
Source: Board of Governors of the Federal Reserve System, *Federal Reserve Bulletin,* selected issues.

later in this chapter when we discuss the prominent role of the federal government in the mortgage market.

A mortgage loan is one of the most difficult of all financial instruments for which to establish a true value. Most mortgages generate multiple cash flow streams—for example: (1) the payment of origination and commitment fees when a mortgage loan is first applied for; (2) the promise of a stream of periodic loan repayments plus interest; (3) the added compensation to a lender for the risk that a mortgage borrower will pay off his or her loan early or perhaps, ultimately, not at all; (4) the servicing income associated with collecting and recording amounts owed and monitoring compliance with the terms of a loan; and (5) the net returns or fees from securitization that arise when a mortgage loan is packaged with other mortgage loans into a pool and income-generating securities are issued as claims against that pool of loans.

Different financial institutions operating in the mortgage market pursue one or more of the foregoing income sources. For example, many locally oriented banks retain new mortgage loans in their asset portfolios and receive the resulting flow of interest and principal payments, while other mortgage lenders may quickly sell any loans they make and instead pursue loan servicing, securitization, and other fee-generating services because of the greater geographic diversification and lower capital requirements involved with these supporting services. Each of these possible cash flow sources

**Key URLs:**
Information for buyers and sellers in the home mortgage market is available through such sites as **buyersresource.com; getsmart.com;** and **houses4sale-online .com**

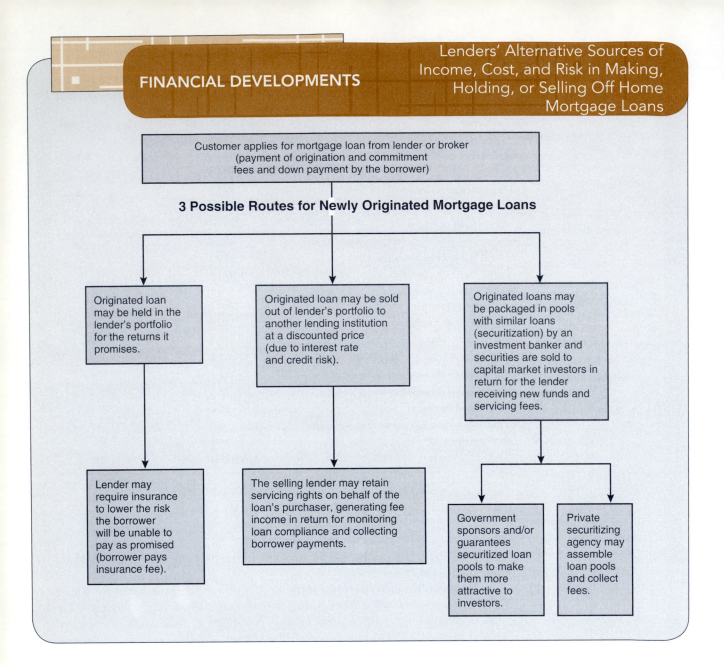

Customer applies for mortgage loan from lender or broker (payment of origination and commitment fees and down payment by the borrower)

**3 Possible Routes for Newly Originated Mortgage Loans**

Originated loan may be held in the lender's portfolio for the returns it promises.

Originated loan may be sold out of lender's portfolio to another lending institution at a discounted price (due to interest rate and credit risk).

Originated loans may be packaged in pools with similar loans (securitization) by an investment banker and securities are sold to capital market investors in return for the lender receiving new funds and servicing fees.

Lender may require insurance to lower the risk the borrower will be unable to pay as promised (borrower pays insurance fee).

The selling lender may retain servicing rights on behalf of the loan's purchaser, generating fee income in return for monitoring loan compliance and collecting borrower payments.

Government sponsors and/or guarantees securitized loan pools to make them more attractive to investors.

Private securitizing agency may assemble loan pools and collect fees.

from a mortgage loan has its own financial advantages and disadvantages in terms of sensitivity to default, interest rate, and liquidity risk, and possible changes in the size of cash flow expected to be received.

## 22.5 The Roles Played by Leading Financial Institutions in the Mortgage Market

Mortgage lenders tend to specialize in the types of loans they grant, and some are far more important to the residential market than to commercial mortgage lending. Moreover, even within the residential lending field, different institutional lenders will favor one type of mortgage (e.g., conventional versus government guaranteed) over another and also desire a certain range of maturities. Some lenders are organized to deal with home mortgage borrowers one at a time, while others may prefer to acquire large packages of mortgages associated with major residential building projects.

## Savings and Loan Associations

*Savings and loan associations (S&Ls)* are predominantly *local* lenders, making the majority of their mortgage loans in the communities where their offices are located. Moreover, S&Ls often service the mortgage loans they make rather than turning that task over to a mortgage bank or trust company. Servicing a mortgage involves maintaining ownership and financial records on the mortgaged property, receiving installment payments from the borrower, checking to ensure the mortgaged property's value is maintained, and in the event of borrower default, foreclosing on the property to collect any unpaid balance.

Historically, S&Ls have preferred single-family home mortgages, lending to help families build their homes and encouraging individuals to save for the future. However, savings associations have diversified their portfolios in recent years to include many new kinds of mortgage-related assets, such as mobile home loans; mortgage credit for apartments and other multifamily housing units; and securities backed by pools of mortgage loans. S&Ls' attempts to diversify and increase their capital in order to lower their risk of failure have brought about a substantial decline in S&Ls' share of the whole mortgage market in recent years. Many savings associations have been purchased by bank holding companies and converted into banks with few mortgage loans or into mortgage companies that make only short-term loans in this market.

## Commercial Banks

In contrast to savings and loans, *commercial banks* have expanded their market share of nearly every type of mortgage loan. Overall, they now rank first as lenders for the purchase of homes, condominiums, and apartments and in the commercial mortgage field. A large share of bank mortgage credit, however, goes for shorter-term loans to finance the *construction* of new commercial and residential projects, with other lenders usually taking on the long-term mortgage loans from these projects. Commercial banks have also shown a strong interest in financing upscale homes purchased by higher-income families in recent years—homes that command significantly higher prices and larger down payments. Finally, banks today are among the strongest supporters of the mortgage-backed securities market, devoting half or more of all their security holdings to these financial instruments which are backed by pools of mortgage loans.

## Life Insurance Companies

*Life insurance companies* make substantial investments in commercial as well as residential mortgage properties. These companies search national and international markets for attractive mortgage investments instead of focusing only on local areas. They often prefer to purchase residential mortgages in large blocks rather than one at a time.

In the past, insurers preferred government-guaranteed home mortgages. In recent years, however, the higher yields available on conventional mortgages have caused some shift of emphasis toward these more risky home loans. Despite the greater flexibility of conventional single-family home mortgages, however, life insurers have been gradually reducing their holdings of single-family home mortgages and emphasizing, instead, commercial and apartment mortgages that often carry "equity kickers", permitting the lending institution to receive a portion of project earnings as well as a guaranteed interest return.

## Savings Banks

Another lender of importance in the residential mortgage market is the *savings bank,* which attracts the public's savings deposits and invests in both government-guaranteed and conventional mortgage loans. Although single-family homes represent the bulk of savings bank mortgage loans, their loans supporting multifamily units (including large apartment projects) have grown in recent years. Like life insurance companies, savings banks often prefer to acquire residential mortgages in large blocks, such as a whole subdivision, rather than loan by loan. Like savings and loan associations, savings banks have tended to lose mortgage market share to other private and governmental lenders.

## Mortgage Bankers

*Mortgage banking houses* act as a channel through which builders or contractors can raise working capital to hire construction workers and purchase materials. In providing this service, mortgage bankers take on portfolios of mortgages from property developers, using mainly bank credit to carry their inventories of mortgages. Within a relatively short time span, these mortgages are placed with long-term institutional investors. Mortgage bankers supply important services to *both* institutional investors and property developers. The developers receive a commitment for permanent financing, which allows them to proceed with planned real estate projects. Institutional investors, especially life insurance companies and savings banks, receive mortgages appropriately packaged to match the timing of their cash flows and risk-return preferences. The mortgage banker often secures servicing (loan management and monitoring) fees from institutional investors who purchase the mortgages he or she packages and sells.

## 22.6  Government Activity in the Mortgage Market

### The Impact of the Great Depression on Government Involvement in the Mortgage Market

**Key URL:**
FHA is a division of the Department of Health and Human Services (HUD) at **hud.gov**

Any attempt to understand how the mortgage market operates today must begin with the Great Depression of the 1930s and the enormous impact that economic calamity had on the market for property loans. The Great Depression generated massive unemployment; for example, an estimated one-quarter of the U.S. civilian labor force was thrown out of work between 1929 and 1933. Few new mortgage loans were made during this period, and thousands of existing mortgages were foreclosed upon, forcing families to leave their homes. With so many forced sales, property values declined precipitously, endangering the financial solvency of thousands of mortgage lenders. The federal government elected to tackle the mortgage market's problems by moving in several directions at once.

## Launching the Federal Home Loan Bank System

**Federal Home Loan Bank (FHLB) System**

In 1932 the first of the U.S. government agencies aimed at improving the availability of mortgage credit to individuals and families—the **Federal Home Loan Bank (FHLB) System**—was created. The FHLB was charged with supervising the activities of savings and loan associations and savings banks and extending loans to these depository institutions, which at the time were threatened with collapse due to heavy withdrawals by panicky depositors. These loans helped to lower the liquidity risk associated with home mortgage lending, spurring private lending institutions to grant more affordable home loans. Prior to the creation of the FHLB System, most home mortgages carried relatively short maturities—3 to 10 years—in contrast to the long-term (15- to 30-year) home loans most common today. Often home loans during the 1930s carried a large balloon payment at the end or required payment of a fee to further extend the loans. Most home buyers could not afford the high payments and fees these short-term, nonamortizable mortgages required.

The FHLB System is organized somewhat like the Federal Reserve System today, with 12 regional home loan banks supervised by the Federal Housing Finance Board. The 12 FHL banks are owned by their members, which today include more than 8,000 commercial and savings banks, savings and loans, credit unions, and insurance companies. These member institutions are eligible to borrow at the FHL bank in their region. Advances to member institutions may be made for terms as short as 24 hours out to 20 years or more. So rapid has been the expansion of FHLB loans to mortgage lenders recently that some observers fear for the soundness of some of the FHL banks.

## Setting Up the Federal Housing Administration (FHA) and the Veterans Administration (VA)

**Federal Housing Administration (FHA)**

In 1934 the National Housing Act was passed, setting up a system of federal insurance for qualified home buyers. The **Federal Housing Administration (FHA)** was authorized to guarantee repayment of acceptable home loans up to a ceiling amount set by the FHA, encouraging lenders to lend a greater percentage of a home's market value, charge lower interest rates, and accept longer-term mortgages. Insurance premiums to fund FHA loan guarantees are deposited in a mutual insurance fund invested in U.S. Treasury securities, standing ready to compensate lenders when loan defaults occur. The FHA's tight insurance rules (including required appraisals and borrowers' credit reports) have encouraged the development of standardized, highly marketable home mortgages.

**Veterans Administration (VA)**

**Key URL:**
The VA home loan insurance program is discussed on the Veterans Administration's Web site: **va.gov**

Shortly before the end of World War II, the **Veterans Administration (VA)** was created with passage of the Servicemen's Readjustment Act (1944). The VA was designed to aid military personnel returning to civilian life find adequate housing for themselves and their families. Like the FHA, the VA offered to insure residential mortgages and helped to lower both loan rates and down payments required on new homes. Thanks to increasing federal standardization of loan procedures and relatively low loan default rates only a small percentage (less than 10 percent) of newly made home mortgages typically carry FHA-VA guarantees today. Private institutions have come to dominate the mortgage lending/insurance process.

### The Creation of Fannie Mae—A Government-Sponsored Enterprise (GSE)

**Federal National Mortgage Association (FNMA)**

The FHA-VA insurance program was an almost instant success and home mortgage lending grew rapidly following its inception. Federal government efforts to create a resale (secondary) market for residential loans took a little longer, however. In 1938, Fannie Mae—the **Federal National Mortgage Association (FNMA)**—was chartered by the U.S. government for the purpose of buying and selling FHA-guaranteed mortgages in the secondary market. In 1948, FNMA was authorized to trade VA-guaranteed mortgages as well, thus encouraging private lenders to make both FHA- and VA-guaranteed loans.

**Government-sponsored enterprise (GSE)**

Beginning in 1968, Fannie Mae was converted to a privately owned mortgage company, now more widely known as a **government-sponsored enterprise (GSE)** instead of a government-owned agency. FNMA's rapidly growing activities added to government spending and Congress decided to remove it from the federal budget. Then Fannie's stock and debt securities could be traded and listed on public exchanges. FNMA began to issue commitments to purchase specific dollar amounts of conventional and insured mortgages at predetermined yields, significantly improving the resale potential of most residential mortgages.

**Key URL:**
To learn more about Fannie Mae's mortgage market activities, see **fanniemae.com**

Fannie Mae raises money for its mortgage market ventures primarily by selling short-term notes and longer-term debentures. In addition, in 1981 FNMA began to issue and guarantee securities backed by conventional mortgage loans purchased from private lenders. Today the majority of Fannie's mortgage-related assets are actually securities backed by various kinds of home mortgages. These FNMA mortgage-backed securities are marketed by lenders that deal directly with FNMA or through security dealers.[1] Most recently Fannie Mae has branched out to purchase mortgage loans on manufactured housing (principally, mobile homes) and to buy subprime mortgages to strengthen this troubled sector of the housing market.

FNMA holds some of the home mortgages it purchases in its own portfolio and *securitizes* the remainder, bundling these loans into pools of similar quality and maturity. Fannie sells claims (securities) against the pooled loans as a way to raise new capital and purchase still more mortgage-related instruments. It guarantees these mortgage-backed securities against default. Today well over half of U.S. single-family home loans have been placed in pools supporting the issuance of mortgage-backed securities.

### The Creation of Ginnie Mae (GNMA)

**Government National Mortgage Association (GNMA)**

When Fannie Mae was converted into a private corporation in 1968, Congress created a new government agency set up within the Department of Housing and Urban Development (HUD)—the **Government National Mortgage Association (GNMA),** or Ginnie Mae. Much of Fannie Mae's portfolio of government-insured mortgages were transferred to GNMA as were any home loan programs requiring government subsidies. In one portion of its current program, Ginnie Mae purchases "assistance"

---

[1]Fannie Mae is the world's largest mortgage bank and for a long time had a virtual monopoly in secondary market trading activities. Early in the 1970s, however, the Mortgage Guarantee Insurance Corporation (MGIC) was organized by a private group in Milwaukee, Wisconsin. Known as Maggie Mae, this corporation pledged to insure conventional home mortgage loans carrying down payments as low as 5 percent. Today, mortgage insurance, provided by a variety of private companies, is often required by lending institutions when the borrower makes a relatively small down payment on the purchase price of a home.

mortgages to finance housing for low-income families and then sells these mortgages to FNMA or to private investors.

### GNMA Mortgage-Backed Securities
Particularly important for the development of the secondary mortgage market has been GNMA's **mortgage-backed securities** program. Backed by the full faith and credit of the U.S. government, Ginnie Mae agrees to *guarantee* principal and interest payments on securities issued by private mortgage institutions if those securities are backed by pools of government-guaranteed mortgages. These so-called **pass-throughs** have been popular with institutional lenders and even individuals as safe, readily marketable securities with attractive rates of return. Mortgage lenders can raise cash to make new loans by selling the pass-throughs against mortgages they place in a mortgage pool.

**mortgage-backed securities**

**pass-throughs**

## The Federal Home Loan Mortgage Corporation—Another Government-Sponsored Enterprise (GSE)

In 1970, the Emergency Home Finance Act gave birth to the **Federal Home Loan Mortgage Corporation (FHLMC),** a government agency known as Freddie Mac. At first FHLMC was set up to purchase home loans originated by thrift institutions. Ultimately, however, in 1989 Freddie gave up its government agency status and became another government-sponsored enterprise (GSE) with publicly traded stock. Freddie combines the mortgages it buys into pools and issues securities against them. Securities issued by FHLMC are guaranteed by that agency and have been popular with investors, particularly savings associations and commercial banks. The creation of Freddie Mac reflected a desire by the federal government to develop a stronger secondary market for *conventional* home mortgages, which it has purchased in huge quantities.

**Federal Home Loan Mortgage Corporation (FHLMC)**

**Key URL:**
Ginnie Mae works to promote affordable housing as revealed in its Web site at
**ginniemae.gov**

### FHLMC Mortgage-Backed Securities
To raise funds to support loan purchases, Freddie Mac sells mortgage participation certificates (PCs) and guaranteed mortgage certificates (GMCs). PCs represent an ownership interest in a pool of conventional mortgages bought and sold by Freddie Mac. FHLMC guarantees the investor's monthly interest and principal payments passed through from the mortgage pool. Guaranteed mortgage certificates (GMCs) are also claims against a pool of mortgages, but they are similar to corporate bonds in that interest is paid semiannually to investors.

**Key URL:**
To learn more about Freddie Mac, see **freddiemac.com**

### Freddie and Fannie Face New Problems
Most recently, both Fannie Mae and Freddie Mac have come under sharp criticism and threats from Congress to remove their long-standing special connection to the U.S. government. Fannie and Freddie's ties to the government are reflected in their (as yet, untapped) lines of credit with the U.S. Treasury Department. Investors in the financial markets appear to interpret this close tie-in between Fannie, Freddie, and the U.S. government as a result of the "too-big-to-fail" character of these mortgage industry giants.

If the U.S. government *has* effectively signaled to the financial marketplace that Fannie and Freddie will not be allowed to fail, this action will tend to raise their credit rating, lower their borrowing cost (by about 30 to 40 basis points), and benefit their stockholders because the perceived government tie grants them a competitive advantage over other mortgage-lending institutions. There probably is some benefit as well to borrowers whose mortgages Fannie and Freddie trade in the form of cheaper mortgage credit, though most experts seem to agree that the *primary* beneficiary of Fannie and Freddie's activities are their stockholders.

Recent objections to Fannie and Freddie's government-related privileges have been spurred on by the rapid growth of both agencies, which have aggressively expanded their market shares of both home mortgage loans and mortgage-backed securities.

Bringing this controversy even closer to the boiling point, these government-sponsored enterprises appeared to be facing higher market risk as the new century began and mortgage interest rates approached record lows. Tens of thousands of home owners refinanced their mortgages to take advantage of the exceptionally low interest rates, reducing the expected return on Fannie and Freddie's asset portfolios and creating a bigger mismatch between the maturities of their assets and liabilities. Recent events appear to have made it more likely that Fannie and Freddie will be more closely regulated in the future, probably either by their principal federal regulator—the Office of Federal Housing Enterprise Oversight (OFHEO)—or perhaps by a newly created regulatory agency. Recently OFHEO and Fannie Mae reached an agreement under which Fannie will increase its capital cushion and carry out a "reaccounting" of its holdings of derivative securities in order to promote greater safety and slow the overall growth of GSEs.

### Collateralized Mortgage Obligations (CMOs) and Real Estate Mortgage Investment Conduits (REMICs)

**collateralized mortgage obligation (CMO)**

Another recent innovation in fund-raising by FHLMC is the **collateralized mortgage obligation (CMO)**—a bond whose value is derived from a pool of mortgages packaged together to back (collateralize) the bond. CMOs differ from other mortgage-backed securities in that they are issued in several different maturity classes (*tranches*) based on a projected schedule for repaying the mortgage loans in back of each CMO. A similar instrument that also partitions the cash flow from a pool of mortgages or mortgage-backed securities into maturity classes is called a **real estate mortgage investment conduit (REMIC).**

**real estate mortgage investment conduit (REMIC)**

**prepayment risk**

CMOs and REMICs offer investors a range of different maturities from long term to short term. They overcome at least some of the cash flow uncertainty investors face when buying home mortgages themselves because a home owner may pay off his or her loan early—known as **prepayment risk**—resulting in a lower rate of return for the investor.[2] More recently, some mortgage-backed securities have been issued as "strips," in which the investor can receive either principal payments (POs) or interest payments (IOs) from a pool of home mortgages, depending on the individual investor's preferences for maturity and risk. Strips make it easier for an investor to reduce interest rate risk using portfolio immunization because their maturity and duration are the same. During the 1990s, CMO trusts began to appear, offering even small investors a share in pools of collateralized mortgage obligations. Unfortunately for enthusiastic investors the CMO market turned down sharply in 2006 and 2007, presenting many CMO buyers with serious losses as the default rate on risky, subprime home mortgage loans soared.

### Impact of Securitized Mortgages

**securitized mortgages**

The development of various types of **securitized mortgages**—debt securities backed by pools of outstanding mortgage loans—by Ginnie Mae, Fannie Mae, and other lending institutions have made mortgage securities more competitive with government securities and corporate stocks and bonds, allowing many mortgage lenders to invade national and international capital

---

[2]For an extended discussion of prepayment risk and the use of portfolio immunization to reduce interest rate risk, see Chapters 7 and 8.

markets for funds. The mortgage-backed securities market has expanded tremendously, rising in volume from less than $25 billion in 1981 to more than $4 trillion as the new century opened. Foreign investors by the thousands have become active in providing new capital to domestic mortgage markets, for example. They have also made it much easier to get old, low-yielding mortgages off lenders' books in order to make room for higher-yielding investments.

On the negative side, however, these new financial instruments have increased the sensitivity of mortgage interest rates to national and international market conditions. Home mortgage rates appear to be more volatile, on average, than in the past. The residential mortgage market has broadened geographically, but at the price of a somewhat less predictable credit market environment, as illustrated by the sharp decline in residential mortgage lending and market values in 2006 and 2007.

**Key URLs:**
Further information on mortgage-backed securities and other collateralized debt obligations (CDOs) is available from such sites as Speculative Bubble at **speculativebubble.com;** Rebuz.com at **rebuz.com;** and investopedia at **investopedia.com/ terms/c/cdo.asp.**

---

### QUESTIONS TO HELP YOU STUDY

5. List the principal *mortgage lending institutions* in the United States. Which is most important? In what particular areas of the market?

6. Identify the following federal agencies and describe their roles or functions: FHA, VA, FHLB, FNMA, GNMA, and FHLMC.

7. How has the federal government's intervention over the past several decades changed the structure and operation of the home mortgage market? For what reason has all of this been done?

---

## 22.7 Innovations in Mortgage Instruments

### Fixed-Rate Home Mortgages—The Oldest Form of Home Loan

Repeatedly in recent years, interest rates have climbed upward, only to fall back during recessions or when inflation subsided, and then move upward again. Each upward movement in market interest rates forced mortgage lenders to cut back on the availability of funds for housing. In part, these cutbacks in mortgage funds were a response to the widespread use of **fixed-rate home mortgages (FRMs),** among the oldest forms of home loans. FRMs return to the lender the same annual interest income (cash flow) regardless of what is happening to inflation or to interest rates. When depository institutions are forced to pay higher rates on their deposits to attract funds, their profits tend to be squeezed because the revenues from FRMs remain unchanged. Of course, these lending institutions are able to charge higher interest rates on *new* mortgage loans, but new loans normally are only a small fraction of an established lending institution's total loan portfolio. The bulk of that portfolio usually is in *old* mortgages, often granted during an era when interest rates were lower.

In short, the use of FRMs has tended to amplify the normal up-and-down cycle of earnings for mortgage-lending institutions, tending toward low or even negative earnings in periods of rising interest rates and to positive earnings in periods of falling interest rates. FRMs require *lenders* to bear the risk of interest-rate fluctuations. An alternative to the FRM was needed that guaranteed lenders a satisfactory real rate of return on mortgage loans and made funds available to home buyers on more reasonable terms.

**fixed-rate home mortgages (FRMs)**

**Key URL:**
Consumers can easily find current home mortgage interest rates and information on available homes at a wide variety of Web sites. One unique site at **mortgagecalculators .info** shows the home buyer what his or her payments will be for a given home mortgage rate.

## *Variable-Rate and Adjustable Mortgage Instruments*

The problems created by fixed-rate mortgages ushered in the development of several new mortgage innovations, led by the **variable-rate mortgage (VRM),** which permits the lender to vary the contractual interest rate on a mortgage loan as market conditions change. Generally, the VRM loan rate is linked to a reference interest rate *not* determined by the lender. For example, the yield on 10-year U.S. Treasury bonds may be used as a reference rate so that, if Treasury bond yields rise, the homeowner pays a higher contractual loan rate.

Alternatively, under a broader **adjustable mortgage instrument (AMI),** the maturity of the mortgage loan may be lengthened or a combination of interest rate increases and maturity changes may be made as market interest rates rise. In some cases, the loan principal can be increased along with interest rate increases, reducing the growth of the homeowner's equity—a process known as *negative amortization.* VRMs and AMIs shift the *risk* of interest rate fluctuations, partially or wholly, from the lender to the borrower.

Under most state and federal laws, changes in the interest rates attached to VRMs are limited as to frequency and amount. However, AMIs, with their options of varying monthly payments, the maturity of a mortgage loan, or the loan principal amount owed as interest rates change, generally face fewer legal restrictions. Many lenders offer *teaser rates* (i.e., loan rates that are temporarily below market levels) in order to get home buyers to commit to a VRM or an AMI instead of taking out a fixed-rate mortgage (FRM) which bears greater interest rate risk for the lender.

## *Interest-Only Mortgages*

The growth of family home ownership and of home mortgage credit early in the twenty-first century threatened to slow drastically as the economy and job growth leveled out after the 9/11 tragedy. Many households found themselves in financial trouble, and housing prices soared out of reach for many families. Leading mortgage bankers fought to keep the housing market rally going with some dramatic innovations. One of the most risky loan types to emerge has been **interest-only mortgages.**

These unique loans offer borrowers the option of only paying the interest on their home mortgages, without retiring loan principal, for an initial time period. For example, the home buyer might pay a few hundred dollars in interest each month for the first five years of his or her loan. These initial loan payments typically are very low, making home ownership more affordable for scores of families. After the initial low-payment period, however, *both* principal and interest must be paid until the loan reaches maturity (normally in 30 years). Unfortunately for the home buyer, the required monthly payment eventually climbs sharply upward because the principal value of the loan must be retired in a shorter-than-usual time period (say, in 25 years rather than the full term of 30 years).

Moreover, the majority of interest-only loans carry an adjustable interest rate. Should market interest rates rise, the home owner faces *both* greater principal payments and higher interest payments at the same time, often amounting to several thousand dollars each month. Particularly for families with weak credit ratings, the risk of losing their home can rise substantially. Careful explanation by mortgage lenders of *both* the advantages and the disadvantages of this unique form of residential mortgage loan appears to be a "must" when dealing with most home loan customers.

**Key URLs:**
Among the leading option adjustable-rate mortgage lenders are Countrywide Financial Corp at **Countrywide.com;** Indy-Mac Bancorp at **indymacbank.com;** and Wachovia Corp at **wachovia.com**

The success of interest-only mortgages has spawned still more innovative mortgage products, such as *option adjustable-rate mortgages,* designed to bring less affordable home purchases within reach for a broader spectrum of borrowers. The home buyer can choose among several different mortgage payment plans each month, including paying interest only, or making a minimum payment less than the interest owed which increases the total amount of the mortgage, or making a conventional loan payment covering principal, interest, taxes, and insurance. Should the borrower choose a minimal payment plan that increases the total mortgage amount ("negative amortization"), most lenders impose a "principal cap" so that total mortgage indebtedness cannot grow to exceed a specified percentage of the original loan amount (such as 115 percent)—otherwise many borrowers may find their loan balances larger than the market value of their homes. Still other lenders began offering home loans stretching out to 40 years instead of the conventional 25- to 30-year loan, thus stretching out and lowering monthly payments but resulting in the borrower paying substantially more in total interest costs.

### Reverse-Annuity Mortgages

Reverse-annuity mortgage (RAM)

A mortgage-financing device that may be of help to older families and retired individuals is the **reverse-annuity mortgage (RAM).** This financial instrument provides income to those who may have already paid off their mortgages but intend to keep their present home. The lender determines the current value of the home and pays the borrower a monthly annuity, amounting to a percentage of the property's value. The loan is secured by a gradually increasing mortgage on the borrower's home. Repayment of the loan occurs when the annuity holder dies, or otherwise leaves the home, with the loan being discharged against the deceased's estate, or when the home is sold. About 90 percent or more of these home loans in the U.S. are called Home Equity Conversion mortgages and are federally insured.

### Epilogue on the Fixed-Rate Mortgage

It is interesting that, with all the new mortgage instruments developed in recent years, fixed-rate mortgages (FRMs) continue to hold a major share of the residential loan market. This is true even though FRMs usually carry a higher interest rate than adjustable mortgages, at least initially, and may also carry higher origination fees and prepayment penalties. One reason appears to be public mistrust of many of the new instruments, coupled with fear of inflation, which would push up the interest rate on a variable-rate loan. Another factor is competition among lenders. It is likely, therefore, that *both* FRMs and VRMs will continue to exist side by side in the home mortgage market, each serving the special needs of individual lenders and homeowners.

**Key URL:**
To discover the possible advantages and disadvantages of reverse-annuity mortgages see **http://library.hsh.com/ articles-hsh.asp**

## 22.8 Pricing and Other Issues in Home Mortgage Lending

### Pricing Home Mortgages and the Treasury Security Market

Whatever type of home mortgage loan we might be looking at today, a key reference interest rate that many mortgage lenders use to determine the appropriate loan

The rapid growth of the housing market in recent years has led to the development of risk hedging tools to protect home builders and capital market investors against plunges in housing values. The Chicago Mercantile Exchange (CME) has been among the leaders in developing tools that allow trading in U.S. real estate values, possibly bringing greater stability to the housing market by protecting against falling home prices and rising mortgage loan defaults.

CME has developed housing futures and options settled in cash and based upon real estate prices in 10 large American cities: Boston, Chicago, Denver, Las Vegas, Los Angeles, Miami, New York City, San Diego, San Francisco, and Washington, D.C. Among the more likely traders in this market are real estate developers and housing lenders (such as commercial and mortgage banks, life insurers, federal mortgage agencies, and pension and hedge funds with large mortgage portfolios).

For example, suppose a subdivision developer in San Francisco anticipates a strong possibility that housing values in that city will decline as mortgage interest rates rise over the next three months. He or she can *sell*

housing futures contracts and then close out the transaction three months later with an equivalent *buy* order, scoring a price gain on these futures contracts and offsetting at least some of the decline in San Francisco's real estate values. Alternatively, the developer might purchase a *put option* on housing futures and subsequently sell these futures contracts to the option writer at their strike price, profiting on the spread between strike price and housing index value. (See Chapter 9 for a comparable example of short futures hedges and put options involving Treasury bonds and money market deposits.)

Each CME Metro Area Housing Index Futures contract is valued at $250 times the S&P/Case-Shiller Home Price Index. For example, if the current index reaches 300, the futures' value approaches $75,000 (or $250 × 300). Housing futures are traded on the CME Globex electronic trading platform, while housing options, each based on the value of a single futures contract, are traded in the CME's GSCI pit with traders on the floor of the exchange using open outcry to find desired prices from other traders.

rate on new home loans is the 10-year U.S. Treasury bond rate. A comparison of recent 10-year T-bond yields to home mortgage contract rates indicates that mortgage rates move closely with T-bond rates and maintain a yield spread of about 1.5 to 2 percentage points above them, as shown in Exhibit 22.5. That yield spread reflects differences in risk (including default risk, liquidity risk, and prepayment risk) between home mortgage loans and U.S. Treasury securities, the latter among the safest and most readily marketable financial instruments in the world. The use of reference rates

| EXHIBIT 22.5 | Comparison of Home Mortgage Loan Rates and the Annual Yields on 10-Year Maturity U.S. Treasury Bonds | | | | |
|---|---|---|---|---|---|
| | **2002** | **2003** | **2004** | **2005** | **2006‡** |
| Effective interest rate on loans for the purchase of newly built homes* | 6.44% | 5.80% | 5.75% | 5.93% | 6.79% |
| U.S. Treasury 10-year bond rate† | 4.61 | 4.01 | 4.27 | 4.29 | 5.11 |
| Yield spread between home mortgage loan rates and 10-year Treasury bond rates | 1.83% | 1.79% | 1.48% | 1.64% | 1.68% |

*The mortgage rates assume repayment of a 30-year home loan at the end of 10 years.
†The 10-year bond rate is the annual average yield from the U.S. Treasury's constant maturity series.
‡2006 figures are averages for June.
Sources: Board of Governors of the Federal Reserve System and Federal Deposit Insurance Corporation.

from the bond market as guides for home mortgage loan rates ties these two huge capital markets close together.

## Mortgage Lock-Ins, Loan Modifications, and Foreclosures

For most types of home mortgages the borrower wants to know before committing to the purchase of a home: What interest rate am I going to pay? Can I afford the monthly payments the lender will require? And what if mortgage loan rates rise after I agree to buy that new home, endangering my ability to pay for it?

**mortgage lock-ins**

This is the purpose of **mortgage lock-ins.** When a borrower "locks in" a mortgage loan rate this means the lender agrees to extend a loan offer at the prevailing mortgage interest rate for a specified period (usually 30 to 60 days and sometimes longer). This mortgage "lock-in" device is designed to protect borrowers from an increase in mortgage loan rates before the borrower takes possession of his or her new home.

However, what if market interest rates *fall* instead of rise? Can a borrower get his or her loan revised to capture the cheaper loan rate? Many "lock-ins" today grant the borrower additional flexibility by including a "float down" option which usually costs extra. With a "float down" clause, if interest rates fall before the closing on the new home loan occurs, the lender will make the home mortgage loan available at a lower interest rate. Otherwise, if the borrower backs out of a loan agreement because interest rates have fallen, the lender may lose a substantial amount in loan fees. Sometimes, however, even without the floating rate feature, a lender will "give a little" if market interest rates fall, knowing the customer may be more likely to run to another lending institution unless there is some flexibility in setting up a new home loan.

What happens if the loan agreement is made and the borrower takes possession of a new home, only to discover he or she can no longer afford the payments? Usually the home owner will try to sell his or her home as quickly as possible, repay the mortgage with the proceeds of the sale, and move into cheaper housing. If this doesn't happen right away and several payments are missed, the lender is likely to *foreclose,* taking possession of the home and selling it to recover the loaned funds.

However, in recent years a new alternative to foreclosure has become popular— a *loan modification agreement.* Loan modifications are designed to assist troubled borrowers avoid foreclosure, remain in a home, and save the lender the costs of foreclosure and repossession. They may also result in additional fee income for the mortgage lender.

Loan modifications usually add any missed loan payments to the remaining balance the borrower still owes on a home and a new payment schedule is worked out. Many such agreements lower the required monthly mortgage payment somewhat by stretching out the maturity of the loan. Modification agreements have slowed outright foreclosures in some markets recently, though home loan foreclosure levels (especially for the riskiest subprime mortgages) soared in 2006 and 2007 with many home buyers facing a dilemma—their homes falling in value while their mortgage payments were climbing under the terms of an adjustable-rate home loan.

## Refinancing Home Mortgages and "Cash Outs"

In recent years, many homeowners have found that it makes economic sense to convert their existing mortgage loans into *new* loans with lower interest costs because market interest rates have fallen substantially since the original loan was taken out. This happens most often to borrowers carrying a fixed-rate mortgage loan. However,

**Key URLs:**
You may find it interesting to explore some of the most popular sites for finding lower-cost home mortgage loans. See, for example, **elcan.com** and **lendingtree.com**

many flexible-rate mortgages also allow the home buyer to convert during the early years of a home loan to a fixed-rate mortgage in return for a fee.

Is refinancing an existing mortgage loan a wise move for a home buyer? The answer hinges upon whether the present value of the interest savings outweigh the costs of refinancing. If mortgage rates have dropped at least a percentage point since the borrower took out the current loan, and the borrower plans to remain in the home long enough to fully recover the costs of refinancing (in many cases about three years), then refinancing through a cheaper new loan is often attractive. The costs of refinancing include the loss of some of the homeowner's interest deduction on federal tax returns due to the lower interest payments on the new loan and the fees ("closing costs") that must be paid in order to set up a new loan. Moreover, loan fees on refinanced property normally are not immediately tax deductible but must be written off gradually over the term of a new loan.

Other than falling market interest rates a strong housing market also can provide an incentive for households to refinance their homes simply to capture some of the additional equity associated with rising home prices. They can pull out substantial amounts of new cash from the increasing market value of their homes.

For example, suppose a homeowner has paid the mortgage on her house down to 50 percent of the original purchase price of $100,000 so that she now owes $50,000 on the current mortgage loan. However, in the interim the home may have doubled in market value. In this case the homeowner would actually own 75 percent of the house, now valued at $200,000. Her equity in the house would have risen to $150,000. In this case, she may elect to extract some of this additional equity through a "cash out" refinancing of the existing mortgage, using the proceeds from the refinancing to pay off credit card debt, start a new business, make home repairs, pay for a college education, or for other financial needs.

Suppose this same homeowner decides to sign on for a *new* mortgage in the amount of 50 percent of her current equity in the home or $75,000. Because she currently owes only $50,000 on the house, she can use the new mortgage to pay off the old mortgage contract and still have $25,000 left over to spend for whatever purposes she desires. Cash-out refinancings can lead to lower mortgage payments provided interest rates have fallen, houses are appreciating in value, and homeowners choose to stretch out the maturity of their new mortgage contract. However, we must caution that while lower interest rates tend to spur refinancings they also tend to increase loan duration which shifts more of the real burden of repaying a mortgage into the future.

The ability of homeowners to obtain refinancing depends critically upon a strong credit history and a significant amount of accumulated equity built up in their home. Increased volatility of interest rates tends to cause homeowners to postpone their plans to refinance their home mortgages. On the other hand, recent structural changes in the home mortgage market (such as greater convenience in finding lenders willing to refinance and in finding the best terms available for getting a new loan) have made it *much* easier for consumers to explore and possibly take advantage of refinancing opportunities.

## Predatory Lending

**predatory loans**

One of the most controversial issues in the history of consumer lending centers on so-called **predatory loans.** Allegedly, some unscrupulous lenders attempt to mislead poorly informed, less well-educated borrowers into taking out high-cost loans, often with their home pledged as collateral. When the borrowers lured into this situation can no longer afford to make their payments, the lender usually either forecloses and takes their home or offers refinancing at an even higher cost to the borrower. Ultimately, the borrowing customer may be forced into home mortgage delinquency and, eventually, into personal bankruptcy.

We know that predatory lending occurs, especially in the form of "subprime" home mortgages that bear the highest interest rates. The current debate centers mainly on how to distinguish predatory from legitimate lending practices and how to protect the most vulnerable consumers. One solution is to educate the public about the risks associated with predatory loans—a process being pursued by such agencies as the Federal Deposit Insurance Corporation and the Federal Trade Commission in the United States. However, public education is a time-consuming and uncertain process.

In the interim, federal and state laws have appeared in an attempt to expose predatory lenders. For example, as discussed in Chapter 21, Truth in Lending laws require lenders to fully inform borrowers of all costs associated with a loan and give consumers the opportunity ("right of rescission") to cancel certain loan contracts (such as home equity loans) up to three business days after the loan agreement is signed where the borrower's home is at risk. The Home Ownership and Equity Protection Act prohibits lenders from selling home equity loans to a consumer without regard to that customer's ability to repay the loan.

**Key URL:**
For further information about the risks associated with predatory lending and how to prevent it, see **fdic.gov/consumers**

## QUESTIONS TO HELP YOU STUDY

8. A number of new mortgage instruments have appeared in recent years. These new financial instruments include variable rate mortgages (VRMs), adjustable mortgage instruments (AMIs), interest-only mortgages, and reverse-annuity mortgages (RAMs), in addition to the more conventional fixed-rate mortgages (FRMs). Describe how each of these home mortgage instruments works and what their advantages are.

9. What is a *mortgage lock-in?* Does it benefit the borrower or the lender? When might it not be a good idea?

10. What is a *loan modification agreement?* What is its purpose?

11. What are the advantages and disadvantages of home refinancings? Under what circumstances should a homeowner consider refinancing a home mortgage?

12. What are *predatory loans?* Why are public policymakers interested in eliminating the practice? How might this be accomplished?

## Summary of the Chapter's Main Points

This chapter has focused on one of the most important markets in the financial system—the market for residential home mortgage credit.

- *Home ownership* has grown in importance in recent years with a record number of households in the United States today (about two-thirds) owning their own homes. The value of homes as a tax-reducing investment and as a hedge against inflation has played a major role in this home ownership trend as has the drive toward more lenient borrowing terms, encouraged by government support of the home mortgage market.

- Among the leading privately owned home mortgage lending institutions today are *commercial banks, savings banks* and *savings and loan associations, life insurance companies, finance companies,* and *mortgage banking firms.*

- U.S. federal government intervention in the home mortgage market began in earnest during the 1930s and 1940s with the creation of several major federal agencies, including the Federal Home Loan Banks (FHLB), the Federal Housing Administration (FHA), the Federal National Mortgage Association (FNMA), the Veterans Administration (VA), and the Government National Mortgage Association (GNMA). These agencies were directed to expand the supply of mortgage credit available and to make mortgages more affordable for a greater proportion of the U.S. population. This was accomplished through such devices as guaranteeing the repayment of selected home mortgages (through FHA and VA) and creating an active resale market for existing home loans (through FNMA and GNMA).

- Later the Federal Home Loan Mortgage Corporation (FHLMC) was created to assist in expanding the supply of home mortgage credit and to aid in the development of security-like mortgage instruments to broaden and deepen the market for mortgage credit.

- Among the most important of new mortgage-related securities developed in recent years to expand the depth and breadth of the residential mortgage market are mortgage-backed securities, collateralized mortgage obligations (CMOs), and real estate mortgage investment conduits (REMICs). Each is based on the notion of pooling together a group of similar home mortgage loans and issuing securities against that pool for sale to investors in the open market. Eventually, these mortgage-backed instruments will be paid off by the principal and interest payments generated from the pooled loans.

- Mortgage-loan-backed security instruments have been used to attract millions of new investors to the home mortgage market and to increase the liquidity of mortgage instruments. *Securitized mortgage instruments* have helped make the market for home mortgages a global capital market rather than a regionally isolated marketplace as it was before their invention.

- In order to encourage individuals and families to consider home ownership, many new home financing devices have been developed, some of them making mortgage credit available on more lenient and affordable terms. Examples include variable-rate mortgages (VRMs), adjustable mortgage instruments (AMIs), interest-only mortgages (IOMs), reverse annuity mortgages (RAMs), and home mortgage refinancings.

- *Refinancings* of existing home mortgages became popular in the 1990s and early in the new century with record low loan rates. Borrowers have become more skilled in using "lock-ins" to protect the interest rate on a new loan from upward interest rate pressures. However, explosive growth in mortgage lending brought in more high-risk borrowers in danger of losing their homes due to *predatory lending*.

- The home mortgage market today has become one of the largest markets for a single financial instrument on the planet. It has helped to make U.S. citizens among the best-housed individuals in the world and in the process has interconnected the market for home loans with those for corporate and government bonds. No longer are mortgage-related instruments insensitive to the broad market trends that affect the global economy and the money and capital markets today.

www.mhhe.com/rose10e

## Key Terms Appearing in This Chapter

conventional home mortgage loan, 691
residential mortgages, 693
nonresidential mortgages, 693
Federal Home Loan Bank (FHLB)
 System, 699
Federal Housing Administration
 (FHA), 699
Veterans Administration (VA), 699
Federal National Mortgage Association
 (FNMA), 700
Government-sponsored enterprises
 (GSEs), 700
Government National Mortgage
 Association (GNMA), 700
mortgage-backed securities, 701
pass-throughs, 701

Federal Home Loan Mortgage
 Corporation (FHLMC), 701
collateralized mortgage
 obligation (CMO), 702
real estate mortgage investment
 conduit (REMIC), 702
prepayment risk, 702
securitized mortgages, 702
fixed-rate home mortgage (FRMs), 703
variable-rate mortgage (VRM), 704
adjustable mortgage instrument
 (AMI), 704
Interest-only mortgages (IOMs), 704
reverse-annuity mortgage (RAM), 705
mortgage lock-ins, 707
predatory loans, 708

## Problems and Issues

1. John George owns a home that he purchased for $100,000 ten years ago with a 30-year fixed-rate mortgage at a 6 percent annual rate of interest. Today he owes $60,000 on the house, which has since doubled in value.

 a. If John George were to refinance his house today, his bank would write a new mortgage for 85 percent of the market value of his house, out of which he would be required to pay fees and points equal to 1 percent of the new mortgage. How much equity could he "cash out" of his house? If he financed the maximum the bank would allow, how much money would he receive in a direct payment from the bank?

 b. Assuming that the new home mortgage in part (a) carries an interest rate of 5 percent and the new loan is for 30 years, by how much would John's monthly mortgage payments change? (Use a financial calculator or go to **lendingtree.com** and use this Web site's online payment calculator.)

 c. What would the payments be on the new mortgage in part (a) if John George were to choose a 15-year mortgage contract at a 4.75 percent annual rate?

 d. What are the advantages and disadvantages of the new mortgage described in part (b) versus the loan described in part (c)?

2. FNMA ("Fannie Mae") and FHLMC ("Freddie Mac") were established by the U.S. Congress during the 1930s and the 1970s to "add liquidity" to the home mortgage market. Explain how they achieve this objective. How does this work to the benefit of consumers?

3. Unlike Fannie Mae and Freddie Mac, which are private firms, GNMA (Ginnie Mae) is a government agency. Why would it not be possible to "privatize" Ginnie Mae and allow it to continue to carry out the function it was originally set up to perform?

4. Which mortgage instruments meet the definitions provided below?

   **a.** A home mortgage loan under which some of the terms of the loan, such as the loan rate or maturity of the loan, vary as market conditions change.

   **b.** A home loan that permits the borrower to pay interest on the loan but postpones repayment of loan principal to later years.

   **c.** Debt securities backed by pools of mortgage loans.

   **d.** Mortgage-backed securities issued in a range of maturity classes so that prepayment risk can be more easily selected to match an investor's particular investment goals.

   **e.** Home mortgage loan carrying an interest rate that varies during the term of a loan, generally depending on the movement of interest rates in the open market.

   **f.** Provides income to those who have already paid off their mortgage but wish to receive a cash inflow (income) based on the value of the equity in their home.

## Web-Based Problems

1. The purpose of this exercise is to gain an understanding of the government-sponsored agency Fannie Mae (the Federal National Mortgage Association, symbol FNM), by comparing its business activities with those of one of the largest commercial banks in the United States—Bank of America (symbol BAC). The information can be found in a combination of **finance.yahoo .com** and the Web sites of the two companies.

   **a.** For each firm obtain a description of the business plan.

   **b.** From the information in part (a) describe how these two financial-service entities differ in terms of their perceived "mission," the markets they serve, and the geographic reach of their operations.

   **c.** For both firms, obtain end-of-year data for each of the following statistics for at least the past three years: (i) Net income; (ii) Total liabilities; (iii) Total assets; and (iv) Total stockholders' equity. Load these data into a spreadsheet.

   **d.** Compute the following financial ratios for each year for both firms: (i) Debt-to-equity ratio = Total liabilities/Total stockholder equity; (ii) Return on assets (ROA) = Net income/Total assets; and (iii) Return on equity (ROE) = Net income/Total stockholders' Equity.

    **e.** Discuss differences between the two firms' financial ratios and whether you can identify any trends in them over time. What explanations might there be for these findings?

**2.** Exploring Web site information on *mortgage lock-ins* (for example, at **pueblo.gsa.gov** and other Web sources), explain the purpose of a mortgage lock-in and who it is supposed to benefit. List the advantages and potential disadvantages of lock-ins for the home mortgage borrower.

**3.** Recently two mortgage industry leaders—Fannie Mae and Freddie Mac—have been at the center of a raging controversy. Using such Web sites as **fanniemae .com, freddiemac.com,** and **federalreserve.gov,** explain the two sides of this controversy—that is, the point of view of the two mortgage agencies and the point of view of competing lenders and the public. The U.S. Congress is debating new legislation to tighten government oversight of Fannie and Freddie as well as other government-sponsored enterprises (GSEs). Based on your review of the arguments, what do you think this legislation should contain?

**4.** Suppose you are searching for a new home and need a mortgage loan to help finance it. Exploring Web sites such as **house4sale-online.com** and **buyersresource.com,** along with other sites you uncover, describe the price range of homes for sale in your area. Using a mortgage rate calculator on the Web, which of these homes could you afford to take on with your current budget and income? With the personal income and budget you hope to have five years from now?

## Selected References to Explore

**1.** Chomsisengphet, Souphala, and Anthony Pennington-Cross. "The Evolution of the Subprime Mortgage Market," *Review,* Federal Reserve Bank of St. Louis, Vol. 88, No. 1 (January/February 2006), pp. 31–56.

**2.** Doms, Mark; Frederick Furlong; and John Krainer. "House Prices and subprime Mortgage Delinquencies," *FRBSF Economic Letter,* Federal Reserve Bank of San Francisco, No. 2007-14 (June 8).

**3.** Emmons, William R. "Cash-Out Refinancing: Check It Out Carefully," *The Regional Economist,* Federal Reserve Bank of St. Louis, July 2005, pp.10–11.

**4.** ———; Mark D. Vaughan; and Timothy J. Yeager. "The Housing Giants in Plain View," *Regional Economist,* Federal Reserve Bank of St. Louis, July 2004, pp. 5–9.

**5.** Garriga, Carlos; William T. Gavin; and Don Schlagenhauf. "Recent Trends in Home Ownership," *Review,* Federal Reserve Bank of St. Louis, Vol. 88, No. 5, September/October 2006, pp. 397–411.

**6.** Krainer, John. "Mortgage Innovation and Consumer Choice," *FRBSF Economic Letter,* No. 2006-38 (December 29), Federal Reserve Bank of San Francisco, 2006.

7. Li, Wendi, and Rui Yao. "Your Home Just Doubled in Value? Don't Uncork the Champagne Just Yet!" *Business Review,* Federal Reserve Bank of Philadelphia, First Quarter 2006, pp. 25–34.

8. Quigley, John M. "Federal Credit and Insurance Programs: Housing," *Review,* Federal Reserve Bank of St. Louis, July/August 2006, pp. 281–309.

9. Wheelock, David C. "Housing Slump Could Lean Heavily on Economy," *The Regional Economist,* Federal Reserve Bank of St. Louis, April 2007, pp. 4–9.

# Part 7

# The International Financial System

Today, no nation can view its financial system as being isolated from the global money and capital markets. In the financial marketplace of the modern era, trading of financial services and assets circles the globe, 24 hours a day, with few impediments to the exchange of information and to the flow of capital from one spot on the planet to another. As the international sector has grown, international financial institutions and the global storage and transfer of financial data have grown and improved along with it. There is greater interest today almost everywhere in the promotion of trade between nations. But global trade depends heavily upon global financial services, especially the efficient transmission of payments and the extension of credit, wherever it is most needed.

Moreover, financial market participants in every corner of the globe follow daily financial developments. Today's lenders and borrowers and savers and investors increasingly recognize that the value of the assets—both financial and nonfinancial—they hold is often sensitive to happenings half a world away. There are few places for financial market players to hide anymore.

In Part 7, we turn initially to a key source of international financial information—a nation's balance of payments—and also examine the fundamental determinants of exchange rates between different national currencies (such as the dollar and the euro). We also explore how international banks are structured and what services they supply to their customers all over the globe. As you will see, despite all the great technological advances reshaping our world today, the international financial system still faces great risks even as it provides great benefits and essential services to businesses and consumers all over the globe.

# Chapter 23

# International Transactions and Currency Values

## What's in This Chapter?
## Key Topics Outline

A Nation's Balance-of-Payments Accounts

Trade Deficits: The Problems They Can Cause

The Problem of Different Monetary Units

The Gold Standard and Managed Float

Character of the Foreign Exchange Market (FOREX)

Exchange Rate Quotations and the Forces That Shape Them

Functions of the Forward Currency and Currency Futures Markets

Currency Swaps

Government Intervention in the Foreign Exchange Markets

## Learning Objectives
## in This Chapter

- You will explore the functions and roles performed by the international markets within the global financial system.

- You will see how international payments for goods and services are made and how international borrowing and lending can be tracked through a nation's *balance-of-payments accounts*.

- You will come to understand how the values of *national currencies* (such as the dollar and the euro) are determined within the modern financial system.

## 23.1　Introduction to International Transactions and Currency Values

In many ways, the world we live in is rapidly shrinking. Jet planes race across the Atlantic between New York and London in less than four hours, about the same time it takes a passenger jetliner to travel across the United States. Broadband transmissions and the Internet, cell phones, and fiber-optic cable move financial information from one spot on the globe to another in seconds. Orbiting satellites bring news of major international significance to home television sets and computer screens the moment an event takes place and make possible direct communication between those involved in international business transactions.

Accompanying these dramatic improvements in communication and transportation is enormous growth in world trade and international investment. For example, in 1965 total exports of goods and services worldwide reached $190 billion. By the twenty-first century, the estimated dollar value of world trade had climbed above $6 trillion, or more than half as much as the U.S. gross domestic product (GDP). Moreover, the United States itself has become increasingly dependent on world trade. For example, imports into the United States represented less than 5 percent of GDP in 1960 but had jumped to about 15 percent of GDP as the twenty-first century unfolded; U.S. exports climbed from 6 percent to about 10 percent of GDP over the same period. Thus, at least a quarter of the value of production and spending in the U.S. economy stems from foreign trade. The international financial markets have had to grow rapidly just to keep up with expansion in world trade.

Actually, international financial markets perform the same basic functions as domestic financial markets. They bring international lenders of funds in contact with borrowers, permitting an increased flow of scarce funds toward their most productive uses. The volume of capital investment worldwide is made larger because of the workings of the global financial system. And with increased capital investment, the productivity of individual firms and nations is increased and economic growth in the international sector accelerates. The international financial markets also facilitate the flow of consumer goods and services across national boundaries, making possible an optimal allocation of resources in response to consumer demand on a global scale. With increased efficiency in resource use, the output of consumer goods and services is increased and costs of production are minimized.[1]

## 23.2　The Balance-of-Payments (BOP) Accounts

**balance-of-payments (BOP) accounts**

One of the most widely used sources of information concerning flows of funds, goods, and services between nations is each country's **balance-of-payments (BOP) accounts.** This statistical report summarizes all transactions between residents of one nation and the rest of the world during a specific period of time. The BOP accounts reflect *changes* in the assets and liabilities of economic units—businesses, individuals, and governments—involved in international transactions. The major transactions

---

[1]These benefits from international trade and finance are most likely to occur if each nation follows the principle of *comparative advantage*. This principle argues that each country will have a higher real standard of living if it specializes in the production of those goods and services in which it has a comparative advantage in cost and imports those goods and services where it is at a comparative cost disadvantage. The principle of comparative advantage seems to work best in an environment of free trade that permits nations to specialize in their most efficient activities.

captured in the BOP accounts include exports and imports of goods and services, income from investments made abroad, government loans and military expenditures overseas, and private capital flows between nations.

In a statistical sense, a nation's BOP accounts are always "in balance," because double-entry bookkeeping is used. For example, every payment made for goods and services imported from abroad simultaneously creates a claim on the home country's resources or extinguishes an existing liability. Similarly, every time a domestic business receives payment from overseas, it either acquires a claim against resources in a foreign country, or a claim that firm held against a foreign individual or institution is erased. In practice, however, imbalances frequently show up in the BOP accounts due to unreported transactions or inconsistencies in reporting. These errors and omissions are handled through a Statistical Discrepancy account.

## The U.S. Balance of International Payments

The U.S. BOP accounts are published quarterly by the Bureau of Economic Analysis. The quarterly figures are then *annualized* to permit comparisons across years. The transactions recorded in the balance of payments fall into three broad groups:

1. *Transactions on current accounts,* which include imports and exports of goods and services and unilateral transfers (gifts).

2. *Transactions on capital and financial accounts,* which include long- and short-term investments at home and abroad and usually involve the transfer of financial assets (bonds, deposits, etc.).

3. *Official reserve transactions,* which are used by monetary authorities (the Treasury, central bank, etc.) to settle BOP deficits, usually through transferring the ownership of official reserve assets (such as gold and foreign currency reserves) to countries with BOP surpluses.

Transactions that bring about an inflow of foreign currency into the home country are recorded as *credits* (+). Transactions resulting in an outflow of foreign currency from the home country are listed as *debits* (−). Thus, credit (+) items in the BOP represent an increase in a nation's buying power abroad. Debit (−) items represent decreases in a nation's buying power abroad. If a country sells goods and services or borrows abroad, these transactions are credit items because they increase external buying power. On the other hand, a purchase of goods and services abroad or a paydown of a nation's international liabilities is a debit item because that country is surrendering part of its external buying power. A summary of the major credit and debit items making up the BOP accounts is shown in Exhibit 23.1.

The international transactions that made up the U.S. balance of payments for 2005 and 2006 (second quarter) are shown in Exhibit 23.2. These U.S. international transactions are subdivided into categories—the current account, the capital and financial accounts, and residual items (including a sizeable statistical discrepancy due to unreported transactions)—that help us understand how the BOP bookkeeping system works.

In summary, the so-called *balance-of-payments identity* applies to the United States and all other nations. It says:

$$\begin{matrix} \text{Transactions in the} \\ \text{current account} \end{matrix} + \begin{matrix} \text{Transactions in the capital} \\ \text{and financial accounts} \end{matrix} = \begin{matrix} \text{The change in the official} \\ \text{reserves account} \end{matrix}$$

For example, if the United States has a current account deficit (which it has run for many years now) and no change in its official reserves, the deficit in its current

| EXHIBIT 23.1 | Principal Credit and Debit Items Recorded in a Nation's Balance of Payments (BOP) |
|---|---|
| **Credit Entries (Inflows of Funds, +)** | **Debit Entries (Outflows of Funds, −)** |
| Exports of merchandise | Imports of merchandise |
| Services provided to citizens of foreign countries | Services provided to domestic citizens by foreign countries |
| Interest and dividends due domestic citizens from business firms abroad | Gifts of money sent abroad by domestic citizens |
| Remittances received from domestic citizens employed in foreign countries | Capital invested abroad by domestic citizens |
| Foreign purchases of securities issued by domestic firms and units of government | Dividend and interest payments to foreign countries on investments made in the domestic country |
| Repayments by foreigners of funds borrowed from domestic lending institutions | |

account must be balanced by a surplus in its capital and financial accounts that covers the deficit. Thus, a country like the United States can consume more than it produces provided it borrows from overseas (such as by issuing government and private securities) to finance that consumption.

## The Current Account

One of the most publicized components of U.S. international transactions in recent years has been the **current account.** Its most important components include:

1. The *merchandise trade balance,* comparing the volume of goods exported to the volume of goods imported.

2. The *service balance,* comparing exports and imports of services.

3. *Net investment income,* measuring income from investments in assets purchased abroad less income from domestic assets purchased by foreigners.

4. *Compensation of employees,* tracking wages for domestic workers employed overseas relative to wages flowing to foreigners working in the domestic economy.

5. *Unilateral transfers,* reflecting the amount of gifts and grants made to foreigners by domestic citizens and institutions less gifts and grants from foreigners to units in the domestic economy.

**current account**

*The Merchandise Trade Balance in the Current Account*   Prior to the 1970s, the United States often reported a positive merchandise trade balance (*surplus*), with goods shipped out of the United States exceeding goods shipped in, due in part to substantial demand for U.S. agricultural products and U.S. equipment overseas. However, since that time, a combination of factors, including rising oil prices, inflation, and the preferences of many Americans for foreign automobiles, TVs, and other goods, has turned what historically were trade surpluses for the United States into substantial *trade deficits*—imported goods far greater in total than exported goods as imports of petroleum, capital and consumer goods have outstripped U.S. shipments of industrial supplies and equipment. This means that recently, U.S. *sources* of external buying power have fallen short of U.S. *uses* of external buying power. The United

**Key URL:**
For a detailed discussion of the components of the BOP, see especially en.wikipedia.org/wiki/ Balance-of-payments

| EXHIBIT 23.2 | U.S. International Transactions for 2005–2006: The Nation's Balance of Payments (million of dollars, seasonally adjusted) | |
|---|---|---|
| **Balance of Payments Components** | **2005** | **2006*** |
| **Current Account** | | |
| Exports of goods and services and income receipts | $ 1,749,892 | $ 2,040,248 |
| Exports of goods | 894,631 | 1,011,372 |
| Exports of services | 380,614 | 412,144 |
| Income receipts from U.S.-owned assets abroad | 471,722 | 613,828 |
| Compensation of U.S. employees abroad | 2,925 | 2,904 |
| Imports of goods and services and income payments | $−2,455,328 | $−2,832,112 |
| Imports of goods | −1,677,371 | −1,853,764 |
| Imports of services | −314,604 | −345,020 |
| Income payments on foreign-owned assets in the U.S. | −454,124 | −633,328 |
| Compensation of foreign employees working in the U.S. | −9,229 | −9,396 |
| Unilateral current transfers, net | −86,072 | −81,776 |
| U.S. government grants and other transfers | −37,665 | −26,772 |
| Private remittances and other transfers | −41,807 | −55,004 |
| **Net Balance on Current Account** | −791,508 | −873,640 |
| **Capital Account** | | |
| Capital account transactions, net | −4,351 | −3,528 |
| **Financial Account** | | |
| U.S.-owned assets abroad, net | −426,801 | −849,356 |
| U.S. official reserve assets, net | 14,096 | 2,240 |
| U.S. government assets other than official reserve assets, net | 5,539 | 5,916 |
| U.S. private assets, net | −446,438 | −853,032 |
| Foreign-owned assets in the United States, net | 1,212,250 | 1,465,588 |
| Foreign-official assets in the U.S., net | 199,495 | 299,496 |
| Direct investments and other foreign assets in the U.S., net | 1,012,755 | 1,166,092 |
| **Net Balance on Capital and Financial Accounts** | $ 781,098 | $ 612,704 |
| Statistical Discrepancy | 10,410 | 260,936 |

*Figures for 2006 are for the second quarter of that year and are annualized.
Note: Details may not add correctly to totals due to rounding error.
Source: U.S. Bureau of Economic Analysis, Department of Commerce.

States' *merchandise trade deficit*—volume of exported goods less than the volume of imported goods—reached just over $780 billion in 2005 according to the figures presented in Exhibit 23.2, nearly doubling in five years as the nominal value of imports into the United States rose significantly.

### The Service Balance in the Current Account
If Americans have purchased a greater volume of goods from abroad than they have sold abroad in recent

years, how has this deficit (debit balance) in the merchandise account been paid for? Historically, part of the needed funds have come from a positive *service balance*—exports of services to foreign entities exceeding imports of services purchased by U.S. individuals and institutions. Services normally included in the BOP accounts include insurance policies covering the shipment of goods, international transportation, royalties and license fees, and hotel accommodations, entertainment, and medical care for persons traveling overseas. Net service income for the United States has been relatively stable in recent years after a period of decline. For example, in 2005 services exported exceeded service imports into the United States by $66 billion and by an estimated $67 billion (when annualized) in 2006, according to Exhibit 23.2.

### Investment Income Receipts and Payments in the Current Account
Americans have invested heavily in foreign ventures of many kinds—from banks to boutiques—generating substantial investment income flowing into the United States each year. However, as the new century dawned, investments of foreigners inside the United States continued to expand rapidly and these assets frequently paid out higher rates of return than many American investments abroad. Nevertheless, the difference between U.S. investment income received from abroad less foreign investment income received from the U.S. has generally been positive, helping to mitigate America's current account deficit somewhat.

**Key URL:**
Foreign-owned businesses investing in the United States have representation in the nation's capital, Washington D.C., in the form of the Organization for International Investment, which is composed mainly of U.S. subsidiaries of companies headquartered abroad.
See especially **ofii.org**

### Compensation of Employees in the Current Account
The BOP's current account also reports the *net* amount of wages earned by U.S. residents working abroad relative to wages paid to foreign workers currently employed inside the United States. The difference between these two income flows is often labeled "compensation of employees, net." We note in Exhibit 23.2 that, during 2005, foreigners employed in the U.S. received $6 billion *more* in wages than U.S. residents at work overseas—one of the consequences of the large volume of investments foreigners have made inside the United States in recent years.

### Unilateral Transfers in the Current Account
Another type of international transaction recorded in a BOP's current account, labeled *unilateral transfers,* consists mainly of gifts and grants from U.S. residents and institutions to foreigners less foreign gifts and grants to U.S. units. These transactions are called "unilateral" because they represent a *one-way flow of resources* with nothing expected in return. Typically, U.S. gift-giving far exceeds the return flow. For example, gifts and grants to foreigners from Americans were an estimated $86 billion larger than foreign gifts and grants flowing into the United States in 2005. Each gift and grant sent overseas represents the *use* of the contributing nation's external buying power and, therefore, is recorded as a debit (−) item in its BOP.

### The Balance on Current Account
When we put the above components—trade in goods and services, investment income receipts and payments, compensation of employees, and unilateral transfers—together, we derive the *balance on current account.* The U.S. balance on current account in 2005 was a debit (−) item balance, estimated at just over $790 billion—a record number in dollar terms and relative to the nation's total output of goods and services (the GDP).

What are some of the possible consequences of persistent current account deficits? A nation running current account deficits surrenders claims on its future income to foreign individuals and institutions. That is, a current account deficit generates net borrowing from abroad. In order to induce foreign investors to lend their funds to help cover a current account deficit, domestic market interest rates may need to be pushed higher, which *may,* in turn, slow domestic purchases of goods and services, increase unemployment, and lower domestic living standards.

## The Capital and Financial Accounts

The flow of funds destined for investment in assets overseas is recorded in the **capital and financial accounts.** These accounts in a nation's BOP are often divided into two major subcategories: *net private capital flows* between private individuals and institutions, and *net official capital flows,* involving governments, central banks, and government agencies of various kinds. Capital investment activity abroad also may be divided into (1) short-term capital flows, (2) direct investments, and (3) portfolio investments. *Short-term capital flows* reflect purchases of financial assets with maturities under a year (principally bank deposits, government and private notes and bills, and foreign currencies). In contrast, *direct investments* and *portfolio investments* represent long-term commitments of funds, involving the acquisition of foreign financial and nonfinancial assets having a maturity of more than a year.[2] For example, a U.S. automobile company building an assembly plant in Germany is making a direct investment abroad, while a U.S. security dealer purchasing the stock of a French company and holding it for two years is making a portfolio investment. When American citizens buy six-month British Treasury bills, they are making short-term capital investments overseas.

Of course, capital investments flow both ways. For example, in 2005, U.S. citizens and private organizations invested about $427 billion in capital assets overseas, while foreign individuals and private institutions invested just over $1.2 trillion in U.S. assets of various kinds. The result was a *net private capital inflow* into the United States from abroad of $785 billion. U.S. banks, hotels, energy companies, port operations, steel plants, and numerous other strategically important firms have been acquisition targets for foreign investors. As a result of these heavy foreign capital flows into the United States in recent years, America's *net investment position*—holdings of foreign assets by U.S. individuals and institutions less holdings of U.S. assets by foreign individuals and institutions—went from positive to negative about two decades ago and has continued to head downward in recent years. On the positive side, this negative investment position has enabled the United States to finance a substantial portion of its trade deficit and has supported the creation of new U.S. businesses and jobs.

## Official Transactions

When a nation has a BOP deficit, it must settle up with other nations by surrendering assets or claims to foreign accounts. *Official capital flows* usually consist of the movement of assets that are readily transferable in order to make international payments—for example, transferring the ownership of gold, convertible foreign currencies (such as the dollar, the euro, and the yen), deposits held in the International Monetary Fund

---

[2]What is the essential difference between *direct investment* and *portfolio investment?* The key factor is *control.* Portfolio investment involves purchasing securities (especially stocks and bonds) to hold in order to earn interest or dividend income. Direct investment, on the other hand, refers to the purchase of a loan or the acquisition of ownership shares in an attempt to control a foreign firm. The U.S. Department of Commerce defines direct investment as ownership of 10 percent or more of the voting stock or the exercise of other means of control of a foreign business enterprise by an individual or corporation. Ownership of less than 10 percent of a foreign firm's stock is usually referred to as portfolio investment.

(IMF) that may be readily transferred from the account of one IMF-member nation to that of another, and special drawing rights (SDRs or "paper gold"), which we will discuss later in this chapter.

When assets available for making international payments *increase,* this represents expanded external buying power by the nation experiencing the increase. On the other hand, a *decrease* in official capital represents a decline in external buying power by the nation experiencing the decrease. If a country has a credit (surplus) balance in its international accounts, its official capital position generally improves, indicating an excess of sales abroad over foreign purchases. Conversely, a nation experiencing a debit (deficit) balance in its international accounts usually finds its official capital position weakening. Such a decline may be temporarily offset, however, by borrowings through its central bank or other government agency.

In 2005, for example, with the United States experiencing a record BOP deficit, foreign governments and central banks increased their holdings of gold, currencies, and other official assets in the United States by almost $200 billion, net. As we noted earlier, most U.S. BOP deficits in recent years have financed themselves primarily through changes in official capital and through private capital inflows from abroad (especially purchases of U.S. stocks and bonds by foreign investors). This preference of foreign governments and foreign private investors for U.S. securities continued to grow over the past decade as the U.S. economy, despite a slowdown, looked relatively strong compared to many weaker economies abroad.

## *Disequilibrium in the Balance of Payments*

**Key URL:**
For an exploration of some of the key issues surrounding balance-of-payments deficits see, for example, The International Monetary Fund at **imf.org** and the Hoover Institute for Public Policy Inquiry at **imfsite.org**

For several years now, the United States has displayed a *disequilibrium* position in its balance of payments. The U.S. has relied on foreign credit, foreign capital inflows, and its stock of gold, foreign currencies, and other official assets to settle U.S. BOP deficits. However, the amount of these financial devices is limited—no nation can go on indefinitely accumulating BOP deficits, borrowing abroad, and using up its official assets. Moreover, relying on foreign capital inflows can be dangerous because the perceptions of foreign investors regarding the desirability of placing funds in the United States may change abruptly due to wars, stock market declines, and so on.

To this point, foreign central banks and foreign investors have regarded U.S. securities and dollar-denominated deposits as good investments and have been willing to extend an increasing volume of international credit to the United States. At some point, however, foreign governments and private investors *may* become satiated with dollar claims; at this point, the value of the U.S. dollar would tend to decline in international markets. U.S. purchases of goods and services abroad also would tend to decline because of the dollar's reduced buying power. The nation's standard of living would tend to fall until equilibrium in its balance-of-payments position was eventually restored.

One factor that gives hope for the future lies in the capital and financial accounts. As we noted earlier, capital inflows into the United States generally have grown faster than U.S. investments abroad, making the United States the world's largest debtor nation. A major factor boosting foreign investment in the United States is the desire to avoid U.S. import restrictions by developing production facilities inside the United States (as many foreign automobile and electronics manufacturers have recently done, for example). Even more significant is the political stability of the United States, offering an attractive haven for international investors concerned about instability abroad. If this capital inflow continues to grow in the future, it will do much to alleviate the future international payments problems of the United States.

**QUESTIONS TO HELP YOU STUDY**

1. Explain what is meant by the term *balance of payments*. Describe and list the principal components of a nation's balance-of-payments accounts.

2. Supply a brief definition of each of the following terms associated with the balance-of-payments accounts:

   *Current account*                          *Service transactions*
   *Merchandise trade balance*                *Official reserve assets*
   *Capital and financial accounts*

3. Describe and then discuss the major trends that have occurred in the following segments of the United States' balance-of-payments accounts in recent years:
   Merchandise trade balance
   Investments in overseas assets by U.S. residents
   Investments in United States' assets by foreign residents.

4. When is a *balance-of-payments* deficit potentially a "bad" sign? In what sense can such deficits sometimes reflect favorable trends.

## 23.3   The Problem of Different Monetary Units in International Trade and Finance

Businesses and individuals trading goods and services in international markets encounter a problem not experienced by those who buy and sell only in domestic markets. This is the problem of different monetary units used as the standard of value from country to country. Americans use the dollar as a medium of exchange and standard of value in domestic markets, while the European Union (EU) relies on the euro as its basic monetary unit. There are more than 100 different monetary units around the world. As a result, when goods and services are sold or capital flows across national boundaries, it is often necessary to sell one currency and buy another.

Unfortunately, the act of trading currencies entails substantial *risk*. Exporters and importers may be forced to purchase a foreign currency when its value is rising and the home country's currency is falling. Profits earned on the sale of goods and services abroad may be outweighed by losses suffered in currency exchange. Differing monetary units also complicate government monetary policy aimed at curbing inflation and ensuring rapid economic growth. Repeatedly in recent years, massive flows of funds surged through foreign and domestic markets from speculative buying and selling of dollars, euros, yen, yuan, and other currencies. These speculative currency flows increased the problems associated with economic recovery, control of inflation, and balance-of-payments (BOP) deficits.

### The Gold Standard

The problem of trading in different monetary units that change frequently is one of the world's oldest financial problems. It has been dealt with in a wide variety of ways over the centuries. One of the most successful solutions prior to the modern era centered on *gold* as an international standard of value. During the seventeenth and eighteenth centuries, major trading nations made their currencies freely convertible into gold.

**gold standard**

Gold bullion could be exported and imported without significant restriction, and each unit of currency was defined in terms of so many grains of fine gold. Nations adopting the **gold standard** agreed to exchange paper money or coins for gold bullion in unlimited amounts at predetermined prices.

One advantage of the gold standard was that it imposed a common standard of value for all currencies. This brought a measure of stability to international transactions, dampened interest rate fluctuations, and stimulated the expansion of commerce and investment abroad. A second advantage was economic discipline. Tying currencies to gold regulated the growth of national economies. A nation experiencing severe inflation or excessively rapid growth in imported goods soon found itself losing gold reserves to settle balance-of-payments deficits. Exports declined and unemployment rose. Eventually, the volume of imports was curtailed, and the outflow of gold slowed.

These advantages of stability and economic discipline were offset by a number of limitations inherent in the gold standard. For one thing, maintenance of that standard depended crucially on *free trade*. Nations desiring to protect their industries from foreign competition through export or import restrictions could not do so. Moreover, the growth of a nation's money supply was limited by the size of its gold stock. Problems of rising unemployment or lagging growth might call for expansion of the domestic money supply. However, such a policy could require suspension of gold convertibility, taking a nation off the gold standard. Thus, the gold standard sometimes conflicted with national economic goals and limited a nation's policy alternatives.

## The Gold Exchange Standard

**gold exchange standard**

Although government policymakers were mainly concerned about the effects of the gold standard on domestic economies, investors and commercial traders found that gold bullion was not a convenient medium of exchange, especially in settling payments between nations. Gold is expensive to transport and risky to handle. Moreover, the world's gold supply was limited relative to the expanding volume of trade. These problems gave rise in the nineteenth century to the **gold exchange standard.** Institutions actively engaged in international commerce began to hold stocks of convertible currencies. Each currency was freely convertible into gold at a fixed rate but also was freely convertible into other currencies at relatively stable prices. In practice, transactions took place in convertible currencies, and gold faded into the background as an international medium of exchange.

Unfortunately, this monetary standard possessed many of the same limitations as the original gold standard. National currencies were still tied to gold, and growth in world trade depended upon growth in the international gold stock. The gold exchange standard collapsed during the worldwide Great Depression of the 1930s.

## The Modified Exchange Standard

**modified exchange standard**

Dissatisfaction with international monetary systems tied exclusively to gold resulted in a search for a new payments system. In 1944, Western countries convened an international monetary conference in Bretton Woods, New Hampshire, to devise a stable payments system. The conference created a new mechanism called the Bretton Woods System, or **modified exchange standard**—and an agency for monitoring exchange rate practices of member nations (known as the International Monetary Fund, or IMF, with headquarters in Washington, D.C.).

The IMF, headed by its Board of Governors with a representative from each member nation, establishes rules for settling international accounts and grants short-term loans to member nations lacking sufficient international reserves to settle their BOP deficits. IMF loans often are accompanied by strict requirements that a member nation receiving credit must adopt stern economic measures to curtail its imports and expand its sales abroad. The IMF's credit guarantee encourages banks and other nations to grant loans to a member nation in trouble. The funds loaned by the IMF come mainly from *quotas,* which each member nation must contribute in dollars or other official reserve assets. A companion organization to the IMF, the *World Bank,* also created at Bretton Woods makes long-term loans to speed the economic development of member nations.

**Key URLs:**
For further details on the important international services provided by the World Bank and the International Monetary Fund, see **worldbank.org** and **imf.org**

The centerpiece of Bretton Woods was the linking of foreign currency prices to the U.S. dollar and to gold. The United States committed itself to buy and sell gold at $35 per ounce on request from foreign monetary authorities. Other IMF member nations pledged to keep their currency's price within 1 percent of its par value in terms of gold or the dollar. In practice, this usually meant that, if a foreign currency fell in value *below* par (the lower intervention point), a central bank would sell its holdings of dollars and buy that currency in the market, driving its price upward toward par. If the price of a nation's currency rose more than 1 percent *above* par (the upper intervention point), the central bank involved would sell its own currency and buy dollars, driving the currency's price down toward par. If a currency fell too far or rose too high, the country involved would simply revalue its currency, establishing a new par value relative to gold or the dollar.

Fundamentally, the success of the Bretton Woods System depended on the ability of the United States to maintain confidence in the dollar and protect its value. One of the weaknesses of the new system was that the U.S. dollar was often in short supply. Later, however, the United States began to export large amounts of capital to Europe, Asia, and the Americas. The result was sizable U.S. trade deficits that were dealt with by drains on the U.S. gold stock and by a buildup of dollar holdings abroad—an indication of fundamental problems developing in the international payments system.

## The Managed Floating Currency Standard

Inflation and other economic problems ultimately forced the abandonment of the Bretton Woods System during the 1970s. The first step in dismantling the old system was taken by President Richard M. Nixon in August 1971, when the U.S. dollar was devalued and the convertibility of foreign official holdings of dollars into gold suspended. Gold became a commodity and not an international monetary medium. Soon, the largest IMF member nations were allowing their currencies to *float* in value, responding freely to demand and supply forces.

**managed floating currency standard**

In 1978, the **managed floating currency standard** was adopted by the 185 member nations of the IMF. Known as the Second Amendment to the International Monetary Fund's Articles of Agreement, the official rules under which today's international money system is supposed to operate allow *each nation to choose its own exchange-rate policy, consistent with the structure of its economy and its goals.* There are, however, three principles each member country must follow in establishing its exchange rate policy:

1. When a nation intervenes in the foreign exchange markets to protect its own currency, it must take into account the interests and welfare of other IMF member countries.

**2.** Government intervention in the foreign exchange markets should be carried out to correct disorderly conditions that are essentially short term in nature.

**3.** No member nation should intervene in the exchange markets in order to gain an unfair competitive advantage or prevent necessary adjustments in balance-of-payments (BOP) positions.

Nations that attempt to keep the exchange value of their currencies within a fixed range around the value of some other currency or basket of currencies are known as *peggers*. (For example, China over the last decade frequently worked to keep the yuan–dollar exchange rate close to 8.3 yuan per U.S. dollar.) The majority of pegging nations are developing countries that have strong commercial links with one or more industrialized trading partners. (Examples include Korea, Guatemala, Hong Kong, Saudi Arabia and Venezuela, which are or have often connected the exchange rate on their currencies to the U.S. dollar.) Frequently, when a developing country has strong trade relations with more than one nation, it uses a basket (group) of currencies to set the value of its own monetary unit in order to "average out" fluctuations in the value of its exports and imports.

A few nations have, from time to time, pegged their currency's exchange rate to a basket of currencies assembled by the International Monetary Fund, known as **special drawing rights (SDRs).** The SDR was created to help settle international claims arising from transactions between the IMF, governments of member nations, and various international agencies. SDRs are really "book entries" on the ledgers of the IMF, sometimes referred to as *paper gold.* Periodically, that organization issues new SDRs and credits them to the international reserve accounts of member nations based on each nation's IMF quota (contributions of currency and other official reserve assets to the IMF). To spend its SDRs, a nation or an institution requests the IMF to transfer some amount of SDRs from its own reserve account to the reserve account of another nation or institution. In return, the country or institution asking for the transfer gets deposit balances denominated in the currency of the country or institution receiving the SDRs. These deposit balances may then be used to make international payments. The value of SDRs today is based on a weighted average of exchange rates for key currencies, including the euro, the U.S. dollar, the Japanese yen and the British pound.

Many of the more developed nations *float,* rather than peg, their currencies. This means the value of any particular currency is determined by demand and supply forces. Usually, a **managed float** is used, in which governments intervene on occasion to stabilize the value of their home currency. The United States has officially adopted a managed float policy, but in practice it often follows a "free" floating exchange rate policy, in which the open market determines the value of the dollar, with U.S. monetary authorities intervening only in emergencies. Most recently the United States has relied heavily on the strength of its economy to achieve an acceptable value for the dollar.

In theory at least, a system of floating currency values should help the United States and other nations experiencing BOP deficits today. For example, if Americans are importing more goods from abroad than they are able to sell to overseas customers, an excess supply of U.S. dollars should build up abroad. The result may be a decline in the dollar's market value vis-à-vis other world currencies, making U.S. exports cheaper and foreign goods sold in the United States relatively more expensive. Ultimately, U.S. exports and imports may become more evenly balanced.

**special drawing rights (SDRs)**

**Key URL:**
To learn more about SDRs—their history and current status— see especially **imf.org**

**managed float**

## QUESTIONS TO HELP YOU STUDY

5. Explain the meaning of *currency risk*. How does currency risk affect exporters, importers, and investors active in the international financial marketplace?

6. Why was the *gold standard* developed? What problems did it appear to solve and what problems did it create? What is the difference between the gold standard and the gold exchange standard?

7. When and why was the *modified exchange standard* created? Explain how this particular monetary system worked to stabilize the value of currencies.

8. The international monetary system we have today has been labeled the *floating currency standard*. Briefly explain what this means. Can you anticipate any problems that might emerge with this standard for handling currency values and risk?

9. What are *SDRs* and what are they for?

10. Why do you think the U.S. dollar is such an important currency within the international financial system? Is the dollar's importance around the globe a matter of history, resources, economic strength, cultural values, or what?

## 23.4   Determining Foreign Currency Values

As we saw in the preceding section, major international currencies have floated with relative freedom since the 1970s and into the twenty-first century, their values dependent primarily on demand and supply forces in the marketplace. With this newfound freedom for currency prices and the expansion of world commerce, the volume of currency trading and the number of financial institutions participating in that trading have exploded. This is especially evident in the London and New York money markets, where exchange brokers bring in currency trading orders from financial institutions worldwide.

However, as the international financial system has moved increasingly toward freely floating exchange rates, currency prices have become significantly more *volatile*. The risks of buying and selling currencies have increased markedly in recent years. Moreover, fluctuations in the prices of foreign currencies affect domestic economic conditions, international investment, and the success or failure of government economic policies. Governments, businesses, and individuals find that it is more important today than ever before to understand how foreign currencies are traded and what affects their relative values.

Consider the problem faced by a corporation headquartered in the United States and selling machinery overseas. This firm frequently negotiates sales contracts with a foreign importer months before the machines are shipped. In the meantime, the market value of the currency the U.S. company expects to receive in payment for its products may have declined precipitously, canceling out expected profits. Similarly, a U.S. importer bringing fine wines into domestic U.S. markets must pay for incoming shipments in the currency demanded by a foreign exporter. The U.S. importer's profits could be significantly reduced if the value of the dollar declined relative to the values of currencies used by the importer to pay for goods purchased abroad. The same problems confront investors in foreign securities, who find that attractive interest rates available overseas must be protected from an erosion in value in one or more

**Key URL:**
Who holds more foreign currency than any other institution or individual in the world? As revealed by the Web site **pbc.gov .cn/english** the People's Bank of China leads the global list, holding well over a trillion dollars in foreign-exchange reserves, reflecting China's rapidly growing exports overseas and its massive inflows of investments from abroad.

foreign currencies. Knowledge of the foreign exchange markets is the *first step* toward successful international business and economic policy today.

## Essential Features of the Foreign Exchange Market

**foreign exchange markets**

The **foreign exchange markets** are among the largest markets in the world, with annual trading volume in the hundreds of trillions of dollars. The purpose of the foreign exchange markets is to bring buyers and sellers of currencies together. It is an *over-the-counter market,* with no central trading location and no set hours of trading. Prices and other terms of trade are determined by negotiation using computer screens linked electronically all over the world. The foreign exchange market is *informal* in its operations; there are no special requirements for market participants, and trading largely conforms to an unwritten code of rules.

## Exchange Rate Quotations

**foreign exchange rates**
**spot market**
**forward market**
**currency futures and options market**

The prices of foreign currencies expressed in terms of other currencies are called **foreign exchange rates.** There are three major markets for foreign exchange: (1) the **spot market,** which deals in currency for immediate delivery; (2) the **forward market,** which involves the future delivery of a currency; and (3) the **currency futures and options markets,** which deal in contracts to hedge against future changes in foreign exchange rates. Immediate delivery is defined as one or two business days for most transactions. Future delivery typically means one, three, or six months from today.

Exhibit 23.3 cites some recent foreign exchange rates between the U.S. dollar and other major currencies. The exhibit shows, for example, that an American importer or investor could obtain pounds sterling (£) that could be used to buy British bonds or British goods and services at a cost of about $1.89 per pound ($1.89/£) in August 2006. Conversely, a British investor or importer seeking to make purchases in the United States would have to pay 0.5291 pounds ($1/1.89 or 0.5291/$) for each dollar needed. Clearly, the exchange rate between dollars and pounds is the *reciprocal* of the exchange rate between pounds and dollars, which is true as well for any other pair of

| **EXHIBIT 23.3** | **Recent Foreign Exchange Rates: The U.S. Dollar vs. Other Key Currencies (figures are currency units per U.S. dollar except as noted)** | | |
|---|---|---|---|
| **Country/Currency Unit** | **2006 Exchange Rate with U.S. Dollars ($)\*** | **Country/Currency Unit** | **2006 Exchange Rate with U.S. Dollars ($)\*** |
| Canada/dollar | 1.1182 | Hong Kong/dollar | 7.7762 |
| China P.R./yuan | 7.9722 | Japan/yen | 115.92 |
| Australia/dollar | 0.7631† | United Kingdom/pound | 1.8941† |
| Switzerland/franc | 1.2318 | European Monetary Union/euro | 1.2810† |

\*Exchange rates are averages for August 2006.
†Exchange rate expressed in currency units per U.S. dollar except for the Australian dollar and British pound, which are expressed in U.S. cents per currency unit. The euro is reported in U.S. dollars per euro.
Source: Board of Governors of the Federal Reserve System.

| EXHIBIT 23.4 | How to Calculate Foreign Exchange Rates |
|---|---|

### Exchange Rate Conversion

Suppose the exchange rate between the European Monetary Union's new currency unit, the euro, and the U.S. dollar ($) is: euro/$ = 1.5000 or euro 1.50/$. What, then, is the $/euro exchange rate?

Answer: 1 ÷ 1.500 = $0.6667/euro

### Exchange Rate Appreciation

Suppose the exchange rate between euros and the U.S. dollar rises from euro/$ = 1.000, or euro 1.00/$, to euro 1.50/$. How much has the U.S. dollar appreciated in percent?

Answer: 1.500 ÷ 1.000 = 0.50, or 50%

Suppose the euro–U.S. dollar exchange rate is euro/$ = 1.5000, or euro 1.50/$. If the dollar appreciates by 3 percent, what is the new euro–U.S. dollar exchange rate?

Answer: 1.5000 × 1.03 = 1.5450, or euro 1.545/$

### Exchange Rate Depreciation

Suppose the exchange rate between euros and U.S. dollars rises from euro/$ = 1.000 to euro/$ = 1.500. How much has the euro depreciated, in percent?

Answer: Note that the $/euro exchange rate has changed from 1 ÷ 1.000 = $1.00/euro to 1 ÷ 1.500 = $0.6667/euro. The ratio of these two exchange rates is 0.6667 ÷ 1.000, or 0.6667. Then, 1 − 0.6667 = 0.3333. Therefore, an exchange rate depreciation of one-third has occurred.

Suppose the euro–U.S. dollar exchange rate is euro/$ = 1.50, or euro 1.50/$, and thus the U.S. dollar– euro exchange rate is $0.6667/euro. If the euro depreciates 5 percent, what is the new euro–U.S. dollar exchange rate?

Answer: Because 0.6667 × 0.95 = 0.6334, the new exchange rate is 1 ÷ 0.6334 = 1.5788, or euro $1.5788/$

Suppose, once again, the euro–U.S. dollar exchange rate is euro/$ = 1.5000. If the U.S. dollar depreciates 5 percent, what is the new euro–U.S. dollar exchange rate?

Answer: 1.5000 × 0.95 = 1.4250, or euro 1.4250/$

### Cross-Exchange Rates

Suppose the euro–U.S. dollar exchange rate is euro/$ = 1.5000, or euro 1.5000/$, and the Japanese yen (¥)–U.S. dollar exchange rate is 1.000, or ¥ 1.000/$. What, then, is the yen/euro exchange rate?

Answer: 1.000 ÷ 1.500 = 0.6667, or ¥ 0.6667/euro

Suppose the euro–U.S. dollar exchange rate is euro/$ = 1.500, or euro 1.500/$, and the U.S. dollar–Japanese yen exchange rate is $/¥ = 1.000, or 1.00/¥ What, then, is the euro/¥ exchange rate?

Answer: 1.500 ÷ (1 + 1.000) = 0.75, or euro 0.75/¥

Source: Based on a similar exhibit developed originally by the Public Information Center of the Federal Reserve Bank of Chicago.

currencies. Exhibit 23.4 illustrates the commonly accepted procedures for calculating exchange rates.[3]

Dealers and brokers in foreign exchange actually post not one, but *two,* exchange rates for each pair of currencies. That is, each trader sets a *bid* (buy) price and an *asked* (sell) price. For example, the dealer department in a New York bank might post a bid price for pounds sterling of £ = $1.89 US (or $1.89/£) and an asked price of £ = $1.91 US (or $1.91/£). This means that the dealer is willing to buy sterling at $1.89 per

---

[3]We note that in each quotation of a foreign exchange rate, one currency always serves as a unit of account (unit of value) and the other currency functions as the unit for which a price is stated. For example a quote of $1.89/£ tells us that one British pound costs $1.89. In this instance, the dollar serves as the unit of account, and the currency whose price is quoted is the pound. It is customary to place the symbol for the currency serving as the unit of account (in this case, $) in front of the stated number and the symbol of the currency whose price is being quoted (in this case, £) following the number.

pound and sell it at $1.91. These two exchange rates are sometimes referred to as "double-barreled" quotations. The dealer makes a profit on the *spread* between the bid and asked prices, although that spread is normally very small.[4]

**Key URLs:**
Data on current and forecasted foreign exchange rates (FOREX) may be found in such sources as **forexnewsletters.com/** and **fxstreet.com**

Dealers in the foreign exchange market continually watch exchange rate quotations in order to take advantage of any *arbitrage* opportunities. A *pure arbitrage* combines long (buying) and short (selling) positions such that the "investor" makes a zero net investment, incurs no risk, and realizes a profit. In the case of foreign exchange markets, arbitrage refers to the purchase of one currency in a certain market and the sale of that currency in another market in response to the price difference between the two markets. The force of arbitrage generally keeps foreign exchange rates from getting too far out of line in different areas around the globe.

## Factors Affecting Foreign Exchange Rates

*BOP Position*    The exchange rate for any foreign currency depends on a multitude of factors reflecting economic and financial conditions in the country issuing the currency. One of the most important factors is the status of a nation's *balance-of-payments (BOP) position.* When a country experiences a deficit in its balance of payments, it becomes a net demander of foreign currencies and may be forced to sell substantial amounts of its own currency to pay for imports of goods and services. Therefore, BOP deficits often lead to price depreciation in a nation's currency relative to the prices of other currencies.

*Speculation*    Exchange rates also are profoundly affected by *speculation over future currency values.* Dealers in foreign exchange monitor the currency markets closely, looking for profitable trading opportunities. A currency viewed as temporarily undervalued quickly brings forth buy orders, driving its price higher vis-à-vis other currencies. A currency considered to be overvalued is greeted by a rash of sell orders, depressing its price as speculators move in.

*Domestic Political and Economic Conditions*    The market for a currency is also greatly influenced by *domestic political and economic conditions.* Wars, revolutions, inflation, recession, and labor strikes have all been observed to have adverse effects on the currency of a nation experiencing these problems. On the other hand, signs of rapid economic growth, rising stock and bond prices, and successful economic policies to control inflation and unemployment often lead to a stronger currency in the exchange markets. Moreover, countries with higher real interest rates may experience an increase in the exchange value of their currencies.

*Purchasing Power Parity*    The theoretical link between each nation's currency value in the international markets and that nation's inflation rate represents an important relationship that has been extensively studied by economists. The **purchasing power parity** theory argues that the exchange rate between two currencies will reflect differences in their countries' inflation rates. For example, if the annual inflation rate stands at 4 percent in the United States and only 1 percent in Great Britain, the value

**purchasing power parity**

---

[4]Dealers will usually quote the bid price first and the asked price second and, as a rule, only the last digits in the price will be quoted to the buyer or seller. Thus, the spot bid and asked rates on British pounds might be quoted by a currency dealer as 40/42 because it is assumed the customer is aware of current exchange rates and knows that the bid price being quoted is $1.8940 and the asked price is $1.8942.

of the U.S. dollar will fall by about 3 percent on an annual basis relative to the value of the pound, reflecting relatively cheaper British goods. Of course, other factors may intervene to upset this expected relationship.

**Key URLs:**
To learn more about the European Central Bank and the euro see such sites as ecb.int; euro.gov.uk/; and ecuactivities.be/

*Central Bank Intervention*    Overshadowing the currency markets is the ever-present possibility of *central bank intervention*. Major central banks around the world, including the Federal Reserve System in the United States, the Bank of England, Bank of Japan, and European Central Bank (ECB) representing the whole European Community, may decide on a given day that their currency is declining too rapidly in value relative to other key currencies. Thus, if the dollar falls precipitously against the euro, support operations by the Federal Reserve System in the form of heavy sales of euros and corresponding purchases of dollars may be employed. Usually, central bank intervention is temporary, designed to promote a smooth adjustment in currency values toward a new equilibrium level rather than to permanently prop up a weak currency. The reason is that no matter how important central banks are, their resources compared to the resources of the whole foreign-exchange market are small—okay for making short-run adjustments, but not likely to be effective over a sustained period of time. Central bank intervention probably will not have a lasting effect on currency exchange rates as long as capital is free to flow from nation to nation. This intervention does not appear to give any nation a lasting trade advantage either.

In the United States, the Treasury Department is the agency designated to pursue market intervention if the U.S. government is dissatisfied with the performance of the U.S. dollar in international markets. The Treasury must decide what to do about the value of the dollar, but it is usually the Federal Reserve System that carries out the buying and selling of currencies on the Treasury's behalf through the foreign exchange desk at the Federal Reserve Bank of New York. The Fed also buys large amounts of currencies for foreign central banks and government agencies abroad.

We must keep in mind that central bank intervention may affect not only relative currency values but also the reserves held by private banks and the money supply. This happens because the central bank generally pays for its purchases of currency by increasing the deposit balances of private banks participating in the transaction with it. Thus, a decision by a central bank to intervene in the foreign currency markets can have *both* currency market and money supply effects unless an operation known as **currency sterilization** is carried out. For example, any increase in bank reserves and deposits that results from a central bank currency purchase can be "sterilized" by using monetary policy tools that absorb reserves and remove deposits from the banking system.

**currency sterilization**

## Supply and Demand for Foreign Exchange

The factors influencing a currency's rate of exchange with other currencies may be expressed in terms of the market forces of demand and supply. Exhibit 23.5, for example, illustrates a demand curve and a supply curve for dollars ($) in terms of British pounds (£). Note that the demand curve for U.S. dollars is also labeled the supply curve for pounds. This is due to the fact that an individual or institution holding British pounds and demanding dollars would be supplying pounds to the foreign exchange market. Similarly, the supply curve for U.S. dollars is identical to the demand curve for British pounds because someone holding dollars and demanding pounds must supply dollars to the foreign currency markets in order to purchase pounds. We recall, too, that the price of dollars in terms of pounds is the reciprocal of the price of pounds in terms of dollars.

To illustrate how demand and supply forces operate in the foreign exchange markets, suppose the current exchange rate between dollars and pounds is £ = 1.90. To

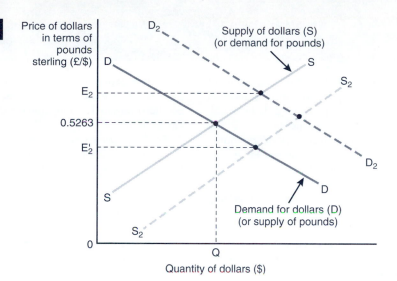

**EXHIBIT 23.5**

**Demand and Supply of U.S. Dollars in Terms of British Pounds**

purchase dollars, we have to pay 0.5263 pounds per dollar; to purchase British pounds costs us $1.90 per pound. This exchange rate between dollars and pounds is set in exchange markets by the interaction of the supply and demand for each currency. Exhibit 23.5 indicates that, at an exchange rate of 0.5263 pounds, the quantity of dollars supplied (S) is exactly equal to the quantity of dollars demanded (D).

If the price of dollars in terms of pounds were to fall temporarily *below* this exchange rate, more dollars would be demanded than supplied. Some buyers needing dollars would bid up the exchange rate toward the point where the demand for and supply of dollars were perfectly in balance. On the other hand, if the price of dollars were temporarily *above* 0.5263 pounds, more dollars would be supplied to the exchange markets. The price of dollars in terms of pounds would fall as suppliers of dollars willingly accepted a lower exchange rate to dispose of their excess dollar holdings. Only at that point where the exchange rate stood at 0.5263 pounds per dollar would quantity supplied equal quantity of dollars demanded. Only at that point would there be no reason for future changes in the exchange rate between the dollar and the pound unless changes occurred in the demand for or supply of either currency.

As we noted earlier, a number of factors affect the exchange rates between currencies, including a nation's BOP position, domestic political and economic developments, changes in real interest rates, and central bank intervention. Each of these factors leads to a shift in the demand for or supply of one currency vis-à-vis another, which brings about a change in their relative rates of exchange.

To illustrate the impact of shifts in currency demand and supply, suppose that consumers in Great Britain increase their demand for U.S. goods and services. As Exhibit 23.5 indicates, the demand curve for dollars would shift from $D$ to $D_2$. This is equivalent to an increase in the supply of British pounds seeking U.S. dollars. The equilibrium cost of dollars in terms of pounds, therefore, will rise to $E_2$. British importers will be forced to surrender a greater quantity of pounds per dollar in order to satisfy the demands of British consumers for U.S. goods and services. Other things being equal, the prices of imported goods from the United States will tend to rise.

The opposite effects would occur if U.S. consumers demanded a larger quantity of British goods and services. In this case, the supply-of-dollars (demand-for-pounds) curve slides downward and to the right from $S$ to $S_2$, as shown in Exhibit 23.5.

On January 1, 1999, the *euro* (€)—the single unit of currency adopted by the majority of nations forming the European Union (EU)—was introduced to the world. While euros were not issued to the public until 2002, deposits and other financial instruments denominated in euros were traded across the European landscape just before the new century began. Nations initially representing the "euro zone" included Austria, Belgium, Finland, France, Germany, Ireland, Italy, Luxembourg, the Netherlands, Portugal, Spain, and Greece.

May 2004 witnessed the addition of 10 new nations to the EU, including the Czech Republic, Estonia, Cyprus, Latvia, Lithuania, Hungary, Malta, Poland, Slovakia, and Slovenia. However, these nations were not immediately added to the euro zone. They were required to meet *convergence criteria* (including the achievement of a "high degree of price stability" and the elimination of "excessive deficits" in their government's financial position) before formally joining the euro-based financial system.

For businesses and households in Europe, the potential benefits of being a part of the euro zone include the likelihood of lower prices for at least some goods and services due to greater cross-border competition, the elimination of currency risk inside the euro zone, and easier access to the financial markets in order to borrow money and thereby improve existing businesses and start new ones. Certainly there is great potential in the growing euro zone. After bringing fully aboard the 10 new member states named in 2004, the euro zone will contain a population of more than 450 million, compared to a U.S. population of approximately 300 million.

**Key URL:**
One interesting financial institution playing a growing role in the expansion of the European Community (EC) and the euro is the European Bank for Reconstruction and Development at **ebrd.com**

Reflecting the increased demand for pounds and associated sales of dollars for pounds by U.S. importers, the dollar's price in pounds sterling falls to $E_2'$. The market prices of British goods and services imported into the United States tend to rise.

What happens if a central bank, such as the Bank of England or the Federal Reserve, intervenes to stabilize the dollar–pound exchange rate at some arbitrary target level? The answer depends, among other things, on which side of the market the central bank enters to intervene, which currency is used as the vehicle for intervention, and the particular exchange-rate target chosen. For example, suppose that increased British demand for U.S. goods and services drove the dollar–pound exchange rate up to $E_1$, as shown in Exhibit 23.6. However, this upward surge in the dollar's value sharply

**EXHIBIT 23.6**

**Effects of Central Bank Intervention to Stabilize the Dollar–Pound Exchange Rate**

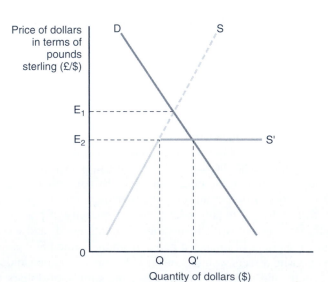

reduced the purchasing power of the pound for dollar-denominated goods and services and threatened to have damaging effects on British foreign trade and industrial output. The Bank of England might intervene to force the dollar–pound exchange rate down to $E_2$ by selling dollars out of its currency reserve and demanding pounds in the foreign exchange market. In effect, the supply-of-dollars curve would be "kinked" at the stabilization price, $E_2$. In order to peg the dollar–pound exchange rate at $E_2$, the central bank would have to spend $Q' - Q$ of its dollar reserves. Otherwise, the price of dollars would again rise toward $E_1$—the level dictated by demand and supply forces in the exchange markets. Conversely, if the dollar were falling to unacceptably low levels against the pound, the Bank of England or the Federal Reserve System might enter on the opposite side of the market, purchasing dollars with pounds and driving the dollar's price higher.

## 23.5 The Forward Market for Currencies

Knowledge of how the foreign exchange markets work and the ways in which currency risk can be reduced is indispensable for business managers today. Of course, the problem of fluctuating currency values is not so serious if payment for foreign goods, services, or securities must be made right away. Spot market prices of foreign currencies normally change by small amounts each day. However, if payment must be made weeks or months in the future, there is considerable uncertainty as to what the spot currency rate will be on any given future date. When substantial sums of money are involved, the rational investor or commercial trader will try to *guarantee* the future price at which currency can be purchased. This is the function of the *forward exchange market*.

### *Methods of Quoting Forward Exchange Rates*

**forward contract**

Trading in the spot market results in agreements to deliver a specified amount of currency at an agreed-upon price, usually within one or two business days and sometimes on the same day. In contrast, a **forward contract** is an agreement to deliver a specified amount of foreign currency at a set price on some future date (usually within 1, 2, 3, 6, or 12 months). The actual delivery date is referred to by traders as the *value date*. In the event customers do not know when they will need foreign currency, an *option forward contract* may be used, which gives its holder the right but not the obligation to take delivery of currency in the future.

There are several different ways of measuring and quoting forward exchange rates. Suppose the spot exchange rate on euros (€) is $1.30US and that dealers in foreign exchange are selling forward contracts for delivery of euros in six months at $1.28US. We may express the *forward* exchange rate for euros simply as $1.28US, or $1.28/euro—known as the *outright* rate.

Another popular method is to express the forward rate as a premium or discount from the spot rate, known as the *swap rate*. In the example above, euros are selling at a 2-cent *discount* in the forward market. Traders in the forward market appear to be signaling an expectation that the euro will fall in value over the next few weeks.

We may also express forward exchange rates in terms of an annualized percentage rate above or below the current spot price. To use the example above, $/€ spot = 1.30 and $/€ forward = $1.28. Then, the discount on forward euros (€) for delivery in six months is figured as follows:

$$\frac{\text{Forward rate} - \text{Spot rate}}{\text{Spot rate}} \times \frac{12}{\text{Number of months forward}} \times 100 \qquad \textbf{(23.1)}$$

$$= \frac{1.28 - 1.30}{1.16} \times \frac{12}{6} \times 100$$
$$= -.02 \times 2 \times 100$$
$$= -4\%$$

Thus, euros are selling at a 4 percent *discount* from their spot in the forward market. Because euros are selling at a discount from their spot price, forward dollars must be selling at a *premium* over spot.

Suppose we know the current spot rate between two currencies and the forward premium or discount. We want to know the actual forward exchange rate. The following will help determine that rate:

$$\text{Spot rate} + \frac{\text{Spot rate} \times [\text{Premium} (+) \text{ or discount} (-) \text{ expressed as an annual rate}] \times \text{Number of months forward}}{100 \times \text{Number of months in a year}} \qquad \textbf{(23.2)}$$

Suppose the \$/€ spot = 1.30 and forward euros for delivery in three months are selling at a 4 percent premium over spot. Using the formula above, we have:

$$1.3000 + \frac{1.30 \times 4.0 \times 3}{1,200} = 1.3130\$ / €\text{ forward}$$

This means €/\$ forward is 0.7616, or € 0.7616/\$.

## 23.6  Functions of the Forward Exchange Market

Contracts calling for the future delivery of currency are employed to cover a number of risks faced by investors and commercial traders. Some analysts group the functions of forward contracts into four categories: commercial covering, hedging an investment position, speculation, and covered interest arbitrage.

### Commercial Covering

The export or import of goods and services usually requires someone to deliver payment in a foreign currency or to receive payment in a foreign currency. Either the payor or payee, then, is subject to currency risk, because no one knows for sure what the spot currency price will be for a given currency at the time payment must be made. The forward exchange market can be used as a buffer against this risk.

To illustrate, suppose that a U.S. importer of cameras has agreed to pay 5,000 euros to a German manufacturer upon receipt of a new shipment. The cameras are expected to arrive dockside in 30 days. The importer has no idea what 5,000 euros will cost in U.S. dollars 30 days from now. To reduce the risk that the price of euros in terms of dollars may rise significantly, the importer negotiates a forward contract with his or her bank for delivery of 5,000 euros at \$1.30/€ in 30 days.

When payment is due, the importer takes delivery of the euros (usually by acquiring ownership of a deposit denominated in euros) at the agreed-upon price and pays the German manufacturer. Because the price is fixed in advance, the risk associated with fluctuations in foreign currency prices has been eliminated. Today, export and import firms routinely cover their purchases overseas with forward currency contracts or other hedging tools (to be discussed later in this chapter).

## Hedging an Investment Position

Thousands of corporations have invested in long-term capital projects overseas, building manufacturing plants, warehouse and dock facilities, and office buildings. In recent years, a large return flow of long-term investments by foreign firms inside the United States has occurred due to the underlying strength of the U.S. economy and a desire to avoid U.S. tariffs. Of course, the market value of these foreign investments may change drastically as currency prices change over time.

To illustrate, suppose a U.S. commercial bank constructed an office building in downtown London. When completed, the office facility had an estimated market value of £2 million. The current spot rate on pounds is, let us say, $1.90/£. The bank values the new building on its consolidated financial statement, therefore, at $3.8 million. However, suppose the pound has declined in value in recent months and some market analysts expect pounds to be selling at $1.75/£ in the near future. In the absence of a hedged position, the bank would take a loss of $300,000 on its building. This is due to the fact that, at an exchange rate of $1.75/£, the office building will have a value of only $3.5 million.

Can this loss be avoided or reduced? Yes, provided the bank can negotiate a sale of pounds *forward* at a higher price. For example, the bank may be able to arrange with a dealer for the sale of £2 million for future delivery at $1.80US ($1.80/£). When this forward contract matures, if the spot price has fallen to $1.75/£, the bank can buy pounds at this rate and deliver them to the dealer at $1.80US as agreed. The result is a profit on the foreign exchange transaction of $100,000, partially offsetting the loss on the building from declining currency values.

## Speculation on Future Currency Prices

A third use of the forward exchange market is speculative investment based on expectations concerning future movements in currency prices. Speculators will buy currency for future delivery if they believe the future spot rate will be *higher* on the delivery date than the current forward rate. They will sell currency under a forward contract if the future spot rate appears likely to be *below* the forward rate on the day of delivery. Such speculative purchases and sales carry the advantage of requiring little or no capital in advance of the delivery date. A speculator whose forecast of future spot rates turns out to be correct makes a profit on the spread between purchase and sale price.

## Covered Interest Arbitrage

One of the most common international transactions arises when an investor discovers a higher interest rate available on foreign securities and invests funds abroad. When the currency risk associated with the purchase of foreign securities is reduced by using a forward contract, this transaction is often referred to as *covered interest arbitrage*.

To illustrate the interest arbitrage process, suppose that a British oil company is selling high-grade bonds with a promised annual yield of 7 percent. Comparable bonds in the United States offer a 5 percent annual return. The bonds are of good quality and there is little default risk, but there *is* currency risk. The U.S. investor must purchase pounds in order to buy British bonds. When the bonds earn interest or reach maturity, the issuing company will pay foreign and domestic investors in pounds sterling. Then the pounds must be converted into dollars to allow the U.S. investor to spend his or her earnings in the United States. If the spot price of sterling falls, the U.S. investor's net yield from the bonds will be reduced. For example, if the spot rate on pounds declines by 2 percent (on an annual basis), the interest gain from the British bonds will be offset by the loss on trading pounds. Clearly, a series of forward contracts is needed to sell pounds at a guaranteed price as the bonds generate a stream of cash for the investor.

## The Principle of Interest Rate Parity

**Key URL:**
For an expanded discussion, see "Extended Mass Layoffs Associated with Domestic and Overseas Relocations, First Quarter 2004," at the Bureau of Labor Statistics Web site **bls.gov/mls/**

**interest rate parity**

The foregoing example suggests an important rule regarding international capital flows and foreign exchange rates: *The net rate of return to the investor from any foreign investment is equal to the interest earned plus or minus the forward premium or discount on the price of the foreign currency involved in the transaction.* The theory of forward exchange states that the forward discount or premium on one currency relative to another is directly related to the difference in interest rates between the two countries involved. More specifically, the currency of the nation experiencing higher interest rates normally sells at a forward *discount* in terms of the currency issued by the nation with lower interest rates. And the currency of the nation with relatively low interest rates normally sells at a forward *premium* relative to that of the high-rate country. A condition known as **interest rate parity** exists when *the interest rate differential between two nations is equal to the forward discount or premium on their two currencies.* When parity exists, the currency markets are in equilibrium and capital funds do not tend to flow from one country to another. This is due to the fact that the gain from investing abroad at higher interest rates is offset by the cost of covering currency risk in the forward exchange market.

To illustrate the principle of interest rate parity, suppose interest rates in a foreign country are 3 percent above those in the United States. Then the currency of that foreign nation, in equilibrium, is likely to sell at a 3 percent discount in the forward exchange market. Similarly, if interest rates are 1 percent lower abroad than in the United States, in equilibrium, the foreign currency of the nations involved is likely to sell at a 1 percent premium against the U.S. dollar. When such an equilibrium position is reached, movements of funds between nations, even with currency risk covered, do not generate excess returns relative to domestic investments of comparable risk. Capital funds tend to stay in the domestic market rather than flowing abroad.

It is when interest rate parity does *not* exist that capital tends to flow across national boundaries in response to differences in domestic and foreign interest rates. For example, suppose that interest rates in a foreign nation are 3 percent above U.S. interest rates on securities of comparable quality and the foreign currency involved is selling at a 1 percent discount against the dollar in the forward exchange market. In this case, investing abroad with exchange risks covered yields the investor a *net* added return of 2 percent per year. Clearly, there is a positive incentive to invest overseas.

Is this situation likely to persist for a long period of time? No, because the movement of funds into a country offering higher interest rates tends to increase the forward discount on its currency and lowers the net rate of return to the investor. Other factors held constant, the flow of funds abroad will tend to subside and capital will tend to stay at home.

## QUESTIONS TO HELP YOU STUDY

11. What are the principal factors affecting the value of any particular foreign currency in the international markets?

12. Distinguish between the *spot and forward markets* for foreign currencies. Why is it necessary to have two markets rather than one?

13. Describe the principal uses of *forward exchange contracts* today and give an example of each use.

14. What exactly are the *advantages* of a hedged position in one or more foreign currencies? What about the *disadvantages* (if any)?

## 23.7 The Market for Foreign Currency Futures

Forward contracts call for the delivery of a specific currency on a specified date in the future at a set price. The intent of buyer and seller in a forward contract is to actually *deliver* the currency mentioned in the contract. In recent years, an important variation of the forward currency contract has developed—*foreign currency futures.* These, too, are contracts calling for the future delivery of a specific currency at a price agreed on today, *but there is usually no intent to actually deliver the currencies mentioned in the contracts.* Rather, *currency futures are traded in the majority of cases to reduce the risk associated with fluctuating currency prices.* Today, currency futures contracts are traded in the United States (for example, at the Chicago Mercantile Exchange) and in a number of other global financial centers, principally on futures exchanges (unlike forward contracts, which are traded mainly in an unregulated dealer market). The most popular currency futures contracts today are for the future delivery of British pounds, Japanese yen, Canadian and U.S. dollars, Eurodollars, and euro currency units (€).

Currency futures are attractive primarily to two groups: foreign exchange hedgers and speculators. The *hedgers,* who typically are banks, trading companies, and multinational corporations, seek to avoid damage to their profits from normal business transactions caused by changes in currency prices. Usually, a hedger seeks out a *speculator* who hopes to profit from changes in relative currency rates by taking on the risk the hedger seeks to minimize. Two basic transactions take place on currency futures exchanges: the buying and the selling hedges.

### The Buying Hedge

Importers of goods typically use the *buying hedge.* In this case, a domestic importer committed to pay in a foreign currency when goods are received from abroad fears that currency may rise in price. He therefore *purchases* a futures contract, agreeing to take delivery of a currency at a set price as near as possible to the date on which the goods must be paid for. Because the price of this contract is fixed, the importer has "locked in" the value of imported goods. As a final step, near the date the goods are paid for, the importer will "zero out" his futures contract purchase by *selling* a comparable currency futures contract, perhaps through a broker trading on the floor of a futures exchange. That is, the exchange's clearinghouse records each transaction taking place on the exchange and requires settlement only in the *net* trades for each trader. Therefore, it will automatically cancel out the importer's obligation both to take delivery of and to deliver a particular foreign currency.

How has the importer protected himself against loss due to currency risk? If a foreign currency rises in value during the life of a futures contract, the importer will experience reduced profits or increased losses on the imported goods themselves because the foreign currency has risen in value relative to his home currency. However, the market value of a currency futures contract also rises when the market value of the underlying currency increases. Therefore, the importer will be able to sell currency futures contracts at a higher price than the price for which they were originally purchased. The resulting profit in currency futures at least partially offsets the reduced gains or losses on the purchase of imported goods.

**Key URLs:**
Additional information on the currency futures market is available from such Web sites as the Chicago Mercantile Exchange at **cme.com** and Business Jeeves at **businessjeeves.com**

### The Selling Hedge

The opposite kind of hedge in currency futures is known as the *selling hedge.* This transaction is often employed by investors who purchase foreign securities and want to protect their earnings from a drop in currency values. In this instance, investors could hedge their expected earnings by *selling* futures contracts in the currency involved at the time the securities are acquired in the cash (spot) market. If contracts are sold in an amount that covers both principal and interest or dividends, investors have "locked in" their investment return regardless of which way exchange rates go. If the foreign currency involved has declined in price relative to the home currency when the security pays out cash or must be sold, a loss will be incurred in cash received, but investors will earn an offsetting futures market profit by *buying* futures contracts in an amount equivalent to those sold earlier.

## 23.8  Other Innovative Methods for Dealing with Currency Risk

The recent volatility of foreign exchange rates has given rise to an ever-widening circle of devices to deal with currency risk. For example, the *currency option* gives a buyer the right, though not the obligation, to either deliver or take delivery of a designated currency at a set price any time before the option expires. Thus, unlike the forward market, actual delivery *may* not occur, but unlike futures trading, no follow-up

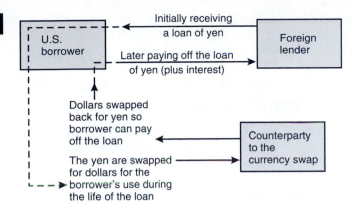

**EXHIBIT 23.7**

**The Currency Swap: Converting a Foreign Currency-Denominated Loan into a Domestic Currency Loan**

purchases or sales are needed to stop delivery. The advantage of the currency option is that it limits downside risk but not upside profits.

A related hedging instrument is the *option on currency futures. Call options* on currency futures give the buyer a way to protect against rising exchange rates by buying a currency futures contract at a fixed price from another investor, thus locking in a desired currency delivery price. On the other hand, *puts* on currency futures give a hedger protection against falling exchange rates by giving him or her the right to sell currency futures at a fixed price, regardless of how market prices change.

**currency swap**          Another innovative device is the **currency swap.** In straight currency swaps, a company that has borrowed a foreign currency (such as Japanese yen) for a designated length of time immediately turns around and exchanges that currency for its home currency (say, dollars) with a counterparty. The counterparty may be a bank or other business firm with an exactly opposite situation—for example, holding dollars but needing yen. As shown in Exhibit 23.7, when the loan comes due, the borrowing company reverses the transaction with the counterparty, swapping its home currency to get back the yen needed to pay off its foreign currency loan. In this case, there is no exposure to the risk of changing yen prices. The borrower has received an inflow of dollars at the beginning of the loan and experienced a dollar outflow when the loan is paid off. The currency swap has merely facilitated the borrower's ability to borrow dollars from foreign markets without currency risk. The advantage of currency swaps is that they can be arranged with longer maturities and more suitable terms of settlement than most standard currency contracts. Central banks frequently use swaps to help protect currency prices.

Innovative new approaches to currency risk continue to emerge each year, and many old methods have been resurrected lately. For example, some multinational firms have expanded their use of *local loans*—that is, securing credit inside the countries where they have sales or production operations. Others have resorted to issuing *dual-currency bonds* with principal and interest payments denominated in two different currencies. Some exporters ship only if *prepayments* are made by an overseas customer that cover all or a substantial portion of the value of a shipment before it is made. Some companies simply *barter* their goods or property directly so that no currency changes hands. *Selective currency pricing* is also employed, in which the seller invoices the buyer in a currency thought to be more stable or easier to hedge.

The ultimate economic response when other risk-reducing methods appear to be too costly or too risky is for a seller to use *risk-adjusted pricing* of goods and services. For example, goods sold to countries where currency risk is unacceptably high may be priced higher to compensate the seller for that added risk. Ultimately, individuals living in those countries where currency risk is unusually high are likely to wind up paying higher prices for goods and services.

## 23.9  Government Intervention in the Foreign Exchange Markets

The value of a nation's currency in the international markets has long been a source of concern to governments around the world. National pride plays a role in this case, because a strong currency, avidly sought by international traders and investors, implies a vigorous and well-managed economy at home. A strong and stable currency encourages investment in the home country, stimulating its development. Moreover, changes in currency values affect a nation's balance-of-payments position. A weak and declining currency makes foreign imports more expensive, lowering the standard of living at home. And a nation whose currency is not well regarded in the international marketplace may have difficulty selling its goods and services abroad, giving rise to unemployment at home.

**Key URLs**
To discover more about currency boards and dollarization see, for example, **iie.com**

The United States has pursued an "on-again, off-again" policy of supporting the dollar in international markets over the years, sometimes supporting the dollar vigorously and at other times merely "signaling" its target value for the dollar with occasional intervention. When the United States has intervened in the currency markets, it has done so mainly out of concern for the condition of the U.S. economy, particularly for the effects of inflation.

**vehicle currency**

Another factor is the key role played by the U.S. dollar in the international financial system. The dollar is a **vehicle currency** that facilitates trade and investment between many nations. For example, international shipments of crude oil, regardless of their origin or destination, are more frequently than not valued in dollars. As noted in Chapter 11, the market for dollar deposits held in banks abroad—Eurodollars—is the world's largest money market, financing commercial projects and even providing operating funds for several foreign governments. For all of these reasons, the United States, as well as foreign governments and central banks, has intervened from time to time in the foreign exchange markets to stabilize currency values and insulate domestic economic conditions from developments abroad.

---

## QUESTIONS TO HELP YOU STUDY

15. What is a *buying hedge* in currency futures? A *selling hedge?* Under what circumstances is each of these hedges likely to be employed?

16. Exactly what is meant by the phrase *interest rate parity?* How does it influence the flow of capital from one nation to another?

17. In recent years central banks have intervened in the foreign exchange markets from time to time to support one foreign currency or another. Why might central bank intervention in the currency markets be a necessity? What impact are central bank operations most likely to have in the short run and the long run?

18. What does the term *sterilization* refer to when talking about central bank intervention in the foreign currency markets?

19. What is the purpose of *currency swaps?* How do they work?

20. Many new *currency hedging techniques* have appeared in recent years. List and define as many examples of these as you can.

## Summary of the Chapter's Main Points

The international financial system performs the same roles and functions that domestic money and capital markets do around the globe. It attracts savings and allocates capital for investment purposes toward the most promising projects, stimulating the international economy to grow.

- One of the most significant sources of information on world trade and the flow of savings (capital) between nations is provided by each country's *balance-of-payments (BOP) accounts,* which summarize economic and financial transactions between residents of a nation and the rest of the world. The principal components of a nation's BOP are the *current account* (which focuses primarily upon flows of merchandise and services between nations), the *capital and financial accounts* (which trace long- and short-term capital flows between nations), and *official reserve transactions* (which are used by governments and central banks to aid in the settlement of BOP deficits).

- One of the most significant risks in the international financial system is *currency or foreign exchange risk.* Crossing national and regional borders with capital or merchandise usually is accompanied by transactions involving two or more different currencies whose relative values can change quickly, threatening losses on trade and in the value of investments.

- Reducing currency risk has been a continuing goal of nations, individuals, and businesses for centuries. Nations have resorted in the past to tying their currencies to assets (such as gold) recognized as having universal appeal and value. However, restrictions on the availability of gold and transaction costs as well as lack of flexibility in a nation's money and credit policy eventually led to a much more flexible currency standard, referred to today as the *managed floating currency standard.* Each nation chooses its own currency standard, taking into account the welfare of other nations.

- The exchange rate between one currency and another is determined by the foreign exchange (FOREX) market through the interplay of the demand and supply for each nation's currency. Currencies are traded over the counter in a relatively informal marketplace and prices are quoted as "double barrel" quotations—the price of one foreign currency expressed in terms of another.

- Foreign currency markets today are multitiered, divided into *spot, forward,* and *futures and options markets.* While spot transactions involve immediate currency exchanges, forward, futures, and options markets are designed to hedge against currency risk.

- The supply and demand forces that shape foreign currency prices are influenced by a few powerful factors, including a nation's balance-of-payments position, speculation over future currency values, domestic economic conditions, and central bank policy.

- The *forward exchange market* is designed to protect against losses due to currency price fluctuations. The functions of forward currency contracts include (a) commercial covering designed primarily to affect export/import values; (b) hedging an investment position against loss in market values; (c) speculation about future currency values; and (d) covered interest

*www.mhhe.com.rose10e*

arbitrage to help protect the yield on an investment instrument (such as a government bond).

- The principle of *interest rate parity* rests on the fact that the net return to the investor from any foreign investment is equal to the interest earned on the investment plus or minus the forward premium or discount on the price of any foreign currency involved in the transaction. The parity principle argues that the interest rate differential between two nations is closely related to the forward discount or premium on their currencies.

- Foreign *currency futures contracts* call for the future delivery of a specific currency at a price agreed upon today and are designed to transfer currency risk to another investor willing to bear that risk. Importers of goods and services typically use a *buying hedge* in currency futures while a *selling hedge* is often employed by investors who purchase foreign securities and want to protect their earnings from a drop in currency values.

- Newer and more innovative methods for dealing with currency risk include *currency swaps,* where two parties exchange payments in different currencies; the use of *local loans* to avoid currency trading; *dual currency bonds,* with principal and interest payments made in at least two different currencies; the *bartering* of goods or property; and the *risk-adjusted pricing* of goods and services in order to take into account foreign exchange risk.

- Government intervention in foreign exchange markets has become less common today. However, many governments intervene to change currency values when emergency shocks occur (such as terrorist attacks or a sudden plunge in the values of stocks or bonds) that could damage a nation's economic welfare.

## Key Terms Appearing in This Chapter

balance-of-payments (BOP) accounts, 717
current account, 719
capital and financial accounts, 722
gold standard, 725
gold exchange standard, 725
modified exchange standard, 725
managed floating currency standard, 726
special drawing rights (SDRs), 727
managed float, 727
foreign exchange markets, 729

foreign exchange rates, 729
spot market, 729
forward market, 729
currency futures and options market, 729
purchasing power parity, 731
currency sterilization, 732
forward contract, 735
interest rate parity, 738
currency swap, 741
vehicle currency, 742

# Problems and Issues

1. The U.S. balance of payments (BOP) is often described in terms of the current account or the merchandise trade deficit or surplus. What is the difference between the current account and the merchandise trade account? Which is the more comprehensive measure of international trade? Is it possible for the current account to be in deficit while the merchandise trade account is in surplus, or vice versa? Explain.

2. The print media regularly report the results of trading in the forward and futures markets for foreign exchange. What are the essential differences between these two markets? Explain what it means to "zero out" a position taken in the currency futures market. Why is it not possible to automatically "zero out" a position in the forward market?

3. Indicate whether each of the transactions below represents a credit (+) or a debit (−) item in a nation's BOP:

   a. General Electric Corporation purchases electric switches from a supplier in Germany.

   b. Bell Helicopter sells new helicopters to a British oil field exploration company.

   c. Universal Studios makes the decision to begin building a new theme park in Singapore.

   d. George Elwin has just received a dividend check for the stock he holds in British Airways.

   e. Citigroup of New York agrees to provide insurance for goods shipped by the International Furniture Mart of Copenhagen to a London wholesale house.

   f. Carlos Mendoza sends his paycheck from San Diego, California, to his family in Mexico City.

4. Suppose the exchange rate between British pounds (£) and U.S. dollars ($) is $1.35 per pound. What is the correct way to write this pound–dollar exchange rate? The dollar–pound exchange rate?

5. Suppose the pound–dollar exchange rate is now 1.3500. Then, the U.S. dollar increases in value by 5 percent. What is the new pound–dollar exchange rate? What is the new exchange rate if the U.S. dollar appreciates by 10 percent?

6. If the pound–dollar exchange rate increases from £/$ = 1.3500 to 1.4000, by what percentage amount has the pound depreciated?

7. If the pound–dollar exchange rate is 1.4000 and the pound declines 10 percent in value, what is the new pound–dollar exchange rate?

8. Suppose the pound–dollar exchange rate is 1.4000 and the yen–dollar exchange rate is 120. What is the yen–pound exchange rate?

9. Suppose the dollar–euro (€) spot exchange rate is 0.8620 and the three-month forward exchange rate for these two currencies is 0.8315. What then is the percentage discount on euros slated for delivery in three months?

10. You are asked to calculate the forward exchange rate on euros (€) versus the U.S. dollar. You find out that the current dollar–euro spot exchange rate is 0.8555 and that forward euros scheduled for delivery in six months are selling at a 3 percent premium over the spot rate. What is the euro–dollar forward exchange rate?

## Web-Based Problems

1. Caterpillar Tractor Company (CAT) is a Fortune 500 multinational company with approximately 50 percent of its product sales outside the United States. The success of its business plan is obviously very dependent upon events that occur around the globe. There are many other multinational companies in other industries that also must confront the challenges of trading in the international marketplace. The purpose of this exercise is to see what insight can be gained from an industry analysis and from knowledge of a multinational firm's business statements regarding its current status vis-à-vis conditions in the overseas markets that it serves.

   a. Visit Caterpillar Tractor's Web site and determine what industry or industries the company is involved in around the globe.

   b. What is the status of the industry (or industries) Caterpillar serves as it relates to the international marketplace? Does the information you obtained suggest that the international business climate is favorable to Caterpillar's business plan, considering the markets in which Caterpillar hopes to compete successfully?

   c. Would you choose to be a buyer of Caterpillar's stock? Why or why not? Does the current international outlook affect your decision in some significant way?

   d. Pick another well-known multinational company from a different industry group and repeat this exercise. Is there a difference in the conclusions that you've drawn for Caterpillar versus the other company you selected? Do these differences relate to the industry group or to the geographic regions that are being serviced by the two firms, or both?

2. As noted in this chapter, the United States has been running merchandise trade and current account deficits for the past several years. The purpose of this exercise is to take a closer look at the data, and compare them with the most recent performance of the U.S. economy in the international trade arena.

   a. Visit the Web site of the Bureau of Economic Analysis at **bea.gov,** which is part of the U.S. Department of Commerce, and locate annual data for the past 20 years for "U.S. International Transactions," which reports regularly on the BOP of the United States.

   b. Download the data from Table 1 that you need to compute the merchandise trade and current account surplus or deficit, along with each of their major components, into a spreadsheet for each of the past 10 years. Graph the merchandise trade and current account surplus (deficit). Do you observe any trends in those graphs?

   c. Produce a graph for the contribution of each major component series in terms of a surplus or deficit. Do there appear to be any major contributors to the trends that you identified in part (b)?

   d. Go to Table 11 and download trade data for Japan and China for as many years as the data are available. Compute the merchandise and current account surplus (deficit) for each of those countries and graph the results. What do you conclude from your graphs?

## Selected References to Explore

1. Broda, Christian, and David Weinstein. "Are We Underestimating the Gains from Globalization for the United States," *Current Issues in Economics and Finance,* Federal Reserve Bank of New York, April 2005, pp. 1–7.
2. Coughlin, Cletus; Michael R. Pakko; and William Poole. "How Dangerous Is the U.S. Current Account Deficit?" *The Regional Economist,* Federal Reserve Bank of St. Louis, April 2006, pp. 5–9.
3. Goldberg, Linda and Eleanor Wiske Dillon. "Why a Dollar Depreciation May Not Close the U.S. Trade Deficit," *Current Issues in Economics and Finance,* Federal Reserve Bank of New York, Vol. 13, No. 5 (June 2007), pp. 1–7.
4. Higgins, Matthew; Thomas Klitgaard; and Cedric Tille. "The Income Implications of Rising U.S. International Liabilities," *Current Issues in Economics and Finance,* Federal Reserve Bank of New York, December 2005, pp. 1–7.
5. Humpage, Owen F. "On the Rotation of the Earth, Drunken Sailors, and Exchange Rate Policy," *Economic Commentary,* Federal Reserve Bank of Cleveland, February 15, 2004, pp. 1–3.
6. Neely, Christopher J. "An Analysis of Recent Studies of the Effect of Foreign Exchange Intervention," *Review,* Federal Reserve Bank of St. Louis, November/December 2005, pp. 685–701,
7. Poole, William. "Chinese Growth" A Source of U.S. Export Opportunities," *Review,* Federal Reserve Bank of St. Louis, November/December 2006, pp. 471–83.
8. Wu, Tao. "Globalization's Effect on Interest Rates and the Yield Curve," *Economic Letter,* Federal Reserve Bank of Dallas, September 2006, pp. 1–8.

www.mhhe.com.rose10e

# Chapter 24

# International Banking

## Learning Objectives

### in This Chapter

- You will understand the important role that large *multinational banks* play in both domestic and foreign markets around the world.

- You will explore the types of physical facilities that multinational banks operate around the globe and be able to identify which financial *services* each banking facility offers.

- You will see how and why international banking is still so closely *regulated* in many areas of the world.

## What's in This Chapter?
## Key Topics Outline

## 24.1   Introduction to International Banking

No review of the international financial system would be complete without a discussion of the role of international banking institutions. Through these banking firms flow the majority of commercial and financial transactions that cross international borders. Along with British, Japanese, German, Chinese, and Canadian banks, U.S. banking institutions have led in the development of international facilities to meet the far-flung financial needs of foreign governments and multinational corporations. Until recently, the international activities of U.S. banks were concentrated principally in their foreign offices, due mainly to federal government restrictions against foreign lending. However, the gradual relaxation of government controls in recent decades, the high cost of maintaining a large network of foreign branches, political instability overseas, and improvements in communications technology have encouraged many international banks to offer more international services from their *domestic* offices.

The development of multinational banking over the past century has resulted in several benefits for international trade. One benefit to the public is greater competition in international markets, lowering the real prices of financial services. It also has tied together more effectively the various national money markets into a unified international financial system, permitting a more efficient allocation of the world's scarce resources. Funds flow freely today across many national boundaries in response to differences in relative interest rates and currency values. Although these developments have benefited both borrowers and investors, they also have created problems for governments trying to regulate the volume of credit, insure a stable banking system, and combat inflation.

## 24.2   The Scope of International Banking Activities

### Multinational Banking Corporations

**multinational corporation**

**Key URLs:**
To learn more about the field of international banking, including career possibilities, see, for example, the Guide to International Banking at **accuity solutions .com** and Guide to Banking Law at **hg .org/banking.html**

The term **multinational corporation** usually is reserved for large nonfinancial companies with manufacturing or trading operations in several different countries. However, this term is equally applicable to the world's leading banks, most of which have their home offices in Canada, the United States, Great Britain, Germany, France, Spain, China, and Japan but have established offices worldwide. These giant banks have accounted for most of the growth in multinational banking in recent decades.

### Types of Facilities Operated by Banks Abroad

**shell branches**

**representative offices**

**Edge Act and Agreement corporations**

**international banking facilities (IBFs)**

**agency offices**

Major banks around the world have used many vehicles to expand their international operations. All major banks have *international departments* in their home offices to provide credit, access to foreign currencies, and other services for their international customers, and many operate *full-service branch offices* in foreign markets as well. Others maintain simple booking offices, known as **shell branches,** on offshore islands such as the Bahamas to attract Eurocurrency accounts while avoiding domestic banking regulations. **Representative offices** help find new customers and give local customers a point of contact with the home office, but they cannot take deposits. U.S. and foreign banks active in the United States have set up **Edge Act and Agreement corporations** across state lines, which are special subsidiary companies that must, under Federal Reserve regulations, devote the majority of their activities to international banking. Many banking firms have also set up **international banking facilities (IBFs)** in the United States, consisting of computerized accounts maintained for international customers and subject to minimal U.S. regulations. **Agency offices**

**Key URLs:**
Two of the most interesting multinational banks in the world are the Hong Kong and Shanghai Banking Corp. Limited and the Deutsche Bank. See their global Web sites at **hsbc.com** and **db.com**

provide specialized services, such as recordkeeping for business transactions and providing customers with liquid balances for spending. In addition, multinational banks often make *direct equity investments* in foreign companies, either alone or as *joint ventures* with other financial firms.

*Choosing the Right Kind of Facility to Serve Foreign Markets*    Which kind of facility is adopted by a multinational bank to serve its customers depends on government regulations and the bank's size, goals, and location. Most banks begin with international departments in their home offices and then, as the volume of business grows, open up representative offices. Ultimately, full-service branches and investments in foreign businesses may be established. A recent trend toward legal liberalization of foreign trade and international lending has stimulated the growth of *home-based offices* that send officers to call on customers overseas or serve clients by satellite, the Internet, and other electronic channels. However, many multinational banks argue that successful international operations require an institution to have a stable presence overseas in the form of agencies, branches, representative offices, or even joint ventures with other banks.

Laws and regulations play a major role in determining the nature and location of multinational banking offices. For example, in some areas of the world, such as the Middle East, fears of political upheaval or outright expropriation of foreign-owned facilities have limited the entry of multinational banks.

For several of the largest U.S. banks, international operations yield from one-third to as much as one-half of their income. Particularly noteworthy has been U.S. bank penetration of foreign consumer banking markets, such as the "money shops" operated by Citigroup in Europe. Personal financial services represent extremely attractive opportunities in many foreign markets, and U.S. banks hold a significant share of consumer loan and deposit markets abroad, especially in Europe, but also a growing market share in Central and South America and in Asia.

**Leading International Banks**

| | |
|---|---|
| ABN AMRO Holding, N.V. Amsterdam, the Netherlands (abnamro.com) | Bank of America Corp. Charlotte, USA (BankofAmerica.com) |
| Bank of China Ltd. Beijing, China (boc.cn/en) | Barclays PLC London, England (barclays.com) |
| Citigroup Inc. New York City, USA (citigroup.com) | Credit Suisse Corp. Zurich, Switzerland (credit-suisse.com) |
| Deutsche Bank AG Frankfurt, Germany (db.com) | HSBC Holdings PLC London, England (hsbc.com) |
| JPMorgan Chase & Co. New York City, USA (jpmorganchase.com) | Mitsubishi UFJ Financial Group, Inc. Tokyo, Japan (mufg.jp/english) |
| Rabobank Nederland Utrecht, The Netherlands (rabobank.nl/) | Resona Holdings, Inc. Osaka and Tokyo, Japan (reson-agr.co.jp/holdings/english) |
| Royal Bank of Canada Montreal, Canada (rbcroyalbank.com) | Sumitomo Mitsui Financial group Tokyo, Japan (smfg.co.jp/english) |

## 24.3   Services Offered by International Banks

Multinational banks offer a wide variety of international financial services to customers. These services are described briefly below. Of course, the particular services offered by each bank depend on its size, location, the types of facilities it maintains overseas, the regulations it faces, and public service demands.

### Issuing Letters of Credit

**letter of credit**

Most banks enter the international sector initially to finance trade because credit is needed to bridge the gap between cash expenditures and cash receipts and to reduce the risks associated with long-distance trading. In these situations, a **letter of credit** is often the ideal financing instrument.

A letter of credit is an international bank's future promise to pay for goods stored overseas or for goods shipped between countries. Such letters may be issued to finance exports and imports or to provide a standby guarantee of payment behind IOUs issued by a customer. Through a letter of credit, the bank substitutes its promise to pay for the promise of one of its customers. By substituting its promise, the bank reduces the seller's risk, facilitating the flow of goods and services through international markets. Occasionally, the seller becomes concerned about the soundness of the foreign bank issuing the letter of credit and asks his or her own bank to issue a *confirmation letter* in which that bank guarantees against foreign bank default.

### Buying and Selling Foreign Exchange (FOREX)

**Key URL:**
Trading in foreign exchange is one of the riskier activities of international banks. For an illustration see **forexnews.com**

Major multinational banks have dealer departments specializing in trading foreign currencies (FOREX). International banks buy and sell currencies on a 24-hour basis to support the import and export of goods and services, the making of investments, the giving of gifts, and the financing of tourism. They also write forward contracts for the future delivery of foreign exchange, as we saw in Chapter 23.

### Accepting Eurocurrency Deposits and Making Eurocurrency Loans

**Eurocurrency deposits**

**Eurocurrency loans**

**Key URLs:**
For more information about the European Central Bank (ECB) and European Monetary Union (EMU), see **ecb.int**; **cepr.org**; and **en.wikipedia.org/wiki/en-largement-of-the-European-Union**

International banks accept deposits denominated in currencies other than that of their home country. As we saw in Chapter 11, these **Eurocurrency deposits** are used to pay for goods shipped between countries and serve as a source of loanable funds for banks. Eurocurrency deposits also may be loaned to corporations and other large wholesale borrowers. The majority of **Eurocurrency loans** carry floating interest rates based on the London Interbank Offer Rate (LIBOR) for three-month and six-month Eurocurrency deposits. Eurocurrency credit normally goes to borrowers with impeccable credit ratings. One important innovation is the *syndicated Eurocurrency credit*, in which one or more multinational banks will put together a loan package accompanied by an information memorandum. Other banks can then participate in the loan without direct communication with the borrower.

### Marketing and Underwriting of Both Domestic and Eurocurrency Bonds, Notes, and Equity Shares

**Eurobond**

For generations international banks have assisted their customers in raising capital through the issuance of new securities—bonds and other forms of debt and equity shares. One of the most well known of these securities is the **Eurobond**—a debt

With the formation of the European Union (EU), the regulation and supervision of international banks selling their services in Europe and the credit policies of the European continent are now conducted and coordinated through a system of central banking institutions—the European System of Central Banks, or ESCB, depicted in this box.

Eleven countries adopted the *euro* as a common currency in 1999—Austria, Belgium, Finland, France, Germany, Ireland, Italy, Luxembourg, the Netherlands, Portugal, and Spain. Greece adopted the euro in 2001 but the three remaining original members of the EU—Denmark, Sweden, and Great Britain—elected to keep their own national currencies. In 2004, 10 additional

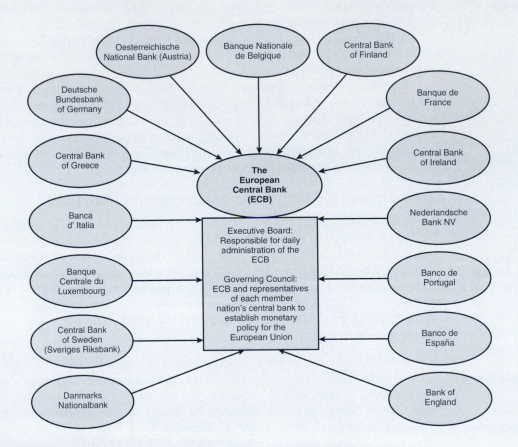

The ESCB is headed by the European Central Bank (ECB). Within the ECB itself there are two key decision-making groups—the Executive Board, which pursues a single monetary policy for all European member states, and the Governing Council, which includes the Executive Board plus the governors of the central banks from each member nation and meets twice monthly. While the ECB is charged to lead Europe's fight against inflation, it does not control exchange rates for the EU. That job is left to the EU's Council of Ministers. Each nation's central bank, not the ECB, examines and supervises the banks headquartered in its home country.

nations were brought into the EU—Cyprus, the Czech Republic, Estonia, Hungary, Latvia, Lithuania, Malta, Poland, Slovenia, and Slovakia. Bulgaria and Romania are scheduled to be added in 2007, eventually bringing to 27 the number of EU-member states. Additional nations under consideration include Croatia, Turkey, Albania, Bosnia, Herzegovina, Montenegro-Serbia, and FYR Macedonia. The central banks of the newest member states are members of the broader ECB system (though they cannot join the ECB's Governing Council until the euro becomes their national currency).

security denominated in a currency other than that of the country or countries where most or all of the security is sold. For example, a U.S. automobile company may desire to float an issue of long-term bonds to raise capital for one of its subsidiaries operating in Greece. The company might issue bonds denominated in British pounds to be sold in Europe through an underwriting syndicate made up of banks and dealers. Alternatively, the borrowing company might issue bonds denominated in euros.

Multinational banks assist the Eurobond market in several ways. Major banks have established international clearing systems to expedite the delivery of Eurobonds. Banks and security brokers are the principal intermediaries through which Eurobonds find their way to the long-term investor. The borrower may contact a multinational bank and ask it to organize a syndicate to place a new Eurobond issue. At this point, a *consortium* is formed, embracing at least four or five U.S., British, Japanese, French, or German banks, and typically at least one bank located in the borrowing country as well. The consortium agrees to subscribe to the Eurobond issue at issue price minus commission and then organizes a large group of banks and dealers as underwriters. Sometimes more than 100 banks are included in the underwriting syndicate. Once formed, the underwriting group gives the borrower a firm offer for its bonds and, if accepted, works to place the issue with investors.

Multinational banks also assist their corporate and governmental customers with medium-term financing through note issuance facilities (NIFs). Under a standard NIF contract, a customer is authorized to issue short-term notes periodically (usually with three to six-month maturities) to interested investors over a designated time span (perhaps five years). The banks involved agree to provide backup funding (standby credit) at a spread over prevailing Euromarket interest rates. For an underwriting fee, the bank agrees to purchase any unsold notes or advance cash to the customers until sufficient funding is obtained.

**Key URLs:**
To further explore the market for Eurobonds, see such Web sites as **finpipe.com** and ISI Emerging Markets at **securities.com**

## Securitizing Loans

Over the past two decades, leading multinational banks have unfurled a new source of funds for themselves and their customers: *securitization,* or the pooling of loans having similar purposes, quality, and maturities and the selling of financial claims (securities) against the pool of loans. Good examples are New York's Citigroup and JPMorgan Chase, among the leading packagers of consumer credit-card receivables, pooling receivables that arise as households borrow on their credit cards and selling securities in the open market as claims against the income those receivables will ultimately bring in. International banks can earn income in several different ways from the securitization process: (1) by securitizing some of their own loans and pocketing the difference in interest earnings between the average yield on the pool of loans and the cost of issuing securities against the loan pool; (2) by agreeing to guarantee the income of investors from pools of securitized loans; (3) by retaining servicing rights on a pool of loans, collecting and recording the income received from the loans in return for a servicing fee; or (4) by acting as adviser or trustee for those customers that desire to securitize any loans they hold in order to generate new capital.

## Advisory Services Provided by International Banks

In addition to the foregoing services, international banks offer extensive *advisory services* to their customers. These include analyses of foreign market conditions, evaluation of sales prospects and plant location sites, and advice on foreign regulations. International banks prepare credit reports on overseas buyers for exporters of goods and services and assist domestic firms interested in entering foreign markets.

## Universal Banking Services and One-Stop Shopping

As the foregoing list of service offerings suggests, the world's largest banking firms, such as Citigroup and Deutsche Bank, are reaching out to diversify their services in many different directions, attempting to offer their customers "one-stop shopping" and becoming what European bankers have, for decades, referred to as "universal banks." Universal banking combines traditional banking, insurance, securities trading, real estate brokering, and a long list of other services under one corporate umbrella. Its alleged advantages include greater stability of revenues and profits, less risk of succumbing to market stress as declines in one service area may be offset by increased revenues from other services, and lower overall fund-raising costs.

However, an international bank may not be able to manage all of its different service areas efficiently, resulting in lower rates of return and loss of market share. A prominent example appeared as the new century opened when Citigroup of New York, which had previously allied itself in the 1990s with Travelers Insurance Company of San Francisco to form one of the largest financial conglomerates in the world, announced that it would sell its Travelers property-casualty insurance affiliate and slow the pace at which it was pursuing the goal of becoming a "one-stop" financial supermarket. Citigroup discovered that its insurance affiliate was earning a lower rate of return than its other businesses and dragging down its overall performance. Citigroup's experience suggests that international banks must proceed cautiously as they proliferate their services and avoid hasty acquisitions that may be difficult to control.

**Key URL:**
Further information on recent developments in international banking can be found at **accuitysolutions.com**

---

### QUESTIONS TO HELP YOU STUDY

1. What exactly is a *multinational bank?*

2. What are the essential differences between the following types of *banking facilities:*

| | |
|---|---|
| International banking departments | Representative offices |
| Edge Act and Agreement corporations | Shell branches |
| Full-service branches | International banking facilities (IBFs) |

3. What factors appear to influence the types of *services* an international banking firm chooses to offer its customers?

4. What are the principal *services* offered by the international banking industry? Make a list of these services and briefly describe what each is about.

---

## 24.4  Foreign Banks Operating in the United States

Banks owned by foreign individuals and companies have entered the United States in great numbers in recent years. The reasons behind the expansion of foreign banking activities in the United States reflect growth in international trade and investments, the opportunity for profit in the huge U.S. market, and a search for safety when overseas markets are in turmoil. Originally, foreign-based banks penetrated U.S. markets for the same reasons U.S. banks established facilities overseas: *to follow their customers who had established operations in other countries.* Once in the United States, however, foreign banks found the possibility of attracting deposits and loans from major U.S. corporations and even from U.S. households irresistible.

**Key URL:**
To learn more about
foreign banking in the
U.S., see especially
FRB: Foreign Banks in
the U.S. at
**federalreserve.gov**

# The Growth of Foreign Bank Activity in the United States

The expansion of foreign bank operations inside the United States has been impressive. Today foreign banks are strong competitors with domestic U.S. banks, especially in the market for business loans. As of year-end 2005, 183 foreign banks from 54 nations were operating 220 state-licensed branch and agency offices inside the United States. At that time, foreign banks accounted for almost 20 percent of total U.S. banking assets. Clearly, foreign banks have become a competitive force to be reckoned with in the United States.

# Federal Regulation of Foreign Bank Activity

Until the 1970s, no federal laws regulated foreign bank activity within U.S. borders. However, Congress has been monitoring foreign bank operations since 1966, when IntraBank, a Lebanese institution, collapsed and several U.S. banks suffered losses. Passage of the Bank Holding Company Act Amendments of 1970 marked an initial step toward federal regulation of foreign banking. Under the terms of these amendments, any corporation controlling one or more domestic banks became subject to supervision by the Federal Reserve Board ("the Fed"). However, with foreign banks in the United States growing more rapidly than domestic banks, the pressure on Congress for more extensive regulation of foreign banks intensified. Proponents of restrictive legislation argued that foreign banks reduced the effectiveness of domestic monetary policy and that the lack of specific regulations applying to foreign banks was unfair to domestic banks, which must conform to an elaborate system of rules.

**International Banking Act (IBA)**

Responding to these pressures, Congress passed the **International Banking Act (IBA),** which became law in 1978. Under the terms of the IBA and subsequent regulations, U.S. branches and agencies of foreign banks with worldwide assets of $1 billion or more became subject to U.S. legal reserve requirements on deposits. Foreign banks that maintain U.S. offices were required to register with the Secretary of the Treasury. In total, the IBA proved to be a more lenient piece of legislation. It did not attempt to punish or discriminate against foreign banks relative to their U.S. counterparts. In fact, the act set in law the principle of *mutual nondiscrimination,* which permits foreign-owned banks to possess the same powers as domestic banks. It is a policy that avoids establishing two sets of banking regulations, one for domestic institutions and the other for foreign-owned banks.

---

**Leading International Bank Regulators**

| | |
|---|---|
| Bank for International Settlements<br>Zurich, Switzerland<br>**(bis.org)** | Board of Governors of the Federal Reserve System<br>Washington, D.C., USA<br>**(federalreserve.gov)** |
| Bank of England<br>London, England<br>**(bankofengland.co.uk)** | Bank of Japan<br>Tokyo, Japan<br>**(boj.or.jp/en/)** |
| European Central Bank<br>Frankfurt, Germany<br>**(ecb.int)** | Peoples Bank of China<br>Beijing, China<br>**(pbc.gov.cn/english/)** |

---

Federal regulation of foreign banks was extended a step further in 1980 when the Depository Institutions Deregulation and Monetary Control Act was passed. All foreign banking organizations offering services to U.S. residents became eligible for

**Key URLs:**
One of the most rapidly growing foreign-bank segments recently entering the United States consists of several leading Chinese banks. The Bank of China and Bank of Communications have operated branch offices for several years in the U.S., but both the Industrial and Commercial Bank of China and China Merchants Bank have recently applied for branch office approval in New York City. See especially **bank-of-China.com/en/static/index.html; en.wikipedia.org/wiki/Bank-of-Communications; icbc.com.cn** and **english.cmbchina.com/** Much of this recent growth is traceable to Chinese business expansion around the world as the Chinese work to internationalize their economy.

**Key URL:**
To explore the international activities of U.S. banks see the recent study by the Federal Deposit Insurance Corporation at **fdic.gov/bank/analytical/regional/r020052q/na/2005summer_03.html**

deposit insurance from the Federal Deposit Insurance Corporation and were required to conform to deposit reserve requirements set by the Federal Reserve Board. When a foreign bank opens an agency, branch, or loan production office in the United States, it must register as a bank holding company and conform with all holding company laws and regulations administered by the Fed. These new requirements even more firmly reflected Congress's intention to place all banks (foreign and domestic) on the same regulatory footing and in the same field of competition.

Finally, on the heels of a scandal involving the Bank of Credit and Commerce International (BCCI) of Luxembourg, which illegally attempted to acquire control of several U.S. banks, the Fed was granted even broader powers to regulate the activities of agencies, branch offices, and subsidiaries of foreign banks inside U.S. territory. Under the terms of the Foreign Bank Supervision Enhancement Act passed by Congress in 1991, the Fed must approve any proposed bank agency, branch, or representative office to be set up in the United States. The Fed was empowered to *close* a foreign bank office if its home country fails to subject the parent bank to comprehensive supervision. Any foreign bank seeking to buy more than 5 percent of the stock of a U.S. bank or bank holding company must receive Federal Reserve Board approval. Moreover, small deposits (less than $100,000 each) can be accepted in the United States by foreign banks only through subsidiary companies that have FDIC insurance coverage and conform to all U.S. banking regulations.

## 24.5 Regulation of the International Banking Activities of U.S. Banks

A more significant problem than regulating foreign banking activities in the United States is the regulation, supervision, and control of U.S. banks offering their services overseas. Indeed, U.S. bank presence abroad is extensive. For example, at year-end 2005, 71 American banks operated nearly 770 branch offices in foreign countries.

The *Federal Reserve Board* has been designated as the chief regulatory agency for U.S. international banking activities. A member bank of the Federal Reserve System choosing to expand its activities abroad through the creation of foreign branches or through investments in foreign firms must secure approval by the Federal Reserve Board. In contrast, state laws govern foreign operations of state-chartered banks. However, most state governments have exerted only nominal control over foreign banking activities.

Of prime concern to the Fed is the *protection of domestic deposits* and the *stability of the domestic banking system.* The Fed has argued that it is difficult to separate a bank's foreign operations from its domestic activities. If a foreign subsidiary gets into trouble, the danger exists that public confidence in the soundness of the controlling domestic bank will be undermined. For this reason, the Fed, in reviewing applications of U.S. banks to expand abroad, examines closely the condition of their domestic offices to determine if their home-based operations are adequately capitalized and if the bank has sufficient management skill to support both foreign and domestic operations.

The regulatory authorities would like to develop ways to insulate foreign activities of U.S. banks from their domestic operations. Such insulation would grant wider latitude to banking activities abroad and at the same time shield domestic banks from hazards associated with foreign operations. Legally, one bank subsidiary is not liable for the debts of another. However, in practice, a domestic bank might feel compelled to aid its affiliates operating in foreign markets. The practical, if not legal, links between foreign and domestic subsidiaries of multinational banks force regulators to keep close tabs on the foreign operations of all banks.

**Key URLs:**
Among the leading sources of information about the past, present, and future of international banking are the combined libraries of the World Bank and the International Monetary Fund at **jolis.worldbankimflib .org**; the Bank for International Settlements at **bis.org**; and the World Bank at **worldbank.org**

## 24.6 The Future of International Banking

The future of international banking is clouded at this time due to the many crosscurrents of economics and politics that pervade our world. Sluggish economic growth and high unemployment in some parts of the world (especially in Japan and parts of Europe), trade barriers, and political struggle and terrorism threaten the flow of international commerce and make bank lending across national boundaries risky. In this section, we take a brief look at these problems and their implications for the future of international banking.

### The Risks of International Lending

*Political and Currency Risk*   Lending funds in the international arena is riskier, on average, than is domestic lending. *Political risk*—the risk government laws and regulations will change to the detriment of business interests—is particularly significant in international banking. Governments are frequently overthrown and confiscation of private property is a frequent occurrence in some parts of the world.[1] There is also *currency risk*—the risk associated with changing prices of foreign currencies. The value of property pledged behind an international loan falls if the currency of the home country is devalued, eroding the lender's collateral. Geography too works against the international lender. The large distances that frequently separate lender and borrower make it difficult for a bank loan officer to see that the terms of a loan are being followed.

The risks of international lending have become a greater concern in recent years because international banks have become the principal source of borrowed funds for

---

[1]Many financial analysts often lump political and other risks in international lending under the general term *country risk.* This is the possibility governments borrowing money from multinational banks may be unable or unwilling to repay and private borrowers may, because of law and regulation, be unable to make payment on their loans. For example, private borrowers may be prevented from paying due to *transfer risk,* a component of country risk in which a nation prohibits outflows of capital, dividends, or interest payments due to an internal shortage of foreign exchange. The other component of country risk—*political risk*—arises when loans cannot be repaid due to war, revolution, or changes in regulatory philosophy that adversely affect the ability of a borrower to fulfill a debt obligation.

International banking, like domestic banking, faces serious ethical issues, especially in the treatment of customers and protecting the assets of clients. For example, the rapid expansion of banking worldwide led to thousands of cases of fraud and financial manipulation annually as some bank employees and government officials have dipped into the burgeoning cash reserves of leading international banks. Many banks overseas are state-owned or are subject to strong pressures from ruling political parties (as in parts of China) that sometimes compel bankers to grant unwise loans that soon turn sour.

Added to the list of problems have been charges of money-laundering activities. International banks are in a key position to rapidly wire funds across international borders. Some of these transactions have been found to aid the drug trade, hide money from taxing authorities, and support terrorist organizations.

Most recently, an ethical controversy has appeared in several prominent areas of the globe, especially in

Australia, Europe, and the United States. Typically the world's biggest banks offer security trading and underwriting along with loans under the same roof. However, government rules often restrict the flow of private customer information from one bank division to another in order to avoid conflicts of interest and avoid damaging disclosures of their customers' private information.

For example, there is a so-called "Chinese wall" separating banks' offering of security underwriting services from their actions as brokers and investment advisors to clients. That wall may have been seriously breached recently as several banks allegedly used information they garnered from their lending and advisory services to help them unload large blocks of stock they were underwriting to their investment clients. No question these trades benefited the banks involved, but may have sacrificed the welfare of investors. Regulators in the international banking community quickly opened an investigation.

**Key URLs:**
An important government-sponsored international bank that facilitates international lending is the Export-Import Bank. See especially **exim.gov** and **tradeport.org**

developing countries as the United States and most other industrialized countries have cut back on their foreign aid programs. Simultaneously, the International Monetary Fund and the World Bank have moved to supply more funds to debtor nations and grant them additional time to adjust their domestic economies to a somewhat harsher economic climate.[2] As the twenty-first century approached, more and more developing nations in Asia, the Americas (especially Argentina), the former Soviet Union, and Africa began to experience credit problems. Some nations periodically threatened to repudiate their international debt (as in the case of Russia) or unilaterally alter the terms of their repayment (as in the case of Argentina). At the same time, some multinational banks began to scale down their international lending operations by selling old loans at deep discounts.

Some banks pioneered *debt-for-equity swaps* in which they accepted shares of stock in some overseas projects as a substitute for holding loans. Debt-for-equity swaps also provided more flexible funding for developing countries, but most troubled nations

---

[2]The relationship between lending activity by the IMF and the World Bank and parallel lending to the same customers by international banks has been a center of controversy in recent years. Some authorities believe that the IMF and the World Bank have actively contributed to international bank lending problems at times. They argue that IMF/World Bank loans have been regarded by some international bankers as a "stamp of approval" for their own extension of credit to troubled international borrowers. In short, loans extended by the IMF or the World Bank may create a "moral hazard" problem for the international banking system, encouraging unsound lending by international banks. Conversely, other observers argue that the IMF and the World Bank have followed lending policies that are too strict, imposing difficult, if not impossible, requirements ("conditionality") on nations asking for help and precipitating financial crises that otherwise might not have occurred. For a reasonably balanced discussion of this ongoing controversy, see especially Globalization.org at **globalization101.org/issue/imfworldbank/4.asp.**

**Key URLs:**
The importance of sound lending policies among international banks for the profitability and growth of these banks has been illustrated recently by the experience of Japan's top three multinational banks—Mitsubishi UFJ Financial Group, Mizuho Financial Group, and Sumitomo Mitsui Financial Group. These institutions have experienced slower loan growth and smaller loan margins, reflecting Japan's comparatively sluggish economy and generally have lost ground compared to several other international banks. See especially **mufg .jp/english/; mizuho- fg.co.jp/english/; and smfg.co.jp/english/**

**Key URL:**
To assess the changing nature of European banking and its possible future, see in particular, **cepr .org/press/ME19PR .htm**

**International Lending and Supervision Act**

sought out restructuring of their existing loans. Some sought outright forgiveness of what they owed.

### Geographic Distribution of International Bank Lending
Beginning in the late 1970s, U.S. bank regulators inaugurated semiannual surveys of foreign lending by U.S. banking organizations. The principal concern of these agencies was that U.S. multinational banks were overly committed to foreign loans where the political and economic risks were unusually high, threatening the confidence of the public in the soundness of the world's largest banks. Recent surveys show that most loans extended by U.S. multinational banks are made to industrially developed nations (including Canada, western Europe, and Japan) and to countries in Central and South America, along with a growing loan commitment to China as it emerges as a major player in international trade. However, close to a third of all foreign loans typically are extended to lesser-developed countries, a number of which have been in serious financial difficulty at various times in recent years (including Argentina, Brazil, and Russia).

Fortunately, loans to distant nations are mainly short term (maturity of one year or less), and many are made to banks themselves. On the whole, multinational banks appear to be relatively conservative lenders, directing their credits to large bank, corporate, and governmental borrowers situated mainly in Europe, more prosperous areas in Asia (such as China, India, and South Korea), and in rapidly growing Latin American markets. The bulk of such loans is concentrated among the largest international banks.

## Public Confidence and Protecting Against Bank Failures

A persistent problem in international banking is the preservation of *public confidence*. Essentially, this means protecting major multinationals against failure. To avert serious financial difficulties among the world's largest banks, regulatory authorities look closely at their *capital positions*. Regulators have often urged a slower expansion of international loans and avoidance of excessive credit exposure in loans to any one country. This is coupled with an insistence on adequate levels of equity capital. One of the first steps in this direction occurred in 1983 when the United States Congress passed the **International Lending and Supervision Act.** This law ordered bank regulatory agencies to prepare new rules requiring U.S. banks to:

1. Maintain special reserves against foreign loans in those cases where the quality of a bank's assets has been impaired by protracted borrower inability to repay loans.
2. Limit loan rescheduling fees charged troubled foreign borrowers.
3. Periodically disclose a bank's exposure to foreign borrowers.
4. Hold minimum levels of capital as protection for an international bank's depositors.
5. Conduct feasibility studies of foreign projects involving mining, metal, or mineral processing before approving a loan to a customer.

Then, as we saw earlier in Chapter 17, in 1988 representatives from the Federal Reserve System, the Bank of England, the Bank of Japan, and the central banks of eight other Western countries signed the Basel Agreement. This historic international contract calls on central banks to monitor the capital positions of international banks and to impose minimum capital requirements on major banks around the world. The

The high risks associated with international banking have pressured multinational banks to find ways of reducing their risk exposure. At the same time, the development of comprehensive trade agreements, such as the formation of the European Union (EU) and NAFTA, have brought banks previously isolated from one another into close contact and increased competition, increasing the risk of failure.

One of the principal ways international banks have dealt with these risk factors is by *merging* into larger, more diversified firms, in terms of both products and geographical locations. Advances in communications technology have overcome barriers to management control and accelerated the "urge to merge." Nowhere has this merger trend been more evident than in Japan where the leading Japanese banks have engaged in dozens of recent mergers and acquisitions.

Examples include the recent combinations of Sanwa Bank with Tokai and Toyo Trust banks, the creation of Sumitomo Mitsui Financial Group from the merger of Sumitomo and Sakura banks, Daiwa Bank and Asahi Bank combined into Resona Group, and the formation of the Mitsubishi Tokyo Financial Group, bringing together the Nippon Trust, Mitsubishi Trust, and the Bank of Tokyo–Mitsubishi. These combinations have created several of the largest banks on the planet. A more dramatic example is Mizuho Bank, composed of Yasuda, Fuji, Dai-Ichi Kangyo, and Industrial banks with well over a trillion dollars in assets.

In Europe, huge mergers have taken place not only between banks, but also between banks, insurance companies, and security firms. Some of these largest combinations crossed national borders in the wake of the formation of the European Union, helping to tie together the financial systems of Germany, France, Italy, and other European countries. Examples include recent mergers involving giant insurer Allianz AG of Munich with Dresdner Bank AG; the acquisition by Germany's Deutsche Bank AG of Bankers Trust Company of New York; the combination of Italy's Unicredit SpA and Capitalia SpA; and the alliance of Verisbank Group with the Bank of Munich. Even larger is the controversial nearly $100 billion bid of Barclays PLC of Great Britain for ABN Amro, a huge Dutch bank—a combination opposed by a group of banks led by the Royal Bank of Scotland.

Recently the European Commission, based in Brussels, was created to review and possibly block future mergers involving European companies. The European Commission currently reviews larger mergers for evidence of "collective dominance," indicating excessive market concentration in a handful of companies. At some point, larger European financial-service firms may run into these competitive and regulatory barriers because banking there is already more concentrated than in the United States. Moreover, several European and Asian nations seem determined to shelter their domestic banks from being acquired by banking companies from other countries.

**Key URL:**
To find additional information on the changing structure of the Japanese banking system prepared by the Japanese Bankers Association at
zenginkyo.or.jp/en

primary objective of this international capital standard is to ensure banks from one nation do not have a competitive advantage over banks from other nations due to more lenient capital rules. Beginning in 1993, all banks subject to the Basel Agreement were required to hold a ratio of core capital (mainly equity funds) to total risk-adjusted assets of at least 4 percent, and a ratio of total capital (core capital plus debt and other temporary forms of capital) to total risk-adjusted assets of at least 8 percent. Thus, the Basel Agreement reduced permissible leverage for banks that might handicap the ability of bankers to meet some international credit needs in the future. Moreover, banks accepting greater risk must hold more capital to preserve public confidence in their long-term viability and prevent failures.

As the new century unfolded, the initial Basel Agreement (known as Basel I) came under revision and a new agreement (referred to as Basel II) was emerging, aimed principally at the largest banks in the world (approximately 20 leading international banks with at least $250 billion in assets or foreign exposure of at least $10 billion). Instead of using rigid formulas to determine how much capital each bank should hold

China, the world's most populous nation, is rapidly emerging as an economic leader around the globe. It has joined the World Trade Organization (WTO), agreeing to open its markets to foreign traders while sharply expanding its exports to the rest of the world. Unfortunately, the banking system of mainland China wrestles today with great problems and issues and, unlike the rest of the Chinese economy, is one of the weaker banking systems in the world.

Part of the reason lies in the nation's *state-owned banks*. These inefficient organizations are saddled with huge amounts of bad loans and currently dominate China's domestic banking system. For example, four Chinese state-owned banks—the Bank of China, Industrial and Commercial Bank of China, China Construction Bank, and the Agricultural Bank of China—control about three-fifths of the more than $2 trillion in assets in the Chinese banking system. They overshadow more than a hundred smaller domestic banks serving towns and cities across the nation. In addition, there are close to 200 foreign banks represented in China, but these banks account for less than 5 percent of the domestic industry's assets and offer principally foreign-currency-based services to their corporate clients trading with China.

Under the terms of admittance to the WTO China must continue to relax its restraints on foreign banking activity. Some of the world's largest banks, led by such international giants as Great Britain's HSBC Holdings, Canada's Bank of Nova Scotia, American Express, Morgan Stanley, and Citigroup from the United States, have selected the Chinese market as their key target in the new century. In response, the *Chinese Bank Regulatory Commission* is considering chartering new domestic, privately owned banks to compete with these foreign entrants, reaching out to the millions of Chinese families and smaller businesses that have few or no relationships with banks. For example, fewer than 5 percent of Chinese adults have credit-card accounts. Interestingly enough, even as China works to expand opportunities for domestic and foreign banks it has also stiffened many of its banking rules—for example, recently demanding that its banks adopt more prudent lending practices.

(as in Basel I), each banking firm will be asked to develop its own internal models for determining its unique level of risk exposure and its corresponding need for capital. Moreover, each international bank will be required to "stress test" its asset portfolio under a variety of possible market conditions. The Basel II Accord is designed to establish a *flexible* system for determining bank capital requirements that can be adjusted to shifting market conditions and to innovations that clever international bankers frequently devise.

## The Spread of Deregulation: How Fast Should We Go?

As we saw in Chapters 14, 15, and 17, the United States began an aggressive program of *deregulating* domestic banking in the 1980s and 1990s. Other nations—such as Great Britain with its Big Bang deregulation of banking and security dealer services 1980s and 1990s—have also made significant strides toward lifting confining government rules permitting their own banks as well as foreign banks operating within their borders to compete more equally. Unfortunately, the pattern of international banking deregulation has been spotty, with some nations (such as China) lowering regulatory barriers to competition slowly in order to protect domestic institutions. The real losers here are domestic consumers of financial services, who have fewer options and probably are paying higher prices until government deregulation takes place. The key issue is how to allow deregulation of financial services on an international scale to proceed rapidly without wholesale bank failures that destroy public confidence.

**Key URL:**
To follow recent developments in Chinese banking, see
Chinadaily.com.cn

**Key URL:**
To learn more about China's Bank Regulatory Commission and some of its rules, see, for example, **china .org.cn/english**

Finding the proper speed and scope for financial deregulation remains a challenging worldwide issue. Nevertheless, there is a growing trend toward relying more on the private marketplace and less on government rule making in order to regulate global banking. Banks that have too little capital or accept greater than normal risks are likely to be punished by the private financial markets, especially when they attempt to raise new funds at reasonable cost.

A related regulatory issue for international banking in the twenty-first century centers on the necessity for regulatory cooperation and for *harmonization* of banking regulations across nations so that no bank entrusted with the public's funds can find refuge in some corner of the world from public scrutiny that ensures respect for law in business dealings. This is especially important in a world increasingly threatened by war and terrorism financed by powerful organizations active on nearly every continent of the globe.

## 24.7 Prospects and Challenges for the Twenty-First Century

These recent trends suggest a somewhat different future for international banking than seemed likely in earlier years. Growth—limited by capital and the availability of experienced management—should be more gradual and loan quality more of a factor in future extensions of credit to businesses and governments abroad. However, continuing expansion of international banking activities in the United States, western Europe, the nations that emerged from the dissolution of the former Soviet Union, Asia (especially China, India, South Korea, Singapore, and Hong Kong), and Latin America can be anticipated as long as risk exposure can be held within acceptable limits.

Certainly, a number of critical questions must be answered for international banking to prosper and grow. For example, to what extent will the regulatory authorities of different nations *cooperate* to control foreign banking activities? How can we *harmonize* different banking rules from one country to the next to promote competition on a level playing field and innovation, but also public safety? Where must regulation end and the free play of market forces be allowed to operate in international banking?

And, what about the rise of strong competitors in the form of nonbank firms—security dealers and underwriters, finance companies, insurance companies, and the like? These firms today are offering parallel services to those offered by many international banks, supplying credit, underwriting new security offerings, securitizing loans, offering long- and short-term savings instruments, and managing customer cash positions, but they are also often burdened with fewer regulations and, therefore, possess a competitive advantage over many banks. Leading international banks have begun to respond to these new competitors. For example, Deutsche Bank of Germany is a leading underwriter of corporate securities on the European continent and in the United States; France's BNP offers savers a product that looks very much like money market fund shares; and Citigroup, JPMorgan Chase, and Bank of America are leading securitizers of receivables emerging from credit-card loans, auto loans, and other forms of lending. As the twenty-first century beckons us forward into a new era, international banks must find innovative ways to adjust to the challenges posed by this "new competition" or suffer erosion of their market share and profitability.

> ## QUESTIONS TO HELP YOU STUDY
>
> 9. What major problems have been encountered by the international banking community in recent years? How have these problems been dealt with?
> 10. What is *political risk?* Why is it important in international banking?
> 11. What is *currency risk?* What types of currency risk exposure are of special concern to international bankers?
> 12. What important principle about international banking was revealed by the global banking crisis of the 1990s?
> 13. How did the International Lending and Supervision Act affect international banks? How about the Basel Agreement? What are Basel I and Basel II?
> 14. Which nonbank financial-service firms are posing a strong competitive challenge to international banking today?

## Summary of the Chapter's Main Points

International banking firms offer financial services around the globe today. Their growth has proceeded at a pace mirroring the growth of international trade and global capital flows as international banks typically follow their largest customers overseas.

- International banks operate many different kinds of *service facilities* across national boundaries today. Among the best known are (a) international banking departments, usually located within the headquarters of a single bank; (b) shell branches in offshore island locations, designed to minimize the burden of regulation in raising funds; (c) representative offices, which funnel service requests to the banks' central facilities; (d) Edge Act and Agreement corporations, which avoid or minimize domestic regulatory restrictions; (e) international banking facilities (IBFs) that keep computerized records of offshore transactions; (f) full-service branches that offer most of the services available from the main office; and (g) agency offices, that assist customers with special transactions, including recordkeeping and cash-management services.

- Among the leading *financial services* provided by international banks are (a) letters of credit to finance international trade; (b) buying and selling foreign currencies for the bank and its customers; (c) issuing acceptances to facilitate trade financing or the purchase of currencies; (d) accepting Eurocurrency deposits and making Eurocurrency loans; (e) marketing and underwriting security sales to help customers raise new funds; (f) securitizing loans to help the bank and its customers generate new working capital and reduce balance-sheet risk; (g) cash management services to provide liquidity for customers; (h) advisory services regarding potential foreign investments and foreign markets that customers might be interested in; and (i) miscellaneous other services.

- *Foreign banks* have come to represent nearly 20 percent of all banking assets in the United States and account for a similar share of business loans made within the American banking system. Foreign bank growth inside the United States has occurred, in part, due to foreign-bank customers entering the United States, the needs of foreign businesses to carry out security sales and other transactions within the U.S. in order to obtain capital and liquidity, and the continuing search for safety in the face of international risks. A bank that can cross national borders offers its customers the chance to enter new markets and diversify business operations, thereby expanding potential revenues and possibly reducing risk.

- *Government regulations* today subject foreign banks to many of the same rules and regulations that domestic banks face. In the United States, recently passed federal laws have led to close supervision and regulation of foreign banks. One example is the Foreign Bank Supervision Enhancement Act passed in 1991, which appointed the *Federal Reserve Board* as the principal supervisor of foreign bank activities in the United States. The Federal Reserve can close a foreign-owned bank office if, in the Fed's opinion, it is not adequately supervised by its home country. The Federal Reserve is also the chief supervisor of U.S. banks' operations in overseas markets.

- The future of international banking presents significant risks today due to recent political and economic changes abroad and unanticipated movements in interest rates and currency prices. International banks also face greater lending risk because overseas loans, on average, are more risky than domestic loans due, in part, to the relative lack of information on the condition of foreign borrowers. In recent years, however, international banks have developed country risk profiles and other advanced tools to help lower the risks inherent in international lending.

- If international banks are to survive and prosper in the future, they must retain the public's confidence and control risk. One of the most important methods used to accomplish these goals in recent years has been to impose common capital rules on major banks in leading industrialized countries through the Basel Agreement on Bank Capital Standards.

- Today there is less emphasis in international bank regulation upon rigid standards and, instead, greater use of risk control models created by each bank to deal with its own unique risk exposures. Moreover, international banking rules are focusing today more and more on the *private marketplace* to impose discipline on bank behavior and risk taking. For example, international banks choosing to take on greater risk often find that the free market forces them to pay more for the capital they must raise to carry on their daily operations.

- International banking is likely to benefit in future years from greater *deregulation* as governments move to liberalize the rules limiting future bank expansion into new markets and allow private markets, rather than government dicta, to play a greater role in shaping the service offerings and performance of international banking corporations.

# Key Terms Appearing in This Chapter

# Problems and Issues

1.  International banking activities have expanded rapidly over the past two decades.

    **a.** Describe the principal forces driving this expansion.

    **b.** What factors may be at work to slow the growth of at least some international banks?

    **c.** If you were investing in a U.S. bank that had extensive international operations, what factors would you need to consider?

2.  Many countries around the world have moved to privatize and/or deregulate their banking systems. As this process continues, why is it essential that these countries strive to harmonize their banking laws? What role have the Basel Accords played in this respect? Why is the principal focus of those accords so crucial to the process of harmonization of banking laws?

3.  A major money-center bank in the United States wishes to expand its presence in the unfolding European Union, where it currently services corporate customers but has no physical facilities. Based on the discussion in this chapter, what initial forms of facilities would you recommend to its management and why? What special problems can you anticipate given recent announcements by the European Union regarding changes in its monetary system and in its regulation of outside financial-service suppliers?

4.  Which services typically offered by international banks:

    **a.** Involve the direct extension of credit to corporate customers?

    **b.** Aid customers in hedging against various forms of market risk?

    **c.** Assist customers in making international payments?

    **d.** Aid customers in restructuring their capitalization?

    **e.** Help customers in obtaining additional capital from the open market or from other lending institutions?

5.  Should the activities of foreign banks be regulated when they enter any particular domestic economy? Why or why not? What could be gained by the nation being entered and what dangers might follow? How would you propose

to deal with the dangers or risks involved? Explain the reasons behind your recommendations.

6. If you were charged with evaluation of *country risk* associated with the following nations, what factors would you want to examine?

    **a.** Brazil    **d.** Japan
    **b.** Korea    **e.** India
    **c.** China    **f.** Argentina

In each case, carefully explain why each factor that you specified relates to the risk exposure faced by an international bank making loans in each nation. What recent developments in each of the above nations suggest that a new assessment of country risk may be in order?

## Web-Based Problems

1. Multinational banks serve essentially the same global marketplace but often differ substantially from bank to bank, in part because they are headquartered in different nations and may be subject to different sets of laws and regulations. In order to get some idea as to how significant this "country effect" can be, compare the profitability, growth, and risk exposure of the following banks using information drawn from their individual Web sites. The banks are: Barclays PLC (BCS) and HSBC Holdings (HSBC) from the United Kingdom; Deutsche Bank (DB) and Dresdner Bank AG (DXBC) from Germany; and Bank of America (BAC) and JP Morgan Chase (JPM) from the United States. Do these banking firms—grouped by country of origin—appear to be more similar to each other in performance and financial condition than they do to banks headquartered in other nations? Do you see any evidence at all for a "country effect"?

2. Because of recent reforms in the regulation of the financial-service industry in Japan, non-Japanese banks and other financial-service providers have made significant inroads into the domestic Japanese marketplace. Describe the pros and cons of these ventures. To put together your answer, consult the Bank of Japan's Web site at **bog.jp** and read about reforms to the Japanese banking system that were adopted in 1998. Have there been any significant Japanese reforms *since* 1998?

3. Explore the Web site of the Bank for International Settlements at **bis.org,** in order to explain the purpose of the BIS and describe the services it provides to the international banking sector. The BIS has been mentioned in the news recently. Can you discover why?

4. Among the most visible of internationally oriented institutions are the World Bank at **worldbank.org** and the Export-Import Bank at **exim.gov.** What are the history and purpose of these two internationally focused organizations and what are their specific links to the international banking community?

5. Consulting such sites as **erisk.com, riskglossary.com,** and **euromoney.com** will help explain the purpose of the original Basel Agreement. What changes in the original agreement will be brought about as Basel II replaces Basel I?

## Selected References to Explore

1. Alm, Richard. "Five Years of the Euro: Successes and New Challenges," *Southwest Economy,* Federal Reserve Bank of Dallas, July/August 2004, pp. 13–18.
2. Craig, Valentine V. "China's Opening to the World: What Does It Mean for U.S. Banks?" *FDIC Banking Review,* Vol. 17, No. 3 (2005), pp. 1–20.
3. Crystal, Jennifer; S. B. Gerald Dages; and Linda S. Goldberg. "Has Foreign Bank Entry Led to Sounder Banks in Latin America," *Current Issues in Economics and Finance,* Federal Reserve Bank of New York, January 2002, pp. 1–6.
4. Curry, Timothy; Christopher Richardson; and Robin Heider. "Assessing International Risk Exposures of U.S. Banks," *FDIC Banking Review,* Federal Deposit Insurance Corporation, Washington, DC, 1998, pp. 13–30.
5. Killgo, Kerry, and Kenneth J. Robinson. "Banking on Basel: An Alternative for Capital Requirements," *Southwest Economy,* Federal Reserve Bank of Dallas, July/August 2006, pp. 11–13 and 16.
6. Pollard, Patricia S. "A Look Inside Two Central Banks: The European Central Bank and the Federal Reserve," *Review,* Federal Reserve Bank of St. Louis, January/February 2003, pp. 11–30.
7. Spiegel, Mark M. "Did Quantitative Easing by the Bank of Japan 'Work'?" *FRBSF Economic Letter,* Federal Reserve Bank of San Francisco, October 20, 2006, pp. 1–3.

www.mhhe.com.rose10e

# Money and Capital Markets Dictionary

## A

**actual maturity**   The number of days, months, or years between today and the date a loan or security is redeemed or retired. *(Chapter 10)*

**add-on rate**   A method for calculating the interest charge on a loan when the interest bill is added to the principal amount of the loan. That sum is divided by the number of installment payments required to determine the amount of each payment needed to eventually pay off the loan. *(Chapter 6)*

**adjustable mortgage instrument (AMI)**   A home mortgage loan under which some of the terms of the loan, such as the loan rate or the maturity of the loan, will vary as market conditions change. *(Chapter 22)*

**agency offices**   Facilities operated in overseas markets by international banks in order to provide customers with selected services (such as cash management). *(Chapter 24)*

**American depository receipts (ADRs)**   Dollar-denominated claims on specific foreign shares of stock that are held in safekeeping by U.S. financial institutions, giving U.S. investors access to selected foreign stock without having to accept or make payments in foreign currencies. *(Chapter 20)*

**annual percentage rate (APR)**   The actuarially determined rate on a consumer loan that Truth in Lending law requires lenders to communicate to borrowers. *(Chapter 6)*

**annual percentage yield (APY)**   The annualized rate of return on a savings account that U.S. depository institutions must report to their customers. *(Chapter 6)*

**arbitrage**   The purchase of an asset in one market and the sale of that asset in another market in response to differences in price or yield between the two markets. *(Chapters 1 and 23)*

**ask price**   The price at which a dealer is willing to sell securities to the public. *(Chapter 3)*

**asset-backed securities (ABS)**   Financial claims backed by a pool of loans or other assets, such as home mortgages or credit-card loans. *(Chapter 19)*

**asymmetric information hypothesis (AIH)**   The concept that different participants in the financial markets often operate with different sets of information, some possessing special or inside information that others do not possess. *(Chapter 3)*

**auction**   A method used to sell assets in which buyers file bids and the highest bidders receive the assets. *(Chapter 10)*

**auction method**   The principal means by which U.S. Treasury securities are sold to the public. *(Chapters 10 and 18)*

## B

**balanced-budget unit (BBU)**   An individual, business firm, or unit of government whose current expenditures equal its current receipt of income. *(Chapter 2)*

**balance-of-payments (BOP) accounts**   A double-entry bookkeeping system recording a nation's transactions with other nations, including exports, imports, and capital flows. *(Chapter 23)*

**bank discount method**   The procedure by which yields on U.S. Treasury bills, commercial paper, and bankers' acceptances are calculated; a 360-day year is assumed and there is no compounding of interest income. *(Chapters 6 and 10)*

**bank discount rate (DR)**   Rate of return measure used in the money market which is based on the par value of a financial instrument and assumes a 360-day year. *(Chapters 6, 10, and 11)*

**bank-dominated financial system**   A financial sector of an economy in which banking firms control a majority of the assets held by all financial-service providers and supply most of the credit provided by the financial system. *(Chapter 2)*

**bank holding company**   A corporation that owns stock in one or more commercial banks. *(Chapter 14)*

**banker's acceptance**   A time draft that a bank has agreed to pay unconditionally on the date the draft matures. *(Chapter 11)*

**banking structure**   The number, relative sizes, and types of banks in a given market or in the industry as a whole. *(Chapter 14)*

**Bankruptcy Abuse Prevention and Consumer Protection Act**   A 2005 U.S. federal law specifying the conditions under which individuals and businesses can apply for debt relief, including participating in an approved credit counseling program and completing a course in personal finance education. *(Chapter 21)*

**base rate**   A loan rate used as the foundation for determining the size of the current interest rate to be charged a borrower, such as the prime rate or LIBOR. *(Chapter 19)*

**Basel I Agreement**   An agreement among the central banks of leading industrialized nations of Western Europe, Canada, the United States, and Japan, formally approved in 1988, that imposed common capital requirements upon all their banks in order to control bank risk exposure. *(Chapters 17 and 24)*

**Basel II Agreement**   Revisions to the Basel I Agreement allowing each bank in leading industrialized countries to determine its own risk exposure and required level of capital based, in part, on stress testing its asset portfolio. *(Chapters 17 and 24)*

**basis**   The spread between the cash (spot) price of a commodity or security and its futures (forward) price at any given point in time. *(Chapter 9)*

**basis point**   A measure of rate of return equal to one one-hundredth of a percentage point. *(Chapter 6)*

**bias**   An element of the policy statement issued by the Federal Open Market Committee (FOMC) that suggests whether future monetary policy adjustments are more likely to consist of raising, lowering, or leaving policy targets unchanged. *(Chapter 13)*

**bid price**   The price a securities dealer is willing to pay to buy securities from the public. *(Chapter 3)*

**Board of Governors**   The chief policymaking and administrative body of the Federal Reserve System, composed of seven persons appointed by the president of the United States and confirmed by the Senate for maximum 14-year terms. *(Chapter 12)*

**bond**   A debt obligation issued by a business firm or unit of government that covers several years, usually over five or ten years. *(Chapter 3)*

**bond-anticipation notes (BANs)**   Short-term securities issued by a state or local government to raise funds to begin a project that eventually will be funded using long-term bonds. *(Chapter 18)*

**book-entry form**   The method by which marketable U.S. Treasury securities are issued, with the buyer receiving only a receipt, rather than an engraved certificate, indicating that the purchase is recorded on the Treasury's books or recorded in another approved location. *(Chapter 18)*

**borrowed reserves**   Legal reserves loaned to depository institutions through the discount windows of the Federal Reserve banks. *(Chapter 13)*

**borrowing**   The change in liabilities outstanding reported by a sector or unit in the economy over a specified time period. *(Chapter 3)*

**branch banking**   A type of banking organization in which services are sold through multiple offices, all owned and operated by the same corporation. *(Chapter 14)*

**budget deficit**   A government's financial position in which current expenditures exceed current revenues. *(Chapter 18)*

**budget surplus**   A government's financial position in which current revenues exceed current expenditures. *(Chapter 18)*

**business cycle**   Fluctuations in economic activity, with the economy passing alternately through expansionary *(boom)* and recessionary *(depressed)* periods. *(Chapter 9)*

# C

**call options**   Grant the buyer the right to purchase a specified number of shares of a given stock or volume of debt securities at a specified price up to an expiration date. *(Chapter 9)*

**call privilege**   The provision often found in a bond's contract (indenture) that permits the borrower to retire all or a portion of a bond issue by buying back the securities in advance of their maturity. *(Chapter 8)*

**capital and financial accounts**   Records of short-term and long-term funds flowing into and out of a nation and included in its balance-of-payments accounts. *(Chapter 23)*

**capital market**   The institution that provides a channel for the borrowing and lending of long-term funds (over one year). *(Chapter 1)*

**carry income**   The difference between interest income and interest cost experienced by a dealer in securities. *(Chapter 10)*

**central bank**   An agency of government that has public policy functions such as monitoring the operation of the financial system and controlling the growth of the money supply. *(Chapters 12 and 13)*

**classical theory of interest rates**   An explanation of the level of and changes in interest rates that relies on the interaction of the supply of savings and the demand for investment capital. *(Chapter 5)*

**clearinghouse funds**   Money transferred by writing a check and presenting it for collection. *(Chapter 10)*

**collateralized mortgage obligation (CMO)**   A type of mortgage-backed security offered in more than one maturity class in order to reduce prepayment risk to investors. *(Chapter 22)*

**commercial mortgage**   A debt instrument used to provide financing for office buildings, shopping centers, and other business ventures involving the purchase or construction of land and buildings. *(Chapter 19)*

**commercial paper**   A short-term debt security issued by a corporation that is not tied to any specific collateral but is secured only by the general earning power of the issuing corporation. *(Chapter 11)*

**common stock**   A residual claim against the assets and earnings of the issuing corporation evidencing a share of ownership in that company. *(Chapter 20)*

**Community Reinvestment Act**   A federal law passed in 1977 that requires depository institutions to designate the market areas they will serve and to provide services without discrimination to all neighborhoods within their designated market areas. *(Chapter 21)*

**competition**   Rivalry between financial-service providers offering the same or similar services. *(Chapter 4)*

**compound interest**   The payment of additional interest earnings on previously earned interest income. *(Chapter 6)*

**Comptroller of the Currency**   Federal regulatory agency that charters national banks in the United States. *(Chapter 17)*

**consolidation**   A trend among financial institutions in which smaller institutions are being combined through merger and acquisition into larger institutions. *(Chapters 14 and 17)*

**contractual institutions**   Financial institutions that attract savings from the public by offering contracts that protect the saver against risk in the future, such as insurance policies and pension plans. *(Chapter 2)*

**conventional home mortgage loan**   Credit funds extended to a home buyer by a private lender without a government guarantee behind the loan. *(Chapter 22)*

**convergence**   The movement of different financial-service providers closer to each other in terms of services offered to the public. *(Chapters 4 and 14)*

**convertibility**   A feature of some preferred stocks and bonds that entitles the holder to exchange those securities for a specific number of shares of common stock. *(Chapter 8)*

**convexity**   The rate of change in an asset's price or value varies according to the level of market rates of interest. *(Chapter 7)*

**corporate bond**   A debt contract (IOU) of a corporation whose original maturity is more than five years. *(Chapter 19)*

**corporate note**   A debt contract (IOU) of a corporation whose original maturity date is five years or less. *(Chapter 19)*

**coupon effect**   The size of a debt security's promised interest rate (coupon) influences how rapidly its price moves with changes in market interest rates. *(Chapter 7)*

**coupon rate**   The promised interest rate on a bond or note consisting of the ratio of the annual interest income promised by the security issuer to the security's face (par) value. *(Chapter 6)*

**credit**   A loan of funds in return for a promise of future payment. *(Chapter 1)*

**credit card**   A plastic card that allows the holder to borrow cash or to pay for goods and services with credit. *(Chapter 21)*

**credit derivatives**   Financial instruments designed to reduce a lender's exposure to default risk. *(Chapter 8)*

**credit enhancements**   Financial devices, such as letters of credit from a bank, that upgrade the credit rating of a borrower and allow that borrower to obtain credit at lower cost. *(Chapter 11)*

**credit scoring techniques**   Statistical models designed to evaluate a prospective borrower's default risk exposure based on variables reflecting the borrower's credit history and financial condition. *(Chapter 21)*

**credit unions (CUs)**   Nonprofit associations accepting deposits from and making loans to their members. *(Chapter 15)*

**cross hedge**   The purchase of a futures contract for a different financial instrument than is being traded in the cash market. *(Chapter 9)*

**currency-deposit ratio**   A ratio that indicates how much cash economic units (such as households) desire to hold for each dollar they maintain in their checking accounts. *(Chapter 12)*

**currency futures and options market**   Trading in agreements that allow businesses or individuals acquiring or selling foreign currencies to protect themselves against future fluctuations in currency prices by shifting currency risk to someone else willing to bear that risk. *(Chapter 23)*

**currency risk**   Possible losses to a borrower or lender or to a holder of assets in foreign markets due to adverse changes in currency prices. *(Chapter 10)*

**currency sterilization**   An action taken by a central bank to offset the impact from government purchases or sales of currencies on bank reserves and deposits through the use of central bank policy tools. *(Chapter 23)*

**currency swap**   A contract designed to reduce the risk of loss due to changes in currency prices by exchanging one nation's currency for another that is of more use to a borrower. *(Chapter 23)*

**current account**   A component of a nation's balance-of-payments accounts that tracks purchases and sales of goods and services (trade) and gifts made to foreigners. *(Chapter 23)*

**current yield**   The ratio of a security's promised or expected annual income to its current market price. *(Chapter 6)*

# D

**dealer paper**   Short-term commercial notes sold by borrowing corporations and issued through security dealers who contact interested investors to determine whether they will buy the notes. *(Chapter 11)*

**debenture**   Long-term debt instruments secured only by the earning power of the issuing corporation and not by any specific assets pledged by the issuing firm. *(Chapter 19)*

**debit card**   A plastic card that is used to identify the owner of the card or to make immediate payments for goods and services. *(Chapter 21)*

**debt management policy**   The refunding or refinancing of the federal government's debt in a way that contributes to broad national goals and minimizes the burden of the debt. *(Chapter 18)*

**debt securities**   Financial claims against the assets of a business firm, individual, or unit of government, represented by bonds and other contracts evidencing a loan of money. *(Chapter 2)*

**default risk**   The risk to the holder of debt securities that a borrower will not meet all promised payments at the times agreed upon. *(Chapters 8 and 10)*

**deficit-budget unit (DBU)**   An individual, business firm, or unit of government whose current expenditures exceed its current receipts of income, forcing it to become a net borrower in the money and capital markets. *(Chapter 2)*

**deflation**   A fall in the average price level for all goods and services. *(Chapters 2 and 13)*

**demand loan**   A borrowing of funds (usually by a security dealer) subject to recall of those funds on demand by the lender. *(Chapter 10)*

**deposit multiplier**   A number that indicates what volume of new deposits will result from an injection of a given amount of excess reserves into the banking system. *(Chapter 12)*

**depository institutions**   Financial institutions that raise loanable funds by selling deposits to the public. *(Chapter 2)*

**Depository Institutions Deregulation and Monetary Control Act (DIDMCA)**   Law passed in 1980 by the U.S. Congress to deregulate interest rate ceilings on deposits and grant new services to nonbank thrift institutions as well as to impose common reserve requirements on all depository institutions. *(Chapters 15 and 17)*

**deregulation**   The lifting or liberalization of government rules that restrict what private businesses can do to serve their customers. *(Chapters 14, 17, and 4)*

**derivatives**   Financial instruments (such as swaps, financial futures, and options) whose value depends upon an underlying financial instrument (such as a stock or a bond). *(Chapters 2 and 9)*

**direct finance**   Any financial transaction in which a borrower and a lender of funds communicate directly and mutually agree on the terms of a loan. *(Chapter 2)*

**direct paper**   Short-term commercial notes issued directly to investors by borrowing companies without the aid of a broker or dealer. *(Chapter 11)*

**discount loan method**   A method for calculating the interest rate on a loan that deducts the interest cost up front from the face amount of the loan with the borrower receiving only the net amount remaining for his or her use. *(Chapter 6)*

**discount method**   A method for calculating the interest charge on a loan that deducts the interest owed from the face amount of the loan, with the borrower receiving only the net proceeds after interest is deducted. *(Chapter 6)*

**discount rate**   The interest charge (in annual percentage terms) set by the Federal Reserve banks for borrowing by depository institutions from the Reserve banks. *(Chapters 11, 12, and 13)*

**discount window**   The department in a Federal Reserve bank that grants credit to depository institutions in need of short-term loans of legal reserves. *(Chapters 12 and 13)*

**disintermediation**   The withdrawal of funds from a financial intermediary by ultimate lenders (savers) and the lending of those funds directly to ultimate borrowers. *(Chapter 2)*

**duration**   A weighted average measure of the maturity of a loan or security that takes into account the amount and timing of all promised interest and principal payments. *(Chapters 7 and 9)*

# E

**Edge Act and Agreement corporations**   Special subsidiaries of U.S. banking organizations authorized by federal law to offer international banking services. *(Chapter 24)*

**efficient market**   A competitive market in which the prices of financial instruments traded there fully reflect all the latest information available. *(Chapters 3 and 20)*

**efficient markets hypothesis (EMH)**   A theory of the financial markets that argues that security prices tend to fluctuate randomly around their intrinsic values, return quickly to equilibrium, and fully reflect the latest information available. *(Chapters 3 and 20)*

**electronic communication networks (ECNs)**   Automated quote-driven market centers that permit trading to take place electronically in stocks listed on virtually all major equity markets. *(Chapter 20)*

**Equal Credit Opportunity Act**   A federal law passed in 1974 forbidding lending institutions from discriminating in the granting of credit based on the age, race, ethnic origin, religion, or receipt of public assistance of the borrowing customer. *(Chapter 21)*

**equities**   Shares of common or preferred stock, with each share representing a certificate of ownership in a business corporation. *(Chapters 2 and 20)*

**Eurobond**   A long-term debt security denominated in a currency other than that of the country or countries where most or all of the security is sold. *(Chapter 24)*

**Eurocurrency deposits**   Deposits of funds in a bank denominated in a currency foreign to the bank's home country. *(Chapter 24)*

**Eurocurrency loans**   Loans made by a multinational bank in a currency other than that of the bank's home country. *(Chapter 24)*

**Eurocurrency market**   An international money market where bank deposits denominated in the world's most convertible currencies are traded. *(Chapter 11)*

**Eurodollars**   Deposits of U.S. dollars in foreign banks abroad or in foreign branch offices of U.S. banks or U.S. international banking facilities (IBFs). *(Chapter 11)*

**event risk**   The probability that changes inside a firm or other security-issuing individual or institution or external happenings will affect the value of the securities involved. *(Chapter 8)*

**excess reserves**   Cash and deposits at the Federal Reserve banks held by depository institutions that are in excess of their legal reserve requirements. *(Chapters 12, 13, and 14)*

**expected yield**   The weighted average return on a risky security composed of all possible yields from the security multiplied by the probability that each possible yield will occur. *(Chapter 8)*

**external financing**   Drawing upon sources of funding, such as the money and capital markets, that lie outside a business firm or other economic unit. *(Chapter 2)*

# F

**Fair Credit Billing Act**   A federal law giving customers the right to question entries on bills sent to them for goods and services purchased on credit and giving them the right to expect that billing errors will be corrected as quickly as possible. *(Chapter 21)*

**Fair Credit Reporting Act**   A federal law that gives credit customers the right to view their credit record held by a credit bureau and to secure correction of any errors in that record. *(Chapter 21)*

**federal agencies**   Departments or divisional units of the federal government empowered to borrow funds in the open market in order to make loans to private businesses and individuals or otherwise subsidize private lending or borrowing. *(Chapter 11)*

**Federal Deposit Insurance Corporation (FDIC)**   Federal agency established in 1934 to insure the deposits of commercial banks and later expanded in 1989 to insure the deposits of savings associations as well. *(Chapters 14, 15, and 17)*

**FDIC Improvement Act (FDICIA)**   Passed by the U.S. Congress in 1991, this federal law provided additional capital and borrowing authority for the Federal Deposit Insurance Corporation (FDIC) and permitted regulatory authorities to restrict the activities of and even close undercapitalized banks. *(Chapters 15 and 17)*

**Federal Financing Bank (FFB)**   A unit of the federal government created in 1973 that borrows money through the U.S. Treasury Department and channels these funds to federal agencies. *(Chapter 11)*

**federal funds**   Funds that can be transferred immediately from their holder to another party for immediate payment for purchases of securities, goods, or services. *(Chapters 10 and 11)*

**federal funds rate**   The market interest rate attached to federal funds loans and a target interest rate for Federal Reserve monetary policy. *(Chapters 11 and 13)*

**Federal Home Loan Bank (FHLB) System**   U.S. federal agency created in 1932 to make loans to mortgage lenders and, thereby, increase the liquidity of home mortgage loans. *(Chapter 22)*

**Federal Home Loan Mortgage Corporation (FHLMC)**   A federal agency created in 1970 to improve the resale (secondary) market for home mortgages. *(Chapter 22)*

**Federal Housing Administration (FHA)**   An agency of the federal government established in 1934 to guarantee mortgage loans for low-priced and medium-priced homes, thereby reducing the risks of lending by financial institutions making qualified home loans. *(Chapter 22)*

**Federal National Mortgage Association (FNMA)**   A federal agency created in 1938 to buy and sell selected residential mortgages in the secondary market and encourage the development of a resale market for home loans. *(Chapter 22)*

**Federal Open Market Committee (FOMC)**   The chief body for setting money and credit policy within the Federal Reserve System, consisting of the seven members of the Federal Reserve Board and the presidents of the 12 Federal Reserve banks (only 5 of whom may vote at any one time.) *(Chapters 12 and 13)*

**Federal Reserve bank**   One of 12 regional banks chartered by the U.S. Congress to provide central banking services to a specific region of the nation. *(Chapter 12)*

**Federal Reserve System**   The central bank of the United States, created by Congress to issue currency and coin, regulate the banking system, protect the value of the dollar, and promote maximum employment. *(Chapters 12, 13, and 17)*

**finance companies**   Financial-service firms that provide both business and consumer credit. *(Chapter 16)*

**financial asset**   A claim against the income or wealth of a business firm, household, or unit of government usually represented by a certificate, receipt, or other legal document. *(Chapter 2)*

**financial disclosure**   The provision of relevant information to the public to aid individuals and institutions in making sound financial decisions. *(Chapters 3, 4, 13, 17, 20, and 21)*

**financial futures contracts**   Contracts that call for the future delivery or sale of designated securities at a price agreed upon the day the contract is made. *(Chapter 9)*

**financial holding companies (FHCs)**   Corporations permitted under the terms of the Gramm-Leach-Bliley Act to acquire and control banks, insurance companies, security underwriters, and other financial firms, all under the sane corporate umbrella. *(Chapters 4, 14, and 17)*

**financial innovation**   A trend in the financial system toward developing new services and new service delivery methods. *(Chapter 4)*

**Financial Institutions Reform, Recovery, and Enforcement Act (FIRREA)**   Federal law passed in 1989 to bail out the U.S. savings and loan industry, strengthen the federal deposit insurance program, and liquidate the assets of failed thrift institutions. *(Chapters 15 and 17)*

**financial intermediaries**   Financial-service firms that simultaneously borrow funds through the issuance of secondary securities and lend funds by accepting primary securities from borrowers. Also referred to as indirect finance. *(Chapters 2, 11, and 14–16)*

**financial market**   An institutional mechanism created by society to channel savings and other financial services to those individuals and institutions willing to pay for them. *(Chapter 1)*

**Financial Services Modernization (Gramm-Leach-Bliley) Act**   A 1999 law of the U.S. government permitting the formation of financial holding companies that bring banks, insurance companies, and securities firms together in the same organization and allow customers to protect their financial privacy. *(Chapters 4, 14, 17, and 21)*

**Financial Services Regulatory Relief Act**   A 2006 federal law designed to eliminate unnecessary and burdensome regulations on depository institutions, including awarding new service powers for banks and thrifts, lowering deposit reserve requirements, and empowering the Federal Reserve to pay interest on legal reserves if warranted. *(Chapters 13 and 17)*

**financial system**   The collection of markets, individuals, institutions, laws, regulations, and techniques through which bonds, stocks, and other securities are traded, financial services are produced and delivered, and interest rates are determined. *(Chapter 1)*

**financial wealth**   Portion of the wealth held by society or by an individual economic unit in the form of stocks, bonds, and other financial assets. *(Chapter 1)*

**fiscal agent**   A role of the Federal Reserve System in which it provides services to the federal government, such as clearing and collecting checks on behalf of the U.S. Treasury and conducting auctions for the sale of new Treasury securities. *(Chapter 12)*

**fiscal policy**   The taxing and spending programs carried out by government in order to promote maximum employment, price stability, and other economic goals. *(Chapter 18)*

**Fisher effect**   The theory of inflation and interest rates that says nominal interest rates respond one-for-one to changes in the expected rate of inflation over the life of a loan. *(Chapter 7)*

**fixed-rate home mortgages (FRMs)**   Mortgage loans that carry an unchanging loan rate. *(Chapter 22)*

**foreign exchange markets**   Channels for trading national currencies and determining relative currency prices. *(Chapter 23)*

**foreign exchange rates**   The prices of foreign currencies expressed in terms of other currencies. *(Chapter 23)*

**forward contract**   An agreement to deliver a specified amount of currency, securities, or other goods or services at a set price on some future date. *(Chapter 23)*

**forward market**   Channel through which currencies, securities, goods, and services are traded for future delivery with the terms of trade set in advance of delivery. *(Chapter 23)*

**fundamental analysis**   A strategy for choosing stocks and other assets based upon an analysis of a security issuer's financial statements and the financial condition of the issuing firm and its industry. *(Chapter 20)*

# G

**Garn-St Germain Depository Institutions Act**   A law passed by the U.S. Congress in 1982 to further deregulate the depository institutions sector and to give federal deposit insurance agencies additional tools to deal with failing institutions. *(Chapters 15 and 17)*

**GDP gap**   The difference between actual gross domestic product (GDP) and potential GDP as a percentage of potential GDP, indicating whether the economy is under- or over-performing relative to its capacity. *(Chapter 13)*

**general credit controls**   Monetary policy tools that affect the entire banking and financial system, such as open market operations or changes in the Federal Reserve's discount rate. *(Chapter 13)*

**general obligation bonds**    Debt obligations issued by state and local governments and backed by the "full faith and credit" of the issuing government (i.e., may be repaid from any revenue source). *(Chapter 18)*

**Glass-Steagall Act**    The National Bank Act of 1933 that created the federal deposit insurance system and separated commercial from investment banking. *(Chapter 17)*

**globalization**    The spreading of financial services and financial institutions worldwide. *(Chapters 4, 23, and 24)*

**gold exchange standard**    A system for making international payments in which each national currency is freely convertible into gold bullion at a fixed price and also freely convertible into other currencies at relatively stable prices. *(Chapter 23)*

**gold standard**    A system of payments for purchases of goods and services in which nations agree to exchange paper money or coins for gold bullion at predetermined prices and allow gold to be exported or imported freely from one nation to another. *(Chapter 23)*

**Government National Mortgage Association (GNMA)**    A federal agency created in 1968 to assist the home mortgage market through such activities as purchasing mortgages to finance low-income family housing projects and guaranteeing principal and interest payments on securities issued by private mortgage lenders that are backed by pools of home mortgages. *(Chapter 22)*

**government-sponsored enterprises (GSEs)**    Insitutions originally owned by the federal government but now privately owned with the authority to borrow from and lend money to private businesses and individuals or to issue loan guarantees. *(Chapters 11, 16, and 22)*

# H

**harmonization**    Regulatory cooperation among different nations. *(Chapters 4 and 17)*

**Harrod-Keynes effect**    The theory of the relationship between inflation and interest rates that argues that inflation affects real rates of return but not necessarily nominal rates of return. *(Chapter 7)*

**hedging**    The act of buying and selling financial claims or using other financial tools in order to protect against the risk of fluctuations in market prices or interest rates. *(Chapter 9)*

**high-powered money**    Often referred to as the monetary base which encompasses liabilities of the central bank, including legal reserves, of the banking system and currency and coin held by the public. *(Chapter 12)*

**holding-period yield (HPY)**    The rate of return received or expected from a financial asset or other investment over the period the asset or investment was held, including the price for which the asset or investment was sold to another investor. *(Chapter 6)*

**home equity loan**    Extension of credit to individuals who own their homes in which the borrowers' homes are pledged as collateral to support the loans and the amount of the loan is based on the difference between the market value of the home and the amount of any home mortgage debt outstanding (i.e., the owner's equity in a home). *(Chapter 21)*

**home mortgage interest rate**    The percentage cost of borrowed funds used to purchase a house or other residential dwelling. *(Chapter 6)*

**homogenization**    The tendency of different financial institutions to offer the same services. *(Chapter 4)*

**hyperinflation**    A condition of rapid price inflation in the economy exceeding 100 percent annually. *(Chapter 13)*

# I

**identity theft**    Using another person's personal, nonpublic data (such as his or her Social Security number) to fraudulently obtain credit or personal assets. *(Chapter 21)*

**implied market forecasts**    The market's expectation about future interest rates as indicated by the shape of the yield curve or by financial futures prices. *(Chapter 9)*

**income effect**    The relationship between interest rate levels and the volume of saving in the economy that argues that the advent of higher interest rates may induce savers to save *less* because each dollar saved now earns a higher rate of return. *(Chapter 5)*

**indenture**    A contract accompanying the issue of a bond or note by a corporation or other borrower that lists the rights, privileges, and obligations of the borrower and the investor who has purchased the bond or note. *(Chapter 19)*

**indirect finance**    Also known as financial intermediation, in which financial transactions (especially the borrowing and lending of money) are carried out through a financial intermediary. *(Chapter 2)*

**industrial development bond (IDB)**    Debt security issued by a local government to aid a private company in the construction of a plant and/or the purchase of equipment or land. *(Chapter 19)*

**inflation**    A rise in the average level of all prices of goods and services traded in the economy over any given period of time. *(Chapters 2 and 7)*

**inflation-caused income tax effect**    The presence of a progressive income tax structure tends to cause nominal interest rates to increase by more than the expected increase in inflation. *(Chapter 7)*

**inflation premium**    The expected rate of price inflation which, when added to the real interest rate, equals the nominal interest rate on a loan. *(Chapter 7)*

**inflation (or purchasing power) risk**    The probability that increases in the average level of prices for all goods and services sold in the economy will reduce the purchasing power of an investor's income from loans or securities. *(Chapter 10)*

**inflation risk premium**    Compensation paid to a lender for that component of inflation that is not expected. *(Chapter 7)*

**insider trading**    Buying or selling the securities of an issuing firm by an employee, director, or by someone under contract with the issuing firm in a fiduciary capacity who acts on the basis of private or privileged information about the issuing firm. *(Chapter 3)*

**installment credit**    All liabilities of a borrowing customer other than home mortgages that are retired in two or more consecutive loan payments. *(Chapter 21)*

**interest-only mortgages (IOMs)**   Residential and commercial mortgage loans that offer borrowers the option of paying only the amount of interest owed each month for a specified number of years early in the term of the loan and then require borrowers to make accelerated payments to retire principal along with interest payments later in the loan's term. *(Chapter 22)*

**interest rate**   The price of credit, or ratio of the fees charged to secure credit from a lender to the amount borrowed, usually expressed on an annual percentage basis. *(Chapter 6)*

**interest rate parity**   A condition prevailing in international markets where the interest rate differential between two nations matches the forward discount or premium on their two currencies. *(Chapter 23)*

**interest rate structure**   The concept that the interest rate or yield attached to any loan or security consists of the risk-free (or *pure*) rate of interest plus risk premiums for the security holder's exposure to various forms of risk. *(Chapter 8)*

**interest rate swap**   A contract between two or more firms in which interest payments are exchanged so that each participating firm saves on interest costs and gets a better balance between its cash inflows and outflows. *(Chapter 9)*

**internal financing**   The use of saving by an economic unit, rather than debt, to support the acquisition of real and/or financial assets. *(Chapter 2)*

**International Banking Act (IBA)**   A U.S. law passed in 1978 to bring foreign banks operating in the United States under regulation. *(Chapter 24)*

**international banking facilities (IBFs)**   A domestically based set of computerized accounts recording transactions of a U.S. bank with its foreign customers. *(Chapter 24)*

**International Lending and Supervision Act**   A federal law passed in 1983 requiring U.S. banks to increase their capital and to pursue more prudent international loan policies. *(Chapter 24)*

**investment**   Expenditures on capital goods or on inventories of goods or raw materials that are used to produce other goods and services, causing future production and income to rise. *(Chapter 1)*

**investment banks or bankers**   Financial firms that assist their customers in raising funds by underwriting their security offerings. *(Chapters 16, 17, 18, 19, and 20)*

**investment companies**   Financial intermediaries that sell shares to the public to raise funds and invest the proceeds in stocks, bonds, and other securities. *(Chapter 16)*

**investment institutions**   Financial intermediaries selling their customers financial assets in order to build up savings for retirement or for other customer uses. *(Chapter 2)*

**investment rate**   Sometimes referred to as the coupon-equivalent or bond-equivalent rate of return on a debt instrument that reflects its par value, purchase price, and days to maturity. *(Chapter 6)*

**IPOs**   Initial public offerings of stocks and other securities as companies convert from privately held businesses to publicly held corporations. *(Chapter 20)*

# J

**junk bonds**   Corporate debt securities bearing credit ratings below investment grade. *(Chapters 8 and 19)*

# L

**leasing companies**   Financial-service firms that provide businesses and consumers access to equipment, motor vehicles, and other assets for a stipulated period of time at an agreed-upon leasing rate. *(Chapter 16)*

**legal reserve requirement**   A law or regulation that calls for a depository institution to hold certain assets (such as vault cash and reserves posted to an account at the central bank) as a reserve backing the institution's deposits and selected other liabilities. *(Chapters 11, 13, and 14)*

**legal reserves**   Deposits held at the Federal Reserve banks by depository institutions plus currency and coin held in the vaults of these institutions. *(Chapters 12, 13, and 14)*

**letter of credit**   An authorization to draft funds from a bank provided stipulated conditions are met. *(Chapter 24)*

**leveraged buyouts**   A form of corporate takeover in which the management of a company or other small group of investors buys the publicly owned stock of the firm, financing the transaction mainly with new debt that will be repaid from planned increases in company earnings. *(Chapter 19)*

**liability management**   The techniques used by banks to control the amount and composition of their borrowed funds by changing the interest rates they offer to reflect competition and the intensity of the bank's borrowing requirements. *(Chapter 11)*

**life insurance companies**   Financial-service firms selling contracts to customers that promise to reduce the financial loss to an individual or family associated with death, disability, or old age. *(Chapter 16)*

**liquidity**   The quality or capability of any asset to be sold quickly with little risk of loss and possessing a relatively stable price over time. *(Chapters 1, 8, and 10)*

**liquidity preference theory of interest rates**   An explanation of the level of and change in interest rates that focuses on the interaction of the supply of and demand for money. *(Chapter 5)*

**liquidity premium**   The added yield (*interest return*) that must be paid to investors to get them to buy and hold long-term instead of short-term securities. *(Chapter 7)*

**loanable funds theory of interest rates**   The credit view of what determines the level of and changes in interest rates that focuses on the interaction of the demand for and the supply of loanable funds (*credit*). *(Chapter 5)*

**London Interbank Offer Rate (LIBOR)**   Short-term interest rate attached to Eurocurrency deposits traded between banks. *(Chapter 11)*

**long hedge**   The purchase of futures contracts calling for delivery of securities or commodities to a counterparty on a specific future date at a set price. *(Chapter 9)*

**long position**   The purchase of assets outright from the seller in order to hold them until they mature or must be sold. *(Chapter 10)*

# M

**M1**   The narrowest definition of the U.S. money supply, consisting of currency outside the U.S. Treasury, Federal Reserve banks, and the vaults of depository institutions; travelers checks of nonbank issuers; demand deposits at commercial banks (except the deposits of other banks, the U.S. government, and foreign banks and official institutions) less cash items in the process of collection and Federal Reserve float; and other checkable deposits (including NOW and ATS accounts at depository institutions, credit union share draft accounts, and demand deposits at thrift institutions). *(Chapter 2)*

**M2**   The definition of the U.S. money supply that includes M1 plus savings deposits (including money market deposit accounts); small-denomination time deposits (each less than $100,000) less individual retirement accounts (IRAs) and Keogh balances held at depository institutions; and balances kept with retail money market mutual funds less IRA and Keogh balances at money market mutual funds. *(Chapter 2)*

**MZM**   The definition of the U.S. money supply that includes M2 plus balances held in institutional money market funds which are excluded from the M2 measure of money; a money measure close to the transactions demand for money. *(Chapter 2)*

**managed float**   An international monetary payments system in which the value of any currency is determined by demand and supply forces in the marketplace, but governments intervene on occasion in an effort to stabilize the value of their own currencies. *(Chapter 23)*

**managed floating currency standard**   System of currency valuation in which each nation chooses its own currency exchange rate policy. *(Chapter 23)*

**margin requirements**   The difference between the market value of a security and its maximum loan value as specified by a regulation enforced by the Federal Reserve Board. *(Chapter 13)*

**market**   An institutional mechanism for trading goods, services, and financial assets. *(Chapter 1)*

**marketability**   The feature of an asset that reflects its ability to be sold quickly to recover the purchaser's funds. *(Chapter 8)*

**market broadening**   A tendency for financial service markets to expand geographically over time due to advances in technology and increased customer mobility. *(Chapter 4)*

**market-dominated financial systems**   Financial marketplaces in which a large portion of borrowing and investment activity is routed through the open market rather than through traditional financial intermediaries (such as banks). *(Chapter 2)*

**market risk (or interest rate risk)**   The probability that the prices of securities or other assets will fall (due to rising interest rates), confronting the investor with a capital loss. *(Chapter 10)*

**market segmentation argument**   A theory of the yield curve in which the financial markets are thought to be separated into several distinct markets by the maturity preferences of various investors so that demand and supply for loans and securities in each market determine relative interest rates on long-term versus short-term securities. *(Chapter 7)*

**master note**   A borrowing arrangement between a corporation issuing commercial paper and an institution buying the paper in which the buying institution agrees to accept new paper each day up to a specified maximum amount. *(Chapter 11)*

**maturity**   Length of calendar time in days, weeks, months, and years before a security or loan comes due and must be paid off. *(Chapter 7)*

**member banks**   Banks that have joined the Federal Reserve System, consisting of all federally chartered *(national)* banks and any state-chartered U.S. banks that meet the Federal Reserve's requirements for membership. *(Chapters 12 and 14)*

**modified exchange standard**   A system of currency exchanges and international payments in which foreign currencies were linked to gold and the U.S. dollar, with the price of gold in terms of U.S. dollars remaining fixed. *(Chapter 23)*

**monetary base**   The sum of legal reserves in the banking system plus the amount of currency and coin held by the public. *(Chapter 12)*

**monetary policy**   The use of various tools by central banks to control the cost and availability of credit in an effort to achieve national economic goals. *(Chapter 12)*

**money**   A financial asset that serves as a medium of exchange and standard of value for purchases of goods and services. *(Chapter 2)*

**money creation**   The ability of banks and other depository institutions to create a deposit, such as a checking account, that can be used as a medium of exchange (to make payments for purchases of goods and services). *(Chapter 14)*

**money market**   The institution set up by society to channel temporary surpluses of cash into temporary loans of funds, one year or less to maturity. *(Chapters 1 and 10)*

**money market deposit accounts (MMDAs)**   Deposits whose interest yields vary with market conditions and are subject to withdrawal by check. *(Chapters 14, 15, and 21)*

**money market mutual fund**   An investment company selling shares to the public and investing the proceeds in short-term securities, such as Treasury bills and other money market instruments. *(Chapter 15)*

**money multiplier**   The ratio of the size of the money supply to the total reserve base available to depository institutions. *(Chapter 12)*

**moral hazard**   When one party to an agreement or relationship uses their position of power or special knowledge to pursue their own self-interest and receives special benefits or rewards at the expense of the other party to the agreement or relationship. *(Chapter 3)*

**moral suasion**   A monetary policy tool of the central bank in which its officers and staff try to persuade bankers and the public through speeches and written communications to conform more closely to the central bank's goals. *(Chapter 13)*

**mortgage-backed securities**   Debt obligations issued by private mortgage-lending institutions using selected residential mortgage loans they hold as collateral; the mortgage loans generate principal and interest payments to repay holders of the mortgage-backed securities. *(Chapter 22)*

**mortgage bank**   A financial-service firm that works with property developers to provide real estate financing and then places the long-term loans with long-term lenders, such as insurance companies and savings banks. *(Chapter 16)*

**mortgage bonds**   Long-term debt secured by a lien on specific assets, usually plant and equipment, held by the issuing corporation. *(Chapter 19)*

**mortgage lock-ins**   Part of a home financing contract that fixes the mortgage loan rate for a designated period of time. *(Chapter 22)*

**multinational corporation**   A large company with manufacturing, trading, or service operations in several different countries. *(Chapter 24)*

**municipals**   Debt securities issued by states, counties, cities, school districts, and other local units of government. *(Chapter 18)*

**mutual fund**   A type of investment company that sells as many shares of interest in a pool of assets as the public demands and invests the proceeds of those sales in a wide variety of assets, particularly such financial assets as stocks and bonds. *(Chapter 16)*

**mutuals**   Depository institutions owned by their depositors, such as savings banks and some savings and loan associations. *(Chapter 15)*

# N

**national banks**   U.S. banking institutions that receive their charter of incorporation from the Comptroller of the Currency, an agency of the U.S. government. *(Chapter 14)*

**National Credit Union Administration (NCUA)**   Federal regulatory agency that oversees the activities of federally chartered credit unions. *(Chapter 17)*

**natural rate of unemployment**   An indicator based on the rate of civilian unemployment of how far the economy is from making optimal utilization of its scarce resources, including capital, labor, and entrepreneurial talent. *(Chapter 13)*

**negotiable certificate of deposit (CD)**   A marketable receipt issued by a bank or other depository institution to a customer acknowledging the deposit of customer funds for a designated period under a specified interest rate formula. *(Chapter 11)*

**negotiated markets**   Institutional mechanisms set up by society to make loans and trade securities in which the terms of trade are set by direct bargaining between a lender and a borrower. *(Chapter 1)*

**net financial wealth**   Portion of wealth held in financial assets less total debt owed. *(Chapter 1)*

**net wealth**   Total assets minus total liabilities held by an economic unit. *(Chapter 1)*

**nominal contracts**   Agreements between contracting parties that fix prices, interest rates, or costs in terms of current (nominal) values; a theory of how inflation may influence the prices of stocks issued by corporations. *(Chapter 7)*

**nominal interest rate**   The published rate of interest attached to a loan or security that includes both a real interest rate component and the inflation rate (inflation premium) expected over the life of the loan or security. *(Chapter 7)*

**nominal value**   The price of assets or other purchasable items measured in terms of their current market price or face value; the price of assets or other items not adjusted for the effects of inflation. *(Chapter 2)*

**nonborrowed reserves**   The largest component of the total legal reserves of depository institutions, consisting of all those legal reserves owned by depository institutions themselves and not borrowed from the Federal Reserve banks. *(Chapter 13)*

**nondeposit funds**   Borrowings in the open market by banks and other institutions in order to supplement monies raised by selling deposits. *(Chapter 14)*

**noninstallment credit**   A loan that is normally paid off in a lump sum rather than in a series of installment payments. *(Chapter 21)*

**nonresidential mortgages**   Loans secured by business and farm properties. *(Chapters 19 and 22)*

**note**   A shorter-term debt obligation issued by a business firm, individual, or unit of government to borrow money with a time to maturity that usually does not exceed five years. *(Chapter 3)*

**NOW account**   An interest-bearing checking account available to individuals and nonprofit institutions from banks and other depository institutions. *(Chapters 14, 15, and 21)*

#  O

**Office of Thrift Supervision**   Federal agency that charters and supervises savings associations. *(Chapters 15 and 17)*

**open market operations**   The buying and selling of selected assets by a central bank to affect the quantity and growth of the legal reserves of depository institutions and general credit conditions in order to achieve the nation's economic goals. *(Chapter 13)*

**open markets**   Institutional mechanisms created by society to make loans and trade securities in which any individual or institution can participate. *(Chapter 1)*

**option contract**   An agreement between contract writers and contract buyers to accept delivery of ("call") securities or place with buyers ("put") securities at a specified price on or before the date the contract expires. *(Chapter 9)*

**option premium**   The fee that the buyer of an option contract must pay to the writer of the contract for the right to deliver or accept delivery of securities at a set price. *(Chapter 9)*

**organized exchanges**   Locations where stocks, bonds, and other assets are traded according to the rules and regulations for trading established by members of the exchange. *(Chapter 20)*

**original maturity**   The interval of time between the issue date of a security and the date on which the borrower promises to redeem it. *(Chapter 10)*

**over-the-counter (OTC) market**   A mechanism for trading stocks and other assets through brokers or dealers operating off the major securities exchanges. *(Chapter 20)*

# P

**pass-throughs**   Securities issued against a pool of mortgage loans held by a financial institution. *(Chapter 22)*

**Pension Benefit Guaranty Corporation**   An agency of the U.S. federal government designed to insure the pension benefits of those participating in qualified defined-benefit pension plans. *(Chapter 17)*

**pension funds**   Financial-service firms selling retirement plans to their customers in which savings are set aside in accounts established in the customers' names and allowed to accumulate interest until those customers reach retirement age. *(Chapter 16)*

**perpetuity rate**   Rate of return on a financial instrument that is perpetual (never matures). *(Chapter 6)*

**policy inertia**   The gradual process by which economic policy proceeds in a series of steps over several weeks or months in a particular direction until there is a consensus on the need for a new policy direction. *(Chapter 13)*

**political risk**   The probability that changes in government laws or regulations will result in a lower rate of return to the investor or, in the extreme case, a total loss of invested capital. *(Chapters 10 and 24)*

**portfolio immunization**   An investment strategy that tries to protect the expected yield from a security or portfolio of securities by acquiring those securities whose duration equals the length of the investor's planned holding period. *(Chapter 7)*

**potential GDP**   A measure of what the level of real gross domestic product (GDP) would be if the economy were fully utilizing its productive resources of capital, labor, and entrepreneurial talent efficiently. *(Chapter 13)*

**predatory loans**   High interest rate loans granted to borrowers with weak credit ratings that substantially increase the likelihood these borrowers will default. *(Chapter 22)*

**preferred habitat**   The theory of the yield curve that claims investors prefer certain maturities of securities over other maturities due to differences in liquidity needs, risk, tax exposure, and other factors. *(Chapter 7)*

**preferred stock**   A share of ownership in a business corporation that promises a stated annual dividend. *(Chapter 20)*

**prepayment risk**   The probability that a loan or security (especially securities that draw their earnings from pools of loans) will be paid off ahead of schedule, lowering the investor's expected yield from the instrument. *(Chapters 8 and 22)*

**present value**   Funds received today are worth more than an equal nominal amount of funds promised in the future. *(Chapter 6)*

**price elasticity**   The ratio of changes in the price of a debt security to changes in its yield. *(Chapter 7)*

**price idexes**   A measure of the cost of a market basket of goods and services which provides an indicator of inflation or deflation in the whole economy or a sector of the economy. *(Chapter 2)*

**price of credit**   The rate of interest that must be paid to secure the use of borrowed funds. *(Chapter 5)*

**primary dealers**   Security firms that are recognized by the Federal Reserve System to buy and sell securities with the Fed. *(Chapter 10)*

**primary markets**   Institutional mechanisms set up by society to trade newly issued loans and securities. *(Chapter 1)*

**primary reserves**   Cash held in a bank's vault plus deposits held with other banks. *(Chapter 14)*

**primary securities**   The IOUs issued by borrowers from a financial intermediary and held by the intermediary as interest-bearing assets. *(Chapter 2)*

**prime bank rate**   Loan rate that many banks use as the base for pricing loans extended to their best customers. *(Chapter 19)*

**private (or direct) placement**   Placing securities with one or a limited number of investors rather than trying to sell them in the open market. *(Chapter 19)*

**privatization**   Placing productive resources and the job of providing services to the public in the hands of privately owned and operated businesses instead of in the hands of governmental departments or agencies. *(Chapter 4)*

**property-casualty insurers**   Financial-service firms selling contracts to protect their customers against losses to persons or property due to negligence, crime, adverse weather changes, fire, and other hazards. *(Chapter 16)*

**public debt**   The volume of debt obligations that are the responsibility of the federal government and therefore of its taxpayers. *(Chapter 18)*

**public sale**   When securities are sold in the open market to any individual or institution willing to pay the price, usually through investment bankers. *(Chapter 19)*

**purchasing power parity**   The currency value of a nation with a higher rate of inflation will tend to fall relative to the currency value of a nation with a lower rate of inflation. *(Chapter 23)*

**put options**   Contracts granting the buyer the right to sell a specified number of equity shares or debt securities at a set price on or before the expiration date. *(Chapter 9)*

# R

**random walk**   A theory of asset price movements that argues that the future path of individual asset prices is no more predictable than is the path of a series of random numbers. *(Chapters 3 and 20)*

**rate of interest**   The price of acquiring credit, usually expressed as a ratio of the cost of securing credit to the total amount of credit obtained. *(Chapters 5 and 6)*

**rational expectations theory of interest rates**   An explanation of the level of and changes in interest rates based on changes in investor expectations regarding future asset prices and returns. *(Chapter 5)*

**real estate investment trusts (REITs)**   Tax-exempt corporations that receive at least three-quarters of their gross income from real estate transactions and devote a high percentage of their assets to real property loans. *(Chapter 16)*

**real estate mortgage investment conduit (REMIC)**   A mortgage-backed security issued in a variety of maturities in an effort to reduce the purchaser's interest rate risk to an acceptable level. *(Chapter 22)*

**real interest rate**   The rate of return from a financial asset expressed in terms of its purchasing power (adjusted for inflation). *(Chapter 7)*

**real value**   The purchasing-power inflation-adjusted price of assets, services, or other items held or available for sale. *(Chapter 2)*

**regulation**   Government enforcement of rules that prescribe permissible and nonpermissible activities for businesses and consumers. *(Chapter 17)*

**reintermediation**   Funds flow from direct and semi-direct finance into financial intermediaries. *(Chapter 2)*

**reinvestment risk**   Probability that earnings from a loan or security will have to be reinvested in lower-yielding assets in the future. *(Chapter 10)*

**representative offices**   Facilities established in distant markets by a bank in order to sell the bank's services and assist its clients; these offices usually cannot accept deposits or make loans. *(Chapter 24)*

**repurchase agreement (RP)** A loan (usually granted to a bank or security dealer) that is collateralized by high-quality assets (usually government securities). *(Chapter 10)*

**required reserves** Holdings of cash and funds on deposit with the Federal Reserve banks by depository institutions that are required by law to backstop the public's deposits held by these same institutions. *(Chapters 12, 13, and 14)*

**reserve requirement ratio** Expressed as a percentage of transaction deposits held by the banking system and set by the central bank. *(Chapter 12)*

**reserve requirements** The percentage of various liabilities (such as deposits received from the public) that must be held by depository institutions, either in vault cash or on deposit at the Federal Reserve banks. *(Chapter 13)*

**residential mortgage credit** Loans provided to support the purchase of new or existing single-family homes and other permanent dwellings. *(Chapters 21 and 22)*

**residential mortgages** Loans secured by single-family homes and other dwellings. *(Chapter 22)*

**revenue-anticipation notes (RANs)** Short-term debt obligations issued by state and local units of government in lieu of expected future governmental revenues in order to meet near-term cash needs. *(Chapter 18)*

**revenue bonds** Debt obligations issued by state and local governments that are repayable only from a particular source of funds, such as revenues generated by a toll road or toll bridge or from user fees derived by selling water or electric power. *(Chapter 18)*

**reverse-annuity mortgage (RAM)** A loan contract based on the unencumbered equity value of a home that provides a stream of income to a homeowner until the homeowner dies or chooses to sell the home. *(Chapter 22)*

**risk-free rate of interest** The rate of return on a riskless asset, often called the *pure rate of interest* or the *opportunity cost of money*. *(Chapter 5)*

**risk-management tools** Financial devices (such as *futures and options*) that permit a borrower or lender of funds to protect against the risks of changing prices and interest rates. *(Chapters 4 and 9)*

# S

**savings** The amount of funds left over out of current income after current consumption expenditures are deducted or, for a business firm, the current net earnings retained in the business instead of paid out to the owners. *(Chapter 1)*

**savings and loan associations (S&Ls)** A leading home mortgage lender in the United States, making predominantly local loans to finance the purchase of housing for individuals and families. *(Chapter 15)*

**savings banks (SBs)** Depository institutions that are owned by their depositors and can be chartered by the federal government and the states. *(Chapter 15)*

**secondary markets** Institutional mechanisms set up by society to trade or exchange loans and securities that have already been issued. *(Chapter 1)*

**secondary securities** Financial claims, such as deposits, issued by a financial intermediary to raise loanable funds. *(Chapter 2)*

**Securities and Exchange Commission (SEC)** Regulatory body of the federal government charged with monitoring the behavior of security brokers, dealers, and investment institutions. *(Chapters 3 and 17)*

**securitization** The selling of shares or certificates representing an interest in a pool of income-generating assets (such as mortgage loans) as a method for raising funds by a financial institution. *(Chapters 14, 19, and 22)*

**securitized assets** Loans are packaged together in a pool and securities representing claims to the income generated by the pooled loans are sold to investors. *(Chapters 14, 19, and 22)*

**securitized mortgages** Securities issued against a pool of mortgage loans whose interest and principal payments are paid to security holders. *(Chapter 22)*

**security brokers and dealers** Financial firms that provide a conduit for buyers and sellers to trade and adjust their asset portfolios. *(Chapters 2, 16, 19, and 20)*

**selective credit controls** Monetary policy tools that affect specific groups or sectors in the financial system. *(Chapter 13)*

**semidirect finance** Any financial transaction (especially the borrowing and lending of money) that is assisted by a security broker or dealer. *(Chapter 2)*

**serialization** The splitting up of a single bond issue into several different maturities (used most often for state and local government bonds). *(Chapter 18)*

**service proliferation** The development and spreading of new financial services so that more financial institutions offer more services. *(Chapter 4)*

**share draft** Interest-bearing checking account offered by a credit union. *(Chapter 15)*

**shell branches** Booking offices of multinational banks, usually set up offshore to attract deposits and avoid certain domestic banking regulations. *(Chapter 24)*

**short hedge** The sale of futures contracts promising the delivery of securities or commodities to another party on a specific future date at a set price. *(Chapter 9)*

**short position** Dealers and other investors promise to sell and deliver in the future assets they do not currently own, hoping asset prices will fall in the interim. *(Chapter 10)*

**simple interest method** A method of figuring the interest on a loan that charges interest only for the period of time the borrower actually has use of the borrowed funds. *(Chapter 6)*

**special drawing rights (SDRs)** An official monetary reserve unit developed by the International Monetary Fund to settle international claims between nations. *(Chapter 23)*

**spot market** Channel through which currencies, securities, commodities, or other goods and services are traded for immediate delivery to the buyer once buyer and seller agree on the terms of trade. *(Chapters 1, 9, 10, and 23)*

**standby letter of credit** Contingent obligations issued by banks or other lending institutions promising to pay off the debt of a borrower if that borrower is unable to pay. *(Chapter 14)*

**state banking commissions** Government boards that charter and supervise banks headquartered in a given state. *(Chapter 17)*

**state-chartered banks**   Banking firms whose charter of incorporation allowing them to open for business is issued by a state governmental body (such as a board or commission) in the United States. *(Chapter 14)*

**stocks**   Ownership shares in a corporation, giving the holder claim to any dividends distributed from current earnings. *(Chapters 2, 3, and 20)*

**strike price**   The price for securities specified in an option contract; also called the *exercise price. (Chapter 9)*

**substitution effect**   Positive relationship between rate of interest and volume of savings in the economy. *(Chapter 5)*

**surplus-budget unit (SBU)**   An individual, business, or unit of government whose current income receipts exceed its current expenditures and, therefore, is a net lender of funds to the money and capital markets. *(Chapter 2)*

# T

**tax-anticipation notes (TANs)**   Short-term debt obligations issued by state and local governments to provide for immediate cash needs until tax revenues come in. *(Chapter 18)*

**tax-exempt securities**   Debt securities issued by state, city, county, and other local units of government or by other qualified borrowers whose interest income is exempt from federal taxation and from most state taxes as well. *(Chapters 8 and 18)*

**tax-exemption privilege**   A feature bestowed by law on some financial assets (such as state and local government bonds) that makes the income they generate free of taxation at federal or state and local government levels, or both. *(Chapters 8 and 18)*

**technical analysis**   A strategy for making buy/sell decisions on stock and other assets based on past patterns in prices and the volume of trading. *(Chapter 20)*

**third-country bills**   Bankers' acceptances issued by banks in one country that finance the transport or storage of goods traded between two other countries. *(Chapter 11)*

**third market**   Mechanism through which securities listed on a stock exchange are traded off the exchange in the over-the-counter market. *(Chapter 20)*

**time draft**   A bank's promise to pay a stipulated amount of funds upon presentation of the draft on a specific future date. *(Chapter 11)*

**TIPS**   Treasury inflation protection securities issued in order to help protect investors in U.S. government securities from lower rates of return due to inflation. *(Chapter 7)*

**transaction accounts**   Deposits (such as a checking account or other accounts offered by financial institutions) that can be used to make payments for purchases of goods and services. *(Chapters 12, 13, and 14)*

**transparency**   Policy used by some central banks today to make their policy goals and actions clear enough so that the public can develop accurate forecasts of where central bank policy is headed for the future. *(Chapters 12 and 13)*

**Truth in Lending**   A law passed by the U.S. Congress in 1968 that requires lenders covered by the law to disclose fully all the relevant terms of a personal loan to the borrower and to report a standardized loan rate (known as the APR, or annual percentage rate). *(Chapters 6 and 21)*

# U

**unbiased expectations hypothesis**   A theory of the yield curve that contends that the curve's shape is determined exclusively by investor expectations regarding future interest rate movements. *(Chapter 7)*

**U.S. Treasury bill**   A debt obligation, one year or less to maturity, issued by the United States government. *(Chapter 10)*

# V

**variable-rate mortgage (VRM)**   Home mortgage loan carrying an interest rate that varies during the term of the loan, generally depending on the movement of interest rates in the open market. *(Chapter 22)*

**vehicle currency**   A monetary unit of a nation that is not only the standard of value (unit of account) for domestic transactions but is also used to express the prices of many goods and services traded between other nations as well. *(Chapter 23)*

**venture capital firms**   Financial firms that gather funds from individual and institutional investors and direct this capital into new or expanding businesses. *(Chapter 16)*

**Veterans Administration (VA)**   A U.S. federal agency set up in 1944 to provide benefits to individuals who have served in the U.S. military, including the promotion of home ownership among veterans by guaranteeing repayment of their home loans. *(Chapter 22)*

# W

**wealth**   Accumulated assets held by an economic unit as a result of saving. *(Chapter 1)*

**wealth effect (of saving and interest rates)**   Contends that the net wealth position of savers (the balance in their portfolios between debt and financial assets) determines how their desired levels of saving will change as interest rates change. *(Chapter 5)*

# Y

**yield curve**   Relationship between short-term interest rates and long-term interest rates (that is, between yield to maturity and time to maturity of a debt security) as reflected in a smoothly drawn curve. *(Chapter 7)*

**yield to maturity**   The interest rate on a debt security that equates the purchase price of the security to the present value of all its expected annual net cash inflows (income) from now until its maturity date. *(Chapter 6)*

# Z

**zero coupon bond**   A long-term debt security that generates no interest (coupon) payments prior to maturity and thus sells at a discount to its face value and tends to rise in value over the life of the bond. *(Chapter 19)*

# Index

Page numbers with n indicate material found in notes.

Lamm, Brian, 688
Lansing, Kevin J., 24
Large-cap funds, 485
Late trading, 488
Laubach, Thomas, 564n2, 600
Law of large numbers, 498
Lawrence, Robert Z., 115
LBOs (leveraged buyouts), 621
Leach, Richard, 24
Leading indicators, 631n2
LEAPs, 270
Leasing companies, 514
Leduc, Sylvian, 600
Legal reserve requirement, 314, 375–379,
    398–402
Legal reserves, 375–379, 386, 445–446
Legislative actions, 64–67, 532; *see also*
    *specific legislation*
Lehman Brothers, 512, 647
Lehmann, Michael B., 79
Lehnert, Andrew, 520
Lemons problem, 61–62, 65
Lending and borrowing, 33–36; *see also*
    Consumer lending and borrowing
Lending institutions, 674–676
Letters of credit, 751
Level of yield curve, 196
Level playing field issue, 111
Level-premium term insurance, 502
Leveraged buyouts (LBOs), 621
Leverage effect, 29n
Levine, Ross, 54
Li, Kai, 638n, 658
Li, Wendi, 714
Liabilities, 28, 31, 568
Liability management, 332, 442
LIBOR (London Interbank Offer Rate),
    327, 623
Life-care bonds, 584
Life-cycle funds, 485
Life-cycle hypothesis, 91, 125, 673
Life Insurance Association of America, 73
Life insurance companies
    assets, 663
    definition and overview, 44, 496–497
    industry structure and growth,
        501–502
    insurance principle and, 498
    investments, 498–500
    as mortgage lenders, 697–698
    new services, 502–503
    September 11 attack claims, 500–501
    sources of funds of, 500–501
LIFFE (London International Financial
    Futures Exchange), 271
Limited partnerships, 647

Lion Capital Group, 305
Liquid assets, 38
Liquidity
    asset prices and interest rates, 218
    definition, 287–288
    demand for, 126–129
    exchange listings and, 643
    money market goals, 286–288
    secondary market role, 14
    Treasury debt management, 565, 575
Liquidity function, 9
Liquidity preference theory of interest
    rates, 126–131
Liquidity premium, 192–193
Liquidity requirements, 441
Liquidity risk, 271
Liquidity trap, 130
Litan, Robert E., 115
Liu, May X., 689
Lloyds Bank PLC, 305
Lloyds of London, 508
Load funds, 486
Loanable funds theory of interest rates,
    132–137
Loan-backed securities, 232–235
Loan limits, 437
Loan loss allowances, 435–439
Loan modification agreements, 707
Loan risk, 435–439
Loans; *see also* Business borrowing;
    Mortgage loans
    consumer, 13, 669–670, 676–677
    demand, 299
    held by commercial banks, 434–435,
        621–623
    local, 741
    predatory, 708–709
    written policies, 441
Loan sales, 460
Loan securitization, 458
Local government expenditures, 580–581;
    *see also* State and local government
    financial market activity
Local loans, 741
Lombard-Wall, Inc., 305
London Interbank Offer Rate (LIBOR),
    327, 623
London International Financial Futures
    Exchange (LIFFE), 271
London International Stock Exchange,
    651
Long hedge, 258–260
Long Island Lighting Company, 592
Long positions, 303
Long-run mean reversion, 249
Longstaff, Francis A., 195, 214

Long-Term Capital Management, 547
Long-term interest rates, 195, 407–408
Long-term securities, 574, 583–584
Lopez, Jose A., 277, 556, 629
Lottery bonds, 585

# M

M1 and M2, 37
Madison, James, 567
Maggie Mae (Mortgage Guarantee
    Insurance Corporation), 700n
Maki, Dean M., 145
Making a market, 303
Maloney Act, 66, 548, 549
Managed float, 727
Managed floating currency standard,
    726–727
Margin requirements, 261, 403–404
Margin risk, 271
Maris, Bryan A., 341, 352
Marketability, 217–218, 568
Market anomalies, 67
Market-based information, 540
Market broadening, 90
Market data, 540
Market discipline, 97, 539–540
Market-dominated financial systems, 48
Market-index CDs, 664
Market-linked accounts, 436
Market microstructure research, 645
Market risk, 287, 539, 565, 648
Markets, 4–5, 12–15
Market segmentation argument, 193–194
Market timing, 488–489
Market values, 87, 567
Marking to market, 261
Marquis, Milton, 146, 383
Master notes, 340
Matched book, 303
Maturity, 188–193; *see also* Yield to
    maturity (YTM)
    lengthening debt, 198, 575
    shortening debt, 575
    yield trade-offs and, 198
Maturity of incoming funds, 46
Maturity preferences, 193
McAndrews, James J., 353
McDonald's, 70
McEneaney, J., 683, 689
McGraw-Hill Companies, 221
McGraw-Hill Publications Company, 74
Mean reversion, 64, 196
Means test, 683
Medium-term notes (MTNs), 340,
    608–609